AMERICAN DECADES

1910-1919

AMERICAN DECADES
1910-1919

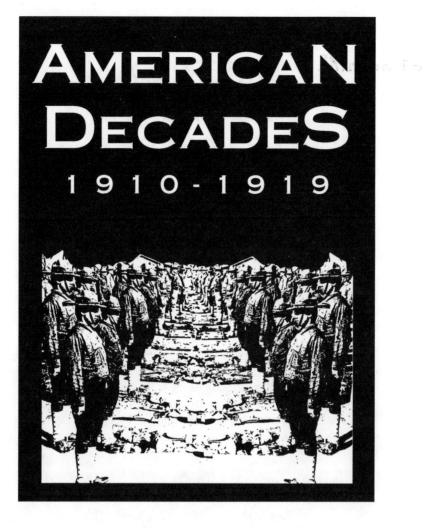

EDITED BY
VINCENT TOMPKINS

A MANLY, INC. BOOK

an International Thomson Publishing company I(T)P ®

AMERICAN
DECADES
1910-1919

Matthew J. Bruccoli and Richard Layman, *Editorial Directors*

Karen L. Rood, *Senior Editor*

Printed in the United States of America

CONTENTS

INTRODUCTION

The Tumultuous Teens. As the United States entered the second decade of the twentieth century, Americans found themselves in the midst of sweeping economic, political, and cultural changes. The United States began the 1910s as the richest nation in the world, and by the end of the decade it had emerged from World War I with an economic output greater than that of all Europe combined. The United States had also become the most important voice for democratic ideals, but Americans drew back from the responsibility of making those ideals a worldwide reality. A decade that began full of what Herbert Croly called "the promise of American life" ended with a year of labor unrest, race riots, and hysteria over the threat of radicalism. In a decade of causes and crusades — for woman suffrage, Prohibition, the rights of workers — Americans tested the pronouncement of one of the decade's brightest young minds, Walter Lippmann, who wrote in 1914 that earlier generations "inherited a conservatism and overthrew it; we inherit freedom, and have to use it." Freedom took many forms in the 1910s, some having little if anything to do with politics: from a looser code of behavior among the young, to an emerging ethic of leisure and consumption among the middle class, to the exhilaration of travel in the increasingly popular automobile. But freedom brought with it uncertainty, restlessness, and conflict, as Americans in peace and war grappled with who they were and what they were becoming.

The High Tide of Progressivism. The surge of political and social movements that began in the 1890s — to advocate reform of government at every level, to push for stronger regulation of big business and public ownership of utilities, to establish settlement houses, trade-union leagues, and child-welfare organizations — crested in the 1910s. Former president Theodore Roosevelt, a progressive Republican who remained the most compelling political figure in the country, made clear the power of progressive ideals in a speech he delivered at Osawatomie, Kansas, on 31 August 1910. There he put conservatives in his own party and nationwide on notice that the rugged individualism of the past "must now give way to the advocate of human welfare, who rightly maintains that every man holds his property subject to the general right of the community to regulate its use to

whatever degree the public welfare may require it." After failing to wrest the Republican presidential nomination from incumbent William Howard Taft in 1912, Roosevelt embarked on a third-party challenge as the nominee of the Progressive (or "Bull Moose") Party. The presidential race that year featured Taft, Roosevelt's handpicked successor, who had prosecuted the trusts even more vigorously than his predecessor; Democrat Woodrow Wilson, who had established a progressive record as governor of New Jersey; Roosevelt, whose "New Nationalism" platform promised a graduated income tax, workers' compensation for industrial injuries, and other progressive measures; and Eugene V. Debs, the candidate of the Socialist Party, who won 6 percent of the popular vote. Between them Wilson, Roosevelt, and Debs won more than 70 percent of the popular vote, giving Wilson a clear mandate to chart a course of reform. During his first term in office — supported by progressives in both the Democratic and Republican parties — Wilson established one of the most impressive legislative records of any American president, passing measures to establish the Federal Reserve System, regulate trusts, provide credit to farmers, curb child labor, and enact a graduated income tax. During the 1910s four amendments to the Constitution were adopted, each reflecting the often conflicting principles of the progressive movement: direct election of senators, the federal income tax, woman suffrage, and Prohibition. In total the reforms of the 1910s established the basic framework for the New Deal of the 1930s and the Great Society of the 1960s.

Growth and Prosperity. Fueled by the growth of new industries, the application new technologies, and a profitable agricultural sector, the American economy expanded rapidly in the 1910s, spreading its benefits to a new middle class of professionals and managers. The most striking example of the astounding productivity of American manufacturing was the automobile industry, which rode a huge wave of consumer demand for its product and implemented innovative production techniques to dominate of the world market in the 1910s. Led by Ford Motor Company, which adopted the moving assembly line to produce its Model T beginning in 1913, American automobile makers were producing more than two million cars a year by 1920, putting what had once been a luxury for the wealthy few within reach of millions of American consumers. In automobile, electrical, chemical, and other industries, the adoption of scientific management and new manufacturing techniques increased productivity and boosted the profits of stockholders. By the end of the decade the growing popularity of "personnel management" was pointing the way toward the welfare capitalism of the 1920s, in which a mix of profit-sharing plans, grievance procedures, company unions, and company-sponsored social activities were used to blunt worker unhappiness and foster loyalty to employers. During the war years, business leaders and government regulators created new arrangements that assured generous profits for business in exchange for cooperation in the expansion of federal involvement in economic planning. Despite industrial growth, however, poverty remained widespread in the rural South, in urban immigrant communities, and among African Americans. For the majority of workers, economic security was a still distant dream, and persistent inflation during the decade eroded their hard-won gains.

An Artistic Awakening. With an expanding economy creating new opportunities for education and leisure among middle-class Americans, a generation of artists and writers emerged in the 1910s, intent on reinventing a national culture. As an editorial in the first issue of *The Seven Arts* magazine declared in November 1916, "It is our faith and the faith of many that we are living in a renascent period, a time which means for America the coming of that national self-consciousness which is the beginning of greatness." Indeed, the 1910s were a decade of awakening in American painting, photography, poetry, drama, fiction, and dance. Inspired by the Armory Show, an exhibition of avant-garde European painters and sculptors in New York City in 1913, young American artists launched their own modernist experiments in form and subject in a burst of creativity not seen since the days of Ralph Waldo Emerson, Henry David Thoreau, Nathaniel Hawthorne, and Herman Melville in the mid nineteenth century. Unleashing themselves from stale traditions and slavish devotion to Old World models that had dominated American taste in the Gilded Age, the young American rebels of the 1910s embraced the cacophony of modern urban life, even as they critiqued the dehumanization of work in the modern factory. Born in the 1880s and 1890s, the new American writers were children of the Industrial Revolution, but they were profoundly skeptical of the premise that the path to happiness lay in thrift, industry, and piety. Instead they drifted to bohemian enclaves in New York, Chicago, and San Francisco, seeking like-minded souls who shared a distaste for the confinements of middle America and rejected the Victorian pieties of their parents. Often they coupled radical politics with radical artistic experiments and through magazines such as *The Masses* and *The New Republic* articulated a vision of America remade in their own image.

America and the World. Since its founding as a nation, the United States has been ambivalent about its role on the world stage. Some Americans believed that it was the nation's destiny and responsibility to serve as a beacon of freedom and democracy; others argued that American policy should consist of little more than heeding George Washington's admonition to avoid "entangling alliances." By 1910 the interest of American manufacturers in competing for markets and raw materials around the globe had involved the country inevitably in affairs beyond its borders, and despite the preference of most Americans to remain neutral, those international economic ties, as well as pro-British sentiment, eventually drew the United States into World War I. In Latin America and the Caribbean presidents Taft and Wilson followed long-established precedents of intervening to assert American influence and protect U.S. economic interests. In 1914 Theodore Roosevelt's dream of an American-controlled passage between the Atlantic and the Pacific was realized when the fifty-mile-long, $352-million Panama Canal was completed. By 1912 one half of all American foreign investments were in Latin America. To Roosevelt's "Big Stick" and Taft's "Dollar Diplomacy" Woodrow Wilson, the son of a Presbyterian minister, added the conviction that the United States was chosen, as he said in 1910, "to show the way to the nations of the world how they shall walk in the paths of liberty." Yet Wilson's moral diplomacy was tempered by his recognition of hard realities: American industries "will burst their jackets," he warned in 1912, "if they cannot find free outlets in the markets of the world." In 1911, when the Mexican Revolution began to create turmoil south of the border, Wilson's moralism did not prevent him from resorting to armed intervention and an attempt to impose American ideals through force. When World War I began in the summer of 1914, Wilson hoped to use moral suasion to bring about a just peace; but when that policy failed, the United States combined force of arms with the principles laid down in Wilson's Fourteen Points in an attempt to create a new world out of the old.

World War I. Compared with the losses of lives and resources endured by the European nations over more than five years of war, American sacrifices in the conflict were slight. But the war nonetheless had a profound impact on American life and American politics from the moment it began. For those bred to believe, as many were, that Europe was the pinnacle of civilization — with its ancient cathedrals and its great literary and artistic traditions — the carnage of war came as a tremendous shock. Though Wilson called on his fellow Americans to remain "neutral in fact as well as in name, impartial in thought as well as action," it was difficult if not impossible for a nation of immigrants to avoid choosing sides in the conflict. As the war continued, ethnic tensions and questions about the loyalty of recent immigrants intensified. At the same time, American bankers and businessmen leaped at the opportunities created by the war.

Trade with the Allies increased from $300 million to $3 billion during the first two years of the war, and loans to the Allies from American banks totaled better than $2 billion by the end of the war. As the novelist John Dos Passos remarked in his novel *1919* (1932), war provided "good growing weather for the House of Morgan."

The War at Home. Once the United States entered the war in April 1917, these effects intensified and multiplied. Three million American men were drafted, and another two million volunteered. Of these five million troops some two million served overseas between 1917 and the armistice in November 1918. More than one hundred thousand Americans lost their lives in the conflict, slightly more than half to diseases that modern medicine had not yet conquered. With millions called into service, the depletion of the labor force created new opportunities for women and African Americans, who had long been relegated to the lowest rungs of the economic ladder. More than four hundred thousand southern blacks heeded the call of the *Chicago Defender* (the leading African American newspaper of the era), which pleaded in an editorial: "I beg you, my brother, to leave the benighted land. . . . Get out of the South." Thus began the "Great Migration" of blacks from the rural South to northern cities, a migration that reshaped not only African American communities and family life but profoundly affected American culture as a whole. Similarly, close to a million women entered the labor force for the first time during the war years, working in hospitals, schools, and factories, and creating the economic basis for the emergence of the independent young "flapper" once the war had ended. In many new ways the war made government a recognizable daily presence in the lives of Americans. Through hundreds of executive agencies and war boards the federal government extended its reach into economic policy, production decisions, labor disputes, and other sectors once considered securely in the private realm. Government propaganda — orchestrated by the Committee on Public Information — encouraged Americans to despise the "Hun," support the troops, buy war bonds, and embrace "100 percent Americanism." In a nation that prided itself on toleration and individualism, conformity with official opinion and popular sentiment was enforced through the Espionage and Sedition Acts of 1917 and 1918 and occasionally by vigilante justice. German Americans found themselves the objects of suspicion and abuse at the hands of local patriots. Radicals of every stripe — anarchists, communists, and socialists — faced similar treatment, particularly in the wake of the Bolshevik Revolution in Russia in November 1917. As historian Barry Karl has written about the war years, "the enemy at home became the most visible enemy to attack."

Nineteen Nineteen. The last year of the 1910s was one of the most tempestuous in American history. In Washington the battle over the Treaty of Versailles and the League of Nations raged through most of the year and contributed to President Wilson's collapse from a stroke in October. For American workers the battle was not over grand plans for peace but over the size of their paychecks. Throughout the decade labor unions had battled employers for improved wages and working conditions, hoping to share the fruits of economic growth. In 1917 there had been more than four thousand strikes, but most workers had put their demands on hold for the duration of the war. Severe wartime inflation, rapid demobilization, and a postwar recession rekindled the fires of discontent. In 1919 hundreds of thousands of workers walked off their jobs in steel, coal mining, and other industries. Boston police went on strike as well, and there was a general strike in Seattle. Though most of the strikes were defeated, they ignited fears of a radical uprising, and by summer 1919 the nation was in the grip of the Red Scare. Alien radicals were deported by the hundreds, radical labor organizers were lynched, and duly elected Socialists were expelled from the New York State legislature. Though the worst of the hysteria was over by summer 1920, the Red Scare helped to dampen the reform energies of progressives who had seen government as a force for good. Their optimistic spirit was further dampened in the bloody summer of 1919 by race riots in Washington, D.C., New York, Chicago, and other cities, as returning black soldiers and workers who had moved north in search of opportunity met resistance and resentment from their white counterparts. When Americans voted for a new president in 1920, they chose Republican Warren G. Harding, who promised "not heroism but healing, not nostrums but normalcy, not revolution but restoration, not agitation but adjustment, not surgery but serenity, not the dramatic but the dispassionate, not experiment but equipoise, not submergence in internationality but sustainment in triumphant nationality."

ACKNOWLEDGMENTS

This book was produced by Manly, Inc.

Production coordinator is James W. Hipp. Photography editors are Julie E. Frick and Margaret Meriwether. Photographic copy work was performed by Joseph M. Bruccoli. Layout and graphics supervisor is Emily Ruth Sharpe. Copyediting supervisor is Laurel M. Gladden. Typesetting supervisor is Kathleen M. Flanagan. Systems manager is George F. Dodge. Laura Pleicones and L. Kay Webster are editorial associates. The production staff includes Phyllis A. Avant, Ann M. Cheschi, Patricia Coate, Joyce Fowler, Stephanie C. Hatchell, Kathy Lawler Merlette, Jeff Miller, Pamela D. Norton, William L. Thomas Jr., and Allison Trussell.

Walter W. Ross and Steven Gross did library research. They were assisted by the following librarians at the Thomas Cooper Library of the University of South Carolina: Linda Holderfield and the interlibrary-loan staff; reference-department head Virginia Weathers; reference librarians Marilee Birchfield, Stefanie Buck, Stefanie DuBose, Rebecca Feind, Karen Joseph, Donna Lehman, Charlene Loope, Anthony McKissick, Jean Rhyne, Kwamine Simpson, and Virginia Weathers; circulation-department head Caroline Taylor; and acquisitions-searching supervisor David Haggard.

AMERICAN DECADES
1910-1919

WORLD EVENTS: SELECTED OCCURRENCES OUTSIDE THE UNITED STATES

1910

- The world population surpasses 1.5 billion people. Of that total, 850 million live in Asia.

- Russian painter Wassily Kandinsky and German painter Franz Marc publish *Der Blaue Reiter* (The Blue Rider) in Munich, Germany, giving birth, and a name, to one of the most influential movements in Postimpressionist Western art. Kandinsky and Paul Klee emerge as the movement's major figures.

- Bertrand Russell and Alfred North Whitehead publish the first volume of their *Principia Mathematica* (1910–1913), a major work on mathematical logic.

- Spanish architect Antonio Gaudi completes one of his best-known buildings, Casa Milá, in Barcelona.

- Lord Robert Stephenson Smyth Baden-Powell, who started the Boy Scouts in 1908, founds the Girl Guides.

15 Jan. French Equatorial Africa is created when the French colonies of Chad, Gabon, Middle Congo, and Ubangi-Shari are brought together as a single administrative unit. Brazzaville is made the capital of the new colony.

28 Apr. The British Parliament adopts the so-called People's Budget, a major step in the creation of a welfare state in Great Britain. The budget increases the level of the British progressive tax structure to pay for a variety of expanded social programs.

6 May Edward VII of Great Britain dies after a reign that has lasted less than a decade. He is succeeded by his son George V.

18 May Halley's Comet, which is visible approximately every seventy-six years, blazes in the night sky. Samuel Clemens (Mark Twain), who was born during the comet's previous appearance (30 November 1835), dies, as he had predicted, during this visit (21 April).

31 May By an act of the British Parliament, the Cape Colony, the Orange Free State, Natal, and the Transvaal are joined to form the Union of South Africa and granted dominion status in the British Empire.

10 Aug. A severe typhoon kills some five hundred people in Japan and leaves approximately four hundred thousand homeless.

22 Aug. Korea signs a treaty formally recognizing its annexation by Japan. Japan occupies Korea until the end of World War II.

15 Sept. In the first elections held in the Union of South Africa, the Nationalist Party, led by Louis Botha, a Boer, defeats the Union Party, which runs on a platform advocating close ties to the British Empire.

4 Oct. Manuel II of Portugal flees to England in the face of a revolt led by the armed forces. The next day a republic is declared and Teófilo Braga is named interim president. Manuel's father, Carlos II, had sown the seeds of rebellion by suspending the Portuguese constitution in 1907.

20 Nov. Francisco Madero leads an armed uprising against Porfirio Díaz, who has been president of Mexico since 1876 and has ruled that country as dictator since 1884.

1911

- American archaeologist Harem Bingham discovers Machu Picchu, a lost city of the Incan Empire, high in the Peruvian Andes.

- Japan, the United States, Great Britain, and Russia agree to empower Canada to regulate the hunting of fur seals in the North Pacific and the Bering Sea. Hunters have lowered the fur seal population from an estimated 3.5 million in the early nineteenth century to a number that approaches extinction.

- Joseph Schumpeter, a Moravian economist at the University of Graz, publishes his *Theory of Economic Development,* a work that exerts wide influence among economists, especially following its translation into English in 1934.

- The last horse-drawn bus operated by the London General Omnibus Company ends its service in London.

- Traveling by rail and ship, André Jaeger-Schmidt sets a new around-the-world record of thirty-nine days, nineteen hours.

- German novelist Thomas Mann publishes *Death in Venice.*

- French artist Georges Braque, one of the founders of Cubism, paints *Man with a Guitar.*

Apr. The Chinese Revolution begins in Szechwan province, sparked by the belief that foreigners dominate the Manchu (Ch'ing) dynasty. By the end of the year fourteen other provinces join the rebellion.

15 May The British House of Commons adopts the Parliament Act, which strips the House of Lords of its ability to veto legislation.

25 May Porfirio Díaz resigns as president of Mexico. Francisco Madero is elected to replace Díaz and takes office on 6 November.

21 June   The SS *Olympic,* the pride of the British White Star Line, arrives in New York City on its maiden voyage. The 892-foot vessel, which can accommodate twenty-five hundred passengers, is the largest ocean liner yet constructed and is the first to have a swimming pool.

22 Aug.   Leonardo da Vinci's masterpiece the *Mona Lisa* is stolen from the Louvre in Paris. It is recovered four months later in Florence, Italy.

Sept.   One hundred thousand people are killed when the Yangtze River overflows its banks.

9 Sept.   Italy declares war on the Ottoman Empire.

14 Sept.   Russian prime minister Pëtr Arkadevich Stolypin is wounded by Mordkha Bogrov, a revolutionary assassin, while attending the opera; he dies four days later from his injuries. The assassination was witnessed by Czar Nicholas II and two of his daughters. Stolypin had acquired many enemies as a result of his repressive policies. On 19 September the czar appointed Vladimir Kokovstev prime minister.

5 Oct.   Italian forces capture Tripoli after bombarding the North African city.

10 Oct.   Chinese imperial troops mutiny at Wu-ch'ang, the capital of Hukwang province.

26 Oct.   A republic is declared in China, bringing to an end nearly three centuries of rule by the Manchu dynasty. Fighting between Republicans and the Imperial Army continues, after Yüan Shih-k'ai returns from exile to assume leadership of the Republican army.

1 Nov.   The Italo-Turkish War becomes the occasion for the first aerial bombardment in history when Italian planes strike an oasis on the Tripoli coast.

5 Nov.   Italy annexes Cyrenaica and Tripolitania, an action Constantinople refuses to recognize. The war continues into 1912.

Dec.   The National Insurance Bill, which includes provisions for unemployment and health insurance for British workers, is passed by Parliament.

4 Dec.   An armistice is declared in China.

6 Dec.   Mongolia is declared a protectorate of Russia after its declaration of independence from China on 18 November.

14 Dec.   An expedition led by Norwegian explorer Roald Amundsen reaches the South Pole. A rival party led by Robert Falcon Scott of Great Britain arrives at the South Pole five weeks later; all five members of Scott's party die on the return trip.

1912

- Fokker Aircraft is founded by Dutch aviation designer Anthony Herman Gerard Fokker.

- German meteorologist Alfred Lothar Wegener postulates the theory of continental drift to explain the movement of the earth's crust. The theory is largely rejected until the 1960s.

- Rowenta, a German firm, introduces the first electric iron.

- French painter Marcel Duchamp completes one of his best-known and most controversial works, *Nude Descending a Staircase.*

- Swiss psychologist Carl Jung publishes *Theory of Psychoanalysis.*

- German poet Rainer Maria Rilke publishes the first collection of his *Duino Elegies,* a work he finally completes in 1922.

- An International Radio-Telegraph Conference adopts the Morse code signal SOS — three dots, three dashes, three dots — as a universal signal of distress.

1 Jan. Sun Yat-sen is made provisional president of the Republic of China.

12 Feb. Hsüan t'ung, the boy emperor of China, abdicates.

14 Feb. Sun Yat-sen resigns as president of China.

7 Mar. Henri Semiet completes the first nonstop flight from Paris to London.

10 Mar. Yüan Shih-k'ai becomes president of China.

13 Mar. Bulgaria and Serbia form an alliance against the Ottoman Empire, weakened by its ongoing war with Italy. The alliance is the first step toward the Balkan revolt that erupts in war in October.

30 Mar. The Treaty of Fez makes most of Morocco a French protectorate with Rabat as its capital.

13 Apr. The Royal Flying Corps, predecessor of the Royal Air Force, is established in Great Britain.

14–15 Apr. The British White Star liner *Titanic,* on its maiden voyage from Southampton to New York, strikes an iceberg in the North Atlantic and sinks within hours, despite the widely held belief that the ship is unsinkable. The ship has inadequate lifeboats for the 2,200 passengers and crew, 1,517 of whom drown. Seven hundred survivors are rescued by the *Carpathia,* whose radio operator had picked up distress signals from the sinking vessel.

1 May *L'Après-Midi d'un Faune* (Afternoon of the Faun), a ballet by Russian dancer Vaslav Nijinsky, premieres in Paris.

5 May The first issue of the revolutionary journal *Pravda* (Truth) is published in Saint Petersburg, Russia.

**5 May–
22 July** The fifth summer games of the modern Olympiad are held in Stockholm, Sweden. More than twenty-five hundred athletes from twenty-eight countries participate.

14 May	Frederik VIII, king of Denmark, dies and is succeeded by his son Christian X.
22 July	The British admiralty recalls its warships from the Mediterranean and sends them to the North Sea in response to Germany's growing naval presence there.
30 July	Japanese emperor Mutsuhito dies and is succeeded by his son Yoshihito, who rules Japan until 1926.
Aug.	Several parliamentary factions unite in China to form the National People's Party, or Kuomintang, under the titular leadership of Sun Yat-sen. Endorsing democratic principles, the party wins a majority in the assembly in the elections of 1912 and 1913, but it is repressed later in 1913.
1 Aug.	Airmail service is initiated between London and Paris.
7 Aug.	Japan and Russia reach an agreement on their mutual spheres of influence in Manchuria and Mongolia.
28 Sept.	In response to the British Liberal Party endorsement of home rule for Ireland, conservative Irish and British political parties sign the Ulster Covenant of Resistance in Belfast.
8 Oct.	Montenegro declares war on the Ottoman Empire and is joined by Serbia and Bulgaria nine days later.
14 Oct.	The Ottoman Turks invade Serbia. By the end of the month Turkish forces are in full-scale retreat.
18 Oct.	Italy and the Ottoman Empire sign a treaty at Ouchy, Switzerland, recognizing Italian control of Tripoli and Cyrenaica.
28 Nov.	Albania declares its independence from the Ottoman Empire. The new Albanian state is recognized by the Treaty of London in 1913.
4 Dec.	The Turks agree to an armistice with Bulgaria and Serbia, but Greece refuses to participate.

1913

- French author Marcel Proust publishes *Du Côte de chez Swann* (Swann's Way), the first volume of his seven-volume modernist novel sequence *A la Recherche du Temps Perdu* (Remembrance of Things Past).

- British novelist D. H. Lawrence publishes *Sons and Lovers,* a novel whose open treatment of sexual themes creates a storm of controversy.

- John Henry Mears, a reporter for the *New York Evening Sun,* sets a new round-the-world record of thirty-five days, twenty-one hours.

23 Jan.	A coup by the nationalist Young Turks ousts Kiamil Pasha and replaces him with Mahmud Shevket Pasha as grand vizier of the Ottoman Empire.
23 Feb.	Francisco Madero, who had been deposed as president of Mexico the week before in a coup led by Victoriano Huerta, is executed, presumably at the behest of Huerta.
6 Mar.	Hostilities flare up again in the Balkans when Greek forces capture Janina and take thirty-two thousand Turks prisoner.

20 Mar.   King George of Greece is assassinated in Salonika and is succeeded by his oldest son, Constantine.

3 Apr.   Radical British suffragist Emmeline Pankhurst is sentenced to three years in prison for inciting arson. She has claimed responsibility for planting a bomb in the home of Chancellor of the Exchequer David Lloyd George. She and other imprisoned suffragists launch a series of hunger strikes, but woman suffrage is again defeated in the House of Commons on 6 May.

8 Apr.   The first parliament in Chinese history opens in Beijing.

26 Apr.   The International Women's Peace Conference opens at The Hague, drawing women from around the world who are concerned by militarism and heightened international tensions in the Balkans and elsewhere.

29 May   Igor Stravinsky's ballet *The Rites of Spring* premieres in Paris, where its modernist dissonance outrages audiences.

30 May   The Treaty of London ends the Balkan conflict. Signatories include Great Britain, Russia, Italy, and Germany, all of whom — with the exception of Great Britain — have taken sides in the conflict.

6 June   The Reichstag passes a measure increasing the size of the German army.

11 June   Mahmud Shevket Pasha, who has recently become grand vizier of the Ottoman Empire, is assassinated.

20 June   Under the terms of the Native Land Act, whites are given possession of more than 80 percent of the land in South Africa, despite the fact that blacks outnumber whites four to one.

24 June   Greece and Serbia end their alliance with Bulgaria because of a border controversy they are unable to resolve.

29 June   Women are granted equal electoral rights in Norway, which thus becomes the first European nation to enact permanent universal suffrage for women.

30 June   Bulgaria attacks Serbia and Greece. The next day Serbia and Greece declare war on Bulgaria.

8 July   Under pressure from western powers, China recognizes the independence of Mongolia.

11 July   Romania declares war on Bulgaria and launches an invasion.

15 July   The British House of Lords rejects a measure granting Ireland home rule.

10 Aug.   The latest outbreak of hostilities in the Balkans is ended by the Treaty of Bucharest.

1 Sept.   Kuomintang forces in China stage an unsuccessful uprising against the repressive measures of Yüan Shih-k'ai's government. In October Yüan is reelected by an intimidated parliament.

23 Sept.   French aviator Roland Garros lands in Tunis, completing the first flight across the Mediterranean Sea.

10 Oct.   The Panama Canal opens.

11 Oct.	Victoriano Huerta, president of Mexico, declares himself dictator.
15 Nov.	Forces led by Mexican rebel Pancho Villa capture Ciudad Juarez, near the U.S.-Mexico border.

1914

- The epic seventy-year immigration of millions of Europeans to the Americas largely comes to an end. Between 1845 and 1914 approximately forty-one million immigrants have settled in North and South America, thirty-three million of them in the United States alone. Despite this exodus the population of Europe has risen by two hundred million during the same time period.

- Irish novelist and short-story writer James Joyce publishes *Dubliners* and *A Portrait of the Artist as a Young Man*.

13 Apr.	British playwright Bernard Shaw's *Pygmalion* premieres in London.
21 Apr.	U.S. Marines occupy the Mexican port city of Veracruz after officials there refused to order a twenty-one-gun salute to the American flag. U.S. ships have been enforcing a naval blockade of Mexico in order to force the ouster of Mexican dictator Victoriano Huerta, who resigns on 15 July and is replaced in August by Venustiano Carranza.
May	Yüan Shih-k'ai establishes himself as virtual dictator of China.
25 May	A bill granting home rule to Ireland (with a six-year exemption granted for the mostly Protestant province of Ulster) is passed by the British Parliament. The act is suspended with the outbreak of World War I, however, and none of its provisions are ever put into operation.
29 May	A Canadian steamship sinks in the Saint Lawrence River after a collision with another vessel. More than one thousand passengers and crew are killed.
28 June	Archduke Franz Ferdinand, heir to the throne of the Austro-Hungarian Empire, and his wife are assassinated in Sarajevo by Serbian nationalist Gavrilo Princip. Austria-Hungary responds by demanding that Serbia accept an ultimatum that would severely limit its sovereignty. With German backing, Austria-Hungary rejects an attempt by Great Britain to mediate the dispute.
28 July	World War I, or the Great War, begins with Austria-Hungary's declaration of war against Serbia.
30 July	Russia mobilizes its army in support of Serbia.
1 Aug.	When Russia refuses to accept a German demand to stop mobilization, Germany declares war on Russia. Switzerland, Sweden, Norway, and Denmark declare their neutrality.
2 Aug.	Germany, having occupied tiny Luxembourg, demands that Belgium allow the passage of troops across its territory, despite a Belgian declaration of neutrality.

3 Aug.	Germany declares war on France and launches an offensive through Belgium the following day.
4 Aug.	In response to Germany's violation of Belgian neutrality, Great Britain declares war on Germany. The United States declares its neutrality, and its 5 August offer to mediate the widening conflict is ignored.
5 Aug.	Montenegro declares war on Austria-Hungary.
6 Aug.	Austria-Hungary declares war on Russia.
8 Aug.	French and British troops mount an offensive against the German army in Lorraine.
12 Aug.	France and Great Britain declare war on Austria-Hungary. Italy is the only major European nation not yet engaged in the conflict.
18 Aug.	Russian forces attack Galicia (in present-day Poland).
20 Aug.	The Anglo-French offensive in Lorraine and along the Franco-Belgian border stalls. Brussels, the capital of Belgium, falls to the Germans, who capture the Belgian city of Namur on the same day, clearing the way for a German invasion of France.
	Pope Pius X dies and is later succeeded by Benedict XV.
23 Aug.	Japan declares war on Germany and attacks Tsingtao, a German-controlled city in the Chinese province of Chiao Hsien.
26–29 Aug.	After fierce fighting along the eastern front, Russian forces led by Grand Duke Nicholas suffer a disastrous defeat in the Battle of Tannenberg at the hands of a German army led by Paul von Hindenburg. The Germans lose 13,000 men; 30,000 Russians are killed or missing, and 92,000 Russian troops are taken prisoner.
28 Aug.	The war at sea begins when the Royal Navy sinks three German cruisers and two destroyers off Helgoland Bight in the North Sea.
29 Aug.	An expeditionary force from New Zealand captures German Samoa and three weeks later takes German New Guinea.
5 Sept.	Russia, Great Britain, and France create a formal alliance against Germany and Austria-Hungary.
6–9 Sept.	The German advance across northern France is halted by an Allied victory in the first Battle of the Marne, north of Paris. French troops are still unable to advance substantially, and, with the Germans unable to take Paris, a nearly stationary western front is established just one month into the conflict.
7–14 Sept.	Russian troops are defeated by German forces in the first Battle of Masurian Lakes, in what is now northeastern Poland.
12 Sept.	Russian forces capture Lemberg, the provincial capital of Galicia.

18 Sept. The German army retreats after intense fighting along the Aisne River in northern France. Following this battle, each side tries to outflank the other in an attempt to control access to the sea. The Germans are prevented from advancing beyond Ypres near the Franco-Belgian border.

1 Oct. Thirty thousand Canadian troops set sail for Europe to join the fighting. Other parts of the British Empire — Australia, New Zealand, and India — also contribute substantial numbers of troops.

10 Oct. The Belgian coastal town of Antwerp is captured by German forces, raising fears in Great Britain of a cross-channel invasion.

21 Oct. In a battle typical of the fighting along the western front during the early months of the war, British, French, and German forces spar at Ypres, launching a monthlong battle that ends in stalemate with 250,000 casualties.

30 Oct. The Ottoman Empire declares war on Russia and Great Britain.

3 Nov. Russia declares war on Turkey after the Ottomans, who are allied with Germany, allowed German naval vessels to enter the Black Sea.

5 Nov. Great Britain declares war on Turkey.

12 Nov. Louis Botha puts down a Boer revolt in South Africa that had been sparked by Boer opposition to an attack on German troops in neighboring South-West Africa.

2 Dec. The Austrians capture the Serbian capital, Belgrade, but the Serbs retake it a month later.

11 Dec. The Royal Navy wins another decisive naval victory when it sinks four German cruisers off the Falkland Islands in the South Atlantic without suffering any losses.

16 Dec. Great Britain establishes a protectorate over Egypt.

1915

- Polish novelist Joseph Conrad, living in England, publishes *Victory.*

- British novelist W. Somerset Maugham publishes *Of Human Bondage.*

- Austrian novelist Franz Kafka publishes *The Metamorphosis.*

- Japanese writer Ryunosuke Akutagawa publishes *Rashomon.*

- Turkey attempts to force the entire population of Armenia to move to Syria and Mesopotamia. The resulting genocide takes the lives of hundreds of thousands of Armenians.

13 Jan. Twenty-nine thousand people are killed during an earthquake in central Italy.

24 Jan. An outmatched German squadron is defeated by the Royal Navy in the Battle of Dogger Bank. British battle cruisers sink the armored cruiser *Blucher,* and nearly two thousand German sailors perish.

18 Feb. Using its force of deadly submarines (U-boats), Germany launches a naval blockade of France and the British Isles, announced on 2 February. German submarine commanders are ordered to fire without warning on any ship attempting to break the blockade, including merchant vessels and passenger liners.

Feb.–
Nov. German and Austrian forces slowly push Russian troops eastward through Poland. By November the German army has pushed the eastern front behind Russia's pre-1800 borders.

1 Mar. In retaliation for Germany's inclusion of foodstuffs in its naval blockade of Britain and France, Great Britain announces a complete blockade of Germany, which includes seizure of neutral ships carrying food to German ports.

22 Mar. The Russian advance is stopped by German troops at the Battle of Przemysl.

22 Apr.–
25 May At the second Battle of Ypres poison gas is used for the first time in World War I when German troops fire mortar shells filled with chlorine gas into the French lines. The battle ends indecisively, though Allied casualties are twice those suffered by the Germans.

25 Apr. In an attempt to capture the strategic Dardanelles Straits from Turkey, Allied troops (including French, British, Australian, and New Zealand forces) land at Gallipoli. Despite earlier bombardment by British naval forces, Turkish troops under Mustafa Kemal hold firm through nine months of brutal fighting, with 50,000 Allied casualties and 250,000 Turkish soldiers killed or wounded.

26 Apr. In London, Russia, Great Britain, and France conclude a series of secret treaties that establish a plan for dividing the postwar spoils. England is to receive most of Germany's colonial holdings; Russia is to have Poland and Constantinople; and France is to extend eastward to the Rhine. The existence of the treaties is kept secret to avoid antagonizing the United States and to preserve the fiction that the Allies are fighting an exclusively defensive war.

7 May A German submarine torpedoes and sinks without warning the British passenger liner *Lusitania,* en route from New York to Liverpool, eight miles off the coast of Ireland. Nearly 1,200 of the 1,806 passengers and crew die, including 128 Americans. The Wilson administration issues a protest, demanding reparations and a pledge that such an attack will not occur again. Germany claims that the ship was carrying munitions. (It is later learned that the cargo included rifles and ammunition.) The attack deepens anti-German feelings in the United States.

23 May In accordance with a treaty signed with the Allies the previous month, Italy declares war on Austria, in return for an Allied promise that Italy will be given Italian-speaking territories in the South Tirol, as well as the city of Trieste, at the end of the war.

25 May In the face of a threatened Japanese invasion, Chinese president Yüan Shih-k'ai accepts the conditions laid down in Japan's Twenty-One Demands of 18 January. The terms expand Japanese commercial and political privileges in China and seriously erode Chinese sovereignty.

The British Liberal and Conservative Parties enter into a coalition government for the duration of the war, with Herbert Asquith staying on as prime minister.

Austrian forces bombard Venice, Italy.

1 June	Germany launches the first of its zeppelin airship raids over London and eastern England, without significant success and at considerable risk to the crews of the airships, which are filled with highly flammable hydrogen gas.
23 June	Italy launches an offensive in hopes of capturing Trieste from the Austrians, but in four battles along the Isonzo River the Italians fail to make headway and suffer 250,000 casualties.
5 Aug.	Warsaw is captured by Austrian and German armies.
30 Aug.	In continued fighting along the eastern front, the Russian fortress at Brest Litovsk is taken by the Germans.
5 Sept.	After watching his army suffer a series of humiliating defeats, Czar Nicholas II takes personal command of the Russian army.
22 Sept.	Allied troops begin an offensive in Artois and Champagne, in northern France. The British capture Loos, a mining town, but suffer 60,000 casualties. The French sustain 145,000 killed or wounded.
6 Oct.	Germany and Austria invade Serbia, driving the Serbian army across Albania and onto the island of Corfu.
14 Oct.	Bulgaria joins the war on the side of the Central Powers when it declares war on Serbia. In return the Central Powers promise Bulgaria Turkish territory according to the terms of the Treaty of Pless, signed on 6 October.
21 Oct.	The first transatlantic radiotelephone call — between Arlington, Virginia, and Paris — is made.
29 Oct.	Socialist Aristide Briand becomes prime minister of France following the resignation of René Viviani.
14 Nov.	Czech nationalist Tomás Masaryk calls for the establishment of a Czech national council as a first step toward independence.
21 Nov.	A British invasion of the Ottoman Empire from India is halted at the Battle of Ctesiphon, near Baghdad.
25 Nov.	Physicist Albert Einstein extends his Special Theory of Relativity (1905) when he completes his General Theory of Relativity.

1916

- Bolshevik leader V. I. Lenin publishes *Imperialism, the Highest Stage of Capitalism,* expanding on ideas first expressed by British liberal John Hobson in his *Imperialism* (1902).

- Edward A. Sharpey-Schafer, an English physiologist, coins the name *insulin* for a hormone produced by the pancreas.

24 Jan.	Great Britain adopts compulsory military service, with exceptions for conscientious objectors.
21 Feb.	German troops begin a major offensive against Allied positions at Verdun, on the Meuse River in northern France. This battle becomes the longest battle of the war, lasting until December and claiming 435,000 German casualties and more than 540,000 French casualties.
5 Mar.	The Allies invade German East Africa.

8 Mar. Mexican rebel Pancho Villa raids Columbus, New Mexico. In retaliation Woodrow Wilson orders U.S. troops commanded by John J. Pershing to pursue Villa into Mexico. The troops are withdrawn in February 1917, having failed to capture Villa.

9 Mar. Germany declares war on Portugal.

Great Britain and France sign the Sykes-Picot Agreement, dividing Asiatic Turkey between them.

24 Mar. A German U-boat sinks the French vessel *Sussex.* Three Americans are among those killed. The incident provokes yet another protest from Secretary of State Robert Lansing and worsens German-American relations.

14 Apr. Allied forces bombard the ancient city of Constantinople in Turkey.

25 Apr. The Easter Uprising begins in Dublin. Sinn Fein leader Patrick Pearse proclaims an Irish Republic, but the attempt to end British rule in Ireland ends in failure a week later, with 450 rebels dead, 2,000 taken prisoner, and 100 casualties among the British troops who put down the rebellion. Pearse is executed by firing squad on 3 May.

29 Apr. After enduring a 143-day siege, British troops at Kut-al-Imara, in present-day Iraq, surrender to the Turks.

May Bowing to protests from the United States, Germany temporarily revokes its order to fire on any ship attempting to break the German naval blockade of Great Britain and France.

12 May James Connolly is the last of the seven leaders of the Easter Uprising to be executed by the British in Dublin.

15 May Austria attacks Italian troops in the Trentino, along the Italo-Austrian border; the assault stalls at Asiago on 17 June.

31 May Both Great Britain and Germany claim victory in one of the epic sea battles of the war, off Jutland (Denmark). The Royal Navy has lost seven ships and close to seven thousand men, while Germany has lost three ships and twenty-three hundred sailors. After this battle Germany keeps most of its fleet in port, surrendering supremacy of the seas, with the exception of submarine warfare, to the British.

6 June Chinese president Yüan Shih-k'ai dies.

23 June The Russians begin an offensive that results in the reconquest of most of Galicia.

24 June The German army initiates a new offensive at Verdun, the scene of some of the bloodiest fighting of the war.

1 July The Allies launch an offensive along the Somme in northeastern France. By the end of the battle in November the Allies had advanced several miles, but failed to achieve a breakthrough. The Germans sustained 650,000 casualties, the French 195,000, and the British 420,000.

9 Aug. Italian troops capture Gorizia (in present-day northeastern Italy).

24 Aug. German socialist leader Karl Liebknecht is jailed for his role in organizing anti-war protests.

27 Aug.	Italy declares war on Germany; Romania declares war on Austria; and Germany declares war on Romania.
	Paul von Hindenburg, hero of the Battle of Tannenberg, is named chief of the German general staff.
Sept.	Tanks are used for the first time in warfare, when the Allies deploy them against German positions in the Battle of the Somme.
3 Sept.	Dar es Salaam falls to the British.
10 Sept.	The Allies begin an offensive in Salonika, Greece.
16 Sept.	German reinforcements of the Austrian army prevent Russia from retaking Lemberg, the provincial capital of Galicia.
	France and Britain recognize a provisional government of Czechoslovakia.
27 Sept.	Greece declares war on Bulgaria, which has declared war on Romania.
17 Oct.	The Allies occupy Athens, and extend official recognition to the rebel provisional government of Eleuthérios Venizélos.
24 Oct.	In fighting at Verdun, French soldiers break through the German lines along a four-mile front.
5 Nov.	In an attempt to establish a buffer between their territory and Russia, Germany and Austria recognize the independence of "Congress" Poland, which had been under Russian rule.
21 Nov.	Emperor Franz Josef, who had ruled the Austro-Hungarian empire since 1848, dies.
7 Dec.	Liberal Party leader David Lloyd George becomes prime minister of Great Britain.
30 Dec.	Russian mystic Rasputin, confidant of Czarina Alexandra of Russia, is murdered.

1917

- Expatriate American poet T. S. Eliot publishes *Prufrock and Other Observations.*

- Guillaume Apollinaire invents the term *Surrealism* to describe art that questions traditional concepts of form, composition, and taste.

- The art journal *De Stijl* is founded by Dutch painter Piet Mondrian.

27 Jan.	The president of Costa Rica is deposed by a military coup, an unusual event on that nation's otherwise peaceful democratic political tradition.
1 Feb.	Germany announces its resumption of unrestricted submarine warfare, which it had suspended in hopes of keeping the United States from entering the war on the side of the Allies.
3 Feb.	In response to the German resumption of unrestricted submarine warfare, the United States breaks off diplomatic relations with Germany. Bolivia, Peru, and Brazil follow suit.

5 Feb.   The Mexican government of President Venustiano Carranza adopts a reformist constitution, promising to end centuries of feudal relations between powerful landowners and peasants in Mexico.

8 Mar.   The Russian Revolution of 1917 begins when rioting and strikes — protesting wartime food shortages and continued Russian participation in the war — erupt in Petrograd (Saint Petersburg). Many of the troops dispatched to quell the rioting mutiny.

11 Mar.   British troops capture Baghdad, capital of present-day Iraq.

12 Mar.   The Russian Duma (parliament) establishes a provisional government, despite Czar Nicholas II's decree disbanding the Duma.

16 Mar.   Czar Nicholas II abdicates the Russian throne, ending three centuries of Romanov rule.

27 Mar.   British troops rout Turkish forces in heavy fighting near Gaza.

6 Apr.   President Woodrow Wilson signs a declaration of war on Germany, bringing the United States into World War I as a combatant against the Central Powers.

16 Apr.   Allied forces initiate an offensive against German units defending the Hindenburg line along the Aisne River.

17 Apr.   Bolshevik leader Vladimir Lenin returns to Russia from a three-year exile in Switzerland and calls for the transfer of state power from the provisional government to workers' soviets. Germany has facilitated Lenin's return to Russia, on a sealed train, hoping that he would foment rebellion and lead Russia to sue for a separate peace.

3 May   Canadian troops capture the Vimy Ridge, bringing to a close the third Battle of Arras.

4 June   Brazil declares war on Germany and seizes German vessels docked in Brazilian ports.

8 June   British forces take the Messines Ridge, south of Ypres.

12 June   King Constantine of Greece, who has allied himself with the Central Powers and has dismissed the pro-Allied government of Venizélos, abdicates the throne under pressure from Allied governments.

16 June   The Congress of Soviets begins in Russia, bringing together Bolshevik leaders from across Russia.

17 June   The British royal family, the House of Saxe-Coburg, renounces its ties to its German relatives and becomes the House of Windsor.

26 June   The first contingent of the American Expeditionary Forces lands in France, commanded by Gen. John J. "Black Jack" Pershing.

29 June   The Ukraine declares its independence from Russia.

6 July   British commander Thomas Edward Lawrence (Lawrence of Arabia) leads a daring and successful attack on Aqaba, capturing the city from the Turks.

14 July   In a move engineered by the German military, Theobold von Bethmann-Hollweg is replaced as chancellor of Germany by Georg Michaelis.

Finland declares its independence from Russia.

16 July   The provisional government of Russia puts down a Bolshevik rebellion, forcing Lenin to flee to Finland to avoid arrest.

17 July   Catholic pilgrims flock to Fátima in Portugal following reports that the Virgin Mary has appeared to several children there.

20 July   Aleksandr Kerensky is named prime minister of the Russian provisional government.

25 July   Mata Hari, an enchanting Dutch dancer, is convicted of spying and is sentenced to death in Paris.

20 Aug.   French troops break through German lines along an eleven-mile front at Verdun.

15 Sept.   Aleksandr Kerensky proclaims Russia a republic.

17 Sept.   Russian troops are routed from Riga, Latvia, on the Baltic Sea by the German army, further unsettling Kerensky's provisional government.

24 Oct.   The Battle of Caporetto begins on the Italian front with an offensive launched by combined German and Austrian forces that drives the Italian army back to the Piave River, inflicting heavy casualties. The advance is halted only after French and British reinforcements arrive. The Italians suffer 320,000 casualties.

6 Nov.   The third Battle of Ypres, in Flanders, ends when Canadian forces capture the town of Passchendaele.

7 Nov.   In a coup led by the Bolsheviks under Vladimir Lenin, Kerensky's provisional government is ousted in Russia. This coup becomes known as the October Revolution because it occurred on 26 October under the Old Style Russian calendar.

9 Nov.   British foreign secretary Arthur Balfour announces plans for a postwar Jewish homeland in Palestine.

16 Nov.   Moscow falls to Bolshevik troops.

17 Nov.   British troops take Jaffa in Palestine.

5 Dec.   Germany and Russia reach agreement on an armistice at Brest Litovsk.

6 Dec.   A collision between a French munitions vessel and a Belgian relief ship in the harbor at Halifax, Nova Scotia, causes an explosion that kills more than sixteen hundred people and levels a large part of the city.

7 Dec.   The United States declares war on Austria.

9 Dec.   British troops capture Jerusalem.

22 Dec.   The Bolshevik government in Russia opens peace talks with Austria and Germany.

1918

- In the worst medical catastrophe since the plague of the fourteenth century, a pandemic of Spanish influenza sweeps the globe, killing more than twenty-one million people, in excess of 1 percent of the world's population. By the time it ends in November 1918, World War I has claimed the lives of another ten million people.

- Spanish fiction writer Vicente Blasco Ibáñez publishes his popular novel *The Four Horsemen of the Apocalypse.*

- British writer Lytton Strachey satirizes cherished myths of Victorian England in *Eminent Victorians.*

18 Jan. Lenin dissolves the Russian Constituent Assembly and proclaims a dictatorship of the proletariat.

6 Feb. Married women older than the age of thirty are granted the right to vote in Great Britain. The same act also removes property requirements as qualifications for suffrage.

24 Feb. Estonia declares its independence from Russia.

3 Mar. The Soviet Union and the Central Powers sign the Treaty of Brest Litovsk, ending hostilities among the signatories and ceding much Russian territory in eastern Europe to the Central Powers. The terms of the treaty are annulled when the Allies and the Central Powers sign the armistice of 11 November.

Allied troops land in Murmansk, in northwestern Russia, claiming that they are there to prevent war materiel from falling into German hands.

5 Mar. The capital of the Soviet Union is moved from Petrograd to Moscow.

21 Mar. A German offensive marks the start of the second Battle of the Somme. The Germans hope to achieve a major advance before fresh American troops arrive at the front in significant numbers. By 5 April the Germans have advanced forty miles, but they are halted before they reach Arras or Amiens.

26 Mar. Ferdinand Foch is appointed supreme commander of the Allied forces in Europe.

1 Apr. The Royal Air Force is created as a branch of the British armed forces.

22 Apr. The Soviet government institutes state control over all foreign trade with Russia.

7 May Having been defeated by the German army, Romania signs the Treaty of Bucharest with the Central Powers.

19 May Five hundred members of Sinn Fein are imprisoned by the British.

27 May In the third battle of the Aisne River, German troops push back Allied forces to capture bridges near Chemin des Dames. To the north, American troops dislodge the Germans in the Battle of Cantigny and by the end of June have extended their gains in the Battle of Belleau Wood.

16 July Czar Nicholas II and his family are executed by local Bolsheviks in the provincial town of Ekaterinburg, in the Ural Mountains. The local authorities have feared that the czar might be liberated by anti-Bolshevik "White Guards."

3 Aug. Allied troops occupy Archangel. They remain on Russian soil until 1920, providing support to the "White Guards."

8 Aug.	In fighting near Amiens, in northern France, the Allies launch an offensive against German troops holding the Paris-Amiens railway. On 10 August they recapture Montdidier.
15 Aug.	The United States ends diplomatic relations with the Soviet Union.
12 Sept.	American troops take the German salient at Saint-Mihiel.
18 Sept.	Great Britain launches its last offensive of the war against the Turks, resulting in the capture of Beirut and Damascus in October.
30 Sept.	Bulgaria surrenders to the Allies.
3 Oct.	In response to growing public unrest over a string of military defeats, Prince Max of Baden is named chancellor of Germany.
4 Oct.	The Austrian foreign minister signals the willingness of Austria-Hungary to sue for peace under the terms laid down in Woodrow Wilson's "Fourteen Points." In November an Allied armistice with Austria-Hungary goes into effect.
6 Oct.	Poland is declared an independent republic, but Russian troops cross into Polish territory as the German army retreats.
15 Oct.	The independence of Czechoslovakia is proclaimed.
17 Oct.	Hungary declares itself independent of Austria.
24 Oct.	In the Battle of Vittorio Veneto, Italian and British troops drive the remaining Austrian forces from Italian territory.
31 Oct.	The Ottoman Empire surrenders, and the Dardenelles are reopened to Allied shipping.
9 Nov.	Kaiser William II abdicates at the insistence of German chancellor Prince Max of Baden, who resigns on the same day. He is replaced by Friedrich Ebert.
11 Nov.	At 11 A.M. an armistice goes into effect, ending the fighting in World War I. Under terms of the armistice Germany agrees to surrender its weapons and withdraw its remaining troops to the eastern side of the Rhine.
12 Nov.	The last of the Hapsburg emperors, Charles I, renounces his throne as ruler of Austria and Hungary.
14 Nov.	Tomás Masaryk is elected first president of the Czech republic.
16 Nov.	Hungary becomes a republic, led by Mihály Károlyi.
18 Nov.	The Republic of Latvia is declared at Riga.
24 Nov.	Representatives of Bosnia, Dalmatia, Croatia, Macedonia, Montenegro, Serbia, and Slovenia proclaim themselves one independent nation. Its boundaries are established by the Treaty of Paris (1920), and in 1931 it takes the name Yugoslavia.
1 Dec.	Iceland is granted independent status by Denmark but remains nominally under the Danish crown.

1919

- British economist John Maynard Keynes publishes *The Economic Consequences of the Peace.*

- Siegfried Sassoon publishes *War Poems.* Sassoon, who was awarded the Military Cross for his service in combat in 1917, has thrown his medal into the sea.

- German architect Walter Gropius founds the Bauhaus school in Weimar, Germany, to promote modern ideas of home construction, furnishings, and design.

5 Jan.   Soviet troops occupy Vilnius, Lithuania, and two weeks later capture the city of Kaunas.

16 Jan.   Rosa Luxemburg and Karl Liebknecht, who led a Sparticist (communist) uprising against the German government on 5 January, are murdered by German soldiers in Berlin.

18 Jan.   The Paris Peace Conference begins as representatives of the so-called Big Four — Vittorio Emanuele Orlando of Italy, Woodrow Wilson of the United States, David Lloyd George of Great Britain, and Georges Clemenceau of France — gather at Versailles. Representatives of the defeated Central Powers are excluded from the conference.

21 Jan.   An unofficial Irish Parliament convenes when twenty-five Sinn Fein members of the British Parliament boycott the House of Commons and meet separately in Dublin.

3 Feb.   White Russian armies, fighting to restore czarist government, defeat the Red Army in a series of clashes in the Caucasus. Though White forces advance to within miles of Petrograd and Moscow, they are eventually routed by Red Army troops commanded by Leon Trotsky. Alekandr Kolchak, commander of the Whites, is captured on 7 February 1920 and executed.

6 Feb.   A German National Assembly meeting in Weimar creates the framework for a republican government. A federal constitution is adopted on 31 July, and Friedrich Ebert is chosen as the first president of the Weimar Republic.

1 Mar.   Nationalist groups declare Korean independence from Japan, but they are quickly and violently suppressed by Japanese troops.

3 Mar.   Bolshevik leaders and representatives from other European Communist parties form the Comintern, or Third International, as a means of coordinating international Communist activity.

11 Mar.   The Allies reach an agreement facilitating the delivery of foodstuffs to famine-stricken Germany.

21 Mar.   Hungarian Communist leader Béla Kun seizes power in a coup.

23 Mar.   Benito Mussolini founds a new political party in Italy, the Fasci di Combattimento, to counter both communism and liberalism.

30 Mar.   Acts of civil disobedience led by Indian nationalist Mohandas K. Gandhi begin in India, in protest against continued British rule and reinstatement of repressive wartime measures known as the Defense of India (Rowlatt) Act. These measures have nullified the Government of India Acts, which were adopted by the British Parliament on 18 March and were designed to move India slowly toward a more democratic system of government.

10 Apr.	Mexican revolutionary leader Emiliano Zapata, the leading advocate of land reform in Mexico, is killed by government troops.
13 Apr.	Troops led by Reginald Dyer fire on peaceful protesters in the northern Indian city of Amritsar, killing four hundred and wounding twelve hundred.
20 Apr.	A Polish army led by Józef Piłsudski captures Vilnius and Kaunas. Sporadic fighting between Poland and Russia over control of Lithuania continues until November 1920.
4 May	Students in China initiate the May Fourth Movement, protesting the decision of the Paris Peace Conference to cede control of China's Shantung province to Japan. Under pressure from the student-led movement, the Chinese government refuses to sign the Treaty of Versailles.
21 June	German sailors manning what remains of Germany's once-powerful navy scuttle the fleet at Scapa Flow, off northern Scotland, to prevent it from falling into Allied hands.
28 June	The Treaty of Versailles is signed by the victorious Allied powers in the Hall of Mirrors, bringing World War I to an official end. Under the terms of the treaty Germany cedes territory to France and Poland, accepts strict limits on the size of its military, is forced to pay reparations, and admits its role in starting the conflict. The treaty also creates a League of Nations, which has been advocated by Woodrow Wilson as a means of arbitrating international disputes.
13 July	The first two-way crossing of the Atlantic is completed by a British airship, the *R-34*.
4 Aug.	Romanian troops oust Hungarian leader Béla Kun, ending his 133-day Communist rule.
25 Aug.	The first international daily air service begins between Paris and London.
3 Sept.	Following the death of Louis Botha, Jan Smuts becomes prime minister of South Africa.
10 Sept.	Austria and the Allies sign the Treaty of Saint-Germain, which sets Austria's borders, prohibits its union with Germany, and forces Austria to recognize the independence of Yugoslavia, Czechoslovakia, Hungary, and Poland. Under the terms of the treaty Austria is also required to cede the regions of Trentino, Gorizia, and Istria to Italy.
23 Sept.	Italian poet, aviator, and war hero Gabriele D'Annunzio leads a band of Italian nationalists into territory disputed by Italy and Yugoslavia, seizing the port city of Fiume.
28 Nov.	Nancy, Lady Astor, is elected to the British House of Commons, becoming the first woman in British history to hold a seat in Parliament.
8 Dec.	Continuing his country's 150-year-old border dispute with Russia, Polish leader Józef Piłsudski leads an army into Ukraine and Belarus. The dispute is settled by the Treaty of Riga on 18 March 1921.

CHAPTER TWO

THE ARTS

by CAROLYN KITCH

CONTENTS

1910

Movies
As It Is in Life, directed by D. W. Griffith, starring Mary Pickford; *Dr. Lafleur's Theory,* starring Maurice Costello and Clara Kimball Young; *The Fire Chief's Daughter,* starring Kathlyn Williams; *His Trust/His Trust Fulfilled,* directed by D. W. Griffith; *In the Days of the Thundering Herd,* starring Tom Mix; *A Romance of the Western Hills,* directed by D. W. Griffith, starring Mary Pickford; *The Saloon Next Door; Ye Vengeful Vagabonds.*

Fiction
Mary Austin, *The Basket Woman;* Finley Peter Dunne, *Mr. Dooley Says;* Hamlin Garland, *Other Main-Travelled Roads;* Joel Chandler Harris, *Uncle Remus and the Little Boy;* O. Henry, *Strictly Business;* Robert Herrick, *A Life for a Life;* Henry James, *The Finer Grain;* Owen Johnson, *The Varmint;* Jack London, *Burning Daylight;* Clarence Mulford, *Hopalong Cassidy;* David Graham Phillips, *The Husband's Story;* Anne Douglas Sedgwick, *Franklin Winslow Kane;* Edith Wharton, *Tales of Men and Ghosts.*

Verse
Robert Underwood Johnson, *Saint-Gaudens, an Ode;* Edwin Arlington Robinson, *The Town Down the River.*

Popular Songs
"Ah, Sweet Mystery of Life," by Victor Herbert; "Any Little Girl That's a Nice Little Girl Is the Right Little Girl for Me," by Fred Fisher and Thomas Gray; "Call Me Up Some Rainy Afternoon," by Irving Berlin; "Come, Josephine, in My Flying Machine," by Fred Fisher and Alfred Bryan; "Down by the Old Mill Stream," by Tell Taylor; "Dynamite Rag," by Russel Robinson; "Every Girl Loves Me but the Girl I Love," by Herbert Ingraham and Beth Slater Whitson; "Grizzly Bear," by Irving Berlin; "Heaven Will Protect the Working Girl," by A. Baldwin Sloane; "Hilarity Rag," by James Scott; "I'm Falling in Love with Someone," by Victor Herbert and Rida Johnson Young; "Let Me Call You Sweetheart," by Leo Friedman and Beth Slater Whitson; "Lovey Joe," by Joe Jordan; "Play that Barber Shop Chord," by Lewis F. Muir and William Tracey; "Put Your Arms Around Me, Honey," by Albert Von Tilzer and Junie McCree; "Stoptime Rag," by Scott Joplin; "Under the Yum Yum Tree," by Harry Von Tilzer and Andrew B. Sterling.

* The Poetry Society of America is founded at the National Arts Club in New York City.

28 Feb.
Russian ballerina Anna Pavlova makes her American debut at the Metropolitan Opera House in New York City.

18 Mar.
The Metropolitan Opera presents its first production of an opera by an American composer, Frederick Shepherd Converse's *The Pipe of Desire.*

21 Mar.
Gustav Mahler conducts for the last time at the Metropolitan Opera.

28 Mar.
Pablo Picasso's first one-man show opens at Alfred Stieglitz's 291 gallery in New York City.

1 Apr.
Some two thousand people attend the opening of the Exhibition of Independent Artists in New York City. The show continues through 28 April.

20 June
Fanny Brice makes her debut in the Ziegfeld Follies.

3 Nov.
The Chicago Grand Opera opens with a production of Giuseppe Verdi's *Aida.*

7 Nov.
Victor Herbert's operetta *Naughty Marietta* has its premiere at the New York Theatre.

10 Dec.
In New York City Ruth St. Denis opens in *Egypta,* a play that features the modern dances she has based on traditional Eastern dance forms.

1911

Giacomo Puccini's *La fanciulla del West* (The Girl of the Golden West), based on David Belasco's play of the same name, becomes the first opera to have its world premiere at the Metropolitan Opera House in New York City.

Movies *Artful Kate,* directed by Thomas Ince, starring Mary Pickford; *Bronco Billy's Adventure* and *Enoch Arden,* directed by D. W. Griffith; *The Fisher-Maid,* directed by Thomas Ince, starring Mary Pickford; *From the Manger to the Cross*; *A Girlish Impulse,* starring Florence Lawrence; *In the Sultan's Garden,* directed by Thomas Ince, starring Mary Pickford; *A Knight of the Road,* directed by D. W. Griffith; *The Last Drop of Water,* directed by D. W. Griffith; *The Lonedale Operator,* directed by D. W. Griffith, starring Blanche Sweet; *A Tale of Two Cities.*

Fiction Frances Hodgson Burnett, *The Secret Garden;* Margaret Deland, *The Iron Woman;* Theodore Dreiser, *Jennie Gerhardt;* Edna Ferber, *Dawn O'Hara;* Zona Gale, *Mothers to Men;* Hamlin Garland, *Victor Ollnee's Discipline;* Ellen Glasgow, *The Miller of Old Church;* O. Henry, *Sixes and Sevens;* Robert Herrick, *The Healer;* Owen Johnson, *Stover at Yale;* Mary Johnston, *The Long Roll;* Jack London, *South Sea Tales;* Kathleen Norris, *Mother;* David Graham Phillips, *The Conflict;* Gene Stratton-Porter, *The Harvester;* Edith Wharton, *Ethan Frome;* Harold Bell Wright, *The Winning of Barbara Worth.*

Verse Ezra Pound, *Canzoni;* George Sterling, *The House of Orchids;* Sara Teasdale, *Helen of Troy.*

Popular Songs "Alexander's Ragtime Band," by Irving Berlin; "All Alone," by Harry Von Tilzer and Will Dillon; "Everybody's Doin' It Now," by Irving Berlin; "Felicity Rag," by Scott Hayden; "Hello, Central, Give Me 603," by Harry Von Tilzer; "I Want a Girl Just Like the Girl that Married Dear Old Dad," by Harry Von Tilzer and Will Dillon; "If You Talk in Your Sleep, Don't Mention My Name," by Nat D. Ayer and A. Seymour Brown; "The Little Millionaire," by George M. Cohan; "Moontime Is Spoontime," by Paul Pratt; "Novelty Rag," by May Aufderheide; "Oh, You Beautiful Doll," by Nat D. Ayer and A. Seymour Brown; "The Ragtime Violin," by Irving Berlin; "Red Rose Rag," by Percy Wenrich; "A Ring on the Finger Is Worth Two on the Phone," by George W. Meyer and Jack Mahoney; "Whirlwind Rag," by Russel Robinson.

- The Irish Players from the Abbey Theatre in Dublin tour the United States. Their repertoire includes John Millington Synge's *The Playboy of the Western World.*

- Pennsylvania becomes the first state to create a board of motion-picture censors.

21 Mar. The Winter Garden Theatre opens at Broadway and Fifty-first Street in New York City.

22 Apr. *Variety* reports that vaudeville-theater owner Marcus Loew has secured backing, largely from the Shubert organization, to expand his chain of theaters and equip them for showing movies.

23 May President William Howard Taft dedicates the New York Public Library.

8 Aug. *Pathé's Weekly,* the first newsreel made in America (produced in New Jersey by the French-owned Pathé company), is released and shown in movie theaters.

9 Dec. John Philip Sousa and his band conclude their yearlong world tour with a concert at the five-thousand-seat Hippodrome in New York City.

19 Dec. The Association of American Painters and Sculptors is founded.

1912

Movies *The Bearded Bandit; Custer's Last Raid,* directed by Thomas Ince; *Father's Flirtation; A Feud in the Kentucky Hills,* directed by D. W. Griffith; *A Girl and Her Trust,* directed by D. W. Griffith, starring Mary Pickford; *The Indian Massacre,* directed by Thomas Ince; *Lena and the Geese,* directed by D. W. Griffith, starring Mary Pickford; *The Musketeers of Pig Alley,* directed by D. W. Griffith; *The Old Actor,* directed by D. W. Griffith; *An Unseen Enemy,* directed by D. W. Griffith, starring Lillian Gish; *War on the Plains,* directed by Thomas Ince.

Fiction Mary Austin, *A Woman of Genius;* Willa Cather, *Alexander's Bridge;* Theodore Dreiser, *The Financier;* Sui Sin Far, *Mrs. Spring Fragrance;* Dorothy Canfield Fisher, *The Squirrel-Cage;* Zane Grey, *Riders of the Purple Sage;* James Weldon Johnson, *The Autobiography of an Ex-Colored Man;* Mary Johnston, *Cease Firing;* Jack London, *Smoke Bellew;* David Graham Phillips, *The Price She Paid;* Edith Wharton, *The Reef.*

Verse Robinson Jeffers, *Flagons and Apples;* William Ellery Leonard, *The Vaunt of Man;* Vachel Lindsay, *Rhymes to be Traded for Bread;* Amy Lowell, *A Dome of Many-Coloured Glass;* Ezra Pound, *Ripostes;* Elinor Wylie, *Incidental Numbers.*

Popular Songs "And the Green Grass Grew All Around," by Harry Von Tilzer and William Jerome; "Be My Little Baby Bumble Bee," by Henry I. Marshall and Stanley Murphy; "The Bunny Hug," by Harry Von Tilzer; "Clover Blossoms Rag," by E. J. Stark Jr.; "Everybody Two-Step," by Wallie Herzer and Earl C. Jones; "Hitchy Koo," by Lewis F. Muir, Maurice Abrahams, and L. Wolfe Gilbert; "It's a Long, Long Way to Tipperary," by Jack Judge and Harry H. Williams; "Melancholy (My Melancholy Baby)," by Ernie Burnett and George A. Norton; "On the Eight O'Clock Train," by Russel Robinson; "Scott Joplin's New Rag," by Scott Joplin; "The Sweetheart of Sigma Chi," by Dudleigh Vernor and Byron D. Stokes; "That Demon Rag," by Russell Smith; "That Mysterious Rag," by Irving Berlin; "The Turkey Trot," by Ribe Danmark (J. Bodewalt Lampe); "Waiting for the Robert E. Lee," by Lewis F. Muir and L. Wolfe Gilbert; "When Irish Eyes Are Smiling," by Ernest R. Ball, Chauncey Olcott, and George Graff Jr.; "Wise Old Moon," by Artie Matthews.

- The Little Theater in Chicago and the Toy Theater in Boston, the first influential little theaters in America, are founded.

- A revival of George M. Cohan's 1906 hit musical, *Forty-Five Minutes from Broadway,* opens in New York City.

- The Dramatists Guild is founded in New York City.

14 Mar. Horatio Parker's opera *Mona,* winner of the Metropolitan Opera's $10,000 prize for the best new American opera, has its premiere in New York City.

22 July The first of the Shuberts' annual *Passing Show* musical revues opens at the Winter Garden Theater in New York City.

Aug. Alfred Stieglitz devotes an issue of his periodical *Camera Work* to modern art, including Gertrude Stein's word portraits of Henri Matisse and Pablo Picasso.

1913

1 Sept.　In Los Angeles the one-thousand-seat Walker Theatre opens — a theater devoted exclusively to showing movies (admission prices range from ten to twenty-five cents).

5 Sept.　*Queen Elizabeth,* a French feature film starring Sarah Bernhardt, opens in Marcus Loew's New York City movie theaters — after Loew pays $25,000 for the American rights to the movie.

23 Sept.　The first Keystone Comedy movie, the split-reel *Cohen Collects a Debt* and *The Water Nymph,* directed by Mack Sennett, is released.

The first issue of *Poetry: A Magazine of Verse,* edited by Harriet Monroe, is published in Chicago, with expatriate Ezra Pound as overseas editor. The magazine is dedicated to publishing the work of American poets.

Movies　*The Adventures of Kathlyn* (serial), starring Kathlyn Williams; *The Battle of Gettysburg,* directed by Thomas Ince; *Caprice,* starring Mary Pickford; *In the Bishop's Carriage,* starring Mary Pickford; *The New York Hat,* directed by D. W. Griffith, starring Mary Pickford; *The Prisoner of Zenda,* starring James K. Hackett; *Tess of the D'Urbervilles,* starring Minnie Maddern Fiske; *A Versatile Villain.*

Fiction　Willa Cather, *O Pioneers!;* Ellen Glasgow, *Virginia;* O. Henry, *Rolling Stones;* Robert Herrick, *One Woman's Life;* Eleanor H. Porter, *Pollyanna;* Gene Stratton-Porter, *Laddie;* Edith Wharton, *The Custom of the Country.*

Verse　Witter Bynner, *Tiger;* Paul Laurence Dunbar, *Complete Poems;* John Gould Fletcher, *Fire and Wine;* Robert Frost, *A Boy's Will;* Vachel Lindsay, *General William Booth Enters into Heaven and Other Poems;* William Carlos Williams, *The Tempers.*

Popular Songs　"American Beauty Rag," by Joseph Lamb; "Danny Boy," by Fred E. Weatherly; "The Dogin' Rag," by Rob Hampton; "Don't Blame It All on Broadway," by Bert Grant, Harry Williams, and Joe Young; "The International Rag," by Irving Berlin; "Junk Man Rag," by Luckey Roberts; "Kismet Rag," by Scott Hayden; "Memphis Blues," by W. C. Handy; "On the Old Fall River Line," by Harry Von Tilzer, William Jerome, and Andrew B. Sterling; "Peg o' My Heart," by Fred Fisher and Alfred Bryan; "Sailing Down the Chesapeake Bay," by George Botsford and Jean C. Havez; "Snookey Ookums," by Irving Berlin; "The Trail of the Lonesome Pine," by Harry Carroll and Ballard Macdonald; "When I Lost You," by Irving Berlin; "You Made Me Love You (I Didn't Want to Do It)," by James V. Monaco and Joseph McCarthy; "You've Got Your Mother's Big Blue Eyes," by Irving Berlin.

- The Jesse L. Lasky Feature Play Company (later Paramount Pictures) is founded in Hollywood, California.

- The New York Motion Picture Company sends director-producer Thomas Ince to California to make Westerns.

17 Feb.　The International Exhibition of Modern Art, commonly called the Armory Show, opens in New York City, with more than thirteen hundred paintings and sculptures. For many Americans the show is their first opportunity to see works of avant-garde modern art.

1914

24 Mar. The million-dollar, eighteen-hundred-seat Palace Theatre opens on Seventh Avenue between Forty-sixth and Forty-seventh Streets in New York City, charging a top ticket price of two dollars, twice that of other vaudeville theaters.

1 Apr. With admission costing as much as one dollar a ticket, *Quo Vadis,* an eight-reel movie made in Italy, opens at the Astor Theatre in New York City, beginning a twenty-two-week run and fueling Americans' desires for longer movies.

13 Apr. Arturo Toscanini conducts his first concert in America, Beethoven's Ninth Symphony at the Metropolitan Opera House in New York City.

26 May The Actors Equity Association is founded.

7 June In New York City more than one thousand striking silk-mill workers from Paterson, New Jersey, march up Fifth Avenue to Madison Square Garden, where they stage a political pageant intended to dramatize the plight of industrial workers, with sets by theatrical designer Robert Edmond Jones and painted under the direction of artist John Sloan.

20 June *Variety* reports that "the feature-length movie is now an establishment. . . . The future will see little else."

1 Oct. Director D. W. Griffith leaves Biograph, the company for which he has made more than four hundred movies in five and a half years.

Movies *The Avenging Conscience,* directed by D. W. Griffith; *The Bargain,* directed by Thomas Ince, starring William S. Hart; *The Battle of the Sexes,* directed by D. W. Griffith, starring Lillian Gish; *Between Showers,* starring Charlie Chaplin; *The Call of the North,* directed by Oscar Apfel and Cecil B. DeMille; *Cinderella,* starring Mary Pickford and Owen Moore; *Dough and Dynamite,* starring Charlie Chaplin; *The Eagle's Mate,* starring Mary Pickford; *The Escape,* directed by D. W. Griffith, starring Donald Crisp, Blanche Sweet, Mae Marsh, and Robert Harron; *The Exploits of Elaine* (serial), starring Pearl White; *Hearts Adrift,* starring Mary Pickford; *Home, Sweet Home,* directed by D. W. Griffith, starring Lillian and Dorothy Gish; *The Horrors of War; In the Latin Quarter,* starring Constance Talmadge; *Judith of Bethulia,* directed by D. W. Griffith; *Kid Auto Races at Venice, California,* starring Charlie Chaplin; *Mabel's Strange Predicament,* starring Charlie Chaplin and Mabel Normand; *The Man from Home,* directed by Cecil B. DeMille; *The Perils of Pauline* (serial), starring Pearl White; *Pool Sharks,* starring W. C. Fields; *The Squaw Man,* directed by Cecil B. DeMille; *Tess of the Storm Country,* starring Mary Pickford; *Tillie's Punctured Romance,* directed by Mack Sennett, starring Marie Dressler, Charlie Chaplin, and Mabel Normand; *The Virginian,* directed by Cecil B. DeMille; *War Is Hell; Wildflower,* starring Marguerite Clark; *The Wrath of the Gods,* directed by Thomas Ince.

Fiction Edgar Rice Burroughs, *Tarzan of the Apes;* George Washington Cable, *Gideon's Band;* Theodore Dreiser, *The Titan;* Hamlin Garland, *The Forester's Daughter;* Robert Herrick, *Clark's Field;* Jack London, *The Mutiny on the Elsinore;* Frank Norris, *Vandover and the Brute;* Booth Tarkington, *Penrod;* Harold Bell Wright, *The Eyes of the World.*

Verse Conrad Aiken, *Earth Triumphant;* Emily Dickinson, *The Single Hound;* Robert Frost, *North of Boston;* Joyce Kilmer, *Trees and Other Poems;* Vachel Lindsay, *The Congo and Other Poems;* Amy Lowell, *Sword-Blades and Poppy Seed;* James Oppenheim, *Songs for the New Age;* Gertrude Stein, *Tender Buttons.*

Popular Songs

"Aba Daba Honeymoon," by Arthur Fields and Walter Donovan; "The Boston Stop — Hesitation Waltz," by Henry Lodge; "By the Beautiful Sea," by Harry Carroll and Harold R. Atteridge; "Chevy Chase (A Rag)," by Eubie Blake; "Chicken Tango," by E. J. Stark Jr.; "Fascination Waltz," by Henry Lodge; "Fizz Water (A Rag)," by Eubie Blake; "Hot House Rag," by Paul Pratt; "The Land of My Best Girl," by Harry Carroll and Ballard Macdonald; "The Lily Rag," by Charles Thompson; "Missouri Waltz," by Frederick Knight Logan and J. R. Shannon; "Oh! You Turkey — a Rag Trot," by Henry Lodge; "Play a Simple Melody," by Irving Berlin; "St. Louis Blues," by W. C. Handy; "The Syncopated Walk," by Irving Berlin; "They Didn't Believe Me," by Jerome Kern and Herbert Reynolds; "When You Wore a Tulip and I Wore a Big Red Rose," by Percy Wenrich and Jack Mahoney; "Yellow Dog Blues," by W. C. Handy.

- Heiress and sculptor Gertrude Vanderbilt Whitney founds the Whitney Studio Club (later the Whitney Museum) in New York City.

13 Feb. The American Society of Composers, Authors, and Publishers (ASCAP) is founded in New York City.

Mar. *Mabel's Strange Predicament,* the Keystone comedy in which Charlie Chaplin's Little Tramp character is introduced, is released.

1 Apr. The Strand Theater opens in New York, designed as a vaudeville and movie house for upscale audiences.

27 Apr. Vernon and Irene Castle begin their twenty-eight-day tour of thirty-two cities, which culminates in a national dance competition held in Madison Square Garden, New York City.

4 June Finnish composer Jean Sibelius makes his first American appearance, conducting the world premiere of his symphonic poem *Oceanides* at a music festival in Norwalk, Connecticut.

3 Nov. The first American show of African sculpture opens at Stieglitz's 291 gallery in New York City.

3 Dec. The Isadorables, six young European dancers trained by Isadora Duncan, appear at Carnegie Hall in New York City, after escaping with her from war-torn Paris.

8 Dec. Irving Berlin's first musical, *Watch Your Step,* starring Vernon and Irene Castle, opens on Broadway.

1915

Movies

The Arab, directed by Cecil B. DeMille; *The Bank,* directed by and starring Charlie Chaplin; *The Battle Cry of Peace,* starring Norma Talmadge; *The Birth of a Nation,* directed by D. W. Griffith, starring Lillian Gish, Mae Marsh, and Miriam Cooper; *The Captive,* directed by Cecil B. DeMille, starring Blanche Sweet; *Carmen,* directed by Cecil B. DeMille, starring Geraldine Farrar and Wallace Reid; *The Champion,* starring and directed by Charlie Chaplin; *Chimmie Fadden,* directed by Cecil B. DeMille, starring Victor Moore; *The Coward,* directed by Thomas Ince; *Esmeralda,* starring Mary Pickford; *The Fairy and the Waif,* starring Mary Miles Minter; *A Fool There Was,* starring Theda Bara; *The Girl of the Golden West,* directed by Cecil B. DeMille; *The Goose Girl,* starring Marguerite Clark; *Graustark,* starring Francis X. Bushman; *Hell's Hinges,* directed by Thomas Ince, starring William S. Hart; *His New Job,* starring and directed by Charlie Chaplin; *The Iron Strain; The Lamb,* starring Douglas Fairbanks; *Mistress Nell,* starring Mary Pickford; *My Valet,* directed by Mack Sennett; *The New Exploits of Elaine* (serial), starring Pearl White; *A Night Out,* directed by and starring Charlie Chaplin; *Rags,* starring Mary Pickford; *The Romance of Elaine* (serial), starring Pearl White; *The Tramp,* directed by and starring Charlie Chaplin; *The Warrens of Virginia,* directed by Cecil B. DeMille, starring Blanche Sweet; *The Whirl of Life,* starring Vernon and Irene Castle; *The Wild Goose Chase,* directed by Cecil B. DeMille, starring Ina Claire; *Work,* directed by and starring Charlie Chaplin.

Fiction

Willa Cather, *The Song of the Lark;* Irvin S. Cobb, *Old Judge Priest;* Theodore Dreiser, *The "Genius";* Dorothy Canfield Fisher, *The Bent Twig;* Jack London, *The Scarlet Plague;* Ernest Poole, *The Harbor;* Booth Tarkington, *The Turmoil;* Harry Leon Wilson, *Ruggles of Red Gap.*

Verse

Stephen Vincent Benét, *Five Men and Pompey;* John Gould Fletcher, *Irradiations: Sand and Spray;* Ring W. Lardner, *Bib Ballads;* Archibald MacLeish, *Songs for a Summer's Day;* Edgar Lee Masters, *Spoon River Anthology;* John G. Neihardt, *The Song of Hugh Glass;* Ezra Pound, *Cathay;* Sara Teasdale, *Rivers to the Sea.*

Popular Songs

"Agitation Rag," by Shelton Brooks; "Babes in the Wood," by Jerome Kern; "Down Among the Sheltering Palms," by Abe Olman and James Brockman; "The Girl on the Magazine Cover," by Irving Berlin; "Hesitating Blues," by W. C. Handy; "I Didn't Raise My Boy to Be a Soldier," by Al Piantadosi and Alfred Bryan; "I Love a Piano," by Irving Berlin; "The Jelly Roll Blues," by Jelly Roll Morton; "Joe Turner Blues," by W. C. Handy; "The Little House Upon the Hill," by Harry Puck, Ballard Macdonald, and Joe Goodwin; "Memories," by Gus Kahn and Egbert Van Alstyne; "Pack Up Your Troubles in Your Old Kitbag and Smile, Smile, Smile" [British], by Felix Powell and George Asaf; "There's a Broken Heart for Every Light on Broadway," by Fred Fisher and Howard Johnson; "Weary Blues," by Artie Matthews; "When I Leave the World Behind," by Irving Berlin; "You'll Always Be the Same Sweet Girl," by Harry Von Tilzer and Andrew B. Sterling.

- Modern dancers Ruth St. Denis and Ted Shawn, who were married on 13 August 1914, found the Denishawn School of Dancing in Los Angeles.

8 Feb.

Despite protests by the National Association for the Advancement of Colored People (NAACP), D. W. Griffith's twelve-reel movie *The Birth of a Nation,* about the Ku Klux Klan in the post-Reconstruction South, has its world premiere at Clune's Theater in Los Angeles.

20 Mar. The Russian Symphony Orchestra plays the premiere performance of Aleksandr Scriabin's symphony *Prometheus* at Carnegie Hall in New York City. The performance includes the projection of color images onto a screen.

21 May *Variety* notes that "the bottom has apparently fallen out" of the market for one-reel movies.

Summer Thomas Ince's Kay Bee studio, Mack Sennett's Keystone studio, and D. W. Griffith's Reliance-Majestic studio are combined to form the Triangle Film Corporation.

15 July The Provincetown Players give their first performance: a double-bill production of *Constancy* by Neith Boyce and *Suppressed Desires* by Susan Glaspell and George Cram Cook, in Provincetown, Massachusetts.

1916

Movies *The Apostle of Vengeance*, starring William S. Hart; *Behind the Screen*, directed by and starring Charlie Chaplin; *Civilization*, directed by Thomas Ince; *The Dream Girl*, directed by Cecil B. DeMille; *The Eternal Grind*, starring Mary Pickford; *The Fall of a Nation*; *Fatty and Mabel Adrift*, directed by Mack Sennett, starring Fatty Arbuckle and Mabel Normand; *The Floorwalker*, directed by and starring Charlie Chaplin; *The Good Bad Man*, starring Douglas Fairbanks; *The Heart of Nora Flynn*, directed by Cecil B. DeMille; *Hulda from Holland*, starring Mary Pickford; *Intolerance*, directed by D. W. Griffith, starring Lillian Gish and Mae Marsh; *Less than the Dust*, starring Mary Pickford; *Maria Rosa*, directed by Cecil B. DeMille, starring Geraldine Farrar and Wallace Reid; *One A.M.*, directed by and starring Charlie Chaplin; *Patria*, starring Irene Castle; *The Pawnshop*, directed by and starring Charlie Chaplin; *Pearl of the Army*, starring Pearl White; *Poor Little Peppina*, starring Mary Pickford; *The Rink*, directed by and starring Charlie Chaplin; *Temptation*, directed by Cecil B. DeMille, starring Geraldine Farrar; *The Trail of the Lonesome Pine*, directed by Cecil B. DeMille; *The Vagabond*, directed by and starring Charlie Chaplin; *The Vixen*, starring Theda Bara; *War Brides*, starring Alla Nazimova and Richard Barthelmess; *The Wharf Rat*, starring Mae Marsh.

Fiction Sherwood Anderson, *Windy McPherson's Son;* James Branch Cabell, *The Certain Hour;* Margaret Deland, *The Rising Tide;* Hamlin Garland, *They of the High Trails;* Ellen Glasgow, *Life and Gabriella;* William Dean Howells, *The Leatherwood God;* Ring W. Lardner, *You Know Me Al;* Booth Tarkington, *Seventeen;* Mark Twain, *The Mysterious Stranger;* Edith Wharton, *Xingu and Other Stories;* Harold Bell Wright, *When a Man's a Man.*

Verse Conrad Aiken, *Turns and Movies;* John Gould Fletcher, *Goblins and Pagodas;* H. D., *Sea Garden;* Robert Frost, *Mountain Interval;* Edgar A. Guest, *A Heap o' Livin';* Robinson Jeffers, *Californians;* Sarah Orne Jewett, *Verses;* Alfred Kreymborg, *Mushrooms;* Amy Lowell, *Men, Women, and Ghosts;* Edgar Lee Masters, *Songs and Satires;* James Oppenheim, *War and Laughter;* Ezra Pound, *Lustra;* Edwin Arlington Robinson, *The Man Against the Sky;* Carl Sandburg, *Chicago Poems;* Alan Seeger, *Poems.*

Popular Songs

"Beale Street Blues," by W. C. Handy; "Bugle Call Rag," by Eubie Blake; "Chromatic Rag," by Will Held; "Everybody Rag with Me," by Gus Kahn and Grace LeBoy; "Have a Heart," by Jerome Kern and P. G. Wodehouse; "Homesickness Blues," by Cliff Hess; "Mama and Papa Blues," by James P. Johnson; "Mother (Her Soldier Boy)," by Sigmund Romberg and Rida Johnson Young; "Nola," by Felix Arndt; "Oh! How She Could Yacki, Hacki, Wicki, Wacki, Woo," by Albert Von Tilzer, Stanley Murphy, and Charles McCarron; "Poor Butterfly," by Raymond Hubbell and John L. Golden; "Pretty Baby," by Gus Kahn, Tony Jackson, and Egbert Van Alstyne; "Prosperity Rag," by James Scott; "Springtime Rag," by Paul Pratt; "There's a Little Bit of Bad in Every Good Little Girl," by Fred Fisher and Grant Clarke; "Twelfth Street Rag," by Euday L. Bowman; "You Belong to Me," by Victor Herbert and Harry B. Smith.

Jan.–May

Sergey Diaghilev's Ballets Russes performs at the Metropolitan Opera House in New York City.

Spring

Charlie Chaplin signs with Mutual for $10,000 a week, plus a $150,000 signing bonus.

12 Apr.

Russian ballet dancer Vaslav Nijinsky makes his American debut.

24 June

Mary Pickford negotiates a new contract with Adolph Zukor's Famous Players Company for more than $1 million over the next two years.

28 July

At the Wharf Theater in Provincetown, Massachusetts, the Provincetown Players stage *Bound East for Cardiff*, the first production of a Eugene O'Neill play.

5 Dec.

The Society of Independent Artists is established.

1917

Movies

The Adopted Son, starring Francis X. Bushman; *Cleopatra*, starring Theda Bara; *The Clodhopper* ; *The Cure*, directed by and starring Charlie Chaplin; *The Fall of the Romanoffs*; *The Gun Fighter*, directed by and starring William S. Hart; *The Immigrant*, directed by and starring Charlie Chaplin; *Joan, The Woman*, directed by Cecil B. DeMille, starring Geraldine Farrar; *Just Nuts*, starring Harold Lloyd and Bebe Daniels; *The Little American*, directed by Cecil B. DeMille, starring Mary Pickford; *A Modern Musketeer*, starring Douglas Fairbanks; *The Poor Little Rich Girl*, starring Mary Pickford; *Rebecca of Sunnybrook Farm*, starring Mary Pickford; *A Romance of the Redwoods*, directed by Cecil B. DeMille, starring Mary Pickford; *The Spirit of '76*; *Thais*, starring Mary Garden; *The Woman God Forgot*, directed by Cecil B. DeMille, starring Geraldine Farrar.

Fiction

Sherwood Anderson, *Marching Men*; Mary Austin, *The Ford*; James Branch Cabell, *The Cream of the Jest*; Abraham Cahan, *The Rise of David Levinsky*; John Dos Passos, *One Man's Initiation*; Edna Ferber, *Fanny Herself*; Henry James, *The Ivory Tower*; Ring W. Lardner, *Gullible's Travels*; Jack London, *Jerry of the Islands*; David Graham Phillips, *Susan Lenox: Her Fall and Rise*; Ernest Poole, *His Family*; Upton Sinclair, *King Coal*; Edith Wharton, *Summer*.

Verse	Conrad Aiken, *Nocturne of a Remembered Spring;* Witter Bynner, *Grenstone Poems;* T. S. Eliot, *Prufrock and Other Observations;* Edgar A. Guest, *Just Folks;* James Weldon Johnson, *Fifty Years and Other Poems;* Vachel Lindsay, *The Chinese Nightingale and Other Poems;* Archibald MacLeish, *Tower of Ivory;* Edna St. Vincent Millay, *Renascence and Other Poems;* Edwin Arlington Robinson, *Merlin;* Sara Teasdale, *Love Songs;* William Carlos Williams, *Al Que Quiere!*
Popular Songs	"Au Revoir, But Not Goodbye, Soldier Boy," by Albert Von Tilzer and Lew Brown; "The Bells of St. Mary's," by A. Emmett Adams and Douglas Furber; "Dance and Grow Thin," by Irving Berlin; "The Darktown Strutter's Ball," by Shelton Brooks; "Efficiency Rag," by James Scott; "For Me and My Gal," by George W. Meyer, Edgar Leslie, and E. Ray Goetz; "Gum Shoe Fox Trot," by E. J. Stark Jr.; "Hail, Hail, The Gang's All Here," by Theodore Morse, Arthur Sullivan, and D. A. Morse; "Harlem Strut," by James P. Johnson; "Magnetic Rag," by Scott Joplin; "Oh, Johnny! Oh!," by Abe Oleman and Ed Rose; "Over There," by George M. Cohan; "The Ragtime Volunteers Are Off to War," by James F. Hanley and Ballard Macdonald; "Smiles," by Lee S. Roberts and J. Will Callahan; "Tiger Rag," by the Original Dixieland Jass Band; " 'Till the Clouds Roll By," by Jerome Kern and P. G. Wodehouse; " 'Till We Meet Again," by Richard A. Whiting and Ray Egan; "When the Boys Come Home," by Oley Speaks and John Hay; "Where Do We Go from Here?," by Percy Wenrich; "Where the Morning Glories Grow," by Richard A. Whiting, Gus Kahn, and Ray Egan; "Whose Little Heart Are You Breaking Now?," by Irving Berlin; "Why Keep Me Waiting So Long?," by Tony Jackson.

- The Supreme Court rules in favor of ASCAP in a test case concerning the payment of royalties to songwriters for public performances of their works.

- Eddie Cantor and Will Rogers make their debuts in the *Ziegfeld Follies.*

- The New York Philharmonic Orchestra celebrates its seventy-fifth anniversary.

- Seventy-two-year-old French actress Sarah Bernhardt makes her last tour of the United States, playing (among other roles) Portia in *The Merchant of Venice.*

1 Apr.	Victor becomes the first record company to release a recording of jazz, by the (all-white) Original Dixieland Jass Band.
9 Apr.	On the opening day of its first exhibition the Society of Independent Artists rejects Marcel Duchamp's *Fountain,* a urinal that he entered as sculpture under the name of Richard Mutt.
11 Apr.	Isadora Duncan, draped in an American flag, performs a modern-dance work called *Star-Spangled Banner* at the Metropolitan Opera House in New York City.
14 Apr.	President Woodrow Wilson appoints a Committee on Public Information (also known as the Creel Committee, after its head, George Creel) to design a code for voluntary censorship of media and arts during the war.

27 Oct. Sixteen-year-old Russian prodigy Jascha Heifetz makes his American debut at Carnegie Hall in New York City.

10 Nov. The Philadelphia Orchestra announces that it will play no works by German composers for the duration of the war.

14 Nov. Acting on orders originating with Secretary of War Newton D. Baker, the mayor of New Orleans closes Storyville — the city's red-light district, where many African American musicians are employed — prompting an exodus of blues and jazz artists to northern cities.

25 Dec. The Jesse Lynch Williams comedy *Why Marry?* opens at the Astor Theatre in New York City.

1918

Movies *Amarilly of Clothes-Line Alley,* starring Mary Pickford; *Beware of Boarders,* directed by Mack Sennett; *A Dog's Life,* directed by and starring Charlie Chaplin; *Fatty in Coney Island,* directed by Mack Sennett, starring Fatty Arbuckle and Buster Keaton; *The Ghost of Rosy Taylor,* starring Mary Miles Minter; *The Great Love,* directed by D. W. Griffith, starring Lillian Gish; *Hearts of the World,* directed by D. W. Griffith, starring Lillian Gish; *Huns Within Our Gates, Johanna Enlists,* starring Mary Pickford; *Mickey,* directed by Mack Sennett, starring Mabel Normand; *Old Wives for New,* directed by Cecil B. DeMille; *One Hundred Percent American,* starring Mary Pickford; *Prunella,* starring Marguerite Clark; *Shoulder Arms,* directed by and starring Charlie Chaplin; *Stella Maris,* starring Mary Pickford; *Tarzan of the Apes,* starring Elmo Lincoln; *Till I Come Back to You,* directed by Cecil B. DeMille; *The Venus Model,* starring Mabel Normand.

Fiction Willa Cather, *My Ántonia;* Theodore Dreiser, *Free and Other Stories;* Mary E. Wilkins Freeman, *Edgewater People;* Zona Gale, *Birth;* Zane Grey, *The U. P. Trail;* Joel Chandler Harris, *Uncle Remus Returns;* Ring W. Lardner, *Treat 'Em Rough;* Jack London, *The Red One;* Ernest Poole, *His Second Wife;* Thorne Smith, *Biltmore Oswald;* Wilbur Daniel Steele, *Land's End;* Edward Streeter, *Dere Mable: Love Letters of a Rookie;* Booth Tarkington, *The Magnificent Ambersons;* Edith Wharton, *The Marne.*

Verse Sherwood Anderson, *Mid-American Chants;* Stephen Vincent Benét, *Young Adventure;* John Gould Fletcher, *The Tree of Life;* Amy Lowell, *Can Grandes Castle;* Edgar Lee Masters, *Toward the Gulf;* Carl Sandburg, *Cornhuskers;* Margaret Widdemer, *Old Road to Paradise.*

Popular Songs "Beautiful Ohio," by Mary Earl (Robert A. King) and Ballard Macdonald; "The Daughter of Rosie O'Grady," by Walter Donaldson and Monty C. Brice; "Dream On, Little Soldier Boy," by Irving Berlin; "Everybody Knows I Love Him," by Russell Smith; "A Good Man Is Hard to Find," by Eddie Green; "Hinky-Dinky Parlez-vous," anonymous; "I'll Say She Does," by Gus Kahn; "I'm Always Chasing Rainbows," by Harry Carroll and Joseph McCarthy; "I'm Gonna Pin a Medal on the Girl I Left Behind," by Irving Berlin; "The Kaiser's Got the Blues," by W. C. Handy; "K-K-K-Katy," by Geoffrey O'Hara; "Oh, How I Hate to Get Up in the Morning," by Irving Berlin; "Rock-a-Bye Your Baby with a Dixie Melody," by Joe Young and Sam M. Lewis; "Snookums Rag," by Charles L. Johnson; "The U.S. Field Artillery March," by John Philip Sousa; "When Alexander Takes His Ragtime Band to France," by Alfred Bryan, Cliff Hess, and Edgar Leslie.

- Italian operatic tenor Enrico Caruso, who is extremely popular in America, records George M. Cohan's wartime hit "Over There."

- The annual O. Henry Awards are created to honor the short-story writer, who died in 1910.

- The first Pulitzer Prizes are awarded for drama (Jesse Lynch Williams's *Why Marry?*) and fiction (Ernest Poole's *His Family*).

15 Feb. Serving as a pilot in the war, dancer Vernon Castle is killed during a training exercise.

Mar. *The Little Review* begins serializing James Joyce's *Ulysses*.

25 Mar. German-born Boston Symphony Orchestra conductor Carl Muck is arrested and imprisoned as an enemy alien.

16 Oct. Congress passes the Alien Act, which allows for the deportation of immigrants and aliens with radical political views. The act is later used to justify the deportation of Muck and the harassment of other German- and Austrian-born artists working in America.

Dec. The Theatre Guild is founded in New York City.

14 Dec. Giacomo Puccini's *Il trittico*, a trilogy of one-act operas — *Il Tabarro*, *Suor Angelica*, and *Gianni Schicchi* — is given its world premiere at the Metropolitan Opera House in New York City.

1919

Movies *Broken Blossoms*, directed by D. W. Griffith, starring Lillian Gish and Richard Barthelmess; *Captain Kidd, Jr.*, starring Mary Pickford; *Daddy Long Legs*, starring Mary Pickford; *A Day's Pleasure*, directed by and starring Charlie Chaplin; *Don't Change Your Husband*, directed by Cecil B. DeMille, starring Gloria Swanson; *The Girl Who Stayed at Home*, directed by D. W. Griffith, starring Carol Dempster; *Girls*, starring Marguerite Clark; *Heart o' the Hills*, starring Mary Pickford; *Kathleen Mavourneen*, starring Theda Bara; *Male and Female*, directed by Cecil B. DeMille, starring Gloria Swanson; *The Miracle Man*, starring Lon Chaney; *Sunnyside*, directed by and starring Charlie Chaplin; *True Heart Susie*, directed by D. W. Griffith, starring Lillian Gish.

Fiction Sherwood Anderson, *Winesburg, Ohio*; James Branch Cabell, *Jurgen*; Finley Peter Dunne, *Mr. Dooley on Making a Will*; Ellen Glasgow, *The Builders*; Fannie Hurst, *Humoresque*; Ring W. Lardner, *Own Your Own Home*; Jack London, *On the Makaloa Mat*; Upton Sinclair, *Jimmie Higgins*; Albert Payson Terhune, *Lad: A Dog*.

Verse T. S. Eliot, *Poems*; Amy Lowell, *Pictures of a Floating World*; Edgar Lee Masters, *Starved Rock*; Ezra Pound, *Quia Pauper Amavi*; John Crowe Ransom, *Poems about God*.

**Popular
Songs**
"Alice Blue Gown," by Harry Tierney and Joseph McCarthy; "Bohemia Rag," by Joseph Lamb; "Castle of Dreams," by Harry Tierney and Joseph McCarthy; "Daddy Long Legs," by Harry Ruby, Sam M. Lewis, and Joe Young; "Dardanella," by Fred Fisher; "How You Gonna Keep 'em Down on the Farm," by Walter Donaldson, Sam M. Lewis, and Joe Young; "Indian Summer," by Victor Herbert; "Liberty Loan March," by John Philip Sousa; "The Little Church Around the Corner," by Sigmund Romberg and Alexander Gerber; "Mandy," by Irving Berlin; "Peace and Plenty Rag," by James Scott; "Peggy," by Neil Moret and Harry Williams; "A Pretty Girl Is Like a Melody," by Irving Berlin; "Rose Room," by Art Hickman; "Swanee," by George Gershwin and Irving Caesar; "You Ain't Heard Nothing Yet," by Al Jolson, Gus Kahn, and B. G. De Sylva.

- *Maid of Harlem,* an all-black musical starring Fats Waller, Mamie Smith, Johnny Dunn, and Perry Bradford, is a hit at Lincoln Theater in New York City.

5 Feb.
United Artists is founded in Hollywood by Charlie Chaplin, Mary Pickford, Douglas Fairbanks, D. W. Griffith, and other investors.

19 Apr.
The Theatre Guild opens its first production, Jacinto Benavente's *The Bonds of Interest,* in New York City.

7 Aug.
The Actors Equity strike begins, soon including more than two thousand actors, stagehands, and musicians.

6 Sept.
The Actors Equity strike is settled, with theatrical management meeting the actors' demands on pay, job security, and control over contracts.

24 Oct.
During the opening performance at Capitol Theatre on Broadway, sixty chorus girls dance to George Gershwin's new song "Swanee," which Al Jolson also sings in his Winter Garden show a few weeks later.

31 Oct.
The Provincetown Players stage Eugene O'Neill's play *The Dreamy Kid* with an all-black cast.

OVERVIEW

"The Little Renaissance." In the second decade of the twentieth century, the American arts experienced what historians call "The Little Renaissance," a period of awakening among practitioners of all the arts and among the reading, viewing, and listening public. New styles and new ideas were born in literature, painting, sculpture, photography, music, and theater that would affect those arts for the rest of the century — and new art forms, including film and modern dance, came into their own. Behind these changes were artists, many of them young and college-educated, who discussed spirituality and the new psychology of Sigmund Freud and who believed that meaning lay in the expression of the inner self. Photographer and gallery owner Alfred Stieglitz spoke for most of the painters, writers, playwrights, and dancers of his time when he explained that his art was "the subconscious pushing through the conscious, driven by an urge coming from beyond its own . . . trying to live in the light, like the seed pushing up through the earth." This new wave of creative talents thought that their work could solve social and political problems; painter Robert Henri believed that art would "keep government straight, end wars and strife, [and] do away with material greed."

The Political Climate. The trust busting of the previous decade, along with ongoing journalistic muckraking that exposed the ills of American society, set the stage for the rise of liberal, even radical, political activity in the early 1910s. The Progressive movement, which was strongest from 1903 to 1917, drew public attention to health, education, and other social issues; suffragists claimed that giving women the vote would ensure the passage of laws to address these concerns. Americans realized that some sort of change was needed to make the country more economically equitable, and most people were suspicious of big business. The antibusiness climate was evident not only in magazines and newspapers but also in literature and drama of the day. George M. Cohan, the quintessential Broadway businessman, portrayed financiers as greedy in his play *Get Rich Quick* (1910). The popularity of alternative political solutions to such problems was clear in the results of the 1912 presidential election, when the Socialist Party candidate, Eugene V. Debs, won nearly a million votes, and in the brief resurgence of the Industrial Workers of the World (IWW), a radical labor union, after industrial crises such as the disastrous 1911 Triangle Shirtwaist Company fire. Socialism was embraced not just by radicals but by millions of Americans, including artists — some of whom contributed their writing and drawing talents to the Socialist magazine *The Masses,* founded in 1911.

Realism and "Cultural Nationalism." One way of changing the world, artists believed, was to expose its realities. In drama, fiction, poetry, painting, photography, and dance, artists sought to strip their work down to the basic truth, to present life as it really was rather than idealizing experience. Visual art and literature were likely to focus on common, often grim, subjects, including charwomen, industrial workers, and slaughterhouses — subjects rarely treated by artists in the nineteenth century. Even works with celebratory themes, such as some of the music written during the 1910s, were rooted in common experiences. Artists agreed that "real life" was a legitimate source of inspiration. As composer Charles Ives put it, art came "directly out of the heart of experience of life and thinking about life and living life." At the same time, American artists increasingly chose native themes. Painter John Sloan, poet Robert Frost, novelist Theodore Dreiser, and songwriter George M. Cohan were among those who found their strongest material in American subjects. New magazines such as *The Seven Arts* and *The New Republic* and books by cultural critics — notably Randolph Bourne's *Youth and Life* (1913) and Van Wyck Brooks's *America's Coming-of-Age* (1915) — called on artists to create a body of native art rather than imitating European traditions. *New Republic* editor Herbert Croly looked forward to the time when "American culture will be invigorated and informed by the same enterprising and co-operative spirit which [has] distinguished its industrial success."

Urban Growth. The 1910s were the pivotal decade of urbanization in America, the time when the bulk of the American population finally shifted from rural areas to cities. By 1920 more than half of all Americans lived in cities with populations greater than twenty-five hundred. This change was acknowledged in the paintings of the so-called Ash Can School of New York, in the poetry of Chicagoan Carl Sandburg, even in the nostalgia for the agrarian past expressed in the fiction of Willa Cather. Some artists emphasized the negative aspects of urban growth: David Graham Phillips's 1917 novel, *Susan Lenox: Her Fall and Rise*, for instance, broached the subjects of prostitution and slum life. Others, however, rejoiced in the city. Discussing his painting of the new Woolworth Building in New York City, watercolorist John Marin said he believed that the skyscrapers themselves were pulsing with life. Beginning in the mid 1910s painters used the new style of Cubism to depict the architectural and engineering aspects of city building.

Cultural Diversity. Urbanization changed not only the physical faces of cities but also their cultural makeup. One reason for the rapid growth of northern cities was the migration of hundreds of thousands of African Americans from the rural South, where they faced discrimination legalized by Jim Crow laws and decreasing economic opportunity. The cultural results of that migration included the transportation of black art traditions, such as jazz and the blues, to the North and the concentration of blacks in geographical centers where other arts would soon flourish as well. (One notable result was the Harlem Renaissance of the 1920s.) Another factor that contributed to urbanization was immigration, which peaked during the first two decades of the twentieth century. Nearly six million immigrants came into the United States during the 1910s, more than two-thirds of them from southern and eastern Europe (including Russia). Many were Catholic or Jewish. Though some tried hard to assimilate, others preserved cultural traditions that influenced the arts, especially theater and music. Some of the greatest talents on Broadway and vaudeville stages and in Tin Pan Alley were either the children of immigrants (Fanny Brice, George Gershwin) or immigrants themselves (Eddie Cantor, Al Jolson, Irving Berlin). Native-born writer John Reed found in New York City "All professions, races, temperaments, philosophies / All history, all possibilities...."

Artists in Control. The 1910s saw the balance of power shift in several of the arts. Against the backdrop of a growing antibusiness climate in the country, artists challenged the power of those who hired them, bought and used their work, and controlled their careers. Actors in movies and theater (which was controlled by a near monopoly) demanded better contracts. Painters and writers created new outlets for their work by staging independent exhibitions and founding new literary journals. Songwriters demanded payment for the use of their works. Artists from all fields formed associations to protect their rights as workers and to increase their opportunities for success. Among such groups founded in the 1910s are the Association of American Painters and Sculptors (1911), the Dramatists Guild (1912), the Actors Equity Association (1913), the American Society of Composers, Authors, and Publishers (1914), and the Society of Independent Artists (1916). In 1919 two thousand members of Actors Equity were among the four million American workers who went on strike for better pay and working conditions. The actors were successful.

Greater Public Access to the Arts. In the 1910s the American public had more access to the arts than ever before. The growth of the "little magazines" and the proliferation of art galleries and exhibitions multiplied the forums through which art reached readers and viewers. The twin forces of artistic innovation and urbanization made American cities thriving cultural centers. Yet people living outside metropolitan areas had nearly as much access to the arts as did city dwellers, thanks to developments such as the regional theater movement; the thousands of vaudeville houses across the country, where touring actors, musicians, and dancers appeared; magazines such as *The New Republic, The Atlantic Monthly*, and *The Smart Set* that published fiction and poetry or essays about the arts; and the increasing availability of phonograph records and record players. Still other trends — the pastime of amateur photography (in 1913 a Kodak camera cost only two dollars), millions of songs published as sheet music or as piano rolls for Pianolas, dance instructions provided in magazines and on records — inspired ordinary Americans to practice artistic pursuits themselves.

The Movies. Of all the developments that made the American arts available to a wide audience during the 1910s, however, the most powerful was the new medium of film. A 1913 article in *The Nation* noted that across the country Americans were talking about "the technique of the moving-picture theatre with as much interest as literary salons in Paris or London discuss the minutiae of the higher drama. The crowd knows how the films are made, and what it costs to make them, and who the leading actors in the show are." The writer noted that movies "converted their entire audience into first nighters." By 1916 movie attendance had grown to nearly twenty-five million Americans per day. For as little as a nickel (the origin of the term *nickelodeon*), a person could see two or three "shorts," and by middecade longer movies were also plentiful and affordable. At the same time they were available to nearly everyone, the movies made "stars" of individuals, creating the concept of truly national celebrity. Stars became valuable properties and were, accordingly, well paid. As moviemakers left New York for the better weather and scenic backdrops of California, they created a new geographic center for the American arts — as well as a truly American cultural phenomenon — in Hollywood.

Interaction among Artists. The 1910s were a remarkable period of cross-fertilization among the various arts. Cultural salons brought artists together in New York, Chicago, and other cities. Playwright George Cram Cook believed that artists were naturally drawn to each other because of their calling in a crucial era: "An American Renaissance of the twentieth century is not the task of ninety million people, but of one hundred. Does it not make them feel like reaching out to find each other — for strengthening of heart, for . . . the kindling of communal intellectual passion?" Individual artists also offered public and private support for each other's work. Abraham Walkowitz made more than five thousand drawings and paintings of dancer Isadora Duncan, whom John Sloan also sketched and whom Edward Steichen photographed. In 1914 composer Charles Ives set to music "General William Booth Enters into Heaven," Vachel Lindsay's best-known poem. Lindsay regularly reviewed movies for *The New Republic,* where he defended D. W. Griffith's *Intolerance* (1916). Others combined disciplines. Painter Max Weber attempted to apply the techniques of Cubism to poetry in his *Cubist Poems* (1914), while poet Gertrude Stein created word pictures of Henri Matisse and Pablo Picasso for Alfred Stieglitz's art magazine *Camera Work* (August 1912). Fiction writers chose artists as subjects: Eugene Witla, the hero of Theodore Dreiser's novel *The "Genius"* (1915), is a realist painter; while Thea Kronborg, the heroine of Willa Cather's *The Song of the Lark* (1915), is an opera singer. Artists also collaborated for professional gain. Dancers Ruth St. Denis and Ted Shawn taught mime and movement skills to silent-movie stars, including Lillian Gish, at their Denishawn school in Los Angeles.

World War I. The 1917 entry of the United States into World War I was an artistic as well as political turning point for the country. Many experiments with art and literature ceased, either because their funding evaporated or because they were considered too politically radical in the new climate of 100-percent Americanism. German art and artists in the United States were vilified and persecuted. The new conservatism was promoted by the Committee on Public Information (known as the Creel Committee because it was headed by former journalist George Creel), which was created to "sell" the war to the American people. George M. Cohan's superhit "Over There" (1917) was one of hundreds of patriotic songs written and sung across the United States during the war. Mary Pickford, Douglas Fairbanks, Charlie Chaplin, and Lillian Russell toured the country selling war bonds. Other artists served in the war and later used their experiences as material for creative work. After the war the cultural climate of the United States remained conservative — a great change from the earlier years of the decade. "One has a sense of having come to a sudden, short stop at the end of an intellectual era," wrote cultural critic Randolph Bourne near the end of the decade.

Sources:

Adele Heller and Lois Rudnick, *1915: The Cultural Moment: The New Politics, the New Woman, the New Psychology, the New Art, and the New Theatre in America* (New Brunswick, N.J.: Rutgers University Press, 1991);

Henry May, *The End of American Innocence: The First Years of Our Own Times, 1912–1917* (New York: Knopf, 1959);

Steven Watson, *Strange Bedfellows: The First American Avant-Garde* (New York: Abbeville Press, 1991);

Arthur Frank Wertheim, *The New York Little Renaissance: Iconoclasm, Modernism, and Nationalism in American Culture, 1908–1917* (New York: New York University Press, 1976).

TOPICS IN THE NEWS

AMERICAN ARTISTS REBEL

Signs of Revolt. Between 1910 and 1920 three fundamental concepts concerning art in America were seriously reconsidered: what "art" is, who makes decisions about standards, and how art is shared with the viewing public. At the start of the decade the American art world was largely controlled by the National Academy of Design, which promoted and exhibited American works in established genres, such as those of landscape painter Winslow Homer, portraitist John Singer Sargent, and impressionist William Merritt Chase. Then, in 1908, a group of artists who became known as The Eight — Robert Henri, John Sloan, William Glackens, George Luks, Everett Shinn, Ernest Lawson, Maurice Prendergast, and Arthur B. Davies — put on an exhibition of their works, nearly all of which (except two by Henri) had been rejected by the academy. In 1910 the group held a larger, open show, the Exhibition of Independent Artists, featuring five hundred American works that had been rejected by the academy. Nearly two thousand people attended its opening. These first independent exhibitions were important not only because they existed outside the academy but also because they broke its traditions: they had no juries and awarded no prizes. Still, the works in these shows (including those of The Eight themselves) seem conventional in comparison with the art of the later 1910s.

The City as Subject. As the decade began, a movement toward realism was already under way in the American art world. Artists in this new movement painted scenes of the less glamorous aspects of modern life, particularly in the cities. Five of The Eight who painted in this style — Henri, Sloan, Glackens, Luks, and Shinn — became known as the Ash Can realists (after Sloan's painting of a woman rummaging through the contents of a trash can). Sloan's *Sunday, Girls Drying their Hair* (1912), *McSorley's Bar* (1912), and *Backyards, Greenwich Village* (1914) depict gritty New York scenery and lower-class residents of the city, as do George Bellows's *New York* (1911) and *Cliff Dwellers* (1913; the title refers to occupants of tenements). Though more of an impressionist than a realist, John Marin chose New York settings for many works, in-

cluding his 1912 watercolors *Woolworth Building* and *Broadway, St. Paul's Church*. So did Cubist painters Max Weber (*Rush Hour, New York*, 1915) and Futurist Joseph Stella (*Brooklyn Bridge*, 1918). Industrialization was also a subject for art: Morton Schamberg's series of eight paintings with a machine motif, finished in 1916, were among many works inspired by new technology. Such themes later dominated the work of precisionists Charles

Brooklyn Bridge (1918) by American Futurist Joseph Stella

Demuth and Charles Sheeler, both emerging talents in the 1910s.

Other "Isms" and an Important Champion. Realism was only one of many "-isms" in American art during the 1910s. In addition to Synchromism, the only one of the artistic "-isms" of the period to originate in America, other new styles were imported from Europe, including Primitivism, Symbolism, Fauvism with its shocking colors, the nihilistic Dadaism, Futurism, which attempted to incorporate motion into art, and — perhaps most important — Cubism. One visionary who embraced all these styles was Alfred Stieglitz, who along with Edward Steichen elevated the craft of photography to an art form.

Remaining an important photographer through the 1930s, Stieglitz made a significant contribution to the art world of the 1910s by championing other artists, both through his New York City gallery, 291 — named for its street address, 291 Fifth Avenue — and his magazine *Camera Work*, which published artistic photographs and photographs of new paintings and sculptures. (In the mid 1910s he briefly published a second magazine, *291*.) Waldo Frank, a cultural critic and writer for *The Seven Arts*, called 291 an "altar at which life was worshipped above the noise of a dead city. . . . a refuge, certain and solitary, from the tearing grip of industrial disorder."

Marcel Duchamp's *Nude Descending a Staircase, No. 2* (1912), one of the most controversial paintings in the influential Armory Show of 1913

The Shows at 291. Stieglitz's gallery was the first to exhibit the abstract paintings of Arthur Dove and the Cubist paintings of Marsden Hartley, Max Weber, and Charles Demuth — all Americans. Other American artists who had their first solo exhibits at 291 included painters Pamela Colman Smith, John Marin, and Georgia O'Keeffe and photographer Paul Strand. Between 1910 and 1913 the gallery also introduced to American audiences several important European artists, including sculptors Auguste Rodin and Constantin Brancusi and painters Henri Matisse, Marius De Zayas, Henri de Toulouse-Lautrec, Henri Rousseau, Paul Cézanne, Pablo Picasso, and Francis Picabia. Stieglitz was not afraid of the unusual or controversial: he gave the earliest-known exhibitions of children's art (1912) and African sculpture (1914), and in 1917, when the Society of Independent Artists rejected Marcel Duchamp's *Fountain*, a urinal he

had entered under the name "Richard Mutt," it was shown at 291. By the time 291 and *Camera Work* ended in 1917, because Stieglitz lost his funding during the war, the gallery and the magazine had played a crucial role in showing Americans the possibilities of art.

Sources:

William Innes Homer, *Alfred Steiglitz and the American Avant-Garde* (Boston: New York Graphic Society/Little, Brown, 1977);

Dickran Tashjian, *Skyscraper Primitives: Dada and the American Avant-Garde* (Middletown, Conn.: Wesleyan University Press, 1975);

Arthur Frank Wertheim, *The New York Little Renaissance: Iconoclasm, Modernism, and Nationalism in American Culture, 1908–1917* (New York: New York University Press, 1976).

THE ARMORY SHOW AND ITS LEGACY

A Revolutionary Event. Of all the art exhibitions during the 1910s, the Armory Show in 1913 issued the greatest challenge to the art establishment. In late 1911 more than two dozen New York painters and sculptors, many of whom had been involved in the independents' exhibitions, organized as the Association of American Painters and Sculptors, with Arthur B. Davies, a member of The Eight, as the first president. The new group decided to hold a major international exhibition. Hoping to include a large number of artworks, they rented the Sixty-ninth Regiment Armory on Lexington Avenue in New York City and spent the next year scouting, especially in Europe, for works to exhibit. When the show opened on 17 February 1913, it included more than thirteen hundred paintings, drawings, and sculptures, some introducing new styles and ideas that both fascinated and shocked the opening-night guests. Reviewers called the show an event not to be missed, and over the next month some seventy-five thousand viewers came to see it.

The Artists. The Armory Show offered a wonderful collection of works by established artists, mostly Europeans (Pierre Auguste Renoir, Claude Monet, Edouard Manet, Vincent van Gogh, Georges Seurat, Auguste Rodin, Paul Cézanne, Camille Pissarro, Paul Gauguin, Henri de Toulouse-Lautrec) and some Americans (Albert Pinkham Ryder, James McNeill Whistler, Childe Hassam, Mary Cassatt). Also exhibited were some works by important American artists then in the beginning or early stages of their careers, including paintings by six of The Eight, as well as John Marin, Joseph Stella, Edward Hopper, Marsden Hartley, and George Bellows. Yet of all the artists represented in the Armory Show, the most notable — and most influential, in the long run — were new European talents, including Francis Picabia, Odilon Redon, Henri Matisse, Constantin Brancusi, Pablo Picasso, and Marcel Duchamp. Some viewers were offended by Matisse's exaggerated nudes, while Duchamp's Cubist painting *Nude Descending a Staircase* was ridiculed as incomprehensible; one reviewer called it "an explosion in a shingle factory." Other Cubist works, including those by Picasso and Picabia, were better received. Some conservative art critics defended the standards of the National Academy of Design and dismissed the Armory Show. Kenyon Cox wrote, "I have no fear that this kind of art will prevail, or even that it can long endure," but overall public response to the show was enthusiastic.

The Middle Years of the Decade. Later in the spring of 1913 the Armory Show traveled to Chicago, and a truncated version went to Boston. Several American writers who saw the show in Chicago or New York — including poets William Carlos Williams, Harriet Monroe, and Wallace Stevens — were profoundly affected by it and later attributed their own creative inspiration to their exposure to Duchamp, Picasso, Cézanne, and other artists whose works were exhibited in the show. More important, by the time the show ended, a quarter of a million people had seen it, and a lasting interest in modern art, particularly Cubism, had been born in America. Encouraged by this friendly climate, the French Dadaists Duchamp and Picabia came to New York to work. During the mid 1910s works by Armory Show exhibitors and other new artists drew viewers to Alfred Stieglitz's 291 gallery and the Whitney Studio Club (later the Whitney Museum), which heiress and sculptor Gertrude Vanderbilt Whitney founded in 1914 to promote new talent. American museums and private collectors were anxious to acquire modern art. Dozens of new galleries were founded to display the new art, and exhibitions were mounted not just in New York but also in Cleveland, Pittsburgh, Baltimore, and other cities.

The Independents' Show of 1917 and Beyond. Internal dissension led to the breakup of the Association of American Painters and Sculptors in 1916. Later that year the Society of Independent Artists was founded with the same goal as the AAPS, discovering and advancing new styles and artists. Its first exhibition, in 1917, was bigger than the Armory Show. More than twenty-five hundred works by some thirteen hundred artists were exhibited at the Grand Central Palace in New York City. It was not as successful critically or financially. Again critics were up in arms over Marcel Duchamp, who, under the pseudonym of Richard Mutt, had submitted a urinal as a piece of sculpture called *Fountain*. The society rejected it, but the considerable publicity surrounding the work, which was subsequently exhibited at Stieglitz's 291 gallery, helped to spread Duchamp's message: there was no difference between "art" and the most common aspects of human life. Though the involvement of the United States in World War I temporarily suspended discussions of aesthetics, the controversies and ideas that were born during the 1910s influenced American artists for the rest of the century.

Sources:

Milton Brown, *The Story of the Armory Show* (New York: Joseph H. Hirschhorn Foundation, 1963);

Martin Green, *New York: 1913* (New York: Macmillan, 1988);

Adele Heller and Lois Rudnick, *1915: The Cultural Moment: The New Politics, the New Woman, the New Psychology, the New Art, and the New Theatre in America* (New Brunswick, N.J.: Rutgers University Press, 1991).

Ted Shawn and Ruth St. Denis performing "Tillers of the Soil" in their *Dance Pageant of Egypt, Greece and India* (1916)

DANCERS BREAK THE RULES

The Professional Dance World. During the 1910s most Americans thought of dance as amusement rather than art. Yet several events in the world of professional dance made headlines — and affected the evolution of dance traditions in the United States. Among them were the first American performances of Sergey Diaghilev's Ballets Russes in 1916 and the debuts of two great Russian ballet dancers, Anna Pavlova in 1910 and Vaslav Nijinsky in 1916. Moved by Pavlova's *Dying Swan*, parents dressed their daughters in tutus and sent them off to ballet school. Modern dance was also taking hold in the United States. The first American pioneer of this dance form, Isadora Duncan, spent most of the decade performing in Europe and South America, but she danced at the Century Theatre in New York City during the 1914 season and performed in New York City and San Francisco in 1917.

Denishawn. More significant than Duncan's contributions to modern dance during this era were those made by Ruth St. Denis and Ted Shawn. The New Jersey–born St. Denis (originally just Ruth Dennis) had spent the first decade of the century dancing in Broadway shows while developing her own exotic style based on Asian traditions. During the early years of the 1910s she toured vaudeville theaters performing dances with names such as *Egypta* and the Japanese *O-Mika*. Denver native Ted Shawn, who began dancing professionally in 1911, was a former theology student who, like St. Denis, believed that spirituality was expressed in movement. When the two met in 1914, each found a soul mate. Despite their age difference (she was thirty-seven and he twenty-three), they married and settled in Los Angeles, where in 1915 they established Denishawn, part school and part dance company, which emphasized the connection of mind, body, and soul. During their seventeen-year professional partnership, the couple choreographed dances that were performed nationally by Denishawn dancers. Some were distinctively American, with themes such as cowboys or industrial workers. More typical of their work, however, were their Oriental dance *Serenata Morisca* and the Aztec ballet *Xochitl,* both of which starred their student Martha Graham. (Doris Humphrey, who also became an important American dancer and choreographer, was another student.) Movie stars such as Lillian Gish went to Denishawn to learn mime skills or improve the grace of their movements. The proximity of Denishawn to Hollywood was fruitful. Ruth St. Denis choreographed the Babylonian ballets for D. W. Griffith's *Intolerance* (1916). Ted Shawn, who during the early 1910s had appeared in an Edison movie called *The Dance of the Ages,* danced around Gloria Swanson in Cecil B. DeMille's *Don't Change Your Husband* (1919).

Dance on the Popular Stage. Both St. Denis and Pavlova took their classical training to Broadway and vaudeville houses, where they drew large audiences. At one point Pavlova was dancing two performances a day at the five-thousand-seat Hippodrome Theater in New York City — and earning $8,500 a week. Elsewhere in vaudeville, the Mosconi brothers, Charles and Louis, delighted theatergoers by dancing halfway up the walls of the stage, while Percy Oakes drew gasps from his audiences when he spun his wife and partner, Pamela Delour, above his head. One version of Florenz Ziegfeld's *Midnight Frolic* show was called "Dance and Grow Thin"; after the show was over, the audience could dance until 4 A.M. In the *Ziegfeld Follies* Fanny Brice's dancing spoofed Nijinsky's, while Vera Maxwell and Leon Errol performed a comic ballroom dance called "The Seasick Dip." The most popular of all dance acts was the husband-and-wife team of Vernon and Irene Castle, who performed their "Castle Walk" and other new syncopated steps based on the rhythms of ragtime on Broadway and in the movies. More important — through the dance clubs they opened, a national contest they headlined and judged, and instructions they gave in magazines — they encouraged Americans to get out onto the dance floor. The

THE "ANIMAL DANCES"

During the middle years of the 1910s, all across the United States — in restaurants and clubs, in contests, at parties, and at home — ordinary people jogged, hopped, and otherwise moved in strange new ways to dances with extraordinary names. Most were named for animals — presumably the creatures dancers resembled when performing the steps. The now-well-known fox-trot was only one of a menagerie of what critics (who thought them immoral) called "animal dances." There were also the grizzly bear, the bunny hug, the turkey trot, the camel walk, the lame duck, the crab step, the kangaroo dip, the fish walk, and the snake.

Source: Irene Castle, as told to Bob and Wanda Duncan, *Castles in the Air* (New York: Da Capo Press, 1958).

Castles' clean-cut image also legitimized public performance of many new dances that had been branded immoral. In October 1913 the magazine *Current Opinion* noted that "people who have not danced in twenty years" were doing so again and reported that "up-to-date restaurants provide a dancing floor so that patrons may lose no time while the waiter is changing the plates."

Dance Clubs and Bands. All across the country restaurants hired dance bands. In New York there were dozens of such places: Bustanoby's, where the house band was initially conducted by operetta composer Sigmund Romberg (who also played ragtime piano with the band); Louis Martin's Café de l'Opéra on Broadway, in whose floor show the Castles had gotten their first American notices; Reisenweber's on Columbus Circle; Murray's on Forty-second Street; Lee Shubert's Palais de Danse; the Jardin de Danse, on the top floor of Marcus Loew's New York Theatre; and the Castles' own Castle House on Forty-sixth Street, where the all-black band of James Reese Europe played. Europe — who cowrote two of the Castles' best-known dance tunes, "The Castle Walk" and "Castle House Rag" — became the first African American bandleader to make a record when his band was featured in a series of dance records released by Victor in 1914. The many dance-music records made during the 1910s gave a crucial commercial boost to the relatively new recording industry and allowed Americans who did not live in major cities to hear music and dance to it at home.

Sources:
Ronald L. Davis, *A History of Music in American Life: Volume II, The Gilded Years, 1865–1920* (Huntington, N.Y.: Robert Krieger, 1980);

Joseph H. Mazo, *Prime Movers: The Makers of Modern Dance in America* (New York: Morrow, 1977);

Walter Terry, *The Dance in America,* revised edition (New York: Harper & Row, 1971).

Sherwood Anderson, whose *Windy McPherson's Son* (1916),
Marching Men (1917), and *Winesburg, Ohio* (1919)
criticized the materialism and sexual repression
of small-town life in the Midwest

LITERATURE: AN AMERICAN VOICE EMERGES

Midwestern Influences. As in art, American literature during the 1910s was dominated by writers trying to break free of older, usually European models, to find their own subject matter in their own country, and to create new forms and styles of writing. If the art, theater, and music worlds revolved around New York City, American literature during the 1910s came primarily from writers of the country's heartland: Willa Cather (Nebraska), Booth Tarkington and Theodore Dreiser (Indiana), Edgar Lee Masters and Carl Sandburg (Illinois), and Sherwood Anderson (Ohio). Hamlin Garland, whose short stories and novels were influential in the first decade of the new century and beyond, published his autobiography, *A Son of the Middle Border* (1917), about growing up in Minnesota, Iowa, and South Dakota. During the 1910s Chicago became an important literary base, giving rise to the literary phenomenon known as the Chicago Renaissance.

Realism in Prose. Developments in fiction resembled art trends in another way: new writers were determined to produce works that reflected the realities of life. The guard was changing in American literature. Henry James and Edith Wharton, now acknowledged as the dominant American literary figures of the previous two decades, were still at work in the 1910s, but both were settled abroad and had limited influence in their native country. Another established talent, Theodore Dreiser, was one of the pioneers of realism. The novels Dreiser published during the 1910s — *Jennie Gerhardt* (1911), the 1911 republication of his *Sister Carrie* (which had been suppressed by his publisher shortly after its appearance in 1900), his antibusiness *The Financier* (1912) and its sequel, *The Titan* (1914), and his novel about a realist painter, *The "Genius"* (1915) — placed him squarely within the emerging philosophy, which held that the most important function of fiction was to tell the truth about the realities of American life. One of Dreiser's main concerns, the ruthlessness necessary to succeed in business, is also the theme of Booth Tarkington's novel *The Turmoil* (1915) and Abraham Cahan's *The Rise of David Levinsky* (1917). Cahan's book, a fictional biography of a Jewish businessman in New York City, was important both as a chronicle of the immigrant experience and as a critique of American business around the turn of the century.

Rural Settings. Though many realistic works of the 1910s have urban settings, small-town and rural life are the subjects of the decade's most important literary prose. Sherwood Anderson's *Winesburg, Ohio* (1919), a collection of interrelated short stories, paints an unflattering portrait of a small midwestern community. Booth Tarkington's juvenile novels *Penrod* (1914) and *Seventeen* (1916) take a more sentimental approach to the experience of growing up in such a setting. Even more rural are the settings of Willa Cather's prairie novels, *O Pioneers!*

Writers and artists associated with the little magazine *Others*, 1916: (seated) Alanson Hartpence, Alfred Kreymborg, William Carlos Williams, and Skipwith Cannell; (standing) Jean Crotti, Marcel Duchamp, Walter Arensberg, Man Ray, Robert Alden Sanborn, and Maxwell Bodenheim

(1913), *The Song of the Lark* (1915), and *My Ántonia* (1918). Cather's realism is somewhat different from that of many of her contemporaries. She acknowledged the emotional and cultural starkness of the prairie and yet celebrated the strength of the people facing those challenges, as well as the beauty of the land itself.

The Literary Legacy of World War I. Though its effect would be fully evident only in later decades, World War I was responsible for a significant body of twentieth-century literature. Some wartime novels, such as Dorothy Canfield Fisher's *Home Fires in France* (1917) and Edith Wharton's *The Marne* (1918), present idealistic pictures of the war, as does Cather's *One of Ours* (1922), a Pulitzer Prize–winning novel about a midwestern boy who finds his purpose in the war. Other literature inspired by the war — particularly that published after its end — is characterized by disillusionment and bitterness. Most significant are the works produced by writers who actually served in the war, including John Dos Passos's *Three Soldiers* (1921); E. E. Cummings's *The Enormous Room* (1922), based on his brief imprisonment in France; William Faulkner's *Soldier's Pay* (1926); and Ernest Hemingway's *A Farewell to Arms* (1929).

Sources:

Warner Berthoff, *The Ferment of Realism: American Literature, 1884–1919* (London: Cambridge University Press, 1965);

Stanley Cooperman, *World War I and the American Novel* (Baltimore: Johns Hopkins Press, 1967);

Henry May, *The End of American Innocence: The First Years of Our Own Times, 1912–1917* (New York: Knopf, 1959).

LITERATURE: THE NEW POETRY

Peak Period. Much of the credit for the identification of the 1910s as a period of literary renaissance must be given to its poets, who revolutionized literature — and whose works had close ties to those of the visual artists of the period. Chicago and New York contributed equally to the flood of new poets and new styles. At least eight periodicals devoted exclusively to poetry were founded during the decade. More-general literary and arts periodicals of the day, such as *The Smart Set, Vanity Fair, The Atlantic Monthly, The Little Review,* and *The Seven Arts,* featured poetry prominently, as did the nation's bookstores.

Regionalism. Like several of their counterparts in prose, the greatest poets of the day chose specific regions of the country as their subjects. The poems in Edwin Arlington Robinson's *The Town Down the River* (1910) describe the residents of a fictional small town in New England. The same region was depicted in the work of the new poet Robert Frost, whose first three books — *A Boy's Will* (1913), *North of Boston* (1914), and *Mountain Interval* (1916) — appeared during the decade and established his reputation. Edgar Lee Masters's *Spoon River Anthology,* a collection of epitaphs for deceased residents of a fictional midwestern small town, was published in 1915; the following year Carl Sandburg's *Chicago Poems* appeared.

New Ideas and Forms. Much as the painters of the 1910s challenged the establishment, poets used verse freely, breaking old rules about meter and form and creating new (and increasingly abstract) styles. Inspired by the interplay among artists working in different media, some even found new functions for their art: poetry not only was to be read but also was to be seen and heard. In 1912 Gertrude Stein published her word portraits of Matisse and Picasso in Alfred Stieglitz's art periodical *Camera Work.* Vachel Lindsay traveled across America reading his poetry in exchange for food and lodging — though after the success of his 1912 poem "General William Booth Enters into Heaven," his recitations took place in more formal settings. T. S. Eliot's "The Love Song of J. Alfred Prufrock," first published in a 1915 issue of *Poetry,* was innovative in form and content. (Seven years later his long poem *The Waste Land* was hailed as a landmark of modern poetry.) By the mid 1910s Eliot, like Gertrude Stein and Ezra Pound, had become an expatriate, he and Pound living in London and Stein in Paris. Yet the work of all three continued to appear in American periodicals.

Imagism. An inveterate inventor and promoter of literary "-isms," Pound created Imagism in 1912 with Hilda Doolittle (H. D.) and British poet Richard Aldington. They agreed on three principles: avoidance of superfluous words, direct treatment of the subject, and avoidance of strict meter in favor of musical phrasing. Pound championed the new movement by editing *Des Imagistes* (1914), which includes poems by the three original Imagists and eight other poets, including Americans Amy Lowell, William Carlos Williams, Skipwith Cannell, and John Cournos. American John Gould Fletcher was also part of the movement. Convinced that Amy Lowell was trying to take over the movement, Pound soon developed new enthusiasms, while Lowell went on to edit three volumes of *Some Imagist Poets* (1915–1917). The wealthy Lowell, a member of the aristocratic Lowell family of Boston (the sister of Harvard president A. Lawrence Lowell and grandniece of poet James Russell Lowell), became a patron of many of the new poets, regardless of their literary styles.

The Little Magazines. Important patronage also came from new periodicals devoted exclusively to poetry, which sprang up all over the country. They included *Poetry*

Actress Florence Lawrence, "The Biograph Girl"

(Chicago, 1912), *The Poetry Journal* (Boston, 1912), *The Glebe* (Ridgefield, N.J., 1913), *Others* (Grantwood, N.J., 1915), *Contemporary Verse* (Philadelphia, 1916), *The Poetry Review of America* (Cambridge, Mass., 1916), *The Sonnet* (New York, 1917), and *Youth* (Cambridge, Mass., 1918). Chief among these magazines — which together signaled the flowering of poetry as an American art form — was *Poetry,* founded and edited by Harriet Monroe, with Pound serving as its overseas editor. This periodical was the first to publish the work of Lindsay and Sandburg; its other contributors during the 1910s included Frost, Robinson, Masters, Lowell, Sara Teasdale, Marianne Moore, Williams, Hart Crane, and Wallace Stevens (some of whom would be better known in the 1920s). Most of these poets — as well as H. D., Fletcher, and Conrad Aiken — also published poems in *Others,* which moved to New York City in 1916. Edited by poet and playwright Alfred Kreymborg, who founded the magazine as a rival to *Poetry* in Chicago, *Others* was influential but short-lived, folding in 1919. Though not exclusively a poetry magazine, *The Little Review* also played an important role in promoting new poets. Founded in Chicago in 1914 by Margaret Anderson, who moved the magazine to New York in 1917 (and to Paris in 1922), *The Little Review* is best known for its publication of parts of James Joyce's *Ulysses* in 1918–1920. As was the case with many arts periodicals and liberal magazines, few poetry journals survived World War I, but *Poetry* continues to be published in the 1990s.

By the mid 1910s feature films were usually preceded by newsreels. In fact, the earliest movie studios were established to produce short films of newsworthy events, including the Spanish-American War of 1898, the funeral of assassinated president William McKinley in 1901, and the San Francisco earthquake of 1906. During the 1910s the production of weekly newsreels was a thriving, competitive component of the movie-studio business. The leaders in the field were Hearst-Selig, Pathé (a French-owned, New Jersey–based company that was the first to make daily newsreels, starting in June 1914), and Fox Studio News. There is little authentic newsreel coverage of the biggest news event of the decade, World War I. Commercial cameramen were kept away from combat, and those who managed to get near it had their films censored by the U.S. government. Lack of real footage did not prevent the movie studios from faking battle scenes and releasing them as dramatic coverage "from the front." A typical newsreel featured a combination of news and entertainment: footage of the president's activities, the woman suffrage campaign, labor strikes, and other "hard news," mixed with coverage of celebrities, sporting events, and the latest craze in clothing, hairstyles, or dances.

Source: Raymond Fielding, *The American Newsreel, 1911–1967* (Norman: University of Oklahoma Press, 1972).

To glamorize plain-sounding monikers, to camouflage ethnicity, or to protect their privacy, dozens of stars in the 1910s (as in other eras) used stage names, including:

Fred Astaire (Fred Austerlitz)
Theda Bara (Theodosia Goodman)
Jack Benny (Benjamin Kubelsky)
Irving Berlin (Israel Baline)
Fanny Brice (Fania Borach)
Eddie Cantor (Isidore Iskowitz)
Vernon Castle (Vernon Blyth)
Marie Dressler (Leila Marie Koerber)
W. C. Fields (Wilbur Claude Dukenfield)
Al Jolson (Asa Yoelson)
Bert Lahr (Irving Lahrheim)
"Jelly Roll" Morton (Ferdinand Joseph La Menthe)
Lillian Nordica (Lillian Norton)
Mary Pickford (Gladys Smith)
Mack Sennett (Michael Sinnott)
Sophie Tucker (Sonia Kalish)
Ed Wynn (Isaiah Edwin Leopold)

Sources:

Harriet Monroe, *Poets and Their Art* (New York: Macmillan, 1926; revised and enlarged, 1932);

Steven Watson, *Strange Bedfellows: The First American Avant-Garde* (New York: Abbeville Press, 1991);

Arthur Frank Wertheim, *The New York Little Renaissance: Iconoclasm, Modernism, and Nationalism in American Culture, 1908–1917* (New York: New York University Press, 1976);

Michael Yatron, *America's Literary Revolt* (New York: Philosophical Library, 1959).

MOVIES: THE BUSINESS, THE STUDIOS, THE STARS

The Early Business in New York. By 1910 the movie business had been in existence for nearly a decade, concentrated in and around New York City. In 1908 the major studios formed what was essentially a trust, the Motion Picture Patents Company, under Thomas Edison, whose inventions had enabled the development of the moviemaking process. The Motion Picture Patents Company had nine production companies — Edison, Biograph, Vitagraph, Essanay, Kalem, Selig, and Lubin, as well as Pathé Frères and Méliès (American subsidiaries of French companies) — and had an exclusive agreement with Eastman Kodak, then the only manufacturer of raw film. By 1912 the trust also controlled nearly sixty film-distribution companies. Two of the first companies to operate successfully outside the trust were Carl Laemmle's Chicago-based Independent Motion Pictures Company (IMP) and the New York Motion Picture Company. During the early 1910s almost all the movies these companies made were one-reel shorts destined for the country's more than ten thousand nickelodeons — storefront theaters where, for a nickel, customers could view two or three short movies, each lasting ten or fifteen minutes.

Longer Movies and New Studios. By 1912, however, major directors were making two- and three-reel films. *Quo Vadis*, an eight-reel Italian film shown during the spring of 1913 in New York, whetted Americans' appetites for feature-length films. A handful of 1915 movies were as long as eight, ten, and even twelve reels. In May of that year *Variety* reported that "the bottom has apparently fallen out of the one-reel subjects." By the mid 1910s the movie business included several newcomers, including Adolph Zukor's Famous Players Company, which gave many stage actors their screen debuts; the Triangle Film Corporation (a combination of the studios affiliated with three major directors: Thomas Ince's Kay Bee studio, Mack Sennett's Keystone studio, and D. W. Griffith's Reliance-Majestic studio); and Jesse Lasky's Feature Play Company (which merged with Famous Players in 1916 and eventually became Paramount Pictures).

THE FIRST CENSORSHIP OF MOVIES

Efforts to censor movies started almost as early as movies themselves. By 1897 citizens were complaining that there was too much sex and violence in the "shorts" shown in storefront movie theaters. The first major legal regulation of motion pictures occurred at the state level, when Pennsylvania created a state board of censors in 1911. Within four years Ohio, Kansas, and Maryland had done the same. A key legal victory for the censors came with a 1915 Supreme Court case, *Mutual Film Corporation* v. *Ohio*, in which the justices ruled that motion pictures were not protected by the First Amendment. (This precedent held until 1952, when the Court ruled that the motion picture is "a significant medium for the communication of ideas" and may be protected by the First Amendment.) In 1922 Hollywood took a proactive stance on the issue of censorship and began regulating itself, appointing Postmaster General Will H. Hays to head the new Motion Picture Producers and Exhibitors of America. The "Hays Office" created a system of codes for decency, violence, and language and imposed a $25,000 fine on violators. These codes were in effect until 1968, when a new movie-rating system was developed.

Sources: Jean Folkerts and Dwight Teeter Jr., *Voices of a Nation: A History of Mass Media in the United States* (New York: Macmillan, 1994);

Garth Jowett, *Film: The Democratic Art* (Boston: Little, Brown, 1976).

The Growth of Hollywood. As early as 1911 and 1912 several New York–based film companies experimented with making movies in California, where there was more land and better weather for filming. Biograph sent D. W. Griffith westward on three trips, and the New York Motion Picture Company established California studios for Ince and Sennett. In 1913 the New York–based Selig Company started a studio in Los Angeles, and Jesse Lasky set up shop in the Hollywood Hills, where director Cecil B. DeMille made all of his pictures. By the following year there were more than fifty movie companies, large and small, based in California. Feature films were still made in New York throughout the 1910s, and some director-producers, including Griffith, worked on both coasts. But by the end of the decade Hollywood had become the hub of the movie business.

Birth of the Star System. Early movie actors were not stars; they were merely employees, acting out parts and receiving no billing. But by 1912 the studios had discovered that ticket sales were higher when a movie featured a recognizable name. At first actors were publicized with reference to their studios — the popular Florence Lawrence was known as "The Biograph Girl," while Florence Turner was promoted as "The Vitagraph Girl." Actress

Mary Pickford changed all that when she made a name with IMP, switched over to Biograph, and then studio-hopped through the 1910s: *she* was the star, not the studio. Both Pickford and Charlie Chaplin translated their fame and popularity into money, demanding higher salaries with every movie they made.

Other Stars. Following the lead of Pickford and Chaplin were other actors and actresses who rose to nationwide celebrity during the 1910s, including Douglas Fairbanks (formerly a stage actor, later Pickford's husband), Lillian Gish (the star of many Griffith films), Mabel Normand (the star of many Sennett films), Geraldine Farrar (an opera singer who moved into film and starred in many of DeMille's early films), and Theda Bara (who during the 1910s made nearly forty films as a "vamp," a kohl-eyed, evil temptress). Other well-known movie actors of the decade included Tom Mix, William S. Hart, Maurice Costello, Francis X. Bushman, Blanche Sweet, Norma Talmadge, Clara Kimball Young, Mae Marsh, Robert Harron, Richard Barthelmess, Miriam Cooper, Wallace Reid, Mary Miles Minter, Ina Claire, Carol Dempster, Edna Purviance, Harold Lloyd, Bebe Daniels, Roscoe "Fatty" Arbuckle, Wallace Beery, and Gloria Swanson — as well as imports from the stage such as Minnie Maddern Fiske, Marguerite Clark, and George Arliss. By the end of the 1910s the star system was firmly in place, with the biggest names making huge salaries: Theda Bara, for instance, earned $4,000 a week, while Pickford and Chaplin were each taking home more than $10,000 a week.

Sources:
William K. Everson, *American Silent Film* (New York: Oxford University Press, 1978);

Garth Jowett, *Film: The Democratic Art* (Boston: Little, Brown, 1976);

David Shipman, *The Great Movie Stars* (New York: Da Capo Press, 1970);

Robert Sklar, *Movie-Made America: A Social History of American Movies* (New York: Random House, 1975).

MOVIES: THE DIRECTORS AND THE PICTURES

The First Great Directors. Despite the rise of the star system, the 1910s were without question a decade of great movie directors. Directors *made* the stars, and the most influential were given their own studios and free rein over the creative aspects of their pictures; most also became producers. The greatest of all was D. W. Griffith, who made more than four hundred short films for Biograph between 1908 and 1913 before turning his attention to the feature films that would make him famous. In *The Birth of a Nation* (1915) and *Intolerance* (1916), both twelve reels long, Griffith pioneered the techniques of close-ups, cross-cutting, and flashbacks; raised the standards for sets and action in films; and made stars of Lillian Gish and Mae Marsh. Another great director who got his start during the 1910s was Cecil B. DeMille, whose films for Jesse Lasky — including *Joan, the Woman*

The Feast of Belshazzar set in D. W. Griffith's *Intolerance* (1916)

(1917) and *Male and Female* (1919) — made stars of Geraldine Farrar, Wallace Reid, and Gloria Swanson. Unlike Griffith, DeMille became more famous in later decades, with extravaganzas such as *The Ten Commandments* (1923; and a sound version in 1956), *King of Kings* (1927), *Cleopatra* (1934), *Union Pacific* (1939), and *Reap the Wild Wind* (1942).

New Film Genres. Though he started as a director of IMP movies starring Mary Pickford, after he moved to California in 1912 Thomas Ince specialized in Westerns. Among his Westerns — which starred William S. Hart, Tom Mix, Howard Hickman, Frank Keenan, and Lew Cody as cowboy-frontier heroes and villains — are *War on the Plains* (1912), *Custer's Last Raid* (1912), *The Bargain* (1914), *Hell's Hinges* (1916), and *The Gun Fighter* (1917). Another new type of movie was the serial, in which the same stars repeated roles from one film to the next, with varying plots. Most such films involve danger but end happily. The first serial was *The Adventures of Kathlyn* (1913), a thirteen-part series starring Kathlyn Williams (billed as The Girl without Fear). The most successful release in this genre was *The Perils of Pauline*, a twenty-part series starring Pearl White as Pauline Mar-

vin, the innocent heroine who survives various dangers, from buzz saws to oncoming railroad trains. The *Perils of Pauline* episodes, released biweekly throughout 1914, were so popular that their plots were printed in newspapers. Pearl White starred in three more serials, *The Exploits of Elaine* (1914), *The New Exploits of Elaine* (1915), and *The Romance of Elaine* (1915).

The Mack Sennett Comedies. The comedy movie was never exclusive to any particular company or set of creators. Yet Mack Sennett was without question the father of film comedy, pioneering physical humor in a silent medium and launching the careers of master comic actors. Trained as a director by D. W. Griffith, for whom he had worked as an actor at Biograph, Sennett began directing his Keystone Comedies in his California studios in 1912, making an average of eight films a month that year. Over the next five years he made more than five hundred comedies. The formula was essentially the same for all these pictures (some of which were about inept policemen, known as the "Keystone Kops"): actors dressed in ridiculous costumes performed slapstick routines, usually ending in a hilarious chase scene. Charlie Chaplin got his start in Keystone Comedies in December

The Original Dixieland Jass Band, the first musicians to make a jazz recording

1913, after Sennett hired him off the vaudeville circuit (where he was performing comic pantomime in a touring British company), and soon became the director, as well as the star, of his Keystone pictures. Most of the Keystone films starred Mabel Normand, though Normand and Chaplin played supporting roles in the six-reel *Tillie's Punctured Romance* (1914), which starred Broadway stage actress Marie Dressler and was one of Sennett's most commercially successful films. Others who worked in Keystone Comedies were Wallace Beery, Gloria Swanson, Roscoe "Fatty" Arbuckle, Buster Keaton, and scenario writer Frank Capra (who would later make such all-American movies as *Mr. Smith Goes to Washington* in 1939 and *It's a Wonderful Life* in 1946).

Movies about the War. Movies with fictional plots about the ongoing war in Europe were also popular during the 1910s. From the outbreak of war in 1914 until about 1916, American movies, like American popular songs, championed pacifism or neutrality, reflecting the feelings of most Americans at the time. Examples of such pictures include *Neutrality* (1914), *War Is Hell* (1914),

The Horrors of War (1914), and *War Brides* (1916). By 1916, however, film plots were more likely centered on fictional war atrocities committed by the "Huns," such as the defilement of defenseless American women by Germans invading the United States. Pictures such as *The War Bride's Secret* (1916), *The Fall of a Nation* (1916), and *Patria* (1917) fueled Americans' prowar feelings. *The Little American* (1917), a DeMille film starring Mary Pickford, is a fictionalized depiction of the May 1915 sinking of the British passenger ship *Lusitania* by a German submarine. *Hearts of the World* (1918), a Griffith picture starring Lillian Gish, is about a French village occupied by German soldiers. Many movies, such as *Huns Within Our Gates* (1918) and *The Kaiser, Beast of Berlin* (1918), are overtly anti-German. Charlie Chaplin's *Shoulder Arms* (1918) is a rare comedic film about military life. The war remained a movie subject even after its end, though pictures such as *The Four Horsemen of the Apocalypse* (1921) reveal some of the ambivalence and disillusionment Americans were feeling about the war by the early 1920s.

Sources:
Ivan Butler, *The War on Film* (New York: A. S. Barnes, 1974);

THE PHONOGRAPH COMES OF AGE

Recording technology began in 1877 with Thomas Edison's "talking machine," and during the first decade of the twentieth century Americans could buy recordings of opera and classical music. In the 1910s the sound-recording business took off, owing in large part to the dance craze sweeping the country. Between 1912 and 1916 the number of commercial recording companies grew from just three — Victor, Columbia, and Edison — to forty-six, and Victor's assets doubled. By 1919 some two hundred companies were manufacturing nearly two million record players a year, and despite their high price (anywhere from $375 to $2,000), public demand exceeded the supply. In addition to the hundreds of dance-music releases, popular records included John Philip Sousa's "Liberty Loan March," recorded by Sousa's band; George M. Cohan's wartime anthem, "Over There," recorded by vaudevillian Nora Bayes and by opera star Enrico Caruso; many versions of Irving Berlin's "Alexander's Ragtime Band"; and — after 1917 — jazz. Though a majority of Americans did not own record players until the 1920s (when prices fell below $100), the machines were rapidly transforming how songs were popularized and how people heard music. Like the new movie industry, the booming recording industry took its toll on other entertainment fields, including sheet-music publishing and vaudeville.

Source: Roland Gelatt, *The Fabulous Phonograph: 1877–1977*, second revised edition (New York: Macmillan, 1977).

Michael T. Isenberg, *War on Film: The American Cinema and World War I, 1914–1941* (Rutherford, Madison & Teaneck, N.J.: Fairleigh Dickinson University Press, 1981);

Ann Lloyd, ed., *The Illustrated History of the Cinema* (New York: Macmillan, 1986);

Gene Ringgold and DeWitt Bodeen, *The Films of Cecil B. DeMille* (New York: Citadel Press, 1969);

Edward Wagenknecht and Anthony Slide, *The Films of D. W. Griffith*, with a foreword by Lillian Gish (New York: Crown, 1975).

THE MUSIC DOWNTOWN

Tin Pan Alley. In its early years during the late nineteenth century, Tin Pan Alley was literally an alley — West Twenty-eighth Street between Broadway and Sixth Avenue in New York City. Later, the phrase was used to identify the dozens of companies in the booming sheet-music business, most of them still based in Manhattan. By 1910 sheet music was so popular across America that the local Woolworth's store in any midsized city was likely to stock more than a thousand titles. Music stores employed pluggers — singers who would perform any song upon a customer's request. The price for the sheet music itself usually ranged from a penny to ten cents. Top songwriters included George M. Cohan, Irving Berlin (who wrote more than three hundred songs during the decade), Jerome Kern, brothers Harry and Albert Von Tilzer, Harry Ruby, Gus Kahn, Eddie Green, Richard Whiting, Harry Carroll, and Percy Wenrich. Between 1910 and 1919 Tin Pan Alley produced thousands of hits. Among the most popular were Berlin's "Alexander's Ragtime Band" (1911), Cohan's "Over There" (1917), Whiting's "'Till We Meet Again" (1917), and George Gershwin's "Swanee" (1919). "Over There" and "'Till We Meet Again" are just two of hundreds of tunes written about World War I. Though songs written in the early years of the European war, such as Al Piantadosi and Alfred Bryan's "I Didn't Raise My Boy to Be a Soldier" (1915), leaned toward neutrality — the prevailing attitude in the United States until early 1916 — later songs of the war era were strongly pro-Ally, prowar, and anti-German. A few, such as Irving Berlin's 1918 hit "Oh! How I Hate to Get Up in the Morning," were about the soldier's life, but most expressed the sentiments of those on the home front.

African American Traditions Converge. Many of the Tin Pan Alley songs that achieved national popularity originated in one of two African American musical traditions, ragtime and the blues. Ragtime — whose black practitioners during the era included Scott Joplin, Scott Hayden, Eubie Blake, and James Scott — was the first of the two styles to be embraced fully by white composers and audiences. "Syncopation is the soul of every American," said Irving Berlin, "and ragtime is a necessary element of American life." Several of Berlin's hit songs were inspired by the ragtime style — though "Alexander's Ragtime Band," ironically, is not one of them. (It is *about* a ragtime band.) Joplin wrote two complete ragtime operas, *A Guest of Honor* (1903) and *Treemonisha* (1911). The blues, made nationally popular by W. C. Handy, descended from two traditions of slavery days, the spiritual and the "field holler" (or work chant). Out of ragtime and the blues came a third form of music: jazz. Many early jazz numbers, played by pianists such as Jelly Roll Morton and James P. Johnson, were actually ragtime numbers played slowly. Jazz musicians also appropriated blues songs, adding instrumental improvisation. Ragtime, blues, and jazz are close musical cousins, and all three became popular with white Americans in the 1910s.

New Music on Tour. Throughout the decade "ragtime jazz bands" toured the United States, bringing what was essentially southern music to audiences in other parts of the country. Among them were several all-black groups — including the Superior Orchestra, the Onward Brass Band, and the Tuxedo Brass Band — as well as the all-white Reliance Brass Band. Blues singer Ma Rainey's Georgia Jazz Band (with a teenage Bessie Smith, who became famous as a blues recording artist in the 1920s) and other black musicians toured on the Negro Vaude-

By the early twentieth century Scott Joplin was nationally known and celebrated for his ragtime compositions, especially his "Maple Leaf Rag" (1899), but in the 1910s he suffered a great disappointment. In 1903 he had written *A Guest of Honor*, a ragtime opera that was neither performed nor published. Undaunted, he began work in 1908 on another such composition, *Treemonisha*, a musical fable set in the post-Reconstruction South and stressing the importance of education for the advancement of African Americans. The three-act work (with twenty-seven musical numbers) became an obsession with Joplin, who published it at his own expense in 1911. Unable to find backing for a full production, he staged one performance — without sets and with only his piano playing as accompaniment — in 1915 at the Lincoln Theater in Harlem. The audience found *Treemonisha* too folksy for their modern, urban taste, and Joplin died in 1917 thinking his beloved opera was an utter failure. *Treemonisha* went unperformed until 1971, when a full-scale production was mounted in Atlanta and revived interest in the work. Since then African America opera stars such as Kathleen Battle have performed selections from the opera.

Sources: Rudi Blesh and Harriet Janis, *They All Played Ragtime* (New York: Knopf, 1950);

Susan Curtis, *Dancing to a Black Man's Tune: A Life of Scott Joplin* (Columbia & London: University of Missouri Press, 1994).

Charles Ives, circa 1917

New Orleans in search of work. Most went north along the Mississippi, taking jazz to Memphis, Kansas City, Saint Louis, and Chicago. Among the migrants was cornetist Joe "King" Oliver, who led the Creole Jazz Band in Chicago in 1918. (Four years later he hired the young Louis Armstrong, who had spent the last years of the 1910s playing the trumpet on a Mississippi riverboat.) All these musicians laid the groundwork for the Jazz Age of the 1920s.

Sources:
Jack B. Buerkle and Danny Barker, *Bourbon Street Black: The New Orleans Black Jazzman* (New York: Oxford University Press, 1973);

David A. Jasen, *Tin Pan Alley: The Composers, the Songs, the Performers, and Their Times* (New York: Donald I. Fine, 1988);

Paul Oliver, *The Story of the Blues* (Radnor, Pa.: Chilton, 1969);

Frank Tirro, *Jazz: A History* (New York: Norton, 1977).

THE MUSIC UPTOWN

The Symphonic Scene. Classical music in 1910s America was still strongly influenced by European traditions. An increasing number of Americans had access to symphonic music, thanks to the proliferation of symphony orchestras in cities and towns across the United States and the growing recording industry. (Both the Philadelphia Orchestra and the Boston Symphony were recording regularly by 1918.) Most major orchestras had been founded in the closing decades of the nineteenth century, and the New York Philharmonic was three-quarters of a century old in 1917. Nevertheless, most

ville Circuit. Leaving New Orleans for New York in 1911, Jelly Roll Morton traveled from the Northeast through Saint Louis, Kansas City, and Chicago, arriving in San Francisco in 1915. Cornetist Freddie Keppard and soprano saxophonist Sidney Bechet, both black jazz musicians, toured during the 1910s, with Keppard traveling to Los Angeles and Bechet to Chicago. By the time Bechet reached the Windy City, however, two all-white jazz bands had already been there (having arrived in 1914). In 1917 one of them, the Original Dixieland Jass Band, became the first band to record jazz.

The Migration North. Reacting to continuing segregation, racial violence, and poverty in the South, African Americans migrated northward in record numbers during the 1910s. The exodus of black musicians from southern states was already well under way by November 1917, when it was hastened by an unexpected turn of events: the closing of Storyville in New Orleans, after four enlisted men from a nearby naval base were killed in a fight in that well-known red-light district. Entertainers who performed in the Storyville sporting houses (brothels that also featured musical entertainment and gambling), almost all of them African Americans, were forced to leave

American musicians and conductors went abroad for their training, and concerts given by American orchestras were dominated by works of European masters and new European composers such as Igor Stravinsky and Sergey Prokofiev. Even the orchestral accompaniment (played live) for early feature films was European music: at the 1915 premiere of D. W. Griffith's *The Birth of a Nation*, for instance, the score included works by Franz Schubert, Wolfgang Amadeus Mozart, Pyotr Tchaikovsky, Gustav Mahler, and Richard Wagner.

A Distinctly American Composer. Ironically, at just this time one of the first major American classical composers was writing his best works, which would not be widely heard for several decades. Connecticut-born Charles Ives wrote music that drew on older musical forms while creating new ones through bold experimentation. Some of his scores, for instance, called for the simultaneous playing of themes in different keys or time signatures. Few of his compositions were performed within twenty years of their composition, and Ives was not taken seriously by the classical-music community until 1947, when his Third Symphony (completed in 1911, first performed in 1945) won the Pulitzer Prize for music. The work that is now his most popular is his *Second Sonata for Piano: Concord, Mass., 1840–1860* (1915), with movements titled "Emerson," "Hawthorne," "The Alcotts," and "Thoreau." Ives published this "Concord Sonata" at his own expense in 1919, and it was not performed until 1939. His Fourth Symphony (1916), which mixed marches, ragtime, square-dance tunes, and hymns and included choral singers, was not performed until 1965, though it is now considered among the greatest American symphonies. Other Ives compositions also drew on American works: *General William Booth Enters into Heaven* (1914) is based on Vachel Lindsay's poem of the same title; *Charlie Rutlage* (1915) derives from a cowboy ballad; *A New England Symphony* (1914) includes refrains from Civil War music; and *Lincoln: The Great Commoner* (1912) includes excerpts from several patriotic tunes. In *A New England Symphony* and *Lincoln, the Great Commoner* Ives also made musical reference to earlier American composers, including Lowell Mason, George Frederick Root, Henry Clay Work, Stephen Foster, and Scott Joplin.

Other Symphonic Composers. A few other American composers of the era chose native themes. John Powell's *Sonata Virginianesque* (1919) draws on southern American folk music. Henry Franklin Belknap Gilbert's *Negro Rhapsody* (1912) is based on African American vocal and dance music. Henry Cowell's *Advertisement* (1915), a frantic-sounding composition for the piano, was meant to convey the annoying intrusion of advertisers on twentieth-century American life. Other American composers were inspired by foreign texts and traditions. Charles T. Griffes, for instance, set several of Oscar Wilde's poems to music in 1912, and later in the decade he wrote *Sho-Jo* (1917), a ballet score influenced by Asian traditions.

American Opera. The foremost opera company in America during the 1910s was the Metropolitan Opera in New York City, though the relatively new Chicago Opera (founded in 1910) quickly became world renowned as well. The programs of American opera companies were heavily dominated by European composers and performers, but several American singers made their marks during the 1910s. Most were women, including Lillian Nordica (who made a series of phonograph records for Columbia in 1911), Rosa Ponselle, Louise Homer, Olive Fremstad, Geraldine Farrar, and Mary Garden. (Farrar and Garden successfully crossed over to the new medium of silent film.) The first major productions of operas by American composers occurred in the 1910s, starting with Frederick Shepherd Converse's *The Pipe of Desire* at the New York Metropolitan Opera House in 1910. Also during the decade the Met began an annual competition (with a $10,000 prize) for the best new opera by an American composer. The first winner was Dr. Horatio Parker of Yale University, whose *Mona* premiered at the Met on 14 March 1912; three years later his *Fairyland* won the top award from the National Federation of Music Clubs and premiered in Los Angeles. Some new American works were first performed outside major cities. For example, William F. Hanson's *Sun Dance*, a five-act opera about Native Americans, had its first production in Utah in 1913. Yet most premiered in New York or Chicago, including Reginald DeKoven's *The Canterbury Pilgrims* and Henry Kimball Hadley's *Azora* in 1917; Hadley's *Bianca* and Charles Wadefield Cadman's *Shanewis* (also with a Native American theme) in 1918; and Joseph Carl Breil's *The Legend* and John Adam Hugo's *The Temple Dancer* in 1919.

European Operas in America. Meanwhile, two great European opera composers were writing music that was not only well received by American audiences but also embraced by vaudeville and Tin Pan Alley. Richard Strauss, whose *Salome* (1905) was widely parodied in burlesque and vaudeville, wrote two new operas during the 1910s that became favorites with American audiences, *Der Rosenkavalier* (1911) and *Ariadne auf Naxos* (1912). Jerome Kern spoofed the latter in his 1915 musical, *Very Good, Eddie*. Giacomo Puccini — whose *Madama Butterfly* (1904) inspired the hit song "Poor Butterfly" — chose New York City as the site of the world premieres of all four works he wrote in the 1910s: *La fanciulla del West* (1910, based on American David Belasco's 1905 play *The Girl of the Golden West*) and Puccini's 1918 triptych, *Il trittico: Il tabarro, Suor Angelica*, and *Gianni Schicchi*.

Sources:

Gilbert Chase, *America's Music from the Pilgrims to the Present*, second edition, revised (New York: McGraw-Hill, 1966);

Ronald L. Davis, *A History of Music in American Life: Volume II, The Gilded Years, 1865–1920* (Huntington, N.Y.: Robert Krieger, 1980);

H. Wiley Hitchcock, ed., *Music in the United States* (Englewood Cliffs, N.J.: Prentice-Hall, 1969).

A 1915 photograph of the Wharf Theater (left), the converted fish house in Provincetown, Massachusetts, where the Provincetown Players staged their first plays in August of that year

THEATER: THE AMERICAN STAGE IN TRANSITION

Abandoning Old Formulas. Writing for *The Theatre* magazine in 1919, Broadway producer Daniel Frohman lamented the passing of what he considered "the two prime requirements" of good theater: "cleanliness and a happy ending." At the beginning of the decade most plays performed in America had both. But by middecade a shift had occurred in the theater, one similar to the advent of realism in American literature and art: instead of portraying how life ought to be, new plays reflected their writers' perspectives on how life *was*. Small theater companies were springing up across the country, experimenting with new themes, new staging, and new styles of acting. The qualities common to turn-of-the-century stage productions — predictable plots, melodramatic acting, and happy endings — gave way to psychological, often gritty, drama, some of it in plays by one of the century's greatest playwrights, Eugene O'Neill.

The Actors. The 1910s were important years for the "Royal Family" of the American theater, the Barrymores. Though she had been featured in Broadway plays since 1901, Ethel Barrymore was not considered a dramatic star until her 1910 appearance in Arthur Wing Pinero's *Mid-Channel*. Her brother John's first important role in a serious stage drama came in John Galsworthy's *Justice* in

1916. The third Barrymore sibling, Lionel, received major acclaim in Augustus Thomas's 1918 play *The Copperhead*. Other theatrical talents of the decade included Minnie Maddern Fiske, Billie Burke, James K. Hackett, George Arliss, David Warfield, Otis Skinner, Alfred Lunt, Douglas Fairbanks, and Frank Bacon. Among American playwrights whose works had their debuts on Broadway during the decade were Edward Sheldon, Percy MacKaye, Owen Davis, Jesse Lynch Williams, Edna Ferber, and Zoë Akins. David Belasco, best known for his earlier plays, was still writing in the 1910s. Glimmerings of the new trend toward dramatic realism could be seen in Sheldon's *Salvation Nell* (1910) and Belasco's *The Governor's Lady* (1912).

The Problems. Still, several factors combined to make the 1910s a relatively unexciting decade for dramatic works on Broadway. Theater ownership — by then virtually a trust — controlled playwrights' and actors' access to existing theaters across the country. Musical revues and vaudeville, which made traditional dramas seem dull by comparison, dominated Broadway. Most of the nonmusical productions on Broadway were light comedies, such as the popular *Peg o' My Heart* (1912), starring Laurette Taylor. Finally, the dramatic stage suffered the defection of many of its stars to the new medium of film during the 1910s. Actors who went from stage to screen included

THE GOLDEN AGE OF YIDDISH THEATER

During the first two decades of the twentieth century, the majority of immigrants pouring into America were from eastern Europe and Russia, many of them Jews fleeing religious persecution and poverty. The Lower East Side of Manhattan was home to the largest population of Jews in America — some 1.4 million by 1915. The new arrivals provided a talent pool and an audience base that made a booming business out of the theatrical tradition known as Yiddish theater, which had existed in the United States since the 1880s. By 1919 New York was home to nearly two dozen Yiddish theaters, where both comedy and serious drama were performed. Among the actors were Jacob Adler, David Kessler, Bertha Kalich, and Paul Muni. Adler and Kessler went on to form their own Yiddish-theater companies, while Kalich and Muni made the transition to mainstream theater (Muni to movies as well). Of the many playwrights who wrote for the Yiddish theater, the one whose legacy has lasted longest is Sholem Aleichem, whose tales of Russian-Jewish life were the source for the 1964 Broadway musical *Fiddler on the Roof*.

Source: David S. Lifson, *The Yiddish Theatre in America* (New York: Yoseloff, 1965).

Fiske, Burke, Hackett, Arliss, Fairbanks, Lily Langtry, James O'Neill (father of the playwright), Elsie Janis, Marguerite Clark, Lillian Russell, and all three Barrymores. One new movie company, Adolph Zukor's Famous Players Company, was founded for the sole purpose of bringing stage actors and plays to the screen.

The Little Theater Movement. As the Broadway theater went into a decline in the 1910s, small theaters appeared across the country. Most of these new companies were staffed by amateurs who shared responsibilities such as writing scripts, acting, set design and construction, and lighting, and they typically produced short (usually one-act) works in tiny theaters. Some little theaters were begun as part of the Progressive reform movement, in settlement houses including Hull House in Chicago and the Henry Street Settlement in New York City (the Neighborhood Playhouse). Others were inspired by the 1911 American tour of the Irish Players from the Abbey Theatre in Dublin, particularly their performances of John Millington Synge's controversial *The Playboy of the Western World*. The earliest little theaters in America, the Toy Theater in Boston and the Little Theater in Chicago, were founded in 1912. Within five years there were more than fifty such companies across the country, in cities including New York, Los Angeles, Cleveland, Detroit, Baltimore, Indianapolis, Madison, Fargo, and Chapel Hill. Among the several little theaters in New York City, two had lasting legacies. One was the Washington Square Players, who presented sixty-two plays between 1915 and 1918, the year they became the Theatre Guild. The other was the Provincetown Players.

The Provincetown Players. The most important little-theater group of the 1910s was named for the place in which it was founded, Provincetown, Massachusetts — a small fishing village at the tip of Cape Cod, where its members spent their summers. The rest of the year they lived in Greenwich Village, New York, where they established their Provincetown Playhouse. Members of the group were radical artists and intellectuals including journalists John Reed, Max Eastman, and Hutchins Hapgood; actress and sculptor Ida Rauh; stage designer (and Socialist activist) Robert Edmond Jones; poet Edna St. Vincent Millay; and novelist-playwrights George Cram Cook, Susan Glaspell, Floyd Dell, and Neith Boyce. *Suppressed Desires* by Cook and Glaspell, *Constancy* by Boyce, *"Change Your Style"* by Cook, and *Contemporaries* by Wilbur Daniel Steele — the four plays produced during the summer of 1915 at the Wharf Theater in Provincetown — focus on the psychological drama of Americans' everyday lives, a new direction for theater. It was this same theme that attracted the group to the unpublished, unproduced works of a newcomer to the group the next summer. In Provincetown on 28 July 1916 the players gave the first performance of a play by Eugene O'Neill, *Bound East for Cardiff*. They performed the play again on 3 November in New York City. They staged a dozen more of his plays there over the next four years, bringing him the critical attention that led to the 1920 Broadway production of his *Beyond the Horizon*, which won a Pulitzer Prize for drama.

The Legacy of the Little Theater Movement. It is a curious footnote to American theater history that the little-theater movement of the 1910s — a movement that arose in response to creative stagnation in the legitimate Broadway theater — produced one of the greatest talents in American drama. O'Neill's pioneering works inspired later American playwrights such as Tennessee Williams, Lillian Hellman, and Arthur Miller. The little theaters of the era left an important legacy as well: an example of success out of the mainstream that served as a model for the Federal Theater Project during the Great Depression of the 1930s and for regional theater companies that still exist across the country.

Sources:
Brooks Atkinson, *Broadway* (New York: Macmillan, 1970);

Adele Heller and Lois Rudnick, *1915, The Cultural Moment: The New Politics, the New Woman, the New Psychology, the New Art, and the New Theatre in America* (New Brunswick, N.J.: Rutgers University Press, 1991);

Benjamin McArthur, *Actors and American Culture, 1880–1920* (Philadelphia: Temple University Press, 1984);

Ethan Mordden, *The American Theatre* (New York: Oxford University Press, 1981).

Will Rogers and the Ziegfeld Girls in the *Ziegfeld Follies* of 1916

THEATER: MUSICALS TAKE CENTER STAGE

A New Theatrical Form. During the 1910s what is now recognized as the American musical was beginning to take shape in Broadway theaters. (It became fully formed with *Show Boat* in 1927.) Musical theater of the 1910s tended to take one of two forms: the musical, a usually thinly plotted play set to music; and the revue, a series of separate musical acts linked by a common theme and ending in a big production number featuring the entire company. Most producers, singers, dancers, and songwriters of the day were involved in both sorts of productions.

Beautiful Girls — and More. The 1910s were the peak decade for the epitome of the musical revue, the annual *Ziegfeld Follies*, which ran from 1907 to 1931. The *Follies* became famous for presenting a stage full of tall, beautifully dressed women, otherwise known as Ziegfeld Girls. Florenz Ziegfeld had a knack for choosing talent as well as beauty. Many of the names connected with his early shows — either his *Follies* or his other revues — later became famous. Among them were Fanny Brice, Will Rogers, W. C. Fields, Eddie Cantor, Irene Castle, and Billie Burke (Ziegfeld's second wife), as well as song-

writers George Gershwin, Irving Berlin, and Jerome Kern. Ziegfeld and the Shuberts — whose annual *Passing Shows*, begun in 1912, gave the *Ziegfeld Follies* their stiffest competition — were responsible for the increased popularity of musical revues during the 1910s. The shows became "upscale" entertainment in theaters where seats cost as much as two dollars.

The Tin Pan Alley Connection. Other popular songwriters of the day also wrote for musical theater. Irving Berlin wrote the score for *Watch Your Step* (1914), which featured, among other numbers, Vernon and Irene Castle dancing to his "Syncopated Walk." A year later Berlin wrote the score for *Stop! Look! Listen!*, a show that introduced his "Everything in America Is Ragtime" and "I Love a Piano." George Gershwin wrote his first full musical score for *La, La, Lucille* in 1919, when he was only twenty-one. The most famous songwriter of the first decade of the century, George M. Cohan, was still creating hits, though in the 1910s he was directing, producing, and acting in plays as well as musicals. His work was not always successful with the critics: in 1911 a reviewer for the humor magazine *Life* called him "the creator of the Star-Spangled drama, the inculcator of the chewing-gum standard of good taste." But Cohan's songs and shows were unqualified commercial suc-

Anyone who has seen the movie *Funny Girl* (1968), starring Barbra Streisand, is familiar with the story of Fanny Brice (1891–1951). When Brice was a sixteen-year-old chorus girl, George M. Cohan fired her, telling her she would never make it on Broadway. So she went into burlesque, where she performed a comic imitation of Eva Tanguay's sultry Salome act — with a Yiddish accent. Her rendition of "Sadie Salome" (1909), written by Irving Berlin, impressed an associate of Florenz Ziegfeld, who invited her to join the 1910 *Ziegfeld Follies*. Brice was a woman doing comedy without a partner, unusual in the 1910s and for years afterward. She was thin and unattractive at a time when most women on the stage were hired for their figures and faces. The daughter of Jewish immigrants, she brought ethnic humor into the mainstream, first through the *Follies*, then through film and radio. She combined motherhood with a career, surviving three unhappy marriages. Her marriage to gambler Julius "Nick" Arnstein inspired her performance of one of her few serious songs, "My Man." During the 1930s she began a twenty-year stint as "Baby Snooks" on the radio. On 29 May 1951, while planning her memoirs, she died of a cerebral hemorrhage at age fifty-nine.

Source: Herbert G. Goldman, *Fanny Brice: The Original Funny Girl* (New York: Oxford University Press, 1992).

cesses. During the 1910s he proved why he had been dubbed "The Man Who Owns Broadway" (a sobriquet derived from the title and title song of his 1909 musical) — and why he earned $1.5 million a year. He wrote, directed, produced, and/or acted in seven plays; two new musicals, *The Little Millionaire* (1911) and *Hello Broadway* (1914); a 1912 revival of his 1906 musical *Forty-Five Minutes from Broadway;* and two musical revues, *The Cohan Revue of 1916* and *The Cohan Revue of 1918.*

The Operetta Connection. Broadway fare included more sophisticated offerings as well. Victor Herbert and Sigmund Romberg, both born and trained in Europe, wrote operettas with songs that became nationwide hits. Herbert's *Naughty Marietta* (1910), which features the popular song "Sweet Mystery of Life," ran for 136 performances at the New York Theatre. Romberg's *The Blue Paradise* (1915) and *Maytime* (1917) were also popular. Another European operetta composer, Rudolph Friml, wrote the scores for the Broadway shows *High Jinks* (1913), *You're in Love* (1917), and *Sometime* (1918). The popularity of such fare led George M. Cohan to try his hand at a comic opera, *The Royal Vagabond* (1919).

The Princess Shows. Equally as sophisticated as operetta were the so-called Princess Shows, created during the second half of the decade by the team of Jerome Kern (music), Guy Bolton (book), and P. G. Wodehouse (lyrics). The British Wodehouse, who lived in New York City and served as the drama critic for *Vanity Fair* magazine, imparted a sophisticated wit to these spare and satirical musicals, which took their name from the intimate three-hundred-seat Princess Theater where they were staged. Among these shows were *Nobody Home* (1915), *Very Good, Eddie* (1915), *Oh, Boy!* (1917), *Oh, Lady! Lady!* (1918), and *Oh, My Dear!* (1918). The Princess Shows produced such enduring songs as "Babes in the Wood" (1915) and " 'Till the Clouds Roll By" (1917).

Sources:

David Ewen, *The Story of America's Musical Theater* (Philadelphia: Chilton, 1961);

Marjorie Farnsworth, *The Ziegfeld Follies* (New York: Bonanza, 1956);

Ward Morehouse, *George M. Cohan: Prince of the American Theater* (Philadelphia: Lippincott, 1943);

Robert C. Toll, *On with the Show: The First Century of Show Business in America* (New York: Oxford University Press, 1976).

THEATER: VAUDEVILLE

The Heyday of Vaudeville. The first two decades of the twentieth century were the heyday of vaudeville, a theatrical form that included performances such as music, dance, light drama, comedy, juggling, magic acts, animal acts. Vaudeville theaters featured several performances a day: in big-time vaudeville performers were expected to present their acts only twice a day, but small-time theaters offered as many as six shows a day. Some performers were lucky enough to get long-term employment in the same theater, but most spent considerable time touring, visiting the thousands of vaudeville theaters in towns all across the country.

The Theaters. In addition to Keith-Albee and the Shuberts, new powers in vaudeville during the 1910s included Marcus Loew and William Fox, whose theaters, like many vaudeville houses of the day, showcased the new feature-length movies as well as live acts. Though some major American vaudeville theaters were outside New York City — such as the Orpheum Theater in San Francisco and the American Music Hall in Chicago — Manhattan was home to the greatest number, including Koster and Bial's, Proctor's, Keith's, and Tony Pastor's. The five-thousand-seat Hippodrome in New York City, built in 1905 for $2 million, was the only truly spectacular theater in Manhattan at the start of the 1910s, but New York soon had other ornate new theaters, including the Palace, which opened in 1913, and the Strand, completed in 1914. The Palace became the most prestigious vaudeville theater. Playing the Palace was proof of making it big.

The Performers. Only a few dozen of the as many as ten thousand vaudeville acts became nationally famous. Eva Tanguay's suggestive performances in white tights (especially her Salome dance and her song "I Don't Care")

Designed and managed by Samuel F. "Roxy" Rothapfel, the Strand Theater in New York City was the grandest of the many fancy vaudeville theaters built during the 1910s to showcase feature films. On its opening night, 1 April 1914, patrons were greeted by uniformed ushers who escorted them through the ornate lobby to cushioned seats inside the theater, which was built to resemble a temple and topped by a lighted dome. The opening-night audience saw quite a show — not just a movie but a wide variety of entertainment typical of the upscale vaudeville theaters of the day. After playing the national anthem, the orchestra performed Franz Liszt's *Hungarian Rhapsody No. 2.* Next the audience enjoyed a newsreel, a travel-documentary film, the performance of a quartet from the Verdi opera *Rigoletto,* and a Keystone Comedy film. Then came the main event: a nine-reel movie, *The Spoilers.* The next morning a *New York Times* critic wrote that the experience "was very much like going to a Presidential reception, a first night at the opera or the opening of the horse show."

Source: Robert C. Allen, *Vaudeville and Film 1895–1915: A Study in Media Interaction* (New York: Arno, 1980).

Comedians Eddie Cantor and Georgie Jessel, circa 1912

earned her $10,000 a year. Other performers used vaudeville — an entertainment form that not only tolerated but encouraged novelty — as a place to try out their acts and get noticed by play and movie producers. Among them were Charlie Chaplin; Jack Haley, who before becoming a popular movie actor played the Palace as half of a song-and-dance comedy team with Charley Crafts; Milton Berle, who was part of a child act; Jack Benny, who as a teenager played the violin with a piano-playing partner named Woods; comedian George Burns; Walter Huston, who had a comedy act with his second wife, Bayonne Whipple; Jimmy Cagney, who at age fourteen was hired as a member of a chorus line of boys dressed as girls; and five teenage brothers named Marks, who soon became the Marx Brothers.

Burlesque. Closely related to vaudeville was burlesque, a theatrical form that included comedy acts as well as scantily clad female dancers. Comedians who got their start in burlesque include W. C. Fields (with a juggling act), Will Rogers (with a rope-twirling act), Ed Wynn, Joe E. Brown, Eddie Cantor, Buster Keaton, Al Jolson, Jimmy Durante, and Bert Lahr. Thanks to talents such as these, and the various charms of the featured women dancers (who in that era sang racy songs but did not strip), the mid 1910s were the high point for ticket sales at burlesque theaters. According to the theater trade publication *Variety,* attendance at burlesque theaters increased by nearly 400 percent between 1900 and 1916. Some shows were "cleaner" than others, and a few made a somewhat successful effort to attract female audience members, especially during the war. One of the most "upscale" burlesque houses, the Columbia Theatre in New York City, reserved its front row for politicians and other well-connected patrons, who paid $1.50 a seat — a higher ticket price than at most big-time vaudeville theaters.

Race and Ethnicity in the Spotlight. Of all the forms of popular entertainment in the 1910s, vaudeville and burlesque were probably the most tolerant of ethnic diversity. Many shows included African Americans and ethnic performers alongside white, native-born performers. While some ethnic theaters thrived apart from the vaudeville circuit, ethnic humor — especially Irish and Yiddish — was a regular feature in burlesque; Fanny Brice took her Yiddish musical-comedy act from burlesque to the *Ziegfeld Follies.* African Americans not only played but succeeded in vaudeville: comedian Bert Williams moved to the *Ziegfeld Follies,* while the song-and-dance team Buck and Bubbles (Ford Lee Washington and John Sublett) played the Palace. All three men, however, were expected to perform wearing burnt-cork blackface makeup — so that audience members, at least theoretically, would not be able to tell that they were really black. In addition to these performers who desegregated mainstream vaudeville stages, hundreds of others — including singers Ma Rainey, Bessie Smith, and Ethel Waters — performed on the Negro Vaudeville Circuit, with stops that included the Booker T. Washington Theater in Saint Louis and the Lincoln Theater in Harlem, where they were seen by mixed-race audiences.

Sources:

Robert C. Allen, *Vaudeville and Film 1895–1915: A Study in Media Interaction* (New York: Arno, 1980);

Bill Smith, *The Vaudevillians* (New York: Macmillan, 1976);

Irving Zeidman, *The American Burlesque Show* (New York: Hawthorn Books, 1967).

"THE VILLAGE," THE SALONS, AND OTHER GATHERINGS

The Birth of "The Village." When the Greenwich Village section of New York City (the part of Manhattan below Fourteenth Street and above Houston Street) was officially designated a residential area in 1916, it was already home to some of the most influential artists and intellectuals in the city. They had moved there partly because the neighborhood was inexpensive — rent for a single room was typically eight dollars a month, or an entire floor of a brownstone house was available for about thirty dollars a month — and partly because of its bohemianism, the prevailing tolerance of a wide variety of lifestyles. The Village was also gaining a reputation as the American Left Bank, a place like the section of Paris where the brightest minds in politics, journalism, and the arts came together. Between 1913 and 1919 Greenwich Village, less than a mile square in size, included the homes of playwrights Eugene O'Neill, George Cram Cook and Susan Glaspell, and Louise Bryant; novelist-playwright Floyd Dell; poet-playwright Alfred Kreymborg; novelists Willa Cather, Theodore Dreiser, Sinclair Lewis, and Sherwood Anderson; poets Hart Crane, Marianne Moore, and Edna St. Vincent Millay; journalists Max Eastman and John Reed; and painters John Sloan, Everett Shinn, William Glackens, Marsden Hartley, George Luks, Maurice Prendergast, Charles Demuth, and William and Marguerite Zorach. Cather was the only one not to participate in the active social life of the Village. One high-spirited night during the late 1910s, a group including John Sloan climbed to the top of the Washington Square Arch and proclaimed Greenwich Village an independent republic — only half in jest. John Reed wrote in a poem, "we are free who live in Washington Square, / We dare to think as Uptown wouldn't dare."

Where Art and Politics Mingled. In New York, Chicago, and elsewhere throughout the 1910s, practitioners of the various arts enthusiastically socialized with radical political thinkers. Many of the artists and intellectuals of Greenwich Village were members of the Liberal Club, formed in 1913 by Henrietta Rodman, a New York City schoolteacher who believed in, among other things, sexual freedom for women. The Liberal Club was billed as "A Meeting Place for Those Interested in New Ideas." It also served alcohol and had dancing. Some members of the club wrote one-act plays that the others staged, and this faction of the club evolved into the Washington Square Players (later the Theatre Guild); the group also included some of the future Provincetown Players. Other meetings of minds in the Village took place at the mural-filled apartment of painters William and Marguerite Zorach and at Polly's Restaurant (which was on the ground floor of the building that housed the Liberal Club and was run by an Illinois-born anarchist named Paula Holladay), where the food was cheap and the politics were radical. In Chicago groups formed around the poet-playwright Floyd Dell and his first wife, Margery Currey (before Dell moved to New York in 1913); cultural critic and economist Thorstein Veblen; Harriet Monroe, the founder of *Poetry;* and Maurice and Ellen Volkenburg Browne, the founders of the Chicago Little Theater.

The Salons. In New York there were two influential salons — regular, planned gatherings of artists and intellectuals. One was at the West Sixty-seventh Street home of art collectors Walter and Louise Arensberg. Their circle included painters Charles Demuth, Joseph Stella, Morton Schamberg, and Man Ray; poets Amy Lowell, William Carlos Williams, and Alfred Kreymborg; and dancer Isadora Duncan. More famous than the Arensbergs' gatherings was the salon of Mabel Dodge, an intellectual socialite who served as hostess, patron, and friend to many of the most important talents of the decade. On Wednesday evenings from 1913 to 1917, her apartment at 23 Fifth Avenue, a block off Washington Square, was filled with guests, including playwrights Eugene O'Neill, Neith Boyce, Susan Glaspell, George Cram Cook, and Floyd Dell; poet Amy Lowell; stage designer Robert Edmond Jones; painter Max Weber; and journalists Max Eastman, John Reed, Walter Lippmann, and Hutchins Hapgood. Dodge's gatherings often had themes — a poetry evening, a magazine evening, a psychoanalysis evening — and guest speakers such as birth-control pioneer Margaret Sanger, radical labor leader William "Big Bill" Haywood, and anarchist Emma Goldman. The radical climate of some of these social events carried over into the political activities of the group members. For instance, Dodge, Jones, and Reed were the masterminds of the Paterson Strike Pageant of 1913, a staged event in which thousands of striking silk-mill workers marched up Fifth Avenue to Madison Square Garden, where they put on a political "pageant" meant to dramatize the plight of the industrial worker. Dodge had been inspired to start her New York salon by her friend Gertrude Stein, an expatriate American poet who held her own salons in Paris. There she befriended and en-

Caricature of Liberal Club members in Polly's Restaurant, circa 1915

couraged American artists working in Europe, including Marsden Hartley and Alfred Maurer, as well as European artists who later came to the United States, including Marcel Duchamp and Francis Picabia. Dodge's New York salon — which ended in 1917 when she moved to Taos, New Mexico, to create an artists' colony — played an important role in bringing together the arts and radical politics during the middle years of the 1910s.

Sources:

Allen Churchill, *The Improper Bohemians: A Re-creation of Greenwich Village in Its Heyday* (New York: Dutton, 1959);

Martin Green, *New York: 1913* (New York: Macmillan, 1988);

Robert E. Humphrey, *Children of Fantasy: The First Rebels of Greenwich Village* (New York: Wiley, 1978);

Steven Watson, *Strange Bedfellows: The First American Avant-Garde* (New York: Abbeville Press, 1991).

WAR AND THE ARTS: THE TWO FACES OF PATRIOTISM

Artists in the War. Some of the young American men who served or lived in Europe during World War I later made their marks in various arts, particularly the writers who used their war experiences as creative material. Several artists with already-established reputations were involved in the war as well. Among those who interrupted successful careers for wartime service were comic actor Buster Keaton, songwriter Irving Berlin, vaudeville cowboy wit Will Ahern, and dancer Ted Shawn. The careers of dancer Vernon Castle and poets Joyce Kilmer and Alan

Seeger ended when they became war casualties. Other artists were involved in a professional capacity. Photographer Edward Steichen supervised aerial photography for the U.S. Army. Short-story writer Ring Lardner was a war correspondent in France for *Collier's* magazine. John Singer Sargent, an American expatriate, served as the offical wartime painter for the British government. (One resulting work, *Gassed,* was exhibited at the Royal Academy in 1919.) John Philip Sousa was put in charge of all U.S. Navy bands. Dance-band leader James Reese Europe, commissioned as an army lieutenant, directed the regimental band of the New York Fifteenth Regiment, an all-black corps that endured 191 consecutive days under fire.

The Home Front. Throughout the war more than twelve hundred American actors traveled to Europe to perform for the troops. Performers also staged wartime fund-raisers and patriotic rallies at home. In 1917 an all-star cast including Laurette Taylor, Minnie Maddern Fiske, George Arliss, George M. Cohan, and James K. Hackett toured the country in a benefit production of *Out There,* a patriotic play about a Red Cross nurse, raising more than $680,000 for the Red Cross. Stationed in the United States, army sergeant Irving Berlin — a Russian-Jewish immigrant who was drafted at age twenty-nine, only a month after he became a naturalized American citizen — wrote, produced, and acted in *Yip, Yip Yaphank,* a fund-raiser with an all-soldier cast that brought in $135,000 when it played at the Century The-

Lillian Gish and Noel Coward in D. W. Griffith's *Hearts of the World* (1918), a movie about German atrocities in an occupied French village during World War I

atre in New York City in 1918. The show included "Oh, How I Hate to Get Up in the Morning," a song that became one of the biggest hits of the war, especially among enlisted men. Director D. W. Griffith chaired the Motion Picture War Service Association, which organized stars' appearances at war-bond rallies. Some celebrities — including Douglas Fairbanks, Charlie Chaplin, Mary Pickford, and Ruth St. Denis — made national tours to sell war bonds. Actress Lillian Russell raised $7,000 in a solo appearance at the Hippodrome in New York City; in Pittsburgh she headlined "Lillian Russell Recruiting Day at the Navy."

Nativism and Intolerance. Amid all this loyalty, there was an ugly side to the patriotism that swept across America during the war. The "Four Minute Men" of George Creel's Committee on Public Information — volunteers who gave four-minute talks on patriotism — made appearances between acts at Broadway and vaudeville theaters, at movie houses, at dance clubs, and even at the opera. Their speeches, along with public-service advertisements from the Creel Committee, warned Americans that the country was full of spies. The Broadway show *Watch Your Neighbors* (1918) echoed this theme. Any person or creative work deemed somewhat less than 100 percent American was suspect. Robert Goldstein, the producer of *The Spirit of '76* (1917), a movie about the Revolutionary War, was arrested and imprisoned under the Espionage Act of 1917 because he depicted the British, allies of the United States in World War I, as evil people. Meanwhile, American movies such as *Huns Within Our Gates* (1918) and *The Fall of a Nation* (1916) — the latter about an invasion of America by brutal Germans — fueled citizens' fears of Americans of German descent. German Americans were vilified during the war years, a time when hamburger was renamed "liberty steak" and sauerkraut became "liberty cabbage."

Anti-German Fervor. The German arts were essentially removed from American culture during the war. German-language theaters in Milwaukee and Saint Louis, cities where there were large German American populations, were shut down. The New York Metropolitan Opera, the Philadelphia Orchestra, and the Pittsburgh Symphony excised the works of German composers from their repertoires, and the Chicago Opera dropped its annual performance of Richard Wagner's Ring Cycle. A wartime patriotic organization called the American Defense Society warned Americans that German music was one of the most dangerous forms of German propaganda because it appealed to the emotions. The cities of Pittsburgh, Washington, Baltimore, and Cleveland canceled recitals by Austrian-born violinist Fritz Kreisler. In California the state government ordered German folk songs cut out of schoolchildren's songbooks; in Marysville, Nebraska, residents removed German-language books, including Bibles, from the school library and burned them.

The Case of Carl Muck. The worst instance of wartime intolerance in the American arts was the internment of Boston Symphony Orchestra conductor Carl Muck. Because of his initial reluctance to open all of the orchestra's performances with "The Star-Spangled Banner" (considering it an inappropriate start for a program of classical music) the German-born Muck — who was actually a naturalized Swiss citizen — became the target of a hate campaign led by the Daughters of 1812 and the Daughters of the American Revolution. His mail was censored, and his home was frequently searched. Even after he added the national anthem to the orchestra's program, his performances in Washington, Baltimore, and other cities were boycotted. On 25 March 1918 he was arrested at his Boston home and sent to Georgia, where he was imprisoned as an enemy alien for more than a year. (Also interned at the same facility was the Austrian-born conductor of the Cincinnati Symphony, Ernst Kumwald.) Muck and his wife were deported in August 1919. In later years several American orchestras asked Muck to conduct, but he refused to return to the United States.

Sources:

Frederick C. Luebke, *Bonds of Loyalty: German-Americans and World War I* (De Kalb: Northern Illinois University Press, 1974);

Paul L. Murphy, *World War I and the Origin of Civil Liberties in the United States* (New York: Norton, 1979).

WORKERS UNITE: ARTISTS ORGANIZE

Stage Set for Action. With a few exceptions, artists remained outside the considerable union activity among American workers in the late nineteenth century. Yet during the first two decades of the twentieth century — as owners, producers, and managers in several creative fields formed business trusts to increase their bargaining power with artists — artists began to organize, seeking control over their work and careers. The political atmosphere of the day was also conducive to union activity, owing in part to the strength of Progressive reform movements and the bargaining power American unions gained during the war years.

Early Organization. Playwrights were among the first artists to organize during the 1910s, forming the Dramatists Guild in 1912 to help individual playwrights bargain with producers. Actors were next, forming the Actors Equity Association on 26 May 1913 in response to what they felt was *in*equitable treatment from theatrical management. By then a few people controlled the majority of the theaters across America. The most powerful of these producer-managers were Abe Erlanger, Mark Klaw, the brothers Charles and Daniel Frohman, Martin Beck, partners B. F. Keith and E. F. Albee, and the Shubert brothers. In 1900 the managers formed a central booking service — later formalized as the United Booking Offices of America (UBO) — to which actors had to pay a fee to get work in affiliated theaters. Actors who chose to work in non-UBO theaters were blacklisted. By the mid 1910s the UBO controlled bookings for nearly fifteen thousand theaters nationwide. Actors Equity was formed not only to fight the booking fee but also to request specific benefits such as rehearsal pay, reimbursement of travel expenses, right of appeal in case of dismissal, and advance notice of closings. Actors Equity, which admitted women as well as men, was strongest in New York City, but it also had chapters in Chicago, Boston, Philadelphia, and Los Angeles.

The Mid 1910s. Throughout the 1910s Actors Equity continued to negotiate these issues with two management groups, the National Association of Theatrical Producing Managers and the United Managers' Protective Association. In 1917 the two sides agreed to institute a standard contract that addressed many of the actors' grievances. After it was drawn up, however, the contract was ignored by the majority of producers. Meanwhile, songwriters had organized as well, forming the American Society of Composers, Authors, and Publishers (ASCAP) in 1914. One of that group's first acts was to sue a New York City restaurant whose orchestra was giving unauthorized performances of numbers from Victor Herbert's operetta *Sweethearts.* Composers believed that they should receive royalties when their works were played in theaters, at concerts, and in other entertainment venues. Ruling on the ASCAP case in 1917, the U.S. Supreme Court agreed. Justice Oliver Wendell Holmes wrote, "If music did not pay, it would be given up."

The Equity Strike of 1919. By the end of the decade actors were still not faring well in their negotiations with theater management, which had formed yet another group, the Producing Managers' Association (PMA). By 1919 almost all American industries were full of unhappy workers who had little bargaining power during a postwar recession. That year four million workers went on strike. Among them were some two thousand Broadway actors, singers, dancers, musicians, and stagehands. On the first day of August nearly fourteen hundred Actors Equity members in New York City signed a petition demanding that the PMA formally recognize their union; five days later nearly twice that number of actors met in the Astor Ballroom and resolved to strike. The walkout, led by Frank Bacon, the star of the extremely popular and profitable play *Lightnin',* began on 7 August, shutting down a dozen Broadway shows immediately and darkening another two dozen theaters within the next two weeks. During that time the Shubert Brothers organization sued Actors Equity for $500,000, and Florenz Ziegfeld secured temporary restraining orders against striking actors in his *Follies.* Both of these attempts to stop the strike were ultimately ineffective. On 12 August, Broadway chorus girls formed an auxiliary union called Chorus Equity, which promptly struck; on 16 August stagehands and musicians joined the action; on 26 August the Teamsters Union backed the walkout.

A Significant Victory. Like the striking actors, representatives of management held demonstrations and claimed loyalty to the theater. (One of them was George M. Cohan, who by then was more invested in the theater world as a producer and director than as a songwriter and actor.) But the strikers won the public's heart by staging a parade down Broadway and giving Actors Equity benefit performances at the Lexington Avenue Opera House. The fact that many of the strikers were stars — W. C. Fields, Eddie Cantor, Ethel and Lionel Barrymore, Lillian Russell, and Ed Wynn were among those who joined the picket lines — also swayed public opinion in the actors' favor. On 6 September the PMA knew it was beaten and agreed to the actors' demands. The Actors Equity strike had a happier ending than most strikes: there was no violence, and from then on the union was formally recognized by management — a victory most unions did not realize until after the passage of the Wagner Act of 1935, which gave federal protection for union activity. Actors Equity is still the main union for Broadway actors.

Sources:

Benjamin McArthur, *Actors and American Culture, 1880–1920* (Philadelphia: Temple University Press, 1984);

Ethan Mordden, *The American Theatre* (New York: Oxford University Press, 1981);

Nell Painter, *Standing at Armageddon: The United States, 1877–1919* (New York: Norton, 1987).

HEADLINE MAKERS

VERNON AND IRENE CASTLE

1887-1918; 1893-1969

DANCERS

A Whirlwind Career. In just three years, 1912 to 1915, Vernon and Irene Castle rose from a nightclub act to the most famous ballroom dancers in the world. Three years after that their partnership ended in tragedy. Yet by 1918 this husband and wife's choreography — together with the high-class aura they lent the new and controversial phenomenon of public dancing — had transformed popular entertainment and brought millions of Americans onto the dance floor.

The Beginning of a Team. Though Vernon Castle preceded his partner into show business, it was Irene Castle's ambition that steered the couple toward stardom. Born Irene Foote on 7 April 1893 in New Rochelle, New York, she spent much of her comfortable, upper-middle-class childhood appearing in local amateur productions and dreaming of acting on Broadway. In contrast Vernon Castle — born Vernon Blyth in Norwich, England, on 2 May 1887 — studied engineering in college and was planning a career in that field when he took a vacation to New York City, where his actress sister was appearing in a play. He got a small part in it and, to avoid appearances of nepotism, chose a made-up last name, Castle, for the program. Vernon Castle remained in New York, appearing in Broadway comedies for the next three years. During the summer of 1910 he met the Foote family, and through his intercession Irene was cast in a small part in a musical in which he was appearing. Their friendship grew to romance, and on Christmas Day 1910 they became engaged. They were married the following May.

First Success. In early 1912 they got jobs in a small show in Paris, for which they improvised a ballroom-dancing act based on American ragtime music (then the rage in Paris). The show flopped, but the Castles did not. They were invited to star at an exclusive nightclub, becoming the darlings of a wealthy European set. In mid 1912 they returned to New York and began a similar career there, dancing regularly at a posh club and at parties given by wealthy Americans. One night they added a variation to their act. As Irene Castle described it later, "Instead of coming down on the beat as everybody else did, we went up — that became known as the Castle Walk." Soon they were making more than $1,000 a night.

Respectable Role Models. In 1913 the couple opened Castle House, an exclusive daytime club on Forty-sixth Street in Manhattan, opposite the Ritz-Carlton Hotel. The enterprise was backed by several society ladies (some of whom were taking private lessons from Vernon Castle). As new dance styles — from the exhibitionist turkey trot to the erotic tango — became extremely popular, they were also widely criticized as immoral. The Castles had a far different image. As Irene Castle explained in her autobiography, "We were clean-cut; we were married and when we danced there was nothing suggestive about it. We made dancing look like the fun it was." They published *Modern Dancing* (1914), a book defending public dancing as moral and good exercise. They won over even the conservative *Ladies' Home Journal,* which ran step-by-step photographs of the Castles demonstrating the steps they had invented.

Nationwide Fame. Irene Castle's fans considered her the epitome of style and class. When she appeared on-stage in simple, flowing dresses (because she could not dance in a hobble skirt, a corset, or a bustle), millions of women copied her dress style. When she cut her hair in 1914 (for convenience while she was hospitalized for an appendectomy), women swarmed to salons demanding Castle Bobs. In spring 1914, during their four-week Whirlwind Tour of thirty-two cities with James Reese Europe's band, their train was greeted by crowds at every stop, and thousands of couples showed up for the dance competitions held along the way. Their popularity peaked that December, when they opened on Broadway in Irving Berlin's musical *Watch Your Step.* In 1915 the Castles starred in a movie version of their story, *The Whirl of Life.* Yet by mid 1915 Vernon Castle was concerned about the war in Europe, and he left the show that fall to enlist.

A Tragic End. In 1916 and 1917 Irene Castle sold Liberty Bonds, acted in several movies — including William Randolph Hearst's pro-American *Patria* (1916) — and danced solo in Florenz Ziegfeld's *Miss 1917.* Work did not alleviate her worry over her husband's dangerous assignments as an aerial photographer of enemy territory in Europe, for which the French government awarded him the Croix de Guerre. Later in the war, while he was training American flyers in Texas, he was killed in a plane crash, on 15 February 1918. The train bearing his body back to New York was met by crowds of mourners all along its route. For a few years after Vernon Castle's death, Irene Castle danced with a new partner, Billy Reardon, but by the end of the 1920s she was no longer dancing regularly, devoting herself instead to animal welfare. She remarried three times and had two children with her third husband. Most of her subsequent entertainment work was related to her past fame, including her service as a technical adviser for *The Story of Vernon and Irene Castle* (1939), in which Fred Astaire and Ginger Rogers played the Castles. She died on 25 January 1969.

Source:
Irene Castle, as told to Bob and Wanda Duncan, *Castles in the Air,* foreword by Ginger Rogers (New York: Da Capo Press, 1958).

WILLA CATHER

1873-1947

NOVELIST

Voice of the Heartland. Willa Cather, whose best-known novels were published during the 1910s, was one of the few major novelists to emerge during that decade. In a period notable for the rise of literary modernism, she wrote fiction that looked back to America's agrarian past. Yet Cather's approach was in accord with the realism of her contemporaries: her celebrations of the pioneer spirit are tempered by compromise, sacrifice, and even suicide.

Early Years. Though she is usually identified as a midwestern writer, Cather lived in Nebraska for only twelve years, albeit formative ones. She was born on 7 December 1873 in Back Creek, Virginia, the first of six children. In early 1883, when she was nine, the family followed relatives to Red Cloud, Nebraska, where her father farmed and opened an insurance business. At first young Willa Cather found Nebraska lonely and depress-

ing and hid away reading the classics in her parents' extensive library. She did enjoy the company of her Norwegian neighbors the Miners, especially when Mrs. Miner, an accomplished pianist, played opera selections. (Though Cather never became a musician, classical music and musicians — violinists, pianists, and opera singers — people her fiction.) Cather studied at the University of Nebraska in Lincoln, where her friends included Louise and Roscoe Pound, later distinguished scholars, and Dorothy Canfield, later a successful novelist. During her last two years at the university, Cather, who graduated in 1895, edited the school literary magazine while writing for the *Nebraska State Journal* (to which she would contribute for the next twenty years, long after she had left Lincoln).

Journalist and Teacher. Between 1893 and 1896 Cather wrote more than two hundred articles — mostly theater, music, and literary criticism — for two Lincoln newspapers, the *Journal* and the *Courier.* In summer 1896 she moved to Pittsburgh, where she worked first as a writer and managing editor of a new women's magazine, *Home Monthly,* and then as an editor and arts critic for the *Pittsburgh Leader,* a daily newspaper for which she also wrote arts criticism. She worked at the *Leader* for three years, also contributing essays and fiction to a Pittsburgh literary magazine, *The Library.* In 1901 she left journalism and took a job teaching high-school English. During this period Cather sold short stories to several major magazines (including *Cosmopolitan, Scribner's, Everybody's,* and *McClure's*) and published a volume of verse, *April Twilights* (1903), and a short-story collection, *The Troll Garden* (1905).

New York. In 1906 S. S. McClure, who had by then published two of Cather's stories in his magazine, offered Cather a job as an editor at *McClure's.* Though Cather had little taste for muckraking journalism — the style of investigative reporting for which *McClure's* was famous — she respected the magazine's fiction offerings and welcomed the chance to move in New York literary circles. Within two years she became managing editor, virtually running the magazine between 1908 and 1912. Cather's job gave her important contacts in the publishing business, but her fiction writing was suffering. She had written twenty-seven short stories during her decade in Pittsburgh but only eight during her first five years in New York. In early 1912 she published *Alexander's Bridge,* a novella with an urban setting that went largely unnoticed by critics. More significant was a story she published in the August 1912 issue of *McClure's,* "The Bohemian Girl," about an ill-fated romance between two young immigrants on the Nebraska prairie. That fall Cather left *McClure's,* and a year later "The Bohemian Girl" reappeared as a tragic subplot in her first major novel, *O Pioneers!*

Novelist. Reviewers nationwide praised *O Pioneers!* and hailed Cather as a major new American writer. The success of the book gave her the income and confidence to devote her remaining thirty-five years to writing novels (after 1915 she wrote little nonfiction and fewer than twenty short stories). Alexandra Bergson in *O Pioneers!* and Thea Kronborg in *The Song of the Lark* (1915), a novel for which Cather drew on both her prairie upbringing and her knowledge of the New York opera world, are heroines in the long tradition of individualists in American fiction. Cather created another memorable character in her 1918 novel, *My Ántonia,* another nostalgic but realistic treatment of midwestern immigrants and agrarian life. The story of Ántonia Shimerda, who is based on a Bohemian woman Cather had known since shortly after her arrival in Nebraska, has been praised for its examination of the American westward migration and the pioneers' relationship to their new environment.

Subsequent Work. Cather changed her fictional focus with *One of Ours* (1922), a novel with a midwestern hero who serves in Europe during World War I. Though it was the only one of her works to win a Pulitzer Prize, the novel is not considered to be among her best. In the seven more novels she produced between 1923 and 1940 — including *Death Comes for the Archbishop* (1927), a historical work set in the Southwest and regarded by some critics as her finest book — Cather explored the territory of the inner self as well as the changing face of the American land. In 1944 she was awarded the Gold Medal for Fiction by the National Institute of Arts and Letters. She died of a cerebral hemorrhage on 13 April 1947, at age seventy-three.

Sources:

Phyllis C. Robinson, *Willa: The Life of Willa Cather* (Garden City, N.Y.: Doubleday, 1983);

James Woodress, *Willa Cather: A Literary Life* (Lincoln: University of Nebraska Press, 1987).

ROBERT FROST

1874-1963

POET

A Poet of New England. When Robert Frost recited his poem "The Gift Outright" at the inauguration of President John F. Kennedy in 1961, he was widely regarded as the greatest living American poet. Having carefully cultivated the image of the grandfatherly farmer-poet for several decades, he had claimed New England as his literary territory and the vernacular of its residents as his poetic voice. Ironically, his public persona tended to blind critics to his accomplishments as a poet and to cause them to overlook how innovative his experiments in capturing the sounds of everyday speech had seemed when he published his second book, *North of Boston,* in 1914.

Background. Robert Lee Frost was born in San Francisco on 26 March 1874. When he was eleven his father died, and Frost, his mother, and his younger sister went to live in Lawrence, Massachusetts, near his paternal grandparents, where Frost's mother took the first of a series of teaching jobs to support her children. At Lawrence High School Frost played on the baseball team, and in his senior year he edited the school *Bulletin,* where his first poem had appeared in April 1890. He and his future wife, Elinor White (whom he married in 1895), were covaledictorians of the class of 1892. Frost entered Dartmouth College in autumn 1892 but dropped out before the end of the first semester. Over the next several years he worked at various jobs, including teacher, mill worker, and newspaper reporter.

A Published Poet. In early 1894 Frost was encouraged when *The Independent,* a prestigious New York magazine, accepted his poem "My Butterfly" for publication. Over the next two decades Frost published a few other poems in newspapers and magazines, but he remained virtually unknown as a poet until the appearance of his first two books in 1913 and 1914. In 1897 Frost enrolled at Harvard University. He did well in his course work but left in spring 1899 suffering from physical and mental exhaustion brought on in part by financial concerns and the stresses associated with a growing family.

The Derry Farm. In late 1900 Frost's grandfather bought him a farm in Derry, New Hampshire, where the poet and his growing family spent the next decade. Frost wrote little poetry during his first few years on the farm, but the landscape and people of Derry provided him with the raw materials he used in many of his finest poems for the rest of his life. In 1911 Frost, who had returned to teaching in 1906, sold the Derry farm, and in summer 1912 the Frosts sailed to England, where Frost intended to devote all his time to writing.

First Success. Soon after his arrival Frost submitted a collection of some of his poems to a British publisher. *A Boy's Will* was quickly accepted and appeared the following spring. In March 1913 Frost met American expatriate poet Ezra Pound, who expressed enthusiasm for the book and wrote two glowing reviews, one for the Chicago little magazine *Poetry,* in which he exclaimed, "This man has the good sense to speak naturally and to paint the thing, the thing as he sees it." Pound also lent his copy of the book to William Butler Yeats, who called it "the best poetry written in America in a long time." Frost subsequently met Yeats, whose poetry he greatly admired, and made other literary acquaintances as well. The closest of his new friendships was with poet and essayist Edward Thomas, who was later killed in World War I.

An Annus Mirabilis. The twelve months that followed the acceptance of Frost's first book were truly a "remarkable year" for the poet. In an enormous burst of creativity he wrote nearly all of the blank-verse dramatic narratives that made his second book, *North of Boston*, a clear step forward in terms of craft and a revolutionary volume in terms of poetic technique. In poems such as "Mending Wall," "The Death of the Hired Man," "Home Burial," and "The Housekeeper" — all set in the rural area of New England "north of Boston" — Frost created intensely psychological word portraits in the everyday rural dialect of his characters. As he explained to an acquaintance at the time, he had "dropped to an everyday level of diction that even Wordsworth kept above." Two decades earlier an editor had suggested that Frost's poems sounded "too much like talk." By 1912 Frost had made that so-called flaw into his greatest poetic strength.

Acclaim at Home. *North of Boston* was published in May 1914 to enthusiastic reviews on both sides of the Atlantic, and later that year the American publisher Henry Holt agreed to publish American editions of Frost's books. Driven home by the outbreak of World War I, Frost and his family arrived in New York City in February 1915. One of the first things Frost saw was a copy of the *New Republic* that included a laudatory review of *North of Boston* by the renowned American Imagist poet Amy Lowell. Frost's reputation was made.

Later Work. Frost's next book, *Mountain Interval* (1916), maintained the high standards set by *North of Boston* with dramatic narratives such as "The Road Not Taken," "An Old Man's Winter Night," "Birches," and "Out, Out — " and lyrics such as "Hyla Brook," "The Oven Bird," and "Putting in the Seed." *New Hampshire* (1922) earned him the first of the four Pulitzer Prizes he won over the next two decades (more than any other poet), and other honors came his way as well. Yet by the time he published *A Further Range* (1936), which won him his third Pulitzer Prize, some critics were faulting the political views that Frost, a conservative Democrat, was expressing in public and in his poems, particularly his reservations about President Franklin D. Roosevelt's New Deal. In the 1940s and 1950s, as Frost's popularity with the public continued to grow, the New Critics, whose literary opinions and methods of analysis were widely accepted in American colleges and universities, tended to dismiss Frost's poetry as too superficial in content and too conventional in its use of traditional poetic meter and rhyme. Yet perceptive readings of Frost's poetry by prominent critics such as Lionel Trilling and Randall Jarrell revealed the psychological complexity and modern sensibility of Frost's poetry and helped to maintain his reputation as a major American poet.

"Like Playing Tennis Without a Net." Beginning with Pound and Lowell in the 1910s, critics often asked Frost why he did not write free verse, for certainly it would be easier for him to capture the sounds of natural, everyday speech if he did not have to be concerned with adhering to a preestablished meter. Frost frequently explained that writing free verse was "like playing tennis without a net." With his great modernist contemporaries Frost shared a worldview in which chaos prevailed and in which no cosmic order was possible. The most a poet could hope to create in a poem, Frost said, was a brief point of order, a "momentary stay against confusion." For him the irregular rhythms of everyday speech were a metaphor for the world's chaos, and traditional poetic form was a means of imposing some momentary order upon it. Such views make Frost an important transitional figure between traditionalism and modernism, but it is the enduring emotional appeal of his poems, not the theory behind them, that ensures his lasting reputation as a poet.

Sources:

William H. Pritchard, *Frost: A Literary Life Reconsidered* (New York: Oxford University Press, 1984);

Lawrance Thompson, *Robert Frost: The Early Years, 1874–1915* (New York, Chicago & San Francisco: Holt, Rinehart & Winston, 1966);

Thompson, *Robert Frost: The Years of Triumph, 1915–1938* (New York, Chicago & San Francisco: Holt, Rinehart & Winston, 1970);

Thompson and R. H. Winnick, *Robert Frost: The Later Years, 1938–1963* (New York: Holt, Rinehart & Winston, 1978).

D. W. GRIFFITH

1875-1948

MOVIE DIRECTOR

Motion Picture Pioneer. One of the first movie directors to explore the creative possibilities of the medium of film, D. W. Griffith made a major impact on the development of the art and techniques of moviemaking.

Background. David Wark Griffith was born on a Kentucky farm on 22 January 1875, the youngest child of a former Confederate officer whose regiment had failed to keep William Tecumseh Sherman from burning Atlanta. In 1889, four years after his father's death, the family moved to Louisville, where David Griffith went to work in a dry-goods store, quitting in 1893 to take a job in a bookstore. While volunteering as an usher and stagehand in various Louisville theaters, he saw stars such as John Drew, Lillian Russell, and Julia Marlowe. In 1896 he got his first acting job, embarking on a career that took him all over the country during the next ten years, a period in which he was also writing plays, poetry, and short stories. On 14 May 1906 he married actress Linda Arvidson, and the two settled in New York, where they were cast in *The One Woman*, a play by Thomas Dixon Jr., author of *The Clansman* (1905), a novel that would play a pivotal role in Griffith's later work.

A Career in the Movies. Determined to be a writer, Griffith sought employment as a scriptwriter for the Edison and Biograph movie companies, only to get work as an actor. By 1908, however, Biograph had begun buying his scenarios and letting him direct movies. Over the next five years Griffith made more than four hundred short films for that company, including melodramas, Westerns, and adaptations of the classics and contemporary literary works. Realizing that the camera could free the motion picture from the natural limitations of stage plays, he experimented with close-ups, long shots, camera angles, editing, and other new techniques. These movies featured Mary Pickford, Mack Sennett, Lionel Barrymore, and the Gish sisters, Dorothy and Lillian. By 1913 Griffith was experimenting with longer films, including the four-reel *Judith of Bethulia* (released in 1914). At the end of that year he left Biograph for Mutual, which offered him more money and freedom to make more-sophisticated movies. During 1914 he directed four movies for Mutual (including a film version of the Edgar Allan Poe story "The Telltale Heart") ranging in length from five to seven reels.

Two Masterpieces. Griffith's next two projects, the ambitious movies *The Birth of a Nation* (1915) and *Intolerance* (1916) — were filmed not in New York but in Hollywood, California, where many independent producers were moving for the weather and scenery. *The Birth of a Nation,* a twelve-reel movie based on Dixon's *The Clansman,* was produced in 1914 at an unprecedented cost of $100,000 and released in early 1915. Today this epic, set in the South during the Civil War and Reconstruction (and strongly influenced by Griffith's father's war experiences), is remembered for its pioneering use of film technique and for the racism of the second part, in which members of the Ku Klux Klan are portrayed as heroes. During its first run (1915–1917) ticket sales totaled $60 million, despite protests from the National Association for the Advancement of Colored People (NAACP). Regardless of its racism, *The Birth of a Nation* is remarkable for its vast scope and complex plot, which was in fact outdone by Griffith's next major motion picture, *Intolerance* (1916). This second epic, which cost $400,000, starred the same actresses Griffith had made famous in *The Birth of a Nation* — Lillian Gish, Mae Marsh, and Miriam Cooper — and told the story of religious and political oppression throughout history. Though audiences of the day found the picture somewhat overwhelming, *Intolerance* is now widely regarded as Griffith's finest work.

War Work and Later Films. Between March and October 1917 Griffith and Lillian Gish visited England and France (at the invitation of the British government) to film scenes against the backdrop of the war for *Hearts of the World,* released in 1918. Over the following thirteen years Griffith directed and produced another two dozen films, distributed by Adolph Zukor's movie companies. Some of these movies starred Carol Dempster, an actress with whom he had become personally involved after separating from his wife in 1912. Several of his later films

were notable, including *Broken Blossoms* (1919), one of Lillian Gish's finest silent movies; the acclaimed *Way Down East* (1920); and two twelve-reel war epics, *Orphans of the Storm* (1921) and *America* (1924). Griffith's first sound film — *Abraham Lincoln* (1930), starring Walter Huston — had mixed success and was followed by a flop, *The Struggle* (1931), the last movie Griffith made.

Final Years. During the 1930s and 1940s Griffith went back to writing poetry and plays (which were not produced). Divorced in 1936, he immediately took a second wife, Evelyn Baldwin, an actress thirty-five years his junior. Also in 1936 he was given an honorary Oscar, and two years later he was named the first honorary life member of the Directors Guild of America. Griffith was unhappy in what he considered forced retirement, and his bitterness led to alcoholism and another divorce. He was living alone in a Hollywood hotel when he died of a cerebral hemorrhage on 24 July 1948.

Sources:

Robert M. Henderson, *D. W. Griffith: His Life and Work* (New York: Oxford University Press, 1972);

Henderson, *D. W. Griffith: The Years at Biograph* (New York: Farrar, Straus & Giroux, 1970);

Paul O'Dell, *Griffith and the Rise of Hollywood* (New York: A. S. Barnes, 1970);

Richard Schickel, *D. W. Griffith: An American Life* (New York: Simon & Schuster, 1984).

W. C. HANDY

1873-1958

BLUES COMPOSER AND BANDLEADER

The Father of the Blues. W. C. Handy is often called "The Father of the Blues," a title he gave himself. Most music historians believe that the blues — songs with three-line verses of woeful lyrics and a melody marked by repeated use of flatted thirds and sevenths (blue notes) — were being performed by African American folksingers before the turn of the twentieth century. While Handy did not invent the blues, he deserves credit for popularizing the genre, because he was the first musician to publish blues sheet music. He also had good timing: the song that made him famous, "The St. Louis Blues," appeared in 1914, a year in which African American music was in vogue nationwide among whites as well as blacks.

Early Years. William Christopher Handy was born on 16 November 1873 to former slaves in Florence, Alabama. From childhood he longed to be a musician, despite the disapproval of his father, a Methodist minister. He sang choral music and learned to play the cornet and the guitar. During his teens he toured with a minstrel show, a vocal quartet, and various brass bands, and in

1896 he joined Mahara's Minstrels, a touring group in which he played solo cornet, arranged orchestrations, and conducted. He received his first press notices with the group, which made a cylinder record in 1897. In 1900 Handy, who had married Elizabeth Price in 1898, took a position teaching music at a black college in Alabama, during which time the first two of his five children were born. He left teaching and returned to Mahara's Minstrels for a final season in 1902.

The Blues. The following year Handy became conductor of the all-black Knights of Pythias Band. During its tours of the southern states, he was drawn to the folk music of local black musicians, songs that, as he later remembered, "consisted of simple declarations expressed usually in three lines and set to a kind of earth-born music that was familiar throughout the Southland half a century ago." He was particularly struck by the haunting quality of the music. By this time Handy had seen enough of the world to feel troubled about his place in it: while both Mahara's Minstrels and the Knights of Pythias Band drew enthusiastic white audiences, they traveled in segregated railroad cars and, especially in the Deep South, frequently faced threats of lynching and other violence.

A Break in Memphis. By 1909 Handy had settled in Memphis, where he conducted a dance band in a popular club. Because the owners were involved in local politics, Handy was enlisted to write a campaign song for E. H. "Boss" Crump, who was running for mayor of Memphis on a reform platform. Initally called "Mr. Crump," this song — a dance tune that incorporated the rhythms of ragtime and the tango (another style Handy believed to be rooted in African traditions) — became Handy's "Memphis Blues," which he published at his own expense in 1912. A year later a New York City publisher offered him fifty dollars for the right to republish it with lyrics, and it became a hit. Handy was happy about the song's success but chagrined that the publisher, not he, was profiting from it. The next year, with a partner named Harry Pace, he founded his own publishing company, for which he wrote "St. Louis Blues," based on his memories of being broke in that city as a young musician. Over the next few years he also wrote and published "Yellow Dog Blues" (1914), "Joe Turner Blues" (1915), "The Hesitating Blues" (1915), and "Beale Street Blues" (1917).

A Power in Tin Pan Alley. While continuing to lead bands, Handy moved his publishing firm to Chicago in 1917 and then in 1918 to New York City. In addition to Handy's own blues music, the company published other popular songs such as "A Good Man Is Hard to Find" (1918), an Eddie Green song made a hit by Sophie Tucker. Handy's "St. Louis Blues" was widely recorded, especially after Tucker sang it in vaudeville. (Over the following decades it would become the most-recorded blues song of all time.) Handy's own band recorded blues in 1917 for Columbia, which promoted the records by declaring Handy Week in towns across the country.

Handy's influence is also evident in the use of blues numbers in popular musicals by white composers, including George Gershwin.

Later Years. Handy continued publishing, writing, arranging, conducting, and recording music during the 1920s and 1930s, though his eyesight was rapidly failing. In 1926 he published *Blues: An Anthology,* an influential work in the Harlem Renaissance. During the last twenty years of his life he was completely blind but continued to work. He made his last recording in 1939 and published his autobiography, *Father of the Blues,* in 1941. His first wife died in 1937, and he was remarried in 1954, to his secretary, Irma Logan. He died on 28 March 1958 in New York City. That year millions of Americans saw the movie version of his life story, *St. Louis Blues,* starring Nat "King" Cole.

Sources:

David Ewen, *Great Men of American Popular Song* (Englewood Cliffs, N.J.: Prentice-Hall, 1970);

W. C. Handy, *Father of the Blues* (New York: Da Capo Press, 1941).

MARY PICKFORD

1892-1979

MOVIE ACTRESS

America's Sweetheart. By the time she was voted the most popular actress in America by the readers of a fan magazine in 1917, Mary Pickford was famous for the juvenile heroines she had played in movies such as *The Poor Little Rich Girl* (1917) and *Rebecca of Sunnybrook Farm* (1917). Despite her childlike appearance she was an astute businesswoman amassing a fortune, the most powerful woman in the film industry.

Background. Pickford's business sense was born of necessity during childhood. The girl dubbed "America's Sweetheart" was a Canadian, born Gladys Louise Smith on 8 April 1892 in Toronto. Her father, who had held various low-paying jobs, died in 1898, leaving his wife and their three children under the age of six — Gladys, Lottie, and Jack — on the verge of poverty. At a friend's suggestion, Charlotte Smith took her daughters to audition for a show that was looking for child actors, and by 1900 all three Smith children were touring the United States with a theater stock company. In 1907 the famous producer-playwright David Belasco cast Gladys in William deMille's new play, *The Warrens of Virginia,* and that job supported her family for two years. When she took the part she changed her name to Mary Pickford. (Pickford was the maiden name of one of her great-grandmothers.)

The Movies. In 1909 Pickford met movie director D. W. Griffith, who offered her five dollars a day to appear in his pictures at Biograph. Pickford asked for twice that amount and got it. During the next two years she appeared in eighty-one Biograph films. In 1911 Pickford married fellow actor Owen Moore, who proved to be temperamental and an alcoholic. In late 1910 she had left Biograph for Carl Laemmle's Independent Motion Pictures Company (IMP), where she made thirty-five films but was unhappy with the directing of Thomas Ince. IMP publicized her name, an unusual move at a time when film actors did not receive billing, and when she rejoined Biograph in 1912, she was no longer just another anonymous actress. Pickford left Biograph again the next year for a brief return to the stage, and then she signed with Adolph Zukor's Famous Players for $500 a week. During her first year with the company she starred in seven pictures, including two big hits, *Hearts Adrift* and *Tess of the Storm Country,* both released in 1914. By 1916 Pickford — still playing child roles — received five hundred fan letters a day, and police had to restrain crowds when she made appearances. In June of that year she negotiated a new contract for more than $1 million over the next two years plus approval of the directors, other stars, and editing of her movies, as well as a percentage of the profits. Under that contract she made some of her most popular films, including *The Poor Little Rich Girl* and *Rebecca of Sunnybrook Farm.*

A Great Love and a New Business. By the time she made these movies, Pickford had been involved in a love affair with actor Douglas Fairbanks for three years. Amid divorce negotiations with their respective spouses, Pickford signed a contract for even more money — $250,000 per picture — with First National, for which she made three films in 1919. In the same year she and Fairbanks joined with D. W. Griffith, Charlie Chaplin, and other backers to form a new movie company, United Artists (UA). Pickford's first film for UA, *Pollyanna* (1920), earned more than $1 million at the box office. On 28 March 1920, two months after its release, Pickford and Fairbanks were married and moved into their new Beverly Hills mansion, Pickfair. During the 1920s Pickford starred in and produced a dozen more films for United Artists. The huge success of *Little Lord Fauntleroy* (1921) and a 1922 remake of *Tess of the Storm Country* — along with Fairbanks's early UA movies, including *The Three Musketeers* (1921) and *Robin Hood* (1922) — helped offset the financial loss after Griffith left the company in 1924. In 1927 Pickford and Fairbanks helped to found the Academy of Motion Picture Arts and Sciences. Two years later Pickford earned one of the new Academy Awards for her performance in *Coquette* (1929), her first talking picture.

Dark Days. After her mother died in 1928, Pickford began to turn to alcohol for comfort. Both Pickford and Fairbanks began having affairs and were finally divorced in 1936. The following year Pickford married Charles Buddy Rogers, with whom she had costarred in *My Best Girl* (1927), her last silent movie. She never got over

Fairbanks and was devastated when he died of a heart attack in 1939. Pickford stopped acting in 1933 but produced films for UA and other companies through the 1940s. In that decade she considered but rejected roles in several movies (including the part of Norma Desmond in *Sunset Blvd.* [1950]). In 1955 she wrote a memoir, *Sunshine and Shadow,* but her alcoholism made an acting career impossible for the remaining years of her life. When she received an honorary Oscar for lifetime achievement in 1976, Pickford, unable to leave Pickfair, had her acceptance speech filmed. She died of a cerebral hemorrhage on 29 May 1979, leaving $7 million to a charitable foundation.

Sources:

Tino Balio, *United Artists: The Company Built by the Stars* (Madison: University of Wisconsin Press, 1976);

Scott Eyman, *Mary Pickford: America's Sweetheart* (New York: Fine, 1989);

Booton Herndon, *Mary Pickford and Douglas Fairbanks: The Most Popular Couple the World Has Ever Known* (New York: Norton, 1977);

Mary Pickford, *Sunshine and Shadow* (Garden City, N.Y.: Doubleday, 1955).

CARL SANDBURG

1878-1967

POET

A Varied Career. Though best remembered for the poetry he wrote during the 1910s, Carl Sandburg is notable for a range of contributions to American letters, including not only poetry but also journalism and biography. A leading figure in a new group of literary talents emerging in the American Midwest, Sandburg, like a handful of his contemporaries, did not go to New York to make a name in literary circles. Instead they remained in the heartland they wrote about. Sandburg repeatedly paid homage to his roots in his work. His literary fame began with a poem named for Chicago and peaked with a biography of the great president from his home state, Abraham Lincoln.

Early Wanderings. The son of Swedish immigrants, Carl August Sandburg was born on 6 January 1878 in Galesburg, Illinois. Though his father, a blacksmith, was illiterate, his mother loved books and encouraged her three children to read. Carl Sandburg dropped out of school after the eighth grade to help support the family, and during his early teens he worked in a barbershop, cut ice, delivered newspapers, and took whatever other jobs he could find around Galesburg. According to his biographer North Callahan, these experiences gave the boy "a kind of Gothic etching of the midwest" that later would appear in his writing. At nineteen Sandburg went to Kansas to work in the wheat fields and then lived as a hobo for a few months, riding freight trains and doing odd jobs in exchange for food. In April 1898, after the outbreak of the Spanish-American War, he enlisted in the army. Though his company was sent to Cuba, they saw no action and returned to Illinois in the fall. Because of his war service, Sandburg was given free tuition at Lombard College in Galesburg, where he studied the poetry of Walt Whitman and edited the campus literary magazine. In May 1902 he dropped out of school and headed east. For two years he worked as a salesman in New Jersey, writing poetry on the side.

Journalism, Socialism, and Marriage. Returning to the Midwest in 1904, Sandburg began nearly thirty years of journalistic work, becoming involved in the Socialist Party and writing for Socialist newspapers in Milwaukee and then Chicago. He met a young party activist named Lillian Steichen, sister of the photographer Edward Steichen, and married her. Over the next decade they had three daughters. The views on the oppression of the working class that Sandburg formed during this period influenced the poetry he was writing.

Chicago Poet and Reporter. During the early 1910s Sandburg wrote his "Chicago Poems" — including "Chicago," which characterized his adopted home as "Hog Butcher for the World." The editors of *The American Magazine* in New York rejected them, but Harriet Monroe, editor of the Chicago-based *Poetry*, published nine of them in the March 1914 issue. Two years later, when these poems were included in his first collection, *Chicago Poems* (1916), Monroe wrote that Sandburg's verse was "as personal as his slow speech or his massive gait; always a reverent beating-out of his subject." Continuing his newspaper work, Sandburg went to Stockholm in 1918 to serve as a war correspondent for the Newspaper Enterprise Association; back in Chicago in 1919, he covered the summer race riots of that year. That same year he won the Poetry Society of America Prize for his second full-length collection of poetry, *Cornhuskers* (1918).

The Lincoln Biography. During the 1920s Sandburg published three more volumes of verse, but his main focus was on his biography of Abraham Lincoln. He had long been fascinated by Lincoln's life: as a young soldier traveling through Washington during the Spanish-American War, Sandburg had visited Ford's Theater, where the president had been shot; in his coverage of the Chicago race riots of 1919, he had quoted the Emancipation Proclamation. By the early 1920s Sandburg had acquired more than a thousand books about Lincoln and had begun work on a biography. The two volumes of *Abraham Lincoln: The Prairie Years* (1926) were followed in 1939 by *Abraham Lincoln: The War Years*, in four volumes. *The War Years* earned Sandburg the Pulitzer Prize for history in 1940 and the Academy of Arts and Letters Gold Medal for history and biography in 1952.

The 1930s and 1940s. During the Depression of the 1930s Sandburg published *The People, Yes* (1936), a long poem in which he echoed President Franklin D.

Roosevelt's belief that the hope for America lay in the strength of its people. This work and the Lincoln biography were evidence of Sandburg's shift away from Socialism and toward the Democratic Party. During World War II he narrated a government movie about the war, did foreign broadcasts for the Office of War Information, and published *Home Front Memo* (1943), a nonfiction work praising responsibility and duty. In 1948, the year he turned seventy, Sandburg published his first work of fiction, a historical novel called *Remembrance Rock*. It received poor reviews, but three years later his *Complete Poems* (1950) won him a second Pulitzer Prize.

Final Years. Sandburg worked well into his eighties. On his seventy-fifth birthday *Always the Young Strangers* (1953), an autobiographical account of his childhood, was published. He was frequently asked to participate in television and radio programs about Lincoln and addressed the U.S. Congress on the 150th anniversary of Lincoln's birth. On his eighty-fifth birthday he published his last volume of poems, *Honey and Salt*. He died four years later, on 22 July 1967, at the North Carolina home to which he had retired in 1945.

Sources:

North Callahan, *Carl Sandburg: His Life and Works* (University Park: Pennsylvania State University Press, 1987);

Penelope Niven, *Carl Sandburg: A Biography* (New York: Scribners, 1991).

JOHN SLOAN

1871-1951

PAINTER

Early Years. John French Sloan was born on 2 August 1871 in Lock Haven, Pennsylvania, a lumber town where his family had a cabinetmaking business. After losing their business and their home during the depression of 1873, they moved to Philadelphia in 1876, when John was five. There he spent hours in a great-uncle's library, reading the classics and paging through magazines such as *Punch* and *Harper's Monthly*. He especially liked the illustrations, keeping a scrapbook of them and illustrating his own copy of Robert Louis Stevenson's *Treasure Island* when he was twelve. As a teenager he began to sell his pen-and-ink drawings; he also earned money by designing calendars and greeting cards.

A New Career and an Important Friend. When he was twenty-one Sloan took a job as an illustrator for the *Philadelphia Inquirer*. That same year he met and became friends with the realist painter Robert Henri and began a year's study at the Pennsylvania Academy of Art. For several years Sloan's artwork took the form of illustrations for newspapers (first the *Inquirer* and then the *Philadelphia Press*) and for literary magazines. But in 1897, under the influence of Henri, Sloan turned his attention to painting, producing portraits and scenes of Philadelphia. Three years later his paintings were shown in exhibitions at the Pennsylvania Academy of Art, the Art Institute of Chicago, and the National Arts Club in New York City, where the exhibit also included works by Henri and some of his other disciples — William Glackens, George Luks, Arthur B. Davies, and Maurice Prendergast. Like Sloan, Glackens and Luks were newspaper illustrators. By 1904 the group, including Sloan and his wife Dolly, had all settled in New York City.

The Eight. In New York Sloan produced etchings and paintings of the city, many of which were shown in galleries and small exhibitions. He briefly substituted for Henri as a teacher at the New York School of Art, where students included George Bellows and Edward Hopper. After their works were passed over by juries for established exhibitions, Sloan and other realists in the Henri circle, which also included Everett Shinn and Ernest Lawson, began to discuss the possibility of showing their own work. In 1908 The Eight, as the group had come to be known, mounted an exhibition in a New York City gallery, creating great public interest and some furor. One reporter called the realists "apostles of ugliness," but high attendance confirmed the value and relevance of their art. In 1910 the group held another show, this one open to other artists. The 1 April 1910 opening of the Exhibition of Independent Artists, which included some five hundred works, was attended by two thousand people. The show's success set the stage for the revolutionary Armory Show of 1913, in which most of The Eight also exhibited. Sloan's contributions to the Armory Show included two of his best-known works of urban realism, *Sunday, Girls Drying Their Hair* and *McSorley's Bar* (both 1912).

Work at *The Masses*. During his first decade in New York, Sloan sold illustrations to *Collier's* and *Century* magazines. Beginning in 1911 he began contributing to a new socialist magazine, *The Masses,* becoming its art editor the next year. Like many Americans at the time, Sloan believed that socialism offered promising solutions to the world's problems. In his two years at the magazine, he produced an impressive body of political cartoons and scenes of city life. In 1913 he supervised the art for the Paterson Strike Pageant, a show that dramatized the plight of striking silk-mill workers in Paterson, New Jersey. When war broke out in Europe in 1914, Sloan's hopes for a better world through socialism began to fade. He left *The Masses* that year.

Ongoing Work and a New Organization. During the mid 1910s Sloan spent his summers in New England, where he concentrated on landscapes. In New York he continued to paint cityscapes, including *Backyards, Greenwich Village* (1914) and *Bleecker Street, Saturday Night* (1918). He had his first one-man exhibition at Gertrude Whitney's Studio Club in 1916, the same year he began a long affiliation with the Art Students League of New

York, teaching there until 1938. He was among the organizers of the Society of Independent Artists, which mounted a large exhibition in the Grand Central Palace in New York City in April 1917; the following year he was elected president of the society, remaining in the office until the society disbanded in 1944. Beginning in the 1920s, John and Dolly Sloan spent part of each year in Santa Fe, New Mexico, where he became an admirer of Native American art. In 1931 he organized the Exposition of Indian Tribal Arts, which toured the country. During the 1930s Sloan began sketching and painting nudes and had several one-man shows in New York and other cities.

Final Tributes. In 1929, the year he was elected to the National Institute of Arts and Letters, Sloan's work was included in the Nineteen Living Americans exhibition at the Museum of Modern Art in New York City. He was frequently asked to speak and write on American art, and in 1941 the Society of Independent Artists held a testimonial dinner in his honor. Sloan continued to paint through the 1940s while living in New York with his second wife, Helen, a pupil whom he had married after the death of his first wife in 1943. In 1950 he was elected to the American Academy of Arts and Sciences and awarded the Gold Medal for painting by the National Institute of Arts and Letters. He died on 7 September 1951 of complications following surgery.

Sources:

Bruce St. John, *John Sloan* (New York: Praeger, 1971);

St. John, ed., *John Sloan's New York Scene* (New York: Harper & Row, 1965).

FLORENZ ZIEGFELD

1867-1932

BROADWAY PRODUCER

A Showman. The son of Dr. Florenz Ziegfeld, who had founded the Chicago Musical College in 1867, Florenz Ziegfeld Jr. was born in Chicago on 21 March 1867. In 1892, hoping to capitalize on the crowds that would be coming to the city for the Columbian Exposition of 1893, Dr. Ziegfeld set up a nightclub in Chicago and sent his twenty-five-year-old son to Europe and New York to find talent. The young scout brought back a Hungarian band, Russian dancers, and the Great Sandow, a German strongman who lifted people and pianos. Sandow was a hit, and Florenz Ziegfeld Jr. made $250,000 by managing Sandow's touring act over the next three years. When public fascination with Sandow faded, Ziegfeld moved to New York, where he managed the career of comedian Lew Weber. In 1896 he found a new client, and a wife: Anna Held, a Polish-born singer who was performing in Paris when Ziegfeld discovered her. Ziegfeld told American reporters that Held bathed daily in milk for her complexion and had won auto races in France; he draped her in diamonds and $20,000 gowns. He believed that money spent on promotion would come back in ticket sales — a philosophy that he maintained for the rest of his career.

The Birth of the *Follies*. In several of the shows he produced for Anna Held, Ziegfeld surrounded the petite actress with tall, beautiful chorus girls, creating a sensational effect. Ziegfeld liked the format, which Held compared to the Parisian Folies-Bergère, and the first *Ziegfeld Follies* premiered in New York City on 8 July 1907. The formula for these shows remained essentially the same for the next twenty-five years: singing, dancing, comedy, and, most of all, beautiful women in big production numbers with elaborate sets and choreography. The "Ziegfeld Girls" became his trademark: while other musical revues of that time used chorus lines of about a dozen dancers, Ziegfeld featured more than a hundred, all tall and exquisitely dressed. The first *Ziegfeld Follies* produced a profit of $120,000. The next year singer Nora Bayes's hit song "Shine On, Harvest Moon" drew audiences. In 1910 Ziegfeld hired two comedians, African American comic Bert Williams, a veteran of minstrel shows and vaudeville, and a young singer named Fanny Brice, whose act was based on Yiddish humor. One of several beauties added to the show in 1909 was singer Lillian Lorraine, the cause of Ziegfeld's divorce in 1912. He remarried in 1914 — not to Lorraine but to the popular dramatic actress Billie Burke, with whom he had a daughter, Patricia, two years later.

The *Follies* Flourish. In 1913 the *Follies* moved into the New Amsterdam Theater. On its top floor Ziegfeld built a posh nightclub, where he staged a smaller show called the *Midnight Frolics*. There, in front of patrons such as William Randolph Hearst and Diamond Jim Brady, new talents tried out their acts. Among them were rope-twirling humorist Will Rogers, who made his *Follies* debut in 1916, and singer-comedian Eddie Cantor, who joined the *Follies* in 1917. Together with Fanny Brice and W. C. Fields (who had debuted in 1915 as a juggling comedian), these comics added a crucial extra dimension to the beautiful-girls show. Sets designed by Austrian painter and architect Joseph Urban grew ever grander. Songwriters Jerome Kern and Irving Berlin began composing for the show in 1911; "A Pretty Girl is Like a Melody," a tune Berlin wrote for the 1919 *Follies*, became the Ziegfeld theme song.

Other Shows. During the 1910s and 1920s Ziegfeld mounted more than three dozen Broadway shows in addition to his *Follies*. Mostly musical comedies, they included *The Century Girl* (1916), with a score by Victor Herbert; *Miss 1917*, starring Irene Castle, with songs by Jerome Kern and Victor Herbert; *Kid Boots* (1924), starring Eddie Cantor; and *Rio Rita* (1927), featuring a score by George Gershwin. *Rio Rita* opened the new Ziegfeld Theatre, which in December 1927 was the scene of Ziegfeld's greatest triumph: his production of Jerome Kern and Oscar Hammerstein II's new musical, *Show Boat*. More musicals followed: *The Three Musketeers, Rosalie,* and *Whoopie* in 1928; *Show Girl* (1929), starring Ruby Keeler; and *Smiles* (1930), featuring brother-and-sister dance team Fred and Adele Astaire.

The Showman Stumbles. Though many of these musicals were box-office hits, the *Follies* began to flounder in the mid 1920s as its stars deserted Broadway for Hollywood. By the end of the 1920s Ziegfeld was in financial trouble. Though his longtime gambling habit and his general extravagance were partly to blame, the price of producing the lavish *Follies* had risen dramatically. Staging the 1927 show cost nearly $300,000, not counting headliners' salaries of up to $5,000 a week. After Ziegfeld suffered a major loss in the stock market crash of 1929, Billie Burke gave him $500,000 of her own savings, but he spent it quickly. In early 1932 he produced a radio version of the *Follies* and mounted a revival of *Show Boat* starring Paul Robeson. Impressed by the success of a film version of *Whoopie*, he considered going into the movie business. But he was sick from worry. Burke took him to California, where she was filming a movie, for a rest. When he died there of a heart attack on 22 July 1932, he was $500,000 in debt. Burke worked to repay the debt and to keep his name in the public eye, continuing (with backing from the Shuberts) to produce the *Follies* for more than a decade. M-G-M made three movies about Ziegfeld's life and work: *The Great Ziegfeld* (1936); *The Ziegfeld Girl*, starring Judy Garland (1941); and *Ziegfeld Follies* (1945).

Sources:

Randolph Carter, *The World of Flo Ziegfeld* (New York: Praeger, 1974);

Marjorie Farnsworth, *The Ziegfeld Follies* (New York: Bonanza Books, 1956);

Richard and Paulette Ziegfeld, *The Ziegfeld Touch: The Life and Times of Florenz Ziegfeld, Jr.* (New York: Abrams, 1993).

PEOPLE IN THE NEWS

On 28 November 1917 brother-and-sister dance team **Fred** and **Adele Astaire** made their Broadway debut in *Over the Top,* starring Ed Wynn and Justine Johnstone.

On 9 April 1919 brothers **John** and **Lionel Barrymore** opened at the Plymouth Theater in New York in Edward Sheldon's play *The Jest,* which became a hit.

On 17 July 1913 **Irving Berlin**'s wife, Dorothy, died of typhoid fever, five months after their marriage; in his grief Berlin wrote the ballad "When I Lost You," which sold two million copies of sheet music.

On 3 October 1910 **Charlie Chaplin,** a twenty-one-year-old member of a British pantomime company, performed his act "The Inebriate Swell" (complete with false moustache) at the Colonial Theater in New York City. He was a hit.

On 6 April 1917, after reading a newspaper report that the United States had declared war on Germany, **George M. Cohan** wrote "Over There," a patriotic song with a chorus based on a bugle call. Over the next several months it sold more than a million copies of sheet music and was widely recorded.

In 1919, at age twenty-two, actress **Marion Davies** got her own movie studio when her admirer, newspaper publisher William Randolph Hearst, formed a production company called Cosmopolitan to create star vehicles for her. Hearst also instructed editors of his newspapers to mention her name at least once in every issue.

On 19 April 1913, during the month when **Isadora Duncan** was dancing to Frédéric Chopin's *Funeral March* in Paris, her two children drowned after the car in which they were riding rolled into the Seine.

On 19 November 1915 **Edna Ferber**'s first play, *Our Mrs. McChesney* — adapted from several of her short stories — opened on Broadway with **Ethel Barrymore** playing the lead role.

In 1915 **W. C. Fields** appeared in his first movie, *Pool Sharks,* based on his act in the *Ziegfeld Follies.*

The 3 July 1915 issue of *Publishers' Weekly* announced the founding of a new publishing company by twenty-three-year-old **Alfred A. Knopf.**

On 21 March 1911 **Al Jolson** made his Broadway debut in *La Belle Paree* at the Winter Garden Theatre in New York City. Wearing blackface makeup, he played a singing and dancing minstrel.

On 7 June 1918 in Dekalb, Texas, **Huddie Ledbetter,** a blues guitar player who later became known as "Leadbelly," was arrested on a murder charge; later that year he was convicted and began serving a seven-year prison sentence.

In January 1916 twenty-one-year-old comic actor **Harold Lloyd** made his movie debut as Lonesome Luke, in a series that proved to be one of the most successful of the many imitations of **Charlie Chaplin**'s popular Little Tramp series.

In October 1914 nineteen-year-old **Anita Loos** sold a screenplay to director D. W. Griffith for twenty-five dollars. It was filmed as *The New York Hat,* the last movie Mary Pickford made for Biograph.

On 29 May 1914 *Reedy's Mirror* of Saint Louis published the first of three installments of *Spoon River Anthology,* free-verse poems about the stark realities of life and death in a midwestern town, written by Chicago attorney **Edgar Lee Masters** under the pen name Webster Ford.

The first one-woman show of drawings by **Georgia O'Keeffe** opened on 3 April 1917 at 291, the gallery of **Alfred Stieglitz,** who later became her husband.

In 1917 twenty-four-year-old wit **Dorothy Parker** was hired as the drama critic for *Vanity Fair* magazine.

On 14 November 1918 American soprano **Rosa Ponselle** made her American debut as Leonora in Giuseppe Verdi's *La forza del destino,* opposite Enrico Caruso, at the Metropolitan Opera House in New York City.

Rutgers University sophomore **Paul Robeson** — an African American scholar-athlete who later won acclaim as an actor and singer — made the 1917 All-American football team.

A charity benefit show, staged on 8 March 1919 at the Waldorf-Astoria Hotel in New York City, featured twenty songs by seventeen-year-old composer **Richard Rodgers** and twenty-four-year-old lyricist **Lorenz Hart.**

After starring together in three films, **Gloria Swanson** and **Wallace Beery** were married in 1916; they were divorced three years later.

In 1912 the theater trade periodical *Variety* reviewed a new burlesque act by nineteen-year-old **Mae West**, billed as "The Baby Vamp" two years before **Theda Bara** popularized the term *vamp* in her movies.

AWARDS

The Pulitzer Prizes were first awarded in 1917 for journalism, biography, and history. Prizes for drama and fiction were added in 1918. In 1918 the Poetry Society of America, founded in 1910, gave its first award.

1918

Poetry Society of America Prize: *Love Songs*, by Sara Teasdale

Pulitzer Prize for fiction: *His Family*, by Ernest Poole

Pulitzer Prize for drama: *Why Marry?*, by Jesse Lynch Williams

1919

Poetry Society of America Prizes: *Cornhuskers*, by Carl Sandburg; *Old Road to Paradise*, by Margaret Widdemer

Pulitzer Prize for fiction: *The Magnificent Ambersons*, by Booth Tarkington

Pulitzer Prize for drama: no award

DEATHS

Henry Adams, 80, historian, teacher, editor, and author of *The Education of Henry Adams*, which was published posthumously in 1919 and won the Pulitzer Prize for biography, 27 March 1918.

Amelia Barr, 87, author of popular romantic novels and short stories, 10 March 1919.

L. Frank Baum, 62, author of children's books, including *The Wonderful Wizard of Oz* (1900), 6 May 1919.

Ambrose Bierce, 72, short-story writer and journalist who disappeared while traveling in Mexico with the rebel army of Pancho Villa, exact date unknown, 1914.

Karl Bitter, 47, Austrian-immigrant sculptor who helped to organize several important American sculpture exhibits, 10 April 1915.

James A. Bland, 56, African American composer of minstrel-show songs, including "Carry Me Back to Old Virginny" and "Golden Slippers," 5 May 1911.

Randolph Bourne, 32, literary radical and cultural critic, 22 December 1918.

Vernon Castle, 30, husband and dance partner of Irene Castle, killed during a training exercise while serving as an aviation instructor, 15 February 1918.

William Merritt Chase, 66, painter, first president of the Society of American Artists, and an influential teacher whose students included Marsden Hartley and Charles Demuth, 25 October 1916.

Bob Cole, 43, African American comedian and songwriter whose hits included "Under the Bamboo Tree," 2 August 1911.

Rebecca Harding Davis, 79, author of *Life in the Iron Mills* (1861), a novella about West Virginia iron workers in the mid nineteenth century, 29 September 1910.

Richard Harding Davis, 51, son of Rebecca Harding Davis, playwright, short-story writer, and journalist, husband of actress-singer Bessie McCoy, 11 April 1916.

Thomas Eakins, 71, painter known especially for his realistic sports scenes and his controversial *The Gross Clinic* (1875), a painting of a surgical operation in progress, 25 June 1916.

James Reese Europe, 38, dance-band leader who was among the first African Americans to make sound recordings, 10 May 1919.

Charles Frohman, 54, powerful Broadway producer, aboard the *Lusitania* when it was sunk by a German submarine, 7 May 1915.

Nat C. Goodwin, 61, popular nineteenth-century comedic actor, 31 January 1919.

Frances Ellen Watkins Harper, 85, African American poet, short-story writer, novelist, and abolitionist lecturer, 22 February 1911.

Scott Hayden, 33, ragtime pianist and composer, 24 September 1915.

Anna Held, 45, Polish-born actress who starred in the first *Ziegfeld Follies* and was the first wife of Broadway producer Florenz Ziegfeld, 12 August 1918.

O. Henry (William Sydney Porter), 47, popular short-story writer, 5 June 1910.

Edmund Milton Holland, 65, nineteenth-century comedic actor, 24 November 1913.

Winslow Homer, 74, painter who specialized in landscapes and seascapes, including *Northeaster* (1895) and *Gulf Stream* (1899), 29 September 1910.

Karl Hoschna, 34, German-born composer of popular operettas and Tin Pan Alley hits, 23 December 1911.

Julia Ward Howe, 91, author of "The Battle Hymn of the Republic" (1862), 17 October 1910.

Henry James, 72, expatriate fiction writer whose works include *Daisy Miller* (1878), *The Portrait of a Lady* (1881), *Washington Square* (1881), *The Bostonians* (1886), *The Turn of the Screw* (1898), *The Wings of the Dove* (1902), *The Ambassadors* (1903), and *The Golden Bowl* (1904), 28 February 1916.

Scott Joplin, 48, pianist and prolific composer of ragtime music, including "Maple Leaf Rag," 1 April 1917.

Benjamin Franklin Keith, 68, owner of hundreds of vaudeville theaters across the country, including the Palace Theatre in New York City, 26 March 1914.

Joyce Kilmer, 32, poet whose best-known work is "Trees" (1913), killed while scouting enemy territory as an enlisted man in World War I, 30 July 1918.

Jack London, 40, fiction writer whose works include *The Call of the Wild* (1901) and *White Fang* (1905), 22 November 1916.

Joaquin Miller, 74, poet, journalist, and playwright, 17 February 1913.

Francis D. Millet, 65, painter who went down with the *Titanic*, 15 April 1912.

Maggie Mitchell, 80, mid-nineteenth-century actress, 22 March 1918.

S. Weir Mitchell, 84, novelist, poet, and physician, 4 January 1914.

William Vaughn Moody, 41, literary scholar, poet, and dramatist whose plays include *The Great Divide* (1906) and *The Faith Healer* (1909), 17 October 1910.

Lewis F. Muir, 32, pianist and songwriter whose hits include "Waiting for the Robert E. Lee," 3 December 1915.

Lillian Nordica (Lillian Norton), 56, operatic soprano, 10 May 1914.

Horatio Parker, 56, opera composer and Yale University music professor whose students included Charles Ives, 18 December 1919.

David Graham Phillips, 43, realist novelist and muckraking journalist, 24 January 1911.

Joseph Pulitzer, 64, Hungarian immigrant who created a newspaper dynasty and endowed the Pulitzer Prizes, established in 1917, 29 October 1911.

Howard Pyle, 58, prolific illustrator and founder of the Brandywine School, 9 November 1911.

Ada Rehan, 56, Irish immigrant who became a popular stage actress, 8 January 1916.

James Whitcomb Riley, 66, popular dialect poet who celebrated ordinary midwestern life in poems such as "When the Frost Is on the Punkin," 22 July 1916.

Monroe H. Rosenfeld, 56, composer of late-nineteenth-century sentimental ballads, credited with having coined the term *Tin Pan Alley,* 12 December 1918.

Albert Pinkham Ryder, 70, painter known for his romantic, allegorical landscapes, which often include literary allusions, 28 March 1917.

Alan Seeger, 28, poet killed in action during World War I, 4 July 1916.

Ren Shields, 45, vaudeville performer, playwright, and lyricist whose hit songs include "In the Good Old Summertime," 25 October 1913.

Mark Twain (Samuel Clemens), 74, celebrated novelist whose books include *Tom Sawyer* (1876), *The Prince and the Pauper* (1881), *Huckleberry Finn* (1884), *A Connecticut Yankee in King Arthur's Court* (1889), and *Pudd'nhead Wilson* (1894), 21 April 1910.

J. Alden Weir, 67, artist who exhibited more than two dozen paintings and etchings in the Armory Show, 9 December 1919.

Ella Wheeler Wilcox, 69, popular poet, 30 October 1919.

PUBLICATIONS

Frances Agnew, *Motion Picture Acting* (New York: Reliance Newspaper Syndicate, 1913);

David Belasco, *The Theatre through Its Stage Door* (New York: Harper, 1919);

Van Wyck Brooks, *America's Coming-of-Age* (New York: Huebsch, 1915);

Carolyn Caffin, *Vaudeville* (New York: Mitchell Kennerley, 1914);

Huntley Carter, *The New Spirit in Drama and Art* (New York: Mitchell Kennerley, 1913);

Vernon and Irene Castle, *Modern Dancing* (New York: Harper, 1914);

Anna Alice Chapin, *Greenwich Village* (New York: Dodd, Mead, 1917);

Sheldon Cheney, *The New Movement in the Theater* (New York: Mitchell Kennerley, 1914);

Francis Collins, *The Camera Man* (New York: Century, 1916);

Kenyon Cox, *Artist and Public* (New York: Scribners, 1914);

Homer Croy, *How Motion Pictures Are Made* (New York: Harper, 1918);

Joseph F. Daly, *The Life of Augustin Daly* (New York: Macmillan, 1917);

Ernest A. Dench, *Making the Movies* (New York: Macmillan, 1915);

Thomas H. Dickinson, *The Case of American Drama* (Boston: Houghton Mifflin, 1915);

Dickinson, *The Insurgent Theatre* (New York: Huebsch, 1917);

Max Eastman, *The Enjoyment of Poetry* (New York: Scribners, 1913);

Walter Prichard Eaton, *Plays and Players: Leaves from a Critic's Scrapbook* (Cincinnati: Stewart & Kidd, 1916);

Arthur Jerome Eddy, *Cubists and Post-Impressionists* (Chicago: McClurg, 1914);

T. S. Eliot, *Ezra Pound: His Metric and Poetry* (New York: Knopf, 1917);

Waldo Frank, *Our America* (New York: Boni & Liveright, 1919);

V. C. Freeburg, *Art of Photoplay Making* (New York: Macmillan, 1918);

Daniel Frohman, *Memories of a Manager* (Garden City, N.Y.: Doubleday, Page, 1911);

Frohman and Isaac F. Marcosson, *Charles Frohman, Manager and Man* (New York: Harper, 1916);

Robert Grau, *The Stage in the Twentieth Century* (New York: Broadway Publishing, 1912);

Grau, *The Theatre of Science* (New York: Broadway Publishing, 1914);

Clayton Hamilton, *Problems of the Playwright* (New York: Holt, 1917);

Hamilton, *Studies in Stagecraft* (New York: Holt, 1914);

Arthur Hornblow, *A History of the Theatre in America*, 2 volumes (Philadelphia: Lippincott, 1919);

Winifred E. Howe, *A History of the Metropolitan Museum of Art* (New York: Metropolitan Museum of Art, 1913);

William Dean Howells, *Years of My Youth* (New York: Harper, 1916);

David S. Hulfish, *Motion Picture Work* (Chicago: American School of Correspondence, 1913);

James G. Huneker, *The Philharmonic Society of New York and Its 75th Anniversary* (New York: Philharmonic Society of New York, 1917);

Huneker, *The Steinway Collection of Paintings by American Artists, Together with Prose Portraits of the Great Composers* (New York: Steinway & Sons, 1919);

Henry James, *Notes on Novelists* (New York: Scribners, 1914);

Arthur Edwin Krows, *Play Production in America* (New York: Holt, 1916);

John Nilsen Laurvik, *Is It Art? Post-Impressionism, Futurism, Cubism* (New York: International Press, 1913);

Michael Bennett Leavitt, *Fifty Years in Theatrical Management* (New York: Broadway Publishing, 1912);

Austin Lescarboura, *Behind the Motion Picture Screen* (New York: Scientific American, 1919);

Vachel Lindsay, *The Art of the Moving Picture* (New York: Macmillan, 1915);

Amy Lowell, *Tendencies in Modern American Poetry* (New York: Macmillan, 1917);

Constance D. MacKaye, *The Little Theater in the United States* (New York: Holt, 1917);

Percy MacKaye, *The Civic Theater* (New York: Mitchell Kennerley, 1912);

Brander Matthews, *A Book about the Theatre* (New York: Scribners, 1914);

Matthews, *Gateways to Literature, and Other Essays* (New York: Scribners, 1912);

Arthur S. Meloy, *Theatres and Motion Picture Houses* (New York: Architects Supply & Publishing, 1916);

H. L. Mencken, *The American Language* (New York: Knopf, 1919);

Mencken, *A Book of Prefaces* (New York: Knopf, 1917);

Hugo Munsterberg, *The Photoplay: A Psychological Study* (New York: Appleton, 1916);

Brett Page, *Writing for Vaudeville* (Springfield, Mass.: Home Correspondence School, 1915);

Albert Bigelow Paine, *Mark Twain, A Biography: The Personal and Literary Life of Samuel Langhorne Clemens* (New York: Harper, 1912);

Henry Rankin Poore, *The Conception of Art* (New York: Putnam, 1913);

John B. Rathbun, *Motion Picture Making and Exhibiting* (Chicago: Thompson, 1914);

John Reed, *The Day in Bohemia, or, Life among the Artists* (New York: Hillacre, 1913);

Edward Renton, *The Vaudeville Theatre* (New York: Gotham Press, 1918);

Edward Le Roy Rice, *Monarchs of Minstrelsy* (New York: Kenny, 1911);

Monroe H. Rosenfeld, ed., *The Tuneful Yankee* (Boston, 1917);

Charles Schwartz and Louis D. Frohlich, *The Law of Motion Pictures and the Theater* (New York: Baker, Voorhis, 1918);

John Philip Sousa, *Through the Years with Sousa* (New York, 1910);

John Ranken Towse, *Sixty Years of the Theater* (New York: Funk & Wagnalls, 1916);

Max Weber, *Essays on Art* (New York: Rudge, 1916);

William Winter, *The Life of David Belasco* (New York: Moffat, Yard, 1918);

Winter, *The Wallet of Time, Containing Personal, Biographical, and Critical Reminiscences of the American Theater* (New York: Moffat, Yard, 1913);

Winter, ed., *The American Stage of Today* (New York: Collier, 1910);

Willard Huntington Wright, *Modern Painting* (New York: John Lane, 1915);

Marius de Zayas and Paul B. Haviland, *A Study of the Modern Evolution of Plastic Expression* (New York: 291, 1913).

Periodicals:

Art in America (1913–);

Christensen's Ragtime Review (1914–1916);

The Dial (1916–1920);

Drama Magazine (1911–1931);

The Glebe (1913–1914);

The Little Review (1914–1929);

Melody (1918–1934);

The Midland (1915–1933);

The Musical Quarterly (1915–);

Others: A Magazine of the New Verse (1915–1919);

Phonograph and Talking Machine Weekly (1916–1930s);

Photoplay (1911–1980);

Poetry (1912–);

Poetry Journal (1912–1918);

The Poetry Review of America (1916–1917);

Rogue (March–September 1915);

The Seven Arts (1916–1917);

Slate (1917);

Soil (1916–1917);

Southwest Review (1915);

Theatre Arts (1916–1964);

291 (1915–1916);

The Unpopular Review (1914–1921);

Vanity Fair (1914–1936).

BUSINESS AND THE ECONOMY

by ROBERT P. BATCHELOR

CONTENTS

Sidebars and tables are listed in italics.

1910

- Nearly one-third of the nation's coal miners are unionized, compared to 10 percent of workers in other industries.

16 May The U.S. Bureau of Mines is established as part of the Department of the Interior, with Dr. Joseph Austin Holmes as its first director.

18 June Congress adopts the Mann-Elkins Act, which enlarges the powers of the Interstate Commerce Commission (ICC) and adds cable, wireless, telephone, and telegraph companies to its responsibilities.

7 Sept. The Hague Court reaches a compromise settling the North American fisheries case between the United States and Great Britain.

1 Oct. Twenty people are killed and seventeen injured when John J. and James McNamara blow up the *Los Angeles Times* building because the newspaper favors the open shop over a closed union shop.

1911

- Air conditioning is invented.

- The first motor-driven hook-and-ladder truck, the "Mack," is introduced.

- Charles Kettering invents the first electrical automobile self-starter.

21 Feb. The United States and Japan sign a navigation and commerce treaty that includes the conditions reached in 1907. The treaty opens both nations to further trade.

15 May The Supreme Court rules that the Standard Oil Company of New Jersey must be dissolved as an unreasonable combination in restraint of trade under antitrust laws.

29 May The American Tobacco Company, the Supreme Court declares, is an illegal combination in restraint of trade and must dissolve.

7 July The sealing industry in the North Pacific is regulated by the signing of a treaty between the United States, Great Britain, Russia, and Japan.

26 Oct. The Taft administration files a suit against the United States Steel Company under the Sherman Antitrust Act, in spite of Theodore Roosevelt's earlier pledge to J. P. Morgan that such a suit would not be brought.

1912

9 Jan. U.S. Marines land in Honduras to protect American companies and property there.

14 Mar. The United States bans arms shipments to opponents of Mexican president Francisco Madero.

1 May Ship safety regulations are issued by federal inspectors following the sinking of the *Titanic*. Steamships are now required to carry enough lifeboats to hold all passengers.

1913

- The Woolworth Building opens in New York City. At a height of 792 feet, it is an imposing symbol of the wealth generated by a national commercial economy.

- Grand Central Terminal is opened in New York City.

- The Panama Canal is completed, opening new possibilities for commerce between Atlantic and Pacific nations.

1 Jan. A new parcel post service begins, giving farmers closer contact with their fellow citizens and improving the rural post system.

Jan.–Feb. Garment workers, led by the International Ladies' Garment Workers' Union (ILGWU), strike in New York and are followed in March by workers in Boston. They demand higher wages, shorter hours, and recognition of their union.

25 Feb. The Sixteenth Amendment to the Constitution is adopted, giving Congress the power to tax personal incomes without apportionment among the states.

28 Feb. A congressional subcommittee, headed by Rep. Arsene Pujo of Louisiana, reports that there is a "growing concentration of control of money and credit."

1 Mar. The Physical Valuation Act gives the ICC the power to determine the physical value of railroad property in order to establish rates and profits.

Despite the veto of President Taft, Congress passes the Webb-Kenyon Interstate Liquor Act, which makes it illegal to ship liquor into states where the sale of liquor is prohibited.

Mar.–Apr. Garment workers' demands are met when their strikes are settled in March and April in New York and Boston.

11 Mar. The new president, Woodrow Wilson, refuses to recognize the Mexican government of Victoriano Huerta, who overthrew the Madero government in February. This action ends the policy of dollar diplomacy.

8 Apr. President Wilson appears before a special session of Congress to deliver a message on the need for new tariff legislation. This is the first time since 1800 that a president has appeared before Congress.

19 June The Supreme Court decides, after hearing the Minnesota rate cases, that a state may establish railroad rates within its own borders if there is no conflict with federal laws on interstate commerce.

23 June Congress is urged by President Wilson to reform laws pertaining to banking and currency.

26 Aug. The Keokuk Dam opens. It is the world's largest hydroelectric dam and spans the Mississippi River from Keokuk, Iowa, to Hamilton, Illinois.

Sept. Coal miners strike in Colorado in response to an open shop drive led by John D. Rockefeller's Colorado Fuel and Iron Company. The strike is called off by the United Mine Workers three months later after much violence and federal intervention.

3 Oct. Congress adopts the Underwood Tariff Act, which reduces duty rates to an average of 26 percent and greatly expands the list of free goods.

23 Dec. The Federal Reserve System is created by the Federal Reserve Act, which divides the country into twelve districts with a Federal Reserve bank in each. The system is controlled by a seven-member Federal Reserve Board. All national banks are required to join the system.

1914

20 Jan. President Woodrow Wilson, in an address to Congress, calls for the strengthening of the nation's antitrust laws.

8 May The Smith-Lever Act provides grants for agricultural extension work to be developed by land-grant colleges and the Department of Agriculture.

15 Aug. The Panama Canal officially opens.

20 Aug. Great Britain issues an order-in-council on wartime trade that makes it increasingly difficult for goods of any sort to reach Germany. The United States protests the measure as an interference of the rights of neutrals.

26 Sept. The Federal Trade Commission Act is adopted. It is designed to bar unfair competition in interstate trade.

15 Oct. The Clayton Antitrust Act becomes law. It is intended to eliminate monopolistic practices that have developed since the passage of the Sherman Antitrust Act. Both companies and individual corporate officers are subject to prosecution. It also states that labor and agricultural organizations are not illegal combinations under the antitrust laws. Boycotts, strikes, and peaceful picketing are no longer subject to injunctions, a major victory for organized labor.

1915

- The taxicab makes its first appearance in American cities. Service costs a nickel, and the popularity of the cabs leads to the development of intercity bus lines.

15 Jan. The first transcontinental telephone line opens for service from New York City to San Francisco.

10 Feb. The United States protests a German declaration of a war zone around the British Isles.

30 Mar. The United States protests the British blockade of German ports, saying that it interferes with legitimate neutral trade.

15 Oct. A $500 million loan is made by private American banks to France and Great Britain.

21 Oct. The first transatlantic radiotelephone communication is made from Arlington, Virginia, to the Eiffel Tower in Paris.

10 Dec. The one millionth Model T automobile rolls off the Ford Motor Company's assembly line in Detroit, Michigan.

1916

- Boeing Aircraft Company designs and produces its first model, the biplane.

17 July The Federal Farm Loan Act, which sets up twelve Farm Loan Banks to extend long-term loans to farmers, is adopted by Congress.

22 July Ten people are killed and many more wounded when a bomb is thrown during the Preparedness Day parade in San Francisco. Thomas Mooney and others involved in the labor movement on the West Coast are arrested. Mooney is sentenced to death; in 1918 his sentence was commuted to life imprisonment. He was pardoned in 1939.

30 July   A munitions dump on Black Tom Island, New Jersey, is blown up by German saboteurs, causing $22 million in damages.

11 Aug.   The Warehouse Act enables farmers to secure loans on the basis of warehouse receipts. In effect the measure adopts one of the central features of the Populist Party platform of the 1890s known as the "sub-treasury" system.

1917

23 Feb.   Federal aid is provided for vocational/educational aid under the Smith-Hughes Act.

31 Mar.   The Council of National Defense establishes the General Munitions Board.

24 Apr.   The Liberty Loan Act is adopted. It provides for the public sale of bonds and the extension of loans to Allied Powers.

28 July   The General Munitions Board is succeeded by the War Industries Board. It effectively runs the economic mobilization effort for the war.

10 Aug.   The Lever Food and Fuel Control Act is passed to increase the production of food and fuel and to provide for their effective distribution. The food program, administered by Herbert Hoover, is particularly effective.

3 Oct.   The War Revenue Act establishes graduated personal income and excess profits taxes and higher postal rates.

6 Oct.   The Trading with the Enemy Act establishes an office of Alien Property Custodian to handle enemy property in the United States, most of which is sold. Trading with the enemy is prohibited, and all imports are placed under control of the War Trade Board.

18 Dec.   Congress proposes the adoption of the Eighteenth Amendment, which prohibits the manufacture, sale, or transportation of intoxicating liquors.

26 Dec.   The U.S. Railroad Administration, under the direction of William Gibbs McAdoo, takes charge of the nation's railroads. They remain under government control until 1920.

1918

21 Mar.   The Railroad Control Act provides for the operation of railroads on a regional basis and the determination of compensation due to railroads while the lines are under federal control.

5 Apr.   The War Finance Corporation is established to help banks finance the operation of war industries.

8 Apr.   The National War Labor Board is established to settle labor disputes and avoid interruption of war production.

10 Apr.   Congress passes the Webb-Pomerene Act. The act allows exporters to combine in export trade associations and not be prosecuted under antitrust laws.

13 May   The Post Office Department issues the first airmail stamps in denominations of six cents, sixteen cents, and twenty-four cents.

16 July   The federal government takes control of the nation's telephone and telegraph systems.

1919

Jan.	Shipyard workers in Seattle, Washington, go on strike to protest poor pay and harsh conditions. A general strike ensues with more than sixty thousand people participating. Nervous national leaders call off the strike before any real gains are made.
29 Jan.	The Eighteenth Amendment to the Constitution is ratified, prohibiting the manufacture, sale, and transportation of intoxicating liquors.
Sept.	Steel workers numbering 250,000 walk out in protest over long hours and low pay. Company owners fight back by using strikebreakers and thugs to stop the strike.
9 Sept.	Boston police go on strike, leaving the city without protection.
28 Oct.	The Volstead Act is passed, enforcing the Eighteenth Amendment.
20 Nov.	The nation's first municipal airport opens in Tucson, Arizona.

OVERVIEW

Great Change. The decade of the 1910s was the age of the great industrialist and financier, the trust-builder and the tycoon. The decade was also the age of the manager and the engineer. From the shop floor to the board room, American corporations were reshaped in the 1910s as scientific management, efficiency, and mechanization took hold. One statistic illustrates the sweeping changes under way in American industry: while the number of wage earners in transportation, mining, and manufacturing grew by more than 27 percent in the 1910s, the number of supervisory personnel grew by more than 66 percent. Perhaps Woodrow Wilson had this transition in mind when he declared during the presidential campaign in 1912 that "We have changed our economic conditions, absolutely, from top to bottom; and with our economic society, the organization of our life."

Science, Efficiency, and Technology. The business engines of the nineteenth century were eclipsed by new businesses that relied on scientific management, efficiency, and technology. The automobile industry became the single largest and most powerful segment in the nation's economy. The sale of cars tripled from 1914 to 1916, and Ford Motor Company alone sold 730,041 cars in 1916–1917. The automobile industry was not alone among emerging businesses. Chemical manufacturers, electrical companies, and electrical appliance and machinery manufacturers grew astronomically. Standardization and efficiency marked the transition from handcraftsmen to the assembly line and provided the consumer goods necessary to satisfy the masses flocking to the urban centers. The relationship between the government and business leaders changed as well to reflect the growing necessity for cooperation and minimal regulation. The United States changed its standing in the world as World War I proved the nation's industrial power. Serving as the source of weaponry for the Allies, the country went from the world's largest debtor to its most powerful creditor. When big business tasted the huge profits generated by the war it thirsted for more and accepted government intervention in the economy in return for larger profit margins. By the end of the decade the new corporate economy had taken shape, and the stage was set for continued economic expansion in the 1920s.

Progressivism and Intervention. The United States entered the tumultuous decade of the 1910s riding a wave of progressive reform that had a tremendous impact on the economy. The dichotomy between progressivism on one hand and government intervention on the other seemed mutually exclusive, but in reality the two went hand in hand to form a business foundation for the 1910s. The successes and failures of the decade laid the foundation for much of what followed in American business history during the twentieth century.

The New Freedom. Woodrow Wilson's election in 1912 insured that the progressive movement would continue, and reformers continued to work for the rights of common people. For progressives the threat to democracy was not the existing government but the failure to use government power wisely. The remedy was to attack the hidden centers of power through banking reform and business regulation. Wilson's reform program, called the "New Freedom," promised to open the economic market. Wilson wanted to eliminate the corporate trusts, which choked off healthy competition among businesses, and sought to use the power of the federal government to protect the people. By combining the ideas of his New Freedom models with the Republican program of big government, Wilson set the tone for the rest of the decade. Wilson acknowledged the power of big business and worked to limit its abusive characteristics. He did not want to accomplish this through heavy government involvement in the economy. In 1914 the administration proposed the cornerstone measure of the New Freedom program: the Clayton Antitrust Act. Then he proposed the Federal Trade Commission (FTC). The Clayton Act outlawed the monopolistic practices of big business, while the FTC was the investigative body enforcing the act. Together these measures worked to protect consumers and open the market for healthy competition among all businesses. The bills symbolized Wilson's acceptance of big business and his recognition that there had to be some regulation of it.

Reform. The successes of the New Freedom encouraged the administration to push forward. The Underwood Tariff Act, passed in 1913, promoted free trade by reducing tariffs on foreign goods. Consumers found merchandise prices unnaturally high because government tariffs deterred the importation of cheaper foreign goods. The Underwood Act encouraged merchants to import by reducing or eliminating tariff rates. To replace the revenues the Sixteenth Amendment to the Constitution became effective on 25 February, which allowed the government to impose a graduated income tax on citizens. Most farmers and factory workers, however, were exempt from the initial tax since incomes less than $4,000 were not taxed. Incomes between $4,000 and $20,000 had to pay a 1 percent tax, and higher incomes paid more taxes to a maximum of 6 percent on wages more than $500,000. The war in Europe and the upcoming 1916 presidential election forced Wilson to push for stronger reform measures. The president backed the Federal Farm Loan Act of 1916 so that farmers could borrow money to sustain production. The act created twelve banks backed by the federal government that would lend money to farmers at a moderate interest rate. The same year Wilson backed the Adamson Act, which gave railroad workers an eight-hour day and prevented a national strike that would have disrupted the nation's shipping and transportation. The administration also backed laws that banned child labor and provided worker's compensation for federal employees who suffered injury or illness.

The Rise of Big Business. The rise of big business in America led to massive social change and was one of the most pervasive factors affecting the economy in the 1910s. Entirely new classes of managers and workers developed to serve the modern corporation. Technology and science were used to meet the need for efficiency and systematic approaches to work and work methods. The modern corporation grew into the dominant element in the expanding urban society in the decade. The entire society, from the European-born immigrant working on the assembly line to the upper-class female labor activist, felt the influence of corporations. By the end of the period, big business affected politics, reshaped labor relations, and generally became a permanent institution in American life. The power of the corporation grew to such a degree that it had to be regulated, and, in fact, the business community itself led the way. Both the federal government and businesses realized that they could benefit from limited regulation. Therefore, the biggest backers of the Federal Reserve System were the member bankers. Likewise, Congress modified the Clayton bill toward the wishes of businessmen. What developed was a system of compromises, not grand social vision or hardened reality.

World War I and the Economy. American involvement in World War I increased government regulation to a degree. The wartime atmosphere created further opportunity for government activism and a partnership with business. President Wilson saw government intervention in the economy as a temporary, but necessary, measure. The American public would not have stood for permanent intervention, their distrust of oligarchical power being too much to allow that. The War Industries Board (WIB), the most powerful of the wartime agencies, was immediately disbanded after the war ended, a sure sign of how the public would not accept permanent economic intervention. Wilson, as well as the general public, saw no further need for the agency after the fighting ended. Wilson feared that regulatory commissions could easily fall under the influence of private interests leading to an elitist economic system. "Dollar-a-year men" flocked to Washington, D.C., during the war, accepting no salaries from the government but retaining their corporate positions. Hundreds of new agencies came into being at this time. The agencies placed controls on the economy and in some instances completely took over segments of the economy, such as the railroads and the telephone and telegraph companies. However, the relationship between government and business remained one of mutual benefit. Each side prospered: the government mobilized the economy for war and won overwhelming public support, while businesses reaped huge profits from government-sponsored programs.

Economic Hegemony. The war allowed the United States to become the world's most powerful nation economically. Farmers enjoyed boom years as they supplied the world with food. The gross income of farmers rose from $7.5 billion in 1910 to $15.9 billion by the end of the decade. Demands on the industrial sector forced companies to increase productivity. The United States alone accounted for 56 percent of the world's manufacturing output by middecade. Steel production benefited greatly, doubling its output compared to the prewar period. However, not all the wartime goals were met. Munitions deliveries were not fulfilled; the War Shipping Board and the Aircraft Production Board were both backlogged by graft and bureaucratic mismanagement; and government-induced inflation pushed the wholesale price index up 98 percent from 1913 to 1918.

Middle Managers. The growing ranks of middle managers and industrial engineers now stood between the owners of large corporations (typically someone holding just a small percentage of a company's stock) and the blue-collar workers in mills and mines, on railroads and freighters. The value of goods and services more than doubled during the decade, from $35.3 billion in 1910 to $91.5 billion in 1920. Exports of American manufactured goods and agricultural products contributed substantially to this astounding achievement, as reflected in the U.S. balance of trade with other countries: in 1910 the United States enjoyed a positive balance of trade of $273 million; by 1920 that advantage had swelled to $2.88 billion. The growth in exports, together with war loans to the Allies, helped turn the United States from a debtor nation at the beginning of the 1910s to a creditor nation by 1920. The increasing number of workers raised the position of the labor movement to a new height. The new relationship between government and business put labor into an position of national importance it had heretofore never held.

Wilson and Labor. The Wilson administration fostered a close relationship with organized labor due largely in part because of labor's support for Wilson in the 1912 and 1916 elections. The American Federation of Labor, under Samuel Gompers, supported Wilson and the war effort. The National War Labor Board was formed to mediate labor disputes and even outlawed strikes, although the wartime atmosphere increased workers' power over management. The number of workers involved in the labor movement grew from 2.7 million in 1916 to more than 5 million by 1920. Although factory workers benefited from the war economy, inflation made their real gains minimal, and the factory worker saw little real economic improvement. Furthermore, the labor unions of the decade excluded the majority of foreign-born workers and paid little attention to women's concerns. However, the ability of labor to organize effectively in the 1910s set the stage for the labor successes of the 1930s.

Science and Technology. The United States entered a period of technological innovation and increasing ties between the science community and the business world. High-technology, science-based industries such as the electric manufacturers, chemical companies, and communications firms expanded during the 1910s. Formal research and development departments at companies such as General Electric, American Telephone and Telegraph, DuPont, and Eastman Kodak introduced new products and led to tremendous growth. Universities entered the fray by supplying the creative minds to quicken this growth. Science and industry were transforming society from the traditional emphasis on classes and interest groups to one large-scale industrial organization. Science found its way into the business world through the scientific management ideas of Frederick W. Taylor and Frank B. Gilbreth and the Ford Motor Company's introduction of the five-dollar day, an attempt to control employees' lives by tying their income to their behavior both on and off the job. Midlevel managers were important to run the new assembly lines, while technicians raced to invent new ways of improving the automation. Science and technology now controlled the worker's time on the job, and sociological and psychological methods were being developed to influence his domestic life.

Progress for Women and Children. Women and children both benefited from the progressive ideas. The National Child Labor Committee, formed in 1904, organized twenty-five branches in twenty-two states demanding that child labor be outlawed. By 1914 every state but one established the minimum working age at fourteen. Women also fought laws that limited their hours and wages in the workforce. In 1912 the first victory came in Massachusetts, when the state created a wage commission to recommend minimum wages for women and make public the names of those employers who did not abide by the recommendations. Women, however, were still discriminated against in the 1910s. The main reason they were hired was that they could be paid substantially lower wages than men doing the same jobs. Even professional occupations dominated by women, such as nursing, teaching, and social work, became lower-paid and lower-status jobs. Women were seen as interlopers by union officials and as transient help by many employers. Thus, while some important strides were taken, women did not reap all of the benefits of the Progressive Era.

BIG BUSINESS: THE MODERN CORPORATION

Big Business. In the early 1910s the United States remained relatively isolated and in the midst of a recession. The majority of Americans still lived in rural areas, and many worked for themselves or in small enterprises. The world of big business, revolving around trusts and holding companies, seemed far removed from the average citizen, but large conglomerates controlled railroads, banks, insurance companies, steel, meatpacking, and oil refining. Despite the federal government's antitrust laws and attempts at regulating large corporations, the government played a relatively small role in the economy.

New Ties. The rise of big business and the triumph of industrial civilization changed the country economically and socially. The United States used its vast resources and technical expertise to become a dominant power in this age. Officials in both business and government realized that to advance their related interests, the ties between corporations and government had to be strengthened and institutionalized. Without great economic power the United States would falter, and this power was increasingly concentrated in the hands of large corporations. In 1913 the country was the leading debtor in the world, but by 1917 it had become the largest creditor. The partnership between large corporations and the federal government served an instrumental role in the turnaround. Big business became representative of American initiative, determination, and expertise, and the nation would flaunt its power later in the decade.

Social Change. The rise of big business and triumph of industrialization led to massive social change in the United States. Corporations spearheaded a new social and economic order. The modern company soon became the dominant element in urban and suburban civilization. The entire society was influenced by the corporate way of doing things. A new managerial class grew by emphasizing efficiency and systematic approaches to business. The new class of corporate managers helped create and then served to strengthen the modern corporation. Big business became a domestic institution in American life and affected politics, reshaped labor, and showed the importance of technology and science.

Louis Chevrolet at the wheel of a 1911 Chevrolet Classic

Government Responds to Fear. Politicians struck a sensitive chord in the general public by criticizing the railroads, giant manufacturers, and influential bankers. Woodrow Wilson, in fact, won the 1912 presidential election running as an opponent of big business. The public feared that the new economic order would destroy America's status as the land of opportunity and individual initiative. The revolution in business worried people. The middle-class dream of running one's own business dwindled as small enterprises were bought up or run out of business by large combinations. The ruthless use of economic power by men such as John D. Rockefeller disturbed people. Progressive legislators countered by outlawing the unscrupulous activities but could not keep up with the plethora of new practices. The government was forced to create regulatory agencies with broad powers to oversee and discipline the competitive behavior of big business. The Federal Trade Commission was established in 1914 to investigate, enforce, and publicize business activity. A new role for government as a watchdog of the private sector developed. The combined efforts of agencies, the Justice Department, and the courts were supposed to prevent the worst misuses of economic power.

Battle for Control. The emphasis on efficiency and production in the 1910s transformed the relationship between labor and management. The factory system changed the nature of work itself by increasing reliance on machines and the assembly line, thus decreasing the ability of factory workers to set their own pace of work. The ensuing conflicts led to many of the strikes and labor violence that punctuated the decade. The changing nature of work in the industrial age brought stresses that bubbled over into heated battles between workers and manufacturers. Systematic management initiatives increased the power of the shop foreman, who often acted like a feudal lord reigning over his minions.

Taylorism. Corporate executives in the 1910s adopted the scientific management principles of Philadelphia engineer Frederick W. Taylor. Taylor offered a method for extracting the maximum efficiency from each worker in a scientific, clinical, and objective manner. Since the only incentive workers responded to was money, Taylor argued, managers should determine a standard day's output from a first-rate worker and then set up pay incentives to reward workers for meeting those standards. The tests to determine the pay scale involved stopwatches and time-and-motion studies that excluded any type of subjectivity on the part of the evaluators. Restructuring the work environment and reducing conflict, Taylor reasoned, would improve efficiency, and by evaluating proficiency on a scientific basis, the worker would be happier in his work. The combination of "Taylorism" with "Fordism" (scientific management and the new assembly system) was perfected at Ford Motor Company's Highland Park plant in Michigan. In the eyes of many observers, Taylorism plus Fordism equaled Americanism. Taylorism, however, completely removed all responsibility and knowledge from the worker, leaving his only goal as greater production.

Psychological Effects. Taylor was not concerned with the psychological impact scientific management had on workers. In fact, he did not care what the employee did after he left the plant, as long as he showed up the next day ready to work. Taylor added, "It is absolutely necessary for every man in our organization to become one of a train of gear wheels." The employers were left to experiment with ways of making life better for workers on and off the job. Companies provided education opportunities, recreation areas, sports leagues, and facilities for employees. Many companies hired welfare secretaries with back-

Carter Glass, senator from Virginia and one of the architects of the Federal Reserve system

grounds in social work to give direction to such activities and to help workers cope with the autonomous nature of their lives in the factories. Modest pension and profit-sharing plans were also initiated to increase the feeling of shared interest between the corporation and employees. H. J. Heinz, Filene's department store, and the National Cash Register Company led the way in providing these services. Once again, Ford provides the best example of the attempt at making the worker's life more tolerable while also increasing productivity with his famous five-dollar day.

New Opportunities. The rise of the modern corporation created millions of new jobs. Middle-level managers, supervisors, clerks, and operatives were needed to regulate the new economic system. Many new avenues were opened for women, and they responded by seeking clerical and professional employment more aggressively. Many people were employed in the new bureaucratic agencies the federal government established to regulate business practices. High tech science-based companies such as General Electric, American Telephone and Telegraph, DuPont, and Eastman Kodak formed research and development (R&D) departments that forged strong ties with the military, engineering companies, and universities. The first true R&D department in the United States was at General Electric and was headed by Willis R. Whitney, a professor of chemistry at the Massachusetts Institute of Technology. Thus, what began as the rise of

On 1 October 1910 the *Los Angeles Times* building exploded under mysterious circumstances. The blast was felt throughout the area. One survivor said, "Frames and timbers flew in all directions. The force of the thing was indescribable." Employees of the *Times* tried to escape the flames, and some jumped from windows without safety nets below. A few hours later, nothing remained but smoldering debris. Twenty people died in the explosion. Harrison Gray Otis, the antiunion publisher of the *Times*, blamed organized labor and dubbed it "The Crime of the Century." Organized labor responded by blaming Otis, asking, "Are his own hands clean?" AFL president Samuel Gompers disavowed union participation in the tragedy, arguing that urban terrorism would actually hurt labor's cause. Famous detective William J. Burns was hired to investigate the blast. He played a hunch and was led to the International Association of Bridge and Structural Iron Workers (BSIW), located in Indianapolis, Indiana. Burns suspected that the union's secretary, John J. McNamara, had directed the attack. The detective set up a trap in a Detroit hotel on 12 April 1912 and arrested McNamara, his brother, James, and another accomplice named Ortie McManigal. In McNamara's suitcase Burns found guns and six lock mechanisms similar to those used in Los An-

geles. On 12 July both brothers pleaded not guilty and set off a chaotic atmosphere in the courtroom. Clarence Darrow, one of America's most famous lawyers, represented the McNamara brothers, although reluctantly, because he felt the prosecution's case was solid. After the first month the attorneys had selected only eight jurors and showed no signs of hurrying the process. On 1 December 1912 the defendants dramatically reversed their pleas. James pleaded guilty to the Los Angeles explosion, while John answered to a lesser charge in a separate bombing. Darrow explained the decision: "It was our only chance . . . It was in an effort to save J. B. McNamara's life that we took the action." Judge Bordwell, reacting to the public's outrage, sentenced James McNamara to life imprisonment and John to fifteen years of hard labor. The McNamara case led to heavy financial losses and declines in membership for all Los Angeles unions. The public backlash hurt the AFL, and Samuel Gompers received criticism for supporting the brothers. Not only had the McNamaras blown up a building and taken lives, they also destroyed the labor movement in Los Angeles.

Source: Graham Adams Jr., *Age of Industrial Violence, 1910–15* (New York: Columbia University Press, 1966).

---

big business led to economic expansion in a vast array of industries.

The New America. Corporations arose and triumphed because they were the most effective instrument yet devised to organize and coordinate productive economic activities in a nation where material progress seemed to be the sole purpose of life. World War I formalized many of the voluntary and regulatory ties between the manufacturers and the federal government. After the 1910s the United States could not return to simpler times abroad or at home despite Wilson's rhetoric of competition among small producers. Wilson's successors as president found themselves at the head of an administrative state with expanded responsibilities and powers for regulating economic growth and activity. While the rhetoric of antitrust remained powerful, the large corporation was in reality a permanent fixture on the economic landscape.

Sources:
Glen Porter, *The Rise of Big Business, 1860–1920* (Arlington Heights, Ill.: Harlan Davidson, 1992);

Robert Sobel, *The Age of Giant Corporations: A Microeconomic History of American Business, 1914–1992* (Westport, Conn.: Praeger, 1993).

CREATING THE FEDERAL RESERVE SYSTEM

Progressive Reform. The fulfillment of many progressive reform goals came after the Democratic Party won both the presidential and congressional elections of 1912. President Woodrow Wilson's "New Freedom" agenda included provisions designed to reshape the nation's financial system, which had long been characterized by instability and occasional chaos, and the government's fiscal policies as well. Wilson immediately began to implement his domestic program by calling a special session of Congress to address the tariff. After successfully rallying the legislature and the public, Wilson signed the Underwood Tariff Act on 3 October 1913, reducing tariffs and opening trade. Tariff reform, however, was only one part of Wilson's overall plan. The president then turned his attention to the nation's banking system, whose structure had not been altered since the Civil War.

Federal Reserve System. The Federal Reserve Act, signed into law on 23 December 1913, established twelve regional Federal Reserve banks, which held the reserves of member banks throughout the country. The Federal Reserve Board (FRB) oversaw the entire system. The

Philander Chase Knox, secretary of state during the Taft administration, who helped devise the policy of "dollar diplomacy"

directors were appointed by the president with the consent of the Senate but were independent of the president. The Federal Reserve performed central banking functions and created a new currency, Federal Reserve notes, issued against collateral. The new currency was flexible and would expand or contract in volume in direct relation to the needs of the economy. District banks would lend money to member banks at a low interest rate, and by adjusting the rate the reserve bank could expand or tighten credit. The Federal Reserve brought both stability and flexibility to the banking system, and by exerting a measure of control over interest rates it made credit less expensive for farmers and other small borrowers. The Federal Reserve Act marked the high tide of President Wilson's New Freedom and was designed to allow public and private interests to work harmoniously.

Inflation. The economic mobilization effort that followed the 1917 entrance of the United States into World War I changed the way the Federal Reserve was used. President Wilson and Treasury Secretary William Gibbs McAdoo used the elasticity of the money supply, which the Federal Reserve Act enabled them to do, to disguise the real costs of the war through a policy of inflation. The banking structure provided a reservoir of financial resources for the government to tap. The system's actions made possible the financing of most of America's war

contribution by the creation of new money. However, without a comparable increase in consumer goods and services the inevitable result was inflation. Between 1916 and 1920 the total money supply increased by 75 percent and the consumer price index nearly doubled. The Wilson administration found hiding the war's true cost through expansion of the currency and of public and private debt more acceptable than increasing direct taxation on the public to pay for the war.

Legacy. The Federal Reserve system was an important step in the federal government's involvement in the regulation of banking and finance. The system helped small borrowers receive better interest rates on loans and gave the country a much-needed central banking structure. But in retrospect, the Federal Reserve did not go far enough in reforming the banking industry. Later historians and economists argued that its shortcomings played a significant role in bringing about the Great Depression in the 1930s. The Federal Reserve did not adequately strengthen the majority of the country's small state banks, and nothing was done to regulate the largest New York City banks that were grossly overcapitalized. The Federal Reserve Board, furthermore, soon fell under the control of Wall Street, at the expense of smaller interests, thus disappointing those who saw it as a panacea for curing all of the nation's financial troubles.

L. L. BEAN

Leon Leonwood Bean liked to hunt and fish in his beloved home of Maine much more than he liked to work. In fact, he spent so much time in the woods and streams that he initially failed as a clothing store owner. In 1913, however, the outdoorsman founded his now famous company, L. L. Bean, in Freeport, Maine. Bean's fortune changed after he invented the famous Maine Hunting Shoe, or "gum shoe," and began selling it through the mail. The uniqueness of the shoe was that it was waterproof. Bean made the top of the shoe leather and the bottom rubber, which prevented water from seeping in. Initially, Bean sold one hundred pairs of the boots, but ninety pairs were returned because the rubber bottoms came off. The owner founded L. L. Bean with the promise of a 100 percent money-back guarantee, so he refunded or replaced every pair of shoes that came back. People respected the guarantee, and word spread about Bean's company. L. L. Bean flourished and made its owner a rich man. Today the company sells more than one hundred thousand pairs of the Maine Hunting Shoes a year and is one of America's most popular mail-order companies, sending out more than five million copies of its color catalogue each year. Leon Leonwood Bean combined his interests as an outdoorsman and clothing store owner and invented a product that made him wealthy and gave him plenty of time to spend hunting and fishing.

Source: Robert Hendrickson, *The Grand Emporiums: The Illustrated History of America's Great Department Stores* (New York: Stein & Day, 1979).

Sources:

Charles Gilbert, *American Financing of World War I* (Westport, Conn.: Greenwood Press, 1970);

David M. Kennedy, *Over Here: The First World War and American Society* (New York: Oxford University Press, 1980);

Arthur S. Link and others, *American Epoch: A History of the United States Since 1900* (New York: Knopf, 1987).

ECONOMIC DIPLOMACY IN THE 1910S

The New Internationalism. By 1910 the traditional American policies of isolationism and noninterference in foreign affairs had clearly ended. The United States protected the Philippines and warded off Japanese aggressions in China, tried to mediate old-world rivalries in Europe, and asserted military and economic dominance in the Caribbean. William Howard Taft and Woodrow Wilson each placed his individual stamp on world affairs, but both operated within the broad policy outlines established by Theodore Roosevelt.

Dollar Diplomacy. President Taft and his secretary of state, Philander C. Knox, tried to overturn many of Roosevelt's diplomatic policies. They abandoned Europe and did not actively pursue goodwill with Japan, but the administration could not reverse Roosevelt's most lasting policy — protecting American interests in the Caribbean. Taft and Knox went beyond the former president's intervention and devised their own strategy called "dollar diplomacy." Dollar diplomacy involved using private American banking resources to displace European creditors and strengthen American influence. When Nicaraguan dictator José Zelaya threatened to take over American mining concessions and made overtures to Japan regarding an alternative to the Panama Canal, the American government helped to overthrow him and install a pro-American president, Aldolfo Díaz. Secretary of State Knox then increased the activity of American banks in the country by controlling the Nicaraguan customs houses. When a revolt against Díaz occurred in 1912, Taft sent twenty-seven hundred marines to suppress the uprising. Taft's dollar diplomacy was an early example of how the United States disregarded the nationalist aspirations of its neighbors in pursuit of its diplomatic goals. Dollar diplomacy was also used in the Far East but was virtually ineffective and caused anti-American feelings in Russia and Japan.

Wilson and the Foundation of Modern Economic Policy. The Woodrow Wilson administration began to revamp the Republican policies of Taft and denounced dollar diplomacy. Wilson believed in democracy as the most advanced, humane, and Christian form of government. All people were capable of being trained in the habits of democracy, according to Wilson, and it was the role of the United States to help them achieve democracy. Wilson's ethical stance was tempered by the economic realities behind foreign policy. The president believed prosperity at home would in part depend on the expansion of overseas exports and investments. The foundations of modern U.S. international economic policy were solidly laid by the Wilson administration, which worked to facilitate the transfer of world financial hegemony from London to New York.

Realpolitik. Finding and protecting foreign markets for U.S. goods became the basic tenet of diplomacy in the 1910s. President Wilson proclaimed, "Our domestic markets no longer suffice. We need foreign markets." The president and Secretary of State William Jennings Bryan intervened in the Caribbean and continued to use private capital to consolidate American influence. Wilson and Bryan believed that they were missionaries of democracy and freedom, but U.S. diplomatic and military involvement continued throughout Central America.

Intervention. American foreign policy was aimed at protecting the future Panama Canal, and Wilson did not remove the troops stationed in Nicaragua by Taft to prevent revolution in an area so close to the canal. In two other cases the United States intervened in the Caribbean to advance Wilson's New Freedom goals. In both the Dominican Republic and Haiti, Wilson sent U.S. troops to save the countries from anarchy and oppression. In 1916 American marine and naval forces were sent to seize Santo Domingo, the capital city of the Dominican Republic. When the Dominicans refused to accept a U.S.-sponsored treaty, the American naval commander established a military government. The United States also occupied Haiti and compelled the National Assembly to elect a pro-American president. The State Department then imposed a treaty on the Haitian government that allowed American supervision of Haitian finances. Anytime hemispheric relations became difficult, Wilson reverted to his basic principles: the virtue of order, the evil of revolution, and the benefits of North American, as opposed to European, enterprises. He used force to protect and institutionalize American economic concerns.

Not So Neutral Policy. When the nations of Europe were drawn into World War I in 1914, the majority of American citizens wanted to remain neutral. Because most citizens sympathized with the British and the French, they grudgingly accepted the British maritime blockade of trade with Germany. Part of Wilson's approval was based on his belief that German actions were morally bereft and would, if left unchecked, eventually threaten the United States. American trade with Germany declined from $169 million in 1914 to $1.2 million in 1916, but the flow of American goods into Allied hands was overwhelming, rising from $825 million to $3.2 billion in the same period. The United States became a warehouse for the Allied powers and sent munitions, food, and goods to Europe. The enormous volume of trade allowed the United States to end its debtor status in the world financial market. After the war the nation would become the world's leading creditor, a remarkable turnaround in a relatively short time span. Wilson then opened the floodgate on private loans to the Allies, led by the House of Morgan extending a $50 million credit to the French. Other private sources gave $1.8 billion to finance the war trade.

Fueling the World Economy. World War I gave the Wilson administration unique opportunities to solidify its international economic goals. The United States continued to fuel the world economy after it entered the war in 1917, and the atmosphere of cooperation between the federal government and big business expanded the domestic economy. Wilson used the New Freedom policies he had implemented in his first term to build a strong international policy based on low tariffs, fair trade, and expanding markets. World War I reduced the imperial presences of Germany and Great Britain in the underdeveloped regions of the world and allowed the United States to concentrate on further developing foreign commerce. The federal government assumed a greater role in directing the nation's foreign trade and searching for new markets for American goods. The policies that Wilson developed fundamentally altered the nation's economic

The magneto assembly line at the Ford Highland Park plant in 1914, the year Ford instituted the five-dollar-day plan

policy by granting the government a large role in coordinating and integrating economic activity. The changes made in the 1910s remained in place long after Wilson left office in 1921.

Sources:

Lloyd C. Gardner, *Safe for Democracy: The Anglo-American Response to Revolution, 1913–1923* (New York: Oxford University Press, 1984);

Walter LaFeber, *Inevitable Revolutions: The United States in Central America* (New York: Norton, 1984);

Arthur S. Link, *The Higher Realism of Woodrow Wilson* (Nashville, Tenn.: Vanderbilt University Press, 1971).

THE FIVE-DOLLAR DAY

Scientific Management. In 1903 Henry Ford, who had started out in his career as a skilled mechanic, founded the Ford Motor Company, and in 1908 he introduced the Model T automobile. From 1910 to 1914 Ford developed the idea of mass production and made the assembly line the symbol of the automobile age. By 1914, six hundred cars a day were rolling off Ford's assembly line, and 90 percent of them were shipped immediately to dealers. Spurred on by the technological superiority of the Highland Park factory, the Ford Motor Company was a remarkable industrial and financial success. The company's net income soared from $25 million in 1914 to $78 million in 1921. Ford was an early exponent of the move toward scientific management, and his company succeeded in part by embracing modern management practices. Ford and his managers experimented with scientific management, worker welfare, and personnel management in an attempt to maximize production. They thought that increased social controls over workers would increase profits. The conscious control of labor and labor processes was an essential feature of Ford's new industrial technology and established practices that other firms would emulate.

Limitations. The Ford Motor Company created the most sophisticated and efficient industrial technology of the period, but there were serious social and psychological limitations to the new technology. Low rates of productivity resulted from what managers labeled the "human element of production." Workers had a difficult time adjusting to the monotonous and repetitive nature of work in the industrial age. Instead of creating products with their own hands and feeling like an important part of the process, workers repeated simple movements over and over again as machines replaced human skill. As one Ford engineer put it, the company "desires and prefers machine-tool operators who have nothing to unlearn . . . and will simply do what they are told to do, over and over again, from bell-time to bell-time." The assimilation of an immigrant workforce, lateness and absenteeism, high turnover rates, output restrictions, and unionization efforts all led to decreased productivity, which management wanted to combat through scientific means. In 1914 Ford stunned the business world by announcing the five-dollar day and acquired the reputation as a humanitarian, philanthropist, and social reformer. Many people began referring to Ford as "the high priest of efficiency."

The Five-Dollar Day. Henry Ford hired John R. Lee to update the company's labor policies in 1913. Lee established an employment department, instituted a "skills-wages" job classification system based on productivity, and sought to connect the workers' desire for upward mobility with management's need for discipline. The company also created an Employees' Savings and Loan Association to alleviate the economic insecurity of immigrant working-class families. Lee's reforms did not solve the labor problems at the Highland Park plant, however, so Ford announced the five-dollar day in January 1914. The program attempted to solve attitudinal and behavioral problems by changing the worker's domestic environment. The company divided the employee's $5 daily income into half wages and half profits. Each worker received his regular wages but only got his profits when he met specific standards of efficiency and improved his home life.

Improving the Domestic Environment. Implementation of the five dollar day required the formation of a Sociological Department and a staff of investigators to examine workers' domestic lives. The investigators,

drawn from social work and academic backgrounds, advised the employee on how to live in order to receive his share of the profits. In essence, the company attempted to change its workers' lives and culture to its preconceived ideal of the "American standard of living," which it felt was the basis for industrial efficiency. As part of the five-dollar day program, Ford started an English school to teach language skills, American values and customs, and the proper habits of work to immigrant workers. According to Ford vice president James Couzens, "Thrift and good service and sobriety will be encouraged and rewarded." Ordering the worker's domestic environment, managers believed, would lead to more efficient and productive work in the factory.

Taylorized. Henry Ford and his managers followed the prescriptions of scientific management researcher Frederick W. Taylor. Ford's engineers standardized the machinery in the Highland Park plant to specialize and routinize the tasks for the worker. They were able to build the ultimate example of an integrated industrial system. Taylor visited Detroit several times and in 1914 spoke to factory managers, superintendents, and foremen. He was pleased that his principles had been adapted to the automobile industry. Taylor believed that intellectual activity should be separated from manufacturing work and all nonproductive movements and motions eliminated from the work routines. Ford managers and engineers "Taylorized" work tasks and routines in the factory. In this environment all thinking would be done by management. The ideal worker became the mindless automaton who applied himself constantly and consistently with little or no need for thought. Taylor's system increased the number of midlevel managers who oversaw the quantity and quality of production. New types of record keeping and inspection were developed to measure the workers' production. The manager became a type of straw boss whose job was to drive and exhort workers to higher and higher levels of production. Labor historian Stephen Meyer concludes that the goal of Taylor's system was that "men, machines, and materials became an intricately interconnected mechanical organism."

The Sociological Department. The essence of the five-dollar day was to use wages to control the lives and behaviors of Ford's workers. One's living conditions and attitudes at home were connected to his industrial efficiency. The company recorded the amount of withheld "profits" on the worker's pay stub so that each payday the worker had a reminder of the money he was losing when his home life was found unsatisfactory by Ford's investigators. If the worker acquiesced to the demands of the Sociological Department (to stop drinking, for example) he could receive a percentage of the lost profits. Thus, the Ford worker traded pride and privacy for economic security and a job with high pay. A company brochure describing the Sociological Department stated that its duty was to "correct the morals and the manner of living" of those workers who did not receive their share of the

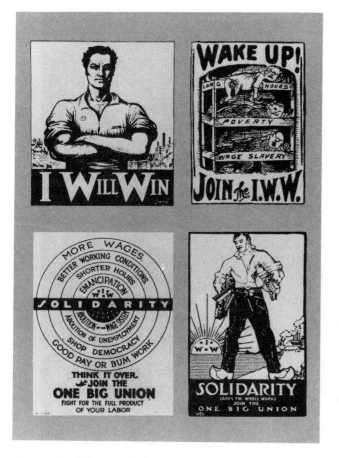

International Workers of the World propaganda stickers from the 1910s

profits and encourage workers to live "under conditions that make for cleanliness, good manhood and good citizenship." It took until early 1916 for the department to formalize a set of instructions that served as a basis for investigating workers and determining their eligibility for profits.

Ford Values. Social workers went into the homes of employees and conducted extensive interviews on a range of subjects from household finances to sexual patterns. Thriftiness was an especially important subject to the investigators. Saving money and trying to improve one's lot greatly increased the worker's chance of receiving profits. In many cases the Sociological Department helped workers improve their lives. Many marriages were saved and homes bought because of the influence of the five-dollar day. The fundamental goal of the department was a middle-class vision of the family and home in the formation of social and cultural values. The intrusion into workers' lives, in the minds of Ford officials, was a small price to pay for increased wages, efficiency, production, and, in the end, profits for the Ford Motor Company.

The War and the Demise of the Five-Dollar Day. World War I undermined the five-dollar day, and the war-induced inflation killed the program. The national mood changed with the outbreak of war, and Ford's pa-

ternalism gave way to authoritarian methods of insuring conformity. The company instituted a program based on militant antiunionism and an extensive spy and informant network at the Highland Park plant. Labor turnover increased during the war and reached 51 percent in 1918, leading to low productivity. Ford's program failed because it could not achieve its principal objective, the control of workers. The five-dollar day could not solve all the problems the factory worker had to endure, and automobile workers increasingly looked to labor unions as a means of regaining control over their lives.

Legacy. The uncertain economic conditions in the postwar period made the five-dollar day obsolete. The Ford Motor Company was first and foremost a money-making institution, and when welfare programs no longer contributed to profits, Ford officials ended them. As new technology spread to other car companies, Ford lost its competitive advantage. By 1919 the wartime inflation had destroyed the incentive nature of the program and the company could not afford to increase greatly the rate of pay. The six-dollar day was introduced in January 1919 and was adopted as the basic wage rate a few years later. Managers increased the speed of the assembly lines and workers faced "the six-dollar speed-up." Ford's creditors demanded payment after the war and the company began a ruthless cost-cutting program. Ford Motor Company officials drastically reduced the size and power of the Sociological Department and then dismantled the outfit during the recession of 1920–1921. The five-dollar day was an important early attempt at implementing a corporate welfare program, and some of its features would be adopted by other companies during the boom years of the 1920s.

Source:
Stephen Meyer III, *The Five Dollar Day: Labor Management and Social Control in the Ford Motor Company 1908–1921* (Albany: State University of New York Press, 1981).

LABOR IN THE 1910s

Servant to the Machine. In the early years of the twentieth century, American industrial workers were confronted with incredible technological advances. The autonomous craftsmen of earlier times were replaced by less-skilled workers who depended on advanced machinery to increase productivity. The assembly line, coupled with the time-motion studies of efficiency experts, allowed manufacturers to increase production by subdividing tasks and making work as mindless, repetitive, and routine as possible. The machinery provided the skill in the new system, not the worker. Henry Ford's reintroduction of the Model T in 1913 remains the shining example of this movement toward greater industrial efficiency. In this era the worker became the servant of the machine that performed the actual work. The American worker was dehumanized in the process and exerted little control over his job. The employee simply carried out the simple, yet endless, tasks assigned to his particular station

Samuel Gompers (center), leader of the American Federation of Labor, with other union officials in 1918

on the line. In the words of labor historian David Brody, "The workplace dwarfed the workingman." Workers turned to unions in an attempt to regain some of the humanity that modern machinery threatened to destroy.

Unions Shaped Workers' Lives. People joined unions for a variety of reasons in the 1910s. Many expected economic gain through collective action, while others hoped for increased job security. Another important reason emerged because of the automated nature of industry — the desire on the part of the wage earner to strengthen his feeling of self-worth and significance within the workplace. In the union the worker could gain a sense of belonging that no longer existed in the factory, or the impersonal city, where he was just another cog among thousands. Unions, in many ways, shaped the worker's life and extended far beyond the factory gate into his home and social life as well. Union journals from the period are filled with accounts of baseball leagues, picnics, dances, lectures, and funerals. The union became an encompassing element in the life of the union man and woman.

Gompers and the AFL. The unionization movement was led by Samuel Gompers and his American Federation of Labor (AFL). Gompers served as president of the AFL from 1886 to 1924. The labor leader asserted that the AFL was the movement of all the nation's workers, but in fact his organizing efforts focused on skilled workers in selected trades. Gompers charted a pragmatic course for the organization, centering on a tighter alliance with the Democratic Party and an emphasis on influencing legislators at the state and local level. Slowly, as the membership of the AFL increased and more socialists joined, the union became more militant. Gompers, however, retained a tight grip on the leadership of the AFL and often worked to moderate the more-leftist elements within the organization. As the nation prepared for and then entered World War I, the AFL played a crucial role in the partnership between big business and the federal government. President Wilson recognized Gompers's help in controlling the labor movement by naming him to several key advisory roles in the wartime government.

The National Union. The dominant unit within the AFL was the national union. Groups such as the United Brotherhood of Carpenters and Joiners and the United Mine Workers represented their specific occupations and led the campaign for collective bargaining within each industry. The resources of the AFL went to the large national unions because of their increasing power, which included total authority within their jurisdictions. It was in the large unions that the dilemma concerning unorganized workers had the most impact. The AFL granted the unions trade autonomy and let them decide where and when to fight for union rights. This narrow view allowed the craft unions to virtually exclude outsiders, especially the unskilled and immigrants. Battles over whom to organize did not boil over until the 1930s but played an important role in the expanding workforce of the 1910s. Immigrants and unskilled workers were attaining an important position in the economy but were discriminated against in the large craft unions, in part because the trade unions believed that unskilled workers were too difficult to organize effectively. However, the AFL still enjoyed boom years at the end of the decade as union membership increased by 2 million from 1917 to 1920 to stand at an all-time high of 5.03 million.

Radical Elements. Unions in the 1910s made important gains in the men's and women's garment fields and consolidated their power in areas such as carpentry, where they already had a stronghold. For the most part, however, corporations had grown too large and powerful. Employers were unyielding in defense of managerial prerogatives, and the leverage unions possessed declined as machinery grew in importance. Unions were often fighting for their most basic rights and their survival prior to World War I. Added support came from the Socialist Party in this period. Led by its remarkable national leader, Eugene V. Debs, the party grew in size and strength, especially in the western and mountain states. The Industrial Workers of the World (IWW) boldly called for a revolution from below and led several important strikes at Paterson, New Jersey (1913); Akron, Ohio (1913); and Lawrence, Kansas (1912). An investigation in California in 1914 revealed that the IWW had forty chapters statewide and a membership of five thousand. The IWW deliberately fought for the rights of groups excluded from the ranks of the AFL. The two labor organizations were bitter enemies, and Gompers publicly rejoiced in the IWW's persecution at the hands of the federal government late in the decade. The crackdown by government officials occurred as the IWW membership, under the leadership of William "Big Bill" Haywood, approached one hundred thousand people.

Labor Gains. World War I improved the fortune of organized labor. The trade union movement was deeply rooted and claimed to speak for all workers but in fact did not reach the majority of industrial workers. The war changed the situation dramatically. The Wilson administration conceded a great deal to organized labor in exchange for labor's enthusiastic cooperation in the war effort. The AFL supported the war effort and joined the government's campaign against the antiwar socialist groups. During the war, labor won the right to an eight-hour workday and could organize without fear of reprisal. From 1917 to 1920 union membership grew by two million and approached 20 percent of the civilian labor force, two times higher than any previous peak. The United Mine Workers became the nation's largest union, boasting a membership of five hundred thousand. Unions were

Cartoon in the *New York Evening World* showing President Wilson's New Freedom reform initiative as an attempt to gain cooperation between the government and big business

even able to begin organizing in the meatpacking, steel, and railroad industries, which had been the strongest antiunion areas.

Corporations Regain Power. Wartime gains were quickly retracted in the last years of the decade, however. The Wilson administration reversed its course and became consumed with the international scene. The Red Scare, furthermore, hurt organized labor. Its leaders were portrayed as Communists, and public opinion seemed to shift in favor of the resurgent corporations. A pitched battle ensued at war's end between labor and capital, with more than three thousand strikes in 1919 involving four million workers. Big business wanted to return to the prewar status quo, with little federal intervention in their practices. The Republican victory in the congressional elections of 1918 brought with it a new antilabor mandate. President Wilson moderated his prolabor stance in hopes of gaining Congress's approval of the Treaty of Versailles; he no longer compelled employers to deal with unions. The postwar situation led to a serious decline in union strength for the next fifteen years. The AFL was forced to adopt a new doctrine based on labor-management cooperation, leading to further declines throughout the 1920s.

Sources:

David Brody, *Workers in Industrial America: Essays on the Twentieth Century Struggle* (New York: Oxford University Press, 1980);

Melvyn Dubofsky, *The State and Labor in Modern America* (Chapel Hill: University of North Carolina Press, 1994);

David Montgomery, *The Fall of the House of Labor: The Workplace, the State, and American Labor Activism, 1865–1925* (Cambridge: Cambridge University Press, 1987).

THE NEW FREEDOM AND THE TRUSTS

Social Responsibility. In 1913 Woodrow Wilson came to office in the midst of the Progressive Era, a time in which a general liberal spirit swept through the nation. Both parties felt a renewed sense of social responsibility and a need for the government to address the problems of industrialization and urban growth. The period facing Wilson was tumultuous, as he had to deal with the trusts, labor disturbances, and the arrival of more than twelve million immigrants since 1900. The election of 1912, furthermore, was a bitter contest pitting these forces against one another. Once elected, President Wilson initiated his "New Freedom" legislation and steered the country along with policies influenced by the reform movement. He exercised a charismatic and principled leadership, often guiding the nation down a middle path that carefully balanced government intervention with controlled reform.

Reform Crawls Forward. Reform came slowly in antitrust legislation because of political cowardice and infighting that allowed a small but vocal minority of conservative Republicans to dominate the issue. These critics had courage in their convictions and stymied the majority in Congress that actually favored reform. President Wilson, on the other hand, pressed for legislation that would improve workers' lives, improve working and living conditions, and allow them to organize. Labor leaders confidently looked forward to a time when injunctions against strikes and conspiracy prosecutions were outlawed. Congress worked to reform the Sherman Antitrust Act of 1890 and to address labor's grievances. The majority in Congress sought to protect labor unions and farmers' organizations from oppressive persecution under the antitrust law.

Brandeis and Wilson. Wilson worked with congressional leaders in the early months of 1914 to draft an antitrust bill. Progressives in Congress wanted an industrial trade commission established that would oversee business activities and suppress unfair labor practices, while the president wanted limited government intervention. The Clayton Antitrust Act, when it was released to the general public, came under tremendous criticism, and President Wilson was visibly shaken by the outburst of negative publicity. The original legislation attempted to outline every possible type of restraint of trade, which both parties denounced as futile. One of Wilson's most trusted advisers, Louis D. Brandeis, came forward in April 1914 with a different proposal. Brandeis proposed outlawing unfair practices in general terms and establishing a regulatory body with the power to enforce the bill. Brandeis's solution had been advanced by an earlier bill introduced by Rep. Raymond B. Stevens of New Hampshire. Wilson agreed with Brandeis's conclusions, and the two fashioned the Stevens legislation into the cornerstone of the new antitrust policy.

Provisions. After the administration shifted its focus the president lost interest in the Clayton bill. The administration let the bill drift in the Senate, and as a result the bill was seriously weakened. The business community ended up quite happy with the Clayton Act. Sen. James A. Reed of Missouri called the act "a sort of apology to the trusts, delivered hat in hand, and accompanied by assurances that no discourtesy is intended." The Clayton Act outlawed monopolistic practices such as price discrimination and the practice of allowing executives to sit on the boards of two or more competing companies. A Federal Trade Commission (FTC) was created to investigate corporations and issue cease-and-desist orders against unfair trade practices. The new law also had important ramifications for organized labor and the rights of workers to strike.

Clayton Act and Labor. The Clayton Antitrust Act added new clauses to help labor. The new law allowed workers to unionize and strike and forbade injunctions against unions and strikes when labor's actions were otherwise legal. The Clayton Act specifically stated that the "the labor of a human being is not a commodity or article of commerce," thus for the first time legitimizing the existence of unions. American Federation of Labor (AFL) president Samuel Gompers hailed the law as the Magna Carta of labor and a final guarantee of workers' rights to organize, collectively bargain, and strike. Critics pointed to the cautious phraseology of the Clayton Act, which to them proved that labor had won few, if any, new rights, but Gompers ignored the criticism and trumpeted the passage as a great day for American workers. The skeptics were soon proved to be correct. The interpretations of the act by various courts showed that the document contained loopholes in exempting unions from the antitrust laws. The new law simply shifted the political responsibility for the struggle over unionism from Congress to unelected federal judges who were insulated from popular pressures. Thus, while the Clayton Act solidified labor's support of the Wilson administration, it had little real effect on the relations between big business and workers.

Regulatory Agency. The Federal Trade Commission Act, passed on 26 September 1914, committed the federal government to a policy of vigorous regulation of all business activities. The FTC outlawed unfair trade practices but did not attempt to define them. As a federal agency, the FTC was given the power to move quickly against corporations accused of suppressing competition; it could first issue cease-and-desist orders and then bring the accused to trial. Brandeis and Wilson wanted to establish the type of environment in which competition could thrive, a tacit acceptance of big business but one that necessitated some regulation. The FTC consisted of five commissioners who were appointed by the president and confirmed by the Senate to seven-year terms. The agency came into existence on 16 March 1915, with Joseph E. Davies named the first chairman. Brandeis, who

Leaders of the IWW: William D. "Big Bill" Haywood, far right; Elizabeth Gurley Flynn, center; and Carlo Tresca, second from left

had been instrumental in the creation of the FTC, argued that an expert regulatory body could do a better job than courts in curbing trusts because it could stay aware of constantly changing technological and business conditions.

Weaknesses. The Wilson administration continued the Roosevelt-Taft policy of moving only against trusts that seemed obviously in restraint of trade. Therefore the case against the United States Steel Company was continued, despite the company's offer to settle out of court. Many companies voluntarily accepted Justice Department proposals to disband, including the American Telephone and Telegraph Company, the New Haven Railroad, and the Southern Pacific Railroad. The successes of Wilson's antitrust policies, however, were short-lived. The FTC was initially hobbled by incompetence, internal dissension, and commissioners who were not serious about pursuing unfair combinations. With the U.S. entrance into World War I the agency had little to do. The fight against trusts was temporarily suspended, and the Wilson administration looked the other way as long as trusts helped the war effort. The two bills ended President Wilson's reform program and, although still in effect today, are severely weakened.

Sources:

Arthur S. Link and others, *American Epoch: A History of the United States Since 1900* (New York: Knopf, 1987);

Susan Wagner, *The Federal Trade Commission* (New York: Praeger, 1971).

ORGANIZED LABOR AND THE WILSON ADMINISTRATION

Labor Growth. The second decade of the twentieth century was a tumultuous time for organized labor. The labor issue frequently divided American society because trade unionism challenged the dominance of traditional economic and political institutions in the nation. Also, the unions contained numerous radical and socialist ele-

ments that frightened business owners and a sometimes timid middle class. Big business never willingly conceded to the demands of unions because the companies had consolidated their power under conservative principles, and unionism in any form threatened those values. Unions, however, were growing in the 1910s, and as the industrial conflict intensified, the battles spread into the larger national arena. Organized labor gained an avenue into nationwide political participation, thus forcing candidates at all levels to recognize their existence. Woodrow Wilson initially distrusted union activity but later became one of the first presidents to court the vote of labor actively. When they backed his candidacy he reciprocated by giving union leaders a voice in national labor policy. Because of political restraints, however, Wilson eventually rescinded his support. The relationship between the president and organized labor began on rocky ground, then blossomed into a close bond, and later fell apart. The interaction between Wilson and the labor movement broke important ground and established the legitimacy of organized labor as a player in American politics and as a representative of industrial workers.

Mutual Support. The Democratic Party needed the vote of organized labor to win the 1912 presidential election. When Wilson won the nomination he was forced to court labor's vote even though he had a distaste for organized labor. AFL demands were incorporated into the 1912 presidential platform, and Wilson offered labor leaders the symbols of influence. The president named former United Mine Workers official William B. Wilson as secretary of labor, and the Department of Labor was staffed with prounion appointees. Wilson then allowed the department to coordinate and formulate labor policy. As a progressive reformer President Wilson wanted to break up corporate monopolies. He believed the trusts weakened the economy from within by eliminating legal competition. His support for the Clayton Antitrust Act, therefore, was a natural outcome of his liberal ideology, and it cemented labor's support. The Clayton Act was heralded by Samuel Gompers, the president of the AFL, as the Magna Carta of labor because it legalized unions and gave them the right to strike. Although historians maintain that the act was not a cure-all, it strengthened the bond between Wilson and labor. Wilson became publicly identified as a friend and ally of the movement, and his critics felt that he had sold out to labor.

Railroad Victory. A dispute between organized labor and the railroads in the summer of 1916 showed Wilson's level of commitment to labor's cause. The federal government could not tolerate a strike on the rails because it would slow the nation's efforts to prepare for World War I. The war scares with Germany and Mexico frightened the public. The scares also forced federal intervention in labor disputes. The unions used this sentiment to threaten national strikes unless they received an eight-hour day and a 25 percent raise in wages. Neither side was willing to compromise, and both knew federal intervention was imminent. Labor gambled that its support for Wilson would be rewarded. In a special message to Congress, Wilson played the consummate politician, appealing to labor and at the same time allaying the concerns of his business critics. Demanding justice, he asked that Congress enact legislation supporting labor and establish a committee to investigate the impact of the measure, promising to give the railroads relief if costs rose substantially. Congress enacted the Adamson Act in response to Wilson's message, granting labor an eight-hour workday and overtime compensation. The Adamson Act guaranteed labor's support for Wilson in the 1916 campaign. Gompers and labor worked hard for the president both publicly and privately. In the western states, which decided the election, organized labor gave more unified support to Wilson than they ever had before. According to labor historian Melvyn Dubofsky, "Labor votes in the Pacific Coast states, most especially California, proved indispensable to Wilson's victory."

Union Militancy. The AFL built a political coalition with the Democratic Party, and Wilson rewarded Gompers with a position on the newly created Council of National Defense. U.S. involvement in World War I, furthermore, created an atmosphere that was conducive to closer ties between the government and labor. Labor leaders, in turn, reacted to the new imperatives by aggressively pursuing better conditions, higher wages, and shorter hours in the factories. Militant workers grew restive, and in the six months after the United States declared war there were more than three thousand strikes. In 1917–1918 more than two million workers struck, even though Gompers signed no-strike pledges for the duration of the war. Leaders simply could not keep followers on the job when employers refused to bargain with unions, increase wages, or reduce hours.

Crackdown on Radicals. The wartime atmosphere of 1917–1918 allowed conservative forces to regain the upper hand over labor. The plethora of businessmen and lawyers who staffed government agencies dwarfed the number of labor leaders in Washington and resisted government attempts to promote trade union growth. Antilabor forces changed tactics and concentrated on the Industrial Workers of the World (IWW), not Gompers, the AFL, or trade unionism. Critics claimed that the IWW was a subversive ally of Germany. Sen. Henry Ashurst of Arizona called the group "Imperial Wilhelm's Warriors." In the West federal troops broke IWW strikes; suspected labor radicals were prosecuted; and local and federal authorities conducted unlawful searches and seizures. Gompers, ironically, joined the outcry against the IWW, believing the radicals drew support away from the AFL. On 5 September 1917 Justice Department agents raided every IWW headquarters in the nation, and by the end of September a federal grand jury had indicted nearly two hundred IWW leaders on sedition and espionage charges.

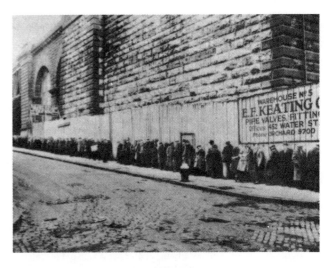

Workers protesting during the Seattle general strike of 1919

The National War Labor Board. The National War Labor Board (NWLB), established in April 1918, helped the cause of labor. The NWLB made the right to unionize real and required employers to recognize the right of workers to bargain collectively. The board reviewed more than eleven hundred cases in less than one year and usually acted on behalf of workers and unions. The NWLB was able to institute the eight-hour day in most industries, raise wages for transit workers, and demand equal pay for women. Labor organizer William Z. Foster commented that the "Federal administration was friendly; the right to organize was freely conceded by the government and even insisted upon. . . . The gods were indeed fighting on the side of Labor." Wartime policies had a tremendous impact on workers and unions. They made huge gains and won basic rights that improved the lives of many workers.

Support Withdrawn. The end of the war and the Republican victory in the 1918 elections stemmed the advance of unionism. President Wilson was forced to moderate his stance in hopes of Senate ratification of the ill-fated Treaty of Versailles. He no longer compelled employers to deal with unions, and his prosecution of radicals led directly to the witch-hunt that became the Red Scare. Unions were left reeling in the wake of Wilson's change of heart and would not return to anything like their wartime influence until the 1930s. The tumultuous relationship between Wilson and labor ended as it began and severely curtailed labor's impact for the next decade.

Source:
Melvyn Dubofsky, *The State and Labor in Modern America* (Chapel Hill: University of North Carolina Press, 1994).

POSTWAR LABOR DISTRESS

Battle Renewed. The end of World War I meant many things to different groups within American society. Some eagerly anticipated the return of loved ones from

Police clearing Pittsburgh streets during the steel strike of 1919

the European front, while others simply rejoiced in the nation's victory in "the war for democracy." Organized labor looked to the future with a great deal of optimism. Federal wartime labor policies allowed the labor movement to achieve tremendous gains. Labor leaders thought that the vast increase in union membership, more than five million members in 1920, as well as labor's growing influence on federal policy, meant the beginning of a better day for American workers. Unions sought to solidify and extend wartime gains but were met head-on by businessmen and employers who had a completely different agenda. They sought to roll back the gains and return to the prewar status quo. The resulting clash between labor and capital led to violence and bloodshed that repulsed the American public and renewed the traditional battle between employers and employees.

Corporations Gain Advantage. The scales tipped back in favor of big business after the war. The Republican Party won control of Congress in the 1918 midterm elections and brought with it a new antiunion mandate that threatened labor. The Wilson administration was forced to moderate Wilson's own prolabor stance in hopes of placating Congress. Wilson's beloved League of Nations hung in the balance. The nation was also experiencing a "Red Scare," and anyone radical was condemned as a Communist, including many labor organizers. Conservative businesses attempted to label union activists as

Bolsheviks, and gradually the general public sided with employers in the name of economic and social stability. Without federal intervention or government agencies to act as arbiters, employers no longer felt compelled to deal with the unions. Labor leaders, therefore, were forced to disregard the wartime truce with business and used strikes to fight for their rights, improved working conditions, and better wages.

Reasons to Strike. More than four million employees, one-fifth of the nation's total workforce, went on strike in 1919. In all, 2,665 strikes took place in the year after the armistice. Much of the immediate problem stemmed from inflation. An unanticipated economic boom in 1919 triggered an insatiable demand for consumer goods. Inflation hit hard as prices rose first by 77 percent and then 105 percent above prewar levels. Workers commanded higher salaries than before the war, but the increases did not keep up with the rising cost of living. Workers looked to their unions for support as their insecurities mounted. These factors led to an unprecedented outbreak of labor-management conflict. In many cases employers were willing to address wage issues but refused to recognize union spokesmen or allow collective bargaining, thus rescinding most of the concessions that had been made under the pressure of war.

Seattle Strike. The Seattle General Strike in early 1919 was the first conflict to arouse public interest and set the tone for the rest of the year. Seattle gained the reputation as a strong union city based on the solidarity of its thirty-five thousand shipyard workers. Their strike, which was launched in January, resulted from a demand for higher wages that was flatly rejected by the local business interests. In reply, Central Labor Committee leader James A. Duncan called for a general strike among all workers in Seattle and more than sixty thousand people joined in. More than 110 local unions took part, and for five days the city was run by the committee. The strike completely paralyzed industry, transportation, and utilities. Labor activists set up twenty-one soup kitchens, made sure that milk delivery for children and laundry service for hospitals would continue, and organized five hundred uniformed war veterans to ensure public safety.

Communist Accusations. Although the Central Labor Committee succeeded in keeping the strike peaceful, Mayor Ole Hanson made national headlines by calling the effort a Bolshevist and Industrial Workers of the World (IWW) attempt at starting a nationwide revolution. In the midst of the Red Scare, public opinion across the country turned against the strikers, and nervous labor leaders at the national level successfully pressured the workers to call off the strike prior to winning their demands. The strike did not provide the workers with the gains they anticipated, but it did demonstrate organized labor's capacity for unity and collective action. The strike also emphasized the impact of the Red Scare on the postwar political climate. Despite this suspicion, many strikes in the postwar years would be waged successfully and help improve the way of life for American workers.

Boston Police Strike. Even more disturbing than the Seattle strike was the walkout several months later by the Boston police. Upset with low wages and other aspects of their jobs, the police formed the Boston Social Club and applied to the American Federation of Labor (AFL) for membership. Police Commissioner Curtis responded by suspending nineteen officers and forbidding further activism. On 9 September 1919 the police went on strike and left the city without protection. The outraged public, which had to endure a wave of theft, violence, and gang disorder, demanded action. President Wilson called the strike a "crime against civilization," and Gov. Calvin Coolidge, a future president, won national recognition by stating, "There is no right to strike against the public safety by anybody, anywhere, anytime." Coolidge then announced that none of the strikers would be rehired and recruited a new force made up from unemployed veterans.

Steel Strike of 1919. The most important strike in 1919 was the national steel strike. The battle in the steel industry foreshadowed the new pattern of conflict that would develop after World War II; if it had been successful, the strike would have changed the entire labor history of the following decade. AFL president Samuel Gompers, encouraged by federal intervention during World War I and assuming public support, led a call for organ-izing the steel industry in 1918 and 1919. The first step was forming a committee made up of representatives of twenty-four unions representing workers in the steel industry. William Z. Foster and John Fitzpatrick, left-wing veterans of the meatpacking union effort in Chicago, were the guiding force within the movement. Foster hired organizers who were fluent in all of the many languages spoken by the steelworkers and created a command network that softened traditional rivalries among the workers. By June 1919 Foster and his committee increased membership to more than one hundred thousand and were ready to test their resolve. The organizing effort was a complete success and even penetrated the Pittsburgh region, the heartland of the steel industry. Black Americans were the only ones not joining in large numbers. Few were willing to join a movement that had so frequently rejected them in the past.

Union Walks Out. The committee attempted to negotiate with United States Steel Corporation chairman Elbert H. Gary, but for months he refused to meet with the workers. Instead, the steel company retaliated by firing union activists, brought in thousands of strikebreakers, and deputized guards to break up union meetings with little care for the workers' civil liberties. The union demanded collective bargaining, the eight-hour workday, and an increase in wages. Otherwise, the workers would strike on 22 September. After receiving Gary's terse reply, 350,000 men in nine states left their jobs. The struggle that followed was characterized by widespread violence, resulting in the deaths of eighteen strikers and the use of federal and state troops to prevent picketing. Violence was held down in some areas by declarations of martial law, but little regard was paid to civil liberties by the companies or local law enforcement officers during the strike. In Pittsburgh sheriffs deputized five thousand U.S. Steel employees and then barred them from holding outdoor meetings, while in Clairton and Glassport, Pennsylvania, state troopers attacked strikers who were holding peaceful gatherings. Such government action enabled companies to keep many mills open throughout the strike.

Company Fights Back. To make this repression successful, the steel companies had to gain public acceptance for their actions. This was not easy, since the companies initially refused to meet with union representatives even after they were requested to do so by President Wilson. The companies used the media to paint the strikers as part of a wider revolutionary movement. Officials used newspaper advertisements to portray the battle as one between the United States and revolutionists, not between the workers and their employers. Because immigrants made up a large number of strikers, the companies played on the public's xenophobia. Immigrants were associated with radicalism. Next, black and Hispanic strikebreakers were brought in to split the strikers along ethnic and racial lines. Back-to-work movements were

Artist's rendering of the twelve-story Wanamaker store, opened in Philadelphia in 1910

aimed at skilled and native-born workers who feared losing their jobs.

Defeat. The steel strike of 1919 ended as a crushing defeat for labor. The organizing unions fought with one another, and money for strike relief slowly ran out. As discouragement spread through the ranks of the strikers the effort fell apart and in January 1920 was called off. However immigrant steelworkers had shown that they were capable of prolonged militancy and discipline for the first time. The steel companies, however, demonstrated their ability to defeat even a monumental, well-organized walkout. Furthermore, craft unionism proved itself unuseful for mass-production industry. Not until the 1930s would a new form of organizing be developed to meet the needs of unskilled workers. The labor turmoil of 1919 also proved that without government intervention unionism could not prevail in the core industries.

Sources:
Lizabeth Cohen, *Making a New Deal: Industrial Workers in Chicago, 1919–1939* (New York: Cambridge University Press, 1990);

Foster Rhea Dulles, *Labor in America: A History* (New York: Crowell, 1966);

Joshua Freeman and others, *Who Built America? Working People and the Nation's Economy, Politics, Culture, and Society* (New York: Pantheon, 1992);

Arthur S. Link and others, *American Epoch: A History of the United States Since 1900* (New York: Knopf, 1987);

David Montgomery, *The Fall of the House of Labor: The Workplace, the State, and American Labor Activism, 1865–1925* (New York: Cambridge University Press, 1987).

THE RETAIL INDUSTRY

Background. The United States was the first country in the world to have an economy devoted to mass production. It was also the first to create advertising and marketing industries, in order to market and sell mass-produced goods. The most prominent symbol of the new consumerism was the department store. Although the department store existed in the nineteenth century, the early decades of the twentieth century witnessed a phenomenal growth in the retail industry that mirrored the trends shaping more-traditional manufacturing industries. The myth of America as the "land of plenty" captured the imagination of people as the economy produced a dazzling array of new consumer products each year. Consumption was everywhere touted as a means to reach personal satisfaction. Millions of dollars were being spent to institutionalize consumerism through advertising and public relations, indoctrinating the idea in the minds of citizens hungry for goods.

Impact on Culture. In 1910 John Wanamaker opened a twelve-story department store in the heart of Philadelphia. It was the most monumental commercial structure

The self-service concept in retailing that supermarkets and discount department stores presently use was not invented until 1916. Clarence Saunders of Memphis, Tennessee, introduced the idea in his Piggly Wiggly chain of small grocery stores in 1916. Saunders set up his stores so that customers passed through a turnstile and followed a predetermined course through the store, exposing them to the appeal of all the merchandise displayed on the shelves. The self-service concept was a revolutionary discovery for retailers. It allowed store owners to concentrate on the presentation of goods and became an integral piece of the scientific management theories used by retailers to increase sales and profits. Saunders's simple idea caught on and developed into a concept that has been a driving force in the retail industry, so much so that consumers believe the self-service aspect of shopping is a fundamental American right, and they would not readily accept any other alternative.

Source: Robert Hendrickson, *The Grand Emporiums: The Illustrated History of America's Great Department Stores* (New York: Stein & Day, 1979).

in the world and served as a fitting headquarters for the leading merchant in the United States and one who revolutionized the retail business. Even Wanamaker, however, probably did not realize the lasting impact that he and his fellow retail mavens would have on U.S. cultural history. The department store developed into so much more than simply a place to buy goods. The stores legitimized fashion, democratized desire and consumption, and helped produce the commercial environment. People began feeling personal loyalty to certain department stores, and the stores would become like a second home for many. The weekend trip to the department store became a permanent fixture in the lives of millions of Americans, a fixture that they would later instill in their children. The stores were pervasive and influential facets of the modern economy in the 1910s.

Efficiency. Store managers attempted to bring to their firms the same attitudes toward production and efficiency that were revolutionizing industries such as steel, automobiles, and meatpacking. Retail executives introduced functional organization, streamlined store designs, and standardized the product offerings. However, the intensive human interaction between salespeople and customers made it difficult to implement mechanized control over the store employee. Retailers wanted to supervise their workers as closely as factory managers but also wished to portray an image of respectability and urbanity. The department store was built on the basis of one sale leading to another, not a dehumanized series of simple

tasks dictated by a conveyor belt on an assembly line. Thus, store managers could change the way of making the space within a store work for the employee but could not force their workers into the radical changes that were taking place in factories.

Organizing Space. Retailers used visual materials of desire — color, glass, and light — to create a stress-free and happy environment within the store. Gradually they perfected the linking between these elements and consumption so that the link seemed natural. Certain colors and lights subliminally gave people the impulse to buy goods. Managers began redefining space within the store. Extensive efforts to redesign or rearrange the elements of stores saved labor, allowed for higher volume, and enhanced an orderly, systematic use of resources. Specialized goods were placed in certain areas. Bargain goods were in the basement, glamour and impulse items on the street level to entice women on their way to the upper floors. Interestingly, men's clothing was also on the street level because it was presumed that men were too timid to venture much farther into the store. Executives calculated the revenues produced by each square foot of selling space and reallocated goods accordingly. Well-trafficked areas were used extensively, while irresistible merchandise was placed in the corners to rehabilitate those areas. Escalators and air conditioning, while not completely accepted, were introduced in the 1910s.

Time-Study Tests. Time studies were introduced that measured the amount of time it took clerks to handle merchandise versus the time they spent with customers. Inefficient fixtures kept salespeople away from customers, defeating their purpose. The coat hanger worked a silent revolution in the department store. It saved time by making the clerk's job easier, decreased the wear and tear on clothing, and displayed the merchandise more appealingly. New fixtures increased customers served and the number of sales by 120 percent over stores without these fixtures. Hangers alone were calculated to boost efficiency by 90 percent. Space became important to retailers by virtue of the size of major stores. The Marshall Field and R. H. Macy Herald Square stores each had more than one million square feet of floor space. In other words, four factories the size of Ford's Highland Park plant would have fit into either store. Stores were built in the center of urban areas; in the minds of store owners space literally equaled money.

Advertising. Investment banks and national corporations helped department store owners by supplying money and strategies for institutionalizing the store as a way of life. Advertising and marketing tools were used to entice consumers. In 1910 big business spent $600 million on advertising, which was 4 percent of the national income for the year. Billboards, electric signs, and window displays were used to lure people into the store. Once inside, retailers were sure they had something for everyone. The trick was getting them into the store. Ad-

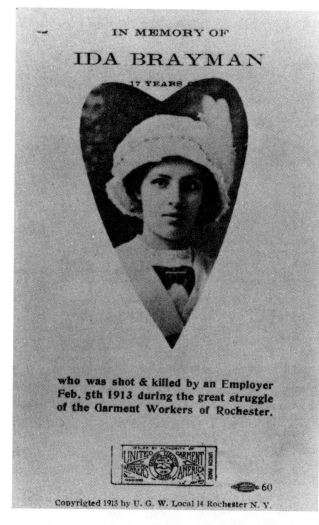

who was shot & killed by an Employer Feb. 5th 1913 during the great struggle of the Garment Workers of Rochester.

Copyrighted 1913 by U. G. W. Local 14 Rochester N. Y.

Postcard printed by the United Garment Workers Union in Rochester, New York, to be sold to pay the funeral expenses of a worker killed during a strike in 1913

Sources:

Susan P. Benson, *Counter Cultures: Saleswomen, Managers, and Customers in American Department Stores, 1890–1940* (Urbana: University of Illinois Press, 1986);

Robert Hendrickson, *The Grand Emporiums: The Illustrated History of America's Great Department Stores* (New York: Stein & Day, 1979);

William Leach, *Land of Desire: Merchants, Power, and the Rise of a New American Culture* (New York: Pantheon, 1993).

SEAMSTRESSES AND STRIKES: WOMEN ORGANIZERS AND THE GARMENT INDUSTRY

Women Unionizing. In 1914 Samuel Gompers, president of the American Federation of Labor (AFL), expressed his regret that women had not joined men in a concerted effort to improve standards in the nation's factories. Gompers's observation, however, was at least partially based in his own bias against women factory workers. If he had looked more closely he would have seen that women were taking important steps toward unionization. Militant women garment workers entered the labor movement in large numbers as organizers, picketers, and negotiators in the 1910s. These brave women willingly met the threats a strike imposed on their livelihood and faced the reality of social ostracism because striking violated the norms of respectability and femininity. Women organizers had to deal with problems that male union organizers did not understand or would not acknowledge.

Grudging Acceptance. Near the end of the decade the International Ladies' Garment Workers' Union (ILGWU) had eighty-two thousand members and was one of the five largest AFL affiliates. Women comprised more than half of the membership list. This was a remarkable figure considering men did not really want to include women in unions. Male members were intent on monopolizing the industry's best jobs and viewed women as competitors for those jobs. It was a grudging acceptance, at best, for women throughout the 1910s. The effort to organize in the garment industry, however, proved that women, both middle class and wage earners, could play an active role in the trade union movement. Ultimately, it would be women themselves who would have to take the responsibility of improving their working conditions, a call often repeated by Gompers and other AFL leaders. Women answered by joining unions and demanding a place within their hierarchy. They demanded a better working environment, improved wages and hours, and safer conditions. The cross-class alliance between middle-class activists and working women, although treated with suspicion by male union leaders, played a major role in bringing about success.

Companies Resist Unionizing Efforts. Factory employers valued women workers for their willingness to accept low wages and terrible working conditions in silence. Therefore, the companies used every method possible in impeding women's attempts to organize. Employers used police assistance, hired thugs and prostitutes

vertising campaigns worked well. According to John Wanamaker, "The time to advertise is all the time."

Human Interaction. Retailers not only tried to control the environment of the store, they also tried to bring the customer under control. They presented the store as a bourgeois home and developed means of persuasion to get people to buy merchandise and build loyalty. The service sector grew at a phenomenal rate to keep up with the drive toward consumerism. Society was based on mass consumption, and the demand for goods increased as the wartime economy inflated salaries for workers. In the department store, however, social interaction replaced production as the means of work. The salespeople had to deal with issues of human interaction and the firm's social role, and the executives tried to increase profits while also forging a community identity. The goodwill of the public was essential. Owners had to balance their roles as cost-conscious businessmen with their roles as cultural agents for a grandiose ethic of consumption.

Taxpayers lining up to pay the permanent income tax for the first time

to harass female leaders, and convinced the judiciary to issue injunctions against strikers and impose heavy fines. Meeting the threats required determination and middle-class support, and garment workers had both in abundance. Young Jewish women dominated the industry and had been infused with socialist idealism encountered by themselves or their families in eastern Europe, combined with a cultural heritage that encouraged opposition to oppression.

Middle-Class Activism. Middle-class women activists tried to interest young women in union participation. They introduced courses on labor topics in settlement houses, instruction in English, social evenings, music, and conferences to bring a social component to the organizing effort. Activists replicated what they saw male organizers doing by attempting to make the union a focal point in women's lives. The female leaders from outside

the factories sanctioned the strike, another important step in fusing the two groups, and their active support won community acceptance for the workers' cause. Agnes Nestor, Rose Schneiderman, Pauline Newman, Dorothy Jones, and Fannia Cohn were among the early leaders of the women's unionizing movement. The young women of eastern European descent on the front lines, however, were the real focal point. They demonstrated a surprising willingness to sacrifice what few comforts they had to fight for a better life for themselves and their children.

Strikes. In 1910 women led strikes in the garment industries in New York, Chicago, and Cleveland. Although the strikes were defeated because of police protection and hired thugs, they set the tone for the rest of the decade. These strikes also proved that women would stand up to the violence that punctuated strikes in the 1910s. Three years later, white-goods workers struck in

New York, led by women as young as fifteen. The strike lasted six weeks, and women won better pay and shorter hours, but not the closed shop they desired. This strike was one of four successful women's strikes in 1913. In the early 1910s unions moved to educate women workers and teach them trade union history in the hope that they would use this knowledge in future uprisings. The period also witnessed some opposition to the assistance of middle-class women. Workers argued that these "outsiders" were becoming too numerous and turning the unions into paper organizations.

AFL Ambivalence. National AFL leaders remained ambivalent toward women in the movement. Embittered delegates to the 1914 national AFL convention even took steps to remove women from the job market completely. Gompers, growing ever more rigid and conservative with age, viewed working women as casual laborers just occupying themselves while they waited for marriage. He refused to take bold action to help improve their situation and straddled the fence in dealing with the Women's Trade Union League (WTUL). Gompers simply did not trust women and continued to question the participation of middle-class activists in the union movement. He was also suspicious of the numerous socialists within the women's movement. The introduction of the suffrage issue infuriated him because he thought that this politically charged issue would create divisions in the ranks of organized labor. Ultimately, it was Gompers's belief that women belonged in the home and not at work that most shaped his view.

Women Wielding Power. While dealing with numerous assaults from outside and internal fighting within the unionization effort, some energetic women were able to gain influential positions in their unions. Unable to move up the AFL ranks, militant women wielded power in other ways. They directed social activities, participated in conventions, led membership drives, and held local offices. Many men were forced to reexamine their assumptions about women when they realized the positive impact the women were having. Men could no longer assume that women were not seriously committed to union work and to the movement to improve the lot of all workers in the United States.

Sources:
Foster Rhea Dulles, *Labor in America: A History* (New York: Crowell, 1966);

Carolyn D. McCreesh, *Women in the Campaigns to Organize Garment Workers, 1880–1917* (New York: Garland, 1985).

TAXATION, TARIFFS, AND THE NATIONAL ECONOMY

Background. Few issues were discussed, dissected, or dramatized in the Progressive Era more than taxation and tariffs. The questions surrounding taxes and tariffs were highly charged politically and divided people along class, sectional, and partisan lines. The tariff debate enabled insurgent Democrats to rise up and capture the

CONCENTRATION OF MONEY AND CREDIT

President Woodrow Wilson and congressional leaders worried about the "money monopoly" in the United States in the 1910s. Congress began an investigation of the money trusts by appointing House Banking and Currency Committee chairman Arsene Pujo of Louisiana to look into the matter. The Pujo Committee held lengthy hearings in 1912 and early 1913, primarily targeting J. P. Morgan and Company, George F. Baker's National Bank, and James Stillman's National City Bank. The three companies worked in "a form of alliance," setting credits for commercial enterprises at terms "which the borrowing corporations must accept." The committee's report, released 28 February 1913, shocked the public. It revealed the enormous concentration of wealth in the hands of a few extremely rich financiers and industrialists like Morgan and John D. Rockefeller. As a result of the hearings held early in the year, the 1912 Democratic platform proposed to revise the banking system and pass legislation to protect the public from the money trusts. Once elected, President Wilson used the committee's findings as justification for progressive programs that established the Federal Reserve system and reinforced the existing antitrust laws through the Clayton Act.

Sources: Benjamin J. Klebaner, "The Money Trust Investigation in Retrospect," *National Banking Review*, 3 (1966): 393–403;

Pujo Committee Report, 62d Congress, 3d Session, House Report No. 1593, pp. 55–103.

House of Representatives in the 1910 midterm election. After 1910 many Republicans then crossed to vote with the Democrats on several issues. The coalition helped generate a groundswell of support at the state level for the Sixteenth Amendment to the Constitution, which established a federal income tax. The new graduated tax on personal incomes provided the federal government with new income to replace the money it had lost by reducing the tariff on goods. The tariff and taxes on consumption generated most of the revenue for the federal government in the early 1910s, but the income tax amendment began revolutionary changes in federal fiscal policy, especially with the expansion of government during World War I.

Tariff Reform. Woodrow Wilson's victory in 1912 brought a Democratic, reform-minded president into office to work with the legislative majority of the same party. The first issue on Wilson's mind was the tariff. He called a special session of Congress on his inaugural day and on 8 April 1913 delivered a message before the legislature, becoming the first president since Thomas Jefferson to appear before Congress. The bill, introduced by House Ways and Means chairman Oscar W. Under-

Members of the War Industries Board, 1917. Standing: Adm. F. F. Fletcher, Hugh Frayne, Col. Palmer E. Pierce, H. P. Ingels, secretary; seated: Daniel Willard, Robert S. Brookings, Robert S. Lovett, and Bernard M. Baruch

wood, fulfilled Democratic promises of tariff reform. It promised to place U.S. industries, which had previously benefited from a protected status maintained by extremely high tariff rates, in a more competitive position in relation to European producers. All products manufactured by trusts, such as iron and steel wares, were placed on the free-trade list, while most raw material, clothing, food, and other items were either put on the free list or given minimal protection. Underwood duties averaged around 29 percent, compared with the previous 40 percent. To compensate for the anticipated loss of revenue, the Ways and Means Committee added a small graduated tax on incomes to the bill.

Political Wrangling. The Underwood bill passed the House with a large majority but still faced a long fight. The bill included a provision ending tariffs on imported sugar and wool, antagonizing Democratic senators from Louisiana, Montana, and Colorado. A swing of these three votes in the Senate would defeat the bill, so President Wilson applied heavy political and personal pressure on wavering Democrats. On 26 May he condemned the large number of lobbyists that he believed infested Washington and adversely influenced tariff reform. Progressive Republican senator Robert La Follette of Wisconsin took Wilson's criticisms one step further and conducted an

inquiry into the actions of lobbyists and compelled senators to reveal personal property holdings that might be affected by tariff legislation. The publicity of La Follette's investigation cleared the way for the bill's passage. Senate Finance Committee chairman Furnifold M. Simmons of North Carolina added food and farm products to the free list and actually reduced the Underwood rates by 4 percent. Progressives also raised the personal income tax from a maximum of 4 percent to 6 percent on individuals with the highest incomes. President Wilson signed the Underwood Tariff Act on 3 October 1913.

Loans to the Allies. World War I created new problems for Wilson and Congress to consider. First, no one knew how much the war effort was going to cost, but the figures started at $33.5 billion. Second, the United States had to inject billions of dollars into Europe to ensure its financial security. The president and Congress had to decide whether to finance the bulk of these expenditures through taxation, which would make the burden felt immediately, or through bonds, which would shift some of the cost onto future Americans. Congress approved the first War Loan Act in April 1917 to provide money for Europe. The bill initially authorized $3 billion for the Allies but was increased as the needs of the U.S. and Allied governments grew. By the end of the decade the government had borrowed $23 billion on a long-term basis and collected $10.5 billion through taxation. The Wilson administration did not want to place large demands on the masses through personal taxation, so the government borrowed against future generations. Wilson originally hoped to finance the war by revising tax laws to raise revenue, but that promised political turmoil over sectional and class issues that Wilson did not want to confront.

Wartime Taxation. Gradually a variety of taxes were raised to offset war costs. The War Revenue Act of 1917 imposed 74 percent of the financial burden of the war on large individual and corporate incomes alone. Mounting costs forced Wilson and Treasury Secretary William Gibbs McAdoo to ask Congress to levy additional taxes on incomes, profits, and luxuries. The Revenue Act of 1918 raised the financial burden on individuals to 80 percent of the war costs. The general effect of wartime taxation was to give people on the bottom of the pay scale a break and to tax the wealthy heavily. The real wages of employees in the manufacturing industries and farming rose substantially. Thus, while the wealthy who purchased government bonds benefited financially from the war, they also for the first time endured substantial taxes on their incomes.

Sources:
David M. Kennedy, *Over Here: The First World War and American Society* (New York: Oxford University Press, 1980);

Arthur S. Link and others, *American Epoch: A History of the United States Since 1900* (New York: Knopf, 1987).

THE WAR INDUSTRIES BOARD

Background. One of the goals of the progressive movement was to create an administrative state capable of regulating business and industry and controlling the business cycles that pitched the country into recessions or depressions with unsettling regularity. But it took a world war to make this goal even a temporary reality. One of the earliest and most ambitious attempts to create an institutional order was the War Industries Board (WIB). The WIB, created in July 1917, was established to mobilize the nation's resources for war while protecting the economy's basic structure and character for the peace that was to follow. The WIB continues to spark debate among historians and economists as a model of the proper relationship between government and the economy. It often elicited both extravagant hopes and exaggerated fears during the war even though it had little formal authority. Social and economic functions that had traditionally been left to private control were suddenly taken up by the government. But fears that the WIB represented a frightening usurpation of private functions by a government bureaucracy proved to be unfounded.

Harness Industry. The Wilson administration realized that the military bureaus were too fragmented to achieve the type of coordination required to mobilize the country for war. Congress, in its preparedness legislation

of 1916, established a Council of National Defense made up of six cabinet members and representatives from business, industry, railroads, and labor. The WIB began as a subordinate body of the council but soon outgrew its parent in importance until President Wilson made it a separate agency in March 1918 and named Wall Street broker Bernard M. Baruch as its new leader. The WIB's goal was to harness the gigantic American industrial machine for the war effort by applying controls over the use of scarce materials and transportation and bringing order to an otherwise unorderly system.

Goals. With Baruch acting as a kind of economic administrator, the WIB set out to implement modern business methods and streamline the production of war materials. The board intervened in every facet of the economy from the national to the local level and in international politics. Individuals and groups had to be either persuaded or forced to cooperate to ensure that production goals were met. Although it was an administrative agency, the WIB at first had no formal authority. Initially the board derived all its power from the fact that President Wilson supported its work. It had to instill its will on the economy through pleading, intimidation, and negotiation. The board tried to inspire businesses to cooperate and operated by request rather than a heavy-handed mandate. The War and Navy Departments continued to make their own purchases of war materiel, for example. Within the confines of the war, individualism and competition gave way to cooperation.

Cooperation and Coordination. Baruch and his staff of "dollar-a-year men" tried to find the ideal balance between public service and the private realm. They donated their services to the government for an annual salary of one dollar to show the importance of the war effort. WIB officials were committed to a common ideology espousing the cooperative ethic in industry, systematic coordination, business-government cooperation, and a gentleman's code rather than government sanctions. President Wilson shared the assumptions held by his business advisers. In summing up Wilson's job, Baruch said he should "encourage, under strict Government supervision, such cooperation and coordination in industry as should tend to increase production, eliminate waste, conserve natural resources, improve the quality of products, promote efficiency in operation, and thus reduce costs to the ultimate consumer."

Middle Ground. The downside to the new relationship between business and government in the mind of the general public concerned the move toward expanded state involvement in the economy on one hand or no government control at all on the other. President Wilson tried to solve the problem between unbridled laissez-faire and full-blown state control by searching out a middle ground. Both Wilson and business leaders were hesitant about expanding state control over the economy. Their dilemma grew into a strange creature actually having little formal power but remarkable real power.

Female worker packing a shell for use in World War I

Legacy. Government-business relations centered on complexity, hesitancy, and ambiguity in the past, but Baruch and his staff achieved some great successes in prioritizing production and distribution in industry and limiting price competition. Business and the government worked together effectively without coercion or federally imposed controls, but often only because the WIB set prices that allowed companies to reap generous profits. Where the WIB had less success was with the military services and the major economic institutions; however, in these instances Baruch relied on compromise and shared power. President Wilson and the WIB could take the risk of bringing government involvement into the economy because of the unique position the United States enjoyed in relation to the belligerents in Europe. The country lacked the urgency of its allies because of its great distance from the actual fighting. Once the United States entered the war the WIB tried to balance delicately coordination with timeless American traits such as pluralism, decentralization, and lax social/economic controls. The amazing aspect is that it worked and did so rather effectively. The most lasting legacy of the WIB is that it brought industry into close and regular relations with congressional committees, cabinet departments, and executive agencies. It left an array of institutions and practices that would be revived by President Franklin D. Roosevelt to bring the country out of the Great Depression, even though the WIB itself went out of existence as soon as the war was over.

Sources:

Bernard M. Baruch, *American Industry in the War* (Englewood Cliffs, N.J.: Prentice-Hall, 1941);

Robert D. Cuff, *The War Industries Board: Business-Government Relations during World War I* (Baltimore: Johns Hopkins University Press, 1973);

David M. Kennedy, *Over Here: The First World War and American Society* (New York: Oxford University Press, 1980).

WORLD WAR I AND THE ECONOMY

Mobilizing the Economy. The United States officially participated in World War I for only nineteen months, but the war had a tremendous impact on domestic America. President Wilson declared that belligerency would require "the organization and mobilization of all the material resources of the country." Indeed, the government worked hard to get both the hearts and minds of the American public behind the war effort.

Benefits of Belligerency. The United States sent a much-needed influx of men and materiel to Europe and insured the defeat of the Central Powers. The war initially cost the U.S. government about $33 billion plus interest, and veterans' benefits would later bring the total to $112 billion. However, this figure hides the great profitability of the war for the nation. Instead of hurting the domestic economy, the war effort strengthened and improved America's competitive position in the world. Farmers enjoyed boom years as agricultural prices rose and the international market for their products expanded. Farmers also used new technological advances that helped them modernize. Real wages for blue-collar workers increased modestly, and all sectors profited from the war. Wartime demands for industrial products raised profits for many companies. The DuPont Company's stock multiplied by 1,600 percent between 1914 and 1918, and DuPont grew from a debtor company to one with a surplus of $68 million at the end of fighting. Steel production reached twice its prewar level by 1917. The standardization effort during the war led to greater postwar industrial efficiency and production.

Arsenal of Democracy. President Wilson encouraged America's changing role in the world economy. Free trade, in his view, promoted both universal prosperity and universal peace. International commerce led to a strong domestic economy, and exports were essential for continued American economic growth. Wilson felt that restrictions on trade, such as tariffs and trade agreements, hindered efficiency and denied the natural cycle of the international economy. The president firmly believed that goodwill flowed along with goods, and that commercial contacts were effective guarantors of peaceful relations among states. American business certainly seemed to benefit from both Wilsonian rhetoric and the new realities created by the war. The war almost instantly reversed the credit standing of the United States. The nation, by the war's end, held billions of dollars in European debt obligations and was the globe's greatest credi-

tor as well as its greatest economic power. By forcing the Europeans to accept goods instead of loans, the Wilson administration guaranteed that the country would be banker, arsenal, and breadbasket to the Allies.

Economic Hegemony. World War I solidified the changes that had been occurring in the economy prior to the war. The United States used its abundant natural resources and technological advances to dominate the world's manufacturing output. Large corporations needed markets to flourish, and the war, by devastating the manufacturing output of the belligerents, gave companies new outlets for their products worldwide. The federal government encouraged and helped businesses increase their presence overseas. The general public, for the most part, did not protest the partnership between big business and the government because most benefited from the war. Annual incomes rose steadily, from $580 in 1914 to more than $1,300 by the end of the decade. Thus, World War I dramatically changed the domestic and international economy and set the stage for the prosperity of the 1920s.

Sources:

Peter Fearon, *War, Prosperity and Depression: The U.S. Economy 1917–45* (Lawrence: University of Kansas Press, 1987);

David M. Kennedy, *Over Here: The First World War and American Society* (New York: Oxford University Press, 1980).

HEADLINE MAKERS

BERNARD M. BARUCH

1870-1965

FINANCIER, CHAIRMAN OF THE WAR INDUSTRIES BOARD

Elder Statesman. Bernard M. Baruch began his career as a Wall Street gambler and evolved into one of the nation's most respected elder statesmen. His skill at predicting stock market fluctuations made him untold millions, but he transcended the financial world using his money and personality to gain political favor with a string of presidents. At the end of his career Baruch gained notoriety for setting up his "office" on a park bench in Lafayette Square across the street from the White House. Baruch's political reputation was solidified in the 1910s when President Woodrow Wilson named him chairman of the War Industries Board (WIB). The speculator's skill at organizing and coordinating the nation's businesses for the First World War won him national acclaim. He parlayed the early success into a cherished position among the country's political elite.

Background. Baruch was born in Camden, South Carolina, and spent the first ten years of his life there. It gave him a taste of country living that would influence his outlook for the rest of his life. No matter how cosmopolitan Baruch became, he still retained his roots in South Carolina. While Baruch was still a child his parents moved the family to New York City, where his mother became a society figure and his father established a medical practice. Baruch attended the City College of New York and had a mediocre academic record. He was intelligent but deathly afraid of public speaking and intellectually lazy. But Baruch excelled in the social aspects of college life, was elected senior class president, and was an outstanding athlete, particularly in baseball and lacrosse. He initially wanted to follow in his father's footsteps and become a doctor, but he felt that business would offer more opportunities.

Wall Street Speculator. Baruch's first two jobs both came from his mother's social connections. The first job was with retired clothing merchant Julius A. Kohn. Baruch was hired to do office tasks and become a student of Wall Street speculation. Kohn taught him well, and Baruch used his own uncanny natural ability to speculate on arbitrage, foreign exchange, and business reorganizations. Baruch liked the gambling aspects of Wall Street, testing his nerve and knowledge on a regular basis. In 1891 he began working for A. A. Houseman and Company in the midst of a depression. This taught Baruch many lessons on the tumultuous nature of the stock market, but he was successful enough to be made a junior partner at age twenty-five. When signs of recovery appeared, Baruch bought a seat on the New York Stock Exchange and married Annie Griffen in 1897, starting a family and a wildly successful career on Wall Street. Baruch spent the next decade increasing his fortune by speculating and gambling on the short-term value of stocks and selling quickly. Baruch's techniques were asocial and disreputable, and many moguls frowned upon public association with him. Instead of investing and building, Baruch was gambling and hustling to make a quick buck. However, the financier's affable personality and charm watered down his competitive nature. An anomaly among Wall Street tycoons because he was not from the Ivy League or old money, Baruch never completely fit in. His standing as an outsider was further enhanced by the anti-Semitism found on Wall Street. Baruch became a symbol of success and the most famous American Jew of his time, but his wealth, fame, and power did not isolate him from the racism in America.

The War Industries Board. World War I changed people's priorities. Baruch and other notable businessmen flocked to the nation's capital to help in the effort. They became known as "dollar-a-year men" because they did not accept a regular salary from the government for their services. President Wilson announced the formation of the WIB on 28 July 1917 to mobilize the nation's economy and resources for the war. Baruch was named the chairman on 4 March 1918. Wilson called Baruch "Dr. Facts" because of his vast business knowledge and stood behind him with the power and the authority of the presidency. Baruch immediately began overhauling the

WIB and sought to achieve its ends, whether that meant cajoling, threatening, or intimidating businesses into co-operation. In fact, Baruch was the perfect choice to head the WIB. He knew many industrialists but was not one of them himself, thus avoiding the charge that he was illegally improving his own fortune masked behind the agency. As a self-made millionaire Baruch commanded the respect of businessmen, and Wilson's support forced the military to succumb to the WIB's goals. Baruch was able to exert leadership in converting the economy for the war, but he did not overstep his bounds and create a system that could not revert to a peacetime economy, although his critics accused him of forming an economic dictatorship. Baruch took deliberate steps to maintain economic order and a stable market.

Legacy. The achievements of the WIB were the high point of Baruch's career as a government adviser. Although his influence and reputation gained him the ear of presidents from Franklin D. Roosevelt to Lyndon B. Johnson, Baruch did not move in and out of government positions like his high-profile contemporaries, such as Robert S. Lovett and W. Averell Harriman. Baruch, however, played as crucial a role as any other American during the war years of the 1910s. He was the perfect person to run the WIB, and he exemplified the spirit of public service and public sacrifice needed to run the war effort.

Sources:

Robert D. Cuff, *The War Industries Board: Business-Government Relations during World War I* (Baltimore: Johns Hopkins University Press, 1973);

Jordan A. Schwarz, *The Speculator: Bernard M. Baruch in Washington, 1917–1965* (Chapel Hill: University of North Carolina Press, 1981).

HOWARD E. COFFIN

1873-1937

ENGINEER

Background. Howard Coffin was born on 6 September 1873 in the small town of West Milton, Ohio. He attended the University of Michigan, majoring in mechanical engineering, and used his proximity to Detroit to get involved in the burgeoning auto industry. From 1902 to 1906 Coffin worked for the Olds Motor Works in Detroit and Lansing, advancing to the position of chief engineer. From 1908 to 1910 Coffin was employed by Chalmers Detroit Motor Company where he served as vice president. At the beginning of the new decade Coffin was named vice president at the Hudson Motor Car Company and spent the next twenty years of his career there. While at Hudson, Coffin worked to standardize parts in the auto industry and became the president of the Society of Automobile Engi-

neers. He was one of the earliest proponents of standardization. Coffin's experience in industry prepared him for his work during World War I, where he helped to lead the effort to gear the national economy for war by spreading the gospel of standardization.

Preparedness Program. Coffin was the most prominent member of a small group of American engineers who pushed for industrial preparedness. Coffin's system centered on gathering data, centralizing administration, and gaining publicity. President Woodrow Wilson appointed Coffin to the Naval Consulting Board in 1915, where he worked diligently to lay the groundwork for the administration's larger preparedness program. With President Wilson's blessing, Coffin enlisted the help of engineering societies and Walter S. Gifford, a statistician at the American Telephone and Telegraph Company. Coffin and Gifford were joined in their effort to develop a national industrial inventory by another engineer, Hollis Godfrey, president of the Drexel Institute in Philadelphia. These men were, as one historian described them, "technocrats who abhorred disorder and loved efficiency with a passion that perhaps exceeded their regard for profits."

Council of National Defense. The work of the engineers gave substance to the nationwide call for preparedness and led in August 1916 to the creation of the Council of National Defense, along with a Civilian Advisory Commission. While the council was a more official agency, composed of various cabinet secretaries, the civilian group brought together representatives from industry, finance, labor, and other sectors. Coffin and Godfrey were original members along with other luminaries, including Samuel Gompers of the AFL; Julius Rosenwald, president of Sears, Roebuck; and Bernard Baruch, who later served as chairman of the War Industries Board (WIB). The group met to coordinate the domestic war effort and to ensure a smoothly functioning partnership between business and the government. President Wilson backed the group, stating that the agency proved the "need of business organization in public matters and for the presence there of the best specialists in their respective fields . . . efficiency being their sole object and Americanism their only motive." The work started by Coffin and his fellow engineers and their relentless call for standardization set the tone for the war effort and the later successes of the War Industries Board.

Failure in Aircrafts. Coffin also took an active role in overseeing the fledgling aircraft industry, serving as the chairman of the Aircraft Board of the United States in 1917–1918. The aircraft industry could not build enough planes to keep up with the needs of the armed forces. Up to 1917, the industry had produced less than two hundred aircraft, but during the war it built more than fifteen hundred by turning to the automobile manufacturers for help. Coffin, who was affiliated with Orville Wright's Dayton-Wright Airplane Company before he joined the WIB, facilitated the cooperation between the two industries. Both Coffin and his successor as chairman of the Aircraft Board,

Edward A. Deeds of Delco, favored the automobile manufacturers when awarding government contracts. For example, Dayton-Wright received $2.5 million, while $6.5 million went to Lincoln Motors. Coffin and Deeds put their hopes in an American-built Liberty engine, but the engine was unusable for aircraft. More than twenty-five hundred Liberty engines were produced, but none was able to be used in the war effort. In fact, by the time of the armistice, not a single American combat plane was in France. Regardless of the enthusiasm showed by Coffin, Deeds, and President Wilson, the attempt to transform the auto industry to airplanes was a failure. The president was so frustrated with the results that he ordered an investigation into the matter headed by Justice Charles Evans Hughes. It showed that Coffin and Deeds abused their power by awarding contracts to their own firms. The airplane industry did not begin to recover until Charles Lindbergh's famous flight in 1927. In the late 1920s only three factories of the forty that had produced airplanes for the military in 1918 were still open.

Influence. Coffin's emphasis on standardization, gathering an inventory of national resources, and combining the efforts of labor, business, and the government set the stage for much of the preparedness effort of World War I. Although Bernard Baruch gained much more fame as chairman of the WIB, a case could be made that without Coffin's influence Baruch's work would have been much more difficult, if not impossible. Coffin and his cadre of engineers focused on industrial mobilization and stuck to the issues, slowly winning both public and private officials to their way of thinking.

Sources:

David M. Kennedy, *Over Here: The First World War and American Society* (New York: Oxford University Press, 1980);

Robert Sobel, *The Age of Giant Corporations: A Microeconomic History of American Business, 1914–1992* (Westport, Conn.: Praeger, 1993).

WILLIAM C. DURANT

1861-1947

FOUNDER OF GENERAL MOTORS

Big Dreams. William C. "Billy" Durant was not the typical automotive executive of the 1910s — an engineer or designer who liked to tinker with cars. Durant, rather, was a man of big dreams, a master stock market manipulator, charmer, and intense individual. He was a wealthy entrepreneur and salesman who fell in love with a Buick in 1904 and decided that he wanted to become a car baron. Fortunately, he had the initiative and access to money to pursue his dream. Durant wanted to create a group of independent car companies that cooperated with one another and could take control of the industry, following the pattern of consolidation in railroads and banking. Durant's greatest trait was as an empire builder. If he did not have the resources to achieve his goals, he would engage the imaginations of others who were powerful and wealthy.

Founds GM. On 16 September 1908 Durant incorporated General Motors (GM) with only $2,000. He then quickly used the profits from GM to acquire Buick, Oldsmobile, Cadillac, and Oakland (later renamed Pontiac). His acquisitions led to a national distribution network and a diversity of product lines. In 1909 he even considered purchasing Ford, but the cost of $8 million in cash was too high. By 1910 Durant had swallowed up thirty companies, including eleven automakers. He dealt on an international level by buying McLaughlin Motor Car Company of Ontario and Bedford Motors of Britain. Like many acquisitional wizards, Durant had much difficulty organizing his empire, and by late 1910 the company teetered on the verge of bankruptcy. No one had placed any controls on Durant's spending spree, and his profits were insufficient to cover his losses when the economy entered a recession. GM was leveraged to the hilt, and Durant faced economic ruin.

Banks Intervene. A GM stockholder, John H. McClement, proposed a plan to save the company, but most people had already given up hope. Durant's bankers circled like vultures and wanted to break the company into parts, selling most and keeping the guaranteed profit-generating divisions, such as Buick. Durant had to convince them that the whole empire was worth saving. He put together a deal that had enough profitable parts to make the whole thing worthwhile. Lee, Higgins and Company of Boston and J. and W. Seligman and Company of New York agreed to underwrite General Motors and provide $15 million. The interest rate was extremely high on the guarantee and produced a $9 million profit during the next five years. A condition of the takeover was that Durant's control had to end. He was given a token vice presidency, but GM was controlled by the banks. Durant's actions had always been fueled by a deep love of the automobile and the thrill of bringing in a new era. GM's new management, on the other hand, was concerned only with the profit margin.

Rebound. During the next five years Durant founded five automobile companies, including his baby, the Chevrolet Motor Company of Michigan. Durant personally commissioned the designing and building of the first Chevrolet models, raised the funds, and put together the factory and sales organizations. He used the profits from his ventures to buy GM stock and urged his friends to do likewise. Durant was setting the stage to take back his company. Durant received support from his close friend Jacob Raskob, who shared Durant's ambition, charisma, and risk-taking. Raskob was the chief financial officer at Du Pont. He convinced Pierre Du Pont to invest in GM because the Du Pont Company would profit by selling paint to the carmaker. Du Pont eventually invested $50 million in GM.

Reclaims GM. In 1915 the bankers controlling GM met to vote whether to renew their arrangement with the automobile company. It was unclear if Durant actually had enough stock to take control of the company, but the bankers had faith in Pierre Du Pont and relinquished control to Durant. In 1916 he replaced the bankers from GM's board with car company managers. When he regained control, Durant set up the General Motors Acceptance Corporation (GMAC), the industry's first company to provide loans for car buyers, car dealers, and dealership owners. By the middle of 1919 GM's common stock was valued at more than $1 billion. The next year, however, led to Durant's second downfall. Farm prices fell; the bond market slumped; and GM could not sell its debt. The market shriveled up, and the company's cash reserves of $100 million vanished; factories closed; and inventories began rusting away in storage yards.

Losing Control. GM once again developed into a sprawling empire of seventy-five factories in forty different cities all under the personal control of Durant, who simply did not possess the management skills required for such a large endeavor. Vice President Alfred P. Sloan Jr. set up an organizational plan for the company, while Durant bought GM shares as the prices were declining, hoping it would create greater demand for the stock. Durant's ploy to manipulate the market failed, and his personal debt grew to $38 million. Instead of stimulating Wall Street, Durant's downfall would take many bankers and brokers with him. The only thing Durant created was market panic. J. P. Morgan Jr. stepped in and formed a company to bail Durant out, and Durant resigned as president of GM in 1920. Ironically, his resignation and the rescue by Morgan abruptly halted the GM stock slide.

Legacy. Durant had a lasting impact on the automobile industry, even if he could not control his empire. Both Chrysler and American Motors Corporation (AMC) were spinoffs from GM. Durant gave both Walter Chrysler and Charles W. Nash their start in the car industry. Durant's passion for acquiring new companies led to many important products being developed. He took over Delco in 1916, and the company still exists as a manufacturer of batteries, starters, and other electrical elements. Durant also refinanced Frigidaire out of his own pocket, renamed its product the "Frigerator," then sold it to the directors at GM for a fraction of its actual cost.

Downfall. Old age was difficult for Durant. At sixty he tried to found Durant Motors but failed. The former multimillionaire was forced into bankruptcy in 1936 and had to sell his wife's jewelry in an attempt to raise money. Two years later he watched as the contents of his New York apartment were auctioned off for a paltry $112,000.

He would have remained penniless if not for donations from Sloan and others at GM in gratitude to the entrepreneur who created, but could not manage, the world's largest industrial company.

Sources:

Maryann Keller, *Rude Awakening: The Rise, Fall, and Struggle for Recovery of General Motors* (New York: Morrow, 1989);

David M. Kennedy, *Over Here: The First World War and American Society* (New York: Oxford University Press, 1980);

Arthur S. Link and others, *American Epoch: A History of the United States Since 1900* (New York: Knopf, 1987);

Bernard A. Weisberger, *The Dream Maker: William C. Durant, Founder of General Motors* (Boston: Little, Brown, 1979).

FRANK B. GILBRETH

1868-1924

PIONEER OF SCIENTIFIC MANAGEMENT

Scientific Management. Frank B. Gilbreth put the "scientific" in Frederick W. Taylor's theories of scientific management in the 1910s. Gilbreth began as a Taylor disciple, but after Taylor died he took up the mantle as one of the leaders in the growing field of industrial engineering. Gilbreth, born in the small town of Fairfield, Maine, in 1868, used his background in bricklaying, a flair for inventions, and a businessman's savvy to build a national reputation and gain the public's acceptance of his work. Gilbreath pioneered the effort to eliminate wasted movements from factory work by studying a worker's movements with special machinery and using the information gained to devise the most efficient means to do the job. Gilbreth advanced the notion that industrial organizations should be built on interchangeable parts and speed work. He developed his ideas independently of Taylor (in part through his experience in construction), but Taylor's methods had a tremendous impact on him. Gilbreth believed that Taylor was the greatest man he had ever met and said that scientific management was the most important thing that had happened in his life.

Motion Study. Gilbreth married Lillian Moller, who held a Ph.D. from Brown University, in 1904, and they began a journey together that Lillian labeled "The Quest of the One Best Way." Every facet of Gilbreth's thinking centered on eliminating waste and finding the perfect set of motions to accomplish a given task. He left the construction business in 1912 and began a career in management consulting. Gilbreth replaced Taylor's stopwatch with a motion-picture camera to get more accurate results in his time-motion analyses. Gilbreth's fascination with motion studies led to a break with Taylor, who believed his young student neglected scientific management as a whole by concentrating on "the minutiae of motion." Gilbreth, however, felt that his work actually surpassed Taylor's and that it could be used in any industry with almost anything that moved.

"Therbligs." The widespread adoption of assembly line techniques in the 1910s changed the face of work in U.S. factories. Managers needed to know how to control problems such as stress and fatigue among workers and called on consultants like the Gilbreths for answers. Using scientific methods, the Gilbreths showed that by eliminating unnecessary motions the worker could eliminate fatigue. The Gilbreths — especially Lillian in *The Psychology of Management* (1914) — also studied how fatigue impacted the mind. They discussed how workers needed "happy minutes" to relieve themselves from the stress and fatigue brought on by assembly work. Frank, however, still concentrated his efforts on motion studies. He broke down the work process into "elementary operations," which he then measured and studied. The former bricklayer believed his studies provided accuracy and objectivity to factory work, and he even invented the micromotion and chronocyclegraph machines to measure fundamental units to the thousandth of a minute. Gilbreth isolated sixteen elementary movements of hand motion, which he called "Therbligs." These fundamental motions were so specific that they did not deviate regardless of the tool used. Whether the worker was using a hammer, scalpel, or an ax, the Therbligs remained constant.

Standardization. Gilbreth wanted to completely reorganize industrial work by classifying all required motions in terms of Therbligs. Every task would be ranked according to necessary motion skills. Gilbreth wanted this done through a U.S. Government Bureau of Standardization of Trades. In their effort to find "The One Best Way To Do Work," the Gilbreths wanted to establish laboratories in the factories and insisted that the "conditions of the shop should be changed until they duplicate the most desirable conditions of the laboratory." The One Best Way was soon applied to every part of the Gilbreths' lives. Lillian became the "One Best Wife and Mother"; they devised the "One Best Way To Raise Children"; and they looked for the "One Best Place To Live." Frank carried on his search for order in a thoughtful and earnest way, which offended some people and led others to see him as an eccentric. Gilbreth was so devoted to his vision that he never questioned whether the type of order he searched for simply might not be what people needed or desired in their own lives.

Efficiency. Frank Gilbreth's version of scientific management meshed with the notions of productivity and efficiency that dominated the 1910s. The government even put Gilbreth to work during World War I to teach soldiers a more efficient way to assemble machine guns. His life's work and his books, such as *Motion Study* (1911), concentrated on increasing the efficiency of workers. Eventually, the Gilbreth's One Best Way became a way of looking at industry in its entirety, from the shop floor to the advertising and sales departments. Gilbreth had a far-reaching influence on the 1910s and embodied the era's faith in science, engineering, and efficiency as the keys to progress.

Sources:

Lillian Moller Gilbreth, *The Quest of the One Best Way: A Sketch of the Life of Frank Bunker Gilbreth* (New York: Society of Women Engineers, 1990);

Samuel Haber, *Efficiency and Uplift: Scientific Management in the Progressive Era, 1890–1920* (Chicago: University of Chicago Press, 1964).

SAMUEL GOMPERS

1850-1924

PRESIDENT OF THE AMERICAN FEDERATION OF LABOR

Leader. Samuel Gompers was the most important labor leader in American history prior to the epic labor struggles of the 1930s. He guided the American Federation of Labor (AFL) through a period in which labor's most fundamental rights were questioned. In an era of intense struggle between labor and capital, Gompers steered a moderate course for the skilled workers in trade unions and helped establish ties between labor and the federal government through his support of the Wilson administration during World War I. He rose from meager beginnings to become a confidant of presidents, politicians, and businessmen. As president of the AFL from 1886 to 1924 Gompers loaded the AFL and the cause of organized labor on his back and carried them into the center of American political and economic thought. His brand of pragmatic unionization appealed to workers because it was not theoretical or difficult to understand. Gompers's "pure and simple" unionism focused on advancing the immediate economic interests of workers in terms of wages, hours, and working conditions.

Background. Gompers was born in London's East End in 1850. He was forced to leave school at age ten to supplement his family's income. In that year young Samuel was apprenticed in his father's trade, cigar making. In June 1863 his family left for New York and the dream of a better life in the United States. Gompers continued working as a cigar maker in New York and as early as 1864 had joined a local union. For the next twenty years he engaged in trade activities and lived on meager wages even after he married Sophia Julian, also a London-born immigrant who worked in his shop stripping tobacco leaves.

Socialist Thought. Gompers learned political and social philosophy in the cigar-making shops. He listened with eager anticipation as his fellow workers talked about socialism and labor reform. Working in the shop of a German political immigrant, David Hirsch, Gompers adopted socialist ideas and began reading all the socialist literature he could find. In the 1880s and 1890s Gompers and his fellow trade unionists believed themselves to be both innovators and followers of the theories and prescriptions of Karl Marx. However, the young activist never became a theorist. He pursued a realistic course in fighting for labor reforms and did not let abstract ideas overwhelm important, short-term gains. It was with this realism in mind that he began to rebuild the Cigar Makers' Union with two other militant leaders, Adolph Strasser and Ferdinand Laurrell, in 1875. Later in life Gompers said that these men were responsible for the future course of American labor and that from them "came the purpose and initiative that finally resulted in the present American labor movement . . . we did create the technique and formulate the fundamentals."

Radical Realist. Early experiences radicalized the labor leader. Watching his craft slowly being destroyed by mechanization led him to support intensely the skills of craftsmen, artisans, and mechanics. Early in his career Gompers was also supportive of blacks and immigrants. But Gompers consistently championed the cause of trade unionism for skilled workers, not the toiling masses. His experience with unskilled immigrants who accepted lower wages in the mechanized age cemented trade unionism in his mind forever.

Toward Conservativism. Time and increased leadership responsibilities dampened Gompers's early radical views. By 1903 he had dropped his belief in class struggle, and by 1913 he was no longer an opponent of the capitalist system. Gompers kept the goals of the AFL centered on helping the skilled worker and completely ignored his own vision of working-class unity from the 1870s and 1880s. Over the years Gompers grew more conservative and rigid. He was ambitious, self-righteous, and bigoted, but he was also scrupulously honest and would drive himself to exhaustion in fighting for the cause of trade unionism.

Political Alignment. The AFL grew tremendously in the 1910s because Gompers aligned the union with the Democratic Party and kept a tight rein over the radical elements within the labor organization. The AFL supported Woodrow Wilson in 1912 and reaped the rewards by gaining a voice in national labor policy. Gompers regularly corre-

sponded with Wilson, and in 1917 the president addressed the annual convention of the AFL. Under Wilson the Department of Labor aggressively advocated trade unionism's case. The department was headed by William B. Wilson, a former official in the AFL's largest affiliate, the United Mine Workers of America. As a result of Gompers's influence within the administration, labor looked upon such positive results as the Clayton Act, the Adamson Act, and a place for Gompers on the Council of National Defense.

World War I. The election of 1916 and America's participation in World War I cemented the relationship between the federal government and organized labor. AFL support in the western states, especially California, helped Wilson win the election. As the principal spokesman for labor, Gompers supported the war effort and used the extraordinary situation surrounding the preparedness movement to increase labor's power. He identified the AFL with American foreign policy and attacked all pacifist and suspected pro-German groups. Gompers assured President Wilson the cooperation of organized labor in the war effort in return for basic concessions from employers regarding wages, hours, and working conditions. The radical Industrial Workers of the World (IWW) did not fall in line, so the AFL president supported government suppression of that labor group. Gompers did not want socialist elements within labor to jeopardize the large gains he achieved for the AFL. In fact, Gompers's irresponsible exaggeration of Bolshevism and radicalism intensified the public's fear of organized labor and the consequent demand for the forceful suppression of strikes during the Red Scare.

Legacy. When Gompers died in December 1924 at the age of seventy-four, both labor and business mourned his death. His moderate policies had won confidence in the general public as well as among business leaders. Gompers held the reins on organized labor for nearly four decades and was instrumental in the gains made on behalf of America's working class. However, the AFL president was also responsible for maintaining a rigid, conservative policy that ignored the needs of many workers, whose needs would not be met until the formation of the broader Congress of Industrial Organizations in the 1930s.

Sources:

Will Chasen, *Samuel Gompers: Leader of American Labor* (New York: Praeger, 1971);

Foster Rhea Dulles, *Labor in America: A History* (New York: Crowell, 1966);

Samuel Gompers, *Seventy Years of Life and Labour: An Autobiography* (New York: Kelley, 1967);

John H. M. Laslett, "Samuel Gompers and the Rise of American Business Unionism," in *Labor Leaders in America*, edited by Melvyn

Dubofsky and Warren Van Tine (Urbana: University of Illinois Press, 1987), pp. 62–88.

JOHN MITCHELL

1870-1919

LABOR LEADER

Background. John Mitchell, a driving force behind the organization of America's coal miners, endured a difficult childhood that included being orphaned at age six and that mixed hard work with irregular schooling. Mitchell was born in Briadwood, Illinois, in 1870. He never finished school; instead he entered the mines at the age of twelve in 1882. For the next several years Mitchell traveled around the West and Midwest from mine to mine. At age fifteen Mitchell joined the Knights of Labor, which was attempting to organize both skilled and unskilled workers in industry, mining, and railroads. The young miner returned to Illinois in 1888, where he found the mining towns filled with immigrants and wages down by 20 percent. Mitchell felt the working conditions in the mines were equal to slavery. After a prolonged but futile strike in 1891, Mitchell returned to the West but only stayed one year. He returned to his home state to marry Catherine O'Rourke and settle in Spring Valley. Mitchell had grown into a sensitive and introspective man by his late twenties, and he often brooded over the conditions miners were forced to endure. His concern with the plight of miners led him to join the United Mine Workers of America (UMWA) in the 1890s.

Meteoric Rise. During the depression of the 1890s Mitchell became the secretary/treasurer of the northern Illinois union subdistrict. In 1897 his hard work as a union advocate earned him a position as a legislative representative for the union in the state capital of Springfield. Mitchell actively participated in the 1897 national bituminous coal strike and grabbed the attention of national union leaders by going into difficult areas of southern Illinois to organize workers. Mitchell attended his first national union convention in 1898 and left as a UMWA vice president. He impressed the delegates with his quiet dignity and proficiency on the state level. Mitchell's meteoric rise to the top of the union culminated in his appointment as acting president in the fall of 1898 and his unopposed run for the UMWA presidency the following year. He was well aware of the tremendous tasks that were ahead and hoped to lead the union ahead cautiously.

Union Leader. Mitchell began a movement to organize the outlying districts and anthracite regions under the auspices of the UMWA. The union leader realized that all miners, regardless of race or ethnic background, labored under cruel and harsh conditions. Most mining families existed in dire squalor. Miners themselves did not present a united front in their fight against the coal mine owners. Native-born American workers despised the new immigrants, and miners were divided by race, religion, and language barriers as well. Mitchell hoped to give the union effort stronger cohesion and devoted himself to helping the most downtrodden workers. Mitchell looked for support wherever he could find it, including local priests and middle-class reformers. The labor president preached a gospel of unionism, dignity of man, and warmth of brotherhood. Under his strong guidance the UMWA improved the conditions of the miners by gaining them wage increases, grievance committees, and shorter work hours.

Strikes. In the early 1900s the UMWA gained enough support to strike against unfair labor practices. Pennsylvania's anthracite workers won an important strike in 1900, returning to work on 29 October and celebrating "Mitchell Day" in the pits. In 1902 Mitchell led a series of strikes aimed at improving the wages and hours of miners. J. P. Morgan, arguably the world's most powerful financier, met with Mitchell to end one strike, and the two men got along quite well, agreeing to a wage increase and the establishment of a grievance committee for the workers. Later the same year, when 150,000 workers struck for more than five months, President Theodore Roosevelt appointed a special Anthracite Coal Strike Committee to resolve the differences. The committee awarded the miners a 10 percent wage increase and a shorter workday. The victory catapulted Mitchell into the national spotlight. Miners idolized him as their Moses. The public praised his temperate and tactful leadership, and President Roosevelt befriended him. The strikes took a great toll on Mitchell, however, and led to a nervous breakdown in 1906. He was forced to yield the presidency to his longtime rival, John L. Lewis, and Mitchell remained in poor health for the rest of his life.

New Activities. Despite his health problems, however, Mitchell remained an important and influential figure in labor and reform circles in the 1910s. From 1911 to 1914 he supported himself by lecturing and writing on the nation's labor problems. The labor leader was quite popular on the lecture circuit. He also participated in the meetings of the National Civic Federation, serving as the chairman of its trade agreement department from 1908 to 1911. From 1914 to 1915 Mitchell served as a member of the New York State Workmen's Compensation Commission and was chairman of the New York State Industrial Commission from 1915 until his death in 1919. In his later years Mitchell became a successful stock market speculator, and when he died of pneumonia in 1919 his estimated assets exceeded $250,000. But the words inscribed on Mitchell's tombstone best epitomize his true influence: "Champion of Liberty — Defender of Human Rights."

Source:
Charles A. Madison, *American Labor Leaders: Personalities and Forces in the Labor Movement* (New York: Ungar, 1950).

EDWARD ALSWORTH ROSS

1866-1951

PROFESSOR AND SOCIAL ACTIVIST

Background. The progressive movement found one of its greatest proponents in Edward Alsworth Ross, a gargantuan man with what contemporaries referred to as a "magnificent" head. He stood six feet six inches tall, and his size mimicked the way the professor loomed over the Progressive Era, always willing to contribute a juicy quote for newspapermen or another article outlining his positions. Professor Ross was a genuinely decent and thoughtful man. He was extremely loyal and generous with his graduate students and colleagues. For years he counseled and gave financial assistance to a worthy scholar who lost his post at a university because of his outspokenly radical views. Ross grew up in the Midwest as an orphan and was raised by many concerned groups. He attended Coe College, a small school where he emerged as a natural leader. He graduated in 1886 and was noted for his intellectual prowess and contagious exuberance. Ross left Iowa in 1888 for graduate study in Germany but returned to the United States and received a Ph.D. in political economy with minors in history and philosophy from Johns Hopkins University in Baltimore.

Spread of Democracy. Ross was an outstanding teacher and held several high-profile posts at universities, including Stanford, the University of Nebraska, and, finally, the University of Wisconsin. While at Nebraska, in only his thirties, Ross associated with William Jennings Bryan and Clarence Darrow, and was close friends with Theodore Roosevelt. Ross's most influential book, *Sin and Society,* published in 1907, solidified his progressive credentials for the next decade. Roosevelt wrote the introduction to the volume and gave Ross a national reputation as a leading academic progressive. When he moved on to Madison in 1905, he was noted for attacking big business in the United States and financier John D. Rockefeller. Although his international books increased his fame, it was his progressive works that solidified his standing in America. Foremost in Ross's belief system was the idea that there should be a worldwide spread of democracy without barriers. Democracy would then elevate the average man above inherited social status. History, in Ross's view, was a recounting of man's struggle to free himself from slavery and serfdom. Democracy stood at the zenith of this development and granted man inalienable rights. The ways to strengthen democracy were through education, low birthrates, industrial abundance, improved communications, and increased leisure time. Ross felt the dignity of the average citizen would be enhanced through education, smaller family size, and technological improvement. The means of Ross's equation were democracy strengthening people and people then strengthening democracy, with the end result of living in a better world based on progressive ideals.

Supporting Farmers. Ross supported industrial democracy in easing the struggle for food and shelter while producing greater wealth. He believed this system provided greater opportunities for the common man and creative individual. Ross's own ties were to rural America, but he enjoyed the dynamic role the city and industry played in fostering human progress and comfort. He held the traditional progressive notion of the West being the land of rugged individualism, similar to Teddy Roosevelt's own view and public persona. In this spirit, he approved of efforts to strengthen the farmer's role in society. He supported the Grange, Farmers' Alliance, Farmers' Union, and agricultural legislation, all as means of securing a greater share of the national wealth for the farmer.

Sympathy for the Factory Worker. The assembly line worker aroused Ross's sympathy. He expressed concern for the quality of the factory worker's life. The scholar worried about the erosion of spiritual values in the family and the rising rates of divorce, adultery, and desertion. Others would later express similar concerns about the worker's life and implement social welfare programs through the company. Henry Ford's famous five-dollar day had strong sociological overtones. Ross looked at the modern factory and saw economic insecurity, a lack of recreational opportunities, and threats to the worker's physical health. Ross could understand alcoholism in people "who scrape pig bristles sixty hours a week and live in mean, dingy little houses" and "seek the ruddy glow of the saloon's good fellowship and drink to forget." Equally depressing was the plight of the female worker.

Commercialization. Ross advocated humanitarian and practical measures to improve workers' lives. He favored legislation to install safety devices in factories, outlaw child labor, limit working hours, establish a minimum wage for women, and award unemployment compensation. Ross called the evils industrialism and capitalism brought to American life "commercialization," which resulted from the intensity of corporate ownership, social and economic stratification, and a growing impersonality between the producer and the consumer. Ross wanted formal controls and regulatory devices installed to thwart aggressive businessmen. Mobilizing religion, public opinion, law, elected officials, experts, and scholars, he believed, would help curb the unsavory practices of corporate America.

Honest Competition. Ross feared that unfair competition in business would increasingly concentrate wealth in the hands of the few and put an end to democratic institutions. Instead, he wanted to steer the middle ground and save capitalism from itself. He believed in Woodrow Wilson's New Freedom and the economic theories of Henry Carter Adams and John Bates Clark, both of which argued for regulating competition in order to preserve it. Honest competition would allow the virtuous, hardworking, and frugal citizen a way up the economic ladder.

Famous Progressive Activist. Edward Alsworth Ross became wealthy and famous by expounding the progressive view with a clarity and elegance few could claim. He perfectly embodied the ideas of the movement and touched upon most of the issues elected officials, unions, and corporate leaders had to deal with throughout the 1910s. A pioneer in economics and sociology and a crusading public reformer, Ross's influence reverberated through the decade.

Source:
Julius Weinberg, *Edward Alsworth Ross and the Sociology of Progressivism* (Madison: State Historical Society of Wisconsin, 1972).

PEOPLE IN THE NEWS

Emily Greene Balch wrote *Our Slavic Fellow Citizens* (1910), the classic study of Slavic immigration; helped found the National Women's Trade Union League; and campaigned for minimum wage legislation.

Historian **Charles A. Beard** published two influential books, *An Economic Interpretation of the Constitution of the United States* (1913) and *Economic Origins of Jeffersonian Democracy* (1915). Beard emphasized an economic interpretation of history and the need to use historical research as a means of reform. He resigned from Columbia University in 1917 in protest over the dismissal of three faculty members who opposed America's involvement in World War I. He later helped found the New School for Social Research in 1919.

On 25 January 1915 the first transcontinental telephone call was made by **Alexander Graham Bell** in New York to **Dr. Thomas A. Watson** in San Francisco. Bell said, "Mr. Watson, come here, I want you."

In 1914 **Jacqueline Cochrane**, the inventor of the dishwasher, introduced a home model. The home dishwasher did not catch on immediately because of the lack of enough hot water in most homes, but Cochrane's company later merged with another to form the successful Kitchenaid Company.

Mary Elisabeth Dreier served as president of the New York chapter of the National Women's Trade Union League from 1906 to 1914. She later turned her attention to the suffrage movement and chaired the New York City Suffrage Party.

Political economist and Yale professor **Irving Fisher** was a skilled mathematical economist and the founding president of the Econometrics Society. Fisher studied income, wealth, and capital stock and saw the link between inflation and interest rates.

Radical and labor leader **Elizabeth Gurley Flynn** helped organize a strike of twenty thousand textile workers in Lawrence, Massachusetts, in 1912 with birth control advocate **Margaret Sanger**. The workers endured beatings and police attacks, but the strike ended with wage concessions for the returning workers.

On 4 December 1915 **Henry Ford** and a delegation of peace advocates sailed from New York to Europe "to try to get the boys out of the trenches and back to their homes by Christmas Day" and stop World War I. Ford returned to the United States, unsuccessful, on 22 December.

Anarchists and labor activists **Emma Goldman** and **Alexander Berkman** were each sentenced to a two-year imprisonment and fined $10,000 on 7 July 1917 for interfering with the registration of soldiers. The Supreme Court upheld the decision on 14 January 1918.

William Dudley "Big Bill" Haywood believed in industrial rather than craft unionism and in 1905 chaired the convention that created the radical Industrial Workers of the World (IWW). He played a leading role in several major strikes in the 1910s, and the federal government prosecuted him and other IWW leaders for conspiracy to sabotage the war effort. Haywood fled to the Soviet Union and died in Moscow.

David F. Houston served as secretary of agriculture in the Wilson administration (1912–1920). He expanded the department's activities and administered programs to help farmers.

Life magazine proposed in 1910 that **J. P. Morgan** was so powerful that he should be crowned U.S. monarch and buy Europe. Morgan asserted his influence by serving on hundreds of corporate boards across the nation.

National Cash Register Company president **J. H. Patterson** and twenty-eight other officials were found guilty in violation of the Sherman Act on 13 February 1913 in Cincinnati and on 17 February received prison sentences ranging from three months to one year. Patterson was sent to prison for one year and fined $51,000.

In 1914 inventor **Mary Phelps Jacob** (later known as **Caresse Crosby**) obtained the first patent for a brassiere. She got the idea by tying together two handkerchiefs with ribbon and cord to substitute for her bulky and heavy corset. Sales were initially slow, and within a few years she sold the rights for $1,500 to a company that went on to make $15 million during the next thirty years.

On 14 May 1913 **John D. Rockefeller** donated $100 million to the Rockefeller Foundation, founded in 1910. It was the single largest philanthropic act in the history of the country.

IWW leader **Frank Tannenbaum** and 189 followers were arrested on 4 March 1914 for invading churches in New York City. On 27 March he was sentenced to one year imprisonment.

Texas lawyer and reformer **Hortense Ward** lobbied successfully in 1913 for state laws guaranteeing married women's property rights, workmen's compensation, and a fifty-four-hour workweek for women. The law concerning property rights is nicknamed the "Hortense Ward Act."

DEATHS

Alexander Agassiz, 75, scientist and engineer, 27 March 1910.

Benjamin Altman, 73, merchant and art collector, founder and chairman of B. Altman and Company, a New York department store, 7 October 1913.

John D. Archbold, 68, president of the Standard Oil Company of New Jersey, 5 December 1916.

George F. Baer, 71, president of the Philadelphia and Reading Railroad, 26 April 1914.

James Gordon Bennett, 77, newspaper publisher, owner of the *New York Herald,* 14 May 1918.

Charlotte Blair, 56, industrial manufacturer, founder and director of the American Cast Iron Pipe Company, 1917.

Samuel Billings Capen, 71, merchant and trustee of Wellesley College, 29 January 1914.

John G. Carlisle, 74, lawyer and statesman, former U.S. secretary of the treasury (1893–1896), 31 July 1910.

Andrew Carnegie, 83, industrialist who founded one of the world's largest steel companies; philanthropist who endowed educational programs, the Carnegie library system, and the Carnegie Endowment for Peace, 11 August 1919.

Robert J. Collier, 42, editor and publisher, *Collier's Weekly,* 8 November 1918.

Katherine Coman, 58, economic historian and professor at Wellesley College; he wrote *Economic Beginnings of the Far West* (1911), 11 January 1915.

Charles A. Conant, 54, international financial expert; he studied monetary reform in Mexico, Nicaragua, and the Philippines, 4 July 1915.

Theodore Cooper, 80, engineer, construction engineer for New York Public Library and the Manhattan Bridge, 24 August 1919.

Samuel D. Coykendall, 75, railroad president, 14 January 1913.

Charles H. Cramp, 85, shipbuilder and naval architect; he designed the *Maine, New York, Indiana,* and *Massachusetts* battleships, 1913.

Zenas Crane, 77, paper manufacturer, Crane and Company, 17 December 1917.

Thomas Y. Crowell, 80, publisher, 29 July 1915.

Samuel Cupples, 81, merchant, manufacturer, and philanthropist; his Samuel Cupples and Company was the largest woodenware dealer in the United States, 1912.

Daniel De Leon, 62, Socialist Labor Party leader, helped organize the Industrial Workers of the World (IWW), 11 May 1914.

John F. Dryden, 72, U.S. senator from New Jersey (1902–1907) and founder and president of Prudential Insurance Company of America, 24 November 1911.

Hiram Duryea, 80, merchant and president of the National Starch Company, 5 May 1914.

George W. Elkins, 61, capitalist and vice president of the Vulcanite Portland Cement Company, 21 October 1919.

Stephen Benton Elkins, 70, wealthy mine and railroad owner, U.S. secretary of war (1891–1893), U.S. senator from West Virginia (1895–1911), and sponsor of the Mann-Elkins Act (1910) strengthening the Interstate Commerce Commission and regulating railroad rates, 4 January 1911.

Joseph Fels, 61, soap manufacturer who devoted time and fortune to the worldwide spread of Henry George's Single Tax doctrine, 22 February 1914.

Henry M. Flagler, 83, financier and associate of John D. Rockefeller and partner in Standard Oil who established steamship service to Key West and built resorts and hotels in the United States and Caribbean, 20 May 1913.

Benjamin O. Flower, 60, reform editor and author, 24 December 1918.

Charles Lang Freer, 63, capitalist and art collector; he was active in the organization of the American Car and Foundry Company and donated the Freer Gallery in Washington, D.C., 25 September 1919.

Henry Clay Frick, 69, chairman of Carnegie Steel Company, he was later associated with J. P. Morgan in the organization of the United States Steel Corporation and served as its director, 2 December 1919.

Washington Gladden, 82, minister and editor who served a term on the Columbus, Ohio, city council (1900–1902) and fought for the welfare of industrial workers, 2 July 1918.

Hetty Green, 81, world's richest woman, turned a $10 million inheritance into a $100 million fortune; nicknamed "the Witch of Wall Street," 3 July 1916.

James B. Hammond, 73, inventor and manufacturer of typewriters, 27 January 1913.

James Harper, 61, publisher, 26 August 1916.

John W. Harper, 84, publisher, 14 August 1915.

John Rogers Hegeman, 74, president of the Metropolitan Life Insurance Company, 8 April 1919.

James J. Hill, 77, railroad financier and president of the Great Northern Railroad, one of the first transcontinental carriers, 29 May 1916.

John A. Hill, 57, publisher and president of McGraw-Hill Book Company, 24 January 1916.

Tom L. Johnson, 57, mayor of Cleveland, political reformer, and industrialist who bought streetcar companies and steel mills, 10 April 1911.

Eben Jordan, 58, merchant, president of Jordan, Marsh and Company, and president of the Boston Opera Company and the New England Conservatory of Music, 1 August 1916.

Francis H. Lee, 77, banker, 7 October 1913.

Miriam Florence Leslie, 78, publisher, feminist, and philanthropist, 18 September 1914.

Craig Lippincott, 64, publisher, president of J. B. Lippincott and Company, 6 April 1911.

James McCrae, 65, former president of the Pennsylvania Railroad, 28 March 1913.

John Griffin McCullough, 80, former governor of Vermont (1902–1904), former president of Chicago and Erie Railroad, and director of Lackawanna Steel Company, 1915.

James McCutcheon, 72, merchant, 20 July 1914.

John R. McLean, 67, newspaper publisher, 9 June 1916.

Darius Ogden Mills, 84, banker and president of the Bank of California at San Francisco; he founded "Mills' Hotels," where people with low incomes could get board and lodging, 3 January 1910.

John Purroy Mitchel, 38, politician and reformer, mayor of New York City (1913–1917) who died while training for service in World War I, 6 July 1918.

J. P. Morgan, 76, financier and capitalist, symbol of the "money trust" in the 1910s, and one of the most powerful men in America, 31 March 1913.

Frances Estelle Moulton, 58, president of Limerick National Bank; she was the first woman to serve as a national bank president in New England, 1 June 1919.

Edgar Gardner Murphy, 44, minister and education reformer who organized the first extensive body of literature on child labor and founded the National Child Labor Committee (1904), 23 June 1913.

Francis G. Newlands, 69, politician and progressive reformer, U.S. senator from Nevada (1901–1917); he was instrumental in the creation of the Federal Trade Commission, Interstate Commerce Commission, and the Adamson Eight-Hour Day Act, 24 December 1917.

Robert C. Ogden, 77, merchant and philanthropist, 6 August 1913.

John S. Ogilvie, 67, publisher, 9 February 1910.

Robert M. Oliphant, 93, former railroad president, 3 May 1918.

Harrison Gray Otis, 80, newspaper owner and publisher; he used his *Los Angeles Times* paper as a conservative force against progressivism; his open-shop stance led to the famous bombings of his building, 30 July 1917.

Walter Hines Page, 63, diplomat and publisher, 21 December 1918.

Robert Treat Paine, 75, philanthropist, 11 August 1910.

Joseph Pulitzer, 64, newspaper owner and journalist, an originator of "yellow journalism" and sensationalism, 29 October 1911.

Ellis H. Roberts, 90, former U.S. secretary of the treasury (1897–1905), 8 January 1918.

Harriet Jane Robinson, 86, merchant, writer, and activist, 1911.

Charles G. Roebling, 69, engineer, 5 October 1918.

Richard Sears, 50, mail-order merchant, advertising innovator, and founder of Sears, Roebuck department store, 28 September 1914.

Isaac N. Seligman, 62, banker and philanthropist, president of J. and W. Seligman and Company, 30 September 1917.

James Seligman, 92, banker, 20 August 1916.

Charles H. Steinway, 62, piano manufacturer, 30 October 1919.

James Stillman, 67, banker and president of National City Bank, 15 March 1918.

Willard Dickerman Straight, diplomat and financier; with his wife, Dorothy, he founded *New Republic* magazine, 2 December 1918.

Josiah Strong, 69, minister and author, he wanted to use liberal Christianity as a means of social reform, but based on Anglo-Saxon superiority; apologist for imperialism and immigration restriction, 28 April 1916.

William Graham Sumner, 70, political economist and writer and defender of laissez-faire and political/economic reforms; he wanted to eliminate the protective tariff, 12 April 1910.

Frederick W. Taylor, 59, engineer, inventor, writer, and founder of the scientific management movement popularized in the 1910s, 21 March 1915.

Catherine Waite, 84, real estate and building executive, 1913.

Sarah Breedlove "Madame C. J." Walker, 52, millionaire; she sold cosmetics and hair straighteners to black women and employed three thousand "Walker Agents" who sold products door-to-door; she also contributed money to the NAACP and women's scholarships at the Tuskegee Institute.

George Westinghouse, 67, engineer, inventor, and founder of Westinghouse Electric Company, 12 March 1914.

Walter Edward Weyl, 46, progressive economist and founding editor of *New Republic*, 9 November 1919.

Peter A. B. Widener, 80, financier and art collector; street-railway owner in Pittsburgh, Baltimore, and Chicago; and an organizer of the United States Steel Company and the American Tobacco Company, 6 November 1915.

Wilbur Wright, 45, inventor and aviator; along with his brother Orville he engineered the first successful flight in a motor-powered airplane, 30 May 1912.

PUBLICATIONS

Leonard P. Ayres, *The War with Germany: A Statistical Summary* (Washington, D.C.: Government Printing Office, 1919);

Roger W. Babson, *W. B. Wilson and the Department of Labor* (New York: Brentano, 1919);

Ernest L. Bogart, *Direct and Indirect Costs of the Great World War* (Washington, D.C.: Carnegie Endowment, 1919);

Maurice J. Clark and others, *Readings in the Economics of War* (Chicago: University of Chicago Press, 1918);

Horace B. Drury, *Scientific Management: A History and Criticism* (New York: Columbia University Press, 1915);

Richard T. Ely, *Property and Contract in their Relations to the Distribution of Wealth* (Port Washington, N.Y.: Kennikat Press, 1914);

H. L. Gantt, *Work, Wages and Profits: Their Influence on the Cost of Living* (New York: Engineering Magazine, 1910);

Frank B. Gilbreth and Lillian M. Gilbreth, *Applied Motion Study* (New York: Sturgis & Walton, 1917);

Gilbreth and Gilbreth, *Fatigue Study* (New York: Sturgis & Walton, 1916);

William I. Hull, *Preparedness: The American Versus the Military Programme* (New York: Fleming H. Revell, 1916);

Walter Lippmann, *Drift and Mastery: An Attempt to Diagnose the Current Unrest* (New York: Kennerley, 1914);

Andrew C. McLaughlin, *America and Britain* (New York: Dutton, 1919);

Thorstein Veblen, *The Higher Learning in America: A Memorandum on the Conduct of Universities by Business Men* (New York: Huebsch, 1918);

Veblen, *The Instinct of Workmanship, and the State of the Industrial Arts* (New York: Kelley, 1914);

Gordon S. Watkins, *Labor Problems and Labor Administration in the United States During the World War* (Urbana: University of Illinois Press, 1919);

Walter E. Weyl, *The New Democracy: An Essay on Certain Political and Economic Tendencies in the United States* (New York: Macmillan, 1912).

EDUCATION

by HARRIETT WILLIAMS

CONTENTS

Sidebars and tables are listed in italics.

1910

- Thirty-nine percent of undergraduates in U.S. colleges and universities are women.

- Admissions directors at Columbia, Harvard, Yale, Princeton, Dartmouth, and Amherst begin discussions about the dramatically increasing number of Jewish male applicants.

- Only eight states have school attendance of 90 percent or higher of children ages six to fourteen: four are in New England, and the remainder are in Iowa, Nebraska, Michigan, and New York.

- Examinations by local officials for teaching certificates are replaced in all states by examinations conducted by state boards or state departments of education.

Feb. The *Journal of Educational Psychology,* a forum for the research of educational psychologists, is founded.

Sept. Dewey, Oklahoma, opens the nation's first nongraded school, with students in grades one to twelve working independently.

The Commission on University Extension Courses is formed by a union of eight Boston institutions of higher education.

The census reports that 550,000 children ages ten to fifteen are at work in factories, shops, and in other nonagricultural positions.

1911

- The average cost of books per pupil enrolled in public schools is about seventy-eight cents.

- The Bureau of Education announces that 1,844 public and society libraries in the United States have been established; 1,005 of these are school and college libraries, and the number of volumes in their collections has increased by twenty million since 1908.

- Tuition at Harvard is $150 per year; at Adelphi $180; and at Colgate $60.

- Research in educational statistics focused on eighth-grade composition reveals that only 60 percent of the eighth graders in Hackensack, New Jersey, schools were able to write an "acceptable" composition on "A Day of My Life" in fifteen minutes.

- New York City public schools offer evening classes in courses such as terra-cotta work, gas and steam engines, boilermaking, printing, and proofreading, signaling a growing emphasis on adult and vocational education.

- Rochester, New York, establishes a Bureau of Research and Efficiency to compile statistical information on public schools.

1912

- A series of conferences on English in the Public Schools of New England, held in Cambridge, Massachusetts, concludes that the study of English grammar and composition in the schools is unsatisfactory.

- In Cambridge, Massachusetts, professors in the Psychology Department at Harvard are so displeased with the academic skills of entering freshmen that they devise an experiment to teach 120 entering freshmen how to improve their study skills.

- New Orleans establishes a Bureau of Research and Efficiency to compile statistics on public schools.

- A study of Wesleyan University graduates reveals that 33 percent had found noteworthy success, defined by their being listed in *Who's Who.* Researchers cite this study as evidence that a college degree is the ticket to success.

- A total of 2,569 students attend New York City evening trade schools.

- The American Federation of Labor announces its position that the technical and industrial education of workers in trades should be a public function and therefore part of the public school system.

1913

- The Bureau of Education distributes 112 issues of its *Bulletin*, more than one million separate copies, to school officials.

- The annual report of the Commission on Education, a public commission, includes sections on "The Junior High School," "Montessori Schools in the U.S.," "Vocational Education," "School Surveys," and "Education for Special Classes of Children."

- The average length of a term for public schools is 158.1 days.

- Forty thousand people enroll in the University of Wisconsin extension departments, including those reached by correspondence courses.

- For the first time, the state of California provides free elementary-school books for all pupils.

16–28 Aug. The annual convention of the National Education Association features keynote addresses on "The Junior College," "Military Training in the Schools," "Sex Morality and Sex Hygiene," "Education of the Negro," and "Education of the Japanese."

1914

- The Bureau of Education estimates that total costs of U.S. public education are $750 million. This amount is less than one-third the national spending for alcoholic beverages and only three times the amount paid for admissions to movie theaters that year.

- Harvard, Yale, Princeton, Columbia, and Cornell announce significant tuition increases. Harvard students in mechanical, electrical, and civil engineering see tuition rise from $150 to $250 a year when Harvard and the Massachusetts Institute of Technology agree to cooperate in offering certain courses.

- Kansas enacts a law providing for the purchase of books for all elementary-school students at a cost to the state of $230,000.

1915

- About one-half of the nation's twenty million schoolchildren attend rural schools.

- Bureaus of Research and Efficiency are established in Kansas City, Boston, Oakland, and Detroit.

- The National Association of Directors of Research is organized.

- New York University offers a new two-year degree program leading toward the degree of doctor of public health.

- Vermont adopts the junior-high-school plan, establishing one hundred separate school buildings to house grades seven to ten.

- Teachers in Minnesota are beneficiaries of a pension bill that allows them to retire after twenty years with an annual pension partially funded by a special state tax.

- A court of inquiry established to investigate a cheating scandal at the United States Naval Academy at Annapolis, Maryland, finds that 63 percent of the first class of midshipmen (seniors) had seen prior copies of examination papers. The affair was recommended to the Navy Department for further review.

1 Apr. A conference is held in Saint Louis on "The Problem of the Feeble-Minded in its Educational and Social Bearings."

July The Boston Board of Health discontinues medical examinations of school-children after the school committee appoints its own doctors to conduct exams.

21 Aug. National Education Day is held at the Panama-Pacific Exposition in San Francisco.

Sept. The Supreme Court of Arkansas declares unconstitutional an act passed by the legislature appropriating $50,000 of common school funds to build high schools.

16 Sept. Stanford University hosts a conference on War, Peace, and International Polity.

11 Nov. The first National Congress on University Extensions meets in Philadelphia.

Dec. In New York City the American Association of University Professors (AAUP) is chartered. John Dewey serves as the first president. One of the organization's first charges is to draft a statement on academic freedom.

1916

- The American Federation of Teachers (AFT), a teacher-only labor union of the AFL, is founded with the aid of John Dewey; the union hopes to fight for the right to create bargaining units in school districts.

- Five states still have no compulsory-education laws.

- The War Aims Course is developed at many American colleges. Its purpose is to explore the issues that are involved in World War I, then called the Great War.

- A study in the schools of Cleveland, Ohio, shows that 27.6 percent of all schoolchildren are "laggards" and that every eighth child repeats at least one grade; 50 percent withdraw before the fifth grade; and 75 percent withdraw before the eighth grade.

- The Children's Bureau of the U.S. Department of Labor publishes a compilation of the exact terms of all child-labor laws enacted up to 1 January 1916.

- A Maryland study finds that two-fifths of all secondary-school teachers in that state are adequately trained; their salaries range from $271 per year in Saint Mary's County to $662 in Baltimore County.

- New York University establishes the first full curriculum (twenty-four courses) to train teachers to work with "mental defectives."

- A study published in *School and Society* cites statistics to support its claim that the country is in grave danger because not enough college-educated women are marrying.

1 Jan. John Dewey, president of the American Association of University Professors, approves a report by the Committee on Academic Freedom and Tenure. The report supports the right of those in the academic profession to speak freely on public issues.

12 Feb. Carnegie Hall in New York City is filled to capacity for a posthumous tribute to the work of Booker T. Washington.

18 Feb. The Emily Blackwell Ward at the New York Infirmary for Women is dedicated. Blackwell was a pioneer in medical education for women.

28 Dec. Twenty-two papers on the subject of mental testing are read at the annual meeting of the American Psychological Association in Chicago.

1917

- All the former slave states except Missouri and West Virginia have established county training schools for African American students by this year.

- The Smith-Hughes Act provides federal grants to the states to prepare students in trade, industry, home economy, and agriculture.

- The state school board in Minnesota rules that pupils and teachers not already immune to smallpox must be vaccinated.

- The school board of Pittsburgh, Pennsylvania, decides to pay the salaries of two women teachers who married in defiance of board policy barring women teachers from marrying.

- In response to wartime patriotic fervor and xenophobia, evening schools open nationwide for "Americanization" classes for immigrants.

- In Winnetka, Illinois, an innovation in school administration occurs when a student council is established to make and enforce school regulations, try pupils for infractions, and fix punishments at New Trier Township High School.

- Cleveland, Ohio, votes to spend $2 million to erect four junior high schools that will be furnished with music rooms, print shops, wood-carving and carpentry shops, botany rooms with greenhouses, drawing rooms, domestic science and household-arts rooms, gymnasiums, and swimming pools.

May Final exams in civics at numerous high schools require students to bring in and analyze copies of President Wilson's 2 April address to Congress seeking a declaration of war.

Sept. Washington University Dental School changes its three-year course to a four-year course.

1918

- President Woodrow Wilson authorizes the Bureau of Education to assist the state officers of education to find teachers for normal, secondary, and elementary schools because of the "national emergency" in teacher shortages.

- The Division of Maps of the Library of Congress issues a several-hundred-page catalogue to schools, titled *A List of Atlases and Maps Applicable to the Present War*.

Jan. The Bureau of Extension of the University of North Carolina announces a series of thirty-eight free lectures on the war to North Carolina communities.

The *Pasadena Star News* publishes "The Great War," its lesson on World War I originally prepared for the Pasadena high schools.

History Teacher's Magazine establishes a public-service information bureau on World War I.

Feb. Indiana high-school boys and girls are urged to form Patriotic Service Leagues to coordinate war activities in the schools.

16 Mar. The Carnegie Institute of Technology hosts a conference on "How Can the Elementary, Secondary and Higher Education Schools Adapt Subject Matter and Methods So As to Help Win the War?"

Apr. The Federal Board for Vocational Education issues a bulletin on mechanical and technological training for men conscripted into the armed services.

5 Apr. The U.S. Bureau of Education issues *Guidelines on the Schools in Wartime*.

14 June On Flag Day Americanization meetings are held nationwide to emphasize the need for educating recent immigrants in American language, citizenship, and ideals.

Oct. The Federal Board for Vocational Education issues an appeal to disabled soldiers and sailors in hospitals to secure an education so that they will be able to lead independent lives once the war is over.

School superintendents and boards are warned by the U.S. Commission on Education to prepare for the next garden season now by employing more garden teachers to step up the programs immediately so that food shortages will not develop.

1 Oct. At 516 colleges and universities throughout the country, 140,000 male students simultaneously become student soldiers when they are inducted into a program called the Students' Army Training Corps (SATC).

Nov. An article titled "The Repulsiveness of the German State" is published in *The Historical Outlook*, a journal for historians, yet another example of the convergence of scholarship and propaganda during the war.

1919

- John Dewey and several colleagues found the New School for Social Research in New York City in an attempt to create a truly independent university run by educators themselves.

- The U.S. Bureau of Education issues a bulletin on "Opportunities at College for Returning Soldiers," a list of institutions and facts about courses of study, tuition fees, and scholarships at each of the nation's colleges.

- The National Education Association (NEA) Committee on History and Education for Citizenship in Schools publishes a model national curriculum for "securing higher intelligence in regard to world affairs and deeper, more fundamental appreciation of the duties and responsibilities of citizenship."

- The NEA campaign for higher teachers' salaries touts New York City's new minimum-wage policy: twenty-one thousand teachers in grades one to six have minimum salaries of $1,005; in grades seven to twelve, $1,350.

- Cleveland's Americanization Committee issues a pamphlet explaining how to nationalize aliens without making them lose their connections with their homelands. The Cleveland Museum of Art stages a Homelands Art Exhibit that features landscapes of twenty-four countries.

Jan. The Progressive Education Association is formed; members cite their dissatisfaction with the "inflexibilities" of traditional schools.

14 Feb. The Agricultural Historical Association is organized "to publish research in the history of agriculture."

Mar. The Women's Committee of the Council of National Defense issues a seventy-seven-page bibliography titled *Women in the War*.

OVERVIEW

Americans Develop Original Theory. Before the second decade of the twentieth century, American educators looked mainly to Europe for the theories to support their concepts of education. Educational philosopher Horace Mann had warned that industrial capitalism after the Civil War threatened educational opportunity for many Americans, but most educators before 1910 solidly arrayed themselves with the forces of conservatism and resisted radical reform. After 1910, however, with a rapidly changing economy and wave after wave of immigration, the American public increasingly found traditional European approaches to education a poor fit. What was needed in this country, many reformers argued, was a form of education that prepared the masses and their children to win a portion of the nation's wealth and mount the socio-economic ladder as high as possible. The calls for reform came from diverse voices and places; but it took John Dewey, psychologist and philosopher, to synthesize the ideas of various reform movements and give them cogent, dynamic expression.

Democracy and Education. One of the most significant educational events of the era was the publication in 1916 of John Dewey's "epoch-making" volume *Democracy and Education.* Hailed by one scholar as "the most important treatise since Plato's *Republic,* the work presented a thorough and systematic philosophy of the educational implications of a democracy. Before this book, few Americans had understood the broad and enduring meaning of late-nineteenth- and early-twentieth-century educational trends; furthermore, Dewey's grasp of the science of psychology gave his work a solid intellectual grounding lacking in the work of earlier reformers. Dewey's theories also appealed to pragmatic businessmen and politicians when he argued that a "stratified society wherein a sharing of ideas was limited to the educated select ruling class must depend in time of crisis on the intellectual and moral resources of a very restricted few." On the other hand, a society with many channels of communication among all its various groups could "mobilize resources of initiative and inventiveness limited only by the numbers and native talents of the whole body politic." Dewey convinced Americans in power, not just educators, that educational reform could benefit the national economy; that democratic education was a logical outgrowth of a society "already made interdependent by the pathways that manufacturing, commerce, transportation and communication in an age of science had already worn down."

Rapid Progress. Once most Americans as well as educators were persuaded that the country would benefit from educational reform, change came rapidly. According to educational historian Edward Reisner in *Twenty-Five Years of American Education* (1924), more educational progress occurred in the decade 1910 to 1919 "than in any period of equal length during our history as a nation and, perhaps, than in all the years of our history preceding." New methods and ideas flourished as schools adapted their curricula to the economic and social needs of children with various aspirations and from varied backgrounds. A voluminous body of educational literature was written; dramatic new work in the scientific study of intelligence and learning took place; and the preparation of teachers was revamped and strengthened. Intensified public interest in the content and quality of the school experience led to the spectacular development of high schools, the growth of technical and higher education, the development of college and university departments of education, and the conversion of so-called normal schools into degree-granting institutions. The reform wave particularly changed high schools by introducing the development of the junior high school and by modifying the secondary curriculum to provide much more extensive vocational training. Although reform in these years was wide-ranging, the American system of local control of schools guaranteed that some systems, particularly in the South and isolated rural areas, would not benefit from the new progressivism. Visiting educators from England, France, and Germany in 1914 were "amazed and amused" to find some American schools far in advance of their own, while others were still using "crude and primitive methods abandoned elsewhere."

Changes in Elementary Education. The concept of elementary education underwent fundamental revision in this decade, as educators increasingly agreed that the function of the elementary school was not merely to give pupils the tools of learning — the three Rs — but to provide the specific factual content necessary to help students succeed in society. Hallmarks of this conceptual change were the greater enrichment of classroom materials, better textbooks, and more practical content for classes. Moreover, the dominant method of instruction shifted from traditional memorization and recitation to methods most educators considered better adapted for younger children. During these years of experiment and change, psychology's scientific study of individual differences heightened educators' emphasis on individuality and strengthened a new demand that students be free to express that individuality. Perhaps as a consequence of what some historians have called the "growing cult of the child," school discipline tended to be significantly milder in this period than it had been in earlier years.

Growth in Secondary Schools. At the secondary level, the rapid and enormous growth in high-school enrollment — a 700 percent increase from 1890 to 1918 — necessitated dramatic changes that accelerated the forces of reform. As the 125,772 high-school graduates in 1910 nearly doubled to 248,199 in 1920, the shortage of existing facilities to house the growing numbers of adolescents triggered both a building boom and a reorganization of the structure of secondary education. Educators who had strengthened compulsory-attendance laws so fewer children would work after elementary school discovered that seventh, eighth, and ninth graders needed to be separated from the elementary schools so that these children could "explore their talents with a view toward selecting a suitable career." This need, combined with the severe shortages of building space, spurred the rise of the junior-high-school movement; by 1919 nearly every state had a building program providing for separate junior- and senior-high schools. Furthermore, the country's burgeoning high-school enrollment forced educators to ask fundamental questions about the nature and structure of the secondary curriculum. A report by the National Education Association (NEA), "Cardinal Principles of Secondary Education" (1918), published and distributed nationwide by the U.S. Office of Education, recommended that high schools reduce the emphasis on purely academic courses and make instruction more functional and pragmatic. The resulting changes in the secondary curriculum were exemplified by the substitution of functional for formal English grammar, direct methods of teaching foreign languages for more traditional methods, applied science for general science, applied mathematics for introductory mathematics, and community civics for traditional courses in history. It was the institutionalizing of industrial, agricultural, and commercial vocational studies, however, that signified the most dramatic change from the high schools of earlier years.

Status of Teachers. The decade 1910–1919 was marked by a severe shortage of teachers, even as teaching, long considered by many to be a relatively unattractive field, was increasingly regarded as a respected profession. Educational requirements for teachers in these years ranged from the bare minimum of an elementary education in some rural areas to a degree in education or some other field for teachers in progressive, urban districts. Pay scales varied wildly, from $100 annually for white female teachers in Little Rock, Arkansas, in 1918, to $1,850 for white male teachers in Cincinnati, Ohio, the same year. In the 1910s teaching continued to be an overwhelmingly female occupation. Male teachers generally were paid about three times the salaries of skilled workers. By 1915 female teachers had improved their wages, compared to laborers and skilled workers in rural areas, and made inroads in approximating the salaries of their male colleagues. The formation of the American Federation of Teachers (AFT) in 1916 signaled a growing professional awareness. (The AFT, affiliated with the AFL, did not adopt the strike as a policy tactic until many years later.) The feminist movement and the rising power of women suffragists led to salary schedules based on the cost of living, the number of professional degrees held, and the teacher's years of experience. In some states equal pay for female teachers was approved by 1919. By 1920 teaching in some parts of the United States was approaching the professional status of lawyers and doctors, if not in salary then at least in terms of establishing new standards of education and competence.

Growth in Higher Education. Students desiring higher education during the decade could choose from the following types of schools: old and distinguished colleges, such as the Ivy League schools, which had recently become universities with graduate departments; the emerging great state universities and land-grant colleges, such as Wisconsin and Michigan, whose extension programs served thousands of their citizens; the municipal colleges that were appearing in nearly every urban area; the growing numbers of vocational and technical colleges; the old-fashioned denominational schools with close ties to their religious backers; or the schools set aside for women and African Americans. "There is a college somewhere in America for everybody," a contemporary observer claimed. In 1910, 355,000 students were enrolled in universities; by 1918 the number had climbed to 441,000. Remarkably, by 1920 more than 598,000 university students were seeking degrees. Tangible evidence of the public's support for higher education was shown in the number of buildings erected on campuses during the era. Patrons, who preferred to have their donations take concrete form, donated millions to erect harmonious groups of buildings at the major universities. The Spanish Colonial buildings in red and yellow that characterize Stanford University (then Leland Stanford Junior University) were built during the decade, as was the unified group of five marble buildings that make up Harvard's medical school. In 1916 the Massachusetts Institute of Technology erected an entirely new site in the classical style on the banks of the Charles River in Cambridge. Campus life was changing as well. Fraternities, once outlawed, were thriving and multiplying, expanding their membership from 72,000 in 1900 to 270,000 (including some 30,000 women in Greek sororities) in

1920. These organizations conducted a building spree of chapter houses during the decade, and by 1920 more than eleven hundred Greek buildings worth more than $8 million had changed the face of American campuses.

Changes in Academia. Expansion of the curriculum accompanied the building boom. The number of students studying the classics grew modestly, but the number of students studying new subjects expanded much more rapidly. Before World War I a significant rise of the social sciences occurred on campuses nationwide. According to John Dewey, this "new body of studies" — economics, political science, and sociology — emerged from the moral philosophy curriculum. A schism soon developed between the modern humanists and the new social scientists. A student in the new field of sociology described the atmosphere in his discipline between 1900 and 1915 as "one of struggle for legitimacy against adversaries." Soon the new field of statistics and mental measurements evolved with dramatic implications for the status of research in many fields. Another new field emerged when some historians, who allied themselves with social scientists, began to use the methods of science in their work. Dubbed the "new history" in 1912 this field's scholars emphasized the present uses of the past, exploiting the practical utility of their discipline's ability to view the past for its use in "illuminating our own times." Regardless of their field, scholars at American colleges and universities during the decade fought for professional status, tenure, and academic freedom. The founding of the American Association of University Professors in 1915 signified a professionalization of scholarship that transcended disciplinary boundaries.

Education for Citizenship. Writers of the period reflected the public's growing faith in public education and linked the promise of economic and social mobility to the expanded opportunities for higher education. America had to educate and assimilate more than one million immigrants a year in the years just before World War I, yet as a postwar editorial read: "The Great War proved what had at times been questioned — that the U.S. was united. In spite of the diversity of racial elements and family connections with all the belligerent nationalities in Europe, the youth here responded with little hesitation to the call to arms. The process of Americanization is more complete than optimists had hoped. The chief credit for that goes to the public schools." Other commentators marveled that "The payroll of an American coal mine or steel mill today reads like an ethnological map of the Balkans, yet the children of workmen are thoroughly Americanized. Feuds of two thousand years, based on racial, religious and linguistic differences, have been wiped out in a single generation." Edward Slosson, in *The University of Today* (1920), mirrored this spirit of optimism and pride in American education, claiming that the system had "eliminated nationalistic and class distinctions so that *real* and personal distinctions may develop. The chief agency for this purpose has been the public school system." For many Americans, particularly African Americans, women, and recent immigrants, this rosy assessment ignored the fact that cultural uniformity was often imposed on a diverse population. Nevertheless, the decade was an era of substantial change and significant progress at every level of education in the United States.

Sources:

John Brubacher, *A History of the Problems of Education* (New York: McGraw-Hill, 1947);

Carol S. Gruber, *Mars and Minerva: World War I and the Uses of the Higher Learning in America* (Baton Rouge: Louisiana State University Press, 1975);

Edward Reisner, "Historical Background," in *Twenty-Five Years of American Education*, edited by I. L. Kandel (New York: Macmillan, 1924).

TOPICS IN THE NEWS

AMERICAN UNIVERSITIES AND WORLD WAR I

Faculties Support Allies. By 1917, when the United States finally intervened in the First World War, most American professors had long favored the Allied powers, primarily because the professors identified with England, but also because most of them saw the war as a genuine contest between good and evil. When President Woodrow Wilson and Congress declared war against the Central Powers, the widespread support from college professors was so enthusiastic that the *New Republic* editors in 1917 labeled the conflict "the thinking man's war" and remarked that "College professors, headed by a President who himself is a former professor, contributed more effectively to the decision to go to war than did farmers, businessmen, or politicians."

Contributions to the War Effort. Professors from all disciplines contributed to the American war effort. At Harvard emerging star chemistry scholar James Conant worked energetically to produce poison gas as well as the gas masks to ward it off. Academics in the social sciences and history were especially eager to serve. When in 1917 the editor of the *National History Review*, Franklin Jameson, organized the National Board for Historical Service, historians across the country wrote that they would "do anything and go anywhere to help the cause." These history professors helped shape public opinion by enlisting speakers to address war topics at high-school commencements and at summer-school courses for high-school teachers. They also prepared a bibliography on war subjects and collections of war prose and poetry for high-school teachers and sponsored essay contests for students and teachers.

Committee for Public Information. Historians and social scientists also contributed to the war effort by volunteering for work with the Committee on Public Information, the official governmental agency that produced tracts and other public announcements aimed at uniting Americans behind the government war policy. Scholars, including some of the best professors in their fields, were enlisted to write "scholarly treatises" that served as propaganda promoting the Wilson administration's view of the war. Agency files indicate there was more academic talent

WAR POLICY IN SECONDARY SCHOOLS

In 1917 the Council of National Defense issued a statement of principles to guide American secondary schools during World War I and added recommendations for adjusting to the rapidly changing economic and social conditions. The document, titled "The War and the Schools," began:

Preamble: In the crisis that confronts us the schools of the Nation should have the single thought to serve their country in the best possible way and in the full extent of their resources, not only in the present emergency but in the years to follow.

Statement of Principles: We accordingly believe, first, that it is of supreme importance that the educational resources of the Nation, and particularly our great public school systems, shall be maintained as fully and completely as possible, in order that our country may not again go thru the sad experiences following the Civil War, or of some of the nations of Europe at the present time, and that the supply of trained and educated men and women may not be largely cut off during the war and after its close. We believe, second, that it is highly desirable that our schools and colleges shall furnish during the war a continuous supply of men fitted to take positions of leadership in the army, in the industrial world, and in social service, and that to that end students should be encouraged to continue their training up to the point of greatest efficiency rather than to enter service prematurely. We believe, third, that the schools should make any changes in their courses of study and methods of instruction that will fit their students to share more effectively in meeting the present crisis and our future needs. We believe, fourth, that in all schools special emphasis should be laid on instruction in thrift.

Source: "The War and the Schools," *American School Board Journal*, 51 (July 1917): 76.

Members of the Student Army Training Corps in combat practice at the University of Denver, 1918

ready and willing to serve the government by writing than could be put to use. University scholars also assisted in a government project to implement the Espionage Act against the foreign-language press of America. More than fifty scholars nationwide were assigned to read foreign-language newspapers in their geographic areas daily and submit verbatim translations of editorials and articles "which might be construed as advocating insubordination or opposition to the U.S. government." The professors' reports influenced decisions about whether to enforce the Espionage Act against particular foreign-language papers.

Campuses and the War. By early 1918 the War Department had enlisted 157 colleges, universities, and technical and trade schools to provide training in such subjects as radiotelegraphy, automobile repair, and sheet metal work to noncollege drafted men. These men were drilled by army officers detached to the schools, and the host institutions were paid a price per man per day for housing and subsistence. In the case of college men, all land-grant institutions had been required under the provisions of the Morrill Act of 1862 to provide military training; accordingly, a mechanism for war preparations was already in place at these schools. In the fall of 1918, the rest of the nation's universities gave their full support to the war effort by turning their intellectual and physical

resources over to the War Department and becoming centers for military training. On 1 October at 516 colleges and universities throughout the country, 140,000 male students simultaneously became student-soldiers when they were inducted into a program called the Students' Army Training Corps (SATC). These men were considered to be on furlough status without pay, not to be called into active service until they received their degrees or turned twenty-one, whichever came first. They were required to spend ten hours per week in military training and six weeks in summer camps in intensive training. The theory behind the SATC was that the army would utilize the buildings, equipment, and organization of American colleges for the selection and training of officer candidates and technical experts. The transformation of colleges into military camps carried over into the classrooms, and nearly every academic department adapted its curriculum to the SATC. Whatever regular courses remained were populated by "women, undersized Jews and cripples," claimed Harvard historian W. S. Ferguson.

Repression. Colleges and universities, ideally sites for reasoned debate and honest disagreement, became hostile environments during the war for anyone who openly dissented from officially held views. Nicholas Murray Butler, the president of Columbia University, declared in

In 1911 Harvard College created a new entrance examination plan for candidates. If a young man's high-school record were approved by the Committee on Admission, he was required to present himself for four examinations — one in English, one in Latin (or, for students desiring the degree of S.B, either French or German), one in mathematics, and one in any of the following subjects except those previously tested: Greek, French, German, history, physics, or chemistry. Of these four examinations for applicants, the examination in English was considered especially significant: the new plan for this exam gave students three hours to complete the following tasks, and students were admonished to "write carefully: the quality of your English is even more important than your knowledge of the subject-matter."

Part A: Answer three of the following six questions:

1. Select from any play which you have read an important character who has one marked weakness, and show into what difficulties this weakness leads him.

2. Quote twenty consecutive lines of poetry and then tell very briefly why you think them good poetry.

3. Suppose a public library, wishing to interest people in good reading, to be composing brief descriptive lists of novels and essays. Suppose the first note to have run thus: " — *Treasure Island*, by Robert Louis Stevenson: an exciting romance of the sea, pirates, buried treasure and other adventures. John Silver, the cook, is one of the great characters in English prose fiction." Write similar brief descriptive notes for any three novels or books of essays that you have read, whether on the prescribed list or not.

4. Identify as many as you can of the characters on the following list by telling in which book each occurs and by describing each in two or three adjectives: Virginius, Sydney Carton, Jessica, Guinevere, "Poor Peter," Dunstan Cass, Madam Eglantine, Ichabod Crane, Malvolio, Squire Thornhill, Apollyon, Locksley.

5. What are the chief differences between prose and poetry?

6. Suppose that you found in one book the statement that Dr. Johnson's manners were very rude and in another book the statement that Dr. Johnson's manners were not rude. Tell as fully as you can what steps you would take and what general principles you would apply in deciding which of these statements were more nearly correct.

Part B: Write a composition on one of the following subjects. Plan your composition carefully, and pay special attention to paragraphing. Allow not less than one hour for this part of the paper.

7. Have you ever read a book which you enjoyed more than any of the books on the prescribed list? Why did you like it?

8. Write a character sketch of any person of your acquaintance who reminds you of any character in a book. Try to explain the resemblances as fully and vividly as you can.

9. Tell, in the form of a letter, the story of some vacation trip or adventure.

10. Write an essay on the sources and uses of rubber.

11. Write an essay on photographic lenses.

12. Tell, from the point of view of one of the chief characters, the story of some narrative poem.

Part C

13. In what period of English literature was this passage written? Why?

Avoid Extremes; and shun the fault of such,
Who still are pleas'd too little or too much.
At ev'ry trifle scorn to take offence,
That always shows great pride, or little sense;
Those heads, as stomachs, are not sure the best.

Source: Chester Noyes Greenough, "The New Plan of Admission in English to Harvard College," *English Journal,* 1 (December 1912): 364–368.

June 1917 that "what had been tolerated became intolerable now. What had been wrongheadedness was now sedition. What had been folly was now treason." Butler dismissed two members of Columbia's faculty, Professor Henry W. L. Dana and Professor James N. Cattell, one for having cooperated with several peace societies, the other for having petitioned Congress asking it to oppose the use of conscripts in the European war. For the duration of the war, and in the Red Scare that followed, those who held radical or unorthodox views were effectively silenced on most campuses, and the concept of academic freedom remained an unfulfilled promise for faculty and students alike.

Sources:

William Clyde DeVane, *Higher Education in Twentieth-Century America* (Cambridge, Mass.: Harvard University Press, 1965);

Carol S. Gruber, *Mars and Minerva: World War I and the Uses of Higher Learning in America* (Baton Rouge: Louisiana State University Press, 1975);

David M. Kennedy, *Over Here: The First World War and American Society* (New York: Oxford University Press, 1980);

Richard Norton Smith, *The Harvard Century: The Making of a University to a Nation* (New York: Simon & Schuster, 1986).

EMERGENCE OF THE MODERN UNIVERSITY

The Elective System. When streams of new students entered American colleges early in the century, they found most colleges in a state of disarray and poorly prepared to educate them. This situation was partially because of a fragmentation in the existing curricula. In the first years of the twentieth century, most colleges and universities had established an elective curriculum. Although Harvard was not the inventor of this system, the university, under the leadership of Charles W. Eliot, had become its chief proponent. Under the elective system students (even freshmen) had been free to study any courses they wanted, and their options had expanded exponentially. Old courses of study had been subdivided into many subjects, and new courses were added to the curriculum. Under the spectacular advances of science, for example, the old courses in natural philosophy were replaced by the whole range of sciences, just as old courses in political economy were subdivided into many different social sciences. These new fields allowed students to learn subjects in a way that was impossible in the old curriculum. However, there were no guarantees that students would choose wisely from the scores of elective choices, and, indeed, the majority of students took the easy and elementary courses, the popular lectures, the classes scheduled at convenient hours. As the example of Harvard's elective system spread throughout the nation, undergraduate scholarship reached a low point during the first decade of the century.

Curricular Changes. Most colleges soon realized they needed to encourage their students to utilize the new freedom of choice in subjects more wisely. Conditions began to improve at several prestigious schools, with

Woodrow Wilson, newly elected president at Princeton in 1902, in the lead. Wilson brought to Princeton fifty promising young scholars to teach the undergraduates in small discussion groups associated with their courses, a plan that promoted serious scholarship. Bryn Mawr became the first college to arrange the new material of learning into group requirements of courses. Then, at his inauguration as president of Harvard in 1909, A. Lawrence Lowell abandoned the elective system and instituted instead a system of distribution and concentration requirements in the curriculum, which soon became the practice followed in most colleges. This shift was the first step in creating a modern curriculum that educators hoped would serve contemporary America as well as the classical curriculum had served the eighteenth century.

The Modern University: Scholarship and Service. Some of the most influential institutions of higher education in the decade had been created as full-fledged universities. Johns Hopkins University and the University of Chicago, for example, provided models for graduate education and professional research. These universities established the modern notion of the importance of creating new knowledge, not merely passing along the best of the past. Both schools established university presses devoted to the advancement of learning and sponsored scholarly journals for the exchange and dissemination of emerging scholarship and research. Another group of large state universities, notably Michigan and Wisconsin, introduced another modern notion about higher education: that the state was obliged to provide higher education for all its citizens. In Michigan the state legislature made an annual grant from the state's tax revenues, allowing the school to have a firm financial footing that ensured its place among other prominent private institutions. Another modern precedent was set by Wisconsin, where the concerns of the state and the university became so intertwined that Wisconsin came to be called the "University State." Because the leaders of the University of Wisconsin envisioned service to the state population as its prime mission, the school provided experts for all aspects of agriculture, as well as for forests and utilities, banks, railroads, and governments.

University Extension. Wisconsin also provided a model for university extension work, making the resources of the university available throughout the state by supplying university courses, lectures, and library services. On the eve of World War I scores of university extension programs had been established in "an organized effort to give to the people not in college some of the advantages enjoyed by the one-half of one per cent who are able to attend campus classes." Columbia University enrolled some two thousand students in regular lectures and recitations leading to academic credit; Pennsylvania State College had forty-eight hundred students in correspondence courses leading to a B.A. degree; the University of Michigan counted more than seventy thousand men and women in attendance at more than three hundred lec-

William Heard Kilpatrick, an American philosopher of education and influential professor to thousands of American graduate students, strongly rejected traditional subjects for the curriculum pattern and originated the project method of education. This innovation, a crystallization of Frank Morton McMurry's *How To Study* and John Dewey's *How We Think,* helped disseminate Dewey's educational philosophy, which emphasized the importance of placing the interests, problems, and purposes of the child at the center of the educational process. In 1918 Kilpatrick popularized the project concept or method, defining it as any unit of purposeful experience or any instance of purposeful activity where "dominating purpose as an inner urge, 1) fixes the aim of the action, 2) guides its process 3) furnishes its 'drive,' its inner motivation for its vigorous prosecution." He outlined four types of projects for a model curriculum: those involving the formation of ideas; projects involving problem solving; projects involving appreciation or enjoying; and those involving knowledge or skills requiring practice or drill. Projects in which a child attacks his own problems were effective means of acquiring rich content as well as the three Rs, Kilpatrick explained, but the teacher must remain the final arbiter and manipulator of the scope and completion of the project. Some critics interpreted this plan as an opportunity to let children do what they pleased, but Kilpatrick disagreed, explaining that "mediation of adults in the learning process" is an essential part of the project method.

The guiding philosophy behind the method was the belief that learning is most effective when children are engaged wholeheartedly in work they need and want to do and have definite purpose in completing that work. Professor Kilpatrick offered many examples of boys and girls "reclaimed" by projects. In one such illustration, he told of a fourteen-year-old Virginia boy in a one-room school who had taken seven years to reach the fourth grade. His teacher claimed he was learning nothing but was too inert to leave school and follow his father into the cornfield. But when given a quarter-acre on his father's farm and told that his project would be to enter a corn-club contest, he came to life. The rules of the contest called for him to measure, compute, keep books, and select and buy his own seed and fertilizer, as well as to make frequent reports to his superintendent and the state and national department of agriculture. The boy came to see the relation of school and social need; he learned that reading, composing, and mathematics were integral to achieving his purposes. As a result of that project, he later graduated from high school and attended his state college.

Sources: J. P. Herring, "Bibliography of the Project Method," *Teachers College Record,* 20 (March 1920);

I. L. Kandel, *American Education in the Twentieth Century* (Cambridge, Mass.: Harvard University Press, 1957), pp. 118;

William A. Maddox, "The Development of Method," in *Twenty-Five Years of American Education,* edited by Kandel (New York: Macmillan, 1924), pp. 144–176.

tures; and the University of Kansas circulated almost five thousand package libraries to high-school debate leagues. Together these developments made the university a central institution in the life of the nation in the twentieth century.

Sources:
W. S. Bittner, *The University Extension Movement* (Washington, D.C.: U.S. Bureau of Education Bulletin No. 84, 1919);

Lawrence A. Cremin, *American Education: The Metropolitan Experience 1876–1980* (New York: Harper & Row, 1988);

William Clyde DeVane, *Higher Education in Twentieth-Century America* (Cambridge, Mass.: Harvard University Press, 1965).

IDEALS OF PROGRESSIVE EDUCATION

Origins of Progressive Education. The term *progressive education* refers to a diverse group of theories and practices that developed in Europe and the United States during the late nineteenth century. The movement's theory was not derived from any single source but from various beliefs united only in their opposition to traditional schooling and their support for schooling that was concerned with the emotional and physical well-being of the child. The principal forerunner of progressive education in the United States was Francis Parker, who opened several schools in the 1880s and 1890s, featuring a flexible curriculum that included self-expression and claimed to teach pupils rather than subjects. John Dewey, a philosopher whose books on educational method provided intellectual foundations for the progressive education movement, was largely responsible for popularizing this new approach to teaching and learning. William Heard Kilpatrick, faculty member of Teachers College, Columbia University, helped make that institution an important center for the dissemination of progressive ideas during his tenure (1909–1930).

Progressive Education Association. In 1919 educators gathering in Washington, D.C., furthered the cause of progressive education by founding the Progressive Education Association. An early leaflet of the organization, by Charles W. Eliot, former president of

Children learning to read and spell by printing labels for their toys (1917), one way in which educators tried to make learning fun

Harvard University, described it as "part of the great liberal tradition in human affairs, akin to other movements in the realms of public health, industrial relations, and social conditions. It is an alliance between the sciences and the idealistic expressions of a new attitude toward childhood and youth." The movement, its founders claimed, was not a plan but "a spirit embodying the appreciation of the nature of young people and the conditions under which they grow most richly and most beautifully." The movement would create schools in which "teachers and students would work together happily, under wholesome and stimulating conditions, living in the fullest sense the life of today to be ready for tomorrow." Founding members included Eugene Smith, Ann George, Mrs. Milan Ayres, Otis Caldwell, and Marietta Johnson.

Principles. The group's first order of business was to work out a set of principles descriptive of the ongoing educational experiments that made up progressive education; they also determined to create a magazine "which should do for education what the *Geographical Magazine* had done for geography." The pioneering members agreed on the following principles to guide their movement:

1. Children should be free to develop naturally. Students should have full opportunities for initiative and self-expression and an environment rich in interesting materials that can be freely used by every pupil.

2. Interest should be the motive for all work. Students should be encouraged to have real, genuine interest in the subjects they explore. A student's interest should be developed through: (a) direct and individual contact with the world and its activities and the use of experiences gained thereby; (b) application of the knowledge gained and correlation between subjects; and (c) the consciousness of achievement.

3. The teacher should be a guide, not a taskmaster. Believing in the progressive ideals, teachers should encourage the use of all the student's senses and train him or her in observation and judgment. Instead of hearing recitations only, the teacher should spend most school time teaching pupils how to utilize varied sources of information, including information from field activities as well as books. Furthermore, the teacher should show students how to reason about the information they acquire, and how to express forcefully and logically the conclusions they reach.

4. Teachers should make a scientific study of pupil development. School records must not be confined to marks given on work but must include objective and subjective reports on the physical, mental, moral, and social development of the child. This information should serve as a guide for the treatment of each pupil and focus the teacher's attention on the all-important work of developing the student rather than merely teaching subject matter.

5. Teachers should give great attention to all that affects the child's physical development. One important consideration is the health of pupils. They should have more room to move about, better light and air, clean and well-ventilated buildings, easier access to the out-of-doors, and frequent use of playgrounds. The teacher must cooperate with parents in the home to promote the child's health.

6. Schools should cooperate with parents to meet the needs of a child's life. The school should provide as much as possible of all that the natural interest of the child demands.

7. Progressive schools should provide leadership in educational movements. Progressive schools should be laboratories where new ideas, if worthy, meet encouragement. Tradition alone should not rule, and the best part of the past must be leavened with modern discoveries.

Impact. The progressive movement in education affected every aspect of schooling, from curriculum to building design. In the course of the decade, interest among educators shifted away from traditional academic subjects to the kinds of knowledge considered most useful and practical in society, as shown in daily life and the printed pages of books, magazines, and newspapers. Arithmetic, for example, became "everyday arithmetic"; science became "the science of everyday life." After World War I reconstructing the curriculum became one of the major projects of progressive educators, as teachers aimed to make education more meaningful to students and to stimulate them to a more independent style of learning. Aspiring to become more "child-centered," progressive schools worked to create opportunities for children to engage in "creative" activities and forms of self-expression. Some schools reflected an exaggerated and excessive cult of freedom for the pupils, a movement John Dewey publicly deplored. One long-lasting effect of the progressive education movement was the institutionalizing of physical education in the curriculum; and many school designs, influenced by progressive ideals, began to recommend fresh air and playground spaces for children.

Sources:

Stanwood Cobb, "An Account of the Beginnings of the Progressive Education Association: 1919," in *Education in the United States: A Documentary History*, edited by Sol Cohen (New York: Random House, 1974), pp. 2167–2168;

I. L. Kandel, *American Education in the Twentieth Century* (Cambridge, Mass.: Harvard University Press, 1957).

INTELLIGENCE TESTING AND STATISTICS

Statistical Analysis. Education administrators collected data for decades before any general attempt was made to state what truths were revealed by their columns of figures; most superintendents counted children, income, expenditures, attendance, and passes and failures annually mainly to have a collection of official statistics. However, in the early twentieth century various mathe-

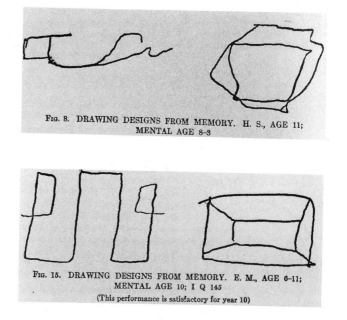

FIG. 8. DRAWING DESIGNS FROM MEMORY. H. S., AGE 11; MENTAL AGE 8-3

FIG. 15. DRAWING DESIGNS FROM MEMORY. E. M., AGE 6-11; MENTAL AGE 10; I Q 145
(This performance is satisfactory for year 10)

Illustrations from Lewis M. Terman's *The Measurement of Intelligence* (1916), demonstrating different levels of intelligence in children of the same age

maticians worldwide clarified and expanded techniques for studying relationships among sets of facts, and their work fired interest in the new field of statistical studies.

A New Discipline. In the United States, Edward Thorndike became a leading proponent of the statistical measurement of social and economic facts, and he offered in 1902–1903, for the first time in this country, a course at Teachers College, Columbia University, called Education 108 — Practicum: the application of psychological and statistical method to education. Soon courses in statistical method were offered at Chicago (1910), Brown (1911–1912), Harvard (1912–1913), and scores of other universities by middecade. In 1904 the results of a statistical study of retardation in the schools of New York appeared in the superintendent's annual report; thereafter, a veritable explosion of research studies occurred in the field of education, and by 1919 statistical studies of nearly every possible topic were conducted at the district level. In city school systems, state systems, normal schools, teachers' colleges, and university schools of education, bureaus of research and statistics devoted to the quantitative study of the schools were established. It is difficult to underestimate the importance of this new development at the college level. In 1910 doctorates awarded in the field of educational research numbered in the tens; immediately after World War I the numbers had risen to the hundreds. Along with this movement toward scientific research in education, growing numbers of educators and members of the public became convinced that human behavior could be positively modified by appropriate nurture and by the directed influences of the environment. For this reason, the public education system became more accepted than ever before as an instrument for social change.

Edward Thorndike was a psychologist, researcher, and innovator in the development and application of mental measurements for humans from infancy to old age. His research, which helped clarify how habits are formed and broken, gave the American public increased faith in the wonder-working power of good schools. After years of careful experimentation with children and animals at Columbia University, Thorndike published *The Original Nature of Man* in 1913, a book dedicated to William James, who had been his teacher. This work contributed to a better understanding of original nature and nurture, of heredity and environment, and was based on biological principles rather than on *a priori* speculation. Thorndike then published a three-volume work, *The Psychology of Learning* (1913–1914), which exercised a profound effect on the development of educational psychology. Convinced that measurement was the key to scientific progress in education, he also made significant contributions to the development of numerous measurement scales. When he explained his core beliefs about the importance of reliable measurements in education, he spoke in laymen's terms:

Whatever exists exists in some amount, and knowing means knowing quantity as well as quality. Education is a change in human beings, and change is the difference in two conditions. Each condition can be known only by the products produced by it — words spoken, acts performed, etc. To measure these products means to define them so that com-

petent persons will know how large they are *better* than they would know without measurement. This information then may be recorded and used.

Thorndike emphasized that only the products produced, not the inner condition of the person, were the proper point of attack for measurement. He also pointed out that scientific measurement was important for students as well as teachers and administrators, that "a pupil must be given information about his own achievement and improvement as a motive and a guide. Neither the idea of mental measurements nor of scales originated with Thorndike, but he was able to bring to them the refinements of statistical methods which he had developed. He soon followed up his handwriting scale with one in arithmetic in 1912, and this scale preceded so many others that by the end of the decade there was hardly any aspect of schoolwork for which scaled tests were not available. Thorndike's work in this field had a significant impact on defining norms and standards of schoolwork for American children. His work in measurement is perhaps best known, however, for the intelligence tests he developed for the U.S. Army for use in World War I.

Sources: "Edward Thorndike on Educational Measurement," in *Education in the United States: A Documentary History*, edited by Sol Cohen (New York: Random House, 1974), pp. 2247–2249;

I. L. Kandel, *American Education in the Twentieth Century* (Cambridge, Mass.: Harvard University Press, 1957), pp. 91–94;

John Ohles, ed., *Biographical Dictionary of American Educators*, volume 3 (Westport, Conn.: Greenwood Press, 1978), p. 545.

Mental Measurements. One of the earliest researchers in the study of the limits of human mental faculties declared that a principal object of measurement was to obtain a general knowledge of the capacities of a person by "sinking shafts, as it were, at a few critical points." To ascertain the best points for the purpose, the sets of measures needed to be compared with an independent estimate of mental powers. By 1905 Alfred Binet actually accomplished this feat when faced with determining who among a group of children were to be considered normal, in terms of mental performance, and who were to be considered below the normal range. The measurement he devised, known as the Binet-Simon scale, was field-tested on two thousand apparently average or above-average children and hundreds of children who were apparently below average and in special schools. By 1912 Lewis Terman, a psychologist and statistician, revised and extended the scale, and in 1916 the Stanford University revision (also by Terman) appeared. With ninety tests in all, six for each age level from ages three to ten, eight for the age of twelve, and six for the age of fourteen,

this revised scale also included six tests for average adults and six for superior adults.

Early Uses of Testing. At first these tests were not widely used in the schools because they had to be administered individually. However, when the United States entered World War I, psychologists were asked to suggest how the relatively new field of psychology might benefit the nation; they subsequently developed two mental tests that could be given to groups. One test was verbal in character and tested literates; the other was a performance test that measured the mental capabilities of illiterates. After the war these group tests, along with the Stanford-Binet measurement scales, were used frequently in American schools; soon, however, although their original purpose was simply to classify children by intelligence, the use of these tests provoked philosophical questions. As early as 1919, some educators debated whether this newly discovered "intelligence quotient," or IQ, was solely an innate inherited characteristic or a composite product of hereditary and environmental factors. The importance of the answer to this question was clear from the start. Immediately the tests were used to select pupils for special and ungraded classes. Then, in most of the state schools for delinquents, mental tests began to be used to classify and determine the types of discipline best suited to various groups of children. Furthermore, as early as 1916, mental tests began to be used in connection with college entrance examinations.

Significance of IQ Testing. Terman, as early as 1916, explained that without IQ tests it could not be known to what extent a child's mental performance was determined by environment and to what extent by heredity. "Is the place of the so-called lower classes in the social and industrial scale," he asked, "the result of their inferior native endowment, or is their apparent inferiority merely a result of their inferior home and school training?" Only intelligence tests, he argued, could distinguish the results of educational efforts with a given child from the influence of the child's original endowment; furthermore, the effects on mental development predicted by the new "progressive education methods" had to be verified by scientific method. Clearly, intelligence testing had a major impact on American education during the decade. As Edward Thorndike wrote in 1918, many administrators were so impressed by educational measurements that they immediately searched for scales that could be used by teachers with little technical training; he warned that an effort was under way to devise tests that could be scored by persons "utterly devoid of judgment concerning the products in question."

Sources:
Jesse B. Sears, "The Development of Tests and Measurements," in *Twenty-Five Years of American Education*, edited by I. L. Kandel (New York: Macmillan, 1924), pp. 115–140;

Lewis Terman, *The Measurement of Intelligence* (Boston: Houghton Mifflin, 1916);

Edward L. Thorndike, "On Educational Measurement: 1918," in *Education in the United States: A Documentary History*, edited by Sol Cohen (New York: Random House, 1974), pp. 2248–2249.

REFORM OF TEACHER TRAINING

Normal Schools. For the greater part of the decade, the so-called normal school continued to be the chief institution for training teachers for America's elementary schools. In some states the normal schools also furnished high-school teachers for rural schools, but most states required high-school teachers to have a college degree and to acquire certification to teach. Normal schools offered a two-year course to young students who usually had little more than an elementary education or two years of high school; the course included academic studies, a review of the material an elementary-school teacher would be expected to teach, and observation and practice teaching in a training school under the supervision of experienced teachers. Critics of normal schools charged that the academic work was weak and too much time was devoted to techniques and methods of instruction instead of con-

---

THE IDEAL TEACHER, CIRCA 1917

In 1917 Elmer Redmond, superintendent of schools in Port Chester, New York, published this twelve-point portrait of the ideal teacher in the *American School Board Journal:*

Voice: should be well modulated, clear and winning with correct pronunciation and wide vocabulary.

Manners: should be that of cultured ladies and gentlemen.

Conduct: should possess a character indicated by irreproachable actions reflecting high ideals and purposes.

Work habits: should be systematic, accurate, prompt, cheerful and masterful in thought and action.

Self Control: should reflect ease, poise and a judicial and thoughtful attitude.

Inspirational Force: should be strong in encouraging, thought-provoking, ambition-arousing, growth-promoting, and success-inspiring action.

Leadership: should be evident in all actions.

Executive Ability: should display initiative and resourceful action.

Cooperation: should be loyal, frank, kind, sympathetic, and helpful.

Common Sense: should display this in refusing to gossip, in conforming to the customs of the community, and in a saving sense of humor.

Attitude: should be optimistic, enthusiastic, respecting the superintendent, trusting the principal, liking associates, loving pupils, while smiling and radiating good cheer.

In Superintendent Redmond's district, the maximum salary for this paragon was $1,000 per year.

Source: Elmer Redmond, "Teaching Efficiency," *American School Board Journal*, 51 (March 1917): 45.

---

tent. In part to counter such criticism, in part to have the right to train secondary as well as elementary teachers, and in part to facilitate the passage of their graduates to liberal arts colleges, normal schools across the country began to improve their standards.

Normal Schools Become Colleges. Educational theorists in the 1910s were redefining the function of a teacher, from one who imparts a defined set of information to a mass of pupils to one who has an understanding

Students in a physical-science laboratory at Oswego Normal School in Oswego, New York

of each pupil as an individual. This shift in roles raised the expectation that teachers would have at least a rudimentary grasp of human psychology. There was also a movement to change the character of the classroom, shifting the emphasis from docile memorization and recitation to a place where pupils were actively engaged in learning with the teacher as a guide, not a taskmaster. This change required teachers to have a broader liberal arts education. These trends, combined with the expansion of the professional literature on education and the accumulation of research studies, prompted the normal schools gradually to assume the title and role of "teachers' colleges." This name change, reflecting a change to a four-year curriculum, allowed the normal schools to place themselves on the same level as liberal arts colleges and to offer degrees attracting candidates wishing to become secondary-school teachers. Wisconsin became a leader in this trend, with eight normal schools there providing opportunities for normal-school students and college students to study in the same classes as early as 1912. By the end of the decade the transition in which institutions changed from normal schools to colleges was widespread, especially throughout the North and Midwest.

Teachers-College Model. Many institutions of higher education based their teacher-training curricula on the model set by Teachers College in New York, which had affiliated with Columbia University in 1890. By 1920 approximately 450 American institutions of higher education and a large number of state teachers' colleges offered degrees in education. After 1910 the field became so wide and the subdivisions within it so highly specialized that no student could master the entire curriculum, and departments evolved in such specialties as psychology, philosophy, administration, methods, law, and even hygiene. At Columbia's Teachers College, a seven-page

catalogue listing in 1919 offered study in such diverse topics as "Industrial Arts for Social and Religious Workers," "Geography for Teachers and Supervisors in Elementary Grades," "Phonetics," "Laboratory Projects in Automobile Mechanics," "Rural Sociology and Economics," and "Psychology of Habit, Skill, Practice, and Memory."

The War and Teacher Training. Opportunities for specialization in elementary, secondary, and rural education were dramatically expanded by developments in psychology, the philosophy of education, and social studies. However, the emergency created by World War I, when a significant mass of data was collected in connection with the organization of the army, revealed deficiencies in American education not previously statistically verified. It was determined, for example, that less than 10 percent of the teachers in the Midwest had more than the equivalent of a high-school education. At the same time, the American public was made aware of the importance and needs of rural education, the prevalence of physical defects in children, the inadequate provision for health education, the problems of immigrant and adult illiteracy, and the low standards of education in general. These dire circumstances, magnified by wartime contingencies, had the effect of galvanizing demands for better and more extensive teacher training and helped lead to the founding of graduate schools of education and other improvements in the 1920s.

Sources:
I. L. Kandel, *American Education in the Twentieth Century* (Cambridge, Mass.: Harvard University Press, 1957);

The Move to Transform Normal Schools into Colleges, Seventh Annual Report of the Carnegie Foundation for the Advancement of Teaching (New York: Carnegie Foundation, 1912);

University Study of Education (New York: Macmillan, 1924).

Southern rural schools for blacks (left) and whites (right), circa 1915

SCHOOLS IN THE SOUTH

Decades of Neglect. The optimistic story of progressive education in the 1910s does not include the seriously impaired educational systems in the South. Beset by economic woes and overwhelming rates of illiteracy, education in the former slave states had failed to develop and advance in the years following Reconstruction. As historian Edgar Knight wrote in 1920, the educational system in the South "bore the odium of bad rule and partisan politics; in consequence, indifference to it was so deadly as to equal outright hostility." Reform efforts had been attempted by the General Education Board, a philanthropic organization formed in 1903 to identify areas of need and render financial assistance. The board promoted secondary education and gave financial gifts to build and maintain hundreds of high schools throughout the South. Through the U.S. Department of Agriculture the GEB in 1906 set up demonstration farms under the supervision of demonstration agents. Despite these ambitious efforts, however, education in the South in 1910 showed the effects of general neglect and disinterest, with the average annual school term lasting only 121 days and no plan of compulsory attendance in effect, even for elementary schools.

Early Advances. The work of the General Education Board in the South helped motivate most of the southern states to attempt some reform, and active campaigns for better schools began to show results by middecade. One of the first reforms was the instituting of compulsory-attendance laws, requiring children of certain ages (usually up through the eighth grade) to attend some or all of the school term. In 1918 Mississippi became the last of the southern states to enact these laws. By 1915 the average school term in the South had lengthened to 130 days (elsewhere in the United States the term was 160 days), and salaries for white teachers in the South had risen to $328 (elsewhere in the nation the average was $543). Southern expenditures per pupil rose from $3 per child at the turn of the century to $8.50 per child in 1915, compared to $22.19 in the North. This expenditure was, however, a major step forward, since the value of property per capita in the South of $18 compared unfavorably to the $79 per capita in other parts of the country. Whereas in the North there was active debate about the best methods of teaching secondary-school students, in the South the debate was over constructing secondary-school buildings where none existed. A 1919 report of the Bureau of Education noted that eight counties in Arkansas, twelve in Florida, sixty-four in Georgia, one in Mississippi, two in Tennessee, four in Louisiana, and two in Virginia had no public high school that met acceptable standards. The status of southern higher education was equally dismal: the total annual budget for higher education in Alabama, Georgia, Kentucky, Louisiana, Mississippi, the Carolinas, and Virginia was $19,000 less than the annual budget of Harvard in 1913.

Hope for the South. Southern leaders were convinced that to build a new South, their schools had to radically improve to prepare southerners to move beyond the needs of an agricultural economy. Between 1900 and 1915 the increase in public-school expenditures nationwide was 180 percent, but in the South it was 280 percent. Child-labor laws, theoretically linked to compulsory attendance, were enacted in all the southern states from 1907 to 1918. Improvement in general health regulation and the physical examination of school children, along with concerted efforts to eliminate adult illiteracy, were also hallmarks of this period. North Carolina in 1919 created one of the most advanced plans in the country to provide for the welfare of all delinquent, neglected, and dependent children under sixteen years of age, and other nearby states made some beginnings in legislation and practices designed to protect children. Education historian Edgar Knight wrote in the 1920s that World War I helped the South to "find herself." He believed that "under the impetus of the call to fight, to give, and to do for others what she had not felt fully able to do for herself, she found fresh hope and new energies." The call for food for the United States and for the soldiers in Europe, the campaigns against waste, and the drives for the Red Cross and Liberty Bonds led the South to "thoughtful consideration of new enterprises and of old ones undeveloped." Despite the fact that the 1918 ranking of their education programs ranked the southern states as the eleven weakest in the nation in terms of attendance at elementary and high schools, length of term, and expenditures, there was some cause for cautious optimism at the end of the decade.

Sources:

Edgar Knight, "Education in the South," in *Twenty-Five Years of American Education*, edited by I. L. Kandel (New York: Macmillan, 1924);

Stuart Noble, *Forty Years of the Public Schools in Mississippi* (New York: Teachers College Press, 1918);

Public Education in North Carolina (New York: General Education Board, 1921);

Booker T. Washington, *Up From Slavery* (Garden City, N.Y.: Doubleday, 1915).

SEGREGATION AND THE SCHOOLS

Southern Problem. The story of black education during the decade was set almost completely in the South. Nine-tenths of the total black population of the United States, according to the census of 1910, resided in the South. About 30 percent of the population of the South was black, while less than 2 percent of the population of the northern states was reported as minority in that census. In South Carolina and Mississippi more than half the population was black at the beginning of the decade. The South was handicapped by dire poverty, with incomes averaging just $3,449 per school-age child in the eleven southern states in 1912 (an amount derived by dividing the states' total incomes by the number of children in those states), compared to the wealth in Iowa at the same time of $13,473 per school-age child. All public schools in the South suffered from decades of poor economic conditions and neglect, but the black schools suffered disproportionately from both poverty and oppression. A second-class system of education existed for blacks, but it was second class to a rudimentary education given to whites. Public schools for blacks in the South were open three to four months per year, and the teachers, earning between $17 and $25 per month, made less than the wages black convicts were paid. According to black educator Booker T. Washington in his 1911 memoir *My Larger Education*, "ten million Negroes in the South would never have an education in the same sense as the white people in the Northern states had." With no standards of curriculum or teaching, the system of education of blacks in the South was "imperfect, incomplete, and unsatisfactory."

Industrial Education. African Americans were themselves divided on the appropriate curriculum for their children. Industrial education, represented best by Booker T. Washington's Tuskegee Institute, favored equipping the black population to make their way materially

and socially in their southern rural environment. This type of training was based on the philosophy, exemplified by Virginia's Hampton Institute, that students must engage in manual labor not merely to defray a part of their school expenses or to learn a trade but to develop mind and character. Washington had determined that northern philanthropy could not possibly support the burden of educating the entire black population of the South. He argued that the only hope for improving the education of black students lay in "arousing the southern people to provide substantial aid from state and local funds." Washington recognized that white southern leaders were especially fearful that northern philanthropists would make blacks discontented with the limited political and economic opportunities accorded them in southern society. He was right. For example, the *New Orleans Picayune* editorialized in 1911 that "just as soon as all the Negroes in the State shall be able to read and write they will become qualified to vote, and it is not to be doubted that they will demand their rights in the primaries with the 14th Amendment to back them up." Washington and powerful white proponents of industrial education, such as Robert Ogden, Edwin Alderman, Charles Dabney, Wallace Buttrick, and George Foster Peabody, pragmatically believed that industrial training was the appropriate form of schooling to assist in bringing racial order, political stability, and material prosperity to the South. Furthermore, these advocates believed that this curriculum was the only possible choice that would receive funding from all-white state legislatures.

Black Opposition to Industrial Education. This conception of education and social order conflicted with the aspirations of many African Americans and their white liberal allies in the North, who hoped to develop an educational system that would extend the emancipation of blacks, not push blacks into a system that presupposed their political and economic subordination. Opposition to Washington, and to "accommodation" to the white majority's vision of a social caste system, coalesced in 1910 in the formation of the National Association for the Advancement of Colored People (NAACP). This organization stood for universal political and civil equality, and among the membership anti-Washington feeling ran high. By 1911 the black intellectual W. E. B. Du Bois, who wrote in *The Souls of Black Folk* (1903) that "every energy is being used to put black men back into slavery, and Mr. Washington is leading the way backward," had convinced many blacks that equal educational opportunities in traditional academic subjects were a minimum necessary complement to Washington's emphasis on manual training. By 1915 even the pro-Washington *New York Age*, *Chicago Defender*, and *Indianapolis Freeman* were becoming increasingly critical of the philanthropists' approach to black education. According to historian James Anderson, "The Du Bois forces had won the ideological war and prevented the Tuskegee-

Students in a domestic-science class at the Marion County Training School in South Carolina. These young women were learning how to be cooks in white people's homes.

Hampton plan of industrial education from becoming the dominant Afro-American educational ideology."

Educating the South's Black Teachers. Problems ran deeper than mere philosophical disagreements, however. In 1910 all proponents of universal elementary education for black southerners agreed that the infrastructure necessary for a viable black public school system did not exist. Nearly two-thirds of the black children of elementary-school age were not enrolled in schools, primarily because there were not enough school buildings or teachers to accommodate them. Northern white missionary teachers, who had contributed significantly to the spread of common schools among former slaves during and after Reconstruction, had no significant presence in the South by 1910. If black children were to learn, whether their curriculum were to be academic or industrial training, they would have to be taught by black teachers. The existing black educational institutions capable of training teachers fell into four groups: 1) the sixteen land-grant and seven state normal schools; 2) approximately fifty public high schools and five city normal schools; 3) approximately sixty private colleges; and 4) the more than two hundred private institutions offering secondary and normal courses. The land-grant colleges did not provide teacher training until after World War I. Before World War I only Virginia, Alabama, Maryland, and North Carolina maintained state normal schools, while city normal schools were located only in

Louisville, Baltimore, Richmond, Saint Louis, and Little Rock. The output annually from all of these sources was insufficient to meet even local demands. The private institutions, which offered a classical liberal-arts curriculum, did not concentrate on developing teachers. Therefore, in 1911, facing the overwhelming need for teachers, legislatures created the county training school, a new system of education for blacks.

County Training Schools. The movement for county training schools began in 1911 with the construction of the Tangipahoa Parish Training School for Colored Children of Louisiana. This industrial boarding school was centrally located, with facilities and teachers to operate seven elementary grades and three years of secondary- and normal-school courses that trained industrial teachers for the small rural schools. Southern-state school superintendents in Alabama, Florida, North Carolina, Tennessee, Texas, and Virginia soon established similar programs, all with financial support from a philanthropic organization, the John F. Slater Fund. By 1917 all of the the former slave states except Missouri and West Virginia had one or more county training schools. From 1911 to 1931 the number of county training schools grew to 390. In its 1917–1918 annual report the Slater Fund's board stated: "There is perhaps no more promising movement in Negro Education than the development of the County Training Schools, which offer seven years of elementary work, with suitable industrial courses, and in addition three years of high school work emphasizing the arts of home making and farm life; the last year includes a simple course in teacher training." Leo Favrot, in a 1920 report on the county schools, noted that school officials in the South were "making the training schools distinctly industrial and agricultural all the way through the courses offered." White southerners supported these schools because graduates of this type of program were not prepared to undertake college-level work. This education, prevalent in all southern states in the decade of 1910–1919, was designed to adjust black southerners to a life of subordination, not emancipation.

Sources:

James D. Anderson, *The Education of Blacks in the South 1860–1935* (Chapel Hill: University of North Carolina Press, 1988);

W. E. B. Du Bois, "The College-bred Negro," *Report of the United States Commissioner of Education*, 1902;

Stuart Noble, *Education of the Negro* (New York: Macmillan, 1924).

VOCATIONAL EDUCATION

Economic and Social Changes. At the turn of the century the changing economy of the United States created new demands on the nation's schools for more vocational training in the new scientific farming methods and in industrial skills. Largely because of improved farm machinery, the total value of agricultural products grew from less than $5 billion in 1900 to nearly $8.5 billion in 1910 and almost $12.5 billion by 1919. At the same time, the growth of manufacturing made the United States the world's leading exporter of manufactured goods in 1910. In northern cities industries were particularly dependent on public schools to provide industrial education for workers because immigration from countries with a high percentage of unskilled and illiterate workers was replacing immigration from countries with skilled and better educated workers. The demand for more industrial training was further increased by the rise of American labor unions, whose restrictions limiting the number of apprentices changed the way workers were trained on the job. The Board of Education in Chicago set a precedent for industrial training when it made provisions in its system for courses in cooperative education; under this plan students could study arithmetic, English, drawing, architecture, and woodworking three months a year, then spend the rest of their school time on vocational instruction. Large commercial establishments, such as National Cash Register; General Electric; Sears, Roebuck and Company; and John Wanamaker, strongly supported the expanding system of vocational education, believing it was well adapted for workers in what one contemporary called modern "highly specialized productive enterprises, such as factories for textiles, locomotives, firearms, jewelry, clothing, furniture, packed meats, books, newspapers, automobiles, shoes, stoves, and buttons."

Agricultural Training. After 1910 the number of agricultural high schools of various forms grew rapidly. In Wisconsin county agricultural schools providing free two-year courses in agriculture and household economy were established. Soon Alabama, Georgia, Virginia, California, Minnesota, Oklahoma, Massachusetts, and New York also established independent agricultural secondary schools. Dozens of other states set up secondary schools in conjunction with agricultural colleges and state universities during the decade. One of the model schools of this type was the Farm Life School of North Carolina. In addition, many other traditional secondary schools offered "courses" in agriculture but did not specialize in the subject. By 1915, 4,665 high schools reported that they were teaching agriculture in some form. Congress was in favor of this expanded emphasis on agricultural education. In 1914 the Smith-Lever Act provided federal aid for extension work in agriculture and home economics. Although this money was not granted directly to the schools, the law provided agricultural education to school-age children through extension services and club work. The 1917 Smith-Hughes Act set a historic precedent when the federal government granted financial aid for the first time directly to schools for agricultural, industrial, and commercial education. The appropriations, which by 1919 totaled more than $3 million, funded a Federal Board for Vocational Education, state boards for states accepting the money, aid for vocational teachers' training and salaries, federal supervision of work and expenditures, and research investigations connected with the field.

Commercial Education. The growing importance of the service sector in the expanding American economy also created a need for more workers in department stores, banks, commission houses, and offices. Separate commercial secondary schools were established in major cities such as San Francisco, Washington, Louisville, Boston, Brooklyn, New York City, and Cleveland. These schools, whose programs were up to five years in length, sought to prepare students for a business career or entrance into a school of commerce at the university level. Their distinguishing feature was the omission of classical studies, with some limitation on other academic subjects. Most traditional secondary schools instituted commercial tracks of one to four years of study in courses such as stenography, bookkeeping, and business English. By 1918 high schools across the nation reported that 278,275 students were enrolled in commercial-education courses.

Sources:

John M. Brewer, *The Vocational-Guidance Movement* (New York: Macmillan, 1922);

"Securing Public Support," in *Education in the United States: A Documentary History*, edited by Sol Cohen (New York: Random House, 1974), p. 2670;

Booker T. Washington, *Up From Slavery* (Garden City, N.Y.: Doubleday, 1915);

W. Thomas Woody, "Vocational Education," in *Twenty-Five Years of American Education*, edited by I. L. Kandel (New York: Macmillan, 1924).

Machine shop class, 1916

WOMEN AND EDUCATION

In Secondary Schools. A key debate during the decade was how to educate women for congenial work and financial independence while fitting them to be homemakers as well. In 1918, 57.9 percent of all students enrolled in secondary schools were girls. Some conservatives lamented that higher education for women and their success in professional training was "disinclining women for marriage and the cares of housekeeping and child rearing." A powerful group of educators, including John Dewey, demanded that the education of women be brought in touch with the vocational needs of the community. Though Dewey was not suggesting that women's studies be confined to home economics, he and other educators held that preparation for a life career and genuine culture were not alien to each other. Most women during this period, however, opted for a traditional classical education. The vast majority of young women enrolled in secondary schools during the latter part of the decade were engaged in academic rather than vocational studies. In the 1917–1918 *Biennial Survey of Education,* published by the U.S. Bureau of Education, 73 percent of girls enrolled in secondary schools opted for the academic track, compared with 10 percent in the home-

economics course and 2 percent in the teacher-training course. Although the percentage of all students electing the academic course work, surrounded as it was "with an aura of prestige," had declined from 80 percent to 70 percent since 1911, the decline was primarily among male students.

Home Economics Movement. Even though relatively few young women were enrolled in high-school programs of "household economy," a powerful impetus was given to this vocational training by the passage of the Smith-Lever Act in 1914 and the Smith-Hughes Act in 1917 — two pieces of legislation that revealed the nationwide interest in the more extensive education of girls in household economy. The first act provided large federal grants to the states for diffusing practical information relating to agriculture and home economics among the people in rural areas. This work was undertaken and organized by the land-grant colleges, and its immediate result was an increase in the number of girls' garden clubs and canning clubs; there was also an increase in useful instruction in the household arts given by county agents to women in farming districts. The Smith-Hughes Act went a step further and provided for the better preparation of teach-

THE NEW WOMAN AND THE CAMPUS SCENE

The third generation of women to be college educated considered themselves to be "new women" — responsive to the progressive causes of social reform but also flouting conventional mores, a foreshadowing of the 1920s flapper. As late as 1907, when men were allowed at women's campus dances, the couples, with dancing forbidden, had to walk to the music. Some of these new women, scoffing at convention, defiantly performed the "forbidden waltz" at Smith College, and by 1913 college men and women everywhere danced together regularly. Campus authorities then had to judge which dance steps should be permitted. The turkey trot was banned at Barnard College in 1915 and the tango was forbidden at Illinois, Wisconsin, and Iowa. At the University of Chicago, where the tango was allowed in 1912, a graduate student was horrified. "This wriggling," he predicted, "will soon lead to a nervous breakdown for innocent girls."

In addition, for female collegians physical exercise became a symbol of "emancipated womanhood." The promotion of sports occurred at all colleges, and females, like males, gladly played. The athletic figure of the Gibson Girl became the ideal image of the new woman. Charles Dana Gibson's sketches of this tall, commanding woman in her shirtwaist and skirt, in constant motion playing tennis, croquet, and other games, inspired women to develop their prowess in sports.

Source: Barbara Miller Solomon, *In the Company of Educated Women* (New Haven: Yale Unversity Press, 1985), p. 102–104.

---

courses in most departments of home economics in colleges as well as universities.

Women and College Attendance. Although there were significant advances in the education of women in the decade, a higher percentage of men had the opportunity to attend four-year colleges. Many women in the 1910s pursued their post-secondary education in commercial or normal schools. Most college women came from families within the expanding middle class, as the wealthy clung to the tradition of preparing their daughters for leisure, not work. A middle-class family could send a daughter to Cornell in 1917 for $150 in tuition and board. Women's progress in respect to numbers in college was striking. In 1898 there were 32,485 women enrolled in colleges and universities, whereas in 1919–1920 there were 128,677 — a fourfold increase in twenty-one years. Statisticians at the time predicted that if this trend continued, collegiate enrollment of men and women could be equal by 1950. However, there were still many colleges and universities that refused to admit women. In the South women (who made up a majority of the high-school graduates there) had limited opportunities for further education unless they left the region. As late as 1910 none of Virginia's four state-supported colleges — William and Mary, Washington and Lee, the University of Virginia, and Virginia Military Institute — admitted women. Campaigns to admit women were met with the prophecy that coeduction would produce a type of woman from whom "we devoutly pray to be spared: boisterous and bold." A women's committee led by Mary Munford produced five bills in the state legislature between 1910 and 1920 urging that women be admitted to the University of Virginia; women did not enroll there, however, for another fifty years.

Women in Professional Schools. A significant growth in the numbers of women in the professional departments of universities, colleges, and technical schools was noted in contemporary educational statistics — from 953 women in 1898 to 2,830 in 1918, "and this in the face of no little discouragement," as one historian noted. However, significant barriers to the education of women remained in the historically male professions of law, medicine, and theology. In 1919, 888 women were taking medical courses; 1,171 were taking law courses; and 874 were taking theology courses. "It is surprising," a female faculty member observed, "that law should attract more women than medicine, which has long been supposed to make a strong appeal to the nurturing instincts of women." She added, "No doubt the small number of women preparing for this work may be partially explained by the great physical demand made upon both the student and the practitioner in medicine, the extended period required to establish one's self in the profession, the restricted facilities open to women in hospitals and clinics, and the popular distrust of, if not prejudice against, women physicians." Nevertheless, World War I gave a real impetus to medical colleges to open their courses to

---

ers of agricultural, trade, industrial, and home economics subjects, work placed under the control of a Federal Board for Vocational Education. In 1918 the Bureau of Education reported that home economics courses in public high schools were expanding at the rate of about one thousand per year. The tendency was to make the work elective for high-school girls but to require it in the upper grades of the elementary schools. Although only 10 percent of the total enrollment of girls in high schools was in the complete course, many girls in other departments still elected to take one or more courses in home economics. By 1919 many schools established practice homes in detached houses or in apartments where girls in high schools or normal schools could obtain practical training in household economy. Some homes even convinced parents to lend their babies to be cared for by the resident students as a part of their course in child hygiene. The increased interest in child welfare that marked the decade manifested itself in the establishment of child-welfare

A household-arts class in a Newark, New Jersey, high school

women. Between 1914 and 1918 several of the largest medical schools in the country took action to admit women, including the University of Pennsylvania (1914), Tulane University (1915), Columbia University (1916), Bellevue Hospital Medical College (1917), the University of Maryland (1917), the University of Virginia (1917), and Harvard University (1918).

Nursing Education. Significant strides in the professional training of women were accomplished in the nursing field. The vocation of trained nurse was elevated into a profession during the decade, requiring years of preparation both in theory and practice. Prof. Adelaide Nutting of Teachers College, Columbia University, provided leadership on a national level in changing the field to one that attracted significant numbers of women with college degrees or with at least two years of college education. By the end of the decade sixteen leading universities, recognizing the growing prestige of the nursing profession as one that required mastery of a considerable body of theoretical and scientific knowledge, had organized their own departments of nursing. In addition, fourteen universities and colleges established some affiliation with schools of nursing and twelve universities offered courses for graduate nurses, chiefly in public-health nursing. By 1920, 54,953 women were in nursing-degree programs.

Lack of Progress in Administration. Women made little progress in these years in advancement to administrative positions in teaching or in appointment to professorships in university faculties. The lower ranks of the teaching profession were largely female, and even 66 percent of the instructors in secondary schools in 1919 were women. However, there were not signficant numbers of women serving in supervisory or administrative positions. The influential committees of the National Education Association (NEA) had no women members. The newly formed Progressive Education Association (1919) had some women members on its roster, but most served primarily as hostesses and/or recording secretaries. At the college level most women who wanted to become professors found themselves shunted into the new departments of home economics and out of the fields in which they had received professional training. The professional career of Florence Robinson, who had earned her Ph.D. at the University of Wisconsin, exemplifies this trend. Despite her degree and stellar academic record in American history, she could find employment only as a home economics instructor at Beloit College. A study in 1911 showed that 60 percent of women professors in coeducational schools were in home economics. A significant proportion of the remaining 40 percent were in colleges of education, nursing, or social work. The movement for the education of social workers, which had begun in earnest at the turn of the century, was well under way by 1910, schools of social work having been established in New York, Boston, Saint Louis, Philadelphia, and Chicago. During the 1913–1914 school year approximately nine hundred students were enrolled in these schools where the majority of professors and students were women. A professor at the Chicago School of Civics and Philanthropy noted at the time that the field's attraction "seems to be especially strong to those women of fine intellectual equipment. No doubt," he continued, "the opportunity to care for the needy, the defective, the unfortunate has proved attractive to many women to whom teaching made little appeal. This new domain of work bids fair to be overwhelmingly a profession for women."

Sources:

Willystine Goodsell, *The Education of Women* (New York: Macmillan, 1925);

Barbara Miller Solomon, *In the Company of Educated Women* (New Haven: Yale University Press, 1985);

Frederick Sykes, "Social Basis of the New Education for Women," *Teachers College Record,* 18 (May 1917): 109–111.

HEADLINE MAKERS

FANNIE FERN PHILLIPS ANDREWS

1867-1950

EDUCATOR, REFORMER, PEACE ACTIVIST

Lifelong Interest in Schooling. Fannie Fern Phillips Andrews was an educator who campaigned tirelessly for an international bureau of education to promote peace studies. Born in Lynn, Massachusetts, she was the daughter of a shoemaker father and a mother who was president of the Women's Christian Temperance Union. Deciding at age three that she wanted to be a teacher, Andrews later attended Salem Normal School in Massachusetts and then taught for six years before receiving her degree in psychology and education from Radcliffe College in 1902. Her work in the public schools of Boston convinced her that students from different ethnic and economic backgrounds had to be taught to communicate and negotiate with each other. Her core belief that men who make war are spurred to conflict by their inability to understand one another's perspectives fueled her interest in "teaching peace."

The American Peace League. In 1908 she founded the American Peace League, an organization that sought to promote peace by teaching the principles of "international justice" in American schools. She extended her influence by organizing the Boston School-Parent Group and serving as president of the Boston Home and School Association from 1914 to 1918. Andrews campaigned nationally for her ideals, and by 1915 league branches had been established in forty states. She envisioned an international bureau of education that would promote understanding among nations. But the era just before the United States entered World War I was an inauspicious time to promote peace. Andrews, who eventually supported American involvement in the war, changed the name of the American Peace League to the American School Citizenship League in 1918, believing that the old title was too provocative during wartime.

International Attention. Andrews and the league received serious consideration from the highest branches of government for her plan to create an international bureau of education. She was engaged in the final planning stages of a multinational conference to consider the logistics of such an institution when World War I erupted. She had caught the attention of President Woodrow Wilson, however, and in 1918 he picked Andrews to attend the Paris Peace Conference. There she lobbied for the emerging League of Nations to include in its covenant a provision for her dream of an international bureau of education, but she was unsuccessful. During the war she received a postgraduate degree in international affairs, never losing sight of her goal of an international school curriculum that would promote justice and understanding. Andrews maintained her dedication to promoting peace studies until her death, serving in the International Law Association, the World Peace Foundation, and the International Guild.

Sources:
J. McKeen Cattell, ed., *Leaders in Education: A Biographical Directory* (New York: Science Press, 1932), p. 48;

Alden Whitman, ed., *American Reformers* (New York: Wilson, 1985), pp. 122–123.

CHARLES AUSTIN BEARD

1874-1948

HISTORIAN

National Reputation. Charles A. Beard has had an enduring influence upon the interpretation of the American past. He was born on a farm in Indiana and educated at a small Quaker academy nearby. After graduatingfrom DePauw University, he undertook graduate study at Oxford, where he helped to found Ruskin Hall, a workingmen's college. He returned to the United States and married Mary Ritter, who later became his lifelong collaborator. After receiving a doctorate from Columbia University in 1904, he accepted a faculty position there, where he was a popular teacher and highly productive scholar until 1917. Among his influential historical texts produced during this period were *American Government and Politics* (1910), *American City Government* (1912), *Outlines of European History* (1912–1914), *The Supreme Court and the Constitution* (1912), *American Citizenship* (1914), and *Economic Origins of Jeffersonian Democracy* (1915). However, his fame began in earnest in 1913 with the publication of *An Economic Interpretation of the Constitution of the United States,* an "intellectual bombshell" in which Beard claimed that the Constitutionwas designed to protect the commercial interests and property rights of the framers.

Controversial View of the Constitution. The book brought Beard both praise and a storm of criticism. According to the historian John Braeman, Beard admired the wisdom and realism of the framers of the Constitution yet insisted in his book that the Constitution was the work of the propertied few and designed to safeguard the economic interests of their class against popular majorities. His book was denounced by conservatives and hailed by reformers, according to Braeman, for "removing a major intellectual obstacle to the program of federal government action to regulate business and assist the less favored numbers of American society." Beard used biographical data and Treasury Department records to conclude that the Constitution was essentially undemocratic, reasoning that the vast majority was unable to participate in its ratification because of the restrictive property qualifications on suffrage. Beard claimed that if the small farmer had been allowed to vote, the Constitution would have been rejected. Later historians believed that much of the data Beard used was inadequate to provide such conclusions; however, few disagreed with his premise that the men writing the Constitution were men of property with a vested interest in the creation of a stable social order. Moreover, many later historians concluded that except for the secession crisis, American politics could most usefully be studied as a series of sharp antagonisms within a class consensus. After Beard's early work, no American historian was able to ignore the role of economics as a potent, although not necessarily singular, influence on the nation's history. Even scholars who profoundly disagreed with Beard could not ignore him.

Champion of Civil Liberties. Beard was a lifelong champion of civil liberties because of his commitment to preserving the free marketplace of ideas. At Columbia University he brought on himself the wrath of the trustees when he spoke out against demands that radical speakers be barred from public schools because one had reportedly declared, "To hell with the American flag." "We could not expect to have liberty without someone's abuse of it," Beard argued, "and between having too much authority or too much liberty, I preferred the latter." Yet he insisted that education inculcate in youth the basic values, that it should "instill in students knowledge of and respect for this country's distinctive and unique heritage." Beard's commitment to civil liberties ended his academic career. In 1917, although Beard supported America's entry into World War I, he resigned from his professorship at Columbia to protest the dismissal of colleagues who had publicly opposed the war. His resignation marked a lifelong commitment to academic freedom, and although he never again held an academic appointment, he did not lose faith in the importance of education in a democracy. In 1919 he helped found the New School for Social Research, based in New York City. Founded as a center for "discussion, instruction and counseling for mature men and women," and offering courses dealing exclusively with matters of concern to the newly emerging social sciences, this was America's first university for adults, and the first to be run by its own faculty, free from the interference of trustees or state legislators. Beard was again embroiled in controversy in the late 1930s and early 1940s when he clung to an isolationist position in the face of Nazi aggression.

Beard's Legacy. Unencumbered by teaching or other academic responsibilities, Beard produced a steady stream of books and articles from the 1920s until his death in 1948, many in collaboration with his wife, Mary. Both *The Rise of American Civilization* (1927), marked by Mary's ardent feminism, and *A Basic History of the United States* (1944), their most popular book (widely used as a textbook), were hailed as landmark publications by historians. Sales of Beard's historical texts totaled more than eleven million volumes. Historians, including Beard's sharpest critics, cited him as one of the most influential figures in twentieth-century American historical thought. At a centennial celebration of his life and work held at DePauw University in 1974, John Braeman explained that "Throughout his life, Beard's overriding commitment was to the fulfillment of the promise of American life. In Beard's own words, he desired 'a high standard of life for the whole mass of the American people, a land without the degradation of poverty and unemployment on one side or the degradation of luxury, rivalry, and conspicuous waste on the other.'" Historian Henry Steele Commager summed up Beard's influence at the centennial celebration: "The contemporary historian has first to dispense with him before he can get on with the job, and that is not true of any other historian of our times."

Sources:

"Charles Austin Beard," in *Thinkers of the Twentieth Century,* edited by Roland Turner (Chicago: St. James Press, 1987);

Richard Hofstadter, *The Progressive Historians* (New York: Knopf, 1969);

David A. Marcell, *Progress and Pragmatism: James, Dewey, Beard, and the American Idea of Progress* (Westport, Conn.: Greenwood Press, 1974);

Ellen Nore, *Charles A. Beard: An Intellectual Biography* (Carbondale: Southern Illinois University Press, 1983);

Marvin Swanson, ed., *Charles A. Beard: An Observance of the Centennial of his Birth* (Greencastle, Ind.: DePauw University Press, 1974).

JOHN DEWEY

1859-1952

PHILOSOPHER, EDUCATOR

Background. John Dewey was an American philosopher, educator, and psychologist whose widely hailed work provided the basis for much of the teaching practice in the United States in the early twentieth century. He had been a prominent national figure since receiving his Ph.D. from Johns Hopkins University in 1884, and his growing reputation was marked by his election as president of the American Psychological Association in 1899 and president of the American Philosophical Association in 1905. His distinctive educational philosophy began to take shape in 1896 when he founded an experimental school at the new University of Chicago. This laboratory school, officially called the University Elementary School, blended and utilized many of the new trends in educational thought and practice at the elementary-school level; it especially encouraged constant experiment and inquiry as the principal learning methods for its children. Dewey consciously intended this Chicago school to be an educational laboratory that could serve as a model for other schools, if its practices were found effective; and the school, which tested educational theories in a real-life setting, became Dewey's first major contribution to the profoundly influential progressive education movement. In later years, especially when he was teaching at Columbia University (1904–1930), Dewey's influence and impact on the American educational establishment reached their height.

Functional Psychology. His *How We Think* (1910) demonstrated his theory of functional psychology, which viewed stimulus and response as the functional and correlative means of organic coordination and direction; in the book he explained how the theory worked in the context of educational and social interactions. Dewey believed that thought arises from efforts to solve problems; when thoughtful action is directed at solving those problems, the learner then uncovers "truth." He wrote extensively on this theory in *Essays in Experimental Logic* (1916). His conception of thinking, known as "instrumentalism," was closely related to the philosophy of pragmatism expounded by William James and Charles Peirce, the philosophy that dominated this era.

Democracy and Education. Dewey's philosophy of thought was eventually translated into specific curricular practices, most notably through the work of his colleague at Columbia, Professor William Heard Kilpatrick. But Dewey's greatest contribution to American education was probably his 1916 volume *Democracy and Education.* In this book he argued forcefully for an American public education system that turned the "ideal of equality of opportunity into reality." Dewey insisted that it was fatal for a democracy to permit the formation of fixed economic classes, to have one system of education for the upper and middle classes and another for children of wage earners. "Over-bookish education for some and over-practical for others brings about a division of mental and moral habits, ideals, and outlooks, he suggested, commenting on the prevailing system of trade-training programs for some versus exclusively academic programs for others. Dewey felt that all children should be exposed to both types of education: "Academic education turns out future citizens with no sympathy for work done with the hands and no training for understanding social and political difficulties. Trade training turns out future workers who may have greater immediate skills than without training, but no enlargement of mind and no insight into scientific and social implications of the work they do." Dewey warned that trade training would never prepare pupils to adjust if the trade they pursued became obsolete. Dewey had great faith in the American public school system, which he called the "only fundamental agency for good." Predicting that the great accumulation of wealth at one social extreme and the conditions of dire necessity at the other in 1916 would make democracy even more difficult in the years to come, Dewey believed that only a system of education that allowed the downtrodden to forge ahead in life could truly support a democracy.

Schools of Tomorrow. Although not as monumental a volume as *Democracy and Education,* Dewey's 1915 book *Schools of Tomorrow,* written in collaboration with his wife, Evelyn, clearly expressed his philosophy of education. It was these tenets that helped clarify the Progressive Education Association's core beliefs in 1919. Dewey wrote, "Conventional education trains children for docility and obedience; the careful performance of imposed tasks because they are imposed regardless of where they lead is suitable only for creating a society in which there is one head to care for and plan the lives and institutions of the people." This training, the Deweys argued, interferes with the successful conduct of society and government in a democracy. "If we train our children only to take orders and fail to give them the confidence to think and act for themselves, we are putting almost insurmountable obstacles in the way of overcoming the defects of the present system and establishing the truth of democratic ideals." As for the curriculum itself, the Deweys insisted that for the great majority of students whose "major interests are not abstract ideas and who must pass their lives in some practical occupation," schools needed to develop a method of education to bridge the gap between the purely intellectual and theoretical side of life and the students' preparation for future occupations. Dewey sharply criticized some vocational training for dispensing with the essential cultural and historical grounding he believed necessary for liberal education in a democracy.

Dewey's Influence. In civic organizations and in national affairs, Dewey was an activist and even a leader in many liberal causes. He served as a trustee for Hull House, the settlement house founded by Jane Addams to serve Chicago's immigrants, and assisted in 1916 with the foundation of the American Federation of Teachers (AFT), a teachers' union within the American Federation of Labor (AFL). Dewey's educational ideas were first put into practice in schools such as the Laboratory Schools, founded by Dewey himself, at the University of Chicago, and the Walden School in New York City, founded by Margaret Naumberg in 1915. Dewey served as the first president of the American Association of University Professors (AAUP) and was a charter member of the American Civil Liberties Union. With the eminent historian Charles A. Beard, he was a founding member of the New School for Social Research in New York City. During his long and prolific career, Dewey's influence on educational thought and the entire American educational establishment was multifaceted and profound. His philosophy of instrumentalism and his numerous books on educational method provided the principal intellectual foundations of progressive education, the influence of which can be traced through the century to the liberal education policies of the 1960s. Significant among his later writings were *Human Nature and Conduct* (1922); *Liberalism and Social Action* (1935); *Freedom and Culture* (1939); and *Problems of Men* (1946).

Sources:

John Brubacher, *A History of the Problems of Education* (New York: McGraw-Hill, 1947);

John Dewey, *Democracy and Education* (New York: Macmillan, 1916);

Dewey and Evelyn Dewey, *Schools of Tomorrow* (New York: Macmillan, 1915);

George Dykhuizen, *The Life and Mind of John Dewey* (Carbondale: Southern Illinois University Press, 1973);

Robert B. Westbrook, *John Dewey and American Democracy* (Ithaca, N.Y.: Cornell University Press, 1991).

HENRY MARTIN MAXSON

1853-1930

SUPERINTENDENT OF SCHOOLS, PLAINFIELD, NEW JERSEY

Theory into Practice. Dr. Henry Martin Maxson was born in Stonington, Connecticut, and graduated from Amherst College in 1877. After receiving his M.A. from Amherst, Maxson taught at and served as the principal of the North Attleboro High School in Massachusetts. In later years, after receiving his Ph.D., he served as superintendent of the Plainfield, New Jersey, school system from 1892 until his retirement in 1926. When Maxson was honored by his colleagues in 1917 at the National Superintendents' Association dinner in Kansas City, his twenty-five-year career exemplified the dramatic progress of education in the United States during these years. With a record that was increasingly emulated by his colleagues, Maxson effectively translated the theories of progressive education into the facts of daily school practice. His accomplishments were even more startling, his champions said, when one realized that "not many years ago, education was limited to the 3 R's." Among his accomplishments, Maxson set the standard by which auxiliary agencies became an established part of the American school district.

Frills Become Requirements. Maxson was one of the nation's first superintendents to recognize the importance of medical and dental inspections and the need for a school nurse. His insistence on an annual physical exam for each pupil became a state law, and he ensured that his schools provided arrangements for proper medical care for those too poor to obtain it. Recognizing the need for physical training, schools in his district measured students in the fall, gave corrective exercises if needed, and reanalyzed the students' progress in June. After Maxson installed a swimming pool in the high school, learning to swim was made a requirement for graduation. He also established manual training classes so that "students who have little capacity for literary work will have an opportunity to develop their talents along industrial lines. The work of such students was judged to meet commercial standards in cabinetmaking, dressmaking, millinery, and cooking. Innovations occurred in academic classes as well when Maxson introduced proficiency examinations to be given two times per year in each academic subject. A trend was started when he hired an attendance supervisor (later called a truant officer), whose job was to follow up student absences to ascertain their causes. Maxson preferred a woman for this post, he said, because she "can get closer to the home and has less of the police character."

Innovative Programs for Nontraditional Students. Maxson established open-air classrooms for anemic children who were "not fitted to do regular work" and created opportunity classes for children with "peculiar mentality who cannot benefit from regular class work." He was praised for his unique plan to train girls of limited mental ability in "various lines of housework." Maxson began yet another trend when he established summer-school classes for students who failed to be promoted because of absences or "other causes"; such classes allowed students to make up deficiencies and catch up with their classmates.

Schools as a Community Resource. Maxson made his district's school buildings widely available for community use. In 1917, for example, nine thousand nonstudent community members used the Plainfield schools outside school hours. The evening-school programs he began for foreign-born community members offered English and civics courses and aided hundreds of immigrants in securing citizenship. Maxson also established free public lecture courses for adults, in which renowned lecturers or musicians performed for audiences of eight hundred to nine hundred people for each event. Although Maxson was not the only school superintendent who turned progressive theory into actual practice, the broad range of innovations and adaptations he brought to the Plainfield schools made his New Jersey district a model for the nation.

Source:
"Dr. Henry Maxson, School Superintendent," *American School Board Journal*, 55 (July 1917): 28–29.

LUCY SPRAGUE MITCHELL

1878-1967

EDUCATOR, FOUNDER OF THE BANK STREET SCHOOL OF EDUCATION

A Different Path. Lucy Sprague Mitchell, writer, teacher, and social reformer, is remembered primarily for her work in building experimental schools and as a researcher who carefully studied children's language-learning patterns. At a time when many educated women who sought careers spurned the notion of marriage and family, Sprague chose to marry economist Wesley Clair Mitchell and raise four children while pursuing a full career.

Background. Lucy Sprague, the daughter of a wealthy Chicago family, grew up in an archetypal Victorian household. She viewed her mother as "ardent but suppressed, delightful but tragic" and eagerly embraced the notion of education as a means of escaping a similar fate. She was largely self-educated before college but attended Radcliffe as an undergraduate and graduated magna cum laude with honors in philosophy (the first honors awarded to a Radcliffe student from that department) in 1900. Like many female graduates of the day, Sprague found herself after four years of exciting college life back at home with her family. At the turn of the century a popular manual for girls titled *After College, What?* warned that for many educated women the answer to the question of the title was "deep and perplexing unhappiness" and "a decided homesickness for the stimulation of college life." Lucy Sprague discovered that this was true in her own case, and when in 1903 she was offered the newly created position of dean of women at the University of California, Berkeley, she eagerly accepted.

Professional Educator. Sprague was a competent, efficient, and pioneering dean. Toward the end of her deanship a wave of education in sex hygiene swept the country, and she was required to become actively involved with issues of sexuality. Under the leadership of reform-minded doctors and women's-rights advocates, a "social purity" campaign had been launched to end the "double standard of conduct and the evils of prostitution and disease. Dean Sprague, who admitted that she had scarcely heard of gonorrhea or syphilis before she conducted research on the topics, held discussion groups on social diseases with women students until all twelve hundred of them had been reached. Although she enjoyed her work in college, Sprague yearned for the opportunity to learn about nonteaching professions for women from some of the leading pioneers of women's work in New York City. Two events affected her decision to leave Berkeley: her father's death and her acceptance of Mitchell's marriage proposal. Sprague's inheritance made her independently wealthy, and Mitchell offered to conduct his profession anywhere she decided she wanted to live. They married in 1912 and settled in New York, where Mitchell joined Columbia University's faculty and Lucy explored her professional options.

Influence of John Dewey and Edward Thorndike. The Mitchells were friends with the philosopher-educator John Dewey and his wife during the years 1913–1917, and Lucy Mitchell and John Dewey often discussed the philosophy of education, especially the ideas Dewey espoused in *Democracy and Education* (1916). Edward Thorndike also influenced her thinking when she attended his classes on the application of science and statistics to education. In 1914 Mitchell worked giving intelligence tests to mentally retarded children, and in January 1915 she convinced the New York Board of Education to establish the Psychological Survey, an agency whose long-range goal was to establish mental and motor performance norms for children from ages eight to thirteen. Through this work during the next two years, she gained expertise as a tester as well as new knowledge about children's abilities and the learning process. Her work in setting up the Psychological Survey established her among the community of experimental, progressive educators in New York.

Contributions to Early Childhood Education. Mitchell then turned her professional interest and her own fortune to the study of early schooling, even at the kindergarten and prekindergarten levels. In 1916, along with her friend Harriet Johnson and others, Mitchell masterminded and sponsored the following innovations in education: a Bureau of Educational Experiments, a school to implement and experiment with the principles of progressive education, a laboratory to record and analyze how and why young children learn, a teachers' college to promote progressive methods, a workshop for writers of children's literature, and a bulletin to disseminate the collaborators' findings from their research. Years later, in 1950, the Bureau of Educational Experiments became certified as the Bank Street College of Education. The school that Mitchell founded served as a model for subsequent early education programs that were considered "developmentally appropriate." But perhaps the greatest contribution of Mitchell and her collaborators was her lifelong focus on the way children learn. Her "Here and Now" stories, published in 1921, set a precedent for realistic children's literature that appealed to prereaders' interest in the things in their world. Programs for young children popularized by Mitchell and other progressives were labeled "flamingly radical" and "loony" during the 1910s, but by the 1950s these same "developmentally appropriate" schools were considered traditional nursery schools. Lucy Sprague Mitchell and her colleagues professionalized the study of early childhood education, and their legacy lived on in programs such as Head Start and in the work of the Bank Street College of Education.

Sources:

Joyce Antler, *Lucy Sprague Mitchell: The Making of a Modern Woman* (New Haven: Yale University Press, 1987);

Polly Greenburg, "Early Childhood Education as Social Reform," *Young Children* (July 1987): 70–84.

ROBERT RUSSA MOTON

1867-1940

COMMANDANT OF CADETS AT HAMPTON INSTITUTE; PRINCIPAL OF TUSKEGEE INSTITUTE

Plantation Childhood. Robert Russa Moton was a leading black American educator in the 1910s who graduated from Virginia's Hampton Institute in 1890, then served as the school's commandant of cadets from 1891 to 1915. He succeeded Booker T. Washington as principal of the Tuskegee Institute in Alabama, a vocational school for blacks, where he raised the curriculum to college level. Moton grew up on a plantation called Pleasant Shade in Prince Edward County, Virginia, where his father, a former slave, had hired himself out to a wealthy white family, the William Vaughans. Moton, with many responsibilities in the Vaughan house, wrote that it was in that home that he "caught my first glimpses of real culture and got my first inspiration as to what I would like to be." Moton was educated by Mrs. Vaughan and also in a free school, one of the first in the country to educate blacks. According to Moton, his childhood was happy and carefree until one of his closest childhood friends, a white neighbor, left to attend Virginia Polytechnic Institute. Moton confronted racial prejudice in a very personal, immediate manner when his friend, returning home at Christmas, refused to shake hands with Moton. Moton decided then that getting an advanced education was the best thing for his future.

Hampton Years. After several long years of hard labor in a lumber camp, Moton left at age eighteen for Hampton Institute, an industrial school for blacks, where he was humiliated by his failure to pass the entrance examinations. However, he resolved to get a job and study until he could meet the requirements, and he began to work in the school's sawmill, where his expertise in grading lumber was appreciated. He was soon admitted to Hampton, working during the day and attending classes at night. During his years at the Hampton Institute he overcame his earlier academic problems and became a successful student. Moton even earned a certificate to practice law after studying on the weekends with the superintendent of schools in Prince Edward County and with a prominent local lawyer who allowed him access to his law library. After graduation Moton was tapped to take over the administration of the school when General Armstrong, the commandant, died in 1893.

Move to Tuskegee. In his autobiography Moton reminisced about the sense of personal loss felt by so many people upon the 1915 death of Booker T. Washington. "The colored people throughout the whole country went about as if they had lost the dearest member of their immediate family, and this feeling was largely shared by the white people as well, especially the older ones." Moton, chosen to succeed Washington as the president of Tuskegee Institute in Alabama, left at once for a $2 million fund-raising drive in northern cities. During the next four years Moton oversaw an extensive effort to build rural schools for blacks in eleven southern states. The extension department of Tuskegee Institute supervised the construction of 720 schools at a cost of $1,133,083, of which $337,192 represented public appropriations; $88,445, private contributions from whites; $430,381, gifts from blacks; and $227,065, the personal gift of Julius Rosenwald, one of Tuskegee's trustees.

War Effort. One of Moton's most lasting contributions was his work for the American war effort in World War I. Tuskegee was selected to train black drafted men who, in contingents of 308 men each, began arriving at the school in May 1918. The last group was trained in October 1918, and all were absorbed into the Student Army Training Corps. In all, Tuskegee trained 1,229 men, most of whom were immediately sent overseas. On 2 December 1918, at the request of President Wilson and Secretary of War Newton Baker, Moton went to France to examine conditions affecting black soldiers. While in France, Moton visited and spoke to black soldiers at every site where they were stationed. Moton had heard rumors to the effect that "morally, the Negro soldier in France had failed" and that many had been guilty of "the unmentionable crime" of rape. Moton investigated these claims and found that only one battalion had displayed questionable behavior, and none of the four officers accused of cowardice in the field was found guilty in a court-martial. Moton reported that Gen. John Pershing said that he believed that "any officers, white or black, under the same adverse circumstances that these men faced, would have failed." Moton also ascertained after numerous investigations that the "unmentionable crime was not more prevalent among colored than among white, or any other soldiers." Moton, who had taken great care to track down every rumor, was proud of his effort to stop the rumors which, as he said, were "defaming a race, threatening to cut down the efficiency of Negro troops, and putting America in a bad light before the world." Throughout his career as Tuskegee principal, Moton continued his efforts on behalf of African Americans for better and more extensive education. Moreover, in 1930 he was appointed to the U.S. Commission on Education for Haiti and the National Advisory Commission on Education in Liberia.

Sources:

Ida Bellegarde, *Black Heroes and Heroines: Robert Russa Moton* (Pine Bluff, Ark.: Bell Enterprises, 1981);

Robert Russa Moton, *Finding a Way Out* (Garden City, N.J.: Doubleday, Page, 1920).

CARTER GODWIN WOODSON

1875-1950

PIONEER IN BLACK HISTORY

Son of a Former Slave. Carter Godwin Woodson, the son of a former slave, rose from humble origins and against steep odds to a remarkable career as a scholar and educator. Though he did not begin high school until the age of twenty, Woodson went on to study at Berea College, the University of Chicago, the Sorbonne, and Harvard University, where he earned a Ph.D. in 1912. Later, from 1919 to 1920, he was dean of the School of Liberal Arts at Howard University.

Framework for the Study of Black History. In 1915 Woodson founded the Association for the Study of Negro Life and History to train black historians and to collect, preserve, and publish documents on blacks. Woodson lived in an era that had completely neglected the history of black Americans, and the absence from textbooks and from historical volumes of any information about the history of blacks in the United States was his motivation for establishing a framework for the scholarly study of black people. What information there was in most history texts on African Americans presented a highly distorted view of their past and their role in the nation's history. For example, the prevailing interpretation of the Civil War and Reconstruction (popularized by D. W. Griffith's 1915 film *The Birth of a Nation*) blamed inept leadership for the conflict and portrayed slaves as well treated and happy with their lot. Reconstruction, in this view, was a dismal episode in the nation's history, with the inept and corrupt black Republicans in control of the South, aided by Northern carpetbaggers interested only in lining their pockets. The rise of the Ku Klux Klan and the imposition of segregation, in this view, was necessary to restore social order. To combat this view Woodson founded the *Journal of Negro History* in 1916 so that other historians who were creating a record would have an outlet for scholarly publishing. Other lasting accomplishments of Woodson were his organization of the first Negro History Week in 1916 and his volume on black schooling, *The Education of the Negro Prior to 1861*, published in 1915. He also published several influential works in the 1920s, including *The History of the Negro Church* (1921), *Free Negro Owners of Slaves in the U.S.* (1924), and *African Myths* (1928). Between 1944 and his death in 1950, he edited the six-volume *Encyclopedia Africana*.

Source:

Carter Godwin Woodson, *Negro Makers of History* (Washington, D.C.: Associated Publishers, 1928).

PEOPLE IN THE NEWS

Edith Abbott of Hull House, and founder of the Chicago School of Social Work, noted in 1918 that the "efforts of the professional woman to realize a new ideal of pecuniary independence constituted a social revolution."

Felix Adler, founder of the Ethical Culture Movement, advocated progressive education, free kindergartens, and vocational training schools in 1910.

Professor **Frank Aydelotte** of the Massachusetts Institute of Technology organized a course on the historic background of the war and the social philosophy of the belligerent nations; called the War Aims Course, it was soon offered at all colleges in the United States training conscripted men.

Charles Caldwell, of the Chicago Tuberculosis Sanitarium, announced in 1917 that approximately 30 percent of Chicago's schoolchildren were anemic, underfed, and possibly affected by tuberculosis.

Dr. P. P. Claxton, of the U.S. Bureau of Education, wrote a foreword in a 1915 pamphlet issued to all rural schools by the Victor Talking Machine Company of Camden, New Jersey, on how to use the machine and its records in country schools.

Andrew Draper, commissioner of education of the state of New York, said in 1910 that the "affairs of the school should be wholly separated from municipal business; the public school system rests upon the taxing power of the state only."

In 1917 **W. E. B. Du Bois** planned a publication called "Black Review" to be published in English, French, and Spanish editions; his goal was for American blacks to learn French and Spanish.

John Erskine helped stimulate the Great Books movement in education in 1916.

Leo Favrot and **Jackson Davis** were appointed in 1917 to write a course guide for the county training schools for blacks nationwide.

Abraham Flexner's Carnegie Foundation study of medical education in the United States and Canada, published in 1910, rated 155 medical schools, and his findings led to closing almost half of them and modifications to many others.

Abraham Flexner's proposal for a model school, published by the Rockefeller Foundation in 1916 as *A Modern School,* led to the founding of the Lincoln Experimental School of Teachers College, Columbia University, patterned after his model.

Guy Stanton Ford, dean of the graduate school at the University of Minnesota, wrote an open letter to the nation's high-school principals urging them to use the 1917 commencement exercises to inspire patriotic fervor for World War I.

Professor **Herbert Foster** of Dartmouth took a leave of absence to travel to France to take charge of all work in history to be written in the aftermath of World War I in 1919.

William Foster, president of Reed College, gave a speech at the 1915 National Education Association meeting titled "Athletics as Education and Athletics as Business."

In 1910 the *Charleston* (S.C.) *News and Courier* expressed editorial outrage at philanthropist **Walter P. Hill's** insistence that blacks could be formally schooled.

William Heard Kilpatrick, known as the "father of progressive education," said in 1918 that textbooks reduce "man to mind and mind largely to memory."

In 1916 Professor **Alexis Lange** of the University of California argued that every college woman should learn home economics so that the liberal arts degree should be "not only for fitness, but for fitness for something."

In 1911 **Bishop Lawrence** of Boston warned Radcliffe women to "stay at their own fireside" and "uplift those at home" rather than the "downtrodden outside."

Etta Leighton, of the National Security League, published pamphlets for teachers on "after-the-war patriotism" in 1919.

Abbott Lawrence Lowell succeeded **Charles William Eliot** as president of Harvard in 1910; Lowell returned the university's curriculum to a structured plan focusing on a major subject and created the system of residential houses.

Abbott Lawrence Lowell of Harvard announced in September 1918 that his institution would accept as a student in Harvard's Students' Army Training Corps any young man older than eighteen who had graduated from a good high school.

President Richard MacLaurin of the Massachusetts Institute of Technology was chosen the educational director of the Students' Army Training Corps in 1918.

Dr. Gustave Mann was dismissed from his chair in physiology at Tulane after criticizing methods and faculty in a public address in 1915.

Robert Russa Moton, formerly commander of cadets at Hampton Institute in Virginia, succeeded Booker T. Washington as principal of Tuskegee Institute in Alabama in 1915. Moton later raised the curriculum of this vocational school for blacks to the college level.

Margaret Naumberg founded the Walden School in New York in 1915; its curriculum was based on progressive ideals of children learning from experience, not memorization.

Fifteen hundred students at the University of Pennsylvania signed petitions protesting the firing of Dr. Scott Nearing, a Wharton School assistant professor fired for critical remarks about the institution and the national economy.

Educator Stuart Noble of Tulane University wrote in 1918 that "psychological research has shown that many full-blooded negroes have ability surpassing that of the median white man, and that there are some negroes of exceptional ability."

George Foster Peabody, a prominent philanthropist and supporter of Booker T. Washington's vision of industrial education, commented on black leaders' attacks on Washington in 1911 by saying, "a great deal of harm is being done, notably by some Negroes in Boston who have never seen the South."

Health Commissioner William Robertson of Chicago announced in 1917 that 80 percent of the 10,760 children between the ages of eight and fifteen who had been examined by volunteer dentists were in dire need of dental treatment.

In Massachusetts Gertrude Simmons reported in 1917 that penny school lunches were financially self-supporting since the children in the upper grades had begun helping wash the dishes.

In 1917 John D. Shoop, president of the Department of Superintendents of the National Education Association, announced the primary issues of concern for their annual meeting in Kansas City: uniform standards in public schools, standardized units of achievement and measurable standards of school administration, vocational guidance based on predetermined mental aptitude, and standards of individual health among pupils.

The state supervisor of Negro Training Schools in Tennessee, S. L. Smith, explained in 1915 that he had equipped his schools with kitchens "as nearly like well ordered kitchens of the city as possible to better prepare the girls to do cooking for the white people of the town."

Lucy Ward Stebbins, a Radcliffe graduate, was named dean of women at the University of California, Berkeley, in 1912.

Carter Godwin Woodson, a pioneer in black history, founded the Association for the Study of Negro Life and History in 1915 to train black historians and to collect, preserve, and publish documents on blacks.

Ella Flagg Young was chosen superintendent of Chicago schools in 1910.

DEATHS

Henry Adams, 80, professor of history at Harvard and the author of *The Education of Henry Adams,* the classic literary autobiography, 27 March 1918.

Clarence Ashley, 67, dean of the New York University Law School, 26 January 1916.

George Willis Botsford, 61, professor of ancient history at Columbia University and author of influential textbooks on the history of Greece and Rome, 14 December 1912.

Professor Francis Cuyler, 58, Van Dyck Chair of Mathematics and Music at Lawrenceville School, Trenton, New Jersey, 25 January 1916.

Martin Luther D'Ooge, 76, professor of Greek at the University of Michigan and former president of the American Philological Association, 14 September 1915.

Charlotte Drinkwater, 84, general superintendent of Boston YWCA and founder of Hillside School in 1901, 2 March 1916.

Edward Kidder Graham, 42, professor at the University of North Carolina, 26 October 1918.

Dr. Karl Guthe, 59, dean of the graduate school at Michigan, 10 September 1915.

Frederick Guion Ireland, 70, charter member of the Schoolmasters Association of New York, 5 February 1916.

John Sinclair, 68, professor emeritus of mathematics at Worcester Polytechnic Institute and the chair of that department from 1869 to 1908, 12 September 1915.

John Stewart, 90, a fifty-seven-year fellow of Middlebury College, 29 October 1915.

Raymond Taylor, 62, professor of civics at Kansas State University and promoter of some of the newer aspects of history teaching, 14 October 1919.

John Howard Van Amringe, dean of Columbia University and professor of mathematics, eulogized by his peers for his influential fifty years of service to the youth at Columbia, 12 September 1915.

Booker T. Washington, 59, first president of the Tuskegee Institute, a trade and vocational school for African Americans, and the most prominent black political and educational leader of his era, 14 November 1915.

PUBLICATIONS

Carter Alexander, *School Statistics and Publicity* (New York: Silver, Burdette, 1915);

Leonard Ayres, *The Public Library and the Public Schools* (Cleveland: Survey Committee of the Cleveland Foundation, 1913);

Lydia Balderston, *Housewifery* (Philadelphia: Lippincott, 1918);

Henry Eastman Bennett, *School Efficiency* (Boston: Ginn, 1917);

Frances Sage Bradley, *How to Conduct a Children's Health Conference, Bulletin No. 23* (Washington, D.C.: Children's Bureau, U.S. Department of Labor, 1917);

J. C. Chapman and Grace P. Rush, *The Scientific Measurement of Classroom Products* (New York: Silver, Burdette, 1917);

Henry Curtis, *Recreation for Teachers, or the Teacher's Leisure Time* (New York: Macmillan, 1918);

Arthur Dean, *Our Schools in War Time — and After* (Boston: Ginn, 1919);

John Dewey, *Democracy and Education* (New York: Macmillan, 1916);

William Dooley, *Vocational Mathematics for Girls* (Chicago: D.C. Heath, 1917);

John Robert Gregg, *Gregg Shorthand* (New York: Gregg, 1912);

John Haaren, *Natural Freehand Writing* (New York: D.C. Heath, 1916);

Warren Horner, *Training for a Life Insurance Agent* (Philadelphia: Lippincott, 1916);

Buford Johnson, *Experimental Study of Motor Abilities of Children in Primary Grades* (Baltimore: Johns Hopkins University Press, 1915);

Frederick Kuenzli, *A Manual of Physical Training and Preparatory Military Instruction* (New York: Macmillan, 1916);

Sterling Leonard, *English Composition as a Social Problem* (New York: Houghton Mifflin, 1919);

Irwin Madden, *A Rural Arithmetic* (Boston: Houghton Mifflin, 1917);

William McAndrew, *The Public and Its School* (Yonkers, N.Y.: World Book, 1914);

Norbert Melville, *Standard Methods of Testing Juvenile Mentality* (Philadephia: Lippincott, 1916);

George Smith, *Longmans' English Lessons* (New York: Longmans, Green, 1912);

Daniel Starch, *Educational Measurements* (New York: Macmillan, 1915);

Eva March Tappan, *The Little Book of the War* (Boston: Houghton Mifflin, 1918);

William Theisen, *The City Superintendent and the Board of Education, Contribution to Education No. 84* (New York: Teachers College of Columbia University, 1916);

Frances Twombley, *The Romance of Labor* (New York: Macmillan, 1917);

Harvey Voorhees, *The Law of the Public School System of the United States* (Boston: Little, Brown, 1916);

Harry Watt, *Health Is Wealth: A Manual for Public Schools* (Ocala: Florida Women's Christian Temperance Union, 1917);

The Wisconsin County Training Schools for Teachers in Rural Schools, Bulletin No. 17 (Washington, D.C.: U.S. Bureau of Education, 1916);

Yearbook for 1916, Carnegie Endowment for World Peace (Washington, D.C.: Carnegie Foundation, 1916).

FASHION

by JESSICA MARSHALL and SILVANA R. SIDDALI

CONTENTS

Sidebars and tables are listed in italics.

1910

- Enormous hats festooned with ostrich plumes and fastened with long hat pins mark the end of the vogue for elaborate millinery creations that began in the nineteenth century.

- Elizabeth Arden (born Florence Nightingale Graham) opens a beauty salon in New York City. In 1915 she opens a branch in Washington, D.C., and by 1939 there are twenty-nine Elizabeth Arden salons.

- Ford Motor Company begins operations at Highland Park in the "Crystal Palace," a trailblazing factory complex designed by Albert Kahn and engineered by Edward Gray.

- Levi Strauss and Company begins making children's clothes, preparing the way for the adoption of casual play clothes for children.

- The first phonograph cabinet, with French cabriole legs and a mansard lid, is patented.

- Frank Lloyd Wright returns from Europe and begins construction on Taliesin, his new studio and house in the farmlands of Wisconsin, where he had lived as a child.

13 July   The first issue of *Women's Wear Daily* is published in New York City.

8 Sept.   Pennsylvania Station in New York City, the largest project ever undertaken by the architectural firm of McKim, Mead and White, is opened to commuter traffic from Long Island, linking the Pennsylvania and Long Island Railroads.

Oct.   Reacting to French fashions — such as the hobble skirt shown by French couturier Paul Poiret the previous spring — as unsuitable for American women's active lifestyles, the American Ladies' Tailors Association stages an exhibition of functional clothing at the Astor Hotel in New York City, showcasing such American originals as the suffragette suit with a divided skirt and aeroplane suits insulated with wool and fur.

1911

- C. H. K. Curtis, publisher of the *Saturday Evening Review* and *Ladies' Home Journal,* hires Charles Coolidge Parlin to conduct the first market research study, which alerts advertisers to the rise of women as consumers.

- Rayon, billed as "artificial silk," is introduced by the American Viscose Company. It does not become popular until 1915, when French couturiere Gabrielle "Coco" Chanel begins using it in her designs.

25 Mar.   A fire at the Triangle Shirtwaist Factory, a sweatshop in New York's Lower East Side, kills 146 female workers.

23 May   Fourteen years after breaking ground, the New York Public Library on Fifth Avenue, designed by the firm of Carrère and Hastings, is opened to the public. Partners John M. Carrère and Thomas Hastings are former employees of the architectural firm of McKim, Mead and White, well known for its Beaux-Arts buildings.

1912

- The dance team of Irene and Vernon Castle starts a craze for ballroom dancing. The simple, lightweight clothing that Irene Castle wears for ease of movement on the dance floor helps to increase the popularity of comfortable clothing among American women.

- Hoping to interest manufacturers in improving American industrial design, the Newark Museum of Art stages an exhibition of commercial productions designed by the Deutscher Werkbund of Germany.

Dec.   *The New York Times* announces that it will sponsor a contest for American fashion designers, leading to the establishment of the Society of American Fashions.

22 Dec.   The prestigious import and custom-design house Thurn of New York City admits it has been sewing French designer labels into its American-made dresses. "American women have been brainwashed into thinking French clothes are superior," complains a Thurn executive.

1913

- The 792-foot-high Woolworth Building, designed by architect Cass Gilbert, opens on lower Broadway in New York City. Until 1930 it holds the record as the tallest building in the world.

- Midway Gardens, an amusement center and concert hall designed by Frank Lloyd Wright, opens in Chicago.

- The architectural firm of Cram, Goodhue and Ferguson completes two Gothic buildings, St. Thomas Church in New York City and the Graduate College at Princeton University.

- Henry Ford's Model T, originally available in a range of colors, is now available only in black.

- Grand Central Terminal, designed by the architectural firms of Reed and Stem and Warren and Wetmore, is completed in midtown Manhattan.

- The first face-powder compact, a cardboard box filled with powder and a puff, is introduced to American consumers.

- Formica is invented.

23 Feb.   *The New York Times* announces the winning designs in its fashion contest. Included among the patriotic winners are a cotton-boll hat and a Quaker-styledress. Department stores trumpet their American-made designs, and *Ladies' Home Journal* claims credit for being first to promote American fashion.

Mar.   *Ladies' Home Journal* features First Lady Ellen Wilson and her daughters modeling American designs.

1914

- The department store Lord & Taylor moves from Fifth Avenue and Nineteenth Street to Fifth Avenue and Thirty-eighth Street in New York City.

- Coco Chanel opens her first dress shop in France.

- The Deutscher Werkbund exhibition in Cologne showcases the buildings of Walter Gropius, Josef Hoffman, and others whose work becomes influential in twentieth-century American architecture.

Fall Anticipating that the outbreak of World War I will shut down the European fashion industry, *Vogue* editor Edna Woolman Chase prepares the New York Fashion Fete to take the place of the Paris shows, but the French couturiers manage to introduce new lines of clothing every season throughout the war.

Nov. Mary Phelps Jacob (later Caresse Crosby) patents her design for the first brassiere. It does not become popular until the 1920s, after she sells the patent to Warner's corset company.

1915

- Helena Rubinstein launches her American cosmetics empire by opening the Maison de Beauté in New York City.

- Two expositions celebrating the opening of the Panama Canal are held in California. The Panama-California Exposition in San Diego, designed by Bertram Goodhue, features a Spanish theme and sparks a Spanish colonial revival. The Panama-Pacific Exposition in San Francisco has a neobaroque Palace of Fine Arts designed by architect Bernard Maybeck.

- Frank Lloyd Wright begins work on the Imperial Hotel in Tokyo (completed in 1922).

1916

- The Colburn Window-Glass Machine of the Libbey-Owens Sheet Glass Company turns out hundreds of square yards of glass in a continuous flow.

- The "hobble skirt" Coca-Cola bottle is introduced.

- Bertram Goodhue begins work on the protomodern Nebraska State Capitol.

- The Massachusetts Institute of Technology moves to new buildings, designed by William Wells Bosworth, on the Charles River in Cambridge.

1917

- Albert Kahn completes Building B of the Ford Motor Company River Rouge Plant in Detroit. The half-mile-long building encloses an entire Ford assembly line.

- Construction begins on Harkness Memorial Tower at Yale University, designed by James Gamble Rogers and completed in 1921. It is one of many examples of a style that becomes known as "collegiate Gothic."

- The striking Hell's Gate Railroad Bridge, a cantilevered steel arch across the Harlem River, is completed in New York City.

23 Feb. The Smith-Hughes Act, promoting industrial education in America, is passed without any provision for education in aesthetics and design.

1918

- St. Bartholomew's Episcopal Church opens at Park Avenue and Fiftieth Street in New York City. Designed by Goodhue, the Romanesque building incorporates the McKim, Mead and White portals from the congregation's previous church on Madison Avenue.

- The Hotel Commodore, designed by Warren and Wetmore, opens near Grand Central Terminal in New York City.

- The Hotel Pennsylvania, designed by McKim, Mead and White, opens near Pennsylvania Station in New York City.

11 Nov. A skyscraper at 27 West Forty-third Street in New York City is the first building completed under the provisions of a 1916 zoning law that created a formula by which upper stories must be "stepped back" to allow more sunlight to reach the streets below.

1919

- William Randolph Hearst's San Simeon, designed by architect Julia Morgan, is begun 100 miles north of Santa Barbara, California.

- The Bauhaus, a design school directed by Walter Gropius, opens in Germany. Gropius becomes a major figure in American architecture after he flees Adolf Hitler's Germany in the 1930s.

- Ludwig Mies van der Rohe joins the Novembergruppe, directing its efforts to revive architecture in Germany, and undertakes the first of his glass skyscraper projects — a design that provides the basis for his history-making Seagram Building (1958) in New York City.

- Art-glass designer Louis Comfort Tiffany goes into semiretirement.

OVERVIEW

Modern Styles for Fast-Paced Lives. By the second decade of the twentieth century Americans had become more active than they had been in the previous century, both on the job and off. The fashions of that more leisurely era restricted movement and were difficult to care for, making them inappropriate for life in the 1910s. Women and men began to look for ways to streamline and simplify their clothing and their households — to become more modern so that they could focus on keeping up with twentieth-century life. Designers began making clothes, houses, furnishings, and cars that looked neat, used a minimum of materials, and worked well — moves that kept American fashion from being derailed by shortages during World War I.

Active Wear for Women. One important social phenomenon that drove the demand for simplified clothes was the rise of activity — professional and recreational — among women. More and more women, many of whom were part of the woman suffrage movement, took to riding bicycles, ice skating, driving cars, dancing, and even flying airplanes. Growing numbers of women were also working outside the home. These women had no intention of pursuing their new endeavors trussed up in the corsets and swaddled in the petticoats of earlier years, and American sportswear designers and mass-market manufacturers began making clothes that suited the needs of the new woman. Suits that went from morning until night and were fitted with belts instead of hundreds of hooks were paired with low-cut shoes that did not require lengthy lacing. Hoping to make money from Americans eager to buy prestigious Parisian labels, American manufacturers throughout these years produced counterfeit French couture, but for the first time European designers found themselves following an American design lead and simplifying their fashions. The war in Europe only hastened a trend that had been evident in the years leading up to the conflict.

Men's Clothing. Men also began to look for more relaxed clothing. Young men had no interest in dressing up in the stiff, overstuffed clothes their fathers had worn. The padding was removed from the shoulders of suit jackets, and slimmer cuts became popular. Trousers were narrower and shorter; oxfords began to replace lace-up boots. Formal clothing also took on trimmer lines, with tuxedo jackets emphasizing men's waistlines and pants cut close to the leg. These stripped-down clothes were little affected by wartime material shortages, and as physically fit American men returned from the war, they were pleased to have comfortable, figure-flattering clothes to wear.

Beaux-Arts Buildings. While clothing began to look more modern, much of commercial architecture still resembled that of the late nineteenth century. The most influential school of architecture remained the historically minded Ecole des Beaux-Arts in Paris. Skyscrapers reached new heights in the 1910s, but they were garnished with bits and pieces from architectures of the past — as though they were Gothic cathedrals or Greek and Roman temples. The architects who designed the great train stations completed in the 1910s also revived old styles rather than creating innovative designs for these modern temples of mass transportation.

Protomodernists. Not all American architects of the 1910s subscribed to the principles of the Ecole des Beaux-Arts, however. Two notable innovators were Frank Lloyd Wright, who completed Midway Gardens in Chicago in 1913, and Albert Kahn, who created two large factory complexes for the Ford Motor Company during the 1910s. These men sought distinctly American solutions to the needs of American business and social life, and they inspired the Europeans who masterminded modernist architecture in the decades to come.

New Home Design. Middle-class American families were also becoming discontented with the rabbit-warren-like rooms of Victorian houses. Instead, with their increasingly healthy paychecks, Americans bought houses with open floor plans that followed the dictates of architects such as Wright. The bungalow with multipurpose rooms was designed to meet the changing needs of modern families. Simplicity and economy were also characteristics of the colonial revival of the 1910s, the evidence of which was apparent in the rapidly spreading suburbs of American cities. The nerve center of the house moved from the formal Victorian parlor to the up-to-date kitchen, where mothers followed the directives of home economists as they tried to rear their children in the most scientifically correct manner possible.

Commercial Design. Although American engineers were creating a host of new products for houses with electricity, running water, and other conveniences, some felt that the aesthetic element was missing from their efforts. Often supported by their governments, European designers tried to make certain that their commercial output was aesthetically pleasing. American manufacturers were more than happy to take advantage of European efforts, often stealing designs when they thought they would be profitable, but they had little interest in funding their own innovations. The federal government also felt that design was not crucial and passed up chances to fund education in aesthetics for industrial engineers.

The Universal Car. The Ford Model T was the apotheosis of American engineering, unhampered by any concern for beauty. In 1909 Henry Ford announced that from that year on his company would manufacture only the Model T and do so in such a cost-efficient manner that everyone in the country would be able to afford one. Ford and his engineers created ever-more-efficient facto-ries and increased the incentives for workers to do their best by shortening the workday and raising wages. Aesthetic considerations, such as color choices, were ignored. (The Model T came in one color, black.) By 1914 the price of the Model T, $440, was a third less than it had been when it was first offered to the public. The Model T dominated the automobile market until well into the 1920s.

Postwar America. The United States emerged from World War I with its confidence and prosperity intact. Americans were making more money and — owing in part to the popularity of the installment plan — spending more of their income than ever before. With the long, lean lines and easy-to-wear cuts of women's and men's clothing marking a break from the stodginess of earlier generations, young Americans were ready to make their mark on the modern world. The hallmarks of the youthful image so widely associated with the Roaring Twenties — jazz music, dropped-waist clothing, the bob haircut (popularized by dancer Irene Castle in 1914), and widespread ownership of automobiles — were all in place as the 1910s drew to a close.

TOPICS IN THE NEWS

ARCHITECTURE: CONFLICTING CURRENTS

The Old versus the New. By the 1910s the two major tendencies in twentieth-century architecture were already evident. One leaned toward the past, reviving styles from bygone eras, often in hopes of reinvigorating the faith and sense of community of older generations that twentieth-century architects feared were gone forever. This inclination was embodied in the work of architects trained at or influenced by the Ecole des Beaux-Arts in Paris and in the neo-Gothic revival. The other looked toward the future, demanding that a new architectural vernacular be developed to meet the needs of technologically advanced, fast-paced, and scientifically enlightened modern life. Students of the Chicago school of urban architecture — and others who demanded that form follow function — were the chief proponents of this movement. Architects following both trends benefited from the vast expansion of the American economy — captains of industry, presidents of colleges, city boosters, new homeowners, and others were looking to put their marks on the landscape and had the cash to do so.

The Ecole des Beaux-Arts. Until the second half of the nineteenth century, there were no architectural schools in America. People who wanted to become architects either apprenticed themselves to individuals engaged in designing and constructing buildings or went to Europe to study. The most prestigious school of architecture was the Ecole des Beaux-Arts in Paris. There American students learned the formal practice of architecture by studying the architectural treatises and creations of great classical and Renaissance architects. Even as American architecture programs began to be established — the first was founded in 1868 at the Massachusetts Institute of Technology — American graduates of the Ecole des Beaux-Arts continued to command the most prestige,

The Woolworth Building, New York City (1913), designed by Cass Gilbert

Stanford White of McKim, Mead and White in New York and the West Coast architect Julia Morgan.

The Skyscrapers of Chicago. The city of Chicago, burned almost to the ground in 1871, was the birthplace of the modern skyscraper. There engineers and architects perfected the elevator and central heating, both critical to the development of buildings more than several stories high. Another major innovation was the discovery of how to distribute the weight of a massive building. In the 1880s architect William Le Baron Jenney abandoned traditional masonry and used a steel frame to anchor a building, covering it with a curtain wall — a decorative, rather than structural, stone facade. Using a steel frame allowed architects to speed construction, to make buildings taller, and to enlarge windows. The prominent Chicago architect Louis Sullivan declared that "form should follow function," calling for an "organic" process in which new buildings should be designed in a way that grew naturally from their projected use. Sullivan, whose actual practice was at its height before 1900, intended this approach as an alternative to the formal, tradition-bound inorganic design process used by students of the Beaux-Arts school. As a result of Sullivan's influence, the historical bric-a-brac that adorned even the tallest buildings began to seem inappropriate to some architects. The organic aesthetic of Sullivan and his students — among them Frank Lloyd Wright — became famous as the main contribution of the Chicago school to American architecture.

Corporate Giants and Tall Buildings. Other architects were happy to provide corporate chieftains with buildings to match their egos. Skyscrapers were considered proof of a successful business endeavor — the more successful the company, the more stories in its skyscraper. City building codes could not keep pace with the challenges presented by buildings that blocked the sun and created new weather patterns. Lower Manhattan in particular suffered from the multiple-story buildings that began crowding along its narrow streets in the early twentieth century. It was not until 1916 that New York was able to pass regulations that required buildings higher than one hundred feet to be tapered away from the street.

The Woolworth Building. Frank W. Woolworth, the mastermind of the dramatic nationwide expansion of five-and-ten-cent stores, set out to build a New York City skyscraper that would steal the spotlight from the forty-seven-story Singer Building, designed by Ernest Flagg and completed in 1907. Woolworth hired architect Cass Gilbert, who served as president of the American Institute of Architects in 1908–1909. Gilbert had been an assistant to Stanford White for two years and was well versed in the Beaux-Arts style, and Woolworth had a model in mind: the Victoria Tower of the British Houses of Parliament. Gilbert obliged Woolworth by melding feathery French and English Gothic styles in a tower that was frosted with colored terra cotta and rose 792 feet over lower Manhattan. After the building was completed in

and their work was widely imitated. The biggest boost to the reputation of the Beaux-Arts style in America came with the opening of the 1893 Columbian Exposition in Chicago. The exposition featured a monumental White City, designed by the Chicago firm of Burnham and Root. These enormous faux-marble Beaux-Arts-inspired buildings surrounding a reflecting pool influenced American civic architecture for decades. Some of the best-known students of the Ecole des Beaux-Arts included

Only the second woman to graduate from the architectural program at the Massachusetts Institute of Technology, Marion Mahony Griffin (1871–1962) was the first licensed woman architect in Illinois and an important exponent of the Prairie Style of architecture developed by Frank Lloyd Wright. In 1895, the year after she graduated from MIT, she went to work at Wright's studio. She quickly gained international recognition for her brilliant architectural draftsmanship and the unusual beauty of her renderings. While she worked for Wright she designed several important projects, not all of which were fully credited to her during her lifetime. (In an unpublished autobiography, "The Magic of America," she discussed her work at Wright's studio and recorded her contributions.) One of her earliest projects was the Church of All Souls (1903), a Unitarian chapel in Evanston, Illinois, which incorporates Gothic design elements with the Prairie Style. Later works include the David M. Amberg house (1909–1910) in Grand Rapids, Michigan; the Adolph Mueller house (1910) in Decatur, Illinois; and the Henry Ford house (1912) in Dearborn, Michigan. All these projects reveal Griffin's enthusiasm for local stone. Griffin also designed furniture, interior accessories, decorative wall panels, mosaics, and murals for Wright. In 1914 she moved to Australia with her husband, architect Walter Burley Griffin, whom she had married in 1911. For the next twenty years she collaborated with her husband on many projects but never produced another solo design.

Sources: H. Allen Brooks, *The Prairie School* (New York: Norton, 1976);

Frederick Gutheim, Entry on Marion Lucy Mahony Griffin, in *Notable American Women: The Modern Period,* edited by Barbara Sicherman and Carol Hurd Green, with Ilene Kantrov and Harriette Walker (Cambridge, Mass. & London: Harvard University Press, 1980), pp. 292–294.

In 1910 Frank Lloyd Wright wrote that Americans in general, and wealthy Americans in particular, had become sycophantic followers of the Beaux-Arts style of architecture: "Painfully conscious of their lack of traditions, our powerful get-rich-quick citizens attempt to buy Tradition ready made and are dragged forward facing backwards." He placed the blame on the sort of education architects were getting, taking a not-too-subtle jab at the pervasive influence of the Ecole des Beaux-Arts on American architecture. Instead of relying on outworn models, Wright said, Americans should rise to the challenges of modern life when they chose the design for their homes. "To thus make of a human dwelling-place a complete work of art, in itself expressive and beautiful, intimately related to modern life and fit to live in," Wright wrote, was the opportunity of American architecture.

Source: Edgar Kaufmann and Ben Raeburn, eds., *Frank Lloyd Wright: Writings and Buildings* (New York: Horizon, 1973).

1913, it was nicknamed "The Cathedral of Commerce Woolworth Building, New York City" and took the record of tallest building in the world away from the New York Metropolitan Life Insurance Building, completed in 1909. "The Cathedral of Commerce" held its record until 1930, when the seventy-five-story Art-Deco Chrysler Building was completed in midtown Manhattan.

Innovation on Hold. Under the conservative influence of businessmen and Beaux-Arts architects, most innovation in American commercial architecture stalled in the 1910s. While the skyscraper was hailed by Europeans as a distinctly American contribution to the history of design,

its basic premises did not evolve far from where the Chicago School had taken them. Not until after World War I, when Eliel Saarinen of Finland took second prize with a semimodern design in the 1922 Chicago Tribune Tower competition, did the skyscraper begin to move away from the Beaux-Arts tradition.

Midway Gardens. There were significant exceptions in areas other than skyscraper architecture. Among them were Frank Lloyd Wright's ziggurat-like Midway Gardens, a restaurant and concert complex that was completed in Chicago in 1913 and was demolished during the Depression. Midway Gardens marked the most comprehensive expression of Wright's aesthetic vision. Along with designing the many-terraced concrete-and-brick building, Wright created the plans for landscaping, lighting, decorating, and furnishing it. His next major public project, the Imperial Hotel in Japan (1915–1922), expanded even further on the ideas he explored in his designs for Midway Gardens.

Albert Kahn. Another innovator was the German-born architect Albert Kahn, who immigrated to the United States with his family when he was eleven years old. When Kahn began designing factories in 1903, he usually competed against junior draftsmen, because architects tended to consider such assignments tedious and undeserving of their talents. Kahn brought the insight of an engineer and the inspiration of a visionary to the task. Using reinforced concrete and steel, he was able to make buildings large enough to contain entire operations under one roof — and soon on one floor. The automobile in-

Midway Gardens, Chicago (1913), designed by Frank Lloyd Wright

dustry was the main beneficiary of Kahn's work: in 1903 he designed the Packard Motor Company Plant in Detroit, and in 1910 his Ford Motor Company plant at Highland Park was completed. In 1917 Kahn created the half-mile-long Building B for Ford's River Rouge plant. The steel-and-glass structure housed an entire Model T assembly line.

The Decade of the Great Train Stations. Although the automobile was rapidly gaining in popularity, railroad travel still reigned supreme in the 1910s. Heedless of the threat cars posed to the industry, passenger railways built their most ambitious and beautiful railway stations during the decade. Like most civic buildings of the era, train stations were designed in the classical Beaux-Arts style that had been popularized by monumental buildings designed for the 1893 Columbian Exposition in Chicago and promoted by the firm of McKim, Mead and White and its students.

Pennsylvania Station. The Manhattan station of the Pennsylvania Railroad was the final stage of an ambitious project to eliminate the obligatory ferry ride for Manhattan-bound rail passengers by connecting the Pennsylvania line, William Gibbs McAdoo's Hudson and Manhattan Railroad, and the Long Island Railroad via tunnels under the East River and the Hudson River (opened in 1907). Pennsylvania Station, completed by McKim, Mead and White in 1910, was an American adaptation of the Baths of Caracalla. The surfaces of the structure were finished in porous white travertine stone, a material widely used in Rome but employed for the first time in American architecture. The huge waiting room had a soaring vaulted ceiling supported by granite Corinthian columns that hid 150-foot steel posts. In the train concourse the massive support system was exposed, awing travelers with a massive grid of steel and glass. In 1965 the once-vaunted station was demolished by the railroad, which replaced it with a new building that also housed offices and a new Madison Square Garden.

Grand Central Terminal. The terminal building for the New York Central and Hudson River Railroad, completed in 1913, was not as ambitious an architectural undertaking as Pennsylvania Station. Yet from the standpoint of civic engineering, it represented an impressive achievement: the terminal, located at Forty-second Street and Park Avenue, was designed to be integrated into the

The Seventh Avenue facade of Pennsylvania Station, New York City (1910), designed by McKim, Mead and White

city around it. Electric train tracks were hidden in tunnels below street level, and Park Avenue was woven around the building so that traffic could continue northward to the new office and apartment buildings planned for the area beyond it. Pedestrian tunnels gave railway passengers access to the sidewalks and the buildings surrounding the terminal. The air rights for the space above the terminal and tracks were leased to commercial developers. In 1929 the New York General Building was erected over the tracks near the terminal, and in 1963 the Pan American (later the MetLife) Building went up above the north end of the terminal. The eighteenth-century French facade of the Grand Central Terminal and its ahistorical concourse were designed by Warren Whitney, an architect in the firm of Warren and Wetmore. His plans echoed those of another monumental building just two blocks west on Forty-second Street, the New York Public Library, designed by the firm of Carrère and Hastings and completed two years earlier.

The Late Gothic Revival. The Boston architectural firm of Cram, Goodhue and Ferguson rose to national stature when its Gothic design for the U.S. Military Academy at West Point won a national competition in 1902. Ralph Adams Cram, the son of a Unitarian minister, preferred the spirituality of pre-Reformation Christianity and hoped to bring it to America through Gothic

architecture. Cram's firm received several important commissions for churches — including the redesign of St. John the Divine Episcopal Cathedral in New York City in 1911. St. Thomas Episcopal Church in New York (1906–1913), which draws on French and English Gothic designs, is thought to be the finest example of Cram, Goodhue and Ferguson's work. Were it not for the new-looking pews and plain tile floors, this church, with its asymmetrical stone exterior and strictly Gothic interior, would look at home in Europe — to the untrained eye. Other Cram, Goodhue and Ferguson buildings are considered by architects to be copies rather than reinterpretations for the twentieth century. For example the Graduate College at Princeton University (1913) has been called a copy of Gothic dining halls in British colleges. Such copies proved popular with American universities. The Harkness Memorial Tower at Yale University, designed by James Gamble Rogers and begun in 1917, is another of the many examples of the so-called collegiate Gothic style.

Eclecticism and Protomodernism. Cram's partner Bertram Goodhue left the firm in 1913 to pursue designs outside the confines of the Gothic revival. He designed the Panama-California Exposition of 1915 in San Diego in a Spanish style, helping to increase interest in Spanish architecture, particularly in California and along the Gulf

Coast. Later, Goodhue created the bulletlike Nebraska State Capitol in Lincoln (1916–1928), which presents an unsettling mix of Beaux-Arts formalism and what would become the streamlined style known as Art Deco. Another architect working in a similar mode, Philadelphian Pasul Philippe Cret, attempted to create a more modern, less historical look by omitting ornamentation from Beaux-Arts buildings. His Indianapolis Public Library (1914), with its bare stone surfaces, demonstrates the tomblike qualities of the buildings that resulted from these early efforts to update the Beaux-Arts style.

Sources:

William Dudley Hunt Jr., *Encyclopedia of American Architecture,* revised by Robert T. Packard and Balthazar Korab (New York: McGraw-Hill, 1994);

Marcus Whiffen and Frederick Koeper, *American Architecture, 1607–1976* (Cambridge, Mass.: MIT Press, 1981).

ARCHITECTURE: DOMESTIC DESIGN

New Ideas. During the 1910s homeowners were somewhat more open to new design ideas than the heads of big businesses. Women's magazines and housekeeping manuals called for the abandonment of outdated ideas in favor of scientific standards for middle-class home life. The architectural manifestations of late-nineteenth-century life, particularly the rambling, eclectic Queen Anne and Eastlake houses, were attacked as benighted, backward settings for growing families. At the same time, the city was judged to be an unsuitable place to rear children, and families were told to take advantage of trolley lines — and, increasingly, automobiles — to settle away from urban areas. Americans who wanted to become homeowners often also took on the role of home builders — and could choose from a range of designs, some published in national magazines or available ready-to-assemble from catalogues.

Prairie Style. One particularly influential school of architecture was the so-called Prairie Style, spearheaded by Louis Sullivan's brilliant and ambitious student Frank Lloyd Wright. Wright, who was influenced by Japanese architecture — as well as by Sullivan's dictum that form should grow organically from function — favored simple, horizontal shapes and open vistas in his home designs, which recalled the expanses of the American prairie. He also took great pains with his materials, choosing wood and stones that would look beautiful essentially unadorned or hand carved. This aspect of his designs shared much with the turn-of-the-century Arts and Crafts movement, started in England, which insisted on quality workmanship and beautiful materials in domestic design in keeping with the standards of the medieval crafts guilds that inspired the movement. Unlike the machine-hating Arts and Crafts advocates, however, Wright believed that modern technology had a vital place in twentieth-century design — and in his foremost goal of creating a distinctly American architecture for domestic and public buildings.

THE PORCH

The most prominent feature of the bungalow was its front porch. Nestled under the heavy eaves, the front porch jutted toward the street. Architects and designers urged bungalow owners to think of the porch as more than just a sheltered passageway to the front door, encouraging families to incorporate the porch into their everyday lives. Chairs, tables, even beds should be set on the porch, they said, so that parents and children could eat meals, read, and sleep in the healthful outdoors. Blinds and screens could be added so that the family could use the porch in less than ideal weather. Some writers called the porch by the names of its foreign equivalents — the *veranda* or the *piazza* — to suggest that the porch would allow bungalow occupants to experience sensual, casual Mediterranean life in the comfort of their own American homes. At the same time, the porch encouraged community interaction. When parents were on the porch, passersby could stop and chat while adults could keep an eye on neighborhood children. After the rise of automobile traffic made the front of the house less attractive as a location for relaxation or contemplation, the front porch became less popular than the back porch and patio.

Source: Clifford Edward Clark Jr., *The American Family Home, 1800–1960* (Chapel Hill: University of North Carolina Press, 1986).

The Bungalow. In 1909 Wright closed his Chicago studio and went to Europe, returning in 1910 to work on larger projects such as Midway Gardens and Taliesin, his Wisconsin home and studio. His assistants, including Walter Burley Griffin, Marion Mahoney, and William Drummond, set about popularizing Wright's ideas. Although it was far from a direct descendant of Wright's work, the bungalow was an outgrowth of his ideas. Named after small, one-story houses in India, the bungalow was the perfect house for a first-time homeowner, particularly in sunny, temperate climes. Bungalows spread across California and the Midwest during the first decades of the century. The low-to-the-ground houses featured shady porches — emphasizing the buildings' connection to nature, as Wright would have it — and cozy inglenooks, recalling Arts and Crafts creations.

Affordable Homes. The average annual income of Americans more than doubled between 1900 and 1917, from $651 to $1505, but the cost of building a new house had gone up as well. Plumbing, heating, and electrical wiring could add 25 to 40 percent to the basic cost of a house. (By the end of the decade 41 percent of American houses had electricity.) Building a bungalow, with its small size and essentially standardized design, was one way to keep construction costs down. As a result of its

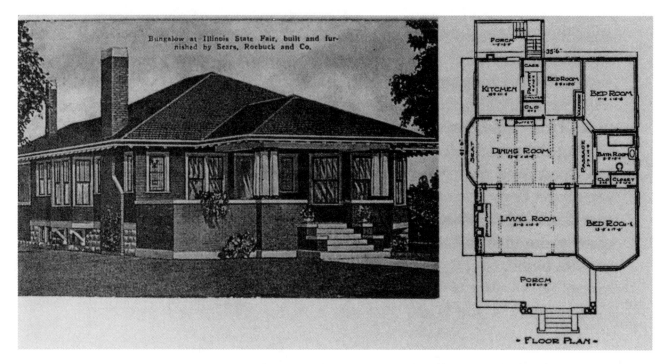

Design for Sears, Roebuck and Company "Modern Home Number 151, Progressive Bungalow" (1914)

popularity, the average price of a new house rose a modest $250, from $2,400 in 1891 to $2,650 in 1910. Newlyweds found the open floor plan and simple but robust-looking wood or stucco exterior of the bungalow the perfect antidote to the fussy, ornate, and oversized houses in which they had grown up. Magazines such as *Ladies' Home Journal* and *The Craftsman* carried bungalow designs for popular consumption. Beginning in 1886 prefabricated bungalows were available from mail-order catalogues, with the largest seller of houses by mail, Sears, Roebuck and Company, offering its first Honorbilt Modern Homes in 1908. Bungalow models were named for romantic wilderness destinations such as "The Alps" and "Yellowstone" — offering buyers a bit of invigorating nature in the midst of burgeoning suburbia at prices ranging from $800 to $3,000. Manufacturers offered the option of a superficially customized bungalow — in Moorish, Japanese, and Dutch Colonial styles, among others — a marketing ploy alien to the Prairie Style aesthetic. In 1919 architect Charles V. Boyd declared the bungalow the most American of styles.

West Coast Creations. Architects in California continued to experiment with modern housing. During the 1910s Bernard Maybeck, who designed the neobaroque Palace of Fine Arts in San Francisco for the 1915 Panama-Pacific International Exposition, was building spare redwood houses, reminiscent of the Arts and Crafts style, in the hills of Berkeley. Julia Morgan, the first woman to study architecture at the Ecole des Beaux-Arts and an engineering graduate of the University of California at Berkeley, was creating eclectic homes in the Bay Area recalling medieval manors and an eclectic mansion, Wil-

liam Randolph Hearst's San Simeon (begun in 1919), on the Pacific coast south of San Francisco. Irving Gill, a self-trained architect, experimented with poured concrete houses, hoping to create timesaving structures. His houses had floors that curved seamlessly into the walls, doing away with angles that collect dust and dirt and thus reducing the labor involved in housecleaning. In 1916 he completed his best-known building, the Walter Dodge House in Los Angeles. The spare, cubist form has been said to prefigure the work of the renowned modern architect Le Corbusier. Gill's influence was limited in the United States because of the rise in popularity of Spanish colonial styles after the 1915 Panama-California Exposition in San Diego and limitations on home building during World War I.

Taliesin. In 1910 Wright returned from Europe, determined to keep his personal and artistic freedom. Abandoning his wife and six children in Chicago, he and the wife of a client settled in the farmlands of Wisconsin, where Wright had grown up, and he set out to build a house and studio that would embody his evolving aesthetic. In the resulting building, which he named Taliesin after a Welsh poet, he attempted to create a garden and farm as well as a house and a studio, embracing the landscape with its low, heavy design. He used native yellow limestone for the patio and pavement, trying to blur the line where the land ended and the structure began. Wright exulted in his creation, which he had to rebuild twice, each time after it was destroyed by fire.

War and Housing. The entry of the United States into the war in Europe ended the housing boom of the 1910s. Labor costs rose as manpower was redirected to the war effort, and materials became scarce or unavailable under government-imposed restrictions. The areas of the country that were most drastically affected by housing shortages were the centers of shipbuilding and weapons production, where the population exploded as employment opportunities expanded. In an attempt to stem the shortage, the federal government embarked on its first attempt to be a home builder for its citizens and created the first federal housing projects. Through government efforts, building standards actually improved for domestic buildings.

Sources:

William Dudley Hunt Jr., *Encyclopedia of American Architecture*, revised by Robert T. Packard and Balthazar Korab (New York: McGraw-Hill, 1994);

Edgar Kaufmann and Ben Raeburn, eds., *Frank Lloyd Wright: Writings and Buildings* (New York: Horizon, 1973);

U.S. Department of Labor, *How American Buying Habits Change* (Washington, D.C.: U.S. Government Printing Office, 1959);

Marcus Whiffen and Frederick Koeper, *American Architecture, 1607–1976* (Cambridge, Mass.: MIT Press, 1981).

Mission Style reclining armchair, designed by Gustav Stickley

ARCHITECTURE: INTERIOR DESIGN

The Up-to-Date Interior. Authorities on the home had been calling for simplified, healthful interiors since the turn of the century. The formal, dark rooms filled with overstuffed furniture that were typical of nineteenth-century houses were vilified as old-fashioned and tasteless. Instead magazines and homemakers' manuals instructed American homeowners to take advantage of the latest technology to create an auspicious atmosphere for family life.

The Flexible Floor Plan. A key component of interior design in the 1910s was the open floor plan, inspired by the work of Frank Lloyd Wright. No longer was each space meant to serve a single, specific purpose, as in Victorian houses, with their parlors, sitting rooms, and library. Instead, the first floor of a house built in the 1910s typically consisted of a porch, a living room, a dining room, and a kitchen, each room open to the next rather than separated by halls and doors. The living room combined the functions of the old-fashioned front hall, parlor, and library. The dining room could become a space for children's projects or a music room. The kitchen was the laboratory for the serious homemaker and a setting for casual family meals. Unlike the stuffy, dull-colored, heavily wallpapered and upholstered rooms of earlier generations, the modern house was uncluttered and airy. Rooms were to be painted bold colors, ornamented only with the dark wood used for window and door frames. Windows were stripped of excessive drapery. Bookshelves, wardrobes, and sideboards were built in, leaving the floor clear so that chairs and tables could be rearranged easily for different activities. Upstairs, the number of bedrooms diminished (in keeping with the smaller family size that was typical of the decade), and the size of the rooms shrank. The vast majority of activities were meant to take place in the communal spaces on the first floor, not in the closed-off rooms upstairs.

The Mission Style. The furniture that most readily complemented the airy, sturdy house of the 1910s was a simple wooden style called Mission because it brought to mind the Spanish missions of California and the Southwest. The roots of this style were in the Arts and Crafts movement, which demanded beautifully cut woods and a minimum of upholstery. Unlike the rather expensive handmade furniture of the Arts and Crafts movement, Mission Style pieces were made by machine in factories and sold at easily affordable prices. Gustav Stickley and (in separate operations) his brothers made the most beautiful machine-aided pieces. Stickley, who began making furniture in 1898, went out of business in 1915, but during the 1910s his furniture was widely copied by many manufacturers, whose pieces were often of inferior quality to Stickley's designs. Usually made of oak, Mission furniture is characterized by vertical slats — used for bedsteads, the backs of chairs, and the sides of desks — and a peg construction that creates square knobs where wooden legs poked through the seats of chairs and the tops of tables. What the furniture lacked in comfort (throw pillows were often added to the seats and backs of chairs) it made up for in durability. Unlike elaborately ornamented and veneered pieces from the late nineteenth century, solid-oak Mission furniture could survive the most boisterous of families without sustaining significant damage — a fact that made it a favorite of educational institutions. One of the most popular Mission items for the home was the turned-oak table, which could hold a few choice family mementos (as opposed to the nineteenth-century tumble of knickknacks that kept maids constantly dusting) or provide a staging ground for games or a spot to serve dinner.

Louis Comfort Tiffany. Upper-class Americans tended to prefer the Art Nouveau style of decoration, which had its origins in the late nineteenth century, to the pared-down Mission Style. A designer they particularly favored was the son of a leading American jeweler and silversmith, Louis Comfort Tiffany, who created lavish leaded-glass lamps and stained-glass windows with painstaking workmanship and jewel-like colors. His firm also made art-glass pieces, mosaics, furniture, textiles, and metalworks. Tiffany, who established his reputation in the 1890s, was a prominent tastemaker, and his work was imitated by several other firms during the first quarter of the twentieth century. (Tiffany himself went into semiretirement in 1919.)

Source:
Clifford Edward Clark Jr., *The American Family Home, 1800–1960* (Chapel Hill: University of North Carolina Press, 1986).

AUTOMOBILES

Goodbye to the Horse-Drawn Carriage. During the 1910s automobiles rapidly replaced horses. Motorcars appealed to the adventurous and the professional — doctors and businessmen were among the first Americans to buy and drive cars. Over this momentous decade the design of the automobile stayed relatively stable: Henry Ford's Model T, introduced in 1908, set the standard, dominating the market and providing a model for its competitors. The wealthy drove cars that looked much like the Model T but were appointed with fur rugs and fine leather. During the 1910s the big changes in automobiles came in their production and engineering. Technological advances made cars easier to drive and maintain, while assembly innovations made them faster and cheaper to make. As costs came down, car dealers came up with a way to put automobile ownership within reach of virtually any adult: the installment plan.

The Model T. Following an alphabet of horseless carriages pioneered by the Ford Motor Company in Detroit, Michigan, the Model T — affectionately nicknamed the "Tin Lizzie" — was Henry Ford's idea of the universal car: reliable and affordable. The touring model cost $850 in 1908. (There were also runabout, town-car, and delivery-car models.) The Tin Lizzie gleamed with brass detailing, a cherry-wood dashboard, and tufted leather seats. By 1913 the car was available in "any color as long as it's black," but the inaugural model was offered in a choice of six colors. Capable of reaching forty-five miles per hour, it featured a twenty-horsepower, four-cylinder engine and a two-speed planetary transmission that was much simpler to use than the sliding-gear transmissions of other automobiles. In 1909, with orders for the car outstripping his ability to provide them, Henry Ford declared that his company would build only the Model T, and henceforth he and his employees devoted their energies to standardizing and perfecting the production of the car.

Technology Reduces Prices. Other automobile companies, such as Oldsmobile and Cadillac, chose to go after a market that could afford to pay $2,000 or more for an automobile, and their few less-expensive vehicles were poorly constructed. Ford wanted to create a vehicle within the price range of average Americans. By 1914 Ford's engineers had developed the first automated assembly line. The company was turning out one car every twenty-four seconds, and the price on the Tin Lizzie fell to $440. Another factor that helped push cars into the mainstream was the standardization of auto parts across manufacturers to make the production and maintenance of cars easier and more reliable. By 1915 the advocates of standardization had won their fight, and consumers saw prices drop as a result of increased competition between parts suppliers.

The Self-Starter. Not every innovation in automobiles came from Ford. Engineer Charles F. Kettering invented the self-starter for Cadillac, which had been looking for a way to get rid of the dangerous hand-crank starter. By February 1911 a Kettering starter had passed all the tests at Cadillac, and three years later 90 percent of American auto manufacturers offered them on their cars. (Ford was a notable exception.)

More Competition. Ford also faced competition from two associates, John and Horace Dodge, who struck out on their own in 1914 and immediately won a loyal following with a tough little car that they priced just above the Model T. In 1916 Charles Nash left General Motors, where he had been president, and bought the Thomas B. Jeffery Company of Kenosha, Wisconsin, which had been turning out a well-liked little car called the Rambler until 1910, and later the Jeffery. Nash turned Rambler/Jeffery into the Nash — a brand that lasted forty years.

Streamlining. Until the 1910s most automobiles looked much like unwieldy carriages that had lost their horses. In 1909, however, a call went out to streamline cars — at least in part for the sake of fuel conservation. By the fourteenth annual automobile show, held in New York City in 1914, streamlining had arrived, made possible by the development of machine presses that shaped pieces of steel and replaced the tedious process of pounding each sheet into the desired configuration by hand. Although important for the increasing production and fuel efficiency, the results of this technical innovation did not make a startling difference in the appearance of automobiles right away. Recognizably streamlined cars did not appear until the 1930s.

Sources:
Warren James Belasco, *Americans on the Road: From Autocamp to Motel, 1910–1945* (Cambridge, Mass.: MIT Press, 1979);

Stephen W. Sears, *The American Heritage History of the Automobile in America* (New York: American Heritage, 1977).

DESIGNS FOR NEW PRODUCTS

American Design Falters. As new inventions were mass-produced, American industrial designers sometimes packaged them in familiar forms. For example, the phonograph cabinet, first patented in 1910, was a hodgepodge of curly French cabriole legs, a stout rectangular box, and a hinged mansard lid. In other cases they allowed the process of manufacture to dictate form without consideration of how the new invention might be used most easily. One example of such a product is the lathe-turned telephone, with its mouthpieces mounted on a simple pillar equipped with a hook for the earpiece.

European Designers Forge Ahead. In the same years that American engineering was turning out new appliances with little consideration for form, European designers were employing styles related to Art Nouveau in a sensual melding of the ornate tendencies of Victorian art with the dictates of organic form to create beautiful, as well as useful, consumer products. Dating from the turn of the century, Art Nouveau splintered into separate styles — all heading toward the streamlined, bold look that would be called Art Deco in the United States. Charles Rennie Mackintosh of the Glasgow school, Lucien Vogel, editor of the French taste-making magazine *Gazette du Bon Ton,* and Josef Hoffman of the Wiener Werkestätten in Vienna were all part of the larger movement to wed form and function in aesthetically pleasing products for the home. In the first decades of the twentieth century most European nations, officially or unofficially, cultivated their own schools of design to foster an aesthetic appropriate to the changing times.

The Struggle to Improve American Design. In 1912 John Cotton Dana, the director of the Newark Museum of Art, invited the Deutscher Werkbund of Munich to exhibit its works in the United States. A group of prominent artists, craftsmen, and businessmen, the Werkbund had been assigned by the German government to improve the country's commercial design. Dana hoped that the inventive, graceful, Art Nouveau–inspired shapes and graphic designs of Deutscher Werkbund products would educate American manufacturers about their aesthetic responsibility to the nation. Instead the message of Dana's exhibition was largely ignored.

Imitation Instead of Inspiration. In 1913, after several angry European manufacturers said they would not be bringing their wares to the Panama-Pacific Exposition in San Francisco, Commissioner of Patents Edward B. Moore called on American manufacturers to stop stealing industrial designs from the Europeans and told Congress that it must take steps to protect what he called *industrial design,* coining the term that from then on was used to designate the distinctive designs of manufactured goods. But Congress refused to act, and American manufacturers insisted that they had to copy European innovations. They pointed to the New York Armory Show of that year, which demonstrated that American artists were out

of touch with modern European trends, as an example of what might happen if American manufacturing had to rely on its own design ideas.

Wartime Opportunity Squandered. The next opportunity to increase the sophistication of American design came in 1917, when Congress passed the Smith-Hughes Act to promote industrial education. With the war cutting off Americans from European influences, some thought the time was ripe for an American school of commercial design. In 1917 the curator of the Metropolitan Museum of Art in New York mounted the first annual exhibition of American industrial art (which would continue until 1931). But despite such attempts to educate the public about the importance of design, the final version of the Smith-Hughes Act omitted a provision for instruction in design and aesthetics. The United States continued to lag behind France, Germany, and England, all of which had started government-supported design programs before the war. In 1919, when an exhibition of French industrial arts was held, American buyers flocked to the event, ignoring the protests of American design advocates.

Source:
Arthur J. Pulos, *American Design Ethic: A History of Industrial Design to 1940* (Cambridge, Mass.: MIT Press, 1983).

FASHION FOR WOMEN

The Birth of the Modern. At the turn of the century a growing middle class, composed primarily of men and women in management and service jobs, was gaining prominence in American life. With the rise of bigger, more-efficient businesses, the triumph of the automobile, and the growth of national magazines, the broad characteristics of twentieth-century America fell into place. Americans grew more prosperous, more mobile, and more alike in their tastes and habits — all of which seemed like progress. One reason for their growing similarity was the national magazine. Although there was a vast array of magazines in nineteenth-century America, none of them commanded a particularly large audience of readers. In the 1910s, however, thanks to a combination of innovations in printing, mailing, and advertising, some magazines began to approach circulations of one million or more. The most successful of these magazines was the *Ladies' Home Journal* (1883–), edited by Edward Bok. Bok's magazine and rivals such as *Vogue* (1892–) and *Harper's Bazar* (1867– ; became *Harper's Bazaar* in 1929) exerted a strong influence in the areas of women's fashion, interior decorating, homemaking, and architecture.

Working Women. Although men headed most women's magazines, women editors, writers, artists, and fashion buyers dominated their staffs. Working women, particularly in cities, were a prominent part of the consumer culture fostered by women's magazines and those who advertised in them. This growing female workforce

Irene Castle was one of the first entertainers to influence American fashion nationwide. As half of the popular ballroom-dancing team Vernon and Irene Castle, she was as well known for her clothing and hairstyles as for her steps on the dance floor. She bought dresses that left her legs free for dancing and favored simple flowing lines. Early in the 1910s her influence led to the popularity of a shorter, slightly bell-shaped skirt made of lightweight chiffon or tulle. She is also credited with getting women to give up their corsets and petticoats for slips and bloomers. Yet her most important fashion statement came in 1914, when she cut her hair to the nape of her neck for practical reasons just before she underwent an appendectomy. After the surgery she appeared in public wearing a seed pearl necklace on her head to keep her bobbed locks in place. As magazines clamored to spotlight her new hairstyle, the look that would define the flapper of the 1920s was born. In her autobiography Castle claimed that 250 women copied her during the week after her first public appearance and that 2,500 followed suit the following week.

Sources: Irene Castle, as told to Bob and Wanda Duncan, *Castles in the Air* (Garden City, N.Y.: Doubleday, 1958);

Caroline Rennolds Milbank, *New York Fashion: The Evolution of American Style* (New York: Abrams, 1989).

Dancers Vernon and Irene Castle, circa 1915. Irene Castle's bobbed hair and simple, flowing dresses were widely imitated during the 1910s.

hoped to use their earnings to create lives for themselves that resembled those they read about in magazines and books. In the nineteenth century there was a marked difference between the dress of working-class women and that of women in the upper classes. By the 1910s, however, the key difference between the clothing of the well-off and that of the working class was quality, not design. Mass-produced versions of the latest styles in clothing and dress were increasingly available and affordable. Where a middle-class woman could wear a fancy dress made of white linen with lace inserts, a working-class woman could afford a simpler cotton version that, to the casual observer, looked much the same.

Ready-to-Wear. In years past women had either made clothes for themselves and their families or, if they could afford it, had their clothes made for them by tailors. The elaborate women's wear of the nineteenth century, which included complicated undergarments, skirts and overskirts, high lace necklines, lace-up shoes, and elaborate hats, were time consuming to create, to put on, and to care for. With the turn of the century clothing and its construction became simpler. A key component in the move toward simplicity was the emergence of clothing manufacturers who turned out streamlined, ready-to-

wear garments. A woman could buy a ready-to-wear suit, inaccurately called a "tailor-made," for ten to twenty dollars, while a custom-made suit could cost hundreds of dollars. Most of the ready-to-wear manufacturing operations — overcrowded, dimly lit, and generally dangerous sweatshops — were located on the Lower East Side of New York City, where eastern European immigrants, many of them Jewish, were desperate for ways to make a living.

The Shirtwaist. The key item in the success of ready-to-wear clothing was the shirtwaist blouse. Created in America at the end of the nineteenth century, the shirtwaist blouse was a simple, inexpensive alternative to elaborate dresses and stiff, high-collared blouses. Worn tucked in, it created a businesslike, clean look for women. Worn pulled out of the skirt, as became the fashion in 1914, it made movement even easier and prepared the way for the dropped-waist look associated with the flapper of the 1920s. Although French fashion authorities — who had called the shots in American style and would largely continue to do so — sniffed in disdain at the shirtwaist, it launched a fashion revolution in the United States. Shirtwaists with ever-simpler necklines were available from mail-order catalogues and in stores, some for less than a dollar.

Success Brings Tragedy. By 1910 the shirtwaist was an empire unto itself, generating $60 million in revenues for ready-to-wear manufacturers. Unfortunately, as this boom increased the demand for the product, more and more women were working under dangerous conditions in sweatshops. In 1911 the Triangle Shirtwaist Factory on the Lower East Side of Manhattan went up in flames. The fire killed 146 female workers, who were trapped in the cramped building that housed the business. Although the tragedy led to improvements in labor laws and building codes, oppressive sweatshops continued to play a key role in the economics of the ready-to-wear industry.

Active Wear for Active Women. The bicycle craze of the late nineteenth century captivated both sexes, and women donned bloomers to participate in the new sport. In 1903 the Wright brothers' successful airplane flight at Kitty Hawk, North Carolina, captured the imagination of a nation obsessed with innovation and invigoration — and by the 1910s outfits had been designed for women who wanted to fly airplanes. Skating, golfing, swimming, automobile driving, and dancing required new feminine attire. American ready-to-wear manufacturers such as Max Meyer and Peter Thompson and catalogue-sales companies such as Lane Bryant profited by offering attire such as fur-trimmed skating outfits and driving veils.

Simplified Clothing. Newly active women demanded simplified clothes that suited their active daily lives. Time spent lacing corsets, layering petticoats, and fastening eyelets — all of which was absolutely necessary to achieve the unnatural S-shaped silhouette of earlier decades — seemed like time wasted. Petticoats and corsets were replaced by bloomers and slips, following the style of the nationally known dancing sensation Irene Castle. The loud color palette of Victorian fabrics gave way to a much more restrained spectrum, reinforced by Europeans' adoption of black and white as fashion mainstays after the death in 1910 of King Edward VII. Women even stopped changing from day dresses into dinner or evening dresses, preferring to add or subtract accessories for formal or informal occasions. *Women's Wear Daily,* founded in 1910, lampooned this "shocking" tendency, deriding the outfit it called "The Transformable Quadruple Gown." Yet by the time America entered World War I, the all-day dress would become a matter of fashion gospel.

Mass Production. The trend toward simplicity suited mass manufacturers. New dresses could be pulled over the head and fitted with a belt. Flounces and detailing added to production costs and manufacturing problems — and middle-class women of the 1910s were

THE RISE OF AMERICAN FASHIONS

In February 1913 the *Ladies' Home Journal* reported, "It looks for the first time as if a distinct movement toward American-designed fashions for American women were under way." When American fashion had made the news in the past, the editors reflected, those instances were just "spasmodic waves." Now that Parisian couturiers were changing styles with the seasons instead of creating timeless clothing, they predicted that things would be different. The American woman needed practical fashions: "In other words when a woman buys a hat or a dress she is entitled to get reasonable wear out of it in return for her money. For her suddenly to discover that the hat or dress is 'out of style,' with the materials still perfectly good, is an injustice." American designers should look to their own heritage and circumstances to find the materials for a truly American style, the editors observed, because "Our architects, our musicians, our artists and our writers have laid a sturdy foundation in their different schools of art adapted to American conditions. Why should American women longer suffer from the ignominious proposition of being told what to wear and how long to wear it by people three thousand miles away?"

Source: "The Coming of American Fashions," *Ladies' Home Journal*, 30 (February 1913): 5.

just as happy without them. The long, flowing skirts of earlier times used excesses of fabric that taxed manufacturers' resources — so skirts grew shorter, up to six inches above the ground, and more streamlined, in a way that suited active women. In ten short years American women went from looking like corseted Victorian matrons to bearing a striking resemblance to the flapper of the 1920s.

Hats. Although hats continued to be an essential part of a woman's public wardrobe, they grew simpler as well. The final year of the mammoth, broad-brimmed hat festooned with plumes from exotic birds was 1910. Foot-long hatpins, which had been necessary to keep those creations from falling from women's heads, disappeared as hats took on manageable proportions. A trim, turban-style headpiece or a neatly geometric hat in pale-colored felt replaced the hats of years past. Dramatic feathers were still used on occasion, particularly for evening wear, but they were never again used quite as lavishly.

Parisian Couture. Wealthy, status-conscious American women had heeded the dictates of Paris-based couturiers for decades. Influential design houses such as those of Paul Poiret, Mademoiselle Paquin, and the Callot

Soeurs used the most sumptuous fabrics and the most elaborate methods of construction to give their rich clients palpably luxurious clothing. But in the 1910s extravagant wardrobes were growing less and less appropriate even for American women in the most self-consciously blue-blooded families. As a result, French couture became increasingly understated to suit the tastes of its patrons.

Conspicuous Consumption. Although most women simply chose their clothing on the basis of cost or practicality, others, mostly college-educated women, avoided French fashions for philosophical reasons. High fashion had been the butt of practical-minded American ridicule since the founding of the country, but a book published in 1899 refocused Americans' attention on the odd and seemingly wasteful ritual of keeping up with fashion. In *The Theory of the Leisure Class* Thorstein Veblen, an academic whose writings mixed sociology, anthropology, and economics, derided Americans' status-conscious conspicuous consumption — which he equated with waste. Prestige, Veblen observed, was conferred in proportion to a person's appearance of leisure. Women's fashions, particularly the confining, nearly crippling nineteenth-century styles in shoes, skirts, and hats, served as prime examples for Veblen, who influenced progressive-minded women's clothing choices by pointing out that extravagant clothing that restricted women's movements signaled that they, like their ancient counterparts, were entirely dependent on men, mere ornaments of their husbands' success. For the educated, independent woman, wearing simple, comfortable clothing was a statement of her independence.

American Fashion Independence. In the 1910s the American fashion industry began to create its own identity separate from the whims of Parisian tastemakers. In December 1912 the head of the newly formed Society of American Fashions pointed out that many other American designers had been sewing Parisian labels into their American-made clothes to attract buyers, and Thurn, one of the most prominent import and custom-made American clothing houses, admitted that it had done just that. Yet the first hint of American fashion independence had come a few years earlier. After spring 1910, when Parisian designers showed the hobble skirt, cut so narrow at the ankles that it severely restricted a woman's ability to walk, the American Ladies' Tailors Association fought back. In October they introduced a "suffragette suit," which featured a skirt that was divided down the middle, allowing the wearer to take long, bold strides.

American Designs. An even bigger boost to American fashion came in February 1913, when *The New York Times* announced the winners of its fashion contest. The winning designs in *The New York Times* contest were self-consciously American, some almost laughably so. The first-prize evening dress, made of putty-colored silk and blue chiffon, was meant to evoke the palette of American expatriate painter James McNeill Whistler.

The second-prize afternoon dress was based on Quaker costumes, and the winning hats were modeled after the cotton boll and the American Beauty rose. Yet such excesses of patriotism did not dim enthusiasm for the event in the fashion world. Society columns reported that society women were proudly sporting the works of American designers. Retailers began to trade on the Americanness of their merchandise instead of emphasizing their connections to European designers. Bloomingdale's, Bonwit Teller, and others featured emphatically American designs in their advertisements. The *Ladies' Home Journal* even took out an advertisement claiming credit for being the first to promote American design and promising to publish pictures of President Woodrow Wilson's wife and her daughters wearing American dresses.

The War in Europe. In 1914, as war threatened to close down the all-important Paris shows, Americans were poised to take over fashion. Edna Woolman Chase, an editor at *Vogue,* arranged the New York Fashion Fete, featuring such American talents as fashion importers and custom-clothing designers Henri Bendel, who had added a ready-to-wear department to his Fifth Avenue clothing store in 1910, and the team of Herman Bergdorf and Edwin Goodman, who opened their own Fifth Avenue store in 1914. But European couture managed to survive the war. Paris designers did not miss a season until World War II. Some observers claimed that World War I seemed to make Parisian fashions more desirable — indeed, when Paul Poiret visited New York in 1916, he found an abundance of counterfeit Poiret clothes. Nevertheless, the most prominent — and extravagant — design houses, such as Poiret, Paquin, and the Callot Soeurs, found their American market much smaller after the war. American tastes ran toward the simpler, sportier designs of Europeans who worked with sensible fabrics such as rayon and wool — young talents including Gabrielle "Coco" Chanel, Jean Patou, and Madeleine Vionnet. The designers who kept up with the needs of modern femininity did a brisk business. By the end of the war American women were at last spending as much on their own clothing as they did on their husbands'.

Sources:

Frances Kennett, *The Collector's Book of Fashion* (New York: Crown, 1983);

Caroline Rennolds Milbank, *New York Fashion: The Evolution of American Style* (New York: Abrams, 1989);

John Peacock, *20th Century Fashion: The Complete Sourcebook* (New York: Thames & Hudson, 1993).

MEN'S AND CHILDREN'S CLOTHING

Men's Clothes. During the 1910s the fashionable silhouette in men's clothing followed the stripped-down look in women's fashions. Men's suits — which had been barrel-chested with thick shoulder padding and wide-legged trousers pegged at the ankle — now followed the body. Shoulder pads were whittled away; trousers had cuffs, and their legs were narrowed, ending just above the

Girls' clothing, circa 1911 (Ella and Doris Lane)

shoe, with creases in the front and back. This slim look, which included a vest (still called a waistcoat), was aided by the decline of the union suit as the underwear of choice. Central heating made it possible to wear simple undershirts and undershorts, cutting down on the bulk under a man's suit. American men dressed formally for work, wearing dress trousers, shirts, vests, jackets, and ties.

Furnishings. Although a more natural look prevailed overall, stiff, detachable shirt collars remained in fashion throughout the decade — with the blunt-tipped high-band Belmont collar leading the way. A collar generally could be worn with an ascot, a bow tie, or a four-in-hand necktie made of silk in many combinations of colors, but the Belmont demanded a tidy, small-knotted necktie. Men still wore garters to keep their socks up. Hats were worn in public and came in several varieties — such as boaters (braided-straw hats with brims and flat crowns), fedoras, Panamas, and derbies — and fabrics — such as felt, silk, or straw — to suit the season and the occasion. Oxford shoes replaced the high-buttoned boots of earlier generations, and the wristwatch, introduced in 1914 and popularized during the war, replaced the pocket watch.

The war also popularized the belt. Until then, dress pants were made without belt loops, and men used suspenders (braces) to keep their trousers up. The war also introduced the Burberry trench coat, which became popular among civilians.

Active Wear. The Norfolk jacket, allegedly based on a hunting jacket worn by an eighteenth-century duke of Norfolk, was the choice for leisure activities such as golfing and horseback riding. Like the new suits, the Norfolk jacket was cut close to the body. It was ornamented with a yolk, a sewn-in belt, patch pockets, and seams running down either side of the wearer's chest. With this jacket men wore whatever trousers were appropriate to the event. The influence of dancers Vernon and Irene Castle led some men to adopt a one-button jacket and slender trousers that were comfortable on the dance floor. Black and white men involved in the development of jazz music took to wearing an extreme version of the popular suit, horrifying fashion conservatives and delighting the avant-garde. The jacket was cut with pinched shoulders, a tight waist, and a twelve-inch vent and was paired with pipe-stem trousers.

Formal Wear. Formal wear was also adapted somewhat to keep up with the changes in men's clothing. Tuxedos and tailcoats became available with natural instead of padded shoulders. One new version of the tuxedo flared over the hips, had close-set buttons clustered at the waist, and had a deep vent up the back. Formal trousers became slimmer, in keeping with the new, narrow look. Pleated shirts with turned-down collars took the place of stiff, high-collared dress shirts. A high silk hat was still worn on formal occasions, day or night.

Wartime Menswear. Because clothes were already streamlined, men's clothing did not change much after the United States entered the war in 1917. Only patch pockets and the second pair of suit pants were lost to wartime austerity measures. Harvard undergraduates had been wearing ankle-length topcoats with folded-down doughboy collars since 1910 — probably because they were just the thing for automobile driving. American military uniforms, however, were cobbled together from bits and pieces of European and American menswear. The Ninety-sixth Aero Squadron, for example, wore wool or khaki-cotton breeches depending on the season; a single-breasted brown wool coat with a high collar, four patch pockets, and bronze buttons; a Sam Browne belt; and reddish leather gloves (styles borrowed from the British army), along with high-laced boots or leg wrappings called puttees. In cold weather members of the squadron wore double-breasted short coats with fur or sheepskin-lined collars — a style that in time would be transformed into the familiar bomber jacket. Pilots and army men wore modified day-workers' outfits, with tan coveralls, black overshoes, and leather gloves. Pilots added goggles and leather helmets. The Marine Corps wore olive drab field uniforms and leather puttees instead of the wrap-around leggings. Helmets with narrow brims were issued to all men in Europe, but several sorts of hats were worn by men in various divisions, including the overseas cap, the dark blue knitted army cap, the small-billed navy cap, and the wide-brimmed Marine Corps field hat.

Children's Clothing. War brought the beginnings of a shift in children's wear. Throughout the nineteenth century children were dressed in smaller versions of adult fashions, particularly for Sundays and holidays. Short pants and decorative short bloomers were fashion's main accommodations to children's needs. The exigencies of war demanded an increase of simplicity. Women were called to fill manufacturing spots left vacant by military men, or they helped by making dressings for wounds and other wartime necessities, and they did not have time to fuss with or make elaborate children's outfits. Ready-to-wear sportswear for both girls and boys pointed the way to a new era of simplicity. The 1910s had seen the advent of the gym slip — bloomers, a white blouse, and tunic belted loosely at the waist — which provided a model for wartime wear. Boys adopted a variation of football outfits — knee-length shorts, open-neck shirts, and long socks. Hats for boys and girls were still obligatory in public, as they were for grown men and women.

Sources:

John Elting and Michael McAfee, eds., *Military Uniforms in America*, volume 4, *The Modern Era — From 1868* (Novato, Cal.: Presidio, 1988);

Frances Kennett, *The Collector's Book of Fashion* (New York: Crown, 1983);

O. E. Schoeffler and William Gale, *Esquire's Encyclopedia of 20th Century Men's Fashions* (New York: McGraw-Hill, 1973).

HEADLINE MAKERS

HENRY BACON

1866-1924

ARCHITECT

Leader in the Beaux-Arts Style. Henry Bacon's greatest accomplishment was designing the Lincoln Memorial in Washington, D.C. (completed in 1917 and dedicated in 1922), a project that reflects his profound commitment to American democratic ideals. In his time Bacon was respected as one of the most talented exponents of the fashionable Beaux-Arts style of architecture, so-called because it was taught at the Ecole des Beaux-Arts in Paris. Based on a careful study of antiquity and often combining an eclectic use of other historic elements, this style placed great emphasis on refinement of taste and made up in elegance and sophistication what it sometimes lacked in vitality and originality. Bacon's contribution to the American interpretation of Beaux-Arts design was a pure classicism born of his great love for ancient Greek and Roman art and architecture. Yet perhaps his most significant legacy to American architecture was his collaboration with some of the foremost sculptors of his day, including Daniel Chester French (who sculpted the statue of Abraham Lincoln for the Lincoln Memorial) and Augustus Saint-Gaudens.

Training and Apprenticeship. Henry Bacon was born on 28 November 1866 in Watseka, Illinois, a village near Chicago. He studied engineering and architecture at the University of Illinois in 1884–1885, leaving to work for Chamberlin and Whidden, an architectural firm in Boston, where he was first exposed to the Beaux-Arts style. Three years later he moved to the celebrated firm of McKim, Mead and White in New York City. His work at Chamberlin and Whidden qualified him to enter the prestigious Rotch traveling-scholarship competition, which he won in 1889 with his design for an "Art College

in a City Park." This scholarship permitted Bacon to spend two years in Europe, where he immersed himself in a study of classical architecture. Returning to McKim, Mead and White in 1891, he remained with the firm until 1897, when he became cofounder of Brite and Bacon. Five years later he formed his own independent firm.

Monuments and Memorials. Although his schools, hospitals, libraries, railroad stations, and banks were also admired, Bacon's memorials and monuments seemed to embody best the classical ideals he brought to his work. Among them are the base of the memorial to Gen. William Tecumseh Sherman in New York and the memorial to Charles Parnell in Dublin, Ireland, one of several on which he collaborated with Saint-Gaudens. Bacon believed that these memorials ought to inspire reverence and mystery in the viewer and often set his monuments in secluded areas, "for then, in quiet, and without distraction of the senses or mind, the beholder is alone with the lesson which the object is designed to teach and inspire." He began preliminary work on the Lincoln Memorial in 1911, chosen because of his extensive training in Beaux-Arts architecture during his association with McKim, Mead and White. With its row of fluted Doric columns, the memorial was inspired by the Parthenon, which Bacon had visited on his European travels. The Lincoln Memorial has become one of the best-loved monuments in America, a symbol of liberty for succeeding generations.

Awards. In 1923 Bacon won the Gold Medal of the American Institute of Architects for his Lincoln Memorial design. He was also a member of the National Academy of Arts and Sciences, as well as the American Academy of Arts and Letters. He died on 16 February 1924.

Sources:

William Dudley Hunt Jr., *Encyclopedia of American Architecture,* revised by Robert T. Packard and Balthazar Korab (New York: McGraw-Hill, 1994);

Christopher Alexander Thomas, "The Lincoln Memorial and Its Architect, Henry Bacon (1866–1924)," dissertation, Yale University, 1990.

RALPH ADAMS CRAM

1863-1942

ARCHITECT

Champion of the Gothic. Ralph Adams Cram was the prime mover behind the revival of Gothic architecture in the 1910s. With his partners at the firm Cram, Goodhue and Ferguson (later Cram and Ferguson), Cram created some of the most influential church and college buildings of his era. Primarily responsible for the overall design and appearance of the firm's buildings, he is widely considered the founder and the foremost exponent of the Eclectic Gothic style in America. While remaining faithful to the pointed arches and delicate stone traceries of English Gothic architecture, this style also borrows from earlier architectural traditions to create structures on the grand scale of newer American buildings. In 1916 a reviewer said of Cram's Gothicism that he "hears its living music, and it is to him not past but eternal."

Proponent of the Spiritual. Cram was born in Hampton Falls, New Hampshire, on 16 December 1863, the son of a Unitarian minister. He displayed an early talent for drawing and toured Europe after high school. In 1881 he went to Boston to work as an apprentice architect for the firm Rotch and Tilden and as the art critic for the *Boston Transcript*. A second European tour in 1886 strengthened his interest in historical styles of art and architecture. During both his pilgrimages to the Old World he was profoundly moved by the spirituality of medieval buildings, particularly as it was embodied in the Gothic style. Becoming a High Church Anglican, he retained an awareness of mystical spirituality and an abiding love of medievalism for the rest of his life. On his return to the United States he and Charles Francis Wentworth formed the firm of Cram and Wentworth in Boston, but it was not until Bertram Grosvenor Goodhue became a partner in 1891 and Frank Ferguson joined the firm in 1899 (the year Wentworth died) that Cram began to get the important commissions that made his reputation. Cram's continued insistence on using the Gothic style eventually caused a rift between him and Goodhue, who left the firm in 1913.

Architecture, Philosophy, and Religion. Cram wrote and lectured on the desirability of medieval-style spirituality and communalism in the face of creeping individualistic materialism, publishing many popular, scholarly, and polemical books and essays. He also expressed unpopular political views, for example urging that the United States enter World War I at a time when most Americans favored neutrality.

Churches and Colleges. Cram is best known for his Gothic churches. He felt strongly that the Gothic style ought to be reserved for "ritualized" churches, but he was versatile enough to design other commissions in eclectic, modern, or neoclassical styles. His best-known work in New York City is his redesign of the Cathedral Church of St. John the Divine. This church had originally been designed in a Romanesque-Byzantine style by the firm of Heins and La Farge in 1891, but Cram, whose firm took over the project in 1911, was able to change the overall design to his characteristic Gothic style. Cram was eventually appointed principal architect of that building, which occupied the majority of his time for the rest of his life. St. John the Divine is well known for its broad nave flanked by high columns that dwarf the visitor and lend a sense of mystery and awe to the interior. Cram also designed the Park Avenue Christian Church (1911) and St. Thomas Episcopal Church on Fifth Avenue (1914) in New York City and the U.S. Military Academy Chapel (1910) and other buildings at West Point. Among his other notable secular buildings are the Watkins House, in Winona, Illinois; the Atwood House in East Gloucester, Massachusetts; and the Princeton University Graduate College in New Jersey, which he designed while he was supervising architect for Princeton University. He worked in a similar capacity at Bryn Mawr, Mount Holyoke, and Wellesley Colleges — becoming the chief architect of the popularity of "collegiate Gothic."

Later Career. Cram's firm continued to "survive in the age of steel and reinforced concrete," as an article in *Fortune* proclaimed in 1931, and he weathered the Great Depression as well. An untiring proponent of the medieval style, Cram was working on East Liberty Church in Pittsburgh, the largest Gothic cathedral in the world, when he died in 1942. (The church remains unfinished.)

Source:
Douglass Shand-Tucci, *Ralph Adams Cram: Life and Architecture* (Amherst: University of Massachusetts Press, 1995).

ELSIE DE WOLFE

1865-1950

INTERIOR DECORATOR

Professional Design. Elsie de Wolfe was the first professional interior designer in America. Before de Wolfe began helping her friends with home decoration around 1900, American homes had never been "designed." Upper-class women called in curtain makers, furniture salesmen, wallpaper specialists, and other craftsmen and then attempted to arrange these elements themselves. De Wolfe, who believed in achieving a single, harmonious, overall design statement, felt that the decoration of the home should reflect the woman's personality, rather than simply the husband's earning power. She introduced a startling freshness to the elaborate, heavily fringed and tasseled Victorian design sensibility of her time. While carrying on the tradition of decorative surfaces and harmonious color combinations, she cleared away the thickly curtained and upholstered look of the nineteenth century. Having spent summers in France, she had come to prefer the light, gilded interiors of Versailles and the delicate lines of eighteenth-century French furniture.

Actress to Designer. Elsie de Wolfe was born in 1865 to a fashionable New York City family. In 1884 she began a career as an actress, appearing in *A Cup of Tea,* and she met Elisabeth Marbury, who would become a lifelong friend and companion. Never an unqualified success in the theater, de Wolfe continued to act (and occasionally star) in various productions in the United States and abroad until she was in her early forties. At one stage of her career, while she had her own theatrical company, she planned all the stage designs, impressing her audiences with her great fashion sense, her fine eye for color, and her ability to create a harmonious environment.

Free Advice. In the late 1890s de Wolfe and Marbury, by then a successful literary agent, moved into Washington Irving's former home in New York City. There de Wolfe first tried her hand at designing an interior from scratch, impressing her visitors. When these women asked for advice in decorating their own homes, de Wolfe gladly helped them in their attempts to create modern, beautiful, and harmonious interiors. Around the turn of the century de Wolfe decided to retire from the stage and launch herself as a professional interior designer. She had cards printed with her logo, a wolf holding a flower in its paw, and opened an office in New York City.

The Colony Club. In 1905 architect Stanford White commissioned de Wolfe to design the interiors of the exclusive Colony Club, a retreat for upper-class ladies. To research the designs for her first large commission, she sailed to England and brought back flowered chintz (then considered an inexpensive, countrified fabric) and simple furniture, which she planned to use in white-painted rooms lined with trellises with real ivy growing on them. Her idea was to re-create an English cottage garden indoors, in a clean, light, comfortable interior. Although her ideas for the Colony Club stirred considerable controversy at first, de Wolfe quickly became one of the most sought-after designers of her generation.

A Signature Style. By the early 1910s de Wolfe had developed her own distinctive style, which included bright colors, fresh paint, and easily maintainable surfaces. One visitor described de Wolfe's home as a "model of simplicity in gold and white." De Wolfe covered dark wood with white paint, removed heavy draperies from windows to let in the light, and covered furniture in chintz. Her book *The House in Good Taste* (1913) has influenced several generations of designers. In addition to the Colony Club, de Wolfe's important design projects include the homes of Mrs. George Beckwith, Mr. and Mrs. William Crocker, Ethel Barrymore, and Henry Clay Frick, as well as a dormitory for Barnard College in New York City.

Lady Mendl. In 1926 de Wolfe married Sir Charles Mendl and moved to Beverly Hills, where she continued to startle her contemporaries with her innovations. She was probably the first woman to dye her hair blue, to perform handstands to impress her friends, and to cover eighteenth-century footstools in leopard-skin chintzes.

Sources:

Elsie de Wolfe, *After All* (New York: Arno, 1974);

Beverly Russell, *Women of Design: Contemporary American Interiors* (New York: Rizzoli, 1992);

C. Ray Smith, *Interior Design in 20th-Century America: A History* (New York: Harper & Row, 1987).

CASS GILBERT

1859-1934

ARCHITECT

Skyscraper Architect. Cass Gilbert, one of the most respected Beaux-Arts architects of the early twentieth century, is most often remembered for designing the Woolworth Building (1913) in New York City, an eclectic Gothic structure that was the tallest building in the world for nearly twenty years.

Out of the Heartland. Gilbert was born in Zanesville, Ohio, on 24 November 1859 and grew up in Saint Paul, Minnesota. After a yearlong apprenticeship with the Twin Cities architectural firm of A. M. Radcliff, which helped him develop what became a legendary skill as a draftsman, he entered the new architecture program at the Massachusetts Institute of Technology, the first of its kind in the country. Leaving school after one academic year, he received the most important part of his training during two years as an assistant to Stanford White, the most prominent member of the Beaux-Arts firm of McKim, Mead and White. In 1883 Gilbert returned to Saint Paul, where he opened a practice with James Knox Taylor, an MIT classmate. Their firm was awarded contracts for residential and commercial projects, as well as churches. Gilbert is considered the first architect to bring the formal and symmetrical Colonial Revival style and other, more sophisticated East Coast architectural styles to the Twin Cities. Examples of his Colonial Revival structures, which were adapted for the harsh Minnesota climate, are the C. P. Noyes House and the Howard Elmer House. Gilbert was also noted for his versatility; some of his residences were designed in the new, less formal Shingle Style, while some of his public buildings reflected the more eclectic Beaux-Arts style.

New York. Throughout the 1890s Gilbert won competitions and public-building contracts in the Midwest as well as in New York City. By 1898 he had opened a branch office in New York City, and the following year, after he won a competition to design the U.S. Customs House in New York City, he relocated there. In New York he executed the most impressive of his many buildings. The famous Woolworth Building, completed in 1913, was a curious example of monumental Gothic architecture, complete with terra-cotta gargoyles, buttresses, and pinnacles.

Professional Success. Gilbert went on to design many public buildings, including the Saint Louis Central Public Library (1912), the Detroit Public Library (1914), and the Allen Memorial Art Museum (1917) at Oberlin College, as well as the U.S. Treasury Annex (1919) and the U.S. Supreme Court building (1935) in Washington, D.C. Throughout his career he worked in an eclectic Beaux-Arts style, rejecting modernizing trends in American architecture. By the time of his death he had been an architect for almost fifty years and had established a nationwide practice. Gilbert was also a member of many professional groups, serving as president of the American Institute of Architects in 1908–1909 and on the National Commission of Fine Arts in 1910–1918.

Source:
Patricia Anne Murphy, *Cass Gilbert: Minnesota Master Architect* (Minneapolis: Minnesota University Gallery, 1980).

ELBERT HUBBARD

1856-1915

MANUFACTURER, PUBLISHER

From Soap to Art. In 1893, at the age of thirty-seven, Elbert Hubbard had already made his fortune in soap manufacturing and abandoned the business world for a life dedicated to educating the American public about the Arts and Crafts movement. Using his business savvy and motivated by a passion for medieval-inspired designs for fabric, paper, ceramics, and furniture, Hubbard turned a small publishing venture into the lifeblood of a community of artists, craftspeople, and workers dedicated to preserving superior craftsmanship in an era of mass production.

Background. Elbert Hubbard was born on 19 June 1856 in Bloomington, Indiana. At fifteen he moved to Buffalo, New York, to help his brother-in-law, John Larkin, start a soap-manufacturing business. He would later say that he had achieved his education in the "University of Hard Knocks." As a charming, handsome, talkative young man, Hubbard was a successful salesman who was willing to experiment with promotional techniques, gimmicks, and prizes at a time when the art of advertising was in its infancy. By the time Hubbard left the company in 1893 it was worth $30 million.

Roycroft. In 1893 Hubbard entered Harvard College to prepare himself for a new career as a writer, but he left after a few months for a trip to England. While there he met artist-designer William Morris, who — along with John Ruskin — was a guiding light of the Arts and Crafts revival in England. Inspired by a tour of Morris's renowned Kelmscott Press, Hubbard returned to upstate New York in 1894 and founded the Roycroft Press, as well as a community of designers and craftsmen dedicated to making handcrafted, useful objects and to restoring the ideals of the medieval guild system. Roycroft Press published several periodicals to spread these ideals, including *The Philistine* and *The Fra* (Hubbard's self-invented nickname, which alluded to his vision of himself as a medieval-style master craftsman). The press specialized in finely crafted books with features such as borders inspired by Morris, hand-colored illustrations, hand-tooled leather covers, and exquisite Japanese papers.

Furniture, Lamps, and Ceramics. Although the overall design concept for goods produced at the Roycroft community was based on the Arts and Crafts style, Hubbard was more concerned with the process of the work and the life of the community than with imposing a single unifying philosophy of design. The profound respect for hand craftsmanship and fine work that characterized the Arts and Crafts movement permitted a wide range of taste and styles. As Hubbard said, his lamps, chairs, and pots were made according to "the principles of artistic quality, sound mechanical construction and good workmanship." In addition the Roycrofters' products were intended to be mass produced. Hubbard's expertise in marketing and advertising enabled him to find a large market for the Roycrofters' wares. By the early 1910s the Roycroft community was producing Morris-style chairs and simple benches and cabinets, some with tooled leather and carved decoration. His furniture designs owed much to Gustav Stickley's "Craftsman" furniture. Hubbard's metal shops produced wrought-iron lamps, copper-and-silver cups, vases, steins, and beautiful jade, silver, and copper jewelry. There were also painters, graphic artists, photographers, and sculptors in the lively and creative Roycroft community. The Roycroft Inn, established in 1903, was a favorite destination for tourists, writers, and craftsmen.

Death aboard the *Lusitania*. Hubbard and his wife died aboard the ocean liner *Lusitania* after it was torpedoed by a German submarine in 1915, but the Roycroft community remained a mecca for artists and writers until 1939, when its shops and inn were sold to Samuel Guard. The Roycroft complex, including many of the workshops, the inn, and gift shops, are now part of a historic-preservation project.

Source:

Marie Via and Margaret Searle, eds., *Head, Heart and Hand: Elbert Hubbard and the Roycrofters* (Rochester, N.Y.: University of Rochester Press, 1994).

GUSTAV STICKLEY

1857-1942

FURNITURE DESIGNER

The Craftsman. Inspired by British art critic John Ruskin and British painter-designer William Morris, Gustav Stickley created a distinctly American approach to furniture design, following their call for a return to the medieval reliance on fine craftsmanship based on solid training and respect for the innate qualities of the craftsman's materials. Founding what became known as the Craftsman movement, he adapted Morris's handmade approach to creating furniture that integrated colonial, Art Nouveau, Mission, and European peasant design into an original, vigorous, straightforward style. Extensively imitated in his own time, Stickley's designs are now recognized as the embodiment of a modern American sensibility that relied primarily on function and the natural beauty of indigenous materials, rather than on design elements of the past and exotic woods.

The Stickley Brothers. Gustav Stickley was born on 9 March 1857 in Osceola, Wisconsin, the eldest of eleven children, six of whom would become furniture makers. After his father abandoned the family during the 1870s, his mother took her children to Brandt, Pennsylvania, where her brother operated a chair factory. There Stickley learned to love working with wood and to appreciate its natural color, texture, and grain, and within a few years he had taken over the business. In 1884 Stickley opened a wholesale and retail furniture store with two of his younger brothers, Charles and Albert, in Binghamton, New York. The shop would have failed without the heavy financial backing from the town of Binghamton, which commissioned him to design and manufacture furniture. Because the Stickley Brothers did not have enough money to buy machinery and were forced to make most of their stock by hand, they designed furniture with simple lines, and emphasized the functionality and plain shapes that recalled some of the elements of colonial furniture design. By the late 1880s Stickley had become interested in Shaker designs, often taking his entire family to visit the Shaker settlement in New Lebanon, Pennsylvania.

Refining the Craft. In 1892 several of Stickley's brothers moved to Grand Rapids, Michigan, where they started another Stickley Brothers factory and produced designs that borrowed heavily from their eldest brother's style. During the same decade Stickley began to experiment with ideas gleaned from his reading of Ruskin, Thomas Carlyle, and Ralph Waldo Emerson. By the late 1890s Stickley had become an expert at creating precise reproductions of colonial furniture. His first trips to Europe at the turn of the century, however, and his association with Irene Sargent, a well-known architectural critic, inspired him to study modern furniture. In France and Germany Stickley met the greatest artists of the Art Nouveau movement. In England he developed a keen interest in the Arts and Crafts style, which, he would later say, was "more in harmony with what I had in mind." From these European designers Stickley learned to appreciate organic, tapered lines and natural form. Yet he rejected exuberant "sculptural" shapes that interfered with the function of the object. For Stickley, furniture that was not primarily functional was absurd.

The Mission Style. Stickley is perhaps best known for the Mission Style of furniture, constructed of quarter-sawn oak that was treated with fumed ammonia to preserve and emphasize the wood grain. Mission Style furniture was functional, beautiful, and easy to care for. He made this furniture at the Craftsman Workshop in Eastwood, New York, established in 1900. The next year Stickley's firm began publishing his magazine, *The Craftsman*, which provided a forum for his philosophy of design, as well as articles on social reform, town planning, and even complete house designs. Early in the first decade of the twentieth century, Stickley also began experimenting with painted Chinese Chippendale furniture. In 1903 he organized an Arts and Crafts exhibition of American and European artifacts and handicrafts in Syracuse and Rochester. He continued to be inspired by a variety of historic, Asian, and modern influences for the rest of his life. By the 1910s Stickley's Mission Style was a fixture in American design and inspired other architects and designers, including Frank Lloyd Wright, who shared Stickley's love of clean, functional lines and the inherent beauty of well-chosen materials. In 1913 Stickley opened his twelve-story Craftsman Building in Manhattan, complete with display areas for his furniture and textiles, gardens, and a restaurant that served food grown on his own farm. Although The Craftsman, Inc., went out of business in 1915, Stickley continued to experiment with wood finishes and designs until his death in 1942.

Sources:

John Crosby Freeman, *The Forgotten Rebel: Gustav Stickley and His Craftsman Mission Furniture* (Watkins Glen, N.Y.: Century House, 1966);

Coy L. Ludwig, *The Arts & Crafts Movement in New York State, 1890s–1920s* (Hamilton: Gallery Association of New York State, 1983).

PEOPLE IN THE NEWS

At the 1918 annual conference of the American Federation of Art, **Richard Bach,** curator of industrial art at the Metropolitan Museum of Art in New York City, said, "It will be an evil day for manufacturers and dealers after the war if American taste must again go to Europe for industrial art products."

In 1912 **Leon Leonwood Bean** founded L. L. Bean, Inc., of Freeport, Maine, a mail-order sporting-goods empire worth $3.5 million by the time of his death in 1967. The casual, sporting clothes sold in his catalogues were a major component of the "preppy" look that became popular during the second half of the twentieth century.

In 1917 **Henri Bendel,** an importer and designer, was one of several influential members of the New York fashion world to write about American and French fashion in *Harper's Bazar.*

On 23 February 1913 **Irma Campbell,** an in-house designer for Lord & Taylor, took second prize for her gray-silk "Quaker dress" in the afternoon-dress division of the American fashion competition staged by *The New York Times.*

In 1913 the architectural firm of **John M. Carrère** and **Thomas Hastings** designed a mansion for industrialist Henry Clay Frick at East Seventieth Street and Fifth Avenue in New York City. After Frick's death in 1919, his magnificent marble mansion became a museum to house the Frick Collection, his extensive collection of art and antiques.

In 1912 interior designer **Elsie de Wolfe** wore a dress hemmed six inches off the floor during a visit to Paris and, she claimed, sparked a craze for "le walking suit" among the French.

In 1912 **W. S. Richardson** of McKim, Mead and White designed 998 Fifth Avenue, an Italian Renaissance–style luxury-apartment building opposite the Metropolitan Museum of Art at Eighty-first Street in New York City. Richardson's building was the first apartment house on Fifth Avenue.

In 1917 **E. M. A. Steinmetz,** a designer for Stein & Blaine in New York City, showed a collection of all-day silk dresses with hemlines just above the shoe.

On 23 February 1913 **Ethel Traphagen,** who was trained in art at the National Academy of Design, took first prize in *The New York Times* American fashion contest with her evening dress inspired by the palette of James McNeill Whistler's *Nocturne.*

DEATHS

John M. Allston, 86, fellow of the American Institute of Architects and a charter member of its Pittsburgh chapter, 17 April 1910.

George M. Anderson, 47, architect who designed the Avondale Presbyterian Church and the Ingalls Building in Cincinnati, 4 October 1916.

Daniel Hudson Burnham, 66, architect, chief of construction for the 1893 Columbian Exposition, 1 June 1912.

Edward M. Butz, 57, architect who designed the Dollar Savings Bank and the Seventh Street Hotel in Pittsburgh, Pennsylvania, 4 September 1916.

J. Cleveland Cady, 82, partner in the architectural firm of Cady, Berg & See, which designed the Brooklyn Academy of Design and the American Museum of Natural History in New York City, 16 April 1919.

Adolph Cudell, 60, architect who designed houses for prominent Chicago families, 18 August 1910.

James A. Darrach, 36, architect who collaborated in the design for Whittier Hall at Teachers College, Columbia University, in New York City, 6 July 1912.

Rudolph L. Daus, 62, member of the Beaux-Arts Society of Architects who designed the Brooklyn Armory for the Second Regiment, 16 October 1916.

Clinton Day, 50, architect who designed the Union Trust Company Bank in San Francisco, 11 January 1916.

Frank Miles Day, 47, president of the American Institute of Architects in 1906 and a specialist in designing academic buildings, including Prudence Risley Hall at Cornell University and Sterling Hall of Medicine at Yale University, 15 June 1918.

George S. Dean, 55, architect who designed the offices and houses at the U.S. Steel Corporation plants in Gary, Indiana; Duluth, Minnesota; and Farrell, Pennsylvania, 18 December 1919.

Ward P. Delano, 49, architect who designed the State Hospital and State Asylum in Worcester, Massachusetts, 25 September 1915.

David C. Lewis, 51, architect who designed the Board of Trade Building and Trinity Church in Portland, 1918.

Edward D. Lindsey, 75, former instructor of applied design at Princeton who designed the Drexel Building in New York City, one of the first fireproof buildings in the city, 30 April 1916.

Alfred Pissus, 60, architect who designed the Hibernian Savings and Loan Association building in San Francisco, one of the few commercial structures to survive the 1906 earthquake and fire, 7 July 1914.

J. Marshall Shirk, 53, student of the Ecole des Beaux-Arts and a prominent designer of homes and hospitals in and around Philadelphia, 2 August 1918.

William R. Ware, 83, architect and founder of the School of Architecture at the Massachusetts Institute of Technology, the first such program in the United States, 9 June 1915.

Edmund March Wheelwright, 58, first city architect of Boston and designer of the Harvard Lampoon Castle in Cambridge, Massachusetts, 15 August 1912.

PUBLICATIONS

"Agitation for American Fashions," *Current Opinion*, 54 (March 1913): 251;

Charles V. Boyd, "An American Bungalow," *Women's Home Companion*, 46 (October 1919): 54.

"Bungalows," *National Builder*, 55 (July 1913): 35;

Charles A. Byers, "Colonial Influence Brings the Bungalow to Greater Perfection," *Art World*, 3 (February 1918): 445–747;

Alwyn T. Covell, "The Real Place of Mission Furniture," *Good Furniture* (March 1915): 359–368;

Herbert D. Croly, "The Country House in California," *Architectural Record*, 33–34 (December 1913): 482–519;

F. J. DeLuce, "How We Built Our Bungalow for $450," *Country Life in America*, 21 (February 1912): 53–54;

Una N. Hopkins, "The Young Folks' First Bungalow," *Ladies' Home Journal*, 30 (May 1913): 39;

Phil M. Riley, "What is a Bungalow?," *Country Life in America*, 22 (July 1912): 11–12;

Henry H. Saylor, *Bungalows: Their Design, Construction and Furnishing* (Philadelphia: Winston, 1911);

Saylor, ed., *Distinctive Homes of Moderate Cost* (New York: McBride, Winston, 1910);

John S. Van Bergen, "A Plea for Americanism in Our Architecture," *Western Architect* (April 1915): 27–28;

Ekin Wallick, *The Small House for a Moderate Income* (New York: Hearst's International Library, 1915);

American Architect and Building News, periodical;

Architectural Record, periodical;

Country Life in America, periodical;

Good Housekeeping, periodical;

Harper's Bazar, periodical;

Ladies' Home Journal, periodical;

Vogue, periodical;

Western Architect, periodical;

Women's Home Companion, periodical.

CHAPTER SIX

GOVERNMENT AND POLITICS

by JOHN LOUIS RECCHIUTI

CONTENTS

1910

17 Mar. Congressman George W. Norris (R–Neb.) introduces a resolution to limit the power of Speaker of the House of Representatives Joseph G. Cannon (R–Ill.) Two days later the measure passes, an indication of the growing strength of progressive Republicans against the "old guard" Republicans represented by Cannon and President Taft.

26 Mar. Congress amends the Immigration Act of 1907 to prohibit criminals, paupers, anarchists, and diseased persons from entering the United States.

18 June Congress passes the Mann-Elkins Act, which extends jurisdiction of the Interstate Commerce Commission to include telephone, telegraph, cable, and wireless companies. It also augments ICC regulation of railroads, and it establishes a Commerce Court (which is abolished in 1913).

20 June Congress authorizes the New Mexico Territory and the Arizona Territory to form state governments and apply for statehood.

25 June Congress establishes the Postal Savings Bank (PSB) system. People who deposit their money in savings accounts with the post office receive 2 percent interest. (The PSB is abolished in 1967.)

Congress passes the Publicity Act, which requires members of Congress to report campaign contributions.

Congress passes the White Slave Traffic Act. Often called the Mann Act because it was introduced by Rep. James R. Mann (R–Ill.), this law prohibits the transportation of women across state lines for "immoral purposes" (prostitution). Between 1910 and 1918 more than two thousand convictions for "white slavery" are obtained in the courts.

31 Aug. Former president Theodore Roosevelt delivers a speech on the "New Nationalism" at Osawatomie, Kansas, calling for government regulation of business and assailing the conservatism of the courts. The speech is interpreted by many as a signal of Roosevelt's break with President William Howard Taft.

8 Nov. In the congressional elections Democrats gain control of the House of Representatives for the first time since 1885. Republicans retain nominal control of the Senate, but in fact Democrats and insurgent Republicans form a bloc against conservative Republicans.

1911

21 Jan. The National Progressive Republican League, founded by Sen. Robert M. La Follette of Wisconsin and other insurgent Republicans, issues its platform, which calls for direct election of U.S. senators, the initiative, the referendum, the recall, and other reforms. Sen. Jonathan Bourne of Oregon is elected league president.

7 Mar. President Taft dispatches twenty thousand U.S. troops to the Mexican border as fighting in the Mexican Revolution occurs so close to U.S. territory that the fighting can be seen from the U.S. side of the border.

15 May Citing the Sherman Antitrust Act of 1890, the U.S. Supreme Court rules that Standard Oil of New Jersey is a monopoly. Though the court orders that the monopoly be dissolved, ties between its various branches continue into the 1920s.

29 May   In *U.S.* v. *American Tobacco Company,* the Supreme Court finds the "tobacco trust" in violation of the Sherman Antitrust Act.

24 June   U.S. troops are recalled from Mexico after Mexican president Porfirio Díaz is deposed by revolutionaries.

7 July   In a move to save seals from extinction the United States joins Great Britain, Russia, and Japan in barring seal killing in the open seas north of the thirtieth parallel.

24 July   The United States renews its commercial treaty with Japan. Among its provisions, the treaty reaffirms the "Gentlemen's Agreement" of 1907, in which President Theodore Roosevelt pledged to see that Japanese residents of the United States were well treated if Japan voluntarily prevented Japanese laborers from immigrating to the United States.

22 Aug.   President Taft vetoes statehood for Arizona because its proposed constitution allows for the recall of judges by popular vote. Arizona omits the offending clause, but after it gains statehood it adopts the recall provision.

16 Oct.   The National Progressive Republican League endorses Robert M. La Follette of Wisconsin for president.

21 Dec.   A joint resolution of Congress ratifies the abrogation of an 1832 treaty with Russia because of Russia's unwillingness to recognize some U.S. passports, including those held by Jews and certain evangelical clergymen.

23 Dec.   In a private letter Theodore Roosevelt states his willingness to run for the presidency in 1912.

1912

6 Jan.   New Mexico becomes the forty-seventh state.

22 Jan.   In response to the Chinese revolution, which began in October 1911, a small contingent of U.S. troops occupies Tientsin, China, to protect American interests.

10 Feb.   Seven Republican governors endorse Theodore Roosevelt to be the Republican candidate for president.

14 Feb.   Arizona becomes the forty-eighth state.

24 Feb.   Roosevelt announces that he would accept the Republican presidential nomination.

27 Apr.   Democratic congressman Arsene Pujo of Louisiana begins House subcommittee hearings into the "money trust."

12 May   The national convention of the Socialist Party of America convenes at Indianapolis. Delegates nominate Eugene Victor Debs of Indiana for president and Emil Seidel, mayor of Milwaukee, Wisconsin, for vice president.

5 June   U.S. Marines land in Cuba to protect American interests.

18–22 June   At the Republican National Convention in Chicago party conservatives committed to Taft manage to exclude many progressive Republican delegates committed to Theodore Roosevelt, ensuring the renomination of Taft and Vice President James S. Sherman.

22 June	Asserting that the Republican Party convention is a fraud, Roosevelt supporters meet and hail Roosevelt as the leader of a third party.
25 June–2 July	At the Democratic National Convention in Baltimore, House Speaker James Beauchamp "Champ" Clark of Missouri and Gov. Woodrow Wilson of New Jersey are the early front-runners for the nomination. On 2 July Wilson is nominated on the forty-sixth ballot. Gov. Thomas R. Marshall of Indiana is nominated for vice president.
10 July	The Prohibition Party holds its national convention in Atlantic City, New Jersey, nominating Eugene W. Chafin of Arizona for president and Aaron S. Watkins of Ohio for vice president.
2 Aug.	Sen. Henry Cabot Lodge (R–Mass.) introduces a resolution — subsequently known as the Lodge Corollary — extending the Monroe Doctrine to obtain to foreign companies and non-European nations.
5 Aug.	Meeting in Chicago, the Progressive Party nominates Theodore Roosevelt for president and Hiram W. Johnson of California for vice president.
11 Oct.	In Milwaukee Theodore Roosevelt is shot and wounded in an assassination attempt but is able to deliver his scheduled speech before being taken to the hospital for treatment.
30 Oct.	Vice President James S. Sherman dies in Utica, New York. Columbia University president Nicholas Murray Butler replaces him as the Republican vice-presidential candidate.
5 Nov.	With the Republican vote split between Roosevelt and Taft, Democratic candidate Woodrow Wilson wins the presidential election, carrying forty of the forty-eight states. President Taft carries only Utah and Vermont. The Democrats win majorities in both houses of Congress.
10 Dec.	Sen. Elihu Root wins the Nobel Peace Prize.

1913

25 Feb.	The Sixteenth Amendment to the Constitution, having been ratified by thirty-eight states, is declared adopted. The amendment legalizes the federal income tax.
28 Feb.	The Pujo Committee issues its report, implicating the "money trust" as restrictive to free-market capitalism.
1 Mar.	Congress overrides President Taft's veto of the Webb-Kenyon Interstate Liquor Act, which prohibits the shipment of liquor into states where its sale is illegal.
4 Mar.	Woodrow Wilson takes the oath of office and becomes the twenty-eighth president of the United States.
	Congress divides the Commerce and Labor Department into two separate cabinet-level departments. William B. Wilson of Pennsylvania, a former miner, becomes secretary of labor; and William C. Redfield, a New York business executive, becomes secretary of commerce.

11 Mar. President Wilson announces that the United States will not recognize the Mexican government of Gen. Victoriano Huerta, whose troops overthrew and assassinated President Francisco Madero in a coup on 18–22 February.

8 Apr. President Wilson delivers a speech on tariff revision before Congress, becoming the first president to appear before Congress since 1800.

24 Apr. In an effort to avoid future wars, Secretary of State William Jennings Bryan submits treaties to all nations with ministers in Washington, D.C., calling for the referral of all international disputes to a permanent court of arbitration and a "cooling off" period. Eventually, the United States signs and ratifies "cooling off" treaties with twenty-one countries.

3 May The California state legislature passes a law preventing Japanese aliens from owning land. The act, opposed by President Wilson, damages U.S.-Japanese relations.

31 May The Seventeenth Amendment to the Constitution, providing for the direct election of U.S. senators, is officially adopted following ratification by thirty-six states. Previously senators were selected by state legislatures.

3 Oct. Congress passes the Underwood-Simmons Tariff Act, which lowers average duties to about 30 percent and allows some raw materials into the country tariff-free. Another section of the bill implements the Sixteenth Amendment by imposing personal-income tax.

16 Oct. Francis Burton, President Wilson's appointee as governor general of the Philippines, announces that the commission that governs the islands will henceforth include a majority of Filipinos.

27 Oct. In a speech in Mobile, Alabama, President Wilson promises that the United States will "never again seek one additional foot of territory by conquest."

23 Dec. President Wilson signs the Federal Reserve Act, establishing the Federal Reserve Board and a system of twelve regional Federal Reserve Banks to control the money supply and regulate the national banking system.

1914

3 Feb. President Wilson lifts the arms embargo against Mexico in an effort to help the forces of Venustiano Carranza, who is working to overthrow the Huerta government.

1 Apr. George W. Goethals is appointed governor of a permanent civilian government in the Panama Canal Zone.

9 Apr. An unarmed group of U.S. sailors from the USS *Dolphin*, stationed in Mexican waters, is arrested in Tampico, Mexico, after they accidentally enter a restricted area while seeking to secure supplies. Without consulting Washington, their commander, Adm. Henry T. Mayo, demands that the Mexicans formally apologize, raise the American flag on their soil, and give it a twenty-one-gun salute. Wilson backs these demands.

21 Apr.	American forces bombard Veracruz, Mexico, and occupy the city as part of a general blockade of Mexico, which is partly aimed at preventing a German ship from landing a shipment of arms at Veracruz. The next day Congress grants Wilson's request to use force against Mexico. Huerta breaks off diplomatic relations with the United States. By 30 April, sixty-seven hundred U.S. troops are engaging Huerta's forces. They do not withdraw from Mexico until 23 November.
8 May	Congress passes the Smith-Lever Act, which establishes a system of agricultural extension work between the Department of Agriculture and land-grant colleges.
25 May	President Wilson accepts the mediation efforts of the "ABC Powers" (Argentina, Brazil, and Chile) in the dispute with Mexico.
24 June	Meeting in Ontario, Canada, representatives from the United States, Mexico, and the ABC Powers decide the U.S.-Mexican dispute overwhelmingly in favor of the United States. Mediators recommend that Huerta resign, that Mexico establish a provisional government, and that the United States pay no indemnity for its invasion of Mexico. Rejected by Mexico, the plan nevertheless puts international pressure on Huerta, and he resigns on 15 July.
28 July	Austria declares war on Serbia.
30 July	Russia begins mobilizing troops to go to the aid of its ally Serbia.
1 Aug.	Germany declares war on Russia.
3 Aug.	Germany declares war on France and invades Belgium.
4 Aug.	In support of its allies Belgium and France, Great Britain declares war on Germany. The United States announces its neutrality.
5 Aug.	Secretary of State William Jennings Bryan signs the Bryan-Chamorro Treaty with Nicaragua, by which the United States leases two Nicaraguan islands and receives the right to build a naval base and a canal in Nicaragua.
6 Aug.	A controversy between the United States and Britain develops after Secretary of State William Jennings Bryan asks the warring nations to accept the Declaration of London as the code for naval conduct during the war. On 20 August Britain agrees to follow the declaration but only after expanding the list of contraband items its navy may justly seize. The British further expand the list on 29 October and 23 December and begin to seize foodstuffs, as well as ships, destined for ports in nations adjacent to Germany.
15 Aug.	The U.S. government announces that war loans to the European nations by U.S. bankers are "inconsistent with the true spirit of neutrality," but by October the U.S. State Department modifies its position, allowing some loans to be made.
	The Panama Canal is officially opened to shipping.
19 Aug.	President Wilson urges Americans to be neutral in "thought as well as in action."
26 Sept.	On President Wilson's recommendation, Congress passes the Federal Trade Commission Act, establishing a bipartisan five-member committee to replace the Bureau of Corporations and investigate the activities of corporations and individuals to prevent unfair business practices.

15 Oct.   Congress passes the Clayton Antitrust Act, which augments the Sherman Antitrust Act of 1890.

3 Nov.   The Democrats gain five seats in the Senate, for a 56–40 majority. In the House of Representatives they lose 61 seats but retain a 230–196 majority; nine seats are held by minor parties.

1915

28 Jan.   Congress establishes the U.S. Coast Guard.

A German ship sinks an American merchant ship carrying wheat to Britain.

10 Feb.   The United States protests a 4 February proclamation by the German government that it would sink merchant ships entering British waters.

18 Feb.   Germany announces that its submarines will sink enemy merchant vessels in the war zone without warning.

4 Mar.   The La Follette Seamen's Act improves conditions for sailors in the merchant marine.

28 Mar.   One American is killed when the Germans sink the British ship *Falaba*.

1 May   Three Americans die when the Germans sink the U.S. tanker *Gulflight*.

7 May   The *Lusitania*, a British passenger liner, is sunk off the Irish coast by a German submarine. The dead include 128 Americans.

11 May   Secretary of State Bryan sends a diplomatic note to Japan stating that the United States will not recognize any impairment of the "Open Door" policy regarding trade in China.

13 May   The first *Lusitania* note to Germany, written by President Wilson and signed by Secretary of State Bryan, demands that Germany stop its unrestricted submarine warfare and make reparation for the U.S. citizens who died in the sinking. Germany asserts that the *Lusitania* was carrying armaments (it was in fact carrying rifles and bullets) and refuses to pay reparations.

7 June   Secretary of State William Jennings Bryan resigns after Wilson asks him to sign a second *Lusitania* note. Bryan fears that the note will draw the United States into the war. Robert Lansing is appointed secretary of state in place of Bryan.

9 June   The second *Lusitania* note is sent to Germany.

15 July   The U.S. Secret Service discovers evidence of German espionage and sabotage efforts by several German Americans as well as members of the German consulate in the United States. The officials are recalled to Germany after their plans are exposed in newspaper articles on 24 July.

21 July   President Wilson personally sends a third *Lusitania* note to Germany warning that similar actions in the future would be regarded as "deliberately unfriendly."

28 July   U.S. Marines go ashore in Haiti following the assassination of Haitian president Vilbrun Guillaume Sam.

5 Aug.   Latin American nations and the United States meet in Washington, D.C., to discuss the problems in Mexico.

10 Aug.	The "Plattsburg idea" — military-preparedness training for civilians — is begun in Plattsburg, New York.
19 Aug.	Two U.S. citizens die when the British passenger ship *Arabic* is sunk by a German submarine.
7 Sept.	President Wilson allows New York bankers to lend $500 million dollars to Great Britain and France.
16 Sept.	Haiti becomes a U.S. protectorate under the terms of a new ten-year treaty, which the Senate approves on 28 February 1916. U.S. Marines remain in Haiti until 1934.
5 Oct.	Germany apologizes for sinking the *Lusitania* and the *Arabic,* offers reparations, and promises that such incidents will not happen in the future.
19 Oct.	The United States recognizes Venustiano Carranza as president of Mexico.
4 Dec.	Chartered by Henry Ford, the *Oskar II,* known as the "peace ship," sails for Norway in an unsuccessful effort to negotiate an end to the war.
7 Dec.	President Wilson addresses Congress on the need for "preparedness."
18 Dec.	President Wilson marries Edith Bolling Galt at her home in Washington, D.C. (Wilson's first wife died in August 1914.)

1916

10 Jan.	Pancho Villa and his band, opponents of the Carranza government in Mexico, kill eighteen U.S. engineers whom Carranza had invited to Mexico to operate abandoned mines.
27 Jan.	President Wilson begins a tour of the country, urging preparedness.
10 Feb.	Secretary of War Lindley M. Garrison resigns over differences with the president.
22 Feb.	U.S. presidential adviser Edward M. House and British foreign secretary Sir Edward Grey sign the House-Grey Memorandum, which states that the United States will initiate a peace conference "on hearing that the moment was opportune."
7 Mar.	Newton D. Baker is appointed secretary of war.
9 Mar.	Pancho Villa and his band raid Columbus, New Mexico, and kill seventeen Americans.
15 Mar.	Fifteen thousand U.S. troops under Gen. John J. Pershing pursue Villa into Mexico. After almost a year of chasing Villa and failing to capture him, the troops are recalled on 5 February 1917.
24 Mar.	A German submarine torpedoes the French passenger ship *Sussex* as it crosses the English Channel; several Americans are injured. Considering the sinking of this unarmed passenger ship a violation of the *Arabic* pledge, Secretary of State Lansing calls for breaking off U.S.-German diplomatic relations.

18 Apr.   President Wilson opposes severing diplomatic relations with Germany and instead calls on Germany to cease its methods of submarine warfare. On 4 May Germany agrees to Wilson's demands.

3 June   Congress passes the National Defense Act, which provides for the expansion of the regular army to 220,000, authorizes a National Guard of 450,000 men, establishes the Reserve Officers Training Corps (ROTC) at colleges and universities, and makes provisions for industrial preparedness.

7–10 June   At the Republican National Convention in Chicago, Supreme Court Justice Charles Evans Hughes of New York is nominated for president, and Charles W. Fairbanks of Indiana is chosen as his running mate.

7–9 June   Also meeting in Chicago, the Progressive Party selects Theodore Roosevelt as its presidential candidate, but he declines the nomination and throws his support to Hughes.

14–16 June   At their national convention in Saint Louis, Missouri, the Democrats renominate President Wilson and Vice President Thomas R. Marshall.

21 June   U.S. troops in Mexico are attacked at Carrizal; seventeen Americans are wounded or killed, and thirty-eight Mexicans are killed.

11 July   Congress passes the Federal Highway Act, authorizing federal assistance to states for road construction.

17 July   Congress passes the Federal Farm Loan Act, establishing twelve regional Farm Loan Banks to provide farmers with long-term loans at low interest rates.

19 July   Meeting in Saint Paul, Minnesota, the Prohibition National Convention nominates J. Frank Hanly of Indiana for president and Ira D. Landrith of Tennessee for vice president.

30 July   German sabotage is believed to be the cause of an explosion of a munitions cache on Black Tom Island, New Jersey, that causes $22 million in damages.

4 Aug.   The United States purchases the Virgin Islands in the West Indies for $25 million from Denmark.

11 Aug.   Congress passes the Warehouse Act, which assists farmers in financing their crops by depositing commodities at licensed warehouses and receiving receipts that can be used as collateral for loans.

29 Aug.   The Council of National Defense (CND) is established to coordinate war-preparedness efforts in American industry.

1 Sept.   Congress passes the Keating-Owen Child Labor Act, which bans goods manufactured by children from interstate commerce. The Supreme Court finds the act unconstitutional in 1918.

3 Sept.   President Wilson signs the Adamson Act, which mandates an eight-hour day for railroad workers and thus averts a nationwide strike planned for 4 September.

7 Sept.   Congress passes the Shipping Act, which authorizes the creation of the U.S. Shipping Board to oversee the requisition of ships through the Emergency Fleet Corporation.

     Congress passes the Workmen's Compensation Act, which offers coverage to half a million federal employees.

1917

8 Sept.	The Emergency Revenue Act doubles the income tax and adds an inheritance tax.
7 Nov.	Woodrow Wilson is reelected president in a close race.
29 Nov.	The United States occupies Santo Domingo and establishes an internal administration in the Dominican Republic. The occupation lasts until 1924.
18 Dec.	President Wilson sends a "peace note" to the warring nations requesting that they state their war aims. Germany refuses to do so, and the Allies put forward a list of demands clearly unfavorable to Germany.

22 Jan.	In a speech before the Senate, President Wilson calls for "peace without victory" in Europe and for an international organization to maintain world peace.
31 Jan.	The German ambassador delivers a diplomatic note to the State Department announcing that on 1 February Germany will renew its submarine warfare against neutral ships.
3 Feb.	The United States severs diplomatic relations with Germany.
	The U.S. ship *Housatonic* is sunk by a German submarine.
5 Feb.	Congress overrides President Wilson's veto to pass a law requiring new immigrants to the United States to pass a literacy test.
23 Feb.	Congress passes the Smith-Hughes Act, which provides funding for agricultural and vocational education.
24 Feb.	The U.S. ambassador to Great Britain is given an intercepted telegram in which the German foreign minister, Arthur Zimmermann, states to the German ambassador to Mexico that if Mexico will ally itself with Germany, much of the southwestern United States would be returned to Mexico after the war.
2 Mar.	Congress passes the Jones Act, making Puerto Rico a U.S. territory and granting its inhabitants U.S. citizenship.
5 Mar.	President Wilson is inaugurated for his second term in office.
8 Mar.	In a special session the Senate votes to change the cloture rule: When two-thirds of the senators present and voting agree to invoke cloture, each senator is limited to one hour of debate.
12 Mar.	The United States announces that its merchant ships in war zones will travel armed and will fire on enemy submarines.
20 Mar.	President Wilson's cabinet unanimously advises that he should ask Congress to declare war on Germany.
31 Mar.	The Council of National Defense establishes the General Munitions Board to orchestrate the purchase of war materiel.
2 Apr.	Jeannette Rankin (R–Mont.) becomes the first woman in the House of Representatives.

2 Apr.	President Wilson addresses a special joint session of Congress to request a declaration of war against Germany. He concludes the speech by calling the American war effort an attempt to make the world "safe for democracy."
4 Apr.	The Senate votes 82–6 for a declaration of war.
6 Apr.	The House of Representatives votes 373–50 for war, and President Wilson signs the war resolution.
14 Apr.	By executive order President Wilson establishes the Committee on Public Information, headed by the journalist George Creel, to disperse propaganda in support of the U.S. war effort.
24 Apr.	Congress passes the Liberty Loan Act, authorizing the secretary of the treasury to issue $2 billion in war bonds at 3.5 percent interest. By the end of the war U.S. war bond drives have collected $21 billion.
18 May	Congress passes the Selective Service Act, which authorizes the use of the military draft to raise troops to fight in World War I. All men ages twenty-one to thirty are required to register.
14 June	Gen. John J. Pershing, commander in chief of the American Expeditionary Forces, arrives in Paris.
15 June	Congress passes the Espionage Act, making it a crime to interfere with recruitment, foster disloyalty in the armed forces, or otherwise engage in disloyal acts. Crimes under the act are punishable by fines up to $10,000 and twenty years imprisonment.
26 June	The first U.S. troops arrive in Europe, landing at St. Nazaire, France.
24 July	Congress appropriates $640 million to develop an army air force. The goal is to build forty-five hundred planes by the spring of 1918.
28 July	The Council of National Defense (CND) creates the War Industries Board (WIB) to orchestrate government purchases and improve wartime efficiency.
10 Aug.	Congress passes the Lever Act, authorizing the creation of a Food Administration and a Fuel Administration to regulate the production, distribution, and costs of food and fuel.
3 Oct.	The War Revenue Act doubles the income tax rates of 1916 and places excise taxes on many goods. Income from taxes pays about 30 percent of the cost of the war effort.
6 Oct.	Congress passes the Trading with the Enemy Act, which authorizes the president to place an embargo on imports, forbids trade with enemy nations, and allows the government to censor foreign mail.
2 Nov.	Secretary of State Lansing and Japanese Viscount Ishii Kikujiro sign the Lansing-Ishii Agreement, in which the United States recognizes Japan's special interests in China, and Japan agrees not to interfere with the "Open Door" policy.
3 Nov.	U.S. forces are involved in their first engagement of the war. While training in the front trenches near the Rhine-Marne Canal in France, three U.S. soldiers are killed by the German forces.
6 Nov.	An amendment to the New York State constitution gives women the right to vote in state elections.

1918

13 Nov.	The Fuel Administration demands that all electric advertising signs be turned off on Thursdays and Sundays to conserve energy.
18 Dec.	The Eighteenth Amendment to the Constitution — prohibiting the sale, manufacture, or transportation of alcohol — is passed by Congress and submitted to the states for ratification.
26 Dec.	President Wilson places the railroads under the administration of the secretary of the treasury.

8 Jan.	In an address before Congress President Wilson puts forward his proposal for peace (the Fourteen Points).
3 Mar.	The Russians, under Bolshevik rule, sign a separate peace with the Germans at Brest-Litovsk.
4 Mar.	President Wilson names Bernard Baruch, a prominent Wall Street businessman, to head the War Industries Board.
19 Mar.	To conserve energy during the war, Congress passes legislation that puts Daylight Saving Time into effect.
21 Mar.	The Railroad Control Act, authorizing federal control of the railroads, is passed by Congress.
5 Apr.	Congress creates the War Finance Corporation and authorizes to make $3.5 billion dollars available in support of war industries.
8 Apr.	The National War Labor Board (NWLB) is appointed as a final board of appeal for labor disputes.
10 Apr.	Congress passes the Webb-Pomerene Act, authorizing cooperation among U.S. exporters by allowing them to work together for the duration of the war without fear of prosecution under antitrust statutes.
16 May	Congress passes the Sedition Act, outlawing any efforts, in speech or action, that hinder the war effort.
20 May	The Overman Act authorizes the president to reorganize the executive branch and other governmental agencies to make the government more efficient in carrying out the war effort.
4 June	On the Western Front U.S. soldiers stop a German advance at Château-Thierry.
6–25 June	In vicious fighting during the Battle of Belleau Wood, France, U.S. forces stop a German advance. Almost eight thousand U.S. soldiers die in the fight.
8 June	The War Labor Policies Board (WLPB) is created to standardize labor conditions in war industries.
15 July	Eighty-five thousand U.S. troops participate in the bloody Second Battle of the Marne, helping to repel an attempted German advance.
18 July–6 Aug.	The Aisne-Marne offensive, employing a quarter of a million U.S. troops along with French forces, pushes the Germans from the Soissons-Rheims salient.

2 Aug. U.S. troops are deployed near Archangel, Russia, in support of the anti-Communist White Russian army, which is mounting opposition to the Bolsheviks. American troops are withdrawn in June 1919.

16 Aug. U.S. troops are dispatched to Siberia to aid the White Russian Army. They are withdrawn in April 1920.

12–13 Sept. U.S. forces at St. Mihiel capture about fifteen thousand German soldiers.

14 Sept. Eugene V. Debs, who has been the Socialist Party presidential candidate in 1900, 1904, 1908, and 1912, is found guilty of making seditious statements that impede recruitment efforts and is sentenced to ten years in prison under the Espionage Act of 1917. His sentence is commuted by President Warren G. Harding in 1921.

26 Sept.–
11 Nov. In the final major battle of the war for U.S. troops, 1.2 million U.S. soldiers join the Allied offensive at Meuse-Argonne.

3 Nov. The Allies sign an armistice with Austria-Hungary.

5 Nov. In congressional elections Republicans gain control of both houses of Congress. In the Senate they have a majority of 49–47, and in the House of Representatives they hold a majority of 240–190 (three seats are held by minor parties). The election results are seen as a repudiation of President Wilson.

11 Nov. On the eleventh hour of the eleventh day of the eleventh month of 1918, the armistice ending World War I goes into effect.

18 Nov. President Wilson announces that he will attend the peace conference in Europe.

21 Nov. Congress passes the Wartime Prohibition Act, banning the manufacture or sale of alcoholic beverages, except for export, during the demobilization.

4 Dec. President Wilson sails for France to attend the peace conference, arriving to a tumultuous welcome from the French people on 13 December.

1919

- The U.S. national debt rises from $2 billion in 1917 to $26 billion in 1919.

18 Jan. President Wilson attends the opening of the peace conference in Paris and urges the Allies to accept his Fourteen Points as the basis for an enduring peace.

29 Jan. The Eighteenth Amendment to the Constitution, banning alcoholic beverages, is ratified. It is repealed in 1933.

14 Feb. President Wilson delivers his proposal for a League of Nations to the Paris Peace Conference.

15 Feb. President Wilson sails for the United States to discuss the peace negotiations with Congress.

4 Mar. Republican senator Henry Cabot Lodge publicizes a list of thirty-seven senators who oppose the League of Nations in its proposed form. Wilson refuses to compromise.

13 Mar. Having sailed on 5 March, President Wilson lands in Europe to continue his efforts on behalf of the peace.

15 Mar.	In Paris, units of the American Expeditionary Forces organize the American Legion.
28 June	The Treaty of Versailles is signed, officially ending World War I.
10 July	President Wilson sends the Treaty of Versailles and the League of Nations agreement to the Senate for ratification.
3 Sept.	President Wilson begins a nationwide tour to promote the Treaty of Versailles and the League of Nations.
22 Sept.	With wartime labor-management agreements at an end, 365,000 steel workers go on strike. The strike is broken within four months with the aid of the military.
25 Sept.	After making his fortieth speech in support of the League of Nations, President Wilson collapses in Pueblo, Colorado, and is forced to return to the White House, where he suffers an incapacitating stroke from which he never fully recovers.
28 Oct.	Congress passes the Volstead Act (the National Prohibition Act) to implement the enforcement of the Eighteenth Amendment.
6 Nov.	Sen. Henry Cabot Lodge announces fourteen reservations to the League of Nations covenant — based on his view that the United States should retain complete sovereignty of action with regard to foreign affairs.
18 Nov.	President Wilson instructs Democrats to vote against the amended treaty.
19 Nov.	The U.S. Senate fails to ratify the Treaty of Versailles.
22 Dec.	Attorney General A. Mitchell Palmer initiates a series of raids against communists, anarchists, and other radicals.

OVERVIEW

The High Tide of Progressivism. The high tide of the Progressive Era occurred during the 1910s, as a profusion of interest groups with competing legislative proposals made the decade one of the most turbulent and exciting in U.S. history. Reforms at the federal level included the lowering of tariffs, the introduction of the income tax, passage of antitrust laws and the Federal Reserve Act of 1913, the direct election of senators, federal child-labor laws, and constitutional amendments prohibiting the consumption of alcoholic beverages and extending the vote to women. During the 1910s reformers at the state level enacted workmen's compensation laws and mothers' pensions (the first government-funded welfare plans for nonveterans). Seeking to break the power of entrenched political interests, reformers also advocated open primaries; the initiative, the referendum, and the recall; and governmental regulation of gas, water, and electrical utilities. Urban reformers sought to weaken political bosses and their machines by implementing commission government and home rule. As the emergence of the modern bureaucratic state continued, various political factions battled for control in a society being transformed by the forces of industrialization, immigration, and urbanization.

Embattled Republicans and Ascendant Democrats. During his single term in the White House, President William Howard Taft, who served from March 1909 until March 1913, continued many of the reformist policies of his predecessor, Theodore Roosevelt. The presidency was Taft's first elected governmental office, and the politically inexperienced Republican leader lacked the necessary skills to hold together a diverse national constituency. Within months of his inauguration, Taft faced significant opposition from insurgents within his own party, and in the elections of 1910 Democrats gained control of both houses of Congress. In the presidential election of 1912 Democrat Woodrow Wilson garnered a plurality of the popular vote and won by a landslide in the Electoral College as many Republican voters, disillusioned by Taft, cast their ballots for the Progressive Party and its reform-minded candidate, Theodore Roosevelt. By the time the Republicans had healed the wounds of their internecine party warfare, the Democrats, under Wilson, had recaptured the presidency by a slim margin

in 1916. In 1918, however, Republicans regained control of both the House and Senate and were soon setting a political course that would lead them to victories throughout the 1920s.

A World Power. During the decade every facet of American politics was shaped by the extraordinary fact that by 1910 the United States had become the wealthiest nation in the world. In the previous quarter century the United States had overtaken the great European powers that had dominated the world for four centuries and established itself as the most productive country in the world. Indeed, by 1919 the U.S. economic output surpassed that of all European nations combined. Proponents of the American political and economic systems argued that the combination of a constitutional republican government and capitalist economy was the basis for their nation's remarkable successes, asserting that U.S. industrial, agricultural, and financial interests were the foundations on which national prosperity was based. Yet the concentration of wealth at the top unsettled others. Capitalists and managerial executives, critics argued, wielded excessive power. Hence one of the major political debates of the 1910s was over what role government should play in the economy. Some feared that too little regulation of corporate power might fuel a growing oligarchy, but others were concerned that too much regulation might destroy the efficiencies of a capitalist system by which America had achieved prosperity. One consequence of this debate was the rise of the philosophy of corporate liberalism, whose advocates argued that government policy ought to gain control of the business cycle, nurture growth, and assist those in society who were not reaping the rewards of modern capitalism. Yet corporate liberals also urged that governmental activism should be limited: government ought not own or control private enterprise, and the regulations it implemented should seek to increase the overall productivity of the economy rather than slow it.

Political Factions. Among the one hundred million U.S. citizens an assortment of factions vied for political power. Farmers, industrial workers, corporate business leaders, small business entrepreneurs, professionals, party bosses and their machines, social scientists, religious leaders, women, immigrants, and African Americans were among the groups who sought to shape local, state, and national policy agendas. Reform to one group was often retrenchment to another. While the decade was rife with the language of reform, there was no single, coherent reform ideology. Urban voters (who were often industrial workers, new immigrants, and Catholics or Jews) tended to cast their ballots for Democrats. Rural voters often backed Republicans, as did Protestants, professionals, and capitalists. Yet the multitude of exceptions to these tendencies demonstrates the complex nature of American politics during the 1910s. In the South voting patterns were fairly easy to discern. Fifty years after its sufferings in the Civil War and Reconstruction — both under Republican presidents — the region remained solidly Democratic, its Republican-voting African American population largely disfranchised by "Jim Crow" laws.

Governmental Activism. *Progress* was a keyword in the early twentieth century. There was astonishing progress not only in the nation's economy but also in its science, medicine, and technology. It is not surprising, then, that politicians seeking a new label with positive valuations decided to call themselves "progressives." The term captured the ethos of the age and represented to many what was best about the nation, but what counted as "progressive" politically was contested terrain. Conservatives, insurgents, socialists, and modern liberals all claimed to be progressive. By the 1910s, however, the predominant political usage of the term was most often associated with political reformers who espoused the expansion of the regulatory powers of government as a means to alleviate social ills. Indeed, as Roosevelt declared in 1912, "The Progressive Movement is greater than the Progressive Party; yet the Progressive Party is at present the only instrument through which that movement can be advanced." During the decade progressives succeeded in using government as a shield to protect citizens, consumers, and workers from powerful corporate and financial interests. They believed that local, state, and national governments ought to perform a variety of new services.

Political Conservatives. Conservatives believed that their programs offered the best hope for true political progress. In "What is Real Political Progress?" (1912) John William Burgess, a political scientist at Columbia University, took aim at the Progressive Party platform. Dismissing socialism as untenable, Burgess asked "whether this [progressivism] is progress, standstill or retrogression in the development of political theory and practical politics." His reply, after a twenty-page history of individual liberty in the western world, was: "we dare not call anything progress . . . which contemplates . . . the expansion of governmental power." Having identified progressivism with an active regulatory welfare state that was, in his view, reactionary and undesirable, he countered with a classic statement of American conservatism.

These so-called progressives, he argued, must "show conclusively that the improvement and development of the system of popular education, the revival of the influence of religion, the restoration of a better family life, producing a more enlightened individual conscience and a more general conscientiousness, would not be the truer way, the American way, *the real progressive way* of overcoming the claimed failure of our system of civil liberty and of fulfilling the hope of history, instead of recurring to the governmental absolutism of earlier times." Nicholas Murray Butler, Burgess's colleague at Columbia University, concurred, arguing in "What is Progress in Politics?" that "limitations on the power of government" were themselves progressive and that to relax those limitations (as the progressives desired) would lead to overbearing government power at the expense of individual civil liberties. Freedom of choice, Butler maintained, could only be maximized through strictures on governmental activism. Instead of building a welfare state on which the poor might rely for assistance, he argued that America "should push forward along the road already traveled . . . . and do so in a spirit that will not lead the individual to lean more heavily upon the community, but rather help him to stand up more surely and confidently upon his own feet." While opposing the rise of the welfare state, however, Butler — like some other conservatives of his day — supported limited regulatory strictures on monopolistic practices. He opposed monopoly on the grounds that it would lead to a diminution of competitive capitalism and to plutocracy in economy and politics, asserting, "We should aim not to bring the government into partnership with monopoly and privilege, but in all our legislation affecting these matters, whether in the State or in the nation, to keep open the channels both of competition and of useful combination by preventing monopoly on the one hand and by punishing specifically unfair and dishonorable business practice on the other."

Taft's Presidency. When William Howard Taft was inaugurated in spring 1909, his political future seemed bright. Yet, three and a half years later, in the election of 1912, he suffered the worst electoral defeat of any incumbent president in the twentieth century, a casualty of the divisive politics that had rent asunder the Republican Party. Secretary of war from 1904 to 1908, Taft had been chosen by Theodore Roosevelt as his successor for the Republican presidential nomination in 1908. Supported by both the Republican Old Guard and by party insurgents, Taft won the nomination and the ensuing national election easily. Within months, however, Taft was caught in a political crossfire within his own party. In 1909 insurgent Republicans (also called reformers or progressives) were battling Republican conservatives for control of the party. On the contentious issue of tariff reform, in a congressional dispute over the power of conservative House Speaker Joseph Cannon's domination of the House of Representatives, and in a high-profile case over control of the nation's conservation policies (the

Ballinger-Pinchot affair of 1909–1910), Taft alienated party insurgents. In the congressional elections of 1910 he made his allegiance to the party's Old Guard clear when he tried to purge insurgent Republicans in the primaries. Unsuccessful at these efforts, Taft incurred the insurgents' wrath, and thereafter he headed a divided party. By January 1911 insurgents, led by Wisconsin senator Robert La Follette, had formed the National Progressive Republican League, and within five months La Follette had announced his candidacy for the Republican presidential nomination. Taft further muddled his political fortunes when, on 27 October 1911, it was announced that his administration, closely adhering to the provisions of the Sherman Antitrust Act of 1890, would prosecute U.S. Steel under that law. In a 1907 meeting with J. P. Morgan, Roosevelt had approved U.S. Steel's acquisition of the Tennessee Coal and Iron Company, the transaction that was the basis for the prosecution. Viewing Taft's actions as a personal slight, Roosevelt used the incident as pretext for reentering the political arena as the presidential candidate of the Progressive Party. Nominated by his party for a second term, Taft, running on a conservative platform, placed third in the general election behind the Democratic winner, Woodrow Wilson, and Roosevelt. To judge Taft's presidency by the measure of his inept handling of the progressive wing of his party would, however, miss his administration's many achievements. Taft was not unsympathetic to the reformers. In one term his administration prosecuted more trusts than Roosevelt had in seven years. He had expanded the nation's forest reserves, supported mine-safety legislation and the eight-hour day, and signed the Mann-Elkins Act of 1910, which regulated the nation's railroads while strengthening the Interstate Commerce Commission. Had he been a more astute politician, Taft might have held his party together and won a second term.

Theodore Roosevelt and the Progressive Party. Though Roosevelt was to hold no political office during the decade, his status as retired president, as well as the American people's abiding affection for him, made him a formidable political force. After completing his second term in 1909 he had embarked on a safari in Africa for several months and then visited European heads of state. Roosevelt returned to the United States in spring 1910 to find many people clamoring for him to reunite a divided Republican Party. On 31 August 1910 Roosevelt delivered a much-heralded speech at Osawatomie, Kansas, espousing the lineaments of the "New Nationalism." After failing to gain the Republican Party nomination from Taft in a hard-fought struggle over delegates at the Republican National Convention of 1912 in Chicago, Roosevelt, backed by reformers, launched the Progressive Party. With the aid of the progressively minded social-scientific community in New York, the new party's mandarins, Roosevelt stood for office on a platform that condemned "the unholy alliance between corrupt business and corrupt politics." Promoting a broad spectrum of social, economic, and political reforms, the Progressive platform proved to be a charter that shaped modern liberal reform for half a century. It called for national medical insurance, old-age insurance, and unemployment coverage. It championed labor's right to collective bargaining, the creation of a department of labor, a minimum wage for women, prohibition of child labor, federal health and safety standards in the workplace, an eight-hour day in many industries, and better educational services for immigrants. The platform advocated graduated income and inheritance taxes, public ownership of natural resources, and federal regulation of securities markets. It supported adoption of votes for women; the direct election of U.S. senators; the initiative, the referendum, and the recall; the short ballot; and primary elections.

Woodrow Wilson's Presidency. Woodrow Wilson was twice elected president during the 1910s. The first and only president with a Ph.D., Wilson had been a professor of political science and history at Wesleyan University and president of Princeton University prior to his election as governor of New Jersey in 1910. Wilson proved to be a moderate reformer. He successfully sponsored tariff reduction, increased government regulation of industry, and extended federal aid to farmers. Yet his presidency was increasingly dominated by foreign-policy issues.

Wilsonian Foreign Affairs. In 1916 the United States sent troops into Mexico, coming close to war with that nation, and by mid decade U.S. relations with Japan and China had improved. Yet beginning in 1914, the war in Europe was the president's major foreign-policy concern. As a new world power and as a nation of immigrants — many of whom traced their origins to one or another of the warring factions — the American people were at first deeply divided over the war, though few at the outset advocated American military involvement. Indeed, it was not clear that the United States had anything to gain by getting involved. At the outbreak of this European conflict, which many wrongly believed would be "over by Christmas," President Wilson declared U.S. neutrality and asked the American people to remain "neutral in thought as in deed." Pacifists in the United States, including Secretary of State William Jennings Bryan, insisted that peace was in the nation's best interest, but U.S. commercial and financial interests, and pro-Allied sympathies across the country, combined to lead America on the path toward war. When Germany returned to unrestricted submarine warfare in the Atlantic in early 1917, President Wilson decided that neutrality was no longer tenable and asked Congress to declare war on Germany. Fighting alongside British and French troops, American soldiers won a series of bloody campaigns against the Germans. By November 1918 the resources and manpower of the United States had been a decisive factor in an Allied victory. Wilson personally conducted the nation's peace negotiations in Paris, and his Fourteen Points were an important part of the deliberations resulting in the Treaty of Versailles. After his achievements in Paris, however, he suffered a massive stroke and remained largely ineffectual during the last months of his presidency.

Conflict amid Success. The 1910s were also a time of domestic turmoil and protest. African Americans, about 10 percent of the nation's population, were disfranchised, segregated, and economically oppressed. Women were struggling for the vote, which they won at the national level in 1920. "New immigrants" — generally from eastern and southern Europe — were pouring into the nation and often found the adjustment to life in their adopted country difficult. During the second decade of the twentieth century, there were scores of race riots and thousands of industrial strikes. The constitutional protection of freedom of speech ensured that American politics was a forum for sharp disagreement and wide-ranging debate over the role of government at every level. Perhaps no other time in American history was such a diversity of opinion expressed in American political discourse, from contemplative conservatism to radical socialism, communism, and anarchism.

TOPICS IN THE NEWS

AMERICA AND WORLD AFFAIRS: DOLLAR DIPLOMACY

A New Player. During the early decades of the twentieth century the United States emerged as a world power. The wisdom and propriety of how it wielded its newfound power in the 1910s have been much debated. Proponents of the U.S. military and international economic policies of that decade have asserted that the country used its influence to promote democracy and economic growth. Critics of those same policies have described them as self-interested military and economic imperialism.

Dollar Diplomacy. In a world that had been dominated by the great European powers for four centuries, the United States sought its share of international influence and world markets. American interventionism during the 1910s took two forms: military action and political-economic intercession. These methods, dubbed "Dollar Diplomacy" during the presidency of William Howard Taft, continued under his successor, Woodrow Wilson. In his final message to Congress (3 December 1912) President Taft summarized this approach to foreign policy as "substituting dollars for bullets," but, as Taft also noted, "While our foreign policy should not be turned a hair's breadth from the straight path of justice, it may well be made to include active intervention to secure for our merchandise and our capitalists opportunity for profitable investment which shall inure to the benefit of both countries concerned." The goal of Dollar Diplomacy was to make the United States a commercial and financial world power. Supporters hailed it as an economic boon, but opponents argued that Dollar Diplomacy effected a not-so-subtle economic imperialism over Latin America and the Caribbean. Under Taft, Secretary of State Philander C. Knox, a former corporate lawyer, used the State Department to assist American businesses on foreign soil; and the United States stood ready to sustain its perceived economic interests with military force.

The Caribbean and Latin America. The Monroe Doctrine of 1823 asserted U.S. hegemony in Latin America and the Caribbean, and the Roosevelt Corollary of 1904 further bolstered U.S. claims in the region. In the late nineteenth century Rear Adm. Alfred T. Mahan had identified naval control of the Caribbean as crucial to American interests, and Latin America and the Caribbean were at center stage in U.S. foreign affairs. From 1910 to 1916 the United States sent troops into Santo Domingo, Haiti, Nicaragua, Cuba, and Mexico. Furthermore, on 4 August 1916 the United States and Denmark signed a treaty by which the United States purchased the Virgin Islands — sixty-eight small Caribbean islands totalling 133 square miles — for $25 million.

Nicaragua. The Taft-Knox approach to Latin American policy is exemplified in U.S. relations with Nicaragua. Longtime Nicaraguan ruler José Santos Zelaya was unpopular with U.S. business interests. When a civil war broke out in Nicaragua in October 1909 the rebels, led by Gen. Juan J. Estrada, had the blessing of American businessmen in the country. Funds from the United States bankrolled the rebellion, and after the Zelaya government executed two U.S. citizens who had been fighting with Estrada's forces, Washington broke off diplomatic relations with the Zelaya government and publicly backed

A MERE MATTER OF HONOUR.

PRESIDENT TAFT. "HERE, SWALLOW THIS!"
AMERICA. "THANKS, I'M AN EAGLE; I'M NOT A VULTURE."

A British view of President William Howard Taft's support
for a bill in which Congress exempted U.S. vessels from
paying tolls to use the Panama Canal (cartoon by F. H.
Townsend, *Punch*, 1912). The British considered
this measure a violation of the Hay-Pauncefote
Treaty of 1901, in which the United States
and Great Britain agreed that all nations
would have equal access to the canal.

the rebels. In the midst of the war U.S. military forces
landed on the east coast of the country to protect U.S.
interests, and by late August 1910 the rebels, with U.S.
backing, had captured Managua, the nation's capital.
In the aftermath of the Nicaraguan civil war the
United States imposed a financial plan on Nicaragua,
forcing the nation to take loans from U.S banks and
seizing control of Nicaraguan customs houses. The
U.S. Senate, however, refused to sanction a treaty that
would have formally instituted U.S. control of Nicaraguan finances. In July 1912, when a second revolution
occurred in Nicaragua, the United States landed
twenty-seven hundred marines to assist in repressing
the revolt. A small U.S. military force remained on
Nicaraguan soil until 1925.

Haiti. Under the pretext of helping to restore democracy and promote economic growth in the poorest nation
of the western hemisphere, U.S. Marines were deployed
to Haiti in 1915. The proximate cause of U.S. intervention was a revolt in the capital city of Port-au-Prince. On
28 July 1915 Haitians rose up against and killed the
repressive dictator Gen. Vilbrun Guillaume Sam, who
had recently executed 167 political prisoners. That same
day U.S. Marines occupied the island. Within two
months the United States had installed a puppet government under President Sudre Dartiguenave. In mid September Dartiguenave signed a treaty with the United
States, placing Haiti's finances, police force, and public
works under the control of Americans appointed by President Wilson. In part these measures were taken to secure
the assets of the National City Bank of New York in
Haiti. Civil liberties were curtailed during the U.S. occupation, which continued until 1934; and — though sanitation was improved, the currency stabilized, and new
roads built — only a small portion of the $16 million loan
promised by National City Bank was ever delivered to the
government.

Cuba. The United States played the central role in
establishing Cuban independence from Spain during the
Spanish-American War of 1898. After the war Cuban
sovereignty was limited by the Platt Amendment to the
U.S. Army Appropriations Act of 1900, which granted
the United States extensive control over the island, including unspecified powers to intervene in Cuba when it
believed "Cuban independence" was threatened. U.S.
forces were withdrawn from Cuba in 1902, but in 1906
President Roosevelt dispatched more than five thousand
troops to Havana "to maintain order," and they remained
there until early 1909. In 1912 and again in 1917 the
United States intervened in Cuba with military force, on
the second occasion to restore order after a fraudulent
election.

Sources:

John J. Johnson, *A Hemisphere Apart: The Foundations of United States
Policy Toward Latin America* (Baltimore: Johns Hopkins University
Press, 1990);

Maurice Matloff, ed., *American Military History* (Washington, D.C.:
Office of the Chief of Military History, United States Army, 1969);

Alonso Aguilar Monteverde, *Pan-Americanism from Monroe to the Present* (New York: Monthly Review Press, 1968).

AMERICA AND WORLD AFFAIRS: THE MEXICAN REVOLUTION

Background. The 1910s were a tumultuous decade in
Mexican politics, and U.S.-Mexican relations were
strained to the limit. Born in poverty, Porfirio Díaz, who
ruled Mexico from 1876 to 1911, had worked against
French efforts to dominate Mexico in the nineteenth
century. For most of his tenure in office he had kept
democratic mechanisms in place, but by 1910 he was
turning increasingly to coercion. Troops under Díaz's
control suppressed strikes by textile workers and miners
with bloody violence, and as many Mexican organizations
began to oppose him, his regime was beginning to totter.
Francisco I. Madero, a member of one of Mexico's ten

U.S. troops searching for Pancho Villa in Mexico, 1916

richest families, ran against Díaz for the Mexican presidency in 1910, lost because of corrupt voting practices, and was imprisoned. Escaping to the United States, Madero rallied his forces, attacked Díaz's ill-disciplined federal troops, and on 25 May 1911 forced Díaz to resign and flee to Paris. On 2 November Madero was declared the winner of a new presidential election. Soon his administration was being charged with broken promises and corruption.

Rebellion. In the Morelos region of Mexico the peasantry, under the leadership of Emiliano Zapata, resisted government pacification efforts with guerrilla warfare and sabotage. Within fifteen months of the election Madero's government was under attack from both the Right and the Left. In February 1913 Victoriano Huerta, commander of the Mexican army, staged a military coup against Madero, who was subsequently imprisoned and assassinated. The Huerta government failed to stabilize Mexican politics, and in northern Mexico Venustiano Carranza soon initiated a democratic opposition to Huerta's military regime.

The Tampico Incident. The United States watched events in Mexico with interest. President Wilson condemned Huerta's regime as "a government of butchers," siding with Carranza. In early 1914 the United States removed an embargo against shipping arms to Mexico in order to bolster Carranza's chances. Wilson also initiated a naval blockade off Veracruz to keep Huerta's government from getting military shipments from foreign allies. Tensions mounted on 9 April 1914, when a small contingent of U.S. sailors from the blockade force went ashore to collect supplies at Tampico, Mexico. The sailors inadvertently wandered into a restricted zone and were arrested. The local Mexican commander promptly released the sailors and tendered an apology to the U.S. naval commander, but the American officer insisted that the Mexicans fire a salute to the U.S. flag. When they refused, President Wilson saw the incident as an opportunity to take action against the Huerta government, and Congress authorized the employment of military force. Using the "Tampico incident" as pretext, U.S. Marines and sailors invaded and occupied Veracruz. Nineteen Americans and more than two hundred Mexicans were killed in the fighting, and the two nations were on the brink of war. In an effort to avoid further conflict the two sides accepted the mediation of three South American countries: Argentina, Brazil, and Chile. Dubbed the "ABC Powers," these governments proposed a settlement favoring the United States in June 1914. The United States should withdraw its troops from Mexico, they asserted, and Huerta should resign. At first Huerta refused to abdicate, but he was forced from office in July, and Carranza came to power in August. U.S. forces withdrew from Mexico in November, and in October 1915 the United States recognized the Carranza government.

U.S. Intervention. During the period between the conclusion of the ABC Conference and U.S. recognition of Carranza's government, Carranza's erstwhile general Francisco "Pancho" Villa called for land reforms and intimated to the Wilson administration that he was willing to follow the lead of the United States. By June 1915 Wilson, badgered by criticisms at home, threatened the use of troops, but by the autumn of 1915 relations between Mexico and the United States had improved. In January 1916, however, Villa's men murdered sixteen U.S. mining engineers, and on 9 March his soldiers razed the town of Columbus, New Mexico, murdering seventeen Americans. With the initial support of the Carranza government Wilson sent a military force under the command of Gen. John J. Pershing to Mexico to pursue and capture Villa. In February 1917 U.S. soldiers withdrew from Mexico without having apprehended Villa. The Mexican Constitution of 1917 included democratic elements, and Carranza was elected president. Yet, as American focus turned increasingly toward Europe, the politival situation remained unstable in Mexico. In 1919 Zapata was killed in an ambush, and the next year Carranza was assassinated as he fled Mexico City during an otherwise nearly bloodless coup. Villa was ambushed and murdered by political opponents in 1923.

Sources:
Robert A. Pastor, *Limits to Friendship* (New York: Knopf, 1988);

Josefina Zoraida Vazquez and Lorenzo Meyer, *The United States and Mexico* (Chicago: University of Chicago Press, 1985);

John Womack Jr., *Zapata and the Mexican Revolution* (New York: Knopf, 1969).

AMERICA AT WAR: FROM NEUTRALITY TO BELLIGERENCY

Outbreak in Europe. World War I began in summer 1914 as a conflict among the five "Big Powers" of Europe: Austria-Hungary, Great Britain, France, Germany, and Russia. In the quarter century leading up to the war the animosities between these powers resulted in a series of entangling alliances. Great Britain and Germany had been locked in an arms race on the seas that fueled their distrust of one another. As early as 1894 Germany, Austria-Hungary, and Italy had formed the Triple Entente, while the French and Russians had concluded a Dual Alliance; by 1904 the British and French had solidified an alliance of their own. The assassination of Archduke Francis Ferdinand of Austria-Hungary by a Serbian nationalist on 28 June 1914 at Sarajevo was the spark that lit the tinder, setting in motion a series of hurried diplomatic maneuverings that failed to prevent war. The economic, industrial, and military forces of the warring factions were at first fairly closely matched, ensuring a protracted war that lasted for more than four years and four months and exacted an enormous toll in human lives. Though wartime death statistics are impossible to calculate accurately, conservative estimates place the war dead

---

THE ZIMMERMANN TELEGRAM

On 23 February 1917 the British relayed to the United States a telegram from German foreign secretary Arthur Zimmermann to the German minister in Mexico. The telegram read:

> We intend to begin on the 1st of February unrestricted submarine warfare. We shall endeavor in spite of this to keep the United States of America neutral. In the event of this not succeeding, we make Mexico a proposal of alliance on the following basis: make war together, make peace together, generous financial support and an understanding on our part that Mexico is to reconquer the lost territory in Texas, New Mexico, and Arizona. The settlement in detail is left to you. You will inform the President [of Mexico] of the above most secretly as soon as the outbreak of war with the United States of America is certain and add the suggestion that he should, on his own initiative, invite Japan to immediate adherence and at the same time mediate between Japan and ourselves. Please call the President's attention to the fact that the ruthless employment of our submarines now offers the prospect of compelling England in a few months to make peace.

Though the authenticity of the telegram was not established at the time, the American press was told of its existence, and its contents helped to push the United States closer to war with Germany.

Source: Thomas G. Paterson and Dennis Merrill, eds., *Major Problems in American Foreign Relations, Volume II: Since 1914* (Lexington, Mass.: Heath, 1993).

---

at more than ten million and the maimed and injured at about twenty million.

The *Lusitania* Incident. President Wilson's hope that Americans would remain "impartial in thought as well as action" was doomed by the rush of events from 1914 to 1917, and by his own policies. Though the British naval forces were the largest in the world, Germany had countered British naval superiority by enlarging its submarine force. The Wilson administration's insistence on freedom of the seas for nonbelligerents was ignored by both the British and the Germans. The British maintained a blockade of much of Europe, and Germany sought to cut off British supply lines through unrestricted submarine warfare against ships on the high seas. American ambivalence was transformed into indignation against Germany after 7 May 1915, when a German submarine torpedoed the British Cunard liner *Lusitania*, en route from the United States to Great Britain, without warning off the Irish coast. The liner sank, and 1,198 people, including 128 Americans, lost their lives. President Wilson protested directly to the German government in a series of

President Woodrow Wilson asking Congress to declare war on Germany, 2 April 1917

diplomatic notes demanding "reparation so far as reparation is possible." Secretary of State William Jennings Bryan, who favored strict neutrality, believed that Wilson's protest was drawing the United States closer to war with Germany and resigned. Before the *Lusitania* had sailed, the Imperial German Embassy had published warnings that it would sink all ships in the Atlantic war zone, and it at first claimed that the torpedoing of the *Lusitania* was justified because the liner was carrying arms to the British. (It was in fact carrying a shipment of rifles and cartridges.) Finally, however, Germany agreed to cease unrestricted submarine warfare, and the Wilson administration was, for a time, appeased.

Mounting Tensions. The British also incurred the anger of the Wilson administration. In their efforts to cut off overseas trade to Germany, the British strengthened their blockade of Europe in spring 1916. On 19 July Britain announced that it was forbidding its citizens to do business with eighty-seven firms in the United States because it believed them to be trading with Germany or its allies. Yet American sympathies were increasingly with the Triple Alliance (Britain, France, and Czarist Russia), and when Germany announced that it would resume unrestricted submarine warfare in the Atlantic on

31 January 1917, it lost much of its remaining support in the United States.

Declaration of War. Tensions heightened on 23 February 1917 when the British gave the United States an intercepted and decoded telegram from German foreign secretary Arthur Zimmermann to the German minister in Mexico. The telegram proposed an alliance between Germany and Mexico in return for which Germany would return to Mexico the territories it had lost to the United States during the Mexican-American War some seventy years earlier. Americans were outraged. The Zimmermann telegram — coupled with the Germans' subsequent sinking of four U.S. ships, with the loss of fifteen American lives — triggered Wilson to action. On 2 April 1917 President Wilson delivered a war message before a joint session of Congress. The House, by a vote of 373 to 50, and the Senate, by a vote of 82 to 6, chose war, and on 6 April the president signed the official declaration. The German high command had gambled that the United States would not enter the conflict, or that, if it did, its military contribution would be too little, too late. Their calculations proved wrong.

Sources:
Robert H. Ferrell, *Woodrow Wilson and World War I, 1917–1921* (New York: Harper & Row, 1985);

The Woman's Peace Party (WPP) was founded in January 1915, with social worker Jane Addams, the founder of Hull House in Chicago, as its first president. Other prominent members included Sophonisba Breckinridge (treasurer), Carrie Chapman Catt, Anna Howard Shaw, and Mrs. Booker T. Washington. Asserting that "the mother half of humanity" needed a voice in world affairs, the WPP political platform called for mediation of the problems among European belligerents, for arms limitations, and for woman suffrage on the grounds that votes for women would bring a quicker peace. The WPP also favored democratic control of foreign policy and removal of the economic causes of war — although the platform was unclear on the meaning of these two demands or how they were to be achieved. The party gained international recognition when Jane Addams presided at the International Congress of Woman held at The Hague, Netherlands, in April 1915. Among the two thousand female participants at the congress, forty-seven (most members of the WPP) were from the United States. During its second year of operation the WPP claimed twenty-five thousand members, but three factions arose within the party as World War I dragged on. The first faction worked for a quick end to the fighting but backed American involvement in the war. The second, behind leaders such as Jane Addams, supported only humanitarian aid. The third, led by militant Crystal Eastman of New York, continued to contest national policy even after the United States declared war on Germany. Once the United States entered the fighting the national leaders of the WPP turned their attention to the postwar world, and at an international conference in Zurich, Switzerland, in May 1919 they helped to found the Women's International League for Peace and Freedom.

Sources: Marie L. Degen, *The History of the Woman's Peace Party* (Baltimore: Johns Hopkins Press, 1939);

Barbara J. Steinson, *American Women's Activism in World War I* (New York: Garland, 1982).

David M. Kennedy, *Over Here: The First World War and American Society* (New York: Oxford University Press, 1980);

Barbara Tuchman, *The Zimmermann Telegram* (New York: Viking, 1958).

AMERICA AT WAR: GOVERNING THE HOME FRONT

An Expanded Military. Prior to World War I the United States defense budget was comparatively small. From 1900 to 1914 the country spent less than 1 percent of its gross national product (GNP) on defense. But in May 1916, with tensions between Mexico and the United States high, and war raging in Europe, Congress had increased U.S. military strength by passing the National Defense Act, authorizing an army of 223,000 and a National Guard of 450,000. This act was augmented on 18 May 1917 with the passage of the Selective Service Act, initiating the wartime draft. By 1918 the U.S. Army reached a peak strength of 3.7 million men (2.8 million of whom had been drafted), and by 1917 only Britain and Germany had more naval tonnage than the United States. U.S. war expenditures eventually totaled $17.1 billion, exceeded only by those of Britain and Germany. At home the executive branch of the federal government gained extraordinary wartime powers. Through a series of executive-agency war boards, the Wilson administration effectively controlled the nation's economy with a careful mixture of voluntarism and compulsion.

Financing the War. The American war effort was financed in large part by five multibillion-dollar federal bond issues. The bonds paid only modest rates of interest (the first, for example, was a thirty-year bond offering 3.5 percent interest — less than market rate). Given such low rates of return, many Americans might well have avoided buying these bonds had it not been for a government propaganda campaign to drum up support for the American war effort. Wilson's secretary of the treasury, William Gibbs McAdoo, dubbed the bond issues "Liberty Loans," and, engaging in one of the biggest federal advertising campaigns in U.S. history, he was able to capitalize on what he called "the profound impulse called patriotism." In 1917–1918, with the help of some 75,000 "four-minute" men and women — who delivered short speeches in theaters, public parks, and other gathering places on patriotic themes such as the importance of purchasing "Liberty Loans" — all five of the government bond issues were oversubscribed.

The Council of National Defense. Organizing the nation for war placed many demands on the Wilson administration and Congress, which responded with a series of measures creating new government agencies, expanding federal power, and limiting dissent. One of the new agencies, established in August 1916, in advance of the declaration of war, was the Council of National Defense (CND). The CND was the parent organization for the bureaus and boards that mobilized industry for the war effort. The CND was directed by six members of President Wilson's cabinet: the secretaries of agriculture, commerce, interior, labor, navy, and war. These cabinet members were aided by an "advisory commission," which actually did much of the work, forming more than a hundred subcommittees in industries across the country and gathering information on production capacities, pricing practices, and transportation availability. The CND allocated federal contracts to manufacturers and coordinated production of goods and services. In summer 1917

President Wilson (second from right) marching in a Liberty Loan parade, Washington, D.C., 1918

the CND created the War Industries Board to continue the move from a free-trade peacetime economy to a planned wartime economy, and thereafter the CND occupied itself with postwar planning and citizen morale.

The War Industries Board. The effectiveness of the War Industries Board (WIB) was greatly enhanced by the president's appointment of Wall Street financier Bernard Baruch as WIB chairman in March 1918. The legal authority of the WIB to dictate policy to the nation's industries remained unclear, but Baruch's masterful mixing of patriotic and personal appeals with profit guarantees resulted in the voluntary cooperation of businesses in the war effort. To administer "commodity sections" of the economy, negotiate production-output agreements, and fix prices, the six-member WIB hired many "dollar-a-year men" (wealthy industrial experts who were willing to work for the government at that nominal salary because they could live well on their corporate profits). Though a creature of the wartime emergency, the board was an example of long-held progressive beliefs in the possibility of gov-

ernment regulation of economic activity guided by impartial "experts" fixed on serving the public interest.

The Overman Act. The Overman Act, passed on 20 May 1918, authorized President Wilson to centralize the governmental bureaucracy. Pressured by exigencies of war, the federal government closely monitored, regulated, and at points took control of the nation's industries, railroads, labor supply, and merchant marine.

The War Labor Board. The War Labor Board (WLB) was formed in April 1918 to oversee labor-management relations in an effort to maximize production and minimize labor disputes that could hamper the war effort. Its members were chosen by national organizations of labor and management. By guaranteeing profits to industrialists, the WLB boosted workers' wages. Permitting union organization during the war while discouraging strikes, the WLB served as a mediator between labor and capital, handling more than twelve hundred cases in its yearlong existence (April 1918–April 1919). While WLB decisions (like those of the WIB) were not legally binding, the WLB effectively used popular sentiment favoring wartime cooperation to place pressure on contesting parties. Unions hailed the WLB for allowing collective bargaining, for acknowledging workers' needs for living wages, and for trying to enforce union-recognition provisions in wartime government contracts, thus allowing unions to grow. In return Samuel Gompers, president of the American Federation of Labor (AFL), made a wartime "no strike" pledge on the part of unions affiliated with the AFL.

The Shipping Act of 1916. The Shipping Act of 1916, which became law on 7 September, allocated $50 million to the federally created U.S. Shipping Board to build or buy merchant ships to serve as "naval auxiliaries" in the advent of war. The Shipping Board was empowered to regulate all U.S. commercial shipping by setting rates and services. The Emergency Fleet Corporation of the U.S. Shipping Board expanded the fleet by ten million tons by war's end. Congress, however, indicated the temporary nature of these measures by mandating that all ships under the board's control be returned to private ownership within five years after the war.

The Federal Railroad Administration. In December 1917, amid nationwide demands for improvements in rail deliveries, President Wilson announced the creation of the Railroad Administration. This administration orchestrated the wartime hauling of passengers, foodstuffs, raw materials, and manufactured goods along more than 250,000 miles of track. It coordinated the efforts of 532 companies with combined assets of more than $18 billion. Though many progressives wanted to see continued government operation of railroads in the peacetime economy, control of the rails returned to private companies with the passage of the Railroad Act of 1920.

The Espionage Act. Following Wilson's request for a declaration of war on 2 April 1917, Sen. Charles Culberson of Texas and Rep. Edwin Webb of North Carolina proposed the Espionage Act, which Congress passed on 5 June 1917. Persons found guilty of obstructing recruitment or military operations were liable for fines of up to $10,000 and prison terms of twenty years; those found guilty of sending seditious materials through the mail could be fined up to $5,000 and be sentenced to five years in prison. On 16 May 1918 the Espionage Act was strengthened by a series of amendments that came to be known as the Sedition Act. These amendments prohibited "any disloyal, profane, scurrilous, or abusive language about the form of government of the United States, or the Constitution of the United States, or the flag of the United States, or the uniform of the Army or Navy." Socialist leader and perennial presidential candidate Eugene V. Debs and anarchist Emma Goldman were among those eventually jailed under the Espionage Act. In all 6,000 arrests were made, and 1,055 convictions were attained under the Espionage and Sedition Acts. Postmaster General Albert S. Burleson used the law to ban Socialist Party literature from the mails. In *Abrams* v. *United States* (1919) the U.S. Supreme Court upheld the constitutionality of the Espionage Act, which expired in 1921.

The Committee on Public Information. The Committee on Public Information (CPI) was established by President Wilson on 14 April 1917. Headed by the journalist George Creel, the committee also included the secretary of state, the secretary of war, and the secretary of the navy. Often called the Creel Committee, the CPI spent more than $2 million in two years on designing and distributing pro-war pamphlets, movies, and posters. It also sponsored the "four-minute" men. As part of its pro-Allied stance, the CPI fanned the flames of anti-German sentiment. One CPI flyer declared: "German agents are everywhere. . . . Do not discuss in public, or with strangers, any news of troop and transport movements, or bits of gossip as to our military preparations." Such caution seemed warranted when, on 24 July 1915, the U.S. Secret Service confiscated documents showing that U.S. resident Dr. Heinrich Albert was paid $28 million dollars by Germany to sabotage American munitions plants and depots. Anti-Germanism was so commonplace that people referred to the German measles as "liberty measles" and to sauerkraut as "liberty cabbage."

Sources:

Robert D. Cuff, *The War Industries Board* (Baltimore: Johns Hopkins University Press, 1973);

Ellis W. Hawley, *The Great War and the Search for a Modern Order*, second edition (New York: St. Martin's Press, 1992).

AMERICA AT WAR: THE AEF IN EUROPE

Stalemate. By 1915 the western front had become bogged down in trench warfare, and within two years the Allied position was becoming increasing tenuous as British, Italian, and French forces sustained massive casualties, mutinies broke out in the French army, and revolutionary forces successfully overthrew the czar in Russia. In April 1917 the Allies' hope was renewed after the United States committed the American Expeditionary Forces (AEF) to the fight, but by the time most of those troops arrived a year later, Britain and France had sustained hundreds of thousands of casulties in four years of brutal trench warfare.

The "Yanks" Arrive. By 1918 the U.S. Army had been expanded into a force of 3.7 million soldiers in sixty-two divisions of 28,000 men. Forty-two of these divisions were deployed to Europe, and within a little more than six months after the first U.S. soldiers entered the fighting, the war was over. The first U.S. action in the war came on 20 April 1918 — slightly more than a year after President Wilson had asked for a declaration of war — when a German regiment attacked part of the U.S. Twenty-sixth Division at the village of Siecheprey. It was a bloody introduction to war on the western front for the inexperienced American forces. They fought fiercely, killing approximately 160 Germans while sus-

Gen. John J. Pershing arriving in France, June 1917

taining 634 casualties; another 135 American soldiers were taken prisoner. A month later, on 28 May, a regiment from the American First Division captured the village of Cantigny from the Germans with U.S. losses of 199 killed and 1,408 wounded. In early June the U.S. Second and Third Divisions assisted Allied forces in repelling a German advance against Paris, and on 6–21 June U.S. Marines counterattacked German positions in Belleau Wood. More than 1,800 Americans were killed; 8,000 other casualties were sustained; and 1,600 Germans were taken prisoner.

The Meuse-Argonne Offensive Tips. By June 1918 a quarter of a millon U.S. troops were arriving in France every month, and Allied morale was greatly bolstered. In July 1918 along the Marne a joint French-U.S. effort repelled what proved to be Germany's final offensive. Soon the U.S. First Army, with French support, was attacking the German salient at Saint-Mihiel. On 26 September the First Army engaged the Germans in in-

tense fighting in the Meuse-Argonne offensive, during which U.S. forces sustained 120,000 casualties. The Meuse-Argonne offensive was the major battle for the AEF, casting doubt on General Pershing's belief that massed troops and speed could break through the stalemate of trench warfare quickly. The offensive also demonstrated that the training of U.S. troops was largely inadequate and that the system for supplying quickly moving troops was not up to the job. The battle also brought out tensions between the American high command and the French. At one point Premier Georges Clemenceau considered asking Wilson to remove Pershing from command, but Marshal Ferdinand Foch talked Clemenceau out of doing so.

Armistice. On 4 October, with the German war effort near collapse, Germany's chancellor cabled President Wilson requesting an armistice in accord with peace terms Wilson had outlined the previous January. France and Britain refused these terms, and Wilson

On 8 October 1918, at the height of the Meuse-Argonne offensive, quiet and unassuming Cpl. Alvin C. York, a thirty-year-old farmer and blacksmith from Tennessee, engaged the enemy in what would become the single most heralded action by a U.S. soldier during World War I. After six of York's fellow platoon members from Company G of the 328th Infantry Regiment were killed by heavy German machine-gun fire, York, a skilled marksman, told his comrades to stay under cover and, finding a strategic position from which to fire on the Germans, killed more than twenty of them. Eight of the remaining Germans attacked the position held by York, but he shot each of them in turn. Then, holding a German major at gunpoint, York marched into the enemy camp and took 132 Germans as prisoners of war. Awarded the Medal of Honor and the French Croix de Guerre, and promoted to the rank of sergeant, York quietly returned to his Tennessee home after the war, saying, "It's over, let's forget it."

Source: Ernest R. May, *War, Boom and Bust* (New York: Time, 1964).

Prime Minister David Lloyd George of Great Britain, Prime Minister Vittorio Emanuele Orlando of Italy, Premier Georges Clemenceau of France, and President Wilson at Versailles, 28 June 1919

rejected the German offer. Turkey quit the war on 30 October, and four days later Austria-Hungary resigned from the conflict. On 9 November Kaiser Wilhelm II of Germany abdicated and fled to the Netherlands. Germany signed the armistice ending the war on 11 November 1918 at 5:00 A.M. The agreement took effect at 11 A.M. The world's bloodiest war to that time was over. U.S. troops had been involved in thirteen major military operations on the Western Front. Among the 3.7 million men who served in the U.S. armed forces there were 116,516 war deaths: 53,402 battle fatalities and 63,114 others, mostly from disease. Perhaps two hundred thousand other American soldiers were maimed or injured in the conflict.

Sources:

David M. Kennedy, *Over Here: The First World War and American Society* (New York: Oxford University Press, 1980);

William M. Leary, *The Progressive Era and the Great War, 1896–1920* (Arlington Heights, Ill.: AHM, 1978);

Arthur S. Link, *The Progressive Era and the Great War, 1896–1920*, second edition (Arlington Heights, Ill.: AHM, 1978).

AMERICA AT WAR: WILSON'S PEACE PLAN

War Aims. In an 8 January 1918 address to Congress President Wilson put forward peace terms that became known as the Fourteen Points. Declaring that the United States had no designs on European territory and no desire for monetary reparations, Wilson made it clear from the outset that the United States wanted no part of the secrecy, intrigue, and imperial ambitions that had created the conditions for war. Instead, he hoped to use the war — and American participation in it — as a means to achieving a just peace maintained by a new international system.

Wilson and Versailles. After the Armistice was signed in November 1918, Wilson gathered together a group of advisers and supporters — together called "The Inquiry" — and sailed for Paris to participate in shaping the terms of the peace. On arrival in Europe he toured western regions ravaged by the war. From Brest to Paris men, women, and children knelt in prayer near the tracks as his train passed, and he was treated as a savior. In the peace conference at Versailles, which convened on 18 January 1919, Wilson was one of the "Big Four" in the negotiations. The other three — David Lloyd George of Great Britain, Georges Clemenceau of France, and Vittorio Orlando of Italy — resented Wilson's high moral tone and disagreed with what they believed to be his overly conciliatory approach to the Germans. Wilson's Fourteen Points did not escape unchallenged. The British and French remained firm in their insistence that Germany pay reparations (later set at $56 billion) for the destruction the war had wrought, and they refused to accept Wilson's proposals for freedom of the seas, free trade, and open negotiations ("open covenants openly arrived at"), and seriously amended his colonial policy of "impartial mediation," as well as the promise of "national self-determination" for the people of Europe. Wilson did, however, succeed in winning a series of concessions on the establishment

In his 8 January 1918 speech before a joint session of Congress, President Woodrow Wilson put forward his view of how the peace in Europe ought to be concluded so that World War I might truly serve as the "war to end all wars," declaring:

We entered this war because violations of right had occurred which touched us to the quick and made the life of our own people impossible unless they were corrected and the world secured once for all against their recurrence. What we demand in this war, therefore, is nothing peculiar to ourselves. It is that the world be made fit and safe to live in; and particularly that it be made safe for every peace-loving nation which, like our own, wishes to live its own life, determine its own institutions, be assured of justice and fair dealing by the other peoples of the world against force and selfish aggression. All the peoples of the world are in effect partners in this interest, and for our own part we see very clearly that unless justice be done to others it will not be done to us. The program of the world's peace, therefore, is our program; and that program, the only possible program, as we see it, is this:

I. Open covenants of peace, openly arrived at, after which there shall be no private international understandings of any kind but diplomacy shall proceed always frankly and in the public view.

II. Absolute freedom of navigation upon the seas, outside territorial waters, alike in peace and in war, except as the seas may be closed in whole or in part by international action for the enforcement of international covenants.

III. The removal, so far as possible, of all economic barriers and the establishment of an equality of trade conditions among all the nations consenting to the peace and associating themselves for its maintenance.

IV. Adequate guarantees given and taken that national armaments will be reduced to the lowest point consistent with domestic safety.

V. A free, open-minded, and absolutely impartial adjustment of all colonial claims, based upon a strict observance of the principle that in determining all such questions of sovereignty the interests of the populations concerned must have equal weight with the equitable claims of the government whose title is to be determined.

VI. The evacuation of all Russian territory and such a settlement of all questions affecting Russia as will secure the best and freest cooperation of the other nations of the world in obtaining for her an unhampered and unembarrassed opportunity for the independent determination of her own political development and national policy and assure her of a sincere welcome into the society of free nations under institutions of her own choosing; and, more than a welcome, assistance also of every kind that she may need and may herself desire. The treatment accorded Russia by her sister nations in the months to come will be the acid test of their good will, of their comprehension of her needs as distinguished from their own interests, and of their intelligent and unselfish sympathy.

VII. Belgium, the whole world will agree, must be evacuated and restored, without any attempt to limit the sovereignty which she enjoys. . . .

VIII. All French territory should be freed and the invaded portions restored, and the wrong done to France by Prussia in 1871 in the matter of Alsace-Lorraine, which has unsettled the peace of the world for nearly fifty years, should be righted, in order that peace may once more be made secure in the interest of all.

IX. A readjustment of the frontiers of Italy should be effected along clearly recognizable lines of nationality.

X. The peoples of Austria-Hungary, whose place among the nations we wish to see safe-guarded and assured, should be accorded the freest opportunity of autonomous development.

XI. Rumania, Serbia, and Montenegro should be evacuated; occupied territories restored; Serbia accorded free and secure access to the sea; and the relations of the several Balkan states to one another determined by friendly counsel. . . .

XII. The Turkish portions of the Ottoman Empire should be assured a secure sovereignty. . . .

XIII. An independent Polish state should be erected which should include the territories inhabited by indisputably Polish populations, which should be assured a free and secure access to the sea, and whose political and economic independence and territorial integrity should be guaranteed by international covenant.

XIV. A general association of nations [the League of Nations] must be formed under specific covenants for the purpose of affording mutual guarantees of political independence and territorial integrity to great and small states alike.

Pickets outside the White House, circa 1919, protesting the imprisonment of political radicals under the Espionage and Sedition Acts

of colonial "trusteeships," and, most important, his plan for a League of Nations was accepted.

The Treaty Defeated. When Wilson returned to the United States he sought, as the Constitution required, the ratification of the Treaty of Versailles by the Senate. But in 1919 the Senate was controlled by Republicans. A leading Republican senator, Henry Cabot Lodge of Massachusetts, was vexed by the president's refusal to include prominent Republicans in the delegation that had accompanied him to the treaty negotiations in Europe. Lodge also believed that Wilson's idea for a League of Nations, which would mediate disputes between sovereign nations in an effort to avoid future wars, would threaten U.S. sovereignty and create entangling alliances — a view shared by progressive midwestern and western senators. Lodge and most of his fellow Republicans refused to support ratification of the treaty on which Wilson had worked so hard, and many of Wilson's liberal allies deserted him, in part because of their frustration with the treaty's harsh reparations. Hoping to generate public pressure in favor of the League of Nations and the treaty, Wilson attempted to by-

pass the Republicans in Congress with a direct appeal to the nation. Against his doctor's recommendations he embarked on a demanding "whistle stop" nationwide train tour. In the middle of this tour he became ill and was forced to return to Washington, where he was felled by a stroke. Opposition in the Senate continued. When the Senate Foreign Relations Committee, chaired by Henry Cabot Lodge, sent their version of the treaty to the floor of the Senate in mid November, it included almost fifty amendments. Because Wilson had instructed his Democratic supporters to accept no amendments, the amended treaty was rejected. Forty-two Democrats and thirteen Republicans joined together to vote down the revised treaty. When a vote was called on the unamended version, the Republicans voted it down, with thirty-seven Democrats standing with their president and voting for it. Though a series of subsequent votes encouraged hope that a compromise could be reached, the treaty was never ratified by the necessary two-thirds of the Senate. The United States did not join the League of Nations, and it did not ratify a formal treaty ending the war with Germany until 1921.

Sources:

Frank D. Fleming, *The United States and the League of Nations, 1918–1920* (New York: Putnam, 1932);

Henry Cabot Lodge, *The Essential Terms of Peace: Speech in the Senate of the United States, August 1918* (Washington, D.C., 1918);

Ralph A. Stone, ed., *Wilson and the League of Nations* (Huntington, N.Y.: Krieger, 1978).

DOMESTIC RADICALISM: THE RED SCARE

Background. Amid the bloodshed of World War I a revolution took place in Russia in February 1917 (according to the old-style calendar then used by the Russians). Czar Nicholas II was overthrown, and the following October (old-style) communist Bolsheviks (colloquially referred to as "reds"), led by Vladimir Lenin, overthrew a provisional government headed by Aleksandr Kerensky. By March 1919 the Soviet Union was seeking to export its revolutionary communism to other countries. Anxieties over Communist influences in the United States were heightened in April, when thirty-six government officials, including Atty. Gen. A. Mitchell Palmer and Supreme Court Justice Oliver Wendell Holmes Jr., were mailed package bombs that were presumed to have come from radicals. By September 1919, after two factions of the Socialist Party of America broke away from that organization to form the Communist Labor Party and the American Communist Party, a "red scare" gripped Americans, for many of whom "radical" was equated with "foreign." The domestic labor unrest that came hard on the heels of the Armistice seemed to signal class warfare, as a general strike in Seattle (January and February), a police strike in Boston (early September), a nationwide steelworkers' strike (late September), and a United Mine Workers strike (November) followed in quick succession.

The Palmer Raids. Fearing the growth of radicalism in the country, Attorney General Palmer initiated a crusade against the "reds," singling out individuals of foreign birth who were not yet naturalized citizens. The "Palmer Raids" began on 7 November 1919. As federal agents made a coordinated sweep of a dozen American cities, they arrested hundreds of suspected Communists and other radicals. In the aftermath of this first raid 249 aliens, including the anarchist Emma Goldman, were deported to the Soviet Union on an army ship dubbed the "Soviet Ark." The "Palmer Raids" continued in January 1920, when four thousand Communists and other radicals were arrested during raids in thirty-five U.S. cities. In the same period the New York State legislature expelled five Socialist Party members who had been legally elected to that chamber, and the anti-Communist Lusk committee in New York began efforts to ferret out subversives.

Antiradical Vigilantes. American Legion posts held antiradical meetings, while concerned citizens formed vigilante commitees. Books considered to be subversive

CHARLES F. MURPHY, POLITICAL BOSS

During the 1910s the Republican and Democratic parties in many cities were dominated by political bosses. To be successful both candidates and legislation had to have the approval of these power brokers. Charles F. Murphy, for example, was the dominant Democrat in New York State politics from 1906 into the 1920s. As *The New York Times* reported, Murphy had "established himself securely as the Dictator of Democratic policies in the State." After 1910, when control of the state Republican Party was captured by conservative forces, New York progressives had to rely on the Democrats, especially Boss Murphy, to get reform measures passed.

As one historian has noted, "Murphy's 'progressivism' was in large part the manifestation of a practical politician's self-defense tactics." Yet, led by Murphy, the Democrats supported woman suffrage, direct election of U.S. senators, the direct primary system for nominations to public office, the federal income-tax amendment, and a compulsory workmen's compensation law. In 1913 they passed a compensation law that labor leader Samuel Gompers called "the best law of the kind ever passed in any state, or in any country." Though the animosity of President Woodrow Wilson curtailed his power for a time, Murphy was a consummate power broker who helped to elect three New York governors during the 1910s: John A. Dix in 1910, William Sulzer in 1912, and Alfred E. Smith in 1918. After Sulzer tried to steer an independent course — refusing to make patronage appointments Murphy sought — Murphy had Sulzer impeached, an object lesson that was not lost on other potential rebels.

Source: J. Joseph Huthmacher, "Boss Murphy and Progressive Reform," in *Urban Bosses, Machines, and Progressive Reformers*, by Bruce M. Stave (Lexington, Mass.: Heath, 1972).

were removed from the shelves of public libraries; radical faculty members were dismissed by university administrators; and a mob vandalized the offices of the socialist Rand School in New York City. In Centralia, Washington, another group of vigilantes pulled an IWW organizer from a jail cell, hanged him, and riddled his lifeless body with bullets. By late 1920 public hysteria had subsided, owing in part to the election of Republican Warren Harding on a platform promising a "return to normalcy."

Sources:

Anthony Gengarelly, *Distinguished Dissenters and Opposition to the 1919–1920 Red Scare* (Lewiston: Mellen Press, 1996);

Robert K. Murray, *Red Scare* (New York: McGraw-Hill, 1964);

John Louis Recchiuti, "The Rand School of Social Science During the Progressive Era: Will to Power of a Stratum of the American Intellectual Class," *Journal of the History of the Behavioral Sciences,* 31 (April 1995): 149–161.

ELECTORAL REFORM

The Initiative, the Referendum, and the Recall. In the 1910s, and earlier, many local and state political parties were run by political machines that controlled both the nominating and the legislative processes. In response to such corruption voters sought to increase direct democracy by furthering a series of electoral reforms that had begun in the late nineteenth century: the initiative, the referendum, and the recall. The initiative and referendum were first established in South Dakota in 1898, and by the 1910s a score of states had established such laws. The initiative and referendum allowed voters to write policy by passing specific laws. The recall, also widely adopted and used during the 1910s, allowed voters to remove an elected official from office if he failed to carry out the wishes of his consitutents. All three measures reflected a progressive belief in the efficacy of the political process: if the means of electing officeholders could be cleansed of corruption, the government would be responsive to the will of the people.

Commission Government. One political innovation was the commission government, usually composed of three to twelve people, which carried out the legislative and executive functions of a city, county, or township. The city commission form of government was first adopted in Galveston, Texas, in 1900, and by 1917 five hundred cities in the United States were run by commission governments. They were effective in small homogenous communities but less successful in governing ethnically diverse urban populations. Often commission government was accompanied by another reform — the city-wide election, which was intended to weaken the power of ward politicians and their ethnic constituents, whose power was frequently concentrated at the neighborhood level.

The Seventeenth Amendment. The Constitution initially provided for direct election of members of the House of Representatives. Senators, however, were to be elected by the legislators of each state. From 1789 to 1866 each state set its own method for electing its two senators, with the result that procedures varied widely, often leading to impasses in state legislatures. After 1866 the U.S. Congress mandated procedures by which states elected their senators. Under congressional guidelines, both houses of a state's legislature were required to vote separately, by roll call. In the event that they were unable to concur on a choice, they were compelled to meet in joint session and continue voting until a candidate was selected. In the late nineteenth and early twentieth centuries, many states initiated primary systems by which the electorate voted for candidates and their state legislators were bound by the results. The Seventeenth Amendment replaced the various state practices by mandating direct election of senators. Proposed on 13 May 1912, the amendment was declared ratified on 31 May 1913. Like other progressive electoral reforms, the Seventeenth Amendment was seen as a vehicle for advancing direct democracy and weakening the grip of special interests (especially big business) and corrupt party machines on the levers of power.

Sources:

Henry Bruere, *The New City Government: A Discussion of Municipal Administration Based on a Survey of the Ten Commission Governed Cities* (New York: Appleton, 1916);

William Bennett Munro, *The Initiative, Referendum, and Recall* (New York: Appleton, 1912).

FEMINISM: THE FIGHT FOR SUFFRAGE

Background. The United States achieved universal male suffrage in 1870 with passage of the Fifteenth Amendment. Women, however, had to educate, agitate, and organize for another fifty years before they obtained the right to vote in federal elections. On 4 June 1919 Congress passed the Nineteenth Amendment, granting women suffrage, and by August 1920 the requisite number of states had ratified it. It had been a long fight, with roots that can be traced back to Abigail Adams's importuning her husband, John Adams, to "remember the ladies" during the Constitutional Convention. Woman's suffrage was proposed at the 1848 Seneca Falls convention, but the drive to achieve it did not begin in earnest until 1869 with the founding of the National Woman Suffrage Association (NWSA) and the American Woman Suffrage Association (AWSA). Susan B. Anthony and Elizabeth Cady Stanton of NWSA focused on national suffrage; Lucy Stone and Julia Ward Howe in AWSA sought state legislation. The merger of NWSA and AWSA into the National American Woman Suffrage Association (NAWSA) in 1890 proved to be an effective combination leading to final victory in 1919.

State Efforts. Between 1896 and 1910 NAWSA initiated scores of campaigns at the state level calling for referenda on the issue of votes for women, but in the few cases in which referenda were held, none resulted in votes for women. Beginning in 1910, however, under the aggressive leadership of Carrie Chapman Catt, a growing roster of states changed their laws to grant women the vote in state elections. Washington State (1910), California (1911), Arizona (1912), Kansas (1912), Oregon (1912), Illinois (1913), Nevada (1914), Montana (1914), and New York (1917) joined Wyoming, Colorado, Utah, and Idaho, which had granted woman suffrage in the late nineteenth century.

The Campaign Intensifies. In 1910 NAWSA claimed seventy-five thousand members; by 1917 it had more than two million. In 1912 twenty thousand suffragists paraded down Fifth Avenue in New York City, and when

A float in a New York City women's suffrage parade, 1915

Wilson arrived in Washington, D.C., for his inauguration in 1913, women marched, carrying banners that declared: "We demand an amendment to the constitution of the United States enfranchising the women of the country." In 1913 Alice Paul, a militant young leader of the movement, left NAWSA and created the Congressional Union, which became the Woman's Party in 1916. Soon after its founding it boasted fifty thousand active members. The Woman's Party picketed the White House and Congress. They especially targeted President Wilson because of his refusal to voice public support for their cause. Beginning in January 1917, the Woman's Party had a perpetual picket stationed outside the White House for a year and a half, standing or marching in an effort to influence public opinion and the nation's chief executive. During this perpetual picket, as one historian has noted, "Women were spat upon, slapped in the face, tripped up, pelted with burning cigar stubs, and insulted by jeers." Sometimes arrested on the charge of obstructing traffic — though they were not doing so — the suffragists usually chose to serve jail time rather than pay small fines. All told, 168 women spent time in jails for picketing, and

several, including Paul, went on hunger strikes while imprisoned. During Paul's three-week hunger strike her jailers resorted to force-feeding her, and when she continued her resistance she was placed in a psychiatric ward for a week. In autumn 1917 President Wilson pardoned the jailed women, but by summer 1918 arrests had begun anew.

A War for Democracy. After Wilson declared that World War I was a war for democracy, women protesters pointed out the limitations of democracy in the United States. When he spoke in public, women from the audience asked, "Mr. President, if you sincerely desire to forward the interests of all the people, why do you oppose the national enfranchisement of women?" On occasions of state, when the president was entertaining foreign dignitaries, members of the Woman's Party displayed banners declaring that the United States was not a democracy. In January 1918 the president capitulated, making a pro-suffrage speech. The following year Congress passed the Nineteenth Amendment, and on 18 August 1920 the floor of the Tennessee House of Representatives in

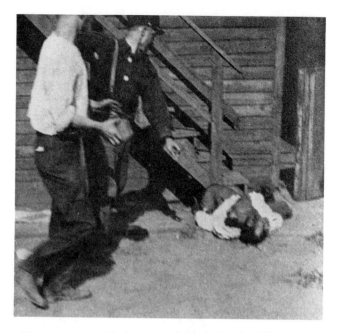

Rioters stoning a black man to death during the Chicago race riots of summer 1919

The basis for legalized social segregation of the races was the Supreme Court decision in *Plessy* v. *Ferguson* (1896), which declared the legality of separate facilities for black Americans. Following this ruling, southern states passed laws forcing black Americans to sit in less desirable seats in theaters (often in back balconies) and in railroad cars (in separate cars or in smoking sections) and to attend black-only public schools, which received much less funding than public schools for whites.

Disfranchisment. States also passed laws that denied African Americans' political rights by disfranchising them. Legislatures across the South passed laws instituting the poll tax and the literacy test and were backed up by white-on-black violence. By 1910 black voters had been effectively disfranchised in all southern states. The denial of black civil, educational, and political rights, together with the economic exploitation of African Americans in the sharecropping system, fueled an exodus of blacks from the South. During the 1910s more than three hundred thousand African Americans fled to northern cities to find work in wartime industries. This Great Migration began broad-based demographic changes that continued for the rest of the century. Amid the horrors of an America divided by racism, African Americans organized and achieved political victories.

Legal Battles. Founded in May 1910, the National Association for the Advancement of Colored People (NAACP) emerged from the Niagara Movement and the National Negro Committee and focused its efforts on education, litigation, and legislation. In November 1910 W. E. B. Du Bois began publishing *The Crisis*, the NAACP monthly journal, and by 1918 the magazine had one hundred thousand subscribers. In 1911 the National Urban League was founded to help southern black migrants adapt to city life and the realities of urban politics. In 1915 the NAACP had its first major victory when in *Guinn and Beale* v. *United States* the Supreme Court declared unconstitutional the "grandfather clause" in the Oklahoma state constitution, which exempted citizens from certain voting qualifications if their grandfathers had voted. The effect of this "grandfather clause" (and others like it) had been to disenfranchise African Americans whose grandfathers had been slaves while giving voting rights to whites who could not meet qualifications (such as literacy) that were enforced for blacks. In *Buchanan* v. *Warley* (1917), another case argued by NAACP lawyers, the Supreme Court struck down segregationist housing laws in Louisville, Kentucky. In *State* v. *Young* (1919) the Court declared that black Americans should be allowed to serve on juries.

The Antilynching Crusade. The NAACP also focused attention on the need for antilynching legislation. The gruesome legacy of vigilante "justice" by lynching is a sordid chapter in American history. There were seventy-six recorded lynchings in 1910, sixty-seven in 1911, thirty-eight in 1917, sixty-four in 1918, and eighty-three in 1919. In 1917 ten thousand African Americans

Nashville was flooded with yellow roses (the symbol of the cause) when Henry Thomas Burns, inspired by a letter from his mother, cast the deciding vote in favor of ratification, making Tennessee the thirty-sixth state to pass the amendment and providing the required three-fourths margin necessary for ratification. Burns later said, "I appreciate the fact that an opportunity as does seldom come to a mortal man to free seventeen million from political slavery was mine."

Sources:

Carrie Chapman Catt and Nettie Rogers Shuler, *Woman Suffrage and Politics: the Inner Story of the Suffrage Movement* (New York: Scribners, 1923);

Marie L. Degen, *The History of the Woman's Peace Party* (Baltimore: Johns Hopkins University Press, 1939);

Eleanor Flexner, *Century of Struggle* (Cambridge, Mass.: Harvard University Press, 1975);

Barbara J. Steinson, *American Women's Activism in World War I* (New York: Garland, 1982).

FIGHTING "JIM CROW": THE BATTLE FOR RACIAL EQUALITY

Segregation. During the 1910s African Americans suffered under a system of legalized race control that sought to deny them equal political, social, educational, and economic opportunity. Invidious methods of racial oppression were in place across the nation but especially in the South. During the 1910s more than 85 percent of African Americans lived in southern states, which had adopted what were known as "Jim Crow" laws in the 1890s and 1900s. While many of their white fellow Americans enjoyed the fruits of the nation's wealth, freedom, and opportunity, blacks were systematically denied civil and political rights, and their labor was exploited.

marched silently down Fifth Avenue in New York City to protest lynchings. Still, Congress passed no anti-lynching legislation, despite an atmosphere of racial violence that sometimes boiled over into race riots.

Race Riots. In 1917 a riot started in Houston after police beat an African American soldier. Seventeen whites and two blacks were killed in the ensuing mayhem. Thirteen blacks were executed, and many more were given life terms in prison for their roles in the riot. (The last African American soldier imprisoned as a result of these riots was released from prison in 1938.) In 1917 race riots in East Saint Louis broke out after African American replacement workers were brought in to take the jobs of white workers who were striking at a defense plant. Spurred by the intense racism of white union leaders and others in the city, tensions were running high when word spread that an black man had shot a white man in a robbery. A vigilante mob gathered and rampaged through the streets beating black citizens and shooting into and setting fire to the homes of many African Americans. Blacks mobilized in response to the violence. The National Guard was called in, and when the riots subsided, thirty-nine black and nine white citizens lay dead. Twenty-five major race riots occurred in 1919 — among them, a riot in Chicago that started when four black youths tried to cross onto a "white" beach on Lake Michigan. A black swimmer was killed, and a week of violence followed. The militia was called out, and thirty-eight people were killed in the rioting. Despite such treatment at home African Americans served their country loyally when called to do so during World War I. The Ninety-third Division — a segregated force of African American soldiers — was the only U.S. contingent allowed to fight as part of the French army.

Sources:

Allen D. Grimshaw, ed., *Racial Violence in the United States* (Chicago: Aldine, 1969);

Donald G. Nieman, *Promises to Keep: African-Americans and the Constitutional Order, 1776 to the Present* (New York: Oxford University Press, 1991).

GOVERNMENT AND AGRICULTURE

Golden Age. For many farmers, especially those in the Midwest and Central Plains states the 1910s were a golden age, particularly in comparison with the lean decades of the late nineteenth century. Though the number of farms rose from two million to 6.4 million between 1860 and 1916, and farm acreage more than doubled, the relative number of farmers (and therefore their electoral power) was diminishing. By 1910 fewer than three in ten workers in the nation were engaged in farming. Productivity and prices rose during the 1910s, and many farmers prospered. The Farmer's Union, established in 1902, sponsored cooperatives for purchasing and storing seed and crops and was active among southern cotton growers and northern wheat farmers during the decade.

Editorial cartoon of President William Howard Taft pleading unsuccessfully with Sen. Nelson W. Aldrich, a powerful conservative Republican, for a substantial reduction in tariffs. Taft's decision to support the Payne-Aldrich Tariff Act of 1909, which kept rates high, angered progressive Republicans and contributed to Taft's defeat in the presidential election.

Farm Legislation. The Smith-Lever Act, passed by Congress on 8 May 1914, added to the farming boom by making federal funds available to educate farmers in the latest technological innovations and farming techniques. Money, in the form of matching grants from the states, was apportioned according to farming population. Agricultural colleges, functioning under the U.S. Department of Agriculture, administered programs of education. Yields rose, and the Farm Loan Act of 1916 made it easier for farmers to get loans to purchase new planting and harvesting equipment.

Farmers and the War. World War I gave farmers a further boost as the price for a bushel of wheat rose from ninety-one cents in 1910 to more than two dollars by 1918. Prices for corn, cotton, and other farm products likewise soared as even marginal lands were cultivated to meet wartime demand. When the war in Europe ended, however, prices tumbled. By the end of 1919 prices for many crops had fallen by a third, and within two years they were as much as 85 percent lower than their wartime peak. During the 1920s farmers experienced persistent economic crisis as a result of oversupply.

Sources:

Richard Hofstadter, *The Age of Reform: From Bryan to FDR* (New York: Random House, 1955);

Russell Nye, *Midwestern Progressive Politics* (New York: Harper & Row, 1959).

At his first inauguration, on 4 March 1913, President Wilson spoke movingly. In part he said:

Our life contains every great thing, and contains it in rich abundance.

But the evil has come with the good, and much fine gold has been corroded. With riches has come inexcusable waste. We have squandered a great part of what we might have used, and have not stopped to conserve the exceeding bounty of nature, without which our genius for enterprise would have been worthless and impotent, scorning to be careful, shamefully prodigal as well as admirably efficient. We have been proud of our industrial achievements, but we have not hitherto stopped thoughtfully enough to count the human cost, the cost of lives snuffed out, of energies overtaxed and broken, the fearful physical and spiritual cost to men and women and children upon whom the dead weight and burden of it all has fallen pitilessly the years through. The groans and agony of it all had not yet reached our ears, the solemn, moving undertone of our life, coming up out of the mines and factories and out of every home where the struggle had its intimate and familiar seat. With the great Government went many deep secret things which we too long delayed to look into and scrutinize with candid, fearless eyes. The great Government we loved has too often been made use of for private and selfish purposes, and those who used it had forgotten the people. . . .

There has been something crude and heartless and unfeeling in our haste to succeed and be great. Our thought has been "Let every man look out for himself, let every generation look out for itself," while we reared giant machinery which made it impossible that any but those who stood at the levers of control should have a chance to look out for themselves.

Source: Leon Fink, ed., *Major Problems in the Gilded Age and the Progressive Era* (Lexington, Mass.: Heath, 1993).

GOVERNMENT AND BUSINESS

Regulating the Economy. The American blend of republican government and capitalist economy, in combination with the nation's vast natural resources, had catapulted the United States into the first rank of world powers by 1910. Nevertheless, the national ideal of freedom had its limits. Enterprising capitalists, free to act as they wished, were amassing vast wealth to the point of monopolizing an entire sector of the economy. Presidents Roosevelt and Taft had used the Sherman Antitrust Act of 1890 to break up some of the most egregious monopolies, but by the 1910s it was clear to many Americans that further regulation of industrial and financial interests was needed. Thus, the Wilson administration, with help from progressives in Congress and political pressure from a variety of organized reform groups, pushed through a series of measures aimed at making the federal government a more efficient and effective regulator of economic activity.

The Pujo Committee. Between 16 May 1912 and 26 February 1913 the House of Representatives investigated the "money trust." Named after the chairman of the House Banking and Currency Committee, Rep. Arsene Pujo of Louisiana, the hearings were conducted by committee counsel Samuel Untermeyer. Many individuals from the largest U.S. financial institutions were called to testify, including representatives from J. P. Morgan and Company, the National Bank, and the National City Bank. The Pujo Committee hearings uncovered astonishing facts about American financial institutions. Most impressive was the discovery that 341 directors of corporations with a net worth of more than $22 billion were controlled by banking interests dominated by J. P. Morgan and the Rockefellers. There could be little doubt that, as Louis D. Brandeis wrote in *Other People's Money and How the Bankers Use It* (1914), "a few men control the business of America."

The Federal Reserve Act. President Wilson had urged controls on "the money monopoly," and as president he worked to implement economic reforms. Prompted in part by the Pujo Committee's findings, he and Congress cooperated in the passage of the Federal Reserve Act of 1913 (or the Glass-Owen Act), which proved to be one of the most important banking and currency reforms of the twentieth century. The complexities of the final provisions of this act were the result of the politics surrounding its passage. Two competing bills emerged in Congress. In the House, Carter Glass, a conservative Democrat from Virginia and chairman of the Committee on Banking and Currency, promoted a reserve system owned and operated by American bankers themselves. In the Senate, however, Robert L. Owen, a progressive Democrat from Oklahoma and chairman of the Senate Banking Committee, advocated a plan that placed control of the national reserve system and the currency in the hands of the federal government. The banking community fiercely opposed Owen's plan. Secretary of State William Jennings Bryan and agrarian interests were equally adamant in opposition to the Glass proposal. Wilson at first was noncommittal. Six months of congressional hearings and debates, coming as they did in the wake of the Pujo Committee's revelations, resulted in a compromise bill that largely resembled Owen's plan. Wilson backed the compromise, telling Congress that control of the new banking system "must be public, not private, must be vested in the Government itself, so that the banks may be the instruments, not the masters, of business and of individual enterprise and initiative." The Federal Reserve Act established twelve regional Federal Reserve Banks and required every national bank to join the system. It also established a Federal Reserve Board to control the money supply. By setting interest rates at which it lends money to member banks, the Federal Reserve Board can — when it uses its power wisely — affect the growth rate of the economy and help ensure robust growth with low inflation.

A Federal Income Tax. The passage of the Sixteenth Amendment to the Constitution in 1913 was one of the most important political reforms in American history. Prior to its passage, the federal government had to rely heavily on the tariff to raise revenue. (In the nineteenth century the other major source of federal funds was the sale of public lands.) Reliance on the tariff for revenue meant that import duties had to be kept relatively high, and — because revenues from even high tariffs were quite limited — government expenditures had to be kept low. The institution of a federal income tax would help to address these limitations, but passage of an income-tax amendment was necessary because the Constitution explicitly forbade the levying of such a tax. In addition to increasing federal revenues and allowing the expansion of the federal government, institution of an income tax would permit the downward revision of tariffs, appeasing southern and western congressmen whose rural constituents suffered under burdensome tariff rates that made manufactured goods more expensive. Proposed on 12 July 1909, the Sixteenth Amendment read: "The Congress shall have power to lay and collect taxes on incomes, from whatever source derived, without apportionment among the several States, and without regard to any census or enumeration." Supporters of the new amendment included tax experts, social reformers, and organized labor, as well as most Democrats and many insurgent Republicans. It was opposed by many industrialists, financiers, Republican regulars, and conservative southern Democrats. Voting tipped in favor of the amendment as a result of the Democrats' electoral victories of 1910 and 1912 in the crucial states of Illinois, Indiana, Ohio, Maine, Massachusetts, New Jersey, and New York. The amendment was declared ratified on 25 February 1913. Implemented in a provision included in the Underwood-Simmons Tariff Act of 1913, the first income-tax rates were low by later standards. Incomes over $3,000 and up to $20,000 were taxed at 1 percent. (Only 4 percent of income earners were in this category in the first year.) Those earning between $20,000 and $500,000 a year (an even smaller portion of the total population in 1913) were taxed at rates between 2 and 6 percent.

The Underwood-Simmons Tariff. The first significant tariff reductions since 1846 were brought about by the Democratic Underwood-Simmons Tariff of 1913. Sponsored by Oscar W. Underwood of Alabama in the House and Furnifold McLendel Simmons of North Carolina in the Senate, the tariff lowered rates from an average 40 percent to about 30 percent. The tariff was also the first significant piece of legislation supported by the new Wilson administration, and in the effort to assure passage of the bill Wilson personally addressed a joint session of Congress on 8 April 1913, becoming the first president to do so since John Adams.

The Clayton Antitrust Act. Another major piece of Wilson's "New Freedom" legislation — fulfilling his pledge to revitalize competition in the marketplace — was the Clayton Antitrust Act of 1914. Introduced by the chairman of the House Judiciary Committee, Democrat Henry D. Clayton, the law augmented the Sherman Antitrust Act of 1890. It forbade interlocking directorates, prohibited a company from holding stock in a competing firm, and in certain circumstances banned the acquisition of competing firms. It also outlawed price discrimination (the practice of charging different customers different prices for the same product) and made it illegal to enter into agreements limiting a distributor to selling products from a restricted number of producers. Corporate officials were to be held personally responsible for violations of the act. Also seen as a major improvement for organized labor, the act declared that "the labor of human beings is not a commodity or article of commerce," a phrase which labor leaders took to mean that labor unions were exempt from antitrust laws, which had been used to weaken unions on the grounds that they, like business monopolies, were "combinations in restraint of trade." Samuel Gompers, president of the American Federation of Labor (AFL), hailed the act as labor's "Magna Carta." Subsequently, however, the courts substantially weakened the labor provisions, holding that the act did not exempt labor from antitrust prosecutions.

The Federal Trade Commission. Further fulfilling his campaign pledge to increase competition in the national economy, President Wilson championed creation of the Federal Trade Commission (FTC), established by Congress in September 1914. The FTC replaced the Bureau of Corporations (which had been in existence since 1903) and was charged with enforcement of the Clayton Antitrust Act. Established as an independent regulatory agency with broad powers to investigate the trading practices of businesses and corporations, the FTC comprised five commissioners who were authorized to file suits against businesses engaged in what they determined to be unfair labor practices and to issue cease-and-desist orders when they believed them necessary.

Regulation of the Rails. One of the greatest assets during the 1910s was the American railroads. By mid decade there were a quarter million miles of rails crisscrossing the country. With the automotive and trucking industries still in their infancy, farmers and manufacturers relied heavily on railroads to transport crops, livestock, raw materials, and finished goods to market. Railroad owners often charged higher per-mile rates for hauling goods short distances than they charged for longer hauls. This price inequity was especially injurious to small farmers and producers, and in 1910 Congress, at the insistence of the Taft administration, passed the Mann-Elkins Act. The act prohibited charging higher rates for short hauls than for long hauls — unless the Interstate Commerce Commission (ICC) ruled otherwise — and gave the ICC power to investigate rate increases.

The Adamson Act. In spring 1916, amid the emerging tensions surrounding the Great War in Europe, American railway unions demanded an eight-hour day and overtime pay for their members. After meeting with both sides of the dispute, President Wilson suggested a compromise, by which the unions would be granted only their first demand. Though labor was willing to comply, railroad owners, who met with the president at the White House on 21 August, refused to accept Wilson's proposal — upon which the president said, "I pray God to forgive you, I never can," and stormed out of the room. The president's next move was to address a joint session of Congress, requesting them to legislate an eight-hour day for railway workers. Representative William C. Adamson, a Democrat from Georgia, sponsored the legislation, and on 3 September 1916, one day prior to the strike deadline set by the railway unions, Wilson signed the Adamson Act into law. The following year the Supreme Court upheld its constitutionality.

Sources:

Louis D. Brandeis, *Other People's Money and How the Bankers Use It* (New York: Stokes, 1914);

John D. Buenker, *The Income Tax and the Progressive Era* (New York: Garland, 1985);

Vincent P. Carosso, *Investment Banking in America, A History* (Cambridge, Mass.: Harvard University Press, 1970);

Earl W. Kintner and Joseph P. Bauer, *Federal Antitrust Law* (Cincinnati: Anderson, 1989);

Arthur S. Link, *Woodrow Wilson and the Progressive Era, 1910–1917* (New York: Harper & Row, 1954);

David Philip Locklin, *Economics of Transportation* (Chicago: Business Publications, 1935);

Richard A. Posner, *Antitrust Law: An Economic Perspective* (Chicago: University of Chicago Press, 1976);

James Weinstein, *The Corporate Ideal in the Liberal State, 1900–1918* (Boston: Beacon, 1968);

Henry Parker Willis, *The Federal Reserve System, Legislation, Organization and Operation* (New York: Ronald, 1923).

GOVERNMENT AND IMMIGRATION

The New Immigrants. The 1910s were the last decade in American history in which immigration to the United States from Europe was unrestricted. The largest groups to immigrate during the 1910s were from eastern and southern Europe. Motivated by a population explosion in Europe and economic opportunities in the United States, Italians, Poles, Jews (from the Russian pale), Czechs, Slovaks, Croatians, Lithuanians, Bulgarians, Greeks, Romanians, Armenians, Serbians, and Hungarians poured into the country. Between 1880 and 1940, the period that historians have labeled the "new immigration," more than twenty-six million people immigrated to the United States from Europe. It was the single largest mass migration of human beings in world history, and many American cities were flooded by the new immigrants. By 1910

Immigrants having their eyes examined at Ellis Island, 1913

in New York, for example, about 40 percent of the population was foreign-born and another 38 percent was first-generation native-born. The new immigrants brought with them religions to which most established "native" Americans were unaccustomed. The United States had traditionally been a land of Protestantism, but the new immigrants were Roman Catholic, Eastern Orthodox, and Jewish. Furthermore, they brought with them their "Old World," often peasant, cultures, and they were frequently disoriented by life in urban-industrial America. These immigrants, and the issue of the nation's immigration laws, shaped American politics during the decade. In cities they often found electoral strength by backing ethnically divisive political machines and bosses and encountered political opposition from many established "native" Americans. As they fueled the industrial and agrarian economies in the United States with relatively cheap labor, helping the dynamic and expansive capitalist economy to grow rapidly, the immigrants encountered resentment from other workers who believed that newcomers willing to work cheaply were taking jobs away from native-born Americans.

Americanization. The spectacle of millions of immigrants arriving on the nation's shores gave many native-born Americans pause. In his *History of the American People* (1902) Woodrow Wilson wrote disparagingly of the new immigrants: "Now there came multitudes of men of the lowest class from the south of Italy and men of the meaner sort out of Hungary and Poland, men out of the ranks where there was neither skill nor energy nor initiative of quick intelligence. . . ." At no time in the nation's history was the push for Americanization stronger than during the 1910s. "Americanization" most often meant the imposition of middle-class Protestant customs and values on immigrants. The Bureau of Naturalization and the Bureau of Education organized educational efforts at the federal level. By 1916 Theodore Roosevelt was hailing "100 percent Americanism" as a desirable goal, and after the United States entered World War I the pressures on immigrants to swear allegiance to their new country were intensified. By the end of the decade thousands of public schools, hundreds of cities, and more than twenty states had established Americanization programs. These classes taught immigrant adults subjects such as English, "American-style" cooking, housekeeping, and child rearing. Another branch of the Americanization effort, run by the National Americanization Committee of the U.S. Chambers of Commerce, taught immigrant laborers that it was "American" to arrive at work on time, to wear clean clothing, and to keep tidy homes.

A Federal Literacy Test. Anti-immigrant feelings grew. In 1917 Congress overrode President Wilson's veto of a law requiring that new immigrants pass a literacy test to prove that they could read and write in some language. Congress restricted immigration into the country even further in 1921 and 1924.

Sources:

Edward G. Hartmann, *The Movement to Americanize the Immigrant* (New York: Columbia University Press, 1948);

John Higham, *Strangers in the Land* (New Brunswick, N.J.: Rutgers University Press, 1955);

Maldwyn Allen Jones, *American Immigration* (Chicago: University of Chicago Press, 1960);

James P. Shenton, *Ethnicity and Immigration* (Washington, D.C.: American Historical Association, 1990).

GOVERNMENT AND LABOR

Prosperity. As a result of growing agricultural yields and increased manufacturing production, the people of the United States in the 1910s were in aggregate the richest in the world. By 1913 the United States was producing nearly a third of the worldwide manufacturing output, and its $37 billion national income in 1914 was more than triple that of its nearest competitors, Great Britain and Germany. The per-capita income of the nearly one hundred million U.S. inhabitants in 1914 was $377, more than one and a half times that of Great Britain, twice that of Germany, and almost ten times that of Russia. As the historian Paul Kennedy has noted, "The United States seemed to have *all* the economic advantages which *some* of the other powers possessed *in part,* but *none* of their disadvantages." America's *aggregate* wealth was enormous, but the distribution of these riches was highly skewed. The richest 10 percent of the popula-

tion controlled well over 50 percent of the nation's wealth, while the poorest fifth lived in relative poverty.

Unions for Skilled Workers. Around 5 percent of the nation's labor force was organized into trade unions in the 1910s. These skilled workers — such as carpenters, steam-pipe fitters, stonemasons, and bricklayers — were affiliated with the American Federation of Labor (AFL). For the most part the AFL and its affiliated unions pursued a "pure and simple" trade unionism and a philosophy of voluntarism. That is, the member unions were largely conservative in politics, seeking only increased wages, better working conditions, and union recognition for organized labor while making few demands on government. AFL affiliates tended to hold the view that state involvement in labor-capital relations was more likely to result in a diminution of labor's power than in its enhancement. Employers, caught up in the demands of a capitalist economy to produce the highest quality product at the lowest competitive price, were often unable or unwilling to meet striking workers' demands. Most strikes were nonviolent endeavors and did not espouse radical ends. Some, however, originated with more radical intentions.

Unskilled Labor. Most workers, especially those who were the unskilled and semiskilled, were not unionized. Their wages were lower and their working conditions poorer than those of unionized workers. Their unregulated working conditions sometimes led to horrible industrial accidents, such as the 1911 fire at the Triangle Shirtwaist Factory in New York City that led to the gruesome deaths of 146 female workers. Organizations of social scientists, such as the American Association for Labor Legislation, did seek government regulation of working environments. In the aftermath of the Triangle fire, for example, the New York State Factory Investigating Commission was established, and fifty-seven laws were passed relating to workplace safety.

Labor Radicalism. Yet unskilled workers remained a seedbed for radical politics. Radicals in the anarcho-syndicalist Industrial Workers of the World (IWW) and in the Socialist Party of America offered an alternative political vision. And, though their successes were modest, curtailed in part by the influx of millions of new immigrants eager to find work at any price, the left wing was a part of the national political landscape. During the 1910s clothing workers on the Eastern Seaboard, loggers in the far western states, and miners from Pennsylvania to Idaho organized under the auspices of the IWW, fighting for shorter working hours and union recognition and at times espousing a need to overthrow capitalism. Labor disputes sometimes turned violent. In October 1910 union activists James and John McNamara bombed the *Los Angeles Times* building, killing twenty-one people in an attempt to silence the newspaper's opposition to union organizing.

The Ludlow Massacre. In September 1913 nine thousand members of the United Mine Workers employed in

Ruins of the striking miners' tent city near Ludlow, Colorado, after company guards set fire to it in April 1914

Colorado mines owned by John D. Rockefeller went on strike, demanding union recognition, improved working conditions, and higher wages. As the strike dragged on for seven months, miners and their families were evicted from company-owned towns and set up tent colonies on the Colorado prairies. Violence erupted between strikers and company guards, and on 20 April 1914 guards attacked a miners' camp near Ludlow. After raking the encampment with gunfire, the guards doused the tents with kerosene and set them afire. When the smoke cleared, twenty-one people lay dead, and one hundred more were wounded. Among the dead were eleven children and two women who had been suffocated as they huddled in a makeshift underground bunker. A fortnight of fighting between strikers and their adversaries ensued, and forty more deaths occurred before federal troops were deployed to restore order. The strikers' demands were not met.

The Lawrence Textile Strike. The Lawrence textile workers' strike was a nonviolent example of IWW activism. Beginning on 12 January 1912 thousands of workers in the mills of Lawrence, Massachusetts, walked off the job in peaceful protest over a wage reduction. Two months into the strike, after a nationwide outpouring of sympathy for strikers and their families, IWW organizers William "Big Bill" Haywood and Joseph Ettor helped the striking workers win restoration of their wages.

The Kern-McGillicuddy Act. Prior to the passage of workmen's compensation laws, workers injured on the job had little recourse but to sue their employers in court. In such cases courts often rendered decisions against workers, declaring that they had "assumed the risk of injury" by taking the job. Workmen's compensation laws,

which award set amounts of monetary compensation for various injuries, brought relief to workers and employers. Workers received recompense for injuries, and employers no longer needed to worry about being sued for work-related accidents. By 1916 thirty-five states had passed such laws, but until that year, when Congress passed the Kern-McGillicuddy Act, there was no system of workmen's compensation for federal workers. A part of a larger federal-government attempt to ameliorate the worst abuses of industrialism, the act was passed at President Wilson's behest during the election campaign of 1916. Drafted by the American Association for Labor Legislation, the Kern-McGillicuddy Act served as a model bill for state laws.

Mothers' Pensions. Government intervention in the lives of children was a further element in the expansion of government efforts to regulate industry and labor during the Progressive Era. Concern for the well-being of children led to the passage of child-labor laws, the opening of public-funded kindergartens and urban playgrounds, and the development of a juvenile-court system. The first statewide government "welfare checks" — called "mothers' pensions" — were distributed during the 1910s. Mothers' pensions were given to families in which the father — through death, desertion, or disability — was no longer able to support the family. Because political and cultural resistance to the notion of government aid or protection for able-bodied men — whether in the form of unemployment insurance or rules governing workplace safety — remained strong, proponents of reform were often more successful in obtaining assistance for women and children. The first mothers' pensions were enacted in Missouri and Illinois in 1911. By 1913 eighteen states had them, and by 1919 thirty-nine states

Anti-Prohibition demonstrators, circa 1915

were disbursing government funds to needy families through mothers' pensions. The federal government did not become involved in aiding families until the 1930s.

Child Labor. One of the most shameful aspects of American labor history was the employment of children in mines, mills, and factories, often for long hours in unsafe, debilitating conditions. Children, of course, had worked on family farms and shops before the twentieth century, but life in the eighteenth and nineteenth centuries had generally afforded children varied work schedules and healthy environments. Repetitive, exacting, often exhausting industrial labor dulled the mind, enervated the spirit, and deformed young bodies. To fight such conditions and to educate the nation about the ill effects of child labor, the U.S. Children's Bureau was established in April 1912. Until 1921 it was directed by Julia Lathrop, the first woman to head a federal agency.

The Keating-Owen Act. Through the efforts of the Children's Bureau and pressure from the National Child Labor Committee, Congress passed the Keating-Owen Child Labor Act in 1916. The act barred the interstate shipment of goods made in whole or in part by children (there were 1.8 million juvenile laborers in 1916); prohibited children under sixteen from working in dangerous locations such as mines and quarries or from working longer than eight hours a day; made the minimum age for other types of work fourteen; and prohibited children under sixteen from night work. Wilson secured passage of the bill through intense lobbying among southern Democrats, who resisted because of pressure from the textile industry, which employed substantial numbers of children. The Supreme Court, however, wary of federal intrusion on the power of the states, found the Keating-Owen Act unconstitutional in *Hammer* v. *Dagenhart* (1918). After the Court's invalidation of the law, Congress took another tack. Later that year it imposed a 10 percent excise tax on products made with child labor — thereby seeking to make the use of such labor unprofitable for employers. In 1922 the Supreme Court invalidated Congress's efforts in *Bailey* v. *Drexel Furniture Co.* (1922). Not until 1941 did the U.S. Supreme Court begin to uphold child-labor laws.

Sources:

Randolph E. Bergstrom, *Courting Danger: Injury and Law in New York City, 1870–1910* (Ithaca, N.Y.: Cornell University Press, 1992);

Samuel Gompers, *Seventy Years of Life and Labor* (New York: Dutton, 1925);

Linda Gordon, *Pitied But Not Entitled* (Cambridge, Mass.: Harvard University Press, 1995);

John Louis Recchiuti, "The Origins of American Progressivism: New York's Social Science Community," dissertation, Columbia University, 1992.

LEGISLATING TEMPERANCE: PROHIBITION

The Problems of Alcohol. The evils of alcoholism and heavy drinking were well known from the earliest days of American society. In the 1830s Americans were consuming 7.1 gallons of alcohol per capita on an annual basis. Since many abstained, and most women, children, and slaves consumed much less than those who regularly "tippled," the alcohol consumption of regular drinkers must have been much higher than the statistics suggest. One historian refers to the United States as "the alcoholic republic." In 1851 a Maine law outlawed the manufacture and sale of intoxicating liquors in that state, and by 1855 thirteen states had adopted such laws. Many believed that outlawing drinking was the only way to curtail the family violence, recklessness, and workplace problems all too common across the country. Protestant congregations and women's groups led the Prohibition movement, while it was opposed by many working-class men, Catholics, and immigrant groups, such as the Irish and the Germans, for whom drinking was a more significant part of their cultures than it was for Anglo-Saxon Protestant Americans.

Outlawing Drink. By the late nineteenth century the campaign for temperance had shifted to a drive for Prohibition — or, as H. L. Mencken put it, antialcohol groups shifted from the "hair-shirt" to the "flaming sword." Backed by the evangelical Protestant movement, the Women's Christian Temperance Union, and the Anti-Saloon League, a constitutional amendment to prohibit intoxicating drink was proposed in 1913. By 1916 twenty-one states had outlawed saloons, and in the national elections of 1916 two "dry" candidates (those who opposed the manufacture and sale of alcohol) were elected to Congress for every "wet." On 22 December 1917 Congress passed the Eighteenth Amendment, which was declared ratified 29 January 1919. Section one read: "After one year from the ratification of this article the manufacture, sale, or transportation of intoxicating liquors within, the importation thereof into, or the exportation thereof from the United States and all territory subject to the jurisdiction thereof for beverage purposes is hereby prohibited." Once Prohibition went into effect on 16 January 1920, no beverage containing more than 0.5 percent alcohol could be sold legally in the United States. (In 1933 the Twenty-first Amendment repealed the Eighteenth Amendment, and drinking was once again made a local issue.)

Sources:

Ruth B. A. Bordin, *Woman and Temperance* (New Brunswick, N.J.: Rutgers University Press, 1990);

Mark H. Moore and Dean R. Gerstein, eds., *Alcohol and Public Policy: Beyond the Shadow of Prohibition* (Washington, D.C.: National Academy Press, 1981);

W. J. Rorabaugh, *The Alcoholic Republic: An American Tradition* (Oxford: Oxford University Press, 1979).

Senate	61st Congress	62nd Congress	Net Gain/Loss
Democrats	32	41	+9
Republicans	61	51	-10
Other	0	0	0

House	61st Congress	62nd Congress	Net Gain/Loss
Democrats	172	228	+56
Republicans	219	161	-58
Other	0	1	+1

Governors	1908	1910	Net Gain/Loss
Democrats	21	25	+4
Republicans	25	21	-4
Other	0	0	0

NATIONAL POLITICS: THE 1910 ELECTIONS

Democratic Resurgence. The close electoral split between Democrats and Republicans in the years following the Civil War was altered in the elections of 1896. In that year the Republican William McKinley won the presidency with a decisive victory over agrarian Democrat William Jennings Bryan. Thereafter, the Republican Party held a majority of congressional seats for twenty-six of the thirty-four years from 1896 to 1930 and, with only two exceptions, won every presidential election from 1896 until 1932. Except for the 1910s the Republicans dominated American politics for the first third of the twentieth century. From 1910 to 1918 the Democratic Party held a majority of seats in Congress, and Democrat Woodrow Wilson won both presidential elections held during the decade.

The Republican Fracture. The Democratic ascendancy in these years was largely the result of the split of the Republican Party into conservative and progressive (or modern liberal) wings. During his presidency Theodore Roosevelt had managed to prevent this fissure from widening, partly through the force of his personality and partly through shrewd political tactics aimed at fulfilling a progressive agenda while mollifying party conservatives. Following the election of William Howard Taft, Roosevelt's handpicked successor, in 1908, the split within the party widened, and progressive Republicans grew increasingly restive.

The Congressional Elections of 1910. Democrats and insurgent Republicans were the big winners in the off-year election of 1910. Democrats came out of the voting with 228 seats in the House of Representatives to the

Republicans' 161 (one socialist, Victor L. Berger of Milwaukee, Wisconsin, was also elected). In the Senate the Republicans maintained a majority, with 51 seats to 41 for the Democrats, but increased insurgent Republican strength mitigated Republican majority strength. After the election of 1908 the Republicans had held a 219 to 172 majority in the House and a 61 to 32 majority in the Senate. Their losses in 1910 were a relative electoral disaster. By the spring of 1910 the Payne-Aldrich Tariff, the Ballinger-Pinchot affair, and the silencing of once-powerful House Speaker Joseph Cannon, made the conservative/insurgent split within the Republican Party impossible to deny. Furthermore, by the end of 1910 the four powerful stand-pat conservative Republicans, Nelson W. Aldrich of Rhode Island, John C. Spooner of Wisconsin, Orville Platt of Connecticut, and William B. Allison of Iowa, had either died or resigned, and Taft's efforts to purge insurgent Republicans in Republican primaries were unsuccessful. Republican support for the protective tariff, which many voters believed had led to an increase in the cost of living, was a major reason given by political pundits for the Republican losses.

State and Regional Results. In the Midwest, in the Mid-Atlantic states, and in New England the Democrats achieved significant gains. In the House of Representatives, Democrats gained eight seats in Ohio, five in Illinois, four in Missouri, twelve in New York, and four each in Pennsylvania, New Jersey, and West Virginia. Of the sixteen governorships that Republicans won in 1910, several were claimed by insurgent (progressive) Republicans. Progressive governors were elected in Wisconsin, New Hampshire, Oregon, Minnesota, and California. Voters elected Democratic governors in ten states, among them Colorado, Kentucky, Maine, Massachusetts, New Jersey, and New York. Reform, it seemed, had arrived on the national stage.

Insurgent Republicans. By 1910 the leading progressive Republican senators were Robert La Follette of Wisconsin, Jonathan Dolliver of Iowa, Albert Cummins of Iowa, Albert Beveridge of Indiana, Moses Clapp of Minnesota, Joseph L. Bristow of Kansas, William E. Borah of Idaho, and Jonathan Bourne of Oregon. In the House of Representatives George Norris of Nebraska was the leading Republican insurgent.

The Tariff Issue. During the second decade of the twentieth century there was a continuing economic war between rural and urban America. Manufacturing (mills and factories) and finance (banks and brokerage houses) were considered by many to be the bedrock of the nation's prosperity. As the party of these interests, Republicans in Congress persistently sponsored (usually successfully) legislation that benefited urban-industrial centers against rural-agrarian interests. A small group of mostly western Republican congressmen, who represented farming interests, worked to counter this trend. Led by Norris of Nebraska, these "Insurgent Republicans" were infuriated by the passage of the Payne-Aldrich Tariff of 1909, which set the average tariff rates to 40 percent, somewhat lower than previous rates (which averaged 57 percent) but still high. High tariffs raise the costs of imported goods. Manufacturers and industrial workers generally favored high tariffs — labeling them "protective" because they protected the profitability of U.S. industries by making competing foreign goods much more expensive. In simple economic terms this increase meant that farmers had to pay urban manufacturers higher prices for goods such as steel plows and other farm implements. Therefore, the Republican insurgents argued, the tariff hurt their constituents by redistributing wealth from the farmers to industrial and financial interests.

Revolt. In the early 1910s insurgent Republicans in the House and Senate focused their energies on tariff reduction and on conservation (another big issue in western states). Insurgent Republicans also turned their political power, modest as it was, against conservative members of their own party. In 1910 they joined with Democrats to break the power of the longtime conservative Republican speaker of the House, Joseph G. Cannon of Illinois. Elected speaker in 1901, Cannon had used his substantial powers to promote legislation that he believed would allow capitalism to flourish unhindered by governmental regulation. Thus, Cannon had supported the Payne-Aldrich Tariff of 1909 and had used his position as speaker to block many regulatory bills from getting to the floor of the House. He also controlled House committee appointments, often denying seats on important committees to House members who failed to conform to his conservative perspective. In March 1910 an alliance of insurgent Republicans and Democrats led by George Norris initiated a major challenge to Cannon's authoritarian control. They succeeded in drastically curtailing the speaker's power by voting to make the all-important House Rules Committee an elective body and to exclude Cannon from its membership. In late December 1910 insurgent Republicans announced that they would form a National Progressive Republican League. Among the leaders of the new organization were Robert La Follette, William E. Borah, and George Norris. On 23 January 1911 the first national organizing meeting of the National Progressive Republican League took place. It was the beginning of a split in the Republican Party that had devastating consequences for the party in 1912.

Sources:

John D. Baker, "The Character of the Congressional Revolution of 1910," in *Journal of American History*, 60 (1973): 679–691;

Lewis L. Gould, *Reform and Regulation* (New York: Wiley, 1978);

Samuel P. Hays, *The Response to Industrialism, 1885–1914* (Chicago: University of Chicago Press, 1957);

Arthur S. Link and Richard L. McCormick, *Progressivism* (Arlington Heights, Ill.: Harlan Davidson, 1983);

John L. Moore, ed., *Congressional Quarterly's Guide to U.S. Elections*, third edition (Washington, D.C.: Congressional Quarterly, 1994).

Democratic candidate Woodrow Wilson, Progressive candidate Theodore Roosevelt, and Republican incumbent William Howard Taft delivering speeches from their campaign trains during the 1912 presidential race

NATIONAL POLITICS: THE 1912 REPUBLICAN NOMINATION RACE

A House Divided. For the Republican Party the 1912 presidential election was a calamity. More than three hundred delegates walked out of the party's national convention and formed the Progressive Party to support Theodore Roosevelt for the presidency. President William Howard Taft, the Republican candidate, retained control of the diminished GOP. Had he been a more astute politician, he might have turned his many accomplishments as president to his advantage. His administration had added more land to the National Parks and National Forests and had broken up more trusts than Roosevelt had done in his seven and a half years as president. (Taft brought ninety legal actions against trusts in his four years as president; Roosevelt had brought forty-four during his nearly two terms.) Farmers were enjoying vast prosperity as prices and profits rose. The economy was dynamic and expansive; unemployment was low; and Wall Street profits were on the rise. Yet by autumn 1912 Taft was beset with political problems. The presidency was the first elective office Taft had ever held, and he lacked the political skill necessary to hold together a divided party. Rather than strengthening a coalition of sup-porters, each of his successes seemed instead to alienate voters.

The Payne-Aldrich Tariff. Taft had proved ineffective on tariff reform, and his indecisiveness over the Payne-Aldrich Tariff of 1909 in particular outraged insurgent Republicans. The Republican Party platform of 1908 had "unequivocally" promised alterations in the tariff structure, buoying hopes of many rural voters. But when the Payne-Aldrich Tariff was introduced in Congress it rapidly became clear that tariffs would be reduced only slightly. Taft signed the bill, which in the eyes of western senators was not sufficient to fullfill his pledge to lower tariff rates. The president further rankled agrarian interests and others who opposed the high tariff rates when he declared the new tariff to be "the best bill that the Republican party ever passed."

Ballinger-Pinchot Affair. In 1909 and 1910 Taft's secretary of the interior, Richard A. Ballinger, following the mandate of law, opened federal lands in Wyoming, Montana, and Alaska to use by private water and mining interests. When Louis Glavis, who worked under Ballinger, claimed that Ballinger had illegally sold mineral and water rights to private interests, Ballinger fired Glavis for exposing the alleged scandal. Chief Forester Gifford Pinchot, a popular figure who had served as Theodore

Roosevelt's adviser on natural resources, considered Ballinger's actions a betrayal of the cause of conservation and appealed directly to the president. After Taft sided with Ballinger, Pinchot went to the press, and Taft fired him for insubordination. A congressional inquiry into the affair further fueled the disagreement. Ballinger was cleared of any wrongdoing, but a minority report published by insurgent Republicans condemned him nevertheless. The taint of scandal remained, embarrassing Taft and deepening the split between Roosevelt loyalists and Taft supporters.

Canadian Reciprocity. Taft's popularity among farmers and insurgent Republicans fell further over his efforts to establish a reciprocal tariff arrangement with Canada. In 1911 Taft summoned Congress to a special session to approve an agreement that would reduce tariffs on goods traded between the two countries. Though the reciprocity agreement was beneficial to manufacturers, who would have access to cheaper raw materials and larger markets for their products, the tariff met a hailstorm of protest from midwestern grain farmers and lumbermen, who stood to suffer economically from Canadian competition. Debate over the Canadian Reciprocity agreement drove insurgent Republicans in Congress even further from their conservative fellow Republicans and practically assured Taft's defeat in the election of 1912. Ironically, Canada refused to ratify the treaty because Taft had affronted its sense of national pride by declaring that the agreement would make Canada an economic satellite of the United States. Speaker of the House Champ Clark had further injured the cause when he stated publicly that the trade agreement would result in Canada's ultimate annexation by the United States.

Roosevelt Runs. Taft faced two challengers in party primaries, Roosevelt and Sen. Robert La Follette. Roosevelt challenged Taft in part because in October 1911 Taft had filed an antitrust suit against U.S. Steel after Roosevelt had given his word in 1907 that the government would not institute antitrust proceedings against the company for its acquisition of the Tennessee Coal and Iron Company. Coupled with Roosevelt's burning desire to return to office (he was only fifty years old in 1912), Taft's actions gave Roosevelt the rationale he sought to pursue his own reelection. By November 1911 Roosevelt was intimating to friends that he was interested in becoming the Republican candidate for president, though he insisted that his nomination appear to be the result of a groundswell of popular support.

Primary Battles. Henry Cabot Lodge, Elihu Root, Henry L. Stimson, and other Republican stalwarts supported Taft. Roosevelt's supporters included most of the progressive Republicans who had previously supported Robert La Follette, friends from his earlier administrations, and political bosses in Ohio, New York, Pennsylvania, Louisiana, and Texas who believed that a Roosevelt victory would be to their benefit. In the

---

ROOSEVELT'S "NEW NATIONALISM"

In a speech delivered on 31 August 1910 at Osawatomie, Kansas, Theodore Roosevelt offered the outline of what became the 1912 Progressive Party platform, the "New Nationalism":

> The right to regulate the use of wealth in the public interest is universally admitted. Let us admit also the right to regulate the terms and conditions of labor, which is the chief element of wealth, directly in the interest of the common good. The fundamental thing to do for every man is to give him a chance to reach a place in which he will make the greatest possible contribution to the public welfare. Understand what I say there. Give him a chance, not push him up if he will not be pushed. Help any man who stumbles; if he lies down, it is a poor job to try to carry him; but if he is a worthy man, try your best to see that he gets a chace to show the worth that is in him. No man can be a good citizen unless he has a wage more than sufficient to cover the bare cost of living, and hours of labor short enough so that after his day's work is done he will have time and energy to bear his share in the management of the community, to help in carrying the general load. We keep countless men from being good citizens by the conditions of life with which we surround them. We need comprehensive workmen's compensation acts, both state and national laws to regulate child labor and work for women, and especially, we need in our common schools not merely education in book learning, but also practical training for daily life and work.

Source: Leon Fink, ed., *Major Problems in the Gilded Age and the Progressive Era* (Lexington, Mass.: Heath, 1993).

---

twelve state primaries held across the country in 1912, Roosevelt received 1,157,397 votes to 761,716 for Taft and 351,043 for La Follette. Roosevelt won the primaries in Illinois, Pennsylvania, California, Minnesota, Nebraska, Maryland, South Dakota, Ohio, and New Jersey. Just prior to the convention 432 delegates were committed to Roosevelt, 326 to Taft, and several dozen to La Follette.

The Convention. If most party delegates had been chosen in state primaries, Roosevelt might well have marched to a first-ballot victory at the convention, held in Chicago on 18–22 June, but in 1912 most delegates were selected by state political machines, and Taft controlled the Republican Party machinery. Thus, Roosevelt's nomination was by no means assured. The Republican National Committee, controlled by President Taft, assigned all but 19 of the 254 contested delegates. After a heated floor fight between delegates supporting the president and the insurgent-progressive challengers, Taft and his vice president, James Sherman, were nominated with 561 delegate votes, while

Organized in 1901, the Socialist Party of America claimed 118,000 members by 1912, with its greatest strength west of the Mississippi River, where the socialists' attacks on financial capital appealed to voters who had earlier supported the Populist Party. Oklahoma was the party's greatest stronghold. Eugene Victor Debs, a former railroad worker and union organizer, was the Socialist Party candidate for president in 1900, 1904, 1908, 1912, and 1920. In 1904 he received 400,000 votes, and between 1910 and 1912 hundreds of Socialist Party candidates were elected to local and state offices. The Socialist Party platform for 1912, which called for many of the same reforms that Theodore Roosevelt and the Progressive Party championed, included the following statements:

> The Socialist Party declares that the capitalist system has outgrown its historical function, and has become utterly incapable of meeting the problems now confronting society. We denounce this outgrown system as incompetent and corrupt and the source of unspeakable misery and suffering to the whole working class.
>
> Under this system the industrial equipment of the nation has passed into the absolute control of a plu-

tocracy which exacts an annual tribute of hundreds of millions of dollars from the producers. Unafraid of any organized resistance, it stretches out its greedy hands over the still undeveloped resources of the nation — the land, the mines, the forests and the water powers of every State. . . .

> It is this capitalist system that is responsible for the increasing burden of armaments, the poverty, slums, child labor, most of the insanity, crime and prostitution, and much of the disease that afflicts mankind. . . .
>
> In the face of these evils, so manifest that all thoughtful observers are appalled at them, the legislative representatives of the Republican and Democratic parties remain the faithful servants of the oppressors. . . .

Though Debs received only 6 percent of the votes cast for president, 1912 proved to be the high point of Socialist Party strength in the United States, not only in its electoral tally but in its influence on the platforms of the major parties.

Sources: *National Party Conventions, 1831–1980* (Washington, D.C.: Congressional Quarterly, 1983).

Nick Salvatore, *Eugene V. Debs: Citizen and Socialist* (Urbana: University of Illinois Press, 1982).

La Follette received a scant 41 votes. Most of Roosevelt's supporters (344) abstained from the balloting, so that Roosevelt received only 107 votes for the nomination. During the convention Roosevelt's supporters on the Credentials Committee and the Republican National Committee resigned. By 20 June Roosevelt had decided to form a third party in his bid for the presidency.

The Republican Platform. The Republican platform was essentially conservative, but it included a few progressive elements: promises of legislation to limit working hours for women and children, workmen's compensation legislation, increased conservation efforts, expanded reclamation of lands, and the establishment of a federal trade commission to regulate interstate commerce. The platform also opposed the recall of judges as "unnecessary and unwise."

NATIONAL POLITICS: THE 1912 PROGRESSIVE PARTY CONVENTION

The "Bull Moose" Party. Theodore Roosevelt's political difficulties in 1912 were of his own making. On election night 1904, amid the excitement of his landslide victory, Roosevelt had pledged himself not to run for

another term as president. By 1910, however, he was reconsidering a bid for another term, and in his "New Nationalism" speech at Osawatomie, Kansas, that August he stunned conservative Republicans with his attack on "the sinister control of special interests" and his call for reforms such as income and inheritance taxes, aid to farmers, and improved working conditions. When he formally entered the race as the Progressive Party candidate in 1912, his campaign proved to be one of the most reformist and progressive in the history of the United States.

Progressive Party Convention. In early August 1912 the Progressive Party held its nominating convention. By then, however, it was clear that most Republican Party officeholders who had supported Roosevelt as a Republican Party hopeful earlier in the year had decided to remain loyal to the GOP. There were, to be sure, a few wealthy businessmen and a few machine politicians who supported Roosevelt, but the great majority of his supporters at the Progressive Party convention were political amateurs, social workers, sponsors of the movement for the initiative and referendum, local good-government campaigners, and progressive social scientists. The convention took on the atmosphere of a crusade. Roosevelt delivered a "Confession of Faith" speech at the convention, importuning that "Our cause is based on the eternal principle of righteousness." And, in his first campaign speech after the Progressive Party convention, Roosevelt announced, "I've been growing more radical. . . . I'm even going further than the platform." Roosevelt's political platform, which he called the "New Nationalism," called for legislation to protect the consumer, votes for women, protection of women and children in the workplace, and the substitution of governmental regulation of corporations in place of trust-busting. He accepted the importance of large corporations to the economy but believed government should regulate them. The platform also promoted labor legislation such as federal workmen's compensation, lower tariffs, conservation, and the initiative, the referendum, and the recall. Robert La Follette, who had been the leader of progressive forces before Roosevelt usurped that role, saw his own presidential aspirations foundered in the face of Roosevelt's immense popularity. An embittered La Follette refused to endorse Roosevelt, and many of his strongest followers threw their support to Democrat Woodrow Wilson. Roosevelt's 1912 campaign brought to fruition the vision of government he had outlined in a speech in 1905. In an address to the Union League Club of Philadelphia in January of that year Roosevelt had argued that the state ought to insure liberty for its citizens in an age of increasingly powerful economic interests — a surprisingly pellucid articulation of the ideology of modern liberalism:

> Unquestionably . . . the great development of industrialism means that there must be an increase in the supervision exercised by the Government over business enterprises. . . . Neither this people nor any other free people will permanently tolerate the use of the vast power conferred by vast wealth, and especially by wealth in its corporate form, without lodging somewhere in the Government the still higher power of seeing that this power, in addition to being used in the interest of the individual or individuals possessing it, is also used for and not against the interests of the people as a whole. . . . No finally satisfactory result can be expected from merely State action. The action must come through the Federal Government.

NATIONAL POLITICS: THE 1912 DEMOCRATIC NOMINATION RACE

Wilson Triumphs. The Democrats held their national nominating convention in Baltimore on 25 June–2 July. As the opening day approached, Speaker of the House James Beauchamp "Champ" Clark of Missouri held the lead in delegates. A former editor, Clark had been a supporter of William Jennings Bryan's populist agrarian politics. Among Clark's challengers was Woodrow Wilson, a relative newcomer to national politics. Though Wilson, a former president of Princeton University, had won the governorship of New Jersey in 1910 with the backing of conservative Democratic bosses, he had proved to be much more liberal than New Jersey party

Senate	62nd Congress	63rd Congress	Net Gain/Loss
Democrats	41	51	+10
Republicans	51	44	-7
Other	0	1	+1

House	62nd Congress	63rd Congress	Net Gain/Loss
Democrats	228	291	+63
Republicans	161	127	-34
Other	1	17	+16

Governors	1910	1912	Net Gain/Loss
Democrats	25	31	+6
Republicans	21	17	-4
Other	0	0	0

regulars anticipated. In 1911, under his leadership, New Jersey's legislature had passed a workmen's compensation act and a corrupt practices act and had established a state commission to regulate municipal utilities and railroads. Another major contender for the nomination was Oscar W. Underwood, a Democratic congressman from Alabama who was House majority leader. Underwood's staunchly conservative views were strongly opposed by the Bryan wing of the party. Bryan himself stood little chance of renomination for the party's top post, but he continued to hope that a deadlocked convention might choose him once again as the party standard-bearer. Champ Clark and Tammany boss Charles Murphy allied early in the convention, and by the tenth ballot Clark had a majority of delegate votes, but he was far short of the two-thirds necessary to win the nomination. On the fourteenth ballot Bryan spoke from the podium in opposition to Clark's candidacy, arguing that the speaker was in cahoots with corrupt Tammany Hall forces. Wilson's managers worked behind the scenes, making a series of deals, including a promise to the Indiana delegation that its favorite son, Thomas Marshall, would be placed on the ticket as vice president. Wilson's Virginia roots helped him win the support of many conservative southern Democrats — called "Bourbons." Finally, after more than forty ballots, Woodrow Wilson became the Democratic presidential nominee.

The "New Freedom." Wilson's "New Freedom" campaign embraced a Jeffersonian vision of government, espousing the notion that federal power should be used only to eliminate privilege, remove roadblocks to individual initiative, and restore and preserve a competitive business climate. With the counsel of Louis D. Brandeis,

Wilson vowed to break up the trusts and return to nineteenth-century competitive capitalism among small producers. The "New Freedom" seemed a sharp contrast to Roosevelt's view that corporate trusts could be regulated, asserting instead that small and midsized business would better serve public interests. During the ensuing campaign, Wilson attacked Roosevelt and the Progressive Party as making "impossible pledges" that would create "a government by experts instead of one of full and open discussion."

NATIONAL POLITICS: THE 1912 ELECTIONS

A Three-Way Battle. The election of 1912 was bitterly fought. Taft attacked Roosevelt and the Progressives as "dangerous," while Wilson's progressive record as governor of New Jersey and the enormous difficulty of mounting an effective third-party challenge diminished Roosevelt's hopes for victory. Bryan successfully canvassed the West for Wilson, allowing Wilson to restrict his campaigning to the East and Midwest. On 14 October Roosevelt was shot before giving a speech in Milwaukee. The bullet traveled through his spectacle case and his folded speech before causing a deep flesh wound, but Roosevelt went on to deliver his prepared speech to an amazed audience. In the week prior to the election, Vice President James S. Sherman died, and the Republican National Committee named Nicholas Murray Butler, president of Columbia University, as his eleventh-hour replacement on the ticket.

Results. With the Republican Party split in two, Wilson won easily, with 435 electoral votes, to 88 for Roosevelt, and only 8 for Taft. One million women voted in a presidential race for the first time. Wilson received 6,293,120 popular votes, Roosevelt 4,119,582, Taft 3,485,082, and Socialist Eugene V. Debs 900,672. Eugene Chafin, the Prohibition Party candidate, received 206,275 votes, and the Socialist Labor Party candidate, Arthur Reimer, got a scant 28,750. Wilson received 42 percent of the votes cast, Roosevelt 27 percent and Taft 23 percent. In Congress the Republican split allowed the Democrats to win a substantial majority in both houses of Congress for the first time since the Civil War. After the 1912 elections the Democrats held 51 seats in the Senate. The Republicans held 44, and the Progressives had one seat. In the House Democrats won 291 seats, the Republicans 127, the Progressives 14, and other minority parties 3.

Sources:
Samuel P. Hays, *The Response to Industrialism, 1885–1914* (Chicago: University of Chicago Press, 1957);

Arthur S. Link and Richard L. McCormick, *Progressivism* (Arlington Heights, Ill.: Harlan Davidson, 1983);

John L. Moore, ed., *Congressional Quarterly's Guide to U.S. Elections,* third edition (Washington, D.C.: Congressional Quarterly, 1994);

George E. Mowry, *The Era of Theodore Roosevelt and the Birth of Modern America: 1900–1912* (New York: Harper & Row, 1958);

Senate	63rd Congress	64th Congress	Net Gain/Loss
Democrats	51	56	+5
Republicans	44	40	-4
Other	1	0	-1

House	63rd Congress	64th Congress	Net Gain/Loss
Democrats	291	230	-61
Republicans	127	196	+69
Other	17	9	-8

Governors	1912	1914	Net Gain/Loss
Democrats	31	29	-2
Republicans	17	18	+1
Other	0	1	+1

Arthur M. Schlesinger Jr., ed., *History of American Presidential Elections, 1789–1968,* volume 3 (New York: Chelsea House/McGraw-Hill, 1971).

NATIONAL POLITICS: THE 1914 ELECTIONS

The GOP Rebounds. Although the Democrats retained control of both houses of Congress, the Republican Party was considered by many to be the big winner in the congressional elections of 1914. Having placed third in the presidential election of 1912, the GOP's successes in 1914 reaffirmed its broad-based electoral support. Republicans charged the Democrats with fiscal mismanagement, while the Democrats ran on the legislative successes of the first two years of the Wilson administration. In the aftermath of the 1914 elections the Progressive Party was on the brink of collapse. Theodore Roosevelt commented that in the East, "there is not a state in which the Progressive party remains in condition even to affect the balance of power between the two old parties." Republicans picked up sixty-nine seats in the House, where they held 196 seats to the Democrats' 230. In the Senate the Democrats fared better, increasing the number of Democratic senators by five, to 56, to the Republicans' 40.

Sources:
John L. Moore, ed., *Congressional Quarterly's Guide to U.S. Elections,* third edition (Washington, D.C.: Congressional Quarterly, 1994);

George Mowry, *Theodore Roosevelt and the Progressive Movement* (Madison: University of Wisconsin Press, 1946).

Wilson campaign truck, 1916

NATIONAL POLITICS: THE 1916 REPUBLICAN NOMINATION RACE

Republican Candidates. By late 1915 the leading Republican presidential contenders were former Ohio senator Theodore Burton, Illinois senator Lawrence Y. Sherman, New York senator Elihu Root, and Supreme Court Justice Charles Evans Hughes. Burton's and Sherman's stars faded rapidly, and Theodore Roosevelt's behind-the-scenes efforts for the nomination were rebuffed. (He was not to be forgiven in 1916 for his apostasy of 1912.) Elihu Root, who was seventy-one in 1916, was generally considered too old. His political luster was further tarnished by his involvement in an ill-fated campaign to rewrite the New York State constitution, and Roosevelt's opposition to Root, who had served him as secretary of war and secretary of state, sealed Root's fate. He was unable to muster the necessary number of delegates to win the nomination. In early 1916 Charles Evans Hughes emerged as the Republican front-runner. As a Supreme Court justice since 1910, Hughes had remained above the fray during the bitter political fighting of 1912 and as a result had alienated neither Republican Party regulars nor progressives. As a Supreme Court justice it would have been improper for him to engage in political posturing, and his silence allowed both progressives and conservatives to believe that he supported their views. Progressives remembered Hughes's record as governor of New York, when he had passed workmen's compensation, child-labor, and election-reform laws, as well as measures to regulate public service corporations. The con-

Antoinette and Charles Evans Hughes visiting a copper mine in Butte, Montana, during his 1916 presidential campaign

servative Taft urged Hughes to run, to "reunite the only party from which constructive progress can be expected."

Republican Convention. The Republican National Convention, held in Chicago on 7–10 June 1916, opened with conciliatory speeches calculated to salve the political wounds of 1912. Sen. Warren G. Harding of Ohio — who would himself become the party's presidential candidate in 1920 — declared, "Let us forget the differences, and find new inspiration and compensation in a united endeavor to restore the country." The party platform, a moderately progressive document, called for a protective tariff, and its attack on Wilson's foreign policy drew praise from both conservatives and progressives. Progressives were further pleased with the platform's call for child-labor laws, a rural-credit system, and workmen's compensation legislation for federal employees.

Nomination Contest. On 9 June Gov. Charles S. Whitman of New York placed Hughes's name before the delegates in a nominating speech praising Hughes as "the man of action, the champion, the idol of the electorate, the faithful public servant, the profound

Senate	64th Congress	65th Congress	Net Gain/Loss
Democrats	56	53	-3
Republicans	40	42	+2
Other	0	0	0

House	64th Congress	65th Congress	Net Gain/Loss
Democrats	230	216	-14
Republicans	196	210	+14
Other	9	6	-3

Governors	1914	1916	Net Gain/Loss
Democrats	29	25	-4
Republicans	18	21	+3
Other	1	2	+1

NATIONAL POLITICS: THE 1916 DEMOCRATIC NOMINATION RACE

The Democratic Convention. The Democrats held their national convention at Saint Louis on 14–16 June 1916 and unanimously declared Wilson their nominee on the second evening. Taking "Americanism" as its central theme, the Democratic platform broke with Wilson's 1912 "New Freedom," declaring instead for more active, regulatory government on a limited number of domestic issues. The platform called for child-labor laws, a living wage, and workmen's compensation for federal employees. In foreign policy the Democrats held that it was "the duty of the United States to use its power . . . to make secure its just interests throughout the world . . . and . . . to assist the world in securing settled peace and justice." This note of internationalism was somewhat contradicted in the speeches delivered by party delegates. Isolationist speeches, especially those stressing that Wilson had kept the nation out of war, were repeatedly cheered, and the phrase "He kept us out of war" was quietly added to the platform.

NATIONAL POLITICS: THE 1916 ELECTIONS

The Campaign. The fifty-four-year-old Hughes put in a fine showing as Republican candidate for the presidency, undertaking a national speaking tour on which he drove home his "America first, America efficient" slogan with verve and attacked Wilson on the economy and foreign policy. He claimed that Wilson's policies had turned Mexico against the United States and that Wilson had failed to protect U.S. maritime rights in the Atlantic against aggressive actions by Great Britain and Germany.

thinker on national affairs." Nicholas Murray Butler, Taft's last-minute running mate in 1912, nominated Elihu Root. Sen. Albert Fall of New Mexico nominated Theodore Roosevelt. While moderate demonstrations of support had been displayed at the nomination of Hughes and Root, the galleries went wild with cheers at the mention of Roosevelt's name. Delegates on the floor of the convention hall, however, were inured to this outpouring of support, and the first ballot proved their resolve. Hughes received 253.5 votes, to 103 for Root, and 638.5 scattered among fifteen other candidates. Hughes was clearly the front-runner. On the second ballot his position strengthened as he received 328.5 votes. With a Hughes victory all but assured, convention organizers suspended further balloting for the day so that they could meet with Progressive Party leaders and invite them to join in nominating Hughes for the presidency. The Progressive Party turned down the GOP offer and nominated Theodore Roosevelt, who refused to run, leaving the Bull Moosers without a candidate. Hughes swept the third ballot with 949.5 electoral votes and was declared the Republicans' unanimous choice. Hughes resigned his post on the Supreme Court to accept the GOP nomination. Encouraged by the 1914 congressional results and by the knowledge that President Wilson had been elected only because their party had been divided in the previous presidential election, Republicans approached 1916 with cautious optimism. If fences could be mended with the Progressives, Hughes stood a good chance of election.

Senate	65th Congress	66th Congress	Net Gain/Loss
Democrats	53	47	-6
Republicans	42	49	+7
Other	0	0	0

House	65th Congress	66th Congress	Net Gain/Loss
Democrats	216	190	-26
Republicans	210	240	+30
Other	6	3	-3

Governors	1916	1918	Net Gain/Loss
Democrats	25	21	-4
Republicans	21	26	+5
Other	2	1	-1

Hughes also called for an expanded military preparedness program. Nevertheless, he was hard-pressed to find issues that would distinguish his campaign from Wilson's, and his failure to cultivate California's progressive governor, Hiram Johnson, on his travels through that state may have cost him the election. During the summer of 1916 Wilson was busy with the affairs of state. The country was on the brink of war with Mexico; relations with Great Britain were worsening; and a national railroad strike loomed. The moderately progressive political campaign that Wilson ran in 1916 helped move the Democrats away from the conservatism of their past and began to transform the party into the vehicle for modern liberalism that it became in the 1930s under Franklin Delano Roosevelt.

Election Results. Wilson's popular vote plurality was reduced from the 2,173,945 mark he had achieved in the multicandidate race of 1912 to only 579,511 in 1916. If a mere 4,000 voters in California had shifted their votes from Wilson to Hughes, Hughes would have become president. Wilson received 277 electoral votes, just 23 more than Hughes. Hughes won in the Midwest, Northeast, Mid-Atlantic, and in Oregon, while Wilson swept the South and the West. Wilson received 9,129,606 popular votes, to 8,538,221 for Hughes, to 585,113 for Socialist Allan L. Benson, and 220,506 for Prohibitionist J. Frank Hanly.

Congressional Results. The Democrats lost three seats in the Senate but retained a 53–42 majority there. They also retained a narrow margin in the House, winning 216 seats to 210 for the Republicans (six seats were held by minor parties).

Sources:
S. D. Lovell, *The Presidential Election of 1916* (Carbondale: Southern Illinois University Press, 1980);

John L. Moore, ed., *Congressional Quarterly's Guide to U.S. Elections*, third edition (Washington, D.C.: Congressional Quarterly, 1994);

James Oliver Robertson, *No Third Choice: Progressives in Republican Politics, 1916–1921* (New York: Garland, 1983);

Arthur M. Schlesinger Jr., ed., *History of American Presidential Elections, 1789–1968*, volume 3 (New York: Chelsea House/McGraw-Hill, 1971).

NATIONAL POLITICS: THE 1918 ELECTIONS

Resurgent Republicans. The election of 1918 was a pivotal contest in American political history. Wilson's efforts to persuade voters to elect Democrats to Congress failed to sway the public and succeeded in alienating Senate Republicans, without whom Wilson's peace plan and the League of Nations were doomed to defeat. For the Sixty-sixth Congress the Republicans regained their majorities in both the House and the Senate. The election was held just prior to the signing of the 11 November 1918 armistice that ended World War I and in the midst a devastating influenza epidemic that killed about five hundred thousand Americans. The campaign was a referendum on Wilson and the Democrats' wartime leadership. Republicans, largely reunited after the collapse of the Progressive Party in 1917, assailed the Democrats' wartime domestic policies and criticized Wilson's wartime diplomacy. Prohibition was also a major issue in the campaign. Most Democrats, especially urban workers and Catholic voters, customarily voted against Prohibition, and Republicans, especially progressives, generally voted for it. The Eighteenth Amendment, which had been proposed on 18 December 1917, was moving toward ratification by the states, and the success of "dry" Republicans in the 1918 elections virtually assured its eventual passage on 29 January 1919.

Sources:
Seward W. Livermore, *Politics is Adjourned: Woodrow Wilson and the War Congress, 1916–1918* (Middletown, Conn.: Wesleyan University Press, 1966);

John L. Moore, ed., *Congressional Quarterly's Guide to U.S. Elections*, third edition (Washington, D.C.: Congressional Quarterly, 1994);

James Oliver Robertson, *No Third Choice: Progressives in Republican Politics, 1916–1921* (New York: Garland, 1983);

Arthur M. Schlesinger Jr., ed., *History of American Presidential Elections, 1789–1968*, volume 3 (New York: Chelsea House/McGraw-Hill, 1971).

HEADLINE MAKERS

Newton D. Baker

1871–1937

Secretary of War, 1916–1921

Mobilization for World War I. As secretary of war for a president who campaigned for reelection in November 1916 on the motto "He Kept Us Out of War," Newton Baker had the unenviable task of rapidly and efficiently mobilizing American troops once the United States declared war on Germany in April 1917.

Background. Born on 3 December 1871 in Martinsburg, West Virginia, Newton Diehl Baker studied political science, economics, and history at Johns Hopkins University from 1888 to 1892. He often ate meals with Woodrow Wilson, then a young instructor at Johns Hopkins, at a boardinghouse near the university — an event they would reminisce about years later. After receiving his law degree from Washington and Lee in 1894, Baker returned home to Martinsburg and established a law practice. In 1896 Baker's father used his friendship with Postmaster General William L. Wilson to secure a position for his son as Wilson's assistant in Washington, D.C., a post which the young Baker held until March 1897, when the Democratic administration of Grover Cleveland was replaced by the Republican administration of William McKinley.

Reform Politics. With his patronage position in Washington a casualty of the election results, Baker took a vacation in Europe. On the return voyage in 1898, Baker made the acquaintance of Martin A. Foran, a Cleveland lawyer who offered him a job in his law firm. In Cleveland, Baker soon became a protégé of reform mayor Tom L. Johnson and served as Johnson's legal counsel, as well as city solicitor from 1902 to 1912, during which time he participated in the politics of reform. Johnson and Baker worked to curb the power of private utility companies, to reduce trolley fares to three cents, and to distribute tax assessments more equitably. In 1911

Baker was elected mayor of Cleveland as a reform Democrat. Serving from 1912 to 1915, he instituted tax reforms, further curtailed the power of the utilities, and gained a "home rule" charter for the city.

Washington and Mexico. In 1912 Baker's vigorous campaigning for Woodrow Wilson within the Democratic Party ranks was a significant factor in helping Wilson capture the party's nomination. When Wilson's first secretary of war, Lindley M. Garrison, resigned his post in 1916 (asserting that the administration's military preparedness efforts were inadequate in the face of war in Europe and ongoing conflicts with Mexico), Wilson turned to Baker. In March 1916, after only a few days on the job, Baker faced his first crisis when the Mexican revolutionary Francisco "Pancho" Villa raided the town of Columbus, New Mexico. Baker ordered Brig. Gen. John J. Pershing and his soldiers to follow Villa's raiders into Mexico. The Mexican government initially gave its blessing to American efforts to capture Villa, but by June 1916, however, the Mexican government was requesting that the United States withdraw its forces. Baker refused to recall the troops, and on 21 June the Mexican army and Pershing's troops clashed in northern Mexico. U.S. troops finally left Mexico in early 1917.

Mobilizing for War. It was the Great War in Europe, however, that defined Baker's tenure as secretary. A pacifist, Baker was slow to build up the nation's military, but once war was declared he oversaw the institution of the draft and an increase of military personnel from 95,000 to 4 million. Baker received a great deal of criticism for the bureaucratic and logistical inefficiencies in the War Department, and in late 1917 a congressional investigation into his handling of the war blamed him directly for many of the problems of the mobilization. By 1918, however, with many of the supply and recruitment problems solved by Baker's reorganization of the War Department, words of praise began to outnumber criticisms. During a year of intense fighting U.S. military reinforcements to the Allied lines on the Western Front turned the tide of the war. By the time the armistice was signed in November

1918, Baker was being praised for his organizational abilities.

Later Life. With the election of Republican Warren G. Harding to the presidency in 1920, Baker returned to the practice of law in Cleveland. During the 1920s he continued unsuccessfully to advocate U.S. membership in the League of Nations. In 1928 President Calvin Coolidge appointed Baker to the Permanent Court of Arbitration at The Hague. In 1932 his name was mentioned as a possible Democratic presidential nominee. He died on Christmas Day 1937.

Sources:

Daniel R. Beaver, *Newton D. Baker and the American War Effort, 1917–1919* (Lincoln: University of Nebraska Press, 1966);

C. H. Cramer, *Newton D. Baker* (Cleveland: World, 1961);

Frederick Palmer, *Newton D. Baker, America at War* (New York: Dodd, Mead, 1931).

EDWARD M. HOUSE

1858-1938

PRESIDENTIAL ADVISER, 1913-1921

Foreign-Policy Adviser. Few men cast a longer shadow in the corridors of power in Washington during the 1910s than Edward Mandell House, who served as President Woodrow Wilson's adviser on European affairs in the years leading up to and during World War I.

Background. Born in Houston, Texas, on 26 July 1858, House entered Cornell University in 1877, leaving before graduation to manage the cotton plantations he had inherited on the death of his father. After he sold the cotton plantations a decade later, he was able to live in financial independence for the rest of his life.

Entry into Politics. In 1892, while living in Austin, House successfully managed the gubernatorial reelection campaign of James S. Hogg, who appointed House to his staff and made him an honorary "Colonel" — a title House retained for the rest of his life. House withdrew from politics in 1902, but he returned for the 1912 presidential election. Working vigorously in support of Woodrow Wilson, House was instrumental in getting William Jennings Bryan to back Wilson's candidacy. During Wilson's two terms as president, House was the president's most intimate adviser, initially helping Wilson choose his cabinet and subsequently acting as Wilson's de facto secretary of state and "silent partner" in the White House.

On the World Stage. While on a summer visit to Europe in 1913, House engaged in foreign policy talks on a range of issues with British Foreign Secretary Sir Edward Grey. During the following spring and early summer House visited London, Paris, and Berlin in an effort to mitigate rising tensions in Europe. After the assassination of Archduke Francis Ferdinand at Sarajevo in June 1914 sparked the outbreak of war, in late July. House acted as Wilson's special emissary to Europe in 1915 and 1916, conducting secret negotiations with the governments of Germany, France, and England in an unsuccessful effort to win a "peace without victory." After the United States entered the war in 1917, House was appointed head of an American mission to Great Britain and France, and he headed the American delegation to the Interallied Conference in December 1917.

Planning the Peace. House was also responsible for gathering together "The Inquiry," the group of intellectuals, foreign-policy experts, social scientists, and politicians that collected facts and drafted policy agendas for the end of the war. In spring 1918 House, at Wilson's behest, drew up the lineaments of a "covenant" for the future League of Nations, which Wilson appears to have used in his subsequent formulations. In October 1918, as the war effort of the Central Powers was collapsing and Germany sought peace negotiations, Wilson chose House to represent the United States at the interallied meetings where the Allied response to the Germans was devised. At these meetings House insisted that Wilson's Fourteen Points be the cornerstone for the peace. These points generated acrimonious debate among the Allies, but House's persistence — and his threats that the United States would make a separate peace with Germany — finally convinced the Allies to adopt the Fourteen Points as a basis for negotiations.

Versailles and the Aftermath. House accompanied Wilson, Secretary of State Robert Lansing, and a large group of U.S. scholars and politicians to the peace talks in Paris, where he continued to be Wilson's closest confidant, taking the president's place at the negotiations when he was absent. During the intense negotiations over the terms of the Treaty of Versailles, however, relations between House and Wilson became strained, largely because of House's willingness to take a more conciliatory position toward the Allies than President Wilson. While Wilson was preparing to return to the United States to promote the Treaty of Versailles and the League of Nations, House — who remained behind in Europe to continue working on peace initiatives — urged the president to seek compromise with Senate Republicans. Though it remains unclear precisely why, the close friendship between Wilson and House ended abruptly on 28 June 1919, and the two men were never to meet again. In 1921 House and Charles Seymour edited *What Really Happened at Paris*, and a few years later some of House's papers were collected in *The Intimate Papers of Colonel House* (1926–1928). House retired from the political scene after his break with Wilson, but he kept up contacts with many European leaders. In the 1932 election Franklin D. Roosevelt consulted House, but House did not contribute to the development of Roosevelt's New Deal.

Sources:

Arthur S. Link, *Woodrow Wilson and the Progressive Era, 1910–1917* (New York: Harper & Row, 1954);

Charles Seymour, ed., *The Intimate Papers of Colonel House Arranged as a Narrative*, 4 volumes (Boston: Houghton Mifflin, 1926–1928).

FRANCES KELLOR

1873-1952

PROGRESSIVE PARTY LEADER

Social Reformer. A social scientist who believed that government was the most effective vehicle for bringing about social reform, Frances Kellor played an important role in Theodore Roosevelt's 1912 presidential campaign. Her career in the 1910s illustrates the new political influence that educated women could exert through the application of their expertise on a range of social issues.

Early Achievements. Born in Columbus, Ohio, on 20 October 1873, Frances Alice Kellor was raised by her mother, Mary Sprau Kellor, in a single-parent household. When Frances Kellor was two, her mother took her two daughters to live in the small town of Coldwater, Michigan, where she supported her two children by working as a housekeeper and washerwoman. Kellor later listed her pastor at the First Presbyterian Church as one of the people who motivated her involvement in social reform. After earning a law degree from Cornell University in 1897, Kellor enrolled at the University of Chicago to study sociology part-time. There she studied aspects of unemployment and crime, arguing in her first book, *Experimental Sociology* (1901), that the origins of crime were to be located in disadvantaged childhoods, low levels of education, and unemployment and asserting the importance of reforming criminals in prisons. In 1900 she traveled in the southern states to study the living and working conditions of African Americans and subsequently published a series of articles recommending improvements in public schooling and the establishment of vocational-training schools, employment bureaus, and labor unions. In 1902 Kellor began studying women's employment bureaus in the urban North. The result of her research was *Out of Work: A Study of Employment Agencies* (1904), which concluded that the federal government ought to become involved in solving the systemic economic problems that led to unemployment. Her emphasis on government as the vehicle by which social reforms could best be achieved was the approach that many social-science-minded reformers took during the Progressive Era.

Municipal Reform. In 1904 Kellor became general director of the Inter-Municipal Committee on Household Research, and the following year she moved to New York City to live with Mary Dreier, head of the organization's legislative committee, which prepared legislative bills on child labor, tenement-house law, and employment agencies. Kellor and Dreier lived together until Kellor's death in 1952. In 1906 Kellor was instrumental in organizing the National League for the Protection of Colored Women, which sought to educate African American women who had recently migrated to New York City and to assist those women in finding places to live and jobs. Kellor served as the first executive secretary of the organization. Appointed to the New York State Immigration Commission in 1908, Kellor joined the other commissioners in investigating urban immigrant living and working conditions, and — finding these conditions to be appallingly poor — they asserted the need for a state bureau to examine further into their problems. Accordingly, in 1910 Kellor was appointed head of the New York State Bureau of Industries and Immigration. Under Kellor's direction the bureau championed worker safety and educational services.

The Progressive Party. The Progressive Party of 1912 was an expression of the will to power of several groups in American society who agreed to work in coalition to further each of their goals. One of the two most important elements in the Progressive Party were social scientists. For years social scientists such as Kellor had been urging the legislation of social reform. Indeed, the Progressive Party platform adopted a plank on "social and industrial justice" that a group of social scientists had put forward at the annual National Convention of Charities and Corrections in June 1912. Kellor was head of the National Service Committee, the Progressive Party administrative board. During the 1912 presidential campaign she led the party's research and publicity committee, prepared campaign statements, and generated support for Roosevelt and the party among other social reformers. She was also instrumental in shaping Roosevelt's campaign agenda. According to historian John Higham, Frances Kellor "did more than anyone else to direct Roosevelt's growing reformist zeal toward the special plight of the urban immigrant."

New Interests. In the 1916 presidential campaign Kellor supported the candidacy of Republican Charles Evans Hughes. In the same year she also directed the National Americanization Committee, and following World War I she became an expert in international arbitration. She was a founding member of the American Arbitration Association in the mid 1920s and published *Arbitration in the New Industrial Society* in 1934.

Sources:

Ellen Fitzpatrick, *Endless Crusade: Women Social Scientists and Progressive Reform* (New York: Oxford Unversity Press, 1990);

John Louis Recchiuti, "The Origins of American Progressivism: New York's Social Science Community," dissertation, Columbia University, 1992.

ROBERT LANSING

1864-1928

SECRETARY OF STATE, 1915-1920

Wartime Cabinet Member. As secretary of state during World War I, Robert Lansing was overshadowed by President Woodrow Wilson, who conducted most important foreign-policy matters himself. As the German ambassador to the United States once commented, "Since Wilson decides *everything,* any interview with Lansing is a mere matter of form."

Background. Born in Watertown, New York, on 17 October 1864, Robert Lansing graduated from Amherst College in 1886. After studying law in his father's law office, he was admitted to the New York State bar in 1889 and became a junior partner in his father's firm in Watertown. In 1890 Lansing married Eleanor Foster, whose father became secretary of state for President Benjamin Harrison in 1892. Reaping the benefits of nepotism, Lansing was appointed associate counsel for the United States in international arbitration and served as counsel on many international arbitration cases over the next sixteen years. In 1907 he became a founding editor of the *American Journal of International Law.* During the opening months of World War I, Lansing worked as a lawyer in the Department of State, serving as acting secretary during Secretary of State William Jennings Bryan's frequent absences from Washington. When Bryan unexpectedly resigned in June 1915 during the *Lusitania* crisis, President Wilson appointed Lansing to the post.

In Wilson's Shadow. Unlike Bryan, who brought to his cabinet position considerable political skills and influence gained as a three-time nominee for the presidency, Lansing, as a career lawyer and diplomat, lacked an independent political base. President Wilson determined all important matters of state. He sent personal notes to foreign powers, conducted informal negotiations via his friend Edward M. House, and at the end of the war in 1918 personally traveled to Europe to conclude the peace. During his tenure in office, Secretary of State Lansing was often relegated to a secondary role in U.S. foreign policy. In November 1917 Lansing and Viscount Ishii

Kikujiro of Japan concluded the Lansing-Ishii Agreement, in which the United States recognized Japanese interests in China, while reaffirming the Open Door policy. During the war Lansing handled protests to the British government over its blacklisting of some U.S. firms, its censorship of U.S. overseas mail, and other issues relating to the British blockade. But the important negotiations with Germany over the sinking of the *Lusitania* and issues of unrestricted submarine warfare were handled by Wilson. Lansing was the official head of the U.S. delegation to the Paris Peace Conference in 1919, but it was soon clear to everyone that his position was only nominal — President Wilson himself was running the American negotiations.

Controversy. Lansing lost Wilson's confidence because he did not view the Covenant of the League of Nations as crucial to the peace treaty. Senators who opposed the treaty used Lansing's opposition to the League of Nations as part of their successful strategy to defeat its ratification. After Wilson was incapacitated by a stroke, Lansing called several meetings of the cabinet to conduct routine business, and Wilson used Lansing's calling of these meetings as a pretext to call for his resignation. On 12 February 1920 Lansing complied with the president's request. Lansing continued the practice of international law in Washington, D.C., until his death on 30 October 1928, and he wrote three books about his experiences as secretary of state, among them *The Big Four and Others of the Peace Conference* (1921).

Sources:

Thomas H. Hartig, *Robert Lansing: an Interpretive Biography* (New York: Arno, 1982);

Robert Lansing, *War Memoirs of Robert Lansing, Secretary of State* (Indianapolis: Bobbs-Merrill, 1935);

Daniel Malloy Smith, *Robert Lansing and American Neutrality, 1914–1917,* University of California Publications in History, volume 59 (Berkeley: University of California Press, 1954).

HENRY CABOT LODGE

1850-1924

U.S. SENATOR, 1893-1924

A Conservative Republican. As a leader of the conservative wing of the Republican Party, Sen. Henry Cabot Lodge of Massachusetts fought the social and political reforms advocated by progressives in his own party and led the successful effort to defeat the Treaty of Versailles in the Senate.

Early Life. Born into a prominent Boston family on 12 May 1850, Henry Cabot Lodge graduated from Harvard College in 1871 and from Harvard Law School in 1874. In 1876 he received the first political science Ph.D. ever granted at Harvard, writing his thesis on Anglo-Saxon land law. From 1873 to 1876, with the backing of

Henry Adams, Lodge edited the *North American Review*. He was a lecturer on U.S. history at Harvard from 1876 to 1879, and for a time it seemed that he would pursue a career in academia. During the 1880s and 1890s he published several biographies and histories, including *Life and Letters of George Cabot* (1877), a biography of his mother's grandfather; *A Short History of the English Colonies in America* (1881); *Alexander Hamilton* (1882); *Daniel Webster* (1882); and *George Washington* (1888).

Entry into Politics. In 1879 Lodge was elected to the Massachusetts House of Representatives on the Republican Party ticket and served there until 1881. In 1883 he managed the Massachusetts Republican Party with great success, and in 1886 he was rewarded for his party loyalty with a nomination for the U.S. House of Representatives. Lodge won the election over his Democratic opponent by a narrow margin in 1886, but his political acumen served him well, and he was reelected to the seat twice with larger majorities each time. Congressman Lodge established himself as an eloquent spokesman for Republican Party interests, championing the protective tariff, the Sherman Antitrust Act of 1890, civil-service reform, and the rights of African Americans to vote.

Senate Career. In 1893 the Massachusetts legislature elected Lodge to the U.S. Senate, a position which he held until his death more than thirty years later. In the Senate Lodge was a proponent of the Spanish-American War, the annexation of Hawaii and the Philippines, the building of the Panama Canal, and the Pure Food and Drug Act of 1906. He was a protectionist on the tariff issue, supported the gold standard, and advocated a strong national defense by supporting increased expenditures for the army and navy. During the 1910s he promoted immigration restriction, was a supporter of William Howard Taft during the 1912 presidential election, and urged preparedness and, along with Theodore Roosevelt, early entry in World War I on the side of the Allies. He was chairman of the Republican National Conventions in 1900, 1908, and 1920 — contributing to party victories in each of these elections. A conservative Republican, Lodge opposed the direct election of senators and woman suffrage, and he voted against the Eighteenth Amendment (Prohibition). But it was his principled and partisan stance against the Treaty of Versailles and the League of Nations at the end of World War I that brought him his greatest notoriety.

The Treaty of Versailles and the League of Nations. Lodge — who became Senate majority leader and chairman of the powerful Senate Foreign Relations Committee after the 1918 elections gave the Republicans majorities in both houses of Congress — had long believed that the United States should master its own fate in international politics and should avoid entangling alliances. Thus, he protested that the treaty Wilson negotiated in Paris would place limits on U.S. sovereignty and involve the nation in exactly the sort of alliances that he believed it should avoid. In March 1919 Lodge led thirty-six Republican senators in signing a resolution objecting to Wilson's peace plan. Wilson, who had angered prominent Republicans by excluding them from the group of intellectuals and politicians he had taken with him to Paris and refusing to consult with Lodge and other Republican senators during the negotiations, now — as required under the Constitution — had to submit his treaty to a Senate controlled by the Republicans. Lodge was adamant that his support for the treaty would come only if specific limits to protect U.S. interests were written into it. Speaking from the floor of the Senate, he called for harsh reparations against Germany. As chairman of the Foreign Relations Committee, Lodge appended a series of amendments, or reservations, to the treaty Wilson had submitted. Enraged by Lodge's opposition, Wilson instructed Senate Democrats to defeat Lodge's initiative, but when the Senate voted on both Lodge's and Wilson's versions of the treaty in November, both versions were defeated, in effect spelling victory for Lodge. Despite attempts at compromise, the Treaty of Versailles and the League of Nations were never ratified by the U.S. Senate. It was not until 1921 that the United States formally signed a separate peace agreement with Germany.

Final Years. Lodge actively supported Warren G. Harding's successful presidential bid in 1920 and was a delegate to the Washington Disarmament Conference in 1921. During the final years of his life he also opposed U.S. participation in the World Court.

Source:
John A. Garraty, *Henry Cabot Lodge, A Biography* (New York: Knopf, 1953).

JOHN J. PERSHING

1860-1948

GENERAL, U.S. ARMY, 1906-1924

AEF Commander. Already well known for his masterful command of troops in Mexico in 1916, Gen. John J. Pershing led American troops in Europe during World War I, tipping the scales in favor of the Allies at a critical point in the war and thus ensuring their victory.

Early Life and Career. Born in Linn County, Missouri, on 13 September 1860, John Joseph Pershing entered West Point in 1882. During his final year he was appointed senior cadet captain and became president of his class, graduating thirtieth in his class in 1886. He served as a cavalry officer in New Mexico during campaigns against Apache chief Geronimo's warriors in 1886 and in South Dakota during skirmishes at Wounded Knee Creek against the Sioux in 1890 and 1891. In 1891–1895 he taught military tactics at the University of Nebraska, where he took a law degree in 1893. In 1897–1898 he taught at West Point, where the cadets nicknamed him "Black Jack" Pershing because of his strict disciplinary approach. He fought in Cuba during the Spanish-American War of 1898, distinguishing himself on the field of battle. His colonel, T. A. Baldwin, said of Pershing that he was "the coolest man under fire I ever saw." From 1899 to 1903 and again from 1906 to 1913 Pershing served in the Philippines, where he headed American efforts to end resistance to American domination of the country by subjugating the Moros, a force of Muslim Filipinos on Mindanao Island. In 1903 he returned to the United States for service with the Army General Staff and attended the Army War College in 1904 and 1905. In February 1905 he married Frances Warren, daughter of Sen. Francis Warren of Wyoming, a member of the Senate Committee on Military Affairs. Pershing's new political connections helped him to secure an assignment as military attaché in Japan during the Russo-Japanese War. President Theodore Roosevelt promoted Pershing to brigadier general in 1906. Pershing was tested by personal tragedy in August 1915, when a fire in the Pershings' home at the Presidio in San Francisco claimed the lives of his wife and two of his three children.

Mexico. Following Francisco "Pancho" Villa's raid across the U.S.-Mexican border in March 1916, Pershing was placed in command of the punitive expedition that pursued Villa in Mexico from 16 March 1916 until 6 February 1917. Though Pershing and his soldiers failed to capture Villa, their relentless pursuit weakened his power and ruined his chances to rule Mexico. Pershing's military competence and his capacity to carry out orders caught the attention of President Wilson, and when the United States declared war on the Central Powers in the spring of 1917, Pershing was called to Washington, D.C.

"Over There." In May he was appointed commander of the American Expeditionary Forces (AEF) in France and began overseeing the training of new military recruits and supplying them for battle. Under Pershing's command (he largely refused to allow U.S. forces to fall under the control of the British and the French) the troops of the AEF fought and died at the Marne, at Belleau Wood, at Château-Thierry, at Saint-Mihiel, and elsewhere on the Western Front. Pershing was determined to prove that his tactic of rapid movement and superior strength could break the stalemate of trench warfare, but at the Battle of Meuse-Argonne and elsewhere the lesson seemed to be that such maneuvers were ineffective against an opponent who was dug in and well-equipped. When swift movement was achieved, it often resulted in a loss of contact with supply lines. The main contribution of the AEF to the success of the Allies may have been that in a brutal war of attrition it contributed tens of thousands of fresh troops at a critical moment.

New Honors. In the aftermath of the victory in Europe, Pershing was appointed in September 1919 to the rank of general of the armies — the highest rank in the U.S. Army and one once held by George Washington. Pershing was army chief of staff from 1921 to 1924, when he retired from active service in 1924 at the age of sixty-four. In 1925 he served briefly as head of a commission seeking to resolve a boundary dispute between Peru and Chile, and during World War II he offered modest counsel to Gen. George Marshall. His *Final Report* (1919) and *My Experiences in the World War* (1931) tell the story of his war years, and the latter book won a Pulitzer Prize for history.

Sources:

Ruth Hill, *John Joseph Pershing* (Boston: Badger, 1919);

Richard O'Connor, *Black Jack Pershing* (Garden City, N.Y.: Doubleday, 1961);

Frederick Palmer, *John J. Pershing, General of the Armies: a Biography* (Harrisburg, Pa.: Military Service Publishing, 1948).

WOODROW WILSON

1856-1924

PRESIDENT OF THE UNITED STATES, 1913-1921

A Wartime President. At the outset of World War I President Woodrow Wilson believed that the United States had no stake in this conflict of imperialist European rivals and promised to keep America out of the war. Yet he ended up presiding over the first total mobilization of American troops for war and winning a Nobel Peace Prize for his role in negotiating the peace treaty that ended that war.

Early Life. Born in Staunton, Virginia, on 28 December 1856, Thomas Woodrow Wilson was named after his maternal grandfather, but in his twenties Wilson dropped Thomas from his name. The son of a Presbyterian minister, he grew up in Georgia, South Carolina, and North Carolina and later recalled that one of his earliest memories was of standing outside a gateway in Augusta, Georgia, at the age of four and "hearing someone pass and say that Mr. Lincoln was elected and there was to be war." As a child, Wilson had a learning disability that kept him from reading until age nine, but by seventeen he was possessed of an able intellect. He entered Davidson College in North Carolina in 1873, receiving high marks in all his subjects with the exception of mathematics. He left Davidson after a year, and in 1875 he enrolled at the College of New Jersey (soon thereafter renamed Princeton University), graduating thirty-eighth in the class of 1879. After studying law for two years at the University of Virginia and completing his studies on his own, he was admitted to the bar in 1882 and briefly practiced law in Georgia before entering graduate school at Johns Hopkins University in Baltimore, Maryland. He completed a Ph.D. in political science there in 1886. (He is the only president to have earned a doctorate.) In 1885, the year he married Ellen Axson, he published his highly regarded *Congressional Government,* the first of seven books on political science and history that he published during his lifetime. After teaching at Bryn Mawr College, near Philadelphia, and at Wesleyan University in Middletown, Connecticut (where for a brief time he coached the football team), he joined the Princeton faculty in 1890. Twelve years later the much-lauded professor of political science and jurisprudence became president of the university. Wilson labored to improve academic life at Princeton, but his efforts to dismantle the elitist eating clubs at the core of school social life and his proposal to restructure the graduate program alienated some alumni and trustees. Wilson resigned in October 1910, having agreed the previous spring to run for the governorship of New Jersey on the Democratic Party ticket.

Governor of New Jersey. Wilson won the general election in November 1910, and during his two years in office he proved to be a moderate reformer. His administration supported enactment of legislation regulating utilities, and he reduced the power of New Jersey political bosses. He championed legislation requiring candidates to file financial statements, pressed for voting reforms (including the direct primary for all elected offices), and instituted the first New Jersey workers' compensation law.

President of the United States. Following a determined fight within Democratic Party ranks, Wilson was nominated for the presidency in 1912. With the Republican Party vote divided between incumbent William Howard Taft and Progressive Party candidate Theodore Roosevelt, Wilson won the election by a landslide in the electoral college though he had garnered only a plurality of the popular vote. During his first term as president, Wilson carried out many of the promises of his "New Freedom" campaign policy agenda, sponsoring tariff reduction, increased regulation of business competition, and expanded federal aid to agriculture and education. In fact, Wilson proved one of the most effective legislative leaders in American presidential history, with a record of accomplishments rivaled only by those of Franklin Delano Roosevelt and Lyndon B. Johnson.

War and Peace. In foreign affairs Wilson's administration lay the groundwork for home rule in the Philippines and Puerto Rico, came to the brink of war with Mexico, and negotiated improved relations with Japan and China. Beginning in 1914, the war in Europe was the president's major concern. Regarding the war as the result of imperialistic European rivalries, Wilson believed that the United States should remain neutral. In the opening years of the war the president sent his trusted adviser and confidant, Edward M. House, to the capitals of the belligerents in hopes of mediating a settlement. When these efforts failed and when it was clear that the Allies were in desperate trouble on the Western Front in 1917, Wilson, using the provocation of German submarine warfare against U.S. shipping as a reason for his change of attitude, asked Congress to declare war on Germany. After U.S. troops had proved to be the deciding factor in winning the war, Wilson traveled with the U.S. delegation to Paris and headed the talks on the American side. His Fourteen Points and proposal for a League of Nations were central to the peace negotiations. The Republican-controlled Senate, however, refused to ratify the Treaty of Versailles and to sanction the League of Nations covenant. Wilson began a nationwide tour to promote the treaty and league directly to the people of the nation, but he was forced to cut the trip short after becoming ill on 25 September, and on 2 October he suffered a massive stroke, which paralyzed his left side and caused severe brain damage. Wilson's doctors and his second wife, Edith Bolling Galt Wilson (whom he had married in late 1915, a year and a half after the death of his first wife), restricted access to the president.

The President's Health Declines. For several months Edith Wilson was the de facto acting president. As she wrote later, "I studied every paper sent from the different Secretaries or Senators and tried to digest and present in tabloid form the things that, despite my vigilance, had to go to the President. I, myself never made a single decision regarding the disposition of public affairs. The only decision that was mine was what was important and what was not, and the *very* important decision of when to present matters to my husband." In 1919 Wilson was awarded the Nobel Peace Prize for his efforts at the Versailles treaty negotiations. He did not seek reelection in 1920, and after the expiration of his term in 1921 he lived with his wife in retirement in Washington, D.C., until his death on 3 February 1924.

Sources:

Kendrick A. Clements, *The Presidency of Woodrow Wilson* (Lawrence: University of Kansas Press, 1992);

Arthur S. Link, *Woodrow Wilson* (Chicago: Quadrangle Books, 1972);

Gene Smith, *When the Cheering Stopped: The Last Years of Woodrow Wilson* (New York: Morrow, 1964);

Arthur Walworth, *Wilson and His Peacemakers: American Diplomacy at the Paris Peace Conference* (New York: Norton, 1986).

PEOPLE IN THE NEWS

In January 1911 Sen. **Jonathan Bourne** of Oregon became the first president of the National Progressive Republican League. In 1907 he had been the first U.S. senator to be elected by popular vote. He lost his reelection bid in 1912.

On 24 April 1913 Secretary of State **William Jennings Bryan** called for a permanent court of arbitration to avoid future wars.

In 1915 **Carrie Chapman Catt** was elected president of the National American Woman Suffrage Association (NAWSA), a position she had previously held from 1900 to 1904. Her leadership skills helped to bring about the passage of the Nineteenth Amendment.

In September 1919 Gov. **Calvin Coolidge** of Massachusetts fired striking police officers in Boston. Coolidge's assertion that "no one has the right to strike against the public safety" made the future president a national political figure.

Following the U.S. declaration of war in April 1917, President Woodrow Wilson appointed **Herbert Hoover** head of the Food Administration. Hoover's efficient and compassionate efforts in supplying surplus American food to Europe brought the future president his first public recognition.

On 5 August 1912 **Hiram W. Johnson** of California was nominated for vice president on the Progressive Party ticket. Johnson, who had been elected governor of California in 1910, served in that capacity until 1916, when he was elected to the U.S. Senate, where he remained until his death in 1945.

In 1914 **Walter Lippmann,** author of *A Preface to Politics* (1913) and *Drift and Mastery* (1914), helped to found *The New Republic*. His incisive political writing made Lippmann the nation's leading American commentator on public affairs for more than fifty years.

On 25 June 1910 Congress passed the White Slave Traffic Act, introduced by Rep. **James R. Mann,** a conservative from Chicago who served in the U.S. House of Representatives from 1896 to 1922. He also cosponsored the Mann-Elkins Act of 1910.

On 2 April 1917 **Jeannette Rankin** became the first woman elected in the U.S. House of Representatives. Having helped to win passage of woman suffrage in Montana in 1914, she was elected to Congress on a woman's rights platform. She also supported Prohibition, tariff revision, and preparedness for war. In spring 1917 she was one of the few in Congress who voted against the declaration of war. Defeated in her bid for reelection in 1918, she was elected to the House of Representatives again in 1940 and cast the sole vote against U.S. entry into World War II.

In 1912 Sen. **Elihu Root** won the Nobel Peace Prize for various efforts in world affairs. Root served as secretary of war from 1899 to 1903 and secretary of state from 1905 to 1909. From 1909 to 1915 he was a U.S. senator from New York.

DEATHS

Nelson W. Aldrich, 73, conservative Republican senator from Rhode Island (1881–1911), coauthor of the Payne-Aldrich Tariff of 1909, and author of the "Aldrich Plan," which laid the groundwork for the Federal Reserve Act of 1913, 16 April 1915.

Randolph Bourne, 32, radical political writer best known for his antiwar essays published in *The Seven Arts* magazine, 22 December 1918.

William E. Chandler, 81, secretary of the navy (1882–1885), secretary of the Republican National Committee (1868, 1872), and Republican senator from New Hampshire (1889–1901), 30 November 1917.

Daniel De Leon, 61, leader of the Socialist Labor Party and a founder of the Industrial Workers of the World, 11 May 1914.

Stephen B. Elkins, 69, railroad and mining magnate, Republican senator from West Virginia (1895–1911), and author of the Elkins Act of 1903, which forbade railroads from offering rebates to shippers, 4 January 1911.

Charles W. Fairbanks, 66, vice president of the United States (1905–1909) under Theodore Roosevelt, 4 June 1918.

Joseph Benson Foraker, 70, conservative Republican senator from Ohio (1897–1909), 10 May 1917.

William J. Gaynor, 65, Democratic mayor of New York City (1910–1913), 12 September 1913.

Washington Gladden, 82, leader in the Social Gospel movement and supporter of the Progressive Party in 1912, 2 July 1918.

John Marshall Harlan, 78, associate justice of the Supreme Court (1877–1911), remembered for his dissent in *Plessy* v. *Ferguson,* 14 October 1911.

Tom L. Johnson, 56, Democratic representative from Ohio (1891–1895) and progressive mayor of Cleveland (1901–1909), 10 April 1911.

Seth Low, 66, reformist Republican mayor of Brooklyn, New York (1882–1885), and New York City (1902–1905) and president of Columbia University (1890–1901), 17 September 1916.

Alfred Thayer Mahan, 74, naval captain, imperialist, and author of *The Influence of Sea Power upon History* (1890), 1 December 1914.

Alexander J. McKelway, 51, leading figure on the National Child Labor Committee (1904–1918), Washington lobbyist (1910–1918), a founder of the Southern Sociological Congress (1912), and framer of twenty social welfare planks in the 1916 Democratic platform, 16 April, 1918.

George Meyer, 59, ambassador to Italy (1900) and Russia (1905), postmaster general (1907), and secretary of the navy (1909–1913), 9 March 1918.

John Purroy Mitchel, 41, Democratic mayor of New York City (1914–1917), 6 July 1918.

John Mitchell, 49, president of the United Mine Workers (1898–1908), New York Workmen's Compensation Commissioner (1914), and chairman of the New York State Industrial Commission (1915–1919), 19 September 1919.

Edgar Gardner Murphy, 43, organizer of the Southern Society to study race relations (1900) and founder of the National Child Labor Committee, 23 June 1913.

William Rockhill Nelson, 74, journalist, editor, and political activist who helped found the Progressive Party in 1912, 13 April 1915.

Francis G. Newlands, 69, progressive representative (1893–1901) and senator (1903–1917) from Nevada, 24 December 1917.

Harrison Gray Otis, 80, conservative Republican editor and political activist, owner of the *Los Angeles Times* (1886–1917), 30 July 1917.

Walter Hines Page, 63, journalist and U.S. ambassador to Great Britain (1913–1918) who urged U.S. intervention in World War I, 21 December 1918.

Walter Rauschenbusch, 56, progressive/socialistic leader of the Social Gospel movement, 25 July 1918.

Theodore Roosevelt, 60, Republican governor of New York (1899–1900), vice president of the United States (1901), and president of the United States (1901–1909), 6 January 1919.

Anna Howard Shaw, 72, physician, Methodist minister, president of the National American Woman Suffrage Association (1904–1915), and head of the Woman's Committee of the Council of National Defense (1917–1919), 2 July 1919.

Willard D. Straight, 38, acting chief of the Division of Far Eastern Affairs in the U.S. State Department (1908–1909), 2 December 1918.

Booker T. Washington, 50, African American political leader, founder of Tuskegee Institute (1881), and author of *Up From Slavery* (1901), 14 November 1915.

Walter E. Weyl, 46, progressive journalist and economist, author of *The New Democracy* (1912), and a founder and editor of *The New Republic* (1914), 9 November 1919.

PUBLICATIONS

John Bertram Andrews, *Labor Problems and Labor Legislation* (New York: American Association for Labor Legislation, 1919);

Charles A. Beard, *American City Government: A Survey of Newer Tendencies* (New York: Century, 1912);

Beard, *American Government and Politics* (New York: Macmillan, 1914);

Beard, *An Economic Interpretation of the Constitution of the United States* (New York: Macmillan, 1913);

Beard and Mary Ritter Beard, *American Citizenship* (New York: Macmillan, 1914);

Henry Bruere, *The New City Government: A Discussion of Municipal Administration Based on a Survey of the Ten Commission Governed Cities* (New York: Appleton, 1916);

Frederick A. Cleveland, *Organized Democracy* (New York: Longmans, Green, 1913);

Benjamin Parke DeWitt, *The Progressive Movement: A Non-Partisan, Comprehensive Discussion of Current Tendencies in American Politics* (New York: Macmillan, 1915);

Rheta Louise Childe Dorr, *What Eight Million Women Want* (Boston: Small, Maynard, 1910);

Samuel John Duncan-Clark, *The Progressive Movement: Its Principles and Its Programme* (Boston: Small, Maynard, 1913);

Pauline Goldmark, Josephine Goldmark, and Florence Kelley, *The Truth About Wage-Earning Women and the State* (Concord, N.H.: Concord Equal Suffrage Association, 1912);

Frank Johnson Goodnow, *Social Reform and the Constitution* (New York: Macmillan, 1911);

Paul Underwood Kellogg, ed., *The Pittsburgh Survey*, 6 volumes (New York: Charities Publication Committee, 1909–1914);

Edmond Kelly, *Twentieth Century Socialism: What It Is Not: What It Is: How It May Come* (New York: Longmans, Green, 1910);

Robert M. La Follette, *La Follette's Autobiography: A Personal Narrative of Political Experiences* (Madison, Wis.: Robert M. La Follette Company, 1913);

Walter Lippmann, *Drift and Mastery* (New York: Mitchell Kennerley, 1914);

Lippmann, *A Preface to Politics* (New York & London: Mitchell Kennerley, 1913);

Charles McCarthy, *The Wisconsin Idea* (New York: Macmillan, 1912);

John J. Pershing, *Final Report of General John J. Pershing, Commander-in-Chief of the American Expeditionary Forces* (Washington, D.C.: U.S. Government Printing Office, 1919);

John Reed, *Ten Days that Shook the World* (New York: Boni & Liveright, 1919);

Theodore Roosevelt, *The New Nationalism* (New York: Outlook, 1910);

I. M. Rubinow, *Social Insurance: With Special Reference to American Conditions* (New York: Holt, 1913);

Thorstein Veblen, *The Place of Science in Modern Civilization and Other Essays* (New York: Huebsch, 1919);

Lillian Wald, *The House on Henry Street* (New York: Holt, 1915);

Gustavus A. Weber, *Organized Efforts for the Improvement of Methods of Administration in the United States* (New York: Appleton, 1919);

Walter E. Weyl, *The New Democracy* (New York: Macmillan, 1912);

Delos F. Wilcox, *Municipal Franchises*, 2 volumes (New York: McGraw-Hill, 1910, 1911);

Woodrow Wilson, *The New Freedom* (New York: Doubleday, Page, 1913).

LAW AND JUSTICE

by G. JACK BENGE

CONTENTS

Sidebars and tables are listed in italics.

1910

5 Mar.   The Chicago Vice Commission is created to combat the prostitution and gambling believed to have reached epidemic proportions because of a lack of vigorous law enforcement.

26 Mar.   The United States amends the Immigration Act of 1907 to bar paupers, criminals, anarchists, and diseased persons from entering the country.

1 May   The National Association for the Advancement of Colored People (NAACP) is founded and six months later begins to publish its journal, *The Crisis*, under the editorship of W. E. B. Du Bois.

2 May   Charles Evans Hughes, former governor of New York, is nominated to the U.S. Supreme Court. He serves on the High Court until 1916 when he is chosen to be the Republican Party's presidential candidate.

16 May   The U.S. Bureau of Mines is established as part of the Department of the Interior. Dr. Joseph Austin Holmes is selected to be its first director.

18 June   The Mann-Elkins Act is passed by Congress. Named after Representatives Stephen B. Elkins of West Virginia and James R. Mann of Illinois, the act increases the authority of the Interstate Commerce Commission to enforce its rulings respecting rate charges and extends the commission's jurisdiction to include telegraph and telephone companies.

24 June   Congress passes a law requiring all American passenger ships to carry radio equipment for reasons of safety.

25 June   The Mann Act, which prohibits the interstate transportation of women for immoral purposes, is passed by Congress.

1 Sept.   New York State enacts one of the first comprehensive sets of traffic and motor vehicle laws. Known as the Callan Automobile Law, the statute requires the registration of all motorcars and establishes regulations controlling speed and setting forth rules of the road as well as penalties for violations.

7 Sept.   In a decision that angers many Canadian fishermen, the International Court of Arbitration extends American fishing rights into the waters off the coast of Newfoundland.

1 Oct.   An explosion destroys a portion of the *Los Angeles Times* building, killing twenty-one people. The publisher of the newspaper blames labor radicals who have been attempting to unionize the newspaper's employees. Union organizers James and John McNamara are arrested and charged with the crime.

8 Nov.   Victor Berger becomes the first member of the Socialist Party of America to win a seat in Congress when he is elected from Wisconsin to the House of Representatives.

10 Dec.   Edward D. White, a member of the Confederate army during the Civil War, former senator from Louisiana, and a Supreme Court associate justice, is nominated by President William Howard Taft to the post of chief justice.

12 Dec.   Willis Van Devanter is nominated by President Taft to succeed former associate justice Edward White on the Supreme Court. His nomination is confirmed by the Senate on 15 December.

1911

18 Jan. Bill Miner robs the Southern Railroad Express of $3,500 near White Sulphur Springs, Georgia. The famous train robber is tracked down and at sixty-six years of age is sentenced for life to the Georgia State Penitentiary, where he dies in 1913.

24 Jan. Judge Kenesaw Mountain Landis begins an investigation of the beef trust in Chicago. The investigation was initiated by complaints of rising meat prices and the abusive business practices of the National Packing Company, among others.

25 Mar. A fire that lasts only half an hour traps 850 people in a New York City garment district factory. Fire and smoke kill 146 employees, mostly women, are killed by the fire and smoke. An angry public demands action, a reaction that results in a revision of the city's building code and the state's labor laws.

11 Apr. The owners of the Triangle Shirtwaist Company are indicted on charges of manslaughter stemming from the deaths of 146 of their employees who were trapped in the company's factory by a raging fire.

1 May In the case of *United States* v. *Grimaud,* the U.S. Supreme Court rules that the federal government, not the states, controls the nation's great forest preserves.

11 June Under pressure brought by the Justice Department, the directors of the American Tobacco Company, which controls 80 percent of the cigarette production in the nation, agree to divide their company into fourteen smaller and independent business entities.

22 Aug. A bill granting Arizona statehood is vetoed by President William Howard Taft because its proposed constitution permits the recall of judges by popular election, a measure the president considers a threat to the traditional independence of the judiciary.

1912

6 Jan. New Mexico is admitted into the Union.

12 Jan. The textile mills of Lawrence, Massachusetts, are closed by a strike that lasts two months. The resulting violence captures the nation's attention and brings the fledgling Industrial Workers of the World to prominence.

14 Feb. By act of Congress, Arizona, after eliminating the provision for the popular election of judges from its proposed constitution, is admitted to the Union and becomes the forty-eighth state.

19 Feb. Mahlon Pitney is appointed by President William Howard Taft to fill a vacancy on the Supreme Court. The appointment of the former New Jersey Supreme Court justice (1901–1908) is confirmed by the U.S. Senate on 13 March.

14 Mar. The Department of Justice announces the beginning of an investigation into the merger of the Southern Pacific and Union Pacific railroads, a combination that is triggered by the Union Pacific's purchase of 46 percent of the stock issued by its rival, the Southern Pacific.

14 Apr. The *Titanic* strikes an iceberg and sinks within hours. The loss of the passenger liner results in an investigation in New York that receives international attention.

1 May In reaction to the sinking of the *Titanic,* federal inspectors issue new regulations requiring ships under their jurisdiction to carry enough lifeboats to accommodate all crew and passengers aboard.

4 June　　Massachusetts enacts the nation's first minimum wage law.

19 June　　Congress passes a law extending the eight-hour day to all workers who are employed by companies receiving federal contracts.

15 July　　Gambler and police informant Herman "Beansie" Rosenthal is shot to death by four assassins as he leaves New York City's Cafe Metropole. Jack Rose later informs police that Rosenthal was ordered to be killed by New York City Police Lt. Charles Becker, head of a graft and kickback ring protecting gambling dens in Manhattan, because Rosenthal refused to pay for police protection. Rose also names the killers, who are quickly caught, convicted, and sentenced to the electric chair. Becker is executed in Sing Sing prison on 7 July 1915.

24 Aug.　　President William Howard Taft signs the Panama Canal Act, authorizing rebates of canal tolls to American coastal ships. The act causes indignation in England and Europe, and the United States is accused of violating the Hay-Pauncefote Treaty of 1901. The law is repealed in 1914.

14 Oct.　　Theodore Roosevelt, the Progressive Party's candidate for president, is shot in the chest while campaigning in Milwaukee, Wisconsin. The bullet is deflected by a manuscript the former president had placed in his coat pocket.

1913

14 Feb.　　An immigration bill requiring literacy testing of all newly arriving immigrants is vetoed by President William Howard Taft.

25 Feb.　　The Sixteenth Amendment to the Constitution becomes effective on this date. Under the authority granted to it, Congress passes an act to impose a 1 to 6 percent tax on all personal income.

　　　　　　A silk workers' strike begins in Paterson, New Jersey. Under the direction of the Industrial Workers of the World, it meets vigorous opposition at the hands of the local authorities and is abandoned after five months.

1 Mar.　　The Webb-Kenyon Interstate Liquor Act is passed over President Taft's veto. The new law prohibits alcohol from being shipped into states where its sale is illegal and represents the first nationwide victory of the Anti-Saloon League.

4 Mar.　　The Department of Commerce and Labor is divided by Congress into two departments having cabinet status. At the same time, Congress passes an act establishing the U.S. Board of Mediation and Conciliation to arbitrate labor-management disputes.

19 May　　The Alien Land Holding Bill is signed into law by California governor Hiram W. Johnson, despite the protests of both President Wilson and the Japanese government. The bill excludes anyone of Japanese ancestry from owning land in California.

31 May　　The Seventeenth Amendment to the Constitution, which provides for the direct popular election of United States senators, becomes effective.

2 June　　The Department of Labor mediates its first strike settlement, resolving a dispute between railway clerks and the New York, New Haven, and Hartford Railroad.

1 July　　The first state minimum wage law takes effect in Massachusetts.

23 Dec. The Federal Reserve Act becomes law. The act establishes the Federal Reserve System, a centralized Federal Reserve Board, and a dozen regional banks. All national banks are required to join the system, and state banks are permitted to join if they wish. The board is authorized to issue currency and to control credit by raising or lowering the discount rate it charges member banks. The purpose of the act is to increase economic stability and make it impossible for speculators to destabilize the nation's economy.

1914

13 Jan. A continuing and increasingly bitter feud over airplane patents is settled by the U.S. Circuit Court of Appeals in favor of Wilbur and Orville Wright and against Glenn Curtiss, the brothers' chief competitor in the fledgling airplane industry.

20 Jan. Wisconsin's circuit court declares the state's marriage law, based on eugenic principles, unconstitutional.

13 Feb. The American Society of Composers, Authors, and Publishers (ASCAP) is organized to improve copyright laws and to protect its members from infringements upon their work.

24 Feb. The constitutionality of the Mann Act is upheld by the Supreme Court in the case of *Hoke* v. *United States*.

20 Apr. National Guardsmen and security forces employed by coal-mining companies shoot into the tents of mine workers near Ludlow, Colorado, killing three men, two women, and seven children as the violence escalates. The workers had been on strike since September of the previous year. Federal troops are eventually required to restore order.

8 May The Smith-Lever Act, providing for a system of agricultural extension work based on cooperation between the Department of Agriculture and the land-grant colleges, is passed. The program incorporates a new form of incentive, federal grants in aid, for colleges willing to become involved in providing the training envisioned by the act.

1 July New York State's Boylin Law takes effect. The law requires all persons dispensing opium, morphine, heroin, or other addictive drugs to keep records of their purchase and sale. It also requires that prescriptions containing any of the drugs identified in the statute include the names of the doctor, issuing druggist, and the patient. Mere possession of these drugs is made a misdemeanor, and court magistrates are given the authority to commit addicts to hospitals where they can receive medical treatment for their addictions.

19 Aug. James Clark McReynolds is nominated to succeed Associate Justice Horace Lurton on the Supreme Court. McReynolds previously had served as an assistant attorney general in charge of the Justice Department's antitrust division and was subsequently, in 1913, appointed to the post of attorney general by President Woodrow Wilson.

26 Sept. The Federal Trade Commission is established to prevent monopolies and to preserve competition and free commerce. The commission is expected to take the place of the Bureau of Corporations.

15 Oct.   The Clayton Antitrust Act, supplementing and strengthing the Sherman Antitrust Act, is enacted to extend the definition of illegal practices under the original act. The new act prohibits price discrimination, anticompetitive contracts, and interlocking directorships. The act also forbids the use of injunctions in labor disputes unless the issuance of an injunction is necessary to prevent irreparable injury to property. The act makes strikes, peaceful picketing, and boycotts legal under federal law.

1915

2 Jan.   Another bill requiring literacy tests for all immigrants is passed by the Senate. The bill is vetoed by President Woodrow Wilson on 28 January 1915.

25 Jan.   In the case of *Coppage* v. *Kansas* the Supreme Court rules unconstitutional a Kansas state law forbidding employers from requiring that the employees be nonunion.

28 Jan.   Congress establishes the U.S. Coast Guard by combining the Revenue Cutter Service, established in 1790, with the lifesaving service. The Coast Guard is placed under the authority of the Treasury Department except in times of war, a reorganization plan viewed as a major step in strengthening the country's Coastal Maritime Services and the Treasury Department's law-enforcement capabilities.

23 Feb.   The Nevada state legislature passes, and its governor signs, a bill that simplifies the state's procedure for divorce. The bill also reduces the state's residency requirement to six months.

15 May   The U.S. Supreme Court finds unconstitutional laws in the states of Oklahoma and Maryland that exempt some voters from the states' literacy requirements. This legislation was intended to permit whites to vote while disenfranchising African Americans. Such amendments usually exempted men who were entitled to vote before 1867 and their lineal descendants, and were known as grandfather clauses.

2 July   A bomb destroys the U.S. Senate's reception room. It was placed there by Erich Muenter, a German instructor at Cornell University who, the following day, shoots and wounds J. Pierpont Morgan in New York. Morgan's company represents the British government in the negotiation of wartime contracts. Muenter commits suicide on 6 July.

13 July   New York State's workmen's compensation law is ruled valid by the New York Court of Appeals. The law had become effective in May.

15 July   Evidence of German espionage in the United States is discovered when Secret Service agents come into possession of a portfolio belonging to Dr. Heinrich F. Albert. The contents reveal Albert to be the head of a German propaganda and espionage ring and implicate several German Americans, members of the German Embassy staff, and officials of a German American steamship line.

17 Aug.   Leo M. Frank, age twenty-nine, is lynched for the 26 April 1913 murder of Mary Phagan, age thirteen, in Atlanta, Georgia. Frank was the superintendent of a factory and was charged with the murder after the girl's body was found on the factory premises. In a sensational trial full of racial and anti-Semitic overtones, Frank was convicted largely on testimony by Jim Conley, the factory janitor. An enraged mob took Frank from a jail in Marietta, Georgia, and hanged him.

1 Nov.	The Arizona Anti-Alien Labor Law, which requires 80 percent of a firm's employees to be native-born, is ruled unconstitutional by the Supreme Court.
19 Nov.	Joe Hill, a composer of radical and labor songs and an organizer for the Industrial Workers of the World, is hanged for a murder to which there are no witnesses and for which there is no motive. President Woodrow Wilson, besieged by pleas for clemency, attempts unsuccessfully to save Hill from execution.

1916

•	Margaret Sanger, a well-known advocate of birth control, is charged with violating New York City's obscenity laws through the distribution of her book, *Family Limitation* (1914), and is found guilty for actions the court finds "contrary not only to the law of the state, but to the law of God."
24 Jan.	In the case of *Brushaber* v. *Union Pacific Railroad Company* the U.S. Supreme Court rules that the new federal income tax is constitutional.
28 Jan.	Louis D. Brandeis is nominated to the Supreme Court to succeed Associate Justice Joseph Lamar. The Senate confirms his appointment on 1 June after considerable debate.
28 Feb.	The Senate approves a treaty that makes the island of Haiti a U.S. protectorate for ten years.
29 Feb.	Child labor legislation in South Carolina raises the minimum age of children employable in the state's mills, factories, and mines from twelve to fourteen.
20 May	A bill authorizing motion picture censorship is vetoed by Gov. Charles S. Whitman of New York.
3 June	The National Defense Act is passed and authorizes the president to increase the size of the nation's standing army to 175,000 men.
11 July	The Shackleford Good Roads Act is signed by President Wilson. The act authorizes the federal government to turn over $5 million to the states for road-building programs.
16 July	John H. Clarke is nominated by President Wilson to become an associate justice of the Supreme Court. Clarke resigns from the Supreme Court in 1922 to promote American participation in the League of Nations.
17 July	The Federal Farm Loan Act is signed by the president. It establishes the Land Bank System to provide loans to farmers who need funds for maintenance or improvements to their farms and equipment.
22 July	A bombing in San Francisco during a preparedness parade kills ten people and wounds forty. Labor organizer Tom Mooney is sentenced to hang, and his alleged conspirator, Warren K. Billings, is sentenced to life imprisonment. President Wilson commutes Mooney's sentence to life imprisonment in 1918, but the case remains an international cause célèbre for many years.
4 Aug.	The United States and Denmark agree to the purchase of what will become known as the Virgin Islands for $25 million. The treaties signed on this date are ratified on 17 January 1917 by the U.S. Senate.
25 Aug.	By an act of Congress, the National Park Service is made a part of the Department of the Interior.

1 Sept. The Keating-Owen Child Labor Act, banning interstate commerce in products made by children younger than the age of fourteen, is passed by Congress. The act also prohibits children younger than sixteen from engaging in mine work, night work, and work in excess of eight hours a day.

3 Sept. The Adamson Act is signed by President Wilson. The act makes an eight-hour workday standard for most railroad workers. The bill had been passed hurriedly by both houses of Congress to stave off the nationwide railroad strike called for 4 September. The strike is narrowly averted, but the president is severely criticized and accused of playing politics during an election year.

16 Oct. The first birth control clinic in the United States is opened by Margaret Sanger, Fania Mindell, and Ethel Burne in Brooklyn, New York.

1917

- An antiprostitution drive in San Francisco attracts huge crowds to public meetings held throughout the month of January. In a conference with the Reverend Paul Smith, the most outspoken foe of vice in the city, three hundred prostitutes make a plea for toleration, explaining that they had been forced into a life of sin by poverty. When Smith publicly asks if they would take honest work at $8 to $10 per week, the women laugh derisively, losing whatever public sympathy they may have had. Within weeks the police close nearly two hundred houses of prostitution.

5 Feb. The Immigration Act is passed by Congress over President Wilson's veto. The law requires a literacy test for immigrants and bars admission to Asian laborers, except those from countries with special agreements or trade ties with the United States.

2 Mar. The Jones Act is passed, making the island of Puerto Rico a U.S. territory and granting U.S. citizenship to its inhabitants.

3 Mar. Congress approves the first Excess Profits Tax to help pay for increased military spending. It is a progressive tax, ranging from 20 to 60 percent on all corporate profit in excess of 7 to 9 percent of capital. The law is replaced on 3 October by passage of the Revenue Act of 1917.

8 Mar. The Senate adopts a cloture rule that permits a majority of its membership to terminate a floor debate. Each senator would be permitted to speak for one hour after the rule is invoked.

9 Mar. President Wilson announces that the legality of arming merchant vessels by presidential order is supported by the attorney general. The president declares that he will issue the order without further delay.

2 Apr. Jeannette Rankin, a Republican from Montana, becomes the first woman to be seated in the U.S. House of Representatives.

6 Apr. Congress passes a declaration of war against the Central Powers, following an address before a joint session of Congress by President Wilson four days earlier in which he had requested such a declaration.

14 Apr. The Committee on Public Information is created by executive order to control the censorship of news and propaganda releases. Journalist George Creel is appointed its first chairman.

18 May Congress passes the Selective Service Act, which authorizes conscription for the nation's armed services and requires all males between the ages of twenty-one and thirty to register for the draft.

15 June The Espionage Act is passed, making it a crime to obstruct recruitment, foster unrest in the armed services, or engage in other disloyal acts.

28 Aug. Ten suffragette picketers are arrested in front of the White House. Four are eventually sentenced to six months in prison. Picketing resumes in November and another forty demonstrators are arrested.

5 Sept. Federal agents, assisted by local police, raid the offices of the Industrial Workers of the World in twenty-four cities and seize the union's records while arresting ten of its leaders, including William Haywood, the organizer of the textile workers' strike in Lawrence, Massachusetts.

6 Nov. The New York State Constitution is amended to allow women to vote in all elections.

18 Dec. The Eighteenth Amendment to the Constitution, outlawing "the manufacture, sale, or transportation of intoxicating liquors," is passed by Congress and submitted to the states for ratification.

26 Dec. The railroads are taken over by the federal government through a presidential proclamation, an arrangement confirmed by the Railroad Control Act, passed into law on 21 March 1918.

1918

- Mississippi becomes the last state to pass a compulsory school attendance law.

7 Jan. The U.S. Supreme Court rules in the case of *Arver* v. *United States* that wartime conscription is constitutionally valid.

10 Jan. A Women's Suffrage Resolution calling for a constitutional amendment passes in the House of Representatives. Despite the president's support, it fails to pass in the Senate.

16 May The Sedition Act is passed by Congress, establishing penalties for those hindering the war effort by making false statements, obstructing enlistment, or impeding the production of war matériels; penalties are also established for disparaging the American form of government, the Constitution, the flag, etc. The act is signed into law by President Wilson five days later.

28 May The American Railroad Express Company is organized under federal supervision by a forced merger of the Adams, American, Wells Fargo, and Southern Express companies. This consolidation is sought by the government to expedite and improve the shipment of war-related materials.

31 May Secretary of War Newton D. Baker orders that conscientious objectors be granted unpaid leave from military service to work on farms.

3 June The Federal Child Labor Law of 1916 is declared unconstitutional by the Supreme Court in the case of *Hammer* v. *Dagenhart* on the ground that it violates rights reserved to the states under the Tenth Amendment. The Court also holds that Congress, in blocking interstate shipments of goods made by underaged children, exceeded its power to regulate interstate commerce.

25 July	Annette Adams begins her term in California as the first woman in the United States to serve as a district attorney.
28 July	The War Industries Board is established to mobilize industry and business in support of America's involvement in the First World War. Bernard Baruch is appointed its first chairman.
14 Sept.	Eugene V. Debs, four times the Socialist candidate for the presidency, is sentenced to ten years' imprisonment for violating the Espionage Act of 1917. Debs was arrested on 30 June 1918 for making allegedly seditious statements against military recruitment in Canton, Ohio. The sentence is commuted in 1921.
21 Nov.	The Wartime Prohibition Act, which is to become effective on 30 June 1919, is signed by President Wilson. The act bans the manufacture or sale of liquor except in instances in which the liquor is designated for exportation.

1919

29 Jan.	The Eighteenth Amendment to the Constitution, prohibiting the transportation and sale of alcoholic beverages, is ratified. It is the first amendment to have a time limit placed on ratification, seven years, and the only one subsequently repealed.
10 Mar.	The conviction of Eugene V. Debs, Socialist Party leader and presidential candidate, for violating the Espionage Act is upheld by the Supreme Court. Debs had received a ten-year prison sentence, which he begins on 13 April.
2 June	An anarchist places a bomb on the front steps of the home of Attorney General A. Mitchell Palmer in Washington, D.C., but the bomb explodes prematurely, killing the anarchist. Palmer, incensed, throws his support behind the notorious "red raids," which result in the arrests of thousands of dissenters across the country and the deportation of some five hundred people who were not American citizens.
4 June	Congress approves the Nineteenth Amendment to the Constitution, which grants the vote to women. The resolution is then presented to the states for ratification.
28–30 July	A seventeen-year-old black youth swims into waters reserved for whites off the Thirty-first Street Beach on Chicago's South Side. Tempers flare and the black youth, who was reportedly hit by stones thrown by whites, drowns. Hot weather and racial tensions, mounting for months as blacks move into traditionally white neighborhoods, fuel a race war that leaves twenty-two blacks and fourteen whites dead, and more than five hundred others wounded. Two days later, units of the state's militia move in to take control of the area, and peace is restored.
14 Aug.	The *Chicago Tribune*, after a much-reported trial, is found to have libeled Henry Ford when it called him an anarchist.
9 Sept.	The Boston City Police go on strike, with 1,117 out of 1,544 patrolmen refusing to report to work. The strike results in widespread looting, which forces Gov. Calvin Coolidge to deploy the state's National Guard throughout the city until replacements for the police can be hired. Coolidge's action catapults him into the national limelight.

28 Oct.   The National Prohibition Act, better known as the Volstead Act, is passed by Congress over President Wilson's veto. The act defines intoxicating liquor as any beverage containing at least 0.5 percent alcohol, and provides for enforcement of the provisions of the Eighteenth Amendment.

11 Nov.   Members of the Industrial Workers of the World in Idaho attempt to defend their union hall from attack by a mob that includes American Legionnaires and members of the Citizen's Protective League. Three of the legionnaires are killed, and the body of one of the Wobblies is found hanging from a tree. Many of the union's members are arrested and jailed.

19 Nov.   The Senate, by a vote of 55–39, refuses to ratify the Treaty of Versailles, making U.S. membership in the newly formed League of Nations all but impossible.

OVERVIEW

In the Throes of Change. The decade of the 1910s was not an especially formative period in American law; it was, however, a period that witnessed significant transitions in perspective, both inside and outside the legal establishment, about the role of the law and the function of the judiciary in American society. During these years the national trends toward greater industrialization and urbanization continued, and a considerable portion of the country's population was experiencing improvement in its standard of living. It was also a time of increasing public anxiety — an understandable reaction to the complexities and dislocations of an expanding industrial economy. Many Americans were troubled by the well-documented abuses of monopolies in industry and transportation and by the increased concentration of corporate wealth. Concerns surfaced about the astounding increase in the flow of immigrants and the often violent upheavals in the relations between management and labor. Responding to what they viewed as a weakening of public morality and traditional social values, state legislatures began addressing such issues as temperance, child welfare, suffrage, and industrial labor reform. Many American reformers, having enthusiastically launched their assaults on the most glaring social problems of the times, discovered the mixed joys of less-than-complete success in the achievement of a more equitable and enlightened society. The reformers learned, too, that their plans required the assistance and cooperation of the government and that they would have to contend with the rigidity of prevailing legal doctrine and judicial methods that were tenaciously resistant to change.

Law and the Legal Profession. In the 1910s the practice of law, at least in the nation's growing urban areas, was marked by significant changes in its methods and attitudes. The law firm itself was restructured to be more businesslike and efficient. At the same time, to upgrade the profession's image and influence, the process of legal training was formalized and standardized, and admission to the bar became more selective. The decade witnessed the dawning of the age of the corporate attorney and his nemesis, the crusading public-interest lawyer; it also saw the appearance of the administrative agency, not only as an enforcer, but as an interpreter and adjudicator of the law. Reacting against the influences of social Darwinism,

progressives in these years strongly believed that they could improve basic conditions for those whom they believed would benefit from their efforts, and their progressive views began to affect many in the nation's government and, though less perceptibly, in the nation's courts, as well.

The Progressive State. The progressive movement, though often divided in its methods and objectives, forced substantial changes in government practice, particularly in the manner and the extent to which government agencies were expected to exercise their authority. Intent on eliminating the excesses of a new and powerful economy and also on remedying social conditions they found threatening to society and morally offensive, reformers threw themselves into redefining the government's basic responsibilities for the social and economic welfare of Americans. Remedial and regulatory legislation was introduced in great abundance, frequently enacted into law, and almost as frequently modified or rejected by a judiciary that claimed a greater allegiance to the immutability of the existing law and controlling precedent. Special agencies were nevertheless created, some of which were empowered to enforce the provisions of the legislation passed. The decade witnessed the establishment of the Federal Reserve System and the Federal Trade Commission, as well as a special court to oversee its operation. Antitrust legislation placed considerable power in the hands of the president and his attorney general, and even that paled in comparison to the authority granted the executive and the courts following the outbreak of hostilities in World War I. The war distracted and eventually redirected the energies of the reform movements and produced postwar conditions that seriously undermined the progressives' influence.

Changes in the Workplace. The flood of industrial accidents and the growing recognition of their social and economic costs produced enormous interest among laborers and employers alike in the nature of working conditions and in how workers were to be compensated for the injuries they suffered. It became clear that neither the courts nor the marketplace was capable of developing uniform solutions to problems that could only be resolved by providing adequate compensation plans, protecting child laborers, and offering workers some assurance of adequate wages and reasonable limits on the length of the workday. Efforts to alleviate workplace conditions, which had begun in the early 1900s, continued to preoccupy many during the first half of the 1910s, with varying degrees of success. For good or ill, the nation's courts were deeply involved in the debates about the American workplace, whether they were searching for some substitute for a common-law theory of liability or aggravating already tense relations between industry and the worker through the employer's use of injunctive relief as a weapon against strikes and efforts to unionize.

Amending the Constitution. Many Americans strongly believed in the progressive values of the 1910s, and few resisted attempts to alter the Constitution. There was little fear that bringing about needed change through a simple modification of the nation's basic charter would render the individual's rights vulnerable. Indeed, the resistance of the courts to any modification of the relationship between the states and the federal government made the prospect of amending the Constitution that much more inviting to those who believed that their concerns were national in scope and needed uniform treatment. Those who feared that the national government's ability to raise revenue would be insufficient to meet the increasing public demand for governmental services, and who argued that changes in tariff policy were insufficient to meet that demand, pushed the Sixteenth Amendment (1913), which instituted the national income tax as a means of more efficiently and fairly allocating the burden of supporting a modern government. Those who believed a true democracy would be better served through popular election supported the Seventeenth Amendment (1913), which provided for the direct election of senators. Prohibitionists, fed up with conflicts among parochial interests and stymied by a Congress that saw temperance as a state issue, believed their concern involved the moral health of the nation and pressed vigorously for the passage of the Eighteenth Amendment (1919). Suffragists, after years of struggle that had changed the perception of women's role in society, were determined not to rest until the right to vote extended to all citizens, regardless of gender, by means of the Nineteenth Amendment (1920).

Managing the Economy. It became clear during the 1910s that the management of the economy could no longer be left to the states and must be considered from a national perspective. Big government was needed to contend with big business. But government first had to decide whether it intended to accommodate the giant corporations whose wealth and power threatened competition or to dispose of such organizations when their monopolistic tendencies became too apparent. Thus began a struggle between those who hoped to eliminate such corporations, principally western populists and the adherents of Theodore Roosevelt's New Nationalism, and those who believed that the nation would be better served by a more discriminating effort to regulate the business activ-

ities of major corporations. The latter group was composed principally of the supporters of President William Howard Taft and, later, of President Woodrow Wilson. The debate became so feverish that the Supreme Court finally took the initiative in the *Standard Oil* cases of 1911 and made a choice for the nation that would remain unchallenged. In these cases, the Court introduced the notion of an "unreasonable" restraint of trade as the ground on which antitrust actions could be initiated. Then with the entry of the United States into World War I and the mobilization of the nation's huge production capacity, any further serious disagreement about the place of big business in a modern, capitalist economy ended.

War. The nation's involvement in World War I shifted the center of power away from the states and toward the federal government, which proved itself capable of raising an enormous army and mobilizing the nation's resources for war production. In the process, the federal government adopted new practices and regulations that remained in place long after hostilities ceased. At the same time, the war brought fear and suspicion to a level and intensity not experienced before in American society. Those who questioned the government's motives in engaging in war, who criticized not just its policies but its leaders and their qualifications, risked severe persecution and punishment. The courts, mindful of the national emergency with which the country was faced, proved particularly tolerant of measures taken by the government to suppress dissent and monitor communication among its citizens. The Supreme Court's decision in *Schenck* v. *United States* (1919), which affirmed the government's power to take extraordinary steps under extraordinary circumstances, served not, as Justice Oliver Wendell Holmes Jr. intended, as a limitation upon the use of such power, but an invitation to extend the government's authority to dangerous lengths. Not even Holmes's dissent in *Abrams* v. *United States* (1919) was sufficient to clarify the issue or to win a majority of the justices over to his position. To those with special regard for the nation's constitutional history, the insensitivity of the judiciary to the civil liberties of those who dared to criticize the government's methods or purposes was appalling.

The Courts. Throughout the 1910s the U. S. courts, as epitomized by the Supreme Court, were rarely far removed from the political consciousness and the political conflicts of the nation. The courts were, however, viewed by many Americans, though not all, as steadfast in their reliance on legal doctrines that were in obvious conflict with the times. Many Americans thought that the nation's courts were proving singularly resistant to change, and, as a result, the courts invited an unprecedented degree of public distrust. There were, nevertheless, some significant changes in American law and judicial philosophy in these years. The common-law rule concerning fault gave way to the concept of liability. No longer was responsibility for causing a workplace injury limited to those directly involved; it now included the employer who controlled work conditions. The philosophy of "let the buyer beware" was replaced, in part, by the theory of a duty of care. Producers were now held to standards of manufacturing and design and responsible for any defects that could have been avoided. New approaches were developed to resolve complaints of workers' injuries, and efforts were made and upheld, though generally for reasons relating to health, to regulate the conditions of the workplace and the use of children in the production of goods. Given the mood of the times, it came as no surprise that the nation's judiciary did give some ground to the changes affecting both society and government; but the retreat was brief. By the end of the decade the courts' natural conservatism returned with a vengeance and remained its guiding light until it was more forcefully confronted in the years ahead.

TOPICS IN THE NEWS

BREAKING TRUSTS AND MONOPOLIES

Search for Effective Public Policy. In 1890, when the United States was poised to take action against the ever-increasing numbers of business trusts and the abusive business practices that often characterized large concentrations of capital, the nation was faced with the task of choosing between two quite different approaches to the problem. Americans could either accept the continuing formation of trusts as a natural outgrowth of modern industry and technological advance and take action solely for the purpose of regulating their activities, or they could pursue a policy calling for the dissolution of all monopolies in the interest of restoring and preserving a competitive market system. With the passage in 1890 of the Sherman Antitrust Act, which prohibited combinations and conspiracies in restraint of trade and outlawed monopolies, the nation appeared to have chosen the latter of the two alternatives.

Busting Trusts. The government, however, was not initially motivated to enforce the antitrust law. Defenders of the trusts pointed out that such combinations actually benefited the nation. Trusts had been successful in eliminating waste and consolidating operations. They had even contributed to the nation's economy through the introduction of some semblance of order and stability. But there was another side to these formidable concentrations of wealth and power that could not help but arouse widespread distrust and deep public resentment. Under Theodore Roosevelt's administration the Justice Department pursued antitrust actions against several of the largest and most powerful monopolies in the nation. Drawing encouragement from the Supreme Court's findings in the 1904 case of *Northern Securities Company* v. *United States*, the Department of Justice's antitrust division challenged monopolies in the meatpacking, tobacco, and oil industries. Much-publicized suits against the Northern Pacific Railroad and Eastman Kodak soon followed. A year later, in *Swift and Company* v. *United States*, the Supreme Court expanded the definition of monopoly to include any organization that, though acting in restraint of trade in only one state, was effectively extending its control to trade in other states by its effect upon the "stream of commerce." However, it soon became apparent that the government did not have the resources to undertake the approach it had adopted in connection with the appearance of the trust, and the government's effort to eliminate such industrial and business organizations began to falter under the weight of the task before it.

Trust-Busting Falters. Ironically, despite the government's aggressiveness in pursuing its antimonopoly goals, those objectives did not fully reflect the sentiments of the president whose name invoked the image of the trustbuster, Theodore Roosevelt. Roosevelt had come to believe in regulation of the trusts, rather than in their elimination, as the wisest course. William Howard Taft, despite his misgivings regarding the practicality of Roosevelt's approach, revitalized and pursued even more vigorously the trustbusting policy of his predecessor. This surge in antitrust activity, however, gave both opponents and proponents of the government's approach an opportunity to renew their debate regarding its effectiveness and also to express their shared concerns respecting the government's capacity to achieve its stated objectives.

Change in Direction. In 1911 the Supreme Court forced the issue, taking steps on its own to rein in the government and thus to compel a reexamination of the government's original assumptions concerning the econ-

Financier J. P. Morgan Jr. testifying at a hearing on business activities, circa 1915

omy and the place of trusts and monopolies within it. In May of that year the new chief justice, Edward D. White, speaking for the majority of the court in what would become known as the *Standard Oil* cases, essentially rewrote the Sherman Antitrust Act by reinterpreting the purpose for which it had been enacted. Fearing that current antitrust policy would irreparably damage the economy and further threaten legitimate property interests, White emphasized that the purpose of the law was not to lay waste to, but to rehabilitate, a system of competition with features of vital importance to the nation's growth. In effect, the Court modified the act to allow some discrimination between trusts whose conduct was considered harmless and those that were guilty of "unreasonable" restraints of trade. The Taft administration, recognizing the obvious impact this new standard would have on future antitrust activity, moved quickly to adjust its position accordingly. Within months of the decision, the Department of Justice settled for a consent decree as a means of concluding its litigation against the American Tobacco Company. The agreement allowed the tobacco conglomerate's reorganization without the burden and delay of a costly trial. It soon became evident that Congress, too, was more than willing to allow the courts to assume responsibility for resolving a dilemma the nation's own economy seemed unable to solve.

Crisis in Antitrust Law. By 1912 the debate had resumed in earnest, eventually engulfing both houses of Congress and providing the presidential election that year with one of its most hotly contested issues. The very nature and purpose of the government's antitrust involvement had become an issue, not only between the two major parties, but also between two warring factions within the Republican Party. In essence, those favoring a strong antimonopoly policy, many of whom were Democrats, feared that the Supreme Court's interpretation and employment of the "rule of reason" standard would render any further effort to protect competition in the marketplace useless. Many business leaders and others who were just beginning to appreciate the nuances of the Court's decision complained that it afforded no guidance as to what was and was not permissible competitive behavior, raising concern that all future antitrust effort would be highly selective and entirely unpredictable. The Republicans supporting President Taft's reelection had proposed amendments to the Sherman Antitrust Act that attempted to define more clearly the conduct proscribed by the various provisions of the act. The progressive Republicans around Roosevelt promoted a plan to shift the burden of antitrust policymaking away from the courts to a new federal agency that would be charged with its development and implementation. The Democrats offered a third alternative, which clearly contemplated the restoration of a climate of competition that would prove ruinous to the trust as a method of conducting business.

Wilson's Policy. Two years after the Democrats succeeded in winning the election, President Woodrow Wilson, recognizing that his party had underestimated the difficulty of achieving the antitrust objectives for which it had campaigned, simply adopted a middle-ground position, borrowing from both factions of the divided Republican Party. Proposing that Congress take a more active role in creating an antitrust policy, Wilson introduced a proposal that prohibited certain practices, such as price

The public's reaction to the growth of large concentrations of industrial wealth and power and the government's increasing regulatory response produced a widespread and sometimes bitter debate over the best way to achieve a balance between the need to control the trusts and the benefits to be derived from them. Increasingly, the trusts' defenders feared that public disenchantment would result in governmental takeovers of industries providing services of great benefit to the majority of Americans, particularly the nation's rail systems. Conditions were thus ripe for the development of some imaginative alternatives, one of which rose to capture briefly the public's interest.

William W. Cook was an attorney and general counsel for the Mackay Cable and Telegraph Company, a sizable corporation. Though widely known as a defender of the trust as a natural outgrowth of a changing economy, Cook was convinced that the public's perception of trusts as contenders for political power would result in disastrous consequences for the nation if allowed to go uncorrected. He feared that such attitudes would lead to government ownership of the nation's railroads, the nation's foremost system of transportation, upon which its economy was clearly dependent.

Cook had no faith in the government's ability to operate the railroads effectively and believed the advantages of his proposal lay in its simplicity. Taking the Bank of England as his model, Cook proposed that the government become involved in the creation of a gigantic public trust through which to gain ownership over the nation's railroads. This public trust would have access to a special fund containing a sum of $25 billion with which to purchase the nation's rail lines and stock. A board of directors would be established under congressional supervision and, to ensure that it remained free from the influence of special interest groups, each board member would be subject to recall by the stockholders. Any attempt to gain control of the holding company through stock manipulation or purchase would be defeated by yet another of the trust's special features: each stockholder would be limited to one vote regardless of the size of his individual holding. Voting by proxy would be strictly forbidden. Controls such as these, Cook believed, would be sufficient to eliminate the public's distrust of large business enterprise and yet retain those corporate leaders whose management skills were vital to the continuation of the railroads' successful operation.

Source: *McClure's Magazine* (January 1912).

---

discrimination, exclusive dealing arrangements, the maintenance of interlocking directorates, and other objectionable conduct. Labor organizations and certain agricultural interests were to be exempted from certain provisions of the act. The president's proposal, which became known as the Clayton Antitrust Act, required a new federal agency to ensure that the provisions of the new act would be strictly enforced. In the late summer of 1914, the Federal Trade Commission was created.

Sources:

Arthur S. Link, *Woodrow Wilson and the Progressive Era, 1910–1917* (New York: Harper & Row, 1963);

John E. Semonche, *Charting the Future: The Supreme Court Responds to a Changing Society, 1890–1920* (Westport, Conn.: Greenwood Press, 1978).

CHILD LABOR

Exploited Resource. When the United States was a nation of farms, shops, and small mills, the use of children to supplement a family's income was so common that it attracted little notice and even less concern. The nation's rapid and dramatic transformation into an industrialized society, however, changed the environment in which children labored and the conditions to which they were exposed. At the same time, changes were taking place in the way the childhood years were perceived. More and more Americans began to regard children as a national resource that deserved society's protection and guidance. Reformers such as Jacob Riis, author of *The Children of the Tenements* (1903), and George Creel, who with the assistance of Denver's juvenile court judge, Ben Lindsey, wrote *Children In Bondage* (1913), helped broaden awareness of the conditions under which many of the nation's poor children were reared. Exhibitions of photographs of children employed in all sorts of economic pursuits, including those considered among the most dangerous and grueling, proved equally successful in pricking the public's conscience. In sharp contrast to these images of child workers worn down by the toil of their labor were the children of the middle class, who led quite different lives and whose progress was measured not in industrial output, but in ways increasingly seen as being vital to their development as productive citizens.

Children operating a bobbin-winding machine at the Yazoo City Yarn Mills in Mississippi, 1911

Early Regulatory Efforts. In the 1880s many states had enacted statutes placing restrictions on the use of child labor. These laws had drawn support from a cross section of the public, including associations of tradesmen, who feared that the growing use of child labor threatened their wages and job security. The exploitation of children as a ready and cheap source of labor, however, continued and remained a source of concern well into the next century. Conditions in the canning industry, the glass industry (where boys were hired to mold glass for hours on end before blistering-hot furnaces), anthracite mining (which used trapper and breaker boys to sort, by hand, the mined coal), and the textile industry began to attract the attention of reformers after 1900. In the South the threefold increase in the number of child laborers in the decade ending in 1900 aroused public sentiment for child labor laws and led to the creation of the Southern States National Child Labor Committee. Elsewhere, interest in improving the legislation that affected children and in pressing for its enforcement resulted in the formation in 1904 of the National Child Labor Committee.

This committee, later chartered by Congress to promote the welfare of America's working children, investigated conditions in many states; it also served as a model for many local child labor committees, who, through mass mailings and intensive lobbying, were successful in securing legislation that placed restrictions on the use of child labor. It soon became apparent, however, that the effort to secure passage of legislation on a state-by-state basis was proving far less effective than expected. In 1910 it was estimated that there were still in excess of two million children employed in an industrial setting.

Absence of Uniformity. The problem stemmed from the fact that there was no uniformity among the child labor laws passed by the various states. Those states prepared to regulate child labor risked finding themselves in an unfavorable competitive position, since under the Constitution they were unable to protect their own markets or industries by excluding goods from states that allowed children to work at cheaper wages. The defeat of Sen. Albert Beveridge's effort to pass the first national anti-child-labor bill in 1907 convinced many advocates

In 1914 the Children's Court of New York City prepared and distributed a report that offered a glimpse into an area of the law about which little had been known, juvenile delinquency and dependency. Progressive reformers were eager to make changes in society and seemed to take a particular interest in documenting the conditions they found. Respecting the treatment of children brought into the court system, they were able to determine that 25 percent of the children appearing before the court had been referred to it for petty offenses; 38 percent were in need of the court's protection because of the lack of proper care or the abuse to which they had been subjected; and 37 percent had been arrested for the commission of serious offenses such as burglary. Of the three thousand children included in the study, 35 percent were the product of "broken homes," where one parent was dead or the parents were separated or divorced. This percentage did not include children who were being raised in extreme poverty or by parents who were ill or alcoholic. The statistics thus compiled allowed the court to identify certain factors that, if addressed, could possibly reduce the numbers of children requiring the court's attention.

The authors of the study concluded that a child's first appearance in juvenile court was his most important one; susceptibility to the rehabilitative influence of the court rapidly diminished with each new appearance (20 percent of the 9,019 children arraigned in the previous year, it was noted, had been in court on prior occasions). Furthermore, children between the ages of fourteen and fifteen were members of the group most likely to engage in delinquent acts (at that age, it was theorized, boredom with school was at its peak and the children were too young to be involved in meaningful work). The study also found that peer pressure was a serious and sometimes decisive factor in whether a child became a delinquent — fully 54 percent of the children detained for the commission of a crime had been involved with others when apprehended.

Source: *Outlook* (11 July 1914): 580.

for children that the solution to the problem lay in a more aggressive program of education and cooperative effort among the states. In 1911 the U.S. Commission on Uniform Laws was encouraged to adopt a uniform child labor law, consisting of fifty sections and establishing minimum standards respecting the employment of children in certain industries and in work considered hazardous to their health. The following year Congress enacted the Children's Bureau Bill, which created a new office within the Department of Labor to serve local governments and state legislatures interested in regulating child labor. By 1915 it had become clear that this approach lacked the strength to overcome the resistance and influence of those who employed children in their mines and factories. These disparities among the laws of the different states were widely condemned as irrational and unjust and resulted in even louder and more pressing demands for federal intervention.

Owen-Keating Bill. With the aid of William Draper Lewis, dean of the University of Pennsylvania Law School, a bill was drafted and introduced in the House by A. Mitchell Palmer (D–Pa.), the future attorney general, and in the Senate by Robert L. Owen (D–Ok.). The proposal moved quickly through the House, but, lacking the support of the president, who had deep reservations about the federal government's jurisdiction in such matters, made no progress in the Senate. The following year the bill was reintroduced by Owen in the Senate and Edward Keating, (D–Colorado) in the House, where it again passed without any difficulty. On this occasion, however, President Wilson, fearful of losing the political initiative to a newly reunited Republican Party and recognizing that such legislation had been one of the more popular planks in his party's platform, used his influence in the Senate to secure its passage. Members of both parties hailed the law as a measure of the nation's social and economic progress, a symbol of its inherent decency and humanitarian tendency. In actuality, the Keating-Owen Act did little more than prohibit shipment in interstate commerce of goods manufactured or processed by child labor. The act forbade the shipment between the states or in foreign commerce of any minerals where, within thirty days prior to such shipment, children sixteen years old or younger had been employed. It also forbade the shipment of any goods produced in factories that, within thirty days prior to shipment, had employed children younger than fourteen years old or where children between fourteen and sixteen years of age had worked more than eight hours a day or six days a week.

Question of Constitutionality. No sooner had the act been passed than opposition to its enforcement appeared. Its first test came when Junius Parker, formerly the general counsel of the American Tobacco Company, was retained to represent Roland Dagenhart, who, together with his two children, ages thirteen and fifteen, was employed by the Fidelity Manufacturing Company in Charlotte, North Carolina. Following his employer's announcement that it intended to abide by the provisions of the Keating-Owen Act, Dagenhart sued to enjoin the company and the government from complying with and enforcing the act. Dagenhart was successful in obtaining his injunction, and the matter was taken up on appeal. The government's position in argument before the Supreme Court was prepared under the direction of Solicitor General John Davis, who also presented the case. Describing the social, economic, and medical costs associated with the employment of children, Davis argued that the public deplored child labor locally, but had been helpless to regulate it, because the problem was essentially national in scope. The states, he explained, were not free to take whatever action they might choose, because they were united under a Constitution providing for and protecting a national market. The problem, he insisted, would require a solution of broad application. Justice William R. Day, however, writing for the majority of the justices, concluded otherwise. There was nothing intrinsically harmful about the goods shipped in interstate commerce, he noted. On the contrary, the objections that had been raised concerned only the manner in which the goods were being produced. Under the Tenth Amendment, Congress had no authority to control the conditions of production in the individual states. Writing in dissent, Justice Oliver Wendell Holmes Jr. challenged the validity of the distinction Justice Day had made between the products of child labor and any other goods shipped in interstate commerce. Had not the Court recently upheld the right of Congress to prohibit the use of commerce for evil or immoral purposes? Holmes asked. For him, the Court's decision was based not on solid reasoning and precedent, but on its reluctance to extend federal power beyond those limits within which it had traditionally been confined.

Stunned Nation Reacts. The Court's ruling took the public by complete surprise. It did not, however, diminish public support for the Keating-Owen Act. *The New York Times* concluded that child labor, like the sale of alcoholic beverages, might better be left to the control of the local authorities; but many others regarded the decision as a blow to justice. Clearly, the Court remained unconvinced that child labor was in itself a social evil. Congress reacted angrily, acting, only months after the opinion had been issued, to amend the Revenue Bill of 1919 to include a prohibitive tax on the products of child labor, a provision later ruled invalid by the child labor tax case of 1922 (*Bailey* v. *Drexel Furniture Company*). During World War I the War Labor Policies Board, under the direction of Felix Frankfurter, inserted a clause in all federal contracts making the provisions of the Keating-Owen Act mandatory for anyone selling equipment and other war matériel to the government. Before long, advocates of child labor reform discovered another alternative by which to achieve a national policy restricting child labor — an amendment to the Constitution. In 1924 an amendment was submitted to the states for consideration but was not ratified. Once again, conditions had begun to change. The introduction of new technologies and innovative manufacturing techniques encouraged the employment of better-motivated and better-educated workers. Hostility toward the use of child labor continued to grow, but the passage of higher state mandatory educational requirements and vigorous enforcement of truancy laws

made employing children increasingly burdensome and uncertain. The 1920 census reflected this situation by recording a decline in child labor, a decline that continued into the 1930s with the passage of the Fair Labor Standards Act of 1938, which, along with establishing minimum wage and hour standards nationwide, discouraged the employment of minors. By setting minimum wages, it decreased incentives to hire children.

Sources:

Editorials, *Outlook*, 94 (29 January 1910): 231-233; 99 (21 October 1911): 401-402; 105 (27 September 1913): 151;

Robert Schnayerson, *The Illustrated History of the Supreme Court of the United States* (New York: Abrams, 1986);

John E. Semonche, *Charting the Future: The Supreme Court Responds to a Changing Society, 1890–1920* (Westport, Conn.: Greenwood Press, 1978).

ESPIONAGE AND SEDITION ACTS

Fears for Internal Security. America's involvement in World War I provoked serious and widespread abuses of civil liberties. While most Americans responded to the call for mobilization with intense patriotic sentiment, there were those who, for a variety of reasons, remained opposed to intervention in the war, and a few, including many pacifists, who resisted the call to arms altogether. In 1917 Congress, under pressure to take some action to protect the nation's security against those who might provide aid to its foreign enemies, passed the much-debated Espionage Act. This act provided the government with extraordinary powers over the rights of free speech and press. Immediately after the nation's declaration of war, the country was filled with rumors regarding the activities of spies and their sympathizers; there were also numerous stories concerning sabotage and plots to render America's industrial might useless. These concerns, however, were not strong enough to dampen fears that the Espionage Act as originally proposed would serve to repress free speech and the right of individuals to debate issues of public concern. The reaction of the nation's press, reinforced by petitions containing some 1.5 million signatures, was so critical of the proposed bill that both houses of Congress were forced to compromise on what became the final version in which it passed.

Espionage Act. The Espionage Act made it a crime to make false reports that might aid an enemy, to incite rebellion within the armed forces, or to obstruct military recruitment. One of its provisions covered the use of the nation's post office system. Any newspaper, pamphlet, book, letter, or other writing advocating insurrection or the forcible resistance to any law of the United States would be punishable by both fine and imprisonment. These last provisions concerning the nation's mail afforded the government an opportunity to suppress dissent of almost every kind. Copies of Georgia populist Tom Watson's newspaper, *The Jeffersonian*, were temporarily delayed en route while government censors studied the headline, "Civil Liberty Dead." It made little difference

Radical Agitators Under Arrest and at Ellis Island

Alleged anti-American agitators with "foreign faces" and radical periodicals depicted in *The New York Times Mid-Week Pictorial*, circa 1919

whether the criticism of the government reflected the views of those not actually opposed to the war, but who stood against conscription as a form of involuntary servitude; or of pacifists who definitely and specifically objected to the country's involvement in the war. Dissent of any kind was regarded as a threat to national unity. Opponents of the draft were among the first to feel the full weight of the act's enforcement. Emma Goldman and Alexander Berkman, both anarchists of some renown, were prosecuted for organizing rallies attacking conscription; despite the absence of credible evidence against them, both were convicted and imprisoned. Those soon to join them included such notables as Roger Baldwin (later the founder of the American Civil Liberties Union), the socialite Kate O'Hare (who would use her experience as a prison inmate to help organize the nation's postwar prison-reform movement), and Victor Berger (a socialist, former congressman, and editor of the *Milwaukee Leader*). Perhaps the best-known American prosecuted under the act was Eugene Debs, a labor leader and head of the American Socialist Party. Debs appeared before a convention of Socialists in Ohio, speaking about

such matters of doctrine as the party's position respecting the economy and about his own views on the war in Europe. He was charged under the Espionage Act, found guilty of violating its provisions, and, at the age of sixty-three, was sentenced to a long term of imprisonment. In 1919 his conviction for obstructing recruitment and inciting mutiny was upheld by a unanimous Supreme Court.

Free Speech and the Supreme Court. The issue of whether or not the Espionage Act violated fundamental freedoms guaranteed under the Bill of Rights was finally presented to the Supreme Court through the arrest and conviction of Charles T. Schenck, general secretary of the Socialist Party. Schenck, convinced that the war was nothing more than an attempt by the wealthy to exploit the working class, advocated peaceful resistance to the draft and condemned conscription as involuntary servitude, a direct violation of the Thirteenth Amendment. The Supreme Court's opinion in *Schenck* v. *United States*, written by Associate Justice Oliver Wendell Holmes, conceded that such exhortations would likely have been considered protected speech under more ordinary circumstances; but, where a condition of national emergency had arisen, such protections as those afforded by the First Amendment could be legitimately curtailed when doing so advanced the nation's interests in meeting a threat to its own security. The Court found that Schenck had indeed intended to obstruct recruitment, an activity specifically prohibited under the act, and could therefore be punished under its provisions. The Court had, in effect, rejected the argument that the right of free speech was absolute. The right to express oneself freely, Justice Holmes wrote, was entirely relative, and therefore subject to a determination of whether or not the words themselves evoked a "clear and present danger." Holmes's standard would become the most significant measure of what constituted protected speech.

The Sedition Act. In May 1918 Congress enacted the Sedition Act, which punished anyone who, during times of war, dared to "utter, print, write, or publish any disloyal or abusive language" regarding the government, the armed forces, the Constitution of the United States, or its flag. If anxiety made Congress more amenable to the passage of such restraints on free speech, the act it passed resulted in some of the worst excesses in the nation's attempt to deal with potential obstruction of its war effort. For example, the movie director Robert Goldstein quickly fell victim to the hysteria the act tended to promote. Goldstein was sentenced to ten years in prison for depicting an ally, Great Britain, in a less-than-favorable light in his Revolutionary War epic, *The Spirit of '76*. Leaders of the International Bible Students' Association, a fundamentalist Christian pacifist organization, were prosecuted for little more than expressing their beliefs about the immorality of war. Not until 1919, after many such actions had occurred, was the constitutionality of the Sedition Act tested before the Supreme Court.

JUSTICE HOLMES ON THE FUTURE

If I am right, it will be a slow business for our people to reach rational views, assuming that we are allowed to work peaceably to that end. But as I grow older I grow calm. If I feel what are perhaps an old man's apprehensions, that competition from new races will cut deeper than workingmen's disputes and will test whether we can hang together and fight; if I fear that we are running through the world's resources at a pace that we cannot keep; I do not lose my hopes. I do not pin my dreams for the future to my country or even to my race. I think it probable that civilization somehow will last as long as I care to look ahead — perhaps with smaller numbers, but perhaps also bred of greatness and splendor by science. I think it not improbable that man, like the grub that prepares a chamber for the winged thing it never has seen but is to be, that man may have cosmic destinies that he does not understand. And so beyond the vision of embattling races and impoverished earth I catch a dreaming glimpse of peace.

Source: Oliver Wendell Holmes Jr., From a speech delivered to the Harvard Law School Association of New York, 15 February 1913.

War on Dissent Continues. In 1918, as Russia convulsed in the throes of a revolution, President Wilson dispatched troops to Russia to demonstrate support for the opponents of the Bolsheviks. Wilson's decision to support Russia's counterrevolutionary forces generated considerable opposition among those in this country who supported the cause of the workingman everywhere. In August of that year five Americans were arrested for distributing leaflets calling for the reversal of the president's policy toward Russia. No evidence was presented at the trial to prove that their leaflets, which condemned German militarism, had, in fact, produced any of the work stoppages that were demanded. There was no proof that the leaflets, printed in a foreign language and thrown out to a city street from an upstairs window, had reached any of their intended audience. In short, the prosecution did not prove that the defendants actually intended to hinder the war against Germany; but even this weakness in the evidence did not prevent the five men from being convicted of violating the Sedition Act. In affirming their conviction, the Supreme Court found that the act did not require proof that the language in question affected anyone or had even produced a harmful result; it was enough that an utterance had been made in the first place. This conclusion was ridiculed by an aroused Justice Holmes, who wrote in his dissenting opinion that no conviction under the act could ever be possible without proof of a specific intent to violate its prohibitory language. The majority of the justices adopted an interpretation, Holmes complained, that

could only result in the suppression of any and all criticism of the government's conduct of the nation's foreign policy, regardless of motive.

War Ends, Fear Remains. Conditions at the conclusion of World War I did not encourage a reexamination of the Espionage and Sedition Acts. Postwar reaction to Bolshevik gains in Russia and the hysteria that led to such outbursts as the Red Scare of 1919 did little to convince either the public or Congress that the powers granted the federal government to maintain domestic security were no longer necessary. It was not until 1921 that the Sedition Act was finally repealed and efforts to secure clemency for those who had been convicted under its provisions began to achieve any measure of success. Moreover, the Espionage Act continued in force until March 1940, when it was modified under conditions that largely resembled those prevalent in this country prior to the country's entry into World War I. Following the end of World War II and the convictions of Ethel and Julius Rosenberg, the act again underwent extensive modification.

Sources:
James W. Hurst, *The Law of Treason in the United States* (Westport, Conn.: Greenwood Press, 1971);

William Preston Jr., *Aliens and Dissenters: Federal Suppression of Radicals, 1903–1933* (Cambridge, Mass.: Harvard University Press, 1963).

EUGENICS AND THE LAW

Theory of Eugenics. In 1883 the English scientist Francis Galton, a cousin of Charles Darwin, coined the word *eugenics* to describe the science that concerned itself with those qualities that contributed to the improvement of the human race. Eugenists, as they were to call themselves, firmly believed, for example, that intelligence was an inherited trait that was relatively independent of any environmental consideration or influence. Eugenists portrayed themselves as being sincerely concerned about the future of the human race and maintained that efforts to ensure that the human race achieved its full potential could be successful only under the following condition: that those who bore the qualities most admired or valued among human beings were encouraged to reproduce those strengths in their progeny. It was, in essence, a theory based upon selective breeding, and it was given some urgency by the eugenists' fears of the reproductive capabilities of those whom they regarded as less qualified to contribute to the advancement of the "race," such as habitual criminals, hopeless paupers, and the "feeble-minded."

Darwinian Connection. The social and moral implications of the eugenists' theories were not as disturbing to many Americans as they later became. This decade was a time in which many people were obsessed with the new field of genetics. The popularization of the laws of heredity by such writers as William E. Castle, a Harvard biologist, was one clear indication of the growing acceptance

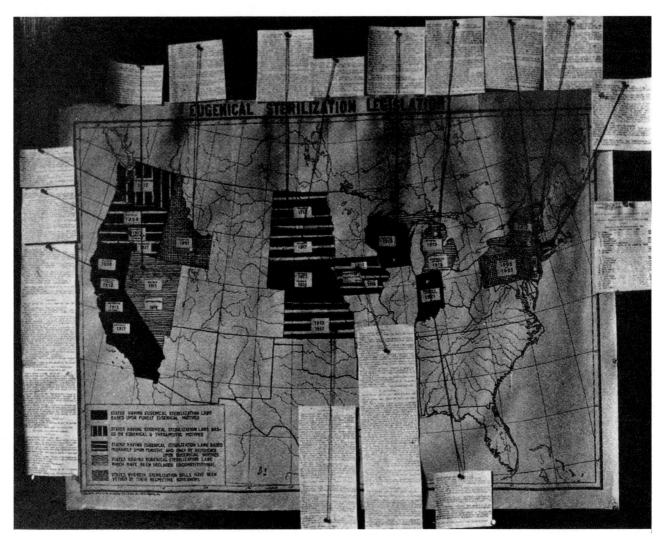

Illustration from *Eugenics in Race and State* (1923). By the late 1910s all the shaded states on the map had passed some form of sterilization law, but some of these laws had been declared unconstitutional.

of the social implications of Darwin's concept of evolution. The word *race* was used broadly at the time, usually to refer to alleged differences among ethnic groups (the "Teutonic race" or the "Anglo-Saxon race," for example) and just as frequently, and often quite openly, to distinguish among social classes and between "naturally" superior and "naturally" inferior groups. While the eugenists acknowledged the importance of environment in the development of the traits they admired, they nevertheless remained firmly convinced that heredity was the key to the "betterment" of a race. This genetic determinism became extremely popular, particularly among those who stood to benefit socially or otherwise from the conclusions drawn and assumptions made. Theorists and academicians such as Madison Grant, chairman of the New York Zoological Society and author of the best-selling book *The Passing of the Great Race* (1916), wrote of the need to protect the nation's interest in producing future citizens whose moral fiber, intellect, and physical makeup would measure up to the nation's ideals and potential. In a country that had watched its population increase by an

astonishing 10 percent in the previous ten years through immigration alone, ideas such as these attracted considerable interest.

Fears Concerning the "Feebleminded." The ideas promulgated by eugenists fueled public concerns that society was becoming increasingly burdened by growing numbers of people who were, in the eugenists' scheme of things, unfit. From eugenic principles social theories had been distilled, frequently under the guise of reform, to deal with individuals who proved burdensome to the public, those who were seen as lacking the intellectual and physical energies to achieve independence in a rapidly evolving society. Those who shared this concern convinced several state legislatures that the state itself had a direct responsibility to protect its citizens from the financial cost of maintaining those deemed unfit, as well as from the impact their reproduction would have on society as a whole. By 1912 thirty-four states had passed laws that deprived the insane of the right to marry. Nine states forbade those who suffered from epilepsy to marry. Fifteen prohibited the mentally retarded from marrying one another. The eugenists were motivated by what they proposed as a utopian vision of the world; they were also motivated by a conviction of the justice of their cause, which they believed was the "betterment" of mankind. What motivated the legislatures in passing such laws, aside from certain economic considerations and arguments, were the concerns many felt about the capacity of the "feebleminded" to assume the responsibilities of parenthood and the likelihood of their producing children who would suffer from similar hereditary conditions.

Institutionalization as an Alternative. The matter, however, did not rest with the passage of state laws and the dissemination of the eugenists' theories; by the early 1910s, feelings against those deemed unfit greatly intensified. In its 30 September 1914 issue *Outlook,* an influential journal of the time, expressed an assumption shared by many when it declared: "Feeble-mindedness has come to be recognized universally as one of the primary causes of crime, vice, and poverty." The connection between "mental deficiency" and "degeneracy," "social stagnation" and "delinquency," now seemed beyond question to many, and the demand for a solution to the supposed problem became louder. One approach entailed a form of segregation or supervision designed to dispose of a problem for which there appeared no more immediate solution. The first step involved the identification of those who met the criteria, a task that involved enlisting the aid of organizations most likely to encounter the people whom society had classified as "mental defectives." Specifically, it was estimated that in the city of New York there were some fifteen thousand such persons, all regarded as a menace "not only through their own irresponsibility, but through their freedom to beget other imbeciles." Once identified, it was hoped that such persons could be sent to an appropriate institution, where they would receive care and be prevented or discouraged from having children. Proposals such as these received financial support from various governmental organizations and were greeted with widespread approval by the majority of the public. But another, more radical approach began to gain favor — one that tried to use the authority of the law in a manner that would provoke debate for years to come.

Another Alternative. In 1907 Pennsylvania became the first state to enact a coercive sterilization statute; three years later the method of forced sterilization had garnered a large and determined following, including such noted persons as Alexander Graham Bell, Margaret Sanger, and a leader of the American Socialist Party, Norman Thomas. This movement in favor of sterilization achieved even greater momentum after it received the unqualified support of the American Association of University Women and was later endorsed by Mary Williamson Harriman, founder of the Eugenics Record Office in New York. Increasingly, forced sterilization became the subject of discussion among many professional and lay organizations, particularly as the practice of institutionalizing the mentally retarded spread and thus dramatized the numbers of people involved. In 1912 Dr. Walter Fernald addressed the Massachusetts Medical Society to emphasize the need to act without delay to ensure that problems associated with the feebleminded would be prevented from plaguing future generations. Studies in this period purported to show that families with histories of antisocial behavior were nearly always of low intellect. Such findings, often cited, offered reasons for many to conclude, as the eugenists had maintained, that heredity was the principal agent of high intelligence and dedication to achievement and civility. Increased interest encouraged greater experimentation with sterilization procedures, which inevitably produced a backlash of sentiment, which found full expression in the nation's courts.

Backlash. In the 1910s, despite the interest such legislation had engendered, governors in Idaho, Nebraska, Oregon, and Vermont vetoed legislation that provided for the sterilization of the mentally retarded. Gov. Thomas R. Marshall of Indiana, later a vice president of the United States, issued an executive order that put an end to sterilization in all hospitals and institutions receiving government support in his state. Between 1913 and 1921 courts in Iowa, Indiana, Michigan, New Jersey, New York, Nevada, and Oregon found the sterilization statutes previously enacted in those states unconstitutional. The courts' reasoning, however, had little to do with considerations of rights to privacy or to what was later referred to as a right to bodily integrity. The principal complaint to which the courts seemed both sensitive and sympathetic concerned issues of due process; that is, whether the statutes favoring sterilization as an extension of public policy adequately provided for certain fundamental procedural safeguards. It was unlikely that the courts were moved by the objections made by the growing number of social scientists who were even then disproving the assumptions basic to the eugenists' theories. Nevertheless, the outcome generally pleased those who opposed such procedures as invasions of the individual's right to conduct his life free of governmental intervention and those who opposed such procedures on moral or religious grounds. The issue would resurface from time to time, most famously in the Supreme Court case of *Buck* v. *Bell* (1927); but, while the authority of the individual states to pursue such policies was not entirely disposed of, protest against such procedures eventually became so strong that further experimentation with sterilization as a solution to the "problem" of feeblemindedness could not be justified.

Sources:

Editorials, *Outlook,* 95 (13 August 1910): 812–813; 111 (18 October 1913): 342–343; 108 (30 September 1914): 243;

Donald K. Pickens, *Eugenics and the Progressives* (Nashville, Tenn.: Vanderbilt University Press, 1968).

EXPERIMENT OF THE COMMERCE COURT

Court of Special Jurisdiction. An early experiment with the concept of a court of special jurisdiction involved the Interstate Commerce Commission (ICC). The ICC had won considerable public support through its efforts to exercise fair but firm control over the railroads, whose activities and political influence had generated much controversy, particularly in the midwestern states. Accordingly, interest in extending the ICC's regulatory powers beyond the narrow field to which they had originally been confined was growing. Moreover, the commission had increasingly benefited from a series of Supreme Court decisions that reinforced its rule-making role and jurisdiction. Some Americans, particularly among the more conservative elements of the Republican Party, were concerned that no process of review had been created to consider the appropriateness of ICC decisions. Sensitive to the interests of the business community, but also desiring to strike a balance between these and the demands of the reformers who championed the commission as a bulwark against the special interests, President William Howard Taft favored the idea of establishing a special court, answerable only to the Supreme Court, that would have the responsibility for reviewing and evaluating the ICC's rulings. The country's experience with national administrative agencies was still somewhat new, and the establishment of a special court would, he was convinced, expedite consideration of the ICC's rulings and provide a process by which their fairness could be expertly judged and provided with the weight of law. The neatness and orderliness of the proposal appealed greatly to the president and clearly reflected the administration's commitment to efficiency and sound management in government.

Presidential Proposal. In 1910 President Taft succeeded in having a bill, later known as the Mann-Elkins Act, amended to include a provision for a special court, the Commerce Court, which would oversee the activities of the ICC. The amending provision, however, attracted the attention of the entire Congress, triggering a bitter debate between the president's supporters and the more progressive elements of both parties. Democrats, who had just recaptured a slim majority of the seats in Congress, feared that the court would soon come under the influence of those whom the ICC regulated — the railroad and other industrial interests whose aggressiveness and abusive conduct had gone unchecked before the establishment of the commission. Insurgent Republicans, who appeared united in their opposition to the president's proposal, were actually divided in the reasons for their objection: some were concerned that the bill would give the court greater powers of review than those authorized by the circuit courts of appeal; other Republicans believed that the amendment deprived the parties appealing the decisions of the ICC the right to be represented by legal counsel. The act, with only slight modification of its more important provisions, eventually became law,

and shortly thereafter the five-judge court began to receive its first cases.

Court in Action. The Commerce Court's first decisions raised considerable alarm among the ICC's supporters and generated renewed interest among some in Congress for the abolition of the court. Of the first five appeals taken from the Commerce Court to the Supreme Court, four were reversed. In rulings that fell like hammer blows, the Supreme Court blocked the Commerce Court's attempt to curb the ICC's investigative powers; it left standing in one case the ICC's finding regarding discriminatory practices; and it pointedly questioned whether the Commerce Court had exceeded its jurisdiction in another case. In 1912 an act abolishing the Commerce Court managed to pass both houses of Congress, but was vetoed by an angry president determined to defend the court against challengers, both within and outside his party. Meanwhile, twenty-two appeals from the Commerce Court's decisions were eventually taken, and fourteen resulted in reversals, an outcome that contributed to the growing distrust of the Commerce Court. But it was not until January 1913, that the court was delivered a body blow from which it could never fully recover. After a much publicized impeachment trial, one of the Commerce Court's judges, Robert Archbald, was convicted by the Senate of improprieties committed while in office. Revelations of his private, secret dealings with companies that were subject to the ICC's regulation, and, in some instances, directly involved in legal challenges of its rulings, badly damaged whatever prestige the Commerce Court retained. These revelations, and the Commerce Court's insensitivity to the high public regard in which the ICC was held, raised powerful questions about its continued usefulness and impartiality. To make matters worse, the court seemed oblivious to the extremely delicate and precarious position in which it increasingly found itself in the ongoing struggle between the forces of reform and an entrenched business establishment.

Experiment Ends. On 22 October 1913, Congress finally succeeded in abolishing the Commerce Court. Newly elected President Woodrow Wilson, who had gone on record in opposition to the political influence of special interests, was not inclined to use his office to protect an institution around which so much suspicion had grown. The court's remaining judges were reassigned to the various circuit courts of appeal, and its offices were closed two months later. Never again would the independence of the ICC be challenged by a means of legal review different from that to which all other agencies of government were subject, the federal courts.

Sources:

Alexander M. Bickel and Benno C. Schmidt Jr., *History of the Supreme Court of the United States: The Judiciary and Responsible Government 1910–1921* (New York: Macmillan, 1984);

Editorial, *Outlook,* 94 (16 April 1910).

The Fellow-Servant Rule and Workmen's Compensation

Changing Workplace. Between 1910 and 1919 the method of compensating employees who suffered injuries during their employment was fundamentally altered. In many respects this transformation was triggered by changes both in the nation's workplaces and in the relationship between labor and management. In times past, when a worker was hired to perform some service for the person hiring him, the arrangement was considered a simple contract. The employer assumed no responsibility for the safety of his employee other than what would be expected of anyone else: that he not deliberately do anything to the employee that would cause harm. Every worker was expected to be held responsible for his own mistakes or negligence, and common law absolved the employer from any responsibility for an injury to one employee caused by the carelessness of another. That, in essence, was the "fellow-servant" rule. But by the beginning of the twentieth century the growth of a complex industrial system had introduced processes of manufacturing, technologies, and scales of operation that far exceeded anything those who first conceived of this rule had ever contemplated. The consequences of such a rule, clearly foreseeable by 1900, were, from the vantage point of a growing industrial society, both costly and entirely unsatisfactory. It was estimated that in the first years of the new century, thirty-five thousand deaths and two million injuries occurred in the nation's workplaces each year. It was estimated further that one-quarter of the annual injuries resulted in the loss of one or more weeks of work. Although the great majority of the workers who suffered injuries could not be blamed for their accidents, the only way they could obtain compensation for their losses was to sue. This was not an option many could afford, given the expense involved in hiring a lawyer and the likelihood that whatever compensation the worker did recover would be far from adequate.

Changing Needs and Attitudes. By the turn of the century the failure of the law to provide for injured workers had become a national scandal. Along with the alarmingly high number of accidents, there were other reasons that encouraged workers to challenge the fellow-servant rule and the protection it afforded the employer. For one, if an injury were severe enough, it often resulted in an employee's discharge, leaving him with little to lose by filing a lawsuit against his former employer. Second, the rising popularity and availability of the contingent-fee arrangement, under which a plaintiff's attorney received a percentage of the settlement, made legal services accessible to more and more workers. As a result, larger numbers of significant recoveries were being recorded, encouraging workers to exercise their right to litigate the issues surrounding their injuries. Finally, in the trial courts themselves, judges and juries were increasingly finding in favor of injured workers and against their corporate adversaries. Whether for reasons of sympathy with individual plaintiffs, or with the working class in general, courts and juries found more and more ways of circumventing the formal and rigid rules of common law.

Common Law in Decline. Many suspected that these doctrines had been designed to preserve the status quo; to protect, under the guise of due process of law, the rights of property holders. When the courts and the legislatures began to find reasons for numerous exceptions to the rules, the respect with which applicable provisions of common law were once regarded began to slip even further. No longer could common-law rule be relied on to restrict the liability of the businessman and industrialist. The rules still prevented many plaintiffs from recovering damages, but the tide was turning, if only gradually. In fact, the chances of businesses losing in such cases had increased to a point where the risks involved began to be taken far more seriously than before. Increasingly, the nation's business and industrial concerns found themselves mired in litigation, facing the costs of settlement, the costs of liability insurance, the expenses associated with the administration and investigation of claims, legal fees, and even the salaries of staff lawyers. This was also a time when the principles of scientific management were becoming more widely accepted, when the benefits of efficiency and planning were becoming more clearly apparent.

Employers Tire of Litigation. Slowly at first, and then with increasing momentum, businesses began to develop a greater receptivity to the idea of workmen's compensation as a system that might offer them the order and systematization they wished to bring to their operations. Clearly, the advantage the legal system had originally provided employers had become far less certain; and it was increasingly apparent that the system in existence was exacting a price industry no longer wished to pay. In the same year the commission released its report, the president of the National Association of Manufacturers, with the full support of his organization, appointed a committee to study the possibility of compensating injured workers without the burdens of time-consuming and costly litigation. By 1911 the association had come to believe that some compensation system was inevitable, and that wisdom dictated that business play a positive role in designing the relevant law. Workers' compensation statutes would eliminate, it was felt, the process of fixing civil liability for industrial accidents through litigation, and the courts could therefore be avoided altogether. Instead, compensation would be based on predetermined schedules, and the responsibility for evaluating claims would rest entirely with an administrative agency.

Workmen's Compensation. The problem of labor unrest also had to be considered. Workers and their unions, already dissatisfied with many aspects of factory management, were especially angered by the relative unconcern with which the issue of workers' safety was treated. In a world where reports of mine, transportation, and industrial accidents were commonplace, issues concerning

One of the issues that rose repeatedly during the first half of the decade concerned the use of convicts as contract laborers. At a time when conditions in penitentiaries throughout the country were being severely criticized, prison administrators found themselves under fire for a time-honored practice that had originally been welcomed as a means of putting idle inmates to work.

In 1912 the Bureau of Labor completed a study of some 296 state prison facilities, noting that of the eighty-six thousand men and women then under confinement in these institutions, fifty-one thousand were employed by private contractors and industry. Almost all of those who were in a position to earn wages were paid below the prevailing rate; none were entitled to set the terms or conditions of their employment; and all were at risk of suffering severe punishment should their performance prove unsatisfactory. Many others were forced into work arrangements designed to benefit the institutions to which they had been committed, a situation ripe for corruption and other abuses. Instances were recorded of prisoners being deprived of food by contractors bent on achieving the greatest savings possible, often with the knowledge of the guards' superiors and the highest officials of the states involved.

Arrayed in opposition to these arrangements were groups representing many different interests: manufacturers who could not compete with those employing this cheap form of labor; labor organizations who viewed such arrangements with disdain and some fear for the security of its membership; and the American Prison Association, which believed nonessential convict labor undermined discipline, fostered ill will, and generally worsened conditions for which prison officials were responsible. It would, however, take a long while before this practice could be eliminated altogether; the contracting for convict labor continued until just after the outbreak of World War II.

Sources: Editorial, *Outlook,* 94 (16 November 1912): 562–563;

Editorial, *Outlook* (25 November 1914): 663;

Roger Sawyer, *Slavery in the Twentieth Century* (New York: Routledge & Kegan Paul, 1986).

---

worker safety invariably affected all facets of labor-management relations, and the lack of compensation for industrial accidents was one obvious weakness in the relationship. Despite the fact that the fellow-servant rule had been seriously weakened over time, most efforts to obtain compensation for industrial-related injuries were still meeting with tenacious resistance on the part of employers. When an employee did recover, the amount paid was often inadequate to meet the needs of the worker and his family. In 1910 the New York Employers' Liability Commission found that in the forty-eight cases of fatality studied in Manhattan, eighteen families received no compensation at all. Only four received more than $2,000, and the remainder were given less than $500. In many instances the cost of supporting the litigation consumed the better part of the recoveries made. This situation was clearly not designed to produce an acceptable outcome for anyone.

Courts Begin to Act. As the courts developed methods to avoid the more unjust outcomes of the common-law tort rules, they began to experience a loss of direction that was aggravated by their deviation from established precedent. Having considered evidence of employer negligence or misconduct and having increasingly adopted many exceptions to the fellow-servant rule, the courts were more and more often at a loss to know what new standard should replace the traditional rule. Clearly, their uncertain approach did not resolve the simmering crisis. Mixed results, primarily because of differences of opinion among various judges, not only added to the confusion but slowed the development of a uniform procedure. As expected, the issues surrounding workers' injuries eventually entered the state appellate courts, many of which were sensitive to the weaknesses of the applicable rules, and thus inclined to legitimize the exceptions the lower courts had carved out. But which exceptions should they favor? The variety of judicial exceptions dramatized the extent to which the courts remained uncertain about where the community's true interests lay in the relations between employer and employee. Even where state legislatures had passed laws addressing this matter, the liability statutes enacted were often ineffective in developing a cohesive body of rules.

And So Do the Legislatures. By 1911 twenty-five states had adopted laws abolishing the fellow-servant doctrine for railroad employees. Their intent had been to impose some form of safety regulation on the railroads, specifically by removing the employer's strongest legal defense — the fellow-servant rule — while weakening if not discarding such defenses as assumption of risk and contributory negligence. Real progress in this regard, however, began in 1913, after the Interstate Commerce Commission developed an interest in the problem of transportation safety and after Congress had acted to temporarily preempt the field with the enactment of legislation requiring interstate railroads to equip themselves with safety equipment.

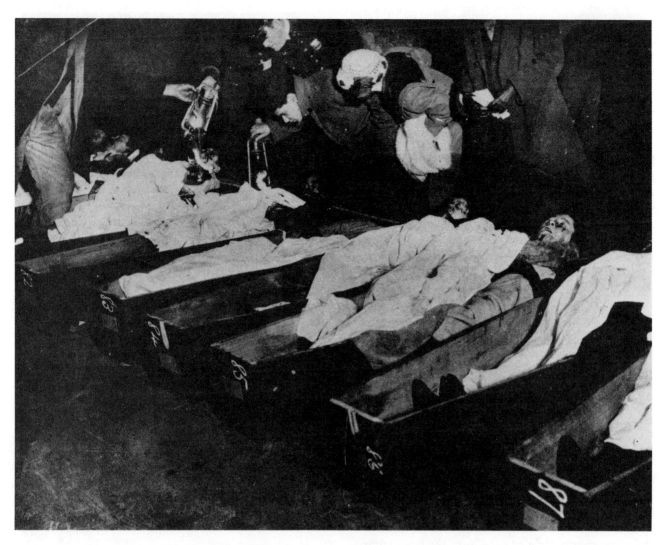

Some of the 146 female workers killed in a fire at the Triangle Shirtwaist factory, New York City, 1911

Setback and Reaction. In 1909 the state of New York enacted one of the country's most watched workmen's compensation laws. The bill as passed made the employer responsible for any accident that might befall one of his employees if the latter were injured while engaged in his employment. In effect, this law rejected the older tort concept completely and replaced it with a theory of liability that was considered somewhat revolutionary in legal circles. This opinion was shared by the state's highest court, which, in its decision in *Ives* v. *South Buffalo Railway Company,* ruled the law an abridgment of the state's constitution. The new law, the court said, had made the employer liable for losses for which he might not have been responsible, since he may have done nothing to have caused them. For that reason, it concluded, the law constituted a taking of property without due process. To what extent the court had been influenced by the Supreme Court's opinion in *Lochner* v. *New York* (1905) — in which state laws governing wages were found to be an interference with the freedom to contract — was uncertain; but the decision surprised many and seemed blatantly to contradict legal developments elsewhere: that

same year, the Supreme Court of Wisconsin had found a similar statute constitutional, and a New Jersey statute modeled after New York's law had survived an early test of its constitutionality. In the following years the *Ives* decision came to be regarded not as the rule but the exception, as other states adopted plans that provided for uniform adjudication of worker claims and also provided for the transfer of the cost of maintaining such insurance to the employers, who were in the best position to control or eliminate the conditions that made such insurance necessary.

Worker's Compensation Comes of Age. The processes adopted in the 1910s for adjudicating worker's claims varied from state to state, but shared many features. Most states made such plans the exclusive remedy for an employee injured on the job. The fellow-servant rule and certain other defenses were eliminated in most statutes, and any employer who did not enroll in the program of insurance established for his workers' benefit was deprived of the protection afforded by many legal defenses. Gradually, such compensatory plans became a common feature in industry, so much so that by 1917 the courts accepted the inevitable, giving constitutional sanction to the changes in the legal doctrines that marked their adoption and enforcement. In that year the Supreme Court upheld state workmen's compensation laws recently passed in New York, in *New York Central Railroad Company* v. *White,* and in 1919 the Court upheld a similar Arizona statute (Arizona Employers' Liability cases), prompting recalcitrant state courts, including those in New York, to follow suit. Upholding such laws, however, was generally as far as the courts were prepared to go in permitting legislative regulation of relations between employers and workers. The reasoning of the *Ives* case continued to command respect in the nation's courts. The due process clause of the Constitution was still seen as defining liberty in a manner deemed immutable and absolute, particularly where property rights were concerned. The Supreme Court's decision in *Hammer* v. *Dagenhart* (1919), invalidating a statute outlawing many forms of child labor as undue interference with the economy and the rights of contract, served as a testament to the strength of conservative judicial views as the decade ended.

Sources:
Lawrence M. Friedman and Jack Ladinsky, "Social Change and the Law of Industrial Accidents," *Columbia Law Review* (1967): 50–82;

Editorial, *Outlook,* 99 (23 December 1911): 924–925.

LAWYERS AND THE LEGAL PROFESSION

New Trends. Two trends characterized the American legal profession in the first decades of the new century. The first involved the increasingly widespread adoption of standards to control admission to the profession, and the second concerned the lawyer's relationship with his clients. Many lawyers, like those in other fields of specialty, had grown seriously concerned with the status accorded their profession, both within their communities and before the courts in which they practiced. Their desire for greater recognition and enhanced stature led to efforts to improve and institutionalize the process of legal training, to remove it from the back offices and libraries in which the clerk traditionally labored to classrooms where the program of instruction could be formalized and the qualifications of instructors assured. Restricting access to the profession also became a popular method of raising the level of public esteem for the profession. The establishment of local, and even, in some instances, state associations, charged with ensuring that certain minimum standards would be maintained among candidates for admission to the bar, constituted a major advancement toward this goal. Efforts such as these reinforced the public's (and the lawyers') perception of the bar as a select group of educated, even scholarly, individuals, whose superior skills and easy access to the courts placed them among society's elite. The early decades of the cen-

Wall Street attorney Paul D. Cravath, creator of the "Cravath System," an organizational model used by most U.S. law firms

tury also witnessed a widening gap between the urban lawyer, in his many versions, and those lawyers whose preeminence in the country's many smaller communities and rural areas had withstood the pressures of the times, which included the changes wrought by specialization and the emergence of new forms and fields of practice. The latter were not backward, just different, and just as faithfully reflected the legal environment in which they labored as did the corporate lawyer in the big city, where competition for clients induced changes in the practice of law hardly imaginable only fifteen years earlier.

The Law Firm in Transition. The scale and complexity of big business and the appearance of a more interventionist government inevitably led to changes in the organization of legal practice. Lawyers were needed to negotiate, defend, or prosecute in the cases heard by a growing number of administrative agencies and courts on both the state and federal levels. Law firms grew rapidly and became more businesslike in their operations, reflecting a trend toward specialization and professionalization in an increasingly regulated society (between 1909 and 1913 more than sixty thousand statutes were enacted by Congress and the various state legislatures). At the same time, the pace of work became more frantic. Many firms, becoming more conscious of the competitive environment emerging within the profession and the need for greater discipline and coordination within their own offices, adopted innovations in professional development that became known as the "Cravath system," an approach to the management of a firm and the cultivation of its collective strengths named after its creator, Paul D. Cravath. The new system was designed to promote loyalty and to ensure that the firm's investment in the professional development of its employees produced significant and rewarding returns for it and served, as well, as an introduction to the firm's distinctive culture. It also helped convert the practice into a business. Partners first supervised their associates' instruction in the general practice of law, a task made easier by the almost universal acceptance of a formal legal education as a prerequisite to entry into the profession; associates then specialized in the more important areas of the firm's practice, such as corporate law, real estate, and trusts and estates. Such specialization often generated larger volumes of business, which, in turn, justified the firm's division into separate departments, where often teams of attorneys, rather than a single practitioner, became responsible for servicing the needs of a single client.

Lawyers and Clients. Corporate clients, a phenomenon of growing importance after the turn of the century, exercised an enormous influence over the development of the modern law firm. The diversity, scale, and complexity of operations characteristic of large corporations forced or seduced law firms into expanding their relationships with their corporate clients to include areas other than litigation. Lawyers could not escape the consequences of their involvement in, and responsibility for, the development of a legal framework for this new economic system. Increasingly, lawyers acted as policy advisers and financial consultants to their corporate clients. These new roles encouraged them to pattern the structure and atmosphere of their own workplaces after those of their corporate clients. Lawyers began to feel that their skills and knowledge as consultants, more than their abilities as litigators, had become the criterion for success. A lawyer's expertise could now be evaluated in terms of his familiarity with a specific area of business endeavor, his "connections," and the relative importance of his clientele. Many, both within and outside the profession, began to feel that the public's regard for the legal profession had seriously declined in the face of this new and commercial influence. Whereas lawyers had once been the social and intellectual leaders of their communities, commanding respect and confidence for their judgment and dedication to the law and the public interest, they were now becoming increasingly viewed, fairly or not, as the representatives of corporate power, driven by greed, and suffering from the loss of vision and of moral direction. In the nation's more industrialized areas, the tendency to view the profession not so much as a calling,

CRIME AND THE EXCLUSIONARY RULE

Responsibility for the enforcement of the laws against crime traditionally fell on the states and the local authorities. The federal government's involvement was, by law and custom, limited mostly to enforcement of laws governing the collection of tariffs and taxes, regulation and operation of the mails, and the maintenance of order in the nation's territories and possessions. In 1914 the Supreme Court inadvertently created a loophole in the rules of evidence that shifted the burden of enforcing the laws even more squarely onto the shoulders of local law enforcement officials, where it would remain for at least two decades more.

When Fremont Weeks was arrested by Kansas City police officers on a gambling charge, he was taken into custody at his place of employment some distance from his home. The evidence the police found was turned over to the federal marshal and used to secure Weeks's conviction under federal law. The judge presiding over the trial had permitted its use despite the fact that it had been taken without a warrant, because no federal officer had been directly involved in its seizure.

The Supreme Court, however, disagreed. In *Weeks v. United States* (1914), in an opinion that took many by surprise, the Court noted that one of the most important duties of the nation's courts was to protect a citizen's fundamental rights against unlawful encroachment and that the courts had a responsibility to exclude any evidence that had been seized in violation of the Fourth Amendment. The Court stopped short of extending the "exclusionary rule" to the local police since their conduct was governed by the evidentiary rules of their respective state courts. Not until years later were the courts of various states required to apply, under the Fourteenth Amendment, the same exclusionary rules as those governing the federal courts.

Source: Alexander M. Bickel and Benno C. Schmidt Jr., *History of the Supreme Court of the United States, Vol. 9: The Judiciary and Responsible Government, 1910–1921* (New York: Macmillan, 1984).

whose independence and values were beyond reproach, but as an extension of the business community, reflective more of its values, its views, and its preoccupation with wealth, was growing. There were many exceptions to this generalization, particularly in regard to those who willingly took up the public cause, both privately and in government, and to the thousands of lawyers who jealously guarded their traditional and community-oriented

Is it possible for a jury to function in cases attracting enormous public scrutiny and in an environment of intense political and industrial strife? This question was raised repeatedly throughout the early stages of one of the most sensational criminal trials of the decade. In October 1910 an explosion demolished a portion of the *Los Angeles Times* building, killing and injuring many of the nonunion printers employed there. Many suspected the explosion had been caused by a bomb. Two bombs, in fact, had been found that same night outside the homes of the newspaper's publisher and the secretary of the city's Merchants and Manufacturers Association. An investigation resulted in the arrests of three men, John J. McNamara, secretary of one of the unions supporting the strike against the newspaper; his brother James; and Ortie McManigal, who would later become a witness for the prosecution and accuse the McNamara brothers and their union of participating in a nationwide plot to intimidate their enemies. For a time this story of industrial conflict and conspiracy divided the nation over the issue of the brothers' guilt or innocence.

Many observers began to express doubt as to whether a jury could ever be impaneled in light of the sensationalism that surrounded the proceedings. The prosecution had announced that it intended to call 350 witnesses; the defense planned to summon 200 of its own. The prospect of a lengthy trial was frightening away many a prospective juror. By the eighteenth day only nine jurors had been picked, and of this number only two had been declared acceptable to both sides. Even the practice of selecting for jury duty only those citizens whose names were to be found on the county's property tax rolls was challenged as being unfair and prejudicial against the defense, since a true cross section of the public would not otherwise be reflected in the jury's composition. Further hampering the selection of a jury, some complained, was the effort on the part of both sides to inject issues involving political motives and industrial strife into what would otherwise have qualified as nothing more than a criminal trial. Even more extraordinary was the judge's decision, unprecedented in California's legal history, to seek two alternate jurors, a step made necessary by the judge's revision of the trial's anticipated length, and yet sure to cause further delay in a proceeding whose outcome, as then uncertain, promised to set the stage for even greater turmoil and conflict.

Source: *Outlook* (2 December 1911): 795.

---

images; but cynicism about the legal profession grew deep among many Americans.

Professional Legal Associations. In 1913 the American Bar Association met in Montreal to consider proposals aimed at reducing delay in court proceedings and also the costs of litigation. Committees to consider reforms in jury selection, application of the rules of equity, and a subject much on the minds of all, the uses and abuses of federal injunctive relief — particularly as it was being applied to labor disputes — submitted their reports and recommendations for the membership's deliberation. But perhaps equally significant as the delegates conferred was the seriousness with which the participants regarded both the occasion and the organization responsible for their assemblage. It had been years since most of those in the nation's bar associations had considered their groups more than social clubs and the bar activities more than an opportunity to cultivate friendships and revel in the exclusivity of their association. Nevertheless, old traditions and attitudes had proved resilient.

Turning Point. The year before had been a watershed for the national bar, when it had been forced to decide whether it would retain its old identity as mainly a social organization or assume a greater responsibility, not just for the conduct of its members, but for its professional standing in the nation it served. By custom, enrollment in the ABA was a matter for the association's executive committee to decide. Among the applicants successful in gaining admission were three lawyers who, unknown to the committee, were African Americans. The uproar that followed this discovery found full expression at the association's annual meeting in 1912 and quickly forced the decision for admission to be rescinded. Deepening the committee's embarrassment was the fact that one applicant had since been appointed by President Wilson to the post of assistant attorney general of the United States. When the matter was put to a vote of the delegates present at the Montreal convention, the delegates voted to admit the black lawyers to the association's ranks. The significance of the vote was not lost on those who had observed it. Not only had the association taken its responsibility as the profession's national organization seriously, but it had assumed the mantle of a semiofficial agency that was committed to a set of principles worthy of its special relationship to the nation's laws, and far greater in importance than the collective attitudes or prejudices of its membership.

Respect for Courts Declines. The judicial system in this country continued to lose the public's confidence during the first decades of the twentieth century. Much

The fundamental rule of the law of torts as it was applied by the courts of the nation in the early years of the twentieth century was a simple one: if a person were without fault for causing another to suffer some injury or damage, he could not be blamed for it, and if he were blameless, he could not be held responsible, that is, made to pay for something he did not do. Such reasoning had been solidly rooted in contemporary standards of morality and fairness and would not begin to change, however, until it became apparent that the standards themselves were losing their relevance in the face of overwhelming social and economic transformation.

In 1912, for example, when the giant Chicago meatpacking firm Armour and Company defended itself against a New York resident who had been poisoned by one of the packer's canned meats, it did so by claiming that it had not knowingly done anything to harm the consumer, had never had any direct contact with her, and should not, therefore, be blamed for her injury. But this traditional interpretation of the law had grown less and less acceptable in a society where consumers and producers had become increasingly separated by middle-men and the advances of technology upon which the consumer, often unaware of dependency upon it, relied. When the federal circuit court upheld the verdict for the consumer, it did so for what it unhesitatingly admitted were purely public policy considerations. To have ruled otherwise, it noted, would have left an aggrieved consumer without any legal remedy with which to pursue the compensation she deserved for her loss. Fault, the traditional standard of judgment, could no longer be defined completely in terms of blame. The concept of "liability" was becoming increasingly useful to the courts in resolving the question of who should be made responsible. As a measure of fault, liability shifted responsibility to the designer, manufacturer, and packager who released a particular product for public consumption. He, and not the consumer, was in the best position to ensure that the product was made as risk-free as possible. The law of torts had been changed to accommodate the realities of a modern, industrial world and to give recognition to the consumer's growing need for protection.

of this sentiment was derived from the public's distrust of the courts whose reactionary philosophies, fixed values, and partiality to the country's monied interests had thoroughly disgusted them. Others, among them many in the progressive movement with its emphasis upon the conscientious discharge of one's public duties, sought to place the blame on the qualifications of those actually sitting on the courts' benches and the process by which they had been placed there, the popular election. By 1905 the public's enthusiasm for the election of the judiciary had peaked — judges were elected to office by popular vote in as many as thirty-six states. In only ten states were they appointed by the governor or the legislature. But efforts were under way to change this situation, to eliminate what was seen as one of the more blatant abuses of the democratic process: namely, the corruption of the judiciary and the weakening of its traditional independence. The movement to raise standards for the selection of judges was initially embraced by progressive reformers whose interests and movements would eventually give the era its name; it was also embraced later, though somewhat more gradually, by the professional organizations of the lawyers themselves. The years that followed witnessed an ironic reversal in a trend once acclaimed as a reaffirmation of the nation's commitment to the spirit of democracy. States began to experiment with other forms of qualifying and nominating judges, among them the Missouri plan, which called for candidates to be screened by a specially appointed commission and then, following the completion of an initial term, to have their performance evaluated periodically through popular election. Changes such as these rarely succeeded in achieving the objectives of their advocates. The low esteem in which the nation's courts were held by many Americans did not rise significantly until later in the decade, after the nation entered World War I and an upwelling of patriotic sentiment shielded public institutions from widespread criticism.

Sources:

John W. Johnson, *American Legal Culture 1908–1940* (Westport, Conn.: Greenwood Press, 1981);

Editorial, *Outlook,* 102 (7 September 1912) p. 1;

Bernard Schwartz, *The Law in America* (New York: McGraw Hill 1974).

THE MANN ACT

Problem of International Concern. The passage in 1910 of the White Slave Traffic Act, better known as the Mann Act, was a product of the sensationalistic stories and lurid details regularly appearing in the nation's newspapers, stories about the abduction of innocent women for the purpose of prostitution. While many reformers had long been engaged in a war against prostitution in their own communities, their efforts had been spurred by the much-publicized success of their counterparts in England, who were reportedly prevailing against the exploi-

Congressman James R. Mann, a Republican from Illinois who sponsored the Mann Act of 1910, barring "white slavery"

tation of women for profit. The release in 1909 of the Immigration Commission's studies of the problems posed by the importation of foreign women to staff the hundreds of brothels scattered throughout the nation's large cities fired the opponents of vice with renewed purpose and energy. Aside from the repulsion and exasperation Americans felt in confronting the evidence of the immorality plaguing their communities was the suspicion — reflecting the prejudices harbored at the time — that the root of the problem was to be found in alien lands, in the hands of the international trafficker who, given the restrictions imposed by considerations of jurisdiction and limited local resources, could act with impunity. In this way the concerns of many reformers directly connected to the issue of immigration control.

Early Efforts. As early as 1875 Congress had attempted to deal with prostitution in that context, enacting a law forbidding the importation of alien women for the purposes of prostitution. In 1903 that measure was replaced by another, extending the prohibition to female children. In 1907 the act was amended to broaden its prohibition against prostitution to include the importation of women for "any other immoral purpose." On an official level, what gave Congress the incentive to pass the Mann Act was the Senate's commitment in 1905 to

abide by the International Agreement for the Suppression of the Trade in White Women. This agreement obligated its signatories to take whatever steps were appropriate to combat the growing international traffic in women for the purpose of prostitution. If that, in fact, had been the act's original purpose, the reason its passage and implementation commanded such wide support in this country was entirely different.

The Mann Act and Public Morals. Since the turn of the century, Americans had begun in increasing numbers to fear for the preservation of their moral values and the familiar symbols of the nation's moral strength. Traditionalists were frightened by trends toward divorce, the political emancipation of women, birth control, and changing attitudes toward sex. From the outset the Mann Act was apparently little more than an attempt to legislate national morality. Pressured by those who believed that local efforts to suppress vice needed reinforcement, the courts were quick to act on the sentiment that had carried this legislation to enactment. Section 2 of the act provided that any person "who shall knowingly transport or cause to be transported, or aide or assist in obtaining transportation for, or in transporting, in interstate or foreign commerce, or in any territory or in the District of Columbia, any women or girls for the purpose of prostitution or debauchery, or for any other immoral purpose, or with the intent to induce, entice, or compel such women or girls to become a prostitute or to give herself up to debauchery, or to engage in any other immoral practice . . . shall be guilty of a felony." Faced with the absence of any clear constitutional authority to legislate moral issues, Congress had relied on its power to regulate commerce among the states to intervene in this area; in doing so, it avoided a problem of a clearly constitutional dimension. Congress had, after all, passed laws prohibiting the use of the mails for gambling or for the distribution of narcotics or as a means of disseminating materials considered obscene; and each law had successfully withstood legal challenges. It would not be long, however, before the Mann Act was challenged in court.

Act Passes Muster. The first case to reach the Supreme Court was that of *Hoke* v. *United States,* decided on 24 February 1913. Effie Hoke and Basile Economides were charged and convicted of transporting two known prostitutes from New Orleans to Beaumont, Texas. Lawyers for the defendants argued before the Supreme Court that Congress had overstepped its bounds in addressing a matter of purely local concern. Their arguments, based on a far more restrictive view of the act, were rejected by the majority of the justices on the Court. The responsibility for the promotion of the general welfare, the majority reasoned, was to be borne either independently of, or in conjunction with, the various states. Congress had been authorized to regulate commerce among the states and could therefore adopt whatever means reasonably served that purpose, even if the method used were more characteristic of the policing power employed by the individual states in enforcing their criminal laws — an area rarely ventured into by the federal government. The cases that followed were equally significant and demonstrated a willingness by the Court's majority to permit the government to extend its regulatory power to a degree that surprised many, in light of the High Court's refusal to do so in other areas of national and congressional concern. In the case of *United States* v. *Holte* the Court effectively ignored the purpose of the act when it validated the conviction of a woman who had permitted herself to be transported across state lines for purposes of prostitution. In *Anthanasaw* v. *United States* the Court upheld the conviction of a man who had arranged for a woman to be employed as a chorus girl, which required her to mingle with the guests in the owner's theater. Nothing but conversational exchanges took place, but the majority interpreted the statute as prohibiting any act that might result in the corruption of morals, whether such corruption had been proven or not.

Unintended Precedent. Not until the Supreme Court issued its decision in *Caminetti* v. *United States*, however, was the full effect and scope of the statute established. Farley Drew Caminetti and his friend, both married men, were charged with violating the act by taking two female acquaintances to Reno, Nevada, for what were alleged to be immoral purposes. The defendants denied that they had taken the women for any consideration of financial profit, arguing that those who introduced and secured passage of the Mann Act had never intended the act and its prohibitions to apply to persons engaged in nothing more exploitive than a tryst. The argument was sufficient to convince several justices that some distinction had to be made between the "occasional immoralities of men and women" and the systematic and commercialized vice envisioned by the title of the act. The majority, however, remained unmoved. Congress's authority to act in the protection of interstate commerce, to ensure that it remained free of immoral exploitation, they reasoned, had already been acknowledged: the act expressly forbade the transportation of women "for any immoral purposes" and contained no legal language limiting the interpretation of the phrase. Congress had, as far as the issue of public morals was concerned, found a welcome but unexpected ally on the part of the Supreme Court. If the Court had resisted the idea of allowing Congress unlimited power in regulating commerce among the states where rights of property or the freedom to contract were concerned, it showed no such reluctance in matters involving public morals. The message was clear: Congress did not have the authority to control all facets of interstate commerce, but it could exercise virtually unlimited power to prevent the use of interstate commerce for what was clearly regarded as a social evil.

Source:
Robert L. Anderson, *The Diggs-Caminetti Case, 1913-1917 (For Any Other Immoral Purpose)* (New York: Edwin Mellen Press, 1990).

PROHIBITION AND THE EIGHTEENTH AMENDMENT

Interest in National Legislation. Despite the fact that some form of Prohibition had been enacted into law in thirty-one states by 1913, interest in the enactment of national Prohibition legislation remained strong. The abuse of alcohol was an issue of great importance in many communities, and it especially galvanized the reformers who were interested in the rehabilitation of criminals and delinquents, the elimination of slums, the alleviation of poverty, and Christian temperance. Many Americans considered alcoholism a serious problem, yet many others were inclined to ignore its personal and social costs. Advocates of reform initially focused on convincing individual communities and states to formulate regulatory policies to advance Prohibition, but these efforts proved to be of limited and often temporary value. For the reformers, the answer was to be found not only in the application of highly restrictive laws that acknowledged the danger consumption posed to the public's social and moral health; reformers decided that they must also work for a more uniform enforcement of the laws against the sale and manufacture of alcoholic beverages.

Reluctant Partner. In the nineteenth century the courts generally granted wide latitude to the states to control or forbid the manufacture and sale of liquor. In 1890 the Supreme Court, however, determined that states could not prohibit the importation of liquor in its original packaging without interfering with the federal government's constitutional authority to regulate interstate commerce. That same year, to sidestep this limitation on a state's regulatory power, Congress passed the Wilson Act, which eliminated the distinction made by the Supreme Court between alcohol manufactured locally and that imported and maintained in its original packaging. Despite this congressional action, the Supreme Court eventually settled on an interpretation of the Wilson Act that protected the interstate shipment of liquor from any restrictions a state might impose on such shipments. The act, the Court decided, did not open shipments of liquor to state regulation until the contents of the shipments in question were placed in the hands of the consumer. There the matter stood until efforts to involve Congress in removing yet another obstacle to state liquor regulation built momentum.

Webb-Kenyon Interstate Liquor Act. In 1913 a bill was introduced in Congress to provide the states with the power they would need to ban the importation of liquor altogether. In those instances where the consumption of alcohol was prohibited locally, enforcement of the law often proved difficult: consumers had only to travel to neighboring towns or counties where no prohibition against liquor existed. Efforts in Congress to exclude from the law liquor intended for strictly personal use was defeated, and the bill was subsequently passed by a large majority in both houses. But President Taft promptly vetoed it, believing the bill gave Congress more power

A 1919 advertisement for a New York City liquor store urging people to stock up before National Prohibition goes into effect

over interstate commerce than the Constitution permitted. Within days Congress overrode the president's veto and the Webb-Kenyon Interstate Liquor Act became law on 1 March 1913. Four years later, in *Clark Distilling Company* v. *Western Maryland Railroad,* the Supreme Court upheld the constitutionality of the act, registering no objection to Congress's decision to share, if somewhat conditionally, its power to regulate this particular aspect of interstate commerce. The states' bid for federal assistance in the preservation of their liquor laws had finally achieved some measure of success, but efforts to involve the federal government further in such regulation, at least on a national level, proved unsuccessful until the coming of the war.

Passing the Eighteenth Amendment. For the advocates of national Prohibition, the advantages of such legislation were clear: the flow of alcohol from outside the country could be shut off; transferring responsibility for the enforcement of Prohibition to the federal government would result in a more efficient and uniform effort to achieve the law's objectives; and federal involvement would insulate the enforcers of the law from corruption and local influence. Whether these arguments by themselves would have proved persuasive in Congress is uncertain. What rekindled congressional interest was the task of mobilizing the nation's resources for war. In August 1917 Congress passed the Lever Food and Fuel Control Act, giving President Wilson the authority to control the use of certain food products, including ingredients used in the production of liquor, for purposes of supporting the nation's war effort. Shortly thereafter, the president issued proclamations directly affecting the manufacture of intoxicating liquors. Much to the dismay of the prohibitionists, he made no decision about the production of beer or wine below a certain alcoholic content. As preparations for the war progressed and the country, in an explosion of patriotic sentiment, committed itself to greater sacrifices, Prohibition advocates proved increasingly successful in equating temperance with the need for order and austerity. On 18 December 1917, despite the determined resistance of the liquor industry's lobby and the reluctance of some congressmen whose constituents viewed such legislation as a form of discrimination against their ethnic or cultural traditions, Congress adopted and submitted to the states for ratification what became the Eighteenth Amendment to the Constitution. Then, a year later, before the amendment was approved by the necessary thirty-six

states, Congress enacted the Wartime Prohibition Act, which made unlawful the sale of liquor for beverage purposes for the duration of the war. Touted as a measure to protect the morals of the millions of men then being conscripted into service, the act was well received throughout the country and helped to create support for bills pending in state legislatures respecting ratification of the amendment. Once the war was over, resumption of the production of alcoholic beverages again drew the attention of Congress. On 28 October 1919 it passed the Volstead Act over President Wilson's veto, thus extending Prohibition to all beverages containing a minimum of 0.5 percent alcohol. Barely three months later, after final ratification by the states, the Eighteenth Amendment became law. The Supreme Court, in a series of cases known as the national Prohibition cases, confirmed the constitutionality of both the Eighteenth Amendment and the Volstead Act, the provisions of which remained in full force throughout the nation until the amendment's repeal in 1933.

Source:
Page Smith, *America Enters the World: A People's History of the Progressive Era and World War I*, volume 7 (New York: Penguin, 1985).

HEADLINE MAKERS

LOUIS D. BRANDEIS

1856-1941

CONSUMER ADVOCATE; ASSOCIATE JUSTICE OF THE SUPREME COURT

Acting in the Public's Best Interest. It seems unlikely that a man who devoted so much of his early career to becoming a successful corporate lawyer would, at the pinnacle of his success, suddenly choose to involve himself in the most controversial issues of his day. Yet that was exactly what Louis D. Brandeis, a man who had become a millionaire before the age of fifty, did, and his decision to pursue a life of service to his fellow countrymen set him on a course that would prove as problematic for him as it was rewarding. In 1916 Brandeis became an associate justice of the U.S. Supreme Court and served with distinction

until his retirement in 1939. His significance as a historic figure during the 1910s, however, has less to do with his appointment to the Court than with his accomplishments as a dedicated and brilliant advocate on behalf of the public interest. He was a man devoted to the highest principles of service and of his profession. Unique among his peers, he became known as the "people's lawyer."

Boston Lawyer. The son of Jewish immigrants, Brandeis grew up in Louisville, Kentucky, where he fell under the influence of an uncle whose work as a lawyer proved fascinating to him. Following two years of study in Germany, Brandeis enrolled in Harvard Law School, from which he graduated in 1877 with the best academic record in the school's history. After a brief stint with his brother-in-law's firm in Saint Louis, he joined with a former classmate to found the law firm of Warren and Brandeis in Boston. He and his partner made much use of the social and professional relationships and associations they cultivated in the interest of enhancing their practice, and the effort proved worthwhile insofar as the firm's fortunes were concerned. By 1890 the partnership had grown and was servicing important business and manufacturing firms throughout New England. Their success eventually brought Brandeis some measure of financial independence, an achievement that gradually freed him to apply himself to interests and pursuits of an entirely different sort.

The People's Lawyer. Brandeis was a brilliant student and legal scholar (Dean Acheson, who served under him as a clerk after Brandeis had become a justice, once remarked that Brandeis wrote the opinions and that he merely contributed the footnotes). He was also an avid reader, well versed in such issues as those concerning the conditions of labor and the poor, who suffered injustices he found intolerable. The writings of reformers Henry George and Henry Demarest Lloyd greatly impressed him, but nothing equaled the impact upon his conscience and his faith in social justice as did the events surrounding one of the most violent strikes in the nation's history. The Homestead strike of 1892 did not actually set him on the path toward legal and social reform for which he became so famous in the early part of the decade — his work with the Public Franchise League in attacking exclusive public utility contracts predated the outbreak of industrial warfare in Pennsylvania — but it did convince him that the public's need for protection was greater than he had ever imagined and required an advocate prepared to make sacrifices on its behalf. Brandeis's work as an unpaid attorney for the holders of industrial life insurance policies in New England, and his success in fashioning a solution that reflected both his legal expertise, and his knowledge of business practices established a pattern in his life from which he did not deviate until his elevation to the Supreme Court. His reputation as a selfless advocate for the worker was strengthened by his involvement in 1906 in the case of *Muller* v. *Oregon,* which ultimately required him to appear before the Supreme Court to convince its justices of the state of Oregon's right to impose and enforce laws governing work hours in the interest of the workers' safety and health.

The Advocate. The methods Brandeis used to protect the interests of his clients were sometimes quite unorthodox, but always practical, and clearly reflected his interest in accumulating as much information as possible as a prelude to action. As the attorney for stockholders in the Boston and Maine Railroad, for example, he had attempted to prevent the railroad's merger with the larger New Haven Railroad in order to prevent the latter from gaining a monopoly over railroad lines throughout New England. Between 1912 and 1913, in an effort to mobilize public opinion against the merger, he wrote a series of articles that appeared in *Harper's Weekly,* documenting many of the unethical practices of those involved in the merger effort. But it was not until the New York City garment strike in 1910 that the genius Brandeis had repeatedly

displayed in his past became more widely recognized. The strike involved some sixty thousand laborers whose protest of conditions in the shops drew nationwide attention and the support of many reform-minded people, but the hardships it brought over time to the strikers made finding some solution to the turmoil all the more imperative. The strikers, many of whom were women, had been subjected to problems ranging from police brutality to harsh treatment at the hands of unsympathetic judges; the respect they had garnered from the public hardly made up for the depletion of their resources. Into this picture stepped Louis Brandeis, who, at the invitation of some of the strikers' sympathizers, proposed a solution that incorporated a provision for the gradual replacement of the nonunion workers with those with union membership and further provided for improved conditions and stepped-up increases in wages. The plan permitted the shop owners time to adjust to the increased cost of doing business. Brandeis also created a protocol that provided a method by which future disputes could be resolved without recourse to strikes, a formula for industrial peace that, along with its author, became much acclaimed in the nation's press.

The Political Arena. Brandeis's prominence and growing circle of reform-minded acquaintances eventually involved him in a political scandal that touched President William Howard Taft, the Ballinger-Pinchot affair. Former president Theodore Roosevelt regarded conservation as his prize domestic achievement, an accomplishment attributable in great part to the efforts of the nation's chief forester, Gifford Pinchot. Roosevelt's successor, Taft, replaced the secretary of the interior, Pinchot's superior, with a man of his own choice, Richard Ballinger. Ballinger, closely associated with those who opposed the expansive conservation program for which Pinchot and Roosevelt had been jointly responsible, used his position to convince President Taft that Roosevelt had acted without proper authority in withdrawing millions of acres of land from development. With the president's approval, Ballinger validated the claims of several companies to the rich coal fields of Alaska in which, unknown to the president, Ballinger's business associates had a stake. Alerted to this plan by one of the department's employees, Louis Glavis, Pinchot went public with the details. Both men were fired for insubordination. During the congressional hearings that followed, Brandeis, who had been retained to represent Glavis, demonstrated, much to the president's embarrassment, that the internal report the president claimed to have relied upon in his decision to fire Glavis had not, in actual fact, been prepared until after the president had discharged him. Brandeis's role in this affair would win him the enmity of many Republican conservatives, the admiration of numerous progressives, and a reputation, in combination with his record as a public advocate, for "radicalism," which would return to haunt him during his confirmation hearings in connection with his appointment to the High Court.

From Presidential Adviser to Associate Justice. Early in 1916 President Woodrow Wilson announced that he was nominating Brandeis to the Supreme Court, a decision that caused enormous controversy, but that clearly demonstrated the president's resolve to fulfill the remaining promises of his New Freedom platform. Brandeis had long served the president as a political adviser and troubleshooter, providing then-candidate Wilson, in 1912, with the benefit of his experience and insight regarding the major issues of the day and speaking for Wilson's candidacy throughout the Northeast. So respected was Brandeis's reputation for fairness and wise counsel that he was asked in 1913 to resolve a conflict that had arisen within the Democratic Party over the structure of the Federal Reserve System, a conflict he resolved in a manner that left virtually no sense of rancor among the disputants. Sometime later, he was prevailed upon to draft what would become the Federal Trade Commission Act of 1914. His appointment to the Court, then, seemed no more than a logical outgrowth of the service he provided the party and its president. However, it frightened many within the business community, who saw Brandeis as a radical representing forces that were inimical to the interests of business. It antagonized others who disapproved of his involvement in the Zionist cause, and it alienated the American Bar Association, which challenged his impartiality and lack of judicial experience. After four months of heated debate during which seven of the ABA's former presidents spoke out against his nomination, the Senate confirmed the appointment by a vote essentially along party lines. Louis Dembitz Brandeis finally took his place on the Supreme Court bench.

Mr. Justice Brandeis. Not until succeeding decades did Brandeis's contributions to the Court and to the nation as a justice achieve the significance with which they would come to be viewed; but that does not diminish his work in the years immediately following his confirmation. Brandeis had been instrumental in conceiving and planning the role of the Federal Trade Commission, believing, as he did, that government had a responsibility to regulate the economy in the public interest. His views did not change after he assumed his duties with the Court, and he consistently proved willing to allow the legislative branch, whether state or federal, wide latitude in its experimentation on behalf of the public interest. Often in the minority in this regard, he would frequently find himself closely allied with yet another great justice, Oliver Wendell Holmes Jr., whose commitment to the doctrine of judicial restraint was unshakable. A believer in social experimentation, as well, he would soon be viewed as the Court's most liberal member, a reputation that would be enhanced by his strong opposition to the government's interference with fundamental civil liberties.

Sources:
Editorial, *Outlook* (11 June 1910);

Alpheus Mason, *Brandeis: A Free Man* (New York: Viking, 1946);

Philippa Strum, *Louis D. Brandeis: Justice for the People* (Cambridge, Mass.: Harvard University Press, 1984).

JOHN WILLIAM DAVIS

1873-1955

SOLICITOR GENERAL OF THE UNITED STATES

Lawyer to Congressman. In 1911 John Davis was elected to represent his West Virginia district in the House of Representatives. A man of great ambition and a lawyer of distinction in his home state, the decision to pursue a political career had not been an easy one for him. He had dedicated himself to the operation of the law office he shared with his father and had become the principal reason for its success. He did become a candidate, however, and won a seat in Congress on his first attempt. As a Democrat he faithfully supported President Wilson's legislative program in spite of the reservations he held with respect to the president's leadership and his liberal ideals. Though highly regarded by his colleagues in the house for his legal acumen, Davis received little recognition for his work outside the Congress until the impeachment trial of Judge Robert W. Archbald brought his advocacy skills well into public view. Davis was selected to deliver the prosecution's summation of the case and delivered an argument that was so forceful and persuasive as to attract the personal attention of the president. On 30 August 1913 Davis, nearing the end of his term and tiring of his legislative role, was offered and eagerly accepted an appointment to the post of solicitor general of the United States.

Solicitor General. As solicitor general Davis argued more cases before the Supreme Court than had any of his predecessors and established his reputation as one of the nation's foremost appellate lawyers. Even the justices before whom he often appeared felt nothing but the highest regard for his technical proficiency and strength as an advocate. Given his involvement in the defense of so many of the most important legislative accomplishments of the Progressive Era, such praise was clearly deserved, even though his efforts did not always meet with success. In one of his most memorable cases, *Hammer* v. *Dagenhart*, he was unable to dissuade the Supreme Court from viewing the nation's first major child labor law as an unconstitutional extension of federal authority. He did, nevertheless, become far better known for his successes, which, given the conservatism of the federal bench, were indeed major accomplishments and often involved issues of exceptionally great interest to the public. Among the cases he handled on behalf of the federal government were those that resulted in the extension of federal regulatory control over public lands, oil company pipelines, and certain utilities. His name appeared in the journals of the day in connection with the Supreme Court's decision finding Oklahoma's attempt to deprive African Americans of their right to vote through the use of a grandfather clause unconstitutional. His defense of the Adamson Act, which regulated the work hours of railroad employees, and, later, of the draft laws of 1917 were considered among his most brilliant, but he would eventually tire of the work that brought him all but what he felt he most needed, material success.

Money, Prestige, and the Man. Davis had been born into a prominent West Virginia family and had received many advantages as a youth, including the finest education available. Sent to Washington and Lee College, he stayed there until he was awarded his law degree in 1895. He returned a year later to teach law, but remained only a short while before leaving to join his father's law firm, where he benefited from the work provided him by the firm's established clientele. Driven by a consuming desire to increase his wealth and establish his position in the firm as its principal counsel, Davis devoted himself entirely to his practice and prospered from the activities of the railroad and mining companies that had come to dominate West Virginia's economy. In 1910, believing public office would bring him greater recognition and expand the firm's list of clients, he somewhat reluctantly sought endorsement of his candidacy for Congress from the Democratic Party, and won the election. This was the first step of a career in government that would culminate in his appointment as ambassador to Great Britain in 1918. Davis remained active on the national scene until his death in 1955.

Presidential Candidate. Following his return to the United States in 1921, he left government service to join a Wall Street firm that counted J. P. Morgan and Company among its prestigious clients. The following year he was elected president of the American Bar Association, and rejected, much to Chief Justice William Howard Taft's disappointment, any further suggestion of his being considered for the Supreme Court. In 1924, on the 103rd ballot, he won his party's nomination for the presidency, but the campaign he conducted revealed his fundamental conservatism, a factor that made him indistinguishable from the incumbent, Republican Calvin Coolidge. Much to his surprise, he was forced to contend with criticism of his service and reputation as a lawyer for the wealthy and powerful. His candidacy revealed more clearly than anything else Davis' deeply held conservatism and his basic prejudices.

Later Career. As a lawyer, he tended to favor a strict constructionist view of the Constitution, and as a man who became fearful of the expansion of federal power and had proven himself a states' rights advocate, he came to feel nothing but disappointment for the changes wrought by the New Deal. Though a witness to the enormous changes in the law and its practice all about him, Davis chose to remain steadfast in his defense of a much more conservative philosophy, attacking the Democratic administration for what he perceived as an emasculation of state authority and its usurpation of power the framers of the Constitution had never envisioned. He was not content merely to criticize, but devoted his energies to the organization of the American Liberty League in 1934 to resist the legal and social changes then well under way. He was, however, still capable of acting somewhat unpredictably, and sometimes with momentous results. In 1931 in the case of *United States* v. *Macintosh,* he represented a theologian who claimed that his selective conscientious objection to war should not disqualify him from citizenship. But in the main, Davis's beliefs and perceptions reflected those of the social and professional milieu he had worked so hard to become a part of and whose values and attitudes he would make his own. In 1952, appalled by President Truman's threat to take over the nation's steel industry and by his forcing it to end the strike and resume production, he successfully defended the industry against the government's seizure of its plants and production properties. Two years later, in his last major case before the Supreme Court, he represented the state of South Carolina in its unsuccessful defense of "separate but equal" school systems for blacks in the case of *Brown* v. *Board of Education.*

Source:
William H. Harbaugh, *Lawyer's Lawyer: The Life of John Davis* (New York: Oxford University Press, 1973).

OLIVER WENDELL HOLMES JR.

1841-1935

ASSOCIATE JUSTICE OF THE SUPREME COURT

A New Age Arrives. The evolution of the Supreme Court as an institution has historically occurred in a series of stages, each of which tends to overlap the next, thus blurring the boundaries between them, and sometimes obscuring the significance of events occurring during these transitional periods. More often than not, these stages serve as a framework within which the forces that have influenced the Court's decisions are to be understood. Occasionally, but rarely, the transition from one era to another has been symbolized by the presence on the Court of a justice whose stature, ability, and performance make him the embodiment of the new age. Oliver Wendell Holmes Jr. was that kind of a justice. Despite his strengths, however, he was never able entirely to escape the Darwinian and Spencerian influences of his formative years as a lawyer. Like the judges he often criticized, Holmes possessed preconceptions of his own, notions and biases reflecting the values by which he had been reared and that represented the views of the age in which he lived. But he developed a deep skepticism for the legal doctrines and precedents that his contemporaries were disposed to treat as truths, both universal in scope and unchanging in nature. This above all sets him apart from his contemporaries and places him well ahead of his time. During his lengthy term as an associate justice, the U.S. Supreme Court issued more than six thousand opinions, only seventy of which were accompanied by the dissents for which he would become so famous. What made these dissents so significant, however, was the fact that in almost every instance they reflected a line of reasoning that foreshadowed things to come. They proved to be the harbingers of a new age in legal thought and constitutional development.

Soldier, Lawyer, Legal Scholar, Educator, and State Supreme Court Justice. Born and raised in Boston, this son of one of the city's established and most distinguished families would forever revere his cultural heritage and the unique history with which his surroundings were so imbued. Though temperamentally and intellectually rooted in his milieu, Holmes possessed a restless mind and was given to ruminations that would often inspire him to view his environment from an entirely different perspective, a trait that would remain with him throughout his long life. In 1857 he enrolled at Harvard University and would have graduated but for the outbreak of the Civil War. Commissioned an officer in the Twentieth Massachusetts Regiment, he served for three years and suffered three wounds, each of which was serious enough to require a period of convalescence before he could to return to duty. No other event would so deeply affect his personality and outlook as his experience on the battlefield, where whatever assurance he had found in the orderliness of his life, in his faith in the inevitability of human progress, had been seriously shaken. For him, nothing could ever again be thought of as unchanging, and change itself could no longer be thought of as being always for the good. In 1864 Holmes somewhat reluctantly took up the study of law, graduating from the Harvard Law School in 1866 and gaining admission to the Massachusetts State Bar the following year. Although he diligently applied himself to the grinding routine so characteristic of the practice of law, it was his work between 1870 and 1873, as an editor of the *American Law Review,* to which he truly and happily devoted himself. Taking what advantage he could of the opportunity to immerse himself in the legal literature of the day, he indulged his interest in the philosophical underpinnings and origins of the law and developed a much-deserved reputation as a legal scholar. In 1880 he completed and published a collection of his essays, *The Common Law,* which came to be regarded as a work of great significance. Holmes's writings revealed him as a man who rejected the traditional view of the law as a fixed and unchanging set of maxims and whose pragmatism placed far heavier emphasis upon the lessons of experience than they did upon blind and unbend-

ing adherence to established rules and concepts. In January 1882 he was appointed to a newly created chair at the Harvard Law School, where he served as an instructor until his appointment to the Massachusetts Supreme Court in December of that year. He remained a highly visible and sometimes controversial figure on that bench until 1902, three years after he had assumed the duties of chief justice of the state's highest court.

The New Associate Justice. At some point Theodore Roosevelt, then president of the United States, was forced to set aside the misgivings he had regarding his nominee for the Supreme Court and to throw his full weight behind Holmes's confirmation as an associate justice. Holmes's record as a state supreme court justice had been impressive and, for the president, somewhat reassuring; but could he be trusted to promote and preserve the administration's program of reform? Many of Holmes's decisions, reaching beyond the conservatism so characteristic of the other members of the Massachusetts high court, had been well received by the progressive circles in the region from which the president had drawn much needed support. It would not be long, however, before Holmes would give Roosevelt reason to regret his choice, to move the president to compare the strength of the justice's backbone with that found in a banana. Though the majority had decided in favor of the government and had extended the reach of the antitrust laws in the case of *Northern Securities Company* v. *United States,* Holmes had found reason to dissent, and did so in a manner that, while infuriating the president, had clearly affirmed his independence as a judge.

The Great Dissenter. As time passed, certain distinctive patterns in Holmes's performance as a justice began to emerge. Holding firmly to his faith in the process of trial and error, Holmes early embraced and became an advocate for the policy of judicial restraint. Unlike his friend and frequent fellow dissenter, Justice Louis D. Brandeis, he did not believe that every exercise of power for or in the public's interest would necessarily result in some measure of progress. Tinkering with the system bore no special attraction for him, but he remained a firm believer in the public's and the legislature's right to tinker, and to do so unimpeded by a judicial process he viewed as often reactionary. Holmes had no regard for the "black letter" approach to the interpretation of the law, the tradition of accepting the dictates of precedent as the only permissible view. He believed, instead, that the Constitution served as a framework within which the most significant issues of the day could be determined, addressed, and, with a little patience, quite possibly resolved. Though increasingly uncomfortable with the results of the political process to which he felt such responsibility, Holmes remained acutely aware of his own small place in that process, striving, as he often remarked, to remind himself that he was not God, nor, necessarily, an effective arbiter between what was good and what was considered bad. There are those who credit him with the introduction of a new age on the Court, with being among the first to appreciate and accept changes in the nation's attitude toward and perception of the government's role in all facets of national life. That is not entirely correct. It would be more accurate to say that he believed all the world and everything in it to be in a state of transition and that he recognized the folly of attempting to bring order to a universe that resisted order and imposed its own will upon the affairs of men. Man's efforts to achieve some degree of order required guidance, a point of reference, and he readily acknowledged that, but the function of law, he believed, was to provide the means by which people could contend with the challenges they faced. At the center of Holmes's insight was his view of the law as an evolving process, which, like the world itself, was in constant movement. He believed that it was the function of the courts to reconcile this process with changes in the country's social, economic, and political life, while scrupulously avoiding the temptation to interfere. Holmes's dissents, for which he gained much fame, often revealed the high regard he held for the principles he believed were embodied in the Constitution. His dissent in the 1919 case of *Abrams* v. *United States*, for example, was a masterful statement of his belief that free expression was the greatest protection any democracy could hope for in controlling its propensity for excess or, as was the case, the repression of opposing or unpopular views. In time the Great Dissenter's perspectives would become those of the majority of the justices, and a new era for the Court would begin.

Source:
Liva Baker, *The Justice From Beacon Hill: The Life and Times of Oliver Wendell Holmes* (New York: HarperCollins, 1991).

GEORGE WILLIAM NORRIS

1861-1944

LEGISLATOR

The Fighting Liberal. During the thirty years that George Norris served in the U.S. Senate, his name became closely associated with a wide range of issues and causes relating to the public development of natural resources, the rights of labor, farm relief, and, to a lesser extent, foreign policy. Lesser known or remembered, however, is the most significant of his many achievements, a contribution he made to this country's history three years before he entered the Senate. In 1910 Norris brought about the most significant procedural changes the House of Representatives, of which he was then a member, had ever experienced; he thus opened the way for the passage of a legislative program with which the Progressive Era became so uniquely identified. A skilled parliamentarian and legislator who valued his independence above almost everything else, Norris rightfully earned his reputation as a champion of the progressive cause and as a determined foe of those whom he suspected of exploiting the nation's natural resources for their private advantage. To his constituents and the public at large, he projected an image of fearlessness and tenacity that belied the fact that he favored compromise and the give-and-take of politics as the preferred means by which to achieve his ends. Norris's opinions and views on any subject of consequence, as opposed to his party affiliation, usually dictated whatever position he took with respect to an issue. The independence he thrived on never allowed him to become indebted to any particular group or interest; his career did not begin, however, so independently.

Congressman Norris. After receiving his law degree in 1883 and gaining admission to the Indiana State Bar, Norris resumed his teaching career, which he pursued for another two years before moving to Nebraska. The upper Midwest was experiencing the heyday of a period of prosperity that was encouraging further development of Nebraska's resources and producing economic conditions that the young attorney, having just started his practice, did not hesitate to exploit. Soon thereafter he was retained as local counsel for the Burlington and Missouri Railroad and divided his attention between service to his principal client and his investments in the milling and mortgage loan businesses he founded. Norris's good fortune, however, suffered a severe blow in the 1890s when both drought and depression struck the state and reduced its economy to a shambles. The situation in which he found himself encouraged him to seek an appointment to a recently vacated and unexpired term as county prosecutor, a position for which he later, in 1892, successfully campaigned. In 1895 he ran as a Republican, an affiliation he maintained throughout his career, in a largely populist region, for a position in the state's Fourteenth Judicial District, a post he won by a narrow margin. Norris remained on the bench until 1902, when he ran as his party's candidate for Congress, again defeating the incumbent by no more than a few votes.

First Term. His first term in Congress was far from being notable. Indebted both to his party and his state's railroad interests, he supported a relatively modest and conservative legislative program and tried to avoid becoming embroiled in the increasingly volatile relations between Nebraska's farming and industrial factions. In 1904 Norris ran for reelection in a campaign the outcome of which was far from certain. Once again, he found himself in desperate need of his party's assistance and welcomed the support of the House Speaker Joseph Cannon, who toured the district on his behalf. Successful in his bid, Norris returned to Washington in 1905 as a man who had been tempered by his experience and who had become far more sensitive to the problems of his constituents, whose efforts to counteract the powerful railroad lobby in the state legislature and to make the state's government more responsive to their needs had attracted his attention and sympathy.

The Coming Storm. During the next two years Norris labored quietly to distance himself from the special interests that had been instrumental in providing him with the support, financial and otherwise, he had needed to secure his place in Congress. Increasingly, he was observed voting with the more progressive elements of his party and in favor of the Roosevelt administration's policies respecting governmental regulation and its struggle against monopolies. This transition did not go unnoticed — or unpunished. In 1908, after Norris announced his intention to run for another term in Congress, he discovered that whatever his expectations may have been, the backing he had anticipated from his party was not forthcoming. Norris won the election with a margin of only twenty-two votes and emerged from the ordeal a somewhat changed man.

Control of the House. This was a period in the history of the House of Representatives when control of its affairs rested almost entirely in the hands of its speaker, Joseph Cannon, whose defense of the status quo and opposition to progressive reform presented a nearly insurmountable barrier to any serious reform. By means of his position as speaker, Cannon controlled the process through which the individual representatives received their committee appointments and was thus able to determine which of any number of proposals pending the House's consideration would ultimately receive its attention. The first attempt to challenge his authority in 1907 had been defeated, and few who had participated in this early rebellion were prepared to resume the struggle. The growing rift between the supporters of President William Howard Taft and those of former president Theodore Roosevelt, however, precipitated another crisis with serious implications for Cannon's continuing domination of the House's membership. The debate among Senate Republicans over the Taft administration's tariff proposals served only to exacerbate the disagreement separating the factions in that party. Like many of his colleagues in the House who represented the midwestern states, Norris felt more inclined to side with the Roosevelt wing against those in his party who remained steadfast in their loyalty to President Taft.

Revolt. On 17 March 1910 Norris, having warned only a few colleagues about his intentions, requested permission to raise what he described as a matter of constitutional privilege. Cannon's caution momentarily failed him, and he granted Norris the opportunity the latter sought to introduce what was immediately recognized for what it was, a proposal of enormous consequences for the House. Norris's proposal called for an expansion of the membership of the House's most powerful committee, the Rules Committee; it also provided for the election of the committee by the House and excluded the speaker from membership. The ensuing debate lasted days and was bitterly fought. The Insurgents, as they became known, were galvanized by Norris's bold move and offer

of leadership and were soon reinforced by the House's Democratic minority, who were quick to appreciate the advantage they would gain by splitting the Republican ranks. By a vote of 191 to 156, Norris's proposal was adopted by the membership, opening the door to a flood of hitherto blocked social and economic legislation.

Senator Norris. Norris's victory brought him to the forefront of the progressive movement and gave him considerably more influence in the development of its program than he might otherwise have had. The election of 1912 provided him another opportunity he had been considering since even before the beginning of his crusade against "Cannonism," running for one of Nebraska's seats in the Senate. Despite the Republican losses that year, Norris was able to succeed in fulfilling his ambition and embark upon a career of service that would garner him a stature accorded few others of his contemporaries. Although a Republican, Norris felt no hesitation in supporting much of the reform legislation supported by President Woodrow Wilson and the Democratic Party. He favored the administration's antitrust policy and the establishment of the Federal Reserve System, and while he opposed the appointments of those whom he believed unqualified for the positions for which they were chosen, or whose interests conflicted with the duties they were to assume, he was quick to recognize talent when he saw it. His perceptiveness explained both his later opposition, as chairman of the Senate Judiciary Committee, to the nominations of Charles Evans Hughes and John J. Parker to the Supreme Court, and his outspoken support of President Wilson's nomination of Louis D. Brandeis as an associate justice.

Foreign Relations and World War I. Norris, however, stopped short of offering the administration an unqualified endorsement, his reservations being nowhere more evident than in the area of foreign policy. The temporary occupation of the Mexican port city of Veracruz by American forces in 1914 gave the senator reason to criticize strongly President Wilson. Norris's dissatisfaction with U.S. policy toward Mexico stemmed in part from the respect he had for the aims of the Mexican Revolution and in part from his belief that U.S. commercial interests were behind the administration's interventionist policy, a suspicion he carried into his views of the country's relations with the warring nations of Europe. In 1917 he joined with several other senators to oppose a resolution that permitted U.S. merchant ships to arm themselves against the threat of submarine and surface raider attacks. Norris's subsequent opposition to the nation's declaration of war against the Central Powers did not prevent him from later supporting Wilson's conduct of the war. This display of wartime unity, however, did not survive long beyond the conclusion of hostilities. Norris was both angered and repulsed by the secret diplomacy in which Secretary of State Robert Lansing and the representatives of the Japanese Empire had engaged and which resulted in the transfer of Chinese territory to Japanese control. Disappointed, as well, in the American response to the Allied nations' claims of colonial rights, he joined those in the Senate who opposed and eventually defeated the president's efforts to enroll the United States in the League of Nations.

"The Knight of American Progressive Ideals." This was the description President Franklin D. Roosevelt used when he referred to Norris following the news of Norris's death from a cerebral hemorrhage in 1944. The 1920s proved to be an excruciatingly long and dismal period for Norris, who, after the death of Sen. Robert M. La Follette of Wisconsin in 1925, became one of the few remaining progressives among the Republicans serving in the Senate. A leading critic within his own party of the Republican administrations that succeeded each other throughout the decade, he spoke out frequently in favor of the rights of the laboring man and the need for a special program for farm relief. Not until after the election of Franklin Roosevelt (whose candidacy he endorsed) in 1932 did Norris recover and expand his influence in the Senate. In short order he introduced and ushered through to passage important legislation that included the Norris-LaGuardia Anti-Injunction Act of 1932, the Norris-Rayburn Rural Electrification Act of 1936, and the Norris-Doxey Farm Forestry Act of 1937. He became the principal author and proponent of the act that created the Tennessee Valley Authority (TVA), and almost single-handedly guided another resolution through Congress that resulted in 1933 in the adoption of the Twentieth "Lame Duck" Amendment to the Constitution. As his biographer would later note, the senator's years in the "wilderness" had come to a distinguished and fitting end.

Sources:

Richard Lowitt, *George W. Norris: The Making of a Progressive 1861–1912* (Syracuse, N.Y.: Syracuse University Press, 1963);

Lowitt, *George W. Norris: The Persistence of a Progressive 1913–1933* (Urbana: University of Illinois Press, 1971).

GEORGE W. WICKERSHAM

1858-1936

U. S. ATTORNEY GENERAL

Trustbuster. When President William Howard Taft appointed George W. Wickersham attorney general in 1909, many were left wondering about the wisdom of the president's choice. As a partner in one of the more established corporate law firms in New York City and a recognized expert on corporate law, Wickersham could not, it was widely felt, be trusted to pursue vigorously the antitrust campaign initiated by the president's predecessor, Theodore Roosevelt. Yet in the four years he served as the nation's attorney general, Wickersham more than doubled the number of antitrust actions brought by his department and was instrumental in settling several major pending cases, two of which resulted in the dissolution of the nation's largest monopolies, Standard Oil and the American Tobacco Company. Wickersham's knowledge of corporate practices and the conditions of the economic marketplace made him invaluable as a leader of the administration's antitrust crusade and obtained for him a place in the President Taft's inner circle of advisers, as well as the confidence of succeeding Republican presidents. For the duration of his distinguished service, he would be regarded as the country's foremost trustbuster.

Attorney General. In March 1909 Wickersham was appointed to the post of the U.S. attorney general by newly elected President Taft. Convinced that he needed to establish a record of achievement distinct from that of his predecessor, Taft, a man of considerable administrative experience himself, was intent on staffing his administration with men of proven executive ability. Taft understood that, unlike Roosevelt, he could not be all things to all people; but he was particularly sensitive to the suspicions of some that he would be less energetic in his pursuit of the malefactors of wealth. Wickersham was among the first of the newly assembled cabinet officers to feel the pressure for action and to understand the nature of his mission. However, the man who eventually became the nation's chief trustbuster was not without misgivings about the government's role in regulating the economy. He believed that forces that were even then leading to greater and more powerful business combinations were inevitable. Size and concentration could not remain, he felt, the principal standards by which his department should determine whether action was justified. The task of government, he believed, was to assess a market on the basis of its relative competitiveness and to determine on that basis whether some form of intervention were necessary or desirable. Wickersham would have much preferred that some other agency, such as the Interstate Commerce Commission, conduct these kinds of regulatory reviews, freeing him and his department to devote their energies to combating monopolies wherever they were discovered. Nevertheless, he pressed on with the job at hand, beginning with a reorganization of the department along divisional lines, which encouraged specialization and improved productivity and simplified direction. Along with the settlements reached in the petroleum and tobacco industries, Wickersham obtained orders dissolving some of the largest trusts then in existence, including that which had been created by the E. I. Du Pont Company. In 1913 he initiated a suit against American Telephone and Telegraph's monopoly of long-distance communication lines, a challenge none of his predecessors had been willing to accept. Wickersham's reputation as a sound adviser and an able drafter of laws became increasingly prized by President Taft as his term progressed. At the president's request Wickersham produced the first draft of the Mann-Elkins Act, which was enacted into law in 1910. He also contributed significantly to many other parts of the president's legislative program, particularly in the area of tariff revision.

The Public Man. President Taft's defeat in the election of 1912 ended Wickersham's career as attorney general and freed him to return to his beloved law firm in New York. He could not avoid, nor did he entirely resist, the many invitations he received to return to public service thereafter. In 1915 he chaired New York's Constitutional Convention's Judiciary Committee. Two years later he was appointed by President Woodrow Wilson as a special commissioner on the War Trade Board. An internationalist, Wickersham found himself in the minority within his party as a result of his support for U.S. involvement in the League of Nations and the World Court. During the 1920s he was elected president of the American Law Institute in recognition for his contributions to the field of international law and his advocacy of mediation of national disputes. In 1929 Wickersham was recalled to service by President Herbert Hoover as the chairman of the National Commission on Law Observance and Enforcement, which had been established in response to growing discontentment with the nation's criminal justice system. In the next two years the commission and its investigators amassed a considerable amount of data, which was carefully divided into specific subject areas and evaluated. Despite the commission's broad scope, the public's attention focused almost immediately on its findings with respect to Prohibition. For well over a year following the release of the commission's report, the debate over its recommendations raged on, earning the commission considerably more criticism than it deserved. Wickersham took it upon himself to defend the commission and its final report, but was unable to respond effectively to some of the inconsistencies it contained, particularly with respect to the enforcement of the Prohibition laws. Toward the end of his life Wickersham, although he remained a critic of some of the New Deal's domestic measures, became a well-recognized supporter of Franklin D. Roosevelt's efforts to improve relations with South America and to lead the nation toward a more active role in international affairs. Illness forced his retirement from his law practice, and shortly thereafter, while convalescing in his home in New York City, he died from a heart attack.

Sources:

Homer Cummings and Carl McFarland, *Federal Justice: Chapters in the History of Justice and the Federal Executives* (New York: Macmillan, 1937);

Arthur S. Link, *Woodrow Wilson and the Progressive Era, 1910–1917* (New York: Harper & Row, 1963).

PEOPLE IN THE NEWS

On 11 July 1912 **Robert W. Archbald,** a circuit judge assigned to the U.S. Commerce Court, was impeached for using his position to advance personal business interests. The sixty-three-year-old judge was accused of making, often under a fictitious name, contracts at advantageous prices for the purchase of coal deposits owned by railroad companies that were litigants before the Commerce Court. The House Judiciary Committee had originally determined that Archbald had developed an improper degree of intimacy with railroad officials and had accepted financial favors from them. The Senate agreed, at least with respect to his conduct as a Commerce Court circuit judge, and removed him from office.

In 1918 **Victor Berger,** a former mayor of Milwaukee, founder of the Socialist Party, and, as an editor of the *Milwaukee Leader,* an opponent of America's involvement in the war in Europe, was indicted for conspiring to violate the Espionage Act. Reelected to Congress shortly before his trial and subsequent conviction, Berger was refused permission by Congress to take his seat, either then or after he was reelected in a special election. In 1921 the Supreme Court reversed Berger's conviction because of the judge's prejudicial conduct during the trial.

After the outbreak of war in 1917, no other member of the president's cabinet caused as much controversy as Postmaster General **Albert Burleson.** In the summer of 1917, under the authority granted him by Congress, Burleson banned numerous publishers, including those of *The New Masses* (formerly *The Liberator*), from distributing their materials through the mails because they were critical of the draft, the government, its foreign policy or the conduct of the war, or advocated for causes, including peace, deemed radical or unpatriotic. Before the end of the year Burleson required all publishers of foreign-language newspapers to submit translations of their contents in advance of publication.

In May 1911 **William J. Burns,** the nation's most famous detective, brought about the arrest of three men whom he identified as being responsible for the October 1910 bombing of the *Los Angeles Times* building and

the deaths of several nonunion printers employed there. Burns's investigation resulted in the indictment of more than forty men for conspiring to carry out acts of terrorism against firms nationwide that opposed the organization of their labor forces by the International Association of the Bridge and Structural Iron Workers.

In March 1910 **Joseph G. Cannon,** one of the most powerful speakers in the history of the House of Representatives, was stripped of his authority by an insurgent group of Republicans who objected to the power he wielded over the House's most important committees — whose membership he and he alone determined. Forty insurgent Republicans, reacting to Cannon's efforts to penalize them for their opposition on other measures, joined with the Democratic minority to break his control by expanding the Rules Committee from five to ten members, all of whom were to be chosen by the House rather than by the speaker. A mere majority of the House could now pass the legislation it wanted.

In 1914 **Anthony Comstock,** a "born-again" moral crusader and head of the New York Society for the Suppression of Vice, again became embroiled in a dispute over the methods he often used in achieving his moralistic ends. Accused of resorting to agent provocateurs and other forms of entrapment to initiate criminal actions against publishers and vendors of a variety of written materials, Comstock was criticized for his efforts to ingratiate himself with the federal judges hearing his cases. One, Judge Charles Benedict, was known to have denied the defense an opportunity to challenge Comstock's evidence and once sentenced a publisher to a year in jail for publishing a title he considered obscene, the Greek poet Ovid's *Art of Love.*

In September 1913 **Maury I. Diggs,** an architect, and **Farley Drew Caminetti,** the son of the commissioner general of immigration, having been convicted of violating the Mann Act, were given sentences ranging from one to two years in prison. They had taken two young women whom they had been dating to Reno, Nevada. The defendants, both of whom were married, had argued that their sexual foibles should not bring them within the prohibitions of the act and protested their being prosecuted under it. Lawyers for the two men appealed their convictions, which were upheld by the U.S. Supreme Court in 1917.

In 1912 **Joseph J. Ettor** and **Arturo Giovannitti,** leaders of a union involved in a strike against the mills of Lawrence, Massachusetts, were arrested for murder during what had become one of the more bitterly fought struggles in labor history. A woman had been killed during one demonstration, and local authorities attributed her death to the violent rioting that had engulfed her — rioting, they charged, that had come about as the direct result of the inflammatory speeches of the two union leaders. For many the trial became a test of the nation's commitment to justice, the issue being whether the courts could distinguish between a rational consideration of the weight of evidence, on the one hand, and the radical political beliefs of the accused, on the other. After hearing the evidence and the final arguments, which were delivered by the defendants themselves, the jury returned a verdict of acquittal.

On 17 August 1915 **Leo M. Frank,** age twenty-nine, was lynched for the murder of Mary Phagan, age thirteen, in Atlanta, Georgia. Frank was the superintendent of the factory in which Phagan had been employed and was charged with her murder after the girl's body had been discovered there. In the sensational trial that followed, Frank was convicted largely on the testimony of Jim Conley, the factory janitor. Outside the South, where the case had gained considerable notoriety, it was widely believed that Frank, a Jew, was a victim of hatred and bigotry. Gov. John Slaton commuted Frank's sentence to life imprisonment, but a vengeful mob removed him from a prison work camp in Marietta, Georgia, and hanged him. In 1982 Alonzo Mann, who had worked as Frank's office boy, revealed that on the day of the murder he had seen Jim Conley carry the body of Mary Phagan to the factory basement and that Conley had threatened him to keep him silent. In 1986, some seventy years after his death, Frank's conviction was overturned.

On 21 December 1919 **Emma Goldman** and 248 other people, all accused of harboring some form of radical beliefs, were marched aboard an old army transport ship and deported from the United States. Goldman had been arrested in 1903 for inciting a riot among New York's unemployed workers. Though no riot had actually occurred, she was convicted and sentenced to a year in prison. By the time of her release, Goldman had become a celebrity as "Red Emma." In 1906 Goldman oversaw the publication of *Mother Earth,* a radical monthly periodical that opposed military conscription and sponsored antiwar rallies. In 1917 she was arrested for obstructing the draft and subsequently convicted, fined, and imprisoned for two years.

On 7 December 1911 the owners of the Triangle Shirtwaist Company, **Isaac Harris** and **Max Blanck,** were acquitted of any criminal responsibility for the deaths of 146 of their employees in a fire that destroyed their factory in New York. The acquittal stunned people throughout the nation, many of whom had received firsthand accounts of the carnage left by the fire and reports of locked doors and barred windows, which prevented escape. The prosecuting attorney, however, found himself confronted with contradictory testimony that left him unable to prove that the owners had actual knowledge of conditions in their factory at the time of the fire.

In 1913 **William "Big Bill" Haywood** and several other leaders of the Industrial Workers of the World were arrested by the Paterson, New Jersey, police for loitering. Many viewed his arrest, which was widely reported, as proof of the police's continuing harassment of the union that had been so instrumental in the recently ended strike at the nearby silk mills. Witnesses testified that Haywood had been doing nothing more than walking down the street when he was arrested. Convicted, Haywood appealed to the state's highest court, which, in a scathing opinion, overturned the conviction as being wholly unsupported by the evidence.

In May 1913 the world heavyweight boxing champion, **Jack Johnson,** was convicted of violating the Mann "White Slavery" Act and sentenced to a year in prison. Johnson, an African American whose highly publicized lifestyle offended conventional notions among whites about the the place of blacks in American society, had been involved in affairs with several white women, one of whom had been abandoned by Johnson in favor of another whom he eventually married. The prizefighter was convicted on his spurned lover's testimony, despite concerns about her credibility, but he fled the country to avoid serving his sentence.

In 1914 the case of Dr. **Thomas J. Kemp** produced an entirely unexpected constitutional debate about the division of powers between the legislative and executive branches of government. Kemp had been convicted of providing information about abortion to patients who had asked him for such information, a felony under federal law. President Wilson was prevailed upon to commute the doctor's sentence, a decision that drew considerable protest from the press and from Congress, which demanded that the president provide it with details concerning the case and the commutation of the doctor's sentence. The president rejected Congress's demand, his claim of privilege being recognized by a narrow majority of the members of the House Judiciary Committee.

In June 1911 the appointment of Boston attorney **William H. Lewis** as assistant attorney general of the United States was confirmed by the Senate. Lewis, a black man, had credentials that were impeccable: a graduate of the Harvard Law School and a former member of the Massachusetts state legislature, he had served since 1903 as an assistant U.S. district attorney in Boston, where he was much respected for his skills as a prosecutor. However, racial prejudice among members of the Senate, particularly those from the southern states, resulted in an unprecedented delay of his appointment.

Throughout much of 1911 the case of Sen. **William Lorimer** of Illinois attracted the nation's attention as another example of the corruptive power of the trusts at the highest levels of government. A product of the city of Chicago's political machine and a recognized champion of the beef trust, Lorimer was accused of rigging his own election to the Congress. Revelations of his and his associates' underhanded and illegal practices gradually moved a reluctant Senate to consider whether it would permit the senator to be seated. In March, by a narrow margin, the senators voted to allow Lorimer to take his seat, and, although the matter was reopened some six months later, nothing more came of the effort to secure Lorimer's impeachment.

In the spring of 1915 typhoid fever struck New York City's Sloane Hospital for Women, resulting in the deaths of two of the twenty-five nurses and staff afflicted. Public health investigators tracked the outbreak to the hospital's kitchen, where they encountered one of the nation's most notorious disease carriers, "Typhoid Mary." Her real name was **Mary Mallon,** and she was the first known carrier of the typhoid fever bacillus in the United States. Quickly detained and isolated, this itinerant cook was later accused of violating the conditions imposed upon her by the courts in exchange for her freedom. Eventually Mary was returned to Riverside Hospital, where she remained until her death in 1938.

In 1913 the imminent arrival of the English suffragist **Emmeline Pankhurst** caused a stir that ultimately involved the president himself. Pankhurst was a known radical who advocated the use of extreme and sometimes illegal measures in support of suffragist aims and women's rights. Convicted in her country of committing arson in the furtherance of her cause, she was released after serving three months of her three-year sentence. Thus, when she proclaimed her intention to embark on a lecture tour of the United States to raise funds for her movement, she was seen as deliberately seeking a confrontation with the American government. Immigration laws in the United States prohibited a convicted felon from entering the country. American officials did, in fact, detain Pankhurst upon her arrival, causing something of a flap, but released her at the president's direction when she agreed to leave the country following the conclusion of her planned tour.

In November 1919 the Lusk Committee of the New York state legislature dispatched seven hundred policemen to raid the offices of suspected radicals. Of the more than five hundred people arrested, one, **Benjamin Pitlow,** was charged under New York's Criminal Anarchy Act of 1902, a law that had been adopted following the assassination of President William McKinley in Buffalo. Pitlow was accused of distributing a thirty-four-page "manifesto" in which he argued that political change could not come through a democratic legislative process and advocated the abolition of democracy and its replacement by another form of government. Pitlow, a former member of the New York state legislature and a leader of the left-wing faction of the Socialist Party, refused, against the advice of his attorney, Clarence Darrow, to defend himself against the accusation or to ask for any consideration in mitigation, defying the jury to find him guilty of anything more than espousing his political beliefs. The jury took less than an hour to convict him, and he was given the maximum sentence of five to ten years in prison.

In February 1912 the House of Representatives passed a resolution directing its Banking and Currency Committee to determine whether the ongoing concentration of wealth in the country posed a threat to the nation's economic security. Rep. **Arsene Pujo** of Louisiana, a lawyer and former member of the National Monetary Commission, was assigned to lead this investigation, which, after highly publicized hearings, resulted in a condemnation of existing banking and credit practices and led the following year to the passage of the Federal Reserve Act.

In April 1914 **Margaret H. Sanger** was indicted for sending information concerning birth control through the mails. A former visiting nurse who had abandoned the practice of her profession to pursue her interest in birth control education full-time, Sanger had launched a movement advocating the use of contraceptives, a subject that brought her into frequent conflict with the authorities and the laws against obscenity. The indictment was quashed by the court some two years later, only a short time before Sanger began to serve a thirty-day sentence for her part in the establishment of the nation's first birth control clinic in Brooklyn, New York.

In October 1913 Gov. **William Sulzer** of New York was removed from office by the state's High Court of Impeachment, consisting of the state senate and the judges of its court of appeals. By a two-thirds vote, the high court found the governor guilty of filing, under oath, a false statement regarding his campaign expenses and of attempting to obstruct an investigation into the contributions which had been made to his campaign.

In July 1915 the Pittsburgh industrialist **Harry K. Thaw** was extradited to New York, and, after a much publicized trial, found sane and released from custody. In 1906 Thaw had shot and killed the famed architect Stanford White in a crowded restaurant above Madison Square Garden. White had been rumored to be having an affair with Thaw's wife. After two trials, Thaw was judged insane and committed to an asylum, from which he escaped. Taking up residence in New Hampshire, he resisted all attempts to have him extradited to New York, claiming that he was wanted for nothing more serious than a misdemeanor (escape), a nonextraditable offense. The Supreme Court disagreed, and Thaw was compelled to return.

In June 1911 Supreme Court Chief Justice **Edward White** formed a committee consisting of himself and Associate Justices Horace Lurton and Willis Van Devanter to revise the rules governing federal courts of equity. Although pressure on the High Court had been mounting for more than a decade, the justices were finally motivated to act by the need to provide guidance in the processing of a flood of applications for injunctions and other emergency relief, a problem they hoped to resolve by implementing new and higher standards that required more detailed descriptions of the conditions or the acts to be enjoined.

In 1912 **Harvey W. Wiley,** the chief of the Department of Agriculture's Bureau of Chemistry, resigned amid much controversy over the issue of the department's responsibility for the enforcement of the food and drug laws. Wiley was almost single-handedly responsible for orchestrating the forces that had helped to dramatize the need for the 1906 Pure Food and Drug Act, but by 1912 his insistence upon rigorous enforcement of the act had managed to antagonize many of the farmers, food processors, and distributors subject to its provisions. The resulting political backlash encouraged Secretary of Agriculture James Wilson to accuse Wiley of improprieties in the management of his office, accusations that were investigated and rejected by both the president and the Congress, but at some cost to Wiley's reputation and influence.

DEATHS

Augustus O. Bacon, 74, chairman of the Senate's Foreign Relations Committee. A onetime member of the Confederate army, a lawyer, and the first senator to be elected under the changes brought about by the adoption of the Seventeenth Amendment, Bacon was an outspoken opponent of intervention in Mexico and a major influence in the formulation of the nation's foreign policy, 14 February 1914.

Lloyd Bowers, 50, former solicitor general under President Taft who achieved enormous success in the cases he handled before the Supreme Court, including those that resulted in the dissolution of the Standard Oil and American Tobacco trusts, 9 September 1910.

David J. Brewer, 72, associate justice of the U.S. Supreme Court between 1890 and 1910, a position to which he had been appointed by President Benjamin Harrison after six years of service as a judge on the Eighth Circuit Court of Appeals, 28 March 1910.

Henry B. Brown, 77, associate justice of the U.S. Supreme Court from 1891 through 1906, 4 September 1913.

Joseph H. Choate, 94, one of the most highly regarded trial lawyers of his time, ambassador to Great Britain between 1899 and 1905, and delegate, in 1907, to the Second Peace Congress at The Hague, 14 May 1917.

Jonathan P. Dolliver, 52, Republican senator from Iowa and a critic of the Payne-Aldrich Tariff Bill. Dolliver valued his independence and was among the first in the Senate to support the Insurgents who dared to challenge the speaker's authority, becoming famous for his remark that an Insurgent member of Congress could easily be distinguished from the rest because he waited to read a bill before voting on it, 15 November 1910.

John Marshall Harlan, 78, associate justice of the Supreme Court from 1877 to 1911; the lone dissenter in that Court's *Plessy* v. *Ferguson* ruling (the "separate but equal" standard) and author of its opinion extending the antitrust act in the *Northern Securities* case, 14 October 1911.

David B. Hill, 66, a charter member of the New York State Bar Association and a politician of enormous influence statewide and nationally, who was closely identified with machine politics in the New York Assembly and served as both the state's lieutenant governor and its senator, 18 November 1910.

John W. Hoyt, 80, lawyer, author, and the former governor of the territory of Wyoming, respected internationally for his contributions to the cause of higher learning, 23 May 1912.

Joseph R. Lamar, 58, former associate justice of the Supreme Court (1910–1916), to which he was appointed by President William Howard Taft, 2 January 1916.

Belva Ann B. Lockwood, 86, the first woman admitted to practice before the Supreme Court of the United States, suffragist and tireless promoter of women's legal rights, 19 May 1917.

Horace H. Lurton, 70, former chief judge of the state of Tennessee and veteran of the Confederate army. Appointed by President Taft in 1909 to sit on the Supreme Court as an associate justice, he retained that position until his death, 12 July 1914.

George Maledon, 76, Judge Isaac C. Parker's chief executioner. After service in the Union army and as a policeman, Maledon became a deputy U.S. marshal for the Western District of Arkansas, which included the Indian Territory in Oklahoma. Maledon gained fame as the "hanging judge's" favorite hangman and was credited with eighty-eight executions.

Henry Martyn, 72, former assistant attorney general and solicitor general for the U.S. Department of Justice; served as counselor to the Department of State, but was best known for his antitrust prosecutions, which included the *Northern Securities* case, 1 December 1910.

William H. Moody, 63, former associate justice of the Supreme Court. After service as the secretary of the navy (1902–1904) and attorney general (1904–1906), Moody was nominated to the Court by Theodore Roosevelt in 1906 and remained on that bench until his retirement in 1910, 2 July 1917.

Carry Nation, 64, a die-hard prohibitionist who resorted to methods that often resulted in her arrest and highly publicized trials, 9 June 1911.

Richard Olney, 81, former attorney general of the United States who unsuccessfully argued before the Supreme Court in support of Congress's power to impose a tax on personal income in the case of *Pollock* v. *Farmer's Loan and Trust,* 8 April 1917.

Theodore Roosevelt, 61, onetime law student, journalist, soldier, legislator, police commissioner, assistant secretary of the navy, governor, vice president, and the twenty-sixth president of the United States, 6 January 1919.

Benjamin R. "Pitchfork Ben" Tillman, 70, U.S. senator from South Carolina, a champion of the farmer and one of the nation's most vocal opponents of the construction of the Panama Canal, women's suffrage, and the annexation of Hawaii, 3 July 1918.

PUBLICATIONS

Benjamin N. Cardozo, *The Growth of the Law* (New Haven: Yale University Press, 1924);

Josephus Daniels, *The Wilson Era: Years of Peace, 1910–1917* (Chapel Hill: University of North Carolina Press, 1946);

Felix Frankfurter and J. M. Landis, *The Business of the Supreme Court: A Study in the Federal Judicial System* (New York: Macmillan, 1927);

Max Lerner, *The Mind and Faith of Justice Holmes* (Boston: Little, Brown, 1943);

George W. Norris, *Fighting Liberal: The Autobiography of George W. Norris* (New York: Macmillan, 1945).

LIFESTYLES AND SOCIAL TRENDS

by NANCY E. BERNHARD and DAVID MCLEAN

CONTENTS

Sidebars and tables are listed in italics.

1910

- The average American worker earns less than fifteen dollars per week and works fifty-four to sixty hours per week.

- Seventy percent of bread consumed in the United States is baked at home, compared to 80 percent in 1890.

- After approval by an act of Congress, the U.S. Post Office inaugurates parcel post service to carry packages up to four hundred pounds.

12 Jan. The House of Representatives passes the Mann Act to curb "white slave" traffic. The act is intended to stop the transportation of women across state lines for immoral purposes.

6 Feb. Chicago publisher William Boyce founds the Boy Scouts of America.

17 Mar. Dr. and Mrs. Luther Halsey Gulick, Mr. and Mrs. Ernest Thompson Seton, and others found the Camp Fire Girls.

26 Mar. Congress amends the 1907 Immigration Act, barring criminals, paupers, anarchists, and carriers of disease from settling in the United States.

18 Apr. Suffragists present a petition with five hundred thousand signatures to Congress, asking that women be granted the right to vote.

1 May The National Negro Committee, founded in June 1909 by W. E. B. Du Bois, becomes the National Association for the Advancement of Colored People (NAACP).

19 June Mrs. John B. Dodd of Spokane, Washington, celebrates the first Father's Day with the support of the Ministerial Association and the YMCA.

20 June Theodore Roosevelt Jr. weds Eleanor Alexander in New York City.

July The tango, sweeping Europe with its South American flavor, begins to catch on in New York City ballrooms.

1911

25 Mar. A fire sweeps through the Triangle Shirtwaist Factory in lower Manhattan, killing 145 workers, most of them young girls. The factory's owners are indicted for manslaughter because of unsafe conditions.

7 May Three thousand women demanding the right to vote march down New York's Fifth Avenue. Only a few hundred women marched the previous year. In 1915, fifteen thousand march.

30 May A new macadam track at the Indianapolis Speedway is inaugurated with a five-hundred-mile race, the first Indianapolis 500, won by retired racing champion Ray Harroun.

10 Nov. Andrew Carnegie establishes the Carnegie Foundation with an initial endowment of $125 million. In 1910 he established the Carnegie Endowment for International Peace with a gift of $10 million.

1912

- The ragtime fad spawns numerous dances named for animals: fox-trot, horse trot, crab step, kangaroo dip, camel walk, fish walk, chicken scratch, lame duck, snake, grizzly bear, turkey trot, bunny hug.

12 Mar. Inspired by the efforts of Sir Robert Baden-Powell, founder of the Boy Scouts in Great Britain, Juliet Gordon Lowe organizes the first American Girl Guide troops.

15 Apr. The *Titanic* sinks on its maiden voyage, killing 1,517 passengers and crew, including members of some of America's most prominent families.

1 May The elegant Beverly Hills Hotel opens in what had once been a bean field. Its bar becomes a famous Hollywood rendezvous.

15 Aug. Deaf and blind from the age of two, Helen Keller announces that she has learned to sing.

9 Oct. Crowds swarm New York's Times Square to see the World Series score on the new electric bulletin board of the *Times.*

1913

- Formal and restrained cotillion dancing gives way to the waltz and the two-step.

- The *New York World* publishes the first crossword puzzle.

2 Feb. Grand Central Terminal opens in New York City, and 150,000 visitors barrage attendants with questions about train locations and departures.

1 Mar. Congress passes the Webb-Kenyon Interstate Liquor Act over President Taft's veto. The act prohibits shipment of liquor into states where its sale is illegal.

14 May John D. Rockefeller donates $100 million to the Rockefeller Foundation.

7 June Socialist journalist John Reed and a crew of labor organizers, anarchists, and Greenwich Village socialites produce the Paterson Strike Pageant at Madison Square Garden. Hundreds of striking workers from the Paterson, New Jersey, silk industry perform a dramatization about their struggle.

7 Oct. Henry Ford opens the first assembly line in Highland Park, Michigan. It can produce a Model T in three hours.

10 Oct. President Woodrow Wilson pushes a button that ignites eight tons of dynamite, opening the Panama Canal and linking the waters of the Atlantic and Pacific Oceans.

5 Nov. The Los Angeles Owens River Aqueduct opens, a feat of engineering that rivals the Panama Canal. It brings water 234 miles, using only gravity, to parched southern California. Critics charge that the government duped Owens Valley farmers into signing away their water rights by promising them an irrigation project.

1914

- Hollywood, California, becomes the center of motion picture production in the United States when filmmaker Cecil B. DeMille establishes his studio there, and other producers follow.

1 Jan. New Jersey sets the minimum wage for women at nine dollars a week.

5 Jan. Henry Ford announces that he will pay his employees a minimum of five dollars per day and inaugurate three eight-hour shifts, rather than two nine-hour shifts, to keep his factories running around the clock. To qualify for the new wage, however, workers must answer questions about their home lives and habits from Ford's new Sociological Department.

7 May Congress passes a resolution to celebrate Mother's Day on the second Sunday in May. President Woodrow Wilson calls on Americans to display flags to express love and reverence.

Dec. The first full-length feature comedy motion picture, *Tillie's Punctured Romance*, stars Marie Dresser, Mabel Normand, and newcomer Charlie Chaplin.

1915

- The United States population passes 100 million.

- Birth control activist Margaret Sanger is arrested on obscenity charges in connection with her book *Family Limitation*. Taken to court by the New York Society for the Suppression of Vice, she is found guilty of circulating a work "contrary not only to the law of the state, but to the law of God" and jailed.

- The Victor Talking Machine Company introduces a phonograph called the Victrola, which soon becomes a generic name. By 1919 Americans spend more on phonographs and recordings than on musical instruments, books and periodicals, or sporting goods.

- The taxicab becomes an established mode of transportation. Short rides cost a nickel, or a jitney. Drivers are known as hackers or hackies in the East and as cabbies in the Midwest.

- Vice President Thomas R. Marshall, during a tedious debate in the Senate, quips, "What this country really needs is a good five-cent cigar."

23 Feb. An easy-divorce law requiring only six months of residence is passed in Nevada.

3 Mar. D. W. Griffith's controversial three-hour film epic, *The Birth of a Nation*, opens in New York. Tickets cost an astronomical two dollars. The film idealizes plantation life in the antebellum South and perpetuates harmful stereotypes of African Americans.

10 Oct. In Chicago a new law restricting liquor sales on Sunday takes effect.

4 Dec. Henry Ford charters the "Peace Ship" for an expedition to Europe. The ship bears the slogan "Out of their trenches and back to their homes by Christmas." The attempt to find a diplomatic solution to the war quickly collapses.

1916

- Auto and truck production in the United States exceeds one million new models this year. The average cost of a new car is slightly more than $600, but Ford's Model T sells for $360. Half a million Model T's roll off the lines in 1916. There are more than 3.5 million cars on the road.

- Trade both within the United States and with foreign countries sets all-time highs. Domestic commerce generates $45 billion, and exports top $8 billion.

- African American self-help advocate Marcus Garvey returns to New York City to establish an American headquarters for his United Negro Improvement Association.

22 July   A bomb explodes along a preparedness parade route in San Francisco, killing six and injuring many more. A Finnish sailor who rushed to the scene and screamed "This is nothing!" is arrested.

8 Sept.   President Woodrow Wilson addresses a suffrage rally in Atlantic City, New Jersey, and tells the cheering crowd that he is on their side, that women will have the right to vote "in a little while."

16 Oct.   The first birth control clinic is opened in Brooklyn, New York, by Margaret Sanger, Fania Mindell, and Ethel Burne.

1917

6 Apr.   The United States declares war on Germany. George M. Cohan writes the song "Over There" to rally public support for sending American troops overseas.

18 May   The Selective Service Act passes, authorizing federal conscription and requiring registration of all male U.S. citizens from ages twenty-one to thirty.

27 June   Maj. Gen. John J. "Black Jack" Pershing arrives in France with the first contingent of the American Expeditionary Forces (AEF) to enter the war in Europe.

8 July   President Woodrow Wilson declares absolute government control over food, fuel, and war materiel exports.

19 Aug.   The War Department announces that the cost of providing each soldier with a uniform, arms, bedding, and eating utensils is $156.30, which people find a startlingly high amount.

23 Sept.   Fifty thousand striking workers from twenty-five unions in factories, shipyards, and machine shops on the Pacific Coast agree to return to work after a special plea from President Woodrow Wilson. The new Shipbuilding Labor Adjustment Board works to resolve the wage disputes that led to the strike.

6 Nov.   A constitutional amendment passes the New York state legislature, mandating women's suffrage.

18 Dec.   Congress passes the Eighteenth Amendment, prohibiting the manufacture, sale, or transportation of alcoholic beverages. It is later ratified by the states on 29 January 1919.

1918

- For one of the few times in American history, the United States population declines. The decline of fifty thousand people is attributed to war casualties, postponed marriages, the lack of immigration, and a devastating influenza epidemic.

- The American Civil Liberties Union is founded, an outgrowth of the Committee Against Militarism and the Committee Against Preparedness.

- A New York toy firm begins manufacturing the Raggedy Ann doll; the doll soon grows into a $20-million-a-year business.

3 Feb. *The New York Times* begins home delivery.

11 May The New York City superintendent of schools asks the board of education to ban the teaching of German in high schools.

18 May New York City's traffic commissioner reports that the city has the world's heaviest traffic.

24 May In New York City 284,114 women register to vote.

2 June The United States sets a new shipbuilding record, launching the destroyer *Ward* in seventeen and a half days.

4 June New York Harbor is closed after nine ships are sunk by U-boats off the Atlantic Coast.

26 July Sugar rations are reduced to two pounds a month per person by the U.S. Food Board.

3–6 Sept. The American Protective League conducts massive "Slacker Raids" in New York City, rounding up fifty thousand suspected draft dodgers. Sixteen thousand are found to have violated the Selective Service Act in ways ranging from administrative matters to draft evasion.

18 Sept. A massive drive to recruit women for farmwork begins, in an effort to compensate for the loss of farm labor that results when large numbers of male farmworkers join the military.

28 Sept. In New York City a shuttle begins service between Times Square and Grand Central Station.

31 Oct. U.S. public health officials predict that the worldwide influenza epidemic will kill twenty million people. By this date, eighty thousand deaths in the United States alone are attributed to the epidemic. In the United States the death toll from influenza eventually reaches between four hundred thousand and five hundred thousand, far exceeding the fifty-three thousand American combat deaths in World War I.

11 Nov. World War I ends. After a parade, 150 tons of paper have to be cleared off the streets of New York City. U.S. combat casualties total fifty-three thousand, with deaths from other causes numbering more than sixty-three thouand. The cost to American taxpayers is $21 billion, in addition to the cost of loans to the Allies.

22 Dec. The federal government ends the last ban on consumption of foodstuffs judged necessary to the war effort.

1919

3 Jan. Herbert Hoover, who had directed the Food Administration during the war, is appointed to lead the effort to help feed the 125 million people left destitute by the war in Europe.

29 Jan.   The Eighteenth Amendment, adopted by the required three-quarters of the states, is proclaimed to be part of the Constitution as of 16 January 1920. Americans have one year to drink legally; some begin stockpiling liquor in anticipation of Prohibition.

27 Apr.   The National Association of the Motion Picture Industry volunteers to submit films for censorship.

2 June   Bombs damage the homes of several leading government officials in Washington, D.C., including those of Attorney General A. Mitchell Palmer and Assistant Secretary of the Navy Franklin D. Roosevelt. Three days later, sixty-seven anarchists are arrested; they face deportation.

20 July   Roaming bands of soldiers, sailors, and marines attack African Americans on the streets of Washington, D.C. The bands claim that African Americans had been attacking white women in the city during the past month.

30 July   U.S. troops are called to help end race riots in Chicago, where whites have burned and pillaged African American sections of the city for two weeks. The riots start when white youths begin throwing rocks at an African American youth swimming near a segregated beach on Lake Michigan. By the time troops are called in, thirty-one people are dead; more than five hundred people have been injured.

Aug.   After race riots in Washington, D.C., and Chicago, similar riots occur in Norfolk, Virginia; Knoxville, Tennessee; Blaine, Arkansas; and Omaha, Nebraska. By summer's end, hundreds of people are dead, mostly African Americans, one hundred of whom have been lynched.

14 Aug.   To help stem rampant inflation, the Wilson administration seizes and distributes food that had been stored in warehouses in several cities. Producers had stored the food as a way of keeping food prices high.

15 Sept.   Massachusetts officials begin hiring replacement workers for striking police in the city of Boston. The state militia had already been called out to help control mobs of looters. Gov. Calvin Coolidge takes the lead in condemning the striking police, thereby catapulting himself into the national spotlight.

26 Oct.   It is reported that nine thousand tractors are in use in the state of Iowa, an indication of the mechanization of farm labor.

28 Oct.   Congress passes the Volstead Act over Wilson's veto. The act defines intoxicating liquor as anything with more than 0.5 percent alcohol and provides for the enforcement of the Eighteenth Amendment, passed on 29 January.

16 Nov.   Since the passage of the child labor provision in the federal tax code in April, child labor has been reduced by 40 percent, particularly in the coal mining and canning industries.

17 Dec.   After meetings among members of Congress, the administration, and motion picture executives, the industry announces it will fight the spread of Bolshevism and anti-Americanism with "all that is within our power."

OVERVIEW

New Definitions. In the 1910s long-term shifts in some of the basic patterns of everyday life in America not only continued but in many cases intensified, ushering in a time of numerous changes in personal behavior and social relations. Dramatic transformations in the ethnic makeup of the country, in race relations, in gender relations, and in the relationship between local and national authorities all raised sharp questions about the forces that governed the increasing complexity of American life. During this ferment some people tried to reestablish the traditional social bonds that had seemed to prevail in past decades; others asserted the need to control individual behavior through new laws; still others mourned the loss of supposedly simpler times. In 1917 America's entry into World War I shook American society in many ways and fostered the unintended effect of a volatility and fluidity in social relations, pitching social tensions into violent conflict by the end of the decade.

Who Is an American? Wholesale changes in the ethnic makeup of the nation's population encouraged many people, perplexed by the shifting social currents around them, to redefine the meaning of being American. The 1910s were the last decade of the "New Immigration" from eastern and southern Europe, the historic population trend that, having started in the 1880s, had by the second decade of the new century radically changed the face of American cities. Meanwhile, fanned by the fears and hatreds unleashed by America's entry into the war in Europe, hostility toward recent immigrants flourished in the later 1910s. The most vicious hatred was aimed at German Americans, who were readily suspected of sympathizing with America's declared enemy; but millions of frightened Americans judged anyone they perceived to be "foreign" as someone insufficiently patriotic, potentially disloyal, and not truly American.

Race. Violent racism against African Americans in these years escalated, resulting in hundreds of lynchings across the rural South. Meanwhile, a historic exodus of black Americans from the states of the former Confederacy began during the war years, when serious industrial labor shortages in the North opened the prospect of higher wages and improved living standards. At the same time, some southern whites, partly in reaction to seeing their cheap farm labor leaving, intensified their terror campaigns; some white Georgians energetically revived the Ku Klux Klan, which had been dormant for nearly fifty years. On the other hand, during the years when blacks were steadily migrating northward and into cities, racial violence flared up in urban areas, where many whites resisted the influx of southern blacks into their industries and neighborhoods. Major race riots erupted in Washington, D.C.; Chicago; Saint Louis; and Houston, proving that whites in the rural South had no monopoly on racism.

Shifting Boundaries of Public and Private Life. During the nineteenth-century, a clear distinction between the private home life of the family and the outside world of work and commerce had begun to seem normal to many Americans, especially in the nation's rapidly growing cities and towns. In the ideal envisioned by the burgeoning middle class, women presided over nurturing and caring activities at home, while men represented the family by going to jobs outside the home and participating in political life. This dividing line blurred significantly during the 1910s, particularly as more and more women entered varied fields of public life. For example, to aid the huge war effort, large numbers of single and married women across the United States worked on factory assembly lines and also in offices, not only gaining many new experiences but also earning wages that, if less than those earned by their male counterparts, were nonetheless significant. By the end of World War I American women had also gained the right to vote, a development that many people predicted would bring a more human and moral tone to the nation's political life. Also in these volatile years, social reformers, various public figures who were reputed experts in moral or social issues, and politicians all tried by various means to extend their influence directly into Americans' private lives. Prohibition, for example, after decades of crusading by temperance groups, became national law. The sexual habits of working-class Americans also became a target for reformers. Sex-education pioneer Margaret Sanger distributed information about birth control to women; her critics judged this work an intrusion into privacy and an offense against nature. Many self-styled experts advised American families how to make their homes more efficient, more businesslike, more American. By the end of the 1910s traditional gender and social roles remained largely intact, but the perception of those roles had begun to change.

Volunteerism. Americans in the 1910s embraced a variety of new voluntary organizations. All kinds of groups, from immigrant-aid societies to bridge clubs, tended to reshape the lifestyles of many Americans, further breaking the traditional barriers between the public and private spheres of individuals' lives. Meanwhile, although recruiters in the early days of the nation's entry into World War I were disappointed by low enlistment rates, the great majority of Americans participated in wartime rationing and conservation programs and bought large numbers of Liberty Bonds to support the war effort. Thousands of volunteer speakers, called "Four Minute Men," appeared at movie theaters throughout the United States, exhorting audiences to support their country and join together in patriotic action. Working with the Justice Department, members of the voluntary American Protective League policed fellow citizens to ensure their correct attitudes and conformity to draft laws. The trend toward volunteerism spread to younger Americans: the scouting movement, imported from Great Britain, became wildly popular, and the decade witnessed the rise of the American Boy Scout, Girl Scout, and Camp Fire Girls organizations.

Rural Life Transformed. The traditional isolation of farm life had been gradually eroding by the turn of the century, but by 1910 a series of new devices and routines fostered a radical change in the patterns of rural living. Probably no technological innovation revolutionized rural lifestyles more than the introduction of automobiles across the American landscape. Not only did motorized tractors replace draft animals and save countless hours of hard labor but automobiles allowed farm families to devote their increasing leisure hours to activities in the towns and cities. Conversely, the ideal of rural home life became more accessible to people who worked in cities, as new railways, streetcars, and the automobile enabled thousands of people to move to suburban areas. At the same time, methods of retailing first introduced in the late nineteenth century were making the rural household more like its up-to-date counterpart in the city. The Sears, Roebuck and Montgomery Ward catalogues made shopping for the latest fashionable clothes or home conveniences as easy as walking to the mailbox. Meanwhile, farm prices, rising dramatically during the war as the American breadbasket fed much of western Europe and American troops as well, enriched many of the nation's farmers. Postwar inflation cut deeply into this booming rural prosperity, but in the meantime, farm life had entered a new modern age. While some resisted the decline of local traditions during these years, most Americans, fascinated by the increased availability of a widening range of goods, services, and experiences, welcomed the changes that were redefining their lives.

City Life. Even while the nation's cities expanded and grew increasingly cosmopolitan in the 1910s, the neighborhood life of the great urban centers remained profoundly local. Ethnic neighborhoods grew rapidly, clustering outward from each immigrant group's stores, churches and synagogues, immigrant-aid societies, unions, and political organizations. Increasingly, each major city was composed of a collection of distinct urban villages. At the same time, a new mass culture was emerging, one that first flourished in these cities, where department stores, movie houses, and mass-circulation magazines depicted a consummately new, modern way of life. Attracted by such images, children in immigrant families increasingly shed their parents' traditional ethnic customs to embrace a sleeker, faster, more defiantly forward-looking lifestyle.

Struggling toward Modernity. American lifestyles in the 1910s often reflected the continuing struggle among the social, industrial, and political forces that were pushing the nation into the modern era and the efforts by many Americans, in the midst of profound upheaval, to preserve the features of their society that they considered desirable. With the introduction of each new technological marvel, a crafts tradition declined. With each expansion in nationwide consumer marketing, the sense of a unique local identity among small communities diminished. Meanwhile, as Americans analyzed and debated the changes permeating their lives, the broad patterns and features of life in the twentieth century were being firmly set. The industrialization and urbanization of the United States accelerated dramatically in these years, as the nation's growing industries and expanding cities attracted larger and larger numbers of workers, drawing their labor force not only from immigrant populations but also from groups that had traditionally lived and worked in rural America. Toward the end of the decade the United States, having entered World War I as a significant but reluctant combatant, emerged from the conflict as one of the small number of undisputed world powers. Most Americans required another generation to accept fully the consequences of their rapidly escalating economic and military might; in the meantime, by the later years of the 1910s American cities had been transformed by a polyglot mixture of languages and by new ideas and new ideologies, and American power had become decidedly international.

TOPICS IN THE NEWS

AFRICAN AMERICANS AND WORLD WAR I

Jim Crow. In 1914, 90 percent of African Americans lived in the states of the former Confederacy, where so-called Jim Crow statutes had legalized the segregation of Americans by race. These statutes had been validated by a series of Supreme Court rulings in the 1890s, culminating in the famous 1896 "separate but equal" doctrine of *Plessy* v. *Ferguson,* which made segregation the law of the United States. To make matters worse, President Woodrow Wilson appointed to his cabinet officials who were openly prejudiced, and who extended segregation within federal departments. Nowhere was the separation of races more strict, more prone to violence, or more hypocritical than in the American armed forces that were supposedly fighting for freedom and democracy in Europe. Nonetheless, the social upheavals created by World War I reshaped race relations in the United States in fundamental ways.

At Home. The war years accelerated the migration of African Americans out of the rural South, where agriculture had been plagued by floods and crop failures, including a devastating plague of boll weevils that decimated the cotton crop. At the same time, factory owners in northern cities sent recruiters to draw workers northward with glowing reports of high wages and good living conditions. During the 1910s the African American population of the North and West grew by 333,000. Meanwhile, the lynchings and racial clashes that blacks faced in the rural South began to spread to southern cities: in 1917 riots occurred in East Saint Louis and Houston; racial tensions spread into the North, as well. As American participation in the war neared, African American leaders split on what approach to take regarding the war effort. The new National Association for the Advancement of Colored People (NAACP) hoped that the war would promote changes in the American legal system, and lobbied to have Congress pass a wartime measure to outlaw lynching. Their effort failed. More-militant activists expected little from the Wilson administration, and parodied patriotic rhetoric with slogans such as "Make America Safe for Democracy." The government responded by threatening to suppress African American

THE GREAT MIGRATION

African Americans began a half-century exodus from the South during the First World War. A series of economic jolts in the middle of the decade, including floods and crop failures, left thousands of black sharecroppers and tenant farmers destitute and homeless. At the same time, the war severely curtailed the number of immigrants arriving from Europe, and a labor shortage in northern industrial cities opened employment opportunities. In 1916 the idea that the North offered a better way of life spread like wildfire through the states of the former Confederacy, and many white southerners became alarmed at the flight of cheap labor from their states. In 1916 the Pennsylvania Railroad hired 10,000 people from Georgia and Florida alone. Between 1910 and 1920 northern and western states registered an increase of 330,000 African American inhabitants. The migration opened industrial employment to blacks, staved off a labor shortage during the war, and changed the face of northern cities. The exodus continued into the 1920s and surged again during the Second World War.

Source: John Hope Franklin and Alfred A. Moss Jr., *From Slavery to Freedom: A History of Negro Americans*, seventh edition (New York: McGraw-Hill, 1994).

periodicals critical of the government and by coercing publishers to quell rumors that black troops were being sent to the most dangerous areas of the front.

Patriotic Service. The vast majority of African Americans displayed loyalty to the war effort, purchasing millions of dollars worth of Liberty Bonds, organizing food conservation programs, and working with draft boards. Large numbers of young black men joined the armed forces, often hoping the nation would reward their service with greater measures of racial justice, a dream that proved elusive. Even the kinds of service African Americans were called on to perform disappointed many of

Troops of the all-black 369th Infantry Regiment, 93rd Division, manning the trenches in 1918. Called the "Hell Fighters" by the Germans, the regiment was awarded the Croix de Guerre.

them. The U.S. Navy employed most of its fifty-three hundred African Americans in noncombat, primarily menial positions (many worked as stewards.) The Marine Corps accepted no blacks in its ranks. The army declined black volunteers, even while drafting blacks in disproportionate numbers. African American doctors and dentists were commissioned as privates; African American soldiers were not allowed to train as pilots. Nearly 90 percent of black troops, whether educated or skilled, worked as laborers in the services of supply. The few white officers who protested the treatment of African Americans troops were told by the secretary of war that blacks should be glad that the service they were rendering was less hazardous than that of white soldiers.

At the Front. The 92nd Division of the United States armed forces was composed exclusively of African American soldiers, although it and all other black units were commanded by white officers. Not only did white officers refuse to share quarters and privileges with black soliders,

but many whites refused to salute black officers or follow their orders. Finally, after agitation from the NAACP, the War Department created a special training facility for African American officers, but these officers were usually regarded with little respect, especially in the South. In France, where black soldiers were cordially welcomed by French troops, American commanders took steps to prevent the French from fraternizing with African Americans and from treating them as equals. To make matters worse, black officers were given second-class accommodations on troopships and in mess tents, and the troops received substandard equipment and training. Not surprisingly, the morale of black soldiers was sometimes low, and the 92nd Division did not always perform well at the front. The 368th Regiment failed to hold the line in the Argonne offensive. But the 369th Infantry out of New York was well regarded, having spent six months at the front with only two weeks rest, more than any other American unit. In recognition of their distinguished ser-

	1910	1920
Alabama	908,000	901,000
California	22,000	39,000
Illinois	109,000	182,000
Kentucky	262,000	236,000
Louisiana	714,000	700,000
Massachusetts	38,000	45,000
Mississippi	1,009,000	935,000
New York	134,000	198,000
Ohio	111,000	186,000
Pennsylvania	194,000	285,000
Tennessee	473,000	452,000

Source: Erik W. Austin, *Political Facts of the United States Since 1789* (New York: Columbia University Press, 1986).

vice, the French government decorated 171 soldiers of the 369th with the Légion d'Honneur and awarded the entire regiment the Croix de Guerre. Despite their wartime service, however, and the hope of black leaders that the ideals of democracy and equality would be strengthened at home, black troops returned to a land still deeply divided by race, with a white majority that refused to pay them the respect they had earned.

Sources:

John Hope Franklin, *From Slavery to Freedom: A History of Negro Americans*, 5th edition (New York: Knopf, 1980);

Ronald Schaffer, *America in the Great War: The Rise of the War Welfare State* (New York: Oxford University Press, 1991).

ANTIWAR SENTIMENT

Europe's Problem. When World War I began in August 1914, most Americans, believing the war was further evidence of the decay of European civilization, were determined to stay out of the conflict. Until 1917 the Woman's Peace Party, the American Union Against Militarism, and many other pacifist organizations that supported American neutrality enjoyed broad public support. Antiwar sentiment peaked in November 1916 when President Woodrow Wilson won reelection with the slogan "He Kept Us Out of War"; during this time the song "I Didn't Raise My Boy to Be a Soldier" swept the nation. But there were those who suspected President Wilson's promise to keep Americans away from European battlefields was disingenuous; whatever his real motivations, in

April 1917, shortly after the election, he requested from Congress a declaration of war.

Blood Ties. While most Americans rallied to the war effort, significant portions of the population, many of whom were the children of European immigrants or recent immigrants themselves, resisted the war effort because of their natural ties to their native lands. Irish Americans who supported Ireland's drive for independence rued fighting on the side of Great Britain. American Poles and American Russian Jews disliked entering an alliance with Russia, from which both groups had experienced persecution. Then, too, millions of German- and Austro-Hungarian Americans hesitated to fight against their countries of origin. Furthermore, African Americans debated the justice of fighting overseas for democracy when the United States itself, in their case, served as such a poor example. In May 1917 Congress passed the Selective Service Act because young American men were not enlisting in the numbers officials had expected; not long after, in tiny New Ulm, Minnesota, ten thousand citizens turned out to discuss the options for resisting the draft.

Organized Opposition. The most determined resistance to the draft was organized by the Socialist Party of America, a major force in American politics at the time. Its symbolic leader, Eugene V. Debs, was jailed for speaking out against the war. Meanwhile, vigilantes raided Socialist Party offices and disrupted their rallies. In Collinsville, Illinois, a young socialist of German descent, who had never spoken publicly against the war, was lynched. At the only campus riot before the Vietnam War era, a Rutgers University student who refused to participate in a Liberty Loan rally was tarred and feathered, then paraded through the streets of New Brunswick, New Jersey. Socialist union organizers William "Big Bill" Haywood and Morris Hillquit, journalist John Reed and anarchist Emma Goldman all vocally opposed American entry into the war, arguing that the war was rooted in the misguided goals of capitalism. Rose Pastor Stokes of Kansas City was sentenced to ten years in jail for a letter she wrote to the *Kansas City Star*, in which she said, "No government which is for the profiteers can also be for the people, and I am for the people while the government is for the profiteers." Her sentence was commuted in 1921.

Conscientious Objectors. The Selective Service Act liberally exempted from battlefield service members of "any well recognized religious sect or organization" with an established pacifist tradition. Local draft boards, however, were often arbitrary in their recognition of such beliefs, and, because the government neglected to indicate suitable alternative service, many conscientious objectors remained stuck in training camps for months. The pressure of remaining in such a martial atmosphere, reinforced by constant taunts and hazing, led sixteen thousand out of twenty thousand of these draftees detained in the camps to elect combat service rather than work to guarantee their status for exemption. Conscientious ob-

Women demonstrating in favor of American neutrality during World War I, circa 1915

jectors unable to prove long-standing, religiously based pacifism were often jailed under the terms of the Sedition Act of 1918.

Breaking the IWW. The Industrial Workers of the World, a radical labor union strong in the mining and lumbering industries of the far West, had long been identifed with pacifism and was known for its disapproval of any extreme forms of patriotism. After 1917 the union concentrated on gaining members in industries on which the war effort principally relied, but the public widely believed that the IWW intended to disrupt the war effort by every means possible. During the war years its strikes were broken and its leaders deported or imprisoned; by late 1918 the union was effectively destroyed.

The American Protective League. To help identify Americans who opposed the war effort, the Justice Department recruited a quarter of a million volunteers into the American Protective League. APL members were issued "Secret Service Division" cards, and often posed as federal agents when they were opening mail, wiretapping telephones, or breaking and entering. They delivered the materials they gathered to the Justice Department's Bureau of Investigation, the predecessor of the FBI. These

APL members conducted tens of thousands of loyalty investigations and lectured civic groups about loyalty and patriotism. In the famous "Slacker Raids" of 3–6 September 1918 the APL rounded up fifty thousand suspected draft dodgers in New York City. Sixteen thousand of these suspects were indeed found to have violated some provision of the Selective Service Act. Assistant Attorney General John Lord O'Brien observed that the United States had never been more effectively policed.

Sources:
Frederick C. Giffin, *Six Who Protested: Radical Opposition to the First World War* (Port Washington, N.Y.: Kennikat Press, 1977);

David M. Kennedy, *Over Here: The First World War and American Society* (New York: Oxford University Press, 1980);

H. C. Peterson and Gilbert Fite, *Opponents of War, 1917–1918* (Seattle: University of Washington Press, 1968);

Ronald Schaffer, *America in the Great War: The Rise of the War Welfare State* (New York: Oxford University Press, 1991).

AUTOMOBILITY

The Model T. In 1908 Henry Ford introduced the model that would become the low-cost automobile every middle-class American could afford, the Model T. By the time it was discontinued in 1927, more than fifteen mil-

Owners of a 1916 Model T Ford picnicking next to their car during an automotive outing

lion Model T's had been sold, and its price had dropped from $850 to $290. Ford's innovative production methods and labor policies revolutionized American manufacturing, just as his product revolutionized American lifestyles. For rural people the Model T became a lifeline to social activity, amusements, and work away from the farm. City people, meanwhile, did not acquire the car habit in large numbers until the 1920s, which was also the period when Ford finally gave up his insistence on thrift and prudence, and allowed his dealers to offer an early form of installment-plan purchases. In the 1910s Ford was not the only company to offer Americans the popular new form of transportation. In 1910 Sears offered its Model L for $370; a Reo Runabout sold for $500; a Maxwell for $600; and the Hupmobile for $700. Cadillacs ranged in price from $1,500 to $2,500.

Ripple Effect. The boom in automobile manufacturing had a powerful effect on the entire American economy. Steelmaking, glassmaking, machine tooling, rubber processing, petroleum distillation and distribution, road construction, and repair shops were some of the corollary businesses the growing automobile industry supported. Indirectly, through its stimulation of suburban sprawl and new forms of leisure, the growing popularity of the

automobile fueled everything from new housing construction to motels and roadside attractions. Billboards sprang up. The real estate booms in California and Florida depended on the exploding rates of automobile ownership. The car insurance industry, having begun when the first liability policy on an automobile was issued in 1896, had created by 1916 the first differentiation of risks in insurance policies, based on the number of cars on the road and the type of driving an individual driver generally did. In New York City, where sixteen thousand cars were insured, the cost of insurance was twelve times more than the cost in Arizona, where two hundred cars were insured.

New and Old Habits. For many Americans, cars provided the freedom to explore the world beyond their local communities. The attractions of the roadhouse and the opportunity for privacy on dates led the more-respectable elements of society to condemn automobiles as "sin wagons." Undoubtedly, courtship practices changed with the increasing popularity of the car. But many people simply integrated their automobiles into their regular routines, using them to go to the market or to attend church on Sundays. Meanwhile, use of automobiles varied widely by social class. The higher the family income, the more likely the car to be a means to leisure activities. For migrant workers at the other end of the income scale, the car often served as a home.

Variety. The number of automobile manufacturers dropped from 253 in 1908 to 108 in 1920, with about 80 percent of the market controlled by the Big Three: Ford, General Motors, and Chrysler. While 1918 production was half what it had been in 1917 because of wartime plant conversions, the 1919 automobile show at Madison Square Garden in New York City displayed hundreds of new models and attracted a crowd that filled the sidewalks for many blocks. The variety of colors, mechanical innovations, and flourishes demonstrated that, despite Ford's insistence on their uniformity, cars were increasingly becoming a mode of self-expression. Buick introduced a blue bridal roadster, decorated with white ribbons, with space for only two passengers. The fancy new Jordan was aimed at the youth market, featuring a sport windshield, a "cocky seat cowl," and velvet rugs. A long Stutz speedster attracted admiring attention, as did the new Hudson, which had a top speed of sixty miles per hour. The highest price tag at the show was attached to the Pierce-Arrow Brougham, priced at $7,800. Cadillac's producers boasted that their vehicles were "the first to cross the Rhine" with the American troops. While most of the new automobiles were loud and dirty, Americans were buying them in increasing numbers. One shrewd manufacturer asked in its advertisements, "Who Denies that Power Gives Pleasure?"

Sources:

Daniel J. Boorstin, *The Americans: The Democratic Experience* (New York: Random House, 1973);

James J. Flink, *The Automobile Age* (Cambridge, Mass.: MIT Press, 1988);

William D. Miller, *Pretty Bubbles in the Air: America in 1919* (Urbana: University of Illinois Press, 1991).

THE FOUR MINUTE MEN

Beginning at the Strand. In March 1917, a month before the American declaration of war against the Central Powers in Europe, a group of young Chicago businessmen followed the suggestion of Sen. Joseph Medill McCormick (R–Ill.) and organized a committee. Their purpose was to send speakers to Chicago movie theaters to explain the new legislation for universal military training. The group named itself the Four Minute Men, referring to their self-imposed time limit for their speeches, and alluding to the Minutemen of Revolutionary War fame. The committee president, Donald Ryerson, gave the first speech at Chicago's Strand Theater in early April.

Creel Jumps on the Bandwagon. After the war began, Ryerson traveled to Washington to gain more information about the draft. Spotting George Creel, the director of the Committee on Public Information,

THE BATHTUB HOAX

In 1917 Baltimore journalist and editor H. L. Mencken was deterred from expressing his admiration for German culture because of wartime hysteria against Germany and anything of a German origin. To gain his sly revenge, Mencken decided to dramatize the gullibility of the average American and the average American journalist. On 28 December 1917 he published a column in the *New York Evening Mail* titled, "A Neglected Anniversary," which purported to be a true history of the bathtub on the anniversary of its introduction to the United States seventy-five years before.

According to Mencken, the story of the bathtub in America began when a Cincinnati-based cotton trader, having seen the tub in England, built one in his new home in 1842. The bathtub required a pump operated by six "Negroes," measured seven feet by four feet, was lined in Nicaraguan mahogany, and weighed 1,750 pounds. Detractors, Mencken wrote, denounced the bathtub as decadent or infectious, but these criticisms probably represented class antagonisms against an indulgence of the wealthy. Bathtub use allegedly spread through the 1850s, and all resistance to it broke down when Vice President Millard Fillmore, an aficionado, ascended to the presidency in 1850 and ordered the construction of a bathtub in the White House.

Mencken delighted in the fact that other writers routinely cited "A Neglected Anniversary" as an authoritative source. Ten years after its publication Mencken finally admitted the article was a hoax, but not before exposing the fact that many of his readers were consummately credulous.

Source: Robert McHugh, ed., *The Bathtub Hoax and Other Blasts and Bravos from the Chicago Tribune by H. L. Mencken* (New York: Knopf, 1958).

in a crowded hallway, Ryerson cornered him. Ten minutes later, Creel created a national program of Four Minute Men with Ryerson in charge. Ryerson returned to Chicago, agreeing to submit all speeches to Creel for approval. By July 1917 there were 2,500 speakers in the program; by November the number had risen to 15,000; by September 1918 there were 40,000. When the program disbanded at the end of that year, there were 75,000 speakers in the program. These Four Minute Men made speeches in all the states of the United States, and also in Alaska, the Panama Canal Zone, Guam, Hawaii, Puerto Rico, and Samoa. It was estimated that, by the end of the war, 755,000 four-minute speeches were heard by 314 million people.

George Creel, head of the Committee on Public Information, who created a national program of Four Minute Men to deliver brief speeches on patriotic topics

Strong Organization. Each town or city had its own staff and executive committee to help with planning and monitoring the speakers. Theater committees also helped and often included theater managers. The Chicago organization also had committees for the public schools, labor unions, amusement parks, churches, and conventions. There were women's auxiliaries, African American branches, and foreign-language sections. New York City boasted 1,600 Four Minute Men, including ten who spoke in Yiddish and seven who spoke in Italian. President Woodrow Wilson wrote a four-minute speech that was delivered by 35,000 speakers across the nation on the Fourth of July, 1918. For all other occasions, bulletins published in Washington directed the speakers on what topics the speeches would address; speakers were instructed to follow their prepared scripts, deliver them in a lively fashion, and ignore questions from the audience.

The Message. The overriding purpose of the Four Minute Men was to define the meaning of the war for their audiences. The speakers tried to move beyond the usual appeals to patriotism, the sense of "my country right or wrong," and to infuse their theatergoing audiences with the feeling that the United States was "supremely right, overwhelmingly right, sacredly right." Appeals were made to immigrants and African Americans to place the cause of their country before all other considerations. Four Minute Men discussed domestic war drives for the Red Cross, food conservation, war bonds, and the details of Selective Service, and the group received great credit for the success of those programs. As a rule, speakers were cautioned to appeal to their listeners with facts rather than emotions, or at least to support emotional appeals with factual information. They were instructed at first that "a statement only of patent facts will convince those who require argument more readily than 'doubtful disputations. . .' No hymn of hate accompanies our mes-

sage." As the war continued, however, the Central Committee advised the Four Minute Men across the country that it was time to appeal to people's fears, noting that, while unity was difficult to obtain when based only on reason, the drive for self-preservation stirred people to fight in common cause.

Sources:

George Creel, *How We Advertised America* (New York: Harper & Row, 1920);

David M. Kennedy, *Over Here: The First World War and American Society* (New York: Oxford University Press, 1980);

Stephen Vaughn, *Holding Fast the Inner Lines: Democracy, Nationalism, and the Committee on Public Information* (Chapel Hill: University of North Carolina Press, 1980).

IMMIGRATION

Two-Way Passage. Tens of millions of "New Immigrants" arrived in the United States between 1880 and 1921. Before 1900 most were young men who had left parents and young families behind to seek economic opportunity in the New World. Between 1908 and 1914, however, one third of the immigrants who arrived in America returned to Europe, with the proportion of Italians, Hungarians, and Croatians who returned to Europe as high as one-half. As time passed, women and children made up larger percentages of the number of immigrants who came to stay, as the vanguard of young men established themselves and then sent for loved ones. Only European Jews, facing political persecution in eastern Europe, consistently remained in America. Beginning in 1913 and 1914, the looming war disrupted emigration patterns and sent more than two million people fleeing

IMMIGRATION BY COUNTRY OF ORIGIN, 1910–1919

	Number	Percent
Northwestern Europe		
United Kingdom (England, Scotland, Wales)	371,878	5.8
Ireland	166,445	2.6
Scandinavia (Norway, Sweden, Denmark)	238,275	3.8
France	60,335	1.0
German Empire	174,227	2.7
Other (Netherland, Belgium, Switzerland)	101,478	1.6
Central Europe		
Poland	N/A	N/A
Austria-Hungary	1,154,727	18.2
Other (Bulgaria, Serbia, Montenegro)	27,180	0.4
Eastern Europe		
Russia	1,106,998	17.4
Romania	13,566	0.2
Turkey	71,149	1.1
Southern Europe		
Greece	198,108	3.1
Italy	1,229,916	19.4
Portugal	82,489	1.3
Other		
Asia	192,587	2.1
Canada	708,715	11.2
Mexico	185,334	2.9
West Indies	120,860	1.9
Central and South America	55,630	0.9
Australia	11,280	0.2
Other	10,414	0.2

Source: N. Carpenter, "Immigrants and Their Children," *U.S. Bureau of Census Monograph*, no. 7 (Washington, D.C., 1927), pp. 324–325, reprinted in *The Huddled Masses: The Immigrant in American Society, 1880–1921*, by Alan M. Kraut (Arlington Heights, Illinois: Harland Davidson, 1982).

from central Europe. At the same time, many immigrants to America streamed back home, fearing wartime restrictions would create forced separations from loved ones. Far from being a one-way passage from the Old World to the New, this new phase of immigration was a dynamic process predicated on political and economic conditions on both sides of the Atlantic.

Arriving. The enormous depot at Ellis Island, New York, completed in 1901, featured a shower facility capable of bathing eight thousand people each day. The famous registry room, or Great Hall, was two hundred feet long and fifty-six feet high. After a "line inspection" by a physician, including a covert test where each immigrant was made to haul his or her luggage up a staircase as a test of strength, those with infirmities were marked with a chalk letter: *L* for lameness, *G* for goiter, *X* for mental illness. Those who failed the exam were detained; some, after a few days of rest and nourishment, were able to pass. Of the average three or four hundred people who passed through Ellis Island each day, about 80 percent were admitted without delay. Those denied admission to the United States were given free return passage by the shipping companies, because the government held these companies responsible for delivering sick immigrants.

Polyglot America. In 1910 more than 75 percent of the populations of New York City, Chicago, Detroit, Cleveland, and Boston consisted of immigrants or their children. More than 70 percent of San Franciscans in 1916 spoke a language other than English as their first language, often Chinese or Japanese. Ethnic groups tended to separate by region. Slavs settled in the mining regions of the upper Midwest and dominated the slaughterhouse industry in Chicago. Italians, many of whom were unskilled laborers, became the driving force in the construction industries and built the New York City subway system and the bridges linking the city's boroughs. Greeks tended to avoid agricultural labor, and by 1910 made up 20 percent of the population in the mill town of Lowell, Massachusetts. Sixty-six percent of the male Jews entering the United States between 1899 and 1914 were classified as skilled laborers, compared to 20 percent of the overall group. These Jewish groups predominated in the needle trades in New York City, where the garment industry employed two-thirds of the working Jewish population.

Assimilation. The first generation of immigrants, especially those from non-English-speaking countries, often experienced isolation and bewilderment in the new nation they had chosen. While ethnic communities supported newcomers when they could, the new immigrants usually underwent transformations as profound as those they effected on the nation that absorbed them. Americanization involved endless compromises between jettisoning traditional ways and adopting new ones. Family names were changed to suit American pronunciation; even traditional recipes were adapted to suit the ingredients available in the United States. Sometimes religious

Workers in a garment industry sweatshop, circa 1910

practices changed, as they did for many Jews when the observance of the Sabbath on Saturday conflicted with the schedules of commerce in the New World. Schools, where children and adults (often at night) learned English, became the first cauldron of Americanization. Reformers such as Jane Addams and Frances Kellor, who founded the Committee for Immigrants in America in 1914, wanted less to "Americanize" immigrants than to help them adapt successfully to life in the United States.

Nativist Backlash. The anti-German hysteria that swept the United States in the years of World War I provoked a backlash against the nation's open immigration policy. Old-stock Americans feared their social position was being jeopardized in the new ethnically mixed America, and mixed a strong anti-immigrant message with the loyalty programs that had been created to support the war effort. Even President Woodrow Wilson, in his third annual message to Congress, declared that some immigrants were dangerous and traitorous: "There are citizens of the United States, I blush to admit, born under other flags but welcomed under our generous natu-

ralization laws to the full freedom and opportunity of America, who have poured the poison of disloyalty in to the very arteries of our national life. . . . Such creatures of passion, disloyalty, and anarchy must be crushed out." By 1921 the United States passed its first legislation restricting immigration. The law was designed to exclude immigrants from southern and eastern Europe, who were by then concentrated in the industrial cities of the eastern United States. For many, the open door had banged closed.

Sources:

Oscar Handlin, *The Uprooted*, 2nd edition (Boston: Little, Brown, 1990);

David M. Kennedy, *Over Here: The First World War and American Society* (New York: Oxford University Press, 1980);

Alan M. Kraut, *The Huddled Masses: The Immigrant in American Society, 1880-1921* (Arlington Heights, Ill.: Harland Davidson, 1982).

THE NEW RETAILING AND ITS DETRACTORS

Speed and Economy. By 1910 three innovations in the way Americans did their shopping were already familiar

Workers at Montgomery Ward filling catalogue orders to be shipped by parcel post, a service established by the U.S. Post Office in 1913

to many people: the department store, the mail-order house, and the chain store. A radical departure from centuries of small local merchants, these mechanisms for mass distribution of mass-produced goods often lowered prices and improved quality. These enterprises bypassed wholesalers and aggressively marketed directly to the consumer. Each store had its own advertising department, and when it purchased name-brand goods from manufacturers, the price included a fee for "cooperative advertising." For the first time, prices were set in advance; there was no bargaining at the sales counter, which made it possible for employers to hire inexperienced and lower-paid workers. Moreover, prices were set low enough so that the profits that were reaped resulted from turning over large inventories.

Service. By 1915 department stores had redesigned themselves as a sort of clubhouse for middle-class women. They offered "silence rooms for never-tired shoppers," beauty salons, restaurants, employment agencies for domestic help, banking and brokerage services, and charge accounts. Wanamaker's in Philadelphia offered twenty-four-hour telephone shopping. For rural consumers the Montgomery Ward and Sears, Roebuck catalogues were part reference work, part indulgence, part

Bible. At the Sears headquarters in Chicago, two thousand people opened and processed more than nine hundred sacks of mail each day. In 1911 the company instituted a card-filing system to keep track of what each customer had ordered, and by 1915 had records on the purchasing habits of six million families. Modern market research began in earnest when product advertisers began asking magazines to describe the people who were reading their ads, and magazines hired researchers to create profiles of their readership. One fact researchers found was that the millions of women who were reading publications such as *Ladies' Home Journal* and *Good Housekeeping* were in fact responsible for 80 to 85 percent of all household purchases. Advertisers used this information to pitch their ads to these women, knowing they were searching for products to make their homes cleaner and more efficient.

The Home Trade League. Meanwhile, proponents of small-town life and the integrity of craftsmanship resisted the steady surge toward mass production. Local businessmen organized "trade-at-home" clubs, and midwestern commercial associations created the Home Trade League of America. William Allen White, editor of the *Emporia* (Kans.) *Gazette* wrote, "There is

After his first wife died, President Woodrow Wilson suffered a serious depression. Rear Adm. Cary Travers Grayson, his personal physician, and Helen Bones, Wilson's cousin and his wife's former secretary, conspired to bring the president together with a vivacious Washington widow, Edith Bolling Galt. Edith Galt and President Wilson first met by accident in a White House hallway, as she was returning from a walk in Rock Creek Park with Helen Bones, and he was returning from a round of golf with Dr. Grayson. As they all took tea in the Oval Room, the president was drawn to Galt's lively conversation and infectious laugh. An ardent courtship ensued, particularly during a lovely summer vacation at the home of American novelist Winston Churchill in Cornish, New Hampshire; but the president took to his bed in anguish when he thought the publicity of the match might deter Galt from marriage. Summoned by Grayson for a discussion of the situation, Galt determined to let love prevail, and an early wedding date was set. She and the president were married at her Washington home on 18 December 1915, with clergy from both her Episcopalian and his Presbyterian denominations officiating.

Sources: Isabel Ross, *Power with Grace: The Life Story of Mrs. Woodrow Wilson* (New York: Putnam, 1975);

Tom Schactman, *Edith and Woodrow: A Presidential Romance* (New York: Putnam, 1981).

such a thing as 'tainted' dry goods, 'tainted' groceries, and 'tainted' furniture. All of such that are not bought at home, of men who befriended you, of men to whom you owe a living are 'tainted' because they come unfairly." Sears shipped its goods in plain brown paper with no return address to protect their customers from such scorn. In 1910 Congress debated the creation of parcel post to carry packages weighing up to four hundred pounds. Proponents argued that parcel post would help modernize farm life; opponents said it would spell the death of local retail merchandising. In 1912 progressives denounced chain stores as creatures of Wall Street interests. Meanwhile, the chains routinely cut prices on standard items, sometimes below cost — a practice that local merchants, as well as some manufacturers, deplored.

Cultural Backlash. The advantages of the new retailing methods to cosmopolitan women, thrift-oriented households, and isolated rural consumers soon overruled most business objections to the new retailing fashions; but a cultural elite resisted the tide of mass marketing for other, less tangible reasons. Condemning the rush to mass pro-

duction as the destruction of a centuries-old crafts tradition, the death knell of the pride of workmanship, and a trend that would encourage the mechanization of the human soul, antimodernists of various stripes embraced and celebrated visions of a preindustrial ideal for the nation. These often wealthy, educated Americans searched for antidotes for a society that was moving rapidly and headlong toward modernization. Many of these critics of the direction of American life demonstrated an increasing fascination with the medieval period of European history. One of their proposed solutions to what they believed to be the imminent crises in American society was a revival of the arts and crafts tradition. Many of them were attracted to and participated in a spiritual and literary movement that encouraged the search for an "authentic" self. Mass society thus came of age with a fierce but largely unheeded critique of its effects on people and social relations.

Sources:

Simon J. Bronner, ed., *Consuming Visions: Accumulation and Display of Goods in America, 1880–1920* (New York: Norton, 1989);

William Leach, *Land of Desire: Merchants, Power, and the Rise of a New American Culture* (New York: Vintage, 1993);

T. J. Jackson Lears, *No Place of Grace: Antimodernism and the Transformation of American Culture, 1880–1920* (New York: Pantheon, 1981);

Susan Strasser, *Satisfaction Guaranteed: The Making of the American Mass Market* (New York: Pantheon, 1989).

OVER THERE: AMERICAN SOLDIERS IN WORLD WAR I

Selective Service. When the United States entered World War I in April 1917, the armed forces were made up of about two hundred thousand volunteers. Because an insufficient number of men signed up in the days following Congress's declaration of war than for any other war in American history, clearly reflecting the public's ambivalence about the war, Congress passed the Selective Service Act. All men between the ages of twenty-one and thirty were required to register for the draft. Secretary of War Newton D. Baker stressed the democratic nature of the process: no one could buy his way out or send a surrogate, as was common practice during the Civil War. On 5 June 1917 nearly 10 million American men registered. During the course of the war the age span was widened to eighteen to forty-five; by the end of the war 24 million men had registered, and 2.8 million had been called for service. Of these, 340,000 men, or 12 percent of those called up for service, failed to show; but most recruits seemed to know that the war would introduce them to other worlds. Theodore Roosevelt called going to war the "Great Adventure," and many training camps assembled in the atmosphere of a college campus on the eve of a big football game.

Keeping the Troops in Line. Controlling the behavior of so many young men proved a challenge. Army psychologists who gave IQ tests to the recruits found that fully 25 percent were illiterate. Progressives in the Wilson

U.S. Marines firing from the trenches, Meuse-Argonne, 1918

administration pressed for using military service as a way to inculcate proper values about education, drinking, and sexuality. The army banned drinking by soldiers in uniform and on military bases, a move which helped fuel the national Prohibition movement. The Commission on Training Camp Activities initiated a vigorous campaign against venereal disease, and lectured troops on the dangers and pains of syphilis and gonorrhea. Its efforts were effective. Venereal disease rates among the troops declined dramatically during the course of the war.

Trench Warfare. The commander of the American Expeditionary Forces, Gen. John J. "Black Jack" Pershing, believed that the goal of the war was the total destruction of the enemy's military power. He expressed contempt for the strategy of trench warfare that both sides employed, but the use on both sides of the battlefields of machine guns and long-range artillery made the trenches necessary. By all reports, life in these trenches was grim: cold, wet, lousy, dirty, and steeped in boredom and sleeplessness. It was surely not the glorious duty many enthusiastic recruits expected.

Final Months. By September 1918 American reinforcements poured into France at the rate of a quarter million a month, and the AEF took control of two hundred miles of the Meuse-Argonne offensive line. In seven weeks of fighting in perpetual rain and deep mud, the

U.S. Army used more ammunition than the North had used in four years during the Civil War. Under this onslaught the Germans soon began to fall back. More than 52,000 American troops, many of whom were sent into the fighting with a minimum of training, died in battle; 200,000 sustained combat wounds. Another 60,000 soldiers died from influenza and pneumonia, many while still in training camps.

On Leave. Most troops spent more time behind the lines in France than they did in battle, and despite the efforts of their commanders, experienced Europe as tourists. Many were overwhelmed by how old everything seemed to them; at the same time, their youth, vigor, and the obvious wealth of their nation appealed to many Europeans, who were worn down by years of war. The beauty of the European landscape and the architecture, the sense of ceremony, and the vivid feeling of history evoked by the European countries all became common motifs in letters home and in the sometimes overwrought musings of doughboy poets. While the literature of World War I is usually regarded to be characterized by disillusionment with the barbarity and brevity of life, the typical American soldier found a surprising richness in his noncombat experience. With twenty-four hours in Paris, Captain (and future president) Harry S Truman of the 129th Field Artillery dined at Maxime's; attended a show at the Folies-Bergère; saw Notre Dame Cathedral,

Napoleon's tomb, the Arc de Triomphe, the Luxembourg Palace, the Tuileries Gardens, and the Louvre; and strolled the Boulevard de l'Opéra. He was also tickled to learn that the most beautiful woman he had seen since he had been in France was an American with the Red Cross.

Sources:
David M. Kennedy, *Over Here: The First World War and American Society* (New York: Oxford University Press, 1980);

David McCullough, *Truman* (New York: Simon & Schuster, 1992).

PROHIBITION

The Eighteenth Amendment. On 18 December 1917 Congress passed the Eighteenth Amendment to the United States Constitution, forbidding the "manufacture, sale, or transportation of intoxicating liquors." By January 1919, forty-six of the forty-eight states had ratified the amendment; only Rhode Island and Connecticut had not. Despite the rapid ratification of the amendment, however, many industrial states never adopted state Prohibition, including California, Connecticut, Illinois, Massachusetts, Missouri, New Jersey, New York, Pennsylvania, and Wisconsin. The opposition of new immigrants to the Prohibition measure proved its undoing in the large cities that rejected state or municipal liquor bans between 1917 and 1919: Boston, Chicago, Cincinnati, Cleveland, San Francisco, Saint Louis, and Saint Paul. In states where Prohibition was unpopular, the state governments assumed the position that the measure was a federal law, and left its enforcement to the federal government. Altogether, the cost to states for enforcing Prohibition was only a quarter of what they spent on administering their parks. Meanwhile, the Eighteenth Amendment produced a decline in federal revenues. The federal government had long benefited from domestic liquor sales: in 1914, one-third of its revenue was derived from liquor licenses and taxes.

The Anti-Saloon League. Founded in Oberlin, Ohio, in 1893, the Anti-Saloon League led the fight for Prohibition. In 1909 there was one saloon for every three hundred people in the United States; indeed, there were more saloons than there were schools, libraries, hospitals, theaters, or parks; and far more saloons than churches. These establishments were not distributed evenly across the United States: there were more bars in Chicago than there were in the entire South, for instance. Generally, Anti-Saloon League members shared a broad program of progressive reform: in addition to temperance, they favored votes for women, an end to monopolies, the improvement of working conditions, and aid to immigrants. They found strong support in Congress for their Prohibition goal. In February 1913 Congress passed the Webb-Kenyon Act, overriding President William Howard Taft's veto, in an effort to stop the transportation of liquor from so-called wet states, where the sale of liquor was legal, into dry states, where it was not. In November 1913, at its twenty-year anniversary jubilee in Columbus, Ohio, the Anti-Saloon League adopted the strategy of

YEARS IN WHICH THE STATES ADOPTED PROHIBITION	
1851	Maine
1880	Kansas
1889	North Dakota
1907	Georgia Oklahoma
1908	Mississippi North Carolina
1909	Tennessee
1912	West Virginia
1914	Arizona Colorado Oregon Virginia Washington
1915	Alabama Arkansas Idaho Iowa South Carolina
1916	Michigan Montana Nebraska South Dakota
1917	Indiana New Hampshire New Mexico Utah
1918	Florida Nevada Ohio Texas Wyoming
1919	Kentucky

Source: Sean Dennis Cashman, *Prohibition: The Lie of the Land* (New York: Free Press, 1981).

lobbying for an amendment to the Constitution, hoping to make the sale and use of alcohol illegal throughout the United States. Meanwhile, workmen's compensation laws in the early 1910s caused many industry leaders to embrace the league's goal. Because companies were required to pay when liquor-related accidents injured or incapacitated their workers, these businesses had gained a strong interest in keeping their workers sober.

ALCOHOL---The Great Enemy

DISEASE

COMMON
HOUSE FLY

The fly, through its germ-spreading proclivities, is said by government experts to cost the nation more than $150,000,000 a year, besides the cost in loss of human life. But we've a greater enemy. In the years 1900-08, 33,000 men, from twenty-five to sixty-five years of age, were reported to have died in the United States, in the "registration area" alone, from alcoholism and from hardened liver due to alcoholism,—11,000 more than died from typhoid fever.

Thirty-Six States Can Stop It By Constitutional Amendment

Series G. No. 16.

An Anti-Saloon League poster

Political Dilemma. The three towering political figures of the age, William Jennings Bryan, Theodore Roosevelt, and Woodrow Wilson, all waited a long time before declaring their positions on Prohibition. Bryan, whose political base was strongest in "dry" areas of the South and Midwest, did not believe that Prohibition was a solution to the complex problems of the cities; not until 1916, when he resigned as secretary of state because of President Wilson's war policies, did Bryan clearly and publicly support Prohibition. Theodore Roosevelt's position was even more ambiguous. Unpersuaded by the social arguments used to support Prohibition, he worried that the proposed law against liquor would infringe on personal liberties; as president from 1901 to 1909, he maintained that Prohibition was primarily a state rather than a federal matter. Indeed, in 1914 both sides in the debate claimed that Roosevelt supported their position. Woodrow Wilson also vacillated, leaving his position unclear in his 1912 campaign for the presidency; then, as president, he declared that supporting the Webb-Kenyon Act was as far as he could go in favoring national Prohibition. The political momentum generated by the outbreak of war, however, pushed President Wilson to strengthen his support for Prohibition.

Rationing Wins the Issue. To win the war in Europe, the United States government exercised unprecedented control over America's railroads, industries, shipping, fuel, and food supplies. It was the government's strict food-rationing program that directly defined Prohibition as a wartime issue. The large quantities of foodstuffs required by the brewing industries that were mainly owned by German Americans, and thus doubly suspect during the war, were needed by the government for the war effort. At the same time, to bolster their case, advocates of Prohibition convinced many politicians that consumption of liquor would undermine the morale and performance of the nation's men in uniform, and succeeded in getting liquor banned from the areas around military camps. Sen. William Kenyon of Iowa asked, "If liquor is a bad thing for the boys in the trenches, why is it a good thing for those at home? When they are willing to die for us, should we not be willing to go dry for them?" Few people were willing to oppose publicly a cause that was identified with the war effort. Like many other issues during the war, Prohibition was quickly reduced to a simple question of morality, of good and evil, and the Congress had little choice but to take the side of good. The Eighteenth Amendment passed. Not until the 1920s would the violence and crime associated with the illegal liquor trade force the Prohibition issue back into public focus.

Sources:

Sean Dennis Cashman, *Prohibition: The Lie of the Land* (New York: Free Press, 1981);

K. Austin Kerr, *Organized for Prohibition: A New History of the Anti-Saloon League* (New Haven: Yale University Press, 1985).

THE SCIENCE OF HOUSEWORK AND CHILDCARE

Home Economics. Nineteenth-century writers on women's role in the home had stressed the sanctity of the household domain as an escape from and an alternative to the hurly-burly of public and commercial life; twentieth-century educators and organizers, in contrast, saw the home as a vital part of the larger society. Not only did they maintain that the household performed functions important to public life — the education of children, the caretaking of workers, the production of food and clothing — but they further argued that those who managed the home should employ the same efficiency methods that were modernizing economic activity in American business. At the turn of the century, a new home economics movement gradually coalesced in the atmosphere of progressive reform, with the result that, in the 1910s, large numbers of American housewives were learning to run their households as if they were professional managers.

Courses of Study. The discipline of home economics found a place in the curricula in the agricultural and mechanical colleges of the Midwest and in a few state universities. At the same time, cooking schools in large cities diversified their curricula to promote professionalization among three distinct classes of women: domestic servants, their employers, and young housewives. Public-school reformers urged home economics education as a

Both Progressive reformers and an emerging cadre of social scientists fostered a new conception of children as a discrete rank within early twentieth century society. The 1910s saw the advent of a separate juvenile court system, compulsory education laws, child labor laws, laws mandating the purity of milk, institutions for delinquent boys and wayward girls, and the prohibition of the sale of alcohol and tobacco to minors. While psychologists disputed about whether bad behavior resulted from faulty genetics or improper upbringing, vast resources were given to studying child development and to creating social conditions that would prevent delinquency.

A host of clubs and activities for children that became popular in the 1910s gained "scientific" sanction for providing the proper kind of influence and necessary structure for healthy socialization. The Boy Scouts and the Girl Scouts of America, with their creeds of honesty, service, and altruism embodied the Progressive ethic of "child-saving." 4-H Clubs (head, heart, hands, health) grew out of a program created by the Congress in 1914, and administered by the Department of Agriculture. Land grant universities and local counties shared the cost of this rurally oriented learn-by-doing program. At the same time that children gained special protections under the law, and a host of new institutions aimed at improving their welfare, they also became test subjects for a wide variety of theories. Children's leisure simultaneously became a social concern, an outlet for progressive organizing, and a subject for the emerging class of professional child workers.

Source: Joseph M. Hawes and N. Ray Hiners, eds., *American Childhood: A Research Guide and Historical Handbook* (Westport, Conn.: Greenwood Press, 1985).

From the turn of the century until the 1930s, when its association with Nazism discredited it, the "science" of eugenics enjoyed great popularity with many social scientists and intellectuals in the United States and Great Britain. The belief that an understanding of human genetics could be used to improve the condition of humankind appealed to a wide variety of people. Birth control advocate Margaret Sanger was deeply influenced by the British authority on human reproduction, and eugenicist, Havelock Ellis. In the years shortly before World War I, eugenics became a popular craze, promoted in newspapers and magazines as the panacea for a variety of social ills. "Fitter Family" contests were held at state fairs; sermon contests on the subject of the family were held in churches and synagogues. The eugenics craze also provided a pseudoscientific justification for right-wing opponents of immigration, such as Madison Grant, whose *The Passing of the Great Race* (1915) warned that Anglo-Saxons were being drowned by a rising tide of "inferior" racial and ethnic types. The eugenics movement became discredited when the theories of eugenics were used to defend racism, and also to defend unequal distribution of property and privilege.

Source: Ellen Chesler, *Woman of Valor: Margaret Sanger and the Birth Control Movement in America* (New York: Simon & Schuster, 1992).

means to Americanize immigrants and to teach thrift, nutrition, and cleanliness to the children of poor families. Paradoxically, despite the strong message of professionalizing women's sphere, the American Home Economics Association was primarily led by men; and the female leaders in the field of home economics tended to be unmarried or childless.

Home as a Business. The principles of Frederick Winslow Taylor, the first modern efficiency expert, had revolutionized factory work since the 1900s; in the 1910s his principles of "scientific management" were extended to the American household. In numerous books and pamphlets, efficiency in the home became the paramount virtue, and its gospel was spread through volumes with titles such as *Increasing Home Efficiency, The Efficient Kitchen,* and *Efficiency in the Household.* Few women went so far as to paint grids on their kitchen floors to conduct time-motion studies of dishwashing, as some experts recommended; but the "string plan," where a child followed its mother around with a ball of string to track her movements and show wasted motion, proved extremely popular. In 1912 the home economics movement's central figure, Christine Frederick, published her system for the modern home in the *Ladies' Home Journal;* this article established her career as a "household engineer." Schedules in the home, she believed, should be made rigorous, but should include planned rest periods; weekly meal plans would make shopping in advance efficient; the kitchen should be strategically organized so that it could be used to maximum advantage. "Today, the woman in the home," Frederick wrote, "is called upon to be an executive as well as a manual laborer."

Century of the Child. In the 1910s those who were regarded as scientific experts began to replace grandmothers and other elders as the source of information on child rearing. Immigrant women far from their mothers, women who bought clothing in stores rather than participating in sewing circles, and women whose children

Draw Your Own CONCLUSION
Which do you prefer, the Hoosier System or the old fashioned way? The Hoosier System groups everything needed in preparing a meal at your fingers' ends—every utensil and every article has its own special place where it is easily reached without taking a single step.
The old fashioned way—you know it only too well.
The Hoosier Kitchen Cabinet
A Pantry—Cupboard—Work-Table Combined
The Hoosier Catalogue—A Valuable Book
THE HOOSIER MFG. CO., 42 Adams St., New Castle, Indiana

Advertisement for a Hoosier Kitchen Cabinet in a 1915 issue of the *Saturday Evening Post*

SAVING TIME AND LABOR

As more jobs became available to women in the 1910s, those who had worked as domestics in private homes increasingly left to explore new opportunities. One result was that the back staircase, formerly used by domestic help, was not built for most new homes in this period; another consequence was that more women were obliged to do more of their own housework, with little or no outside help. Into these households came a flood of time-saving devices, often with unwieldy designs but always with new, practical applications to the daily housework routines. Large iceboxes, ornate gas-cooking ranges, hefty hot-water heaters, spindly telephones, and almost Gothic-looking hand-cranked washing machines all helped in various ways to reduce the number of hours required to run an average household. Furthermore, electricity became increasingly available in the 1910s; according to a government survey of family expenditures from 1917 to 1919, 41 percent of American houses were using electricity by the end of the decade — electricity that made possible many new appliances and conveniences.

Source: Clifford Edward Clark Jr., *The American Family Home, 1800–1960* (Chapel Hill: University of North Carolina Press, 1986).

were delivered by doctors rather than midwives needed new information to replace the traditional sources they had lost; and the experts readily stepped in to fill the knowledge gap. In 1909 an English edition of the work of Swedish writer Ellen Key became a best-seller in the United States. Key called for motherhood to be redefined as work, and for society to provide services to support this crucial occupation. She also called for the application of scientific methods to solving common problems, and believed that scientific methods could be applied to the practices of child rearing. Another influential guide of the period was G. Stanley Hall, the leading figure in the child-study movement, a founder of the American Psychological Association and the *American Journal of Psychology;* Hall contended that children were born as savages and had to be civilized in a process that was essentially a recapitulation of human evolution. The most popular advice manual, Mrs. Max West's *Infant Care,* available through the Government Printing Office for twenty-five cents, stressed that parents should never play with children who were less than six months old; furthermore, according to West, although it might appear cruel, the establishment of regular habits and strict schedules should take precedence over all other activities, creating forms of discipline that would benefit the child all through its life.

Source:
Susan Strasser, *Never Done: A History of American Housework* (New York: Pantheon, 1982).

VOTES FOR WOMEN

Middle-Class Movement. In 1910 the decades-old fight for women's suffrage was led by middle-class women who subscribed to the progressive agenda for social reform. The movement benefited from progressive organizing and the popularity of the progressive movement in the 1900s. The most prominent national organization, the National American Woman Suffrage Association (NAWSA), grew from seventeen thousand members in 1905 to seventy-five thousand members in 1910. Despite resistance to suffrage in eastern states — where it was linked to the Prohibition movement — many western states passed forms of suffrage legislation between 1910 and 1915. In 1912 the Progressive Party, led by Theodore Roosevelt — who had long vehemently opposed women's suffrage — endorsed the suffragist position; when that party dissolved, Republicans and Democrats began to support voting rights for women in order to woo former Progressive Party members. Even propo-

Women making bullets during World War I

nents of women's right to vote feared the consequences of extending the franchise to blacks, immigrants, or the less educated. Many women favored a literacy test for voting rights. The crusade for women's suffrage was sustained in part by racism and nativism.

Catt Takes Over NAWSA. An excellent organizer, Carrie Chapman Catt became the leader of NAWSA in 1915. Before America's entry into World War I, most feminist leaders, including Catt and settlement-house activist Jane Addams, strongly opposed the war; but in 1917 Catt made a strategic decision to reverse herself and support American involvement. Stressing women's contributions to the war through selling war bonds, working in factories, and volunteering for the Red Cross, Catt continued to lobby Congress for a constitutional amendment to allow women to vote. But her support of the war split the women's movement into two camps, between moderate NAWSA supporters and more-militant pacifists; nevertheless, the tactic allowed President Wilson to favor the moderates' position, and after long hesitation, in 1917 he threw his support behind the amendment as "vital in winning the war."

National Woman's Party. Alice Paul, a Quaker who categorically opposed war of any kind, brought radical new tactics to women's fight for the vote. Having spent several years learning from the suffrage movement in England, she returned to the United States in 1913 and formed a Congressional Union within NAWSA. Soon, however, she tired of the large organization's moderation and orderliness. In 1916, together with western women voters, she formed the National Woman's Party (NWP). Copying methods of British suffragists, the NWP staged dramatic demonstrations, picketing the White House and burning President Wilson's speeches. Its members chained themselves to the White House fence, and when jailed began a hunger strike. Their militancy alienated legislators, but forced the government to act.

The Nineteenth Amendment. The U.S. House of Representatives finally passed a women's suffrage amendment in January 1918, and the more conservative Senate followed suit in 1919. Another year of political organizing was needed to move the measure through the requisite three-quarters of state legislatures, but in August 1920 the state of Tennessee gave the final vote necessary for ratification. The war, Carrie Chapman Catt wrote,

Headquarters of an antisuffrage organization in New York City, circa 1918

had "a tremendous effect on woman suffrage by revolutionizing the whole sphere of women."

Sources:
Nancy F. Cott, *The Grounding of American Feminism* (New Haven: Yale University Press, 1987);

Eleanor Flexner, *Century of Struggle: The Women's Rights Movement in the United States*, revised edition (Cambridge, Mass.: Harvard University Press, 1975).

WOMEN, WORK, AND THE WAR

Stepping In. When more than two million young men departed for military service in 1917 and 1918, the labor shortage that resulted brought more than a million women, most of whom had never worked outside their homes, into the labor market. For women who had previously worked outside their homes, primarily as domestics, seamstresses, and laundresses, the war years presented an opportunity to move into better-paying industrial occupations. The number of female servants dropped by a quarter of a million, while there was a corresponding rise in the number of women doing clerical work. Two and a quarter million of 9.4 million workers in war-related industries were women, and the number of women in industrial jobs rose more than 100 percent between 1910 and 1920. Nearly forty thousand women served in the armed forces as nurses, in National Guard camps, and as navy "Yeomanettes."

A Stir. While relatively few women stepped into visible positions that appeared to challenge traditional gender roles, these exceptions received great attention. Six women who joined the New York police force, and female traffic cops in other locations, were almost celebri-

ties in their communities. For the first time, women found work as train and streetcar conductors, a step which raised many eyebrows and protests. Unions in Cleveland and Detroit went on strike because of these hirings and forced the intervention of the National War Labor Board. Among the few women conductors, several were literally holding jobs for male relatives in the service, and did not see themselves in any kind of vanguard, as some suggested they were.

Equal Work, Unequal Pay. Factory managers, meanwhile, routinely praised women's efficiency. A motor company reclassified the job of inspector as women's work because it found women more accurate and efficient than men in that capacity. Notices in the want ads in Cleveland, Ohio, targeted women for such traditionally male positions as bookkeeper, cashier, elevator operator, chocolate dipper, and sweeper. Many employers preferred female workers because they accepted lower pay: on average, about half what males were paid. While there were no laws mandating equal pay for equal work, the government created a Women in Industry Service to regulate working conditions. This group limited work to eight hours a day and mandated provision for rest periods, meals, and restrooms. While women's wages lagged seriously in comparison to men's, they nevertheless doubled during the war period because of the availability of work in manufacturing.

Weaker and Stronger. Many employers, reflecting the common prejudice of the era, assumed that African American and foreign-born women would perform heavy manual tasks more easily than white or native-born women. Two ice plants in Philadelphia employed females, one preferring "Russians and Polacks" because they appeared to be the strongest and the neatest, also for the reason that they had come from countries with long winters. The other company favored African Americans because they had not "undergone the enervating influences of civilization." Such discrimination, coupled with widespread sexual harassment and tedious work, often made working conditions for women deplorable. Discipline could be harsh and crude: doors were taken off toilets to prevent socializing and lagging, and girls who failed to accept dates with managers often found themselves unemployed. African American women often found themselves excluded from the new opportunities afforded white women during the war. Eighty percent of black women in nonagricultural jobs in 1920 were employed as maids, cooks, or washerwomen. When they did find jobs in industry, they were typically on the lowest rung of the ladder. As *World Outlook* admitted in October 1919, wartime gains were short-lived, for "in most cases, the colored woman is the 'marginal worker.' She is the last to be hired, the first to be fired."

Lasting Change. Many women who stepped into the American workforce out of a sense of duty, or to supplement family income during the war, stepped out again when the troops returned home. The lasting changes in female employment happened for those who had worked at menial jobs before the war. For the most part, these women maintained the advances they made into better-paid and more-prestigious positions; advances that had started before the war for women moving into white-collar positions also held firm. Women also kept their jobs as telephone operators, clerks, and typists. The number of married women who worked outside the home hardly changed once the wartime workers left. They represented less than a quarter of the women who worked. Overwhelmingly, the culture deemed motherhood women's most vital occupation.

Sources:

Jacqueline Jones, *Labor of Love, Labor of Sorrow: Black Women and the Family, From Slavery to the Present* (New York: Vintage, 1988);

Neil A. Wynn, *From Progressivism to Prosperity: World War I and American Society* (New York: Holmes & Meier, 1986).

HEADLINE MAKERS

CARRIE CHAPMAN CATT

1859-1947

SUFFRAGIST

Early Years. Carrie Chapman Catt, a leader during the 1910s of the movement for a women's suffrage amendment to the Constitution, was born on a family farm in Ripon, Wisconsin, in 1859. In 1866 her family settled in Charles City, Iowa, where Carrie attended a one-room schoolhouse until entering high school. In March 1877 she entered the Iowa State Agricultural College, where she paid her tuition with the money she had earned while teaching at a country schoolhouse. She graduated in 1880, the only woman in her class of eighteen students, and began reading for the law. But she abandoned her legal education to accept a teaching job in Mason City, Iowa, and in her second year at the school she became its superintendent. In 1885 she married Leo Chapman, a suffragist and editor of the local weekly, *Republican*, and she began writing about women's issues for the paper. She also began attending women's suffrage meetings, traveling that year to Des Moines, Iowa, for a conference of the American Association of Women, chaired by suffragist Julia Ward Howe. In May 1886 Chapman arrived in San Francisco to find that her husband had died of typhoid fever while awaiting her arrival. She remained in the city for a year before returning to her family in Charles City.

Lecturer and Activist. While in the West Chapman began lecturing as a means of supporting herself. Many of her lectures focused on the dangers that immigrants posed to American society. She particularly disapproved of the fact that male immigrants were given the vote within six months of arriving in America, while women born and raised in the United States were denied the same right. She took a firm stance against Native Americans for the same reason — that Native American men could vote. In the 1900s and 1910s she recanted these positions and became a staunch supporter of racial and ethnic equality.

NAWSA. In 1890 the National American Woman Suffrage Association (NAWSA) formed from two suffragist factions that had been divided for twenty years. Chapman, present at the first meeting, became within ten years president of the organization. Meanwhile, in June 1890, after formalizing a prenuptial agreement that allowed her to remain active in the suffrage movement, she married George Catt, who was a strong supporter of his wife's work until his death in 1905. Between 1890 and 1910 Carrie Chapman Catt was a leader of NAWSA and specialized in organization and coordination of the group's field work. She was president of NAWSA from 1900 to 1904, when she resigned to care for her dying husband.

National Figure. In October 1909 Catt and other activists launched the Woman Suffrage Party. She had mainly devoted the 1900s to two endeavors — campaigning for women's suffrage in New York State and helping organize the International Woman Suffrage Alliance. This alliance had formed in 1902 in Washington, D.C., and later held conferences in Berlin (1904), Copenhagen (1906), Amsterdam (1908), and London (1909). Though Catt remained an international figure, she devoted most of her energy in the 1910s to the cause of women's suffrage in the United States. After a world tour from 1911 to 1912, she returned to America in November 1912, arriving in San Francisco just as women in that city were voting for the first time in a national election. (California and nine other states had passed suffrage laws by 1912).

Success. In 1915 Catt again became president of NAWSA, at a time when the organization was deeply divided by Alice Paul's more radical Congressional Union (renamed the Woman's Party in 1916), which challenged NAWSA's methods. Catt's organizational skills helped bridge the gap between the group's two factions by combining NAWSA's emphasis on state suffrage rights with Paul's insistence on a federal amendment. Catt's program, named the "Winning Plan," won approval, and within two years of its adoption by NAWSA, President Woodrow Wilson, after years of reluctance, requested a suffrage bill from Congress. The bill passed the House on 10 January 1918 and the Senate on 4 June 1919. On 26 August 1920 the Nineteenth Amendment was ratified; it mandated that women could vote in every state and in every election.

War Years. In 1915, as the United States prepared for a possible entry into World War I, Catt helped found the Woman's Peace Party. This party called for opposition to militarism, a general disarmament, an international police force, and women's suffrage as a means of "feminizing" governments, a process which she believed would reduce the possibility of wars. Eventually, in a reversal, she threw the support of NAWSA behind the U.S.

government's "preparedness" position — an act for which she was vilified by other pacifists; but her support of President Wilson later proved invaluable in the drive toward women's suffrage. Catt had offered NAWSA's support for the war effort despite the fact that she continued to believe, as she said, that "war is ... barbarism, a relic of the stone age." While continuing her critically important work in the suffrage movement, she served on the Woman's Committee of the Council of National Defense.

Final Years. Carrie Chapman Catt's work did not end with the passage of the Nineteenth Amendment. At NAWSA's convention in 1919 she organized the National League of Women Voters, which became the logical successor to NAWSA. After the suffrage amendment passed, some twenty-seven million women were suddenly eligible to vote, but many of them were unfamiliar with the world of politics. Thus, the league's first function was to educate these new voters. Catt also continued her international peace work, calling on the women of the world to end the barbarism of war. In 1925, in Washington, D.C., she participated in the first "Conference on the Cause and Cure of War," which met annually until 1939, and for which she served as conference chairperson until 1937. In her later years she received numerous honorary degrees, and was given a citation of honor by President Franklin D. Roosevelt in 1936. In 1933 she won the American Hebrew Medal for her efforts on behalf of German-Jewish refugees. In 1947 Catt died of a heart attack in New Rochelle, New York, at the age of eighty-eight.

Source:
Jacqueline Van Voris, *Carrie Chapman Catt: A Public Life* (New York: Feminist Press, 1987).

MABEL DODGE

1879-1962

MEMOIRIST, ARTS PATRON, BOHEMIAN

Self-Invention. In *Movers and Shakers* (1936), the third book of a four-volume autobiography, Mabel Dodge Luhan described her years in New York City during the 1910s in these words: "in the first place I wanted to know everybody, and in the second place everybody wanted to know me. I wanted, in particular, to know the Heads of things. Heads of movements. Heads of Newspapers. Heads of all kinds of groups of people. I became a Species of Head Hunter, in fact." She also became the best-known hostess in New York's Greenwich Village, which during the 1910s was teeming with artists, writers, intellectuals, and radicals. From the time of Dodge's arrival in the city in 1912 to her departure in 1918, her salon at 23 Fifth

Avenue was the gathering place for the intellectual and artistic elite, the most famous salon of its kind in America. Dodge was at its center, bringing the "heads of things" together, so that she could observe them while also inventing her apparently elusive self. Her New York years were probably her best-known period, but even before this time, and then through the odyssey of her later years, Dodge was regarded by many friends and observers as an embodiment of the much-discussed New Woman, who repudiated stale traditions, searched for more-fulfilling roles than those society had usually permitted her, and demonstrated the power of women in a male-dominated society.

Background. By her own account, Dodge, born in Buffalo, New York, in 1879, grew up in the sterile, loveless household of a wealthy, stodgy Victorian family. She attended St. Margaret's girls' school from 1886 to 1894, then Miss Graham's Young Ladies' Boarding School in Manhattan in 1895, completing her formal education in 1896 at a finishing school in Chevy Chase, Maryland. The following year she was presented at a "social debut" in the Victorian style. In later years, she thoroughly rebelled against her upper-class upbringing and spent her life filling the psychic void that she claimed to have developed as a youth. In 1900 she secretly married Karl Evans, who she later claimed had tricked her and forced her into marriage. A short time later they married publicly, and in 1901 Dodge gave birth to her only child, whose rearing she essentially neglected. Karl Evans was killed in a hunting accident in 1902, and in 1904 Dodge traveled to Europe to recover her physical and mental health. During this journey she met Boston architect Edwin Dodge, whom she married in Paris.

Florence. She and Edwin Dodge settled in Florence, Italy, in 1905. Florence proved to be a kind of dress rehearsal for Mabel Dodge's New York years: her Villa Curonia et Atcetri became a popular stopping place for artists and intellectuals who were traveling through Italy. Describing these years at Villa Curonia in her memoirs, Dodge noted that among her guests in Florence were Leo and Gertrude Stein and Alice B. Toklas, stage designer Gordon Craig, Italian actress Eleanora Duse, artist Jo Davidson, composer Arthur Rubinstein, and surrealist André Gide. Dodge herself became the subject of numerous portraits by her visiting artists, and Gertrude Stein wrote "Portrait of Mabel Dodge at the Villa Curonia" (1911), which Dodge published herself.

New York. By the early 1910s the marriage to Edwin Dodge, who had not fit well into Mabel Dodge's discovered role of society hostess, was failing. She later wrote that "the inner separation was pretty complete, made so by my selfish ego, long before I left him." In 1912, returning to New York with trepidation after her years away, Dodge imagined the city would be "dreary"; in fact, by her energy in cultivating friendships and acquaintances, she quickly established her Fifth Avenue salon. Her stature in New York was greatly enhanced by Stein's

"Portrait of Mabel Dodge at the Villa Curonia," which Dodge enthusiastically distributed. Soon, the guests began arriving at her second-floor flat, which was decorated mostly in stark white, and the most famous gathering place of the decade was established.

The Salon. The elite in art, journalism, and labor activity swirled around Mabel Dodge for more than five years. Among her close friends were writer Hutchins Hapgood, poet Edwin Arlington Robinson, music critic Carl Van Vechten, anarchist Emma Goldman, radical editor Max Eastman, and radical journalist John Reed, all contributing to what Dodge later referred to as "the particular thing we all created there for a moment." For Dodge, John Reed was probably the most important member of this circle. In 1913 she helped him organize a Madison Square Garden pageant in support of a Paterson, New Jersey, silk workers' strike. Before the pageant the IWW strike had generated little publicity. The spectacle of the pageant, however, drew huge press coverage. Fifteen thousand people attended; strike songs and stage plays were featured; the letters *IWW*, ten feet tall in electric lights, blazed on the outside of Madison Square Garden. Shortly thereafter Reed and Dodge became lovers, openly living together after the autumn of 1913. Their affair continued sporadically until 1915, while Reed traveled the world to cover labor and political unrest. Meanwhile Dodge continued other pursuits. She was a guest editor of Eastman's *The Masses* in 1914. In February 1913 she gave financial support to and served as a hostess for Alfred Stieglitz's remarkable Armory Show, which changed American art history by introducing modern European art to the United States. In 1914 Dodge provided financial backing for Isadora and Elizabeth Duncan's school of modern dance, which brought expressionistic dance to America. In 1915 and 1916, while enjoying great success as a hostess, she began undergoing psychotherapy and dabbling in mind cures. In 1917 Dodge married her third husband, Maurice Sterne, a painter whom she tried to convince to become a sculptor.

Taos. In 1918 Dodge and Sterne moved to Taos, New Mexico. Their marriage ended quickly; by the year's end Sterne was back in New York and Dodge had met Tony Luhan, a full-blooded Pueblo Indian. Dodge underwent a conversion experience and began living an American Indian way of life. She married Luhan in 1923 and remained in Taos until her death in 1962. While in Taos she lobbied for Indian rights and again served as hostess of an artistic community that included Georgia O'Keeffe, Leopold Stokowski, D. H. Lawrence, and Alfred Stieglitz. In 1924 she began writing her memoirs, which were published in four volumes in the 1930s. In 1935 she published *Winter in Taos*, in tribute to her personal Eden, where she finally found peace. Her memoirs, greeted with praise and interest, provided a singular portrait of a singular woman at the center of an important time.

Sources:

Winifred L. Frazer, *Mabel Dodge Luhan* (Boston: Twayne, 1984);

Mabel Dodge Luhan, *Movers and Shakers*, volume 3 of *Intimate Memories* (New York: Harcourt, 1936);

Lois Rudnick, *Mabel Dodge Luhan: New Woman, New Worlds* (Alberquerque: University of New Mexico Press, 1984).

LEO FRANK

1884-1915

MANUFACTURER, LYNCHING VICTIM

Lynched. Among the most notorious events in America during the 1910s was the lynching of Leo Frank on 16 August 1915 in the woods outside Marietta, Georgia. Frank had been convicted of murder in August 1913, but as his case gained notoriety, his guilt was increasingly questioned, and the anti-Semitic fervor that had surrounded his trial received increasing news coverage, especially in the North. Governor John M. Slaton, after reviewing the case, commuted Frank's death sentence in June 1915, but a frenzied mob refused to accept Slaton's judgment. Frank was abducted from prison and hanged.

Background. Born in Texas in 1884, Frank was raised in New York City. He attended the Pratt Institute, then graduated from Columbia University in 1906 with a degree in mechanical engineering. After briefly working in Boston, he moved to Atlanta, where he became superintendent of the National Pencil Factory. In 1910 Frank married into a wealthy Atlanta family and in 1912 was elected president of the local B'nai B'rith.

The Murder. In the early morning of 27 April 1913 Newt Lee, a night watchman at the National Pencil Factory, found the body of thirteen-year-old Mary Phagan in the basement of the factory. Phagan, a factory employee, had been beaten and choked to death. Even in an Atlanta with large areas of squalor and slums, and where recently violent race riots had occurred, the news of Phagan's murder shocked the city. It also seemed to focus a combination of volatile social currents and undercurrents, many generated by the rapid changes taking place in the South that had left many bewildered. The agrarian South was becoming urban, even as black southerners were emigrating to the North. Atlanta's working poor were mostly white tenant farmers who had moved to the city to work in factories, many of which had been established by northerners. Mary Phagan, from small, rural Marietta, Georgia, was in many ways a typical child in the Atlanta of this period, a part of Atlanta's huge child labor force, which was utterly unregulated by local government. After her brutal murder the local police were under intense pressure to find her killer; they picked up Leo Frank two days after the body was discovered.

Hysteria. The hysteria that followed Phagan's death and the arrest of Frank was provoked largely by Atlanta's three newspapers, the *Atlanta Constitution*, the *Atlanta Journal*, and the *Atlanta Georgian*. The *Georgian* in particular focused on the Phagan murder. This paper had been purchased by William Randolph Hearst in 1912 and quickly established itself by using the Hearst methods of yellow journalism. Its lurid coverage of the Phagan murder made the *Georgian* the top-circulating newspaper in the South, with daily sales tripling during the Frank trial. Allegations, misinformation, and rumor dominated the news. Among the rumors that appeared in the papers were tales of Frank's perverse sexual and religious practices: the Jewish faith allowed for the violation of Gentile women, the papers said; Frank's wife knew he was guilty and refused to visit him in jail; Frank had another wife in New York; he had illegitimate children; he was a pervert who preyed on young girls; he was a Mason; he was Catholic. In short, Frank was portrayed as a monster, an outsider, an alien to southern culture, preying upon a young Christian Georgia girl. The hysteria followed the case to trial.

Trial and Appeal. The tragic irony of the Frank case was that the evidence pointed to the prosecution's primary witness, Jim Conley, as the actual murderer. Conley worked as a sweeper in the factory. Later records indicated rampant perjury, coercion, and suppression of evidence on the prosecution's part, but Frank's lawyers performed badly, missing numerous opportunities to damage the prosecution's case. The case was finally decided by issues beyond mere legalities and evidence. Mob rule seemed to be in effect. A public filled with sensationalistic news stories and bent on avenging Mary Phagan's death seemed prepared to accept Frank's guilt unconditionally, and exerted great pressure for conviction. Jurors were intimidated, and some were themselves prejudiced against Frank and his Jewish heritage. The case remained confined to Georgia until the fall of 1913, when Louis Marshall, president of the American Jewish Committee, heard of the miscarriage of justice. When Frank's lawyers appealed the case, Jews in the North began rallying support, albeit privately, certain that overt support would produce even more of a backlash against Frank.

National News. The story broke widely in the national press in late 1914. Newspapers in Baltimore, Kansas City, and New York City began reporting the Frank case. *Collier's* magazine covered the case in December 1914 and *Everybody's* covered it the following March. Meanwhile Frank's lawyers, their appeals for a new trial denied, began lobbying Governor Slaton to commute Frank's death sentence. Most Georgians, meanwhile, continued to be convinced of Frank's guilt, and public emotions were greatly exacerbated by Tom Watson, an anti-Semitic newspaper correspondent, whose paper, *The Jeffersonian*, called for vigilante justice if Frank were set free.

Petitions. By the spring of 1915 the appeals in Frank's favor were massive. More than one hundred thousand letters reached the Georgia governor's office; among them were letters from the governors of Arizona, Louisiana, Michigan, and Mississippi. U.S. senators urged commutation of the death sentence. Meetings were held in Boston, Chicago, New York, and Minneapolis. More than a million signatures on numerous petitions poured into Georgia, and newspapers began lobbying on Frank's behalf. Even ten thousand Georgians petitioned Governor Slaton. In June 1915, near the end of his term as governor, Slaton began studying the notorious case, fully aware how politically charged it was. Then, despite receiving more than a thousand death threats while he reviewed the case, Slaton announced on 21 June that he would commute Frank's sentence to life in prison — fully expecting, he later explained, an eventual new trial and Frank's acquittal.

Aftermath. While the national press responded with jubilation to Slaton's announcement, most Georgians fumed. Meanwhile, the governor had Frank moved secretly to a prison farm near Marietta, where Frank had special living quarters that were barricaded and heavily guarded. Demonstrations against Slaton's commuting of Frank's sentence lasted for more than a week: both Slaton and Frank were burned in effigy, while a group calling itself the Knights of Mary Phagan swore revenge. In July Frank was brutally attacked in prison by other inmates; then, on the morning of 15 August a group of vigilantes stormed the prison farm. After leading Frank into the woods they hanged him.

Source:
Leonard Dinnerstein, *The Leo Frank Case* (New York: Columbia University Press, 1968).

MARCUS GARVEY

1887-1940

BLACK NATIONALIST, EDITOR

Early Years. Although he lived in the United States a mere eleven of his fifty-three years, Marcus Garvey had a tremendous impact on African American consciousness after 1917, as well as in the years after his death in 1940. He was born in Jamaica in 1887 and raised in Saint Ann's Bay. In 1901 he left school and began life as an apprentice printer with his father in Kingston. By 1907 he was a master printer working at a large Kingston print shop, where he led an unsuccessful strike that year. Blacklisted, he spent the next years traveling. In 1910 he was in Costa Rica working for the United Fruit Company; he then traveled to Peru and Panama. In all three places he witnessed the harsh and difficult life of working blacks. In 1912 Garvey moved to London, where he met the Egyptian activist Duse Mohammed Ali, publisher of *Africa Times and Orient Review*. The interest in Africa that later defined

Garvey's life came from Ali. Garvey also read Booker T. Washington's *Up from Slavery* (1901) at this time and was deeply influenced by its message of black progress through vocational and technical training.

UNIA. In 1914 Garvey returned to Kingston and formed the Universal Negro Improvement and Conservation Association and African Communities League, later shortened to UNIA. "My brain was afire," Garvey later wrote, with "unifying all the Negro peoples of the world into one great body to establish a country and Government absolutely their own." Following Washington's methods, Garvey tried to establish educational and industrial colleges for blacks, and although he found some support, he also encountered strong resistance. The motto of the association, "One God! One Aim! One Destiny!" was soon carried to the United States, where Garvey found his greatest successes and greatest failures. His trip was intended to be a short visit during which he hoped to garner financial support from Washington and his allies; but when Garvey arrived in Harlem, New York, on 23 March 1916, Washington was dead. Garvey decided to stay and try to sell his program on his own.

Negro World. Garvey began speaking in the streets of Harlem, and by May was noticed and mentioned in *The Crisis*, the magazine of the NAACP, edited by W. E. B. Du Bois. He then embarked on a tour of thirty-eight states, observing the living conditions of blacks in America. In June 1917 at New York City's Bethel African Methodist Episcopal Church, Garvey was introduced and made an impassioned speech in which he hoped to create support for the UNIA, which had about fifteen hundred members in 1917. By 1919 Garvey claimed two million members, though half that total was probably more accurate. In January 1918 Garvey established the *Negro World*, a weekly newspaper that reached a circulation of more than sixty thousand and survived until 1933. Poet Claude McKay, a critic of Garvey, called it "the best edited colored weekly in New York," and within months of its inception, it was a leading African American weekly, spreading Garvey's program nationwide. *Negro World* was aimed at and priced for lower-income blacks, especially in the newly burgeoning urban centers which were absorbing a substantial migration of rural southern blacks in the 1910s. The paper presented notable leaders and achievements in African and African American history, editorials on contemporary black life, and even published sections in Spanish and French for its West Indian and Central American readership. Although Garvey eventually relinquished editorship to William H. Ferris, *Negro World* remained a propaganda vehicle for Garveyism. Garvey also expressed in the paper his dislike of African American intellectuals such as Du Bois, who, Garvey believed, relied too much on the support and acceptance of whites, while ignoring the plight of poor urban blacks.

Black Star Line. In addition to *Negro World*, Garvey's other great experiment was his establishment in 1919 of the Black Star Line, a steamship company owned, managed, and operated solely by black Americans. Garvey envisioned the line as a trading and traveling connection between blacks on all continents. Garvey was applying Washington's philosophy of self-empowerment, independent of white capital. The plan was mocked by most, including the elite black press, but Garvey was remarkably successful, selling shares at an affordable five dollars each to working-class blacks, making them for the first time shareholders in an enterprise. Shares were sold only to blacks and no one could buy more than two hundred shares. To the amazement of his critics, Garvey actually bought a ship in September 1919, and in November prepared for its first voyage. Five thousand blacks cheered as the ship was launched, but the Black Star Line soon became an utter disaster. In its brief history the line managed to purchase three ships that made six ill-fated voyages, all marred by breakdowns and financial problems. Despite Garvey's success in selling shares, the Black Star Line was terribly mismanaged, and Garvey was indicted in 1922 for mail fraud. Convicted the following year, he was imprisoned from 1925 to 1927, and then deported to Jamaica.

The Vision. Garvey's vision survived, however, despite the disastrous failures of his plans. His UNIA conventions in 1920, 1921, and 1922 were hugely successful, especially the first, at which the "Declaration of the Rights of the Negro Peoples of the World" was issued. His Negro Factories Corporation, founded in 1919, had created black-run co-op grocery stores, a restaurant, a laundry, a tailor shop, and a publishing house. His vision of a free, postcolonial Africa and a mass return to Africa by American blacks was not realized; but it greatly influenced later black activists, such as Malcolm X. "Every time you see another nation on the African continent become independent, you know Marcus Garvey is alive," Malcolm X wrote; he also credited contemporary freedom movements in America to Garvey's influence.

Later Years. Garvey, an enigmatic figure, was by most accounts autocratic and difficult to work for. In 1922 he infuriated blacks by meeting with Edward Young Clarke, leader of the Ku Klux Klan, with whom he agreed on certain points. His critics accused him of preying on poor blacks by selling them shares in his company; his supporters saw the positive psychological impact Garvey's work had on many African Americans. Garvey returned to Jamaica in 1929, and in 1935 moved to London to operate the UNIA. He died in London in 1940, leaving behind a legacy of black initiative, pride, and empowerment that spoke to the everyday needs and the highest aspirations of many in the African American community.

Source:
David Cronon, *Black Moses: The Story of Marcus Garvey and the U.N.I.A.* (Madison: University of Wisconsin Press, 1969).

JOE HILL

1879-1915

SONGWRITER; LABOR ACTIVIST; FOLK HERO

Death in the Morning. On 19 November 1915, at 7:44 A.M., Joe Hill, strapped to a chair in the Utah State Penitentiary in Salt Lake City, was pronounced dead. Hill had been shot in the heart minutes before by a five-man firing squad, ending a yearlong struggle by his supporters to have his sentence commuted or a new trial declared in what may have been the trial of the decade. Hill's case had, since its beginning in January 1914, grown from a dubious murder charge for a local crime to an international cause célèbre that symbolized the violent ongoing struggle between the forces of capital and the much hated Industrial Workers of the World (IWW), of which Joe Hill was a member. Before his death, Hill, an itinerant worker known throughout his workers' union as a songwriter, had remained in prison, professing his innocence while the storm raged around him. "I have absolutely no desire to be one of them what-ye-call-em-martyrs," he wrote in a letter in August 1915; but as his execution neared, he became a martyr, nevertheless, and his name became a prominent labor rallying point in the 1910s, when his case achieved the status of folklore.

Early Years. Although his later life achieved a myth-like status, little is known about Joe Hill before his arrest for murder on 13 January 1914. He was born Joel Hägglund in Gävle, Sweden, in 1879 (even this information was not known until 1949.) His family was poor, especially after his father, a railroad conductor, died in an accident when Hill was eight. The young Hill worked in a rope factory and then as a fireman on a steam-powered crane. He had been raised in a musical family and had learned to play guitar, piano, and violin. In 1902 his mother died and Joel immigrated to America with his brother. All that is known about his life between 1902 and 1910 is that he worked and traveled. He sent a Christmas card from Cleveland in 1905, and in 1906 witnessed the San Francisco earthquake, about which he wrote a letter to a Gävle newspaper, describing the devastation. He is known to have joined the IWW in 1910 in San Pedro, California, and by many accounts was in Tijuana, Mexico, in 1911 when the Wobblies (the nickname for members of the IWW) rallied around the Magón brothers, who were plotting against the Mexican government. Hill was in Hawaii in 1911, where he apparently lived as an itinerant worker.

Songwriter. Were it not for his music, Hill would probably have died in anonymity. But his songs, especially the classic "The Preacher and the Slave," had made him famous among IWW members. Usually set to an already popular folk tune, Hill's songs were hard-bitten stories of the workers. He also wrote songs about his own plight to survive against the forces of capital, and about the necessity of his writing; he also wrote parodies about his enemies. His songs were made popular in the IWW's "Little Red Song Book," which first appeared in August 1909. Hill's contributions began appearing in the third edition in 1911, and many quickly became standards for rallying workers. "The Preacher and the Slave" was his best-known song. Others, such as "Casey Jones," "The Union Scab," and "Where the Fraser River Flows," directly addressed and interpreted IWW strikes of the time, at some of which Hill had apparently been present. These songs were an important weapon that the IWW used to build morale and unity among strikers. Hill's works, poignant in their depiction of working people, harshly satirized the leaders of industry and memorably supported the IWW's work. By March 1913 Hill had placed more than a dozen songs in the different editions of the "Little Red Song Book."

The Charge. On 10 January 1914, at about ten o'clock at night, two men entered the Salt Lake City grocery store of John G. Morrison, who, with his two sons, was closing his shop for the night. Morrison and his eldest son Arling were shot and killed, while thirteen-year-old Merlin Morrison watched. Ninety minutes later Joe Hill arrived at a doctor's office with a bullet hole through his chest. He maintained to his death that he had been shot in an argument about a woman. Police officials believed otherwise; Hill was arrested three days after the Morrison shooting and charged with murder. At the time of his arrest, his affiliation as a Wobbly was unknown. But by April the IWW, through its paper *Solidarity*, was calling for support of their fellow member and songwriter, citing trumped-up charges and a Utah vendetta against the IWW. Between 1912 and 1914 the IWW presence had begun to have an impact in Utah, especially in the copper mines. The year 1912 had seen strikes in Bingham Canyon and Park City. In 1913 a strike in Tucker, Utah, led directly to violence at an IWW rally in Salt Lake City. Though Hill's IWW affiliation did not become widely known until the trial began in June, the union had taken the offensive and rallied around Hill, while at the same time using his case to support their cause.

Awaiting Execution. The case went to trial on 17 June 1914. Despite dubious circumstantial evidence, Hill was found guilty and on 8 July 1914 was sentenced to die. Given the choice of execution by shooting or hanging, he chose the firing squad. Although his verdict was based on questionable evidence, it was never certain that Hill was convicted because of his IWW affiliation. Nonetheless, his cause snowballed over the next sixteen months, becoming a national and later an international story. While Hill's lawyers appealed the decision of the court, the IWW promoted his case. Meetings and marches were held in his honor in New York City, Minneapolis, San Francisco, and other cities. The IWW branch in London began a fund-raising campaign. By the summer of 1915 threats were pouring in from the IWW and others. Utah Gov. William Spry hired the famous security man William Pinkerton for protection. Pleas for clemency arrived from across the country. The Swedish government lobbied for Hill, who was still a citizen of Sweden. Even President Woodrow Wilson asked Governor Spry to reconsider the case, an extraordinary request that many Utah citizens believed to be an act of federal interference in state business. After appeals, Hill was resentenced two more times, and scheduled to die on 19 November 1915. Hundreds of letters and telegrams arrived daily in support of Hill. On 8 November a "Joe Hill Protest Meeting" was held in New York City, featuring radical journalist John Reed and IWW activist Elizabeth Gurley Flynn as keynote speakers. American Federation of Labor president Samuel Gompers wired President Wilson on behalf of Hill, as did Helen Keller. But all these actions were futile. The protests had bought Hill some extra months of life, but on 19 November 1915, as scheduled, he was executed by firing squad. The day after his execution, Hill lay in state in Salt Lake City; one day later, a funeral in the city drew thousands of people. Hill had a second funeral in Chicago on 23 November, Thanksgiving Day, and again thousands came, including Bill Haywood, head of the IWW. Hill's body was later cremated.

The Legend. Joe Hill, the legend, the martyr, the working-class hero, remained for the rest of the decade a rallying cry for the IWW, even after America's entry into World War I reduced Wobbly membership. In 1925 a young poet, Alfred Hayes, published "I Dreamed I Saw Joe Hill Last Night," a poem which, after being set to music a few years later, became a classic among labor folk songs. Upton Sinclair used Joe Hill's songs in a 1924 play, *Singing Jailbirds*. Notable writers such as Carl Sandburg referred to Joe Hill, and Hill's songs continued to be labor standards through the tumultuous 1930s. In 1950 Wallace Stegner published *The Preacher and the Slave* (later published as *Joe Hill*), a novel about Hill's life. Other plays, poems, and songs about Hill appeared, confirming what the poet Hayes had written: "Joe Hill ain't never died." Hill was also remembered for his own work as a songwriter and for his contribution to labor legend and history. On the eve of his execution he wrote short messages to many people. Perhaps sensing his future place in labor legend, he wrote to Bill Haywood: "Goodbye Bill: I die like a true rebel. Don't waste any time mourning — organize!" These words remain a rallying cry for union men and women around the country.

Sources:

Gibbs M. Smith, *Joe Hill* (Salt Lake City: University of Utah Press, 1969);

Wallace Stegner, *Joe Hill, A Biographical Novel* (Boston: Houghton Mifflin, 1950).

PAUL KELLOGG

1879-1958

EDITOR, REFORMER

Survey. "The *Survey*'s work is," Paul Kellogg wrote in 1915, "as an investigator and interpreter of the objective conditions of life and labor and as a chronicler of undertakings to improve them. The points of view of those who contribute is almost as diverse as their places of residence." Kellogg was more than editor in chief of this prominent journal of social work, reform, progressive politics, and opinion. The *Survey* was inextricably tied to his name, from his early work as a contributor, to his becoming editor in chief in 1912, to the journal's demise from lack of funding in 1952. In the 1910s Kellogg and the writers for the *Survey* were at the forefront of progressive reform, leaders in taking social work — which had previously focused on amelioration of existing conditions — to the level of constructive planning for policies to prevent the creation of the difficult conditions routinely faced by the poor, laborers, immigrants, and minorities. Kellogg's journal grew from a small professional journal in social-work practice to a large and influential instrument for interpreting America in the 1910s.

Background. Kellogg, born in 1879 in Kalamazoo, Michigan, grew up on close terms with his brother Arthur, who was a year older and who also devoted his later life to the *Survey*. After a family business failed in the early 1890s, Kellogg's father left the family and Mary Kellogg was forced to raise her sons alone. The teenage brothers helped support their mother, while also editing and writing their high-school newspaper. In 1897 they graduated from high school together, but were too poor to afford college. Paul began working in a bookshop, but quickly found a job as a reporter and then as the city editor of the *Kalamazoo Daily Telegraph.* Arthur joined him, and for four years they worked while living at their family home. In 1901 Paul moved to New York City and enrolled at Columbia University. In the summer of 1902 he took a six-week course in the Summer School in Philanthropic Work at Columbia, whose faculty included social-work pioneers such as Edward T. Devine, Homer Folks, Lee K. Frankel, and Zilpha D. Smith. Devine was impressed with Kellogg and hired him as an assistant editor of *Charities Review,* the magazine of the New York Charity Organization Society. In 1903 Arthur Kellogg would also work for the journal. Paul was only twenty-three, but he quickly suggested to Devine that *Charities* was too narrow, that a broader focus with more-readable articles was needed to expand the journal's

readership. Devine followed this advice, and the journal grew in the 1900s, offering practical articles for social workers in departments such as "Care and Relief of Families in Their Homes," "Public Care of Dependent Classes," and "Housing Reform." It also began publishing periodically special issues on topics such as immigration, race relations, and even venereal disease. By December 1907 the journal, by then known as *Charities and the Commons* (and after 1909 as the *Survey*) had quadrupled its circulation, giving it ten thousand readers.

Reformer. In September 1907 Paul Kellogg, at the request of officials in Pittsburgh, moved to that city and launched what became the *Pittsburgh Survey,* published as a six-volume report between 1910 and 1914. Kellogg and his staff gathered data on the lives of workers and the poor in this gritty steel town. Included in the survey were reports on industrial accidents, employment among women, family life, sanitation, nutrition, and alcoholism. The exhaustive survey surprised even its data collectors by the poor level of working and living conditions they unearthed. As the *Pittsburgh Survey* was published in the early 1910s, Kellogg began organizing efforts to improve living and working conditions for laborers. The era was one of great activity for reformers in many fields, with activists such as Jane Addams and Florence Kelley working tirelessly for the urban poor. In 1911 Kellogg led an effort to address the conditions of workers. He helped to form the Committee on Occupational Standards and to craft its proposals, many of which became the basis for Theodore Roosevelt's Progressive Party platform in 1912. *Survey* published a symposium in 1911, which included the work of Edward T. Devine, Florence Kelley, Rabbi Stephen Wise, and Kellogg, all calling for a congressional Committee on Standards of Living and Labor. The committee was established, but newly elected President Woodrow Wilson disappointed reformers with his appointees, and the committee ultimately performed unsatisfactorily. Nevertheless, *Survey* continued to lobby for reform. Between 1910 and America's entry into World War I in 1917, *Survey* presented articles on topics as diverse as tenement conditions, racism, lynching, school reform, city planning, juvenile court reform, prison life, and birth control, while also keeping track of social-work methodology for practitioners. Some readers complained that *Survey* was becoming too much like an opinion magazine, like the *Nation* or the recently founded *New Republic* (1914); but on the whole Kellogg succeeded in shaping a journal that combined articles about theoretical analyses with articles about social-work practice, while keeping opinion to a minimum.

Survey **and the War.** The start of World War I in 1914 provided a new challenge to Kellogg and the *Survey.* A pacifist at heart, Kellogg focused his commentary on the potential of the United States as a mediator and peacemaker, not as a military force. In 1915 the *Survey* published articles on "War and Reconstruction," emphasizing the need for a postwar rebuilding of Europe and for internationalism, even while arguing that America should remain neutral in the conflict. Prominent figures such as Jane Addams, economist Simon Patten, Emily Greene Balch, and Frederic Howe contributed articles. "Reconstruction" became a key concept for Kellogg before and during America's involvement in the war. His magazine focused on a postwar America in which the lessons of the war years would be applied to conditions of peace. War expenditures dramatized the abundance of America; there was no reason for poverty. Rehabilitation of wounded soldiers could provide methods for rehabilitating injured workers. Blacks and women had made gains during the war. Why not continue their contribution? Kellogg also saw the role of the *Survey* as one of protecting the voices of antiwar dissenters. Civil liberties suffered during the inflamed passions of the war, and while Kellogg eventually supported the U.S. intervention, he argued eloquently for the rights of pacifists. The magazine also published practical articles on how social workers could adjust to wartime conditions, such as coping with food and energy shortages, caring for the crippled, and dealing with the heavy migration of southern African Americans to jobs in northern factories. In short, Kellogg kept the *Survey* focused on constructive solutions, tolerance, and reform. He traveled to France in 1917 to work for the Red Cross, while his brother kept the *Survey* operating. Paul Kellogg sent occasional reports to the *Survey* from the war, before returning to the United States in March 1918.

After the War. After the armistice Kellogg lobbied for a fair settlement with Germany and for an international political organization such as the proposed League of Nations. Kellogg's own League of Free Nations Association publicized its support of Wilsonian principles, but ultimately Kellogg was disappointed by the Treaty of Versailles and the failure of the League of Nations. For the next thirty years he would edit the *Survey*, all the while continuing his reform activities. In 1923 he founded the *Survey Graphic*, a monthly offshoot of the *Survey*. He was a strong supporter of Nicola Sacco and Bartolomeo Vanzetti, of free speech, and a free press. He backed Franklin D. Roosevelt's New Deal and helped design the Social Security Act of 1935. He served as president of the National Conference of Social Work in 1939. After the *Survey* ceased publication in 1952, Kellogg lived at the Henry Street Settlement House in New York City until his death in 1958 at age seventy-nine.

Source:
Clarke A. Chambers, *Paul U. Kellogg and the* Survey (Minneapolis: University of Minnesota Press, 1971).

ALICE PAUL

1885-1977

SUFFRAGIST

Background. In December 1912 Alice Paul, age twenty-seven, arrived in Washington, D.C., to work for women's suffrage. She arrived alone, having convinced the National American Woman Suffrage Association (NAWSA) that she should begin lobbying for a federal amendment guaranteeing women's suffrage throughout the nation. NAWSA had for years concentrated its efforts on individual states, and, in fact, had seen nine states, all in the West, grant women the right to vote. But Alice Paul did not want to wait for the other states to follow. By 1912 she was already an experienced organizer in suffrage work.

Education. Paul was born in 1885 in Moorstown, New Jersey, into a Quaker family, which, like other Quakers, ardently believed in women's suffrage. After attending Quaker schools, Paul graduated from Swarthmore College with a B.S. in biology in 1905. In 1906 she attended the New York School of Philanthropy, and the following year finished her M.A. in sociology at the University of Pennsylvania. She then traveled to England on a fellowship and became involved in the British suffrage movement, which was led by Christabel, Emmeline, and Sylvia Pankhurst. In England she met fellow American suffragist Lucy Burns, with whom she worked throughout the 1910s. Like many in the Pankhurst movement, Burns and Paul were arrested numerous times in England, where the militant movement demanded the right to vote. By the time Paul returned to the United States in 1910, she was a veteran of suffrage work. After completing her Ph.D. in sociology at the University of Pennsylvania, she began her work for NAWSA.

Congressional Union. When Paul arrived in Washington, D.C., suffrage as a federal issue was dead. NAWSA had no plans to push for a federal amendment to the Constitution and provided no money to its Congressional Committee in the capital. Alice Paul forcefully changed these facts, and her militancy created a rift in the suffrage movement. Three generations of activists had lobbied for suffrage in a polite fashion. Paul recognized the need to demand suffrage, and had a plan to do so. She was a decisive leader and a tenacious fund-raiser. She also knew how to gain publicity for her cause. Within three months of her arrival in Washington, on the eve of Woodrow Wilson's inauguration, about eight thousand women walked in a procession from the Capitol to the Hall of the Daughters of the American Revolution. The disruption caused by the procession and the crowd remained in the news for weeks. Paul had struck her first blow for a federal amendment. During the next years she would "educate" President Wilson on the issue, while also keeping the press and the public informed about the cause of suffragists. After the successful march Paul convinced NAWSA that an auxiliary organization, the Congressional Union for Woman Suffrage, was needed to work exclusively for a federal amendment. She formed the group from her Congressional Committee of NAWSA. The group's colors of purple, white, and gold became regular sights in the nation's capital for the next six years.

Separation. In November 1914 the Congressional Union began publishing *Suffragist*, its weekly newspaper covering party activity. In early 1914 Paul decided to disassociate the Congressional Union from NAWSA, in part because of disagreements on tactics but also because of financial considerations. The Congressional Union did not wish to pay NAWSA a 5 percent tax on its budget, reasoning that the money was of more use in their campaign in Washington. Paul's strategy for 1914 was to attack the Democratic Party. The Democrats controlled the House, the Senate, and the presidency, yet had made no strides on addressing suffrage. Paul felt that holding the party accountable for blocking suffrage work would pressure it into addressing the issue. Thus, in 1914 she made the Congressional Union a national organization, and instituted an anti-Democrat campaign in the nine states in which women could vote, while continuing to press President Wilson for action. Despite backlash from the Democratic Party, the Congressional Union began to be heard in Congress. On 12 January 1915 the Susan B. Anthony Amendment was debated for more than six hours in the House, before failing by seventy-eight votes to reach the two-thirds needed for passage. Still, the Congressional Union had made progress, and Paul decided on a next, even bigger step.

National Woman's Party. "We want to have Congress open in the midst of a veritable Suffrage cyclone," Paul wrote in March 1915. With the election completed, the focus of the Congressional Union's energy was again Congress, not state election work. After a June conference in California, a group from the Congressional Union traveled across the country to much fanfare in order to present a petition with some half million signatures to the president, who now said that he supported suffrage, but insisted that it was still a state issue. The following year the Congressional Union initiated another bold step. Paul asked that a new political party be formed consisting of women voters who could enter candidates in the election of 1916. The National Woman's Party was formed that summer, for the sole purpose of pressing the Susan B. Anthony Amendment. Paul succeeded brilliantly in keeping the suffrage issue in the news. In 1916 the Progressive Party became the first national party to endorse women's suffrage; meanwhile, the Republicans and Democrats continued to support the states' rights

platform. The National Woman's Party had no real aspirations of winning congressional seats. What Paul did know was that in the West, the NWP campaign would keep the debate alive and force the Democrats to consider suffrage. When her advisers asked her to withdraw rather than face a humiliating defeat, she refused, explaining that "if we withdraw our speakers from the campaign, we withdraw the issue from the campaign. We must make this such as important thing in national elections that the Democrats will not want to meet it again."

Picketing and Victory. On 10 January 1917, twelve women began picketing the White House, while carrying banners of purple and gold and large signs that read, "Mr. president what will you do for woman suffrage?" For the next eighteen months they became a daily sight in Washington, embarrassing the president at home as he championed liberty and democracy abroad. The picketers achieved nearly mythic status in the women's movement, enduring miserable weather, hostile crowds, and violence, even from police. In June police began to arrest the picketers, including Paul; she was tried in October 1917 and sentenced to seven months in jail. She told the judge, "We do not wish to make any plea before this court. We do not consider ourselves subject to this court since, as an unenfranchised class, we have nothing to do with the making of the laws which have put us in this position." She went to prison on 20 October, where she was isolated and prevented from communicating with the Woman's Party organization. But on 28 November she and all suffrage prisoners were released. Privately, President Wilson had instructed Congress to pass a suffrage bill. Paul's education of the president and the political pressure she had created had had a decisive impact. In 1919 the Nineteenth Amendment passed Congress, and swept through the states for ratification.

Beyond Suffrage. Alice Paul was only thirty-five years old when women gained the right to vote. In the fifty-seven years that she lived after passage of the Nineteenth Amendment, she remained active. She earned three law degrees — an LL.B. in 1922, an LL.M. in 1927, and a D.C.L. in 1928. She headed the Woman's Research Foundation from 1927 to 1937. She authored the Equal Rights Amendment in 1923, and in the 1930s she founded the World Party for Equal Rights for Women (also called the World Women's Party). In 1972 her Equal Rights Amendment, for which she had campaigned for nearly fifty years, passed the Congress and went to the states for ratification. At the time of her death in 1977, the amendment needed only three more states for ratification, but in the conservative political climate of the early 1980s, it failed to be adopted.

Sources:
Nancy F. Cott, *The Grounding of Modern Feminism* (New Haven: Yale University Press, 1987);

Eleanor Flexner, *Century of Struggle: The Woman's Rights Movement in the United States,* revised edition (Cambridge, Mass.: Harvard University Press, 1975).

A. PHILIP RANDOLPH

1889-1979

EDITOR, LABOR LEADER

Most Dangerous. In the latter half of the 1910s, when any dissent against American government policy could be punished by a long prison term, A. Philip Randolph was one of the nation's most vociferous dissidents, criticizing American policy in World War I and American capitalism as a whole. A radical activist, Randolph was editor of the *Messenger*, which issued its first monthly volume in November 1917. Randolph and his partner, Chandler Owen, were among a group known as the New Negroes, who were strong voices against American racism throughout the decade, particularly during the war years. By 1919 Randolph and Owen, nicknamed "Lenin and Trotsky" around Harlem, were referred to as "the most dangerous Negroes in the United States," and the *Messenger* was called by the U.S. Department of Justice "the most able and the most dangerous of all the Negro publications."

Background. Asa Philip Randolph was born in Crescent City, Florida, in 1889, and raised in Jacksonville, Florida. His father was an African Methodist Episcopal minister with a small congregation. Asa and his older brother, James, were raised in the church; later they would disavow its teachings even while recognizing the necessary social functions of black churches. The brothers, two years apart in age, entered the Cookman Institute in 1903. The school had been built by Methodist missionaries in 1872, becoming the first high school for African Americans in Florida. Its teachers were northern white missionaries and southern blacks. The Randolph brothers performed well in school, and Asa was the valedictorian at graduation in 1907. He was a fine singer and actor, and the idea of becoming a professional performer led him to New York. In 1911, after four years of working jobs such as delivery driver, sales clerk, and laborer on the railroad, Randolph moved to Harlem.

Harlem. There was no better place in America for an eager, intelligent, twenty-two-year-old black man in 1911. Black Harlem had been expanding for years as the first great wave of southern black migration began to flow north. Throughout the decade Harlem was the nation's capital of black intellectual life, in the early years of what would later be called the Harlem Renaissance. Randolph immediately began seeking company and conversation, while pursuing a theater career. In 1912 he was offered an acting job, but refused the job after his parents wrote of their displeasure. Instead of the stage, Randolph found politics. In February 1912 he

began attending City College of New York, and formed a circle of radical friends as he studied history, philosophy, and economics. He founded the Independent Political Council in 1913, a current-affairs group, and worked on the campaign of Socialist John M. Royal, who was a candidate for the city council. Randolph also came under the influence of street orator and pioneer Harlem radical Hubert Harrison.

Radical. Randolph met Ernest T. Welcome in 1914 and began working for Welcome's Brotherhood of Labor, an organization that brought workers from the South and helped them find jobs in New York. He also met and married Lucille Campbell that year. She was crucial to his development as a radical, supporting him economically as he pursued his political activism. In early 1915 Randolph met Owen, a Columbia student and fellow radical. The two worked closely for years, becoming dominant voices in the New Negro movement. Through 1915 and 1916 Randolph and Owen followed and participated in Harlem radical politics. They became well-known soapbox orators at Harlem's notoriously radical speakers' corner of 135th Street and Lenox Avenue. Eventually, they quit college and reorganized Randolph's IPC, issuing a platform that would "combine and distribute literature; . . . conduct public lectures on vital issues affecting colored people's economic and political destiny; . . . examine, expose and condemn cunning and malicious political marplots." Their first opportunity to do these things in print came in January 1917 when William White, president of the Headwaiters and Sidewaiters Society, asked them to write and edit *Hotel Messenger*, his union's newsletter. Randolph and Owen produced the magazine for eight months, until they angered White by exposing an internal union scandal. The *Hotel Messenger* ceased publication, but Randolph and Owen continued their work.

The *Messenger*. The two young radicals were busy in 1917. They organized the United Brotherhood of Elevator and Switchboard Operators, and worked on the mayoral campaign of Socialist Party candidate Morris Hillquit. Their crowning achievement in 1917 was the first issue of the *Messenger*. Funded largely by Lucille Randolph, the *Messenger* quickly became what Randolph referred to as "the first voice of radical, revolutionary, economic and political action among Negroes in America." The first issue appeared in November 1917. At the time, America had been in the war for seven months, and Russia's October Revolution had just taken place. "Our aim," Randolph wrote in the first number, "is to appeal to reason, to lift our pens above the cringing demagogy of the times, and above the cheap peanut politics of old reactionary Negro leaders. Patriotism has no appeal to us; justice has." The journal was quickly singled out as one of the finest of the era, with its regular contributors named "Messenger" radicals. The group included Robert Bagnall, William Pickens, William Colson, Wallace Thurman, Theophilus Lewis, and George

Frazier Miller; by the early 1920s the journal was publishing Langston Hughes, Claude McKay, and Countee Cullen. The *Messenger* addressed socialism, labor unions, violence against African Americans, and racism; and it vehemently protested the war raging in Europe. It celebrated the Bolshevik Revolution and the Industrial Workers of the World, and was bitingly critical of the elite black leadership in America, especially after W. E. B. Du Bois supported the war effort in the pages of the NAACP's *Crisis.* Until lack of funds forced its closure in 1925, the *Messenger* was perhaps the strongest voice in defending the rights of African Americans as laborers as well as citizens.

The War and Beyond. Opposition to World War I — at a time when any dissent was fraught with serious risk — was perhaps the strongest message of the *Messenger.* On 4 August 1918 Randolph and Owen were arrested in Cleveland at an antiwar rally. The judge in the case, thinking that Owen and Randolph were too young to have produced the *Messenger* alone, dismissed the case with a warning, but the *Messenger* was banned from the mails. Randolph continued his attacks on the war effort, and especially on Du Bois. Many blacks thought that their participation in the war would earn them respect at home. Randolph argued otherwise, and was proved correct during the summer following the war's end, known as the "Red Summer" because of the outbreak of race riots around the country. Hundreds of blacks died in these riots, and the *Messenger* began advocating "violent defense of rights and life." As the decade closed, Randolph was just beginning to be heard. In the following decades he became a major labor organizer and major advocate for the rights of American blacks, especially through the Brotherhood of Sleeping Car Porters, organized in 1925, and his unionization of the Pullman Company in 1937. The radical voice of the 1910s eventually consulted Presidents Roosevelt, Truman, Kennedy, and Johnson, and helped lead the civil rights movement of the 1960s. Randolph died in 1979.

Source:
Jervis Anderson, *A. Philip Randolph: A Biographical Portrait* (New York: Harcourt Brace Jovanovich, 1972).

PEOPLE IN THE NEWS

Thirty-nine-year-old historian **Charles Beard** revolutionized the writing of American history with the 1913 publication of his controversial *An Economic Interpretation of the Constitution.* Beard argued that the founding fathers were men of considerable property, and acted to protect their wealth from an excess of democracy.

As a choreographer of parade drill teams with the American army in France in 1917 and 1918, **Busby Berkeley** perfected the crisscrossing precision that moviegoers would come to love.

In 1919 **Edward L. Bernays** founded the world's first public relations firm. Bernays dispensed advice to clients well after his one hundredth birthday, until his death in 1995.

Cornelia Foster Bradford, the founder of the Whittier Settlement House in Jersey City, New Jersey, became estranged from her eastern European immigrant constituency after 1915 when she took an increasingly nativist stance.

On a business trip in London, Chicago publisher **William Boyce** lost his way in a fog. A British Boy Scout helped him, and on 6 February 1910 Boyce founded the Boy Scouts of America.

Edith Terry Bremer established the International Institute in Greenwich Village in 1910 to work with second-generation immigrant girls. The institute offered English classes, job counseling, and housing.

In September 1910 New York architect **Arnold W. Brunner** called on leading citizens to demonstrate their sense of good taste by supporting his campaign to halt the proliferation of neon billboards in Times Square.

Ida Maud Cannon became the chief of social work at Massachusetts General Hospital in 1914, a post she held for thirty-one years. Her 1912 course at Simmons College was the first in medical social work.

The Unity Centers of the International Ladies' Garment Workers Union offered union workers the biggest and best courses in labor problems, history, government, and literature. As executive secretary of the union's education department after 1918, **Fannia Cohen** was one of the nation's foremost labor educators.

In 1915, along with Eugene O'Neill and Ida Rank, **George Cram Cook** founded the legendary acting troupe, the Provincetown Players.

The first female commissioner of corrections in New York in 1914, **Katherine Davis** fought against segregation and unfair classifications of prisoners. John D. Rockefeller Jr. deemed her "the cleverest woman I ever met."

The nation's foremost expert on minimum wage legislation, **Molly Dewson** succeeded in shepherding the nation's first minimum wage law through the Massachusetts legislature in 1912.

Although the communal "Peace Mission" he established at Sayville, Long Island, in 1916 did not last, forty-two-year-old evangelist George Baker, known as **Father Divine,** attracted thousands of followers with his strict morality and promise of salvation.

In 1913 **John** and **Henry Dodge** left the Ford Motor Company to start their own manufacturing firm, but retained a major block of Ford stock.

In 1911 day nursery pioneer **Josephine Marshall Jewell Dodge** became the president of the National Association Opposed to Woman Suffrage.

The former head of General Motors, **Will Durant,** together with Swiss-born American race-car driver Louis Chevrolet, began producing Chevrolet automobiles at a plant at Fifty-seventh Street and Eleventh Avenue in Manhattan in 1910.

Boston socialite and reformer **Elizabeth Evans** raised funds and joined the picket lines with striking Lawrence, Massachusetts, textile workers in 1912 and 1917.

The sisters **Josephine** and **Clara Goldmark,** believing "human problems are not insoluble to educated intelligence," served on public commissions investigating the 1911 Triangle Shirtwaist fire and the effects of long workdays on defense workers during World War I, and on a major Rockefeller Foundation study on nursing education. In 1918 Josephine became the national manager of the U.S. Railroad Administration's Division of Labor, and was responsible for more than one hundred thousand workers.

In 1914 **Malke** and **Selik Grossinger** started a vacation boarding house in the Catskill town of Ferndale, New York, that catered to Manhattan's garment workers. It grew into a resort that handled twenty-five hundred people a week.

A political cartoonist for the *Indianapolis Star,* **John Gruelle** found a ragdoll in his attic and made up stories about her to amuse his daughter Marcella, who had been infected with tuberculosis by a contaminated needle. Drawing on neighbor James Whitcomb Riley's

Little Orphan Annie and Raggedy Man, Gruelle created Raggedy Ann. Marcella died in 1916, but in 1918 a New York firm began marketing the doll, which grew into a $20–million-dollar-a-year business.

Twenty-five-year-old Polish American **Nathan Handwerker** and his nineteen-year-old wife, Ida, started a hot dog stand at the corner of Stillwell and Surf Avenues in Coney Island, Brooklyn, in 1917. They charged only five cents, half the price of the competition, which started rumors that the meat was impure. Handwerker hired college students to dress in white coats and stethoscopes and eat his hot dogs. The legendary Nathan's Hot Dog was born.

In 1915 Atlantan **Eugenia Burns Hope** became the chairwoman of the Drive for French War Babies by the Colored American Society for Relief of French War Orphans.

Judge **Franklin Chase Hoyt** served as president of the Big Brother Movement from 1911 to 1925, and in 1918 was made honorary president of the Boy Scouts of America.

Mary Phelps Jacob patented the brassiere in 1914, a contraption she had devised, with the assistance of her French maid, from two pocket handerchiefs and some pink ribbon before a dance. It quickly replaced the corset.

Allegations of impropriety against prizefighter **Jack Johnson** led to the 1910 passage of the Mann White Slave Traffic Act, making it a crime to transport women across state lines for immoral purposes.

Florence Kelley, executive director of the National Consumers' League from 1898 to 1932, led the successful fight to defend the constitutionality of legislation limiting working hours in the 1918 landmark Supreme Court case *Bunting* v. *Oregon.*

Julia Lathrop, one of the founders of Hull House, the legendary settlement house in Chicago, became the first woman to head a bureau of the federal government in 1912 when President William Howard Taft appointed her as chief of the new United States Children's Bureau.

Public relations pioneer **Ivy Ledbetter Lee** persuaded John D. Rockefeller Jr. to travel to Colorado in 1913 to speak with miners striking against one of his family's firms. It proved a successful strategy, and Lee urged the family to take a greater interest in philanthropy.

Pioneer juvenile court judge and muckraker **Benjamin Barr Lindsay** took eighth place in a national 1914 poll to determine who was the greatest living American. He tied with Andrew Carnegie and the Reverend Billy Sunday.

Edward McLean purchased the 44.5-carat Hope diamond in 1911 for his wife, heiress to a gold mining fortune, to wear as a head ornament. She would be guarded by three men, but they could not protect her from the stone's uncanny history of madness and violent death. Her son Vinson, born six months after the stone's purchase, was struck by a car and killed when he was nine years old.

The 1919 Lawrence textile strike established pacifist **Abraham J. Muste** as the first nationally prominent clergyman organizer. His doctrine of nonviolent resistance made the strike a peaceful one, and he influenced many later activists, including Martin Luther King Jr.

Harriet Quimby was the first American woman to earn a pilot's license, which she received at the Moisant Aviation School on Long Island in August 1911. She died in a plane crash the following year.

After crisscrossing the state of Montana on horseback, proclaiming that the spirit of the pioneer was still alive, Republican **Jeannette Rankin** beat her opponent by twenty-five thousand votes and became the first woman in the House of Representatives. She took her seat on 2 April 1917, and was one of a handful of representatives that voted against the declaration of war just four days later.

After studying fashion and beauty in London and Paris, **Helena Rubinstein** in 1915 opened a salon in New York, where she introduced many new products, including foundation and waterproof mascara as well as all-day spa visits. She carried on a vicious, fifty-year rivalry with **Elizabeth Arden**.

On Thanksgiving night 1915 at Stone Mountain, Georgia, **William Joseph Simmons** revived the Ku Klux Klan, moribund since the 1860s. He dedicated it to white supremacy, the protection of southern womanhood, and Americanism. Within six years, membership reached one hundred thousand.

Because Hull House cofounder **Ellen Gates Starr** often endured arrest for the sake of striking workers, the Amalgamated Clothing Workers of America awarded her an an honorary lifetime membership in their organization in 1915.

Henrietta Szold founded Hadassah, a Zionist women's organization in New York in 1912. She headed it until 1926.

An American Indian of Sac and Fox ancestry, **James Francis "Jim" Thorpe** won both the pentathlon and the decathlon at the fifth Olympic Games in 1912. When he admitted that he had played semiprofessional baseball the previous summer, he lost his medals, but retained his reputation as the greatest football player and all-around athlete of the early twentieth century.

In 1912 **Frank Woolworth** bought out his four silent partners in the five-and-dime business, and incorporated the F. W. Woolworth Company. In 1913 he built the sixty-story "Cathedral of Commerce" in New York; it was the world's tallest building until 1931.

DEATHS

Henry Adams, 80, American historian, 27 March 1918.

Col. John Jacob Astor, 48, drowned aboard the *Titanic* after helping his ailing wife and other women to lifeboats, 15 April 1912.

Hubert H. Bancroft, 85, American historian, 2 March 1918.

Isabel Hayes Chapin Barrows, 68, physician and social reformer, 15 October 1913.

Clara Barton, 90, founder of the American Red Cross, 12 April 1912.

Frank Baum, 63, author of the Oz books, 6 May 1919.

John Shaw Billings, 74, physician, social reformer, and sanitarian, 11 March 1913.

Elizabeth Blackwell, 89, first American woman to earn a medical degree; also a noted public health advocate and medical educator, 31 May 1910.

James Buchanan "Diamond Jim" Brady, 60, famously lavish railroad equipment entrepreneur and Broadway bon vivant, 13 April 1913.

Simon Brentano, publisher, 15 February 1915.

Andrew Carnegie, 83, steel baron and philanthropist, 11 August 1919.

William F. "Buffalo Bill" Cody, 71, army scout, Indian fighter, land speculator, expert rifleman, symbol of the Old West, 10 January 1917.

Katherine Coman, 57, Wellesley professor of political economy and sociology, 11 January 1915.

Grace Hoadley Dodge, 58, social worker and educator, 27 December 1914.

Edward Miner Gallaudet, 80, president of the National Deaf-Mute College in Washington, D.C., renamed for him, 26 September 1917.

Elgin Ralston Lovell Gould, 55, political economist and urban reformer who advocated model tenements, 18 August 1915.

Charles Richmond Henderson, 66, Terre Haute, Indiana, minister who pioneered local charity organizing societies, 29 March 1915.

Abraham Jacobi, 89, the "father of American pediatrics," 10 July 1919.

Mary Morton Kimball Kayhew, 58, social worker and champion of Boston's working women, president of the Women's Educational and Industrial Union for twenty-five years, 13 February 1918.

William Pryor Letchworth, 87, child welfare reformer and mental health advocate, 1 December 1910.

Alexander J. McKelway, 51, leader in the protection of child labor, editor of the North Carolina Presbyterian, 14 April 1918.

Thomas Maurice Mulry, 61, Catholic philanthropist who helped to professionalize social work and to reform charitable institutions, 10 March 1916.

Edgar Gardner Murphy, 43, Episcopal priest who worked for racial equality in the Deep South, 23 April 1913.

Florence Nightingale, 90, the "angel of the wounded" and "lady of the lamp"; British nurse who brought sanitary conditions to the Civil War field hospital, 13 August 1910.

Robert Treat Paine, 74, lawyer and philanthropist who launched the Associated Charities of Boston, the Workingmen's Building Association, and the Wells Men's Institute, 11 August 1910.

C. W. Post, 59, cereal magnate, committed suicide, 9 May 1914.

Franklin Benjamin Sanborn, 85, teacher, abolitionist, and social reformer, whose career spanned the era of the transcendentalists and the late-nineteenth-century empiricists, 24 February 1917.

Helen Campbell Stuart, 79, home economist and companion to Charlotte Perkins Gilman, 22 July 1918.

Frederick Winslow Taylor, 50, engineer, and innovator of scientific management, 21 March 1915.

Harriet Tubman, 92, abolitionist and Underground Railroad organizer, 10 March 1913.

Montgomery Ward, 69, department store founder, 7 December 1913.

Booker T. Washington, 57, eminent African American, founder of the Tuskegee Institute, author of Up from Slavery (1901), 14 November 1915.

George Westinghouse, 68, inventor of electrical appliances, 12 March 1914.

Ellen Louise Axson Wilson, 54, first lady, wife of President Woodrow Wilson, 6 August 1914.

Wilbur Wright, 45, pioneering aviator, 30 May 1912.

PUBLICATIONS

Henry Adams, *The Education of Henry Adams* (Boston: Houghton Mifflin, 1918);

Jane Addams, *The Long Road of Woman's Memory* (New York: Macmillan, 1916);

Addams, *A New Conscience and an Ancient Evil* (New York: Macmillan, 1912);

Addams, *Twenty Years at Hull House* (New York: Macmillan, 1910);

Addams, Emily Balch, and Alice Hamilton, *Women at the Hague: The International Congress of Women and Its Results* (New York: Macmillan, 1915);

Emily Greene Balch, *Approaches to the Great Settlement* (New York: Huebsch, 1918);

Balch, *Our Slavic Fellow Citizens* (New York: Charities Publication Committee, 1910);

Charles Austin Beard, *An Economic Interpretation of the Constitution of the United States* (New York: Macmillan, 1913);

Sophonisba Breckinridge and Edith Abbott, *The Delinquent Child and Home* (New York: Charities Publication Committee, 1912);

Breckenridge and Abbott, eds., *The Housing Problem in Chicago* (Chicago: University of Chicago Press, 1910);

John Graham Brooks, *American Syndicalism* (New York: Macmillan, 1913);

Richard Clarke Cabot, *The Christian Approach to Social Morality* (New York: Young Women's Christian Association, 1913);

Cabot, *Social Work: Essays on the Meeting-ground of Doctor and Social Worker* (Boston: Houghton Mifflin, 1919);

Cabot, *What Men Live By: Work, Play, Love, Worship* (Boston: Houghton Mifflin, 1914);

Ida Maud Cannon, *Social Work in Hospitals* (New York: Survey Associates, 1913);

Christian Carl Carstens, *Public Pensions to Widows with Children: A Study of Their Administration in Several American Cities* (New York: Russell Sage Foundation, 1913);

Joanna Carver Colcord, *Broken Homes: A Study of Social Desertion and Its Social Treatment* (New York: Russell Sage Foundation, 1919);

Robert Fulton Cutting, *The Church and Society* (New York: Macmillan, 1912);

Charles Alexander Eastman, *From the Deep Woods to Civilization: Chapters in the Autobiography of an Indian* (Boston: Little, Brown, 1916);

Eastman, *The Indian To-day: The Past and Future of the First American* (Garden City, N.J.: Doubleday, Page, 1915);

Eastman, *The Soul of the Indian: An Interpretation* (Boston: Houghton Mifflin, 1911);

John A. Fitch, *The Steel Workers* (New York: Charities Publication Committee, 1910);

Mary Parker Follett, *The New State: Group Organization and the Solution of Popular Government* (New York: Longmans, Green, 1918);

Marie Francke, *Household Engineering: Scientific Management in the Home* (Chicago: American School of Home Economics, 1919);

Francke, *Opportunities for Women in Domestic Science* (Philadelphia: Association of Collegiate Alumnae, 1916);

Christine Frederick, *The New Housekeeping* (Garden City, N.Y.: Doubleday, Page, 1913);

Effie Price Gladding, *Across the Continent by the Lincoln Highway* (New York: Brentano, 1915);

Madison Grant, *The Passing of the Great Race, or, The Racial Basis of European History* (New York: Scribners, 1916);

William Healy, *Honesty, A Study of the Causes and Treatment of Dishonesty Among Children* (Indianapolis, Ind.: Bobbs-Merrill, 1915);

Healy, *The Individual Delinquent: A Textbook of Diagnosis and Prognosis for All Concerned in Understanding Offenders* (Boston: Little, Brown, 1915);

John Haynes Holmes, *New Wars for Old: Being a Statement of Radical Pacifism in Terms of Force Versus Non-*

resistance, With Special Reference to the Facts and Problems of the Great War (New York: Dodd, Mead, 1916);

Robert Hunter, *Why We Fail as Christians* (New York: Macmillan, 1919);

James Weldon Johnson, *The Autobiography of an Ex-Colored Man* (New York: Knopf, 1912);

Wilford I. King, *The Wealth and Income of the People of the United States* (New York: Macmillan, 1919);

Susan Myra Kingsbury, *Licensed Workers in Industrial Home Work in Massachusetts* (Boston: Wright & Potter, 1915);

Paul H. Marley, *Story of an Automobile Trip from Lincoln, Nebraska, to Los Angeles* (N.p., 1911);

Eleanor Martin and Margaret A. Post, *Vocations for the Trained Woman: Agriculture, Social Service, Business of Real Estate* (New York: Longmans, Green, 1914);

James McLaughlin, *My Friend, the Indian* (Boston: Houghton Mifflin, 1910);

Mary Pattison, *Principles of Domestic Engineering: or, the What, Why, and How of a House* (New York: Trow Press, 1915);

Emily Post, *By Motor to the Golden Gate* (New York: Appleton, 1916);

Mary Ellen Richmond, *The Good Neighbor in the Modern City* (Philadelphia: Lippincott, 1913);

Richmond, *The Inter-relation of Social Movements* (Boston: American Unitarian Association, 1911);

Richmond, *Social Diagnosis* (New York: Russell Sage Foundation, 1917);

Edward Alsworth Ross, *Changing America: Studies in Contemporary Society* (New York: Century, 1912);

Isaac Max Rubinow, *Social Insurance: With Special Reference to American Conditions* (New York: Holt, 1913);

Bertrand Russell, *Our Knowledge of the External World* (Chicago: Open Court, 1914);

John Augustine Ryan, *Distributive Justice: The Right and Wrong of our Present Distribution of Wealth* (New York: Macmillan, 1916);

Margaret Sanger, *Family Limitation* (New York, 1917);

Sanger, *What Every Girl Should Know* (New York: Max Maisel, 1915);

Vida Dutton Scudder, *The Church and the Hour: Reflections of a Socialist Churchwoman* (New York: Dutton, 1917);

Scudder, *Socialism and Character* (Boston: Houghton Mifflin, 1912);

Marion Talbot and Sophonisba Breckinridge, *The Modern Household* (Boston: Whitcomb & Barrows, 1912);

Hugo Alois Taussig, *Retracing the Pioneers from West to East in an Automobile* (San Francisco: Privately printed, 1910);

Women's Educational and Industrial Union, *Industrial Experience of Trade-School Girls in Massachusetts* (Washington, D.C.: U.S. Government Printing Office, 1917);

Robert A. Woods, *A Handbook of Settlements* (New York: Charities Publication Committee, 1911);

Woods and Albert J. Kennedy, eds., *Young Working Girls: A Summary of Evidence from Two Thousand Social Workers* (Boston: Houghton Mifflin, 1913);

Good Housekeeping, periodical;

Ladies' Home Journal, periodical.

CHAPTER NINE

MEDIA

by NANCY E. BERNHARD

CONTENTS

Sidebars and tables are listed in italics.

1910

- Robert R. McCormick, known after World War I as the Colonel, becomes editor and publisher of the *Chicago Tribune,* turning it into the most consistently ultraconservative paper for the next several decades.

- Oswald Garrison Villard, at work as a reporter for his father's *New York Evening Post,* investigates the Republican majority leader of the New York state legislature. His exposés lead to the first conviction of a legislator for graft in New York history.

- Rheta Childe Dorr publishes *What Eight Million Women Want,* an account of the suffrage movements in Great Britain and the United States.

10 Mar. The *Pittsburgh Courier* begins publication.

13 July The first issue of *Women's Wear Daily* appears, under the editorship of journalist Edmund Fairchild.

1 Oct. A bomb explodes at the offices of the *Los Angeles Times,* killing twenty. Two union leaders, John and James McNamara, later confess to planting the bombs to protest the conservative antilabor policies of the paper's owners, the Chandler family.

Nov. The first issue of *The Crisis,* the monthly publication of the new National Association for the Advancement of Colored People (NAACP), is published, with W. E. B. Du Bois as editor.

1 Dec. The city of Miami, with a population of under six thousand, gets its first daily newspaper, the *Miami Herald.*

1911

- The Curtis Publishing Company, publisher of the *Saturday Evening Post,* builds new headquarters on Washington Square in Philadelphia.

- Hearst Magazines acquires the household monthly *Good Housekeeping* from newspaper publisher Charles W. Bryan. Hearst begins emphasizing fiction, publishing name authors such as W. Somerset Maugham, James Hilton, Sinclair Lewis, Daphne du Maurier, and John P. Marquand.

- Victor Berger founds the *Milwaukee Leader.* During World War I its third-class mail privileges are suspended under the Espionage Act.

- James R. Quirk founds *Photoplay,* the first motion picture fan magazine. It includes articles, interviews, and photographs of stars, but its film reviews are honestly critical.

Jan. The socialist weekly *The Masses* is founded. In 1912 Max Eastman becomes editor and lines up contributors such as Randolph Bourne, Floyd Dell, and John Reed. The publication is suppressed by the government in 1918 for opposition to the war.

Collier's begins publication of the fourteen-part landmark series by Will Irwin, "The American Newspaper."

28 Sept. The *Chicago Day Book* is founded by E. W. Scripps as an experimental tabloid, taking no advertising. It comes near to financial success until increased newsprint costs due to World War I bankrupts it.

Oct. With the death of Joseph Pulitzer, Frank I. Cobb becomes editor of the *New York World.*

1912

- The School of Journalism opens at Columbia University with a $2 million bequest from Joseph Pulitzer. It becomes one of thirty universities offering courses in journalism.

- Gertrude Battles Lane becomes editor in chief of the *Woman's Home Companion*, a post she will hold until 1941.

16 Mar. A record is set for a wireless transmission — fifty-five minutes from London to New York.

15 Apr. The *Titanic* sinks after striking an iceberg, killing 1,517 people. Seven hundred people are saved because another ship, the *Carpathia*, receives a radio distress call and steams to the site of the disaster. A closer ship missed the call because its radio operator was asleep.

Oct. The magazine *Poetry: A Magazine of Verse* is founded in Chicago by Harriet Monree. Carl Sandburg, Hilda Doolittle (H. D.), Amy Lowell, Ezra Pound, T. S. Eliot, Vachel Lindsay, and Hart Crane are among its early contributors.

1913

- *Southern Women's Magazine* is founded.

- *Dress and Vanity Fair* is founded in New York City by Condé Nast as a sophisticated monthly. In 1914 Frank Crowninshield becomes editor and shortens the name to *Vanity Fair*, making it at least the fourth publication with that name.

- The Associated Press inaugurates the first teletypes, which print the news automatically, replacing the telegraph.

- Bell Syndicate is founded by John N. Wheeler, featuring "Mutt and Jeff," the first daily cartoon strip, first drawn by H. C. "Bud" Fisher of the *San Francisco Chronicle* in 1907.

- Cartoonist George Herriman introduces a spinoff to his popular "The Dingbat Family" comic strip called "Krazy Kat," which will prove to be one of the most popular and influential strips in the history of the art.

1914

- The number of newspapers in the United States reaches a record high of fifteen thousand.

- Thirteen hundred foreign-language newspapers are published in the United States, including 160 dailies. There are 55 in German; 12 each in French, Italian, and Polish; 10 each in Japanese and Yiddish; and 8 each in Bohemian and Spanish. Total circulation is 2.6 million, with more than 800,000 German and more than 750,000 Yiddish readers. The largest daily is the *New Yorker Staats-Zeitung* with 250,000 readers.

- King Features Syndicate, the first major distributor for comic strips, is founded by William Randolph Hearst. The "Katzenjammer Kids" is its leading color comic.

- H. L. Mencken and George Jean Nathan become coeditors of *The Smart Set*.

- *Pearson's* publishes muckraker Charles Edward Russell's series on the business pressures that brought an end to muckraking.

13 Feb. The American Society of Composers, Authors, and Publishers (ASCAP) is founded in New York with Victor Herbert as director.

Mar. *The Little Review* is founded in Chicago by Margaret Anderson to showcase experimental art, literature, and music. Its serial publication of James Joyce's *Ulysses* leads to Anderson's conviction for publishing obscenity.

3 July The first telephone line is completed between New York and San Francisco.

9 Sept. *The New York Times* establishes its *Mid-Week Pictorial* featuring pictures of the European war.

7 Nov. *The New Republic* is founded by Herbert Croly, Walter Weyl, and Walter Lippmann with financial backing from Willard and Dorothy Straight. Croly serves as editor in chief of this liberal journal of public affairs until 1930.

1915

- The number of daily newspapers in the United States reaches a record high of twenty six hundred, but circulation for those remaining will continue to climb for decades.

- The Associated Press allows members to subscribe to other news services for the first time.

- Five hundred U.S. correspondents cover the war in Europe, with another fifty covering the American Expeditionary Forces after they are formed in 1917.

- American Telephone and Telegraph Company sends a radio signal across the Atlantic from the naval station at Arlington, Virginia.

Jan. *Midland,* a significant review featuring work about the Midwest and the West, is founded.

June The *Texas Review* is founded.

1916

- William Randolph Hearst inaugurates the *City Life* arts supplement to his Sunday newspapers.

- Lee De Forest commences daily music broadcasts from his home in New York City.

- The experimental radio station 8XK begins broadcasting in Pittsburgh but is shut down for the duration of the war. It will reopen in 1919 and receive the first Department of Commerce commercial radio license in 1920, as KDKA.

Nov. David Sarnoff, the commercial manager of the American Marconi Company, predicts that the future of commercial broadcasting will be in homes rather than for point-to-point communication.

7 Nov. De Forest broadcasts presidential election returns, incorrectly reporting the victory of Charles Evans Hughes over Woodrow Wilson.

1917

- President Woodrow Wilson establishes the Committee on Public Information, known as the Creel Committee because of its chairman George Creel. It promulgates official information and a voluntary censorship code.

- The first Pulitzer Prizes are awarded to the *New York Tribune* for its editorial on the first anniversary of the sinking of the *Lusitania* and to Herbert Bayard Swope of the *New York World* for his series "Inside the German Empire."

17 Feb. Floyd Gibbons of the *Chicago Tribune* sails for England on the *Laconia*. When the ship is torpedoed only thirteen passengers perish, and Gibbons's account of the sinking and rescue establish his reputation as a brave and vivid reporter.

6 Apr. The United States enters the war in Europe. All nongovernmental radio operations are closed for the duration.

15 June The Espionage Act enables prosecution of people opposed to the war, including those who make statements that undermine morale. In its first year seventy-five publications lose mailing privileges or agree to change their editorial positions.

Sept. John Reed and Louise Bryant arrive in Petrograd, Russia, in time to witness the October Revolution.

15 Sept. Bertie Charles Forbes founds the general interest business weekly *Forbes*.

Oct. The president establishes a Censorship Board to monitor foreign communication.

1918

- *Puck*, the humor magazine, ceases publication.

- Max and Crystal Eastman found *The Liberator*.

Feb. The price of Sunday papers in New York rises from five cents to seven cents and shortly thereafter to ten cents. Each hike is followed by a brief dip in circulation.

18 Feb. *Stars and Stripes* is founded in France for the American Expeditionary Forces and continues until June 1919 with Harold Ross, later of *The New Yorker*, as editor.

May The Sedition Act amends the Espionage Act of 1917, making it a crime to publish writing opposed to the government of the United States.

25 Aug. The War Industries Board declares moving pictures an "essential industry."

11 Nov. The United Press International (UPI) falsely reports an armistice.

1919

- Upton Sinclair publishes *The Brass Check*, a novel replete with criticism of the newspaper industry.

Jan. Bruce Barton, Roy Durstine, and Alex Osborn start the Barton, Durstine, and Osborn Advertising Agency in New York City and meet with almost instant and overwhelming success.

18 Jan. *Justice*, the largest labor magazine, a publication of the International Ladies' Garment Worker's Union, is founded. It reaches a peak circulation of almost four hundred thousand.

Feb. *The Watch on the Rhine* newspaper is founded for the Army of Occupation in Germany.

May   Bernarr Macfadden, publisher of *Physical Culture*, founds the confessional magazine *True Story* with the motto "Truth is Stranger than Fiction."

26 June   Cousins Robert R. McCormick and Joseph Medill Patterson found the tabloid *New York Illustrated Daily News*, soon dropping the word *Illustrated* from the title. It becomes the most widely read paper in the country.

Aug.   The *Chicago Tribune* is found guilty of libeling Henry Ford.

Oct.   Encouraged by the navy, American Telephone and Telegraph, Westinghouse, General Electric, and United Fruit together found the Radio Corporation of America to prevent foreign control of American broadcasting. David Sarnoff becomes commercial manager.

OVERVIEW

Business and Taste. In the second decade of the twentieth century, newspaper and magazine publishing decisively left behind the era of personal journalism and became big business. The 1910s witnessed the birth of the tabloid newspaper and the confessional magazine, two hallmarks of twentieth-century popular culture. These formats targeted the growing constituency of urban working people and reflected a basic change in social codes and attitudes. The era of the consumer was dawning: in order to lure the largest possible number of readers and advertisers, publishers developed editorial formulas to shock and titillate. While pandering to questionable tastes was nothing new, the widespread acceptance of such material as normal and suitable by great numbers of people was. Popular tastes were changing. Respectability was no longer the most crucial measure of culture. Instead, people asked: Is it new? Is it exciting? Does it sell?

The End of Muckraking. The spirit of reform that had dominated journalism during the first decade of the century began to ebb during the second with little fanfare. People tired of hearing about the abuses of big business and the corruption of government. Publishers, themselves often tied to the fortunes of such elites, had little reason, in the absence of reader interest, to keep the muckraking movement alive. Advertisers began to spend more money on slick and splashy illustrations, and they needed fashionable magazines to carry them. The "Smart Magazines" — *The Smart Set, Vanity Fair,* a revamped *Vogue* — focused on the fast, clever, insouciant lifestyles of the urban rich. What Frederick Lewis Allen later called the "Ballyhoo Years" of the 1920s was foretold by this trend in mass circulation magazines.

The Birth of Modern War Journalism. The dominant event of the decade was World War I. Journalism grew and matured in response to the demands of reporting a mammoth and horrifying spectacle and to accommodate new technologies and techniques in the dissemination of information. Hundreds of American correspondents covered the war in Europe even before the United States entered the fray in 1917. The principles of a free press were tested as never before. Each belligerent nation tried its best to control the flow of information about its political goals and military failures and successes. The American public undoubtedly received more and better war news than the people of any other country, whether ally or enemy. But that is not to say it received full or frank information at all times: for the first time the U.S. government at home and the military in the field engaged in systematic censorship and propaganda.

At Home. President Woodrow Wilson created the Committee on Public Information (CPI) to manage the distribution of information to the public. Headed by temperamental newspaperman George Creel, the CPI gained a notorious reputation among defenders of the free press. Not only did it limit and slant the information it distributed, the CPI engaged in outright propaganda, whipping the American people into an anti-German frenzy. While it asked for voluntary cooperation from the press and the motion picture industry rather than enforcing its censorship codes, the CPI managed information more effectively than many official censors. It was aided in the spirit of suppression by two pieces of legislation, the Espionage Act of 1917 and the Sedition Act of 1918. Under these laws it became a crime to oppose U.S. entry or participation in the war. Many German American and socialist papers were shut down or had their mailing privileges revoked by the government because of their political views. Between 1914 and 1917 — when the United States had not yet entered the war — a range of opinion was at least tolerated by the government and by mainstream public opinion. After 1917 intolerance and enforced patriotism took over, and the media had little choice but to cooperate.

At the Front. The military enforced a clear code of censorship among the reporters covering the American Expeditionary Forces (AEF) in Europe, but the correspondents chafed under these restrictions. At least as independent-minded and resourceful as any other reporters, the war correspondents often found ways to evade military discipline. Required to wear military uniforms and armbands with a *C* for correspondent, they were decidedly more rumpled than the average soldier. The number of accredited correspondents rose above five hundred, with more than fifty covering the AEF's expeditions on the Western Front. While Gen. John J. "Black Jack" Pershing's censor, a former wire-service reporter named Frederick Palmer, tried to keep the correspondents in a group monitored by a press officer, they often evaded such hand-holding and covered the fighting their own way. Still, military information was restricted to that which had been released by official communiqués, and much brilliant reporting was trashed by the censor.

New Technologies. The telegraph made transatlantic reporting of war news far speedier than it had ever been before. Carr Van Anda, the legendary managing editor of *The New York Times*, encouraged his war correspondents to use the technology even at premium rates to ensure that the *Times* would print a complete and authoritative account of the military and diplomatic news. The wireless telegraph, or radio, also figured prominently in the news and in its dissemination. Most notably, the sinking of the *Titanic* in 1912 showed both the lifesaving possibilities of the technology and the need for regulation of its use. During the war the navy took over the entire radio spectrum, and its scientific innovations, spurred by necessity,

led to a flourishing of commercial broadcasting after the armistice.

On the Verge of the Modern. The 1910s were a transitional decade for the American media. Moving from the nineteenth century's preoccupation with political power and industrial growth, the public's attention seemed to shift to matters of personal style and popular culture. A thirst for the new came in tandem with skepticism about any given proposition. New technologies promised to transform media thoroughly in the coming decades, even as the experience with wartime propaganda revealed how easily both professional journalists and the public could be manipulated. An ironic mood, so prevalent in the fiction of F. Scott Fitzgerald, Ernest Hemingway, and John Dos Passos, found ample expression as well among journalists such as H. L. Mencken, who could write after the war that the United States was "essentially a commonwealth of third-rate men" and get away with it. The modern sensibility was widely felt in the media.

TOPICS IN THE NEWS

THE AMERICAN NEWSPAPER

Muckraking Comes Home. Between 1903 and 1910 muckraking magazines had exposed corruption in American government and business with great fervor and to great acclaim. The magazine publisher Robert J. Collier began to wonder why the newspapers in American cities had not unearthed those stories. He asked Will Irwin, a veteran reporter for the *New York Sun* and former *McClure's* magazine editor, to investigate the American newspaper industry. Irwin spent a year traveling around the country interviewing publishers, editors, reporters, and readers. He found that while some newspapers held to strict professional codes of independence and courage, others shaped their news coverage to the tastes and beliefs of their advertisers or their owners. His fourteen-part series, published in 1911 in *Collier's* as "The American Newspaper," was far more than an exposé; it was a major history of American journalism.

A Varied Industry. Observing that the power of the press had clearly shifted from owners to editors in the twentieth century, Irwin looked at how editors selected the news. There was no standard method of selection or even a shared sense of the role of the newspaper in society. Oswald Garrison Villard, editor of the *New York*

Evening Post and *The Nation*, felt a moral obligation to improve the world. Adolph S. Ochs and Carr Van Anda of *The New York Times* aspired to produce a newspaper of superior merit, one that could claim to report the news fairly and objectively. Other publishers admitted more mercenary, profit-oriented goals. Business-oriented editors concerned themselves with what the public wanted, while professionally oriented editors thought about what the public needed.

The Mixed Legacy of the Yellow Press. Despite its reputation for fouling the waters of public discourse, Irwin lauded the sensationalistic yellow journalism of the late nineteenth century for improving the quality of writing in journalism and for attracting more-educated practitioners. He concluded that this type of publishing was on the decline, in part because its chief embodiment, William Randolph Hearst, had used his newspapers to further his own political ambitions, and people had soured on him. Irwin also observed that most people did not long remain readers of the yellow papers: immigrants learned English; youngsters grew up; women became more discriminating; and they all moved on to other kinds of papers after about six years.

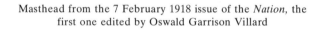

The Nation

FOUNDED 1865

Published Thursdays. Owned by THE NATION PRESS, INC.,
OSWALD GARRISON VILLARD, President.
EMIL M. SCHOLZ, Publisher, Secy. and Treas.

Entered at the New York City Post Office as second class mail matter.

OSWALD GARRISON VILLARD, EDITOR
HENRY RAYMOND MUSSEY, MANAGING EDITOR
R. B. McCLEAN, BUSINESS MANAGER
WILLIAM G. PRESTON, ADVERTISING MANAGER
ROBERT R. CLELAND, CIRCULATION MANAGER

SUBSCRIPTION RATES.—Four dollars per
annum, postpaid, in United States and Mexico;
to Canada, $4.50, and to foreign countries com-
prised in the Postal Union, $5.00.
Address, THE NATION, 20 Vesey Street.
P. O. Box 794, New York.

LONDON OFFICE: 16 Regent St., S. W.; WASHINGTON OFFICE:
Home Life Building; CHICAGO OFFICE: People's Gas Building.

Masthead from the 7 February 1918 issue of the *Nation*, the
first one edited by Oswald Garrison Villard

A Growing Professionalism. Irwin also noted an
emerging code of professional ethics for journalists, now
being cultivated in new departments and schools of journalism in American colleges and universities. Scrupulous
reporters gained consent from the people they wrote
about and never printed information learned in social
settings. The newspaper should be a watchdog, this new
breed of journalist believed, but it should also be a "gentleman." Irwin singled out the influence of big business as
the greatest threat to the industry's integrity, both
through the power of advertisers to influence the news
and by the association of publishers and editors with
prominent members of their communities. The antidote
was a strong sense of professionalism among reporters, an
awareness of their responsibility to the American people
to keep the press the freest in the world, the guardian of
liberty.

Sources:
Marion Marzolf, *Civilizing Voices: American Press Criticism, 1880–1950*
(New York: Longman, 1991);

Michael Schudson, *Discovering the News: A Social History of American
Newspapers* (New York: Basic Books, 1978).

THE ANTIWAR PRESS

A Variety of Resisters. Though the "war to end all
wars" and the "war to make the world safe for democracy" — were the official slogans of the war effort, not
everyone in the United States believed that World War
I would accomplish these noble goals. Isolationists believed that the United States had no business meddling
in the problems of Europe. Religious pacifists opposed
any war on moral grounds. Black Americans found it
hypocritical to fight for a cause abroad that served
them badly at home. Immigrants from Germany and
Austria were torn between support for their ancestral

THE AMERICAN NEWSREEL DURING WORLD WAR I

The American newsreel industry was in its infancy when World War I began in Europe, but
each belligerent government forbade cameras on
its battlefields. Enemy troops often mistook large
camera tripods and long lenses for newfangled
weapons, and made them particular targets. Some
British officers in Belgium even gave orders to
shoot anyone with a camera. Given the doubled
risks of trying to get combat footage, plus the
common practice by theater owners of excising
graphic war images to protect the fragile sensibili-
ties of their customers, few newsreel photographers attempted to film real battles. Instead, they
staged elaborate mock fights, complete with bayo-
nets that sprung backwards and exploding water
bottles. Still, many cameramen lost their lives.
One Frenchman was shot on his inaugural outing
with a new hand-held Aeroscope camera. The
camera, with its efficient stabilization mechanism,
went on recording the Battle of Verdun after its
operator was dead.

Once the United States entered the war, a far
more complete film record began to accumulate
due to the large and well-organized Army Signal
Corps. Censorship all but eradicated civilian newsreel efforts in Europe, and the little film movie
audiences saw was straight propaganda filtered by
the Committee on Public Information. The Signal Corps provided a training ground for an entire
generation of newsreel cameramen, and Hollywood
cinematographers and directors.

Source: Raymond Fielding, *The American Newsreel, 1911-1917* (Norman: University of Oklahoma Press, 1972).

homes and loyalty to their new one. Socialists believed
the war only furthered imperial and capitalistic ambitions. The struggles of all of these groups found expression in their newspapers and magazines. For their
opposition to the war, some suffered persecution and
prosecution under the 1917 Espionage Act and the 1918
Sedition Act.

The Black Press. Most black newspapers and periodicals met U.S. entry into the war with mixed responses.
Why, some editors asked, given all the discrimination
and violence blacks confronted at home simply because of
their race, should they go thousands of miles away to
defend democracy? One Virginia weekly was suppressed
for publishing such views. Other black journalists realized that opposing the war could do irreparable harm to
black causes at home. The large and influential black
papers, led by the *Chicago Defender,* focused on the issue

"Come on in, America, the Blood's Fine," a cartoon by R. Kempf that appeared in *The Masses*, June 1917

of segregation and discrimination within the military and urged the training of black officers. Even when presented in a prowar context, however, these criticisms were viewed by the wider white society as unpatriotic. The federal government's Committee on Public Information (CPI) claimed that assertions of discrimination in the armed services were lies disseminated by German agents infiltrating the black community.

Divided Loyalties. While the United States remained officially neutral between 1914 and early 1917, the German-language American press rejoiced in German victories. As the United States moved closer to the Allied camp and finally declared war in 1917, many editors said nothing rather than criticize their country. Most supported the United States as the present and future home of their children. The anti-German hysteria that swept the country turned on these newspapers, and editors were required to file translations of all the stories they published related to the government and the war effort.

Socialists Silenced. Max Eastman, editor of *The Masses,* wrote in 1917, "It is not a war for democracy." Pointing to the ties between prominent industrialists and bankers in the United States and England, socialists contended that the war was being fought to protect investments. Three major socialist publications, *The Masses, Appeal to*

Reason, and Victor Berger's *Milwaukee Leader,* were silenced by the government. Many papers voiced the notion that no matter which side won, workers would lose.

Suppression. All sorts of organizations sprang up to enforce "correct" thinking about the war. The American Defense League, the American Protective League, the Sedition Slammers, and the Terrible Threateners formed patrols that roamed the streets looking for people espousing antiwar views. *The New York Times* urged readers to report anything suspicious to the authorities. (The brother of *Times* publisher Adolph S. Ochs, whose family came from Germany, legally changed his name to Oakes to Anglicize it.) But the government was the official censor. Under the Espionage and Sedition Acts, the postmaster general had the right to confiscate any material violating the acts. In the first six months after the passage of the Sedition Act, more than 1,000 people were arrested, and 130 were imprisoned under its provisions. More than eighty newspapers and periodicals were suppressed for antiwar articles, including most of the major socialist papers and many foreign-language papers. Supreme Court Justice Oliver Wendell Holmes wrote in defense of a raid on a bookstore, "When a nation is at war many things that may be said in peace are of such a hindrance to its efforts that their utterance will not be endured." The United States failed to protect unequivocally the civil liberties of its citizens during wartime.

Sources:
Lauren Kessler, *The Dissident Press: Alternative Journalism in American History* (Beverly Hills, Cal.: Sage, 1984);

H. C. Peterson and Gilbert Fite, *Opponents of War, 1917–1918* (Seattle: University of Washington Press, 1968).

CENSORSHIP AT THE FRONT

Few Choices. In the years when the United States remained officially neutral, the British, French, German, and Austrian governments rarely allowed their own reporters, let alone those representing neutral countries, to travel with their armies. It was difficult for writers to get access to the front or to get their stories past the official censors. Ernest Hemingway wrote, "The last war, during the years of 1915, 1916, 1917 was the most colossal, murderous, mismanaged butchery that has ever taken place on earth. Any writer who said otherwise lied. So the writers either wrote propaganda, shut up, or fought."

Winners Are More Accommodating. The European belligerents worked hard to seduce reporters into writing favorable stories and to prevent them from writing unfavorable ones. At first the German army prevailed on the Western Front; while it did it allowed neutral reporters to observe battles and let them write what they wanted. The Austrians provided each correspondent with a guide, free wine and cigarettes, and elaborate meals, all served with promises of free trips to the front, but this access never materialized. On the Eastern Front the Russians provided two railway cars to show reporters the lines in

Floyd Gibbons of the *Chicago Tribune*, one of a group of journalists who fought the efforts of the chief American wartime censor, Frederick Palmer

FLOYD GIBBONS ABOARD THE UNITED STATES LACONIA

In early 1917, just before the United States entered the European war, twenty-nine-year-old Floyd Gibbons, a correspondent for the *Chicago Tribune* who had already covered the Mexican revolution, was assigned by the paper to the European theater. Instead of booking passage on a neutral ship, he looked for one that was likely to get torpedoed. He sailed from New York on 17 February 1917 on the Cunard liner the *Laconia*, with a special set of supplies provided by the *Tribune*. It included a life preserver, flasks of brandy and water, and multiple flashlights.

On 25 February a German submarine torpedoed the *Laconia*, and it sank. Only thirteen of the three hundred people aboard were lost, and the survivors were rescued after six hours on open water. The next day, just as President Wilson was telling Congress that the Germans had not yet committed an overt act of war on the high seas, the *Tribune* carried Gibbons's first-person account, and the country edged closer to war. A wound he incurred later in the war on the Western front required Gibbons to wear an eye patch, and his image as a fearless, heroic war correspondent became indelible.

Source: John Hohenberg, *Foreign Correspondence: The Great Reporters and Their Times*, second edition (Syracuse: Syracuse University Press, 1995).

Galicia, but the battle turned against them, and the cars never reached the action. The French said simply that any correspondent found near the front would be executed as a spy. And the British stipulated that neutrals covering their armies would be considered spies and shot if they subsequently covered the Germans. The Germans also followed this policy, so American reporters tended to cover one side or the other.

"Gentlemen of the Press." Once the United States entered the war, each American reporter, to receive accreditation, had to appear before the secretary of war and swear to report the truth but also to refrain from disclosing facts that might aid the enemy. He then had to write (with a pen, not a typewriter) an account of his life, work, experience, character, and health and an itinerary and set of plans for his European trip. His paper had to pay $1,000 to the army to cover equipment and offer a $10,000 bond to promise that he would act as a "gentleman of the press." Correspondents overseas were also obligated to wear green armbands with the letter *C* in red.

Major Palmer. Frederick Palmer had been the only American correspondent accredited to the British army before U.S. entry into the war. He had written for the Associated Press and the United Press. When his personal friend Gen. John J. "Black Jack" Pershing was made commander in chief of the U.S. forces, Palmer turned down $40,000 a year (then an astronomical sum) to cover the American forces for the *New York Herald* and its syndicate in order to become the chief American censor. Palmer had already covered five wars and was impressed with the British army's control of its press. He did not expect his American colleagues to put up a big fight, but this assumption was gravely mistaken. His spare and sporadic releases of information did not satisfy the correspondents. Among this group were several legends: Floyd Gibbons of the *Chicago Tribune;* Will Irwin and Heywood Broun of the *New York Tribune;* Herbert Bayard Swope of the *New York World;* Wythe Williams and Jimmy James of *The New York Times;* Paul Scott Mowrer and Junius Wood of the *Chicago Daily News;* Damon Runyon of the *New York American;* Irvin S. Cobb of the

On 4 July 1917 Gen. John J. Pershing, the commander in chief of the American forces in France, went to Little Picpus cemetery on the outskirts of Paris to lay a wreath on the tomb of Lafayette, the French general who had come to the aid of the American revolutionaries in 1776. A troop of reporters with nothing better to do tagged along. Maj. Charles E. Stanton, the army paymaster, was a gifted public speaker and made a preliminary set of remarks, working himself up to a fever pitch and concluding with the ringing proclamation, "Lafayette, we are here!" General Pershing came next and made some inaudible murmurings as he laid the wreath on the tomb.

Far back in the crowd the correspondents mistakenly thought the general had made the effusive and dramatic remark. Floyd Gibbons of the *Chicago Tribune* and several others filed their 4 July stories with praise for Pershing's eloquence. Paymaster Stanton later wrote that their mistake dogged the general for the rest of his career, creating false expectations for his skill as a speaker.

Source: John Hohenberg, *Foreign Correspondence: The Great Reporters and Their Times,* second edition (Syracuse: Syracuse University Press, 1995).

Saturday Evening Post; and the youngest, at twenty-three, Westbrook Pegler of the United Press.

Rules Made to Be Broken. Palmer implemented several stringent rules. Correspondents would be required to wear uniforms and would travel together under the control of press officers. All copy had to be cleared by Palmer's office, and there was no right to protest his censorship decisions. Many other minor regulations were imposed. Long before the reporters reached the front, open war was declared between Major Palmer and the correspondents. Gibbons and Broun often fled the reporters' bivouac to track down their own stories. Broun's accreditation was revoked, but he did not care. The reporters often disregarded the strict rules, and managed to function nearly normally. Despite the efforts of the American military, the American public received more and better war news than the citizens in its Allied countries, but World War I was not a banner time for the free press.

Sources:
John Hohenberg, *Foreign Correspondence: The Great Reporters and Their Times,* second edition (Syracuse, N.Y.: Syracuse University Press, 1985);

Phillip Knightley, *The First Casualty: From the Crimea to Vietnam: The War Correspondent as Hero, Propagandist, and Myth Maker* (New York: Harcourt Brace Jovanovich, 1975).

THE CREEL COMMITTEE

The Committee on Public Information. In March 1917, when United States entry into the war seemed inevitable (the declaration came one month later), rumors circulated in Washington that military leaders were again advocating censorship of the press. Beginning in June 1916 President Woodrow Wilson's attorney general, Thomas Gregory, had pushed for measures to punish members of the press found guilty of espionage and strictly limit freedom of the press and of speech. He tried again in February 1917, but on each occasion Congress balked. The administration tried again following the declaration of war and found the mood in Congress much more receptive. Newspaperman, muckraker, and Wilson adviser George Creel sent the president a memo urging a voluntary agreement with the press to control information rather than the institution of formal censorship. Wilson agreed and created the Committee on Public Information (CPI), with Creel as its chairman. The other members of the committee would be the secretaries of war, state, and the navy, who had themselves suggested such a committee to the president on 13 April 1917, writing that Americans ought to be "given the feeling of partisanship that comes with full, frank statements concerning the conduct of the public business." Given Creel's background as a crusader and his fiery temperament, many observers felt that putting him in charge of rallying public opinion for the war was most unwise. Wilson's stated fear — that once into war the American people would "forget that there was ever such a thing as tolerance" — was realized in part because of the work of the CPI. It prevented formal censorship on the home front (not in the combat theater, where strict censorship reigned) but raised serious questions about where the line lay between public information and propaganda.

Expert Communication or Propaganda? The CPI organized a speaker's bureau of seventy-five thousand people, known as the "Four-Minute Men." They traveled all over the country making short speeches to rally the public for the war effort. By 1918 they were being told to make liberal use of war atrocity stories in their speeches. Creel recruited advertising experts and prominent journalists such as Ida M. Tarbell, Ernest Poole, Ray Stannard Baker, and Will Irwin to publish a daily newspaper with a circulation of one hundred thousand, known as the *Official Bulletin.* A government wire service supplied official information from all over the world. To some observers Creel expertly mobilized every form of communication in the cause of the war. To others he incited the "righteous wrath" of the public against the "Hun" and the "Boche." Writer Raymond B. Fosdick (who was also head of the Commission on Training Camp Activities) summarized the attitude of the American people: "We hated with a common hate that was exhilarating." Fosdick observed a church meeting where a speaker demanded that the kaiser be boiled in oil, and the congregation rose to its

Covers for four of the most famous publications of George Creel's Committee on Public Information

feet in hysterical approval. Such spectacles chilled civil libertarians.

Pamphlets, Publications, and Movies. The CPI regularly issued publications with titles such as "German War Practices" and "The German Whisper," written as exposés of enemy tactics. They certainly inflamed the public. At the outset of the publicity campaign, the committee made films with innocuous titles such as *Our Colored Fighters* and *Pershing's Crusaders.* By war's end they had turned to producing movies such as *The Kaiser: The Beast of Berlin,* and *The Prussian Cur.* Creel sent the writer Lowell Thomas to Europe to collect stories that could be used to stir appropriate sentiment. When the Western Front proved too gory for good recruiting material, he went on to the Middle East where T. E. Lawrence was fighting along with the Arabs against the Turks. Thomas's romanticized dispatches about Lawrence helped to shape one of the indelible myths to come from the war, that of Lawrence of Arabia. Lawrence called Thomas, who grew rich off creating the legend, "the American who made my vulgar reputation; a well-intentioned, intensely crude and pushful fellow."

Terrible Legacy. While avoiding formal censorship, the CPI's *Official Bulletin* certainly blacked out information that did not reflect favorably on the war effort. In the aftermath of the war the public and Congress grew progressively more outraged over having been, as they saw it, "duped" into war in the first place. Despite all the criticism Creel received personally for his temper during the war, the CPI became far more notorious as a source of foul and misleading propaganda after it had been disbanded. When the United States mobilized for World War II, President Franklin D. Roosevelt designed his public information policies in large measure by trying not to duplicate the mission and the spirit of the CPI.

Sources:

George Creel, *How We Advertised America* (New York: Harper, 1920);

David Kennedy, *Over Here: The First World War and American Society* (New York: Oxford University Press, 1980);

Stephen Vaughn, *Holding Fast the Inner Lines: Democracy, Nationalism, and the Committee on Public Information* (Chapel Hill: University of North Carolina Press, 1980).

On 1 October 1910 a dynamite blast destroyed the *Los Angeles Times* building. Fifteen men died, and half a million dollars in damage resulted. The brothers, John and James McNamara, officers in the Structural Iron Workers' Union, had been fighting against *Times* owner Gen. Harrison Gray Otis and his open-shop policy. They advocated "direct action" against repressive capitalists but at first claimed their innocence. The city of Los Angeles seemed ready to square off in a class war.

Just when the famous muckraker Lincoln Steffens had persuaded many of Los Angeles's most powerful politicians that to put the McNamara brothers to death would only intensify the bitter division in the city, their defense lawyer, Clarence Darrow, was accused of trying to bribe a member of the jury. Then, before their trial concluded and before election day, when many socialist candidates expected to win, the McNamara brothers confessed to the bombing, dealing a great blow to the labor movement in California.

Source: Louis Filler, *The Muckrakers* (University Park: Pennsylvania State University Press, 1979).

Front page of the first issue of Joseph Medill Patterson's *New York Daily News,* under its original title

THE FIRST AMERICAN TABLOID

Born of a Family Split. The *New York Illustrated Daily News* made its debut on 26 June 1919. Two grandsons of *Chicago Tribune* founder Joseph Medill served as copublishers of their family paper, and both served in World War I. Col. Robert R. McCormick was as conservative as his grandfather, but Capt. Joseph Medill Patterson had imbibed the reform spirit of the early twentieth century. As a young man he had enrolled at Yale University but took time off to become a *Tribune* correspondent in China, where he covered the Boxer Rebellion. After graduating from Yale in 1901, he defended the rights of the common people against political corruption in his reporting and won election to the Illinois legislature. His politics never meshed with those of the conservative paper, and he left the daily to write socially minded novels and plays. Before the United States entered World War I he became a European correspondent for the paper, and he joined the military when Congress declared war.

Lord Northcliffe Recommends. In 1903 the British public saw its first tabloid paper, the *Daily Mirror.* The paper began as a publication for women but soon changed into a "half penny illustrated," printed on paper half the size of a regular newspaper and full of pictures and sensational crime and sex stories. By 1909 its circulation reached one million, and the *Daily Sketch* and the *Daily*

Graphic had been introduced as competitors. Joseph Patterson met the *Mirror* publisher, Lord Northcliffe, in London during the war. When Northcliffe told him of the enormous profits to be made in tabloid publishing, Patterson saw a way to avoid future conflict with his cousin McCormick and to serve the immigrant and semiliterate population whose welfare most concerned him.

Innovations. With a $1 million loan from the flush Chicago Tribune Company, the new tabloid began printing in 1919. Its cover, true to its British inspiration, showed the Prince of Wales, who was soon to visit the United States. The *Daily News* sponsored its own beauty contest and in an ad enjoined readers of *The New York Times* to "SEE NEW YORK'S MOST BEAUTIFUL GIRLS EVERY MORNING IN THE ILLUSTRATED DAILY NEWS." The paper was largely tailored for women but appealed to men with unprecedented attention to the latest sports news. It started a long tradition by publishing photographs of boxing, baseball, and other events on the back page, but Patterson initially tried to keep the news content of the paper serious.

"A Daily Erotica for the Masses." Almost as soon as the *Daily News* dropped the word *Illustrated* from its title (a few months after it first appeared), it gave up its goal of being a smaller, more pictorial alternative to the large papers and became thoroughly sensational. Its brief news stories concerned titillating and grisly crimes and sex scandals, capitalizing on a more generalized postwar assault on traditional morality. The *News* seemed particularly adept at securing pictures and love letters from divorce proceedings and love-nest scandals. As the first and still the strongest American tabloid, the *Daily News* set far-reaching precedents for newspaper publishing.

Sources:

Edwin Emery and Michael Emery, *The Press and America,* fourth edition (Englewood Cliffs, N.J.: Prentice-Hall, 1978);

Sidney Kobre, *Development of American Journalism* (Dubuque, Iowa: William C. Brown, 1969).

THE HINDENBURG CONFESSION

A Solemn Pledge. On Armistice Day four reporters who had witnessed the horrors and brutality of the war shook hands and pledged that they would spend the rest of their lives writing the truth about the war so that the bloodshed would never be repeated. The millions of soldiers and civilians dead from combat and disease, the unprecedented pain and suffering — each man felt he would give his life to prevent such massive injustice from happening again. The four reporters were Herbert Corey, George Seldes, Lincoln Eyre, and Cal Lyon.

And So Much for Military Discipline. At the same time, the four young men decided that the rules of military discipline no longer applied to newspaper correspondents. They decided to drive into Germany to observe conditions and to try to interview Field Marshal Paul von Hindenburg, the (former) commander of the German army. They drove through France into Germany and soon came upon the German army in full retreat. The soldiers were frightened and surprised to see Americans (correspondents wore military uniforms), and a colonel gave a brisk order, "Take them into the woods and shoot them." Eyre frantically tried to explain in German that they were reporters.

Rescue. A soldier with a red armband arrived and took control of the situation. This man was a member of the Arbeiter und Soldenrat, the Workers' and Soldiers' Council, a group from Kiel that had mutinied against their overseers in the last days of the war and whom the Allies had appointed to help administer Germany after the surrender. He sent them to Frankfurt, where a friend of his could arrange transportation to Kassell, where Hindenburg was stationed. After the field marshal refused to see the reporters, the council representative called to set up the interview and arranged for Hindenburg's personal automobile to pick them up.

An Astonishing Evaluation. Seldes asked Hindenburg what he thought had ended the four years of stalemate on the Western Front. Hindenburg replied directly that it was the arrival of the U.S. infantry. Until 1917 he

THE LOST BATTALION

Just a few weeks before the armistice, during the advance of the entire American army, the Second Battalion of the 308th Infantry, Seventy-seventh Division, was reported missing. The United Press scooped the story, which remained page 1 news for almost a week. Where were they?

In fact, the battalion had been trapped at the edge of a steep precipice by German soldiers. They held off the Germans for five days. While Major Whittlesey, the officer in command, was reported to have replied "Go to Hell" to the German demand for surrender, this was a myth. He made no reply but did order his men to cover two white airplane panels lying on the ground, lest they be mistaken for a sign of surrender.

Some enterprising reporters from the army publication *Stars and Stripes* investigated the fate of the "Lost Battalion," and found that nearly 200 of Major Whittlesey's soldiers had marched out of the Charlevaux Valley; 107 had died; and 378 had been evacuated on stretchers. The five-day stand of the Lost Battalion became known as one of the most heroic deeds of any American unit during the war.

Source: George Seldes, *Witness to a Century: Encounters with the Noted, the Notorious, and the Three SOBs* (New York: Ballantine, 1987).

believed Germany could have won the war on land. When the Allies could replace their divisions with fresh troops from the United States rather than from their own weak and broken divisions, he knew Germany's cause was lost. "The Americans are splendid soldiers," he said. The American attack in the Argonne Forest won the war, according to the German military commander. Having said that, Hindenburg wept.

Quite a Burden. Seldes believed that had the American censor allowed the four reporters to file their story, it would have made headlines in every newspaper in the Western world and would have made a lasting impression on millions of people, including the Germans. He wrote, "I believe it would have destroyed the main planks of the platform on which Hitler rose to power, it would have prevented World War II, the greatest and worst war in history, and it would have changed the future of all mankind." It becomes particularly poignant, in light of the promise that the four correspondents made to one another, that they were prevented from making Hindenburg's confession public. And Seldes also made a painfully frank personal confession. Had he, or any of the others, been willing to endanger his position in journalism in order to publish that story, he might have prevented World War II all by himself. While that seems improbable, the story of Hindenburg's confession and its suppression does raise irresistible historical "what-ifs."

Source:

George Seldes, *Witness to a Century: Encounters with the Noted, the Notorious, and the Three SOBs* (New York: Ballantine, 1987).

THE MOST HATED MAN IN AMERICA

Against Entry. William Randolph Hearst, the larger-than-life publisher of the *New York American,* the *San Francisco Examiner,* and many other major papers and magazines, opposed U.S. entry into World War I, both before and after it occurred. Hearst was no pacifist, as his enthusiasm for the war against Spain in 1898 had demonstrated. But from the beginning of war in 1914, and through the three years of official American neutrality, he and his papers argued that it was Europe's war, that the Allies would lose, and that there was no sense getting involved and sacrificing American lives. He was called anti-British (true), pro-German (false), and the most hated man in the country. His publications lost circulation, advertising revenue, and respect. Hearst was burned in effigy, not for the first or last time.

Anti-British. Hearst disliked the English for several reasons. His wife was Irish American, and he thus supported Ireland's resistance to British rule. Also, he had sympathy for all peoples fighting for their freedom. Hearst detested President Woodrow Wilson, who was a confirmed Anglophile and whose ostensibly neutral policies slid closer and closer to the Allies between 1914 and 1917. He objected to the loans made by American banks to the British, in effect wagering the health of the American economy on the victory of the Allies and providing a compelling reason to guarantee it. A longtime dislike for anything Japanese also fueled Hearst's opposition: Japan was allied with the British. Finally, the infusion of British propaganda into the United States riled Hearst: as a master propagandist himself, he hated to see an adversary succeed.

Not Especially Pro-German. Although he took pleasure in German beer, castles on the Rhine, and the therapeutic waters at Bad Neuheim, Hearst had never shown particular political sympathy for the Germans. He had even advocated making war against the kaiser when a German admiral insulted Admiral Dewey in Manila Bay. He hired a former *New York Times* correspondent, William Bayard Hale, and sent him to Germany but did not know that Hale was in the pay of the Germans. Critics charged that he took his determinedly unpopular and, after 1917, when the United States declared war, unsafe position in order to attract German American and Irish American readers. While it is true that these groups bought his papers in greater numbers during the war, overall Hearst lost a fortune because of his diehard stand.

The 18 May 1918 issue of the *New York Tribune* featured this article attacking William Randolph Hearst and his antiwar efforts.

Let Them Come to Us. Once President Wilson declared war, Hearst took his most bizarre position. Since England would surely lose, he said, the United States should not act simply as an adjunct to the British armies. He argued that to transport an army across the Atlantic, infested with German submarines, was to consign it to the bottom of the sea. "Let Germany come to us," he said, "or it will be a bloody sacrifice." Theodore Roosevelt branded Hearst "one of the most efficient allies of Germany on this side of the war" and stressed that the "Huns within" were more dangerous than the "Huns without."

Pilloried in the Press. The *New York Tribune* began a weekly series titled "Coiled in the Flag — Hears-s-s-s-t," likening the publisher to a snake and quoting from his editorials. Roosevelt denounced President Wilson for failing to use the power of the government to suppress the Hearst papers. A mob in Poughkeepsie burned copies of the *New York American.* To fight back, Hearst took advertisements in rival papers listing "What Hearst Papers Have Done to Help Win the War." In 1918 he invited 250 senators and congressmen to New York at his expense to witness a demonstration on 4 July of his patriotism, but only thirty-four legislators and their families accepted the invitation.

A Loan or a Bribe? Shortly after the war ended, it was revealed that a consortium of thirteen wealthy German American brewers had loaned Arthur Brisbane, Hearst's

Herbert Croly, a founder and the editor of the *New Republic*

close ally and editor, $375,000 in 1917 so that he could purchase the *Washington Times*. A congressional investigation ensued to determine if Brisbane, and by extension Hearst, had been paid to act as the mouthpiece for these investors. The *Times* coverage of the war had paralleled that of the Hearst papers. When asked by a congressman if Germans dictated the content of the Hearst papers, Brisbane replied that nobody could tell the sovereign publisher what to print. Hearst's willingness to take wildly unpopular positions seems to bear this out.

Source:
W. A. Swanberg, *Citizen Hearst* (New York: Scribners, 1961).

THE NEW REPUBLIC

Herbert Croly's Insurrections. In 1909 a young intellectual, the son of two newspaper writers, published an influential political polemic titled *The Promise of American Life*. Herbert Croly argued that while the laissez-faire philosophy of keeping government out of the marketplace held great appeal for a small-scale society, the advent of big business meant that a strong central government was needed to protect the weak. And to avoid being overtaken by special interests, government required strong leadership. Theodore Roosevelt became an early convert to Croly's "New Nationalism." Croly is also credited with inspiring Woodrow Wilson's "New Freedom." Though painfully shy, Croly, along with some like-minded colleagues, determined to start a magazine, a "journal of opinion" that would start "little insurrections" in the minds of its readers.

A Straight Fortune. Willard and Dorothy Straight became Croly's financial backers. Dorothy was a Whitney by birth and received royalties from Standard Oil. Willard was a Morgan banker who had served as a consul in China and believed in American internationalism. After reading Croly's book, the Straights decided that rather than giving money to schools or hospitals, they wanted to fund a magazine to disseminate Croly's views. The Straights purchased a townhouse in New York to house the magazine, complete with a library and a French chef for the staff's comfort. The magazine began publication in 1914 under the editorial direction of Croly; Walter Weyl, a noted muckraking journalist; and the brilliant young journalist and political philosopher Walter Lippmann, who by age twenty-five had already published two influential books, *A Preface to Politics* (1913) and *Drift*

The colorful and controversial publisher of *Physical Culture*, Bernarr Macfadden, started a new magazine in 1919 called *True Story*. Readers sent in accounts of their triumphs and tragedies in love, and Macfadden and a panel of young readers selected those that best held their interest. They received seventy thousand to one hundred thousand entries per year. Each entry had to be accompanied by an affidavit from someone other than the writer that the story was true, but many readers nonetheless found the tales so shocking that they refused to believe they were genuine.

Despite the titillation that these stories of girls gone astray, jealous husbands, and love triangles provoked, each one had to end with a strong moral lesson. Macfadden maintained a five-person advisory board made up of three ministers, a priest, and a rabbi. With its bold tabloid format, *True Story* influenced many other magazines and introduced a new confessional style to advertising.

Source: Roland Marchand, *Advertising the American Dream: Making Way for Modernity, 1920–1941* (Berkeley: University of California Press, 1986).

---

cal intrigues of the Versailles Conference and eventually opposed U.S. entry to the League of Nations as a betrayal of Americans' goals in entering the war. Though its circulation dropped off after the war, the magazine continued throughout the century as one of the foremost outlets for liberal political journalism.

Sources:

Charles Forcey, *The Crossroads of Liberalism: Croly, Weyl, Lippmann, and the Progressive Era, 1900–1925* (New York: Oxford University Press, 1961);

David W. Levy, *Herbert Croly of the New Republic: The Life and Thought of an American Progressive* (Princeton: Princeton University Press, 1985);

Theodore Peterson, *Magazines in the Twentieth Century* (Urbana: University of Illinois Press, 1964);

Ronald Steel, *Walter Lippmann and the American Century* (New York: Vintage, 1981).

A NEW WORLD OF BOOKS

Selling Books. As the mass market for books continued to grow in the second decade of the twentieth century, old-fashioned publishers lamented that the quality of the writing and the paper on which it was printed were both declining. Literary merit certainly brought some books to light, but salability became the paramount concern for the modernizing publishing business. To fill an established marketing niche, publishers went to established writers with plans and formulas for projected books rather than waiting to choose among completed manuscripts. The biggest problem facing the industry was distribution. Even the biggest houses employed no more than four salesmen, with territories such as all the major cities east of the Mississippi, or the entire South, or, in one busy fellow's case, New England, part of the Midwest, and the Pacific Coast. In 1914 there were 3,501 bookstores in the country to call on, statistically one for every twenty-eight thousand people, but these were concentrated in cities and large towns. The rural population was woefully underserved. Before World War I, 90 percent of all books were sold by subscription salesmen, who traveled door to door, with the rest sold by direct mail.

The Next Generation. While in 1911 the older generation of publishers began a Publishers' Lunch Club that met on the first Thursday of each month, a new generation of publishing entrepreneurs was blazing new trails in the business. B. W. Huebsch, Alfred A. Knopf, and Albert and Charles Boni were all learning the trade in other houses or establishing their own firms. With the money that his father sent Albert to pay for Harvard Law School, the Bonis opened Washington Square Bookshop on MacDougal Street in 1912 and were at the center of bohemian life in Greenwich Village. They cut an opening into the Liberal Club next door and made a big impression on the publishing industry with their Little Leather Library, thirty titles with excerpts from the classics bound in imitation leather, which sold by mail order for $2.98 for a complete set of all thirty volumes. Woolworth's sold

---

and Mastery (1914). Although Willard Straight died in 1918, the Straight family continued to subsidize the magazine for forty years, at an average of $100,000 a year, and never interfered with its editors' prerogatives.

A Distinguished Staff. The *New Republic* staff in its first years included Francis Hackett, who had created the book supplement for the *Chicago Evening Post* and became literary editor of the *New Republic*. Learned Hand, a powerful federal judge, acted as adviser and brought aboard Felix Frankfurter, a future Supreme Court justice. Croly served as editor until his death in 1930. Other early and notable contributors included Randolph Bourne, Malcolm Cowley, Edmund Wilson, and John Dewey.

Peace without Victory. The magazine's staff was largely inexperienced with foreign relations when World War I broke out. The *New Republic* initially took a neutral stance, which was the officially stated position of the Wilson administration. By February 1917, two months before the United States declared war, the magazine was advocating U.S. entry. Lippmann was widely credited with having won Wilson over to the cause of war. Many people believed the *New Republic* represented the views of the Wilson administration, and its circulation soared to 45,000, actually making a profit. It pushed for U.S. participation in the League of Nations, coining the phrase "Peace Without Victory" as the goal of the peace conference. But the editors were dismayed by the politi-

Horace Liveright, who joined with Alfred and Charles Boni in 1917 to form the publishing firm of Boni and Liveright

David Sarnoff, who helped the commercial development of radio while working for the Marconi Company. After World War I he became commercial manager of the Radio Corporation of America.

a million sets in a single year. In the spring of 1917 they incorporated a new firm in partnership with Horace Liveright and introduced the Modern Library of the World's Best Classics, later shortened to the Modern Library. The first eighteen titles were reprints, followed by original works by Leon Trotsky and Fyodor Dostoyevsky, plays by August Strindberg, and *The Picture of Dorian Gray* (1891), by Oscar Wilde.

War Books. Boni and Liveright attracted the attention of military intelligence officers during the war for their publication of pacifist and antiwar authors. Several of its titles were suppressed. Other publishers showed restraint or rushed to profit from public interest in the war. In 1913 Scribners published a prescient work, *The Last Shot*, by Frederick Palmer, which correctly predicted the sudden beginning of the war the following year, the battle lines, the broken treaties, and the importance of big guns in changing the style of warfare. When the war began, it became a runaway best-seller, the only war book to sell well before U.S. entry in 1917. Scribners published war-related books by Richard Harding Davis and the unlikely correspondents Edith Wharton and Mary Roberts Rinehart but preferred to leave the exploitation of the war to others. Houghton Mifflin, the ultraconserva-

tive Boston-based house, published more than one hundred war-related books between 1914 and 1919.

Source:
John Tebbel, *Between Covers: The Rise and Transformation of Book Publishing in America* (New York: Oxford University Press, 1987).

THE RADIO MUSIC BOX

Sarnoff. A young immigrant from Russia named David Sarnoff spent the thirteen years from 1906 to 1919 working for the American branch of the Marconi Wireless Company. As one of the company's most skilled telegraph operators, he often forwarded memos with suggestions for company operations to E. J. Nally, the vice president and general manager. In November 1916 Sarnoff wrote a memo to Nally on the subject of the "Radio Music Box." None of the Marconi executives who read it gave it a second thought, and if they did it was to consider Sarnoff a screwball. But the memo foretold the

Lee De Forest was one of the truly innovative pioneers in radio broadcasting. His invention of the three-element grid audion tube, or triode, greatly advanced the technology of radio reception and was the forerunner of the vacuum tube, which would be central to mass-produced radios. In 1915 he erected a 125-foot tower on top of his factory and workshop in the Bronx and began nightly half-hour "concerts" of phonograph music. That fall he broadcast the Harvard-Yale football game.

On Election Day 1916 De Forest provided six hours of coverage of the neck-and-neck presidential race between the sitting president, Democrat Woodrow Wilson, and Republican Charles Evans Hughes. When De Forest signed off at 11 P.M., he declared that Hughes had been elected president, only to learn in the morning, with the rest of the nation, that Wilson was the victor.

Source: Susan Douglas, *Inventing American Broadcasting, 1899–1922* (Baltimore: Johns Hopkins University Press, 1987).

Add Sports and Talks. In addition to music, Sarnoff proposed that other forms of entertainment and information could be transmitted through the air. Lectures on any subject could be broadcast, as well as sports scores: a transmitter could be set up at the Polo Grounds. He predicted that such a service would be of immense interest to farmers and other people living in isolated places. They could enjoy the cultural activities taking place in the nearest city.

$75 Million. Sarnoff discussed the prices and profits to be made in such a venture. If one million families out of fifteen million in the country bought radio music boxes, and each was priced at $75, the manufacturer would earn $75 million, minus manufacturing and distribution costs. With the outbreak of World War I, the Marconi Company was taken over by the government. It was reconstituted in new form after the war as the Radio Corporation of America, with Sarnoff as commercial manager. He did not become its president until thirteen years later, but in many ways he ran it from the beginning, and radio made much more than $75 million for its pioneering companies.

Source:
Carl Dreher, *Sarnoff: An American Success* (New York: Quadrangle, 1977).

future of the radio industry at a time when the technology was still used exclusively as a means for point-to-point communication. While radio pioneer Lee De Forest was already transmitting music from a phonograph from his home in the Bronx, his audience was made up of those who already had receivers. It would be left to others, including Sarnoff, to induce the public to buy radio receivers in great numbers.

Broadcasting Envisioned. Sarnoff proposed to develop radio as a "household utility" along the lines of a piano or a phonograph. "The idea is to bring music into the home by wireless," he wrote. While similar plans using wires had failed, Sarnoff proposed that a transmitter with a range of twenty-five to fifty miles could be installed in a central place, where singers and musicians would work their magic. Hundreds of thousands of families could receive simultaneously from the single transmitter.

Simple. A radio receiver in 1916 was a complicated apparatus, operated by people with at least minimal engineering experience. Sarnoff conceived a simple appliance for the novice. "The receiver can be designed in the form of a simple 'Radio Music Box,'" he wrote, "and arranged for several different wavelengths, which would be changeable with the throwing of a single switch or the pressing of a single button." An amplifier eradicated the need for headphones, and a circular antenna could be sealed inside the box. Sarnoff even foresaw the box "placed on a table in the parlor or the living room."

THE "SMART MAGAZINES"

From Society and Comedy. A new class of magazines began to publish during the 1910s, which writer George Douglas has dubbed the "Smart Magazines." The principal examples from this era were *The Smart Set* and *Vanity Fair*. Later additions to the fold included *The New Yorker* and *Esquire*. They grew out of two separate strains in magazine publishing: the urban society journal and the humor magazine. Urban society journals published news about the "Four Hundred" high-society families, their parties and charities, their debutantes, weddings, and travels. Humor magazines such as *Life* (not to be confused with a later publication by that name), *Punch,* and *Judge* published satire, cartoons, and comedic fiction. The "Smart Magazines" catered to an elite audience but set out to amuse, entertain, and provoke, to be the fodder of conversation at parties.

Vanity Fair. *Vogue* publisher Condé Nast bought two dying society journals in 1913, *Dress* and *Vanity Fair*. He originally combined the two as *Dress and Vanity Fair,* but when he hired Frank Crowninshield as editor, Crowninshield immediately dropped the first part of the name. Crowninshield was a dapper man-about-town who knew so many prominent people in the arts and belonged to so many society clubs that the magazine sometimes resembled an outlet for his friends. He was unapologetic about the magazine's pretensions, saying, "My interest in society — at times so pronounced that the word 'snob' comes to mind — derives from the fact that I like an immense number of things which society, money, and

"THE SIREN", by G. Vere Tyler—A

The SMART SET

A Magazine of Cleverness

"The End of Ilsa Menteith",
by Lilith Benda
"The Three Sailors' Gambit",
by Lord Dunsany
"I'm a Stranger Here Myself",
by Sinclair Lewis
"The Duel of Sex", by Owen Hatteras

AUGUST 1916
25 Cents

Cover for the August 1916 issue of *The Smart Set* magazine

position bring in their train: painting, tapestries, rare books, smart dresses, dances, gardens, country houses, correct cuisine, and pretty women." *Vanity Fair* was beautifully published on slick paper and was what a later era would call a "coffee-table" magazine. Crowninshield's vision was of a publication that people could not stop talking about. He managed to present serious issues with a light touch. *Vanity Fair,* if not the best magazine ever, as critic Cleveland Amory called it, certainly reflected the spirit of its age and printed the work of outstanding writers and artists.

The Smart Set. Started in 1900 by William D'Alton Mann, the publisher of the society tattle sheet *Town Topics, The Smart Set* bore the subtitle, "The Magazine of Cleverness." While it had a steep newsstand price of twenty-five cents, it was a commercial success from the beginning because advertisers were eager to reach the highbrow carriage trade that read it. Mann wanted *The Smart Set* to be for the Four Hundred, but also by and about them. If the idle rich never wrote for the publication (ghost writers took on aristocratic names instead), they did embrace its innovative fiction, features, and de-

sign coverage. Looking to revivify the magazine in 1908, Mann recruited two of the most promising young men of letters in the nation, who met for the first time in the New York office of *The Smart Set.* George Jean Nathan and H. L. Mencken started as the magazine's drama and literary reviewers and became its coeditors from 1914 until 1923, after a succession of changes in ownership. Mencken wrote to Ellery Sedgwick, editor of the prestigious *Atlantic Monthly,* that he intended *The Smart Set* to be a "magazine for civilized adults in their lighter moods. A sort of frivolous sister to the *Atlantic.*"

"The Aristocrat Among Magazines." Both Nathan and Mencken styled themselves as iconoclasts, working against the tides of popular enthusiasm. They supported and attacked their prejudices with gusto and delight and seemed to find amusing spectacles everywhere. *The Smart Set* published a new generation of European writers, including D. H. Lawrence, Joseph Conrad, W. Somerset Maugham, and William Butler Yeats. Americans such as Theodore Dreiser, Floyd Dell, Edna St. Vincent Millay, F. Scott Fitzgerald, and Robinson Jeffers also made their appearances. *The Smart Set* was part of the cultural renaissance triggered by the famous Armory Show of paintings and the introduction of "little" magazines such as *Poetry. The Smart Set* soon became one of the premier literary magazines in the United States. It limped along financially, but the sheer force of the coeditors' personalities and wit, their industry (they sometimes wrote half the issue under pseudonyms), and their nerve carried it forward until they abandoned it in 1923 to launch the *American Mercury.*

Sources:

George H. Douglas, *The Smart Magazine: Fifty Years of Literary Revelry and High Jinks at Vanity Fair, The New Yorker, Life, Esquire, and The Smart Set* (Hamden, Conn.: Archon Press, 1991);

Theodore Peterson, *Magazines in the Twentieth Century* (Urbana: University of Illinois Press, 1964).

STARS AND STRIPES

Military Journalism. The nearly two million soldiers of the American Expeditionary Forces (AEF) frequently complained that they could get no reliable news from home. The Paris editions of the *New York Herald* and the *Chicago Tribune* printed society news rather than sports scores. AEF leaders saw an opportunity to disseminate information about military decorum and orders. Once it was determined that the costs of printing an eight-page weekly could be covered by selling subscriptions and advertising, the AEF began to publish its own newspaper, the *Stars and Stripes,* on 8 February 1918. It ran through June 1919, for seventy-one weeks, and eventually reached a circulation of more than one hundred thousand. Its staff swelled to more than three hundred.

Civilians in Uniform. The newspaper's foremost writers were journalists in civilian life and conducted the paper's business as ordinarily as possible. Harold Ross, who would later become the longtime editor of *The New*

The staff of *The Stars and Stripes* working on the "Victory Edition" of the newspaper

Yorker, became chief editor, and he was assisted by distinguished journalists Grantland Rice, Alexander Woollcott, and Franklin P. Adams. While one of the paper's chief purposes was to keep morale high among the troops — with stories selected and slanted in ways most favorable to the efforts of the United States — the quality of writing in the paper made it much more than a propaganda sheet. It provided useful information on everything from hygiene to grief, from politics to baseball.

Doughboy Doggerel. The *Stars and Stripes* constantly printed light verse composed by the servicemen on every subject from death to beer. The difficulties of living in a foreign country made for some clever verse, as did the required deference to officers. These two topics combined in a typical (anonymous) poem titled "Its Pronounced Foch," about the French commander's name:

> The French will think it is a joke
> When bungling Yanks pronounce it Foch,
> Yet we will make a sadder botch
> If we attempt to call it Foch;
> Nor can we fail to pain and shock
> Who boldly try to say it Foch.

In fact, we have to turn to Boche
To find the word that rhymes with Foch.

War Orphans. The most touching project the *Stars and Stripes* undertook was a war orphans program. The brainchild of Harold Ross, it linked orphaned French children with American soldiers. For Fr 500 (about $88 at the then current exchange rate) the Red Cross would provide and monitor the child's care and education. The soldier (or often unit) would receive a picture of the child and updates on his or her progress. The project generated tremendous goodwill with the French population and continued to do so as the children themselves came to maturity. People and companies in the United States also participated, and altogether Americans "adopted" thirty-five hundred children.

Something Human. Doughboys and officers praised the paper as something human in the dreary trenches, and as an efficient morale booster, as one small thing that made them feel closer to home. Newspapers in the United States also praised the paper for its high standards and service to the average soldier. *Stars and Stripes* veterans held high-ranking positions throughout the field of

An airbrushed photograph of David Sarnoff at a telegraph; the faked picture was used by the staff at RCA to back up the false claim that Sarnoff had been the only person to relay news of survivors in the *Titanic* disaster.

A WARNING FOR LUSITANIA PASSENGERS

On the morning that the British-owned passenger liner the *Lusitania* was set to sail from New York harbor, readers of several New York dailies found startling advertisements in their newspapers. The Imperial Germany Embassy had taken out full-page notices warning travelers that they boarded the *Lusitania* at their own risk.

In early 1915 the German navy had declared that all ships entering British territorial waters would be fired upon. Even unarmed passenger ships sailing the North Atlantic were at risk from German submarines, or U-boats. President Wilson found this an intolerable situation and vigorously defended freedom of the seas for neutral nations.

Several days after the *Lusitania* left New York, when the ship was just twenty miles off the British coast, a torpedo struck it and it sank like a stone, thanks in part to its illicit cargo of weapons. Of the 1,924 people aboard, 1,198 drowned, including 114 of 188 Americans. Despite obvious illegal aid to Britain by a supposedly neutral nation, the sinking of the *Lusitania* helped shift American public opinion toward war.

Source: Robert D. Schulzinger, *American Diplomacy in the Twentieth Century* (New York: Oxford University Press, 1984).

journalism, from the *New York Tribune* to the *Ladies' Home Journal,* and between them published dozens of books. A weekly *Stars and Stripes,* edited in Washington, D.C., was published for a few years after the armistice. The name was revived during World War II to denote a dozen publications for units all over the world. None matched the distinction of the first to use the name.

Source:
Alfred A. Cornebise, *The Stars and Stripes: Doughboy Journalism in World War I* (Westport, Conn.: Greenwood Press, 1984).

THE TITANIC AND THE RADIO ACT OF 1912

Unsinkable. On 10 April 1912 one of the largest and most luxurious ocean liners ever built sailed for New York from England. Full of prominent people whose pictures filled the newspapers in stories of this maiden voyage, the *Titanic* represented all the arrogance of technology and wealth. The captain, believing his ship impervious to the dangers of nature, sped through an ice field, an ice field through which other ships would have proceeded with extreme caution. On 15 April the *Titanic* struck an iceberg and began taking on water.

Distress Signals. Jack Phillips, one of the wireless operators on the *Titanic,* immediately began broadcasting distress signals and the ship's position. Tragically, most ships, including those closest to the *Titanic,* employed only one operator; when that man was away from his station, no one monitored the wireless. By sheer coincidence, Harold Cottam, the operator of the *Carpathia,* had returned to his station to complete a "time rush" (in which two ships check the agreement of their clocks). The *Carpathia* was fifty-eight miles away, and it took three and a half hours to get to the site of the disaster, by which time the *Titanic* was gone. The *Carpathia* rescued seven hundred people, mostly women and children, who had made it into the insufficient number of lifeboats. More than fifteen hundred others died, including the wireless operator Jack Phillips, who remained at his station as the ship went down. The *California* was less than twenty miles away, but its wireless operator was asleep.

Confusion. Shortly after the initial distress message from the *Titanic,* wireless stations all along the East Coast of North America clogged the air with traffic. The Marconi Company complained about the interference, and out of this congestion finally emerged the false news that the *Titanic* was moving safely toward Halifax. In the aftermath of the tragedy many people hoped the perpetrator of what they thought was a hoax would be caught and executed. One calmer explanation is that a message from the steamship *Asian*, "Towing oil tank to Halifax," was mistaken for a message about the *Titanic* passengers. Still, the press and government officials took this incident as an incentive to begin more-systematic regulation of the airwaves.

The Radio Act of 1912. In the aftermath of the disaster new regulations for shipboard wireless were proposed in Congress. The bill required that the wireless be manned at all times and that auxiliary power be available in the event of engine failure. It also called for implementation of a strict protocol for receiving distress signals; each ship radio had to have a range of at least one hundred miles. The Radio Act of 1912 also began to purge the airwaves of all the amateurs who had confused official operators on the night of 15 April. Operators had to be licensed and adhere to certain band widths, and large portions of the spectrum would be set aside for the navy. Amateurs could listen to any transmissions but could not broadcast over them. They could only transmit on the shortest waves, considered useless.

Sarnoff Writes Himself a Hero's Role. David Sarnoff, a crack wireless operator for the Marconi Company atop Wanamaker's Department Store in New York City in 1912, went on to become chairman of the powerful Radio Corporation of America. He claimed to have heard the signal of the *Titanic*, given the information to the press, and alerted other possible rescue ships. How he learned of the disaster is not known, but he did rush to his station and spent a long vigil in contact with the *Carpathia*, getting the survivors' names to frenzied families and friends of the passengers assembling at Wanamaker's. He stayed at his post for seventy-two hours. Both Sarnoff and his boss Marconi were lionized for their roles in the *Titanic* disaster, and in two days the Marconi Company's stock zoomed from $55 to $255.

Sources:
Susan Douglas, *Inventing American Broadcasting, 1899–1922* (Baltimore: Johns Hopkins University Press, 1987);

Carl Dreher, *Sarnoff: An American Success* (New York: Quadrangle, 1977).

HEADLINE MAKERS

EDNA WOOLMAN CHASE AND CONDÉ NAST

1877-1957/1873-1942

EDITOR OF VOGUE/PUBLISHER OF VOGUE

Attracting the Gold Tips. Born in New York to parents whose social standing exceeded their accomplishments, the fastidious young Condé Nast attracted the notice of a wealthy aunt who put him through Georgetown University. As advertising manager for his friend Robert Collier's weekly *Collier's,* Nast pioneered several business strategies. He believed that advertisers would pay premium rates for the most affluent readership. He explained his approach with a metaphor of 2 million needles, only 150,000 of which had gold tips. Rather than searching through the pile, he proposed it would be more efficient to devise a magnet for gold. Just so with elite society publications, he concluded. In 1909 he purchased the small society gazette called *Vogue,* whose ad manager was already attempting to turn it into a fashion magazine and shopping guide in order to lure lucrative fashion ads. Here was his gold magnet. Readers were at least as interested in the ads as in any copy in the magazine. *Vogue* has since maintained a symbiotic relationship with its advertisers, highlighting their products in its features.

Fancy Dress Balls and Fashion Shows. Edna Woolman Chase came to *Vogue* in 1895 to address envelopes for three weeks. The child of divorced parents, raised by her maternal grandparents in Asbury Park, New Jersey, in her youth Edna emulated the wealthy girls she read about in the society sheets. She became editor of *Vogue* in 1914, and over the course of her career she became the grande dame of American fashion. In 1911 she persuaded a reluctant Nast to allow *Vogue* artists to design gowns for fancy dress balls to accompany the photographs of women in their costumes borrowed from the Metropolitan Opera. The designs were a sensational hit. In 1914, when the outbreak of war disrupted the Parisian fashion industry, Chase proposed to stage the first New York fashion show. The leading design houses were happy to participate, but no one knew if the ladies of society would attend. Chase agreed to donate proceeds from the admission charge to the Committee of Mercy to aid women and orphans of the Allied nations. When Mrs. Stuyvesant Fish, the leading light of the social scene, agreed to participate after lengthy and fawning persuasion by Chase, the "Fashion Fete" became a success.

Arbiters of Expensive Taste. Nast liked to throw lavish parties at his Park Avenue triplex and mixed Astors and Vanderbilts with Groucho and Harpo Marx. He gave large bonuses to employees who pleased him, including $100,000 to Chase to furnish a home she was building on Long Island. One Christmas she found a gold piece under every candy in a box of chocolates he gave her. *Vogue* became the fashion industry's bible, previewing forthcoming styles and shaping national tastes. Chase's presence at a showing made it an important event. Many people found her rigid and snobbish, which she was, but her exquisite taste and infallible editorial judgment served *Vogue* and Nast well.

Expansion. By 1913 Nast had acquired two other publications and found for them superb editors: Frank Crowninshield for *Vanity Fair* and Richardson Wright for *House and Garden.* In 1915 he launched a British edition of *Vogue,* followed by a French edition in 1920. His gold-tipped strategy was an unmitigated success. By 1926 *Vogue* had the highest income of all American magazines, even though its circulation was just 10 percent that of the largest publications. Nast lived to be sixty-nine, dying of a heart attack in 1942. Chase retired in 1952 at the age of seventy-five; wrote her autobiography, *Always in Vogue*, with her daughter's assistance; and died on vacation in Sarasota, Florida, in 1957.

Sources:

Edna Woolman Chase, *Always in Vogue* (Garden City, N.Y.: Doubleday, 1954);

Theodore Peterson, *Magazines in the Twentieth Century* (Urbana: University of Illinois Press, 1964);

Caroline Seebohm, *The Man Who Was Vogue: The Life and Times of Condé Nast* (New York: Viking, 1982).

FRANK I. COBB

1869-1923

EDITOR

A Handpicked Successor. In 1904 Joseph Pulitzer, legendary publisher of the *New York World* and the *St. Louis Post-Dispatch*, surveyed his editorial staff. While John Heaton, William H. Merrill, Horatio Seymour, and Pulitzer's own son Ralph were all able men, the publisher wanted to find someone more like himself: a leader, a bold writer, and someone with deep knowledge of American history. He sent his personal secretary Samuel M. Williams on a nationwide hunt. In Detroit the editorials of the *Free Press* caught Williams's eye. They were clear and concise. He found that they were written by Frank Cobb, a man still in his early thirties. Over a series of lunches Williams quizzed Cobb on his knowledge of history and government and his views on journalism, and he assessed everything from his temperament to his table manners. Williams reported to Pulitzer that he had found his man. Born in rural Kansas and a veteran of Michigan sawmills and lumber camps before his twentieth birthday, Cobb had gone to Michigan State Normal School while supporting his wife and son. At twenty-one he was made superintendent of the high school at Martin, Michigan. He soon found work at the *Detroit Evening News* and then the *Free Press*. It took some persuading by Williams, but Cobb moved his family to New York City, unaware of Pulitzer's plans for him.

Harsh Standards. Determined to turn Cobb into the nation's outstanding editor, Pulitzer subjected the young writer to constant criticism. Not until he had been with the paper for five years did Pulitzer confide in Cobb that he expected him to represent the traditions of the *World* for the next generation. At one point the pressure became so intense that Cobb asked to be excused from his contract. He had an offer to return to the *Detroit Free Press* with an interest in the paper. By the time he met with Pulitzer, the old man had determined to sweet-talk Cobb into staying, and he apologized for his impossible standards. He explained that he considered Cobb the best editorial writer in the country and was just encouraging him to fulfill his potential.

Ascendancy. Within a year of his arrival in New York City, Cobb became chief editorial writer for the *World*. At Pulitzer's death in 1911 he became the paper's editor, a post he held for twelve years. During that time the paper was the most important outlet for opinion in the nation. Cobb shared Pulitzer's belief that a great newspaper should serve the public interest first and that it should serve the interests of its owner only incidentally. He used his incomparable platform to campaign for human rights and to advocate political liberalism and freedom. During the first decade of the century the *World* campaigned against corruption in business and government, and in 1911 the paper successfully fought off a libel suit brought by Theodore Roosevelt for its investigations of improprieties in the construction of the Panama Canal. In a ringing defense of freedom of the press, Cobb wrote, "Long after Mr. Roosevelt is dead, long after all the present editors of this paper are dead, the *World* will still go on as a great independent newspaper, unmuzzled, undaunted and unterrorized."

Against Tyranny. Cobb's views on American entry into World War I were restrained. Though close to President Wilson, he retained his independence. He penned a lasting editorial for 1 August 1914 titled "An Indictment of Civilization." Noting that the fate of the world hinged on three men: a "doddering old man" in Vienna; a "weak, well-meaning neurotic" in Saint Petersburg, and a "brilliant, talented, ambitious manipulator" in Berlin, he concluded, "The thing would be laughable, ridiculous, if it were not so ghastly." Concluding that this state of affairs was an indictment of civilization itself, Cobb lamented that "Human progress is slow indeed when a whole continent is ready to fight for anything except the right to life, liberty, and self-government." Cobb was a member of the Inquiry, a group of analysts that advised President Wilson at the Versailles Peace Conference.

Impeccable Legacy. Cobb is credited with inaugurating the modern style of editorial writing. Florid, imprecise phrases gave way to direct expression of independent thoughts. He died young, on 21 December 1923, at the age of fifty-four. In his eulogy Woodrow Wilson said that Cobb had "a peculiar genius for giving direct and effective expression to the enlightened opinion which he held."

Sources:

William David Sloan, "Frank I. Cobb," in *Dictionary of Literary Biography*, volume 25: *American Newspaper Journalists, 1901–1925* (Detroit: Gale Research, 1984);

W. A. Swanberg, *Pulitzer* (New York: Scribners, 1967).

RICHARD HARDING DAVIS

1864-1916

WAR CORRESPONDENT

Dashing. When World War I erupted in 1914, Richard Harding Davis was America's preeminent war correspondent. The son of an editor of the *Philadelphia Public Ledger* and the well-known writer Rebecca Blaine Harding Davis, Richard went to Lehigh University where he became a star halfback but neglected his studies. Asked to leave, he became a journalist. He had covered Cuban attempts to gain independence from Spain for two years before the United States intervened in 1898. His articles for the Hearst press, including the graphic "The Death of Rodriguez" — describing the execution by firing squad of a captured rebel — strengthened American opinion to come to the aid of the Cubans. Davis's good looks and personal flamboyance contributed in large measure to the romantic image of the war correspondent. H. L. Mencken called him the "hero of our dreams." In addition to the Spanish-American War, he covered the Boer War, the Russo-Japanese War, and the Mexican Revolution.

Out of Retirement. By 1914 Davis had retired to his home in Mount Kisco, New York, to write plays and stories, when the papers began telling of the mobilization in Europe. Davis was offered the princely sum of $600 a week plus expenses by the Wheeler syndicate and $1,000 apiece for four articles by *Scribner's*. He accepted both offers and took his wife to London. The Wilson administration refused to name him as the one American correspondent who would be allowed to accompany the British troops (Davis was a friend and supporter of Wilson's rival Theodore Roosevelt), so he went to Brussels, just in time to witness the entry of the German army into the defeated city. King Albert had ordered the Belgians not to oppose the occupation, and Davis's description of the stream of German soldiers as "one unbroken steel-gray column . . . twenty-four hours later is still coming . . . not men marching, but a force of nature like a tidal wave, an avalanche" became a classic of war reportage.

Arrested. Davis was arrested on three separate occasions for following the German army without proper credentials. In his passport picture Davis was wearing a (British) West African Field Force uniform. He persuaded a series of German officers that despite the uniform he was indeed American, but without credentials he would inevitably be detained again. Finally he proposed a plan: a German major would put a statement in his passport that he was a "suspected spy" and set him on the road to Brussels, fifty miles away. If he was found off the road, or failed to reach Brussels in two days, he was to be shot on sight. He bluffed his way past three guard posts and,

exhausted, flagged down a German car, prepared to be arrested. The driver was old and somewhat dense and simply delivered Davis to Brussels, where he arranged for better credentials.

The Western Front. Davis observed the utter destruction of cities such as Louvain and Soissons. In his 1914 book, *With the Allies,* he wrote of the unattended piles of bodies: "After death the human body is mercifully robbed of its human aspect. You are spared the thought that what is lying . . . in the wheatfields staring up at the sky was once a man. It appears to be only a bundle of clothes, a scarecrow that has tumbled among the grain it once protected." He found the deliberate shelling of the ancient cathedral at Rheims shocking. German officers claimed that the placement of French batteries had made it unavoidable, but Davis determined that the French positions were a mile away and that the Germans had methodically shelled the cathedral for four days. By the end of his first tour in Europe, Davis no longer saw the war as a conflict over imperial interests but as a clash between the forces of good and evil. He promoted American entry as a moral duty and became one of the foremost advocates of intervention.

Home, Briefly. In 1915, at age fifty, Davis returned home to see his newborn daughter and to train with the army at Plattsburgh in upstate New York. That experience weakened him physically, as he suffered from angina. He returned to Europe for the late fall and early winter of 1915–1916, spending time in France and Greece but, increasingly ill, returned home in February. On 11 April 1916, just short of his fifty-second birthday, he suffered a fatal heart attack in his study at Crossroads Farm. His reputation for both bravery and integrity assured the persistence of his reputation as one of the great war correspondents of all time.

Sources:

Phillip Knightley, *The First Casualty: From the Crimea to Vietnam: The War Correspondent as Hero, Propagandist, and Myth Maker* (New York: Harcourt Brace Jovanovich, 1975);

Arthur Lubow, *The Reporter Who Would Be King: A Biography of Richard Harding Davis* (New York: Scribners, 1992).

RHETA CHILDE DORR

1868-1948

WAR CORRESPONDENT

Feminist. As a child in Nebraska, Rheta Childe routinely disobeyed her parents. At age twelve she sneaked out of the house to attend a women's rights rally led by Elizabeth Cady Stanton and Susan B. Anthony. Her parents found out when the newspaper printed the names of those who had joined the National Woman Suffrage Association. She began working at the age of fifteen, over the objections of her parents, so that she could become independent and prove her industry. She was conservative by nature but became a rebel upon viewing a tombstone inscribed "Also Harriet, wife of the above."

Self-Expression. In 1890 Childe went to New York City to study at the Art Students' League and decided that she would become a writer. When John Pixley Dorr, a man twenty years older than she, visited from Lincoln, they fell in love and were soon married. She was swept away by his good looks and love of books. They lived in Seattle for two years, where their son Julian was born. Rheta wrote articles for the New York newspapers, which her husband found an unacceptable activity. They soon parted by mutual consent, and Rheta returned to New York with their young son, determined to make a living as a journalist.

Cads and Editors. Dorr was shocked at how she was treated in New York City. Editors would not put her on staff simply because she was a woman, and when she complained that the rates they paid for freelance articles could not support a family, they said they could find other women to work for those rates. She finally got a break by persuading Theodore Roosevelt to be photographed (something he hated) and was rewarded with an ill-paying job on the *New York Evening Post*, which she left within a year. Her first overseas assignment was to cover the coronation of a new king in Norway, and on the way back she attended the International Woman Suffrage Alliance meeting in Copenhagen, where she met prominent British suffragists.

"The Woman's Invasion." Returning to New York almost penniless, Dorr resolved to be done with the society pages that passed for women's journalism. She proposed to the editor of *Everybody's* that she go underground as a worker and write about her experiences. She spent a year working in a laundry, a department store, on an assembly line, and as a seamstress but was often too exhausted to do more than make notes about her experiences. A cowriter named William Hard was assigned to help her, but Dorr resisted giving her notes over to him. She was shocked to see the magazine begin a series with her title, ideas, and experiences but with the byline of William Hard. She hired a lawyer and was at least able to prevent the publication of a book by Hard exploiting her work.

International Suffrage. In 1910, with the assistance of *Hampton's Magazine*, Dorr published *What Eight Million Women Want*, an account of the suffrage clubs, trade unions, and consumer leagues that had sprung up all over Europe and the United States. In 1912 she went to Sweden, Germany, and England to interview leaders in the women's movement, and she spent the winter of 1912–1913 in Paris assisting British suffragist Emmeline Pankhurst in writing Pankhurst's autobiography, *My Own Story*. When she returned to the United States she went to work for the *New York Evening Mail* and wrote a daily column, "As a Woman Sees It." Not everyone was moved by her arguments: interviewing President Wood-row Wilson in 1914, she asked him about woman suffrage. He replied, "I think that it is not proper for me to stand here and be cross-examined by you."

The Russian Revolution. Having twice been to Russia, Dorr was anxious to observe the 1917 revolution. One night she lay in her hotel bed listening to the murder of a general in the next room. When she tried to leave the country after five months, all of her notes were confiscated by the authorities, so she wrote *Inside the Russian Revolution* (1917) entirely from memory. In her opinion, Russia had become "a barbarous and half-insane land. . . . Oratory held the stupid populace spellbound while the Germans invaded the country, boosted Lenin into power and paved the way for the treaty of Brest-Litovsk. . . . Russia was done."

War Correspondent. Since her son Julian was serving in the army in France, she asked her editors to send her back to Europe. When the French government refused to grant her press credentials because she was a woman, she signed on as a lecturer with the YMCA. She walked into a mess tent where her son was eating. Astonished, he cried, "Mother!" and no soldier would sit down until she had been found a chair. Mothers were unquestionably better received than female war correspondents. Later Dorr covered the Women's Death Battalion in Russia and described an incident in which fellow soldiers broke into their barracks in order to rape them but were held off by the women at gunpoint. In addition to her many wartime articles, she also wrote *A Soldier's Mother in France* (1918) for women on the home front. Dorr, along with Louise Bryant, Mary Roberts Rinehart, and Bessie Beattie, pioneered the way for women to become war correspondents. After spending many more years in Europe and writing more books, including her autobiography, *A Woman of Fifty*, Dorr died in Bucks County, Pennsylvania, in 1948 at age eighty.

Sources:

Rheta Childe Dorr, *A Woman of Fifty* (New York: Funk & Wagnalls, 1924);

Julia Edwards, *Women of the World: The Great Foreign Correspondents* (New York: Ivy Books, 1988);

Ishbel Ross, *Ladies of the Press* (New York: Harper, 1936).

GEORGE HERRIMAN

1880-1944

COMIC STRIP ARTIST

One of the Greats. Born to French-Creole parents in New Orleans, George Herriman grew up in the rich culture of the southern bayous. A lifelong animal lover and vegetarian, his comic strips usually featured talking animals. He began cartooning in 1901, and when "Krazy Kat" became an independent strip in 1913, he created one of the most enduring characters of the century. Herriman was the most celebrated, and in many people's minds the greatest, comic strip artist of his time.

Crusades. Herriman's characters often went on quixotic crusades, following their plans at the expense and ruin of everyone around them. From 1904 to 1910 he drew a strip for the *New World* called "Major Ozone's Fresh Air Crusade." In 1909 and 1910 he played with another called "Gooseberry Sprig." It featured talking animals, off-center plots, and barely sketched settings. In 1910 he began drawing "The Dingbat Family" for the *New York Evening Journal.* It included a substrip or parallel story that unfolded along the bottom with smaller characters making comic commentary. Krazy Kat began in the substrip of "The Dingbat Family."

A Wise Fool. The Kat spoke in obtuse near nonsense. He turned imbecilic phrases based on his own skewed logic. His nemesis was usually a mouse, and someone usually ended up with a rock or a brick to the head. Connoisseurs dubbed it a more "literate" version of Bud Fisher's "Mutt and Jeff" strip, where a confidence man always has his plans foiled by his nincompoop sidekick. Krazy Kat grew steadily more philosophical as the strip matured.

Cabinet Meetings. In 1916 William Randolph Hearst gave "Krazy Kat" a full page in his Sunday papers, but not in the comic section. He built a new section, a sophisticated arts supplement called "City Life," around it. President Woodrow Wilson took such delight in "Krazy Kat" that he read it to cabinet meetings. Herriman drew many other strips simultaneously, but none lasted as long or drew as much praise as "Krazy Kat." In 1927 Krazy Kat's most enduring adversary, Ignatz Mouse, came to life from a prehistoric cave painting. Herriman died in 1944 at the age of sixty-four.

Sources:

Arthur Asa Berger, *The Comic-Stripped American: What Dick Tracy, Blondie, Daddy Warbucks and Charlie Brown Tell Us About Ourselves* (New York: Walker, 1973);

Richard Marschall, *America's Great Comic-Strip Artists* (New York: Abbeville Press, 1989).

JOHN REED

1887-1920

REPORTER

Busy at Harvard, and After. Born in Portland, Oregon, in 1887, John Reed entered Harvard University with the illustrious class of 1910 that included Walter Lippmann and T. S. Eliot. He studied writing and found time to write for the *Lampoon,* help edit the literary *Monthly,* captain the water polo team, sing in the glee club, and write lyrics for Hasty Pudding theatricals. After graduation he traveled to Europe, settled among a bohemian circle in New York's Greenwich Village, and wrote for the muckraking *American Magazine* and for the radical *Masses* after its founding in 1911.

The Stories of Workers and Peasants. Reed wrote with great passion about domestic social problems. His moving account of a strike by twenty thousand textile workers in Paterson, New Jersey, attracted widespread attention. In 1913 *Metropolitan* magazine sent him to Mexico to cover Pancho Villa's peasant revolution against the dictator Victoriano Huerta. When he found Villa's forces in the mountains of Chihuahua, Reed began to fight alongside them. His vivid dispatches inspired Walter Lippmann, who had also already achieved renown, to say that "with Jack Reed reporting begins." After returning from Mexico, he wrote an account of a miners' strike in Colorado that culminated in the "Ludlow Massacre," in which mine owners burned a tent city constructed by the strikers and twenty-five people died. Reed habitually stepped over the line between reporting and advocacy, a tendency that lent great power to his writing, even if it called his impartiality into question.

Russia, Portland, Provincetown. In 1914 Reed went to Europe with illustrator Boardman Robinson to report on the war for *Metropolitan.* They received a cool reception in czarist Saint Petersburg because of Reed's socialist views, which would become his ticket to great access to the leaders of the Russian Revolution three years later. In 1916, on a visit to his parents in Portland, he met the wife of a local dentist. Louise Bryant followed him back to New York, where they eventually married. They spent their time in Greenwich Village and Provincetown, Massachusetts, where Reed had helped to found the Provincetown Players.

Revolution. In 1917, as revolutionaries came closer to ousting Czar Nicholas from his throne, Reed decided to return to Russia. It took him six months to raise enough money and to secure the impractical sponsorship of the left-wing *Call, The Masses,* and *Seven Arts* magazine. Bryant earned accreditation from the Bell Syndicate. She and Reed arrived in Saint Petersburg in September, where they witnessed the October Revolution firsthand. Their best contact was Alexander Gumberg, a well-connected Russian. Reed kept a daily diary and spent every possible hour conversing with well-educated leaders and peasant radicals alike. He witnessed Vladimir Lenin's return and proclamation of the victorious "Workers and Peasants Government" at the Great Hall of the Smolny Institute. While some foreign correspondents were ignored or attacked, Reed was treated as a comrade and worked more effectively than his peers.

Troubles. Reed was not allowed to return to the United States in January 1918 because of a sedition charge. He stayed in Norway and wrote *Ten Days That Shook the World* (1919), an account of the revolution in Russia that stands as one of the great books of journalism. His close proximity to the events of the October Revolution makes it an indispensable guide, full of vivid sights and sounds, as well as insights into the principal players. For a decade it was the standard work on Bolshevism, and Lenin's wife translated it into Russian. On his eventual return to the United States, Reed abandoned journalism and began to organize the Communist Labor Party, a competitor to the Soviet-sponsored Communist International. He returned to Russia in the fall of 1919 on a fake passport but was disappointed when the Comintern failed to recognize his Communist Labor Party.

A Hero's Burial. In 1920 Reed gave a speech to the Congress of the Toilers of the East in Baku on the Caspian Sea. He contracted typhus, and with Bryant at his side he died in Moscow on 17 October 1920, just before his thirty-third birthday. He was buried at the foot of the Kremlin wall, facing Red Square, the only American and one of the few foreigners ever accorded such an honor. In the 1960s his remains were moved to a new site within the Kremlin designated for the "fallen heroes" of the Russian Revolution.

Sources:

Whitman Bassow, *The Moscow Correspondents: Reporting on Russia from the Revolution to Glasnost* (New York: Morrow, 1988);

Robert A. Rosenstone, *Romantic Revolutionary: A Biography of John Reed* (New York: Vintage, 1975).

CARR VAN ANDA

1864-1945

EDITOR

An Unknown Force. As a child in Wapakoneta and Georgetown, Ohio, Carr Vattel Van Anda showed equal enthusiasm for mechanical tinkering and publishing. At age ten he built his own printing press and published his *Boy's Gazette,* and he spent his profits on chemistry and physics experiments. He went to college at age sixteen and worked as a typesetter and reporter. In 1904, after fifteen years as a reporter and editor for the *New York Sun,* Van Anda became managing editor of *The New York Times.* He worked twelve hours a day, seven days a week, and hardly took a day off for the twenty-one years he held that position. Van Anda's genius in selecting news and finding ways to get information quickly, as well as his remarkable intelligence, set standards for news gathering. While reporters respected him for his fairness, his disapproving glance was known as the "death ray." It was Van Anda, perhaps even more than the paper's publisher, Adolph Ochs, who made the *Times* into the newspaper of record for the twentieth century. As he shunned all personal publicity, he remains less celebrated than his accomplishments warrant.

First on the *Titanic.* In 1912 the *Times* received an Associated Press bulletin the day before the *Titanic* was due to reach New York on its maiden voyage. The message said that the "unsinkable" ship had struck an iceberg and required assistance. While the first edition of the paper had already gone out, Van Anda and his staff checked all available information. Based in part on the ship's failure to send other messages, Van Anda concluded that the massive ship was sinking, and the last city edition of the paper carried a banner headline saying so. By taking this calculated risk, the paper beat all its competitors. Even the company that owned the liner did not confirm its loss until twelve hours later. Later that week a *Times* reporter accompanied Guglielmo Marconi when he boarded the rescue ship *Carpathia* to interview the surviving telegraph operator of the *Titanic* and the operators of the *Carpathia.*

Scientific Hobbies. As a child Van Anda had shown prodigious mathematical abilities. Throughout his life he showed a fascination for scientific voyages of discovery, a passion he shared with Ochs, and the paper sponsored pioneering excursions. In 1910 the *Times* scooped the *New York World* on a story the *World* had sponsored when it reported the first plane flight from Albany to New York. Van Anda bought the exclusive rights to the stories of competing explorers Roald Amundsen and Robert Falcon Scott about their race to the South Pole. He even saved Albert Einstein from an embarrassing transcription error, noting that one equation the professor gave in a lecture did not match a manuscript that Van Anda was editing for publication in the *Times.*

The Newspaper of Record. In 1914 Van Anda published in full the British "White Paper," a set of diplomatic correspondence between the British Foreign Office and the Central Powers that had led to the declaration of war. This he managed before an official copy of the documents had reached Washington. Soon he published the German equivalent, after the translators for the *Times* raced to transcribe it. All during the war the *Times* reprinted unofficial documents such as speeches by officials of the major warring nations, including those of the Central Powers. On Sundays a special section carried war photographs. Van Anda's insistence on making as complete a record of the war as possible established the reputation of the *Times* as the newspaper of record and earned it the first Pulitzer Prize awarded to a newspaper for "disinterested and meritorious public service" in 1918. In 1919 Van Anda arranged for twenty-four telephone and telegraph lines to transmit the complete text of the Treaty of Versailles from Washington. It ran eight full pages in the *Times,* which was the only paper to carry it.

Planes and Tombs. During the 1920s Van Anda continued to encourage innovations in aviation and science. In 1922 the discovery of the tomb of King Tutankhamen in Egypt fascinated him, and he gave it front-page coverage. Viewing photographs of tomb inscriptions, his language skills gave him the ability to correct the translation in the accompanying captions. He took an unofficial retirement in 1925 because of illness, but his name remained on the masthead of the *Times* as managing editor until 1932. He pursued his interests in science until 1945, when, in reaction to learning of his daughter's death, he died of a heart attack at the age of eighty.

Sources:

Meyer Berger, *The Story of the New York Times* (New York: Times Books, 1950);

Barnett Fine, *A Giant of the Press: Carr Van Anda* (Oakland: Acme Books, 1968).

OSWALD GARRISON VILLARD

1872-1949

EDITOR

Family Fame and Fortune. As the grandson of abolitionist William Lloyd Garrison and the son of Civil War correspondent, publisher, and railroad magnate Henry Villard, Oswald Garrison Villard inherited both crusading liberal views and the means to promote them. He was born in Wiesbaden, Germany, and educated in private schools in New York. After earning undergraduate and graduate degrees from Harvard in 1893 and 1896 respectively, he became a newspaper reporter and then took over as the editor of his father's *New York Evening Post.* He was dedicated to the advancement of blacks, equal rights for women, birth control, prison reform, and civil liberties. He opposed American entry into both world wars.

Unsettling New York. Villard's greatest exposé occurred in 1910, when his investigation of the New York State legislature president and Republican majority leader, Jotham P. Allds, uncovered rampant graft. It led to the first graft conviction of a New York legislator. In 1911 Villard was one of a handful of men to join in the first woman suffrage parade in New York City, and he gleefully suffered jeers from members of his own University Club as the parade passed under its windows. Villard supported Woodrow Wilson for president in 1912 but withdrew his support when the new administration mandated segregation for federal workers.

Against War. Villard applauded Wilson's restraint after the sinking of the *Lusitania,* when many people called for revenge against Germany. Later Villard blamed Wilson for drawing the United States unnecessarily into war through his increases in defense spending and preferential treatment for the Allies. He founded the League to Limit Armaments and campaigned against universal military service. When Wilson declared war, Villard proclaimed that his loyalty to American traditions mandated that he remain at peace. He wrote in dismay of the war's effects on his cherished agenda for domestic reform: "From the moment we embarked upon that crusade it was marked by a bitterness, a vindictiveness, a rage against all who opposed it, which in themselves should have given pause to those who really believed that out of such passions, out of wholesale murder, would come an all-cleansing spiritual victory." Villard feared prosecution for his views but only met with unofficial scorn and hostility.

A New *Nation.* After bitter disputes with the prowar staff of the *Evening Post,* Villard sold the paper in 1918, but he kept the *Nation,* which was part of the Post company. It had long been a liberal political magazine but had recently turned more to fiction. Spending $150,000 the first year, he set out to restore political reporting to the weekly, adding foreign correspondents to the staff, as well as a widely admired book section. The editorial stance of the *Nation,* which argued that the United States should not interfere with the Russian Revolution, precipitated censure from the government. An issue criticizing labor leader Samuel Gompers was censored outright: postal workers supported Gompers's stand against labor unrest for the duration of the war. Villard himself covered the Versailles Conference and, despite his distaste for Wilson, was impressed with the reception the president received in Europe. He witnessed rampant political violence throughout Europe in 1919 and concluded that this was the natural result of four years of war. The *Nation* stood consistently and articulately against the political repression that overtook the United States in 1919 and 1920 and was known as the "Red Scare."

Against the Concentration of Power. Villard railed against concentration of power until well into the mid twentieth century, whether agglomeration of business interests in the form of huge corporations or the increased power of the president in government. He did not greatly admire Franklin Delano Roosevelt but embraced the New Deal heartily. His opposition to U.S. entry into World War II sent him closer to the ranks of conservatives and isolationists than he had ever been in his long life. He died in 1949 at the age of seventy-seven, bitter that his principles had not been better realized.

Source:

Michael Wrezin, *Oswald Garrison Villard: Pacifist at War* (Bloomington: Indiana University Press, 1965).

PEOPLE IN THE NEWS

In 1914 a beautiful, eager, and arrogant young woman from the backwoods of Indiana founded the *Little Review*. **Margaret Anderson** made it into one of the most influential literary journals of the first decades of the twentieth century.

While he would receive greater notoriety with his liberal column "It Seems to Me" and as an organizer of the American Newspaper Guild in the 1920s and 1930s, **Heywood Broun** reported World War I for the *New York Tribune* and found innovative ways to get around military censorship. In December 1917 he exposed inferior supply operations for the American Expeditionary Forces in France that endangered the troops, and his paper was fined $10,000 by the War Department.

James Middleton Cox, publisher of the *Dayton Daily News,* was elected governor of Ohio in 1912. He had bought the paper with help from his boss, Congressman **Paul J. Sorg,** in 1898 and began his political career in 1908 when he was elected to Congress as a Democrat. He failed to win reelection as governor in 1914 but won again in 1916 and 1918. He gained the Democratic nomination for president in 1920, with **Franklin Delano Roosevelt** as his running mate.

W. E. B. Du Bois was named the first editor of *The Crisis,* the monthly magazine of the National Association for the Advancement of Colored People, for its first issue in November 1910. He remained its editor until 1934, championing the cause of racial equality and promoting the careers of African American writers, artists, and intellectuals of the Harlem Renaissance.

In 1913 radical intellectual and pacifist **Max Eastman** founded *The Masses,* which was suppressed by the government during the war. Eastman was tried twice for sedition, and each trial ended in a hung jury. In 1918, with his sister Crystal, he founded *The Liberator.*

As Sunday editor of the *New York Journal* from 1896 to 1922 and the creator of the Sunday supplement called the *American Weekly,* **Morrill Goddard** suffused Sunday journalism with bizarre pseudoscience, mild sex stories, and wild illustrations.

In a widely varied career, **Charles H. Grasty** became president and general manager of the *Baltimore Sun* in 1910, a post he held for four years. He published the *Baltimore Evening News* from 1892 to 1908, later served as a war correspondent for the *Kansas City Star* and the Associated Press from 1915 to 1916, was treasurer of *The New York Times* from 1916 to 1917, and was a special editorial correspondent for the *Times* from 1917 to 1924.

In 1912 **Gertrude Battles Lane** was named editor of the *Woman's Home Companion,* a post she would hold until her death in 1941. Lane argued that women should do less housework so that they would have time for intellectual and artistic pursuits.

As a columnist and humorist with the *New York Evening Sun* from 1912 to 1922 and the *Tribune* from 1922 to 1925, **Don Marquis** created Archy the Cockroach and Mehitabel the Cat, intertwining the humorous with the melancholy.

Robert R. "Bertie" McCormick edited and published the *Chicago Tribune* from 1910 until 1955. Ultraconservative and isolationist, he nonetheless served on **John Pershing**'s staff in World War I with the rank of colonel. After the war he issued military style orders and often rode in a bulletproof car.

While working as a political reporter and columnist for the *Baltimore Sun,* **H. L. Mencken** also served from 1914 until 1923 as the coeditor of *The Smart Set* with **George Jean Nathan.** During World War I his pro-German views led to his voluntary departure from the *Sun,* but the cautious Mencken refused to print any antiwar material in the pages of *The Smart Set,* preferring to battle the censors with irony and sarcasm.

Declaring in 1912 that "A Milton might be living in Chicago today and be unable to find an outlet for his verse," **Harriet Monroe** started *Poetry,* which proved to be the most lasting of the "little" magazines. She remained editor until 1935.

In 1919 **Lucius W. Nieman** and his newspaper won a Pulitzer Prize for service to Americanism. He headed the *Milwaukee Journal* for more than fifty years, from 1882 to his death in 1935. His widow endowed $1 million for the Nieman fellowships, which allowed journalists to spend a year at Harvard University without the pressure of daily deadlines.

It was said that **Fremont Older,** editor of the *San Francisco Bulletin* from 1895 until 1918, influenced more journalists than anyone else in the profession. His protégés included **Sinclair Lewis, Rube Goldberg, Bruce Bliven,** and **Maxwell Anderson.**

In November 1916 **James Oppenheim** and **Waldo Frank** founded the *Seven Arts* magazine with funding from **Annette Rankine,** a wealthy patron. During its brief existence the magazine was a central feature of the artistic and intellectual community in New York City and the nation at large. The magazine folded in 1917 after Rankine withdrew support, largely because the *Seven Arts* had published the bitter antiwar essays of critic **Randolph Bourne.**

The immensely talented political cartoonist **Boardman Robinson** drew for the *New York Tribune* and the radical publications *The Masses* and *The Liberator* in the 1910s. He accompanied **John Reed** to Russia in 1916.

Beginning in January 1914, **Charles Edward Russell,** a leading muckraker, wrote a series for *Pearson's* on how business pressure had brought muckraking to an end. Russell was a founding member of the National Association for the Advancement of Colored People and a member of the Socialist Party who ran for governor, mayor, and senator from New York. In 1919 he represented the Creel Committee in Great Britain.

Ellery Sedgwick, editor of the *Atlantic Monthly* from 1909 until 1938, brought attention to contemporary issues — economic, social, political, and scientific. The magazine's circulation increased to one hundred thousand by 1921.

Called the greatest reporter of his time, **Herbert Bayard Swope** covered World War I for the *New York World* and won the first Pulitzer Prize for reporting in 1917. He went on to become executive editor of the paper.

AWARDS

PULITZER PRIZES FOR JOURNALISM (FIRST AWARDED IN 1917)

1917

Editorial Writing: *New York Tribune*

Reporting: Herbert Bayard Swope, *New York World*

1918

Meritorious Public Service: *The New York Times*

Reporting: Harold A. Littledale, *New York Evening Post*

Newspaper History Award: Minna Lewinson and Henry Battle Hough

1919

Meritorious Public Service: Lucius W. Nieman, *Milwaukee Journal*

DEATHS

Henry Mills Alden, 82, personally all but unknown but influential editor of *Harper's Monthly*, 1869–1919, 7 October 1919.

James Gordon Bennett Jr., editor and publisher of the *New York Herald* and sports patron, 14 May 1918.

Ambrose Bierce, 72, caustic columnist for Hearst newspapers and popular writer of short stories; known as "Bitter Bierce"; he disappeared on 11 January 1914.

Randolph Bourne, 32, well-respected contributor to the *New Republic* and the *Seven Arts*, 23 December 1918.

Samuel Bowles IV, 63, editor and publisher for four decades of the *Springfield* (Mass.) *Republican*, 16 March 1915.

Henry Richardson Chamberlain, 52, London correspondent for the *New York Sun* from 1892 to 1911 who predicted that a Balkan conflict would ensnare Europe in a general war, 15 February 1911.

Samuel S. Chamberlain, 65, editor and publisher with Hearst who played a key role in revitalizing the *San Francisco Examiner*, the *New York American*, and the *Boston American*; he also served as editor of *Cosmopolitan*, 25 January 1916.

Robert J. Collier, 41, editor and publisher of *Collier's* and the *National Weekly* and president of P. F. Collier and Son, 17 April 1918.

James Creelman, 55, famous reporter and foreign correspondent who wrote for Hearst, Pulitzer, and Bennett during his career, 12 February 1915.

Homer Davenport, 45, political cartoonist for the Hearst newspapers who supported William McKinley and Theodore Roosevelt and campaigned for municipal reform, 2 May 1912.

Richard Harding Davis, legendary war correspondent known for his honesty, courage, and classic good looks, 11 April 1916.

Theodore Lowe DeVinne, 86, outstanding printer of magazines and a founder of the Grolier Club, a society of bibliophiles, 16 February 1914.

Legh Richmond Freeman, 72, itinerant frontier publisher known as the "press on wheels," 7 February 1915.

Elbert Hubbard, publisher of the iconoclastic *Philistine* and *Fra* magazines who was a casualty of the sinking of the *Lusitania*, 7 May 1915.

Miriam Florence Leslie, 80, successor to her husband Frank Leslie as editor of *Frank Leslie's Illustrated Weekly* who changed her name to Frank Leslie, 18 September 1914.

Alfred H. Lewis, 57, Washington correspondent of the *Chicago Times*, 1891–1894; Washington bureau chief of the *New York Journal*, 1894–1898; editor of *Verdict*, 1898–1900; he was a prolific practitioner of yellow journalism better known for his fiction, 23 December 1914.

John R. McLean, 67, owner and editor of the *Cincinnati Post* and the *Washington Post* known for his managerial skill, 9 June 1916.

William Rockhill Nelson, 74, founder and editor of the *Kansas City Star* from 1880 to 1915 who crusaded for municipal improvements, 13 April 1915.

Harrison Gray Otis, 80, owner of the *Los Angeles Times* from 1886 until his death, 1914.

Walter Hines Page, 63, genteel southerner who briefly edited the *Atlantic Monthly* and then joined Frank Doubleday to form the publishing firm of Doubleday, Page, and Company; he established the magazine *World's Work*, which he edited from 1900 to 1913, and served as ambassador to Great Britain, 21 December 1918.

George W. Peck, 75, editor and publisher who also served as mayor of Milwaukee and governor of Wisconsin, 16 April 1916.

David Graham Phillips, 44, London correspondent, editorial writer, and muckraker for the *New York World*, author of *The Treason of the Senate*, who was murdered by an insane musician who thought his sister had been insulted by one of Phillips's novels, 27 January 1911.

Joseph Pulitzer, publisher of the *New York World* and the *St. Louis Post-Dispatch,* and one of the most influential figures in the history of journalism, 29 October 1911.

Whitelaw Reid, 75, famous Civil War correspondent and diplomat who owned the *New York Tribune* and was seen as a transitional figure between personal and corporate journalism, 15 December 1912.

Herman Ridder, 64, manager and owner of the *New Yorker Staats-Zeitung,* which became the cornerstone of a major newspaper chain built by his three sons, 1 November 1915.

Jacob Riis, 65, photographer and social reformer who was the author of *How the Other Half Lives* (1890), 26 May 1914.

Harvey W. Scott, 72, editor of the *Portland Oregonian* and director of the Associated Press who was known as the "schoolmaster," 7 August 1910.

George W. Smalley, 82, distinguished Civil War correspondent for the *New York Tribune* who established the paper's European bureaus after the war, 4 April 1916.

Cy Warman, 58, who established the *Creede* (Colo.) *Chronicle* in 1892 and worked as a railroad man, poet, and songwriter; his "Sweet Marie" (1892) sold one million copies, 7 April 1914.

Horace White, 80, editor in chief of the *Chicago Tribune* and the *New York Evening Post* who kept a low profile but had as much influence on American journalism as Charles Dana or Whitelaw Reid, 16 September 1916.

PUBLICATIONS

Samuel G. Blythe, *The Making of a Newspaperman* (Philadelphia: Altemus, 1912);

Grant Milnor Hyde, *Newspaper Reporting and Correspondence* (New York: Appleton, 1916);

John Reed, *Insurgent Mexico* (New York: Appleton, 1914);

Reed, *Ten Days That Shook the World* (New York: Boni & Liveright, 1919);

Reed, *The War in Eastern Europe* (New York: Scribners, 1916);

Charles G. Ross, *The Writing of News: A Handbook* (New York: Holt, 1911);

Merle Thorpe, ed., *The Coming Newspaper* (New York: Holt, 1915);

Walter Williams and Frank L. Martin, *The Practice of Journalism: A Treatise on Newspaper Making* (Columbia, Mo.: E. W. Stephens, 1911);

Chicago Day Book, periodical;

The Crisis, periodical;

Forbes, periodical;

Justice, periodical;

The Liberator, periodical;

The Little Review, periodical;

The Masses, periodical;

Miami Herald, periodical;

Midland, periodical;

Milwaukee Leader, periodical;

The New Republic, periodical;

New York Daily News, periodical;

Pittsburgh Courier, periodical;

Poetry: A Magazine of Verse, periodical;

Seven Arts, periodical;

Southern Women's Magazine, periodical;

Stars and Stripes, periodical;

Texas Review, periodical;

True Story, periodical;

Vanity Fair, periodical;

Women's Wear Daily, periodical.

MEDICINE
AND
HEALTH

by JOAN LAXSON

CONTENTS

Sidebars and tables are listed in italics.

1910

- The Flexner Report on medical education, presented by the American Medical Association's Council on Medical Education and Hospitals, leads to the closing of many inadequate medical schools and the merging of others.

15 Jan. The first meeting of the directory of the Rockefeller Sanitary Commission for hookworm prevention is held.

- The Hospital of the Rockefeller Institute opens.

- The drug salvarsan comes into use against syphilis.

- The National Association for the Study and Prevention of Infant Mortality is formed, leading to the creation of baby clinics.

- The School of Medicine of the University of Pennsylvania establishes the nation's first medical research chair.

- The New York School of Chiropody opens in New York City.

- Columbia University offers the country's first course in optics and optometry.

- The University of Michigan awards the first American degree in public health.

3 Oct. The first U.S. course for dental assistants and nurses is offered by the Ohio College of Dental Surgery in Cincinnati.

1911

- Measles is discovered to be a viral infection.

6 Feb. The first Old Age Home for Pioneers opens in Prescott, Arizona.

3 May Wisconsin enacts the nation's first workmen's compensation insurance law.

30 June The first army flight surgeon reports for duty.

1912

- The United States Public Health Service is created by act of Congress.

- The National Organization for Public Health Nursing is founded.

- Vitamin A is discovered.

- Phenobarbital, a sedative and anticonvulsant that effectively suppresses epileptic seizures, is introduced.

- The Sherley Amendment to the 1906 Pure Food and Drug Act attacks fraudulent claims of patent medicine effectiveness.

- Local medical boards form a voluntary association, the Federation of State Medical Boards.

- Alexis Carrel, who immigrated to the United States from France in 1904, becomes the first American to win the Nobel Prize in medicine or physiology.

- The Progressive Party includes a proposal for compulsory health insurance in its platform.

9 Apr. Congress creates the Children's Bureau to investigate and report on "all matters pertaining to the welfare and child life among all classes of people."

13 June The first graduation ceremony of a university school of nursing is held at the University of Minnesota in Minneapolis.

12 Aug. The Dental Corps of the U.S. Navy is authorized.

30 Sept. The Cooperative Safety Congress holds its first national convention, in Milwaukee.

25 Nov. The American College of Surgeons is incorporated in Springfield, Illinois.

7 Dec. James B. Herrick publishes the first diagnosis of a heart attack in a living patient in the *Journal of the American Medical Association*.

1913

- The American Cancer Society is founded.

- The Rockefeller Foundation is chartered in New York.

- Full-time clinical professorships begin at Johns Hopkins Medical School with the appointments of professors of medicine, surgery, and pediatrics.

- The Association of Experimental Pathology is founded.

- Mammography, an X-ray technique for detecting breast cancer, is developed.

- Congress again amends the Pure Food and Drug Act of 1906 to make it more effective.

- Pellagra kills 1,192 in Mississippi.

- The U.S. Children's Bureau publishes a pamphlet on prenatal care.

- The National Safety Council is created.

- The Phipps Psychiatric Clinic at Johns Hopkins Hospital opens.

5 May The American College of Surgeons is organized in Washington, D.C.

19 June The first immunology society, the American Association of Immunologists, is organized in Minneapolis.

13 Nov. The first annual convention of the American College of Surgeons takes place in Chicago.

17 Nov. The first course in the U.S. for dental hygienists begins at the A. C. Fones Clinic in Bridgeport, Connecticut.

1914

- The Council of Medical Education of the American Medical Association (AMA) sets minimum standards for medical schools. To receive the AMA's Class A rating, medical schools must require at least one year of college work as a prerequisite for admission.

- The AMA publishes its first listing of hospital internships.

- The pasteurization of milk begins in large cities.

- Congress passes the Harrison Anti-Narcotic Act.

- The Association of Immunologists is founded.

- The hookworm control program begun in the South by the Rockefeller Foundation reaches its peak of activity, but in many areas barefoot victims are soon reinfected.

- The Life Extension Institute, an insurance association, begins offering preventive health examinations.

- The Mayo family opens its Mayo Clinic building in Rochester, Minnesota.

- The American Public Health Association adds an Industrial Hygiene section.

22 June The first annual meeting of the American Association of Immunologists is held in Atlantic City, New Jersey.

The American College of Surgeons admits its first women members.

1915

- The U.S. Bureau of the Census establishes forms to measure births and infant mortality rates.

- Death certificates come into general use.

- Joseph Goldberger demonstrates that pellagra is the result of a dietary deficiency rather than a bacteria-borne disease.

- Thyroxin, an iodine-containing hormone later used to treat thyroid disorders, is isolated and identified.

- The Mayos give $1.5 million to endow the Mayo Foundation for Medical Education and Research.

- Modern virology is born with the development of a simple procedure for culturing and assaying viruses that attack bacteria.

- The American College of Physicians is incorporated.

- The United States Public Health Service Division of Industrial Hygiene and Sanitation is created.

Jan. The first issue of the *International Journal of Orthodontia* is published in Saint Louis, Missouri.

19 May Connecticut enacts the first state dental legislation to regulate dental hygienists.

14 June The first Protestant Church for Lepers is dedicated in Carville, Louisiana.

20 Sept. Temple University opens the first chiropody school (a system of healing involving spinal manipulation) as a regular division of a university.

1916

- Antitoxin is introduced for treatment of gas gangrene by William T. Bull.

- The anticoagulant property of the drug heparin is accidentally discovered by a medical student, William H. Howell.

- A polio epidemic strikes 28,767 victims in midsummer; about 6,000 die, and thousands more are crippled.

- The practice of refrigerating blood for transfusion is begun.

- To relieve angina pectoris, sympathectomy, or the surgical interruption of sympathetic nerve pathways, is performed for the first time.

- The Medical Division of the Council of National Defense is created by President Woodrow Wilson.

- The National Board of Medical Examiners holds its first examinations in Washington, D.C.

- The American Association of Industrial Physicians and Surgeons is incorporated.

2 May   The Harrison Drug Act requires all persons licensed to sell narcotic drugs to file an inventory of their stocks with the Internal Revenue Service.

5 June   The Supreme Court rules that users and sellers of opium are liable for prosecution.

16 Oct.   Margaret Sanger, Ethel Byrne, and Fania Mindell open the first birth control clinic in the United States in Brooklyn, New York.

1917

- Vitamin D is isolated from cod-liver oil.

- Harvard Medical School establishes a Department of Applied Physiology.

23 Feb.   The American Society of Orthodontists, the first for the profession, is incorporated.

June   The AMA House of Delegates approves a final report endorsing health insurance.

1918

- S. R. Benedict devises a test to measure the basal metabolism rate.

- The American Medical Association increases the prerequisite for Class A medical school admission from one to two years of college.

- Some 46 percent of fracture cases in the U.S. Army result in permanent disability, chiefly by amputation; 12 percent of fracture cases result in death.

- The American College of Surgeons begins an effective program to evaluate hospital standards.

- Congress adopts the Chamberlain-Kahn Act for the study and control of venereal disease.

May   The first issue of the *Journal of Industrial Hygiene* is published.

25 May   The Army School of Nursing is authorized by the secretary of war.

27 Aug.   The "Spanish" influenza epidemic begins its sweep through America with two sick sailors in Boston; nearly 25 percent of Americans come down with the disease, and some five hundred thousand die.

1 Oct.   The Johns Hopkins School of Hygiene and Public Health, the first of its kind, opens in Baltimore.

1919

- President Woodrow Wilson initiates the White House Conference on the Care of Dependent Children.

- Ohio enacts the first law for statewide care of handicapped children.

- The curative effect of sunlight on rickets is discovered.

- Kellogg's All-Bran, proclaimed as a healthy source of dietary fiber, is introduced by the Battle Creek Toasted Corn Flakes Company.

29 Jan. The Eighteenth Amendment to the Constitution prohibiting the sale of alcoholic beverages is proclaimed. The amendment will go into effect 16 January 1920.

27 Feb. The first national social organization for the hearing impaired, the American Association for the Hard of Hearing, is formed in New York City.

23 Dec. The first ambulance ship, the *Relief,* designed and built as a hospital, is launched.

OVERVIEW

The Spirit of Reform. During the first two decades of the century, the country was alive with the spirit of reform. Advancements in medicine coincided with sociopolitical reforms as Progressive Era reformers demanded that government take more responsibility for Americans' health. In the first decades of the century the people of the United States saw extraordinary advances in medical science and technology. In the second decade, especially, enormous improvements were made in the ways physicians were trained and hospitals were organized. World War I highlighted many of the health and medical issues of the country even as, it accelerated improvements in medical care at great cost. But though American life and health was improving overall, not all Americans benefited equally. In the 1910s the country was still struggling with many pressing health issues and would face its single most devastating health crisis of the twentieth century in the great influenza pandemic of 1918 to 1919, which resulted in over a half-million deaths.

Syphilis. The example of syphilis in the 1910s indicated both the promise of medical research and the difficulty health workers faced in effecting widespread change. Victims of syphilis had little cause for hope until German scientist Paul Ehrlich's discovery of a compound named salvarsan, which stopped the organism that caused syphilis from multiplying in the body. The arsenic-based compound marketed in 1910 (also named 606 for the number of experiments needed to produce it) was one of the few drugs in existence for a specific malady. Salvarsan was the first antibacterial therapeutic drug and marked the beginning of chemotherapy, but it could not solve the country's problem of preventing syphilis, which remained a major health problem and a widely feared disease.

Children's Health. By 1910 the public health movement had made great inroads into many health problems. Clean water, improved sanitation, and new laws requiring that food and drink no longer be adulterated led to increases in life expectancy, especially for children. But bacterial infections still attacked every household, and doctors were helpless against such maladies as rheumatic fever, a bacterial infection that affected the heart valves. Children suffered and sometimes died from measles, whooping cough, and scarlet fever.

Continued Threats. Despite the efforts of researchers and public health workers, physicians still lacked the means to protect Americans from many diseases adequately. Smallpox remained a health threat, with an outbreak occurring in Milwaukee in 1914. Although a sound scientific picture of poliomyelitis had taken shape by 1910, the disease continued to plague Americans during the ensuing decade, with epidemics occurring in Iowa, Ohio, and New York. While the Public Health Service could report in 1917 that polio was an exclusively human disease transferable directly from one human to another by some still-undetermined mechanism, an effective vaccine was yet decades away. Influenza, pneumonia, and tuberculosis remained the primary diseases of death. Evidence of tuberculosis infection could be revealed with X-ray technology, but without any vaccine or other effective medication, isolation, rest, and gentle exercise were the prescribed treatments. Tuberculosis was treated in rest centers, or sanitariums, until the discovery of effective antibiotics in the 1940s. The death rates for the disease, however, showed a steady decline from 150 per 100,000 in 1910 to 120 in 1920, largely due to increased public knowledge and awareness of the disease fostered by organizations such as the National Tuberculosis Association.

Unhealthy Americans. The growing emphasis on medical examinations in the 1910s revealed that most Americans had some kind of health problem. Of 3.76 million men examined for service in World War I, about 550,000 were rejected as unfit; and of the 2.7 million called into service, about 47 percent had physical impairments. In one study examining 10,000 workmen, not one was reported in perfect health. Ten percent were slightly impaired, and the other 90 percent were in varying stages of poor health: 41 percent had problems requiring minor treatment; 35 percent had conditions requiring medical supervision; 9 percent had serious physical impairments requiring systematic treatment; and 5 percent had grave problems requiring immediate medical attention. Among 5,000 citizens of Framingham, Massachusetts, examined as part of a Metropolitan Life Insurance demonstration project to control tuberculosis, 77 percent were recorded as ill with some disease; two-thirds of the defects discovered were supposedly preventable.

But Americans did not see themselves as unhealthy. The physicians' examinations found twelve times as much illness as did a house-to-house survey of self-reported sickness.

Revolutionary Trends. Two major trends continued to revolutionize the delivery of health care in the United States. First, scientific advances in bacteriology increasingly permitted physicians to understand the causes and origins of disease — a major element in the development of modern diagnostic and therapeutic procedures. Second, the advancement of medical knowledge naturally led to the increasing specialization of medical practices. Both trends were accelerated by World War I, which stimulated research and resulted in refinements in many specialities, especially surgery. Once mainly holistically concerned with their patients' well-being, physicians were more and more often choosing to become experts in specific illnesses.

Reform in Physician Training. Higher standards of medical performance required consistent, systematic training in both basic science and clinical work. American physicians who had studied medicine abroad created a growing movement to reconstruct the medical profession in the United States along European lines. In the first decade of the century, the American Medical Association (AMA) established a Council on Medical Education. The council began to publicize the poor scores that candidates from weak schools made on state board examinations and initiated a comprehensive review of standards. Abraham Flexner's report, published in 1910, indicted American medical education and the standard of competence of American physicians. It recommended a European model and generated immediate and powerful changes. Many private, fee-supported proprietary medical schools, including many that had trained African American and women physicians, could not meet the new standards and closed. Quality as measured by the AMA rating system improved, but both the ratio of physicians to the population and the evolving profession's diversity declined.

Better Techniques and Technology. Advancements in operating techniques as well as improvements in avoiding infection and controlling pain were changing surgery from an emergency or a treatment of last resort into a therapeutic aspect of medicine and an acceptable, even ordinary method for dealing with diseases. By the middle of the second decade, Harvey Williams Cushing's work as the country's first neurosurgeon established a foundation for brain surgery and defined techniques that would be further refined. A variety of chest operations were tried with steady improvements. While early efforts to suture stab wounds had resulted in high death rates from infection, by 1914 mortality was reduced to 45 percent, and further advances were made during World War I. In 1912 the French-born surgeon Alexis Carrel won America's first Nobel Prize in medicine or physiology for his work in connecting blood vessels. In 1913 American

scientist William D. Coolidge developed the first efficient X-ray tube (one form of the tube is still called a Coolidge tube).

Hospitals. The recognition of the importance of well-organized, skilled nursing care and the more functional designs of hospitals led to an extraordinary increase in the number of hospitals in the first two decades of the twentieth century. While in much of the nineteenth century hospitals had been the last resort of the poor, they rapidly assumed a central position in the care of the sick of all classes. One reason for hospitals' growing acceptance was that they were exercising much better control of infection by antiseptic and aseptic methods. The increasing reliance on surgical procedures also produced a need for well-designed, well-equipped, and competently staffed operating rooms. In addition physicians quickly realized the advantages in centralizing expensive laboratory and X-ray equipment.

Mental Health and Psychiatry. In the United States the crusade for the proper care and prevention of mental disease, begun in the nineteenth century by Dorothea Dix, was continued in the twentieth century by Clifford W. Beers and others. A young businessman who had recovered from a severe mental upset, Beers in 1909 led the organization of the National Committee on Mental Hygiene, which would be instrumental in promoting the improvement of hospitals and in arousing public concern for the proper treatment of all mental cases. In the same year American interest in psychoanalysis and psychology was sparked when Sigmund Freud and Carl Jung lectured at Clark University in Massachusetts. During the 1910s research became an accepted responsibility in most state and private psychiatric hospitals. The Stanford-Binet test to determine mental age stimulated the development of scientific methodology in the measurement of mental processes. The attempt to measure intelligence was forced into America's public consciousness during World War I, when some 1.7 million U.S. recruits were given the famous Army Alpha and Beta tests under the direction of Col. Robert M. Yerkes. World War I also introduced a new term, *shellshock,* and stimulated interest in the psychiatric problems created by war. In addition, Henry H. Goddard's study of the Kallikak family called public attention to the relation between social problems and mental deficiencies.

The Government and Medical Research. Except for research conducted by the army, the navy, the Department of Agriculture, and the Public Health Service, the federal government provided few funds specifically for medical research before World War I. During the war the military's medical needs were generally administered by the Medical Division of the Council of National Defense, which was created by President Wilson in 1916. Facing the major wartime problem of rampant venereal disease in army camps, the Medical Division recommended the first substantial federal appropriation specifically designated for research, which led to the Chamberlain-Kahn Act of 1918 for the study of venereal disease control.

The Medical Profession and the Future. In the first two decades of the twentieth century, the profession of medicine began to establish its scientific credentials. The revision of medical education, which entailed the adoption of higher entrance standards and the requirement of a demanding course of study, helped to advance the medical profession to a position of leadership and respect. The nation's transformation into a modern industrialized society created a wider market for medicine and led to the expansion of hospitals, clinics, and scientific research. By 1919 the medical profession had won stronger licensing laws; turned hospitals, drug manufacturers, and public health officials into strong supporters; and seen new developments in technology and medical specialization. Over the next few decades the advent of antibiotics and other advances would give medicine increased mastery of disease and pave the way for the future growth of the profession.

TOPICS IN THE NEWS

THE GREAT INFLUENZA EPIDEMIC OF 1918-1919

A Little Bird. America was still at war on 27 August 1918 when two sailors reported to sick bay at Commonwealth Pier in Boston. By 31 August the Navy Receiving Ship had 106 flu cases. In September an estimated eighty-five thousand people in Massachusetts had contracted the disease, and hundreds died of flu and pneumonia. Little girls at school in Massachusetts jumped rope to a new ditty at recess, not knowing that within the coming month seven hundred people would die in Philadelphia in a single day:

> *I had a little bird*
> *And its name was Enza.*
> *I opened the window*
> *And in-flew-Enza.*

The Terrible Pandemic. In early May of 1918 news coming from Madrid told of a mysterious malady that was raging through Spain in the form of what was often called "the grippe." Symptoms included much sneezing, reddening and running of the eyes and nose, chills followed by a fever of 101 to 103 degrees, aching back and joints, loss of appetite, and a general feeling of debility. It differed from the grippe in that it was more severe and more likely to lead to pneumonia. Soon after, a similar epidemic struck in Switzerland, France, England, and Norway. Carried from Europe in ocean liners and troop transports, the flu would spread all over the East Coast by mid September. By the end of October flu deaths had occurred throughout the country and on both coasts. When it had run its course, it would be the worst pandemic to afflict mankind since the Black Death of the mid fourteenth century. Sweeping through Europe, America, and Asia, the disease would kill 21.64 million, more than one percent of the world's population.

The Spanish Flu. Popularly known as "Spanish" influenza (although it actually began in China), the epidemic affected 80 percent of the people in Spain and nearly one out of every four Americans. Influenza epidemics were familiar to Americans, but the Spanish flu developed into pneumonia and secondary complications with incredible rapidity. Death quickly followed, often within forty-eight

Police in Seattle, Washington, wearing medicated masks to ward off the Spanish flu.

hours of the first signs of illness. More than 550,000 Americans died. Influenza killed infants, young adults, and old people more readily than older children and the middle-aged. Schools were closed; parades and Liberty Loan rallies banned; hospitals jammed; and coffin supplies exhausted in Baltimore and Washington, D.C. Emergency tent hospitals went up throughout America as the epidemic overwhelmed regular hospital facilities. Although officials in World War I were able to protect against such military plagues as typhoid and typhus, neither prevention nor cure was found for the flu or pneumonia. Those who were active in the effort to check the disease found themselves almost as helpless in the face of the pandemic, even with all their modern equipment, as did early physicians in the presence of the plague.

Response. The deadliness and speed of Spanish influenza were unprecedented. Nothing else — no infection, no war, no famine — has ever slaughtered so many in such a short time. Yet the government and the American people were not awed by the magnitude and tragedy of the disease. They ignored it to an amazing extent. The government had a war to fight, and efforts to research and fight the flu were uncoordinated, underfinanced, and feeble. The flu was viewed as a minor obstacle, a problem to be solved in the process of winning the war. Congress made no special appropriation for influenza research at all. The pandemic received meager newspaper coverage and only made the front pages of the New York newspapers while it was killing five and six hundred people a day in New York City. The disease moved fast, killed, and was gone before people had time to realize fully the danger it posed. And unlike other frightening diseases, the flu did not kill all of its victims. While contracting a disease such as rabies was a death sentence, most who caught the Spanish flu were able to recover. Unlike the epidemics of polio or AIDS later in the century, the flu had little impact on organizations and institutions. Its greatest impact was on individuals who lost friends and loved ones.

Where Did the Flu Go? The causes of the pandemic are still debated. Although the causal agents that produce influenza have been identified, there is a great deal concerning its origins and epidemiology that is still unknown. The key factor cited in explaining the intensity of the outbreak is the virulence of the virus strain involved. Some theories suggest that while the virus was present before 1918 it developed its greater virulence through mutation. Other theories postulate animal reservoirs of influenza, where the disease lurks between epidemics. The reason for the deadliness of Spanish influenza clearly lies in the balance of two factors, each of which defines the other: the virulence of the virus and the vulnerability of its victims. But the influenza of 1918–1919 still keeps its final secrets — where did the flu go? Could it return?

Sources:

Alfred W. Crosby Jr., *Epidemic and Peace, 1918* (Westport, Conn.: Greenwood Press, 1976);

Richard Harrison Shryock, *The Development of Modern Medicine: An Interpretation of the Social and Scientific Factors Involved* (Philadelphia: University of Pennsylvania Press, 1936);

"Spanish Influenza Much Like Grippe," in *Medicine and Health Care*, edited by Saul Jarcho and Gene Brown (New York: Arno, 1977), pp. 27–28;

THE GROWTH OF GROUP PRACTICE

Private Group Practices. Private group medical practices, constituting a middle road between the individual practice common in the early 1900s and the prospect of nationalized medicine predicted by some, found growing acceptance during the 1910s. Arising mainly in the Midwest, private group practices, also called private group clinics or group medicine, collected physicians into a single organization, often with business managers and technical assistants. These clinics were usually made up of not more than ten physicians who used common equipment, were jointly responsible for patients, and pooled their incomes. Advocates claimed that such clinics improved the quality of service without increasing fees and saved the patient's time. Some doctors contributed capital and became owners, while other physicians remained employees. The period from 1914 to 1920, and especially from 1918 to 1920, saw a high rate of growth in private group practices.

The Mayo Clinic. Group practice originated in America with the Mayo Clinic. The Mayo family practice began when brothers William and Charles Mayo joined their father in building up a popular general practice beginning in the 1880s. The family specialized in surgery and as years passed invited other doctors, young physicians who were proficient in the new diagnostic techniques, to join them. The Mayos and their partners selected patients who would be the most likely to benefit from their surgical expertise. As the practice matured, diagnostic work and research gradually became as important as surgery. When the clinic opened its building in Rochester, Minnesota, in 1914, there were seventeen doctors on the permanent diagnostic staff. The clinic also evolved into a center of medical education; in 1915 the Mayos gave $1.5 million to endow the Mayo Foundation for Medical Education and Research, which later became affiliated with the University of Minnesota as a graduate medical school. In the beginning, the Mayo Clinic's practice was strictly private, but in two stages, beginning in 1919, the Mayos gave up ownership and converted the clinic into a nonprofit organization.

A Small City Phenomenon. Group clinics most often sprang up in small cities in the Middle and Far West. An American Medical Association (AMA) survey in 1932 found half of some three hundred groups (median size between five and six physicians) in cities with fewer than twenty-five thousand people and two-thirds in cities with fewer than fifty thousand. Private group clinics were rare in the East because established voluntary hospitals and their affiliated physicians were available to perform specialized services. The absence of large hospitals in the West created an opportunity for the development of proprietary clinics.

Reactions. Although William Mayo said in 1910 that medical care had become a "cooperative science" and

DEATH RATES ACCORDING TO AGE GROUPS

The table below indicates the death rates in various age groups based on the estimated midyear population. Note the rise in the death rate among young people in the population as opposed to the very young and the very old during 1918, the year of the influenza epidemic.

Deaths per 1,000:	1910	1915	1918	1919
Under one year	131.4	102.4	111.7	91.0
1–4	14.0	9.2	15.7	9.3
5–14	2.9	2.3	4.1	2.7
15–24	4.5	4.1	10.7	5.3
25–34	6.5	5.8	16.4	7.5
35–44	9.0	8.3	13.4	8.6
45–54	13.7	13.1	15.2	12.3
55–64	26.2	25.5	26.5	23.1
65–74	55.6	55.6	55.0	50.0
75–84	122.2	120.1	113.0	107.8
85+	250.3	240.3	222.1	222.2
All ages	14.7	13.2	18.1	12.9

Source: *Historical Statistics of the United States 1789–1945* (Washington, D.C.: Bureau of the Census, 1949), pp. 48–49.

"individualism in medicine" could no longer continue, many doctors were hostile to group practice. Solo practitioners in communities where doctors had formed group practices tended to be antagonistic, often complaining that the groups cut fees below the common rates. Even the Mayos were under fire from colleagues in Minnesota who accused them of underselling and publicity seeking. The AMA was unwilling to take a position either for or against group practice. The organization did not go so far as to condemn group practice, but it expressed unease about its impact and editorialized about its disadvantages.

Slowdown. After rapid growth following World War I, the spread of group practices slowed as hospitals started to appear in the medium-sized cities of the West. Because of the rapid growth of medical technology, the diagnostic services and facilities only hospitals could provide were desired throughout the nation. As hospitals proliferated, the demand for private group practices declined.

Sources:

Richard Harrison Shryock, *The Development of Modern Medicine: An Interpretation of the Social and Scientific Factors Involved* (Philadelphia: University of Pennsylvania Press, 1936);

Paul Starr, *The Social Transformation of American Medicine* (New York: Basic Books, 1982).

HEALTH INSURANCE

Beginnings. Compulsory health insurance began in Germany in 1883 when Chancellor Otto Bismarck introduced it along with other social rights in lieu of granting wider political rights. It was adopted in modified form in Britain through the efforts of David Lloyd George in 1911. But a consciousness of the need for medical relief was slow to develop in the United States. Most American sickness benefits were provided by small immigrant benefit societies and local chapters of fraternal orders and unions. While American workers bought life insurance policies from commercial insurance companies, they spent their money to insure their escaping a pauper's funeral, not to buy better health. Reformers outside government rather than political leaders took the initiative in calling for health insurance measures. The first workmen's compensation law in the country was enacted in Wisconsin on 3 May 1911. By 1915 workmen's compensation laws had been passed by some twenty states. Such laws applied only to disabilities arising from employment. There was no other form of legally required health insurance.

The American Association for Labor Legislation. The American Association for Labor Legislation (AALL), founded in 1906, was at the center of the push for health insurance. The AALL's major concern was occupational disease, and its first major success came in the campaign against "phossy jaw," a bone-eroding disease of the face common among workers in match factories. In 1907 the AALL called for a broad program of social legislation that included sickness insurance, and by 1915 it announced that it was preparing a standard bill, which it intended to introduce into state legislatures in 1916. The bill called for compulsory health insurance for employed people earning $1,200 or less and for other employees who wanted to subscribe. The bill would provide hospitalization with necessary medical, surgical, and nursing care and cash payments equal to two-thirds of the employee's wages for up to twenty-six weeks of illness. Although some labor leaders endorsed the bill, it was opposed by the powerful president of the American Federation of Labor, Samuel Gompers, who criticized the belief that the government needed to supervise the nation's health when the trade unions were already raising the workers' standard of living. Official studies of health insurance were made in eight states between 1915 and 1918. Special commissions appointed in Massachusetts, California, and four other states approved the prin-

Theodore Roosevelt delivering his New Nationalism speech at Osawatomie, Kansas, in August 1910. Roosevelt's Progressive Party agenda included health-care reform.

ciple of health insurance, but the legislatures failed to act.

Two Objectives. The AALL pressed its campaign for health insurance while the progressive reform impulse was beginning to wane. The Progressive Party's nominee, former president Theodore Roosevelt, supported social and health insurance in the belief that no country could be strong whose people were sick and poor. But his defeat in 1912 by Woodrow Wilson meant that compulsory health insurance in the United States would not have a national political sponsor. Progressive reformers such as the AALL put forward two objectives for health insurance. First, reformers argued that poverty caused by illness would be reduced by providing support to families with ill breadwinners. Second, reformers claimed that the total costs of illness and insurance to society would be lessened by encouraging more effective medical care, creating financial incentives for disease prevention, and eliminating the wasteful expenditures on industrial insurance.

From Pro to Con. The arguments for health insurance reflected a Progressive belief in the ability of public health and medical care to prevent and cure disease. In general physicians at first supported the attempts to secure health legislation. In 1915 the American Medical Association responded positively to the AALL's push. By late 1916 social insurance bills had been introduced into state legislatures, and Congress was holding hearings on social legislation that included health insurance. In January 1917 the *Journal of the American Medical Association* again made favorable editorial comments about social insurance, pointing out that among the large industrial nations the United States was almost the only one that had failed to adopt compulsory health insurance laws. But there were disagreements between the reformers and the physicians, especially where the Progressive program conflicted with the physicians' defense of their income and professional autonomy. Searching for efficiency, some reformers encouraged the growth of group practices and suggested paying doctors by salary or capitation (per patient per year) instead of by the traditional fee-for-service method. This led to increasing negativity from physicians, and during 1917 the journal began to swing away from favorable comments on social insurance toward opposition.

The Death Knell for Social Insurance. Fearing that sick pay could encourage malingering, employers rejected the argument that health insurance would increase productive efficiency. To the great annoyance of the reformers, the American Federation of Labor opposed social insurance as an unnecessary, paternalistic reform that would create a system of state supervision of the people's health. The private insurance industry, which feared the loss of an important source of profit, also fought the concept of compulsory health insurance. But the entry of the United States into World War I in April 1917 proved to be the final undoing of the Progressives and their social insurance movement. Anti-German sentiment in the country left social insurance vulnerable to the charge that it was "a dangerous device, invented in Germany, announced by the German Emperor from the throne the same year he started plotting and preparing to conquer the world." The Red Scare immediately after the war, when the government challenged the last vestiges of radicalism, meant opponents of compulsory health insurance would associate it with Bolshevism and communism. The health insurance movement dissipated in the complacency of the 1920s and the negative stance of the American Medical Association.

Sources:
James Bordley III and A. McGehee Harvey, *Two Centuries of American Medicine, 1776–1976* (Philadelphia: W. B. Saunders, 1976);

Paul Starr, *The Social Transformation of American Medicine* (New York: Basic Books, 1982).

IMPROVING HOSPITALS

The American College of Surgeons. The 1910s marked a major period of reform in hospitals. In few countries was the growth of the modern hospital so rapid as it was in the United States. Many new hospitals were built in American cities throughout the nineteenth century, as the population rapidly increased, and anesthesias, antisepsis, and medical technology began to make the hospital a necessity. In the twentieth century every community, regardless of size, seemed to believe that it must have its own hospital. In 1912 Congress recognized the increasingly important work of hospital laboratories by a special act, authorizing them to "study and investigate the diseases of man." The American College of Surgeons

(ACS), founded in 1913, provided the major impetus for improving the work done in American hospitals in the 1910s. Under the college's strict membership requirements, surgeons desiring membership had to submit one hundred case histories of operations. Many surgeons could not do so because their hospitals kept no detailed case records and often lacked laboratories and X-ray equipment. The ACS then created a whole system of requirements for the accreditation of hospitals.

New Requirements. The American College of Surgeons required hospitals to have an organized medical staff; keep accurate clinical records for each patient; maintain adequate diagnostic and therapeutic facilities, including a laboratory or laboratories for chemical, bacteriological, serological, and pathological work and an X-ray department providing both radiographic and fluoroscopic services; hold clinical staff conferences at least once a month; and provide a pathologist's report on every organ removal. Each year a list of approved hospitals was published by the ACS and appeared in newspapers. Patients could see for themselves how their hospital fared in the eyes of professional judges. Institutions wanted this type of accreditation, and within little more than a decade, the influence of the College of Surgeons proved to be a catalyst for standardizing American hospital equipment and procedures. Of 692 large hospitals examined in 1918, about 13 percent were approved, but the percentage would rapidly increase in ensuing years.

Approved Hospitals for Intern Training. Prodded by the Flexner Report, the Council on Medical Education of the American Medical Association also established requirements that encouraged the standardization of hospitals. According to the AMA, only hospitals with competent clinical supervision and guidance would be granted the privilege of training interns. The council published its first list of approved hospitals in 1914. To be accredited by the AMA a hospital had to have a clinically competent staff organized to provide a planned educational program; a well-equipped and readily accessible medical library; a system for recording and maintaining complete case histories of all patients; adequate laboratories and X-ray equipment; and the services of a pathologist. In addition, at least 15 percent of the patients who died in the hospital had to have autopsies.

Consequences of Accreditation. Because of the desirability of accreditation, hospitals more and more began to offer standardized services regardless of the overall needs of their communities. The resulting lack of coordination of services to communities contributed to rising medical care costs, and the number of small hospitals became a target for critics. "If many hospitals in each city could pool their interests," wrote a hospital superintendent in 1911, "the result would be greater efficiency and greater economy — and yet nothing is more unlikely than that independent, privately controlled hospitals will pool interests." Nevertheless, accreditation raised the overall level of care provided by hospitals. No longer places of

DEATH RATES BY DISEASE

The table below shows death rates based on the estimated midyear population. Pneumonia and influenza rates are included for the year 1918 to show comparative data for the influenza epidemic. The dramatic death-rate decline of tuberculosis, diphtheria, and typhoid fever was perhaps more attributable to the public health and sanitation efforts of the time than to available vaccines. The death rate for cancer, however, rose during the decade and has steadily increased since the beginning of the century. (The data for heart disease do not include diseases of the coronary arteries.)

Deaths per 100,000:

	1910	1915	1918	1919
Tuberculosis	153.8	140.1		125.6
Diseases of the Heart	147.9	158.9		163.9
Pneumonia and Influenza	223.0	155.9	145.9	588.5
Cancer	76.2	80.7		81.0
Diphtheria	21.1	15.2		14.9
Typhoid and Paratyphoid fever	9.2	22.5		11.8

Source: *Historical Statistics of the United States 1789–1945* (Washington, D.C.: Bureau of the Census, 1949), pp. 48–49.

dreaded impurity filled with the poor and destitute, hospitals were becoming citadels of science and bureaucratic order. As major hospitals gained ties to research universities surgery, modern medicine, and education all came to reside in a single institution. By the end of the 1910s hospitals had been established at the center of medical education and medical practice.

Sources:

James Bordley III and A. McGehee Harvey, *Two Centuries of American Medicine, 1776–1976* (Philadelphia: W. B. Saunders, 1976);

Richard Harrison Shryock, *The Development of Modern Medicine: An Interpretation of the Social and Scientific Factors Involved* (Philadelphia: University of Pennsylvania Press, 1936);

Paul Starr, *The Social Transformation of American Medicine* (New York: Basic Books, 1982).

MEDICINE IN WORLD WAR I

Preparation. By the time the United States entered World War I in April 1917, improvements in medical education, medical skills, and medical resources meant that the country was far better prepared to grapple with the problems that would arise. In 1916 President Wood-

row Wilson appointed a Council of National Defense that included a medical division headed by Dr. Franklin Martin of Chicago. With the cooperation of the American Medical Association and the American College of Surgeons, Dr. Martin organized the medical profession for the war effort. Once war was declared, much of the work of the medical division was planned and controlled by its executive committee, which included the three surgeons general of the army, the navy and the U.S. Public Health Service, together with noted physicians from major medical centers throughout the country.

Poor Health and Death from Disease. The physical examinations of U.S. recruits for the war revealed a startling amount of general poor health. More than one-third of the young men drafted were rejected on physical grounds. Many of these rejected men had problems that could have been corrected had they had timely and proper medical attention. For those who were healthy enough to enter military service, disease contracted in one of the military's thirty-two training camps threatened health more than battle wounds or injuries. Sixty-three thousand soldiers and sailors died from disease, nearly ten thousand more than those who died as a result of combat wounds. The camps were lethal because they mixed together some thirty to forty thousand recruits, including many rural men previously unexposed to the contagious diseases more commonly found among city dwellers.

Communicable Diseases. Although the camps would turn out to be breeding grounds for disease, the medical personnel attending the troops were better prepared than ever before. Typhoid fever was kept in check by monitoring sanitation procedures and water supplies and through the routine use of typhoid vaccine. Venereal diseases among the troops in the camps and in Europe were a serious problem, but the availability of arsphenamine for treating syphilis made its long-term effects less damaging than they might have been. But doctors and planners were not prepared for the men's vulnerability to unanticipated disease threats. Measles, a minor childhood disease for most, presented one of the major health threats in the camps because it reduced resistance to other bacterial infections. Complications arising from measles included laryngitis, tracheitis, and bronchopneumonia, the most common cause of death where measles occurred. Thousands of soldiers came down with measles; some camps experienced 100 to 500 cases a day. Of every 1,000 men with measles, 44 developed pneumonia and 14 died. Large outbreaks of mumps and of cerebrospinal (meningococcal) meningitis had a high mortality rate, but pneumonia, either as a primary disease or as a complication of other diseases, was the main cause of death. In the winter months of 1917 to 1918, 13,393 cases of pneumonia led to 3,110 deaths. The high mortality from disease was largely due to the influenza epidemic that struck U.S. camps in the fall of 1918. When the epidemic entered the camps, the cases of pneumonia rose to 61,199, with 21,053 deaths. Had it not been for influ-

Ambulances evacuating wounded at Beau Desert, France, during World War I

enza, the death rate from disease in the military forces would have been unusually low.

Combat Wounds. Of the 1.4 million United States military men who saw active combat service, 53,400 were killed outright or died of their war injuries while 204,000 survived their wounds. World War I saw a major improvement in the treatment of combat wounds as a result of better surgical methods and antisepsis, the use of X rays, tetanus antitoxin and blood transfusions, and the more rapid evacuation of the wounded by motorized ambulances to hospitals. Although surgical methods were greatly improved over earlier wars, many of the wounded died of shock. The nature of shock was not then adequately understood, and its treatment consisted mainly of first-aid measures. The casualty was given hot sweet tea to drink, wrapped up, and kept warm by stoves under his stretcher during the hours of waiting. Ambulance journeys aggravated shock by increasing the anxiety, hemorrhage, and pain of the wounded. The result was sometimes fatal when broken bones were allowed to grate together.

Transfusions. Blood transfusions were given to replace lost blood, but the procedure did not always go smoothly. The concept of blood types was known, but problems from incompatibility were still encountered. Blood was transfused in insufficient quantities by a form of syringe technique directly from donor to recipient. Three-quarters of a pint was considered a large transfu-sion. If the patient died, a condition of "irreversible shock" was diagnosed, rather than inadequacies of the transfusion technique. One major problem was the clotting of the donor's blood in the syringe or in the tubing through which the blood was injected. This was solved when it was discovered that the addition of a citrate solution to the blood would prevent clotting. By 1917 the citrate method of anticoagulation was sufficiently developed and standardized to save thousands of lives.

The Fight against Infection. Nearly 90 percent of combat wounds were caused by shell fire, and shrapnel carried particles of mud-caked clothing and equipment deep into wounds. Surgeons who had been trained in "clean" surgery performed under aseptic conditions were faced with war casualties with terribly contaminated wounds. In the improvised operating theaters there was no possibility of adequate asepsis. Tetanus and gas gangrene were two types of infection that often complicated wounds, especially when battles were fought over fertilized farmland. The incidence of tetanus in 1914 was 1,500 to 3,000 per 10,000 wounded, and the mortality rate was generally higher than 60 percent. With the introduction of tetanus antitoxin injections toward the end of 1914, the infection rate fell to about 7 per 10,000. Gas gangrene was a serious condition, and it was necessary to remove all dead and dying tissue from wounds. In 1916 it was discovered that the gas produced by the infection would show up on X rays, and when this was seen surgical intervention, with possible amputation, was urgent. Toward the middle of the war an anti–gas gangrene serum was introduced that greatly improved the chances of those infected, although it did not replace early and adequate surgery as effective treatment. The search for a suitable antiseptic for wounds led Alexis Carrel and Henry Drysdale Dakin to create an irrigation treatment of wounds with Dakin's antiseptic solution. The Carrel-Dakin treatment of wounds became the preferred antiseptic for the next twenty years.

Poison Gas. Medical personnel during World War I also had to contend with the first large-scale poison gas attacks in history. The most dramatic accounts of gas use came from Ypres, Belgium, on 22 April 1915. Both British and French soldiers noticed a curious blue-white mist — the tear gas xylyl bromide — rising from the parapet of the German trenches and drifting before them. The sentries were the first to begin to cough and choke. The tear gas sank into the Allied trenches, and soon soldiers were streaming to the rear, tearing at their collars, vomiting, and gasping for breath. The Germans also bombarded the Allies with a variety of poison gases in artillery shells marked with a yellow (mustard gas), blue (the arsenical compounds), or green (phosgene) cross. Mustard gas and phosgene were the most widely known poison gases used during the war. Mustard was an oily liquid that at average temperatures produced enough evaporation to create a gas that severely blistered and burned the skin and was a deadly cell poison. Damage to lung cells by mustard led to a rapid loss of fluid from the blood, which flooded into the lungs and caused severe edema and often death. Phosgene also acted on the lungs and could also have lethal effects. Prevention, using gas masks, was the most effective solution against gas attacks, but artificial respiration devices were also used to treat victims.

Base Hospitals. Hospitalizing the wounded was one of the most difficult problems the military faced. Base hospitals, organized and staffed by medical schools and civilian hospitals in the United States, evolved to meet the need. The local communities of the parent civilian hospitals were proud of them and held large fund-raising campaigns to provide equipment. One such base hospital was #18, organized by the Johns Hopkins Hospital and Medical School. All of its surgical dressings, operating gowns, sheets, pillowcases, and towels were made by Baltimore women volunteers, and a group of Baltimore businessmen raised $30,000 to equip the unit further. Base Hospital #18 took over a one-thousand-bed hospital from the French and in September and October 1918 gave primary surgical care to the wounded who arrived at the hospital by ambulance after receiving first-aid treatment at the front. Several medical students who had volunteered as enlisted men toward the end of their third year were awarded their M.D. degrees while the unit was still in France. Two of these degrees were awarded posthumously since one student died of scarlet fever and another died of typhoid fever.

PHARMACY AND THE WAR

Before World War I American drug companies made few synthetic drugs of their own. Drugs in bulk, or the license to manufacture them under American labels, were purchased from Germany. The war gave the American drug industry its start by ending the German domination of the American market. Congress suspended the German patents, allowing American firms to copy the German drugs. Local manufacturers of such basic chemicals as acetone and phenol began to provide them as the British blockade interrupted shipments from Germany. The price of the enormous domestic surplus of bulk chemicals dropped after the war, and these building blocks of pharmaceuticals were available and cheap.

The Abbott Laboratories company began its great boom by duplicating German drugs whose patents had been canceled. After the war it started making a local anesthetic similar to the German drug Novocain, simply because the price drop of the raw chemicals had made it possible. American pharmaceutical companies journeyed a long way during the decade from their humble origins in small, dusty "mixing" rooms to become giants of industry.

Source: Edward Shorter, *The Health Century* (New York: Doubleday, 1987), pp. 16–17.

Medical Advances. Although the devastation of World War I was unprecedented, in the long run, according to Maj. George A. Stewart of the War Demonstration Hospital of the Rockefeller Institute for Medical Research, "The war . . . taught us how to save more lives than the war . . . cost." He believed that medicine and surgery took giant strides and that the science of medicine advanced half a century in the four long years of war. The use of chlorine and the development of the "Carrel-Dakin" method of treating infected wounds by periodic irrigation with Dakin fluid (a noncaustic hypochloride) marked an advance in the treatment of infection. The lessons learned in surgery, in X-ray work, in the treatment of the gas bacillus, and in the serum treatment for prevention or cure of such diseases as typhoid fever, lockjaw, pneumonia, and meningitis were some of the compensations for the tragedy of war.

Sources:
James Bordley III and A. McGehee Harvey, *Two Centuries of American Medicine, 1776–1976* (Philadelphia: W. B. Saunders, 1976);

John F. Fulton, *Harvey Cushing, A Biography* (Springfield, Ill.: Charles C. Thomas, 1946);

Robert G. Richardson, *Surgery: Old and New Frontiers* (New York: Scribners, 1968);

"World to Benefit by War Medicine," in *Medicine and Health Care*, edited by Saul Jarcho and Gene Brown (New York: Arno, 1977), p. 83.

NURSES IN WORLD WAR I

Nurses and Wars. The history of nursing is also the history of war, for times of war have seen the major advances and achievements of nursing. The English nurse Florence Nightingale, pioneer and founder of modern nursing, became the "Lady with a Lamp" in the Crimean War (1854–1855). During the Civil War the United States produced women such as Clara Barton who greatly influenced nursing. World War I, the first conflict in which nurses had professional training, made the nation realize its reliance on nurses and the crucial need to prepare them to meet the medical needs of war. When the United States declared war on Germany in April 1917, the American Red Cross Nursing Service, under the direction of Jane Delano, began to serve as a recruitment and training agency, equipping nurses for overseas duty. Approximately twenty thousand nurses were assigned to military service, many of them remaining abroad after the war to assist with postwar relief programs.

Nurses' Training. Government authorities insisted that only trained nurses be sent to France with the army, but as the war progressed the supply of nurses was too small to meet both military and domestic needs. To meet the demand and maintain training standards, M. Adelaide Nutting, Annie Goodrich, and Lillian Wald met on 24 June 1917 and formed the National Emergency Committee on Nursing, which eventually became known as the Committee on Nursing of the General Medical Board of the Council of National Defense. It created the Vassar Training Camp in 1918 to train college graduates under a three-month intensive program to enter schools of nursing. Other universities offered similar programs, all bringing college recognition to nursing. In May 1918 the secretary of war authorized the establishment of the Army School of Nursing at Walter Reed Hospital, Washington, D.C., with branches in other military hospitals across the country.

In the War. Nurses and other medical personnel were confronted with communicable diseases, shock, hemorrhaging, infected wounds, and cases of poison gas inhalation. Although nurses did not serve at the advanced dressing stations on the front lines, they did serve at the three other types of hospitals organized for treating the wounded: field hospitals, just behind the front (occasionally); evacuation hospitals (clearing stations), ten miles back from the front; and base hospitals, located safely away from the front, where all of the wounded were eventually sent. Although the peak strength of the Army and Navy Nurse Corps was nearly twenty-three thousand, nurses had no military rank. They were not designated by Congress

as either officers or enlisted personnel, but they were governed by military discipline. Since they had no official military authority, nurses could not direct orderlies or corpsmen or handle administrative problems as heads of wards and nursing services. It was not until after the war, on 4 June 1920, that relative rank was granted to members of the Army Nurse Corps through an amendment of the National Defense Act. Nurses were given officer status, but their pay and allowances were not the same as for men.

Recognition. Although women nurses were not allowed directly on the front and no nurse in World War I died as a result of enemy action, 260 died in the line of duty, many because of the influenza epidemic of 1918. Many women won awards for their contributions. Three nurses were presented with the Distinguished Service Cross, and four navy nurses won the Navy Cross, the highest navy decoration. (One of the four, Lenah S. Higbee, the second superintendent of the corps from 1911 to 1923, had a destroyer named in her honor on January 1945. This was the first time a fighting ship was named after a woman in the military service.) The war dramatized the role played by nursing and the need for more and better prepared nurses. The whole system of nursing education gained a firmer footing as standards of admission and training were raised to create schools that were educational institutions in fact, not just in name.

Source:
M. Patricia Donahue, *Nursing, The Finest Art* (Saint Louis: C. V. Mosby Company, 1985).

WORLD WAR I AND KOTEX

The technology of war often has unexpected results. In 1918 the first sanitary napkins were introduced under the name "Celucotton" by Kimberly & Clark Co. Ernst Mahler, a German American chemist, had developed a wood-cellulose substitute for cotton to fill the need for dressings and bandages in World War I's European field hospitals. Red Cross nurses began to use Celucotton for sanitary napkins, and when the Neenah, Wisconsin, company discovered this, it began the development of the first commercial sanitary napkins, which were sold as "Kotex" beginning in 1921.

PREVENTIVE MEDICINE AND PUBLIC HEALTH

The United States Public Health Service. The discoveries of Louis Pasteur and Robert Koch in the 1870s provided a scientific foundation for preventive medicine and public health. Early public health efforts were directed at cleaning up the environment, and public health

Jane Delano surrounded by Red Cross nurses about to depart for service overseas, 12 September 1914

was more closely associated with engineering than with medicine. With the development of bacteriology in the late nineteenth century, the theory and practice of public health and its relationship to medicine changed. Although American physicians were relative latecomers to the field of microbiological research, they led their European counterparts in applying the new science to the advancement of public health. As originators of the public health bacteriological laboratory, American public health officials concentrated their battles on particular pathogenic organisms, and attention shifted from the environment to the infected individual. The earliest bacteriological laboratory was established at the Staten Island Marine Hospital in 1887. The next year Victor C. Vaughan founded the Michigan State Hygiene Laboratory in Ann Arbor. In 1892 the New York City Bacteriological Laboratory formed a diagnostic laboratory that was highly effective during the cholera epidemic in New York City during that year. In two stages, in 1902 and 1912, Congress expanded the Marine Hospital Service into the United States Public Health Service. The Act of

1912 provided for: 1) investigation and research, 2) improvement in methods of public health administration, 3) distribution of federal aid to state and local health departments, and 4) interstate control of sanitation and communicable diseases.

Government Involvement. In the 1910s most public health matters were still left to the state and local governments, and at those levels the general approach was to rely on private and voluntary action as much as possible. States organized state boards of health, and by 1914 all of the states except New Mexico and Wyoming had established public health laboratories in connection with their boards of health. These laboratories diagnosed communicable diseases and provided free vaccines and antitoxins to doctors and public health officers. While the reliance on local jurisdictions to perform public health functions led to a hodgepodge of federal agencies and offices created to deal with specific problems, major progress was nevertheless made on some public health problems. The first substantial federal appropriation for medical re-

A dispensary for hookworm diagnosis and treatment in Lincoln County, North Carolina

search for a public health problem was the Chamberlain-Kahn Act of 1918 for the study and control of venereal disease.

Universities and Public Health. Within the medical profession, public health was becoming an acknowledged specialization and began to have its own professional schools. In 1910 the University of Michigan was the first institution in the United States to award a specific degree in public health. In September 1913 Harvard Medical School and the Massachusetts Institute of Technology together established a School for Health Officers, which functioned until a court ruled in 1922 that the granting of a joint degree was not permitted under the charters of the two schools. Harvard then assumed full responsibility for the school as the Harvard School of Public Health. In October 1918 Johns Hopkins University created the first separate Institute of Hygiene and Public Health within an established university, under the direction of William H. Welch. The school was created to train physicians to work in public health and had a variety of disciplines related to sanitation, preventive medicine, and public health. Courses were offered in physiology, epidemiology, bacteriology, immunology, virology, vital statistics, chemistry, and nutrition.

Pellagra. Although public health researchers originally concentrated on diseases caused by microorganisms, scientists in the early years of the twentieth century also recognized that factors other than microorganisms could cause disease. A classic example of a noninfectious endemic disease is pellagra. In 1914 the U.S. Public Health Service became interested in pellagra because of its prev-

alence in the southern states and because at the time it was thought to be an infectious disease. Joseph Goldberger, an infectious disease expert of the Public Health Service, took on the search for the causative microorganism. In an experiment conducted in 1915 with volunteers from the Rankin State Prison Farm in Mississippi, Goldberger proved that pellagra was not caused by a microorganism but by a dietary deficiency. He believed at first that the disease was caused by the lack of certain amino acids found in protein foods. However, he discovered that pellagra could not be prevented by adding the protein casein but could be prevented by adding dried yeast to the diet. In 1926 he named this factor the P-P (pellagra-preventive) factor. In 1929 the factor was named vitamin G as a tribute to Goldberger, who died that year.

Hookworm Disease. Hookworm disease is caused by the presence of the worm in the human intestinal tract. Tiny larvae hatch out of eggs in soil contaminated by feces and penetrate the skin of bare feet. They find their way to a blood vessel, are carried to the lungs, enter the sputum, and are swallowed with the sputum. In the intestines the larvae grow to adult worms and feed on the blood of their host, causing anemia and sometimes death. Children afflicted with hookworm often suffer impaired physical and mental development. A U.S. Public Health Service research zoologist, Charles Wardell Stiles, was the first to cite the problem of hookworm infestation in the southern states. In the hookworm campaign sponsored by the Rockefeller Sanitary Commission, 39 percent of the half-million children examined in eleven

INFANT AND MATERNAL MORTALITY RATES

These figures indicate the death rate for infants under one year of age (exclusive of stillbirths). Stillbirth ratios were not recorded before 1922.

Deaths per 1,000 live births

Year	Total	White	Nonwhite
1915	99.9	98.6	181.2
1919	86.6	83.0	130.5

The rates below indicate the maternal mortality rate.

Deaths per 1,000 live births

Year	Total	White	Nonwhite
1915	6.1	6.0	10.6
1919	7.4	7.0	12.4

Source: *Historical Statistics of the United States 1789–1945* (Bureau of the Census, Washington, D.C., 1949), p. 46.

southern states between 1910 and 1914 were found to have the disease. Incidence was high among adults as well. The survey also revealed that most of the physicians in the affected areas did not know of the problem nor did they know the methods for diagnosing and treating the disease. To make people aware of the hookworms and of methods for prevention and treatment, a publicity campaign was mounted involving printed leaflets and through newspapers, schools, and local boards of health. The best means of prevention entailed encouraging the construction of sanitary outhouses to prevent the eggs in human feces from reaching exposed soil as well as convincing people to wear shoes to keep the larvae from reaching the skin. The medical organizations of the South cooperated with the commission in establishing free outdoor clinics where diagnoses could be made and a course of medication of capsules of thymol and salts over a period of eighteen hours started for each patient. The campaign against hookworm brought rapid results and improved the morale, physical development, and sense of well-being of the people of the southern states.

Baby Clinics. By 1915 there were 538 baby clinics in America, five times more than in 1910 when the National Association for the Study and Prevention of Infant Mortality was formed as part of the emphasis on hygiene and medical examinations. The high infant mortality rate had dictated a comprehensive program of "baby saving" that included prenatal care, instruction for mothers in feeding and raising their children, sick and well baby care at local

clinics, and the provision of pasteurized milk. Voluntary agencies operated some clinics, but city health departments ran most of them. The clinics were an outgrowth of the old-style dispensaries and infant hygiene movements of the turn of the century, but the shift from "dispensary" to "clinic" reflected the increased use of diagnostic techniques and a reorientation to the complex task of promoting changes in child care, diet, and living patterns. By the end of the 1910s some progress had been made in reducing both the infant and the maternal mortality rates.

The Golden Age of Public Health. The turn of the century and its first few decades were a golden age for the public health movement. Death rates declined with better nutrition, more efficient quarantine practices for communicable diseases, and improvements in the physical environment, especially from the conquest of waterborne diseases through public health measures. During the Progressive Era, American society celebrated science and efficiency, while reformers and muckrakers called for strict professional licensing and drug regulation. With this emphasis on scientific and medical expertise and cooperative action, public health and preventive medicine gained greater legitimacy. But later in the twentieth century the discovery of antibiotics and other drugs for tuberculosis and ailments such as venereal diseases would lead Americans to rely again on private physicians. Public health would be given a secondary status, and the artificial separation of preventive from curative medicine would contribute further to what later critics would describe as the "fragmentation" of the American medical system.

Sources:
James Bordley III and A. McGehee Harvey, *Two Centuries of American Medicine, 1776–1976* (Philadelphia: W. B. Saunders, 1976);

Nan Richardson, Catherine Chermayeff, and Thomas K. Walker, eds., *Medicine's Great Journey. One Hundred Years of Healing* (Boston: Little, Brown, 1992);

Paul Starr, *The Social Transformation of American Medicine* (New York: Basic Books, 1982);

Francis Wilie, *M.I.T. in Perspective: A Pictorial History of the Massachusetts Institute of Technology* (Boston: Little, Brown, 1975).

PSYCHOLOGICAL TESTING IN THE MILITARY

Measuring Intelligence. The measurement of intelligence forced its way into Americans' public consciousness during World War I, when some 1.7 million U.S. recruits were tested by the army under the direction of Col. Robert M. Yerkes. The findings provided the first large-scale evidence from the "science of mental testing" that American-born blacks and some of the foreign-born draftees scored lower on intelligence tests than did American-born whites. After the war the army's system of scoring was translated into mental age levels, and the results were made public. According to the scales and the method of calculation then in use, it was estimated that the average army draftee had a mental age of about four-

The psychologists who designed the intelligence tests administered by the army, including Col. Robert M. Yerkes (center, second row) and Lewis M. Terman (far right, second row)

teen years. These tests initiated a debate that has gone on ever since. What is intelligence? Can it be measured?

The Army Alpha Tests. The army had no intention of committing itself to a definition of intelligence. To achieve the goal of classifying recruits quickly — weeding out the "feeble-minded" and identifying candidates for officers' training — the army asked a committee of psychologists to assemble a series of tests by drawing on the different existing systems, including the Stanford-Binet test. The committee tried their series of tests out in a few camps, timing the participants. The number of text items and the time limits were then fixed so that only about 5 percent of an average group would be able to finish the entire test in the time allowed. This determined the "A" man — a man supposedly with "very superior intelligence." Between one hundred and two hundred men were ordered to report for testing at a time. After a five-minute literacy test, those who could not read or write English were withdrawn, and the rest were given pencils

and printed forms of the Army Group Examination Alpha. A senior officer stood at the front of the room and read the general directions — one time only. Then the men were given the tests.

Administering the Beta Test. While the Alpha tests were devised for literate, English-speaking recruits, the Beta tests were devised to compensate for language differences among groups of poorly educated soldiers. The Beta tests were constructed so that the directions could be given in pantomime. Test I, for example, was a maze. An assistant demonstrated by tracing through the sample maze on a blackboard at the front of the room with a piece of chalk. When he purposely went into a blind alley and crossed over a line, the officer shook his head, said, "No, no" and took the demonstrator's hand back to the place where he could get on the right track again. Then he traced an imaginary line with his finger through each maze on the sheet and said, "All right. Go ahead. Do it. Hurry up." Speed was emphasized as orderlies walked

THE ARMY INTELLIGENCE TESTS – A SAMPLE

During the war the nature of the army's intelligence tests was a military secret. Anyone caught revealing their contents faced a $10,000 fine, a two-year prison term, or both. However, the March 1919 issue of *The American Magazine* carried what it called a specimen set of the Army Alpha under the heading "Try These Tests on Yourself and Others":

With your pencil make a dot over any one of these letters FGHIJ, and a comma after the longest of these three words: boy mother girl. Then, if Christmas comes in March, make a cross right here . . . but if not, pass along to the next question, and tell where the sun rises. . . . If you believe that Edison discovered America, cross out what you just wrote, but if it was some one else, put in a number to complete this sentence: "a Horse has . . . feet."

The entire version of this sample took the average adult 125 seconds. Fifty percent of average educated adults came somewhere between 100 seconds and 150 seconds. Those taking less than 100 seconds were ranked in the superior 25 percent. Those taking more than 150 seconds were labeled in the poorest 25 percent. No one taking the text scored the maximum. Scores were ranked on the following scale:

Ranking	Points Right
A Very Superior	135–212
B Superior	105–134
C+ High Average	75–104
C Average	45–74
C- Low Average	25–44
D Inferior	15–24
D- Very Inferior	0–14

An E rating was reserved for those considered unfit for duty because of mental inferiority and discharged (about .5 percent).

Source: Evelyn Sharp, *The IQ Cult* (New York: Coward, McCann & Geoghegan).

about the room motioning to men who were not working and telling them to "Do it. Do it. Hurry up, quick."

Flawed Test. The Beta test came under criticism and was not as successful as the Alpha. For example, the Beta test taker was expected to know what was missing in a picture of an electric light bulb without the filament or a tennis game without a net. For many recruits in 1917 and 1918, however, electricity was not available and tennis was a sport for the well-to-do. Despite the flaws in the test, the individual's score did affect his army career. Men who scored low were assigned to labor battalions. In May 1918 Beta scores became the basis for putting men in special development battalions for intensive training to see if ways could be found for using them in the army.

Intelligence, Culture, or Education? When psychological tests were first created early in the century, little allowance was made for cultural or educational differences. Such tests were developed to find out what kept children from learning and progressing in schools. The committee that constructed the army tests thought at the time that they were measuring innate intelligence, not schooling. But test results were closely connected to the amount of schooling a man had received. College men were at the upper end of the scale, and the majority of those who had not advanced beyond grade school were concentrated in the middle and lower end. In the uproar that followed publication of the test results, Lewis M. Terman, the creator of the Stanford-Binet tests, pointed out that the mental age standards for the army were established by giving both the Alpha and the Beta tests to groups of schoolchildren. It came as no surprise to test critics that the average fourteen-year-old student in school did as well as or a little better than soldiers who on average had less formal education.

Immigration Controversies. After the war the low scores of recent Polish, Russian, Jewish, and Italian immigrants — well below the scores of the thoroughly acculturated immigrants from England and Western Europe — fueled the arguments of those professing that the new immigrants were genetically inferior. Members of the Eugenics Research Association and members of the House Committee on Immigration and Naturalization of the United States Congress claimed that the tests had taken the national debate about immigration, which had simmered during and after the war, "out of politics" and placed it on "a scientific basis." In 1924 Congress passed a law restricting the total number of immigrants and favoring those from northern and western Europe. Immigration from the European Continent had become partitioned by geography.

New Questions. In the 1920s some investigators pointed out that scores of African American draftees from some northern states exceeded the scores of white draftees from some southern states on the Alpha test. Literate African Americans from Illinois, for example, achieved a higher median than the literate whites from nine southern states. Some scientists argued that "The level of effective intelligence in any group of whatever race can be substantially raised through education." But many cited the test results as proof of white intellectual superiority, marking the beginning of a long controversy. Despite the questionable validity of the army tests, they certainly succeeded in bringing new questions to public attention: Can intelligence, ability, and learning be separated? Is intelligence inborn? Is it racial in nature? To what extent can intelligence be affected by environment? Should intelligence testing affect public policies? The great legacy of the tests is the continuing debate over such questions.

Sources:

Theodora M. Abel, *Psychological Testing in Cultural Contexts* (New Haven, Conn.: College and University Press, 1973);

William C. Bagley, "The Army Tests and the Pro-Nordic Propaganda," *Educational Review*, 64 (1924): 179–187;

N. J. Block and Gerald Dworkin, eds., *The IQ Controversy, Critical Readings* (New York: Pantheon, 1976);

C. C. Brigham, *A Study of American Intelligence* (Princeton: Princeton University Press, 1923);

R. J. Herrnstein, *I.Q. in the Meritocracy* (Boston: Little, Brown, 1971);

Evelyn Sharp, *The IQ Cult* (New York: Coward, McCann & Geoghegan, 1972);

Robert M. Yerkes, ed. *Psychological Examining in the U.S. Army*, in *Memoirs of the National Academy of Science*, volume 15 (Washington, D.C.: U.S. Government Printing Office, 1921).

REGULATING MEDICINE

The Pure Food and Drug Act. The Pure Food and Drug Act passed by Congress in 1906, in part as a response to muckraking reporter Samuel Hopkins Adams's exposés in *Collier's Weekly*, did not have as great an effect as was hoped on the patent medicine market that Adams estimated to be worth $75 million a year. While the law discouraged the adulteration of foods and drugs and the misrepresentation of claims on labels and also led to somewhat improved sanitary conditions, it directly affected only the most brazen abuses. It did not call for the reporting of all ingredients, except in the case of narcotics; it only banned statements on the label of a drug about its composition that were "false and fraudulent." The 1906 act also did not apply at first to claims about the effectiveness of drugs or to statements made in newspaper advertisements. Unintimidated nostrum manufacturers believed the existence of the act would lead consumers to think that whatever was sold had received some form of government approval.

Amendments to the 1906 Act. The 1906 law did not cover cosmetics, obesity cures, the newer habit-forming drugs, or curative devices of a mechanical nature. In 1910, for example, Albert Adams could market his "spondylotherapy" cancer treatment with impunity. Adams sold an electrical "dynamizer" on which a patient was directed to deposit a drop of blood. To effect a cure, the cancer sufferer was to place an electrode from the dynamizer on the forehead of a healthy person, who was then to face west in a dim light. Such continued quackery quickly revealed the limitations of the original law, and further legislation was approved. In 1912 the Sherley Amendment changed the federal law to cover fraudulent claims of drug effectiveness, but it burdened the government with the task of proving such claims false and fraudulent, and the law had little effect. Other legislation in-

MAIL-ORDER "BABY KILLERS"

Every year the American public spent between $75 million and $100 million on medical frauds, many mail-ordered by women. Many of these nostrums were aimed at children and sold as teething "sirups," sweet powders, cough killers, croup remedies, "children's comforts," and "babies' friends." They depended for their effectiveness on alcohol, opium, morphine, and/or chloroform. Used to excess on a fussy child, they killed outright; even in moderation they could gradually become addictive. The United States government investigated seven of these widely advertised drugs but could not legally prevent their sale. All it could do was make the manufacturers take the word "harmless" from the labels and tell the public about the quantity of opiates contained in these "baby killers." The manufacturers responded by substituting for the familiar morphine and chloroform equally dangerous drugs such as codeine and heroin that were less well known. In 1913 all of these "sirups" and similar concoctions were still on the market.

Source: Edith Rickert, "The Meanest Business in the World: How Many Sick Women are Tricked," *Ladies' Home Journal*, 30 (September 1913): 10+.

cluded the Gould Amendment of 1913, which required quantity labels on packaged goods.

The Role of the AMA. The American Medical Association (AMA) played an important role in the battle to exercise control over the patent medicine market. Its Council on Pharmacy and Chemistry published Adams's articles from *Collier's Weekly* in a booklet and by 1911 had distributed 150,000 copies around the nation. The editor of the *Journal of the American Medical Association* firmly stated in 1912, "there is no such thing as an unobjectionable 'patent medicine' advertisement in a newspaper." Despite the loss of a lucrative source of income, many newspapers began to censor patent medicine advertisements, forcing many patent medicine manufacturers to give up their fraudulent claims. By 1915 the Pinkham company, fond of marketing its goods to women suffering from "female complaints," had stopped referring to the prolapsed uterus in its advertising. The AMA suggested that Pinkham's labels might just as usefully read: "For Those Who Like This Sort of Thing, This is the Sort of Thing That Those People Like."

Foreign Drug Monopolies. The AMA council also criticized the high cost of certain drugs. It was especially critical of the Bayer Company, a German firm that was the original producer of aspirin, or acetylsalicylic acid, an easily manufactured chemical. The Bayer Company's exaggerated advertising claims for "Aspirin-Bayer" led the council to banish it from *New and Nonofficial Remedies*,

"I am not Well enough to Work."

How often these significant words are spoken in our great mills, shops, and factories by the poor girl who has worked herself to the point where nature can endure no more and demands a rest! The poor sufferer, broken in health, must stand aside and make room for another.

The foreman says, "If you are not well enough to work you must leave, for we must put some one in your place."

Standing all day, week in and week out, or sitting in cramped positions, the poor girl has slowly contracted some deranged condition of her organic system, which calls a halt in her progress and demands restoration to health before she can be of use to herself or any one else.

To this class of women and girls Mrs. Pinkham proffers both sympathy and aid. When these distressing weaknesses and derangements assail you, remember that there is a remedy for them all. We have on record thousands of such cases that have been absolutely and permanently cured by **Lydia E. Pinkham's Vegetable Compound**, restoring to vigorous health and lives of usefulness those who have been previously sorely distressed. Here is one of them.

Miss Junglas' First Letter.

"DEAR MRS. PINKHAM:—As I have heard and read so much about your wonderful medicine I thought I would write to you and tell you about my sickness. I have been sick for four years with womb trouble, have whites, sick headache, pain in my back, and in right and left side of abdomen, feeling of fullness in vagina, am dizzy, weak and nervous. I have used many patent medicines, but found very little relief. Please give me your advice."—Miss KATIE P. JUNGLAS, New Salem, Mich. (May 4th, 1898.)

MISS KATIE P. JUNGLAS

Miss Junglas' Second Letter.

"DEAR MRS. PINKHAM:—I write to thank you for the good **Lydia E. Pinkham's Vegetable Compound** and Sanative Wash have done me. It is now six years since I was taken sick. I had falling of the womb and ovarian trouble. I suffered untold pains, sometimes was so bad that I thought I could not live. I used the Vegetable Compound faithfully and am now well. If you like, you may use my letter for the benefit of others,"—Miss KATIE P. JUNGLAS, New Salem, Mich. (May 12th, 1900.)

$5000 REWARD

Owing to the fact that some skeptical people have from time to time questioned the genuineness of the testimonial letters we are constantly publishing, we have deposited with the National City Bank, of Lynn, Mass. $5,000, which will be paid to any person who will show that the above testimonial is not genuine, or was published before obtaining the writer's special permission.—LYDIA E. PINKHAM MEDICINE CO.

A Pinkham advertisement featuring a customer's claim that the company's vegetable compound had righted her prolapsed uterus

its annual volume for physicians containing carefully documented information about drugs. In 1917 the AMA tried to prevent the Bayer Company from renewing its patent on aspirin, which had given the company a monopoly on the manufacture and sale of acetylsalicylic acid in the United States. Partly as a result of the AMA disclosures, the Bayer patent was not renewed in 1917, and other drug companies were able to enter the aspirin market.

The Demise of the Patent Medicines. As public opinion shifted and the new laws gave physicians more authority, the patent medicine companies slowly gave in to the medical profession. The AMA's own regulatory system extended the federal effort to control drugs while also shifting drug purchasing from purely an individual choice to one contingent on the recommendation of the physician. The campaign against patent medicines continued to build the confidence and authority that the medical profession had begun to gain in the Progressive Era. But consumers would still need to wait for a further law, the Pure Food, Drug, and Cosmetic Act of 1938, to expand federal protection over many other harmful items.

Sources:

James Bordley III and A. McGehee Harvey, *Two Centuries of American Medicine, 1776–1976* (Philadelphia: W. B. Saunders, 1976);

James T. Patterson, *The Dread Disease. Cancer and Modern American Culture* (Cambridge, Mass.: Harvard University Press, 1987);

Paul Starr, *The Social Transformation of American Medicine* (New York: Basic Books, 1982).

THE REVOLUTION IN MEDICAL EDUCATION

Medical Education. Once it was easy to become a doctor. During the nineteenth century the United States saw the emergence of an estimated four hundred proprietary medical schools. Set up to offer medical degrees as part of profit-making ventures, these schools generally had low standards of instruction, poor facilities, and admitted anyone who could pay the tuition. Since the proprietary schools competed with so many other for-profit schools as well as schools affiliated with universities, they advertised incentives to get students for their programs. One school gave free trips to Europe upon graduation to any students who regularly paid fees in cash for three years. Anyone who had the money could get a medical degree and practice medicine. In many of the private proprietary schools, degrees were granted after one year of courses that consisted chiefly of listening to lectures.

Flexner's Tour. At the turn of the century some members of the medical profession were concerned that a great discrepancy had opened up between medical science and medical education. In 1904 the American Medical Association (AMA) contracted with the Carnegie Foundation for the Advancement of Teaching to undertake a comprehensive study of medical education. The Carnegie Foundation commissioned Abraham Flexner, the dean of Johns Hopkins University, to do a survey by visiting schools of medicine in the United States and Canada. Flexner spent over a year and a half visiting all the medical schools in the two countries and

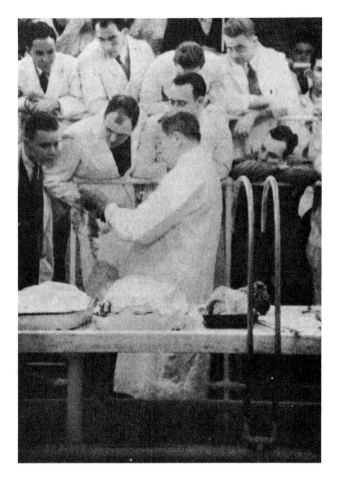

A surgeon exhibiting pathological specimens to Johns Hopkins University medical students

preparing his report. "Amusing incidents" were frequent. In Salem, Washington, Flexner asked the dean of the medical school whether the school possessed a physiological laboratory. "Surely," he replied. "I have it upstairs; I will bring it to you," and he fetched down a small sphygmograph — an instrument designed to register the movement of the pulse. When he toured an osteopathic school in Des Moines with the dean of the school, Flexner found that the doors labeled ANATOMY, PHYSIOLOGY, and PATHOLOGY were all locked. The janitor was not to be found. But Flexner waited until the dean was out of sight at the train station, returned to the school, found the janitor, and gave him five dollars to open the doors. Every room looked the same. There was a desk, a small blackboard, some chairs, and nothing more.

Evaluation. Published in 1910, Flexner's *Medical Education in the United States and Canada* rated 155 medical schools — 148 in the United States and 7 in Canada. Although he was a layman, Flexner was much more severe in his judgment of the medical schools than the AMA had been. Through careful detail and biting humor he demonstrated that the vast majority of medical schools provided little or no training in the basic sciences. Most were not linked to universities or hospitals, and many provided only apprenticeship training. Some were mere

diploma mills, trading credentials for cash. Medical training was inadequate and in many cases fraudulent. Only three medical schools — Harvard, Western Reserve, and Johns Hopkins — were given full approval; many other schools were characterized by Flexner as "plague spots," "utterly wretched," or "out-and-out commercial enterprises." He strongly recommended that medical schools have full-time faculty and extensive laboratory and hospital facilities. He urged that standards concerning the admission of students to medical schools be established and that medical education be conducted by universities on a graduate level. The best example of a modern medical school for Flexner was Johns Hopkins University, which included a medical school, a nursing school, and a university hospital. Johns Hopkins insisted on the bachelor's degree or its equivalent for admission as well as specific premedical college-level courses in the sciences.

Reform. As Flexner himself said, "such a rattling of dead bones has never been heard in this country before or since." Although widespread protests came from the affected schools, the Flexner Report brought about needed improvement in medical education. The better schools improved their programs, and many inferior schools collapsed thanks to bad publicity, financial problems, and their failure to meet the requirements of state licensing boards. A 1912 Flexner report on "Medical Education in Europe" promoted further reform when it implied that even the improved medical schools in the United States could not compare with their European models. In Europe clinical teaching was the backbone of medical education, but in the United States in 1912 students could still receive the degree of doctor of medicine by studying textbooks rather than the sick. By 1915, 39 percent of the 155 schools inspected had closed. By 1920, 45 percent had closed. In 1905 only five schools required college preparation, but by 1915 eighty-five schools required a college background. By 1925 all state boards mandated that candidates for a license examination be from an accredited medical college.

Great Strides Forward. Flexner's report led to the modern model of medical schools that was based on the organization and facilities of Johns Hopkins, Harvard, and German schools. Flexner made several proposals that set basic standards and were widely adopted. The curriculum and organization of the modern medical school largely resulted from demands pushed through state legislatures by the AMA:

1. Basic training must include two years of biological and physical sciences.

2. Clinical training must include two years of closely supervised experience in a hospital.

3. Medical schools should be affiliated with universities to take advantage of faculties in the sciences.

Dr. T. H. Weisenburg, a neurologist at the Philadelphia General Hospital, accumulated more than two miles of "cinematograph" film that recorded the actions and expressions of patients suffering from nervous disorders. In the 28 December 1912 *Journal of the American Medical Association* Dr. Weisenburg reported on his use of motion photography in studying nervous diseases and his use of the films in his medical school course on nervous diseases. In his classroom discussions of epilepsy, he first lectured on the disease and then showed the reel that contained the different types of epilepsy. His students had the advantage of seeing many more different types of epilepsy than Dr. Weisenburg thought they would see from their clinical experience. The films also provided a means of diagnosis, especially in the case of certain epileptic spasms where the actual movements were too swift to be detected by the naked eye but could be slowed up for recognition on the picture by reducing the speed of the film.

Source: "The Moving Picture in Medicine," *Literary Digest* (25 January 1913): 178.

4. Graduates of medical schools must pass a rigorous examination before being allowed to practice medicine.

The report called for emphasis on biological research with science at the base of medical education. Some schools filled its requirements; others were mere imitations; but all tried to follow it.

Consequences. There were obvious positive consequences of the changes in medical education. The education of physicians was upgraded; the latest scientific findings and theory were more effectively related to medical practitioners; and the number of physicians relative to the population was limited, causing competition for patients to decrease. But there were unexpected drawbacks as well. The poorest equipped and staffed schools were obviously the hardest hit by the new accreditation requirements. Many of these were the schools that had been training women and African American physicians at a time when discrimination prevented them from being admitted to mainstream schools. Many of these colleges were closed, since they could not afford the improvements necessary to meet the accreditation requirements. As a result, the proportion of women and minority physicians in medical practice remained relatively low throughout the remainder of the twentieth century. Other types of school closed by the new requirements was the part-time and night school. Students from poor backgrounds attended these schools and worked days while they attended part-time or at night. But with the closing

of such schools, medical education became an increasingly expensive and time-consuming process that required extensive financial support. As a consequence, the medical profession became increasingly dominated by members of the middle and upper classes. The Flexner Report, nevertheless, led to great strides forward in the quality of research and the quality of medical practice in the United States. Rarely has the work of one individual had such a major impact on a particular institution.

Sources:
James Bordley III and A. McGehee Harvey, *Two Centuries of American Medicine, 1776–1976* (Philadelphia: W. B. Saunders, 1976);

William C. Cockerham, *Medical Sociology* (Englewood Cliffs, N.J.: Prentice Hall, 1989);

John A. Denton, *Medical Sociology* (Boston: Houghton Mifflin, 1978);

Abraham Flexner, *Abraham Flexner: An Autobiography* (New York: Simon & Schuster, 1960);

Andrew C. Twaddle and Richard M. Hessler, *A Sociology of Health* (New York: Macmillan, 1987).

SURGERY

The New Surgery. The discoveries of anesthesia in 1846 and antiseptics in 1865 as well as the rapid expansion of radiology not only set the stage for further developments in established surgical procedures but also opened new fields for surgeons. Because of improved methods and technology, surgical procedures that a generation before had been contemplated with anxiety were viewed in 1910 as almost routine. By the beginning of World War I a surgical revolution established new directions for surgical practice, especially in the realm of neurosurgery, and by the war's end other new contributions to surgery had been made.

Cushing. Modern neurosurgery began in 1907 when Harvey Williams Cushing performed an operation for trigeminal neuralgia (tic douloureux) at Johns Hopkins. Cushing's main contribution to the field of neurosurgery was to develop precision techniques that steadily improved operative effectiveness. One of the main difficulties faced in early brain surgery was almost uncontrollable bleeding; because the texture of brain tissue differed from that of other body tissues, it was not possible to stop bleeding in the brain by already established methods. Cushing developed tiny silver clips for bleeding points in the brain to achieve bloodless operations. Always teaching his students to handle tumors and brain material with gentleness, he also reintroduced simple trephining, sometimes called palliative decompression, to relieve headache and other tumor-related symptoms. Cushing's surgical skill made it possible to save the lives of people who would have died in an earlier era. Through his career as a surgeon and a teacher of surgeons, Cushing established a new basis for brain surgery and defined the techniques for future developments.

World War I and Brain Surgery. In 1912 Cushing became professor of surgery at Harvard and the first surgeon-in-chief of the Peter Bent Brigham Hospital.

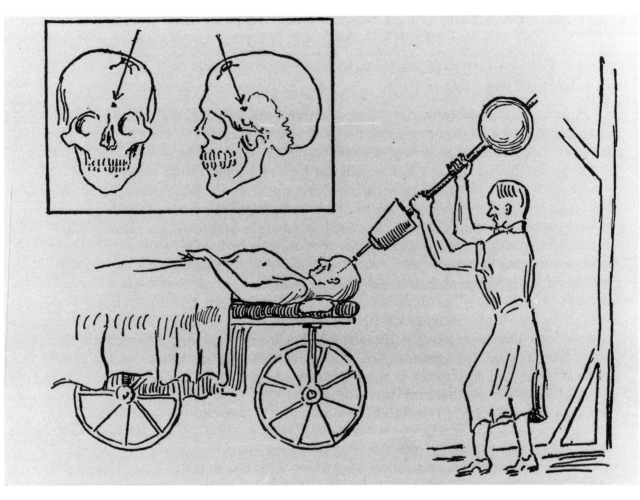

A diagram showing Harvey Williams Cushing's use of a magnet and a nail to remove shrapnel from the base of the brain during World War I

Early operations to remove brain tumors were discouraging, with many fatalities. But as Cushing gained experience and developed better methods for localization of tumors, he achieved a 90 percent reduction in the brain surgery mortality rate. By 1915 he had removed 130 tumors with 8 percent mortality. During World War I he put his extensive knowledge of the surgical treatment of brain injuries to work in France. In his war journals Cushing described his medical habits. When the wounded came pouring in, he would not permit himself to be rushed into giving up the slow, painstaking methods that were the mainstay of his success. Each time he operated on a wounded soldier, it was a personal matter between that patient and himself — the needs of war were to him insufficient reasons for abandoning the things he had fought for throughout his professional career. The greatest test of his inventive capabilities came one day when a man came in with a shell fragment at the base of his brain. Cushing tried to use a large magnet as well as different instruments and probes to extract the steel shrapnel, but with no success. Finally he inserted a nail with a rounded-off end down three and a half inches to the base of the brain, and the magnet was swung into

position. Slowly the nail was withdrawn, but there was nothing on it. Three times he tried it, carefully, slowly, but each time without success. Cushing was about ready to give up, but after he took his gloves off, he decided to try once more. After he gloved up, again the magnet was swung into position, and this time when the nail was withdrawn, there was a small fragment of rough steel on its tip.

Reconstructive Surgery. Until World War I the techniques of plastic surgery were so primitive that such surgery was rarely performed. With the advances made in general surgery and the control of sepsis, however, men were surviving their wounds with features and limbs so shattered and distorted that a return to ordinary life was almost impossible. The need to repair such injuries became a necessity. British and French surgeons led the field, their teams composed of dental surgeons, artists, and physicians skilled in skin and bone grafting. In 1915 New York surgeon F. H. Albee introduced the important reconstructive technique later known as Albee's graft, which he had originally designed for the repair of damage caused to the vertebrae by tuberculosis. Medical personnel returning from the war told of the wonderful results achieved in reconstructive surgery by the surgeons of the American and other Allied armies. One Red Cross worker described a man who had come into the American Red Cross Hospital in Neuilly, France, with the greater part of his face intact but with no nose:

> It had been shot off completely, she said, leaving his flesh flat from chin to forehead. We made him a nose to fit him. From the place where his nose had joined to his forehead there hung a little wisp of skin. This was pulled down, stretched every day, and kept dry and healthy by an antiseptic powder. Finally it grew to the correct length for a nose. Then we opened his wrist and grafted a piece of bone to the place where his nose should have been, binding arm and face together until the operation was completed. Then we adjusted the skin, which filled out with healthy flesh, and there was a new nose!

Urology. Another field that witnessed important advances in the 1910s was urology, the branch of medicine that deals with the diagnosis and treatment of diseases of the urinary tract and urogenital system. Hugh H. Young, a Johns Hopkins surgeon, won international fame for his perineal prostatectomy technique, first performed in 1896. He also invented the "punch operation" for removal of tumors of the small median lobe of the prostate. In 1912 he performed this surgery with such success on a wealthy patient, "Diamond Jim" Brady, that the grateful patient provided the funds to construct and partially endow the James Buchanan Brady Urological Institute, a separate unit of the Johns Hopkins Hospital. In 1917 Young founded the *Journal of Urology.* He continued to train many of the outstanding urologists in the United States in his institute and remained a leader in the field until his death in 1945.

Surgery at the Mayo Clinic. The Mayo Clinic in Rochester, Minnesota, was one of the most famous surgical clinics in the country. By the end of World War I the facilities and achievements of the Mayo Clinic were admired throughout the country and the rest of the world. Its corridors featured a system of colored lights that showed the whereabouts of the senior doctors. Outside the six operating theaters, where up to forty major operations could be performed in a morning, were illuminated signals showing the nature of the operation in progress. Visitors were able to observe without creating a disturbance. The clinic was laid out so that all necessary specialties were close at hand. For example, a pathology laboratory adjoined the theaters; the urology department was next to an X-ray room. The two founding Mayo brothers were brilliant surgeons who traveled throughout the world, watching surgeons at work in distant countries and bringing back to the clinic the best they had seen. Charles Mayo specialized on the abdomen, breast, thryoid, and prostate; and William J. Mayo was interested in the intestines and urinary tract. It was a smooth functioning clinic where all facilities were available, whatever the need of the patient, and was a model for others throughout the country.

Sources:

James Bordley III and A. McGehee Harvey, *Two Centuries of American Medicine, 1776–1976* (Philadelphia: W. B. Saunders, 1976);

"Broken Men Remade by Army Doctors," in *Medicine and Health Care,* edited by Saul Jarcho and Gene Brown (New York: Arno, 1977), p. 84;

Frederick F. Cartwright, *The Development of Modern Surgery from 1830* (New York: Crowell, 1967);

John F. Fulton, *Harvey Cushing, A Biography* (Springfield, Ill.: Charles C. Thomas, 1946);

Robert G. Richardson, *Surgery: Old and New Frontiers* (New York: Scribners, 1968);

Elizabeth H. Thomson, *Harvey Cushing, Surgeon, Author, Artist* (New York: Collier, 1961).

TECHNOLOGICAL AND MEDICAL RESEARCH ADVANCES

The Artificial Kidney. Among the milestones in medical technology in the 1910s was the first successful application of renal dialysis to living animals in 1913. Three physicians from Johns Hopkins University — John J. Abel, Leonard G. Rowntree, and B. B. Turner — devised an apparatus to pass all the blood out of the body of a living dog through a branching network of collodion tubes immersed in a bath. They "cleansed" the blood by rinsing out toxic amounts of acetylsalicylic acid (aspirin) while the blood was outside the body and restored the blood to the body without danger to the animal's life. The device was so similar in its action to the function of the kidney that the three physicians referred to it as the "artificial kidney." While the doctors did not apply their dialysis method to humans, they predicted that an artificial kidney would one day be used to treat acute renal failure in human beings. One of the problems the doctors had to solve in their experiment was preventing the blood from clotting while it flowed through the artificial vessels. Leeches were known to secrete an anticlotting factor as they sucked blood, so Abel ground up the heads of thousands of leeches to use their anticoagulant properties in order to keep the dog's blood from clotting in the collodion tubing. Before the technique could be used on humans, researchers would need to find a more readily available anticoagulant and a more convenient and plentiful material for making the permeable membrane. While the work of Dr. William H. Howell in Baltimore led to the discovery of the anticoagulant heparin in 1916, it would yet be decades before suitable semipermeable membranes were made from cellophane.

Contrast Radiography. Many new surgical procedures depended upon the use of contrast radiography. Neurosurgeons, for example, had been handicapped by their inability to localize many brain tumors. William Stewart Halsted, a Johns Hopkins surgeon, indirectly suggested the method that would lead to nearly every tumor being properly located. He frequently remarked on the way bubbles of gas in the intestines would stand out as negative shadows in X-ray pictures of the abdomen, and his comments impressed Walter E. Dandy, a neurosurgeon at Johns Hopkins who had worked under Harvey Cush-

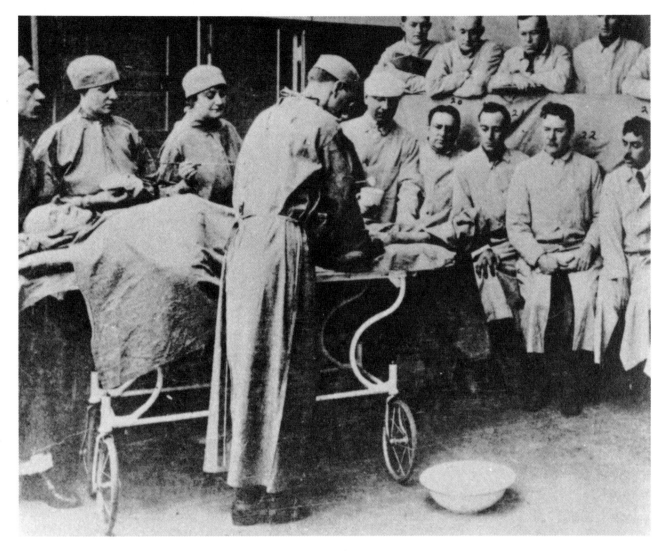

Alexis Carrel demonstrating his surgical techniques at the Rockefeller Institute for Medical Research, January 1918

ing. Dandy reasoned that if intestinal gas showed in X-rays, it should be possible to outline the ventricles of the brain by the injection of air. He did this in 1918 with satisfactory results and so created the method of pneumoventriculography or pneumoencephalography. When air was injected into the brain, X rays would clearly reveal the shape of a brain tumor or other space-occupying lesions. After its introduction the technique was widely adopted by brain surgeons and neurologists.

Electrocardiography. Americans made important contributions to the developing field of electrocardiography in the 1910s. The electrocardiogram (EKG) records the sequence of electrical events that goes with each cycle of cardiac contraction. The contraction of the muscles of the heart is stimulated by a tiny electrical current, originating in the neuromuscular tissue near the base of the heart and passing to the atria and the ventricles. When the current reaches the muscle cells, it causes them to contract. The first European-invented EKG apparatuses

were heavy and clumsy and took up a great deal of laboratory space. While early clinical work using EKGs focused on obvious abnormalities in cardiac rhythm, American contributions to electrocardiography began in 1909 after attention had shifted to the conduction system within the heart. The first American-designed electrocardiograph was created by Alfred Cohn and Horatio B. Williams and installed at the Rockefeller Hospital in New York in March 1911. This apparatus was so well made that it continued in operation for the next thirty-two years. During the decade EKGs were used to study atrial fibrillation — the rapid twitching movements that could replace the normal rhythmic contraction of the heart, causing a weak circulation and pulse and sometimes leading to complete heart blocks. In 1919 James Bryan Herrick published the first electrocardiogram of myocardial infarction — the death of part of the heart's left ventricle from a deficiency in the heart's blood supply — and suggested that the EKG might be useful in the diagnosis of these myocardial infarcts or heart attacks.

Orthopedics. Although orthopedics had its most significant development in Europe, American orthopedic surgeons by the 1910s were well established and had done some original work. Initially New York and Boston were the most important centers. Between 1911 and 1915 in New York, Fred H. Albee did important work on bone transplantation and the use of bone grafts in treating Pott's disease, fractures, and deformities. In New England, Edward H. Bradford, Robert W. Lavell, and James W. Sever promoted the treatment of scoliosis, or spinal curvature, by plaster jackets. E. G. Abbott of Portland, Maine, also treated this lateral curvature of the spine by applying jackets.

Radium Therapy. While Europeans experimented with radium therapy in the early years of the twentieth century, work lagged in the United States because the country lacked an adequate supply of radium. In 1913 large-scale trials of radium therapy began in Baltimore when Howard A. Kelly, a professor of gynecology at Johns Hopkins, acquired a supply of radium and began to use it for the treatment of cervical and vaginal carcinoma in his small private hospital. In June 1915 he reported that there had been at least a temporary regression of the cancer in some of his patients. Work continued throughout the decade at other research centers, including Harvard University and the Memorial Hospital in New York City. These researchers reported that their results varied widely with the type of cancer treated. Good results were secured with cancer of the skin and the cervix, but cancer of the pharynx resisted successful treatment. Better methods were developed during the decade for measuring the amount of radiation so that the results of treatment could be related to the dosage. Scientists at the Memorial Hospital concluded that the tissues of malignant tumors were more susceptible to radiation than were normal tissues.

Tissue Culture. Alexis Carrel was a French surgeon who had immigrated to New York in 1905 to work at the Rockefeller Institute. In 1912 he received the first Nobel Prize in medicine given to an American in recognition of his work on the suturing together of blood vessels and the transplantation of blood vessels and organs. The development of this technique laid the foundation for vascular surgery, heart surgery, and the transplantation of organs. In the course of his surgical work on the healing of wounds, Carrel became curious about how cells of the skin, connective tissue, blood vessels, and nerves grew out to fill the gaps and close the wounds created by disease, injury, or surgery. His work and that of others in grafting tissues and transplanting organs gave him hope that future surgeons might learn to keep human tissues alive in storage and possibly even to grow them as replacements for damaged elements of the body. His methods of growing cells in "bottles" soon attracted public attention. To convince skeptics of the potential of his tissue culture method, and to prove that these tissues could even long outlive the animal from which they originated, Carrel decided to keep alive cells from the heart of an embryonic chick by transplanting them every two or three days to a fresh nutrient medium. His famous culture was started on 17 January 1912. By May 1914 it had been transplanted 358 times, and the press followed his reports with avid interest. The chicken heart culture even outlived its scientific maker: the cells continued to be kept alive and growing until 26 April 1946, two years after Carrel's death and thirty-four years after the tissue was taken from the chick embryo. In addition to this demonstration of the relative ease with which one could cultivate the tissues of warm-blooded animals, Carrel's most important contributions were the introduction of strict surgical asepsis in the handling of the tissues and the perfection of the instrumentation for tissue culture, including a specialized flask that bears his name.

X Rays. In 1895 Professor William Conrad Roentgen made an accidental discovery in his laboratory at the Physical Institute of the University of Wurzburg, Germany, that would revolutionize medicine. He observed that barium platinocyanide crystals across the room fluoresced whenever he turned on a Crooke's, or cathode-ray discharge, tube. He correctly hypothesized that a previously unknown form of radiation of very short wavelength was involved and christened them X Rays. Within a few weeks of the news scientists in the United States were producing X rays and carrying out experiments with them, and it was not long before some of their injurious effects, such as X-ray burns and cancer-producing overexposures, came to light. By the end of the first decade of the twentieth century, however, radiology was becoming recognized as a medical specialty, and X rays were being used for therapy and diagnosis. Radiologists improved their diagnoses by checking their X-ray pictures and fluoroscopic findings against the results of operations and autopsies. A great advance in radiology occurred when the first efficient tube was developed in 1913 by William David Coolidge at the Massachusetts Institute of Technology. One form of X-ray tube is still called a Coolidge tube. The old gas tubes had conventional cathodes plus hot filaments to supply electrons, but the cathode in Coolidge's tube was itself the electron-emitting tungsten filament. The Coolidge tube made possible more accurate adjustment, better stability and flexibility, the exact reproduction of results, and higher output. During the war Coolidge's improved tubes were shipped from General Electric in Schenectady, New York, to the battlefields of France. The need for X rays in the treatment of the wounded led army training schools to turn out additional radiologists and technicians. Physicians returned to civilian practice after the war more aware of the value of this diagnostic technique and the other medical technologies that had developed during the decade.

Sources:

James Bordley III and A. McGehee Harvey, *Two Centuries of American Medicine, 1776–1976* (Philadelphia: W. B. Saunders, 1976);

"New Aid to Surgery in Carrel Discovery," in *Medicine and Health Care*, edited by Saul Jarcho and Gene Brown (New York: Arno, 1977): 81–82;

Robert G. Richardson, *Surgery: Old and New Frontiers* (New York: Scribners, 1968);

Van Buren Thorne, "Machine Purifies Blood and Restores it to the Body," in *Medicine and Health Care*, edited by Saul Jarcho and Gene Brown (New York: Arno, 1977): 23–26.

THE WAR ON TUBERCULOSIS

Contagious Killer. Tuberculosis, also known as consumption and "the Great White Plague," was a thoroughly democratic disease. The poor were especially susceptible, but the rich and famous could not escape its ravages. Tuberculosis is a highly contagious, bacteria-borne illness. Its victims inhale a droplet of liquid or speck of dust bearing a few virulent tubercle bacilli. When these organisms succeed in entering one of the tiny air sacs in the lung, they are in an ideal breeding ground. Within a few weeks the tubercle bacilli spread, first to the lymph nodes and then into the bloodstream and throughout the body. Most of the time the body's white blood cells can fight off the infection, but in 10 to 15 percent of the cases the disease gradually begins to dissolve the lung tissue, and symptoms such as coughing begin to occur. The severely infected cough up bright red blood, show a daily fever, lose weight, and tire easily. If the disease remains untreated, it often leads to death. At the end of the nineteenth century tuberculosis accounted for a seventh of all deaths, and in the 1910s it continued to cause more deaths than any other contagious disease.

Treatment. By 1910 enough scientific information had been collected to describe completely how the bacterial disease affected the lungs and other tissues. But scientific research had not and would not yield a cure during the decade. The contagious nature of tuberculosis led to the isolation of tubercular patients, under conditions as pleasant as possible, from the general population. This rest cure gave rise to the sanatorium culture familiar to Americans of the 1910s, and sanatoriums were constructed across the country, reaching their peak on the eve of World War I. Patients rested, read, slept, ate wholesome meals, and gazed out at the scenery. A frequent component of their sanatorium stay was artificial pneumothorax, a surgical procedure invented in Italy and officially endorsed by the International Congress of Tuberculosis at Rome in 1912. If the lung rested, proponents argued, it could more readily recover from the disease. Artificial pneumothorax was an invasive method designed to help the lung rest. Nitrogen was injected between the ribs into the chest cavity, causing one lung to collapse and be momentarily inactive. It was hoped that healing would occur while the other lung carried on the work of respiration. The procedure was never adequately evaluated. Some of the

DARKEST CINCINNATI

In the popular view consumption was a disease of a victim's surroundings; many blamed the crowds and bad air of poverty-stricken areas in cities. Health crusaders attacked social conditions as well as the disease. In 1913 the Cincinnati Anti-Tuberculosis League produced a movie, *Darkest Cincinnati*, with graphic scenes of misery and unambiguous commentary about its causes.

In one scene the narrator describes "A Sunday view of a court in this neighborhood. Filth and garbage from end to end. The stench is awful. Note the little girls carrying babies in their arms over piles of rotten garbage. Nearly all the property around this court belongs to one man." The film portrayed the landlord as a villain increasing his income at the expense of human life and promoted the cause of the Anti-Tuberculosis League to large and enthusiastic crowds at every showing.

In a later scene the narrator comments on a child sitting on her front step sobbing: "And now we come to the other side of the picture where the hand of the good people through its agents is extended to distress caused by these conditions. Poor little Marie with a rose in her hand waiting for the nurse's call on mamma. How her face brightens when she sees the nurse from the Anti-Tuberculosis League."

Source: Mark Caldwell, *The Last Crusade. The War on Consumption, 1862–1954* (New York: Atheneum, 1988), pp. 34–35.

12 to 15 percent of the patients who apparently benefited may have recovered anyway.

The Antituberculosis Movement. The sanatorium movement was aided by a vigorous public campaign against consumption. The use of the tuberculin test, introduced around 1890 and refined in 1907, showed that latent tuberculosis infection was widespread. Many people were infected but not ill, indicating that strengthening resistance by improving nutrition, housing, and working conditions might help to prevent infection. Physicians and interested laymen organized themselves in the first voluntary association in 1892, the Pennsylvania Society for the Prevention of Tuberculosis. The national press publicized the cause, and voluntary antituberculosis associations began forming across the country. On 6 June 1904 the National Association for the Study and Prevention of Tuberculosis met for the first time in Atlantic City. In the absence of any firm treatment beyond rest and pneumothorax, the emphasis was on hygiene. The antituberculosis

Tubercular children meeting in an outdoor classroom

movement of the 1910s was concerned with social and environmental improvements as well.

Health and Politics. The 1915 pamphlet *A War on Consumption,* published by the Metropolitan Life Insurance Company, illustrated all the popular understandings of the disease. Hygeia, her flowing robe bearing the double-barred cross of the National Tuberculosis Association, led the masses from the smoke-shrouded landscape of the city into a sunlit meadow, shaded by flowering trees. Hygeia's white banner bore the symbol of the Metropolitan Life Insurance Company as a reminder to the reader that although fresh air and sunlight could help in the battle against tuberculosis, it was the benevolent corporation that was the shining light in the crusade. By the eve of the World War I, tuberculosis was a national obsession, and every state and territory had its own tuberculosis society by 1917. The public concern aroused by the National Tuberculosis Association and other individuals and organizations contributed to a steady decline in tuberculosis mortality from 150 per 100,000 in 1910 to 120 per 100,000 in 1920. Another contributing factor in this decline was the widespread care in the four hundred private sanatoriums and state and municipal tuberculosis hospitals that existed by 1910. These provided medical supervision and at the same time removed the patient from contact with other individuals whom he might infect. Death rates from tuberculosis would continue their steady decline as other medical procedures and treatments came into use, culminating in the 1940s with the discovery of effective antibiotic treatments that brought the sanatorium movement to a close.

Sources:

Barbara Bates, *Bargaining for Life: A Social History of Tuberculosis, 1876–1938* (Philadelphia: University of Pennsylvania Press, 1992);

James Bordley III and A. McGehee Harvey, *Two Centuries of American Medicine, 1776–1976* (Philadelphia: W. B. Saunders, 1976);

Mark Caldwell, *The Last Crusade. The War on Consumption: 1862–1954* (New York: Atheneum, 1988);

Paul Starr, *The Social Transformation of American Medicine* (New York: Basic Books, 1982).

WHAT COULD WE DO ABOUT CANCER IN 1913?

Educating the Public. By 1910 advances in public health began to bring many deadly communicable diseases under control. But it would be the chronic illnesses such as heart disease and cancer that would pose the most alarming and challenging medical problems of the century. Cancer was a mysterious and feared disease, but as the professional standing of physicians rose, they began to define cancer as a problem solvable by medical management. In May 1913 the *Ladies' Home Journal* published an article titled "What Can We Do About Cancer? The Most Vital and Insistent Question in the Medical World," by Samuel Hopkins Adams, famous from the preceding decade for his work against medical fraud and patent medicines. This was the first publication about cancer aimed at the general public, and it reflected the level of knowledge about the disease at that time. When Adams asked a group of specialists, "What causes cancer?" everyone made the same reply: "I do not know." But when he asked, "What is to be done about it?" the answer was again unanimous: "Educate the people save themselves." For Americans in the 1910s cancer had risen to the fifth or sixth leading cause of death and in some areas was as high as third, surpassed in the number of its victims only by tuberculosis and pneumonia. According to Dr. Thomas S. Cullen, the chairman of the Cancer

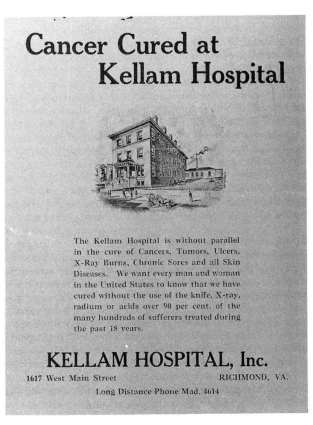

Cancer Cured at Kellam Hospital

The Kellam Hospital is without parallel in the cure of Cancers, Tumors, Ulcers, X-Ray Burns, Chronic Sores and all Skin Diseases. We want every man and woman in the United States to know that we have cured without the use of the knife, X-ray, radium or acids over 90 per cent. of the many hundreds of sufferers treated during the past 18 years.

KELLAM HOSPITAL, Inc.

1617 West Main Street   RICHMOND, VA.

Long Distance Phone Mad. 4614

While the medical establishment promoted early surgery as the cure for cancer, institutions such as the Kellam Hospital continued to promote less invasive treatments.

Campaign Committee of the Congress of Surgeons of North America, cancer was in its early stages a "local process" and not a blood disease. When the cancer was still small, the surgeon could totally remove it and "with one-fourth the amount of labor, accomplish ten times the amount of good." The task, as Adams framed it, was to educate the public:

No cancer is hopeless when discovered early. Most cancer, discovered early, is curable. The only cure is the knife. Medicines are worse than useless. Delay is more than dangerous; it is deadly. With recognition of and prompt action upon early symptoms, the death rate can be cut down at least a half, probably more. The fatalism which says "If it's cancer I might as well give up" is foolish, cowardly and suicidal.

The Nature of Cancer. Some scientists believed cancer was caused by a germ. Others believed it could be attributed to diet or the environment or heredity. But there was no proof. All that was really known in 1913 was that for some inexplicable reason one of the many cells of the human body got out of its proper place and lodged among the cells of another kind, where it multiplied abnormally, destroying the structures around it and forming a malignant tumor. The growing tumor spread through the lymphatic glands until death inevitably resulted. Irritation, the medical profession erroneously suggested, started the trouble by weakening the tissues and leaving them unable

to resist the onslaught of the invading cell. It was falsely claimed that no skin cancer ever developed except at a spot where there was some previous and persistent irritation. As proof, they pointed out that men who smoked clay pipes were peculiarly liable to cancer of the lip. This form of lip cancer was rare in women, unless the woman was a smoker. Cancer of the tongue was said to develop from the slight chafing of a jagged tooth, suggesting that a visit to the dentist could well be a life-saving measure. By analogy, doctors inferred that internal cancers developed only after some prolonged irritation and warned that no irritation internal or external, should be permitted to last for a long time. Today, physicians consider a sore that does not heal to be a warning sign of cancer.

Signs of Cancer. Since early detection and surgery were thought to be the keys to survival, cancer victims had to be suspicious enough to realize they needed expert advice. The danger signs were weight loss and weakness, an abnormal growth, a persistent irritation, or a suspicious discharge. Breast self-examination was recommended for women as "simply a matter of laying the hand flat upon the surface and pressing firmly in upon the chest." To wait for the occurrence of pain was "the gravest of errors. Pain is a late symptom in cancer. It may come only when the damage is beyond repair."

Postsurgical Survival Rates. The most common cancer for both men and women was cancer of the stomach. In their parents' generation stomach cancer was inoperable, but victims of 1913 could be reassured that their surgeon knew his business better. He no longer had to be afraid to cut out enough of the cancer for fear that the small portion of the stomach left could not function. Although only a third of these surgical patients survived, Adams again warned that many of those who died came to the operating table in the late stages of the disease, "when there is perhaps only one chance in a hundred." For women, breast cancer was the most likely cancer after stomach cancer, followed by cancer of the uterus. In its very early stages the survival rate after surgery for breast cancer was 50 to 75 percent. Surgeons removed the lump, and if a microscopic examination determined it to be cancerous, the entire breast was removed while the woman was still under anesthesia. Surgery survival rates for uterine cancer were lower. A woman had only a 25 percent chance of surviving if a tumor was removed from the womb, but the survival rate increased to 70 percent if the entire uterus was removed. Carcinoma of the lip was the most curable, because it was the most obviously seen and therefore easiest to excise at an early stage. More than 90 percent survived. Half of intestinal cancer victims survived after surgery. Surgery in 1913 was much less painful than it had been ten years earlier. Readers were assured the pain following the operation was negligible compared to the slow and gnawing agony of the cancer itself.

Three 1913 Truths about Cancer. There were, said Adams, three general truths always to remember about

CHEMOTHERAPY AND WORLD WAR I

Ironically, the mustard gas attacks of World War I led to the use of chemotherapy for cancer. When autopsies were performed on mustard gas victims, pathologists noted that their lymph glands were destroyed and their bone marrow wiped out. Because bone marrow makes white and red cells for the blood, there were few white cells remaining. Around 1930 James Ewing, a cancer specialist at New York's Memorial Hospital, suggested to colleagues that they try mustard gas on various cancers. It was too toxic for internal use, but it did work on skin cancer.

Source: Edward Shorter, *The Health Century* (New York: Doubleday, 1987), p. 184.

cancer: "First, cancer usually develops from previous and continued irritation. Second, if the cause of that irritation be removed in time the cancer will be averted. Third, if the development of cancer be determined in the early stages the patient can probably be cured by operation, but not by any other method." Remember, Adams told his readers, the words of Dr. Charles H. Mayo, one of the greatest surgeons in America: "The risk is not in surgery, but in *delayed* surgery." In 1913 the only solutions to cancer were the patient's self-awareness and the surgeon's knife.

Current Thinking on Cancer. Cancer is not one single disease but more than one hundred different diseases with a common outcome: abnormal cellular growth that can spread throughout the body, invading and destroying normal organs and tissues. Scientists have identified several causes of cancer, including certain chemicals, viruses, and some rare, genetically determined cancers. There are three effective forms of treatment: surgical removal of the cancer, X ray and other controlled forms of radiation treatment, and chemotherapy. Cure rates vary according to the different types of cancer. As in 1913, the outlook is much more favorable if the tumor is removed or treated while still localized. Physicians consider a cancer "cured" if a patient survives at least five years after treatment without recurrence of the disease. The percentage of cancer patients who survive five years after diagnosis is about 49 percent. Cancer has become a leading cause of death in the United States, second only to heart disease.

Sources:
Samuel Hopkins Adams, "What Can We Do About Cancer? The Most Vital and Insistent Question in the Medical World," *Ladies' Home Journal,* 30 (May 1913): 21–22;

James T. Patterson, *The Dread Disease. Cancer and Modern American Culture* (Cambridge, Mass.: Harvard University Press, 1987).

HEADLINE MAKERS

JOSEPH B. GOLDBERGER

1874-1929

THE PELLAGRA DETECTIVE

The Microbe Hunter. Joseph Goldberger was a Hungarian who immigrated to the United States with his family at the age of seven. They lived in the East Side of Manhattan and ran a grocery store where Joseph worked as a delivery boy. A bright student, he entered the City College of New York at age sixteen. Goldberger first planned to become a civil engineer, but two years after he dropped in on a lecture at Bellevue Hospital Medical College, he changed his mind and decided to become a doctor. After graduating from Bellevue Hospital Medical College in 1895, he had a private practice until he joined the United States Public Health Service in 1899. For the next fourteen years he was a microbe hunter, fighting yellow fever, dengue fever, typhus, and typhoid in the United States and Mexico. His most important battle, however, remained ahead.

A Mysterious Malady. The disease pellagra was first described in the United States during the Civil War and was probably one of the causes of the high death rate in the Southern prison camps. Pellagra is characterized by an extreme form of dermatitis, digestive disorders that include diarrhea, and nervous and mental abnormalities. Between 1909 and 1913 two surveys confirmed that pellagra was widespread in the South and also seemed to support the view that the disease was infectious. The United States Public Health Service decided to investigate the disease, and in 1914 the surgeon general selected Goldberger to take charge.

Investigating Pellagra. Goldberger investigated pellagra at two orphanages in Mississippi. In each orphanage more than half of the children had pellagra in spite of a diet that was nutritious by the standards of that day. Goldberger decided that the disease could not be infectious: the adult attendants did not have pellagra; not all of the children had the disease; and there was no evidence of

transmission from the affected to the healthy even though they lived closely together. He noted that the disease affected mostly children over three years old and saw that their diet was deficient in meat and other protein foods. Children under three in the institutions received milk, but the older ones did not. The healthy adult attendants received meat as part of their diet. Goldberger got funds from the Public Health Service, fed the children milk and meat, and in the next few months pellagra disappeared.

The Disease Detective. To determine that the cause of pellagra was dietary and not infectious, Goldberger observed carefully who in a community had the disease and who did not, and then he tried to see how the two groups differed. In the field he was tireless. Nearly every night he went to a different community and quizzed the local doctors or asylum supervisors. He asked people what they ate and whether their privies were screened (in case pellagra did turn out to be a contagious malady spread by flies). In 1915 he selected two groups of patients for study in a state sanatorium in Georgia where pellagra was frequently found. Both groups were kept under similar conditions, but one group continued to receive the regular institutional diet while the other group was given a diet higher in protein. Pellagra did not occur in the group receiving the supplement. Goldberger and his associates attempted unsuccessfully to transmit pellagra to volunteers with bodily materials obtained from patients who had the disease, but they could discover no risk factor other than diet.

The Deficiency Disease. Later work by other scientists would show that pellagra developed from a lack of the B vitamin niacin or the body's own synthesis of it from the amino acid tryptophan. Poor people in the South were always heavy cornbread eaters, but in normal times they got their niacin and tryptophan requirements from meat, milk, and vegetables. As pre–World War I economic circumstances brought hardship on southern workers, a diet lacking these essentials became the norm on southern tables and brought about the appearance of an epidemic. As a result of Goldberger's work thousands of lives were saved, and pellagra eventually vanished from the South.

Sources:

James Bordley III and A. McGehee Harvey, *Two Centuries of American Medicine, 1776–1976* (Philadelphia: W. B. Saunders, 1976);

Edward Shorter, *The Health Century* (New York: Doubleday, 1987).

EDWARD CALVIN KENDALL

1886-1972

HORMONE HUNTER

Research Chemist. Edward C. Kendall was born on 8 March 1886 in South Norwalk, Connecticut, the third of eight children. He received his Ph.D. in chemistry from Columbia University in 1910 and then worked for a year as a research chemist for Parke, Davis and Company in Detroit, where he took on the task of extracting the thyroid hormone from the thyroid gland. Hormones are natural secretions of the endocrine glands that serve as the chemical messengers of the body; they are potent substances that activate, coordinate, and regulate the phenomena of life. Although scientists had theorized that the thyroid gland must produce some substance that was directly delivered into the blood, no one had yet succeeded in isolating and chemically identifying the thyroid hormone.

Mayo Biochemist. Unhappy with his experience in a commercial laboratory, Kendall accepted an offer to set up a new biochemical laboratory at Saint Luke's Hospital, New York, where he continued his work on the thyroid. At Saint Luke's, Kendall found the closer association with physicians and patients that he felt was necessary for his research on medical problems. He suffered a setback when Saint Luke's Hospital ran out of funds for his research. In 1914 he wrote to Louis B. Wilson, the chief of the Laboratory Division of the Mayo Clinic, and was offered a position as biochemist at the Mayo Clinic, where he found that several members of the medical staff were intensely interested in thyroid disease. Surgery was then a well-established treatment for the goiters produced by hyperthyroidism, or Graves' disease.

The Discovery of Thyroxin. From the work of Eulgen Baumann, a German scientist, Kendall was aware that a unique feature of thyroid tissue was its high iodine content, and he knew the thyroid hormone would contain iodine. Less than a year after renewing his work at the Mayo Clinic, Kendall succeeded in isolating the pure crystalline thyroid hormone, containing 65 percent iodine, to which the name *thyroxin* was given. His discovery was made by a fortunate accident. After preparing an extract of thyroid tissue in ethanol, he inadvertently left it in his laboratory for several hours while the ethanol evaporated, leaving a pure crystalline form of thyroid hormone. He reported his accomplishment in May 1915 at a meeting of the Association of American Physicians.

Nobel Prize Winner. Kendall would go on to become a world-renowned hormone chemist at the Mayo Clinic.

His work with Dr. Philip S. Hench on the "Compound E" hormone, which they renamed cortisone, enabled rheumatoid arthritis cripples to walk again and would win them the Nobel Prize for physiology or medicine in 1950.

Sources:

James Bordley III and A. McGehee Harvey, *Two Centuries of American Medicine, 1776–1976* (Philadelphia: W. B. Saunders, 1976);

Tyler Wasson, ed., *Nobel Prize Winners* (New York: Wilson, 1987).

WILLIAM JAMES MAYO AND CHARLES HORACE MAYO

1861-1939; 1865-1939

FOUNDERS OF THE MAYO CLINIC

A New Way of Practicing Medicine. Brothers and outstanding surgeons, William James Mayo and Charles Horace Mayo along with their father, William Worrall Mayo (1819–1911), founded the world-famous Mayo Clinic in Rochester, Minnesota, one of the nation's first efforts at practicing medicine through group practice. The clinic began as part of Saint Mary's Hospital, which was opened in 1889 by the Sisters of Saint Francis with the help of the William Worrall Mayo, who had immigrated to the United States from England in 1845 and settled in Rochester as a country doctor. The three Mayos named their part of Saint Mary's the Mayo Clinic in 1903. Although the Mayo Clinic began as a surgical clinic, it became a full medical center in 1915 when the clinic's facilities were expanded, and the brothers began to attract other renowned physicians from all over the world. At that time they also founded the Mayo Foundation for Medical Education and Research as part of the University of Minnesota.

Boyhood Apprenticeships. William James Mayo was born in Le Sueur, Minnesota, on 29 June 1861. His brother, Charles Horace, was born four years later on 19 July 1865. Both brothers' training for the medical profession began in their boyhoods. Their father took his two sons with him on professional visits, explaining his diagnoses and methods of treatment and encouraging them to express their opinions freely. The brothers assisted their father in his surgical operations, anatomical dissections, and postmortems. Their father also directed their premedical reading and study and gave them instruction in chemistry, osteology, anatomy, and laboratory techniques. William graduated from the University of Michigan medical school in 1883 and also took medical degrees at the New York Post-Graduate Medical School and Hospital in 1884 and at the New York Polyclinic in 1885. He joined his family in practice at Rochester, as did Charles after his graduation from the Chicago Medical School in 1888.

Joint Service. William recalled, "From the very beginning Charlie and I always went together. We were known as the Mayo boys. Anyone that picked on one of us had the two to contend with." William was quiet and reserved, and Charles was lively and sociable, with a gift for anecdote and a penchant for practical jokes. Professionally they were known fondly as "Dr. Will" and "Dr. Charlie." When the Committee of American Physicians for Medical Preparedness was organized in 1916 as a step in the Wilson administration's "preparedness for peace," William was named its chairman and Charles one of its members. When the committee became the General Medical Board of the Council for National Defense, William was made a member of its executive committee and Charles his alternate. William Mayo was commissioned as a first lieutenant in the medical reserve corps in 1912. He was called to active duty and commissioned a major when the United States entered the war. He later was promoted to colonel. During the war he was chief surgical consultant for the surgical services of the U.S. Army in the office of the army's surgeon general. Charles was also a colonel in the army medical corps and alternated with William as the associate chief consultant for all surgical services of the U.S. Army. The two brothers divided their time between the Mayo Clinic in Rochester and their duties in Washington so that one of them might always be on duty in Rochester. The strain of their war service, added to the additional effort of keeping the Mayo Clinic going, took its toll on the health of both men. Charles contracted pneumonia during one of his turns in Washington, and William came down with a severe case of jaundice in the fall of 1918 that kept him off duty for more than two months. In William's absence Charles filled his post in Washington, making this the first time that the brothers were both absent from the clinic for any extended period.

The Mayo Clinic during the War. During World War I the Mayo Clinic was kept busy with draftees to examine and a war training school to run for incoming members of the medical corps. William and Charles designed short courses to bring doctors-up-to-date on the latest developments in scientific medicine and surgery. Before the war the United States was almost wholly dependent on Germany for medical equipment and materials, and when the German supply was cut off, American medical personnel found it difficult to adjust to the poorer quality of American-made slides, stains, lenses, and drugs. In 1918 the flu epidemic put extra strains upon the Mayo Clinic. Everyone was called into service, including relatives and friends with any time to spare. A small hotel building

next door to the hospital had been remodeled and opened for use in June 1918, so it was ready when the influenza arrived in September. The flu broke out in the community in a mild form at first, then suddenly and virulently in the hospital itself. The clinic was quickly overwhelmed with patients.

Postwar Prejudices. After the signing of the armistice, the prejudice stirred up by the war was not easily dissipated. For decades American medical men had taken for granted that part of their training would take place in Germany and Austria, in the classes and laboratories of the European masters of surgery and medical science. But post war prejudices against anything German dismissed the vaunted German medical curriculum as only a propaganda myth. German scientists and physicians were accused of being shameless in developing and exploiting ideas picked up from British and American thinkers. While William and Charles shared in the general antagonism toward Germany, they were not willing to see such feelings translated into action against individuals. When the 1918 meeting of the American Surgical Association proposed that the German and Austrian honorary members be dropped from the list of members, William, in uniform, strongly opposed the action, insisting that political and military hostility should not extend into the world of science. The resolution failed to pass at that session but was adopted at the next one, which William could not attend.

Group Practice. War service gave many physicians their first taste of teamwork in medical practice. Many did not like it, but those beset with problems of increasing costs, not enough patients, and unpaid bills were led to consider group organization by the example of the Mayo Clinic, the inspiration for the growth of group practices in the Middle and Far West. The story of the Mayo Clinic and the Mayo Foundation for Medical Education and Research made the Mayos national celebrities. The national news services picked up and publicized anecdotes such as the one about the pompous millionaire who, seeing William cross the lobby, bustled up to ask importantly, "Are you the head doctor here?" "No," William replied soberly, "my brother is the head doctor. I'm the belly doctor."

Honors. In 1919 William received the U.S. distinguished service medal, a medal Charles was awarded in 1920. Each medal bore the same citation: "In addition to the manifold service to the surgeon-general . . . he distinguished himself by exceptionally meritorious service to the government in his work in the organization of surgical service and his invaluable assistance in the reorganization of the medical department." Both brothers continued to practice medicine and perform surgery until they were well into their sixties. William retired in 1928, and a series of strokes brought Charles's career to an end a year and a half later. Many of their colleagues debated which of the brothers was the greater surgeon; but in medical history they are best remembered as complementary parts of a team whose legacy was the great clinic built upon their surgical partnership. The famed physicians who had worked so closely together died within a few months of each other in 1939, Charles Mayo on 26 May and William Mayo on 28 July.

Sources:
Helen Clapesattle, *The Doctors Mayo* (Minneapolis: University of Minnesota Press, 1941);

Paul Starr, *The Social Transformation of American Medicine* (New York: Basic Books, 1982).

ADOLF MEYER

1866-1950

A LEADER OF AMERICAN PSYCHIATRY

Psychobiology. Adolf Meyer was the leading non-Freudian psychiatric theorist in the United States. He was born on 13 September 1866 in Niederweningen, Switzerland, the son of a minister and the nephew of a doctor, and grew up in an atmosphere of liberalism and reflection. Meyer was trained in neurobiology and neurophysiology at the University of Zurich, where he received his M.D. degree in 1892. He had hoped for the post of assistant to the professor of medicine at Zurich, but when this was denied him he decided to go to the United States. His first appointment was as a pathologist at the Illinois Eastern Hospital for the Insane at Kankakee, Illinois. Meyer soon became acquainted with the work of psychologist William James, the philosopher-educator John Dewey, and others who were molding psychology and philosophy. He blended these different influences into a concept of human behavior that he called ergasiology or psychobiology, which sought to integrate the psychological and biological study of human beings.

The Phipps Clinic. In 1910 Meyer became a professor of psychiatry at Johns Hopkins University. In 1914 he was named the first director of the Henry Phipps Psychiatric Clinic, a position he held until his retirement in 1941. Under his leadership the Phipps Clinic became one of the most important centers in the world for training psychiatrists. Rejecting the traditional view that separated the mind from the body, Meyer taught his students to be concerned with the whole human being. He rejected simple biological explanations of mental illness and worked to develop formulations of "reaction patterns." He argued for the individuality of the patient and suggested, for example, that schizophrenia was a personality disorder. Before the widespread acceptance of Sigmund Freud's work, Meyer began to contend that childhood sexual feelings could lead to serious mental problems.

Case Histories. Meyer's psychobiological studies showed that thoughts and feelings affected a person's physiological state. He became the first American psychiatrist to compile voluminous case histories of his patients, creating a behavior chart for the day-by-day notation of each patient's conduct. Containing data on hereditary and environmental details, social and economic circumstances, and conscious and unconscious factors, Meyer's case histories became the main research material of the Phipps Clinic.

Influence. During the first half of the twentieth century Meyer exercised a major influence on psychiatric research. Much of his teaching has been incorporated into psychological theory and practice in the United States, Britain, and other English-speaking nations. He can be credited with giving American psychiatry a pragmatic bent by maintaining a view of psychiatry as a biological science while incorporating many psychoanalytic principles. Through his illustrious career Meyer impressed generations of students with the idea that in the diagnosis and treatment of mental illness the whole person must be taken into account.

Sources:
James Bordley III and A. McGehee Harvey, *Two Centuries of American Medicine, 1776–1976* (Philadelphia: W. B. Saunders, 1976);

Alfred Lief, ed., *The Commonsense Psychiatry of Dr. Adolf Meyer* (New York: McGraw-Hill, 1948).

THOMAS HUNT MORGAN

1866-1945

FATHER OF MODERN GENETICS

Science and the Fruit Fly. After the Moravian monk Gregor Johann Mendel's discoveries in the mid nineteenth century, the next major contributor to the understanding of genetic principles was Thomas Hunt Morgan. Morgan was born in Lexington, Kentucky, on 25 September 1866 and received his college degree from the State College of Kentucky. He received his Ph.D. in comparative anatomy and physiology from Johns Hopkins in 1890 and then became professor of biology at Bryn Mawr College. In 1904 he went to Columbia University where he became a professor of experimental zoology. Morgan's extensive experiments in genetics began in 1909 when, following a suggestion made by Professor W. E. Castle of Harvard, he began his lifelong work with the fruit fly, *Drosophila melanogaster.*

The Mystery of Genetics. Mendel was the first to recognize that inherited characteristics were transmitted by discrete units as opposed to the theories of the blending of body fluids that existed in his time. But it would remain for Morgan to reveal the mystery of heredity.

Working with fruit flies, Morgan found that he could accumulate an enormous amount of hereditary data in a short time. Fruit flies could be easily studied in laboratories; their reproduction rate was rapid; and male and female were easily distinguished. They had only four pairs of chromosomes, which simplified genetic study. In 1910, about a year after he had begun studying these flies that are drawn to ripe fruit, a male fly with white eyes appeared in one of the milk bottles Morgan used for incubators. Wild flies have red eyes, so Morgan was sure that this was a mutation. He bred the white-eyed male to a red-eyed female and in a short time had hundreds of red-eyed offspring, just as Mendel's mathematic studies of heredity would lead him to expect. With additional matings and research Morgan was able to demonstrate that the individual units of heredity, genes, were arranged in a line on the chromosomes, those "colored bodies" that are found in the nuclei of cells. This theory, known as the chromosome theory of heredity, was presented in 1915 in *The Mechanism of Mendelian Heredity*, which Morgan wrote with his coworkers A. H. Sturtevant and C. B. Bridges.

Nobel Prize Winner. Morgan's experiments established the chromosome as the storehouse of the hereditary material that is passed on from cell to cell, from parent to offspring, from generation to generation. After thousands of fruit fly experiments, Morgan constructed a "chromosome map" indicating which genes were responsible for certain traits and establishing their location. Chromosomes were easy to count, to stain for microscopic study, and to describe, but the elusive genes, which Morgan considered to be the basic units of heredity, were not. These would await further studies by other scientists in future decades. Thomas Hunt Morgan was awarded the 1933 Nobel Prize for physiology or medicine for his work in establishing the chromosomes as the bearers of hereditary traits.

Sources:

James Bordley III and A. McGehee Harvey, *Two Centuries of American Medicine, 1776–1976* (Philadelphia: W. B. Saunders, 1976);

Bernard G. Campbell, *Humankind Emerging*, sixth edition (New York: HarperCollins, 1992);

Ian Shine and Sylvia Wrobel, *Thomas Hunt Morgan: Pioneer of Genetics* (Lexington: University Press of Kentucky, 1976).

MARGARET SANGER

1879-1966

BIRTH CONTROL REFORMER

A Father's Injunction. Margaret Sanger almost single-handedly founded the birth control movement in America and was the driving force in the development of modern contraceptives. Her efforts to make birth control universally available to American women saved the lives of countless women by ending the nightmare of constant pregnancy that often burdened families with more children than they could support. Sanger was born as Margaret Louisa Higgins in Corning, New York, on 14 September 1879, the middle child in an Irish American family of eleven children. She often quoted her father, a sculptor of graveyard art and an avowed socialist, that the only obligation he expected of his children was to "leave the world a better place."

Maternity Ward Nurse. While she nursed her tubercular mother, Sanger borrowed several medical books that fired her own ambition to become a physician. But Sanger could not afford medical school, so after her mother's death she enrolled in a school of nursing, an occupation at that time considered more menial than professional since nurses were not much more than servants to their patients. The great challenge of her training at the White Plains, New York, hospital in 1900 was in the maternity ward. Some patients, who already had many pregnancies and children, begged her to tell them how to prevent another pregnancy. "Miss Higgins," they pleaded, "what should I do not to have another baby right away?" When she asked the doctors, they were indignant that anyone would raise the question with a girl. Sanger, in her autobiography, told of one woman in the White Plains Hospital who had several miscarriages and six babies. The doctors and nurses knew every time she went out that she would soon be back again, but it was no one's business; it was just "natural."

Fundamental Change. After she completed her training, Sanger and her young architect husband, William Sanger, and their three children moved to New York City where she found work as a visiting nurse and midwife in order to help make ends meet. By 1910 New York City was caught up in the national spirit of reform, and the Sangers became active socialists in the movement's heyday. Working part-time with poverty-stricken immigrants in New York's Lower East Side, Margaret Sanger experienced an epiphany when one of her patients, a young Jewish immigrant, died of septicemia from a self-induced abortion after pleading with her unresponsive doctor for a reliable means of contraception. Sanger resolved to abandon "the palliative career of nursing in pursuit of fundamental social change."

The First Birth-Control Clinic. During the early 1910s Sanger lectured and wrote papers on sex education and health for *The Call,* New York's popular socialist daily newspaper. But the culture at large was reticent about open discussions of sex, and for a woman to flaunt this taboo and write about such topics as defloration, pregnancy, abortion, masturbation, and menstruation was especially provocative. In March 1914 she published her first edition of her magazine, *The Woman Rebel.* Arrested in August on four criminal counts carrying a maximum sentence of forty-five years for sending "indecent" materials through the mail, Sanger continued to write while preparing for her trial. Her pamphlet, *Family Limitation*, with its straightforward language and diagrams, discussed familiar and unfamiliar means of contraception. In October, after a trial postponement was denied, she fled to Europe under an alias to buy herself time and sympathy. Returning a year later, she found that contraception was now a public controversy. After all charges were dropped, Sanger rented space in Brooklyn, New York, and along with Ethel Byrne and Fania Mindell opened America's first birth-control clinic on 16 October 1916.

Mother of the Pill. Ten days later Sanger and a volunteer worker were arrested for maintaining a public nuisance, and her clinic was closed. Impatient with the postponements of her trial, Sanger reopened the clinic on 20 November. Two days later the police raided it a second time and forced the landlord to evict her. The clinic was closed for good, and a trial date was finally set. Found guilty, she was sentenced to thirty days in prison. On her emergence she once again pursued her goal of empowering women to live independent, self-fulfilled lives. Having founded the National Birth Control League in 1914, she organized the Planned Parenthood Foundation of America in 1921 to inform the general public about family planning. Frustrated with existing birth control technology, Sanger in 1950 enlisted the aid of Gregory Pincus, a reproductive biologist at the Worcester Foundation in Massachusetts. Pincus's research led to the development of the birth control pill, and Sanger would be credited as one of the "mothers" of "the pill."

A Legacy of Social Change. Many years ahead of her time, Sanger was a radical activist and liberated woman whose fellow sympathizers included Emma Goldman and John Reed and whose lovers included Havelock Ellis and H. G. Wells. Sanger dedicated more than half a century of her life to ensuring that women had access to a safe and reliable means of preventing pregnancy, and she lived to see the realization of her efforts when the Supreme Court made a landmark 1965 ruling in *Griswold* v. *Connecticut,* which guaranteed the private use of contraceptives as a constitutional right.

Sources:

Ellen Chesler, *Woman of Valor. Margaret Sanger and the Birth Control Movement in America* (New York: Simon & Schuster, 1992);

Emily Taft Douglas, *Margaret Sanger: Pioneer of the Future* (New York: Holt, Rinehart & Winston, 1970);

David M. Kennedy, *Birth Control in America: The Career of Margaret Sanger* (New Haven: Yale University Press, 1991);

Margaret Sanger, *An Autobiography* (New York: Norton, 1938).

LEWIS MADISON TERMAN

1877-1956

PIONEER OF INTELLIGENCE TESTS

Educational Psychology. Lewis Madison Terman was an educational psychologist known for his long-term study of highly intelligent individuals. Born in Johnson County, Indiana, on 15 January 1877, Terman received his Ph.D. at Clark University in Worcester, Massachusetts, in 1905. (Clark University, under the leadership of psychologist G. Stanley Hall, was at that time a hotbed of American psychology.) Terman's thesis was based on his investigation of the differences between groups of bright and dull children on a wide range of tests. After graduating from Clark, Terman, who had tuberculosis, went west on the advice of his physician. He settled in California and joined the faculty of Stanford University in 1910, where he stayed until his retirement in 1942.

The Stanford-Binet Intelligence Test. In 1916 he revised the Binet-Simon intelligence test, which then became known as the Stanford-Binet test, and introduced the term *intelligence quotient* (IQ). Performance on the original Binet test, originated by the French psychologist Alfred Binet in 1905, was expressed on an age scale. A basal age was established by an individual's ability to pass an initial set of tests; additional months of credit were applied for tests passed above the basal age level. The result was a designation of "mental age." Terman considered it necessary to have an index that related the mental age level to the typical performance of the individual's age group. For this purpose he adopted the intelligence quotient, or IQ, in his modified test. The ratio of mental age (MA) to chronological age (CA) provided an index of relative performance. An average adult would have an IQ of 100, with a mentally defective IQ defined as 40 or below and a gifted IQ as 160 or above.

Revisions. The first Stanford-Binet test, published in 1916, was based almost entirely on the results of Terman's experiments with one thousand children and four hundred adults in his sample group. He then added new items, including a vocabulary test. *The Literary Digest* ran Terman's vocabulary as a sort of do-it-yourself intelligence test in its 16 February 1918 issue, titled, "Of Course You Are a Superior Adult." Terman created his vocabulary list by selecting the last word of every sixth column in a dictionary containing 18,000 words and arranging them roughly in the order of their difficulty. He calculated that each word in his list represented 180 words of vocabulary; therefore a person who knew 50 of these would in all probability have a working vocabulary of about 9,000 words.

IQs of the Deceased. Terman put great emphasis on his figuring of the numerical score, or IQ. He was convinced that the IQ stayed the same throughout an individual's life, and so adult intelligence could be predicted in early childhood. He and a Stanford associate, Catherine Cox, decided that they could estimate the IQs of a group of three hundred famous people who were long dead. Not only did they say that these individuals had high IQs, but they assigned each an exact number: Da Vinci, 180; Galileo, 185; Lincoln, 150; and Goethe, 210. Since the "science of the IQ" was held in high regard, their study was solemnly received.

Large-Scale Studies. The Stanford-Binet scale and its subsequent revisions by Terman and Maud A. Merril became the most widely used of all mental tests for children. An adaptation of it was put together in a period of a few weeks for U.S. Army recruits in 1917. In the 1920s Terman began his studies of fifteen hundred of the brightest children in California, with IQs of 135 and up, and traced their careers and accomplishments in four volumes of *Genetic Studies of Genius* (1925–1959).

Controversy. Results of the Stanford-Binet test have been fairly consistent with respect to individual performance over a period of years. This stability led to the test's acceptance and its widespread application as a measure of intelligence. Some critics claim the test was oversold in the beginning and had capabilities attributed to it that it never had. For years the Stanford-Binet test was common in schools, and individual lives hinged on its outcome. "Scientific" data derived from such testing was cited as support for the restrictive immigration quota of 1924, which clearly discriminated against southern Europeans, a group Terman considered to be the "least prolific of gifted children." The test came under criticism later because it did not account for developmental and environmental factors in intelligence levels. Terman himself continued to believe that "in the main, native qualities of intellect and character, rather than chance determine the social class to which a family belongs."

Sources:

N. J. Block and Gerald Dworkin, eds., *The IQ Controversy* (New York: Pantheon, 1976);

May V. Seagoe, *Terman and the Gifted* (Los Altos, Calif.: W. P. Kaufmann, 1975);

Evelyn Sharp, *The IQ Cult* (New York: Coward, McCann & Geoghegan, 1972).

VICTOR CLARENCE VAUGHAN

1851-1929

COMMUNICABLE DISEASE SPECIALIST IN WORLD WAR I

Scientist and Doctor. Dr. Victor Clarence Vaughan played an important role in easing epidemics in military camps during World War I, a war in which more Americans succumbed to disease than to combat injuries. Vaughan was born in Mount Airy, Missouri, on 27 October 1851 and led an idyllic childhood on his parents' farm surrounded by horses and playmates. Four years of his childhood were spent in the middle of the Civil War, and Vaughan learned "to hate war and to love peace so dearly that I have been willing to do my small bit in fighting for it." He graduated from Mount Pleasant College, a Baptist school in Huntsville, Missouri, in 1872, learning Latin and teaching himself chemistry after finding the laboratory closed at the school. Vaughan nurtured his fascination with chemistry at the University of Michigan, receiving a Ph.D. and entering medical school in 1876, where he also began teaching chemistry. He received his M.D. in 1878 and continued doing postgraduate work under Robert Koch at the University of Berlin.

A Personal Interest. In his middle years Dr. Vaughan turned to the study of communicable diseases, especially tuberculosis. He was personally familiar with communicable disease, having suffered from both tuberculosis and malaria as a young man. When he was twenty-one, years before Robert Koch identified and isolated the tubercle bacillus in 1882, his great uncle diagnosed him with pulmonary tuberculosis. Vaughan adopted a "heroic" treatment, standing in a sulfur spring with a local reputation for medicinal qualities even though both he and his uncle were skeptical of the spring's healing reputation. During the summer and fall he immersed himself up to his chin daily in the cold water, and soon his symptoms faded, leaving him with only a lesion in one apex of his lung as evidence of his disease.

An Expert in Public Hygiene and Sanitation. In 1891 Vaughan became the dean of the University of Michigan Medical School. By World War I he had established his expertise in public hygiene and sanitation, having already seen medical service during the Spanish-American War. As one of a three-member commission that studied typhoid fever in the military camps in 1898, he was familiar with epidemiological studies of the spread of disease through a population. In the case of typhoid fever the commission recognized the role played by contaminated water and food but made an important new discovery: that the common housefly served as an agent to transmit typhoid bacilli from feces to food. As a result of Vaughan's findings, many new sanitary measures were taken in the camps, and the annual death rate among the troops fell from 879 per 100,000 in 1898 to 107 per 100,000 in 1899. Vaughan himself contracted yellow fever in 1898.

The War against Disease. In 1916, anticipating the likelihood that the United States would become involved in the war raging on the Continent of Europe, President Wilson appointed a Council of National Defense, which included a medical division. After Congress declared war in April 1917, the Medical Division's Executive Committee planned and controlled much of the medical work of the war. As a member of the committee, Vaughan was placed in charge of the biggest medical problem of the war — communicable diseases.

The Health Challenge of World War I. Vaughan's greatest challenge in World War I was the thirty-two military camps, each with thirty thousand to forty thousand soldiers, many of whom were susceptible to all sorts of common contagious diseases. Epidemics of measles, mumps, cerebro-spinal meningitis, and pneumonia became serious problems. It was as if the men had pooled their diseases, each picking up illnesses to which he had never been exposed. The process of transmission was greatly assisted by the faulty layout of camps, poor administration, and lack of adequate laboratory facilities and hospitals. In the fall of 1917 at Camp Wheeler, Georgia, one hundred to five hundred cases of measles developed a day, with each case predisposing the patient to pneumonia. Measles itself was not a deadly disease, but of every one thousand men with measles, forty-four had pneumonia and fourteen died.

Pneumonia and Influenza. Vaughan improved the sanitation and water supplies in the World War I camps and with the routine use of typhoid vaccine virtually eliminated typhoid fever as a serious wartime problem. In 1912 vaccination against typhoid fever was made compulsory for the military, and "in 1917 the civilian who wished to escape typhoid fever could find no safer place than the army." Pneumonia, however, was the great killer of World War I. When Vaughan charted the pneumonia morbidity and mortality in each of the large camps, he was struck by variations in the cases in several of the camps. He found the incidence of pneumonia was lower among the urban recruits than the rural men and attributed this to the degree of immunity to respiratory diseases urban dwellers gained from their more constant exposure to these infections. Vaughan worked to solve problems of overcrowding in the camps and insure adequate supplies of clean water, warm clothing, blankets, and medical supplies. But there was one problem that seemed insoluble, the influenza epidemic of 1918. Science could provide no cure, and the epidemic continued to rage even after camps were disbanded. Vaughan felt the influenza epidemic "flaunted its red flag in the face of

science" and refused to discuss it in his memoirs. Nevertheless, Vaughan received the United States' distinguished service medal in 1919 for his work during the epidemic.

Sources:

James Bordley III and A. McGehee Harvey, *Two Centuries of American Medicine, 1776–1976* (Philadelphia: W. B. Saunders, 1976);

Simon Flexner and James Thomas Flexner, *William Henry Welch and the Heroic Age of American Medicine* (New York: Viking, 1941);

Victor C. Vaughan, *A Doctor's Memories* (Indianapolis: Bobbs-Merrill, 1926).

LILLIAN D. WALD

1867-1940

PUBLIC HEALTH NURSE

A Baptism of Fire. Lillian D. Wald is regarded as the founder of what is now called public health or community nursing, and she was known for her contributions to school nursing and child welfare. Wald was born to a wealthy family in Cincinnati, Ohio, and raised in Rochester, New York. Educated at Miss Crittenden's English and French Boarding and Day School for Young Ladies and Little Girls, she was encouraged by her physician relatives to become a nurse. She spent a year nursing at the New York Juvenile Asylum and then entered Woman's Medical College in New York. During medical school Wald was asked to go to New York's Lower East Side to instruct immigrant mothers on the care of the sick. Like Margaret Sanger, she was shocked by what she saw there. One day, as she was teaching a hygiene lesson in the slum, a little girl approached her for help. The child led her through filthy, crowded tenements to where her mother lay untended in a bed soiled with the hemorrhage of childbirth. Wald referred to that morning's experience as her "baptism of fire." Never returning to medical school, she began her career in public health nursing and her battle against poverty and disease.

The House on Henry Street. In 1893 Wald persuaded a classmate to go into the tenement district with her to live and work. Their house on Henry Street eventually became the Henry Street Visiting Nurse Service. She fought for legislative reforms, coining the phrase "public health nursing," and served on the New York State Immigration Commission. In addition to the creation of the United States Children's Bureau in 1912, she established the Rural Nursing Service of the American Red Cross in the same year. In 1912 she also became the first president of the National Organization for Public Health Nursing, the nation's third national nursing association. By 1913 she and Mary Adelaide Nutting had established an educational program in public health nursing in which nurses would receive theoretical course work at Teachers College and Columbia University and practical experience at the Henry Street Settlement.

The U.S. Children's Bureau. The history of pediatrics is closely associated with the history of public health. In the first two decades of the twentieth century infant mortality fell dramatically as public health workers turned their attention to prevention as a key to saving babies' lives. In 1908 New York City set up the first division of child hygiene in the world with astounding results. Twelve hundred fewer deaths were recorded from one year to the next as new mothers were identified and visited by public health nurses who taught them how to care for their babies. The New York experience inspired others and led to Congress's creation in 1912 of the U.S. Children's Bureau, the brainchild of Wald and fellow health activist Florence Kelley. The bureau specialized in prenatal and maternal care, and its 1913 pamphlet on prenatal care became one of the government's most popular publications.

World War I. After the United States entered World War I, Wald joined in a powerful nursing triumvirate with Mary Adelaide Nutting and Annie Goodrich to form the National Emergency Committee on Nursing. Fearing that the war's acute need for nurses would force nursing schools to lower admission and graduation requirements, the committee stated that its purpose was to develop "the wisest methods of meeting the present problems connected with the care of the sick and injured in hospitals and homes; the educational problems of nursing; and the extraordinary emergencies as they arise." Wald's social vision, initiative, and skill in acquiring support for new ideas and new plans made her one of the most influential health workers of her day.

Sources:

M. Patricia Donahue, *Nursing, The Finest Art* (Saint Louis: C. V. Mosby Company, 1985);

Lillian Wald, *The House on Henry Street* (New York: Holt, 1915);

Wald, *Windows on Henry Street* (Boston: Little, Brown, 1934).

WILLIAM HENRY WELCH

1850-1934

RESEARCHER AND EDUCATOR

A Family Tradition. William Henry Welch, the early twentieth century's greatest statesman in the field of public health, was born on 8 April 1850 in Norwalk, Connecticut. His father, uncles, grandfather, and great-uncle had all been doctors, but Welch was reluctant to conform to the family tradition. He grew up as the child of a country practitioner, and there had been sick people in his house all day as well as raps on the door at night. When Welch received his A.B. degree from Yale College in 1870, nothing pointed toward a career either in science or medicine; his real enthusiasm was for the classics. After graduation he taught Cicero and German in an academy in Norwich, New York, but the job petered out in the spring of 1871, and Welch had to confront the problem of a career. He turned to medicine as the last resort of a man thwarted in his ambitions.

A New Kind of Medicine. Welch's career would be in medical research, a new kind of medicine, with no precedent among his older physician relatives and not much precedent in medical history. One of a small group of students who finished college before entering medical school, Welch further prepared for medical school by working as his father's apprentice. After graduating from the College of Physicians and Surgeons (now part of Columbia University in New York) in 1875, he followed the pattern of many American physicians of his time and studied for three years in Europe. At Breslau he witnessed the historic demonstration by Robert Koch of the infectivity of *Bacillus anthracis.* Inspired by the new ideas in medicine that he saw being born in Europe, Welch returned to the United States in 1878 and established the country's first pathology laboratory at Bellevue Hospital Medical College. He returned to Berlin to study under Koch, concentrating on the new bacteriology. With Simon Flexner he demonstrated the pathology of diphtheria, and in 1892 with George H. F. Nuttall he discovered the cause of the gas gangrene that would affect wounded troops in World War I (*Bacillus aerogenes capsulatus,* known as Welch's bacillus). He also contributed to the knowledge of embolism and thrombosis.

Johns Hopkins. In 1884 Welch began as a professor of pathology at Johns Hopkins University, where he laid the foundation for his greatest contribution to medicine. Through his establishment of sound training methods and his part in the founding of the Johns Hopkins Medical School in 1893 as well as in directing the school's development as its first dean, he played a major role in the establishment of modern medical practice and education in the United States. Virtually single-handedly he constructed a curriculum that revolutionized American medicine by demanding of its students a rigorous study of physical sciences and an active involvement in clinical duties and lab work. In his famous 1910 evaluation of the nation's medical schools, Abraham Flexner gave only three schools — Harvard, Western Reserve, and Johns Hopkins — his full approval. Under Welch's leadership Johns Hopkins became a model for the changes in the nation's medical schools during the second decade of the twentieth century.

Public Health Education. Welch helped to shape the Rockefeller Institute for Medical Research and headed its board of scientific directors from 1900 until his death in 1934. In addition to serving as the first dean of Johns Hopkins's medical faculty, he established the first full-time clinical professorships at Johns Hopkins Medical School with the appointments of professors of medicine, surgery, and pediatrics in 1913. He became director of the first university School of Hygiene and Public Health at Johns Hopkins in 1918, which marked a turning point in public health education in this country and throughout the world.

Service in World War I. During World War I Welch participated in the Medical Division's Executive Committee, which planned and controlled much of the medical work of the war. On 16 July 1917 Welch was appointed a major in the Medical Section, Officers' Reserve Corps, and served as a liaison between America's medical laboratories and the army. In July 1917 he began visiting the many training camps that were undergoing epidemics of communicable diseases. All during the war he conducted his strenuous trips of inspection even though he was approaching seventy. Little by little conditions in the camps improved until the major object of his inspections changed from solving crises to "stimulating the medical staff to better work and clearer thinking." Shortly after Welch had convinced himself that the camps were in such good condition that he might retire, he was called to investigate a mysterious epidemic. A fellow physician remarked, "the only time I ever saw Dr. Welch really worried and disturbed was in the autumn of 1918, at Camp Devens, near Boston." The continuous line of sick soldiers coming in from the various barracks to the hospital and the great numbers of deaths and autopsies caused Dr. Welch to remark, "This must be some new kind of infection or plague." His colleague recalled, "he was quite excited and obviously very nervous. . . . It was not surprising that the rest of us were disturbed, but it shocked me to find that the situation, momentarily at least, was too much even for Dr. Welch." Welch was witnessing the beginning of the great influenza epidemic that would soon sweep across the country.

A Famous Portrait of a Giant of Medicine. Today students and visitors to the medical library at Johns Hopkins University may see William Henry Welch's portrait appearing in John Singer Sargent's famous painting of the *Four Doctors* of Johns Hopkins. The other subjects include Sir William Osler, Howard A. Kelly, and William S. Halsted.

Sources:

James Bordley III and A. McGehee Harvey, *Two Centuries of American Medicine, 1776–1976* (Philadelphia: W. B. Saunders, 1976);

Donald Fleming, *William Henry Welch and the Rise of Modern Medicine* (Boston: Little, Brown, 1954);

Simon Flexner and James Thomas Flexner, *William Henry Welch and the Heroic Age of American Medicine* (New York: Viking, 1941).

PEOPLE IN THE NEWS

John Jacob Abel isolated amino acids from blood by vividiffusion in 1913.

In 1911 John F. Anderson and Joseph Goldberger for the first time produced measles in an animal by injecting monkeys with cell-free blood filtrate from a human measles patient, suggesting that measles was a viral infection.

In 1910 John Auer demonstrated the bronchial spasm in acute anaphylaxis, and Samuel J. Meltzer suggested that this reaction characterized bronchial asthma.

Oswald T. Avery and Alphonse Dochez described the specific soluble substance of pneumococcus in 1917.

S. R. Benedict devised a basal metabolism test in 1918.

Francis Gilman Blake and James Dowling Trask demonstrated the viral origin of measles in 1919.

In 1910 Washington University at Saint Louis president Robert Somers Brookings was inspired by the Flexner Report and began a program to elevate his university's medical school.

On 22 June 1914 A. G. Bryant and F. W. Duckering became the first women members of the American College of Surgeons.

In 1916 William T. Bull introduced antitoxin for treatment of gas gangrene.

Walter B. Cannon published *The Mechanical Factors of Digestion* in 1911. In 1912 Cannon began work on the effect of adrenal secretions on the emotions. He published *Bodily Changes in Pain, Hunger, Fear and Rage* in 1915.

The 1912 Nobel Prize for medicine or physiology was awarded to Alexis Carrel for his work on vascular suturing and organ transplantation. In 1914 Carrel performed the first successful heart surgery on a dog.

In 1915 the Alexis Carrel-Henry Drysdale Dakin treatment of infected gunshot wounds was introduced.

Rufus Cole and Raymond Dochez developed in horses a serum for use against type I pneumococcus in humans in 1912.

Robert A. Cooke introduced an intracutaneous diagnostic test for hypersensitivity to allergens in 1915.

In 1910 General Electric researcher William D. Coolidge announced a new and improved X-ray tube. In 1915 Coolidge revolutionized X-ray technology with his patent of a hot-cathode X-ray tube, the prototype for all future tubes.

Harvey Cushing, Samuel J. Crowe, and J. Homans developed experimental hypophysectomy in 1910. In 1912 Cushing advanced knowledge of the pituitary gland and its relation to diabetes with his book *The Pituitary Body and Its Disorders.*

In 1914 Walter E. Dandy demonstrated pathogenesis of hydrocephalus. Dandy in 1918 used air injections in the ventricles of the brain to diagnose and localize brain tumors.

Alphonse Dochez and Oswald T. Avery identified the forms of pneumococci (1913–1916).

In 1919 the Eastman School of Medicine and Dentistry was founded at the University of Rochester by photography pioneer George Eastman.

At the Massachusetts General Hospital in Boston in 1912 David Linn Edsall organized a research ward that emphasized clinical investigation.

Charles Elsberg introduced insufflation anesthesia under pressure into clinical practice in 1910.

John Miller Turpin Finney of Baltimore was elected the first president of the American College of Surgeons on 13 November 1913.

Dr. Simon Flexner, director of the Rockefeller Institute for Medical Research and the brother of Abraham Flexner, declared on 12 March 1911 that infantile paralysis was caused by a germ.

In 1910 Chicago physician James Bryan Herrick made the first diagnosis of sickle-cell anemia (it will be given that name in 1922). In 1912 Herrick published his classic description of coronary thrombosis.

William H. Howell discovered the anticoagulant heparin in 1916.

On 30 June 1911 J. P. Kelly, the first army flight surgeon, reported for duty in College Park, Maryland.

On 4 June 1912 Julia C. Lathrop was appointed as the first chief of the U.S. Children's Bureau.

Emanuel Libman published an important description of bacterial endocarditis in 1910.

In 1919 Robert F. Loeb introduced mammary cancer by ovariectomy in mice.

Physicians David Marine and Edward C. Kendall conducted the first large-scale study of iodine's effect on human goiter in 1916.

In 1912 biochemists Elmer Verner McCollum and Marguerite Davis discovered the fat-soluble nutrient that would later be called Vitamin A in butter and egg yolks; Thomas B. Osborne and Lafayette B. Mendel independently made the same discover. McCollum isolated Vitamin B in 1916.

In 1910 California physicians George Walter McCoy and Charles Willard Chapin identified tularemia, a disease of wild rabbits and other animals that is communicable to humans; tularemia was the first distinctly American disease to be identified.

In 1919 Edward Mellanby found that rickets was not an infection, as had been widely believed, but a dietary vitamin deficiency.

In 1918 Yale biochemists Lafayette Benedict Mendel and B. Cohen showed that guinea pigs could not develop Vitamin C and contracted scurvy even more readily than did humans.

In 1916 Colorado Springs dentist Frederick S. Motley traced his patients' discolored but cavity-free teeth to the city's drinking water that contained fluoride salts.

Hideyo Noguchi demonstrated the presence of the syphilis spirochete in the brains of paretics and in the spinal cords of tabetics in 1910.

In 1910 Adelaide Nutting established a course of public health nursing at Columbia University in New York City.

Inventor Morgan Parker patented a disposable scalpel in 1915.

In 1910 Professor Richard Mills Pearce was named the first medical research chair at the School of Medicine, University of Pennsylvania in Philadelphia.

Charles H. Peck reported in the September 1913 *Journal of the American Medical Association* that continuous insufflation of air into the lungs would sustain life for many hours when all respiratory movements have ceased; the technique diminished surgical shock and permitted more control of anesthesia.

Howard Taylor Ricketts published his investigations of tabardillo in 1910.

Peyton Rous published his study of viral cancer in chickens in 1911. In 1915 Rous developed a trypsin digestion method for isolation of individual cells from tissues for study.

Leonard G. Rowntree introduced the PSP test of renal function in 1910.

In 1913 at New York's Mount Sinai Hospital, Hungarian American physician Bela Schick developed the Schick test to determine susceptibility to diphtheria.

Maude Slye performed experiments regarding hereditary susceptibility to and immunity from cancer (1913–1927).

Charles Rupert Stockard and George N. Papanicolaou demonstrated vaginal epithelian changes during the estrus cycle in women in 1917.

In 1911 Lucius Lincoln Van Slyke began the development of a method for estimating amino nitrogen.

In 1910 E. B. Vedder demonstrated the amebicidal effect of emetine.

Gerald Bertram Webb became the first temporary chairman of the American Association of Immunologists on 19 June 1913.

AWARDS

NOBEL PRIZE WINNERS IN MEDICINE OR PHYSIOLOGY

1912

Alexis Carrel (U.S.A., born in France) for his work in the transplantation and suturing of blood vessels.

THE EBERT PRIZE

The Ebert Prize is given for the best original paper published during the preceding year in the *Journal of Pharmaceutical Sciences*. It was first awarded in 1874.

1910

Harry M. Gordin

1911

W. A. Puckner with L. E. Warren

1912

No award

1913

No award

1914

No award

1915

E. N. Gathercoal

1916

John Uri Lloyd

1917

No award

1918

No award

1919

No award

THE REMINGTON HONOR MEDAL

The Remington Honor Medal is given each year to the individual who has done the most for American pharmacy during the year or whose contributions to the advancement of pharmacy over a period of years have been outstanding. It was first awarded in 1919.

1919

James Hartley Beal

DEATHS

Dudley Peter Allen, 63, professor of surgery at Western Reserve University, whose *Wounds from Blank Cartridges* (1903) resulted in the prohibition of the sale of blank cartridges in Cleveland, 6 January 1915.

David Alfred Amoss, 58, Rockefeller Institute physician noted for his work in organizing the tobacco growers of his Kentucky region into a tobacco trust, 3 November 1915.

William Henry Baker, 69, surgeon and professor of gynecology at Harvard Medical School who was known especially for his skill in plastic surgery and abdominal surgery, 26 November 1914.

Clara Barton, 82, founder of the American Red Cross, whose Civil War nursing earned her the name "Angel of the Battlefield" and set the standard for American nursing, 12 April 1912.

John Shaw Billings, 75, surgeon who served with the Army of the Potomac and was present at the battles of Chancellorsville and Gettysburg, 11 March 1913.

Elizabeth Blackwell, 89, the first woman to obtain a medical degree from an American medical school and a founder of the New York Infirmary for Women and Children and the London School of Medicine for Women, 31 May 1910.

Emily Blackwell, 84, cofounder with sister Elizabeth Blackwell of the New York Infirmary for Women and Children that was staffed entirely by women, 8 September 1910.

Joseph Decatur Bryant, 69, surgeon and crusader against pulmonary tuberculosis and cholera who in 1893 performed a secret operation on President Grover Cleveland's jaw for a malignant growth that saved the president's life, 7 April 1914.

Robert Lowell Burrage, 54, tuberculosis expert, one of the founders and organizers of the Widows' and Orphans' relief society, and medical director of the Prudential Insurance Company, 29 October 1911.

Arthur Tracy Cabot, 60, one of the leading American specialists in genitourinary surgery and author of 120 medical papers who was also active in organizing and directing antituberculosis work, 4 November 1912.

Bukk G. Carleton, 57, author and chair of genitourinary and kidney diseases at the Metropolitan Postgraduate School of Medicine in New York City, 20 October 1914.

Herbert William Conn, 58, bacteriologist and dedicated public health worker who proved that typhoid fever could be transmitted by oysters and took an active role in the work of the New York milk committee, 18 April 1917.

Ephraim Cutter, 85, physician and inventor of surgical and medical instruments who was also a pioneer in the field of microphotography, 24 April 1917.

Francis Delafield, 73, professor of medicine at New York's College of Physicians and Surgeons who classified the group of diseases subsumed under pulmonary consumption, 17 July 1915.

Jane Arminda Delano, 57, Red Cross director of nursing who died while on a tour of inspection of the American Red Cross Nursing service overseas, 15 April 1919.

Samuel Gibson Dixon, 66, bacteriologist and the first professor of hygiene at the University of Pennsylvania who produced immunity to tuberculosis in lower animals and discovered the involution form of the tubercular virus, 26 February 1918.

Louis Adolphus Duhring, 67, the author of the first American textbook on skin diseases who was one of the founders and twice the president of the American Dermatological Association, 8 May 1913.

Maj. **Clarence Fahnestock,** 44, physician and big-game sportsman who, although beyond the age limit, was one of the first men to volunteer to fight when the United States entered World War I, 5 October 1918.

Grace Falkinburg, 22, Red Cross nurse, 6 October 1918.

Francis L. Galt, 83, Civil War surgeon, 17 November 1915.

Emil Gruening, 71, ophthalmologist and otologist who developed the techniques of mastoid operations and was the first to call attention to the danger of blindness from wood alcohol poisoning, 30 May 1914.

Alan McLane Hamilton, 71, one of the foremost American authorities on nervous diseases who was the first to use and recommend nitroglycerine in nervous and vascular diseases; he also participated in many celebrated criminal trials including that of President Garfield's assassin, Charles J. Guiteau, where he testified as an expert on behalf of the government, 23 November 1919.

Mrs. Lucy Hart, 77, Civil War nurse, 19 January 1919.

George Jacob Helmer, 51, osteopath pioneer who opened the George J. Helmer Infirmary of Osteopathy in New York City and was one of the organizers of the American Association for the Advancement of Osteopathy, 15 March 1917.

Joseph L. Hicks, 81, surgeon in the Civil War, 19 April 1915.

Philip Hanson Hiss Jr., 45, bacteriologist who became famous for his process of detecting typhoid bacilli and as the original refiner of the diphtheria antitoxin first used by the New York board of health, 27 February 1913.

Edward Gamaliel Janeway, 69, professor in the medical departments of New York University and Bellevue Hospital Medical College who was active in the New York health department, 10 February 1910.

Theodore Caldwell Janeway, 45, a leading diagnostician who concentrated on cardiovascular diseases and therapeutics and was an authority on nephritis, 27 December 1917.

Benjamin Joy Jeffries, 82, ophthalmic surgeon and author who in 1872 demonstrated conclusively before the international ophthalmological congress the superiority of ether over chloroform in ophthalmic surgery, 21 November 1915.

Charles Jewett, 67, an eminent gynecological specialist who performed the first symphyseotomy in America, 6 August 1910.

Adoniram Brown Judson, 79, orthopedic surgeon and author, 20 September 1916.

Walter Kempster, 77, insanity specialist and author who established the first laboratory for the study of the histology and pathology of the brain at the State Lunatic Asylum at Utica, New York, 22 August 1918.

David Braden Kyle, 53, author and specialist in diseases of the ear, nose, throat, and chest, 23 October 1916.

George Hudson Makuen, 61, laryngologist who invented several improved surgical instruments, 21 February 1917.

John B. Murphy, 58, surgeon who was the first to recognize the disease actinomycosis hominis in the United States and whose invention of the anastomosis button reduced the danger of many abdominal operations, 1916.

Richard "Dare Devil Dick" Norton, 46, professor of the history of fine arts at Harvard University who in 1914 organized the American Volunteer Motor Ambulance Corps to serve on the French front, 2 August 1918.

Thomas Opie, 72, physician and surgeon who organized the College of Physicians and Surgeons of Baltimore, 6 October 1914.

Robert Maitland O'Reilly, 68, U.S. surgeon general who introduced the antityphoid serum into the army, 3 November 1912.

Isaac Ott, 68, neurologist and professor who discovered thermogenic center, 1 January 1916.

Roswell Park, 61, cancer specialist and professor of surgery in the medical department of the University of Buffalo who was the first surgeon in the country to establish a private bacteriological laboratory, 15 February 1914.

William Louis Rodman, 58, surgeon and advocate of the excision of the ulcer-bearing area in cases of gastric ulcers who in 1915 founded the National Board of Medical Examiners, 8 March 1916.

Linus Eli Russell, 69, lawyer and surgeon who became the chair of clinical surgery and operative gynecology in the Eclectic Medical Institute in Cincinnati, 2 August 1917.

John Shrady, 84, author, Civil War surgeon, and editor of the New York Medical Register, 11 November 1914.

Edward Charles Spitzka, 61, neurologist and alienist who was the only expert witness at the 1882 trial of Charles J. Guiteau, the assassin of President Garfield, to testify to the defendant's insanity, 13 January 1914.

Thomas Henry Tomlinson, 82, physician and surgeon who was a member of the original staff of Muehlenberg Hospital in Plainfield, New Jersey, 22 June 1919.

Walter Wyman, 63, surgeon general of the U.S. Navy who in 1899 established the first government sanatorium for consumptives at Fort Stanton, New Mexico; he conceived and put into operation measures to prevent the introduction of cholera, yellow fever, and other contagious diseases into the United States, 21 November 1910.

PUBLICATIONS

———

J. J. Abel, L. G. Rowntree, and B. B. Turner, "On the Removal of Diffusible Substances from the Circulating Blood by Means of Dialysis," *Transactions of the Association of American Physicians*, 28 (1913): 51;

American Medical Association, Committee on Social Insurance, *Statistics Regarding the Medical Profession* (Chicago: American Medical Association, 1916);

Leonard P. Ayres, "What American Cities Are Doing for the Health of School Children," *Annals*, 37 (March 1911): 250–260;

M. T. Boardman, *Under the Red Cross Flag at Home and Abroad*, (Philadelphia: Lippincott, 1915);

Lawrason Brown, *Rules for Recovery from Pulmonary Tuberculosis*, second edition (Philadelphia: Lea & Febiger, 1916);

Thomas S. Carrington, *Tuberculosis Hospital and Sanatorium Construction*, third edition (New York: National Association for the Study and Prevention of Tuberculosis, 1914);

Charles V. Chapin, *How to Avoid Infection* (Cambridge: Harvard University Press, 1917);

W. E. Dandy, "Ventriculography Following the Injection of Air into the Cerebral Ventricles," *Annals of Surgery*, 68 (1918): 5;

Michael M. Davis Jr., "Organization of Medical Service," *American Labor Legislation Review*, 6 (March 1916): 18;

Davis Jr. and Andrew W. Warner, *Dispensaries: Their Management and Development* (New York: Macmillan, 1918);

William H. Davis, "The Influenza Epidemic as Shown in the Weekly Health Index," *American Journal of Public Health*, 9 (January 1919): 52+;

H. Havelock Ellis, *The Task of Social Hygiene* (New York: Houghton Mifflin, 1912);

Gertrude Farmer and Janet Schoenfeld, "Epidemic Work at the Boston City Hospital," *Boston Medical and Surgical Journal* (29 May 1919): 608–609;

George O. Ferguson Jr., "The Intelligence of Negroes at Camp Lee, Virginia," *School & Society*, 9 (14 June 1919): 721–726;

Irving Fisher, "The Need for Health Insurance," *American Labor Legislation Review*, 7 (March 1917): 23;

Abraham Flexner, *Medical Education in the United States and Canada*, Bulletin No. 4 (New York: Carnegie Foundation for the Advancement of Teaching, 1910);

Arpad Gerster, *Recollections of a New York Surgeon* (New York: Paul B. Hoeber, 1917);

Henry H. Goddard, "The Binet-Simon Measuring Scale for Intelligence," *Traning School Bulletin* 8 (1911): 56–62;

Goddard, "The Binet Tests in Relation to Immigration," *Journal of Psycho-asthenics*, 18 (1913): 105–107;

Goddard, *The Kallikak Family: A Study in the Heredity of Feeblemindedness* (New York: Macmillan, 1912);

Dr. H. W. Hill, *The New Public Health* (New York: Macmillan, 1914);

Henry Hurd, "The Hospital as a Factor in Modern Society," *Modern Hospital*, 1 (September 1913): 33;

James I. Johnston, "History and Epidemiology of Epidemic Influenza," *Studies on Epidemic Influenza. Publications from the University of Pittsburgh School of Medicine* (1919);

Anna Kalet, "Voluntary Health Insurance in New York City," *American Labor Legislation Review*, 6 (June 1916): 142–154;

James J. King, "The Origin of the So-Called 'Spanish Influenza,'" *Medical Record* (12 October 1918): 632–633;

S. Adolphus Knopf, "The Ideal Sanatorium, the Ideal Physician, the Ideal Nurse, the Ideal Patient," *New York Medical Journal* (18 October 1919): 9;

E. R. LeCount, "The Pathologic Anatomy of Influenzal Bronchopneumonia," *Journal of the American Medical Association* (1 March 1919): 650+;

Ward MacNeal, "The Influenza Epidemic of 1918 in the American Expeditionary Force in France and England," *Archives of Internal Medicine* (June 1919): 675+;

Josiah Morse, "A Comparison of White and Colored Children Measured by the Binet Scale of Intelligence," *Popular Science Monthly,* 84 (January 1914): 75–79;

Mary Adelaide Nutting and L. L. Dock, *A History of Nursing* (New York: Putnam, 1912);

R. V. Pierce, *The People's Common Sense Medical Adviser in Plain English; or, Medicine Simplified* (Buffalo, N.Y.: World's Dispensary Medical Association, 1918);

Sidney L. Pressey and G. F. Teter, "A Comparison of Colored and White Children by Means of a Group Scale of Intelligence," *Journal of Applied Psychology,* 3 (September 1919): 277–282;

Proceedings of the Eighteenth Annual Convention of the American Society of Superintendents of Training Schools for Nursing (New York: Society, 1912);

W. L. Rathbun, *The Municipal Sanatorium at Otisville,* second edition (New York: Department of Health, 1914);

I. M. Rubinow, *Social Insurance* (New York: Holt, 1916);

Sadie Fuller Seagrave, *Saints Rest* (Saint Louis: Mosby, 1918);

Dr. R. M. Smith and Mrs. H. C. Greene, *The Baby's First Two Years* (New York: Houghton Mifflin, 1915);

L. L. Stanley, "Influenza at San Quentin Prison, California," *Public Health Reports* (9 May 1919): 996–998;

Dagny Sunne, "A Comparative Study of White and Negro Children," *Journal of Applied Psychology,* 1 (March 1917): 71–83;

Edgar Sydenstricker, "Existing Agencies for Health Insurance in the United States," in U.S. Department of Labor, *Proceedings of the Conference on Social Insurance, 1916* (Washington, D.C.: U.S. Government Printing Office, 1917), pp. 430–475;

Douglas Symmers, "Pathologic Similarities between Pneumonia of Bubonic Plague and of Pandemic Influenza," *Journal of the American Medical Association* (2 November 1918): 1482+;

L. M. Terman, *The Measurement of Intelligence* (Boston: Houghton Mifflin, 1916);

H. M. Thomas and others, "Symposium on the Development of the Johns Hopkins Medical School and Osler Influence," *Johns Hopkins Hospital Bulletin,* 30 (1919): 105;

Marion R. Trabue, "The Intelligence of Negro Recruits," *Natural History,* 19 (December 1919): 680–685;

U.S. Council of National Defense, *First Annual Report of the Council of National Defense, Fiscal Year, 1917* (Washington, D.C.: U.S. Government Printing Office, 1917);

Lillian D. Wald, *The House on Henry Street* (New York: Holt, 1915);

Edward E. Weaver, *Medicine, Hygiene: Mind and Health* (New York: Macmillan, 1913);

S. Burt Wolback, "Comments on the Pathology and Bacteriology of Fatal Influenza Cases, as Observed at Camp Devens, Massachusetts," *Johns Hopkins Hospital Bulletin* (April 1919): 104+;

Paul G. Wooley, "The Epidemic of Influenza at Camp Devens, Massachusetts," *Journal of Laboratory and Clinical Medicine* (March 1919): 339+.

RELIGION

by DAVID MCLEAN and MONICA SIEMS

CONTENTS

Sidebars and tables are listed in italics.

1910

- The Presbyterian General Assembly adopts a declaration of "essential" doctrines, to be used in examining theology professors and students for doctrinal orthodoxy. The "five points" included in the declaration are the inerrancy of Scripture, the Virgin Birth of Christ, his substitutionary atonement (the idea that his death provided forgiveness of sins), his bodily resurrection, and the authenticity of the miracles.

- A census records 540,000 Jews living in New York City, with most on the Lower East Side. This figure represents approximately 25 percent of the country's total Jewish population.

- Jane Addams, whose Chicago settlement house had provided the model for many Social Gospel churches and missions, publishes a retrospective, *Twenty Years at Hull House.*

- Stephen Theobald, the first black diocesan priest to be accepted and trained in a seminary in the United States, is ordained by Archbishop John Ireland in Saint Paul, Minnesota.

Feb. The Fundamentalist movement in American Protestantism begins to take shape with the publication of the first volume, edited by Amzi C. Dixon, of *The Fundamentals: A Testimony to the Truth.*

June John R. Mott of the Student Volunteer Movement presides over the World Missionary Conference in Edinburgh, Scotland, attended by more than twelve hundred delegates.

25–28 Sept. The National Conference of Catholic Charities holds its first meeting, at the Catholic University of America. Bishop Thomas Shahan, the rector of the Catholic University, is elected president. The conference, organized largely by lay members of the St. Vincent de Paul Society, is designed to coordinate the efforts of lay and diocesan social work agencies nationwide.

9 Oct. Charles Taze Russell, founder of the International Bible Students' Association (later known as Jehovah's Witnesses), delivers a speech before thousands of Jews at the Hippodrome in New York City advocating the return of the Jews to Palestine. His prophetic interpretation of the Bible had led him to support Zionism, gaining him the support of many Jews.

1911

- Vida Scudder, a professor at Wellesley College, cofounds the Episcopal Church Socialist League.

15 Apr. *Collier's* magazine publishes a letter from former president Theodore Roosevelt defending Mormons, who had been under attack in several magazines for their alleged desire to "take over" the United States. Later that year, President William Taft invites the Mormon Tabernacle Choir to sing at the White House.

27 Apr. The Catholic Foreign Mission Society of America, popularly known as Maryknoll, is approved by American archbishops in Washington, D.C. The Society will be authorized by Pope Pius X on 29 June. Maryknoll priests and nuns are most active in mission work in Central America and South America.

6 June The city of Baltimore honors James Cardinal Gibbons, Catholic archbishop, in a jubilee celebrating the twenty-fifth anniversary of his elevation to the cardinalate and the fiftieth anniversary of his ordination to the priesthood. Twenty thousand people attend the celebration, including President Taft and Theodore Roosevelt.

Summer   William Jennings Bryan, three-time Democratic nominee for president, delivers an address titled "The Old-Time Religion" at the annual interdenominational Winona Bible Conference in Indiana. The speech marks Bryan's continuing commitment to evangelical Christianity in the face of progressive trends.

29 Nov.   Archbishops John Farley of New York and William O'Connell of Boston are named cardinals by Pope Pius X .

1912

- The Methodist General Conference issues a statement asserting that lynching, which has been a persistent problem for twenty years, should become a federal crime.

- Jacob Schiff, a prominent Jewish industrialist, donates fifteen thousand volumes of Hebraic literature to the Library of Congress.

- Father Divine, an enigmatic black preacher about whose background almost nothing is known, launches his first preaching mission in Americus, Georgia.

7 Mar.   Zionist Henrietta Szold founds Hadassah, the Jewish welfare organization, in New York City.

14 Apr.   Abdul Baha, the major purveyor of the Baha'i faith (a Persian offshoot of Islam) to the United States, delivers a sermon on the "fundamental unity of all religions" at the Church of the Ascension in New York City. The sermon is part of Abdul Baha's tour of the United States, which culminates in the breaking of ground for the massive Baha'i Mother Temple in Wilmette, Illinois, a suburb of Chicago. The temple is not dedicated until 1953.

Fall   At the opening meeting of the Princeton Seminary, J. Gresham Machen, a rising star among conservative Presbyterians, calls on scholars to reassert the intellectual foundations of the faith, which he feels have been neglected by advocates of the Social Gospel.

1913

- Under the leadership of Solomon Schechter and Mordecai Kaplan, twenty-two congregations leave Orthodox Judaism and unite to form the United Synagogue.

- The Jewish Anti-Defamation League is founded.

- Moderate conservative Baptists establish the Northern Baptist Seminary in Chicago to combat the liberal influence of the Divinity School at the University of Chicago.

- Rev. Reverdy Ransom, editor of the *AME Review,* founds the Mission Church of Simon of Cyrene to minister to the poor in the "Black Tenderloin" section of Manhattan.

- Noble Drew Ali (Timothy Drew) forms the Moorish Science Temple of America in Newark, New Jersey, the first mosque in the United States. Ali preaches emancipation for American blacks through the adoption of Islam as their religion and Moorish, which he identifies as "Asiatic," as their ethnicity.

26 Aug.   Leo Frank, president of B'nai B'rith in Atlanta, is sentenced to death for the murder of fourteen-year-old Mary Phagan, who worked in his pencil factory. Many suspect that anti-Semitism played a major role in his conviction and sentencing, and his conviction elicits worldwide protest. In June 1915 the governor of Georgia commutes Frank's sentence, but two months later he is abducted from the state penitentiary by a band of armed men and hanged.

Oct. Father John A. Ryan and Morris Hillquit begin a series of debates on socialism in *Everybody's Magazine.* The series runs for seven issues, concluding in April 1914. The debates are excerpts of a book, *Socialism: Promise or Menace,* published in 1914.

20 Dec. Eudorus N. Bell, in an article in *Word and Witness,* calls for the establishment of a national organization of Pentecostals.

1914

- The Philadelphia Yearly Meeting of the Society of Friends (Quakers) goes on record as the only U.S. religious body to endorse woman suffrage.

- Twenty-five Buddhist centers are active in the United States, with the largest located in San Francisco.

11 Jan. Charles Taze Russell's "Photo-Drama of Creation," a multimedia production that includes motion pictures, slides, music, and phonograph recordings, opens at the International Bible Students' Association Temple in New York City with five thousand people in attendance. By the end of the year, the Photo-Drama has toured the United States, Europe, Australia, and New Zealand.

Feb. The Church Peace Union is created with a $2 million endowment from philanthropist Andrew Carnegie. Its initial board of twenty-nine trustees include Protestant, Catholic, and Jewish leaders. Carnegie writes a clause into the deed of this endowment stating that if "the time shall come when peace is fully established, and no more need be done in that cause, the income of the grant may be spent for the alleviation of poverty or other good causes."

Apr. At a conference in Hot Springs, Arkansas, a new Pentecostal denomination is organized as the Assemblies of God. Only sixty-eight delegates sign the charter of incorporation, but by the end of the year most white ministers of the Church of God in Christ, as well as many independent Pentecostal ministers, join the Assemblies.

20 Aug. Pope Pius X dies in Rome. He is succeeded by Giacomo Cardinal della Chiesa as Benedict XV.

30 Aug. The Federation of American Zionists (FAZ) convention takes place at the Hotel Marseilles in New York City. Louis D. Brandeis is chosen as chairman of the Provisional Executive Committee. FAZ membership rises from 12,000 in 1914 to 176,000 in 1919.

4 Oct. At the request of the Federal Council of Churches of Christ in America, President Woodrow Wilson declares a day of prayer. In cooperation with the Church Peace Union, standard prayer texts are issued, along with a "peace hymn" written by Unitarian minister John Haynes Holmes. By 1917 Holmes will be widely denounced for his pacifist beliefs.

1915

- Patrick Henry Callahan, director of the Roman Catholic fraternal organization the Knights of Columbus, works with Rev. John A. Ryan, the famous Catholic economist and reformer, to develop a profit-sharing plan for the Louisville Varnish Company, of which Callahan is the president. Under the plan the company's surplus revenues are divided between stockholders and employees.

Jan. The Church Peace Union issues a questionnaire to ten thousand ministers, asking their opinion on a military buildup in preparation for the possibility of U.S. entry into the European war. When the results of the survey are published in May, 95 percent of the clergy polled are on record as opposing an arms buildup as a threat to peace.

9 June   William Jennings Bryan's strict pacifist beliefs lead him to resign as President Woodrow Wilson's secretary of state when the two men clash over how the United States should respond to German submarine attacks on American ships and citizens.

8 July   Baptist theologian Walter Rauschenbusch and Congregational pastor Charles Aked publish *Private Profit and the Nation's Honor: A Protest and a Plea.* They call for the prohibition of arms shipments to any party involved in World War I. The book receives a strong negative reaction for its failure to support military preparedness wholeheartedly.

9 Sept.   Two black Baptist ministers, Rev. Richard H. Boyd and Rev. C. H. Clark, split from the National Baptist Convention U.S.A., Inc., to form the National Baptist Convention of America. At issue is the control of the National Baptist Publishing Board, which plays a major role in the success of the new black Baptist denomination.

4 Dec.   The Ku Klux Klan is revived in Atlanta, Georgia, by William J. Simmons, under a charter granted by the state. Anti-Catholicism and anti-Semitism are joined with the original Klan's white supremacist views, and for the first time the Klan has chaplains and specially adapted Protestant hymns. The revival is spurred in part by the case of Leo Frank; members of the Knights of Mary Phagan, who had lynched Frank, join with Simmons in the revived Klan.

1916

- Martha G. M. Avery and David Goldstein found the Catholic Truth Guild in Boston, which becomes the most extensive lay mission movement in American Catholicism.

4–6 Jan.   Representatives of fifteen Protestant denominations convene in Garden City, New York, for the Conference on Faith and Order for North America. Participants discuss the nature and functions of the church in modern America, as well as issues of doctrine and the administration of missionary and social functions.

28 Jan.   President Woodrow Wilson nominates Louis D. Brandeis for the position of associate justice of the Supreme Court. Following his confirmation by the Senate, Brandeis becomes the Court's first Jewish justice.

Mar.   Eighty-three ministers from various Christian denominations sign a letter, published in *The New York Times,* expressing support for American military preparedness. The letter is intended as a rebuttal to a Church Peace Union petition against the buildup in armaments.

May   Representatives of three different Norwegian Lutheran bodies (the Norwegian Synod, Hauge's Synod, and the United Norwegian Synod) meet in Minneapolis to unite as the Norwegian Lutheran Church in America. The new denomination serves 3,000 churches with 1,300 ministers and 310,000 communicants.

13 May   In a parade for military preparedness in New York City 130 clergymen march as a division. The following day, many other ministers preach on the event and the topic of preparedness in their pulpits.

Aug.   The Commission on Religious Prejudices, an arm of the Knights of Columbus, a Roman Catholic fraternal organization, issues a report on religious prejudice. The commission had been founded in 1914 by Patrick Henry Callahan, the Knights' director.

21 Aug.   The National Committee on Public Morals, a division of the American Federation of Catholic Societies, condemns "alien radicalism," meaning socialism, divorce, and immoral films.

6 Dec.   The Federal Council of Churches of Christ in America, the great Protestant ecumenical body, meets in Saint Louis under president Shailer Mathews of the University of Chicago Divinity School. The council reaffirms its goals of "improving social and civic conditions" and "promoting the moral and religious interests of the laboring class." Relief efforts pertaining to the war in Europe are also discussed, and Frank Mason North is elected as the council's new president.

1917

- The Mennonite Church of North America votes to withdraw from the Federal Council of Churches of Christ in America when its pacifist beliefs clash with the council's growing involvement in the war effort.

- The Federated Colored Catholics is founded by Thomas Wyatt Turner, a biology professor, to target segregation in Catholic schools and universities.

3 Feb.   William Jennings Bryan gives a speech on peace that leads to the formation of the Emergency Peace Federation to fight growing sentiment for war preparedness.

14 Apr.   The Supreme Board of Directors of the Knights of Columbus meets in Washington, D.C., and pledges to provide volunteer recreational and religious workers in army camps. The Knights had performed similar services during the Mexican border campaign the previous year.

26 Apr.   The War Department's Commission on Training Camp Activities meets and officially places the Young Men's Christian Association in charge of recreational activities in U.S. Army camps.

30 Apr.   Representatives of various Society of Friends (Quaker) meetings hold a conference in Philadelphia to discuss the possibilities for Quaker service in wartime. The conference results in the founding of the American Friends Service Committee, officially named at a 4 June meeting. Rufus Jones is appointed chair of the committee, which focuses on opportunities for noncombatant service and support for conscientious objectors.

8–9 May   The Federal Council of Churches calls a special meeting in Washington, D.C., in conjunction with the YMCA, the YWCA, the American Bible Society, several mission boards, and other organizatons, to discuss cooperative war work. A total of some thirty-five Protestant denominational and interdenominational bodies are represented at the session.

11 Aug.   John Burke, a Paulist priest and the editor of *Catholic World,* calls a meeting at the Catholic University of America in Washington, D.C., to discuss coordinating Catholic war efforts. Delegates from forty dioceses, twenty-eight lay organizations, and the Catholic press attend. The meeting results in the organization of the National Catholic War Council.

20 Sept.   The General War-Time Commission of the Federal Council of Churches meets for the first time in New York City.

1918

- In March, John Cardinal Farley, archbishop of New York, launches a New York Catholic War Fund drive. The campaign generates more than twice its $2.5 million goal in revenue.

- The Central Conference of American Rabbis (Reform Judaism) argues for a "fundamental reconstruction of our economic organization." They advocate workers' compensation insurance, labor's right to organize and bargain collectively, social insurance for the elderly, establishment of a minimum wage, and the abolition of child labor.

- African Methodist Episcopal minister Reverdy Ransom is nominated by the United Civic League of New York as a candidate for the twenty-first congressional district. Although a technicality keeps him off the actual ballot, he receives 456 write-in votes.

- Edward T. Demby of Arkansas becomes the first black bishop in the Episcopal Church.

- Aimee Semple McPherson arrives in Los Angeles with $100, a tambourine, and a car with a sign reading "Jesus is Coming Soon — Get Ready." Her dynamic preaching leads to the founding of the Church of the Foursquare Gospel in 1927.

1 Mar. The first government-run school for the training of army chaplains opens at Fort Monroe, Virginia.

May The Committee on National Prohibition as a War Measure, a division of the Federal Council of Churches' General War-Time Commission, submits a petition to the president and Congress calling for a law to prevent the manufacture, importation, and sale of all intoxicating beverages.

28–30 May At the Philadelphia Prophecy Conference, premillennialists speak on how the events of World War I represent "signs of the times" that correspond to biblical prophecies about the coming of the millennium.

30 May President Woodrow Wilson declares Decoration Day to be a day of fasting and prayer for victory in the war.

June At a convention in Pittsburgh, the Federation of American Zionists adopts a policy regarding the future Jewish state in Palestine. The platform calls for public ownership of land, cooperative economic development, and political equality for all inhabitants.

21 June Seven "Russellites," or Jehovah's Witnesses, are sentenced to twenty years each in the federal penitentiary in Atlanta for circulating and teaching the doctrines laid out by founder Charles Taze Russell in *The Finished Mystery*, published earlier that year. Their actions were held to be in violation of the Espionage Act of 1917. In the book Russell argued that he found no biblical support for patriotism as a duty, and he denounced the coercion of citizens into participating in wars. A substantial number of Witnesses had applied for conscientious objector status at the beginning of the war.

5 Sept. The United War Work Campaign, a massive fund-raising effort to benefit all Protestant, Catholic, and Jewish war work organizations, is announced by President Wilson. The drive kicks off on 11 November, Armistice Day, but nonetheless pledges a total of $205 million by 20 November. Of those pledges, a total of $188 million are ultimately collected and distributed.

1919

- Wentworth Arthur Matthew, a former Pentecostal minister who was active in Marcus Garvey's Universal Negro Improvement Association, founds the Commandment Keepers Congregation of the Living God, a black Jewish group in New York. He argues that the Hebrew patriarchs were black, making blacks representatives of the "true" Jewish race. Matthew also denounces Christianity as a "white man's religion" and adheres to Orthodox Jewish practices, including the use of Hebrew in the services and the keeping of kosher laws.

- Father Divine establishes a misson in Sayville, Long Island, with his wife and about twenty followers. He preaches hard work (many of his followers are employed as domestic help in nearby estates), honesty, sobriety, racial and gender equality, and sexual abstinence. The mission, later named the Peace Mission Movement, provides food and shelter to anyone in need and opens its membership to whites as well as blacks. He is regarded as the Second Coming of Jesus by his followers, and the mission's neighbors soon complain about the people coming by busload from across the country to see Father Divine.

- At an "All American Convention" in Pittsburgh, Pennsylvania, the Russian Orthodox Church in America declares that it will be independent of the Russian Orthodoxy in the newly formed Soviet Union, in order to distance itself from the Bolsheviks.

- A Pentecostal preacher named Elder Micheaux organizes a Church of God movement in Newport News, Virginia, and begins broadcasting services over local radio. By 1928 he gains considerable fame as a radio evangelist.

29 Apr. The General War-Time Commission of the Federal Council of Churches of Christ in America is disbanded at its final meeting.

May The first conference of the World's Christian Fundamentals Association is held in Philadelphia. Speakers denounce the "Great Apostasy" and the rejection of biblical doctrines by liberal Protestants. The association was founded by William Bell Riley, the pastor of a prominent Baptist church in Minneapolis, Minnesota.

Methodist minister and suffragist Anna Howard Shaw is awarded the Distinguished Service Medal for her work as chair of the Women's Committee of the Council of National Defense, a position she had held since 1917. She is the first American woman to receive this honor.

24 Sept. The National Catholic Welfare Council is established in response to a call from Pope Benedict XV for American bishops to "join him in working for the cause of peace and social justice in the world." The Council represents the transformation of the National Catholic War Council into a peacetime organization devoted to social action.

OVERVIEW

The Progressive Spirit. The progressive movement in politics provided a keynote for a dominant voice in American religion in the early years of the twentieth century. Much of the country's white, middle-and upper-middle-class, Protestant establishment believed that America had a special role to play in the destiny — even the salvation — of the world, and the years prior to World War I gave them ample reason for confidence. The prevailing scientific mood of the times fostered a belief in progress toward bigger and better things, and the religiously liberal as well as the politically liberal in the United States thus embraced the new and the modern as evidence of such evolution. They also believed they had the ability and a duty to aid in the betterment of society, so a "crusading," reformist spirit characterized the time. Theodore Roosevelt's Progressive Party platform of 1912 dovetailed nicely with the Social Gospel movement that had grown up in American Christianity since the 1880s. The call for social and industrial reforms issued by the progressive movement was based on a deeply held conviction about what constituted a just and moral society, and while Roosevelt failed to capture the White House in 1912, his surprising draw in the election illustrated the power of such a vision. American exceptionalism had reached a high point. Through progress, guided by moral principles, the United States could become the world's exemplar of a Christian civilization.

The World Stage. This progressive spirit extended beyond the borders of the United States, manifesting itself abroad in the ambitious foreign missionary movements launched by American religious bodies around the turn of the century. At the opening of the century's second decade, America's greatest missionary organizer, John R. Mott of the Student Volunteer Movement, presided over a massive world missionary conference in Edinburgh, Scotland, thus illustrating the leadership of the United States in the propagation of Christianity across the globe. When war broke out in Europe in 1914, the sense of missionary duty was made all the more urgent for some. Mott felt that the only solution to Europe's present crisis lay in "the worldwide spread of Christianity in its purest form," so that the spirit and moral fiber of the warring nations would be transformed. Other American religious leaders focused on the need for America to remind her European peers of the Christian imperative for peace. In 1914 an unprecedented number of peace organizations existed in the United States, and most of the country's prominent pastors belonged to at least one such union. The Federal Council of Churches of Christ in America, the great Protestant ecumenical body that had been founded in 1908, had issued a statement in 1912 urging that American Christians "rise at this time and demand that all nations learn again the first principles of the teachings of Jesus Christ, that membership in his kingdom should bind them together in mutual love and . . . that the thought of engaging with each other in deadly combat shall become abhorrent and impossible forever." The council put this demand into practice in 1914 when it established a Commission on Peace and Arbitration, which worked to support various peace plans that were being negotiated in Europe. For at least the first few years of the decade, the United States occupied the moral high ground with regard to Europe, thus reinforcing its special place on the world stage.

A True Crusade. But as the war dragged on in Europe, it contradicted the ideals of civilizational progress so many Americans held dear. As America looked on, arguing for peace, Europe seemed to be growing more, rather than less, barbaric in its conduct. When Germany began conducting submarine warfare in 1915, the war expanded in ways that the United States could not ignore, and the duty of America to the rest of world was increasingly seen as military rather than moral. By the time President Woodrow Wilson asked Congress to declare war on Germany in April 1917, a majority of the country's religious leaders had accepted the new proposition that the only way for America to fulfill its task of "making the world safe for democracy" was to fight; that this war had to be fought to end the need for war once and for all. The crusading spirit had found a true military expression. Pacifists, Christian and otherwise, were disgusted by the churches' support for the war, tinged as it often was with wartime propaganda and hysteria. What had happened, they wondered, to the call to all nations to honor the precepts of Christ? When the war ended and America's progressive religious leaders had a moment to reflect on their own, and their government's, conduct, many of them would ask the same question. Prominent members of the clergy, including Reform Jewish rabbi Stephen S. Wise and Methodist minister and suffragist Anna Howard Shaw, toured the country lecturing in support of the League of Nations and Wilson's peace proposals. Clinging to what they could of the ideals of progress, they hoped that the peace agreement might yet demonstrate that something good had come from the fighting. The Federal Council of Churches went so far as to cable Wilson, while he was in Paris for the treaty talks, to express their belief that the League of Nations represented the "political expression of the Kingdom of God on earth," showing how devoted they still were to the notion that such a kingdom could be brought about through human effort. But the failure of the United States to participate in the League of Nations and the punitive Treaty of Versailles struck another blow to American optimism. The decade that had started in such faith closed with many American religious leaders facing bitter disillusionment, wondering anew at the prospects for a truly Christian civilization.

"100 Percent Americanism." At home, meanwhile, though the liberal progressive vision may have held a certain privilege throughout the 1910s, it hardly had a monopoly on notions of America's Christian principles and Christian duty. Conflict is implicit in the notion of a crusade, and no one vision of America's destiny could go unchallenged for long in the complex social atmosphere of the 1910s. The very term *American* allowed for shades of meaning, and ethnic diversity continued to complicate the issue. Immigrants from Europe continued to pour into the United States — nearly six million arrived between 1911 and 1920, following the nine million of the previous decade — so assimilation remained a hotly contested issue in many religious bodies. While the Protestant establishment, along with already assimilated elements within Roman Catholicism and Judaism, urged the "Americanization" of immigrants to introduce them to all the benefits of American society, many of the new arrivals insisted that religious liberty and tolerance were the most salient features of America's Christian civilization. The issue came to a head during World War I, when dual loyalties and anything less than "100 percent Americanism" were regarded as suspect. Catholics suffered perhaps more than any other religious group in this wartime fervor. Millions of the immigrants were Catholics from southern and eastern Europe, and they joined German American Catholics who had been struggling to maintain their ethnic identity since the late nineteenth century. These factors, combined with the long heritage in the United States of anti-Catholic nativism, led to the singling out and persecution of ethnic Catholics during the war, to which they responded with a concerted effort to demonstrate their patriotism by performing wartime service. America's Russian Orthodox communities faced a similar challenge after the Bolshevik Revolution of 1917. By the end of the decade American Orthodox churches had taken steps to dissociate themselves from the church in Russia; they had even gone so far as to censure some of their more outspoken progressivist priests, for in the minds of many Americans, influenced by the Red Scare of 1919, labor reformism was only a short step from insidious Bolshevism. As the decade passed, then, the tension caused by international conflict and upheaval put increasing pressure on America's millions of immigrants to assert their patriotism and their adherence to the mainstream Protestant vision of what it meant to be American. On that view, loyalty seemed to have replaced liberty as the country's cardinal virtue. American confidence was shaken by the events of the 1910s, so American identity was guarded all the more closely.

Labor Strife. Immigration and antiforeign sentiment related to another area of religious conflict in the 1910s, the question of the proper Christian response to ongoing labor abuses and strife. Large numbers of immigrants concentrated in the urban centers of the East Coast, often joining the masses of the laboring poor already there. The Social Gospel, a theological movement developed in the 1880s that sought to infuse the American economic system with the principles of Christian love and cooperation, had attained a certain maturity by the 1910s. The major theorists of the Social Gospel, Congregationalist Washington Gladden and Baptist Walter Rauschenbusch, were both in their final decade of life, but they continued to refine the principles of the movement. Rauschenbusch published three of his most highly regarded works in this decade: *Christianizing the Social Order* (1912), *The Social Principles of Jesus* (1916), and the definitive *A Theology for the Social Gospel* (1917). Social Christianity also had scores of representatives at the level of urban missions, settlement houses, and Young Men's Christian Associations (YMCA) across the country, but labor unrest was getting worse rather than better in the century's second decade. Strikes gripped key industries, and workers organized to express their grievances in ever more-radical ways. One growing labor union, the Industrial Workers of the World (IWW), launched a concerted media attack against the Christian churches, criticizing their failure to make good on their reformist ideals. The churches, for their part, feared the IWW's radicalism and its socialist leanings. As the decade wore on, the IWW came to be viewed as part of the "foreign peril" of communism and anarchism that Americans so dreaded, and the chance of a rapprochement between the churches and the labor movement grew slimmer. Thus, labor remained another instance where progressive Christianity, with its ideals of what would be best for America and its privileged position as the impulse of the established Protestant mainstream, failed to extend its promise far beyond its own sphere.

Modernism. The question of what it meant to be a Christian civilization had clear theological implications, and it thus engendered serious debate within American Protestantism during the 1910s, as the seeds for the explosive Fundamentalist/Modernist controversy of the

1920s were sown. For many conservative Protestants, who until this decade were only loosely allied through conferences and publications, the progressive spirit and agenda relied too heavily on the scientific theory of evolution, which, to the conservatives, was a completely unacceptable departure from their own reliance on the Bible as the ultimate source of truth about this world and the next. The Fundamentalist movement, although it would not technically receive that name until 1920, took shape in the 1910s primarily as a crusade to rescue the Bible from the liberal Protestant tendency to read the Scriptures allegorically and as a testimony only of faith, not of scientific truth. Eloquent defenses of the Bible appeared in *The Fundamentals,* a twelve-volume collection of conservative theology published between 1910 and 1915. The movement took greater shape in 1919 with the formation of the World's Christian Fundamentals Association, and by this time the fundamentalists' aims and concerns had become more complex. As the decade had progressed, the conservatives correlated the liberals' flexibility in theological matters with the moral breakdown of society, evidence of which they found in the war and communism, both examples to them of the anarchy and chaos that seemed to be shaking the world to its very foundations. The correlation of moral and doctrinal decline fit especially with the fact that America's liberal Protestants had long been heavily influenced by trends in German theology; when conservatives observed what they considered Germany's utter moral depravity during the war, they pointed to it almost triumphantly as the logical consequence of liberal theologizing. Thus, the old debates about evolution and the Bible were revived with new force. For the fundamentalists, the very survival of civilization depended on the repudiation of the new ideas and a return to a straightforward dependence on the Scriptures. The battle that had once been waged in America's seminaries and pulpits had gained a new urgency, which would translate into an unprecedented prominence in the 1920s.

Roman Catholicism. American Catholics had entered the twentieth century with two major problems demanding their attention. The first was the great ethnic diversity within the American church. The English and French elements of the church had been established since colonial times, and in the first half of the nineteenth century these had been augmented by massive waves of Irish immigration. After 1850 the tide of immigration shifted, bringing millions of German Catholics to America's shores and setting the stage for intense conflict with the Irish over questions of language, custom, parochial schools, and temperance. The Irish-German controversy had barely settled down when the church faced new ethnic challenges with the arrival of many Italian and eastern European immigrants around and after the turn of the century. Ethnic conflicts likewise rearranged themselves; in 1916, when a German-born bishop was installed in the diocese of Chicago, a German-Polish

Catholic controversy began that would linger for several years. The issue of assimilation, so pressing for all immigrants, thus posed unique problems for the Catholic Church in America.

Patriotism. But in the 1910s that issue took a back seat to the church's other major challenge of long standing, acceptance by American Protestants, who had a long history of nativist prejudice against Catholics. Church leaders such as James Cardinal Gibbons, archbishop of Baltimore, and John Ireland, archbishop of Saint Paul, Minnesota, had worked since the 1880s on a program of Americanization for the Catholic Church in an effort to quell anti-Catholic prejudice, and as the war demanded the support of all loyal patriots they redoubled their efforts in this cause. Gibbons was particularly instrumental in this regard, seizing upon the war as an opportunity for American Catholics to distinguish themselves through loyal service. Thus, he oversaw the formation of the National Catholic War Council, which raised money for and coordinated all kinds of Catholic volunteerism. There was scarcely a pacifist priest or conscientious objector to be found among the country's fourteen million Catholics, and the efforts of the Catholic War Council went a long way toward reassuring Protestants that Catholics could, in fact, be devoted patriots. The Catholic War Council had another part to play in the further assimilation and acceptance of American Catholics as well. In 1919, rather than disbanding, as the Protestant General War-Time Commission did, the Catholic War Council was transformed into the National Catholic Welfare Conference (NCWC), the first national Catholic organization dedicated to social reform. By adopting a social creed and providing a means to coordinate hitherto scattered and small-scale Catholic expressions of the Social Gospel, the NCWC became a defining force for an emerging reality: the *American* Catholic Church.

Judaism. Like Catholicism, Judaism in America was shaped largely by issues of ethnicity within and prejudice without. Two of American Judaism's three main divisions were constituted largely on the basis of ethnicity, with Reform representing the highly assimilated descendants of nineteenth-century German immigrants and Orthodox consisting largely of newly arrived immigrants who were fleeing persecution and violence in eastern Europe. Conservative Judaism, as it took shape after the turn of the century, provided another angle on the question of national identity and assimilation, stressing the idea of the peoplehood and nationhood of Israel as an ethnicity in itself. This notion, expressed by Mordecai M. Kaplan after 1916 in the phrase "Judaism as a civilization," did much to foster the burgeoning Zionist movement in America. In the 1910s all three branches of Judaism increased their support for a political, as well as a spiritual, home for the people of Israel.

Anti-Semitism. But while Zionism helped bring together some of the diverse elements of American Jewry, anti-Semites seized on any implication that Jews were a people set apart. The lynching of Leo Frank, an Atlanta businessman and B'nai B'rith leader convicted of murdering a fourteen-year-old girl in his employ, illustrated the extent to which anti-Semitism still lingered in the American consciousness, just as anti-Catholicism did. In fact the Frank case was a major factor in the revival of the Ku Klux Klan in Atlanta in 1915, which for the first time added anti-Catholic and anti-Semitic rhetoric to the white-supremacist platform its nineteenth-century incarnation had embraced. Perhaps there was ample reason, then, for American Jews to look to a homeland where Jews were free of such prejudice and persecution.

Social Service. Another similarity between American Catholics and American Jews was the opportunity for at least some degree of acceptance through social service. The Jewish Welfare Board, created in April 1917, spearheaded a wartime effort analogous to those of the Protestant General War-Time Commission and the National Catholic War Council, including providing chaplains to serve the two hundred thousand Jewish soldiers in America's armed forces. After the war the Jewish Welfare Board became active in the creation of Jewish Community Centers in cities across the country. Nor was the Jewish Welfare Board the only Jewish body working for social reform. In 1918 the Central Conference of American Rabbis (a Reform Jewish body) adopted its own social creed, advocating workmen's compensation, collective bargaining, minimum wage, and unemployment insurance. Reform rabbi Stephen S. Wise became one of the most prominent crusaders of the day, often working in conjunction with such Christian reformers as the Unitarian minister John Haynes Holmes and Paul Kellogg, the editor of the *Survey* magazine. The progressive spirit, then, provided a means for traditionally marginalized religious groups such as Roman Catholics and Jews to join in the American mainstream and contribute to the shaping of the American social agenda.

Black Americans. For black Americans the mainstream was never so accessible. Racial barriers remained in place well into the twentieth century, following the rise of Jim Crow laws in the South and the persistence of lynching as a real danger to American blacks. Moreover, race was one issue that the progressive Protestants overlooked almost entirely; the giants of the Social Gospel were virtually silent on the question. Protestantism was the religion of a vast majority of American blacks, but they were concentrated in separate institutions, independent from white denominational bodies. As a result, black Americans after the turn of the century developed their own Social Gospel movement. Reverdy Ransom, an African Methodist Episcopal minister who worked in Chicago and, later, New York City, was a pioneer in this effort. A close friend of reformer Jane Addams, Ransom had established an institutional church on the model of Addams's Hull House settlement in Chicago in 1900. His work continued into the 1910s as he moved to New York and established a similar church, the Mission Church of Simon of Cyrene, in the depressed "Black Tenderloin" section of Manhattan. Through the efforts of Ransom and his peers, black American Christians thus addressed another failure of the progressive Protestants to realize their ideals among disenfranchised sectors of the American populace.

Black Nationalism. Black Americans could also respond to the plague of racism by assertions of solidarity and nationalism, a trend that found its first explicitly religious expression in the 1910s. Marcus Garvey's Universal Negro Improvement Association was taking up the cry for black autonomy based on a recognition of the unity of "all the Negro peoples of the world" and calling for a return to Africa and the establishment of independent black nations. But it was the introduction of a new religious option for blacks that would have a more enduring effect on black nationalism in America. In 1913 a man named Timothy Drew established what he called the Moorish Science Temple of America in Newark, New Jersey, thus sowing the first seeds of Islam among blacks. The basis of Drew's movement was the assertion of a new black American identity — no longer "Negroes, black folk, colored people, or Ethiopians," they were now to be known as Moors, which Drew considered an "Asiatic," rather than an African, designation. Not an orthodox sect of Islam (Noble Drew Ali, as he came to be known, promulgated his own version of the Islamic scriptures, the *Holy Koran*, which included Christian and Eastern esoteric elements), Moorish Science clearly centered on the liberating power of the "ethnic transformation" of black Americans into "Asiatics." Drew provided his followers with identification cards to certify their new status, a system that led to legal skirmishes when members of a Chicago temple began brandishing their cards in the faces of whites, explaining their newfound freedom from "European domination." And although the Moorish Science movement remained small, with temples only in scattered cities, it bears great significance for black American religious history: after Drew's death in 1929, members of a Moorish Science Temple in Detroit turned to Wallace D. Fard for leadership, signaling the beginnings of the Nation of Islam. Thus, while some blacks found in Christianity the promise of liberation and redemption, as well as an avenue for social improvement, from this decade onward others would follow Drew's lead in denouncing Christianity as a "white man's religion" and turning to Islam in protest and in hope.

Women. Protest was also a salient feature of the religious experience of American women throughout the 1910s. Often denied acceptance into the established ministry of Protestant churches (and, at the time, always denied such access in Judaism and Roman Catholicism), women who shared the reforming spirit had long since explored other opportunities for exhorting their fellow Americans to moral greatness. Sometimes, as in war relief efforts, they worked side by side with men, but in other cases they stood clearly in the forefront. The drive for temperance had often been spearheaded by women, especially through the workings of the Women's Christian Temperance Union (WCTU), which continued active until the passage of the Eighteenth Amendment instituting Prohibition in 1919. But in the 1910s women were most occupied with issuing a more radical moral challenge to their countrymen, the extension of the right to vote to women. Two of the most prominent women engaged in this cause were, in fact, early pioneers in the ordination of women to the ministry — Anna Howard Shaw was a Methodist minister, and Olympia Brown was a Universalist and perhaps only the second or third woman in the United States ordained by a Protestant body. Brown's speeches in particular explicitly provided a religious ground for woman suffrage, representing yet another challenge to the male progressives to take their ideals to their logical conclusion. Men were not the only ones, it seemed, who could lead crusades.

The Challenge and Promise of Progress. Thus, the idea of progress indeed informed most of the major trends in American religion in the 1910s. But progress meant different things to different people. The Social Gospel found its political expression in the Progressive Party's calls for labor reforms but failed to address the problems of poverty that were associated with racism. Similarly, when the military defeat of Germany brought the extension of democracy in Europe, American women pointed to a full half of the population in the United States that was denied access to that same democracy. In fact, almost any time the progressive Protestant mainstream reaffirmed its commitment to Christian ideals such as brotherhood, equality, and cooperation, some other segment of America could point to some sphere in which those ideals were not being realized. Progress was the great promise of the new century. But as the 1910s began, it had become clear that it was also the great challenge of modern American religion.

TOPICS IN THE NEWS

FUNDAMENTALISM

Calm before the Storm. In the decades following the Civil War, liberal theology made substantial inroads into Protestant seminaries and universities in the United States. The primary feature of this liberalism was an acceptance of and reliance upon scientific methods for the discovery of truth. This view of truth contrasted sharply with the traditional Christian commitment to revealed truth, especially as the Bible contained it. Instead of looking to the Scriptures to determine the truth of a matter, liberals often held biblical texts up for comparison with scientific theories, such as Darwinian evolution. When they found disagreement, liberals began to reinterpret the Bible not as a source of knowledge about the physical world but as a record of faith composed by human beings at different historical intervals, causing inconsistencies and errors where knowledge had been deficient. This method of reading the Bible became known as the "higher criticism." Many prominent American theologians had spent some time studying at German universities, the intellectual source of this new theology. As a result of this European influence, higher criticism had taken root in most major American seminaries and divinity schools by the turn of the twentieth

century. But conservative Protestants, who still looked to the Bible as the source of literal truths about the world, did not stand quietly by while this shift took place. In the last decades of the nineteenth century many Protestant denominations conducted heresy trials against well-known professors who were thought to have gone too far in accepting the "modernist" ideas of the liberals. Conservatives also maintained a firm hold on some of the nation's most illustrious divinity schools, especially Princeton, the bastion of conservative Presbyterianism. But clearly neither side could claim victory; by 1900 it had become apparent that an intractable split had opened up in American Protestantism. To the liberals, the conservatives were dinosaurs whose inflexibility in matters of doctrine threatened to cause massive defections from the faith as more and more people, clergy and lay people alike, came to accept the truth of scientific knowledge. The conservatives, on the other hand, saw the liberals as nothing short of heretics whose theological innovation seemed designed to destroy the faith itself from within. In the first two decades of the twentieth century, an uneasy truce seemed to be in effect between these two sides. They tended to work in their respective spheres, with only a few volleys being fired in their publications. But this was merely the calm before a great storm. The

Foreword to volume 2 of *The Fundamentals: A Testimony to the Truth*, the series of apologetics that invigorated traditional Protestant Christianity during the 1910s

groundwork was being laid, especially on the conservative side, for the massive fundamentalist versus modernist controversy of the 1920s. Although the term *Fundamentalism* was not officially coined for the movement until 1920, the 1910s clearly saw a conservative marshaling of forces as diverse factions coalesced into a movement of surprising strength and influence.

The Fundamentals. In August 1909 Union Oil magnate Lyman Stewart heard Amzi Dixon, then pastor of Dwight L. Moody's church in Chicago, preach a sermon in which he lambasted "one of those infidel professors" at the University of Chicago Divinity School, the stronghold of liberalism in the early twentieth century. Stewart realized that he had found in Dixon a man who could help him to fulfill his aim of publishing sophisticated Christian apologetic literature, works designed to provide "warning and testimony" to anyone who might be seduced by modernist ideas. Stewart and his brother, Milton, offered to put up $250,000 to finance a series of volumes to be edited by Dixon and a committee of his choosing. Dixon agreed, choosing the great revivalist Reuben A. Torrey and a Jewish Christian evangelist, Louis Meyer, as his coeditors. They solicited articles from all the leading scholars of American and British conservative theology, gathering all the contributions into a twelve-volume series titled simply *The Fundamentals: A Testimony to the Truth*. The first volume appeared in February 1910, and the others followed periodically until 1915. The Stewarts distributed three million copies

of these volumes free of charge to pastors, professors, missionaries, Young Men's Christian Association (YMCA) and Young Women's Christian Association (YWCA) officials, and other religious professionals. But despite this massive effort, which caused many to regard *The Fundamentals* as the classic statement of Fundamentalism, these volumes neither attracted significant attention in the religious press nor contained many of the elements that the fundamentalist movement of the 1920s considered essential. Many of the articles consisted of personal testimonies of religious experience, and although the volumes contained pieces attacking a series of "isms" — Russellism (Jehovah's Witnesses), Mormonism, Eddyism (Christian Science), Spiritualism, and Romanism (Roman Catholicism) — they displayed a notable lack of commentary on political and ethical issues. What the articles were about demonstrates the extent to which the editors had boiled the liberal/conservative controversy down to a single fundamental issue, biblical literalism. A full one-third of *The Fundamentals* was devoted to defenses of scriptural truth and attacks on higher criticism. Creedal loyalty and doctrinal orthodoxy were becoming easier and easier to measure as the issues were painted in ever-simpler terms: one either accepted the Bible or did not. While much of *The Fundamentals* is moderate in tone, especially when compared to later fundamentalist statements, its publication clearly helped erode whatever middle ground may have been left between liberal and conservative theologians.

Christianity and Culture. A diversity of conservative opinions stood behind the silence of *The Fundamentals* on some issues, most notably those dealing with the attitude Christians ought to take toward social and political trends in America. The authors of *The Fundamentals* represented a broad spectrum of views on this question of "Christianity and culture," a question that could include anything from card-playing and dancing to the perceived "menace" of socialism. Among the contributors were some strict "separationists," such as Arno C. Gaebelein, the editor of the independent *Our Hope*, who saw both modern society and the modern church as thoroughly corrupt and advocated as extensive a withdrawal from both as one could manage. But many of the early fundamentalists had roots in the great revival tradition of nineteenth-century evangelical Christianity, a tradition noted as much or more for its moral crusading as for its theological conservatism. William Jennings Bryan expressed the continuation of this approach to religion in a 1911 Bible conference lecture when he spoke of all the things Christianity had to offer modern civilization by way of moral and social reform. A fellow Presbyterian, J. Gresham Machen of Princeton, gave an address in 1912 in which he explicitly associated the theological battle being fought in the seminaries with the changing cultural conditions of the time. "What is to-day a matter of academic speculation, begins tomorrow to move armies and pull down empires," Machen argued, calling for a full-fledged effort to infuse all aspects of culture with the word of God. By 1920 such views would clearly represent the majority opinion within the fundamentalist movement; the battle against modernism would not distinguish its theological from its cultural aspects. World War I had a galvanizing effect on this wing of the movement, pushing it to create by 1919 mature statements about the relationship between Christianity and culture.

The War Years. The war also helped to solidify the influence of premillennialism in the fundamentalist movement, a development related to the clarification of cultural values. Premillennialism was a long-standing Protestant movement, based on a literal reading of prophetic texts from the Bible that led believers to expect the imminent personal return of Christ to initiate his thousand-year reign of peace. Premillennialists were enjoying great success as the European war seemed to testify to the accuracy of their biblically founded prophecies, and liberal theologians launched a major offensive in the religious and secular press to counter the growing influence of this wing of conservative Protestantism. Shirley Jackson Case of the University of Chicago Divinity School led the charge, making a major tactical error when he attempted to paint the premillennialists as German sympathizers. The premillennialists responded in force by pointing out the clear link between American and German liberal theologians. By 1918 German theology, biblical criticism, and philosophy were being blamed by many conservative preachers for what they saw as Germany's moral bankruptcy, evidenced by the war. Howard Kellogg, a staunch premillennialist, gave a speech on this theme in the summer of 1918 at the Bible Institute of Los Angeles, an institution supported by Lyman Stewart. He put the issue in the starkest terms possible. "Loud are the cries against German Kultur. . . . Let this now be identified with Evolution, and the truth begins to be told." Kellogg apparently blamed acceptance of Darwinism for Germany's current appearance as "a monster plotting world domination, the wreck of civilization and the destruction of Christianity itself."

Fundamentalism Takes Shape. This development in premillennial argumentation led to the crystallization of American Fundamentalism in its "classic" form as a movement that was conservative not only theologically but also socially, with a strong commitment to preserving traditional values — preserving a civilization that fundamentalists believed was on the brink of moral, if not actual, collapse. World War I, liberal and conservative Protestants seemed to agree, was being fought to preserve civilization itself. But while the liberals spoke of civilization in terms of democratic values and freedom from tyranny, premillennialists and their fellow travelers identified those same traits as the near anarchy that needed to be eradicated.

The Red Scare. Following the war, fundamentalists found ample reason to transfer their concerns about German civilization to America. With the end of the war,

---

THE FUNDAMENTALS

In 1910 the first of the twelve volumes of *The Fundamentals* was published by the Testimony Publishing Company in Chicago. Subtitled "A Testimony to the Truth," the book was presented "compliments of two Christian laymen," its title page proclaimed. With Amzi Dixon as editor in chief and the financial backing of oil magnate Lyman Stewart and his brother, Milton, the new publication had both a sweeping goal and the money required to meet that goal. The Stewart brothers expressed the aims of the series in their foreword to the first volume:

This book is the first of a series which will be published and sent to every pastor, evangelist, missionary, theological professor, theological student, Sunday school superintendent, Y.M.C.A. and Y.W.C.A. secretary in the English speaking world, so far as the addresses of all these can be obtained.

Two intelligent, consecrated Christian laymen bear the expense, because they believe that the time has come when a new statement of the fundamentals of Christianity should be made.

Their earnest desire is that you will carefully read it and pass its truth on to others.

Source: George M. Marsden, ed., *The Fundamentals: A Testimony to Truth,* volume 1 (New York: Garland, 1988).

---

social and economic displacement struck many Americans, leading to an unstable period of labor unrest, violent confrontations, and even scattered terrorist bombings. The threat to American values had a new name — Bolshevism — and fundamentalists became caught up in the Red Scare that gripped the country immediately after the war. Socialism and anarchy were thought to go hand in hand, and the response of many conservative Protestants was to urge strict isolationism in American policy. Many cautioned against joining the League of Nations; they perceived in the reconstruction taking place in Europe the threat of a "World Communist Internationale," as Gaebelein expressed it.

Culture Wars. Seeing personal and national values as closely intertwined, fundamentalists also redoubled their efforts to combat moral laxity wherever they saw it. Smoking, public dancing, and moving pictures were among the many targets attacked from pulpits and in the pages of fundamentalist publications. Oliver Van Osdel, a pastor in Michigan, gave a sermon in November 1919 in which he argued, "when you find people indulging in worldliness they become loose in doctrine, then apostasy easily creeps in, the union of Christendom becomes possible, and probably will be united through corrupt doctrine under one head, the Pope of Rome," often identified by fundamentalists as the Antichrist. The same ideas had been expressed in May 1919 in Philadelphia by speakers at the first conference of the World's Christian Fundamentals Association, an organization founded by William B. Riley, a Minneapolis pastor. The WCFA was committed to biblical literalism, premillennialism, and the preservation of traditional Christian values as normative in American culture. It held conferences in several cities during 1919, drawing audiences that totaled in the tens of thousands. Fundamentalism had spent the decade of the 1910s finding its voice. With many of the diverse strands of conservative Protestantism united under the program of the WCFA, Fundamentalism — though still a year shy of officially receiving that name — had by 1919 gained the strength it would need to make its voice heard in the raucous debates of the 1920s.

Sources:

George M. Marsden, *Fundamentalism and American Culture: The Shaping of Twentieth-Century Evangelicalism, 1870–1925* (New York: Oxford University Press, 1980);

Ernest R. Sandeen, *The Roots of Fundamentalism: British and American Millenarianism, 1800–1930* (Chicago: University of Chicago Press, 1970);

Timothy P. Weber, *Living in the Shadow of the Second Coming: American Premillennialism, 1875–1982*, revised edition (Grand Rapids, Mich.: Academie Books, 1983).

RELIGION, SOCIALISM, AND THE INDUSTRIAL WORKERS OF THE WORLD

An Army of Church Invaders. "Six hundred unemployed men crept into the Labor Temple at Second Avenue and Fourteenth Street last night, while the lights were out for a moving picture show," *The New York Times* reported on 1 March 1914. When asked what they wanted, their leader, Frank Tannenbaum, replied, "We have come to take possession of this place for the night. We intend to stay. . . . If you try to put us out, the floor of this place will run with blood." The church capitulated somewhat to the demand, agreeing to house sixty-five men who said they had nowhere else to sleep for the night and peacefully dispersing the rest. Between 1 March and 5 March, Tannenbaum led his "army of the unemployed" into a series of churches in New York City, demanding food and shelter. They were welcomed by the pastor of St. Mark's Protestant Episcopal Church on behalf of the parish's socialist fellowship, but elsewhere, including a tony Fifth Avenue Protestant church, they were turned away or even arrested. Many churches simply postponed their regularly scheduled evening meetings that week and locked their doors, because "they feared a visit from Tannenbaum's army." *The New York Times* editorialized against these invaders, charging Tannenbaum with inciting lawlessness and anarchy. Tannenbaum had struck a nerve; he brought sharply to the public eye the growing struggle between established religion and the burgeoning socialist labor movement in America. At the age of twenty-one, Tannenbaum already served as the perfect symbol for this battle. An active

CHURCH MEMBERSHIP IN THE 1910S

Between 1911 and 1918 total church membership in the United States increased from 36 million to 41.5 million, with most religious bodies enjoying modest growth. Catholicism continued to expand at the most prodigious rate, adding two million members in this seven-year period.

Denomination	Members in 1911	Members in 1918
Seventh-Day Adventist	95,808	123,768
Baptist	5,775,358	7,213,922
Congregationalist	738,761	815,396
Disciples of Christ	1,533,962	1,511,160
Eastern Orthodox	424,000	472,794
Episcopal	947,320	1,072,321
Society of Friends (Quakers)	122,796	119,233
Latter-Day Saints	400,650	435,797
Lutheran	2,289,897	2,443,812
Methodist	6,819,660	7,579,311
Presbyterian	1,944,181	2,259,358
Roman Catholic	12,778,707	14,927,466

Sources: *The American Year Book, 1912* (New York: Appleton, 1913); *The American Year Book, 1919* (New York: Appleton, 1920).

leader of a radical new union, the Industrial Workers of the World (IWW), Tannenbaum marched his army into New York City's churches demanding Christian charity — and, as he had suspected would be the case, often found the churches unresponsive.

A Foreign Peril. Tannenbaum threw into bold relief the contrast that had existed implicitly within mainstream Protestantism since the founding of the IWW. On the one hand the Social Gospel movement continued to expand in the 1910s, calling for labor and economic reforms to ameliorate the conditions under which people lived and worked. On the other hand, even liberal Protestant ministers took care to distance themselves from the IWW and the socialism and "anarchy" it represented.

Frank Tannenbaum of the Industrial Workers of the World addressing a crowd of strikers in Union Square, New York City, in 1913. In 1914 Tannenbaum led a large group of the unemployed to New York City churches demanding food and shelter.

The New York church "invasions" served only to deepen this division, particularly after Tannenbaum expressed sentiments such as, "If it is against the law to break windows behind which is bread, then I say that when I am hungry I refuse to be a law-abiding citizen." By the time World War I broke out, the IWW had become a symbol for every foreign peril feared by Americans. Many pacifists, including some famous pacifist ministers, had socialist leanings or sympathies; some, like the Congregationalist Sydney Strong, had expressed their support for the IWW. Thus, aside from not supporting the war effort, such men and women faced questions about their patriotic loyalty for other reasons as well. The symbolic connections between pacifism and anarchism were well established but also highly flexible. Thus when Shirley Jackson Case, a liberal theologian and committed patriot, wanted to attack premillennialists for not supporting the war, he published an article in June 1918 titled "The Premillennial Menace," in which he charged that premillennialism was "a short step" from the IWW and anarchy — despite the fact that many premillennialists were staunchly opposed to socialism (as their response to the

Red Scare of 1919–1920 would show). In a time when Christianity and civilization were equated by many Protestants, so that religion and patriotism went hand in hand, the IWW represented a serious challenge to both. It was a challenge that, by and large, religion did not meet gracefully.

"Sky-Pilots." Nor, for that matter, did the IWW issue its challenge subtly. The church invasions under Tannenbaum were only a small part of a much larger campaign launched by the IWW to call Protestant churches to task for their "hypocrisy." They seemed to accept Christianity in a general sense — indeed, Jesus, the radical carpenter from Nazareth, provided them with a powerful role model — but felt that established religious bodies utterly failed to embody Christ's teachings. The "Wobblies," as the IWW members were called, took to the pages of their publications to lambaste any and all religious leaders who failed to live up to Jesus' ethical demands. The IWW press denounced religious leaders from Gen. William Booth of the Salvation Army to evangelist Billy Sunday, all of whom, it was charged, amassed

"THEY HAVE NOT WHERE TO LAY THEIR HEAD"

The 28 March 1914 issue of the IWW magazine *Solidarity* printed a poem by James P. Hayes. Addressed to "Mr. Sky Pilot," the poem summed up the Wobblies' attack on the complacency of the Christian churches.

They Have Not Where to Lay Their Head

When you've lauded all the captains

who rule the ship of might,
And exhorted all your hearers to
walk the path of right,
Here's another text I give —
the gospel of the cross,
Go feed and clothe the naked! Go
Seek the one that's lost!

His name? Their names are legion:
their names you never knew;
You passed them by in silent scorn,
to reach the chosen few;
For what avails the homage of the
lowly, hungry mass:

They have no viands to feed you, no
wines to fill your glass?

But a better song is in their ears
than ever Christian heard,
A higher praise in their hearts than
preacher's golden word;
For they have learned the church's
mission; twas learned at bitter cost,
Those men who lived and suffered,
those men who loved and lost.

And throughout the world they'll
wander, those outcasts at your gate;
They have done with all your customs
they have learned your creed of hate;
And they'll preach another gospel;
a truer faith they'll spread:
Go ye and eat of what ye reap —
let each one earn his bread.

Source: James P. Hayes, "They Have Not Where to Lay Their Head," *Solidarity* (28 March 1914): 4.

---

small (or large, in Sunday's case) fortunes in the course of their religious work. Such religious leaders were compared by the Wobblies to Judas Iscariot, the betrayer of Jesus; and Ananias, a figure from the New Testament book of the Acts of the Apostles who was struck down for refusing to turn all his property over to the early Christian church. Tannenbaum and his fellow IWW members also resented the preaching that often went along with relief work in the early twentieth century — the before-meal sermons delivered at urban missions throughout the country, in which the unemployed and downtrodden were exhorted to examine their own moral track records and look to salvation in the next life rather than in this one. This led the Wobblies to coin their pejorative nickname for ministers: "sky-pilots." It also made the preachers tools of the status quo, in the eyes of the IWW; it was no wonder, one editor wrote, that when Billy Sunday toured the state of Washington, "some of the sawmill companies allowed their slaves to attend the services at the tabernacle on the company's time." When Tannenbaum led his army into New York's churches, then, he was insisting on receiving Christian charity without what he considered Christian claptrap. "He complained that on the night before religion had been forced on them at the Bible Study Class Mission, after they had received food." He exhorted his followers, in his own kind of sermon, "And, men, don't go to the missions. Don't become men who are converted every night for the sake of a place to sleep. We're tired of that, too."

War and Peace. The Wobblies were also tired, they discovered as the decade wore on, of religion being used to glorify war. This was another respect in which they felt they had caught the churches red-handed in hypocrisy. "We claim to worship the Prince of Peace, / But trust in the sword and gun" ran part of one IWW poem. The editor of the *Industrial Worker* made it even clearer: "Even the devil, bad as his reputation is, would not be guilty of the crimes with which they are trying to saddle God. No God or devil would ever fall so low as to fight for the American munition trusts." The Protestant mainstream had, to a large extent, thrown its lot in wholeheartedly with progressive American culture as a perfect meshing of values. Some conservative Protestants claimed that this alliance made the churches every bit as corrupt as the culture was. For almost exactly the opposite reasons, the IWW came to much the same conclusion in the 1910s. American Christianity was clearly, to them, far too comfortable in a valueless economic system. The churches unintentionally helped to prove the point by locking their doors when the Wobblies came, in the name of the carpenter of Nazareth, the great friend of the poor and of the peacemakers, seeking food and a place to spend the night.

Sources:
"Unemployed Invade the Labor Temple," *New York Times*, 1 March 1914, p. 1;

"Urges Workless on to Anarchy," *New York Times*, 3 March 1914, p. 1;

Donald E. Winters Jr., *The Soul of the Wobblies* (Westport, Conn.: Greenwood Press, 1985).

WORLD WAR I: A CALL TO ARMS

A Chorus of Support. In January 1918 Sydney Strong, a Congregational minister in Seattle, Washington, distributed a questionnaire to his fellow clergymen, asking what they would like to see happen after the war. A fellow Congregationalist, Charles Aked of San Francisco, responded with a call for "the repentance in sack cloth and ashes of ten thousand ministers of Christ who have howled for blood and raved the ravings of the jingopress." Aked could have cited numerous examples of such sins, for America's religious leaders had demonstrated that they were not immune to the "war fever" that swept the nation, especially after the United States declared war on Germany in April 1917. Rhetorical excesses characterized many of the sermons, articles, and even hymns put forth by some of the country's most prominent preachers as they offered up a "chorus of support" for the war, causing some observers to question whether the term *Christian* could be honestly applied to their conduct. After the war many religious leaders would find ample reason to reflect and wonder at how they had allowed themselves to get caught up in what was at times a rather unseemly fervor — and some would indeed feel compelled to repent.

A Rising Tide. The tide of militaristic sentiment among the clergy was clearly rising in the years after 1914, a trend that was documented in a series of surveys issued by various organizations and newspapers. In January 1915 the Church Peace Union sent a questionnaire to ten thousand ministers of all denominations. When the results were published in May, 95 percent of the clergy polled opposed any increase in armaments as a threat to peace. But the British ocean liner *Lusitania* had been sunk by a German submarine in May 1915, an event that made war seem more likely and led many to favor a strategy of military preparedness. By the fall of that year, another survey of ministers found that the majority favored preparedness, and in March 1916 a group of eighty-three ministers signed their names to a letter voicing these sentiments. The letter, which ran in *The New York Times,* was intended as a rebuttal to a Church Peace Union petition against military buildup. In another year opinion shifted still further. On 11 March 1917 the New York Federation of Churches issued an appeal, urging other clergymen to support the proposition that "the President will be justified in recommending to Congress the most extreme measures." Of the churches that responded to this appeal, those in favor of war outnumbered those opposed by a margin of three to one. The federation then published a statement justifying action against Germany. Clerical warmongering had begun in earnest.

Evangelist Billy Sunday, who used his provocative style to win converts to Christianity, to support the war effort, and to convince his followers to hate Germans

Propaganda. When the war began in Europe, the British had control of the transatlantic cables, allowing them to censor effectively the flow of news about the war to America. As a result, Allied propaganda exerted a deep influence on the American news media during the war years. American ministers, of course, read the same newspapers as everyone else in the country, and many came to repeat and even embellish the stories they saw and heard. After the United States entered the war, some of the country's most prominent ministers also became the leading voices in a series of tirades against Kaiser Wilhelm II and German militarism, represented in the pro-Allies press as the "Hun." Lyman Abbott, a Congregationalist known throughout his life as a doctrinal liberal, used the pages of his popular magazine *Outlook* to denounce Germany. "I do not hate the Predatory Potsdam Gang because it is my enemy," he wrote. "I hate it because it is a robber, a murderer, a destroyer of homes, a pillager of churches, a violater of women. I do well to hate it." Newell Dwight Hillis, pastor of the prestigious Plymouth Congregational Church in Brooklyn, New York, launched a much more extensive campaign. Raised a Quaker, he once claimed that he "deeply sympathized" with the pacifist movement; but that sympathy did not stop him, early in 1917, from criticizing the Woodrow Wilson administration for dillydallying about entering

THE CHALLENGE OF THE PRESENT CRISIS

Despite the level of hysteria attained in the preaching of some of America's most prominent ministers after 1917, a great majority of clergymen did not come by their decision to support the war easily. One of the most sophisticated treatments of the possibility of harmonizing Christian principles with the need for war was Baptist preacher Harry Emerson Fosdick's *The Challenge of the Present Crisis*, published in 1917. The war struck a forceful blow to the optimism and progressivism of the age, and Fosdick's question was "In what mood shall a Christian, or for that matter an idealist of any kind, face the catastrophe? . . . And how can he harmonize his ideals with his necessities of action in a time of war?" He recognized the possibility that faithful Christians would slip into despair: "the horrors of Verdun, the mutilated bodies of Belgian boys, the bleaching bones of countless children left by the Russian retreat along the military roads of Poland, and, after sixty generations of Christian opportunity, some five million wounded men in the hospitals of Europe — how shall we keep heart in the face of this?" Fosdick argued that the answer lay in Christians' accepting the "present crisis" as a challenge to meet the need for force without excessive belligerence. And the need for force was clear in Fosdick's mind:

The gradual substitution of moral for physical force in international relations is as certain as human progress, for there can be no assured human progress without it, but mankind is not yet so free from elemental sin that any nation can count on spiritual sweetness as a safeguard against rampant greed. Even Jesus did not bless the peaceful; he blessed the peace-makers; and peacemaking in any human relationship may any day involve resort to force." Fosdick closed his essay with a prayer for all Christians in wartime. "O God, bless our Country! We lament before Thee the cruel necessity of war. But what could we do? . . . we plead before Thee that we have not wanted war, that we hate no man, that we covet no nation's possessions, that we have nothing for ourselves to gain from war, unless it be a clear conscience and a better earth for all the nations to live and grow in. . . . And now we lay our hand upon our sword. Since we must draw it, O God, help us to play the man and to do our part in teaching ruthlessness once for all what it means to wake the sleeping lion of humanity's conscience.

Source: Harry Emerson Fosdick, *The Challenge of the Present Crisis* (Philadelphia: Westminster Press, 1917).

the war. Once the United States had committed its troops, Hillis gained vast popularity on the lecture circuit and in fund-raising efforts such as the Liberty Loan drives by detailing German atrocities, often with photographs as visual aids. His wartime lectures were collected into two books, *German Atrocities* (1918) and *The Blot on the Kaiser's Scutcheon* (1918). Magazines such as *Christian Work* and *The Christian Century* reprinted them, editing out only the most graphic of Hillis's many examples. In *The Blot on the Kaiser's Scutcheon* Hillis mentioned approvingly a proposal by a group of surgeons calling for the sterilization of ten million German soldiers, so that "when this generation of Germans goes, civilized cities, states and races may be rid of this awful cancer that must be cut clean out of the body of society." Indeed, said Hillis, "All civilization must unite to kill" the German soldiers, whom he called "mad dogs."

Billy Sunday. While some members of Hillis's audiences, including the clergy, no doubt thought he went too far both in his rhetoric and his penchant for explicit detail, other preachers matched or outdid him with their own sermons and publications. A Unitarian newspaper declared that American soldiers need have no qualms of conscience about the fighting, because Jesus Christ could serve as their example even on the battlefield. Indeed, there was "not an opportunity to deal death to the enemy that he would shirk from or delay in seizing! He would take bayonet and grenade and bomb and rifle and do the work of deadliness against that which is the most deadly enemy of his Father's kingdom." But perhaps no other preacher outranked evangelist Billy Sunday in fiery wartime preaching. The 1910s saw the peak in Sunday's popularity: he drew record audiences and, by decade's end, claimed to have secured even more conversions than the premier nineteenth-century revivalist Dwight L. Moody. To the thousands gathered at his meetings, Sunday preached about the war, sometimes in shirtsleeves, in a style often described as "roughhouse." (At a revival in Atlanta in 1917, he even came to blows with a "German sympathizer" who rushed the platform during one of his tirades.) The prose was undoubtedly colorful: German soldiers were "that weazen-eyed, low-lived, bull-neck, low-down gang of cutthroats of the Kaiser," the "dirty bunch that would stand aside and see a Turk outrage a woman," a "great pack of wolfish Huns whose fangs drip with blood and gore," and "that bunch of pretzel-chewing, sauerkraut spawn of blood-thirsty Huns." Sunday also made it clear that this was a holy war: "I tell you it is Bill against Woodrow, Germany against America, hell against heaven." In one of his most famous statements, Sunday asserted that "If you turn hell upside down, you will find 'Made in Germany' stamped on the bottom." He reserved some of his choicest words for the "shirkers" who did not lend their full, unqualified support to America's participation in the war. "Either you are loyal or you are not," he said. "You are either a patriot or a black-hearted traitor. There is no sitting on the fence at this time."

Against Pacifism. Sunday was not alone in denouncing pacifists. Many ministers took to the pulpit or the editorial page to denounce their "cowardly" colleagues, and several ecclesiastical governing boards asked for, and received, the resignations of ministers who refused to stop voicing their doubts about the righteousness of the war. On 9 April 1918 the American Unitarian Association passed a resolution declaring "that any society which employs a minister who is not a willing, earnest and outspoken supporter of the United States in the vigorous and resolute prosecution of the war cannot be considered eligible for aid from the Association." When the board of trustees of one Unitarian congregation, the Church of the Messiah in New York City, defied this order by supporting its pacifist minister, John Haynes Holmes, much of the congregation withdrew its membership. The clergy, after all, did not generate but only reflected the war fever that had swept the country starting in 1915. They were also citizens of the United States as well as servants of the Lord, and separation of church and state could go only so far in helping them to navigate conflicting duties. One of the most prominent liberal Protestant theologians of the day, Shailer Mathews of the University of Chicago Divinity School, published his *Patriotism and Religion* in 1918, attempting to dissolve the conflict by merging the two forms of duty. "For an American to refuse to share in the present war," he argued, "is not Christian." In the end, the majority of the clergy seemed to follow Mathews's lead, drawing an equation between being a good Christian and being a good citizen. They seemed to agree with former president Theodore Roosevelt, who declared in 1917 that "the clergyman who does not put the flag above the church had better close his church and keep it closed."

Sources:

Ray H. Abrams, *Preachers Present Arms* (Scottsdale, Penn.: Herald Press, 1969);

Sydney E. Ahlstrom, *A Religious History of the American People* (New Haven: Yale University Press, 1972);

"Billy Sunday Fires Hot Shot at Kaiser," *New York Times,* 19 February 1918, p. 11;

"Sunday, Coatless, Flays Kaiserism," *New York Times,* 28 May 1917, p. 9;

"Sunday in Fist Fight with Pro-German," *New York Times,* 21 December 1917, p. 9.

WORLD WAR I: A CALL FOR PEACE

Peace Advocates. In 1914, when Andrew Carnegie put forth a $2 million endowment for the founding of the Church Peace Union, talk of world peace was all the rage. The Church Peace Union, whose board of trustees included Protestant, Catholic, and Jewish leaders, took its place among some thirty other peace societies working toward the goals of a league of nations and a system of arbitration for the resolution of international conflicts. The Federal Council of Churches, the major Protestant ecumenical body, established a Commission on Peace and Arbitration in the same year and worked to help secure a diplomatic solution to the rising tensions in Europe. Several progressive religious leaders, including John Haynes Holmes and Rabbi Stephen Wise, joined prominent reformers such as Jane Addams, Lillian Wald, Frederic C. Howe, and Florence Kelley in founding the American Union Against Militarism late in 1915. Many were optimistic; belief in progress and confidence in human nature ran high. Charles MacFarland, the general secretary of the Federal Council of Churches, published a pamphlet in 1912 expressing the hope "that the thought of engaging with each other in deadly combat shall become abhorrent and impossible forever." The same year Frederick Lynch issued a stronger statement, saying, "It looks as though this is going to be the age of treaties rather than the age of wars, the century of reason rather than the century of force." But perhaps the most extravagant display of optimism came from Andrew Carnegie himself when he wrote the charter for the Church Peace Union. "If in the judgment of the trustees," he wrote, "the time shall come when peace is fully established, and no more need be done in that cause, the income of the grant may be spent for the alleviation of poverty or other good causes." A clear majority of American religious leaders were, like Woodrow Wilson, "peace advocates," working in some way or another to secure international peace and hoping to see their labor come to fruition.

Peace through Victory. But a peace advocate was not the same thing as a principled pacifist. The distinction would become clearer and more divisive throughout the war years. When the outbreak of war in Europe ended the hope for a settlement through arbitration (and, coincidentally, prevented two World Peace Congresses from meeting), most American peace societies kept up the call for American neutrality and opposed any military buildup. But by 1917 the peace advocates, almost without exception, shifted their support to the preparedness strategy and acknowledged the necessity not only of the war in Europe but also of American involvement there. Still maintaining that they hated war, they saw this as the "war to end wars" and thus began to call for "peace through victory," hoping that the war's end would bring the lasting peace to which they had looked forward. "True" pacifism, then — that is, opposition not only to war in the abstract but also *this* war in particular — was left to a small minority of the clergy who had been peace advocates, most of whom joined together in new organizations after the old peace societies had thrown in their lot with war. On 3 February 1917 William Jennings Bryan, a conservative Presbyterian and devout pacifist (he had resigned as President Wilson's secretary of state in 1915, as soon as it began to seem likely that the United States would eventually enter the war), gave a speech in New York City pledging that the United States would not "get down and wallow in the mire of human blood." Bryan and his audience subsequently organized the Emergency Peace Federation, whose branches held meetings throughout the country during the next two months, hoping to stave off the entry of the United States into the European war. Two other organizations had formed in 1915, as soon as public opinion began to shift toward

One of America's most prominent and influential theologians of the early twentieth century, Walter Rauschenbusch of Rochester Theological Seminary, suffered terribly in the strong anti-German (and antineutrality) atmosphere of the times. Rauschenbusch, though born in the United States, was a German American, and, along with several other German American ministers, had trouble swallowing the denunciations of Germany so prevalent at the time. Some Lutheran ministers had begun as early as 1914 to issue statements attempting to defend Germany's conduct in the European war, and Rauschenbusch, a Baptist, followed similar lines. The *Congregationalist* published an article by Rauschenbusch, titled "Be Fair to Germany," in October 1914, in which he attempted to demonstrate that Germany was not the only nation that had behaved aggressively. Instantly labeled "pro-German," Rauschenbusch only made things worse for himself when he collaborated with Charles Aked in 1915 on a statement that criticized America's military buildup as turning the nation into a "workshop of death." Rauschenbusch became involved with the Fellowship of Reconciliation, and his reputation remained in question until the summer of 1918. At that time the press released a personal letter in which Rauschenbusch explained to a friend that he was not a "pro-German," for he hoped the war would cause "the downfall of all autocratic government in the Central Empires." For many of Rauschenbusch's ministerial colleagues, this statement sufficed to assure them of his patriotism. In fact, though, he never experienced a change of heart, and friends even suggested that the anguish he felt over the war contributed to his death on 25 July 1918, less than four months short of the armistice.

Sources: Ray H. Abrams, *Preachers Present Arms* (Scottsdale, Penn.: Herald Press, 1969);

Paul M. Minus, *Walter Rauschenbusch: American Reformer* (New York: Macmillan, 1988).

preparedness. The Association to Abolish War was founded by Charles Dole, a retired Unitarian minister, and Wilbur Thomas of the American Friends Service Committee. It experienced a defection of many of its members after the declaration of war in April 1917, but continued to function until the war's end. John Mott of the YMCA and the Student Volunteer Movement played a large role in the formation of the Fellowship of Reconciliation, the most influential group of Christian pacifists throughout the war. They may have been a minority, but the pacifists were determined not to be silent, no matter how loud the cries for war became.

Conscientious Objectors. The Association to Abolish War, the Fellowship of Reconciliation, and the American Friends Service Committee (founded in 1917) all found themselves occupied with a major task following America's entry into the war, expressing concern and support for conscientious objectors. The Selective Service Act of 1917, which initiated the wartime draft, provided exemptions from service not only for all clergy and theological students but also for members of certain designated "peace churches," whose basic creeds included opposition to war. Some 64,000 young men claimed conscientious objector (CO) status under this law, and most came from the peace churches: the Society of Friends, the Mennonites, and the Brethren. Another one-third of the objectors were members of the International Bible Students' Association, which would later become organized as the Jehovah's Witnesses. Of the 64,000 who applied, 57,000 were granted CO status, exempting them from combatant service. Twenty-one thousand of these objectors were later inducted through the draft, and many of these eventually accepted combat duty. In fact, only about four thousand of the inducted objectors actually tried to use their certificates of exemption, showing that even members of traditional peace churches could be swayed from their beliefs by wartime ideals and intense public and official pressure. Of those who presented their certificates, 1,300 accepted noncombatant service in the Medical Corps, Quartermaster Corps, or Engineer Service; 1,200 were furloughed to agricultural work; 99 went to the Friends Reconstruction Unit; and 450 were sent to prison by courts-martial for refusing even alternative service. These last, along with many political prisoners, were the focus of the peace organizations' efforts.

Prison Treatment. Roundly decried in the press as traitors and sometimes subjected to harsh treatment in prison, the conscientious objectors struck many as clear evidence that America had betrayed its ideals of free speech and the rights of conscience. Even the country's major religious bodies, dedicated as they were to other forms of wartime service, seemed to take little sustained interest in the plight of conscientious objectors. The Federal Council of Churches had passed a resolution early in 1917 pledging to use its power to safeguard the freedoms of expression and conscience, but when, only a few months later, the American Civil Liberties Bureau asked the council to investigate the objectors' situation and bring the matter to the attention of the War Department, the council dragged its feet. It did not pass a resolution addressing the issue until March 1919, and its report concluded that, while the objectors should be granted amnesty as soon as the peace was signed, it could find no evidence of ill treatment the prisoners had received at the hands of the War Department. John Haynes Holmes, the prominent Unitarian minister and pacifist who supported the American Civil Liberties Bureau, expressed his disgust at the "hypocrisy" the council had shown in refusing to confront seriously the plight of the objectors. To the small number of Christian pacifists engaging in relief efforts for the prisoners, freedom of conscience seemed to come perilously close to becoming another casualty of the war.

Pacifist Ministers. Beginning in 1917 pacifism increasingly became not only a minority viewpoint but also a persecuted one. The imprisonment of conscientious objectors and political dissenters was only the most obvious example of a sustained pattern of suppression of nonconformist views. Under the Espionage and Sedition Acts (1917, 1918), the postal service began to bar the delivery of certain publications, including John Haynes Holmes's *Unity* and the Fellowship of Reconciliation's *The New World*, because they posed difficult questions about the morality of America's involvement in the war. When the Association to Abolish War began to circulate a pamphlet in Boston containing the biblical text of the Sermon on the Mount — which proclaims, "Blessed are the peacemakers" — without any editorial comment, the Justice Department warned them against continuing its distribution. Pacifists were routinely denounced as both traitors and cowards; a group of buildings belonging to the Mennonite Church in central Illinois were painted yellow. Ministers who remained true to their beliefs, denouncing America's war involvement, often found themselves unemployed or worse. Two Presbyterian ministers, William Fincke and Edmund Chaffee, wrote a sermon titled "A Ministry of Reconciliation," to be delivered at Fincke's church on 2 April 1917. When they proposed to "work for the peace of the world through understanding," they were dismissed by their presbytery. A Unitarian minister in Dorchester, Massachusetts, resigned his pastorate when the governing board of his church insisted that he not deliver a proposed sermon on "The Conscientious Objector." An Episcopalian pastor on Long Island was forced to resign following a public outcry after he took down an American flag that some small boys had hung in his church; and in the most extreme case, another Unitarian, Charles Joy of Portland, Maine, used one of his sermons to call the war "unrighteous" and deplorable, only to find his congregation burning him in effigy that night in front of the church. Again, religious congregations and governing boards alike demonstrated the extent to which they had been caught up in the spirit of the times. Even a colleague could be a "traitor" if he did not toe the line in his preaching.

Sitting on the Fence. "There is no sitting on the fence at this time," Billy Sunday had said; and, following his lead, many other ministers began to expand their condemnation of pacifists even to their colleagues who supported the war, but only reluctantly or with doubts about the "righteousness" of the cause. Perhaps the best example of this type of treatment is Robert E. Speer, a Presbyterian, a secretary of the Board of Foreign Missions, and the chairman of the Federal Council of Churches' General War-Time Commission. As chair of the commission, Speer bore the ultimate responsibility for coordinating all the major Protestant wartime service efforts. Yet he came under public fire after giving a speech on 18 February 1918 at Columbia University under the auspices of the Intercollegiate YMCA. Speer's address, titled "World Democracy and America's Obligation to Her Neighbors," touched on five things that hindered the progress of world democracy. Among these elements was "the persistence of race prejudice and suspicion," which Speer illustrated with examples not only from contemporary Germany but also from the not-too-distant past of the United States. He used a similar technique to substantiate his other points, and soon enough *The New York Times* ran a letter denouncing Speer for his "insidiously corrupting" speech, which "breathed throughout the spirit of pacifism and minimized the infamies that Germany had perpetrated." Speer was labeled "pro-German," and the *Times* continued to publish comments on the address, some from ministers, the vast majority of which castigated Speer. He was "amazed and indignant" at the response his words had received, and the *Times* ran his own response to the criticisms. Despite his insistence that he believed "this is a war against war and that it must be waged in order that war may be destroyed," Speer had little luck salvaging his reputation with his subsequent admission that he did not feel it was necessary for a patriot to affirm the "impeccability" or "perfection" of his nation's past or present. His work with the commission did not suffer appreciably from the controversy, but his case provides a clear indication that, at the height of war, to sit on the fence was viewed as tantamount to siding with the enemy. This was true even if the doubter was a minister or someone guaranteed the right to object to the war by law — even if, in other words, one balked at supporting the war on the strongest grounds of faith.

Sources:

Ray H. Abrams, *Preachers Present Arms* (Scottsdale, Penn: Herald Press, 1969);

Sydney E. Ahlstrom, *A Religious History of the American People* (New Haven: Yale University Press, 1972);

Marvin B. Endy Jr., "War and Peace," in *Encyclopedia of the American Religious Experience*, edited by Charles H. Lippy and Peter Williams (New York: Scribners, 1988);

C. Roland Marchand, *The American Peace Movement and Social Reform, 1898–1918* (Princeton: Princeton University Press, 1973);

John F. Piper Jr., *The American Churches in World War I* (Athens: Ohio University Press, 1985).

WORLD WAR I: A CALL TO SERVE

Middle Ground. As chairman of the Federal Council of Churches' General War-Time Commission, Robert Speer represented the middle ground between the extremes of militarism and pacifism. Like much of the population, Speer and his colleagues in the council felt a profound sense of duty to their country and committed themselves to furthering the war effort in whatever ways they could. As the controversy over Speer's YMCA

Troops depositing money with the YMCA secretary at Camp MacArthur, Waco, Texas

speech illustrates, however, many were perfectly able to perform this service without engaging in German-bashing. They had pledged their loyalty to their country and acknowledged the United States as the last great hope in what seemed to be a war "to save civilization itself." The result was, in effect, a temporary suspension of the separation of church and state. Religious bodies became virtual subsidiaries of the War Department, providing a variety of services that the military was not equipped to handle as the nation faced a war the likes of which it had never even imagined before.

Commissions and Councils. The wartime service of America's religious bodies was overseen by impressive administrative structures, which were either founded or reorganized specifically for this purpose. The Federal Council of Churches, which in 1916 represented more than two-thirds of all Protestants in the United States, with 103,113 affiliated ministers serving nearly eighteen million communicants, sought to coordinate the efforts not only of various denominational bodies but also of the many interdenominational agencies that had undertaken various social services in this, the era of the Social Gospel. At a special meeting in Washington, D.C., on 8 and 9 May 1917, the council conferred with representatives from more than thirty organizations, including the YMCA, YWCA, the American Bible Society, and numerous mission boards. This meeting resulted in the formation of the General War-Time Commission, a body of one hundred members representing the full scope of these organizations' war work, which met for the first time on 20 September of the same year. Roman Catholics, for their part, created a new administrative body to help

facilitate the efforts of many lay social service organizations. The brainchild of a Paulist priest, Father John Burke, who served as the editor of *Catholic World*, the National Catholic War Council came into being in 1917 but foundered until a reorganization in January 1918 placed it under the authority of the nation's archbishops. In a similar fashion, sixteen smaller groups joined together as the Jewish Welfare Board. From these administrative bodies, smaller committees and commissions proliferated at an astonishing rate, addressing every aspect they could think of relating to war conditions at home and abroad. Most of the men and women who worked in these organizations expressed temperate views about the enemy and the war but focused on doing all they could to help the members of their congregations (and their families) who were doing the fighting.

Chaplains. One of the most visible avenues for religious service in the military was in the office of chaplain in the armed services. But as the United States prepared to enter World War I, the army and the navy were both woefully short on staff and supplies to fulfill that function. In May 1917 Charles MacFarland, secretary of the Federal Council of Churches, had convened a General Committee on Army and Navy Chaplains. The committee, which later became part of the General War-Time Commission, focused on recruiting men to serve in that capacity. Aside from recruiting, however, there was the issue of supplies. Most denominations had independent agencies to equip their chaplains with books, Bibles, tracts, and any materials needed for the celebration of religious services in the soldiers' camps. After June 1918 the War-Time Commission acted as the central store for many of these denominations. For Catholic chaplains, the Chaplain's Aid Association, formerly a local organization overseen by Father Burke in New York City, became national and supplied each Catholic chaplain with a kit containing sacramental supplies and money. But the actual service of chaplains from all religious bodies faced obstacles in the governmental appropriations process. In May 1917, when Congress passed a military budget, the president was able to assign one chaplain to each regiment of twelve hundred men. But within a year the army had restructured its regimental system along the French model, so that a regiment now contained thirty-six hundred men whose needs were still to be met by a single chaplain. Protestants and Catholics joined together to submit a legislative petition to restore the former ratio of ministers to troops, and Congress increased the appropriation to two chaplains for every regiment. Religious leaders also banded together to establish training schools to prepare their ministers for military service. Theological schools in the Cambridge and Boston area allowed themselves to be used for this service, and on 1 March 1918 the first government-run school for chaplains opened at Fort Monroe in Virginia. In order to address the continuing personnel shortage, however, the churches began to encourage the service of voluntary, nonenlisted "camp

"Charged with spreading doctrines calculated to promote unrest and disloyalty among the men of the army and navy, six leaders of the International Bible Students' Association, which was founded by the late 'Pastor' Charles T. Russell, were arrested yesterday afternoon in Brooklyn," reported *The New York Times* on 9 May 1918. Although stationed well off the Protestant mainstream, the Russellites (later to be called Jehovah's Witnesses) did have a premillennial vision that caused them to be branded as disloyal and unpatriotic, as were many other premillennialists. And perhaps because they were a marginal group to begin with, the Bible Students faced a more serious attack during the war than premillennialists in established denominations. Joseph Rutherford, Russell's successor, and seven other men ultimately faced charges of "unlawfully and willfully conspiring to cause insubordination, disloyalty, and refusal of duty of the military and naval forces of the United States." Part of the evidence brought against them was a posthumous collection of Russell's writings, published as *The Finished Mystery*, which "reeked with passages condemning war and referring to patriotism as a delusion which caused men to kill each other." Another piece of the prosecution's case was a letter from Ruther-

ford to a conscientious objector, supporting his protest and commenting, "We know that the present order is Babylon, and that the day has come for it to go down in a great tide of revolution and anarchy which shall follow the war." The jury found the eight Russellites guilty on four counts of conspiring to subvert the purpose of the Selective Service Act of 1917, and the presiding judge, H. B. Howe, sentenced seven of the men to four terms of twenty years, to be served concurrently in a federal prison in Atlanta. The eighth defendant received a sentence of ten years. Editorializing from the bench, Judge Howe commented that the Bible Students were "worse than traitors." "If they had taken guns and swords and joined the German Army, the harm they could have done would have been insignificant compared with the results of their propaganda," he said.

Sources: Ray H. Abrams, *Preachers Present Arms* (Scottsdale, Penn.: Herald Press, 1969);

"Arrest Russellites on Sedition Charges," *New York Times*, 9 May 1918, p. 22;

"Letter to Russellite Favors Opposing War," *New York Times*, 7 June 1918, p. 13;

"Russellites Guilty of Hindering Draft," *New York Times*, 21 June 1918, p. 7;

"20 Years in Prison for 7 Russellites," *New York Times*, 22 June 1918, p. 18.

pastors." But just as the General War-Time Commission was preparing a handbook to guide the conduct of these volunteers, the War Department issued an order calling a halt to this form of civilian service, arguing that the recent increase in the number of chaplains made the camp pastors' work superfluous. Thus, the efforts of religious bodies to ensure that soldiers would have enough ministers in their camps met with mixed results during the war. But it was largely because of the churches' persistence on this issue that, when the army was reorganized in 1920, a chief of chaplains was appointed, marking the first step on the way to the establishment of an official chaplains' corps — although that goal would have to wait until another world war had ended for its attainment.

Huts in Hell. Chaplains were not the only individuals providing service to the soldiers in the camps. In fact, a far more extensive wartime ministry came in the form of lay religious organizations working to provide recreational activities for military personnel. Acknowledging that the conditions of war made the camps potential hotbeds of vice, the YMCA and YWCA launched a massive effort to operate canteens and recreational facilities in camps here and abroad. Four days after the declaration of war on Germany, John Mott convened a YMCA Conference on Army Work in Garden City,

New York. The conference created the National War Work Council to carry out their aims, which they defined as "to promote the physical, mental and social and spiritual welfare of the more than one million men of the military forces of the United States, to strengthen the hands of the Chaplain's Corps and to serve the Churches." The alacrity with which the YMCA had responded to the declaration of war so impressed government officials that the War Department ultimately put the organization officially in charge of all camp recreational activities, and President Wilson recognized it as "a valuable adjunct and asset to the service." But the YMCA's priority in this regard did not go uncontested, as the major Catholic lay organization, the Knights of Columbus, also submitted a bid to be officially recognized for camp service. On 14 April (just a few days after the YMCA meeting), the Supreme Board of Directors of the Knights of Columbus met in Washington to pledge its support and its volunteers for recreational and religious activities in the camps. The Knights had experience in this line of duty, which they had gained in military camps during the border campaign against Mexico in the previous year. The Knights had to fight anti-Catholic bias in seeking to be officially sanctioned for war work, as well as the YMCA's disapproval of the well-funded campaign by the Knights to give things away for free in the camps, instead of selling them as the YMCA workers did. Eventually, the Knights dropped the "everything free" campaign and were admitted to the camps. They were followed by the YWCA, the Jewish Welfare Board, the American Library Association, the War Camp Community Service, and the Salvation Army, as well as, ultimately, Catholic women's groups, who established "Visitors' Houses" in France on the model of those operated by the YWCA. Some religious leaders spoke disparagingly of the activities of these groups, using as a symbol the time they spent "selling cigarettes" in their canteens. These efforts were, after all, carried out by lay men and women who could not perform many religious services. But they clearly devoted large amounts of their own time and energy to seeing that the troops did not stray into sin.

Fund-Raising. Outside the camps, there were still many arenas for service for the religious civilian population. One of the more-extraordinary achievements of the various wartime councils was the raising of large sums of money to finance their own activities, as well as the general national war effort. "Liberty Loan Sundays" were proclaimed, days on which pastors used their pulpits to exhort their congregations to buy government Liberty Bonds. Liberty Bonds were also advertised in religious periodicals, with slogans such as "Kill the Hun — Kill His Hope" calling to mind the more salacious propaganda of the day. But the sums these organizations raised in their own behalf were truly staggering. The Christian Scientists alone raised $2 million for their War Relief Committee, and in New York City alone, a Catholic War Fund drive launched in March 1918 by Archbishop Cardinal Farley generated more than twice its $2.5 million goal. The crowning achievement of wartime fund-raising was the United War Work Campaign, a joint effort by the General War-Time Commission, the National Catholic War Council, and the Jewish Welfare Board. As had happened when the Knights of Columbus tried to enter the camps, anti-Catholic prejudice initially stonewalled the attempts to organize such a campaign. But after months of ironing out the details, on 5 September 1918 President Wilson announced the United War Work Campaign. The overall goal was $170 million, to be divided between Protestant, Catholic, and Jewish agencies. Although the public effort to secure contributions did not begin until 11 November — Armistice Day — by 20 November pledges totaling $205 million had been received. Of the amount pledged, a total of $188 million was ultimately collected from this effort and continued to be distributed after the war. Members of congregations across the country seemed to share their leaders' devotion to service in the nation's time of need.

The Preservation of the Social Gospel. With all that was happening, the religious bodies did not lose sight of the goals they had been pursuing for the betterment of American society prior to the war. They endeavored to maintain the message of the Social Gospel that had been a central component of liberal Christianity since the turn of the century. As the country geared up for a massive military effort, some Social Gospelers feared that the gains that had been made in labor conditions would be sacrificed in the interest of victory. The General War-Time Commission created a Committee on Industrial Conditions to make sure that wartime was not engendering labor abuses. The increasing militancy of labor organizations, especially the burgeoning Industrial Workers of the World (IWW), spurred their efforts to discover what could "make men discontented and so ready to be misled by self-interested or lawless agitators." They also turned their attentions to newly formed centers of industrial production, makeshift communities with few or no facilities outside the factories and housing projects. The General War-Time Commission, in response to this situation, created a Joint Committee on War Production Communities, which, with financial support from the Home Missions Council, set about building at least one church — a "Liberty Church" — in every such settlement. Though these efforts did not produce substantial results, they did represent an attempt to make sure that peacetime values were maintained even in the frenetic conditions of wartime production. This drive for continuity in service continued even after the war's end. The General War-Time Commission disbanded at its final meeting on 29 April 1919, but the Federal Council of Churches remained intact and continued to work for the ideals expressed in the Social Creed of the Churches it had adopted at its formation in 1908. The National Catholic War Council was transformed into the National Catholic Welfare Council (later Conference), the first nonlay, national Catholic organization for social service. Its policy statement was written by Father John A. Ryan of Catholic University, whose *A Living Wage,* published in 1906, had earned him a place as perhaps the leading Catholic spokesman for the Social Gospel. When the bishops signed Ryan's statement, they agreed to his call for a minimum wage; unemployment, health, and old-age insurance; child labor laws; public housing; and legal support for organized labor. Catholic social activism had attained a new maturity with the council. The Jewish Welfare Board underwent a similar transformation after the war, staying in existence but turning its attention to the establishment of Jewish community centers in major cities. While the specific circumstances of war were complicated with moral questions, in general World War I served to galvanize the spirit of service that had taken shape earlier in the Social Gospel movement. Within the major religious bodies, social action had been worked into organizational structures by the war's end, and it was there to stay.

Sources:

Ray H. Abrams, *Preachers Present Arms* (Scottsdale, Penn.: Herald Press, 1969);

Sydney E. Ahlstrom, *A Religious History of the American People* (New Haven: Yale University Press, 1972);

Marvin B. Endy Jr., "War and Peace," in *Encyclopedia of the American Religious Experience*, edited by Charles H. Lippy and Peter Williams (New York: Scribners, 1988);

John A. Mayer, "Social Reform After the Civil War to the Great Depression," in *Encyclopedia of the American Religious Experience*, edited by Charles H. Lippy and Peter Williams (New York: Scribners, 1988);

John F. Piper Jr., *The American Churches in World War I* (Athens: Ohio University Press, 1985).

WORLD WAR I: A FULFILLMENT OF PROPHECY

A Prophetic Script. World War I also served to galvanize the premillennial wing of conservative Protestantism. A growing movement since the late nineteenth century, premillennialism focused on the second coming of Jesus to initiate the millennium, the thousand-year reign of peace predicted in the biblical book of Revelation. Most premillennialists expected these events, which would mark the end of human history, to occur imminently. They read the Bible carefully, especially prophetic books such as Daniel and Revelation, and interpreted it literally, looking for clues that would help them recognize the onset of this cataclysmic time. The events of the European war corresponded strikingly well to a set of these prophetic "signs of the times" that premillennialists had agreed upon and had been anticipating for years prior to 1914. Foremost among the premillennialists' prophecies was the expectation that ten European nations would join together in a revived Roman Empire, a kingdom headed by the Antichrist. This would be one of the signs that marked the coming end of the "age of the Gentiles," the era or dispensation humankind had been living in since the birth of Christianity. They also looked for the return of the Jews to Palestine, since the reconstitution of the nation of Israel was a key ingredient in the prophetic formula. A northern confederacy of nations, whose leading power would be Russia, would rise up to challenge the new Roman Empire. The battle between those two kingdoms would eventually escalate into Armageddon, the final battle between the forces of good and evil. These elements formed the basic outline of a "prophetic script" that premillennialists had crafted well before 1914. When war broke out in Europe that year, they recognized its significance and began to compare the events of the day to their predictions.

Prophetic Success. When premillennialists set about refining and filling in the details of their prophetic system, one of their primary tasks was to envision the shape Europe would take after the war. Fully counting on the revival of the Roman Empire, and committed to a literal reading of the Bible, they did not expect any nation that had not been part of the original Roman Empire to take part in the new southern European confederacy. Germany and Austria-Hungary, therefore, would need to be broken up, so that the territories now controlled by them that had once been under Roman control would be free to join the new league of nations, while northern Germany and Austria-Hungary's Slavic provinces would fall under Russian influence. As for Russia itself, its current cooperation with the Allies would end as it prepared to take the reins of the northern confederacy. It would play, wrote one premillennialist, "a prominent, and to herself fatal, part during the predicted end of this age." In addition, Ireland, which Rome had never penetrated, would have to gain its independence from Britain, while, in order to allow for the return of the Jews, the Ottoman Empire would need to lose control of Palestine. The events that actually transpired during and after the war, then, lent substantial credence to the premillennial prophecy. But while some argued that the same outcomes might have been predicted by any perspicacious student of politics and history, the premillennialists were quick to assert that they had reached their conclusions *strictly* on the basis of a literal reading of Scripture. As a result, premillennialists enjoyed an unprecedented surge in their popularity.

Wars and Rumors of Wars. Some premillennialists threatened that popularity by making extreme statements. One, William Blackstone, attempted to fix a specific date for the events to come. He applied old mathematical formulas for converting biblical time into Gregorian calendar time to arrive at a prediction of sometime between 1916 and 1934 for the end of the age of the Gentiles. Other premillennialists then distanced themselves from Blackstone, for such specific predictions, when they failed, often brought not only disappointment but also defection from the movement. Another extreme expression was that of F. C. Jennings, who predicted that only the rapture (gathering and lifting) of the saved into heaven by Christ could end the fighting. The warring nations would be so confused by the sudden disappearance into the air of thousands of Christians that massive political instability would follow, allowing the Antichrist to take over and form the southern confederacy. Most premillennialists, however, found that the more cautious they were — that is, the more closely they stuck to literal readings and the agreed-upon script — the more likely their predictions were to be successful. Thus, when asked whether World War I was Armageddon, they tended to say no on two grounds. First, the term *Armageddon* itself was the name of a valley northwest of Jerusalem where this great battle would occur, so the fighting in the fields and forests of Europe did not correspond to the prophecy. Second, World War I was surely not the last war the world would see, contrary to the prevailing optimistic belief. As proof of this, the premillennialists pointed to a text in the gospel of Matthew where a list of signs are given to help believers recognize when the end is near. "And ye shall hear of wars and rumours of wars," the King James text reads. "See that ye be not troubled: for all these things must come to pass, *but the end is not yet.*" The traumatic events of World War I marked only the beginning of worse things to come, one premillennialist argued — "not because we wish it to be so . . . but because we believe the statements of a very old and very much neglected book called the Bible."

The Liberal Response. Many, if not most, liberal Protestants at this time were not premillennialists. Rather, they were postmillennialists, meaning that they did not expect to see the return of Christ until after human efforts and progress had realized the kingdom of God on earth. They tried to craft their own prophetic interpretation of the war, casting it in as positive a light as they could to preserve the idea that humanity was evolving into higher and higher states of consciousness. They argued that the war brought the kingdom of God one step closer by breaking the power of political tyranny in Europe once and for all, reminding people that this war was being fought to preserve the only form of civilization advanced enough to usher in the kingdom. But as the war dragged on and American lives began to be lost, such positive views became more untenable. Civilization seemed to be growing more brutal rather than more refined; notions of inevitable human progress had less and less evidence to support them. Shailer Mathews, a leading liberal theologian of the day, later reflected that the war "argued a breakdown of forces which we believed were shaping up a new world order." In the disillusionment that ensued, liberal theologians found themselves on the defensive against the growing premillennial tide. They lashed out in a series of antipremillennial publications with unprecedented vigor. What most liberal Protestants had seen as an insignificant theological fringe group now posed a threat that had to be opposed. Mathews and his colleague at the University of Chicago Divinity School, Shirley Jackson Case, wrote extensively on the subject, publishing books such as *Will Christ Come Again?*, *The Millennial Hope: A Phase of War-Time Thinking* (1918), and *The Revelation of John* (1919). Other authors entered the fray, and prominent journals of the day took up the issue as well. Case's "The Premillennial Menace" joined a host of antipremillennial articles in *Biblical World* in 1918 and 1919, while *The Christian Century* printed a twenty-one-part series with the same theme. With an impressive record of prophetic accuracy, premillennialists had earned the right to be heard. The liberals had to take to the presses to urge people not to listen.

Unpatriotic. One of the charges the liberals most often leveled against the premillennialists was that they were "unpatriotic" for not supporting America's war effort. The charge had some truth to it, although by the end of 1917, with American troops overseas, most premillennialists had joined the majority and at least expressed their loyalty to the American government. But

that loyalty was always superseded by a total dependence on God and a belief that current events represented God's direct intervention in history and international relations. This led them to remain moderate when it came to advocating American involvement. The argument that the war would foster democracy in Europe was not apt to sway them, either. Prominent revivalist Reuben Torrey wrote in *Christian Workers Magazine* in July 1917 that "we are reminded by the inspired prophets that the ascendancy of democracy, though certain, is not lasting." In fact, democracy seemed to represent the kind of breakdown of authority that would allow the Antichrist to exercise tyranny over southern Europe. As a result of these views, premillennialists were branded as disloyal, with some even facing legal charges. Shirley Jackson Case incited an antipremillennial fervor when he leaked a rumor to the *Chicago Daily News* that the premillennialists spent $2,000 a week, possibly from "German sources," to promulgate their views in this country. But with this accusation, Case unwittingly provided his opponents with the perfect means for a counterattack. Torrey responded to Case's comments by proclaiming the patriotism of premillennialists and noting that "while the charge that the money for premillennial propaganda 'emanates from German sources' is ridiculous, the charge that the destructive criticism that rules in Chicago University 'emanates from German sources' is undeniable." While he argued against calling Case, Mathews, and their colleagues traitors, Torrey nonetheless opened up a vulnerable spot in the liberal theologians' armor. Many of them had been trained in German universities; Germany was, in fact, the source of much of the biblical scholarship that viewed Scripture as written by human beings who were conditioned by their social and historical circumstances. This "higher criticism," as it was known, argued against looking to the Bible for the literal truth about historical and scientific questions. This single issue of biblical literalism placed liberals and conservatives on the opposite side of a widening doctrinal chasm in early-twentieth-century American Protestantism. So during the war, premillennialists took full advantage of the "German connection" exposed by the teaching of higher criticism at American universities and seminaries. Liberal theology, in fact, came to represent for the premillennialists a lurking peril to America's Christian civilization; Germany itself provided evidence of that fact. One conservative theologian blamed "corrupt German Biblical scholarship" for the "astounding moral collapse of German civilization." The result of this war of words between liberal theologians and premillennialists during World War I was surprising. Premillennialists who had previously stressed the absolute sovereignty of God, cautioning against overinvolvement in worldly affairs, came to see themselves as part of the larger fight conservative Protestants (of whom the premillennialists were only a minority) were waging to preserve civilization from the peril of "modernism" in all its guises. They became, in other words, an active and powerful part of the fundamentalist movement that would blossom in the 1920s.

Sources:

Sydney E. Ahlstrom, *A Religious History of the American People* (New Haven: Yale University Press, 1972);

George M. Marsden, *Fundamentalism and American Culture: The Shaping of Twentieth-Century Evangelicalism, 1870–1925* (New York: Oxford University Press, 1980);

Timothy P. Weber, *Living in the Shadow of the Second Coming: American Premillennialism, 1875–1982,* revised edition (Grand Rapids, Mich.: Academie Books, 1983).

ZIONISM

Balfour and Allenby. At the outbreak of World War I, Palestine lay under the control of the Ottoman Empire. The cherished hopes of the World Zionist Organization (WZO) for a Jewish homeland in Palestine seemed impossible to realize while the Holy Land remained in Muslim hands. But 1914 brought new hope with the British declaration of war on the Ottoman state. Long sympathetic to the Zionist cause (its offer to help procure land in Africa for Jewish settlement had been rejected by the WZO in 1905), Britain now adopted the reclamation of Palestine and its opening for Jewish immigration as an official part of its foreign policy. The Balfour Declaration of November 1917, named for foreign secretary Arthur Balfour, epitomized Britain's stand on Zionism at the time. "His Majesty's Government view with favour the establishment in Palestine of a national home for the Jewish people, and will use their best endeavours to facilitate the achievement of that object," the declaration read. When the British general Edmund Allenby captured Jerusalem from the Turks on 8 December 1917, Zionists had reason to celebrate and to believe that they might soon see their dreams realized. Progress turned out to be slow, of course, and the British became bogged down in their efforts to honor another part of the declaration, which pointed out that nothing could be done "which may prejudice the civil and religious rights of existing non-Jewish communities in Palestine." But in the decade of the 1910s as a whole, the Zionist movement was clearly on the rise. Nowhere was this more true than in the United States, where membership in Zionist organizations skyrocketed and leaders of the movement persuaded President Woodrow Wilson, reluctant because the United States had never declared war on Turkey, to express his support for the Balfour Declaration. Suddenly Zionism, which twenty years earlier had failed to attract more than a small minority even of the U.S. Jewish population, was exerting an influence on American foreign policy. The cry for a Jewish homeland in Palestine was clearly being taken up by unprecedented numbers of people in sometimes surprising spheres of society.

Brandeis. The story of the transformation of American Zionism in the 1910s is largely the story of one man, Boston attorney Louis Dembitz Brandeis. Brandeis took

COLONEL ROOSEVELT'S MESSAGE TO THE TROOPS

The marriage of Christian ethics to America's democratic principles in justifying America's entry into World War I was illustrated by an article in *The New York Times* on 17 June 1917. "A message from Theodore Roosevelt to American soldiers in France will be inserted in all Bibles given to the fighters by the New York Bible Society, according to an announcement made yesterday in a plea for funds to buy 100,000 books." Roosevelt's message read thus:

> The teachings of the New Testament are foreshadowed in Micah's verse: 'What more doth the Lord require of thee than to do justice, and to love mercy, and to walk humbly with thy God?'

> Do justice: and therefore fight valiantly against the armies of Germany and Turkey, for these nations in this crisis stand for the reign of Moloch and Beelzebub on this earth.

> Love mercy: treat prisoners well; succor the wounded; treat every woman as if she was your sister; care for the little children, and be tender with the old and helpless.

> Walk humbly: you will do so if you study the life and teachings of the Saviour.

> May the God of Justice and Mercy have you in his keeping.

Source: "Colonel's War Texts" *New York Times*, 17 June 1917, p. 6.

the helm of American Zionism on 30 August 1914, when an "emergency meeting" of the Federation of American Zionists (FAZ) offered him the chairmanship of its Provisional Executive Committee for General Zionist Affairs. The FAZ's immediate concern in August 1914 was to raise funds for the support of Jewish settlers already living in Palestine, who suddenly found themselves cut off from European import and export markets as a result of the Ottoman Empire's alliance with Germany. But Brandeis expanded both the organization's aims and its clout in extraordinary ways. Perhaps no other American Jew was in as favorable a position to influence public policy as was Brandeis; his personal relationship with Wilson led to his appointment as the Supreme Court's first Jewish justice in 1916. Thus, it was Brandeis, along with prominent Reform Jewish rabbi Stephen S. Wise, whose lobbying encouraged Wilson to embrace the Balfour Declaration. But equally important for the cause was Brandeis's ability to increase the appeal of Zionism among America's diverse Jewish population.

Diversity. Conservative Judaism, centered at New York's Jewish Theological Seminary and under the leadership of Solomon Schechter and, later, Mordecai Kaplan, provided the major basis of support for American Zionism. With an understanding of Judaism as what Kaplan would call the "religious civilization of the Jewish people," Conservatives saw the need for a homeland where that civilization could be established independently, providing a center from which Jewish life around the world could draw strength and direction. But with this view the Conservatives stood in stark contrast to the large Reform Jewish population of the United States. Products of the emancipation of Jews from Germany's ghettos in the nineteenth century, Reform Jews had worked hard to erase the stigma so often attached to their religion. Arriving in the United States, they had assimilated quickly and thoroughly into the mainstream Protestant religious culture they found here. English had replaced Hebrew as the language of the synagogue; church schools had been established; and, perhaps most important, the Pittsburgh Platform, a statement of Reform principles issued in 1885, had declared that Judaism was only a religion and not an ethnicity, thus implicitly denying the need for a home for the "people." At the other end of the Jewish spectrum, newly arrived Orthodox Jews from eastern Europe also grappled with the issue of assimilation and the adoption of "American" as an ethnic identity. Already experiencing persecution because of their obvious "foreignness," Orthodox Jews became hesitant to voice their support for a far-off Jewish homeland. It was up to Brandeis to craft a Zionist vision broad enough to draw in all these segments of American Judaism.

The American Synthesis. Brandeis met the challenge, developing the first uniquely American vision for the Jewish homeland. He did this by stressing the compatibility of Zionism with American ideals. American Zionists did not advocate the creation of a Jewish theocracy overseas, Brandeis argued; instead, they merely sought the establishment of a state where worldwide Jewry could enjoy all the benefits of democracy, just as American Jews already knew them. At a convention in June 1918, the FAZ issued a new Pittsburgh platform, expressing its distinctly American vision for the new Palestinian society. The Jewish state, according to this platform, should guarantee "political and civil equality of all inhabitants of Palestine, regardless of race, sex, or faith; equality of opportunity, with public ownership of land, natural resources, and utilities; free public education; the cooperative principle in economic development; and Hebrew as the national language." The retention of the last plank showed the continuing influence of the Conservative understanding of the Jewish people, bound in part by a common language. But the other tenets demonstrated the new attempt to cast the net more widely — equality and liberty, the founding principles of the United States, were included to appeal to Reform Jews, and enough of a hint of socialism was added to attract some of the many Jews who had adopted that political ideology since their arrival in the United States. The results of this Brandeisian synthesis were astounding. The appeal of the new ideas was evidenced in part by the return of Reform rabbi Stephen S. Wise to the fold of Zionism, which he had left in bitter disagreement some years before. The rank and file apparently followed; the FAZ, which could claim only 12,000 members when Brandeis took the helm in 1914, swelled in size to 176,000 by 1919, the year in which it was reorganized as the Zionist Organization of America (ZOA). The restructuring was significant because it introduced individual membership, whereas the FAZ had been a loose alliance of small, local Zionist groups. Brandeis had come up with a simple formula to express his belief that Americanism, Judaism, and Zionism were complementary, rather than conflicting, loyalties. "To be good Americans, we must be better Jews," he argued, "and to be better Jews, we must become Zionists!"

Other Expressions. But the ZOA, powerful as it was by the end of the decade, was not the only voice in the United States for Zionism. In fact, the idea of a Jewish return to Palestine had supporters from such unlikely quarters as premillennialist Protestantism, which saw the reconstitution of the nation of Israel as a crucial element of God's plan for the last days of the world. But within Judaism, the two major expressions of Zionism outside the ZOA were Po'ale Zion and Hadassah. Po'ale Zion represented a wing of Jewish socialism and was known as "Labor Zionism" because of its involvement in the broader struggle for the unionization of American labor. But as a result of its deep political activism and sometimes radical Marxist views, Po'ale Zion ultimately gained little support from either the socialist party or the ZOA, working instead as an independent voice on behalf not only of Palestinian settlers but also of Jewish workers in America. For its part, Hadassah represented the efforts of women's groups, usually local "Daughters of Zion" chapters, to do relief work in Palestine. It came into being through the auspices of Henrietta Szold, who had seen firsthand the lack of medical care available to Jewish settlers in the Holy Land. She returned from her trip there in 1910 and began discussing the settlers' plight with the women in her study circle at a New York synagogue. By 1912 the groundwork had been laid for a national women's Zionist organization. Meetings on 24 February and 7 March 1912 led to the creation of the national group, the Daughters of Zion, and an affiliated New York organization, the Hadassah Chapter of the Daughters of Zion. In 1914 the name of the national organization was changed to Hadassah, the Women's Zionist Organization of America. In early 1914 Hadassah sent its first two nurses to minister to the settlers in Palestine; ultimately it raised the funds and coordinated personnel for a major medical relief effort. Hadassah would also become the single largest Zionist organization in the world, although Szold herself resigned as its president in 1916 to found a similar organization, the American Zionist Medical Unit. By 1919, then, Zionism encompassed the efforts of a broad range of America's Jewish population to realize the deepest principles of Jewish peoplehood and philanthropy, both in Palestine and in the United States.

Sources:

Isidore S. Meyer, ed., *Early History of Zionism in America* (New York: Arno, 1977);

Ezekiel Rabinowitz, *Justice Louis D. Brandeis: The Zionist Chapter of His Life* (New York: Philosophical Library, 1968).

HEADLINE MAKERS

LYMAN ABBOTT

1835-1922

CONGREGATIONAL MINISTER, WRITER, EDITOR

Outlook. As the 1910s opened, Lyman Abbott was seventy-five years old and had already fit several careers into a single lifetime. He had ended the nineteenth century by resigning from his position as pastor of Brooklyn's Plymouth Congregational Church in 1899. His life in the twentieth century was focused on writing and editing his enormously successful and influential paper *Outlook;* lecturing at universities; and shaping public debate on a variety of political, social, and religious topics of the turn of the century. Under Abbott's direction *Outlook* had grown from a circulation of 15,000 (when it was known as the *Christian Union*) in 1876 to 30,000 in 1893, to 100,000 in 1900, and to a peak of 125,000 in 1910, when Theodore Roosevelt was a member of its staff. It was among the strongest voices in political, social, and religious thought. Through it Abbott was a strong supporter of liberal causes, of progress, and of the presidency and later candidacy (in 1912) of Theodore Roosevelt. Abbott repudiated strict Darwinism but accepted many tenets of evolution, adapting them to Christian thought and making them more palatable for skeptical Christians. As war neared in Europe, Abbott became a vociferous champion of U.S. involvement, joining what in retrospect appears to have been a deeply prejudiced campaign against the German people. But this position defied Abbott's usual progressive stances on political and religious issues and sounds an unfortunate ending note to an otherwise stellar career of thoughtful analyses, synthesis, and opinion on some of the central religious and theological issues of his time.

Origins. Abbott was born in Roxbury, Massachusetts, in 1835 but grew up primarily in Farmington, Maine, until 1843, when, upon the death of his mother, the family moved to New York City. He was educated in schools operated by his uncles and at fourteen entered New York University. At age eighteen he graduated and joined the law firm of his brothers, Austin and Vaughn. He practiced law for six years before abandoning it in order to fulfill a boyhood desire to become a minister. He was ordained in Farmington in 1860 at the age of twenty-four and promptly began his second career two weeks later at a Congregational church in Terre Haute, Indiana.

Reconstruction. He served in Indiana throughout the Civil War and became a strong advocate of reconciliation and Reconstruction. In 1865 he resigned as pastor of the church to become a secretary of the American Union Commission, a group dedicated to cooperating with the government on the Reconstruction of the South. While working for the commission he was also pastor of the New England Congregational Church in New York City. He remained in both positions for four years. By this time he had begun to write book reviews for *Harper's Magazine* while developing his own ideas about Christian duty and society. He also began to practice journalism as well as other writing.

Editor. In 1870 Abbott became the editor of a new periodical called *The Illustrated Christian Weekly,* for which he worked until 1876. He then became associated with Henry Ward Beecher as coeditor of the *Christian Union,* the position in which he would remain for forty-six years. After Beecher's departure from the paper in 1881, Abbott became editor in chief and changed the paper's name to *Outlook* in 1893. But Beecher left Abbott something else as well. The great preacher died in 1887, and Abbott was invited to become the temporary pastor of Beecher's church, the Plymouth Congregational Church in Brooklyn. He was well received and became the permanent pastor in 1890. He served in this position for ten years while also retaining control of the ever-growing *Outlook*. He was a prolific author during the 1890s, publishing six books in nine years. He and Washington Gladden became two of the most prominent popularizers of liberal theology and practical Christianity. Among his books during this decade were *The Evolution of Christianity* (1892), *Christianity and Social Problems* (1896), and *The Theology of an Evolutionist* (1897). While many Christians were denouncing Darwinism and some scientists were dismissing religion, Abbott looked for a compromise position. Though he found natural selection unpleasant and considered it simply wrong, he chose to use evolutionary thought as a basis for reaffirming faith. "For the question whether God made the animal man by a mechanical process in an hour or by a process of growth continuing through centuries is quite immaterial to one who believes that into man God breathes a divine life," he wrote in 1915.

The Christian Rationale for War. The focus of Abbott's work in the 1910s was primarily in justifying preparedness for war on Germany for Christians who were troubled by religious scruples against war. His opinions regarding World War I, at the time popular, defensible, and commonplace, in retrospect are difficult to understand from a man who had urged reconciliation and rebuilding after the Civil War and whose career had been grounded in liberal theology. After the sinking of the *Lusitania* in May 1915, Abbott pressed for war on Germany. In a speech in May 1916 Abbott, citing Christ's words that those who live by the sword should perish by the sword, said, "We have that sword given us by our Master, and we will not sheathe it until the predatory Potsdam gang has perished from the face of the earth." The speech was telegraphed throughout the country. In 1918 Abbott published *The Twentieth Century Crusade*, in which he "contends that our participation in this world war furnishes a striking evidence of the power of Christianity, and the extent with which its spirit has pervaded the nation." He approved of the Espionage Act of 1917 and the Sedition Act of 1918, measures that effectively curtailed freedom of expression for those who did not support the war. He opined that pacifists had no rights of assembly, that banning German music was "not unreasonable," and vehemently opposed the notion of forgiveness for Germany at the war's end. In short, the war against Germany was a holy war against evil, and Abbott, among many others in positions of religious leadership, fanned public opinion against Germany and worked to curtail dissent at home. In the midst of the decade he published his *Reminiscences* (1915), the story of a singular life, long and controversial, that bridged an old world to a new one. He died in 1922.

Sources:

Lyman Abbott, *Reminiscences* (Boston: Houghton Mifflin, 1915);

Ira V. Brown, *Lyman Abbott: Christian Evolutionist* (Cambridge, Mass.: Harvard University Press, 1953).

OLYMPIA BROWN

1835-1926

UNIVERSALIST MINISTER, SUFFRAGIST

The Final Push. On 2 November 1920 Olympia Brown, at the age of eighty-five, cast a ballot for the first time in her long, distinguished life when she voted in a presidential election. That simple act was the culmination of a lifetime of fighting for women's rights as well as achieving personal goals against much resistance. The 1910s had seen the suffrage movement reenergized, and Brown, although she was seventy-five when the decade began and had faced numerous disappointments in her career as an activist, again became focused on the goal, knowing that the time was ripe and the era would provide a final chance for women to achieve the vote in her lifetime.

Youth. Brown's beliefs and her strong personality came from her mother, Lephia Brown. Olympia was born in a log cabin near Schoolcraft, Michigan, in 1835 in what was then still frontier country. Lephia Brown believed in equality and education, teaching her children herself until her husband, Asa, built a schoolhouse on his farm and arranged to have a teacher brought there. Brown's aunt and uncle, Thomas and Pamela Nathan, were ardent abolitionists, and their home nearby served as a stop on the Underground Railroad, which helped runaway slaves escape to Canada. Brown was raised in an atmosphere of equality, with her mother stressing the need for education. In 1854, unable to attend college in Michigan, Olympia and her sister Oella traveled to South Hadley, Massachusetts, to attend Mount Holyoke College, founded eighteen years earlier as a women's college. Brown found the school suffocating and restrictive. One year later she entered Horace Mann's Antioch College in Yellow Springs, Ohio, where her education blossomed. She graduated in 1860 and began applying to theological schools. Only one would consider a woman. Brown went there.

Pastor Brown. Brown entered the Universalist St. Lawrence Theological School in Canton, New York, in the fall of 1861. She found much resistance from the other students — all men — and several faculty wives. The resistance that she would face from other women frustrated her throughout her career. Despite the opposition, Brown excelled at St. Lawrence. In summer 1862 she worked as a pastor in Vermont, where much of her family lived. On 25 June 1863 she became the first woman to be ordained in the United States and was graduated from St. Lawrence weeks later. She found a church in Marshfield, Vermont, and became its pastor after a trial visit. She began to attract the attention of women's rights activist Susan B. Anthony, who wrote to her to inquire if she would be interested in helping the cause. Brown, intent on succeeding as a pastor, declined the offer, even though she had shown a talent for such work in 1860–1861 in Cleveland getting signatures for a women's property bill. But Brown felt the need to further her career in the ministry. In 1864, after taking voice improvement lessons in Boston, Brown became the pastor of a Universalist church in Weymouth Landing. Massachusetts newspapers carried the story. She was the only woman minister in the United States. She stayed at Weymouth Landing for five years while also launching her second career, that of a suffragist.

Activist. In 1866 Brown attended a women's rights convention in New York City. There she met Susan B. Anthony and Elizabeth Cady Stanton, as well as Henry Ward Beecher and Frederick Douglass. The group organized the American Equal Rights Association, which was to work for the rights of black men as well as all women. Later that year Brown spent six weeks on the campaign trail with Anthony, Lucy Stone, and others. She developed a schism with many of the male activists who supported the vote for black men (the Fifteenth Amendment) but did not believe that women should vote. This equality-for-some attitude frustrated her throughout her career, causing her to debate vehemently with the likes of Frederick Douglass in person as well as President Woodrow Wilson from afar. Brown's fervent work on behalf of women's equality had gained her national attention, and she was offered a full-time position by Anthony. She rejected it, however, in order to return to Weymouth Landing and continue with her now-flourishing church. In late 1867 she participated in the ordination of Phoebe Hanaford in Hingham, Massachusetts. She had broken the barrier alone and was now helping others to do so. She helped to found the Massachusetts Woman Suffrage Association and in 1868 helped found the New England Woman Suffrage Association. She was succeeding in both careers, becoming known not only as a hardworking organizer but also as a fine orator.

Principles. In 1869 Susan B. Anthony formed the National Woman Suffrage Association and asked Brown to work for her. She again said no. She became increasingly concerned about factionalism within the women's movement, and when Lucy Stone formed the American Woman Suffrage Association, Brown wrote to Stone in November 1869 that "For my own part I wish to work for principles, not individuals or cliques." Instead, she took a pastorate in Bridgeport, Connecticut. In 1873, at the age of thirty-eight, she married John Henry Willis and within three years had given birth to a son and a daughter. Her pastorate, meanwhile, was foundering, because

of resistance to her based on her sex. She began to devote more time to suffrage work. In January 1876 she delivered a strong speech before a congressional committee in Washington, D.C. "Women from the rank and file, law-abiding women, desire the ballot," she told them. "Not only that they desire it, but they mean to have it." Congress remained unmoved. She would have to wait another forty-four years.

Wisconsin. In 1878 Brown reenergized her career as a pastor when she took a position in Racine, Wisconsin. It was her final congregation. Her family followed her west, and her husband founded a newspaper, *The Racine Times-Call.* Brown became instantly active in Wisconsin suffrage work as well as making her church an educational and social center. She founded a Sunday school, a women's club, and youth groups and brought speakers in to discuss issues, especially women's issues. She organized and raised funds for major building repairs to her church while becoming president of the then-slumping Wisconsin Woman Suffrage Association. In 1885 Wisconsin passed a vague and limited woman suffrage bill. Brown decided to test it and in 1887 resigned her pastorate in order to work full-time as a suffragist. She tried to vote, was refused, and filed a lawsuit against ballot inspectors who would not permit women to vote. Ironically, some inspectors had allowed it and many women across the state had their votes counted. A circuit court judge ruled in favor of the suffrage group, but the state Supreme Court struck down the ruling. Brown again faced defeat, and though she would continue her work and, after the death of her husband, take to editing his newspaper, the women's movement settled into a valley. Anthony and most of the others of her generation would not live to cast the ballot themselves. Only Brown and Antoinette Brown Blackwell, an early inspiration to Brown, would survive long enough to cast a vote.

Victory. The year 1912 had seen a woman suffrage bill passed by the legislature of Wisconsin, where Brown resided, though in a popular referendum the bill failed. At the same time, Kansas voted to give women the vote, forty-five years after Brown had canvased the state alone supporting such a bill. In 1913 Brown joined the Congressional Union, a new party dedicated to getting the Susan B. Anthony amendment through Congress. The Congressional Union, inspired by English suffragette Emmeline Pankhurst and her more militant approach, began picketing the White House. Brown had already testified before Congress and had seen one vote defeated. Women took to the street before the White House and campaigned vehemently against President Woodrow Wilson, who, while speaking frequently about justice and human rights, was staunchly opposed to women voting. Protesters spent months through the winter of 1917 marching in the streets, the eighty-two-year-old Brown among them. Women of the Congressional Union, now known as the Woman's Party, were arrested and thrown in jail. Even other suffragists, such as Anna Howard

Shaw, disliked their tactics, criticizing them as unladylike and even unpatriotic for pushing the issue during the war years. But Brown had seen how "ladylike" activism had failed, that demanding rights instead of reasoning for them was what was needed. In December 1918, with President Wilson at the peace talks in France, Brown participated in a protest in Washington at which a pile of Wilson's books and speeches were burned. Six months later the Anthony bill passed through Congress. Within twenty months the amendment had been ratified by the states. Brown, as well as all American women, had the right to vote. Brown survived to cast another vote in the 1924 election. She had had a remarkable career and life — active, stubborn, cantankerous, and indomitable, in conflict with a male world throughout and even the younger generation of suffragists during the 1910s. When she died in 1926, tributes poured in from across the nation.

Source:
Charlotte Coté, *Olympia Brown: The Battle for Equality* (Racine, Wis.: Mother Courage Press, 1988).

ARNO C. GAEBELEIN

1861-1945

FUNDAMENTALIST EDITOR

The Fundamentals. With the publication, between 1910 and 1915, of *The Fundamentals,* the fundamentalist Christian movement became a more organized and prominent Protestant voice in American religion during the 1910s. Conservative Protestants such as Reuben A. Torrey and Amzi Dixon, an editor of *The Fundamentals,* hotly debated modernist and liberal theologians such as Shirley Jackson Case and Shailer Mathews, both of the University of Chicago Divinity School. Among the strongest voices of fundamentalist Christianity was that of Arno C. Gaebelein, the editor of one of fundamentalism's sturdiest platforms, the monthly magazine *Our Hope.* Gaebelein was himself a contributor to *The Fundamentals,* with interpretation of biblical prophecy as his specialty. He had been active in the nascent fundamentalist movement during the 1890s and remained vehemently attached to dispensational premillennialism (the belief that human history is divided into seven ages, or dispensations, and that the present one will end with the return of Christ to establish his millennial kingdom) until his death in 1945.

Early Years. Gaebelein took a circuitous route to Fundamentalism. He was born in Germany in 1861 and immigrated to America in 1879, where he procured work in a woolen mill in Lawrence, Massachusetts. In 1880 he joined the German Methodist Episcopal Church and made the acquaintance of Augustus Wallon, whose father was a pastor in New York City. In 1881 Gaebelein moved to New York to become Louis Wallon's assistant. Wallon was postmillennial in belief and led young Gaebelein through a home study of church history and theology,

while leading him away from seminary study. Gaebelein instead became a preacher, first in Bridgeport, Connecticut, on weekends and then in 1882 at a church in Baltimore after he had passed a candidacy exam for the Methodist ministry. He made language study his specialty, learning Greek, Hebrew, and Latin while also studying Aramaic, Arabic, Syrian, and Persian. He was successful as a pastor and in 1884 was ordained as a deacon. He married in 1885, and in 1886, at the age of twenty-five, he became an elder of the Methodist Episcopal Church and was assigned to a church in Hoboken, New Jersey.

The Mission. In 1887 Gaebelein met Sam Goldstein, a Jew who had converted to Christianity. Goldstein suggested that Gaebelein travel to New York and preach to the growing Jewish immigrant population there. Reluctant at first, Gaebelein began to preach at Jacob Freshman's Hebrew Christian mission. The experience changed both Gaebelein's thinking and the direction of his life. Gaebelein became a convinced premillennialist as a result of his exposure to Orthodox Judaism, which taught that a literal messiah would come to claim King David's throne. Gaebelein began studying the Bible in a new light and became convinced that his future work should be with the Jews. In 1891 he moved to New York City and began preaching to Jews full-time while studying their culture. Though he met with some resistance, he drew large crowds to his "mission," to which he later gave the name Hope of Israel. In 1893 he began publishing *Tiqweth Israel — The Hope of Israel Monthly,* a magazine in Hebrew. The following year Gaebelein was joined by professor Ernst F. Stroeter, another German Methodist. Together they formed *Our Hope,* an English-language monthly that served their mission as well as other Hope of Israel missions that had sprung up in Baltimore, Philadelphia, and Saint Louis.

Our Hope. The purpose of the Hope of Israel missions was evident in *Our Hope.* Besides serving the poor immigrant communities of the economically depressed 1890s, Gaebelein and Stroeter both believed that the Jewish people, as prophesied in the Bible, were the key to the Scriptures. Zionism became a focus of *Our Hope.* Gaebelein criticized Christians who were anti-Semitic and who acted "triumphant" in regard to the Jews. For Gaebelein, Christian prophecy could not be realized without Jewish "help." Thus, he became a supporter of the Jewish people, though much later in his life he began to have doubts about these sentiments. His vehicle for spreading his belief was *Our Hope,* which was in existence from 1894 to 1957. *Our Hope* was among the early supporters of Jewish colonization in Palestine. It supported the founder of Zionism, Theodor Herzl, though it disagreed with his plan to purchase Palestine. The journal castigated Christians who remained ignorant of Jewish customs, while following closely all international developments regarding the Jewish people. In 1895 Gaebelein traveled to Russia, Germany, Poland, Romania, and England to observe the situation of the Jews and report for

Our Hope. By 1897 *Our Hope* had become independent of the Methodist Episcopal Church's Missionary Society. That same year, however, Gaebelein changed his thinking on a major aspect of his work, sending his career in a different direction.

Fundamentalist. Prior to 1897 Gaebelein had made the acquaintance of early fundamentalist leaders such as James M. Gray, Cyrus I. Scofield, and George L. Alrich. In 1898 he participated in the Niagara Bible Conference along with Reuben A. Torrey and William G. Moorehead, the president of the United Presbyterian Theological Seminary. By 1899 Gaebelein, now influenced by fundamentalist teachings, was forced to confront the question that was challenging the Hope of Israel's founding principles. Essentially, he came to discard the idea that a Jew converted to Christianity was still a Jew. From this point on, he believed that Jews could no longer be part of "Christ's body," the church. He now argued that converted Jews became Gentiles, and that "ordinances, etc. are no longer in existence for a believer in the Lord Jesus Christ." Stroeter disagreed and left *Our Hope.* Gaebelein resigned from the Methodist Episcopal Church. *Our Hope* essentially became a fundamentalist organ with an emphasis on interpreting scriptural prophecy. At the start of the new century Gaebelein was a rising fundamentalist leader who, now removed from mission work, began to write and publish in abundance. He published a series of commentaries on books of the Bible, beginning with *Studies in Zechariah* (1900) and following up with *The Gospel of Matthew* (1903–1907), *The Prophet Daniel* (1911), *The Prophet Joel* (1909), *The Prophet Ezekiel* (1918), *The Book of Revelation* (1915), and *The Gospel of John* (1925). He worked on Cyrus I. Scofield's *Reference Bible*, published in 1909, and in 1912 he began ten years of work on his own *Annotated Bible*. He published *The Jewish Question* in 1912, which affirmed what Gaebelein thought was the Christian church's failure in dealing with Judaism while advocating the need for a Jewish homeland.

1910s and Beyond. Gaebelein remained active through the 1910s and beyond. His article for *The Fundamentals,* titled "Fulfilled Prophecy, A Potent Argument for the Bible," was the only chapter that dealt specifically with prophecy. He became a featured fundamentalist speaker, participating in the Fifth International Prophetic Conference at the Moody Bible Institute in Chicago in 1914 and acting as president of the sixth conference in 1918. Gaebelein led the charge in defense of Fundamentalism against vehement attacks from liberal theologians. His response to World War I was one of both horror and caution. While many saw the carnage in Europe as an expected sign of Armageddon, Gaebelein pointed out that, according to the book of Revelation, "Armageddon is in Palestine and not in Europe." He also pointed out that the Jews had not been "restored to their land nor do we see anything of Anti-Christ." He saw, in fact, the capture of Jerusalem

from the Turks in 1917 as a significant sign, anticipating the eventual return of the Jews, though he would not live to see the state of Israel established in 1948. After the war Gaebelein became an ardent anticommunist and spent the 1920s and 1930s vehemently opposing Bolshevism. His own prophecy seemed to anticipate the horrors of World War II, while at the same time, his anticommunism often seemed tainted with anti-Semitism when Jews were acting on behalf of the forces of the Left. He wrote that "too often the Jews have brought disaster upon themselves by meddling with the politics of the countries into which the Lord has scattered them." He considered leftist Jews "apostate," thinking that they did not fit neatly into his interpretations of the Bible. In light of his career, however, and the genuine horror he felt at the Holocaust, charges of anti-Semitism seem only loosely founded. Gaebelein died on Christmas Day in 1945, his influence on the fundamentalist movement well established.

Source:
David A. Rausch, *Arno C. Gaebelein, 1861–1945: Irenic Fundamentalist and Scholar* (New York: Mellen, 1983).

JAMES CARDINAL GIBBONS

1834-1921

ROMAN CATHOLIC CARDINAL AND ARCHBISHOP OF BALTIMORE

Elder Statesman. As the archbishop of Baltimore, the oldest Roman Catholic see in the United States, as well as the only U.S. cardinal between 1886 and 1911, James Cardinal Gibbons enjoyed the status of the unofficial leader of American Catholicism in the early part of the twentieth century. Although he had passed the prime of his life before the 1910s — he was seventy-five when the decade began — little could be accomplished by Catholic organizations except under his auspices. Gibbons also possessed another talent that was even more important than his leadership skill. His tact and diplomacy won him the respect and affection not only of Catholic officials in Rome but also of his Protestant peers and public officials in America. By the time he orchestrated the organization of the National Catholic War Council in 1917, he was universally recognized as American Catholicism's elder statesman.

A Calling. James Gibbons was born in 1834 in the city that would forever be associated with his name. The son of Irish immigrants who had come to Baltimore just a few years previously, Gibbons would not really discover the city until he was twenty. When he was three, his family returned to a farm in Ireland where young James was raised and educated until he was thirteen. After the death of his father in 1847, the Gibbons family returned to the United States and settled in New Orleans, where Gibbons worked as a grocery clerk during his teen years. Although he had been a good student and had impressed the owner of the grocery store with his intelligence, there had yet to be any indication of the man who would grow to be a force not only in the Catholic Church but on the political and social scene as well. It was in 1854, at the age of nineteen, that James Gibbons received his calling, a call that took him back to Baltimore and ultimately to the highest place he could reach in Catholic America. In January 1854 at St. Joseph's Church in New Orleans, Gibbons heard a sermon by Rev. Clarence Walworth. Gibbons decided then to become a priest and decided to pursue the calling in the city of his birth.

Priest. Gibbons enrolled at St. Charles College in Baltimore in the autumn of 1855. He was an outstanding student and upon graduation entered St. Mary's Seminary in Baltimore. Seven years after the sermon by Woolworth, Gibbons was ordained a priest on 30 June 1861. He rose through the church hierarchy at a remarkable rate. In July 1861 Gibbons became an assistant pastor at St. Patrick's in Baltimore. Only six weeks later he was given a full pastorate at St. Bridget's in Canton, Maryland. The Civil War had recently begun, and among Gibbons's duties was ministering to both Union soldiers and Confederate prisoners of war at nearby Fort McHenry. He showed early on the energy that would characterize his work throughout his life. In 1865 Gibbons was asked to become secretary to the archbishop of Baltimore, Martin Spalding. He so impressed the archbishop and others at the Second Plenary Council in 1866 that he was again quickly promoted. The same year, at the age of thirty-two and only five years beyond his ordination, Gibbons was nominated as bishop of the new Vicariate-Apostolic of North Carolina. His days as a parish priest were over. The church had larger plans for him.

Bishop. In 1868 Gibbons became the youngest Roman Catholic bishop in the world when he was consecrated bishop of Adramyttum. Few Catholics lived in North Carolina at the time, and Gibbons traveled widely, serving those who were settled there while doing mission work in the territory. He converted many, built new churches, and preached in Protestant churches as a guest and in civic buildings when no churches were available. His energy and zeal paid off personally when he was called to Rome in 1870 for the Ecumenical Council of the Vatican. He was the youngest of more than seven hundred delegates, but there he made the acquaintances that would forge his future by meeting Henry Cardinal Manning of England and Gioacchino Cardinal Pecci, who would eventually become Pope Leo XIII. Upon his return to the United States, Gibbons was named bishop of Richmond when that bishopric was vacated in 1872. He served there for five years before returning to Baltimore as archbishop. In 1876, while serving in Richmond,

Gibbons wrote his first and most famous book, *The Faith of Our Fathers,* published in 1877. Hailed as the finest available explanation and defense of Roman Catholic practices, the book became an immediate success, selling more than two million copies during the next forty years. Gibbons's work in predominantly Protestant regions had led him to understand the source of opposition to his faith and to write a defense of the most commonly misunderstood aspects of it. The same year it appeared, Gibbons was called to Baltimore as coadjutor with right to succession to Archbishop Bayley. Bayley died within weeks of Gibbons's arrival, and Gibbons resettled in Baltimore, where he remained for forty-three years. At the time of Bayley's death, Gibbons was forty-three years old.

Archbishop. As archbishop of the oldest Catholic see in the United States, in the vicinity of the nation's capital, and for a faith whose followers had been pouring into the country at a rate that had alarmed much of the Protestant population, Gibbons became a man of great influence and tremendous stature not only in America but in the worldwide Roman Catholic hierarchy as well. He knew personally every president between Andrew Johnson and Woodrow Wilson. He was instrumental in promoting the celebration of the Thanksgiving holiday. In 1880 he visited Rome and met with Pope Leo XIII, with whom he would work for years to further establish Catholicism in the United States. During his years as archbishop he more than tripled the number of churches in his diocese. He built parochial schools and colleges and helped create the Catholic University of America in Washington, D.C. He became an important figure in support of the nascent labor organization the Knights of Labor, which many Catholic leaders had condemned as a secret society. He supported workers' rights and Archbishop John Ireland's controversial educational experiments in Minnesota in the 1880s. He became a strong advocate of Americanizing the church, a strategy intended to meet the dual pressures of anti-Catholic prejudice among Protestant Americans and the determination of different Catholic ethnic groups to preserve their own languages and customs. In 1903 he became the first American to take part in a papal election, supporting Cardinal Sorto, who became Pope Pius X. He published *Our Christian Heritage* (1889), *The Ambassador of Christ* (1896), and *Discourses and Sermons* (1908). In 1886, after the death of John Cardinal McCloskey in 1885, Gibbons traveled to Rome to become the second American cardinal.

Cardinal for a New Century. James Cardinal Gibbons was perhaps the most important and influential American Catholic, as well as an important public figure, through World War I and to his death in 1921. Just prior to the war Theodore Roosevelt told him, "Taking your life as a whole, I think you now occupy the position of being the most respected, and venerated, and useful citizen of our country." The cardinal was eighty years old when the war started but immediately began working at home in preparation for U.S. involvement. While the drums beat for a declaration of war after the sinking of the *Lusitania*, Gibbons remained a cool, neutral figure. But by 1917 he supported the war and pushed for Catholics to enlist. The issues of ethnicity and assimilation continued to plague the church, especially as the war engendered a new wave of nativism. Gibbons saw in the war effort an opportunity for American Catholics to prove their patriotic loyalty. Although it was John Burke, a New York priest and the editor of *Catholic World,* who chaired the National Catholic War Council, Gibbons had been instrumental in the council's organization, and he led the committee that oversaw its transformation into the National Catholic Welfare Council in 1919. In addition, during the war he served as the church's official spokesman in all matters of policy. He issued statements supporting the American Red Cross, the U.S. Food Administration, the Liberty Loan, the United War Work Campaign, and the Committee on Public Information. When Pope Benedict XV declared 29 June 1918 a day of prayer for Catholics worldwide, Gibbons took advantage of the opportunity to invite American Catholics to pray for victory in what he now clearly saw as a just war. "If we fight like heroes and pray like saints soon will America overcome mere force by greater force, and conquer lust of power by the nobler power of sacrifice and faith." In 1916 he published his *Retrospect of Fifty Years.* James Cardinal Gibbons died in 1921 at the age of eighty-six. An estimated two hundred thousand people viewed his body when it lay in state in Baltimore's cathedral.

Source:
Albert E. Smith and Vincent Fitzpatrick, *Cardinal Gibbons: Churchman and Citizen* (Baltimore: O'Donovan Brothers, 1921).

RUFUS JONES

1863-1948

QUAKER TEACHER, MINISTER, AND LEADER

A Small-Town Boy. In his autobiographical works, *A Small Town Boy* (1941) and *Finding the Trail of Life* (1943), Rufus Matthew Jones presented a picture of his idyllic childhood in the small Quaker village of South China, Maine. He wrote that "sunset and evening stars produced a spell on my young mind" and of how he enjoyed the sound of "the swish of my scythe in the grass wet with morning dew." The mystical beauty of nature and the joys of hard work were staples in his young life. The story goes that his Aunt Peace, upon the birth of Rufus, held up the newborn and proclaimed, "This child will one day bear the message of the Gospel to distant lands and to peoples across the sea." She was right, of course, but she might have added much more. Rufus Jones became a Quaker leader, a professor, a historian of the faith, an organizer

and unifier of the Society of Friends, and the first leader of the American Friends Service Committee during World War I.

Background. Jones was the son of Edwin and Mary Jones, relatively prosperous farmers at the time of Rufus's birth in 1863. The Joneses were a religious family who often had itinerant preachers staying in their home. Religion was a daily topic of discussion. Even more influential on Jones, however, was his uncle, Eli Jones, a minister and community leader. Eli Jones and his wife, Sybil, had traveled to Africa to help the nascent black African Republic of West Africa and had taken the gospel to the Holy Land. They were close friends of the poet John Greenleaf Whittier, and Eli Jones had served in the Maine state legislature. His life as a "noble citizen, valiant man, a living example of what a Christian ought to be" influenced Rufus greatly. Rufus's school years were typical of the times. He attended nearby Oak Grove Seminary from 1877 to 1879, then at age sixteen won a scholarship to attend the highly regarded Friends School in Providence, Rhode Island. Prior to his leaving for Providence he had never traveled more than twenty miles from home. In 1882, having graduated from the Friends School, he was awarded a scholarship to attend Haverford College in Philadelphia. Three years later he received his B.A. His thesis work had been on mysticism, a topic that would interest him greatly all his life. He was offered a teaching position at the Friends Boarding School in Union Springs, New York, and took the offer, the first of his many years of teaching.

Finding the Trail. He taught for one year but needed to take time away. His eyesight was poor and was giving him great trouble. He decided to travel to Europe and borrowed the money for the journey. Although his uncle Eli and his Quaker schooling had set him on his path in life, it was this journey abroad that truly showed him the trail he was to take. He traveled first to England, where he visited Friends schools and meetings and met the English Quaker and Member of Parliament John Bright. In London, Jones met well-known Quaker Charles Taylor and William Charles Braithwaite, son of prominent Quaker Bevan Braithwaite. He would make early plans with William Braithwaite to write a history of the Quakers, a goal that would be achieved more than twenty years later. Weeks later, while in France, Jones would have a mystical experience that would help him to define his future life. While on a solitary walk near Nîmes he "felt the walls between the visible and invisible grow thin." He saw that his future life must be "an unfolding in the realm of mystical religion . . . interpreting the deep nature of the soul and its relations to God." In a more practical development, he found in Germany a doctor who could alleviate his eye trouble with the correct lens. He returned to the United States in 1887 and began his teaching career at the Friends School in Providence.

Teacher. From 1887 to 1893 he taught, for two years at the Friends School and later at the Oak

Grove Seminary in Vassalboro, Maine, where he was also school principal. He married Sarah Hawkshurst Coutant in 1888 and became a father in 1892, when his son, Lowell, was born. In 1890 he was recorded as a minister of the Society of Friends and began to lecture and preach. In the summer of 1892, while on a second visit to Europe, he met John Wilhelm Rountree, with whom he struck up a great friendship. Rountree was influential in convincing Jones that a new type of Quaker ministry was needed, one that combined inspiration with interpretation. Primary to achieving this goal was a fresh historical interpretation of what Quakerism had meant and could continue to mean. Jones again realized that he wanted to write a history of Christian mysticism that found "the roots of Quakerism to these movements before the birth of George Fox," the founder of the Society of Friends. Rountree and Jones would meet annually to discuss their ideas, but only upon the death of Rountree in 1905 did Jones begin seriously to research his history of the Society of Friends. Jones intended to begin graduate work at Harvard in the fall of 1893, but he was offered the editorship of the *Friends Review* and a position in the Philosophy Department at Haverford College. He accepted both and began a new role, as a leader in the Society of Friends.

Editor. In 1893, when Jones became editor of the *Friends Review*, Quakerism was foundering. Jones saw four separate movements in the Society of Friends each with its own ideas and publication. The groups ranged from the ultraliberal "Hicksites" (publisher of *The Friends Intelligencer*), to the ultraconservatives of Philadelphia (*The Friend*), to the moderate liberals of Haverford (*Friends Review*), to the evangelical Quakers of the West (*The Christian Worker*), who ran Dwight Moody–inspired revivals that were markedly different from the traditional contemplative quietism of the Quaker church. Jones saw his mission as unification, and he began to use his editorial voice to support it. He refused to support any one sect and instead used his skills as an historian to discover what the essential aspects of Quakerism should be. Within a year of beginning his role as editor he merged the *Friends Review* with *The Christian Worker* and founded *The American Friend* in 1894. The orthodox group in Philadelphia changed slowly and reluctantly, however. To further unify the church Jones proposed in 1900 a "Constitution and Discipline" and a national organization to which all Quakers would belong. After some changes the Yearly Meeting of Friends for New England adopted the constitution. This gathering was followed by many other Yearly Meetings. Jones's vision was catching on. Meanwhile, during his editorship he faced two

tragedies. In 1898 his wife died after a long illness, and in 1903, at the age of eleven, his son, Lowell, died. Jones was devastated but found solace in Saint Francis of Assisi, whom he would consider as one of his "major guides" for the remainder of his life.

American Friends Service Committee. Jones had much more work ahead of him. In 1906 he began serious work on the six-volume *History of Quakerism*. William Braithwaite would write volumes three and four while Jones wrote the first two (*Studies in Mystical Religion* and *Spiritual Reformers in the Sixteenth and Seventeenth Centuries*) and the final two (*The Quakers in the American Colonies* and *Later Periods of Quakerisms*). All four of the volumes would appear by 1921. Jones did remarry in 1906, to Elizabeth Bartram Cadbury, who gave birth to their daughter, Mary Hoxie Jones, in the same year. Rufus continued to teach, but in 1912 he resigned the editorship of *The American Friend*. He also continued to lecture and remained involved in Quaker affairs. In 1917 he helped to found what for many is his crowning achievement. As the war in Europe raged on, the United States moved toward involvement in the fighting. The Quakers' belief in pacifism should not exempt them from providing a service, Jones believed. On 30 April 1917 the Yearly Meeting in Philadelphia proposed a plan for service during the war. Rufus Jones was named chairman of the new American Friends Service Committee, an organization that not only supported conscientious objectors to the war but also allowed them to perform useful work, often in harm's way, without their engaging in the fighting. The Friends Service Committee sent men to France to work with the Red Cross, and after the war, at the request of Herbert Hoover, who was organizing postwar relief efforts, the Friends Service Committee sent money and personnel to feed German children in the Weimar Republic. The committee was, in Jones's view, his "cathedral," a "translation of Christianity . . . greater than any cathedral builders ever made." He would live until 1948, continuing to teach until 1934. He published fifty-four books and personally oversaw Friends' work during World War II. He was chairman of the second World Conference of Friends in 1937 and addressed the world via radio hookup. "The Quaker philosophy of life," he said, "sees in a human spirit something that of all things in the universe is most like that ultimate reality we call God, who is spirit. Spirit like ours cannot come from anything else than Spirit."

Sources:
David Hinshaw, *Rufus Jones, Master Quaker* (New York: Putnam, 1951);

Elizabeth Gray Vining, *Friend of Life: The Biography of Rufus M. Jones* (Philadelphia: Lippincott 1958).

MORDECAI KAPLAN

1881-1983

RABBI AND THEOLOGIAN

Youth. Mordecai Kaplan was born in Lithuania in 1881, the year the pogroms began against Jews in czarist Russia. His biographer, Mel Scult, referred to 1881 as "the year of the beginning of the modern Jew," thus making Kaplan's birth in that year appropriate. He would live 102 years and be as representative of modern Jewry, its thought, conflicts, and community as anyone in the twentieth century. He arrived in the United States in 1889, part of the great Jewish immigration to America that had begun a few years before. His father, Orthodox rabbi Israel Kaplan, lacked a stable position in Lithuani and had taken a rabbinical job in New York. The rest of the Kaplan family followed a year later to join New York's burgeoning Jewish immigrant community. In 1895, at the age of thirteen, Mordecai Kaplan began attending the Jewish Theological Seminary as well as the City College of New York, from which he received his B.A. in 1900. Two years later he graduated from the seminary, just prior to the arrival in America of Solomon Schechter, the man who would remake the Jewish Theological Seminary into a graduate institution and a center of Conservative Jewish thought. In 1900 Kaplan had also begun attending graduate school at Columbia University, where he first encountered the modern ideas that would challenge his Orthodox beliefs. Among these ideas were Darwinian evolution, the early development of social sciences such as anthropology and sociology, and the philosophical study of ethics and pragmatism. His master's thesis covered ethical philosopher Henry Sidgwick. Kaplan the dissenter had begun to emerge.

Rabbi. In 1902 Kaplan, recently graduated from the seminary, assumed a rabbinical position at Kehilath Jeshurun, an Orthodox synagogue in New York. Despite his developing thought, Kaplan remained Orthodox in behavior. As early as 1904 he was using the phrase "a theology of Reconstruction" to describe the needs of Jewish thought and practice in the United States in the new century. Yet he remained at Kehilath Jeshurun until 1909, presiding over a divided congregation. The major division of the times was over the questions of keeping the religion preserved as it had been in Europe or adapting it to the New World, for instance by using English in services. Kaplan came down on the side of modernism. "I believe that Judaism need not and must not be afraid to meet and absorb all that is good in modern culture," he wrote in 1904. Yet he was critical of Reform Judaism, which to him discarded too much of Jewish nationalism in favor of a general "cosmopolitanism." While at Kehilath Jeshurun, Kaplan continued his graduate studies at Columbia, coming under the influence of Felix Adler, who had left the Jewish faith to form his own Ethical Culture, a universalist society that eschewed the religious

practices of a single ethnicity. Kaplan felt deeply ambivalent about Adler's thought while at the same time absorbing much of its universal emphasis. This emphasis would later appear in Kaplan's controversial Reconstructionist thought, which focused on Judaism more as a culture than as a religion. In 1908 Kaplan married Lena Rubin and planned his honeymoon as a trip to Europe, where he received *smicha* from Rabbi Jacob Reines, thus making Kaplan an official rabbi.

Teacher and Community Leader. Kaplan began teaching at the Jewish Theological Seminary in 1909, marking a turning point in his career. Since his arrival in 1902, Solomon Schechter had remade the JTS from a struggling seminary into an acclaimed graduate school with some of Jewish New York's finest thinkers on the faculty. Kaplan would join the group at the JTS and become a more prominent voice while also beginning to write out the philosophy that would make him so controversial. He was busy during the 1910s, giving speeches and developing the Teaching Institute of the JTS. He would remain at the JTS for fifty-four years. He played a role in the founding of Schechter's United Synagogue in 1913, a group of twenty-two synagogues that were not part of the Union of American Hebrew Congregations. Kaplan served as a vice president of the organization. Kaplan also performed services for New York's Young Men's Hebrew Association (YMHA) from 1913 on and worked with New York's *Kehilla*, a Jewish community organization that tried to "govern" all of the city's Jewish sects and educational institutes. He helped found the Central Jewish Institute in 1915, a combination of social and recreational programs with a school at its center. In all the 1910s were an active decade for Kaplan, but this activity did not prevent him from developing some of the most influential ideas of his long career.

Menorah Journal. In 1915 Kaplan began to publish a series of articles in the new *Menorah Journal* that would develop his own ideas about Judaism in America and eventually lead to his magnum opus, *Judaism as a Civilization*, published in 1934. The first article was titled "What Judaism is Not" and was followed by a second article, "What Is Judaism?" The articles began to spell out Kaplan's controversial views of the Jewish religion as seen through sociological investigation. His views would form the basis of the Reconstructionist movement, which sought a means of being both Jewish and American. In 1920 he published "A Program for the Reconstruction of Judaism" in the *Menorah Journal*. Many viewed this article as the seminal text in Reconstructionist Judaism, though Kaplan himself resisted calls for a "new" party. He believed strongly in a unified community, not sectarianism. The quest for a community was the major thrust of Kaplan's Judaism, though his definition of the community enraged Orthodox Jews, who thought he was throwing the religion out of Judaism.

In a sense they were right. Kaplan had dismissed some of the core beliefs of Orthodox Judaism. He did not believe that Jews were a chosen people, but only one of many civilizations worldwide. He thought that a Jewish homeland in Palestine was needed as a center for this great civilization. This belief in community above synagogue caused him to be active in creating Manhattan's Jewish Center in 1918 as well as the Society for the Advancement of Judaism (SAJ) in 1920. Through the decade of the 1920s, while continuing to teach, Kaplan focused on developing the SAJ, even publishing the *SAJ Review*, which covered all aspects of Jewish life.

Judaism as a Civilization. In 1931, in response to a contest that sought essays concerning an "effective functioning of the Jewish community in America," Kaplan wrote his greatest work, *Judaism as a Civilization*. The book was among three "winners" of the contest, though so controversial that the judges could not agree to sanction its thought. The ideas discussed in Kaplan's *Menorah Journal* articles were fully developed in *Judaism as a Civilization*, which was published in 1934. The book is a landmark of Jewish thinking, defining not only Jewish nationalism but also redesigning the Jewish religion for the twentieth century. The book was praised and reviled, though all seemed to recognize its importance. Kaplan followed up its publication by launching a biweekly journal, the *Reconstructionist*, in January 1935, which served as a forum to debate the ideas in Kaplan's book. Kaplan was fifty-one when he wrote *Judaism as a Civilization*. He would spend much of the second half of his life detailing his ideas by reworking the faith in Reconstructionist terms. He coedited *The New Haggadah*, a Passover text, in 1941. In 1945 he published a new *Sabbath Prayer Book*, which was burned by the Union of Orthodox Rabbis, who promptly excommunicated Kaplan. Undeterred, Kaplan published a succession of reinterpreted prayer books. He meanwhile continued to write original material. His first book remains his most important, but others that followed continued to define his thinking and influence his coreligionists. *The Meaning of God in Modern Jewish Religion* (1937), *The Future of the American Jew* (1948), *The Faith of America* (1951), and *The New Zionism* (1955) are among his subsequent works. Kaplan retired from the Jewish Theological Seminary in 1963, taught at the new Reconstructionist Rabbinical College after 1968, and spent many of his final years living in Israel. Kaplan died in 1983 at the age of 102, among the giants of Judaism in America as well as the world in the twentieth century.

Sources:

Mel Scult, *Judaism Faces the Twentieth Century: A Biography of Mordecai M. Kaplan* (Detroit: Wayne State University Press, 1993).

Emanuel S. Goldsmith, Mel Scult, and Robert M. Seltzer, eds., *The American T. A. Judaism of Mordecai M. Kaplan* (New York: New York University Press, 1990).

JOHN R. MOTT

1865-1955

DIRECTOR OF THE YOUNG MEN'S CHRISTIAN ASSOCIATION, AND LAY MISSIONARY

Pledge. John Mott was born just weeks after the end of the Civil War and would live beyond America's conflict in Korea. Along the way John R. Mott would lead an extraordinary life dedicated primarily to the one goal he established in his youth, that of spreading the gospel to those who had never heard it. He had an ordinary, comfortable childhood in Postville, Iowa, the son of a lumberyard operator and a mother committed to the Methodist Church. At the age of thirteen, under the influence of evangelist J. W. Dean, Mott professed Methodism and with the help and guidance of his local pastor, Rev. Horace E. Warner, entered Upper Iowa University at the age of sixteen. Two years later he transferred to Cornell University in Ithaca, New York. He was considering a legal career and had lost some interest in his church when he had a conversion experience on 14 January 1886. English cricket player J. Kyngston Studd, in a thundering speech, asked, "Seekest thou great things for thyself? Seek them not. Seek ye first the Kingdom of God." Mott's course in life was determined shortly after the speech. In the summer of 1886 Mott, who had become active in the Young Men's Christian Association at Cornell, represented the college at Dwight L. Moody's College Students Summer School at Mount Hermon, Massachusetts. He was among two hundred fifty representatives from eighty-nine colleges, but by the end of the two weeks' time Mott had become a member of the select group known as the "Mount Hermon 100." Exactly one hundred students left Moody's camp having pledged, "God permitting, to become foreign missionaries." None of that group would do so much or be so committed to that goal as John Mott, who for the next sixty-nine years would dedicate his life to taking the gospel to those people of the world who had not had the chance to hear it.

Student Volunteer Movement. Moody's summer school also provided Mott with his first job after his graduation from Cornell. He had, at Mount Hermon, been noticed by Richard Morse of the Young Men's Christian Association (YMCA). Upon graduating from the university in 1888, Mott went to work as the secretary for the YMCA, traveling and organizing with student leaders. He also became the chairman of a new movement. The "Mount Hermon 100" had in two years become the Student Volunteer Movement for Foreign Missions (SVM) and had increased its membership to twenty-two hundred students. The goal of the SVM was nothing less than the "evangelization of the world in this generation," a phrase that became the title of Mott's most famous book, published in 1900. Mott, though a layman, was committed to bringing together Christian forces worldwide to spread the gospel, not necessarily to convert everyone but simply to give them the chance to hear the gospel. He organized a Foreign Missions Conference of North America in 1893 and remained associated with the group for the remainder of his life. He also remained head of the SVM for thirty-two years, until 1920, overseeing its work through the great period of missionization around the turn of the century. By 1920 more than forty-seven thousand students from more than eight hundred campuses belonged to the Student Volunteer Movement, and eighty-one hundred missionaries had actually been sent out to work abroad. Mott traveled extensively himself, organizing movements in China, Japan, India, Australia, and the Near East. By 1920 some three hundred thousand students were involved in Mott's World Student Christian Federation. Mott also wrote extensively, publishing such works as *Strategic Points in the World's Conquest* (1897), *The Evangelization of the World in This Generation* (1900), *The Pastor and Modern Missions* (1904), and *The Future Leadership of the Church* (1908). He organized "Quadrennials," SVM missionary conferences held every four years in different cities, and continued to organize Moody's summer conferences at Mount Hermon.

World Missionary Conference. In June 1910 Mott served as chairman of the first World Missionary Conference in Edinburgh, Scotland. More than twelve hundred delegates participated. The conference, which organized commissions to study and plan stages of missionary endeavors, made Mott an internationally known figure. His own commission at Edinburgh became the Edinburgh Continuation Committee, which later became the International Missionary Council. Mott chaired this commission until 1941. In 1912–1913 Mott toured the Far East organizing regional conferences and speaking to large crowds. In 1912 he was offered the position of ambassador to China by his close friend, President Woodrow Wilson. Mott declined many opportunities over the years, in order not to detract from his mission work. Princeton offered him its presidency; Yale offered him the deanship of its Divinity School; yet Mott chose to bypass them all for his own work. He did, however, become general secretary of the YMCA in 1915, a seat he would hold until 1928. The World Missionary Conference had displayed his leadership to an international audience and his diplomacy to a world in need of such men during the World War I years.

The War. In 1914, as the First World War erupted in Europe, Mott declared that the "only program which can meet all the alarming facts of the situation is the worldwide spread of Christianity in its purest form." On the day that the United States declared war on Germany, Mott telegraphed President Wilson and offered the services of the YMCA for the war effort, and within days he called a Conference on Army Work in Garden City, New York. At that conference YMCA officials pledged "to promote the physical, mental, social, and spiritual welfare of the one million and more men of the military and naval forces of the United States." They pledged to raise money, help industry, assist prisoners of war, and serve the churches. To fulfill these goals the group formed the National War Work Council. Mott, always a busy man, remained even busier during the war, continuing his missionary work along with his war effort. He chaired the United War Work Campaign (a massive fund-raising enterprise) and served on a special diplomatic mission to Russia in 1917. Mott's wartime activities culminated in his role as an adviser to America's delegation to the Paris Peace Conference of 1919. He was, like President Wilson, strongly in favor of a fair peace and restored relations with Germany, though representatives of other Allied nations at the conference thought otherwise.

Honors. After the war Mott, while continuing his work, began to collect the honors bestowed upon a man of his stature. He was awarded high honors by Japan, Poland, Greece, Siam, France, Sweden, and Italy. He received numerous honorary doctorates during the next thirty years. However, he did have periods of disillusionment with the failure of Christianity to reach as far as he had hoped. The social aspects of Christianity, so popular in the first two decades of the century, began giving way to a less progressive view of how religion could imbed itself in all aspects of political and social relations. Religion became more focused on the individual and less on the amelioration of society. Mott's enthusiasm and work in the ecumenical movement made him an obvious choice as the first president of the World Council of Churches, formed in 1948. In 1946 a lifetime of work for international peace and the spread of Christian ideals led to his sharing the Nobel Peace Prize (with Emily Greene Balch). He died at the age of eighty-nine in 1955, largely successful in fulfilling the pledge he had made sixty-nine years before.

Sources:

Edwin S. Gaustad, *A Religious History of America*, revised edition (New York: HarperCollins, 1990);

Charles H. Lippy, ed., *Twentieth Century Shapers of American Popular Religion* (New York: Greenwood Press, 1989).

REVERDY C. RANSOM

1861-1959

BISHOP, AFRICAN METHODIST EPISCOPAL CHURCH

The Other Social Gospel. The late nineteenth and early twentieth centuries were marked in American religion by the rise of a movement called the Social Gospel among Protestant clergy. Men such as Josiah Strong, Walter Rauschenbusch, and Washington Gladden developed the idea of the church as a social force helping to ameliorate the difficult living conditions of urban immigrants as well as supporting nascent labor movements. Less well remembered and studied were the Social Gospel thinkers of the African Methodist Episcopal Church. In fact, critics often point to the lack of awareness of race issues on the part of white Social Gospel theologians. Reverdy Cassius Ransom, however, a black African Methodist Episcopal pastor and strong voice for equality in America, had a remarkable career as a pastor, Social Gospel activist, black rights activist, editor, and eventually bishop in his church. He ranked among the major voices and activists in the 1910s for the black churches and people.

Formative Years. Reverdy Ransom was born in Flushing, Ohio, in 1861. His mother, Harriet Johnson, would be a major influence on his thinking as well as his early career. He never knew his father but took the name of Ransom after his stepfather, whom his mother married shortly after his birth. Ransom was raised primarily in Cambridge, Ohio, where the African Methodist Episcopal Church was a major force in the lives of blacks. Ransom, barred from white schools, was educated in AME churches, which provided space in which public schools for blacks could operate. His mother attempted to enroll him in a white public school more than once but each time was rebuffed. She insisted that he be educated, however, and began performing extra work in order to pay white tutors to teach Reverdy privately. In 1881 Harriet Ransom mortgaged her home in order to send Ransom to Wilberforce University in Xenia, Ohio. He officially joined the AME Church that year. The following year he transferred, with the help of a small scholarship, to the famous Oberlin College in Oberlin, Ohio. Ransom admitted in his autobiography that he did not yet trust black institutions like Wilberforce to provide for his education. At Oberlin, however, a school noted for its liberalism, he found segregation and had his scholarship withdrawn after he organized a protest. He returned to Wilberforce where he completed his B.A. in 1886. He had seen the importance of black institutions. Men such as Daniel Payne and sociologist Benjamin W. Arnett (later an AME bishop and an adviser to President William McKinley), both professors at Wilberforce, became major influences on his thought during these years. Ransom was singled out as a gifted orator, earned a license to preach, and became the pastor of an AME Church in Selma, Ohio, in 1885. He was ordained in 1886.

Pastor and Social Gospeler. The first ten years of Ransom's career as a pastor were spent in smaller cities, as he developed his Social Gospel thinking. He held pastorates in Altoona and Hollidaysburg, Pennsylvania (1886–1888); Allegheny City, Pennsylvania (1888–1890); Springfield, Ohio (1890–1893); and Cleveland, Ohio (1893–1896). Ransom was married in 1881 but divorced in 1886. He then married a second time in 1887, a union that lasted fifty-four years, and he began his early work as an advocate of the Social Gospel. In 1890 he organized a Men's Club in Springfield, the first such club in the AME Church. In Cleveland he became a supporter of women deaconesses and organized the first AME board of deaconesses. In 1893 he attended the World's Parliament of Religions in Chicago with Arnett, where he was exposed to ecumenical ideas in religion. He would, throughout his life, support the unification of the AME Church and the AME Zion Church, though he would be disappointed that it never occurred. The 1890s saw the beginning of the great black migration from the rural South to the urban North. Though the migration would not really explode until after World War I, Ransom recognized early on the social conditions that would block the progress of urban blacks, and that the church could not confront alone. He saw the need for social institutions, not simply religious ones, in urban centers.

Chicago. In 1896 Ransom, who had been remarkably successful as an orator, organizer, and leader in his previous pastorates, was assigned by Bishop Arnett to the Bethel AME Church in Chicago, America's second largest city. Ransom's boldest social initiatives as a pastor would take place in Chicago, making him a well-known thinker as well as a preacher. With Jane Addams's Hull House and through friendships with Social Gospeler Frank Gunsaulus and lawyer Clarence Darrow, Ransom would begin to attack directly the new problems of the urban poor, much to the dismay of other AME pastors in the city. In 1900 he formed the Institutional Church and Social Settlement (ICSS), a kind of Hull House for Chicago's black community and the first settlement house in the country owned and operated by African Americans. W. E. B. Du Bois called it the "most advanced step in the direction of making the church exist for the people rather than the people for the church." The ICSS offered among its services day care for the children of working mothers, a gymnasium, various classes in practical crafts as well as music, men's clubs, women's clubs, Bible study groups, and an employment bureau. But Ransom faced opposition. Many AME pastors challenged Ransom's views of the church and resented his popularity as a preacher. At one point he was banned from preaching on Sunday mornings because other preachers feared losing their regular congregations. Others challenged the ICSS because they feared it would displace the emphasis on the spiritual. In 1904 Ransom left Chicago, and the ICSS was returned to being a "normal" AME Church, with religion as its emphasis.

Niagara. Ransom moved to Massachusetts in 1904, working in New Bedford for two years before becoming pastor of the prestigious Charles Street AME Church in 1905. The early years of the twentieth century saw a debate among blacks between the popular and powerful Booker T. Washington and his "conservative" approach to racial and social questions and the more "radical" groups led by Du Bois and Ida B. Wells. Ransom was among the radicals, and in 1906 he attended the second annual meeting of the Niagara Movement, which had been formed a year earlier. Ransom gave his famous speech "The Spirit of John Brown" at the conference in Harpers Ferry, West Virginia, a speech that Du Bois would later claim was the driving force behind the formation of the National Association for the Advancement of Colored People, organized in 1909 and founded in 1910. In the speech Ransom outlined both the conservative and radical viewpoints of the ongoing debate with Washington but then called for action, saying that "the Negro should assert his full title to American manhood, and maintain every right guaranteed him by the Constitution of the United States." J. Max Barber, editor of the *Voice of the Negro,* called it "the most eloquent address this writer has ever listened to." Ransom also spoke at the founding meeting of the NAACP, presenting the group's case for active protest, particularly against the epidemic of lynchings and race riots in the early twentieth century. In the meantime Ransom had left Boston in 1907 for his final pastorate in New York City, which he would keep until 1912.

Editor. In 1912 Ransom became the editor of the *AME Review.* His twenty-six years as an active pastor were over, and he moved into the realm of politics and writing. He became involved in presidential politics, influencing the black vote in the elections of 1912, 1916, and 1920. In 1912 he supported but then withdrew from Progressive Party candidate Theodore Roosevelt, switching to Democrat Woodrow Wilson instead after Roosevelt slighted black southern delegates. But after Wilson continued segregation in government offices (which had begun under Taft) and did nothing to stop the problem of lynching, Ransom, feeling betrayed, returned to the Republican Party (the party of Abraham Lincoln) in 1916 and 1920. He did not believe in the party but saw no other alternative. He continued his social work during the decade by forming the Church of Simon of Cyrene in New York, a mission created to minister to Manhattan's poor black community. The *AME Review* expanded its outlook and coverage of events under Ransom's guidance through the 1910s. Major voices such as William Monroe Trotter, Booker T. Washington, Kelly Miller, W. S. Scarborough, and Fenton Johnson published in the *Review,* while Ransom used his editorials as a place to address injustices to the African American community as well as discuss church-related issues.

Bishop. In 1924 Ransom was made a bishop of AME Church. He was sixty-three years old and would live another thirty-five years, continuing his role as church leader and spokesman for American blacks. He served over the years as bishop for three separate districts covering Kentucky and Tennessee (1924–1932) and Ohio, Pennsylvania, and West Virginia (1932–1952) and was a delegate to the World Methodist Conference in Massachusetts in 1947. He served as the president of Wilberforce's Board of Trustees from 1932 to 1948 and was the first president of the National Fraternal Council of Negro Churches. Among his books were *The Spirit of Freedom and Justice: Orations and Speeches* (1926), *The Negro: The Hope or Despair of Christianity* (1935), *The Pilgrimage of Harriet Ransom's Son* (1949), and *Preface to History of the AME Church* (1950). He died in 1959 at the age of ninety-eight, one of the most important voices and religious leaders of the first half of the twentieth century.

Source:
Calvin S. Morris, *Reverdy C. Ransom: Black Advocate of the Social Gospel* (Lanham, Md.: University Press of America, 1990).

WALTER RAUSCHENBUSCH

1861-1918

BAPTIST MINISTER AND THEOLOGIAN

Youth. For Walter Rauschenbusch, becoming a pastor was not only a matter of finding a calling but also a family tradition. He was the seventh in a line of pastors that reached back to seventeenth-century Germany. But Rauschenbusch, born in 1861 in the United States, became the most liberal and best known in his family lineage. His father, August Rauschenbusch was one of the great patriarchs of American Baptists after shocking his family by converting from Lutheran to Baptist after he moved to America in 1846. Walter followed in his father's footsteps, though he would eventually approach Christianity differently from the conservative Baptists of the Rochester Seminary, where his father was a professor from 1857 to 1888. Despite his father's altered faith in the New World, Walter Rauschenbusch developed strong ties to Germany, ties that would later cause him grief as World War I began, and German Americans were treated with suspicion and found their loyalty questioned. Rauschenbusch developed these ties with two extended visits in his youth. The first was in 1865–1869, when August Rauschenbusch sent his family to Germany to create a bond between them and his home country. The second visit, with his father, took place in 1879. Walter had earlier in that year undergone a conversion experience and had been baptized in Rochester. He stayed in Germany for four years, attending the Evangelische

Gymnasium zu Gutersloh, from which he graduated *primus omnium* in 1883.

Hard Work for God. Rauschenbusch returned to Rochester in 1883, having decided to become a pastor. He later described the experience that had followed his baptism: "Very soon the idea came to me that I ought to be a preacher, and help save souls . . . I wanted to do hard work for God." The hard work began at the Rochester Seminary, the only place to study for those interested in working with German Baptists. While attending seminary he also began a course of study at the University of Rochester, from which he was awarded a degree in 1885. Rauschenbusch felt the need to fill gaps in his education. He also wanted the college degree because all of the family's long line of pastors had also been university-educated. The Rochester Theological Seminary was a bastion of conservative theology at the time of Rauschenbusch's study there. For three years Rauschenbusch studied under men such as Howard Osgood and Augustus Hopkins Strong, who disdained the "New Theology," which included critical approaches to the Bible and some acceptance of Darwinian evolution. Osgood was familiar with contemporary critical analyses of Scripture but would have none of it. Despite theological differences, Strong and others recognized the talent and intelligence of the young Rauschenbusch and in fact invited him back to teach in the German department two years later. But Rauschenbusch refused. He was well into what would be his life's work, developing his brand of the Social Gospel.

Pastor. In June 1886 Walter Rauschenbusch moved to New York City to take over as pastor of the Second German Baptist Church, which lay on the northern edge of the city's notorious Hell's Kitchen district. Living conditions for the urban, immigrant poor were abominable at this time as New York was swelling with new arrivals from Europe. Church attendance was poor, with only 125 regular members at the Second German Baptist. He preached his first sermon on Jesus' words "Thy Kingdom Come," a metaphor that would become his dominant theme as his social gospel developed. The young pastor impressed his flock, and attendance grew quickly. Ministering to this church would be Rauschenbusch's major occupation for the next five years and a key period in developing his theological ideas. In the summer of 1888 Rauschenbusch attended a ten-day revival held by the popular Dwight L. Moody in Northfield, Massachusetts. Following the revival, he collaborated with Moody's hymn writer, Ira Sankey, on a book of hymns in German, which was published as *Evangeliums Leider* (1891). By 1889 Rauschenbusch had begun his social preaching, taking the message of salvation beyond the individual and applying it to society. Prompted by the living conditions of his congregation, he had taken to studying economics and social conditions. Economist Richard Ely's *Social Aspects of Christianity,* which merged economic theory with social theology, had influenced him greatly, and in 1889 Rauschenbusch embraced socialism, though he would never become a member of a socialist party. Later that year he launched his *For the Right,* a journal of Social Gospel thought that he would not publish until 1891. He had in the meantime led the drive to build a new church for his congregation, which had increased in membership by more than 50 percent in five years. Rauschenbusch's "hard work" was paying dividends.

Beyond New York. In January 1891 Rauschenbusch announced his resignation and his intent to travel abroad. He wanted to study and write, but, also, his hearing, which had faltered badly in his early years as a pastor, was still failing, and his functions as a pastor were affected by his inability to hear. The church did not accept his resignation and instead offered Rauschenbusch a paid leave and an interim pastor to help him in his duties when he returned. Rauschenbusch accepted, with the result that after he returned from abroad, he remained with his church until 1897. He traveled to England first. He had been deeply interested by Fabian socialist leaders such as Sidney Webb, who advocated an extension of equality into the economic realm through education and systematic change, but not through radical or violent overthrow. He viewed enthusiastically the work of William Booth's Salvation Army, in which the working classes were recruited to help the poorer classes. From England Rauschenbusch traveled to Germany, where his ideas took a more theological turn and his views began to ripen. The idea of the Kingdom became the center of his thought and where he thought the energy of the church should be focused. Rauschenbusch wrote that the Kingdom "responded to all the old and all the new elements of my religious life. The saving of the lost, the teaching of the young, the pastoral care of the poor and frail, the quickening of starved intellects, the study of the Bible, church union, political reform, the reorganization of the industrial system, international peace — it was all covered by the one aim of the Reign of God on earth." He returned to the United States on Christmas Day 1891 with his greatest work ahead of him.

Brotherhood. Rauschenbusch remained with the Second German Baptist Church on a part-time basis until 1897. In the interim, however, he continued to study and work for reform. The economic depression that occurred during the 1890s only strengthened his beliefs in a social view of religion. In 1892 he met with Leighton Williams, Nathaniel Schmidt, and Samuel Batten at a Baptist congress in Philadelphia. Together they formed a "society of Jesus," which they later called the Brotherhood of the Kingdom, dedicated to a "better understanding of the Kingdom of God on earth." The group's goal was to be an active brotherhood, applying their theories toward religion and social reform. They were the first group of American Christians to put forth such a comprehensive agenda of reform. Among the group's ideals were international peace, rigorous study of Scripture, better municipal government, and the rights of workers. For five years the Brotherhood of the Kingdom was the focus of

Rauschenbusch's work. Thinkers such as Richard Ely, Henry George, Josiah Strong, W. D. P. Bliss, Jacob Riis, and Washington Gladden presented papers and talks for the Brotherhood as it attempted to advance its agenda with a missionary fervor. The Brotherhood met some resistance from conservative Baptists but remained an active force for some two decades.

Teacher and Writer. In 1897 Rauschenbusch took a position in the German Department at the Rochester Theological Seminary, where he would remain until his death. In a sense his church work at the congregational level was over. Walter Rauschenbusch the teacher, the theologian, the lecturer, and the writer would emerge as the Social Gospel grew into the twentieth century. His power as an orator made him a speaker in high demand, but it was the publication of his first book, *Christianity and the Social Crisis*, in 1907 that made him a nationally known figure. The book was a great success critically as well as commercially. In it Rauschenbusch collected sixteen years of thought, practice, and theology in a warm, graceful style that made the book powerful as well as readable. The book combined history and economics with Rauschenbusch's interpretation of the Kingdom of God, arguing, for instance, for workers' rights, "for human life against profits," for turning Christianity's power "against materialism and mammonism," and for the individual to place his integrity above his income. During the next three years it would be the best-selling religious book in America, with some fifty thousand copies sold. Rauschenbusch followed this with several other books that solidified his position as a preeminent religious figure of the Social Gospel movement. *Prayers of the Social Awakening* (1912), *Christianizing the Social Order* (1912), *The Social Principles of Jesus* (1916), and a *Theology for the Social Gospel* (1917) all furthered Rauschenbusch's prominence as a theologian. However, one other issue made news as well, causing Rauschenbusch much grief for his ideals as well as his reputation.

The War. The anti-German fervor that accompanied the advent of World War I could not be ignored by a man such as Rauschenbusch. He had relations on both sides of the war in Europe. He was a pacifist disturbed by the butchery of the war, and he was a German American, troubled by the obvious hatred of Germany that had sprouted in America. Rauschenbusch took the role of dissenter in an effort to gain fairness for Germany. In 1914 he published "Be Fair to Germany," an article that accepted claims of German brutality and aggression but noted that Germany was not the only country to practice such things. The article tried to present a neutral view of England and Germany, but was perceived widely as a defense of German aggression. Reaction was strong in the anti-German atmosphere of the times. Still, Rauschenbusch could not keep quiet. In July 1915 he published a joint statement with Charles Aked of San Francisco criticizing America's failure to remain neutral in the war. *Private Profit and the Nation's Honors: A Protest and a*

Plea was published nationwide. The reaction to this piece was even stronger than the first, and Rauschenbusch was forced to withdraw even further. Though he continued to write, including his widely popular *The Social Principles of Jesus*, Rauschenbusch remained a controversial figure for America during the war and personally felt disappointed in a world seemingly gone mad with war. He died on 25 July 1918 with the war still raging and his own reputation sadly still in question. But his writing and activities left an indelible impression on the relations between church and society in the United States.

Source:
Paul M. Minus, *Walter Rauschenbusch: American Reformer* (New York: Macmillan, 1988).

GEORGE SANTAYANA

1863-1952

PHILOSOPHER

Who Is Santayana? In an article titled "Who Is Santayana?" published in the *Saturday Review of Literature* in January 1956, Charles Frankel wrote, "I am inclined to believe that what happens to Santayana's reputation will be the touchstone of the quality of our culture, and of our growth in maturity and wisdom." That George Santayana, Spanish by birth and passport, American "in practice" as a writer and teacher, and resident of Italy during the final twenty-eight years of his life, could inspire such a quote, along with poems of tribute from Wallace Stevens and Robert Lowell, indicates that he was a man of letters of enormous stature. He is known as a philosopher, but in essence he was a little of everything in the writing trade, an ascetic man who resisted a move by one man to nominate him for a Nobel Prize by asking, "In what science or art could I be said to have accomplished anything? Literature? Philosophy? It is doubtful." What is not doubtful is his stature as a prolific writer and thinker, among the giants of twentieth-century American thought.

Spain and Boston. He was born in Madrid, Spain, in 1863 and was raised in Avila, Spain, until the age of nine. His mother and his two sisters moved to Boston in 1869, leaving George with his father, though three years later Agustin Santayana followed his wife, reuniting the family in Boston in 1872. George was nine years old and spoke no English. Despite his age, he was initially placed in a kindergarten in order to learn English, but eventually he learned the language from his sister Susana, with whom he would maintain a close relationship. His father returned to Spain a year later, the same year that George entered a public school. In 1874, already fluent in English, George entered the prestigious Boston Latin School, from which he graduated in 1882. That fall he began attending Harvard College, with which he would be affiliated for the next thirty years. The young Santayana blossomed at Harvard. He drew cartoons for the *Harvard Lampoon,* and joined several clubs including art, chess, and Phi Beta Kappa. He acted on the stage, was a founding member of the *Harvard Monthly,* and was president of the Philosophical Club. His Harvard years included visits to his father in Spain in 1883 and travels through Europe. He studied at Harvard under William James, who influenced him greatly. Following graduation in 1886, Santayana and classmate Charles Strong traveled to Germany to study, but Santayana returned a year later and pursued a Ph.D. in philosophy. He finished in 1889 and his formal education ended, though he had not really decided on a career. In a sense learning was his career. Teaching was simply a necessity.

Professor. Santayana was offered a course to teach when William James became overburdened with work in 1889. Thus began Santayana's twenty-three-year teaching career in the Philosophy Department at Harvard. Once a student of James's, Santayana became a colleague. Among his students over the years would be poets Robert Frost, Wallace Stevens, Conrad Aiken, and T. S. Eliot and political essayist Walter Lippmann. Though most remembered him as a good teacher, Santayana was quick to retire from the work once he had the opportunity. His real love was writing, and his years as a Harvard professor were marked by mixed successes as a poet and the early development of his early philosophical ideas. His first published book, *Sonnets and Other Verses* (1894), was not well received, but his second, *The Sense of Beauty* (1896), an attempt at a complete statement of aesthetics, was praised by critics. The influence of James was present in Santayana's use of psychology to conceive a philosophy. Beauty was "pleasure objectified," in Santayana's words, a three-part combination of the materials of an art-work, its form, and its ability to display expression. Material and form were intrinsic to the object, while expression is a result of mental associations that result from the suggestions of the work. Santayana would further develop his aesthetic ideas in *Reason in Art* (1905), volume four of his five-volume *The Life of Reason, or the Phases of Human Progress* (1906–1917). *The Sense of Beauty* made Santayana's reputation and prior to *The Life of Reason* was his most successful work. He wrote another unsuccessful book of poetry and a failed drama in the 1890s and furthered his study at King's College, Cambridge, during a leave of absence from Harvard. In 1893 the deaths of a close friend, Warwick Potter, and his father put Santayana through a "passage through dark night," as he called it. The period made Santayana look even more inward. He began to live a simple life free from material concerns, a self-sufficient life of the mind. His chance to do so permanently came in 1912 with the death of his mother. She left him a small inheritance of $10,000, enough to allow Santayana to resign from Harvard and free himself for travel and learning. His years as a wandering student and writer began.

Influence. Even though Santayana's career as a teacher ended in 1912, he remained throughout the 1910s one of the most influential American philosophers. His ethical idealism served as a counterpart to the pragmatic philosophy of James and the instrumentalism of John Dewey, both of which emphasized the necessity of testing truth through experience. Young cultural radicals such as Randolph Bourne, Lewis Mumford, and Van Wyck Brooks, who in the 1910s were critiquing the moral underpinnings of industrial capitalism, found in Santayana a guide and a soul mate.

Wanderer. The period between Santayana's resignation from Harvard and the outbreak of U.S. involvement in World War I in 1917 was one of restless traveling. He likened himself to a student in the Middle Ages, wandering from city to city in order to learn, with no practical applications for his knowledge. He would settle in England during the war and witness its horrors at relatively close range, wavering before choosing to support the Allies. In 1914 he published *Appearances: Notes of Travel, East and West,* and during the war he wrote *Egotism in German Philosophy,* an analysis and critique of the German nation, but as a whole, the war years were his least productive. The publication of *The Life of Reason* in 1905–1906 seemed to have closed out the first stage of his philosophical work, to which he would return in the early 1920s. When the war ended, Santayana traveled to Spain, only to find disillusionment. Politics strained his relations with his sister Susana, who had been an ardent supporter of Germany. Though he would always keep his Spanish passport, Santayana rarely visited again, and never again after 1928.

Philosopher Again. In 1922 Santayana published *Scepticism and Animal Faith,* one of his major philosophical statements and a recasting of his previous work. The work is transitional in that it serves as an introduction to the ideas that Santayana would discuss in his four-volume *Realms of Being,* published between 1927 and 1940. Essentially, he argues against logic and the senses. They cannot be trusted. But such deep skepticism is dangerous; thus, Santayana argues, a confidence, what he calls "animal faith," must be created by each individual in order to function meaningfully in the world. The work was an introduction to what Santayana would deem "essence," the cornerstone of his *Realms of Being.* Essences were concepts, unknowables, that could still be used in existence. In fact, the first volume of *Realms of Being,* titled *The Realm of Essence,* expands the notion and attempts to complete Santayana's philosophy. The subsequent volumes are mere addenda to this first important volume. Santayana had settled in Rome in 1924 in order to work on his final major philosophical statement. Rome would be his home until his death in 1952, though he continued to travel extensively between the two world wars.

An Old Philosopher in Rome. Rome proved to be a fruitful place for Santayana to settle through the 1930s. As Europe careened toward yet another major war, Santayana worked vigorously on *Realms of Being* while also writing the best-selling novel *The Last Puritan,* published in 1936. Its subtitle, *A Memoir in the Form of a Novel,* indicated that it was as much biography as fiction. It was hugely successful, and Santayana's career had managed to surprise again. He was shown on the cover of *Time* magazine. He had become an international celebrity, and celebrity brought visitors. Santayana became the old philosopher in Rome, receiving visitors frequently and generously as long as they did not disrupt his work schedule. He began his autobiography, *Persons and Places,* and when the war broke out he found refuge in a nursing home convent, operated by the Blue Nuns in Rome. It would be his final home. Santayana had one more bestseller in him. In March 1947 he published *The Idea of Christ in the Gospels,* which sold out the day of its publication. During the war he had begun reading the Bible again. Santayana's book found the life of Christ a poetic force, not an historic one. Though he believed Jesus of Nazareth was based on some historic figure, he refuted the Protestant insistence on the veracity of the gospels. The work was an application of Santayana's early religious philosophy applied to a text. He had always seen religion as poetry and myth, inspirational and beautiful but not to be taken literally. "Religion is a symbolic representation of moral reality," he had written in *Reason in Religion.* He identified God with the natural world, not nature as wildness, but natural as in that which exists. He was sympathetic to pantheism and held no denominational beliefs. His naturalism was summed up in a tribute by Spanish poet Jorge Guillén:

> He looks to matter for his faith,
> And Spanish by birth, English by language,
> In the solitude of his eminence
> Untrammeled, he is aware of the lay world
> Without gods. Truth gives him serenity.

Santayana died in 1952 at the age of eighty-nine.

Source:
John McCormick, *George Santayana: A Biography* (New York: Knopf, 1987).

PEOPLE IN THE NEWS

In October 1919 **Evangeline Booth,** commander of the Salvation Army in America, was awarded a Distinguished Service Medal from President **Woodrow Wilson** for the services performed by the Salvation Army in military camps during the war.

Louis Dembitz Brandeis, a prominent Boston attorney, was chosen as the chairman of the Provisional Executive Committee at a Zionist convention on 30 August 1914. The Federation of American Zionists, the major Zionist organization in the United States, grew under Brandeis's leadership from 12,000 members in 1914 to 176,000 members in 1919, at which time the group was restructured as the Zionist Organization of America. Brandeis was nominated to the Supreme Court by President Woodrow Wilson in 1916, becoming the first Jew to serve in the nation's highest court.

On 29 November 1911 Archbishops **John M. Farley** of New York and **William O'Connell** of Boston were elevated to the cardinalate in Rome by Pope Pius X. Farley later created the New York Catholic War Council, which staffed canteens for members of the armed forces and established hospitals for victims of shell shock.

Eminent Baptist preacher **Harry Emerson Fosdick,** a professor of theology at Union Theological Seminary after 1915, published *The Meaning of Prayer* (1915) and *The Meaning of Faith* (1917), the first two parts of a trilogy on what it meant to be a Christian, a series completed in 1922. Fosdick also published *The Challenge of the Present Crisis* (1917), a moderate defense of the need for America to take up arms in World War I. In 1918 Fosdick, crossing denominational lines, became associate pastor of the First Presbyterian Church in New York City. He also visited and spoke to American troops on the front in France and Flanders during the war.

Father John Kedrovsky, a Russian Orthodox priest in Hartford, Connecticut, drew sharp criticism after 1917 for his progressive politics. Following the October Revolution in Russia, American Orthodox leaders became anxious to distance themselves as much as possible from Russia's Communists. **Archbishop Alexander** thought that priests used the language of "reformation and progressiveness" to cover their real intent to "destroy the church with axes, hammers and sickles," and seven priests in New York who supported Kedrovsky were suspended.

The dean of the University of Chicago Divinity School since 1908, Baptist **Shailer Mathews** served as president of the Federal Council of Churches of Christ in America between 1912 and 1916 and also held the presidency of the Northern Baptist Convention in 1915. He also published *Will Christ Come Again?* (1917), followed up by a series of articles in *Biblical World* in 1918 on the same subject. Also in 1918, Mathews published the influential *Patriotism and Religion,* in which he argued that "for an American to refuse to share in the present war is not Christian."

Thousands of Jewish residents of New York gathered at the Hippodrome on 9 October 1910 to hear a speech by the founder of the International Bible Students' Association (later Jehovah's Witnesses), **Charles Taze Russell**. His advocacy of a Jewish homeland in Palestine had won him the support of many Jews. In October 1911 Pastor Russell sued the *Brooklyn Daily Eagle* for $100,000 after its stories about his selling "Miracle Wheat" in church caused a scandal. After his death in 1916, some of Russell's sermons and writings were collected and edited into a volume entitled *The Finished Mystery.* The book contained negative statements about both war and patriotism in general, and its distribution was later deemed subversive of the Selective Service Act of 1917. In 1918 Russell's successor, former judge **Joseph Rutherford,** and seven other members of the International Bible Students' Association were sentenced to twenty years in prison each after they were found disseminating Russell's pacifist teachings.

Throughout the 1910s **Vida Scudder,** a professor of English at Wellesley College, was the country's most vocal and active supporter of Christian socialism. In 1911 she cofounded the Episcopal Church Socialist League, and in the same year she joined the Socialist Party. In 1912 she published her influential book *Socialism and Character,* whose success led striking workers at a textile mill in Lawrence, Massachusetts, to ask her to speak on their behalf. When she and a Wellesley colleague did so, the *Boston Evening Transcript* called for their resignations. Wellesley did not ask her to resign but did suspend her famous course on "Social Ideals in English Letters" for one year. She lectured widely at colleges as a member of the Intercollegiate Socialist Society. Her support for the war led to strife within the Church Socialist League, so in 1919 she organized the Church League for Industrial Democracy to accommodate adherents of many different political views committed to social reform.

On 2 May 1917 Methodist minister and suffragist **Anna Howard Shaw** became chairwoman of the Women's Committee of the Council of National Defense, which coordinated the war relief efforts of scores of women's organizations nationwide. She was awarded the Distinguished Service Medal by President **Woodrow Wilson** in May 1919, the first American woman ever to receive that honor. On 19 May of that year, Shaw embarked on a tour of fourteen states with former president **William Howard Taft** and **A. Lawrence Lowell,** the president of Harvard University, speaking in support of President Wilson's peace plan. The tour ended on 5 June, and Shaw died of ill health just four weeks later, on 2 July.

The chairman of the Federal Council of Churches' General War-Time Commission, **Robert E. Speer,** came under fire for a speech he delivered at Columbia University on 18 February 1918. The speech, "World Democracy and America's Obligation to Her Neighbors," offered examples from the history of the United States, along with many other nations, of the five greatest hindrances to world democracy. Following the address, *The New York Times* was flooded with letters denouncing Speer as "pro-German" and his speech as "insidiously corrupting." Though the *Times* printed Speer's rebuttal, in which he insisted that he believed that the war "must be waged in order that war may be destroyed," the issue took some weeks to subside.

Billy Sunday was sued in 1918 by **Hugh A. Weir,** who claimed to be the ghostwriter of Sunday's book *Great Love Stories from the Bible and Their Lessons for Today.* Although Weir eventually settled out of court for an undisclosed sum, the scandal that followed, along with complaints about Sunday's accumulated fortune, led to his declining popularity in succeeding decades.

The founder of Hadassah, a women's Zionist organization, **Henrietta Szold,** resigned in 1915 as president of that group to found the American Zionist Medical Unit, which established itself in Palestine in 1916. In 1919 Szold went to Palestine herself to become director of the unit, which provided much-needed medical care for Jewish settlers in Palestine.

In 1913 Reform rabbi **Stephen S. Wise** and his close friend, Unitarian minister **John Haynes Holmes,** worked together to fight corruption in New York City's Tammany Hall, the Democratic political machine. Wise was influential in securing the election of the Republican candidate, **John Purroy Mitchel**. In 1912 Wise and Holmes had experienced a political disagreement when Wise endorsed Woodrow Wilson's candidacy instead of Theodore Roosevelt's Progressive Party. Wise toured Palestine in 1913, returning to the United States with a new dedication to Zionism. He rejoined the FAZ under **Louis Brandeis**'s leadership and, with Brandeis, helped convince President Wilson to support the Balfour Declaration.

DEATHS

Peter Abbelen, 74, German American vicar general of the archdiocese of Milwaukee who, in 1886, submitted a memorial to Pope Leo XIII requesting that Catholic parishes in America be drawn up along ethnic lines, 24 August 1917.

Amelia Edith Huddleston Barr, 88, popular religious writer and novelist, 10 March 1919.

Harrison D. Barrett, 47, first president of the National Spiritualist Association; he once defended in court a medium accused of witchcraft, 12 January 1911.

Borden Parker Bowne, 63, professor of philosophy at Boston University, 1 April 1910.

Phineas Bresee, 76, founding father of the Holiness Church of the Nazarene, 13 November 1915.

Charles Augustus Briggs, 72, theologian and biblical scholar tried for heresy by the Presbyterian Church in 1892, 8 June 1913.

Henry Harrison Brown, 77, Unitarian minister and founder of "Now" Folk, an early New Thought group, 8 May 1918.

Francis Xavier Cabrini, 67, Roman Catholic nun and founder of the Institute of the Missionary Sisters of the Sacred Heart; in 1946 she became the first American canonized by the Roman Catholic Church, 22 December 1917.

Beverly Carradine, 71, Holiness evangelist and religious writer, 1919.

Benajah Harvey Carroll, 70, preacher and educator; he founded the Southwestern Baptist Theological Seminary, 11 November 1914.

Paul Carus, 66, German-born philosopher, author of several books on Buddhism, and editor of the *Open Court Journal*, 11 February 1919.

Gaston Barnabas Cashwell, 66, pioneer Pentecostal preacher, converted at the Azusa Street Revival, who introduced Pentecostalism in much of the American South, 1916.

John Wilbur Chapman, 59, popular Presbyterian evangelist who worked with Dwight L. Moody and influenced Billy Sunday, 25 December 1918.

Thornton Chase, 65, one of the first converts to the Baha'i faith in America; he wrote *The Baha'i Revelation* in 1909, 13 September 1912.

Charles Edward Cheney, 80, bishop of the Chicago synod of the Reformed Episcopal Church for thirty-eight years, 15 November 1916.

William Newton Clarke, 70, Baptist theologian and champion of modernism, 14 January 1912.

Fanny Muriel Jackson Coppin, 76, former slave, teacher and executive of African Methodist Episcopal Church, and president of Women's Home and Foreign Missionary Society, 21 January 1913.

Fanny Crosby, 94, poet and popular hymn writer, 12 February 1915.

Andrew Jackson Davis, 83, father of American Spiritualism and author of *The Principles of Nature* (1847), 13 January 1910.

William Porcher DuBose, 82, Episcopal theologian, 18 August 1918.

William Durham, 39, independent Pentecostal minister converted at Azusa Street revival; publisher of *Pentecostal Testimony*, 7 July 1912.

Mary Baker Eddy, 89, founder of the Church of Christ, Scientist, 3 December 1910.

John Murphy Farley, 76, cardinal of the Roman Catholic Church and the archbishop of New York since 1902; he initiated publication of the *Catholic Encyclopedia*, 17 September 1918.

George Burnham Foster, 60, Baptist theologian and professor of philosophy at the University of Chicago, 22 December 1918.

James Marion Frost, 68, founder of the Sunday School Board of the Southern Baptist Convention, 30 October, 1916.

Wesley John Gaines, 71, former slave, bishop of the African Methodist Episcopal Church, 12 January 1912.

Washington Gladden, 82, Congregational minister and Social Gospel theologian, 2 July 1918.

Raphael Hawaweeny, 54, first Russian Orthodox bishop consecrated in the United States, 27 February 1915.

Eliza Healy, 72, first black nun to become the superior of a convent (the Congregation of Notre Dame), 13 September 1919.

Patrick Francis Healy, 75, first African American to be accepted by the Jesuits in North America, to be awarded a doctorate in the United States, and to be appointed president of a Catholic college (Georgetown University in 1874), 10 January 1910.

Max Heindel, 53, astrologer and Theosophist who founded the Rosicrucian Fellowship in 1908, 6 January 1919.

John Ireland, 80, Roman Catholic archbishop of Saint Paul, Minnesota, 25 September 1918.

Samuel Macauley Jackson, 61, Presbyterian minister and scholar whose works include the *Dictionary of the Bible* (1880), 2 August 1912.

Jenkin Lloyd Jones, Unitarian minister and prominent pacifist, 12 September 1918.

Edward Judson, 69, Protestant reformer who initiated the institutional church movement in America, 23 October 1914.

John Joseph Keane, 78, Roman Catholic archbishop; cofounder and first rector of the Catholic University of America, 22 June 1918.

George William Knox, 58, Presbyterian theologian who served as a missionary in Japan, studied Japanese religions, and founded the Union Theological Seminary in Tokyo, 25 April 1912.

Ulrik Vilhelm Koren, 84, Norwegian American minister of the Norwegian Synod of the Lutheran Church and cofounder of Lutheran College in Decorah, Iowa, 20 December 1910.

David Lipscomb, 86, minister in the Church of Christ; he edited the *Gospel Advocate* for forty-seven years, 11 November 1917.

John William McGarvey, 82, Churches of Christ minister, editor of the conservative *Apostolic Times,* and pacifist, 6 November 1911.

Benjamin Fay Mills, 58, liberal Presbyterian minister, Social Gospel advocate, popular revivalist, and author of *Twentieth Century Religion* (1898), 1 May 1916.

Stephen Mitropolsky (Bishop John), 78, Russian Orthodox bishop of Alaska who moved the seat of the church in America from Sitka, Alaska, to San Francisco, 3 May 1914.

Joanna Patterson Moore, 83, Baptist missionary to former slaves; first person commissioned by the Women's American Home Missionary Society, 15 April 1916.

Henry Lyman Morehouse, 82, Baptist Home Missionary secretary for thirty-eight years, 5 May 1917.

Virginia E. Moss, 44, evangelist and founder of an early Pentecostal Bible college, Beulah Heights Bible and Missionary School, 1919.

L. T. Nichols, 67, independent preacher and founder of Meggido Mission Church, a riverboat mission, 28 February 1912.

Stephen Ortynsky, 50, Roman Catholic bishop; born in the Ukraine, he served as bishop for Ukrainian American Catholics (known as Ruthenians), 24 March 1916.

Quanah Parker, 66, Comanche chief and founder of the Native American Church, the pan-Indian peyote religion that incorporated elements of Christianity, 23 February 1911.

Arthur Tappan Pierson, 74, Presbyterian minister, independent evangelist associated with Dwight L. Moody and the Keswick Movement and missionary and editor of *Missionary Review* since 1890, 3 June 1911.

James E. Quigley, 60, Roman Catholic bishop of Chicago, 10 July 1915.

Walter Rauschenbusch, 56, Baptist minister and Social Gospel theologian, 25 July 1918.

Charles Taze Russell, 64, founder of Jehovah's Witnesses, 31 October 1916.

Solomon Schechter, 65, Conservative Jewish rabbi and president of the Jewish Theological Seminary in New York, 20 November 1915.

Anna Howard Shaw, 72, first woman ordained by the Methodist Protestant Church; active in temperance and woman suffrage movements, 2 July 1919.

Andrew B. Shelly, 79, president of the General Conference Mennonite Church and editor of *Mennonitischer Friedensbote*, 26 December 1913.

Amanda Smith, 78, evangelist and missionary in the African Methodist Episcopal Church, 24 February 1915.

Hannah Whitall Smith, 79, popular religious writer and cofounder of the Women's Christian Temperance Union, 1 May 1911.

Joseph Fielding Smith Sr. 80, nephew of Joseph Smith, Jr., the founder of Mormonism; he was the sixth president of the Church of Jesus Christ of Latter-Day Saints, 19 November 1918.

Joseph Smith III, 82, president of the Reorganized Church of Jesus Christ of Latter-Day Saints, a group of Mormons who stayed in Nauvoo, Illinois, and did not travel to Utah after the death of founder Joseph Smith Jr., 10 December 1914.

John Lancaster Spalding, 76, Roman Catholic bishop of Peoria, Illinois, 25 August 1916.

James Woodward Strong, 79, founder, trustee, and president of Carleton College, a Congregational college in Northfield, Minnesota, 24 February 1913.

Josiah Strong, 69, Congregational minister, Social Gospel advocate, and author of the highly influential *Our Country* (1885), 28 April 1916.

Milton Spencer Terry, 74, Methodist theologian and Bible scholar, 13 July 1914.

Crawford Howell Toy, 83, liberal Southern Baptist theologian, biblical scholar, and pioneer in the history of religions at Harvard University, 12 May 1919.

Henry McNeal Turner, 81, African Methodist Episcopal bishop, editor, and outspoken activist for black rights, 9 May 1915.

Benjamin Franklin Underwood, 75, Free Thought lecturer and editor at Open Court Publishing, 10 November 1914.

Margaret Newton van Cott, 84, first American woman licensed to preach by the Methodist Episcopal church; never ordained, she worked as a traveling evangelist, 29 August 1914.

Alexander Walters, 58, bishop of the African Methodist Episcopal Zion Church and activist for black rights, 1 February 1917.

Muhammad Alexander Russell Webb, 69, early convert to Islam who organized the first Muslim mosque in the United States and founded *Moslem World Magazine,* 1 October 1916.

Anna White, 79, Shaker elder and spokeswoman for international disarmanent, vice president of the Alliance of Women for Peace, and coauthor of *Shakerism: Its Meaning and Message* (1904), 16 December 1910.

Ellen Gould Harmon White, 87, cofounder, with her husband, James, of the Seventh-Day Adventists, 16 July 1915.

William Heth Whitsitt, 69, Southern Baptist church historian and president of the Southern Baptist Theological Seminary, 20 January 1911.

Ella Wheeler Wilcox, 69, nationally known poet, writer, and New Thought metaphysician, 30 October 1919.

John Roel Zook, 62, traveling evangelist for the Brethren in Christ Church; he helped found Messiah College in Grantham, Pennsylvania, 6 November 1919.

PUBLICATIONS

Lyman Abbott, *Reminiscences* (Boston: Houghton Mifflin, 1915);

Abbott, *The Spirit of Democracy* (Boston: Houghton Mifflin, 1910);

Abbott, *The Twentieth Century Crusade* (New York: Macmillan, 1918);

Peter Ainslie III, *The Message of the Disciples for the Union of the Church* (New York: Revell, 1913);

Ames, *The Divinity of Christ* (Chicago: New Christian Century, 1911);

Ames, *The Higher Individualism* (Boston: Houghton Mifflin, 1915);

Ames, *The New Orthodoxy* (Chicago: University of Chicago Press, 1918);

Ames, *The Psychology of Religious Experience* (Boston: Houghton Mifflin, 1910);

Charles Palmerston Anderson, *Letters to Laymen* (Milwaukee: Young Churchman, 1913);

Robert Archibald Ashworth, *The Union of Christian Forces in America* (Philadelphia: American Sunday School Union, 1915);

William Walker Atkinson, *Your Mind and How to Use It* (Holyoke, Mass.: Elizabeth Towne, 1911);

Harrison D. Barrett, *Pantheistic Idealism* (Portland, Oreg.: Glass & Prudhomme, 1910);

Samuel Z. Batten, ed., *The Moral Meaning of the War* (Philadelphia: American Baptist Publication Society, 1918);

Batten, ed., *The New World Order* (Philadelphia: American Baptist Publication Society, 1919);

Antoinette Brown Blackwell, *The Social Side of Mind and Action* (New York: Neale, 1915);

Charles Albert Blanchard, *Getting Things From God* (Chicago: Bible Institute Colportage Association, 1915);

Borden Parker Bowne, *The Essence of Religion* (Boston: Houghton Mifflin, 1910);

Charles Augustus Briggs, *History of the Study of Theology*, 2 volumes (New York: Scribners, 1916);

Briggs, *Theological Symbols* (New York: Scribners, 1914);

William Jennings Bryan, *The First Commandment* (New York: Revell, 1917);

Bryan, *Heart to Heart Appeals* (New York: Revell, 1917);

John Wright Buckham, *Progressive Religious Thought in America: A Survey of the Enlarging Pilgrim Faith* (Boston: Houghton Mifflin, 1919);

Frank J. Cannon, *Brigham Young and His Mormon Empire* (New York: Revell, 1913);

George Quayle Cannon, *The Latter-Day Prophet: Young People's History of Joseph Smith* (Salt Lake City, Utah: Deseret Books, 1914);

Paul Carus, *The Canon of Reason and Virtue* (Chicago: Open Court Publishing, 1913);

Carus, *The Dawn of a New Religious Era* (Chicago: Open Court Publishing, 1916);

Shirley Jackson Case, *The Evolution of Early Christianity: A Genetic Study of First Century Christianity in Relation to Its Religious Environment* (Chicago: University of Chicago Press, 1914);

Case, *The Historicity of Jesus* (Chicago: University of Chicago Press, 1912);

Lewis Sperry Chafer, *Salvation* (Findlay, Ohio: Dunham, 1917);

Chafer, *True Evangelism* (New York: Gospel Publishing House, 1911);

Warren Akin Chandler, *Wesley and His Work* (Nashville, Tenn.: Publishing House of the Methodist Episcopal Church, South, 1912);

John Wilbur Chapman, *When Home Is Heaven* (New York: Revell, 1917);

Charles Edward Cheney, *A Neglected Power and Other Sermons* (New York: Revell, 1916);

William Newton Clarke, *The Ideal of Jesus* (New York: Scribners, 1911);

Catharine C. Cleveland, *The Great Revival in the West, 1797–1805* (Chicago: University of Chicago Press, 1916);

George Albert Coe, *The Psychology of Religion* (Chicago: University of Chicago Press, 1916);

Coe, *A Social Theory of Religious Education* (New York: Scribners, 1917);

Henry Sloane Coffin Sr., *In a Day of Social Rebuilding and Lectures on the Ministry of the Church* (New Haven: Yale University Press, 1918);

Leopold Cohn, *A Modern Missionary to an Ancient People* (New York: American Board of Missions to the Jews, 1911);

Irving Steiger Cooper, *Theosophy Simplified* (Los Angeles: Theosophical Book Concern, 1915);

Algernon Sidney Crapsey, *The Rise of the Working Class* (New York: Century, 1914);

Sister Devamata (Laura Franklin Glenn), *Development of the Will* (Boston: Ananda Ashrama, 1918);

Ralph Eugene Diffendorfer, *Missionary Education in Home and School* (New York: Abingdon Press, 1917);

Horatio Willis Dresser, *History of the New Thought Movement* (New York: Crowell, 1919);

William Porcher DuBose, *The Reason of Life* (New York: Longmans, Green, 1911);

William H. P. Faunce, *The New Horizon of State and Church* (New York: Macmillan, 1918);

Faunce, *Religion and War* (New York: Abingdon Press, 1918);

Harry Emerson Fosdick, *The Challenge of the Present Crisis* (Philadelphia: American Baptist Publishing Society, 1917);

Fosdick, *Finishing the War* (New York: Association Press, 1919);

Fosdick, *The Meaning of Faith* (New York: Association Press, 1917);

Fosdick, *The Meaning of Prayer* (New York: Abingdon Press, 1915);

George Burman Foster, *The Function of Death in Human Experience* (Chicago: University of Chicago Press, 1915);

James Marion Frost, *The School and the Church* (New York: Revell, 1911);

The Fundamentals: A Testimony to the Truth, 12 volumes (Chicago: Testimony Publishing, 1910–1915);

Arno Gaebelein, *The Jewish Question* (New York: Publication Office of Our Hope, 1912);

James Cardinal Gibbons, *Beacon Lights* (Baltimore: John Murphy, 1911);

Gibbons, *Catholic Loyalty* (New York: Paulist Press, 1917);

Gibbons, *A Retrospect of Fifty Years*, 2 volumes (Baltimore: John Murphy, 1916);

Frederick Carnes Gilbert, *From Judaism to Christianity* (Concord, Mass.: Good Tidings, 1911);

Washington Gladden, *Present Day Theology* (Columbus, Ohio: McClelland, 1913);

Edgar Johnson Goodspeed, *The Story of the New Testament* (Chicago: University of Chicago Press, 1916);

George Angier Gordon, *Revelation and the Ideal* (Boston: Houghton Mifflin, 1913);

James Martin Gray, *Christian Worker's Commentary on the Old and New Testaments* (New York: Revell, 1915);

Roy Bergen Guild, *Practicing Christian Unity* (New York: Association Press, 1919);

Frank Wakeley Gunsaulus, *The Minister and Spiritual Life* (New York: Revell, 1911);

Isaac Massey Haldeman, *Why I Preach the Second Coming* (New York: Revell, 1919);

Max Heindel, *The Rosicrucian Mysteries* (Oceanside, Cal.: Rosicrucian Fellowship, 1911);

Wilson Thomas Hogue, *History of the Free Methodist Church of North America*, 2 volumes (Chicago: Free Methodist Publishing House, 1918);

Horace Hotchkiss Holley, *Baha'ism — The Modern Social Religion* (New York: Kennerly, 1913);

John Haynes Holmes, *New Wars for Old* (New York: Dodd, Mead, 1916);

Holmes, *The Revolutionary Function of the Modern Church* (New York: Putnam, 1912);

James Walker Hood, *Sketch of the Early History of the African Methodist Episcopal Zion Church*, 2 volumes (N.p., 1914);

John Horsch, *Infant Baptism, Its Origins Among Protestants* (Scottsdale, Penn., 1917);

Edwin Holt Hughes, *The Bible and Life* (New York: Methodist Book Concern, 1915);

Jesse Lyman Hurlbut, *Bible Atlas: A Manual of Biblical Geography and History* (Chicago: Rand, McNally, 1910);

Yemyo Imamura, *Democracy According to the Buddhist Viewpoint* (Honolulu: Honpa Hongwangi Mission, 1918);

Edgar DeWitt Jones, *The Inner Circle* (New York: Fleming H. Revell, 1914);

Robert Jones Sr., *Bob Jones' Sermons* (Montgomery, Ala.: Paragon Press, 1911);

Rufus Matthew Jones, *The Inner Life* (New York: Macmillan, 1916);

Jones, *The Quakers in the American Colonies* (London: Macmillan, 1911);

Jones, *Spiritual Reformers of the 16th and 17th Centuries* (Boston: Beacon Press, 1914);

Henry Churchill King, *The Ethics of Jesus* (New York: Macmillan, 1910);

King, *Fundamental Questions* (New York: Macmillan, 1917);

King, *The Moral and Religious Challenge of Our Time* (New York: Macmillan, 1911);

Albert Knudson, *The Religious Teachings of the Old Testament* (New York: Abingdon Press, 1918);

Kaufmann Kohler, *Jewish Theology Systematically and Historically Considered* (New York: Macmillan, 1918);

Kenneth Scott Latourette, *The Christian Basis of World Democracy* (New York: Association Press, 1919);

J. H. Leuba, *A Psychological Study of Religion, Its Origin, Function and Future* (New York: Macmillan, 1912);

David Lipscomb, *Salvation from Sin* (Nashville, Tenn.: McQuiddy Printing, 1913);

William Douglas MacKenzie, *Christian Ethics and the World War* (New York: Association Press, 1918);

Kathleen Mallory, *Manual of the Woman's Missionary Movement Methods* (Nashville: Broadman, 1917);

Jasper Cortenus Massee, *The Second Coming* (Philadelphia: Philadelphia School of the Bible, 1919);

Shailer Mathews, *Patriotism and Religion* (New York: Macmillan, 1918);

William Fraser McDowell, *In the School of Christ* (New York: Revell, 1910);

McDowell, *A Man's Religion* (New York: Eaton & Mains, 1913);

Arthur Cushman McGiffert, *Protestant Thought Before Kant* (New York: Scribners, 1911);

McGiffert, *The Rise of Modern Religious Ideas* (New York: Macmillan, 1915);

Henry Pereira Mendes, *Esther and Harbonah* (Boston: Gorham Press, 1917);

Daniel Long Miller, *Some Who Led* (Elgin, Ill.: Brethren Publishing House, 1912);

Edward C. Moore, *An Outline of the History of Christian Thought Since Kant* (New York: Scribners, 1912);

Henry Clay Morrison, *The Simple Gospel* (Louisville, Ky.: Pentecostal Publishing, 1919);

John Mott, *The Decisive Hour of Christian Missions* (Edinburgh: Foreign Missions Committee of the Country of Scotland, 1910);

Mott, *The Present World Situation* (New York: Student Volunteer Movement for Foreign Missions, 1914);

Edgar Young Mullins, *Baptist Beliefs* (Louisville, Ky.: Baptist World Publishing, 1912);

Mullins, *The Christian Religion and Its Doctrinal Expression* (Philadelphia: Judson Press, 1917);

Mullins, *The Life of Christ* (New York: Revell, 1917);

Franz August Otto Pieper, *Conversion and Election: A Plea for a United Lutheranism in America* (Saint Louis: Concordia, 1913);

Daniel Alfred Poling, *Huts in Hell* (Boston: Christian Endeavor World, 1918);

James Morgan Pryse Jr., *The Apocalypse Unsealed* (Los Angeles, 1910);

Pryse, *The Restored New Testament* (Los Angeles, 1914);

Walter Rauschenbusch, *Christianizing the Social Order* (Boston: Pilgrim Press, 1912);

Rauschenbusch, *Prayers of the Social Awakening* (Boston: Pilgrim Press, 1912);

Rauschenbusch, *The Social Principles of Jesus* (New York: Association Press, 1916);

Rauschenbusch, *A Theology for the Social Gospel* (New York: Macmillan, 1917);

Charles Mason Remey, *The Baha'i Movement* (Washington, D.C., 1912);

William Bell Riley, *Evolution of the Kingdom* (New York: C.C. Cook, 1913);

Riley, *The Menace of Modernism* (New York: Christian Alliance, 1917);

Archibald Thomas Robertson, *John the Loyal, or Studies in the Ministry of the Baptist* (New York: Scribners, 1911);

Charles Taze Russell, *Pastor Russell's Sermons* (Brooklyn, N.Y.: Peoples Pulpit, 1917);

Russell, *What Pastor Russell Taught* (Chicago: Leslie W. Jones, 1919);

Joseph Franklin Rutherford, *A Great Battle in the Ecclesiastical Heavens, As Seen By a Lawyer* (New York, 1915);

John Augustine Ryan and Morris Hillguit, *Distributive Justice* (New York: Macmillan, 1916);

Ryan and Hillguit, *Socialism: Promise or Menace* (New York: Macmillan, 1914);

Elias Benjamin Sanford, *Origin and History of the Federal Council of the Churches of Christ in America* (Hartford, Conn.: Scranton, 1916);

Solomon Schechter, *Seminary Addresses and Other Papers* (Cincinnati, Ohio: Ark Publishing, 1915);

Anna Howard Shaw, *The Story of a Pioneer* (New York: Harper, 1915);

Gipsy Smith, *Bearing and Sharing* (New York: Doran, 1913);

E. Hershey Sneath, *Religion and the War* (New Haven: Yale University Press, 1918);

Robert E. Speer, *The Christian Man, The Church and the War* (New York: Macmillan, 1918);

Speer, *The New Opportunity of the Church* (New York: Macmillan, 1919);

William Ambrose Spicer, *The Hand of God in History* (Washington, D.C.: Review & Herald Publishing, 1913);

Spicer, *Our Day in the Light of Bible Prophecy* (Washington, D.C.: Review & Herald Publishing, 1918);

Augustus Hopkins Strong, *A Tour of the Missions: Observations and Conclusions* (Philadelphia: Griffith & Rowland Press, 1918);

Josiah Strong, *My Religion in Everyday Life* (New York: Baker & Taylor, 1910);

Strong, *Our World: The New World Life* (Garden City, N.Y.: Doubleday, Page, 1913);

Strong, *Our World: the New World Religion* (Garden City, N.Y.: Doubleday, Page, 1915);

Strong, *Union With Christ* (Philadelphia: American Baptist Publication Society, 1913);

Billy Sunday, *Billy Sunday's Sermons in Omaha* (Omaha, Neb.: Omaha Daily News, 1915);

Sunday, *Burning Truths from Billy's Bat* (Philadelphia: Diamond, 1914);

Sunday, *Great Love Stories from the Bible and Their Lesson for Today* (New York: Putnam, 1918);

Ethelbert Talbot, *A Bishop Among His Flock* (New York: Harper, 1914);

Talbot, *A Bishop's Message* (Philadelphia: G. W. Jacobs, 1917);

James Edward Talmage, *The Vitality of Mormonism* (Boston: Richard G. Badger, 1919);

Charles Lemuel Thompson, *The Religious Foundations of America* (New York: Revell, 1917);

Thompson, *The Soul of America* (New York: Revell, 1919);

Worth Marion Tippy, *The Church and the Great War* (New York: Revell, 1918);

Tippy, *A Methodist Church and Its Work* (New York: Methodist Book Concern, 1919);

Reuben Archer Torrey, *The Person and Work of the Holy Spirit* (New York: Revell, 1910);

Elizabeth Lois Jones Towne, *How to Use New Thought in Home Life* (Holyoke, Mass.: Elizabeth Towne, 1915);

Crawford Howell Toy, *Introduction to the History of Religions* (Boston: Ginn, 1912);

Toy, *Studies in the History of Religions* (New York: Macmillan, 1912);

Ralph Waldo Trine, *The Higher Powers of Mind and Spirit* (New York: Dodge, 1917);

Trine, *The Land of Living Men* (New York: Crowell, 1910);

Trine, *This Mystical Life of Ours* (New York: Dodd, Mead, 1919);

Henry Clay Vedder, *The Gospel of Jesus and the Problems of Democracy* (New York: Macmillan, 1914);

Vedder, *Socialism and the Ethics of Jesus* (New York: Macmillan, 1912);

Alexander Walters, *My Life and Work* (New York: Revell, 1917);

Harry Frederick Ward, *The Labor Movement, From the Standpoint of Religious Values* (New York: Sturgis & Walton, 1917);

Ward, *The New Social Order — Principles and Programs* (New York: Macmillan, 1919);

Ward, *Poverty and Wealth from the Viewpoint of the Kingdom of God* (New York: Methodist Book Concern, 1915);

Ward, *Social Creed of the Churches* (New York: Eaton & Mains, 1912);

Ward, *Social Evangelism* (New York: Missionary Education Movement of the United States and Canada, 1915);

Benjamin Breckinridge Warfield, *The Plan of Salvation* (Grand Rapids, Mich.: Eerdmans, 1915);

Sidney Weltmer, *The Healing Hand* (Nevada, Miss.: Weltmer Institute of Suggestive Therapeutics, 1918);

Ella Wheeler Wilcox, *The Art of Being Alive: Success Through Thought* (New York: Harper, 1914);

Wilcox, *My World and I* (New York: Doran, 1918);

Stephen Samuel Wise, *How to Face Life* (New York: Huebsch, 1917);

Elwood Worcester, *Religion and Life* (New York: Harper, 1914);

Richard Robert Wright Jr., *The Centennial Encyclopedia of the African Methodist Episcopal Church* (Philadelphia: Book Concern of the AME Church, 1916);

AME Review, periodical;

American Journal of Theology, periodical;

Bible Champion, periodical;

Biblical World, periodical;

Bibliotheca Sacra, periodical;

Catholic World, periodical;

Christian Advocate, periodical;

Christian Century, periodical;

Christian Herald, periodical;

The Christian Socialist, periodical;

Christian Work, periodical;

Christian Workers Magazine, periodical;

Harvard Theological Review, periodical;

Lutheran Quarterly, periodical;

Methodist Review, periodical;

Missionary Review of the World, periodical;

Our Hope, periodical;

Outlook, periodical;

Pilot, periodical;

The Presbyterian, periodical;

Religious Education, periodical;

The Theosophical Path, periodical;

The Word, periodical;

Zion's Herald, periodical.

SCIENCE AND TECHNOLOGY

by JOHN LOUIS RECCHIUTI

CONTENTS

Sidebars and tables are listed in italics.

1910

- Following the increased availability of electricity in American homes, electric washing machines begin to capture widespread public attention.

- The number of telephones in the United States exceeds seven million.

- The potential for air and water pollution problems, a result of rapid technological innovations, industrialization, and increased population density, are highlighted in Charles Steinmetz's *Future of Electricity*.

- Halley's comet is observed "as a giant headlight" in the night sky across America. Believed by astronomers to have first entered the inner solar system around 239 B.C., the comet completes its long elliptical orbit every seventy-six years.

- Maj. Frank Woodbury of the U.S. Army introduces tincture of iodine as a disinfectant for wounds.

1911

- After Dutch scientist H. Kamerlingh Onnes discovers superconductivity — the property of some metals, when cooled to extremely low temperatures, to lose virtually all resistance to the flow of electrons — scientists in the United States begin to study the phenomenon.

- The British scientist Ernest Rutherford theorizes that the atom is composed of a positively charged nucleus surrounded by negatively charged electrons.

- Physicists from around the world meet at the first Solvay physics conference — named for the Belgian industrial chemist and philanthropist who founded the Solvay institutes at Brussels — and discuss recently developed atomic theories.

- The Bell Telephone Company creates a research and development division. Similar corporate R and D labs become a major development of the decade, providing the foundation for many important breakthroughs.

- A. A. Campbell Swinton describes a theoretical model for the television that incorporates the cathode-ray tube.

- The massive Roosevelt Dam on the Salt River is completed; its reservoir supplies a quarter-million acres of land surrounding Phoenix, Arizona, with fresh water.

- Charles Franklin Kettering invents an electric starter for automobiles. The development of the electric self-starter means that cars can be started with a switch or key instead of requiring the motorist to stand in front of the vehicle and turn a large crank.

- The gastroscope, which allows physicians to look into the stomach and digestive track, is developed by William Hill, a London doctor.

- Thomas Hunt Morgan, a professor of experimental zoology at Columbia University, plots the first genes on chromosomes; A. H. Sturtevant makes the first chromosome maps.

- The world's first escalators are introduced at London's Earl's Court subway station.

- Franz Boas publishes *The Mind of Primitive Man,* a groundbreaking work of cultural anthropology.

- The word *vitamin* is coined by the Polish American biochemist Casimir Funk. Previously vitamins were called "accessory food factors."

14 Dec. Norwegian explorer Roald Amundsen becomes the first person in history to reach the South Pole. A month later the British explorer Robert Scott and his party also reach the South Pole, but they perish on the return journey.

1912

- Astronomer Henrietta Swan Leavitt studies variable stars (stars that vary in brightness) in the Southern Hemisphere's Magellanic Cloud.

- Dr. Sidney Russell invents the electric heating pad.

- The portable typewriter is introduced to the U.S. market by the Corona Company.

- Lee De Forest uses three of his triode tubes to develop an amplifier that can boost audio signals 120 times.

- Albert Einstein stirs interest in the U.S. physics community with his theory of photons and electrons (the law of photochemical equivalence). The laser is subsequently developed using Einstein's theory.

- The Morse code SOS (. . .- - -. . .) is adopted internationally as the universal signal for a ship in distress.

- German scientist Alfred L. Wegener proposes the theory of continental drift in his *The Origins of Continents and Oceans.*

15 Apr. The SS *Titanic,* believed "unsinkable" because of its compartmentalized interior design, sinks on its maiden voyage after striking an iceberg and sustaining a three-hundred-foot gash.

1913

- Elmer Ambrose Sperry receives a patent for his stabilizer gyroscope.

- Henry Ford introduces the assembly line for the manufacture of automobiles, one of the most significant applications of technology in the twentieth century.

- Irving Langmuir vastly improves the lightbulb by introducing coiled tungsten filaments and inert gas.

- Robert Andrews Millikan determines the charge of the electron. Millikan's study of the electron and his work on the photoelectric effect will be recognized with the Nobel Prize in physics in 1923.

- Telephone signals are boosted by the use of Lee De Forest's amplifier, vastly improving telephone communications between New York and Baltimore.

- Edouard Belin introduces the "Belino," or portable facsimile machine.

- Construction on the 792-foot Woolworth Building, then the tallest office building in the world, is completed in New York City.

- Construction is completed on the Los Angeles aqueduct, which carries fresh water 215 miles to the city from the Owens Valley high in the Sierra Nevada.

- Stainless steel, which has a high tensile strength and is resistant to abrasion and corrosion, is developed in England by adding a relatively high chromium content to the alloy of iron, carbon, and other elements that compose traditional steel.

- Hungarian American Béla Schick develops the "Schick test" for diagnosing diphtheria.

- Igor Sikorsky, a Russian-born aeronautical engineer, builds and flies the first multimotored plane.

- Rejecting psychologies of introspection as well as the theory of the unconscious, John B. Watson develops his theory of behavioral psychology, which emphasizes the study of observable responses.

- Henry N. Russell publishes his theory of stellar evolution. Combined with the work done in 1905 by Danish astronomer Ejnar Hertzsprung, Russell's theory leads to the Hertzsprung-Russell diagram, which traces the life cycle of stars.

- The French physicist Charles Fabry discovers the ozone layer in the Earth's stratosphere.

- The British scientist Henry Gwyn-Jeffreys uses X-ray spectrography to conclude that the number of electrons in a chemical element is the same as its atomic number.

- William D. Coolidge invents the hot-cathode X-ray device.

Jan. William Burton invents a new process for refining oil, "thermal cracking," that employs high temperatures and pressures to convert petroleum to gasoline by "cracking" large molecules into the smaller molecules of gasoline, without the aid of catalysts.

1914

- American Theodore W. Richards wins the Nobel Prize in chemistry for determining atomic weights.

- Henry Ford introduces the five-dollar day for his workers on his new automobile assembly lines.

- Edwin H. Armstrong, while a student at Columbia University, patents his radio receiver with regeneration (positive feedback) that greatly improves radio reception.

- The first transcontinental telephone line is completed.

- Gasoline companies begin distributing free road maps to customers.

- A near-perfect vacuum is created by American scientist Irving Langmuir's mercury-vapor pump.

- The modern stapler is introduced by the Boston Wire Stitcher Company.

- Tony Jannus pilots his plane in Florida on scheduled flights from Saint Petersburg to Tampa for three months, establishing the first passenger airline.

- Robert Goddard begins development of an experimental rocket.

- The red-green traffic light is introduced in Cleveland, Ohio.

- Harlow Shapley publishes a detailed explanation of the correlation between luminosity and distance in Cepheid variable stars, a class of stars that regularly brighten and dim.

14 Aug.   The fifty-one-mile Panama Canal is opened to shipping.

1915

- Manson Benedicks uses a germanium crystal to convert alternating current into direct current.

- Pyrex (80 percent silicon oxide and 12 percent boron oxide) is created at the Corning Glass Works in New York. The new glass is soon used in kitchens and in laboratories.

- The all-metal airplane is developed in Germany.

- The British lead the development of the tank as a weapon against barbed wire on the western front during World War I.

- French scientist Paul Langevin invents sonar to detect icebergs and other objects submerged in water.

- August Fruehauf, a blacksmith from Detroit, invents the tractor-trailer, a truck with its cab and engine separate from the main cargo body.

- Albert Einstein completes his general theory of relativity.

25 Jan.   Alexander Graham Bell makes the first transcontinental telephone call, from New York to San Francisco, to his assistant Thomas A. Watson.

Oct.   The first transatlantic radiotelephone conversation is held between the Eiffel Tower in Paris and Arlington, Virginia.

1916

- Working from Albert Einstein's theory of relativity, German astronomer Karl Schwarzchild posits the theoretical existence of "black holes," intense gravitational fields from which nothing, not even light, can escape.

- The first all-steel automobile body is crafted by the Dodge Company.

- Windshield wipers are introduced on American cars.

- Physicist Robert Andrews Millikan uses the photoelectric effect to confirm Planck's constant, a fundamental constant of quantum theory posited by German physicist Max Planck.

- Gilbert Newton Lewis, professor of physical chemistry at the University of California, explains chemical bonding and the valence structure of chemicals with his theory of shared electrons, or covalent bonding.

1917

- Building on Albert Einstein's theories, Dutch astronomer Willem de Sitter asserts that the universe is expanding.

- Clarence Birdseye develops a technique for preserving foods, the beginning of the frozen food industry.

- The first commercial use is made of the plastic Bakelite. It is soon used to make handles for frying pans and in other home and industry applications.

- Herbert D. Curtis calculates the distance from Earth to the Andromeda galaxy.

1 Nov. George Ellery Hale uses the Hooker Telescope, a reflecting telescope with a one-hundred-inch mirror installed at Mount Wilson Observatory in Pasadena, California, for the first time.

1918

- Edwin H. Armstrong's development of a superheterodyne circuit, which lowers the frequency of electromagnetic waves and subsequently amplifies them, will make getting good amplitude modulation (AM) reception as easy as turning a dial. The first radio station, KDKA in Pittsburgh, is still three years from its first broadcast.

- Electric mixers for the kitchen are marketed.

- Alexander Graham Bell develops a sixty-foot-long high-speed hydrofoil, the HD-4, that can achieve seventy miles per hour.

- The nation's first three-color traffic light (red, amber, green) is installed in New York City.

- The first diamond-edged drills for oil exploration go into production.

- Harlow Shapley plots the shape and dimensions of the Milky Way galaxy, the home galaxy for our solar system.

- Herbert Evans claims that human cells contain forty-eight chromosomes (the number is later found to be forty-six).

1919

- Shortwave radio is invented, and amateur radio "hams" begin to take to the airwaves.

- The Radio Corporation of America (RCA) is founded.

- Charles F. Jenkins of Dayton, Ohio, patents a mechanical system for transmitting television pictures.

- Lockheed produces the hydraulic braking system for cars.

- Robert Goddard develops his theory of extreme altitude rocketry and posits the theoretical possibility of its use for sending a rocket to the moon.

- Thomas Hunt Morgan publishes *The Physical Basis of Heredity.*

- Ernest Rutherford confirms the existence of the proton as a product of the disintegration of the atomic nucleus.

29 May Astronomers confirm Albert Einstein's theory of general relativity by observing the bending of a star's light around the sun during a total eclipse.

OVERVIEW

The Best and Worst of Times. The automobile assembly line, new atomic theories, Einstein's general theory of relativity, advances in radio technology, and continuing developments in the social sciences are among the many scientific and technological advances of the 1910s. Modern science was in full bloom. New inventions made life less arduous and more comfortable for millions of urban and rural Americans. Many new products found their way into homes, factories, farms, and hospitals. The decade, however, also bore witness to the devastation of World War I. From 1914 to 1918 the Great War showed that technological advancements, so wondrous in peacetime, could have horrible consequences in war. The first extensive use of submarines in sea battle, the invention of the tank, and the gruesome toll of the machine gun each played its part in the maiming and killing of millions. World War I showed that the achievements of the scientist and engineer could cause immeasurable pain and suffering, a dark lesson that humanity would be taught again at the dawn of the atomic age.

Scientific Internationalism. An essential feature of science and technology in the second decade of the twentieth century was its international character. The story of science and technology in the United States in the 1910s would be incomplete without reference to achievements elsewhere. In the decade that saw the first transatlantic radiotelephone communication, European and American scientists could share ideas and results rapidly. The international exchange of theories and inventions via journals, papers, missives, and conferences makes the story of scientific and technological advancement truly cosmopolitan, but the United States was beginning to assert itself. In 1910 the United States was seen as a worthy partner of the great scientific powers of England, France, and Germany. By the end of the decade the United States was poised to take the lead in many fields.

Research and Development. The growth of industrial laboratories for research and development (R and D) was an important facet of American science and technology. Development of institutionalized engineering in the United States can be traced back into the nineteenth century, when universities opened the first engineering schools and professional engineering associations were formed. The American Society of Civil Engineers was founded in 1852, the American Institute of Mining Engineers in 1871, the American Society of Mechanical Engineers in 1880, and the American Institute of Electrical Engineers in 1884. In 1901 General Electric was the first corporation in the United States formally to found a research laboratory — though Thomas Alva Edison's laboratories had set the benchmark for R and D in the closing years of the nineteenth century. Following Edison and General Electric, scores of R and D facilities, often with staffs numbering no more than a dozen, cropped up across the nation. In the century's second decade their numbers grew apace. By 1917 there were more than 350 industrial research labs in the United States. By 1918 General Electric's R and D facility, begun so modestly at the beginning of the century, had grown to employ more than three hundred researchers and staff. The independent inventor or tinkerer was increasingly being replaced by engineers and scientists on corporate, university, and sometimes government payrolls.

Technological Innovation. The variety of technological achievements in the 1910s was impressive. Hoover vacuum cleaners, an electric-mechanical calculator called the "Millionaire," electrically powered washing machines, the world's first portable facsimile (fax) machine (invented by Edouard Belin of France in 1913), and the tank (initially produced in England) were all introduced or developed during the decade. Bakelite, a hard durable plastic, was invented and put to use in electrical circuits as an insulator as well as in parts for automobiles and airplanes. Rotogravure was used in newspapers for the first time in printing the 1912 Christmas issue of *The New York Times*. In 1913 the Woolworth Building, the tallest office building in its day at 792 feet, was completed in New York City. In 1914 a combination plow and harrow was developed; the plow tilled the soil while the harrow was drawn behind to cover the seed and break up the plowed earth. By 1916 the miles of railroad track crisscrossing the nation reached approximately 253,000 miles (thereafter mileage was reduced by consolidations of rail company lines). In these and many more ways, technology touched every facet of American life and every American.

TOPICS IN THE NEWS

THE AIRPLANE

Early Flight. Although powered flight was achieved at Kitty Hawk, North Carolina, in 1903, the airplane industry did not take off until the advent of World War I. The years before the war, however, did see impressive achievements in aviation. In January 1910 the first aviation competition in America was held in Los Angeles. Also that year Glenn Curtiss flew from Albany to New York City in 150 minutes to set a new long-distance speed record. In 1911 there were only about four hundred airplanes in the United States, but the airplane was in the news: Curtiss built the first practical plane with pontoons instead of wheels; Galbraith Perry Rogers flew from New York to California in forty-nine days in sixty-eight segments, with an average airspeed of 51.5 MPH (not until 1913 would speeds in excess of 100 MPH be achieved in flight); and Harriet Quimby, an editor at *Leslie's Magazine,* became the first woman licensed as a pilot. In 1912 Ruth Law flew nonstop from Chicago to New York. The war years, though, brought a great leap forward in aviation. Toward the decade's end a few passenger and mail delivery routes had been established in the United States. By 1919 aircraft technology had advanced enough to allow John Alcock and Arthur Whitten-Brown to make the first nonstop transatlantic flight.

Airplanes in War. In 1914 there were only about five thousand airplanes in the world, but by the end of World War I there were an estimated two hundred thousand planes worldwide, most of which had been manufactured for military service. During the war airplanes were used for reconnaissance, as bombers, and to strafe enemy infantry. The first dogfights between fighter pilots captured the imagination of many Americans. Germany's Baron Manfred von Richthofen (the "Red Baron") had eighty successful air engagements with enemy planes. The Frenchman Rene Fonck (with seventy-five successful engagements) and British airman Edward Mannock (with seventy-three) were not far behind. There were no aircraft carriers during World War I. The few planes that took off from ships at sea (at times aided by catapult devices) had either to ditch in the sea near their ship and be pulled from the water or fly to a land base. During the war U.S. engineers designed pilotless bomb-carrying air-

THE FIRST INTERCITY AIRPLANE RACE

The 19 August 1911 edition of *Scientific American* recounted the first airplane race from New York to Philadelphia, which was flown on 5 August: "The first aeroplane race across country from New York to Philadelphia was flown on Saturday, August 5th, when Messrs. Bechy, Ely, and Robinson of the Curtiss force started from Governors Island, flew up the Hudson to Thirty-Third Street, circled over the roof of the Gimbel building, and headed for Philadelphia. Bechy, who has already made a name for himself by his flight over Niagara Falls a short time ago, won the race, his time from store to store for the 90 miles being 3/4 minutes less than two hours, including a stop at Trenton, in order to take on fuel. . . . Just before reaching Philadelphia Bechy was soaked as he circled above the Gimbel building in Philadelphia. . . . The prize was $5,000 in cash."

craft, but the armistice was signed before the designs could be put into production.

The V-12 Liberty Engine. At the opening of World War I the United States trailed Europe in the manufacture of airplanes. During the war, however, U.S. engineers developed the famous V-12 Liberty engine, twenty thousand of which were produced for the military. Mainly designed by engineers in the automobile industry (especially at Packard Motor Company in Detroit), the V-12 proved the ability of American scientists and engineers to respond swiftly in a crisis. The V-12 went from drafting table to production in six months, from May to November 1917. Engineers tested prototype airplane engines by bolting them to truck beds and "driving" the propeller-powered trucks in the streets of Detroit. As one observer noted, "The air-propelled truck could travel faster than any man would care to drive it." An automotive plant was retooled to produce the new engines in

A reconnaissance plane taking off from the USS *Pennsylvania,* 18 January 1911

quantity, and engineers at Ford Motor Company developed cylinders forged from steel tubing — replacing the slow and laborious method of boring cylinders directly into a metal block — that allowed for more efficient engine production at a much reduced cost. Another innovation of the V-12 was its use of water rather than air as an engine coolant.

Sources:

John Batchelor and Bryan Cooper, *Fighter: A History of Fighter Aircraft* (New York: Scribners, 1974);

"The True Story of the Liberty Motor," *Scientific American* (1 June 1918): 500, 515.

ASTRONOMY

Yardsticks of the Universe. As the result of her work in the Harvard Observatory on Cepheid variable stars in the Magellanic Cloud, Henrietta Leavitt in 1912 made an important contribution to astronomers' attempts to understand the size of the universe. (Cepheids are the class of variable stars that brighten and dim with constant periods.) Leavitt discovered that the period of time it takes for a Cepheid variable to complete its bright-dim cycle is related to the star's luminosity. In 1914 Harlow Shapley used Leavitt's work in his detailed explanation of

the correlation between luminosity and distance in Cepheid variable stars. Such insights led astronomers to develop the means of gauging large interstellar distances that could not be calculated by parallax, the method for measuring planetary and stellar distances by triangulation. Appropriately, Cepheid variables have been called the "yardsticks of the universe." It is now understood that Cepheid class stars, which take their name from Delta Cephei, the first such star discovered in 1784, are yellow supergiants. The variation in the intensity of the light from a Cepheid results from the star's physical pulsation.

The World's Largest Telescope. Another important contribution to American astronomy was made by George Ellery Hale. A professor of astrophysics at the University of Chicago, Hale was the key person behind the making of the era's greatest telescope, the giant one-hundred-inch reflecting telescope at Mount Wilson Observatory in Pasadena, California. It was Hale's enthusiasm and his ability to excite an interest in non-astronomers for astronomical research that led him to entice John Daggett Hooker, a wealthy American businessman, to contribute the initial money to build the telescope, which was originally called the Hooker Telescope. When the project appeared to be floundering —

The completed 100-inch telescope at Mount Wilson Observatory in Pasadena, California

RUSSELL'S PARADOX

British mathematician-philosophers Bertrand Russell and Alfred North Whitehead collaborated on their monumental three-volume *Principia Mathematica* (1913). Setting out to establish mathematics as a branch of logic, they constructed their arguments from the most basic definitions, axioms, and postulates of math and logic. Though their effort was ultimately found to be unsuccessful, the mathematical, philosophical, and scientific communities were abuzz with discussions of their work throughout the decade. Russell's famous paradox — "is there a mathematical set of all sets not self-members?" — was a troubling problem for mathematicians until in the 1920s the Austrian-born mathematician Kurt Godel, inspired in part by Russell's Paradox, proved the most influential theorem of twentieth-century mathematics: Godel's incompleteness theorem.

Sources: John Dawson Jr., *Logical Dilemmas* (New York: A&K Peters, 1995);

Jean Van Heijenoort, ed., *From Frege to Godel* (Cambridge, Mass.: Harvard University Press, 1958).

Sources:
Isaac Asimov, *Eyes on the Universe: A History of the Telescope* (Boston: Houghton Mifflin, 1975);

Marcia Bartusiak, *Thursday's Universe* (New York: Times Books, 1986);

Richard Berendzen, Richard Hart, and Daniel Seeley, *Man Discovers the Galaxies* (New York: Science History Publications, 1976);

Fred Hoyle, *Astronomy* (Garden City, N.Y.: Doubleday, 1962);

A. Pannekoek, *A History of Astronomy* (Totowa, N.J.: Barnes & Noble, 1961);

Frederick Slocum, "George Ellery Hale: America's Foremost Solar Physicist," *Scientific American* (8 July 1911): 23, 37–38;

Otto Struve and Velta Zebergs, *Astronomy of the Twentieth Century* (New York: Macmillan, 1962).

the casting process at first left bubbles and other imperfections in the glass — Andrew Carnegie contributed the funds necessary to finish the project.

The First Look. Hale oversaw construction of the observatory and installation of the mirror. The telescope was mounted in a dome one hundred feet in diameter and one hundred feet high. On the evening of 1 November 1917 the ninety-thousand-kilogram telescope was found to move smoothly in its mounting, but the initial efforts to observe Jupiter were alarming. Rather than seeing a single crisp image of the planet in the eyepiece, Hale saw six overlapping images. Realizing that the multiple images might be being caused by temperature variations within the observatory dome, Hale and his assistants waited for several hours and were greatly relieved to see but one image in the eyepiece after the atmosphere surrounding the telescope had stabilized. The new telescope made it possible for astronomers to observe three hundred million stars as well as faint nebulae. It remained the world's largest reflecting telescope until 1948, when the great two-hundred-inch telescope was installed at the Mount Palomar Observatory. Hale was also the driving force in that project, but he died before its completion.

ATOMIC PHYSICS

What is an Atom? Atomic physics was making rapid strides during the second decade of the twentieth century. By the turn of the twentieth century, there was general acceptance among physicists of the molecular theory of matter. Molecules were believed to be composed of still smaller units of matter, atoms. However, it was also becoming clear that the "unsplittable" atoms were composed of even smaller parts. While the properties of electrons were beginning to be understood, the structure of the atom itself remained a mystery.

Rutherford's Experiments. Various theories of atomic structure were ventured, but the one given the most credence was the model proposed by Professor Ernest Rutherford of England. From about 1906 Rutherford had been firing alpha particles (positively charged particles

The participants at the Solvay Council in 1911 included Ernest Rutherford, H. Kamerlingh Onnes, and Albert Einstein (standing, fourth, third, and second from right, respectively)

consisting of two protons and two neutrons that are emitted by several radioactive substances) at sheets of matter in hopes that the record of how they passed through or were deflected by the sheets would help to suggest a picture of the atom. In 1908 Rutherford fired alpha particles at a sheet of gold only two thousand atoms thick (a thickness of 1/50,000th of an inch). He found that most of the alpha particles passed through the gold and were recorded on a photographic plate behind it. This seemed to indicate that the atoms were mostly empty space (we now know that the size of a proton is only 1/100,000th of the diameter of an atom). A comparatively small number of alpha particles, Rutherford noticed, were deflected from the main stream at a substantial angle.

The Nuclear Atom. By 1911 Rutherford had collected enough data to put forward his revolutionary theory of the nuclear atom. In a paper delivered on 7 March 1912 in Manchester, England, Rutherford described his dis-

coveries, and soon thereafter he explained his theory before American physicists at Princeton University's Physics Colloquium. He argued that the center of the atom was composed of protons (from the Greek word for "first") and that it was surrounded by electrons. In Rutherford's view, the atom was "built up like a solar system on an extremely small scale. The positive electricity is concentrated into a very small nucleus, which takes the place of the sun, and the negative electrons revolve around this like planets. It seems probable that they are arranged in rings, like the rings of Saturn."

The Electron's Charge. Another pioneer in the study of the atom was American physicist Robert A. Millikan, who set out in 1906 to find the absolute charge of the electron. His earliest efforts involved charting the course of water droplets as they fell through the air while the pull of a charged plate above them countered the force of gravity. The evaporation of the droplets resulted in poor results, and in 1911 he switched to oil droplets. By pass-

Atom is a word derived from ancient Greek. The philosophers Leucippus and Democritus had conceived of the universe as being constructed from tiny bits of hard matter, of differing shapes, that could not be broken into parts. Since the ancient Greek prefix for "not" is "a" and the word for "splittable" is "tomoi," these pre-Socratic natural philosophers called these tiny building blocks "atomoi." Modern scientists simply adopted the word in describing the tiny bits of fundamental matter from which, they believed, all things were made.

Source: Philip Wheelwright, ed., *The Presocratics* (Indianapolis, Ind.: Bobbs-Merrill, 1966).

ing X rays through the chamber in which the oil droplets were raining down, Millikan was able to attach extra electrons to the falling droplets. When a droplet absorbed electrons the charged plate above had a noticeably greater effect. The descent of such droplets was slowed, and if the positive charge above was great enough the droplets even rose. The change was due, Millikan reasoned, to the additional electrons. By calculating the effects of gravity pulling the droplet down and the positive plate pulling it upward he was able to determine the charge of a single electron. (Millikan's result closely approximates the now accepted value of sixteen-quintillionths of a coulomb.) For this discovery Millikan was awarded the Nobel Prize in physics in 1923.

The Puzzling Electroscope. The electroscope used in the early twentieth century to detect the presence of radiation posed an intriguing problem for physicists. At the time electroscopes consisted of two thin wafers of gold joined at the upper end and suspended inside a jar so that they were separated by a small distance. When the gold wafers were electrically charged from an outside source they would repel each other (since they had the same charge) and form an inverted *V*. When radiation penetrated the glass of the jar, scientists discovered, it would carried off the electric charge and the wafers would slowly fall back to their original place. Yet even when scientists kept all known radiation sources away from the jar the gold plates would eventually return to their original state. An undetermined source of radiation was apparently entering the electroscope.

Cosmic Rays. The Austrian physicist Victor Hess believed that the Earth itself might be the source of the radiation. In 1911 he made ten balloon flights with an electroscope in hopes of achieving a height at which the hypothesized radiation from the Earth would become negligible. To his amazement, the gold wafers, instead of remaining apart for a longer duration, collapsed toward

each other much more rapidly. The radiation affecting them was coming not from the Earth but from space. At the suggestion of Millikan the newly discovered rays from space were dubbed "cosmic rays." Hess won the Nobel Prize in physics in 1936 for his discovery.

The Genesis of Quantum Physics. Based on Rutherford's theory, and the earlier work of Max Planck, the 1910s witnessed the genesis of quantum physics. The first of the famous Solvay Congresses, attended by many American physicists, on quantum physics was held in 1911 in Brussels. In 1912 the Danish physicist Niels Bohr explained how, in Rutherford's atomic nuclear theory, the electron orbiting the central proton did not simply spiral downward into the nucleus. He proposed the notion that the orbital momentum of the electron is quantized, and that radiation is emitted when electrons jump between valences around the nucleus. Bohr, in Europe, became director of the new Institute for Theoretical Physics in 1916, and many American scientists traveled to the institute to discuss Bohr's work. In 1913 the English scientist Frederick Soddy further excited American chemists and physicists with his theory of isotopes. Soddy showed that atoms of different atomic weights could act in chemically identical ways. Excitement over atomic theory electrified the American scientific community in the 1910s, and by 1919 American Irving Langmuir was deeply involved in studying the structure of electronic valances around the atomic nucleus. Yet it would remain for those who followed to unlock the atom's secrets further.

Sources:

Isaac Asimov, *Understanding Physics* (New York: Walker, 1966);

Barbara Lovett Cline, *The Questioners* (New York: Crowell, 1965);

Arthur H. Compton, "What is Matter Made Of?," *Scientific American* (15 May 1915): 451–452;

Daniel J. Kevles, *The Physicists: The History of a Scientific Community in Modern America* (New York: Knopf, 1971);

Emilio Segre, *From X-Rays to Quarks: Modern Physicists and Their Discoveries* (San Francisco: Freeman, 1980);

James S. Trefil, *From Atoms to Quarks: An Introduction to the Strange World of Particle Physics* (New York: Scribners, 1980).

THE AUTOMOBILE

Innovative Industry. New Year's Day 1910 saw the opening of Henry Ford's Highland Park factory, where innovations in the manufacturing process would help to make the Ford Motor Company's revolutionary Model T, introduced in 1908, the car of the decade. In 1910 458,500 motor vehicles were registered in the United States, and motor vehicle manufacturing was rapidly growing into one of the nation's major industries. Ancillary industries produced innovative technologies in rubber, glass, and petroleum refining. The decade witnessed important improvements in automotive engineering, as the all-steel automobile body was introduced and the front-mounted engine that drove the rear axle by means

Traffic jam at Bryant Park, Forty-second Street in New York City in 1919

of a turning shaft (rather than by chain as in some early cars) became the industry standard. Perhaps the most important innovation of the early 1910s was Kettering's development in 1911 of the electric starter, which meant that engines no longer had to be started by a cranking mechanism. The innovation made automobiles a much more alluring product and drove their popularity to new heights.

Steam-Powered Cars. Although they were overwhelmed by the internal combustion engine in the 1910s, steam-powered vehicles and electric cars contended for market share in the early years of the automobile industry and continued to be produced in the decade. Working on the same principles that drove locomotive trains, steam-powered cars ran more smoothly than did gas engines — dubbed by their critics "nasty explosion engines." Steam-powered engines freed the driver and passengers from irritating vibrations and difficult, often jerky, gear-changing procedures. Steam engines, however, were difficult to start since the water had to be boiled until pressure within the system reached 180 to 200 pounds per square inch. One model came with lengthy instructions for starting, beginning with "head the car into the wind." As well as being inconvenient, steam-powered cars were expensive. In 1918 the Stanley Steamer was selling for $2,750 while Ford's Model T cost less than $400. (The

In a quiet ceremony in Washington, D.C., the one millionth patent was awarded by the U.S. Patent Office on Tuesday, 8 August 1911. Frank Halton of Cleveland received the patent for an improved automobile tire. As William Taft noted in the August issue of *Scientific American,* "It was fitting that this patent, in itself a monument to progress, should have been awarded to an improvement on the automobile, for there is probably no single recent invention which has done so much to mark American progress or to show the world the prosperity of the United States." Patents had been granted since the beginning of the Republic, but few were granted in the early years. In 1790, for example, only three patents were issued — and all were signed by President George Washington. Before the system for granting patents was overhauled in the mid 1830s, 9,902 patents had been issued; these, however, were not consecutively numbered. In July 1836 the patenting process was overhauled; a commissioner of patents was appointed; and the new U.S. Patent Office granted the first numbered patent. Patent No. 1 was awarded to John Ruggles on 13 July 1836 for a locomotive engine. As *Scientific American* noted, "It is rather a strange coincidence that Patent No. 1 and Patent No. 1,000,000 should both have been awarded to improvements in the foremost mode of locomotion for their times and that these inventions mark the progress of two machines which represent the highest form of power transference then known."

Stanley Company continued to sell steam-powered cars until 1927.)

Early Electric Autos. Electric cars were used during the 1910s (as they had been during the previous decade) for local trips. Because their batteries had to be recharged after relatively short distances, such vehicles were generally limited to shopping trips or for visits to nearby friends. The typical 1914 electric car was run by forty cells. Its speed was controlled by a pedal that, when released, caused the car to speed up and, when pressed, stopped the vehicle. By 1920 the difficulties associated with charging electric vehicles had not been surmounted, and electric cars fell into disuse.

The Assembly Line. Henry Ford revolutionized production of the automobile with the introduction of the assembly line in 1913. As a result of the economies of scale and the quickened, more efficient work done on the assembly line, Ford reduced the hours of work for his employees from ten to eight while increasing wages to $5 a day for some workers at a time when wages averaged $2.50 a day in the industry. So successful was Ford's assembly-line production in its division of labor, delivery of components to workers on the line, and the "planned, orderly, and continuous progression of the commodity through the shop" that assembly-line production was called "Fordism." The assembly-line came to symbolize U.S. technological and manufacturing efficiency. Increased production with lower production time and lower unit cost was hailed as a great technological achievement. Complaints from workers about the repetitious, mind-numbing labor on the rapidly moving line were drowned out by its successes. The assembly line reduced assembly time for a Model T from twelve and a half hours to two hours and forty minutes by December 1913. By 1914 the assembly line had reduced to one and a half hours the time required to assemble a car. Ropes for hauling materials along on the line were replaced with an endless chain in January 1914. By 1914 it was reported that there were 15,000 machines — among them specially designed milling machines — at work on Ford's assembly line. Even with the rise in wages and decrease in work hours, Ford was able to lower the price of his product dramatically. In 1910 a Model T sold for $850; by 1916 it cost only $345. (The purchase price of the Model T reached a low of $290 in 1927.)

Model T. In its first year of production in 1908, 1,200 Model T cars were sold. In 1910 Ford produced 32,053 Model T's, but after the introduction of the assembly line production soared, and 734,811 cars were produced in 1916 — at which time Ford controlled about half of the U.S. market. Mass production of the low-cost cars did lead to some constraints. Henry Ford remarked that the consumer could have any color of car "so long as it was black." Model T owners joked about their cars' lack of aesthetic qualities but often bragged about their efficiency. In all, 15,458,781 Model T's were produced between 1908 and 1927.

An Age of Motor Vehicles. During the 1910s the United States was becoming a nation of automobiles. Four-cylinder cars were the norm, but some six-cylinder engines were introduced, and beginning in 1914 the V-8 was put into production by Cadillac. The V-12 became popular from 1915 to 1923. Although Ford was by far the most successful producer of cars, he was facing increasing numbers of competitors. In 1916, when Ford produced nearly 735,000 cars, the Willys-Overland company produced 140,000, Buick 124,834, and Dodge 71,400. There were also scores of smaller automobile manufacturers. *Scientific American* reported in its 18 April 1914 issue that motorized taxicabs in New York City covered 819,000 miles annually — roughly twice the distance to the moon and back. By 1916 there were over three million autos in the United States.

Trucking. Most deliveries in the 1910s were still made by horse-drawn vehicles, but trucks were beginning to displace horses. In 1915 August Fruehauf, a blacksmith from Detroit, invented the tractor trailer, a truck with its cab and engine separate from the main cargo body. With the outbreak of World War I trucks were needed to fill gaps in transportation that neither horse nor railroad could perform. During the war "Ship By Truck" became a marketing slogan, and three hundred thousand trucks were made in 1917.

Good Roads. For the motor vehicle industry to live up to its potential, reliable roads were needed. In 1912 a Good Roads Convention was held in the nation's capital. Delegates importuned for federal financing of new interstate road systems. In 1913 Carl G. Fisher of Indianapolis led a movement to build a hard-surface transcontinental highway. In an effort to rouse support for the idea he proposed the patriotic name "Lincoln Highway." Congress appointed a Committee on Roads in 1913 and after studying the question brought about the Federal Aid Act of 1916. President Wilson was committed to vetoing the act, for in his view the Constitution left such "internal improvements" to the individual states rather than to the federal government. However, on the day Wilson was going to deliver his veto, a German submarine appeared in the harbor at Baltimore, having eluded the Allied navies. The presence of the submarine on the eastern seaboard, while no immediate military threat, was disconcerting and led Wilson to reconsider his position. He then signed the legislation, arguing that improved roads were a matter of national defense.

Sources:

Henry Ford, with Samuel Crowther, *My Life and Work* (Garden City, N.Y.: Doubleday, 1923);

Robert Lacey, *Ford: The Men and the Machine* (Boston: Little, Brown, 1986);

Stephen Meyer III, *The Five Dollar Day: Labor Management and Social Control in the Ford Motor Company, 1908–1921* (Albany: State University of New York Press, 1981).

BIOLOGICAL SCIENCES AND PUBLIC HEALTH

The First Genetic Map. The 1910s saw important work in the biological sciences that often had both immediate and long-term consequences. Building on the base provided by the Austrian botanist Gregor Mendel, who in the mid nineteenth century had shown that "hereditary factors" in plants were passed on to their progeny in predictable ways, Thomas Hunt Morgan and his colleagues published the first chromosome map in 1911. The diagram identified the location of five sex-linked genes from the salivary glands of the fruit fly (*Drosophila*). Morgan found that the genes were arranged like beads on a necklace. In 1919 he published his *Physical Basis of Heredity,* and by the decade's end almost two thousand genes had been mapped, setting the stage for future advancements.

A Cure for African Sleeping Sickness. Among the outstanding women scientists of the period was Louise

THE ELECTRIC HAND DRIER

The increasing awareness in public health circles of the transmission of microparasites and disease in public places led to the outlawing of the public drinking cup. Soon thereafter it was realized that repeated use of hand towels by public lavatory users also spread disease. In 1913 Massachusetts, Ohio, and Michigan passed laws prohibiting the use of common towels. In 1914 the "Air Towel," an electric hand drier, was invented by J. M. Ward. First installed in public rest rooms in the District Building in Washington, D.C., the air towel allowed patrons to dry their hands by placing them over heated coils across which air was blown by an electric fan.

Pearce, a Ph.D. graduate of Johns Hopkins University in 1909. Pearce's discovery of a cure for sleeping sickness was a godsend to the tens of thousands of Africans who annually contracted the disease. Caused by a microparasite carried by the tsetse fly, patients stricken with the disease experienced inflammation of the brain and persistent lethargy. Pearce discovered that Salvarsan — a drug then used as a cure for syphilis — stopped the disease in laboratory animals. Soon after her discovery of the cure, she traveled to Africa to oversee the successful administration of the drug personally.

Safer Food. As advances in microbiology and other sciences increased understanding of bacterial agents, measures to improve the processing and preservation of foods improved. Americans increasingly relied on canned foods as a part of their diet. The healthfulness of canned foods was improved by the founding of the National Canning Association (NCA) in 1913. The NCA's establishment of safe canning standards contributed to expansive growth in the industry. Millions of cans, a safe and economical form in which to transport food over long distances, were shipped from the United States to the Western Front during World War I. The processing of milk was also much improved in the decade. Raw milk can easily become a carrier for bacteria. The pasteurization of milk, a process whereby it is heated to 145 degrees Fahrenheit and then cooled rapidly, kills bacteria. In 1914 New York City's sanitary code required all milk to be pasteurized, and the consequent reduction of illness in the city paved the way for pasteurization to become a common national practice.

Refrigeration and Frozen Foods. The first modern electrical refrigerators were introduced into the United States when A. H. Goss's popular Kelvinator refrigerator was marketed between 1912 and 1914. Refrigeration led to a major advance in the modern food industry when Clarence Birdseye of Brooklyn, New York, developed a

Clarence Birdseye on the Labrador coast, where he was inspired to experiment with freezing food

technique for preserving foods by freezing them. On a vacation trip to Canada with his wife and child, Birdseye had observed that frozen foods retained their freshness. Upon his return to the United States, Birdseye developed refrigeration techniques by which to freeze foods on a mass scale, thus creating the multimillion-dollar frozen food industry.

Emphasizing Cleanliness. Though biologists had known of the infectious nature of germs for decades, an article by Dr. W. L. Mallinson of Michigan State College on "The Invisible World" of germs was widely reprinted during the 1910s and awakened Americans to the need for cleanliness in food preparation. Emphasis on the reduction of bacteria through refrigeration gave the refrigeration industry a major boost.

A "Flyless City." Public health officials in the decade strived to increase public awareness that diseases were caused by microparasites. Since insects were often carriers, various efforts were made to eradicate insect pests in many towns and cities. In Cleveland, for example, a municipal "Battle Against the House-Fly" was waged from 1913 to 1915. The campaign to eradicate the housefly — an annoyance and potential disease carrier in houses, gro-

ceries, and fields — became a symbol of the increasing public awareness of the spread of germs. Public health officials sought to "put Cleveland on the map as a flyless city" by removing the "organic filth" within which flies bred, by setting out poison traps, by teaching farmers and grocers about insect breeding habits, and by draining stagnant pools of water. A vigorous newspaper campaign of public awareness along with the distribution of two hundred thousand flyswatters to the city's schoolchildren resulted in a measurable decrease in the fly population. Cleveland never became a "flyless city," but its efforts highlighted the important link between scientific laboratories and public health efforts in the nation's cities and towns.

Sources:

Harry Carlton, *The Frozen Food Industry* (Knoxville: University of Tennessee Press, 1941);

Jean Dawson, "Eliminating a City's Filth and Flies: Cleveland Battles Against the House-Fly," *Scientific American* (11 July 1914): 28–29;

Maitland Edey and Donald C. Johanson, *Blueprints: Solving the Mystery of Evolution* (Boston: Little, Brown, 1989);

Thomas Hunt Morgan, *Evolution and Genetics* (Princeton, N.J.: Princeton University Press, 1925);

Alfred Henry Sturtevant, *A History of Genetics* (New York: Harper & Row, 1965).

BUILDING THE PANAMA CANAL

The Choice of Panama. The Panama Canal was one of the great engineering triumphs of its era. For decades shipping interests had dreamed of shortening the trip from the Atlantic to the Pacific, which until the canal was completed required an arduous journey around South America's Cape Horn. In the nineteenth and early twentieth centuries the United States contemplated building a canal across Nicaragua but after much debate settled on the Isthmus of Panama as the best site. A railroad constructed by a New York firm had been completed there in 1855, and its existence and profitability were major factors in the choice of Panama. A French firm that had begun digging a canal at the site in 1881 had abandoned its efforts in 1889 — in large part because of the horrendous death toll to its workers caused by malaria.

Political Maneuvering. On 22 January 1903 representatives from the United States and Colombia signed the Hay-Herrán Treaty, but the Colombian Senate refused to ratify it. On 3 November 1903 a group of Colombians living near the canal site declared their independence from Colombia. Within three days the Roosevelt administration, eager to complete the canal project, recognized the sovereignty of Panama. A week later Panama's minister to the United States signed the Hay-Bunau-Varilla Treaty giving the United States the right to operate a canal in the new nation. The treaty also granted control of land on either side of the canal for five miles, the Canal Zone, to the United States.

Work Begins. Construction on the canal began in 1904. The decade-long project was a massive undertak-

Steamer *Ancon* passing through the Culebra Cut on the first official transit of the canal, 15 August 1914

ing. A railroad system to haul equipment to the site and earth from the dig had to be constructed; and terminals, wharves, coaling stations, dry docks, machine shops, and warehouses had to be built. The builders encountered many obstacles, among the worst of which was the high death rate caused by yellow fever. Walter Reed, William Gorgas, and other doctors and researchers, having identified the mosquito as the main carrier of the deadly illness, were able to triumph over yellow fever, reducing the death rate from 17.6 percent to 0.6 percent. In the torrential rains common in the Canal Zone — in some years during construction over ten feet of rain fell annually — mud slides and rock avalanches were commonplace. Repeated avalanches, which could bury shovels, railroad tracks, locomotives, and men under tons of rock and dirt, were especially worrisome on the east bank of the Culebra Cut. As one observer noted, "No one could say when the sun went down at night what the condition of the Cut would be when the sun arose the next morning. . . . The work of months and years might be blotted out by an avalanche of earth or the toppling over of a small mountain of rock." Temperatures at the bottom of

the Culebra Cut were seldom under 100 degrees and sometimes reached 130 degrees.

Engineering Triumph. The canal was completed under the able leadership of George Washington Goethals, who headed the project from 1907 to its completion. Goethals engineered a series of canal locks and a reservoir system by which ships were raised and lowered through the canal. The amount of earth removed from the fifty miles of the construction site would have been enough to construct sixty-three pyramids the size of the Great Pyramid of Cheops. Formed into a shaft with a base the size of a city block, the column of earth removed from the canal would tower nineteen miles into the air. Through his personable management style, Goethals inspired camaraderie and motivated workers to finish the canal nearly a year ahead of schedule. Asked by a journalist how he had achieved results where those before him had failed, Goethals replied, "The pride everyone feels in the work."

Early Years. The fifty-one-mile canal opened to shipping on 14 August 1914, though formal ceremonies opening the canal were not held until 12 July 1915. With

The effects of the dreaded yellow fever were recorded by James Stanley Gilbert in his 1911 poem:

Yellow Eyes
You are going to have the fever,
Yellow eyes!
In about ten days from now
Iron bands will clamp your brow;
Your tongue resemble curdled cream,
A rusty streak the center seam;
Your mouth will taste of untold things,
With claws and horns and fins and wings;
Your head will weigh a ton or more,
And forty gales within it roar!

Source: James Stanley Gilbert, *Panama Patchwork* (New York: Trow Press, 1911).

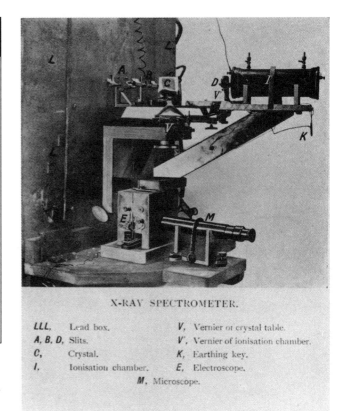

X-RAY SPECTROMETER.

LLL,	Lead box.	*V,*	Vernier of crystal table.
A, B, D,	Slits.	*V',*	Vernier of ionisation chamber.
C,	Crystal.	*K,*	Earthing key.
I,	Ionisation chamber.	*E,*	Electroscope.
	M, Microscope.		

An early instrument used to observe the effect of passing X rays through crystals

World War I consuming Europe, traffic on the canal remained relatively light. During its first three years of operation only four or five ships a day passed through the canal. With the war's end, however, the canal came into heavy use. In July 1919, for example, an armada of thirty U.S. ships returning from the war zone traveled through the canal in just two days. A trip around South America's Cape Horn would have delayed their journey by weeks.

Source:
David McCullough, *The Path Between the Seas: The Creation of the Panama Canal: 1870–1914* (New York: Simon & Schuster, 1977).

DEVELOPMENTS IN CHEMISTRY AND PHYSICS

The Genesis of Modern Plastics. The decade from 1910 to 1919 was notable for many discoveries that would lead to startling technological advancements later in the century. One of the most notable developments was the beginning of the modern age of plastics, which originated with the work of the Belgian-born American chemist Leo Hendrik Baekeland. As is the case with many important breakthroughs, Baekeland's discovery was serendipitous. Chemists in 1909 often faced the difficult problem of removing chemical residues from their equipment, and Baekeland thought that he might be able to invent a solvent that could do the job. But first, because he did not have any chemical residue at hand, he set about creating some difficult residue to experiment on by combining phenol with formaldehyde. When he tried to dissolve the substance he created, no solvent worked. It then occurred to Baekeland that the substance he had created might itself have useful applications, and he set about improving the resinous mass to make it harder and tougher. Placing the reagents under suitable temperatures and pressures, he discovered that he could create a liquid that when cooled took on the shape of its container. He named the resultant plastic after himself, and Bakelite, marketed in 1917, was the first thermosetting plastic (a plastic that will not soften under heat once it has set).

Neon Lights. In 1910 the French chemist Georges Claude demonstrated that electricity passed through noble gases (monoatomic, chemically inert gases, also called inert gases) produced light. The red light produced by running an electrical current through neon produced the most spectacular result. Glassmakers and advertising executives soon recognized that glass tubing filled with neon and shaped into letters could be used as those bright roadway signs that advertise shops.

Superconductivity. In 1911 H. Kamerlingh Onnes, a Dutch scientist, unexpectedly discovered superconductivity in his Cryogenic Laboratory at the University of Leiden. He found that at temperatures approaching absolute zero metals lose resistance to the flow of electric current. Once a current is started in such a supercooled metal, the electron flow will continue almost unimpeded. For his discovery Onnes won a Nobel Prize in 1913. European and American scientists would continue to search for methods and materials that could expand the practical applications of superconductivity.

X-Ray Crystallography. The German physicist Max von Laue demonstrated in 1912 that when X rays were passed through crystal structures they were scattered in

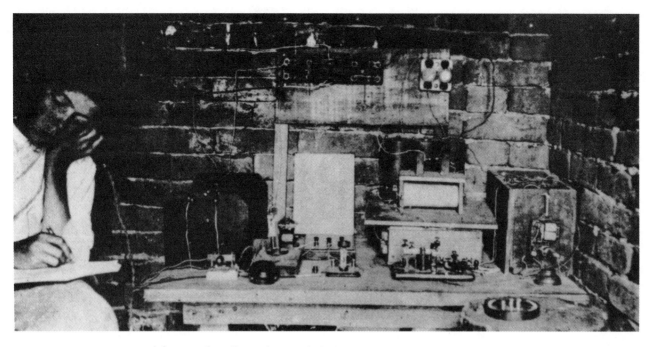

A homemade radio receiver, typical of thousands being set up in the 1910s

discrete patterns that could be identified on photographic plates. English physicists William Henry Bragg and his son William Lawrence Bragg successfully argued that the patterns on the photographic plate could be used to identify the exact location of atoms in the crystal. The science of crystallography was born. Laue won the Nobel Prize in physics in 1914 for his discovery.

Sonar. French physicist Paul Langevin revolutionized oceanography with the invention of sonar in 1917. In 1880 Pierre Curie had discovered the piezoelectric effect, which he demonstrated could generate ultrasonic sound waves. Langevin reasoned that ultrasonic sound waves (sound waves of extremely short wavelengths) would reflect off objects and bounce back to the sender. (Common sound waves are much longer than ultrasonic waves, bend around physical obstructions, and reflect back to the observer less efficiently.) The time it takes for the emitted ultrasonic waves to travel to the reflecting object and return could be used to fix the distance of the object. Since ultrasonic sound can easily travel through water, Langevin's sonar worked superbly to detect schools of fishes well as German submarines (a serious problem to Allied shipping interests during World War I). Today sonar is used by fishermen to find their prey and by oceanographers to map the ocean's floor.

Sources:

William H. Bragg, *X-Rays and Crystal Structure*, in *Physical Sciences*, volume 7, edited by W. L. Bragg and G. Porter (Amsterdam: Elsevier, 1970);

Tibor Zoltai and James H. Stout, *Mineralogy: Concepts and Principles* (Minneapolis: Burgess, 1984).

DEVELOPMENTS IN RADIO

Development of Radio. Founded on the work of such men as James Clerk Maxwell, Heinrich R. Hertz, and Guglielmo Marconi, radio technology advanced rapidly in the first decade of the century. In 1901 Reginald A. Fessenden invented a high-frequency alternator (a device that produces alternating current) to produce a continuous radio wave instead of the spark-generated pulses Marconi had managed in his Morse code transmission. Fessenden also discovered a way to modulate the amplitude of radio waves, and on Christmas Eve 1906 he broadcast the first voice radio transmission. That same year Lee De Forest invented the triode vacuum tube, or audion. Edwin H. Armstrong in 1912 used the audion to create a "regenerative circuit" by which incoming radio signals could be amplified to such a degree that they could be played over audio speakers. (The early history of radio was rampant with lawsuits. Armstrong's invention was soon challenged in court by De Forest, who claimed that he had actually invented the regenerative circuit three years earlier.)

Superheterodyne. The broadcast radio revolution of the 1920s owed much to Armstrong's improvements on his 1912 discovery. In 1918 he developed the superheterodyne radio receiver, which would allow for the reception of a wide range of radio transmissions. In 1919 Armstrong's receiver went into mass production. That same year shortwave radio was invented, and the Radio Corporation of America (RCA) was founded. The industry was poised for the explosive growth it would experience in the 1920s. Although De Forest had for a brief

The power of radio was demonstrated in 1912 during the sinking of the *Titanic*. The White Star liner *Titanic* (American owned but with a British crew), then the largest ship in the world, sank on its maiden voyage from Southampton, England, to New York City on the night of 14 April 1912. Dubbed "unsinkable," the ship symbolized the advances in technology and engineering that made its construction possible. Yet, when another ship signaled the radio operator on the *Titanic* of the perils of icebergs ahead, he ignored the warnings, signaling back that he was busy with other matters. Soon thereafter, at 11:40 P.M., the ship sideswiped an iceberg in the North Atlantic, its starboard bow plates buckled under the impact, and it began to sink. The 882-foot-long luxury liner, whose eight decks rose to the height of an eleven-story building, would go down in just two hours and forty minutes. Believing the ship invincible, ship designers had supplied lifeboats for only about half its passengers. As the passengers scrambled aboard the lifeboats, the ship's previously lackadaisical radio operator frantically signaled for help using the SOS Morse code signal. Fifty-eight miles away the radio operator on board the *Carpathia* picked up the call for help from the *Titanic* and raced to the rescue. Three and a half hours later the *Carpathia* was able to pick up 705 lifeboat survivors who otherwise faced certain death by exposure, but 832 passengers and 685 crew members were drowned. In New York, Guglielmo Marconi, who had invented the radio used by the two ships, was hailed as a hero in newspaper editorials.

Sources: Steven Biel, *Down With the Old Canoe: A Cultural History of the Titanic Disaster* (New York: Norton, 1996);

Michael Davie, *Titanic: The Death and Life of a Legend* (New York: Knopf, 1987);

Stephen Kern, *The Culture of Time and Space, 1880–1918* (Cambridge, Mass.: Harvard University Press, 1983).

Science thrives on inquiry, and scientists must often reevaluate their firmly held beliefs. In his article titled "The Past and Present Status of the Ether" appearing in the August 1910 edition of *Popular Science Monthly,* professor Arthur Gordon Webster of Clark University addressed the anxiety caused by widespread reevaluation: "many persons believe that physics is now undergoing a sort of crisis, in which many of our most cherished ideas are about to be relegated to the scrap-heap." One such idea was the belief in an interplanetary vaporous ether, which was, Webster noted, "becoming unfashionable." As the decade progressed more and more scientists came to realize that the reason they were having trouble detecting the elusive interplanetary ether was that it did not exist. Indeed, as early as 1887 American physicists Albert Michelson and E. W. Morley had conducted an experiment — known as the Michelson-Morley experiment — that failed to detect any difference in the speed of light caused by the Earth's motion, something that would be expected if ether existed in interplanetary space.

EINSTEIN'S THEORIES

Einstein and Relativity. Albert Einstein electrified the physics community in the United States with his special theory of relativity in 1905 and his general theory of relativity in 1916. In his special theory of relativity Einstein posited that space and time are not absolute and independent realities. Indeed, the word *relativity* indicates that motion, space, and time cannot be measured from a fixed point but are relative to the observer measuring them. The speed of light, however, is a constant in all frames of reference. As an object approaches the speed of light, it appears to contract in the direction of motion; its mass increases; and time, as measured by a clock moving with the object, slows. Einstein asserted that mass and energy are interchangeable properties: $E=mc^2$, where energy is said to be equivalent to mass times the square of the speed of light. Since the speed of light is 186,000 miles per second, Einstein's theory suggested that a small mass could be transformed into a enormous amount of energy (his theory was shown to be true with the fission reaction of the atomic bomb). His 1905 theory applied only to systems that move at a constant velocity relative to each other.

The General Theory of Relativity. Einstein's general theory of relativity extended his work of eleven years earlier to account for systems moving relative

time broadcast a radio program of music and news prior to 1910, the 1910s did not see the advent of commercial radio. That would have to wait until 1920 when Pittsburgh's KDKA began broadcasting.

Sources:
Gleason Archer, *History of Radio to 1926* (New York: American Historical Society, 1938);

Tom Lewis, *Empire of the Air: The Men Who Made Radio* (New York: HarperCollins, 1991);

W. Rupert Maclaurin and R. Joyce Harman, *Invention and Innovation in the Radio Industry* (New York: Macmillan, 1949).

to each other at any velocity, even if those velocities are changing. It is principally concerned with the large-scale effects of gravitation. Recognizing that inertial mass (the mass derived from measurements of acceleration) and gravitational mass (mass from measurements of gravitation intensity) were the same, Einstein asserted that material bodies — planets, stars, and other masses — produce curvatures in space-time. The space surrounding massive bodies is distorted, or curved. Einstein's general theory holds that clocks run more slowly in stronger gravitational fields and even light is bent in the curvature of space associated with a powerful gravitational field.

A New Physics. Einstein noted that the laws of classical physics, developed by Sir Isaac Newton in the seventeenth century, usually gave results close to those predicted by general relativity. But in some instances he suggested that there might be observable differences in the two theories. Einstein predicted that the perihelion (closet point of orbit) of a planet's orbit would be slightly further from the body it orbited than classical physics predicted. Just such a difference in perihelion was observed in the orbit of Mercury. The views of the general theory were given further credence when A. S. Eddington measured the curvature in starlight passing near the sun during a solar eclipse in May 1919.

Sources:

Peter G. Bergmann, *The Riddle of Gravitation* (New York: Scribners, 1968);

Albert Einstein, *Relativity: The Special and General Theory*, fifteenth edition (London: Methuen, 1954);

Einstein and Leopold Infield, *The Evolution of Physics: The Growth of Ideas from Early Concepts to Relativity and Quanta* (New York: Simon & Schuster, 1938);

Max Jammer, *The Conceptual Development of Quantum Mechanics* (New York: McGraw-Hill, 1966).

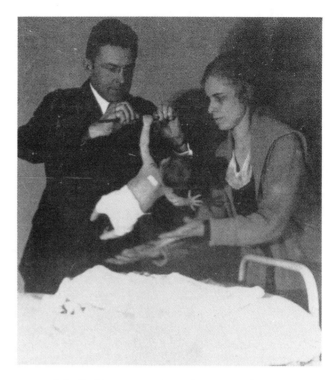

John B. Watson tests the tonic grasp reflex in a newborn in 1916

THE FERMENT IN SOCIAL SCIENCE

A Science of Society? Science and technology captured the imaginations and improved the lives of millions of Americans in the decade following the turn of the century. Since science could make communication across vast distances instantaneous, revolutionize transportation, and cure diseases, many Americans believed that scientific methods could also improve individuals, societies, and governments. During the 1910s the hope that social scientists could transform society was very much alive. Psychologist John B. Watson's theory of behavioral psychology suggested that man had the ability to learn to control human behavior. Frederick Winslow Taylor's *The Principles of Scientific Management* (1911) proposed new routines to increase worker efficiency and industrial productivity. In 1919 the sociologist Thorstein Veblen published *The Place of Science in Modern Civilization* as well as a series of articles in the *Dial* that were to become the basis for his *The Engineers and the Price System* (1921). Veblen suggested that "an effectual revolutionary overturn in America," a technocracy, could be shaped by the nation's engineers and technicians. Science in this way could help achieve tangible social progress.

Popularizing Darwin. During the 1910s the impact of Darwin's theory of evolution (which by then had been accepted by the great majority of biologists and geologists) was still churning up vigorous discussion in the scientific community and widespread debate in society at large. *American Naturalist, Scientific American,* and *Popular Science Monthly* were among the journals that published articles on Darwinism. In 1910 the articles in *Popular Science Monthly* on Darwinism included "Darwin's Place in Future Biology" and "The Evolution of Man and Its Control." James Arthur Thompson's *Darwinism and Human Life* (1910) was one of the many books read by Americans that popularized Darwin's theory and, as some social scientists held at the time, its implications for "social selection" through eugenics.

Eugenics. The eugenics movement was a vibrant and controversial topic in the 1910s. Eugenics holds that intelligence, like other human traits (such as hair color), is passed on from parents to offspring through the genes. Professor Edward L. Thorndike of Teachers College, Columbia University, argued that intellectual differences "are due in large measure to original, inborn characteristics." Supporters of eugenics held that criminality, imbecility, and laziness were also inheritable traits and that those who demonstrated these traits should be discouraged, or prohibited, from reproducing. Dr. C. B. Davenport argued the eugenicist position in the January 1911 issue of *Popular Science Monthly:* "Our only hope, indeed,

Sources:

Peter J. Bowler, *The Non-Darwinian Revolution* (Baltimore: Johns Hopkins University Press, 1988);

Dr. C. B. Davenport, "Euthenics and Eugenics," *Popular Science Monthly*, 78 (January 1911): 16–20;

Howard A. Knox, "Measuring Human Intelligence: A Progressive Series of Standardized Tests Used by the Public Health Service to Protect Our Racial Stock," *Scientific American* (9 January 1915): 52–53;

Dorothy Ross, *The Origins of American Social Science* (New York: Cambridge University Press, 1991);

Edward L. Thorndike, "Eugenics: With Special Reference to Intellect and Character," *Popular Science Monthly*, 83 (August 1913): 125–138.

for the real betterment of the human race is in better mating. If any one doubts this let him ask the agriculturalist. Let him ask the Florida orange grower, who no longer fears the frost, if heredity is a 'terrible' fact ... let him ask the breeder of improved Holstein cattle whether he would, if he could, annihilate the fact of transmission of qualities; they would laugh in your face; they would assure you that heredity is their main reliance and their most precious tool. So to the eugenist heredity stands as the one great hope of the human race; its savior from imbecility, poverty, disease, immortality."

Application of Eugenics. Thorndike argued that "we already know enough to justify us in providing for the original intellect and character of man in the future with a higher, purer source than the muddy streams of the past." And, as was often the case among eugenicists, he intimated that social and governmental policies should derive from eugenics. In its response to massive immigration the American government was often not far from endorsing such views. During the 1910s the U.S. Public Health Service at Ellis Island sorted out immigrants "who may, because of their mental make-up, become a burden to the State or who may produce offspring that will require care in prisons, asylums, or other institutions." Many times such "mental defectives" were refused admission into the country.

FREUDIAN THEORY

Freud's Visit. In September 1909 Sigmund Freud traveled from Europe to the United States and delivered a series of five lectures at Clark University in Worcester, Massachusetts. Freud's lectures to his American audience stimulated interest in psychoanalysis among many in the lecture hall audience, including G. Stanley Hall, the psychologist who was president of Clark, while others in the United States were exposed to his ideas through their reading of books and articles.

Popularizers. Though Freud's work was only just beginning to be known in the America of the 1910s, his theories did have American popularizers. One such American account of Freudian psychology was made by Professor H. W. Chase of the University of North Carolina. In an article in *Popular Science Monthly* of April 1911, Chase explained "Freud's Theories of the Unconscious" to his readers: "By unconscious action, we understand action which goes on without our being aware of it, and yet which seems intelligent, adapted to a purpose." Freud, Chase noted, "In the course of a long practice with neurotic patients ... arrived grad-

Sigmund Freud in 1916 with his sons Ernst and Martin at home on leave

ually at theories of the mechanism of the unconscious." Ideas that are too disturbing or distressing to the conscious mind are repressed into the unconscious mind, but they do not disappear. Repressed ideas and desires influence our thoughts and actions at every turn. In dreams, in verbal slips (Freudian slips), and through psychoanalysis the unconscious desires reveal themselves. Once a person's repressed desires are brought into the conscious mind, Freud's popularizers explained, those desires could either be accepted and acted upon, rejected and dismissed, or sublimated (that is, rechanneled into other efforts). Freud's views on infantile sexuality, the id, superego, and ego, as well as his emphasis on "the talking cure" of psychoanalysis as a means to treat neurosis were increasingly discussed in the United States during the decade (though whether or not Freudian psychoanalysis was "scientific" remained in question).

Impact of the War. In 1910 the International Association for Psychoanalysis was founded, and by 1914 psychoanalytic societies existed in the United States, England, Germany, Switzerland, and else-

where. The need to treat soldiers suffering from shell shock and civilians suffering traumas of war spurred an interest in Freudian analysis as well as other schools of psychology. As one journalist noted in 1919, "Perhaps in no field of science has the war stimulated such sudden and such notable advances as in that of the psychologist. He has had unprecedented opportunity to observe the behavior of men under conditions of stress; and he has been called on to make tests, and perforce to devise machines and methods of test, on a scale never before contemplated. He has proved his technique to himself and to others, so that he now stands on a level of achievement and recognition that he would not have attained in years of normal activity."

Sources:
H. W. Chase, "Freud's Theories of the Unconscious," *Popular Science Monthly,* (April 1911): 355–363;

Sigmund Freud, *The Origin and Development of Psychoanalysis* (South Bend, Ind.: Gateway, 1965);

Nathan G. Hale Jr., *Freud and the Americans: The Beginnings of Psychoanalysis in the United States, 1876–1917* (New York: Oxford University Press, 1971);

"Review of the Year 1918," *Scientific American* (4 January 1919): 9.

Robert Goddard posing with the first liquid-fueled rocket in 1926

GEOLOGY

Continental Drift. U.S. geologist Frank Bursley Taylor first put forward the theory of continental drift in a lecture in 1908. (People had never seriously questioned the permanence of the earth's continents until Sir Francis Bacon, in 1620, noted that the coastlines of South America and Africa, if pushed together, appeared to fit into each other like the pieces of a puzzle.) In 1912 the German geologist and meteorologist Alfred L. Wegener daringly proposed that about two hundred million years ago all the earth's land was a single gigantic land mass, which he called *pangaea* (Greek for "all-earth"). His theory set off a scientific debate that continued for many years. Wegener argued that the Earth's crust floated on a basalt layer and that over millions of years the original single supercontinent had broken up into the seven continents. Wegener was able to demonstrate that mountain chains on separate continents were composed of similar rock, and he cited as evidence the unusual presence of coal deposits in Antarctica as well as the glacial features in the topography of land near the equator. His detailed studies showed that the west coast of North America was moving six feet a year, and that in the course of a century Greenland had moved a mile further away from Europe. It was not until American geologist Harry Hammond Hess developed his theory of spreading sea floors in the 1960s that Wegener's views became widely accepted.

Earth's Core. In 1914 the German-born American geologist Beno Gutenberg put forward his theory that the Earth's core is liquid. He asserted that the Earth's mantle and lithosphere surround a molten core of heavy metals (now believed to be composed of nickel and iron in a 1-to-9 ratio). Gutenberg based his conclusion on his studies of earthquakes. Large earthquakes send off massive waves of energy. These vibrations are sometimes large enough to be measurable everywhere on Earth. Gutenberg found that there were shadow zones on the planet where no waves are found. By studying large earthquakes and the resultant pattern of resonant waves measured around the world, he argued that a liquid core of about forty-two hundred miles in diameter refracted the energy waves and caused the shadow zones. The line dividing the molten core and the mantle is named the "Gutenberg discontinuity" in his honor.

Sources:

Alfred Lothar Wegener, *The Origin of Continents and Oceans* (New York: Dutton, 1924);

Peter J. Wyllie, *The Dynamic Earth: Textbook in Geosciences* (New York: Wiley, 1971).

ROCKETRY

Robert Goddard and Space Travel. Robert Goddard's first trailblazing experiments in rocketry, the initial steps toward space exploration, were conducted in the 1910s. While a professor of physics at Clark University in Massachusetts, Goddard designed and tested almost every element of modern rockets. During 1915 and 1916 he experimented with rockets fueled by solid chemical propellants but found this means of propulsion unsatisfactory. Prior to his experiments with solid chemical rockets, Goddard was already contemplating the possibilities af-

A 1915 kerosene tractor designed for small farms

forded by liquid propellants. In July 1914 the U.S. Patent Office issued Goddard two patents for "Rocket Apparatus," which contained the essential features of rockets used for late-twentieth-century space travel: liquid propellants that could sustain much higher thrust than solid propellants and a nozzle and combustion chamber configuration.

A Military Rocket. In a 25 July 1915 letter Goddard wrote the secretary of the navy requesting that the navy consider developing a rocket torpedo. His inquiry was rebuffed. By January 1917, however, the Smithsonian Institution had granted Goddard $5,000 to continue his research. Shortly after receiving the grant the United States entered World War I, and Goddard put aside his liquid rocketry efforts to work for the U.S. Army Signal Corps in the development of a small rocket for use by the infantry. He successfully demonstrated a prototype of the rocket five days before the war ended on 11 November 1918.

The Liquid Launch. With the war's end, he returned to Clark University and continued his researches. His 1919 paper "A Method of Reaching Extreme Altitudes," published in the *Smithsonian Miscellaneous Collections,* offered an extensive statement of the theory and practical importance of rockets. Goddard even suggested the possibility of flight to the moon. His efforts culminated in the first liquid-propelled rocket launch in history on 16 March 1926 and many successes thereafter.

Source:
Mitchell Wilson, *American Science and Invention* (New York: Simon & Schuster, 1954).

SCIENCE ON THE FARM

Modernizing the Farm. In 1910 more than a fifth of the nation's population worked on farms, and farming remained the nation's leading business. Farm yields grew in the decade by leaps and bounds, largely because of, as Secretary of Agriculture James Wilson recognized, "the application of scientific methods in all branches of farming." The farmer with hoe and scythe had been transformed in many regions into the farmer with a harvester.

Fertilizers. The use of chemical fertilizers had doubled between 1900 and 1910, and during the 1910s the growth of the fertilizer industry continued unabated. One of the greatest achievements in the history of chemistry — judged from the practical perspective of its utility for the population at large — was the invention by German scientists of a process for "fixing" atmospheric nitrogen into chemical fertilizers. Used in the United States and around the world, the new process made high-quality fertilizers both more readily available and lower in cost.

Outreach. Advances in agricultural methods are of little value if farmers are not made aware of them. Along with farming periodicals and broad ranging advertising by some manufacturers of farming equipment, the Department of Agriculture distributed leaflets and other short tracts on a wide range of farm issues. In 1912 the department printed ten million copies of bulletins for farmers. The efforts of the Farm Bureau Federation, land grant colleges, and the Hampton Institute and Tuskegee Institute (which trained African American farmers in scientific agriculture) accelerated the introduction of science and technology on the nation's farms.

A tank leading the way for members of the U.S. 107th Infantry

Source:
Ian McNeil, *An Encyclopedia of the History of Technology* (London: Routledge, 1990).

THE TECHNOLOGY OF WAR

Deadly Inventions. The four years and four months of war that consumed Europe from the summer of 1914 until the armistice of 11 November 1918 redirected the focus of much science and technology. The death struggle in Europe slowed the progress of the pure sciences, but technology, at least insofar as it supported the war effort, flourished. Many European and American scientists and engineers served in the war effort. New products were developed for the war, including plastics, rayon, cellulose acetate (for film), and aluminum alloys. The machine gun, invented in the mid nineteenth century and substantially improved and refined by Hiram Maxim during the 1880s, became one of the most deadly weapons of World War I. Col. I. N. Lewis developed a lightweight machine gun that was a significant improvement over those in use, and within a year of entering the war in 1917 the United States was outproducing every other country in the manufacture of machine guns and grenades. Tanks were developed in Britain with the support of Winston Churchill, then first lord of the admiralty. The vehicle's code name during its development was "water tank," a name that was used both to confuse the enemy as to the secret weapon's actual purpose and to appease officials within the government who otherwise might have questioned the propriety of a land-based vehicle being overseen by the admiralty office. Brought into production in Britain in 1915, the tank was first deployed at the Battle of the Somme in September 1916.

U.S. Engineers' Wartime Efforts. A small contingent of U.S. troops arrived in France along with Gen. John J. Pershing, commander of the American Expeditionary Forces, in June 1917. By that time the war in Europe had dragged on for nearly three years, and the soldiers and weapons of both the Allied forces and Central Powers were wearing thin. The American technological ability to make high explosives and gunpowder as well as field artillery was crucial in the final year of the war. In Nashville, Tennessee, the largest explosives factory in the world turned out more than one hundred thousand pounds of explosive powder daily, and there were scores of smaller plants across the country dedicated to similar pursuits. Technological innovations — such as a centrifugal method for drying finished powder and a cyanamide process for making nitric acid — were developed by American scientists. Incendiary bombs, flamethrowers, and colored rockets were invented or improved upon. University of Chicago professor of astronomy Forest Ray Moulton designed a more aerodynamic artillery shell. Heavy guns mounted on railroad cars — an innovation

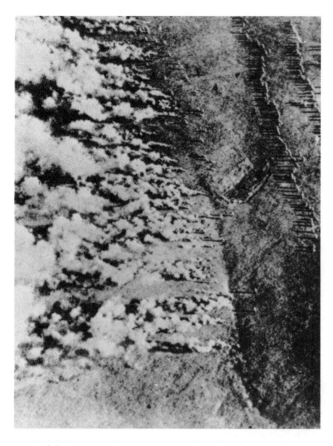

Aerial view of a German gas attack on the eastern front

novelty of their invention was the use of a long copper wire running out from the mine that, when coming into contact with the metal hull of a passing ship, closed an electrical circuit and detonated the explosion. In 1917 the U.S. Army had only fifty-five airplanes and thirty-five pilots, but by war's end the United States had forty-five squadrons of planes and more than seven hundred pilots. On 4 July 1917 the first "Liberty engine" for an aircraft was delivered at Washington, D.C., and was soon in widespread production and use. Not a single U.S.-made aircraft ever made it to the front, as all aerial combat was conducted in French or British planes.

The Scientists' War. Trench warfare and modern science combined to make World War I the most costly war ever fought. A report in 1915 noted that each step in the "methods of destruction . . . is a further application of scientific knowledge. Indeed, in the present European war the application of such knowledge seems to be reaching the utmost limit of ingenuity. It may almost be called a chemist and physicist war with its application of physics in aerial navigation and its use of submarines, of telephones, wireless telegraphy, searchlights, and range-finders, and the application of chemistry in the manufacture of its many explosives, the manufacture of hydrogen for airships, its illuminating bombs and flares and latest of all in the manufacture of poisonous gases to be used for tactical purposes."

Gas Warfare. For much of the war mustard gas was the chemical weapon of choice. A greenish-yellow gas with a pungent odor, its high density meant that it could be especially effective against soldiers hunkered down in trenches on a windless day. The gas would stay suspended just above the ground, sink into the trenches, and torment victims through the agonizing process of burning the mucous membranes of their lungs and eyes until they collapsed in searing pain and died. Though the Germans had initiated the use of poison gas in April 1915, the Allies soon followed suit, and by the end of the war U.S. chemists had experimented with more than two dozen deadly gases for use in the war.

Sources:

John Batchelor and Bryan Cooper, *Fighter: A History of Fighter Aircraft* (New York: Scribners, 1974);

Ezra Bowen and others, *Knights of the Air* (Alexandria, Va.: Time-Life Books, 1980);

"Chlorine Gas on the Battlefield," *Scientific American* (15 May 1915): 452;

Charles G. Grey, *The History of Combat Airplanes* (Northfield, Vt.: Norwich University, 1942);

S. L. A. Marshall, *World War I* (New York: Houghton Mifflin, 1964).

first used by Americans during the Civil War — were shipped to France. Trucks and Caterpillar tractors were also shipped overseas. Combatant and noncombatant engineers were used in every aspect of the U.S. war effort. Some helped build roads, bridges, and lightweight railroads, while others worked in electrical and mechanical repair.

Sea and Air. U.S. submarines were filled from bow to stern with new technologies. Among their innovations were electric engines that allowed U.S. subs to remain submerged longer than German U-boats. Utilizing radio technology, scientists William D. Coolidge and Max Mason developed long- and short-range listening devices, which helped to fix the range of enemy guns. Ford Motor Company produced "Eagle boats" as submarine chasers, and though only a few dozen were in use before the war ended, Ford engineers and laborers were hailed for their efficiency in production. Naval engineers, led by Ralph C. Browne, invented an improved sea mine. The

HEADLINE MAKERS

IRVING LANGMUIR

1881-1957

CHEMIST AND PHYSICIST, NOBEL LAUREATE

Education. Born in Brooklyn, New York, on 31 January 1881 to an insurance executive and his wife, Irving Langmuir studied chemistry, physics, and mathematics at Columbia University and received a degree from the university's School of Mines in metallurgical engineering in 1903. Langmuir studied under the future Nobel laureate Walther Nernst at the University of Göttingen in Germany, receiving the Ph.D. in 1906 for his dissertation on the study of heated platinum wire and low pressure gases. Upon his return to the United States he taught at the Stevens Institute of Technology.

Research Scientist. In 1909 Langmuir took a full-time position as a researcher at the General Electric Company's research laboratory in Schenectady, New York. At GE Langmuir made a major contribution to the development of the modern lightbulb when he proved that adding inert gas to the bulb enhanced the life of the tungsten filament and made the lightbulb more energy efficient. His work on a mercury vacuum pump, which created a vacuum more than one hundred times better than those in use at the time, became an important element in the development of radio tubes. He made improvements to electrical stoves and developed a hydrogen welding torch. Langmuir also investigated atomic structure and engaged in groundbreaking research on electrically charged gases that he dubbed "plasma." His plasma research was subsequently used by physicists in the development of thermonuclear fusion. During World War I he worked on nitrate production and antisubmarine defense projects. In World War II he dedicated himself to smoke-screen research and to the chemical deicing of airplanes.

The Chemistry of Surfaces. At GE during the 1910s Langmuir began his studies of surface chemis-try that led in 1932 to his becoming the second American to win the Nobel Prize in chemistry. He developed several experimental techniques for studying surface chemicals only a single molecule in thickness and developed a theory of absorption to describe the interaction of surface molecules. As the first scientist employed by an industrial research lab to receive the Nobel Prize, Langmuir's career demonstrated the usefulness of the R and D facilities in both industry and applied science.

Cloud Seeding. Toward the end of his career he became fascinated with atmospheric science, and along with V. J. Schaefer he developed techniques for "seeding" clouds with dry ice and silver iodine to make rain. Over the course of his career Langmuir, a popular public speaker, was granted sixty-three patents, published more than two hundred papers, and was awarded fifteen honorary degrees. He died of a heart attack on 16 August 1957 and has since been heralded as one of the greatest chemists in United States history.

Sources:

Thomas P. Hughes, *American Genesis: A Century of Invention* (New York: Viking-Penguin, 1989);

Leonard S. Reich, "Irving Langmuir and the Pursuit of Science and Technology in the Corporate Environment," *Technology and Culture* (October 1983): 199–221.

HENRIETTA SWAN LEAVITT

1868-1921

ASTRONOMER

Two Courses. Henrietta Swan Leavitt was born in Lancaster, Massachusetts, on 4 July 1868, one of seven children of a Congregationalist minister and his wife. She studied at Oberlin College in Ohio from 1885 to 1888. She transferred to the Society for the Collegiate Instruction of Women (later Radcliffe College of Harvard University) in Cambridge, Massachusetts, where she finished her A.B. degree in 1892. It was in Cambridge, occasioned by two courses, that Leavitt became intrigued by astronomy. Soon after graduation she suffered an illness that left her profoundly deaf.

Cataloguing Variable Stars. By 1895 Leavitt had received an appointment as a research assistant at the Harvard College Observatory in Cambridge. By 1902 she was a member of the permanent staff of the observatory and soon thereafter became the head of the observatory's photographic photometry department. As a researcher at Harvard she established a method for ranking star magnitudes on photographic plates that became a standard in the profession. She also discovered more variable stars than any other astronomer. The twenty-four hundred variables that she catalogued during her years at Harvard were about half the known variables at the time.

The Luminosity-Brightness Relationship. While studying hundreds of photographic images of Cepheid variable stars in the Southern Hemisphere's Magellanic Clouds, Leavitt made an important discovery. She observed that the brightness of a Cepheid variable star correlated with the period of its variability. She published her findings in 1908: "It is worthy of notice," she wrote, "that the brighter variables have longer periods." She worked for four more years, collecting more data and analyzing it. By 1912 she was able to assert confidently that the apparent magnitude of a Cepheid variable increases linearly with the logarithm of the period.

New Horizons. Leavitt's discovery was central to the determination of extragalactic distances. Before Leavitt's work, astronomers determined the distances between stars by the parallax method, which was effective for determining distances of up to one hundred light-years. In 1913 the Danish astronomer Ejnar Hertzsprung was able to determine the distances of a few Cepheids. Leavitt's period-luminosity correlation could then be applied to any such star to calculate its distance. Harlow Shapley also amplified upon Leavitt's groundbreaking work to calculate the relation between absolute brightness and period. Because of Leavitt's insight, astronomers had a method by which to measure accurately immense extragalactic distances of ten million light-years and more. A member of the American Association for the Advancement of Science and the Astronomical and Astrophysical Society of America, and an honorary member of the American Association of Variable Star Observers, Leavitt died of cancer on 21 December 1921.

Sources:
G. Kass-Simon and P. Farnes, eds., *Women of Science* (Bloomington: Indiana University Press, 1990);

M. B. Ogilvie, *Women in Science* (Cambridge: MIT Press, 1986).

THEODORE WILLIAM RICHARDS

1868-1928

CHEMIST, NOBEL LAUREATE

Life in Academia. Theodore William Richards was born on 31 January 1868 in Germantown, Pennsylvania. His mother, who educated him at home until he was fourteen, was a writer and poet, and his father was a painter. At fourteen he enrolled at Haverford College, and he graduated first in his class three years later. He took a second undergraduate degree summa cum laude from Harvard University in 1886 and completed the Ph.D. at Harvard two years later at the age of twenty. During the 1888–1889 academic year Richards studied in several European laboratories while on a fellowship from Harvard. In 1901 he was made professor of chemistry at Harvard, and he was director of the Wolcott Gibbs Lab there from 1912 until his death.

Precision in Atomic Weight. Richards's fascination with the precise calculation of atomic weights led to his painstaking measurement of the atomic weight of water. Though the current theory called for the ratio of oxygen to hydrogen in water to be precisely 16, Richards demonstrated that the ratio was actually 15.869, indicating that the then-current theory was in error. Previous measurements of some chemicals, Richards found, had been calculated upon impure samples. He also discovered that the atomic weight of lead that had been exposed to radioactive uranium differed from that of unexposed lead. For his determination of physical constants in atomic structures Richards in 1914 became the first American to be awarded the Nobel Prize in chemistry.

Further Achievements. Richards was an exceptional influence on the development of analytical and physical chemistry in the United States. He directed research in physical chemistry at Harvard, and many of his graduate students became distinguished professors. He also invented an improved calorimeter that measured the heat given off by chemical reactions. He made important contributions to thermochemistry, publishing more than fifty papers in the discipline. He died in Cambridge, Massachusetts, on 2 April 1928.

Sources:
Helen M. Burke, "Theodore William Richards," in *The Nobel Prize Winners: Chemistry*, edited by F. N. Magill (Pasadena, Cal.: Salem, 1991);

Sheldon J. Kopperl, "Theodore William Richards," in *American Chemists and Chemical Engineers*, edited by W. Miles (Washington, D.C.: American Chemical Society, 1976).

HENRY NORRIS RUSSELL

1877-1957

ASTRONOMER

A Princeton Professor. Henry Norris Russell was born at Oyster Bay, New York, on 25 October 1877. He was educated at home by his mother, an accomplished mathematician, and his father, a Presbyterian minister, until the age of twelve. At nineteen he graduated from Princeton insigne cum laude, the highest academic honor awarded at the university. Two years later he earned the Ph.D. in astronomy at Princeton for research on the orbits of binary stars. After a period of illness Russell continued his studies at Kings College, Cambridge University (1902–1904), where he did research at the Cavendish Laboratory. Along with Arthur R. Hinks, Russell developed a method for determining stellar parallax from photographic plates. Their technique enabled astronomers to determine more accurately the distances to far-off stars. In September 1904 Russell, again taken ill, returned to Princeton, where in 1905 he was appointed instructor of astronomy. He became professor of astronomy in 1911 and the following year was made director of the university's observatory. He remained at Princeton until he retired in 1947. Following his retirement he continued his research at the Lick Observatory and at Harvard.

Hertzsprung-Russell Diagram. Russell's most acclaimed achievement was the charting of stellar evolution. Drawing on the work of several astrophysicists, especially that of Danish astronomer Ejnar Hertzsprung, he published his famous conclusions on the origin and evolution of stars in 1913. Adopting Hertzsprung's insights into dwarf and giant stars, Russell challenged the accepted paradigm of stellar development, which held that stars evolved from blue (hot) to red (cool) stars. Russell asserted instead that red stars represented both the beginning and the ending of stellar evolution. Collecting data on hundreds of stars, Russell was able to demonstrate that when the absolute magnitude of stars was plotted against their spectral class, most stars fell on an S-shaped curve that he called "the main-sequence." Russell maintained that initially stars would heat up and contract, while later in their life cycle they would expand and cool. The Hertzsprung-Russell diagram remains the basis for astronomers' understanding of stellar origin and evolution.

Versatile Scientist. In 1912 Russell published the first analysis of light variation in eclipsing binary stars. From 1914 to 1921 he published papers on the orbits and masses of many binary stars. During World War I he worked to improve aircraft navigation for the Bureau of Aircraft Production of the army's Aviation Service. In the 1920s Russell's study of the absorption-line spectra of the sun led to the accurate hypothesis that hydrogen is the main element in stars. He was also able to analyze correctly many gases in the solar atmosphere. In 1927 he published a book of philosophical and religious speculation, *Fate and Freedom*, based on a series of lectures in religion he delivered at Yale University. Russell also studied the age of the Earth by analyzing radioactive uranium as well as thorium and lead in its crust, estimating the planet's age to be between two and eight billion years old.

Celebrated Career. Russell published hundreds of scientific papers during his career. A member of many scientific societies, he was the president of the American Philosophical Society (1931–1932), the American Association for the Advancement of Science (1933), and the American Astronomical Society (1934–1937). His most famous book is *The Solar System and Its Origins* (1935), a classic in the field. Upon his death in 1957 Russell was hailed as "the most eminent and versatile theoretical astrophysicist in the United States if not in the world."

Sources:

James B. Kaler, *Stars* (New York: Scientific American Library, 1992);

Henry Smith Williams, *Great Astronomers* (New York: Simon & Schuster, 1930).

VESTO MELVIN SLIPHER

1875-1969

ASTRONOMER

Flagstaff. Vesto M. Slipher was born into a farming family on 11 November 1875 in Mulberry, Indiana. After high school Slipher taught in a small country school. At twenty-one he enrolled at Indiana University, graduating in 1901 with a B.A. in celestial mechanics and astronomy. During the summer after graduation Slipher began work as an assistant to the renowned astronomer Percival Lowell in Flagstaff, Arizona. Slipher's position soon became permanent, and he continued working in Flagstaff for the rest of his career.

Planet Investigations. From 1901 to 1915 Slipher was Lowell's assistant. In 1902 Slipher installed a spectrograph at Lowell's observatory, and, under Lowell's guidance, used the device to search for evidence of water and oxygen on Mars and to measure the length of a day on Venus. From 1905 to 1907 he unsuccessfully searched for life on Mars, looking especially for the existence of chlorophyll. In 1909 Indiana University granted Slipher the Ph.D. on the basis of his work at Lowell's observatory. In 1912 Slipher found that Uranus's spectrum indicated that it rotated once every 10.8 hours, and he was also able to determine rotation periods for Mars, Jupiter, and Saturn through spectrographic analysis.

Interstellar Stuff. Slipher was among the first astronomers to offer evidence of the existence of both interstellar gases and interstellar dust. In 1908, during spectral studies of a binary star, Slipher found that a spectral line of calcium did not change as the rest of the observed spectrum of the binary did. He surmised that the unchanging spectral line gave evidence of interstellar gases between the binary and Earth. Furthermore, in 1912 Slipher analyzed the dust of the cloudlike nebulosity surrounding the open star cluster Pleiades. He found that clouds surrounding the bright stars of the nebula exhibited the same dark-line spectra of the stars themselves and concluded that the clouds' luminescence resulted from their reflecting the light of their companion stars. Slipher's finding showed that matter, other than planets and stars, existed in the universe, and this opened the door to further study of nebular emission and absorption patterns.

Slipher Finds That Galaxies Are Receding. In 1909 Lowell and Slipher began the study of the spectra of spiral nebulae. Many scientists held that the spiral nebulae were in the Milky Way galaxy, and Lowell believed that they might be solar systems in formation. Slipher's 1913 study of the spectra of the Andromeda nebula revealed that its spectra was consistent with the Doppler shift of an object moving toward our sun at a speed of 125 miles per second, which at the time was the greatest radial velocity known. By 1914 Slipher had made observations of fourteen spiral nebulae and had found that the majority were receding from our solar system at high rates of speed. Though many astronomers remained skeptical of Slipher's findings, Danish astronomer Ejnar Hertzsprung wrote Slipher on 14 March 1914 with congratulations: "It seems to me, that with this discovery the great question, if spirals belong to the system of the Milky Way or not, is answered with great certainty to the end, that they do not." Slipher further measured the rotational velocities of spiral nebulae and found them to be on the order of a few hundred kilometers per second. He also made spectrographic studies of the aurora and of comets.

Discovery of Pluto. In 1915 Slipher became assistant director of Lowell's observatory, and a decade after Lowell's death in 1916 he became director of the observatory, a position he held until 1952. As director he supervised the search for a ninth planet that culminated in the discovery of Pluto in 1930 by Clyde Tombaugh, a staff member at the observatory. Slipher was a member of the American Academy of Arts and Sciences and the American Philosophical Society. He was the recipient of the Paris Academy of Sciences's Lalande Prize in 1919, the National Academy of Sciences's Draper Gold Medal in 1922, and the Royal Astronomical Society's gold medal for his work in planetary spectroscopy in 1933.

Sources:

Richard Berendzen, Richard Hart, and Daniel Seeley, *Man Discovers the Galaxies* (New York: Science History Publications, 1976);

Barry Parker, "Discovery of the Expanding Universe," *Sky & Telescope* (September 1986): 227–230.

ALFRED HENRY STURTEVANT

1891-1970

GENETICIST

Meeting Morgan. Alfred Henry Sturtevant, the youngest of six children, was born on 21 November 1891 in Jacksonville, Illinois. Sturtevant's grandfather was a founder and president of Illinois College, where his father taught. Sturtevant was seven when his family moved to a farm in Alabama. In 1908 Sturtevant entered Columbia University and moved in with his oldest brother, Edgar, who taught Greek and Latin at Barnard College. Encouraged by his brother, Sturtevant submitted a paper on the inheritance patterns of the coloring of horses — an interest inspired by his days on the family farm in Alabama — to the renowned geneticist Thomas Hunt Morgan. Deeply impressed with the young undergraduate's enthusiasm for genetics, Morgan encouraged him to publish his findings in the *Biological Bulletin* in 1910.

Researcher. Morgan invited Sturtevant to join his genetics research laboratory in the autumn of 1910. Dedicated to the study of fruit flies (*Drosophila*), the small lab, dubbed the "fly room," was a fount of excitement and discovery during the ensuing decade. Morgan and his students freely exchanged experimental techniques and theories as they studied genetic inheritance patterns in fruit flies. After earning his Ph.D. under Morgan in 1914, Sturtevant stayed on as a researcher in the lab.

The First Genetic Map. Sturtevant was the first geneticist to realize that the frequency of crossing-over between genes is an index of the distance between them. With this understanding he was able to produce the first rudimentary genetic map. He later recounted that he "went home, and spent most of the night (to the neglect of my undergraduate homework) in producing the first chromosome map, including the linked genes, y, w, v, m, and r, in that order, and approximately the relative spacing, as they still appear on the standard maps." He also discovered that double crossing-over between genes can occur and that the frequency of such events is equal to or less than the sum of two single crossing-over occurrences. He published his findings in 1913.

Mutant Genes. In 1915 Sturtevant published the results of his experiments with mutant genes in fruit flies. He found that with the use of genetic mutants he could trace inheritance patterns in the flies. This work was the basis for much subsequent research that made use of mutant genes to understand genetic behavior in many organisms. In 1919 Sturtevant discovered that intersexuality in fruit flies could be accounted for by the presence of certain recessive genes. He later discovered that female fruit flies could be made to exhibit male characteristics by the introduction of a specific gene onto the chromosomes. In 1920, still working with *Drosophila*, he discovered the first reparable genetic defect.

Subsequent Career. In 1928 Sturtevant accepted an appointment with the California Institute of Technology, becoming the school's first professor of genetics. In 1929 Sturtevant found a gene that when present resulted in the production of X sperm in flies, causing the progeny of such flies almost always to be female. In the 1930s genetic researchers confirmed that the genetic maps that Sturtevant had drawn in the 1910s were accurate in their prediction of linear ordering of genes in chromosomes. During the 1940s he studied the genetic mutations in fruit flies and their effects on the development of subsequent generations. In 1951 he published a chromosome map of the fourth chromosome of *Drosophila*, in its day a significant genetic achievement. In his later career he also wrote papers on the implications of genetic research for society, and in a 1954 paper he described the possible devastating consequences of nuclear war on human genes. During the early 1960s he wrote his *A History of Genetics* (1965). In 1968 he was awarded the National Medal of Science for his many accomplishments in the field of genetics. Today he is considered by some to be the father of the Human Genome Project.

Sources:

Elof Axel Carlson, *The Gene: A Critical History* (Philadelphia: Saunders, 1966);

Maitland Edey and Donald C. Johanson, *Blueprints: Solving the Mystery of Evolution* (Boston: Little, Brown, 1989);

S. Emerson, "Alfred Henry Sturtevant," *Annual Review of Genetics,* 5 (1970): 1–4.

PEOPLE IN THE NEWS

John Jacob Abel, often called the father of modern American experimental pharmacology, isolated amino acids from blood in 1914.

In 1915 astronomer **W. S. Adams** used a spectroscope to show that giant and dwarf stars can be distinguished by differences in their spectra.

In 1915 physicist **Manson Benedicks** found that a germanium crystal converts alternating current (AC) into direct current (DC).

In 1910 **William D. Coolidge** developed a method for producing drawn tungsten filaments. His method was a major improvement over the pressed filament in use at the time.

In 1910 **Eugene Ely** became the first pilot to fly an airplane from the deck of a ship. His achievement stimulated interest in the development of aircraft carriers.

Engineer **John Fisher** was credited with the development of the modern washing machine in 1916.

In 1917 **Henry Ford** introduced a lightweight, reliable, and inexpensive farm tractor.

In 1913 the German **Hans Geiger** and British physicist **Ernest Rutherford** built a device for detecting alpha particle radiation. The apparatus was subsequently called a Geiger counter.

In 1911 **Herman Hollerith** merged the Tabulating Machine Company with two other companies to form the Computing Tabulating Recording Company. In 1924 this firm was renamed International Business Machines (IBM).

Mary Phelps Jacob, a New York socialite, developed a brassiere incorporating elastic into its structure in 1914.

In 1919 **Charles Francis Jenkins** applied for a patent on a prototype television system using spinning disks.

Engineer **Frederick Kolster** introduced a radio-compass system with transmitters on the East Coast in 1913. The innovation has been credited with saving many ships.

In 1916 the African American inventor **Garret Augustus Morgan**, along with his brother Frank, donned lifesaving gas masks that he had invented and rescued twenty people trapped in a tunnel 228 feet beneath Lake Erie. Morgan also invented the four-sided traffic signal. He was awarded a gold medal at the Second International Exposition of Sanitation and Safety in New York City for his inventions.

In 1914 **William T. Price** invented a diesel engine in which the fuel is ignited by an electrically heated Nichrome filament.

Harry Ralph Ricardo, a British engineer, demonstrated in 1913 that the knock in gasoline engines results from the spontaneous detonation of the gas mixture in the cylinder. Improvements to the octane of gasoline eventually followed.

In 1912 Dr. **Sidney Russell** invented the heating pad.

In 1913 **A. Salomen,** a German surgeon, invented mammography for the diagnosis of breast cancer.

In 1914 the autopilot was developed by **Elmer Ambrose Sperry,** but the device was not used in commercial aircraft for another two decades.

In 1910 **Charles P. Steinmetz** published his *Future of Electricity,* which warns the nation about air pollution from coal-burning plants and water pollution from untreated sewage.

AWARDS

Nobel Prize

1914

Theodore W. Richards of the United States is awarded the Nobel Prize in chemistry for determining the atomic weights of some sixty chemical elements, leading to the identification of isotopes, atoms with the same number of protons but with different numbers of neutrons. Dr. Richards was professor of chemistry at Harvard University.

DEATHS

Cleveland Abbe, 77, meteorologist who initiated daily weather reports in Cincinnati in September 1869, 28 October 1916.

Charles C. Abbott, 76, naturalist who demonstrated that human beings had lived in the Delaware River Valley during the glacial era, 27 July 1919.

Andrew T. Apple, 59, astronomer, mathematician, and professor at Franklin and Marshall College who wrote academic and popular articles on the sciences, 15 February 1918.

George F. Atkinson, 64, botanist who studied mushrooms, fungi, and ferns, 14 November 1918.

William W. Bailey, 70, botanist and author of *Botanical Collector's Handbook* (1881), 20 February 1914.

John Sellers Bancroft, 75, mechanical engineer who made improvements to the monotype machine and held about one hundred patents for various electrical and mechanical inventions, 29 January 1919.

Adolph F. Bandelier, 73, archaeologist of various sites in New Mexico, Arizona, Mexico, and Central America who wrote *The Delight Makers* (1890), a novel about Pueblo Indian life, 19 March 1914.

Joseph Barrell, 49, professor of structural geology at Yale University from 1908 until his death, 4 May 1919.

Lindon Bates Jr., 31, engineer and author of *The Russian Road to China* (1910) and *Path of the Conquistadores* (1912), 7 May 1915.

George F. Becker, 72, geologist who explored gold and diamond mines in South Africa and wrote books on the gold fields of Appalachia and Alaska, 20 April 1919.

Charles E. Bessey, 69, botanist and author of *The Essentials of Botany* (1884), 25 February 1915.

Francis Blake, 63, inventor of the Blake Transmitter in 1878, which was important in the development of the telephone, January 1913.

Lewis Boss, 65, astronomer who researched comets, solar motion, and star fields, 5 October 1912.

Cyrus F. Brackett, 81, professor of chemistry and physics at Bowdoin College and Princeton University, 29 January 1915.

Roberdeau Buchanan, 77, astronomer and author of *The Mathematical Theory of Eclipses* (1904), 18 December 1916.

Samuel J. Buck, 82, mathematician and natural philosopher at Grinnell College, 10 May 1918.

George D. Burton, 62, inventor who held more than five hundred U.S. and foreign patents, among them a process using electricity to tan hides, 7 January 1918.

Charles A. Catlin, 66, chemist who patented chemical processes relating to the manufacture of phosphates for dietetic use, 2 April 1916.

Seth Carlo Chandler, 67, astronomer and editor of the *Astronomical Journal*, 31 December 1913.

Moses T. Clegg, 41, bacteriologist who researched leprosy and other public health problems, 9 August 1918.

Aaron H. Cole, 57, biologist and popular University of Chicago lecturer who developed a method of showing the movement of sap in plant leaves, 31 December 1913.

James M. Crafts, 78, dean of chemistry at Cornell University who published *Qualitative Chemical Analysis* (1870) and *Thermometry* (1913–1915), 20 June 1917.

Theodoor De Booy, 36, archaeologist and explorer who worked for the Museum of the American Indian in New York and conducted archaeological expeditions in Cuba, Venezuela, and the Virgin Islands, 18 February 1919.

Samuel G. Dixon, 66, bacteriologist who was a professor at the University of Pennsylvania and a president of the Academy of the Natural Sciences in Philadelphia, 26 February 1918.

Charles L. Doolittle, 75, astronomer and mathematician who wrote *A Treatise on Practical Astronomy* (1885), 3 March 1919.

William L. Dudley, 55, chemist who devised a process for electroplating with iridium and also conducted spectrographic studies on tellurium, 8 September 1914.

Robert K. Duncan, 45, chemist who developed a new process for manufacturing phosphorus and made early studies of radioactivity; he wrote *The New Knowledge* (1905) and *The Chemistry of Commerce* (1907), 18 February 1914.

Caleb W. Durham, 64, inventor who developed the hot-air heater in 1875 and also developed a drainage system for houses that became known as the Durham System, 28 March 1910.

Stephen D. Field, 67, inventor of the multiple call distribution telegraph box in 1874; he also developed the electric elevator and the modern trolley in 1878, 18 May 1913.

Edward L. Greene, 72, president of the International Congress of Botanists who wrote *Landmarks of Botanical History* (1909), 10 November 1915.

Karl E. Guthe, 49, physicist who wrote *College Physics* (1911) and *Definitions in Physics* (1913), 10 September 1915.

Charles M. Hall, 51, chemist and inventor of an electrolytic process for the manufacture of aluminum, 27 December 1914.

James B. Hammond, 83, inventor who contributed to the development of the typewriter, 27 January 1913.

John P. Holland, 74, submarine designer who built *The Plunger* for the United States Navy in 1895 and later built submarines for Great Britain, Japan, and Russia, 12 August 1914.

Samuel A. King, 85, who made the first ascent in a balloon in 1851 and subsequently made a career of ascending in balloons at fairs, 3 November 1914.

Hiram S. Maxim, 76, inventor of an early machine gun, the "Maxim gun," on which the recoil served as the power for reloading; he also developed cordite, a smokeless gunpowder, 24 November 1916.

Robert H. McCormick, 69, who developed the McCormick reaper and self-binder agricultural machine that in 1875 was billed as "the greatest labor-saving device for the age," 14 March 1917.

W. J. McGee, 59, an anthropologist and geologist who studied the Tiburon Islanders and wrote many books, including *The Siouan Indians* (1897), *The Seri Indians* (1898), and *The Potable Waters of Eastern U.S.* (1895), 4 September 1912.

John McTammany, 69, developer of the player piano as well as machines to make perforated paper to play in the pianos; in 1892 he patented the first voting machine that pneumatically registered votes by making perforations in rolls of paper, 26 March 1915.

Edward C. Pickering, 72, astronomer and director of the Harvard College Observatory who studied the light and spectra of stars, 3 February 1919.

Edward S. Renwick, 89, inventor and patent expert who published the *Practical Inventor* in 1893, 19 March 1912.

Wallace C. Sabine, 50, physicist and dean of the Science School at Harvard, 10 January 1919.

John B. Smith, 53, entomologist who took the lead in the effort to eradicate the mosquito pest on the eastern seaboard; he was the author of *Economic Entomology* (1896) and *Our Insect Friends and Enemies* (1909), 12 March 1912.

Frederick Winslow Taylor, 59, engineer and theorist of scientific management who wrote *The Principles of Scientific Management* (1911), 21 March 1915.

John M. Van Vleck, 79, mathematician and astronomer who prepared astronomical calculations for the *American Ephemeris and Nautical Almanac* from 1855 to 1896, 4 November 1912.

George Westinghouse, 67, inventor and manufacturer who patented the air brake in 1868; he also took a leading role in the development of the induction motor, the gasoline engine, and the steam turbine, 12 March 1914.

Wilbur Wright, 45, inventor of the airplane along with his brother Orville, 30 May 1912.

PUBLICATIONS

G. R. Agassiz, ed., *Letters and Recollections of Alexander Agassiz* (Boston: Houghton Mifflin, 1913);

Roald Amundsen, *The South Pole*, 2 volumes, translated by A. G. Chaler, (London: Murray / New York: Keedick, 1913);

Edwin H. Armstrong, "A New Method of Receiving Weak Signals for Short Waves," *Proceedings of the Radio Club of America* (December 1919);

Armstrong, "Theory of Tuned Circuits," *Proceedings of the Radio Club of America* (May–December 1913);

Franz Boas, *The Mind of Primitive Man* (New York: Macmillan, 1911);

William Heally Dall, *Spencer Fullerton Baird* (Philadelphia: Lippincott, 1915);

Fabian Franklin, *The Life of Daniel Coit Gilman* (New York: Dodd, Mead, 1910);

George Ellery Hale, "Preliminary Results of an Attempt to Detect the Magnetic Field of the Sun," *Astrophysical Journal*, 38 (1913): 27–98;

David Starr Jordan, ed., *Leading American Men of Science* (New York: Holt, 1910);

Charles R. Mann, *A Study of Engineering Education*, Bulletin #11 (New York: Carnegie Foundation for the Advancement of Teaching, 1918);

Robert A. Millikan, *The Electron: Its Isolation and Measurement and the Determination of Some of Its Properties* (Chicago: University of Chicago Press, 1917);

Thomas Hunt Morgan, *A Critique of the Theory of Evolution* (Princeton: Princeton University Press, 1916);

Morgan, *The Physical Basis of Heredity* (Philadelphia & London: Lippincott, 1919);

Morgan, "Sex-Limited Inheritance in Drosophila," *Science*, 32 (1910): 120–122;

Morgan, A. H. Sturtevant, H. J. Muller, and C. B. Bridges, *The Mechanism of Mendelian Heredity* (New York, 1915);

Henry Norris Russell, "On the Determination of the Orbital Elements of Eclipsing Variable Stars," *Astrophysical Journal*, 35 (1912): 315–340;

Ernest Rutherford, *Radioactive Substances and Their Radiations* (New York: Cambridge University Press, 1913);

Arthur Schuster, *The Progress of Physics During Thirty-Three Years* (Cambridge: Cambridge University Press, 1911);

Harlow Shapley, "The Distances, Distribution in Space, and Dimensions of 69 Globular Clusters," *Astrophysical Journal*, 48 (1819): 154–181;

Shapley, "On the Determination of the Distances of Globular Clusters," *Astrophysical Journal*, 48 (1918): 89–124;

Shapley, "Remarks on the Sidereal Universe," *Astrophysical Journal*, 49 (1919): 311–336;

Vesto M. Slipher, "The Radial Velocity of the Andromeda Nebula," *Lowell Observatory Bulletin*, no. 58 (1913): 56–57;

Elmer Sperry, "Gyroscopic Stabilizers for Ships," *Scientific American*, 75 (1913): 203–205;

Alfred Henry Sturtevant, *An Analysis of the Effects of Selection* (Washingon, D.C.: Carnegie Institution of Washington, 1918);

Sturtevant, "The Himalayan Rabbit Case, with Some Considerations on Multiple Allelomorphs," *American Naturalist*, 47 (1913): 234–238;

Sturtevant, "The Linear Arrangement of Six Sex-Linked Factors in Drosophila," *Journal of Experimental Zoology*, 14 (1913): 43–59;

Sturtevant, *The Mechanism of Mendelian Heredity* (New York: Holt, 1915);

Frank Bursley Taylor, "Bearing of the Tertiary Mountain Belt on the Origin of the Earth's Plan," *Geological Society of America*, 21 (1910): 179–226.

CHAPTER THIRTEEN
SPORTS

by ADAM HORNBUCKLE and MARTIN MANNING

CONTENTS

Sidebars and tables are listed in italics.

1910

16 Mar. Barney Oldfield sets a new land speed record of 131.7 MPH at Daytona Beach, Florida.

Apr. William Howard Taft becomes the first president to throw out the first ball of the baseball season at a game between the Washington Senators and the Philadelphia Athletics.

19 Apr. Fred L. Cameron of Amherst, Nova Scotia, wins the fourteenth Boston Marathon in 2:28:52.6.

7 May Jockey R. Estep rides Layminster to victory in the thirty-fifth annual Preakness Stakes.

10 May Fred Herbert rides Donau to victory in the thirty-sixth annual Kentucky Derby.

29 May Glenn H. Curtiss wins the $10,000 prize offered by the *New York World* when he flies from Albany, New York, to Governors Island, New York, in 2 hours, 46 minutes, an average speed of 54.2 MPH.

30 May Jimmy Butwell rides Sweep to victory in the forty-fourth annual Belmont Stakes.

18 June Alex Smith wins the U.S. Open Golf Tournament in an eighteen-hole play-off after regulation play had ended in a three-way tie with Smith, John J. McDermott, and Macdonald Smith.

26 June Hazel Hotchkiss wins the women's singles at the U.S. Lawn Tennis Association Championship.

4 July Jack Johnson successfully defends his world heavyweight boxing title against Jim Jeffries.

2 Sept. William A. Larned wins the men's singles at the U.S. Lawn Tennis Association Championship.

10 Sept. The first Pendleton, Oregon, Round-Up begins, becoming the second oldest rodeo in the United States.

17–23 Oct. The Philadelphia Athletics win the World Series, defeating the Chicago Cubs four games to one.

1911

19 Apr. Clarence DeMar wins the fifteenth annual Boston Marathon in 2:21:39.6.

13 May Meridian, ridden by jockey George Archibald, wins the Kentucky Derby.

30 May Ray Harroun wins the first Indianapolis 500 automobile race with an average speed of 74.59 MPH.

17 June Hazel Hotchkiss repeats as the women's singles champion of the U.S. Lawn Tennis Association Championship.

24 June John J. McDermott wins the U.S. Open Golf Tournament, defeating Michael Brady and George Simpson in a play-off round to become the first American-born champion.

3 Sept. William A. Larned repeats as the men's singles champion of the U.S. Lawn Tennis Association Championship.

**17 Sept.–
5 Nov.** In a Wright biplane, Calbraith P. Rodgers completes the first transcontinental airplane flight by flying from New York City to Pasadena, California.

14–26 Oct.   The Philadelphia Athletics win the World Series, defeating the New York Giants four games to two.

24 Oct.   Orville Wright establishes a glider flight record of 9:45.

11 Nov.   The football team at Carlisle Indian School, led by Jim Thorpe, defeats Harvard University, 18–15.

1912

- George Horine of Stanford University sets a world record of 6′ 7″ in the high jump using the newly developed western roll technique.

- Eddie Collins of Philadelphia Athletics, twice steals six bases in nine-inning games.

- Robert A. Gardner of Yale University becomes first pole vaulter to surpass 13′ with a vault of 13′ 1″.

- The Amateur Fencers League of America holds its first women's national fencing championship, won by A. Baylis. The women's competition is limited to foils only.

9 Feb.   The U.S. Lawn Tennis Association rules that the defending men's singles champion must play through the entire tournament rather than gaining a bye until the challenger was decided.

22 Feb.   In San Francisco, Johnny Kilbane outpoints Abe Attell in twenty rounds for the featherweight boxing title.

11 Apr.   Rube Marquard and the New York Giants defeat the Brooklyn Dodgers, the first of Marquard's nineteen consecutive wins in the season.

19 Apr.   Michael J. Ryan of New York City wins the sixteenth annual Boston Marathon in 2:21:18.2.

20 Apr.   Fenway Park opens in Boston. In the first game played in the new stadium the Red Sox defeat the New York Highlanders, 7–6.

5 May   The 1912 Olympic Games begin in Stockholm, Sweden.

11 May   Carol Shilling rides Worth to victory in the Kentucky Derby.

30 May   Joe Dawson wins the Indianapolis 500, averaging 78.72 MPH.

20 July   Hawaiian swimmer Duke Kahanamoku establishes a world record of 61.2 seconds in the 100-meter freestyle.

2 Aug.   John J. McDermott wins the U.S. Open Golf Tournament.

26 Aug.   In the U.S. Lawn Tennis Association Championships, Maurice E. McLoughlin wins the men's title and Mary K. Browne wins the women's.

Fall   The Carlisle Indian School football team, led by Jim Thorpe's twenty-two points, defeats Army 27-6.

8 Oct.   The Boston Red Sox win the World Series, defeating the New York Giants four games to three.

28 Nov.   Willie Ritchie wins the lightweight boxing title in sixteen rounds on a foul by Ad Wolgast, in San Francisco.

1913

- Frank Klaus wins the middleweight title over Billy Papke in 15 rounds.

- Harriet D. Hammond, of Wilmington, Delaware, forms the first women's trapshooting club.

- Daytona Beach hotel owner Robert Ball introduces shuffleboard to his guests.

- Walter Johnson of the Washington Senators pitches fifty-six consecutive scoreless innings.

- Christy Mathewson of the New York Giants pitches sixty-eight consecutive innings without allowing a base on balls.

5 Feb. The New York State Athletic Commission votes unanimously to prohibit inter-racial boxing competition, in part because of racial disturbances caused by the victory of Jack Johnson, an African American fighter, over former champion Jim Jeffries.

14 Feb. The U.S. Lawn Tennis Association, though an amateur organization, fails to re-strict payment of expenses for transportation, board, and lodging.

19 Apr. Fritz Carlson of Minneapolis wins the seventeenth Boston Marathon in 2:25:14.8.

10 May Roscoe Goose rides Donerail, a 91–1 long shot, to victory in the Kentucky Derby.

30 May Jules Goux of France wins the third annual Indianapolis 500, averaging 75.93 MPH.

7 June Hudson Stuck, an Episcopalian clergyman, completes the first officially recog-nized ascent of Mount McKinley in Alaska, the highest peak in North America (20,320 feet).

13 June Mary K. Browne wins the women's title at the U.S. Lawn Tennis Association Championship.

25–28 July The United States wins the Davis Cup for the first time since 1902, defeating Great Britain three matches to two.

14 Aug. Maurice E. McLoughlin wins the men's title at the U.S. Lawn Tennis Associa-tion Championship.

Sept. Coal magnate James A. Gilmore becomes president of the minor Federal League and plans to challenge the National and American Leagues for the best baseball players.

20 Sept. Francis Ouimet, a twenty-year-old amateur, defeats two British professionals, Harry Vardon and Ted Ray, in an eighteen-hole play-off round to win the U.S. Open Golf Tournament.

7–11 Oct. The Philadelphia Athletics win the World Series, defeating the New York Giants four games to one.

1 Nov. Notre Dame wins its first football game with Army, 35–13.

23 Dec. George Chip knocks out Frank Klaus in five rounds to win the middleweight title in Pittsburgh.

1914

- E. G. "Cannonball" Baker establishes a transcontinental motorcycle speed record of 11 days, 12 hours, 10 minutes.

- James A. Gilmore's Federal League plays its first season in competition with the National and American Leagues. Gilmore offers established players substantial salary increases to join his fledgling organization.

- The Pacific Coast League of Canada admits the Portland Rosebuds, a hockey team from the United States.

- The Yale Bowl, a new stadium capable of accommodating sixty-one thousand spectators, opens in New Haven, Connecticut.

21 Mar.   In the first U.S. Figure Skating Championship Norman N. Scott of Montreal, Canada, wins the men's division, Theresa Weld of Boston wins the women's division, and Jeannie Chevalier and Scott win the pair's competition.

7 Apr.   In Brooklyn Al McCoy knocks out George Chip in the first round for the middleweight title.

20 Apr.   James Duffey of Hamilton, Ontario, wins the eighteenth Boston Marathon in 2:25:01.

9 May   John McCabe rides Old Rosebud to victory in the fortieth annual Kentucky Derby.

16 May   The Grand League of American Horseshoe Players organizes in Kansas City, Kansas, and standardizes equipment, procedures, and rules for the sport.

30 May   Rene Thomas, averaging 82.47 MPH, wins the fourth annual Indianapolis 500.

9 June   Kid Williams takes the bantamweight title by knocking out Johnny Coulon in three rounds in Vernon, California.

4 July   Eight men from Harvard win the Grand Challenge Cup at the Henley Royal Regatta in England, marking the first victory of an American crew in the event. The Union Boat Club of Boston takes second place.

15 Aug.   Australia defeats the United States in Davis Cup competition, three matches to two.

21 Aug.   Walter Hagen wins the U.S. Open Golf Tournament, defeating amateur Charles Evans Jr.

1 Sept.   Mary K. Browne wins the women's division of the U.S. Lawn Tennis Association Championship, and Richard Norris Williams wins the men's title.

9–13 Oct.   The Boston Braves win the World Series, defeating the Philadelphia Athletics four games to none.

1915

- Charles C. Pell captures the first of twelve national racquets singles titles he will win in the next nineteen years.

- Norman Taber establishes a world record of 4:12.6 for the mile.

- The Pacific Coast League of Canada admits a hockey team from Seattle, Washington, the Seattle Metropolitans.

- Ty Cobb sets a major league record of 96 stolen bases in a season, which stood until Maury Wills stole 104 bases in 1962.

- William B. Huey of Chicago wins the three-cushion billiard title to become the only amateur billiard player to gain a professional championship.

5 Apr.   Jess Willard knocks out Jack Johnson in the twenty-sixth round for the world heavyweight boxing championship in Havana, Cuba.

19 Apr.   Edouard Fabre of Montreal, Canada, wins the nineteenth annual Boston Marathon in 2:31:41.2.

6 May   George Herman "Babe" Ruth, a Boston Red Sox pitcher, hits the first home run of his career against the New York Yankees at the Polo Grounds in New York City.

8 May   Joe Notler rides Regret to victory in the forty-first Kentucky Derby.

31 May   Ralph De Palma, averaging 89.84 MPH, wins the fifth annual Indianapolis 500.

12 June   Molla Bjurstedt, a Norwegian, wins the women's division of the U.S. Lawn Tennis Association Championship. She becomes the first foreigner to win the title.

18 June   Jerome D. Travers becomes the second amateur to win the U.S. Open Golf Tournament.

27 July   The American Lawn Bowls Association organizes in Buffalo, New York.

8 Sept.   William M. Johnston wins the men's division of the U.S. Lawn Tennis Association Championship. The event moves from Newport, Rhode Island, to the West Side Tennis Club in Forest Hills, New York.

Fall   Professional football teams from Toledo, Youngstown, Akron, and Dayton join Canton, Massillon, and Columbus in the Ohio League.

8–13 Oct.   The Boston Red Sox win the World Series, defeating the Philadelphia Phillies four games to one.

21 Dec.   U.S. District Court judge Kenesaw Mountain Landis settles an antitrust suit between the Federal League and the American and National Leagues.

1916

1 Jan.   In the second Tournament of Roses Association football game (first played in 1902), Washington State University defeats Brown University 14–0. This annual football contest will become known as the Rose Bowl in 1923.

17 Jan.   The Professional Golfers' Association (PGA) is organized.

1 Apr.   The Amateur Athletic Union (AAU) holds both the first women's indoor and outdoor national swimming championships.

19 Apr.   Arthur V. Roth of Roxbury, Massachusetts, wins the Boston Marathon in 2:27:16.4.

13 May   Johnny Loftus rides George Smith to victory in the Kentucky Derby.

30 May   Dario Resta, averaging 84 MPH, wins the Indianapolis 500, the distance of which was reduced to three hundred miles. The race is not held in 1917 and 1918 because of World War I.

12 June   Molla Bjurstedt wins the women's division of the U.S. Lawn Tennis Association Championship.

30 June   Charles "Chick" Evans Jr., an amateur, wins the U.S. Open Golf Tournament. His 286 total stood as a record until 1936. Competition was suspended because of World War I and resumed in 1919.

22 July   The Bethlehem Steel Company soccer team wins the National Challenge Cup. Earlier in the year the same team had won the American Challenge Cup.

30 July   *The New York Times* reports that women golfers are allowed only restricted access to most courses in New York and New Jersey.

6 Sept.   Richard Norris Williams wins the men's division of the U.S. Lawn Tennis Association Championship.

30 Sept.   The Boston Red Sox defeat the New York Giants 8–3, ending the longest winning streak in major league baseball history at twenty-six games.

7 Oct.   Georgia Tech defeats Cumberland College of Lebanon, Tennessee, 222–0, the most lopsided college football game in history.

7–12 Oct.   The Boston Red Sox win the World Series, defeating the Brooklyn Dodgers four games to one.

24 Oct.   In Boston "Battling Levinsky" outpoints Jack Dillon in twelve rounds to win the light heavyweight boxing title.

29 Nov.   The Women's National Bowling Association organizes in Saint Louis.

21 Dec.   *The New York Times* reports rapid growth in trapshooting. The sport attracts 675,000 participants, members of some five thousand clubs nationwide, who spend $12 million a year on ammunition.

1917

- The Seattle Metropolitans capture the Stanley Cup, the first U.S. professional hockey team to accomplish the feat, when they defeat the Montreal Canadiens.

1 Jan.   The University of Oregon defeats the University of Pennsylvania, 14–0, in the third annual Tournament of Roses Association football game.

19 Apr.   William K. Kennedy wins the twenty-first Boston Marathon in 2:28:37.

2 May   Jim Vaughn of the Chicago Cubs and Fred Toney of the Cincinnati Reds both pitch no hitters for nine innings. The game is finally decided when the Reds score one run in the tenth to win.

12 May   Charles Borel rides Omar Khayyam to victory in the forty-third annual Kentucky Derby.

28 May   Benny Leonard wins the lightweight boxing championship, knocking out British title-holder Freddy Welsh in the ninth round of a bout in New York City. Leonard held the title until he retired in 1924. He fought 209 times and lost only five bouts in his career.

23 June   Molla Bjurstedt wins the women's title at the U.S. Lawn Tennis Association Championship.

19 Aug.   John McGraw, manager of the New York Giants, and Christy Mathewson, manager of the Cincinnati Reds, are arrested when their teams violate a New York prohibition against playing baseball on Sunday.

25 Aug.   Robert Lindley Murray wins the men's singles in the Patriotic Tournament, held in place of the regular U.S. Lawn Tennis Association Championship.

6–15 Oct.   The Chicago White Sox win the World Series, defeating the New York Giants four games to two.

14 Nov.   Mike O'Dowd knocks out Al McCoy in six rounds for the middleweight boxing title, in Brooklyn.

1918

1 Jan.   The Mare Island Marines defeat the Camp Lewis Army Team, 19–7, in the fourth annual Tournament of Roses Football Game.

7 Mar.   In the U.S. Figure Skating Championships, Nathaniel W. Niles of Boston wins the men's singles division and the pairs division with Theresa Weld of Boston. Mrs. Seton R. Beresford of Great Britain wins the women's singles division.

11 May   Willie Knapp rides Exterminator to victory in the Kentucky Derby.

15 May   The forty-third annual Preakness Stakes is run in two sections. The first is won by War Cloud, with a time of 1:53.6. The jockey was Johnny Loftus. The second is won by Jack Hare Jr., with a time of 1:53.4. The jockey was C. Peak.

22 June   Molla Bjurstedt wins the women's title at the U.S. Lawn Tennis Association Championship.

2 Aug.   Secretary of War Newton D. Baker orders major league baseball to end its season on 1 September but permits the World Series to be played.

3 Sept.   Robert Lindley Murray wins the men's title of the U.S. Lawn Tennis Association championship.

5–11 Sept.   The Boston Red Sox win the World Series, defeating the Chicago Cubs four games to two.

16 Dec.   William Harrison "Jack" Dempsey knocks out Carl Morris in fourteen seconds in a heavyweight bout in New Orleans. On 27 July Dempsey had knocked out Fred Fulton in eighteen seconds.

1919

- Major league baseball adopts a 140-game schedule.
- Babe Ruth of the Boston Red Sox sets a new major league baseball home run record of twenty-nine in a single season.
- The Inter-Allied Games are held in Paris, France, after World War I.
- Sir Barton, ridden by Johnny Loftus, becomes the first triple crown champion, winning the Kentucky Derby, the Preakness Stakes, and the Belmont Stakes.

- The 1919 influenza epidemic causes the cancellation of the Stanley Cup Championship series between the Seattle Metropolitans and the Montreal Canadiens.

- Earl "Curly" Lambeau organizes the Green Bay Packers franchise in Wisconsin, laying the groundwork for the American Professional Football Association.

1 Jan. The Great Lakes Naval Training Station defeats the Mare Island Marines, 17–0, in the fifth annual Tournament of Roses football game.

17 Mar. Jack Britton knocks out Ted Lewis in nine rounds in Canton, Ohio, to capture the welterweight boxing title, which he will retain until 1922.

19 Apr. Carl W. A. Linder wins the twenty-third Boston Marathon in 2:29:13.

28 Apr. Leslie Irvin successfully performs the first delayed parachute jump near Dayton, Ohio.

31 May Howard Wilcox, averaging 88.05 MPH, wins the seventh Indianapolis 500.

11 June Walter Hagen wins the U.S. Open Golf Tournament in a play-off against Michael Brady.

21 June Hazel Hotchkiss Wightman wins the women's title at the U.S. Lawn Tennis Association Championship.

4 July In Toledo, Ohio, Jack Dempsey defeats Jess Willard in three rounds for the world heavyweight boxing championship.

4 Sept. William M. Johnston wins the men's title at the U.S. Lawn Tennis Association Championship.

20 Sept. Jim Barnes defeats Fred McLeod in the final round of the PGA tournament.

1–9 Oct. The Cincinnati Reds win the World Series, defeating the Chicago White Sox five games to three. The series would soon become the focus of the infamous "Black Sox" scandal.

OVERVIEW

An Overlooked Decade. The second decade of the twentieth century is one of the most overlooked periods in the history of American sport. Overshadowed by the 1920s, the "Golden Age" of American sport, the 1910s saw many of the developments that laid the foundation for that fabulous decade, and if the sports of the 1910s had not been interrupted by World War I, the decade might have earned greater notoriety than did the 1920s. During the 1910s the amateurism of the nineteenth century continued to give way to professionalism. While tennis and track-and-field events remained wholly amateur sports and basketball and football continued to thrive on college campuses, professional basketball and football, though not organized to the extent they would be in the 1920s, gained greater acceptance in the cities. Above all, the 1910s was a decade for many firsts in American sport, such as the first Indianapolis 500 automobile race in 1911, the first American Stanley Cup champion in 1917, and the first Triple Crown thoroughbred horse racing champion in 1919. After World War I Americans embraced their sports in greater numbers and with greater enthusiasm than ever before, and the decade would have ended on a high note had it not been for the Black Sox Scandal, in which eight Chicago White Sox players accepted bribes to throw the 1919 World Series. The players were banned from baseball for life in 1921.

Baseball. The 1910s in baseball were extraordinarily eventful off the field, for in addition to the Black Sox Scandal, players unionized for higher salaries, and a rival league, the Federal League, formed to compete for baseball profits against the American and National Leagues. On the field the decade was the last of the deadball era, and teams with precise pitchers and crack base runners were dominant. The final years of the decade, however, saw the rise of the superstar of the Golden Age, George Herman "Babe" Ruth, who swatted a record twenty-nine homers for the Boston Red Sox in 1919 and would go on to establish the dominance of the slugger. The decade also saw the American League, only a decade old in 1911, win eight of ten World Series titles from the established National League. The American League probably would have garnered nine titles had the White Sox not thrown the 1919 series.

Increasing Professionalism. While baseball remained the main professional sport in the United States, other sports moved toward professionalism in the 1910s. Professional football, although confined largely to Ohio, became more and more popular as interest was sparked by the play of its first superstar, Jim Thorpe of the Canton Bulldogs. The regional success led promoters to organize a league of national proportions in the 1920s. Basketball went through a similar transformation during the 1910s, as the professional game gained increasing acceptance, and the foundation was laid for a national professional league in the 1920s. In golf, Walter Hagen promoted professionalism, and professional players began to gain acceptance within country clubs, which had long been bastions of the amateur character of the game.

Golf and Tennis Go Public. The 1910s saw golf and tennis, sports that had long been confined to the country club elite of the late nineteenth and early twentieth centuries, become sports for the middle classes. The turning point in the transformation of golf came in 1913 with the stunning victory of Francis Ouimet, a twenty-year-old American amateur, in the U.S. Open Golf Tournament. In tennis, the move of the U.S. Lawn Tennis Association Championship from the elite Casino Club in Newport, Rhode Island, to the West Side Tennis Club at Forest Hills, in the Queens borough of New York, signaled the USLTA's effort to attract a wider audience. Moreover, interest in tennis grew during the late 1910s because of the athletic game of Californian William Johnston.

Track and Field. Besides tennis, the foremost amateur sport in America was track and field. The 1910s saw Americans dominate track and field, setting world records in many events and introducing new techniques. During the course of the decade John Paul Jones and Norman Taber established new amateur world records in the mile, which was becoming one of the glamour events of track and field. Taber's mark of 4:12.6 marked the first time an amateur record for the distance surpassed the professional record set by Walter George of Great Britain in 1885. Americans introduced new techniques in the high jump and pole vault, setting world records in those events. Also, several Irish Americans set world records in the hammer throw.

Olympic Games. As in the 1900s the showcase for American track and field talent was the Olympic Games. In 1912 Stockholm, Sweden, hosted the fifth Olympiad, the first modern Olympics held independently of a World's Fair. Although Swedish athletes won the most medals, American athletes performed well, especially in track and field, swimming, cycling, and shooting. Native American athletes Jim Thorpe and Louis Tewanima produced exceptional performances in the Stockholm Olympic Games. Thorpe won gold medals in the decathlon and the pentathlon, and Tewanima won the silver medal in the 10,000-meter run. The 1916 Olympic Games, scheduled for Berlin, Germany, were canceled because of World War I.

Boxing. The Swedes hosted the Olympic Games with the provision that boxing, an outlawed sport in Sweden, not be included in the Olympic program. Although it was also illegal in most parts of the United States, boxing flourished, with the heavyweight title drawing great attention. The decade began with African American Jack Johnson as the world heavyweight champion and white America's search for the "Great White Hope" to take the heavyweight title from him. White America finally found its champion in Jess Willard, who knocked out Johnson in a bout held in Havana, Cuba, in 1915. Boxing had gained greater acceptability by the end of the decade, as the military used it for training during World War I and Jack Dempsey gave the sport a new face for the 1920s.

College Football. Brutality in sport, especially in boxing and college football, continued to be a much debated issue in the 1910s. Although college football authorities introduced rule changes to curb the injuries and deaths that had plagued the sport since the late nineteenth century, it was not until the introduction of more effective protective gear that the casualities in football finally declined. Nevertheless, some California institutions substituted rugby for football to avoid the carnage. Despite its brutal reputation college football continued to grow in popularity. The 1910s witnessed the last years of supremacy for Ivy League teams as schools in the Midwest, West, and South began to dominate the game.

TOPICS IN THE NEWS

AUTO RACING: THE INDY 500

Early Days. Auto racing began at the end of the nineteenth century but had only a small following by the early 1900s. The first organized motor race was sponsored by the Paris newspaper *Petit Journal* and ran over public roads from Paris to Rouen on 22 July 1894. Inspired by the publicity from this race, H. H. Kohlsatt, publisher of the *Chicago Times-Herald,* sponsored the first motor race in America on Thanksgiving Day 1894. During the next ten years, there were hundreds of motorized competitions in the United States and abroad, many organized by newspapers hoping to generate publicity and create stories for reporters to cover. The most famous of these races were run in Paris, which became the center of the world automobile industry in the early days. Racing became increasingly dangerous as the speed and power of the automobiles increased.

Indy Beginnings. In the United States the Automobile Club of America, later the American Automobile Association, became the first governing body for the sport. On Thanksgiving Day 1908, the club sponsored a Grand Prize Race at Savannah, Georgia, that drew more than two hundred thousand spectators. The popularity of the automobile and racing led to the construction, beginning in 1909, of America's first speedway, nicknamed the "Brickyard," and the commencement of an American tradition, the Indianapolis 500, which would become one of the greatest automobile races in the world. The two-and-a-half-mile track, built on 320 acres of farmland just outside Indianapolis, Indiana, originally served as a testing ground for the rapidly growing automotive industry, where new designs and innovations were tested and improved.

First Races. The first series of races at Indianapolis took place on 19 August 1909. They were sponsored by a group of manufacturers headed by Carl G. Fisher, James A. Allison, Arthur C. Newby, and Frank H. Wheeler, the speedway's four founders. These men operated the track successfully until the summer of 1922 when it was purchased by former race driver and World War I flying ace Edward V. Rickenbacker. Because the oval roadway was originally paved with crushed rock and tar, the speeding cars tore holes in its surface. Four peo-

ple were killed when two cars hit the holes, went out of control, and crashed. The potholes were especially dangerous since tires crudely made from cotton cord with only a thin coating of rubber were prone to blowouts. Fisher immediately had the track resurfaced with more than three million paving bricks in time for another speed program three months later. Three weekends of racing also were presented during 1910, with events ranging in distance from five to three hundred miles before management decided to hold a single annual five-hundred-mile race. The Indy 500 would offer thousands of dollars in prize money and would feature cars with a maximum piston displacement of six hundred cubic inches that weighed no less than twenty-three hundred pounds.

First 500 Race. The first Indianapolis 500 auto race was held on Memorial Day (a tradition that continues) in 1911 and attracted participants from across the United States. The cars were generally big racers with blunt noses and wooden-spoked wheels that had two seats, one for the driver and one for a mechanic. David Bruce-Brown's red Fiat led much of the first half, followed closely by Ralph Mulford, but Ray Harroun was in front when it counted. He drove a Marmon Wasp, a trim yellow and black six-cylinder single-seater, with a cone-shaped tail. Harroun bolted a stabilizer to the top of the cone, one of the first attempts to streamline a car for faster, smoother performance, and installed a rearview mirror, the first, on the cockpit cowling. Harroun averaged 74.59 MPH, completing the race in six hours, forty-two minutes, eight seconds, and collected $14,250 for his victory. His famous car is now on display at the Indianapolis Motor Speedway Hall of Fame Museum.

Controversy. Harroun's victory, however, became the subject of much debate. During the race, one driver had lost control of his car and slammed into the scorekeepers' stand. Although no one was hurt in the accident, the scorers lost track of the leader in the ensuing confusion. When they refocused on the race, the scorers were unsure whether Harroun or Mulford was in front. While Mulford seemed to be ahead to some, the scorers made a guess and declared Harroun the winner. The decision triggered a heated argument among fans, who split be-

Joe Dawson receiving the congratulations of Gov. Joe Brown after winning the Savannah Challenge Trophy,
11 November 1910

tween Harroun and Mulford. The argument was never
settled.

DePalma's Push. The second Indianapolis 500 race
was won by Joe Dawson in six hours, twenty-one minutes, six seconds, at an average speed of 78.72 MPH.
Ralph DePalma led from lap 3 through 198, at which
point his Mercedes put a rod through the crankcase.
DePalma and his mechanic pushed the car more than a
mile to the pits to become an enduring symbol of true
grit. In 1912 the Indy 500 was not yet a nationally known
event, but the story of DePalma's "great push," reported
in hundreds of newspapers and read by millions of sports
fans, drew much attention to the event.

The Tradition Builds. At the 1913 race Frenchman
Jules Goux cruised to victory in his revolutionary Peugeot
while his rivals shredded their primitive tires in a futile
attempt to catch him. Goux and his riding mechanic
downed champagne at each of his six pit stops. In 1914
Rene Thomas, whose Delage weighed the minimum
twenty-three hundred pounds and could top 100 MPH
with ease, won by averaging 82.47 MPH. The top four
finishers, all Europeans, drove French automobiles. The
unfortunate Ray Gilhooley flipped his Isotta and gave the
world a new slang expression, "to pull a real Gilhooley."

Front row starters DePalma and Dario Resta competed
for the entire five hundred miles at the 1915 race. Just as
in 1912, DePalma's Mercedes put a rod through the
crankcase on lap 197. This time, however, DePalma's car
was able to crawl around the track on three cylinders,
finishing less than four minutes ahead of Resta.

The War Years and After. Because of the war in
Europe, the 1916 race was shortened to three hundred
miles (five hundred kilometers). This race had the small-
est starting field and the fewest spectators of any Indy
500. Resta dominated the race in the same Peugeot he
had driven in the previous year's race. This was the last
event at Indianapolis until after World War I. The seventh Indianapolis 500 was held on 31 May 1919. Howard
Wilcox cruised to a win in a prewar Peugeot, completing
the course in at an average speed of 88.05 MPH. Most of
the competition either crashed or broke down. Three
men were killed and two were critically injured. Qualifying speeds broke 100 MPH for the first time, with racer
Rene Thomas averaging almost 105 MPH.

Qualifying Grid. Qualifying times for the Indy 500
between 1912 and 1919 consisted of the best out of three
timed laps. The starting grid was determined by order of
entry in 1911 and in 1912 and by a blind drawing in 1913

Ralph DePalma in his Vauxhall before the start of the 1914 French Grand Prix

and in 1914. In 1915 a grid determined by qualifying speed was used for the first time.

Winner's Purse. For winning the first race, Ray Harroun earned $10,000 plus $4,250 in contingency money. The total purse of $27,550 paid only through twelfth place. It was almost doubled to $52,225 in 1912, with the winner getting $20,000 plus contingency money. The purse was increased to $60,000 in 1924; the additional money was split by drivers who finished below tenth. Beginning in 1920, a group of Indianapolis businessmen paid $100 to the leader of each lap.

DePalma Record. Although Ralph DePalma, the best driver of his era, missed most of the money, he led a total of 613 out of 1,400 laps in the seven races he competed in between 1911 and 1921 for an incredible outfront percentage of .438. This feat was unsurpassed until Al Unser broke the record for most career leading laps in 1988, but it took him four times as many races. In his twenty-five-year career, DePalma won more than two thousand races. In 1919 he held the world land speed record of 149 MPH. His courage and his gallantry made him a hero to fans and to competitors alike.

Sources:

Edward F. Dolan, *Great Moments in the Indy 500* (New York: Watts, 1982);

Jay Schleifer, *Indy! The Great American Race* (New Jersey: Crestwood House, 1995);

Rich Taylor, *Indy: Seventy-five Years of Racing's Greatest Spectacle* (New York: St. Martin's Press, 1991).

BASEBALL OFF THE FIELD

Legacy of the National Agreement. Prior to the early 1900s baseball had experienced nearly a quarter-century of turmoil with rival leagues competing against each other and team owners and players contending for profits. In 1903 the National Agreement between the American League (AL), newly formed in 1901, and the older National League (NL), established in 1876, brought peace to baseball. The leagues agreed to recognize each other's territorial and reserve-clause rights, which gave teams the power to control their players' careers, and establish a three-man National Commission to govern the game. The National Commission, which consisted of the NL and AL presidents and a third individual selected by them, would serve as a judicial body to resolve disputes between the major leagues as well as controversies involving the minor leagues. From 1903 to 1921, the National Commission succeeded because of the cooperation and service of Ban Johnson, the AL president, and August Garry Herrmann, the chief stockholder in the Cincinnati Reds of the National League. Johnson and Herrmann provided the commission with needed stability during a period when the turbulent National League had four different presidents, all of whom were figure-

Garry Herrmann, National Commission chairman, and Ban Johnson, American League president, attending the 1914 World Series at Fenway Park, Boston

heads until 1919. Although Herrmann served as the chairman of the commission, Johnson dominated it. He ruled the American League as a fiefdom, appointing, as he had since the league's inception, club owners and managers who remained his loyal vassals.

Discontent over Salaries. Until the mid 1910s the major leagues faced relatively few problems, with the exception of player discontent over their salaries. In the wake of the National Agreement, team owners, as they had following the demise of the Players' League in 1890, slashed players' salaries. While salaries steadily increased after 1903 — the average baseball salary stood at $3,000 in 1910 as compared to $700 for a steelworker or $1,200 for a skilled craftsman — they did not rise proportionately with owners' profits. Baseball players had only three options: play for the salary offered, hold out for more generous terms, or quit organized baseball. Unable to market their skills to another league, many players held out for a better deal. Team owners countered a holdout by flattering the player, appealing to the player's sense of team loyalty, and spelling out the disastrous financial effects his actions might have upon his family. Finally, team owners exercised their most potent weapon, the reserve clause, against holdouts. Frank Navin, owner of the Detroit Tigers, warned Ty Cobb when he held out in

1913: "You will play for Detroit or you won't play for anybody."

Rise of a Players' Union. Discontent over salaries and other labor practices, such as the buying, selling, and drafting of players and the lack of uniformity of player contracts, led to the formation of a players' union in 1912. Organized by David Fultz, an attorney and former big league player, the Players' Fraternity claimed seven hundred members, including minor leaguers. After filing several lawsuits against various clubs for contract violations, the union presented the National Commission with a list of seventeen reforms in 1913, most of which concerned contract uniformity, player releases, and severance pay. The commission, faced with the possibility of players joining the recently established Federal League (FL), agreed to some of the demands. The most significant of the concessions won by the Players' Fraternity was the right of big league veterans of ten years to negotiate with the clubs of their choice. Although this measure provided players with a kind of free agency, it did not abrogate the reserve clause nor undermine the right of owners to buy and sell players. The fraternity continued to represent effectively both major and minor league players in contract disputes until the fall of the Federal League weakened its bargaining position.

Challenge of the Federal League. James A. Gilmore, a Chicago coal magnate, and other wealthy Chicago, New York, and Saint Louis businessmen organized the Federal League as a rival to the established major leagues for the 1914 season. Offering generous salaries, the FL lured away more than one-third (eighty-one) of the AL and NL rosters. The two older leagues responded by blacklisting the players that joined the FL, raising the salaries of their players, and suing the FL for violation of the reserve clause. Average baseball salaries more than doubled, from $3,187 in 1913 to $7,327 in 1915. The salary of Ty Cobb, who stayed with the Detroit Tigers, increased from $9,000 in 1910 to $20,000 in 1915. Connie Mack, the owner-manager of the Philadelphia Athletics of the American League, however, held out against the pressure exerted by the Federal League. He refused to raise salaries and sold or released his best players. Desperate to dispose of the FL, especially before it penetrated the crucial New York market, major league owners offered its financial backers lucrative buyouts. Harry Sinclair, the owner of the Newark club in the Federal League, received $10,000 annually for fourteen years from major league owners. Owners of FL clubs in cities not in direct competition with the AL or NL received nothing except revenue from the sale of their players back to major league teams. Major league baseball's buyout of the FL, which cost nearly $5 million, tarnished the image of organized baseball and led to the bankruptcy of many minor league clubs as some major league teams reduced their farm organizations.

World War I. When the United States entered World War I in April 1917 major league owners proudly proclaimed their patriotism but neither canceled the 1917 or 1918 seasons nor called upon their players to enlist in the armed forces, since a massive enlistment of players would have ravaged team rosters. Owners supported the war by offering servicemen free tickets, sponsoring pre- and postgame military parades, and encouraging fans to buy war bonds. Johnson ordered AL players to conduct daily military drills. Fans enjoyed the pregame spectacle of players, under the direction of a military sergeant assigned to each team, marching in drill formation with their bats slung over their right shoulders. In 1918 Secretary of War Newton D. Baker issued a "work-or-fight" order, which required all men of draft age, regardless of their deferment status, to work in an "essential" wartime industry or join the armed forces. Baker rejected baseball's claim of essential industry status and insisted that players must also work or fight. While 227 players joined the armed forces, others found employment in the draft-exempt industries of farming and shipbuilding. Shipbuilders employed baseball players mainly to strengthen their semipro baseball teams. Major league owners filled out their rosters with available lesser-skilled and overaged players and completed the 1918 season a month earlier than scheduled. World War I had a more

BASEBALL ATTENDANCE

Unlike the first decade of the century, which saw a twofold increase in baseball crowds, the 1910s saw relatively steady attendance. The dips in 1914 and 1915 were caused by the competition with the Federal League; in 1918 American involvement in World War I caused a general attendance drop. The American League led the National League in attendance each year, with the Philadelphia Athletics, Chicago White Sox, Boston Red Sox, and Detroit Tigers drawing the biggest crowds. Among National League teams, the Chicago Cubs, New York Giants, Boston Braves, and Philadelphia Phillies had the greatest fan support.

Year	American League	National League	Total
1910	3,270,689	2,935,758	6,206,447
1911	3,339,514	3,231,768	6,571,282
1912	3,263,631	2,735,759	5,999,390
1913	3,526,805	2,831,531	6,358,336
1914	2,747,591	1,707,397	4,454,988
1915	2,434,684	2,430,142	4,864,826
1916	3,451,885	3,051,634	6,503,519
1917	2,858,858	2,361,136	5,219,994
1918	1,707,999	1,372,127	3,080,126
1919	3,654,236	2,878,203	6,532,439

Source: John Thorn and Pete Palmer, *Total Baseball: The Official Encyclopedia of Major League Baseball*, fourth edition (New York: Viking, 1995).

devastating effect on the minor leagues, however, as only the International League finished its season.

Sources:
Bill James, *The Bill James Historical Baseball Abstract* (New York: Villard, 1988);

Benjamin G. Rader, *Baseball: A History of America's Game* (Urbana & Chicago: University of Illinois Press, 1992);

David Quintin Voigt, *American Baseball: From the Commissioners Game to Continental Expansion* (University Park & London: Pennsylvania State University Press, 1983).

BASEBALL ON THE FIELD

American League Dominance. American League teams captured eight of ten World Series titles from 1910 to 1919. Leading the American League in its World Series romp over the National League were the Philadel-

Frank Baker, third baseman in the celebrated infield of the Philadelphia Athletics, led the American League in home runs four consecutive years, (1911–1914), though he never hit more than twelve in a season.

phia Athletics in 1910, 1911, and 1913; the Boston Red Sox in 1912, 1915, 1916, and 1918; and the Chicago White Sox in 1917. The National League's 1914 Boston Braves "Miracle Team," rising from the cellar in mid July to win the pennant and sweep the Athletics in the series, and the 1919 Cincinnati Reds prevented an American League sweep. Although the New York Giants did not win the series in the decade, they were undoubtedly the National League's strongest, most consistent team, winning the pennant four times, from 1911 to 1913 and in 1917. The other National League champions who lost the series were the Chicago Cubs (1910 and 1918), the Philadelphia Phillies (1915), and the Brooklyn Dodgers (1916).

Connie Mack Leads Philadelphia. The success of the Philadelphia Athletics was largely because of Connie Mack, who was manager and part owner of the team from 1901 to 1950. In 1905 the Athletics confronted the New York Giants for the World Series, losing the title four games to one. For the remainder of the 1900s, Mack built the team into a formidable World Series contender, mainly through the recruitment of strong pitchers. In 1910, when the Athletics defeated the Chicago Cubs in

the World Series, Philadelphia's bullpen consisted of Jack Coombs, who won thirty-one games; Chief Bender, who won twenty-three games; Cy Morgan, who won eighteen; and Eddie Plank, who won sixteen. However, the key to Mack's World Series championships in the early 1910s was the "$100,000 infield." The most outstanding of this group was second baseman Eddie Collins, who contemporaries compared to former Philadelphia great Napoleon Lajoie for his ability to swing a bat. Jack Barry at shortstop, Frank Baker at third base, and John McInnis at first base rounded out the celebrated infield. After losing the World Series to the Boston Braves in 1914, Philadelphia declined as an American League powerhouse. Mack sold his all-star lineup because he refused to increase their salaries to match those offered by the rival Federal League.

Reign of the Boston Red Sox. After floundering in fifth place in 1911, the Boston Red Sox captured the American League pennant in 1912, and went on to secure the World Series title, four games to three, over the New York Giants. Boston's phenomenal rise and World Series triumph was in part because of the pitching of Joe Wood, whose fastball was considered the equal of the Washing-

Ty Cobb left his mark on baseball in the 1910s. In every year except 1916, when Tris Speaker hit .386, Cobb won the American League batting championship. The "Georgia Peach," as he was nicknamed by Garland Rice, posted a lifetime batting average of .366, which remains the major league record. He batted better than .400 three times. Playing during the "deadball" era, Cobb also excelled as a base runner. In 1915 he stole 96 bases, which remained a major league record until 1962, when Maury Wills stole 104. Cobb, though, stole home thirty-five times, which remains a major league record.

Sources: Benjamin G. Rader, *Baseball: A History of America's Game* (Urbana & Chicago: University of Illinois Press, 1992);

David Quintin Voigt, *American Baseball: From the Commissioners' Game to Continental Expansion* (University Park & London: Pennsylvania State University Press, 1983).

---

ton Senators' Walter Johnson, the leading hurler of the decade. In 1912 Wood led American League pitchers, winning thirty-four games and losing five. That year he and Johnson both won sixteen straight before Wood snapped Johnson's winning streak in a 1–0 Boston win. Wood led Boston to the 1912 World Series title by winning three games. Pitching continued to be the mainstay of Boston's success throughout the decade. From 1914 to 1919 Babe Ruth hurled for the Red Sox, posting a league-best earned run average of 1.75 in 1916. In three starts as a World Series pitcher, Ruth was undefeated. After giving up a first inning homer in his first World Series start against Brooklyn on 9 October 1916, Ruth went on to pitch thirteen scoreless innings for a 2–1 victory. He ran his scoreless-inning streak to a record twenty-nine in two victories against the Chicago Cubs in the 1918 World Series, winning the first game 1–0 and the fourth 3–2. Ruth's power as a slugger was also on display, as he led the American League in home runs with eleven in 1917 and twenty-nine in 1919.

New York Powers the National League. The National League powerhouse New York Giants were managed by the indomitable John J. McGraw. The Giants who won the World Series over the Philadelphia Athletics in 1905 were fueled by pitchers Joe McGinnity and Christy Mathewson. By 1910, however, all of the Giants' superstars had either retired or were past their prime, and McGraw had to rebuild his team. He quickly picked up the players who made up the core of his pennant-winning teams of the 1910s: Fred Snodgrass and Josh Devore in the outfield; Art Fletcher, Larry Dole, Charles Herzog in the infield; Rube Marquard, pitcher; and John Meyers, catcher. Of the players from the 1905 championship team, there remained only Mathewson, who piled up

---

Rube Marquard of the New York Giants set a major league record of nineteen consecutive victories in 1912. His winning streak started with an 18–3 victory over the Brooklyn Dodgers on 11 April, the opening day of the season. It continued until 8 July, when the Chicago Cubs upended the Giants by the score of 7–2.

Date	Opponent	Score	Losing Pitcher
11 April	Brooklyn	18–3	Nap Rucker
16 April	Boston	8–2	Lefty Tyler
24 April	Philadelphia	11–4	Grover Alexander
1 May	Philadelphia	11–4	Tom Seaton
7 May	Saint Louis	6–2	Bill Steele
11 May	Chicago	10–3	Lew Richie
16 May	Pittsburgh	4–1	Marty O'Toole
20 May	Cincinnati	3–0	Art Fromme
24 May	Brooklyn	6–3	Pat Ragan
30 May	Philadelphia	7–1	Tom Seaton
3 June	Saint Louis	8–3	Slim Sallee
8 June	Cincinnati	6–2	Rube Benton
12 June	Chicago	3–2	Lew Richie
17 June	Pittsburgh	5–4	Marty O'Toole
19 June	Boston	6–5	Otto Hess
21 June	Boston	5–2	Hub Perdue
25 June	Philadelphia	2–1	Grover Alexander
29 June	Boston	8–6	Buster Brown
3 July	Brooklyn	2–1	Nap Rucker

Source: Fred Menke, *The Encyclopedia of Sport*, fourth revised edition (New York: Barnes, 1969).

---

seventy-three victories in the pennant-winning years from 1911 to 1913. The Giants complemented their power in the bullpen with outstanding hitting: they led the league with team batting averages of .279 in 1911, .286 in 1912, and .273 in 1913. Moreover, they outdistanced the second-place team in their league by large margins, winning by 7½ games over the Chicago Cubs in 1911, 10 over the Pittsburgh Pirates in 1912, and 12½ over the Philadelphia Phillies in 1913. After losing the pennant to the Boston Braves in 1914, the Philadelphia Phillies in 1915, and the Brooklyn Dodgers (also known as the Robins) in 1916, the Giants returned to the top of the National League in 1917.

White Sox Tarnish Baseball. Having won the World Series in 1917 and fallen to sixth place in the American League in 1918, the Chicago White Sox returned to baseball's premier event in 1919. Although Chicago's record of eighty-eight wins and fifty-two losses was less impressive than the National League's Cincinnati Reds' ninety-six wins and forty-four losses, Chicago was favored to win the series on the strength of its 29- and 23-game winning pitchers, Eddie Cicotte and Lefty Williams. After winning four of the first five games, Cincinnati seemed invincible, but Chicago battled back and captured the next two games. In the eighth game of the series, Cincinnati defeated Chicago in Chicago 10–5 to win the series. Although rumors of a "fixed" series spread among baseball aficionados, the *Spalding's Guide* dismissed them as unfounded and emphasized Cincinnati's teamwork, the pitching of Dutch Ruether, Slim Sallee, and Jim Ring, as well as the batting of Ed Roush. The rumors might have been suppressed had not Chicago sportswriter Hugh Fullerton pursued the question and published his findings. Fullerton's story led to a grand jury investigation in 1921 on the conspiracy to throw the World Series. Eight Chicago players, including Cicotte, Williams, and Joe Jackson confessed their involvement in the conspiracy, but their confessions disappeared before the end of the trial, and all eight denied their involvement. Although the grand jury trial ended without a single guilty verdict, the newly appointed commissioner of baseball, Kenesaw Mountain Landis, convicted the eight Chicago players of throwing the World Series and banned them from major league baseball for life.

Sources:
Bill James, *The Bill James Historical Baseball Abstract* (New York: Villard, 1988);

Benjamin G. Rader, *Baseball: A History of America's Game* (Urbana & Chicago: University of Illinois Press, 1992);

David Quintin Voigt, *American Baseball: From the Commisssioners Game to Continental Expansion* (University Park & London: Pannsylvania State University Press, 1983).

BASKETBALL

Early Days. Basketball, the creation of Dr. James Naismith, is the only major sport that originated solely in the United States. Two peach baskets fastened to a gymnasium balcony in the winter of 1891 provided its humble beginnings and suggested the sport's name. The Springfield Young Men's Christian Association (YMCA) arbitrated the rules for the game's first two years. The YMCA then joined with the Amateur Athletic Union

Walter "Doc" Meanwell, whose system of short passes and crisscross patterns made Wisconsin a dominant team

(AAU) to govern the game. In 1908 the National Collegiate Athletic Association (NCAA) assumed charge of the college rules, and in 1915 the YMCA, the NCAA, and the AAU formed a joint committee.

College Basketball. While small gyms limited crowd size, the potential for basketball as an intercollegiate sport was becoming apparent by the turn of the century. Since existing facilities could be modified to accommodate the sport and since a few good players could make a team competitive, small colleges found that basketball allowed them to take on larger schools and also discovered that the game could gain attention for their institutions. Conference play between colleges began as early as 1902 in the Eastern League; the Western Conference followed in 1906, the Missouri Valley in 1908, the Southwest in 1915, and the Pacific Coast in 1916. Early powers outside of the East included Wabash College in Indiana, which was 66–3 from 1908 to 1911, as well as Wisconsin, which under coach Walter Meanwell won or shared the Western Conference title from 1912 to 1914 and took the title outright in 1916 and in 1918. Other powerhouses included Kansas, coached by Forrest C. "Phog" Allen; Purdue under Ward "Piggy" Lambert; and Missouri.

COLLEGIATE BASKETBALL NATIONAL CHAMPIONS

1910 — Columbia (Harry A. Fisher, coach)

1911 — St. John's, Brooklyn (C. B. Allen, coach)

1912 — Wisconsin (Walter Meanwell, coach)

1913 — U.S. Navy (Louis P. Wenzell, coach)

1915 — Illinois (Ralph R. Jones, coach)

1916 — Wisconsin (Walter Meanwell, coach)

1917 — Washington State (J. F. Bohler, coach)

1918 — Syracuse (Edmund Dollard, coach)

1919 — Minnesota (Dr. L. J. Cooke, coach)

NATIONAL AMATEUR ATHLETIC UNION BASKETBALL CHAMPIONS

The AAU, which held its first basketball championship in 1897, did not hold a championship game from 1902 to 1909; the AAU Championship resumed in Chicago in 1910, was suspended for two more years, then was permanently reestablished in 1913. YMCA teams dominated the early tournaments but were supplanted by college teams in the early 1920s. The first open-bottom nets, made as early as 1906, were approved for championship play in the 1912–1913 season.

1910 — Company F, Portage National Guard (Wisconsin)

1911 — No competition

1912 — No competition

1913 — Cornell (Armour Playground), Chicago

1914 — Cornell (Armour Playground), Chicago

1915 — Olympic Club, San Francisco

1916 — University of Utah, Salt Lake City

1917 — Illinois Athletic Club, Chicago

1918 — No competition

1919 — Los Angeles Athletic Club

Source: *Modern Encyclopedia of Basketball*, edited by Zander Hollander (New York: Four Winds, 1969).

Professional Development. Organized professional basketball began at the tail end of the nineteenth century. The National Basketball League, with teams in Philadelphia, New York City, Brooklyn, and southern New Jersey, was formally organized in 1898 and lasted for two seasons. The first two decades of the twentieth century saw many professional teams and leagues begin in the East, but organization was fluid. Players often appeared in different leagues and teams within a season. Many professional teams started out as YMCA clubs. The Buffalo Germans, for example, turned pro in 1905 after winning the national AAU title and demonstrating basketball techniques at the 1904 Olympics. From 1895 to 1925 the Germans took on all challengers, winning 792 games while losing only 86.

Original Celtics. At the end of World War I, professional basketball was a collection of loosely organized leagues comprised of teams whose players could shift allegiances easily, taking the best offer they could get. This changed with the emergence of the Original Celtics. Named for the New York Celtics, a pre–World War I settlement-house team, the Original Celtics were organized in 1918 by Jim Furey, a New York promoter, and his brother, Tom. After the Celtics' unexceptional first season, the Fureys lured such players as Nat Holman and Chris Leonard from the New York Whirlwinds and built a team around Henry "Dutch" Dehnert, a talented pivot man with no high school or college experience; Joe Lapchick, one of the finest big men of the game; Swede Grimstead; and Johnny Beckman, considered the finest free-throw shooter of his time. These players were signed to the first individual contracts in the game's history and were paid by the season instead of by the game, which ended the practice of switching teams or leagues for the first good offer.

Celtic Dominance. The dominant team in the New York region, the Original Celtics not only sparked interest in basketball as a professional sport but also contributed to the development of the game. At a time when basketball was seen as strictly an individual game in which each player considered himself responsible for the person opposite him at the center jump, the Celtics played as a team. Each Celtic guarded the nearest man, regardless of whose personal opponent he was. Along with teamwork, the Celtics developed refinements to the game, including the pivot play, the switching defense, and the give-and-go offense. Superb showmen and excellent athletes, they experimented constantly, frequently staging brilliant passing exhibitions in games against overmatched opponents.

Philadelphia SPHAs. Another formidable team was the Philadelphia SPHAs, named for the South Philadelphia Hebrew Association. Beginning play in 1918, the SPHAs won seven local championships in thirteen seasons. The all-Jewish team played most of the top independent teams of the era and won more games than they lost, but their fame was confined mostly to the East. The SPHAs were coached by Eddie Gottlieb, who later founded the Philadelphia Warriors.

Early Players. Notable early professional players were Max Friedman, who turned pro in 1909 and played in every pro league until 1927; Barney Sedran, who turned pro in 1911 and played for many teams in a fifteen-year career; and Nat Holman, who played for Germantown, the New York Whirlwinds, and the Original Celtics. Holman and Sedran were the two premier little men of the game, making the Whirlwinds probably the best pro team of the early period until the advent of the Original Celtics. These and other players helped to popularize professional basketball and exposed more people to the developing skills of ball-handling, team play, and accurate shooting. The pro teams introduced barnstorming, playing college, high school, AAU, and YMCA teams, mostly along the East Coast.

Sources:

Modern Encyclopedia of Basketball, edited by Zander Hollander (New York: Four Winds, 1969);

Douglas A. Noverr and Lawrence E. Ziewacz, *The Games They Played: Sports in American History, 1865–1980* (Chicago: Nelson-Hall, 1983);

The Official NBA Basketball Encyclopedia, second edition, edited by Alex Sachare (New York: Villard, 1994).

BOXING

Unpopular Beginnings. While there have always been amateur fist fights in which contestants for recreation or in anger match skills in the "manly art of self-defense," the sport of boxing for money, or prizefighting, did not enjoy wide popularity for much of America's history. Until John L. Sullivan popularized the sport in the late nineteenth century by using boxing gloves, fights were staged with bare fists under London Prize Ring Rules. Such encounters, held in isolated spots and watched by small crowds, were illegal, and the police were constantly alert to trouble.

The Sport Looks Ahead. By the beginning of the century's second decade the sport had gained a measure of popularity and legality if not respectability. In 1910 Johnny Coulon defeated Jim Kendrick, the British bantamweight titlist, in nineteen rounds in New Orleans. Both weighed in at 116 pounds, and after their fight that became the official weight for the bantamweight class. That same year, Jimmy Clabby and Jimmy Gardner both claimed the welterweight title, but Clabby was recognized as champion when he defeated Dixie Kid in a ten-round no-decision bout in New York. On 22 February 1910, Ad Wolgast won the lightweight title from Oscar "Battling" Nelson when the referee stopped the match after forty rounds of a forty-five-round match in Port Richmond, California.

Violent Reactions. The events of October 1910 did little to allay claims of boxing opponents that the sport

John L. Sullivan meeting Jack Johnson in 1910

inspired violence beyond the rules. During the match between Abe Attell, the featherweight champion of the world, and Eddie Kelly in New York, the referee demanded more action from both men. When the referee continued his admonishments and was joined by the crowd, Attell "accidentally" punched the referee in the jaw. He then knocked out Kelly in the fourth round. That same month, Stanley Ketchel, one of the best and hardest-hitting middleweights of all time and the middleweight champion of the world, was murdered in Conway, Missouri, by farmhand Walter Dipley, the boyfriend of a woman to whom Ketchel allegedly made advances.

Jack Johnson. Because boxing is a sport of individuals and personalities, its champions often evoke intense feelings in fans. Boxers often became working-class heroes, and African American pugilists were especially powerful symbols of self-worth and inspiration to blacks in an era of deep-rooted prejudice and discrimination. Few black heroes were as well-known or gave African Americans more pride than Jack Johnson, the first black heavyweight champion (1908–1915). After Johnson defeated Tommy Burns, the reigning champion, in Sydney, Australia, fight promoters and newspapermen launched a hunt for a "Great White Hope" to recapture the crown from Johnson. Whites were angered by a black man who defeated white fighters instead of "going down" as blacks were expected to do. Johnson also triggered strong feelings because of his flamboyant lifestyle, which included elegant clothes and relationships with white women, both of

Jess Willard standing over Jack Johnson, whose gesture of shielding his eyes from the sun led some to argue that he faked being knocked out

which violated racial taboos. Ultimately, Johnson represented an important threat to the entire superstructure of racial segregation.

Bitter Victory. On 4 July 1910 Johnson defended his world heavyweight title against James J. Jeffries, a popular former heavyweight champion who came out of retirement to rid boxing of the "black menace." A skilled boxer with fast, punishing fists and feints that confused his opponents, Johnson handily outclassed Jeffries, who had not fought for six years and was out of shape, verbally taunting him as he administered the beating. In the fifteenth round, Johnson floored Jeffries with a left to the jaw. After the match, Johnson's mother reportedly remarked, "He said he'd bring home the bacon, and the honey boy has gone and done it." Jeffries's humiliating defeat sparked black celebrations and white violence against blacks across the country, in which at least eight persons were killed. Fear of race riots led many cities, including Atlanta, Baltimore, Cincinnati, Saint Louis, and Washington, D.C., to ban screenings of the Johnson-Jeffries fight films in local theaters.

Troubles Continue. In 1913 Johnson was charged with violating the Mann Act, a law passed 25 June 1910 to prohibit the interstate transportation of women for immoral purposes. Despite highly questionable testimony and strong concern that he was framed, he was sentenced to a year and a day in federal prison. During an appeal of his sentence, Johnson jumped bail and fled to Canada and then to Europe, where he performed in vaudeville and fought second-rate challengers. In the aftermath of the Johnson-Jeffries bout, the New York State Athletic Commission banned "mixed" bouts between black and white boxers on 5 February 1913.

The career of heavyweight champion Jack Johnson inspired Howard Sackler's Pulitzer-winning play, *The Great White Hope*, a thinly veiled depiction of Johnson's life (he was called Jack Jefferson in the drama). Although Sackler took some liberties with Johnson's story, all of its major events were depicted: his 1910 victory in Reno, his conviction under the Mann Act and flight from the United States, and his loss of the heavyweight title in Havana. In both the play and a subsequent motion picture, the leading roles were played by James Earl Jones and Jane Alexander. Premiering at the Arena Stage in Washington on 12 December 1967, the play's exploration of the prevailing racial attitudes of Johnson's era resonated with audiences then struggling with the ramifications of the Civil Rights movement. *The Great White Hope* was subsequently performed on Broadway, where it opened on 3 October 1968 at the Alvin Theatre and ran for 556 performances until 31 January 1970. Later that year Twentieth Century Fox made it into a motion picture.

Emergence of Willard. On 5 April 1915 Jess Willard won the world heavyweight boxing championship when knocked out Jack Johnson in a bout in Havana, Cuba. Johnson had become fat and rusty while he enjoyed his popularity and world fame. The Kansan Willard, the "Pottawatomie Giant," was six feet seven inches tall and in superb fighting condition. In the twenty-sixth round, he knocked Johnson down although it was not clear whether a blow by Willard or the blazing sun caused Johnson's descent to the canvas, which was described as a slow sinking. Later Johnson claimed that he threw the fight for $50,000 and an exemption from his prison sentence, but few believed him.

Dempsey Triumph. Willard defended his title once in 1916 and did not fight again until 4 July 1919, when he was defeated by William Harrison "Jack" Dempsey. After the third round Willard's cheekbone was split, his nose smashed, and his body covered with welts from the power of Dempsey's unmerciful body attack. Willard did not come out for the fourth round, and the shortest heavyweight title fight up to that time was over. Dempsey held the crown until he was defeated by Gene Tunney in 1926, and eventually became one of the most popular sports heroes of the 1920s, defending his title in million-dollar fights before enormous crowds.

New Popularity. The social status of prizefighting was helped by World War I, which softened the traditional public animosity toward the sport. During the war the army used boxing as part of the training of doughboys.

After the war states dropped many legal barriers to boxing, often at the instigation of the American Legion, and it became an accepted sport. Secret fights on barges, in backrooms of saloons, or in isolated rural areas attended by slummers, roughnecks, and the "lower elements" of society were replaced by bouts in glittering arenas and in huge stadiums with the middle-class and "high society" turning out for the spectacle. Boxing matches were becoming big social events, and the audience often came to see attending celebrities as well as the fight.

The Rise of the Promoter. Another development in the 1910s was the rise of the boxing promoter. During John L. Sullivan's reign as heavyweight champion, fight promoters were practically unknown. Pugilists or their backers put up side bets, winner take all, and it was customary to pass the hat among spectators, the funds collected going to the winner or being split 50–50. During the 1910 Jackson-Jeffries fight, Edward "Tex" Rickard acted as both promoter and referee. In 1916 he staged a bout between the heavyweight champion Willard and Frank Moran. Willard won $30,000 from this match, then doubled it by betting on Woodrow Wilson to win the 1916 presidential election. In 1919 Rickard promoted the Dempsey-Willard match and became the nation's premier sports impresario. When Dempsey defeated Willard, boxing entered its Golden Age.

Sources:

Graeme Kent, *Boxing's Strangest Fights* (London: Robson, 1991);

Douglas A. Noverr and Lawrence E. Ziewacz, *The Games They Played: Sports in American History, 1865–1980* (Chicago: Nelson-Hall, 1983);

Gilbert Odd, *Encyclopedia of Boxing* (New York: Crescent, 1983);

Benjamin G. Rader, *American Sports: From the Age of Folk Games to the Age of Televised Sports,* second edition (Englewood Cliffs, N.J.: Prentice Hall, 1990);

Bert R. Sugar, *The Great Fights: A Pictorial History of Boxing's Greatest Bouts* (New York: Gallery, 1981).

FOOTBALL: COLLEGE

Changing a Brutal Game. The game of football was still going through fundamental change in the early years of the twentieth century. The game's brutality — eighteen collegiate players were killed in 1905 — caused President Theodore Roosevelt to threaten to outlaw the sport and led to new rules, such as the creation of a neutral zone between offensive and defensive lines, the increase of yardage required for a first down from five to ten yards, and the legalization of the forward pass. The changes did not stem the violence, though, as there were 113 fatalities between 1905 and 1910. In 1910 seven men were required on the line of scrimmage and such practices as the flying tackle, the interlocking of arms in running interference, and the pushing and pulling of the ball carrier to advance the ball were deemed illegal. Also, the football game was divided into four quarters of fifteen minutes each, with a one-minute break between the first and second and third and fourth quarters and a thirty-minute break between halves. In 1912 teams were allowed four downs to achieve a first down; an end zone was created behind each goal; and the value of a touchdown increased from five to six points. The evolving rules helped to change the character of the game. Although football remained a brutal sport throughout the 1910s, injuries and deaths declined, especially as new types of protective equipment, such as improved helmets and pads, were introduced.

Harvard Leads the Ivy League. In the 1910s Ivy League football teams continued to set the standard for college play, as they had since the late nineteenth century. From 1908 to 1916, Harvard University, coached by Percy Haughton, dominated the Ivy League, posting a record of seventy-one wins, seven losses, and five ties. In 1910, 1912, and 1913, the Crimson won the national title, going without a loss in 1912 and 1913. For Haughton the especially memorable year was 1912, as Harvard spoiled both Princeton's and Yale's bids for undefeated seasons. In 1913 Harvard's strength came from the leg of Charlie Brickley, a superbly accurate kicker who scored five field goals to defeat Yale. In 1914 Harvard destroyed Yale by the score of 36–0, despite the efforts of Yale's new coach Frank Hinkey, a former Yale defensive standout. (As a player Hinkey had won the nickname "Tonowanda Terror" because he hailed from the Tonowanda region of upstate New York and was known for terrorizing offenses.) In 1915 the outcome of the Harvard-Yale encounter was even more devastating, as Harvard won 41–0. Harvard would have enjoyed another undefeated season in 1915 had it not played Cornell University. Buttressed by the play of running back Charlie Barrett and receiver Murray Shelton, Cornell defeated Harvard 10–0, going on to an undefeated season and the national championship.

The Rise of Notre Dame. The decade also witnessed the rise of Notre Dame, one of the most dominant college football teams of the twentieth century. In 1911 and 1912, Notre Dame enjoyed undefeated seasons under coach Jack Marks, a former Dartmouth football standout. Marks relied upon a strong running game, but he was succeeded in 1913 by Jesse Harper, who utilized the forward pass to put Notre Dame in the forefront of college football. In that year Notre Dame stunned Army with the forward pass, as quarterback Gus Dorais completed 13 of 17 passes for 243 yards, including several throws to the sure-handed Knute Rockne, in a 35–13 victory. In one play Rockne, running down the field for a pass, stumbled and fell but quickly got up and turned around, directly facing Dorais, who threw the ball to him. The Army defenders had abandoned Rockne after he fell, leaving him open for Dorais's pass. The play may have inspired the "button hook," in which the receiver races downfield then stops quickly to catch the ball. Following Harper's retirement in 1917, Rockne, who had become a chemistry instructor at Notre Dame, became the football coach. His first year as coach produced a 3–1–2 record, before the sport was canceled until 1921 because of World War I.

IVY LEAGUE FOOTBALL RIVALRIES

The 1910s marked the last great decade of Ivy League football. Yale, led by Walter Camp, dominated college football throughout the late nineteenth and early twentieth centuries. In the 1910s, under Percy Haughton, Harvard dominated the Ivy League. Intense rivalries developed among the schools, especially Harvard, Yale, and Princeton.

Year	Harvard-Yale	Harvard-Princeton	Yale-Princeton
1910	0–0	No Game	5–3
1911	0–0	6–8	3–6
1912	20–0	16–6	6–6
1913	15–5	3–0	3–3
1914	36–0	20–0	19–14
1915	41–0	10–6	13–7
1916	3–6	3–0	10–0
1917	No Game	No Game	No Game
1918	No Game	No Game	No Game
1919	10–3	10–10	6–13

Source: Frank G. Menke, *The Encyclopedia of Sports*, fourth revised edition (New York: Barnes, 1969).

Rockne then coached Notre Dame until 1930, posting a career coaching record of 103 wins, 12 losses, and 5 ties.

The Western Conference. While Michigan and Chicago were the strongest teams of the Big Ten Conference of the Midwest in the previous decade, other powers, especially Illinois, Minnesota, and Ohio State, came to the fore in the 1910s. In 1913 Robert Zuppke, who had been a Wisconsin second-stringer, became the coach at the University of Illinois. The Illini caught national attention that year by holding Purdue to a scoreless tie. In 1914 Illinois had an undefeated season, scoring 224 points and holding opponents to 22. After posting another undefeated season in 1915, Illinois slumped in 1916 and 1917, rising back to the top of the Western Conference in 1918 and 1919. The Illini's brightest moment in 1916 came against a strong Minnesota team, which had in its four games that season scored 236 points. In a game featuring precision passing from Bart Macomber to Dutch Sternaman, Illinois defeated Minnesota by the score of 14–9. Undeterred by the loss to Illinois, Minnesota won its last two games with scores football teams rather than practice law. After enjoying successful coaching stints at Oberlin College, Akron University, Auburn University, and Clemson University, Heisman joined Georgia Tech in 1904 and built the Engineers into a national power. In 1915 Georgia Tech started a thirty-two-game winning streak that lasted more than five seasons. In 1916 Georgia Tech defeated Cumberland College 222–0, the most lopsided score in the history of college football. Georgia Tech gained national acclaim in 1917 by shutting out the University of Pennsylvania 41–0 and clinched the national championship by defeating Auburn University 68–7. Heisman, who coached Georgia Tech until 1919, posted a record of 101–28–6, before becoming football coach at his alma mater, the University of Pennsylvania.

Washington Leads the West. The University of Washington dominated football on the West Coast during the decade. Washington's success stemmed from the coaching of Gilmour Dobie, who had been the quarterback the University of Minnesota from 1899 to 1902. After successfully coaching North Dakota State University to two consecutive undefeated seasons in 1906 and 1907, he joined the University of Washington in 1908. Under Dobie, the Huskies did not lose a game from 1908 to 1916; during this remarkable stretch they won fifty-eight games, including thirty-nine in succession, and tying three. Washington's streak, which started in 1907 before Dobie's tenure, extended to sixty-three by 1917, and remains the longest in college football. During the whole of its streak Washington did not have the opportunity to play the University of California at Berkeley or Stanford University. Because of the brutality of the game, these teams chose to play rugby instead of football from 1906 to 1919. Despite these important defections, football thrived in California, where it was highlighted in the Rose Bowl, a permanent New Year's Day event beginning in 1916.

Sources:

Allison Danzig, *The History of American Football: Its Great Teams, Players, and Coaches* (Englewood Cliffs, N.J.: Prentice-Hall, 1956);

Danzig, *Oh, How They Played the Game: The Early Days of Football and the Heroes Who Made It Great* (New York: Macmillan, 1917);

Ivan N. Kaye, *Good Clean Violence: A History of College Football* (Philadelphia: Lippincott, 1973).

Knute Rockne during his playing days at Notre Dame

of 54–0 over Wisconsin and 49–0 over Chicago. Despite its record, Minnesota lost the Big Ten Conference championship to the Ohio State Buckeyes, who enjoyed an undefeated season under coach Dr. John W. Wilce. Ohio State enjoyed yet another undefeated season in 1917.

Heisman and Georgia Tech. The credit for Georgia Tech's emergence as the best college football team in the South was given to John Heisman, an 1892 University of Pennsylvania Law School graduate, who chose to coach

FOOTBALL: PROFESSIONAL

Limited Beginnings. Teams began paying players to play football in the 1890s, but professional football remained a largely disorganized sport from 1900 to 1920, with most teams clustered in Pennsylvania, Ohio, and the Chicago area of Illinois. The popularity of pro football was strictly local or regional as the teams of athletic clubs challenged each other for city or state supremacy. Unlike college football, early pro football was dominated by ethnic, Catholic, and working-class players.

African American Players. Although both the professional and collegiate ranks were dominated by whites in the 1910s, black players participated in the professional game in this early period. Doc Baker played four seasons with the Akron Indians as halfback, the last in 1911; Henry McDonald played backfield for the Rochester Jeffersons (1911–1917); and Fritz Pollard, a Brown University star who was the first black to make Walter Camp's first-team All-American, played for four different professional teams from 1919 to 1926 and was the first black pro coach when he was player-coach at both Akron and Hammond.

Jim Thorpe. The star of the decade in professional football was Jim Thorpe, the Olympic champion from the Carlisle Indian School who turned pro in 1913. In 1915 Thorpe signed with the Canton, Ohio, Bulldogs for $250 a game. His appearance in the game between Canton and Massillon that year drew fourteen thousand fans. In the 1916 season, Thorpe led his team to ten straight wins and the Bulldogs became the pro champions of the world. Thorpe remained the premier attraction in pro football into the 1920s.

Problems. Despite some success, professional football suffered internal problems that greatly undermined its advancement. Many teams refused to organize into leagues or abide by uniform rules, and they routinely raided talent from other teams and even from colleges, which irritated many college coaches. Players jumped from team to team during the season to maximize their pay. The constant player turnover, betting and gambling scandals, and uneven competition turned off many potential fans. As early as 1914 college coaches and fans began to berate the professional game. It was a discouraging struggle for the pros, for though they had exciting players they could not match the respectability of the college game or draw its crowds. Hoping to reverse the tarnished image of professional football, and to improve its profitability, representatives from mostly smaller Ohio cities gathered at the Hupmobile automobile agency showroom at Canton in 1920. There they formed a new pro league that officially became the National Football League in 1922.

Sources:
William S. Jarrett, *Timetables of Sports History: Football* (New York: Facts On File, 1989);

Douglas A. Noverr and Lawrence E. Ziewacz, *The Games They Played: Sports in American History, 1865–1980* (Chicago: Nelson-Hall, 1983).

GOLF

Taft's Game. Golf was played in the United States before 1888, but the U.S. Golf Association (USGA), with five charter clubs, was not established until 1894 as the governing body of U.S. play. By 1900 there were more than 1,000 courses in the United States, with Massachusetts and New York each having more than 150. The game spread rapidly from 1900 to 1920. A 25 June 1909 *New York Times* story reported a boom in golf when President William Howard Taft began playing the game to keep up his health. The number of players at some public links was reported to have doubled following media coverage of Taft's interest.

The 1910 Open. On 18 June 1910 Alex Smith (one of five brothers, all of whom were professional golfers) won the USGA Open Golf Tournament after an eighteen-hole playoff round against John J. McDermott and Macdonald Smith, the first three-way play-off in the Open's history. In the same year, he also won the Metropolitan Open. Alex Smith was considered one of the fastest putters in the game. He urged golfers to "go up to the ball and knock it into the hole" and he coined the phrase "miss 'em quick."

An American-Born Champion. British players seemed to have a lock on the U.S. Open title until June 1911, when McDermott, who learned the game in the caddy ranks, became the first American-born champion by defeating Michael Brady and George Simpson in a play-off round. He repeated his victory in August 1912. McDermott's legendary iron play was matched by his ego; he believed that he could beat anyone and could generally carry out his boast. His wins ended British supremacy of the game, but he did not fulfill his potential as a golfer as mental illness led to his permanent confinement in an institution.

Amateurs. In the amateur ranks, youth moved forward. Jerome D. Travers, an amateur from Long Island, New York, won his first U.S. Amateur championship in 1907, then captured the U.S. Open in 1915, the second amateur to earn this distinction. He was the game's most prominent figure from 1906 to 1915. Before Travers ended his career, he won four U.S. Amateur championships, five Metropolitan Amateur championships, and one U.S. Open title.

Ouimet Victory. On 20 September 1913 Francis Ouimet, a twenty-year-old amateur, won the U.S. Open Golf Tournament at the Brookline Country Club in Massachusetts. His upset victory after a three-way play-off remains the most significant win in the development of golf in the United States. His opponents were the two leading British professionals, Harry Vardon and Edward "Ted" Ray, the 1912 British Open champion. Ouimet played the last six holes two under par to tie Vardon and Ray. In the eighteen-hole play-off round Ouimet bested them by five and six strokes, respectively. It was one of the most dramatic play-offs in the history of the U.S. Open and was considered one of golf's most thrilling moments. A record number of entrants necessitated the first qualifying round in the history of the event. At least three thousand people witnessed this great upset and victory for native American talent.

Increasing Popularity of Game. The achievements of American golfers led to golf's increasing popularity. In 1913 there were 350,000 American golfers; in ten years the figure would grow to more than two million. As 1914 ended the Executive Committee of the U.S. Golf Association reported a membership of 88 active member clubs and 303 allied clubs, an increase of 33 over the previous year. After World War I the number of good American professionals grew along with the number of top-flight players capable of winning big tournaments. Unlike the British, the Americans were quick to build up the financial side of tournament play, particularly in the 1920s.

Walter Hagen. The U.S. Open held at the Midlothian Country Club in suburban Chicago in August 1914 was a watershed event. The last open before World War I took its toll on British golf, the tournament was distinguished as the final stand of the famous British "triumvirate" of Vardon, James Braid, and John H. Taylor. It also marked the first U.S. Open victory of American Walter Hagen, who defeated his fellow American, the amateur Charles "Chick" Evans Jr. Hagen's contribution to golf at Midlothian, however, surpassed his notable achievements as a player, as his actions helped to make professional golf a respectable occupation. Considered socially inferior to the club members, the first golf pros were mostly Englishmen and Scots who designed the early courses, kept the grounds, made and repaired the hickory-shafted golf clubs, trained and managed caddies, and instructed novices. Before Hagen pros received little money from tournament earnings, product endorsements, or paid exhibitions. During open tournaments, they were barred from the clubhouses. Hagen, with his pleasing personality, sartorial elegance, and supreme confidence, challenged this social discrimination directly, precipitating the "Midlothian Incident." Feigning ignorance of rules barring pros, Hagen made himself at home in the clubhouse and in the

Francis Ouimet spraying himself with water as he saves his ball from a hazard

locker room. The country club soon gave up its attempt to enforce its rules, thus quietly acceding to "a social revolution in American golf."

Endorsements. Throughout his career Hagen broke down social barriers in both the United States and Europe. Rather than rely upon tournament winnings, Hagen made his money on tours and product endorsements, hiring a business manager, Robert "Bob" Harlow, hailed as the "founder of professional golf," to guide his career. Harlow capitalized on Hagen's popularity by lining up endorsements for golf equipment and arranging profitable golf tours that netted Hagen between $30,000 to $50,000 annually.

American Triumvirate. On 18 June 1915 Travers, then America's leading amateur, became the second amateur to win the U.S. Open and to stand off the pros. Ouimet, Evans, and Travers were often called the great amateur triumvirate of America. In the 1916 U.S. Open Evans established a record low of 286, which was not matched until 1932, when Gene Sarazen tied it. The prize money was increased to $1,200 in 1916, with the winner getting $500 (if professional) and a gold medal. Evans also won the 1916 National Amateur, the first time both events were captured in the same year by one golfer.

Professional Golfers' Association. On 17 January 1916, the Professional Golfers' Association (PGA) began at a luncheon in New York City given by Rodman Wanamaker, of the Wanamaker department store family, and attended by many top golfers. The organization developed from a desire of the early professionals to foster interest in the game, to raise the standard of living for the sport's pros, and to maintain a high standard of professional ethics. On 7 February an organizing committee established the new association, drew up tentative bylaws, and chose a permanent committee. Its first president was Robert White. Three months later the first national PGA tournament was held at the Siwanoy Golf Course in Bronxville, New York, on 10 April. It was won by Jim Barnes, of Great Britain, with a one-stroke victory over Jock Hutchison. Wanamaker donated a total prize of $2,580 with $500 going to the winner. World War I stopped play in 1917 and in 1918 but Barnes successfully defended his PGA crown in 1919 by defeating Fred McLeod in the final round.

Women. Women's interest in golf in the 1910s continued to develop, though the only major championship for women was the U.S. Women's Amateur, first held in 1895 in Hempstead, New York. Because of discrimination, progress for women in the game was slower than it might have been. On 30 July 1916 *The New York Times* reported that women golf players had only restricted access to most courses in New York and in New Jersey. The Garden City Golf Club in New York allowed women to play only on Monday and Friday mornings, and they had to tee off by 11 AM. The twenty or so women members of the Upper Montclair Country Club in New Jersey were not allowed to play on holidays; they were restricted to Saturday mornings and to Sundays after 3 PM.

World War I and After. When the United States entered World War I in 1917, all golf tournaments were canceled. However, the PGA sponsored an "open patriotic tournament" in 1917 at the Whitemarsh Country Club in Philadelphia to benefit the American Red Cross and charged admission to spectators, a practice copied by the U.S. Open in 1921. The Whitemarsh tournament was probably the first tournament played as a fund-raiser, but it was not the last as many exhibitions were staged throughout the war. In 1919 all major U.S. tournaments were resumed and on 11 June 1919, Walter Hagen won the first postwar U.S. Open Golf Tournament at Brae Burn Country Club in West Newton, Massachusetts, with a 301 total and a play-off victory over Michael Brady. The USGA increased the prize money in the U.S. Open to $1,745, which provided purses for the first twelve players though first prize remained $500. By the end of the 1910s, golf was well established in appeal and popularity in a nation that increasingly valued exercise and open air sports. Emphasizing etiquette and polite manners, the game appealed to businessmen and the upper classes who found it challenging and diverting.

HORSE RACES AND PURSES, 1909-1913

Year	Racing Days	Races	Purse Distribution	Average Purse
1909	724	4,510	$3,146,695	$698
1910	1,063	6,501	$2,942,333	$453
1911	1,037	6,289	$2,337,957	$372
1912	926	5,806	$2,391,625	$412
1913	969	6,136	$2,920,963	$476

Sources:

Gerald Astor, *The PGA World Golf Hall of Fame Book* (Englewood Cliffs, N.J.: Prentice-Hall, 1991);

Al Barkow, *The History of the PGA Tour* (Garden City, N.Y.: Doubleday, 1989);

Nevin H. Gibson, *The Encyclopedia of Golf* (New York: Barnes, 1958);

Douglas A. Noverr and Lawrence E. Ziewacz, *The Games They Played: Sports in American History, 1865–1980* (Chicago: Nelson-Hall, 1983);

Robert Sommers, *The U.S. Open; Golf's Ultimate Challenge* (New York: Atheneum, 1987);

David Stirk, *Golf; the History of an Obsession* (Oxford: Phaidon, 1987).

HORSE RACING

Beginnings. During the 1910s horse racing emerged from a period of financial instability. Formerly dependent on admission charges for their prize money, major tracks began to conduct stake races in which horse owners paid an entry fee that became part of the purse. Stake races included the Saratoga Cup, the Belmont, the Champagne, the Alabama, the Preakness, the Withers, and the Kentucky Derby.

Betting. Just as thoroughbred racing was expanding, it was threatened by a nationwide reform movement directed at gambling. Bookmakers, who paid a fee to the track owner for the privilege of handling track betting, were a particular target. A Kentucky law passed in 1908 specifically prohibited bookmaking. Churchill Downs remained open by adopting pari-mutuel betting, which was legal, while other tracks in Kentucky as well as those in Maryland, which had a similar law against bookmaking, began to take pari-mutuel bets. In New York, racing shut down for two years after bookmaking and gaming devices were prohibited in 1910 under the Director's Liability Act, and racetracks were made responsible for its enforcement. New York antigaming measures affected even pastimes such as hog-calling contests, since fair management feared that patrons would bet on the outcome.

Maryland and Kentucky. The New York racing blackout did not adversely affect racing in other parts of the

Man O' War, the chestnut colt who lost only one race in his career

country. During the 1910 and 1911 seasons, there was actually more racing in America than in the years before or after. Tracks in states where racing was still legal tried to benefit from the New York situation, and in Maryland and Kentucky racing increased during the two-year period. Helped by a Maryland pari-mutuel law in 1912, the Pimlico racetrack in Baltimore, one of the most popular and prosperous tracks in the East, became a perennial leader among American tracks in daily purse distribution in the 1920s. Baltimore developed its own racing circuit with the opening of Laurel in 1911, Havre de Grace in 1912, and Prince George Park (later Bowie) in 1914. In Kentucky, racing gains were offset by severe damage to the state's more important breeding industry as the market for thoroughbreds was weakened when breeding efforts were begun in other states.

Roamer. In 1913, after unsensational starts at Pimlico and in Kentucky, two-year-old Roamer, one of the original "horses for courses," won the Saratoga Special, his only stakes victory that season. Five years later in August 1918, Roamer crowned his career in an exhibition race at Saratoga by beating the previous record time of 1:35.5 for the mile. Carrying 110 pounds, Roamer quickly left his pacesetter behind and clicked off quarter-mile fractions of 23.6, 46.0, 1:10.2, and 1:34.8 to set a new record. This was the last mark for a popularly run distance established in a race against time. All subsequent records were set during actual competition.

Regret. In May 1915 Regret, considered one of the greatest mares in the sport, became the first filly to win the Kentucky Derby. Fighting the traditional wisdom that no three-year-old filly could beat colts at a mile and a quarter, she went to the post a strong favorite and stayed in the lead throughout the race. Regret retired with nine wins and one place in eleven starts for total earnings of $35,093. No other filly ever finished in front of her.

Exterminator. On 11 May 1918 Exterminator, an ungainly three-year-old gelding, made his debut at the Kentucky Derby and won by a length. In fifteen starts that year, he was out of the money only once. During his career Exterminator started one hundred races, won fifty, placed in seventeen, and showed in seventeen for earnings of $252,996. For four straight seasons Exterminator

THE TRIPLE CROWN

The Triple Crown is the most coveted and elusive prize in American thoroughbred horse racing. The inspiration for the American Triple Crown came from England, where the Epsom Derby, the St. Ledger, and the Two Thousand Guineas races were considered the three jewels in the crown. In the 1930s Charles Hatton, a turf reporter for the Morning Telegraph, first applied the term *Triple Crown* to the Kentucky Derby, the Preakness Stakes, and the Belmont Stakes. In 1950 the Thoroughbred Racing Association decided to award a Triple Crown trophy retroactively to Sir Barton, the winner of the three races in 1919, and the 1948 champion Citation. At the association's awards dinner, Sir Barton was recognized with a three-sided silver trophy designed by Cartier as the first horse to win the American Triple Crown.

Source: Marvin Drager, *The Most Glorious Crown* (New York: Winchester Press, 1975).

was the leading money winner of the handicap division, which penalized a horse for winning by assigning it higher weights in subsequent races. The horse won at sixteen different racetracks in three different countries and dominated long routes.

Sir Barton. On 10 May 1919 Sir Barton, ridden by Johnny Loftus, won the forty-fifth annual Kentucky Derby with a time of 2:09.8. Loftus also rode Sir Barton to wins in the Preakness and in the Belmont Stakes, making the horse the first Triple Crown champion in racing history. Since the derby was his first race, Sir Barton's weight assignment was so low (110 pounds) that his jockey was two-and-one-half pounds overweight in the race. Taking the lead immediately, Sir Barton never looked back and scored the first victory of his career by five lengths. It was a happy victory for trainer H. G. "Hard Guy" Bedwell, the leading trainer of 1916, and for owner J. K. L. Ross, a wealthy Canadian businessman, yachtsman, and war hero. Their other horse in the race, Billy Kelly, finished second, the first one-two result in Derby history. Eternal, a slight favorite in the betting, finished tenth. Sir Barton went on to become the biggest money winner of the season. He never finished out of the money in thirteen starts, eight of which he won, including the Derby, the Preakness, Withers, Belmont Stakes, Potomac (Maryland), and two Pimlico fall serial races.

Man o' War. One of the greatest legends of horse racing got his start at the end of the decade. Man o' War, described as having the "look of eagles" and a "living flame," appeared upon the scene at the same time as Bill

Tilden and Jack Dempsey and got racing in the 1920s off to a roaring start. He suffered his only defeat on 13 August 1919 at the Sanford Stakes in Saratoga to a horse named Upset. In his remarkable career he won twenty races in twenty-one starts and retired as America's leading money winner. Man o' War was the first stud to command a $5,000 service fee. He seemed to set all of his eight record times effortlessly: three world records, two American records, and three track records.

Sources:
Marvin Drager, *The Most Glorious Crown* (New York: Winchester, 1975);

William H.P. Robertson, *The History of Thoroughbred Racing in America* (Englewood Cliffs, N.J.: Prentice-Hall, 1964);

Suzanne Wilding and Anthony Del Balso, *The Triple Crown Winners: The Story of America's Ten Superstar Race Horses*, revised edition (New York: Parents' Magazine, 1978).

OLYMPIC GAMES

The Selection of Stockholm. In 1896 the first modern Olympic Games were held in Athens, the site of the original games. Subsequent Olympic Games were hosted by Paris in 1900, Saint Louis in 1904, and London in 1908. These Olympic Games were held in conjunction with World's Fairs, events that often overshadowed the athletic contests. Meeting in Berlin in 1909, the International Olympic Committee (IOC) selected Stockholm, Sweden, as the site of the fifth Olympic Games. "Of all the countries in the world," remarked Baron Pierre de Coubertin, the founder of the modern Olympic movement and secretary-general of the IOC, "Sweden is at the moment best qualified to host a great Olympic Games." Although Stockholm's award was largely because of a strong campaign by Sweden's longtime IOC representative, Col. Victor Balak, who would become the chairman of the Swedish Olympic Organizing Committee, Germany ensured the selection of the Swedish capital by withdrawing Berlin as a candidate for the host city. In order to hold the Olympic Games in Stockholm, however, the IOC dropped boxing from its schedule of events, because Sweden prohibited the sport.

The Swedish Success. The Games of the fifth Olympiad, according to historian John Lucas, were "the best organized and most pacific international games since the original Athens' celebration." Held from 5 May to 22 July, the Stockholm Olympics were the largest since the revival of the Games in 1896, with 2,490 athletes from twenty-eight nations participating. Sweden, the host nation, finished as the unofficial team champion with sixty-five medals — twenty-four gold, twenty-four silver, and seventeen bronze. The United States finished second to the Swedes, garnering sixty-one medals, of which twenty-three were gold, nineteen silver, and nineteen bronze. Great Britain, the team champion of the 1908 Olympic Games held in London, was third with forty-one medals — ten gold, fifteen silver, and sixteen bronze. Scandinavian athletes, on the whole, performed well in

Ralph Craig, the sprinter who led the American domination of the track-and-field events in the 1912 Olympics

the 1912 games. Swedish athletes, who won medals in nearly all sports, were particularly strong in the triple jump, cross-country, equestrian, modern pentathlon, shooting, diving, Greco-Roman wrestling, and yachting. Finnish runners initiated their pre–World War II dominance in long distance events.

American Triumphs. As in previous Olympic Games, American athletes dominated track and field. Ralph Craig of the University of Michigan won both the 100 meters, leading an American medal sweep, and the 200 meters. Syracuse University's Charles Reidpath won the 400 meters in an Olympic record of 48.2 seconds. James Meredith, a prep-school runner from Pennsylvania, captured the 800 meters in a world record of 1:51.9, narrowly defeating countrymen Melvin Sheppard and Ira Davenport by a hundredth of a second. Louis Tewanima, a Hopi Indian, finished second to Finland's Johannes Kolehmainen in the 10,000 meters. Jim Thorpe, a Native American of Sac and Fox descent, won the decathlon and pentathlon events. Americans swept the medals in the 110-meter high hurdles, pole vault, and shot put. Hawaiian swimmer Duke Kahanamoku won the 100-meter freestyle, his first of five Olympic medals spread over four Olympic Games. Americans performed surprisingly well in shooting, winning four gold medals, three silver, and one bronze. In the three-day equestrian team event, Americans won the bronze medal. American cyclists also won bronze in the individual and team road races.

Furor over Women's Aquatics. The IOC expanded women's sports to include swimming and diving at the 1912 games. Many in the United States and Australia opposed this expansion of women's events on the Olympic schedule. James E. Sullivan, the head of the AAU in the United States, opposed women's sports altogether, and did not permit American female swimmers and divers to compete in Stockholm. Australian feminist Rose Scott opposed female participation in swimming and diving because, as historian Allen Guttmann put it, she "feared that the presence of shapely young women in swimsuits might attract more voyeurs than sports spectators." Scott's protests aside, Australian women went to Stockholm and returned with the gold and silver medals in the 100-meter freestyle. Sarah Durack, the gold medalist, won the event in a world record of 1:22.2. In the 4-by-100-meter freestyle relay the British won in a world record of 5:52.8. Greta Johansson and Lisa Regnell, both of Sweden, dueled in platform diving, with Johansson gaining the gold and Regnell the silver. Despite the pre-Olympic furor over the women's swimming and diving events, Everett C. Brown, an AAU associate of Sullivan, viewed and approved of the new events, noting that any criticism of them must "have been brought about by foul minds."

Berlin Plans for the 1916 Games. In 1909, when the IOC met in Berlin and decided upon Stockholm as the site for the 1912 Olympic Games, it also told the German Olympic Committee to "begin serious planning for the 1916 Olympic celebration." This announcement inspired the Germans to make Berlin the ultimate site for the Olympic Games. Since 1896, when the German Olympic Committee had returned from the first modern Olympic Games in Athens, they had campaigned vigorously to host the event in Berlin. Immediately upon learning that the German capital would most likely be the site for the Games of the sixth Olympiad, the Berliners started construction of a thirty-four-thousand-seat stadium, complete with a four-hundred-meter running track and six-hundred-meter cycling track, as well as a one-hundred-meter swimming pool with a gallery for four thousand spectators. In 1911 the IOC announced officially that Berlin would host the 1916 Olympic Games, but national elation turned into disappointment after German athletes failed to perform well in the 1912 Olympic Games. In response, the Germans visited the United States to study military and collegiate athletic

Maurice E. McLoughlin moving toward the net against Richard Norris Williams III in the championship match at Newport, Rhode Island, in 1913

training systems. They hired Alvin C. Kraenzlein, a German American who coached track at the University of Michigan and an Olympic gold medalist from 1900, to prepare German Olympians. Once in Germany, Kraenzlein told *The New York Times* in 1913 that German "life could only benefit from the healthy enthusiasm and rivalry found in athletic competition and Olympic sports."

The Games Canceled by War. In addition to unfurling the five-ringed flag that has come to symbolize the Olympic Games, the IOC finalized the program for the 1916 Olympic Games at the 1914 IOC convention. After the convention Robert Thompson, the president of the American Olympic Committee, remarked that "the Berlin Games would be the greatest ever held," because of the thoroughness of the Germans' organization and preparation. Less than a month after Thompson made that remark, war broke out in Europe. Germany, allied with Austria-Hungary, declared war on Russia and France. Coubertin believed that the Germans, as the host nation for the 1916 Olympic Games, would sue for a peaceful end to the war, but Germany soon invaded Belgium, and Great Britain entered the war against the Central Powers, Germany and Austria-Hungary. Anticipating a quick end to the conflict, the German Olympic Committee continued to prepare for the Games, but other national Olympic Committees urged Coubertin to change the

venue for the Games. In a letter to *The New York Times* in 1915 Coubertin stated his position: "The Sixth Olympic Games remain and will remain credited to Berlin, but it is possible that they will not be held." With European civilization on the brink of destruction during the summer of 1916, Berlin's Olympic Games were canceled.

Sources:

John Findling and Kimberly Pele, eds., *The Historical Dictionary of the Olympic Games* (Westport, Conn.: Greenwood Press, 1996);

Allen Guttmann, *The Olympics: A History of the Modern Games* (Urbana & Chicago: University of Illinois Press, 1994);

David Wallechinsky, *The Complete Book of the Olympics*, revised edition (New York: Viking, 1988).

TENNIS

Rich Game. The sport of tennis was largely confined to the East Coast before 1900. It was seen as a private or club sport played by the wealthy. As the sport grew more popular, courts on public playgrounds were built with hard surfaces of cement, clay, or asphalt rather than the high-maintenance grass courts popular with the rich. In the 1910s, tennis was still generally viewed as a sport of the well-to-do and upwardly mobile. The ambitious middle class and nouveau riche were in the taking control of the U.S. Lawn Tennis Association (USLTA), the regional associations, and many of the tennis clubs.

Molla Bjurstedt (Mallory), who won eight U.S. singles' championships

Hotchkiss and Larned. In 1910 and 1911 Hazel V. Hotchkiss (later Hazel Hotchkiss Wightman, the donor of the Wightman Cup) won the USLTA singles championship in the women's division for the second and third years in a row, and William A. Larned brought his total number of men's singles titles to seven (1901–1902 and 1907–1911). Hotchkiss's aggressive forecourt play added a new dimension to women's tennis. In 1910 she also won the women's and mixed doubles championships, losing only five games in all three finals. As Hazel Hotchkiss Wightman, she would win her final singles title in 1919, defeating Molla Bjurstedt.

Triumph of McLoughlin. The year 1912 was the first in which the defending USLTA champion was required to play through the entire tournament instead of only having to play the tournament survivor in a challenge match. On 26 August 1912 the singles championships were won by Mary K. Browne and Maurice E. McLoughlin, the "California Comet." McLoughlin also won the championship the next year, and Browne won in 1913 and 1914. McLoughlin, who learned his sport on the public courts of San Francisco, played with dash and style. His power serves, dashes to the net, strategic vol-

leying, and daring shots down the line were a refreshing change from the cautious backline game of serve and lob in which the forecourt was almost an unknown area of play. McLoughlin electrified tennis prior to World War I, transforming the game from the staid, restrained sport epitomized by Larned, an unspectacular player who relied on careful placement and steady service, rarely scoring an ace.

Exploits on the World Court. McLoughlin made his only European appearance in the 1913 Wimbledon, where he thrilled spectators with his cannonball serves. He completed the all-comers' singles and challenged Tony Wilding, the titleholder since 1910, for the crown. McLoughlin lost all three sets, but Wilding's reign ended in 1914 with his defeat by his Australian Davis Cup colleague, Norman Brookes. In 1914 McLoughlin defeated Brookes in what was considered one of the greatest sets in Davis Cup history. McLoughlin won 17–15 in the first set and then took the next two sets easily. McLoughlin and Hotchkis changed the style of tennis and helped popularize the sport among the middle class.

A Foreign Champion. At the Stockholm Olympics in 1912, Norwegian Molla Bjurstedt won the bronze medal for the women's singles on indoor courts. She became the first foreigner to win the women's USLTA singles championship in 1915, the first of four titles in a row. As Molla Mallory, she also won the American championship from 1920 to 1922 and in 1926.

Shifting Play. In 1915 the USLTA moved the men's championships from Newport, Rhode Island, to the West Side Tennis Club in Forest Hills, in the New York borough of Queens, to attract a larger audience. The women's championships would be moved there from Philadelphia in 1921. In 1914, the last year at Newport, Richard Norris Williams II defeated McLoughlin to take the national men's singles championship. The Newport Casino, the home of America's most prestigious tennis event for thirty-four years, remained as a tourney site and became home to the Tennis Hall of Fame, but the exclusive era in tennis it represented was in the past.

McLoughlin's Successor. In September 1915 Californian William M. Johnston succeeded McLoughlin as the game's premier player. Like McLoughlin, he had an easy smile and a genial disposition that won him much loyal support. He played a power game but was more deliberate and balanced than McLoughlin. In 1915 and in 1919 he claimed the men's singles championships. A great doubles player as well, he won national championships in 1915, 1916, and 1920 when he teamed with Clarence Griffin. Johnston and McLoughlin were the first heroes of tennis and brought many fans to their dynamic sport.

International Lawn Tennis Federation. Prior to 1913 the British Lawn Tennis Association (BLTA), with members from all over the world, was as close as tennis could come to a world governing body. Intended to replace the BLTA, the International Lawn Tennis Federation (ILTF) was founded by Australia, Austria, Belgium, the British Isles, Denmark, France, Germany, Netherlands, Russia, South Africa, Sweden, and Switzerland. The United States did not formally join the new organization but was informally represented by one of the British delegates at the ILTF's first meeting in Paris on 1 March 1913. The American absence resulted in the Davis Cup organization developing as a parallel but separate entity to the ILTF (the two bodies did not merge until 1978). The separate international organizations led to various "world championship" titles ("World Championship on Grass," "World Championships on Hard Court"), which were abolished after World War I when the United States became an ILTF member. The Davis Cup organization continued to boost tennis as an international sport. Prior to World War I, which temporarily halted the competition, nine nations, including the United States, participated.

The Game's Golden Future. In 1918, a tall, ungainly man from Philadelphia, William Tilden, made his third bid for the national singles title at the West Side Tennis Club, but he was beaten by Robert Lindley Murray, a left-hander with a big serve, who had also won the event the year before. In 1919 "Big Bill" Tilden stepped on to the court with "Little Bill" Johnston in the first of six meetings in the national finals that *The New York Times* billed as the battle for the title "William the Conqueror." Johnston won the first of the six clashes, but Tilden was the victor in all the rest. He was soon being called the greatest player of all time.

A French Champion. At the World's Hard Court Championships in Paris in 1914, Suzanne Lenglen, a promising young French girl from Picardy, won the women's doubles with a Californian partner, Elizabeth Ryan. Lenglen would go on to be considered by many the greatest player in the history of the women's game. Ryan's career also deserves mention. In 1914, she joined with Agatha Morton to win the women's doubles, the first of nineteen titles she gained at Wimbledon, a record that held until 1979 when Billie Jean King won her twentieth doubles match with Martina Navratilova.

Sources:

Bud Collins' Modern Encyclopedia of Tennis, edited by Bud Collins and Zander Hollander (Detroit: Gale Research, 1980, 1994);

Douglas A. Noverr and Lawrence E. Ziewacz, *The Games They Played: Sports in American History, 1865–1980* (Chicago: Nelson-Hall, 1983);

Benjamin G. Rader, *American Sports: From the Age of Folk Games to the Age of Televised Sports,* second edition (Englewood Cliffs, N.J.: Prentice Hall, 1990);

Alan Trengove, *The Story of the Davis Cup* (London: Stanley Paul, 1985).

TRACK AND FIELD

Drew's Decade. The 1910s witnessed the rise of Howard P. Drew, the first in a long line of African American sprinters during the twentieth century who earned the title of "the world's fastest human." In 1910 and 1911 he first gained national attention by winning national junior championships in the 100- and 220-yard dashes. Drew became a favorite for a gold medal in the 1912 Olympic Games by defeating Ralph Craig of the University of Michigan in the 100 meters at the Eastern Olympic Trials. In the Olympic Games at Stockholm Drew won his semifinal in 10.7 seconds, but declined to compete in the final because of an injury sustained in the semifinal. Craig, the 1910 and 1911 collegiate champion at 100 and 220 yards, won the Olympic gold medal in the 100 meters, defeating compatriot Donald Lippincott, who set world and Olympic records of 10.6 seconds in the semifinal. Craig, who had twice run world records of 21.2 seconds for 220 yards in 1910 and 1911, also won the gold medal in the 200-meter dash. Drew, however, returned to the United States and captured the first of two consecutive Amateur Athletic Union (AAU) 100-yard dash titles; in 1913, he also captured the AAU 220-yard dash title. As a student at the University of Southern California, Drew equaled the world records of 9.6 seconds for 100 yards and 21.2 seconds for 220 yards in 1914. Charles Paddock, America's foremost sprinter in the 1920s, hailed Drew as "the smoothest piece of running machinery the world has ever seen."

Patrick J. McDonald, Olympic and three-time American shot put champion

three consecutive collegiate titles. His 1911 victory resulted in a world record of 4:15.4, and his 1913 triumph resulted in a world record of 4:14.4, the first world record for the distance recognized by the International Amateur Athletic Federation, an organization formed in 1912 to govern track and field. Jones's world records, however, were inferior to the professional record of 4:12.8 set by Walter George of Great Britain in 1885. While Jones ruled collegiate mile running, Abel Kiviat, a Jewish athlete representing the Irish American Athletic Club, captured AAU mile titles in 1911, 1912, and 1914. In 1912 he established a world record of 3:55.8 for the 1,500 meters, making him a favorite for the Olympic gold medal. Jones, Kiviat, and Norman Taber of Brown University represented the United States in the 1,500 meters in the 1912 Olympic Games. Arnold Jackson of England, however, bested the American trio in the Olympic final. Taber, who had tied Jones in the 1912 collegiate mile run championship, established an amateur world record of 4:12.6 for the mile in 1915. In that year, Joie W. Ray won the first of a record eight AAU mile championships.

High Jump. American high jumpers revolutionized their events during the 1910s. George Horine developed the "western roll," a more economical style of high jumping than the traditional scissors technique. Whereas the traditional jumper would maintain an upright position and clear the bar with his legs cutting through the air in a scissorlike, clipping motion, the innovative Horine would roll over the bar with his body parallel to the ground. In 1912 he utilized the western roll to establish world records of 6′ 6 1/8" and 6′ 7". At the 1912 Olympic Games, however, Horine garnered only the bronze medal, as fellow American Alma Richards won the gold medal in an Olympic record jump of 6′ 4". Another innovator in the high jump was Clinton Larson, who introduced a face-up, back-to-the bar style, similar to the "flop" popularized by Richard Fosbury in the 1960s. Larson used the technique to win the 1917 AAU title.

Pole Vault. In the pole vault Marc Wright developed the techniques that other twentieth-century pole-vaulters have followed, Wright used a thirty-meter run-up, a prolonged swing, a single-hand release (first with the left hand, then the right hand), and an arch position over the bar. Wright won the 1912 Olympic Trials in a world record of 13′ 2 1/4". Like Horine in the high jump, Wright's innovations failed him in the Olympic Games, as he garnered only the bronze medal in the pole vault. Harry Babcock, the 1912 AAU champion, won the gold medal in an Olympic record of 12′ 11 1/2". Frank Foss, the 1919 AAU champion, introduced the "jackknife" clearance position over the bar.

Irish American Catapults. The 1910s was the last decade in which Irish Americans dominated in the shot put, discus throw, and hammer throws. Patrick J. McDonald, an Irish-born New York policeman, who won the 1911, 1912, and 1919 shot put titles, defeated Ralph Rose, the defending Olympic champion in the 1912

Middle Distances. In the early twentieth century, the 440-yard dash was not considered a sprinter's race but rather a middle distance event, more akin to the 880-yard run than to the 220-yard dash. In the 1912 Olympic Games, Charles Reidpath, the 1910 and 1912 collegiate champion in the 440 from Syracuse University, won the 400 meters in an Olympic record of 48.2 seconds. James "Ted" Meredith defeated compatriot and defending Olympic champion Melvin Sheppard in the 800-meter event. Meredith's winning time of 1:51.9, a new world record, eclipsed the standard set by Sheppard in the 1908 Olympic Games. As a member of the United States 1,600-meter relay team, which established a world record of 3:16.6, Meredith won a second Olympic gold medal. For the remainder of the 1910s, the 440- and 880-yard runs belonged to Meredith, who enrolled at the University of Pennsylvania after returning from the 1912 Olympic Games. He won three consecutive collegiate 440 titles from 1914 to 1916, and two straight 880 titles in 1915 and 1916. Meredith captured two consecutive AAU titles in the 440 in 1914 and 1915; his latter victory, on a straight course, resulted in an astounding, but unofficial, world record of 47 seconds. In 1916 he established a legitimate world record of 47.4 for the 440 as well as a world mark of 1:52.5 in the 880.

A Trio of American Milers. A trio of Americans rose to the forefront of mile running during the decade. From 1911 to 1913, John Paul Jones of Cornell University won

Olympic Games, setting an Olympic record of 50′ 4″. In 1912 James Duncan established a world record of 156′ 1 3/8″ in the discus throw but failed to garner the Olympic gold medal that year, winning only the bronze medal in Stockholm. Matthew McGrath, who won his first AAU hammer throw title in 1908, garnered the national championship in 1910, 1912, and 1918. At the 1912 Olympic Games, he won the gold medal in the hammer throw, setting an Olympic record of 179′ 7″. McGrath's rival, Patrick J. Ryan, won seven AAU championships (1913–1917 and 1919–1920). McGrath and Ryan battled over the world record in the event. In 1913 McGrath achieved a distance of 190′ 10″, which was not recognized as a world record because it came during an exhibition meet. Four days later Ryan claimed an official world record with a toss of 189′ 6 1/2″.

Sources:

Roberto L. Quercetani, *A World History of Modern Track and Field Athletics* (New York: Oxford University Press, 1964);

David Wallechinsky, *The Complete Book of the Olympics*, revised edition (New York: Penguin, 1988).

HEADLINE MAKERS

JAY GOULD

1888-1935

COURT TENNIS CHAMPION

A Court Master's Education. From 1906 to 1925 Jay Gould dominated court tennis, one of the more obscure sports in the United States during the late nineteenth and early twentieth centuries. Court tennis is a completely different game than tennis: players use the walls and ceilings in making their shots. Whereas lawn tennis gained much popularity during the 1910s and 1920s, court tennis remained the game of a wealthy elite because of the cost of maintaining the indoor, enclosed court. Exclusive urban athletic clubs usually maintained court tennis facilities, but some individuals, such as Jay Gould's father, George Gould, a wealthy industrialist, constructed their own courts. In 1900 Jay and his brother Kingdon began to take lessons in racquets and tennis from Frank Forester. After a year of instruction in racquets (a forerunner of modern racquetball), Forester introduced the boys to the rigors of court tennis. Although they at first received an hour of instruction in each game, the boys preferred court tennis and soon began practicing it daily for two hours. Jay quickly mastered the fundamentals of court tennis and, according to tennis authority Allison Danzig, offered Forester "fairly strong opposition." In 1902 Jay won his first official match, two sets to none, against James Henry Smith, one of the better players at both the New York Racquet and Tennis Club and the Tuxedo Club. Later that year Smith arranged for Gould to play Pierre Lorillard Jr., one of the nation's top players, at the Tuxedo Club. Although Lorillard won their 1902 meeting, Gould triumphed in 1903.

"So Young and Capable a Player." In the three years prior to his first national court tennis championship, Gould continued to learn from Forester and gained experience from playing and often defeating many of the world's best players. In 1903 Ernest A. Thomson, one of the leading players in New York, played Gould on the latter's home court in New Jersey. Thomson defeated Gould by using the "railroad service," a technique unfamiliar to the teenager. Gould, according to Danzig, "was so taken with it that he immediately asked to be taught it." Thomson showed him how to hold the racquet and deliver the serve. Gould quickly mastered the technique and soon developed his own variations. In 1905 Gould was considered one of the leading court tennis players in the United States and played in the Godl Racquet Tennis Tournament at the Tuxedo Club. Although he reached the finals, he lost the championship, three games to one, to Charles E. Sands, the reigning national champion. Later that year he played Peter Latham, who held the world's title from 1896 to 1905. Latham gave Gould a handicap of fifteen points, and Gould defeated him in two straight matches, nine games to seven, and six games to two. Afterward, Latham remarked: "Young Gould is the finest player for his years I have ever known."

The National Champion. In 1906 Gould won the first of eighteen straight national court tennis singles championships. He prefaced his first with a victory over Lorillard in the Gold Racquet tournament at the Tuxedo Club. On the eve of the national championships at the Racquet and Tennis Club in New York City, Gould, wrote Danzig, "created great uneasiness among the old guard lest the monopoly of New York and Boston in winning the title be broken up." In the finals, it seemed the "old guard" could rest assured that the New Jersey teenager would be denied the title as Joshua Crane led Gould two sets to one and five games to three in the fourth and deciding match. Then, an event occurred that altered the mood of the game. A pair of spectacles fell from the gallery onto the court, and while play was suspended for the glass to be swept up, Gould relaxed and regained his composure while Crane stiffened up. Gould took the fourth set and the right to challenge Sands for the national title after defeating Crane six sets to two. In the challenge round, Gould defeated Sands three sets to one, and claimed the national championship.

The World's Best. Shortly after winning the U.S. national court tennis title Gould, with Forester as his coach, sailed to London to challenge Eustace Miles for the English championship. The young American qualified for the final round in which he had to face V. H. Pennell, the 1905 runner-up, before playing Miles for the championship. Although Gould defeated Pennell three sets to one, he lost to Miles four sets to one. When Gould returned to England in 1907, thousands jammed the Queen's Club to see the championship match, which Gould won, becoming the first American to win the British court tennis title. In 1908 Gould solidified his place as the world's best tournament player by winning the gold medal in court tennis in the Olympic Games in London.

Gould Retires a Champion. Except for 1918 and 1919, when World War I led to the cancellation of the national court tennis championships, Gould successfully defended the national championship to 1925. His reign as the singles champion came to an end in 1926, when he announced he would not defend his title because of poor physical condition after a serious bout with influenza. Although he gave up singles, Gould continued doubles play. Previously, he had teamed with W. T. H. Huhn for eight championships (1909 and 1911–1917) and with Joseph W. Wear for six (1920–1924 and 1926); he won five more doubles titles with W. C. Wright (1927–1929 and 1931–1932).

Sources:

Allison Danzig, *The Racquet Game* (New York: Macmillian, 1930);

Danzig, *The Winning Gallery* (Philadelphia: United States Court Tennis Association of America, 1985).

JOE JACKSON

1887-1951

BASEBALL PLAYER

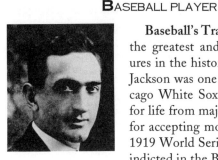

Baseball's Tragic Hero. One of the greatest and most tragic figures in the history of baseball, Joe Jackson was one of the eight Chicago White Sox players banished for life from major league baseball for accepting money to throw the 1919 World Series. Of the players indicted in the Black Sox Scandal,

as it came to be known, Jackson was indeed the most tragic. Even though he took $5,000 after the completion of the Series, he had played exceptionally well and maintained that he played to win during the entire championship. His tragedy seems all the greater because of his rise from impoverished beginnings in the rural South and his status as one of the greatest ever to play the game. As a hitter Jackson was surpassed perhaps only by Babe Ruth, who adopted Jackson's batting stance and swing. Asked why he fashioned his style after Jackson, Babe remarked, "Why not? Joe had the most perfect swing I ever saw." No less a judge than Ty Cobb maintained that Jackson was the best outfielder in the game.

Mill Boy. Joseph Jefferson Jackson was born on a rundown plantation in Pickens County, South Carolina, where his father, George Jackson, worked as a sharecropper. When Joe turned six years old, his father moved the family to Brandon Mill, a cotton mill town run by northern industrialists in search of cheap southern labor. The entire Jackson family, Joe, his father, six brothers, and two sisters, worked in the Brandon Cotton Mill. The mill was a dangerous place to work. Joe's brother Davey was caught in the mill machinery and maimed for life. The Jacksons, like other mill town families, earned such small paychecks that they were persistently in debt to the company for rent, groceries, and clothes. The mill, however, did organize a baseball team, giving its players less hazardous jobs and time off to practice each day. Moreover, the baseball team was paid to play games against other mill town teams. For Jackson the baseball team would open his way to an easier life in the mill and eventually a way out of poverty.

From the Mill to the Majors. The thirteen-year-old Jackson joined the Brandon Mill baseball team in 1901. He began as a catcher on the team but was soon moved to pitcher because of his strong throwing arm. Jackson pitched so hard that he broke a catcher's arm, after which he moved to the outfield. In 1907 he joined a semipro team in nearby Greenville, South Carolina. Jackson's play for the semipro team caught the eye of Tom Stouch, a former major league second baseman, who was the manager of the Greenville team in the recently organized Carolina Association. Stouch did not think much of Jackson until he saw him swing the bat. "He didn't appear to have much in him, but he drove the ball . . . like a bullet out of a gun," Stouch recalled. "I thought to myself, if this rube hits 'em like that every time, he must be some whale." Stouch signed Jackson to a seventy-five-dollar-a-month contract, nearly twice his pay at the mill. In 1908, after batting .346 for Greenville, Jackson caught the attention of Connie Mack, the manager of the Philadelphia Athletics of the American League, who bought the southern ace for $900. Jackson, who had never been away from his family, had reservations about going to Philadelphia, and remarked to Stouch, "I hardly know as how I'd like it in those big Northern cities." Jackson failed to play well in Philadelphia, in part because the fans taunted him for his unsophistication. Mack tried to provide him with instruction in reading and writing, but Jackson, out of embarrassment, would not cooperate. After the 1909 season, Mack released Jackson to play with a minor league club in Savannah, Georgia, in the South Atlantic League. In Savannah, Jackson met and married Katherine Wynn, who remained his wife until his death forty-two years later. At home in the South, Jackson batted .358 for Savannah.

A Star in Cleveland. In 1910 Mack sent Jackson to play for New Orleans in the Southern League. Jackson led the Southern League in batting, with an .354 average. In the meantime, Mack concluded that Jackson was not meant to play in Philadelphia, so he sold Jackson to the Cleveland Indians. Jackson blossomed in Cleveland, batting .387 for the last twenty games of the 1910 season. From 1911 to 1915 Jackson competed with Ty Cobb of the Detroit Tigers for the American League batting title. In 1911 he batted .408 while Cobb batted .420, giving Jackson the distinction of being the only American Leaguer to hit more than .400 and not win the batting title. Despite his success on the baseball field, his illiteracy continued to complicate his life. Hugh Fullerton, the most influential baseball critic of the decade, wrote that Jackson was a poor example for American youth, asking "why should they study when Joe Jackson showed them it was possible to be a star even when you could not read your own press clippings."

On to Chicago. In 1915 Cleveland sold Jackson to the Chicago White Sox for $65,000. White Sox owner Charles Comiskey's purchase of Jackson was one of many deals made by Comiskey to construct a club capable of winning the World Series. In 1916 Jackson almost singlehandedly carried the White Sox to the American League pennant by batting .341 and scoring ninety-one runs. On the strength of the pitching of Eddie Cicotte and Lefty Williams, Chicago in 1917 won the American League pennant with one hundred victories. No Chicago team has won as many games since. In the 1917 World Series, the White Sox rolled over the New York Giants four games to two. Jackson hit .307 and made several game-winning catches in the championships. Chicago was on the verge of building a dynasty when World War I intervened. Several of Chicago's key players left the team to serve in defense industry jobs or the armed forces overseas in 1918.

The Black Sox. After World War I the White Sox regained the strength that propelled them to victory in the 1917 World Series. They appeared to be a likely candidate to win another world championship, although their National League opponents, the Cincinnati Reds, had a better regular season record, with ninety-six wins and forty-four losses. In the World Series, however, the White Sox never seemed to get the right playing combination together and lost five games to three. In 1920, it was revealed that eight players were guilty of deliberately losing the World Series in return for payoffs by gamblers who had bet on the outcome.

Jackson's Role. What was Joe Jackson's role in the 1919 World Series debacle? According to Eliot Asinof, author of *Eight Men Out*, Jackson was involved in the scheme from the beginning, but at the last minute changed his mind and tried to inform Comiskey of the plot. Sadly, Jackson never managed to schedule a hearing with the team owner. Others maintain that Jackson became part of the plot through his association with Claude "Lefty" Williams, and that the $5,000 that Jackson received was half of Williams's payoff to his roommate, who half-heartedly went along with the plan. Some argue that the real culprit in the affair was Comiskey himself, who left his players vulnerable to gamblers' bribes by paying them such low salaries.

Later Life. In 1921 Jackson and the seven other Black Sox were banned from major league baseball by Kenesaw Mountain Landis, the newly appointed commissioner. Although Jackson tried to stay in baseball by playing in the minor leagues under assumed names, he eventually retired from the game and returned to Savannah, Georgia, his wife's hometown, where he opened a successful dry-cleaning business. In 1951, several weeks before he was to appear on national television to plead his innocence once again, he died of a heart attack.

Sources:

Eliot Asinof, *Eight Men Out* (New York: Ace, 1963);

Jack Kavanagh, *Shoeless Joe Jackson* (New York: Chelsea, 1995).

WALTER JOHNSON

1887-1946

HALL OF FAME PITCHER

History's Hardest Thrower. Although there were no reliable devices available to measure the velocity of a blazing pitch, the fastball of Walter Johnson is generally considered to be one of the hardest of all time. Johnson was born on 6 November 1887 in Humbolt, Kansas, the son of Frank and Minnie Johnson, Swedish farmers who moved from Pennsylvania to Kansas by wagon train. In 1901 the Johnsons moved to Olinda, California, where they hoped to strike it rich in the oil fields. Although no oil bubbled up for the Johnsons, they made a good living providing mule teams for the oilmen. At fourteen Johnson was playing baseball for the local Oil Field Juniors baseball team. Strong and athletic, he probably would have been the team's pitcher had he not pitched so hard that nobody would catch for him. In 1907 Johnson was working for the Idaho Telephone Company, digging postholes, and playing semiprofessional baseball in Waiser, Idaho. His fastball attracted the attention of a traveling salesman who wrote about him to Joe Cantillon, the manager of the Washington Senators. Cantillon sent his catcher Cliff Blankenship to Idaho to scout out Johnson. Blankenship saw Johnson fire his fastball for twelve innings in a 1–0 loss and offered the righthander a $100 signing bonus and $350 a month, plus traveling expenses to Washington, D.C.

Early Years in Washington. The Washington Senators were one of the worst teams in major league baseball. In 1907 the Senators lost 102 games while their rookie pitcher compiled a record of five wins and nine losses, striking out seventy batters and walking sixteen in 111 innings. Johnson's fastball was his signature pitch, though he developed a fair curveball. Johnson's breakthrough season was 1910. He won twenty-five games and lost seventeen, the first of ten consecutive seasons in which he won twenty or more games. Pitching eight shutouts and striking out 313 batters, he captured the first of twelve strikeout titles on his way to a career record of 3,503 strikeouts.

His Finest Season. Johnson won twenty-five games in 1911 and thirty-two in 1912. The Senators, under new manager Clark Griffith, had become a respectable club, finishing second in the 1912 American League pennant race. The Senators had another good year in 1913, finishing six and a half games behind the Philadelphia Athletics. During the 1913 season, Johnson enjoyed winning streaks of fourteen, eleven, and ten games on his way to a remarkable 36–7 season. He pitched twelve shutouts and five one-hit games. From April 10 to May 14, he pitched fifty-six consecutive shutout innings. In addition to leading the league in most games won that year, he led in innings pitched (346), strikeouts (243), and winning percentage (.837). Moreover, 1913 marked the first season in which earned run averages (ERAs) were computed, and Johnson set a record of 1.14, which remained unsurpassed until Bob Gibson of the Saint Louis Cardinals posted an ERA of 1.12 in 1968. Johnson's 1913 season was one of the best in the history of major league baseball and he was recognized as the Most Valuable Player that year.

Federal League Offers. Johnson followed his stellar 1913 season with twenty-eight wins, including ten shutouts, 225 strikeouts, and a 1.72 ERA in 1914. Although his salary was $12,000, he believed that he was worth more, and so did the newly formed Federal League. In 1914 the Federal League offered Johnson a contract worth $16,000, plus a $10,000 signing bonus to play for the Chicago Whales. The Senators could match the salary offered by the Whales but not the additional $10,000 bonus. To pay Johnson's increased salary, the Senators' owner turned to Charles Comiskey of the Chicago White Sox, arguing that if Johnson played for the Whales the attendance at White Sox games would decline. Comiskey paid the money to keep Johnson in Washington.

Pennant Winner. In 1924 the Senators won the American League pennant and met the New York Giants

in the World Series. In that year, Johnson won twenty-three games and lost seven, leading the American League in strikeouts (158), winning percentage (.767), shutouts (5), and earned run average (2.72). Although Johnson won one game and lost two in the World Series, Washington defeated New York for the world championship for its only World Series title. The Senators won the pennant again in 1925, but lost the World Series to Pittsburgh. In the Series Johnson won two of three decisions. After 1926 Johnson's pitching declined. He managed the Senators (1929–1932) and the Cleveland Indians (1933–1935). In 1936 he joined Ty Cobb, Honus Wagner, Babe Ruth, and Christy Mathewson as the first inductees into the Baseball Hall of Fame in Cooperstown, New York. After baseball, Johnson retired to a farm outside Bethesda, Maryland, and in 1940 lost his bid for election to the U.S. Congress.

Source:
Martin Appel and Burt Goldblatt, *Baseball's Best: The Hall of Fame Gallery* (New York: McGraw-Hill, 1980).

FRANCIS OUIMET

1893-1967

AMATEUR GOLF CHAMPION

A Golfer for the Common Man. Until Francis Ouimet, a young man of working-class origins, won the U.S. Open Golf Tournament in 1913, golf had been seen as a sport for the privileged classes in the United States. His victory gave the sport mass appeal and transformed it into popular recreational activity.

Beginnings as a Caddy. The youngest of Louis Ouimet's two sons, Francis was born 8 May 1893 in Brookline, Massachusetts. His father, a French Canadian immigrant who worked as a gardener, moved his family into a house across the street from The Country Club, one of the nation's oldest and most prestigious country clubs. Francis and his brother, Wilfred, became caddies at The Country Club and, although the rules prohibited caddies from playing on the course, the Ouimet boys often sneaked in some practice strokes when Alex Campbell, the club pro, was not watching. On the weekends Francis and his friends would golf at Franklin Park in Boston on the public nine-hole course.

Ouimet's Rise. In addition to caddying at The Country Club, Francis worked at a dry-goods store to earn money for tournament entrance fees. As a student at Brookline High School he won the Boston Interscholastic Championship in 1909. Ouimet failed to qualify for the U.S. Amateur Championship three times (1910–1912). At the state level he fared better, however, making the final round of the Massachusetts State Amateur

Championship in 1912 and winning the State Amateur title in 1913.

U.S. Open Champion. In 1913 Ouimet qualified for the U.S. Amateur Championship and reached the second round, where he lost to the eventual champion, Jerome Travers. In the U.S. Open that year, played at the Country Club, he raised eyebrows by shooting a credible 74 in the third round to move into a three-way tie with English standouts Harry Vardon and Ted Ray. In the final round Ouimet played with remarkable composure; he displayed, as he had throughout the entire tournament, the cool determination of a professional. He later acknowledged, however, that "his nerves were strumming like guitar strings." On the last hole of the final round, Ouimet successfully made a five-foot putt to tie Vardon and Ray, sending the tournament into a fifth, tie-breaking round. In the play-off round Ouimet shot a one-over-par 72 to win the U.S. Open, becoming the first amateur to capture the tournament.

America's Greatest Amateur. In 1914 Ouimet finally won the U.S. Amateur Championship, defeating perennial favorite Jerome Travers. For the young Bostonian, winning the U.S. Amateur Championship was a greater thrill than his triumph in the U.S. Open the previous year. (He would not win his second U.S. Amateur title until 1931, when he defeated Jack Westland.) Ouimet also achieved international acclaim by winning the 1914 French Amateur title. He was unable to repeat his championship performance in the U.S. Open, in which he tied for fifth. Ouimet, who worked as a stockbroker, remained an amateur throughout his career. He lost to Bobby Jones in three semifinal rounds in the U.S. Amateur (1924, 1926, and 1927) and later called Jones "the greatest golfer who ever lived." In 1925 he tied for second in the U.S. Open. Ouimet also played on the U.S. Walker Cup team against Great Britain, from 1922, when the tournament began, until 1934. From 1936 to 1949 he served as the nonplaying captain of the team.

Later Accolades. Retiring from amateur golf in 1949, Ouimet established the Francis Ouimet Caddy Scholarship Fund, which provided caddies with the funds to seek a college education. In 1951 he was elected captain of the Royal and Ancient Golf Club of Saint Andrews in Scotland. Ouimet celebrated his achievement with a solid drive from the first tee on the famous old course, where golf supposedly had originated. As the first non-British citizen elected to the post, he joined the Duke of Windsor and the King of England as captains of the Royal and Ancient Golf Club. In 1955 Ouimet was awarded the Bob Jones Trophy for distinguished sportsmanship by the U.S. Golf Association. He authored three books on golf: *Golf Facts for Young People* (1921), *A Game of Golf* (1932), and *The Rules of Golf* (1948).

Sources:

Will Grimsley, *Golf: Its History, People, and Events* (Englewood Cliffs, N.J., 1966);

Herbert Wind, *The Story of American Golf* (New York, 1956).

SIR BARTON

1916-1937

TRIPLE CROWN CHAMPION

Prestigious Pedigree. Sir Barton, a Kentucky thoroughbred, became the first Triple Crown champion when he won the Kentucky Derby, the Preakness Stakes, and the Belmont Stakes in 1919. His sire was Star Shoot, an English stallion that came to the United States to stud in 1901 when he showed signs of difficult breathing after ten successful races on English tracks. Star Shoot had a prestigious pedigree, including his sire, Isinglass, a winner of the English Triple Crown. Star Shoot's dam, Astrology, was sired by Hermit, an English Derby champion. Siring many winning horses in the United States, Star Shoot in 1912 became the number one stud for John E. Madden, the owner of Hamburg Place, near Lexington, Kentucky. In 1912 Madden introduced Star Shoot to Lady Sterling, a seventeen-year-old mare, who bore Sir Barton the following spring.

Owner and Trainer. Believing a two-year-old too young for full competition, Madden raced Sir Barton infrequently in 1918. Although Sir Barton only placed once in his first six races, he impressed horse racing aficionados, especially Madden's friend, Comdr. John Kenneth Leveson Ross, a wealthy Canadian who owned a stable near Bowie, Maryland. Ross, who inherited a fortune from his father, one of the founders of the Canadian Pacific Railroad, indulged himself in horse racing and yachting. He bought Sir Barton for $10,000 and hired Harvey Guy Bedwell, one of the most successful trainers in the country, to prepare the young chestnut colt for the upcoming racing season. Bedwell, a former Oregon cowboy, had enjoyed great success racing horses at the local fairgrounds in Grand Junction, Colorado, where he owned and operated a livery stable. In the early 1910s he began racing horses at the Empire City racetrack in New York. Bedwell joined Ross as his chief trainer in 1918, and horses from the Ross stables garnered more than $99,000 in winnings that year.

Conditioning of Sir Barton. Although Sir Barton contributed only $4,113 to the Rosses' earnings in 1918, Bedwell began his process of conditioning and adjusting the colt to his training theories. One of Bedwell's techniques was to have his horses stand in pails of mud, which he believed prevented their hooves from drying out and becoming brittle. This practice was especially beneficial for Sir Barton, who had very tender hooves that stayed sore from shoeing. Blacksmiths fashioned special shoes for Sir Barton and placed a pad of piano felt between the hoof and shoe. His sore hooves may have contributed to the horse's ill temper. Sir Barton would kick and bite the cats and dogs that lived in the stable and would not let most humans approach him. Sir Barton, however, trusted Bedwell, who nursed the horse through a bout of blood poisoning that nearly took his life.

Triple Crown. In 1919 the Ross stable, with Sir Barton and his stablemate, Billy Kelly, dominated American thoroughbred horse racing. Ross entered both Sir Barton and Billy Kelly, "a small, skinny gelding that looked more like a polo pony than a race horse," in the 1919 Kentucky Derby. Neither of the Ross stable horses were picked to win the Derby. Eternal, owned by John McClelland, was the favorite. Sir Barton received a "twelve-pound maiden-allowance" for coming into the race without a win and Billy Kelly received a "three-pound gelding allowance." It rained on Derby Day, so the Churchill Downs track was wet and soggy, presenting poor conditions for Eternal — who excelled on a hard dry track — but optimal conditions to Sir Barton, who performed better in mud than on hard tracks because of his tender hooves. In the race, Sir Barton entered the homestretch in the lead and jockey Johnny Loftus rode him to victory with Billy Kelly finishing a distant second. In the Preakness, Sir Barton, jockeyed again by Loftus, won by four lengths over Eternal. Loftus again rode Sir Barton to victory in the Belmont Stakes, setting a record of 2:17.4 for the mile and three-eighths course. In 1919 Sir Barton raced thirteen times and won eight times, winning $88,250. In all, the Ross stable won $209,303 that year.

Sir Barton's Retirement. In 1920 Sir Barton raced twelve times, finishing first five times, second twice, and third three times. In 1922 Ross sold Sir Barton to the Audley Farm in Virginia, where the horse stood to stud until 1933. Sir Barton sired a few winners, but none of his offspring matched his exploits. He spent his final days on the United States Remount Ranch, a government-owned horse-breeding farm in Douglas, Wyoming.

Sources:

Marvin Drager, *The Most Glorious Crown* (New York: Winchester, 1975);

Suzanne Wilding and Anthony Del Balso, *The Triple Crown Winners: The Story of America's Ten Superstar Race Horses,* revised edition (New York: Parents' Magazine, 1978).

JIM THORPE

1888-1953

OLYMPIC CHAMPION

America's Greatest Athlete? Jim Thorpe, who many believe was America's finest all-around athlete, was certainly the nation's greatest Native American sportsman. The son of Hiram Thorpe, a farmer of mixed Irish and Sac and Fox Indian descent, and Charlotte Vieux Thorpe, of French and Chippewa heritage, Jim was born in the Oklahoma Indian Territory. As a boy he attended the Sac and Fox Reservation School and the Haskell Institute for Indians at Lawrence, Kansas. Thorpe, who preferred outdoor activities like horseback riding, swimming, hunting, and baseball over books, often found himself in classroom brawls. When Thorpe was orphaned at age sixteen, authorities enrolled him in the Carlisle Institute in Pennsylvania, the nation's foremost school for Indian youth, renowned for its strict discipline and code of conduct.

College All-American. At Carlisle, Thorpe was trained as a tailor and a farmer. He came under the tutelage of the legendary football coach Glenn "Pop" Warner. In 1908 he scored two touchdowns in Carlisle's tie with the University of Pennsylvania. Despite his gridiron success, Thorpe left Carlisle in 1909 to play semiprofessional baseball in Rocky Mount, North Carolina. In 1911 he returned to Carlisle and led the football team to 11 victories in 12 games, including an 18–15 triumph over Harvard University, in which Thorpe dashed seventy yards for a touchdown and booted four field goals. Walter Camp named Thorpe to his annual All-American team that year.

Olympic Triumph and Tragedy. Thorpe, an all-around track and field athlete at Carlisle, participated in the 1912 Summer Olympic Games at Stockholm, winning both the pentathlon and the decathlon. Thorpe's score in the decathlon was a world record of 8,412 points. Upon presenting him with the gold medal for the decathlon, King Gustav V of Sweden said, "Sir, you are the greatest athlete in the world," to which Thorpe replied, "Thanks, King." Thorpe returned to a hero's welcome in America, led Carlisle to another fabulous football season and was named to another Camp All-American squad. In 1913 the IOC learned that he had played semiprofessional baseball from 1909 to 1911. In response to his violation of the Olympic amateur code, the IOC barred Thorpe from future Olympic competition and demanded that he return the medals.

A Professional Athletic Career. Unable to compete as an amateur, Thorpe left Carlisle and embarked on a career in major league baseball and professional football. He played six seasons as an outfielder for the New York Giants (1913–1915, 1917–1919), Cincinnati Reds (1917), and Boston Braves (1919). His best season came in 1920, when he batted .358 and drove in 112 runs for Akron, Ohio, of the International League. He also played professional football for the Canton Bulldogs (1915–1920) and for the New York Giants and other teams in the fledgling National Football League in the early 1920s.

An Athlete Down and Out. Throughout his professional athletic career, Thorpe drank and caroused excessively. After retiring from sports he remained dependent on the charity of friends and admirers, since he had squandered his earnings and lacked the skills to hold gainful employment. For income Thorpe often starred in B-movies and lectured on Indian life and his athletic career. During World War II he served in the U.S. merchant marine. Thorpe, who was married three times and divorced twice, fathered seven children. In 1950 an AP poll of American sportswriters named him the outstanding male athlete and the best football player of the first half of the twentieth century. Three years later Thorpe died of a heart attack in Lomita, California. In 1982 the IOC returned Thorpe's 1912 gold medals to his family.

Source: Robert W. Wheeler, *Jim Thorpe: World's Greatest Athlete*, revised edition (Norman: University of Oklahoma, 1979).

PEOPLE IN THE NEWS

One of baseball's greatest pitchers, **Grover Cleveland Alexander** of the Philadelphia Phillies led the National League in victories in 1911 (28), 1914 (27), 1915 (31), 1916 (33), and 1917 (30). He posted the best earned run average in 1915 (1.22), 1916 (1.55), 1917 (1.86), and 1919 (1.72).

Philadelphia Athletics third baseman **John Franklin "Home Run" Baker,** who ranks as one of baseball's greatest sluggers, led the American League in home runs in 1911 (9), 1912 (10), 1913 (12), and 1914 (8).

Cincinnati Reds outfielder **Bob Bescher** led the National League in stolen bases in 1910 (70), 1911 (80), and 1912 (67).

Pittsburgh Pirates outfielder **Max Carey** led the National League in stolen bases in 1913 (61), 1915 (36), 1916 (63), 1917 (46), and 1918 (58).

Philadelphia Phillies outfielder **Clifford Carlton "Cactus" Craveth** led the National League in home runs in 1913 (19), 1914 (19), 1915 (24), 1917 (12), 1918 (8), and 1919 (12).

George Gaidzik reigned as the first national platform diving champion from 1909 to 1911.

John W. Heisman, for whom the Heisman Trophy is named, coached football at Georgia Tech from 1905 to 1919, leading his team to three undefeated seasons from 1915 to 1917.

Willie Hoppe captured the world 18.1 balkline billiards championship in 1906, 1910, 1911, 1913, and 1914, and the world 18.2 balkline billiards championship in 1908, from 1910 to 1920, and from 1922 to 1924.

After riding George Smith to victory in the Kentucky Derby in 1916, **Johnny Loftus** jockeyed Sir Barton to wins in the Kentucky Derby, Preakness Stakes, and Belmont Stakes, to win history's first Triple Crown in 1919.

In 1915 **Charles C. Pell** won the first of twelve national racquets singles championships during a nineteen-year period.

AWARDS

1910

Major League Baseball World Series — Philadelphia Athletics (American League), 4 vs. Chicago Cubs (National League), 1

Kentucky Derby Winner — Donau (Fred Herbert, jockey)

Collegiate Football National Champion — Harvard University, 8–0–1

U.S. Golf Association Amateur Champions — W. C. Fownes Jr.; Dorothy Campbell

U.S. Golf Association Open Champion — Alex Smith

U.S. Lawn Tennis Association Singles Champions — William A. Larned; Hazel V. Hotchkiss

1911

Major League Baseball World Series — Philadelphia Athletics (American League), 4 vs. New York Giants (National League), 2

Indianapolis 500 Champion — Ray Harroun (Marmon) 74.59 MPH

Kentucky Derby Winner — Meridian (George Archibald, jockey)

Collegiate Football National Champion — Princeton University, 8–0–2

U.S. Golf Association Amateur Champions — Harold H. Hilton; Margaret Curtis

U.S. Golf Association Open Champion — John J. McDermott

U.S. Lawn Tennis Association Singles Champions — William A. Larned; Hazel V. Hotchkiss

1912

Major League Baseball World Series — Boston Red Sox (American League), 4 vs. New York Giants (National League), 3

Indianapolis 500 Champion — Joe Dawson (National) 78.72 MPH

Kentucky Derby Winner — Worth (Carol H. Shilling, jockey)

Collegiate Football National Champion — Harvard University, 9–0–0

U.S. Golf Association Amateur Champions — Jerome D. Travers; Margaret Curtis

U.S. Golf Association Open Champion — John J. McDermott

U.S. Lawn Tennis Association Singles Champions — Maurice E. McLoughlin; Mary K. Browne

1913

Major League Baseball World Series — Philadelphia Athletics (American League), 4 vs. New York Giants (National League), 1

Indianapolis 500 Champion — Jules Goux (Peugot) 75.93 MPH

Kentucky Derby Winner — Donerail (Roscoe Goose, jockey)

Collegiate Football National Champion — Harvard University, 9–0–0

U.S. Golf Association Amateur Champions — Jerome D. Travers; Gladys Ravenscroft

U.S. Golf Association Open Champion — Francis Ouimet

U.S. Lawn Tennis Association Singles Champions — Maurice E. McLoughlin; Mary K. Browne

1914

Major League Baseball World Series — Boston Braves (National League), 4 vs. Philadelphia Athletics (American League), 0

Indianapolis 500 Champion — Rene Thomas (Delage) 82.47 MPH

Kentucky Derby Winner — Old Rosebud (John McCabe, jockey)

Collegiate Football National Champion — Army, 9–0–0

U.S. Golf Association Amateur Champions — Francis Ouimet; Mrs. H. Arnold Jackson

U.S. Golf Association Open Champion — Walter Hagen

U.S. Lawn Tennis Association Singles Champions — Richard Norris Williams II; Mary K. Browne

1915

Major League Baseball World Series — Boston Red Sox (American League), 4 vs. Philadelphia Phillies (National League), 1

Indianapolis 500 Champion — Ralph DePalma (Mercedes-Benz) 89.84 MPH

Kentucky Derby Winner — Regret (Joe Notler, jockey)

Collegiate Football National Champion — Cornell University, 9–0–0

U.S. Golf Association Amateur Champions — Robert A. Gardner; Mrs. C. H. Vanderbeck

U.S. Golf Association Open Champion — Jerome D. Travers

U.S. Lawn Tennis Association Singles Champions — William M. Johnston; Molla Bjurstedt

1916

Major League Baseball World Series — Boston Red Sox (American League), 4 vs. Brooklyn Dodgers (National League), 1

Indianapolis 500 Champion — Dario Resta (Peugeot) 84.00 MPH

Kentucky Derby Winner — George Smith (Johnny Loftus, jockey)

Collegiate Football National Champion — University of Pittsburgh, 8–0–0

U.S. Golf Association Amateur Champions — Charles Evans Jr.; Alexa Stirling

U.S. Golf Association Open Champion — Charles Evans Jr.

U.S. Lawn Tennis Association Singles Champions — Richard Norris Williams II; Molla Bjurstedt

1917

Major League Baseball World Series — Chicago White Sox (American League) 4, vs. New York Giants (National League), 2

Indianapolis 500 Champion — no competition

Kentucky Derby Winner — Omar Khayyam (Charles Borel, jockey)

Collegiate Football National Champion — Georgia Tech, 9–0–0

U.S. Golf Association Amateur Champions — no competition

U.S. Golf Association Open Champion — no competition

U.S. Lawn Tennis Association Singles Champions — Robert Lindley Murray; Molla Bjurstedt

1918

Major League Baseball World Series — Boston Red Sox (American League), 4 vs. Chicago Cubs (National League), 2

Indianapolis 500 Champion — no competition

Kentucky Derby Winner — Exterminator (Willie Knapp, jockey)

Collegiate Football National Champion — University of Pittsburgh, 4–1–0

U.S. Golf Association Amateur Champions — no competition

U.S. Golf Association Open Champion — no competition

U.S. Lawn Tennis Association Singles Champions — Robert Lindley Murray; Molla Bjurstedt

1919

Major League Baseball World Series — Cincinnati Reds (National League), 5 vs. Chicago White Sox (American League), 3

Indianapolis 500 Champion — Howard Wilcox (Peugeot) 88.05 MPH

Kentucky Derby Winner — Sir Barton (Johnny Loftus, jockey)

Collegiate Football National Champion — Georgia Tech, 9–0–0

U.S. Golf Association Amateur Champions — S. D. Herron; Alexa Stirling

U.S. Golf Association Open Champion — Walter Hagen

U.S. Lawn Tennis Association Singles Champions — William M. Johnston; Hazel Hotchkiss Wightman

DEATHS

Willie Anderson, 30?, four-time U.S. Open Golf champion (1901 and 1903–1905), 1910.

Roscoe Conkling Barnes, 64, one of the leading batters for National Association and National League teams during the 1870s, 8 February 1915.

Jacob Peter Beckley, 50, first baseman who played 2,377 games at his position from 1886 to 1904, 25 June 1918.

James Gordon Bennett Jr., 77, owner and editor in chief of the *New York Herald* who promoted amateur and professional sporting events and sponsored the Gordon Bennett Trophy, 14 May 1918.

Francis Gordon Brown Jr., 31, Yale University football player from 1897 to 1901 who remains one of only four men selected to four consecutive first All-American teams, 10 May 1911.

John Tomlinson Brush Jr., 67, owner of the New York Giants (1902–1912) and designer of the rules that govern the World Series, 26 November 1912.

Robert Lee Caruthers, 47, one of baseball's leading pitchers from 1883 to 1911 who compiled a winning percentage of .692, 5 August 1911.

Clarence Algernon Childs, 43, one of baseball's leading second basemen and hitters from 1888 to 1904, 8 November 1912.

Michael Joseph Donovan, 70, middleweight boxing champion from 1878 to 1883, 24 March 1918.

James Dwight, 64, five-time national tennis doubles champion (with Richard Sears) who served as president of the U.S. Lawn Tennis Association (1882–1884 and 1893–1911), 13 May 1917.

Charles Follis, 40?, the first African American professional football player, 1919.

John W. Fowler, 54, first African American professional baseball player, who batted more than .300 from 1878 to 1895, 26 February 1913.

Robert Fitzsimmons, 55, boxing champion in the middleweight, heavyweight, and light heavyweight divisions, 22 October 1917.

Andrew Freedman, 54, owner of the New York Giants baseball team from 1895 to 1902, 4 December 1915.

Joe Gans, 35, lightweight boxing champion from 1902 to 1908, 10 August 1910.

Frank Alvin Gotch, 39, world professional wrestling champion from 1908 to 1917, 16 December 1917.

Luther Halsey Gulick, 52, promoter of basketball who helped to guide the sport in its early years through his work with the Young Men's Christian Association and Amateur Athletic Union organizations, 13 August 1918.

James Joseph Hogan, 35, three-time All-American at Yale University (1902–1904), 20 March 1910.

James Wear Holliday, 43, outfielder who in his nine-year career (1885–1894) posted a career fielding percentage of .934, 15 February 1910.

Adrian Joss, 31, pitcher who from 1902 to 1911 compiled history's second-best lifetime ERA of 1.88, 14 April 1911.

Henry Van Noye Lucas, 53, organizer and owner of baseball's Union Association, a rival major league in 1884 that lasted one season, 15 November 1910.

Joseph Terrance McGovern, 37, featherweight boxing champion from 1900 to 1901, 26 February 1918.

Edward John McKean, 55, one of the leading batters of the 1890s, who compiled a lifetime average of .302, 16 August 1919.

William Monroe, 39, star in the Negro Leagues from 1903 to 1915, where he compiled a .333 batting average, 16 March 1915.

James Henry "Orator Jim" O'Rourke, 66, baseball's most versatile player, who played every position in his nineteen-year career, 8 January 1919.

David L. Orr, 55, batter with a lifetime average of .342 in eight-year career, 3 June 1915.

Ralph Waldo Rose, 28, shot-putter who won two Olympic gold medals (1904 and 1908) and three AAU championships (1907, 1908, and 1909); he was the first man to put the shot more than fifty feet, 16 October 1913.

James Bentley "Cy" Seymour, 47, pitcher and outfielder from 1896 to 1913, 20 September 1919.

Martin Joseph Sheridan, 37, Olympic gold medalist in the discus throw (1904, 1906, and 1908) and shot put (1906), 27 March 1918.

Lewis M. Sockalexis, 42, first Native American major league baseball player, who played for the Cleveland Spiders from 1897 to 1899, 24 December 1913.

Albert Goodwill Spalding, 65, one of the leading pitchers of 1870s, who became a successful baseball entrepreneur and president of the Chicago Cubs from 1882 to 1891, 9 September 1915.

James Edward Sullivan, 53, one of the founders of the Amateur Athletic Union who served as its secretary (1889–1896), president (1906–1909), and secretary-treasurer (1909–1914); the James E. Sullivan Memorial Trophy has been awarded to the nation's most outstanding amateur athlete since 1930, 16 September 1914.

Oliver Wendell Tebeau, 53, baseball manager for National League's Cleveland and Saint Louis teams who had a .556 winning percentage from 1891 to 1900, 15 May 1918.

Michael Joseph Tiernan, 51, outfielder who batted .311 lifetime in thirteen-year career (1887–1899), 9 November 1918.

Christian Frederick Wilhelm Von Der Ahe, 61, an organizer of the American Association baseball league in 1882 and owner and manager of the Saint Louis Brown Stockings, 7 June 1913.

George Edward "Rube" Waddell, 37, one of the leading pitchers from 1896 to 1911, 1 April 1914.

Arthur Ledlie Wheeler, 44, Princeton guard who was a three-time college football All-American from 1892 to 1894, 20 December 1917.

William Henry "Whoop-La" White, 56, pitcher who had a career ERA of 2.28 from 1877 to 1889, 30 August 1911.

Nicholas Emanuel Young, 76, an organizer of the National Association of Professional Base Ball Players in 1871, who became the secretary of the National League in 1876 and president of the NL from 1885 to 1901, 31 October 1916.

PUBLICATIONS

Thomas Andrews, *1919 Championship Records, Pocket Sporting Compendium* (Milwaukee, 1919);

Gustav Axelson, *"Commy": The Life Story of Charles A. Comiskey* (Chicago: Reilly & Lee, 1919);

Walter Camp, *The Book of Football* (New York, 1910);

Camp, *Walter Camp's Book of Sports* (New York: Century, 1910);

Ty Cobb, *Busting 'Em and Other Stories,* (New York: E. J. Clode, 1914);

Park H. Davis, *Football: The American Intercollegiate Game* (New York: Scribners, 1911);

William H. Edwards, *Football Days* (New York: Moffat, Yard, 1916);

Hugh Stuart Fullerton, *Jimmy Kirkland and the Cascade College Team* (Philadelphia: J. C. Winston, 1915);

Fullerton, *Jimmy Kirkland and the Plot for a Pennant.* (Philadelphia: J. C. Winston, 1915);

Fullerton, *Jimmy Kirkland and the Shasta Boys Team* (Philadelphia: J. C. Winston, 1915);

Fullerton, *Touching Second: The Science of Baseball* (Chicago: Reilly & Britton, 1910);

Christy Mathewson, *Pitching in a Pinch; or, Baseball from the Inside* (New York: Bodmer, 1910);

George Moreland, *Balldom* (New York: Balldom, 1914);

Michael C. Murphy, *Athletic Training* (New York: Scribners, 1914);

Herbert Reed, *Football for Public and Player* (New York: Frederick A. Stokes, 1913);

George S. Robbins, *Frank A. Gotch: World's Champion Wrestler* (Chicago: J. B. Bowles, 1913);

Albert G. Spalding, *America's National Game* (New York: American Sports, 1911);

Alfred H. Spink, *The National Game: A History of Baseball* (Saint Louis: National Game, 1911);

Marshall Stillman, *Mike Donovan: The Making of a Man* (New York: Moffat, Yard, 1918);

Jerome Travers, *Travers' Golf Book* (New York, 1913);

Travers and Grantland Rice, *The Winning Shot* (Garden City, N.Y.: Doubleday, Page, 1915);

Hallenbeck Wynkoop, *Weston and His Walks* (New York: Crawford, 1910);

Paul Withington, *The Book of Athletics* (Boston: Lothrop, Lee & Shepard, 1914);

American Lawn Tennis, periodical;

American Physical Education Review, periodical;

Outing, periodical;

Physical Culture, periodical;

Wright and Ditson Official Lawn Tennis Guide, periodical.

GENERAL REFERENCES

GENERAL

Frederick Lewis Allen, *The Big Change: America Transforms Itself* (New York: Harper, 1952);

Daniel Boorstin, *The Americans: The Democratic Experience* (New York: Vintage, 1973);

Gorton Carruth, *The Encyclopedia of World Facts and Dates* (New York: HarperCollins, 1993);

Mary Kupiec Cayton, Elliott J. Gorn, and Peter T. Williams, eds., *Encyclopedia of American Social History*, 3 volumes (New York: Scribners, 1993);

John Chambers II, *The Tyranny of Change: America in the Progressive Era, 1900–1917* (New York: St. Martin's Press, 1980);

Chronicle of the Twentieth Century (Mount Kisco, N.Y.: Chronicle, 1987);

John Milton Cooper Jr., *Pivotal Decades: The United States, 1900–1920* (New York: Norton, 1990);

John W. Dodds, *Everyday Life in Twentieth Century America* (New York: Putnam, 1965);

Irving S. Kull and Nell M. Kull, eds., *An Encyclopedia of American History*, revised and updated by Stanley H. Friedelbaum (New York: Popular Library, 1965);

Charles D. Lowery and John F. Marszalek, eds., *Encyclopedia of African-American Civil Rights: From Emancipation to the Present* (Westport, Conn.: Greenwood Press, 1992);

Iwan W. Morgan and Neil A. Wynn, *America's Century: Perspectives on U.S. History Since 1900* (New York: Holmes & Meier, 1993);

Thomas J. Schlereth, *Victorian America: Transformations in Everyday Life, 1876–1915* (New York: Harper-Collins, 1991);

Barbara Sicherman and Carol Hurd Green, with Ilene Kantrov and Harriette Walker, eds., *Notable American Women: The Modern Period, A Biographical Dictionary* (Cambridge, Mass.: Harvard University Press, 1980);

Statistical History of the United States from Colonial Times to the Present (Stamford, Conn.: Fairfield, 1965);

Mark Sullivan, *Our Times* (New York: Scribners, 1930);

This Fabulous Century (New York: Time-Life Books, 1988);

James Trager, *The People's Chronology*, revised edition (New York: Holt, Rinehart & Winston, 1994);

Robert Wiebe, *The Search for Order, 1877–1920* (New York: Hill & Wang, 1967).

ARTS

Robert C. Allen, *Vaudeville and Film, 1895–1915: A Study in Media Interaction* (New York: Arno, 1980);

Brooks Atkinson, *Broadway* (New York: Macmillan, 1970);

Alfred L. Bernheim and Sarah Harding, *The Business of the Theatre: An Economic History of the American Theatre, 1750–1932* (New York: Blom, 1932);

Warner Berthoff, *The Ferment of Realism: American Literature, 1884–1919* (London: Cambridge University Press, 1965);

Eileen Bowser, *The Transformation of Cinema* (New York: Scribners, 1990);

Oscar G. Brockett and Robert R. Findlay, *Century of Innovation: A History of European and American Theatre and Drama Since 1870* (Englewood Cliffs, N.J.: Prentice-Hall, 1984);

Milton Brown, *The Story of the Armory Show* (New York: Joseph H. Hirschorn Foundation, 1963);

Jack B. Buerkle and Danny Barker, *Bourbon Street Black: The New Orleans Black Jazzman* (New York: Oxford University Press, 1973);

Ivan Butler, *The War on Film* (New York: A. S. Barnes, 1974);

Gilbert Chase, *America's Music from the Pilgrims to the Present*, second revised edition (New York: McGraw-Hill, 1966);

Stanley Cooperman, *World War I and the American Novel* (Baltimore: Johns Hopkins University Press, 1967);

Joseph Csida and June Bundy Csida, *American Entertainment: A Unique History of Show Business* (New York: Watson-Guptill, 1978);

Ronald L. Davis, *A History of Music in American Life, Volume II, The Gilded Years, 1865–1920* (Huntington, N.Y.: Krieger, 1980);

Isadora Duncan, *The Art of the Dance*, edited by Sheldon Cheney (New York: Theatre Arts, 1928);

Emory Elliott, ed., *Columbia Literary History of the United States* (New York: Columbia University Press, 1988);

Lewis Erenberg, *Steppin' Out: New York Nightlife and the Transformation of American Culture, 1890–1930* (Westport, Conn.: Greenwood Press, 1981);

William K. Everson, *American Silent Film* (New York: Oxford University Press, 1978);

David Ewen, *All the Years of American Popular Music* (Englewood Cliffs, N.J.: Prentice-Hall, 1977);

Ewen, *The Story of America's Musical Theater* (Philadelphia: Chilton, 1961);

Marjorie Farnsworth, *The Ziegfeld Follies* (New York: Bonanza, 1956);

William H. Gerdts, *American Impressionism* (New York: Abbeville Press, 1984);

Martin Green, *New York: 1913* (New York: Macmillan, 1988);

Horace Gregory and Marza Zaturensha, *A History of American Poetry, 1900–1940* (New York: Harcourt, Brace, 1946);

Katrina Hazzard-Gordon, *Jookin': The Rise of Social Dance Formations in African-American Culture* (Philadelphia: Temple University Press, 1990);

Adele Heller and Lois Rudnick, *1915: The Cultural Moment: The New Politics, The New Woman, The New Psychology, The New Art, and The New Theatre in America* (New Brunswick, N.J.: Rutgers University Press, 1991);

H. Wiley Hitchcock, ed., *Music in the United States* (Englewood Cliffs, N.J.: Prentice-Hall, 1969);

William Innes Homer, *Alfred Stieglitz and the American Avant-Garde* (Boston: New York Graphic Society/Little, Brown, 1977);

Homer, *Alfred Stieglitz and the Photo-Secession* (Boston: Little, Brown, 1983);

Robert E. Humphrey, *Children of Fantasy: The First Rebels of Greenwich Village* (New York: Wiley, 1978);

Michael T. Isenberg, *War on Film: The American Cinema and World War I, 1914–1941* (Rutherford, N.J.: Fairleigh Dickinson University Press, 1981);

David A. Jasen, *Tin Pan Alley: The Composers, the Songs, the Performers, and Their Times* (New York: Fine, 1988);

Garth Jowett, *Film: The Democratic Art* (Boston: Little, Brown, 1976);

Paul Kuritz, *The Making of Theatre History* (Englewood Cliffs, N.J.: Prentice Hall, 1988);

Paul Lauter, ed., *The Heath Anthology of American Literature*, volume 2 (Lexington, Mass.: Heath, 1990);

Richard Lingeman, *Theodore Dreiser: An American Journey*, 2 volumes (New York: Putnam, 1986, 1990);

Ann Lloyd, *The Illustrated History of the Cinema* (New York: Macmillan, 1986);

Glenn Loney, *20th Century Theatre*, volume 1 (New York: Facts On File, 1983);

Paul Magriel, *Chronicles of American Dance* (New York: Holt, 1948);

Gerald Mast, *A Short History of the Movies*, revised by Bruce F. Kawin (New York: Macmillan, 1992);

Henry F. May, *The End of American Innocence*, revised edition (New York: Columbia University Press, 1992);

Joseph H. Mazo, *Prime Movers: The Makers of Modern Dance in America* (New York: Morrow, 1977);

Walter Meserve, *An Outline History of American Drama* (New York: Feedback Theatre Books/Prospero Press, 1994);

Ethan Mordden, *The American Theatre* (New York: Oxford University Press, 1981);

Thomas L. Morgan and William Barlow, *From Cakewalks to Concert Halls: An Illustrated History of African-American Popular Music from 1895 to 1930* (Washington, D.C.: Elliott & Clark, 1992);

Charles Musser, *Before the Nickelodeon: Edwin S. Porter and the Edison Manufacturing Company* (Berkeley: University of California Press, 1991);

Musser, *The Emergence of Cinema* (New York: Scribners, 1990);

Paul Oliver, *The Story of the Blues* (Radnor, Pa.: Chilton, 1969);

David Perkins, *A History of Modern Poetry: From the 1890s to the High Modernist Mode* (Cambridge, Mass.: Harvard University Press, 1976);

Christina Peterson, *Alfred Stieglitz's Camera Notes* (New York: Norton, 1993);

Barbara Rose, *American Art Since 1900* (New York: Praeger, 1968);

Nancy Lee Chalfa Ruyter, *Reformers and Visionaries: The Americanization of the Art of Dance* (New York: Dance Horizons, 1979);

Maxine Schwartz Seller, ed., *Ethnic Theatre in the United States* (Westport, Conn.: Greenwood Press, 1983);

David Shipman, *The Great Movie Stars* (New York: Crown, 1970);

Robert Sklar, *Movie-Made America: A Social History of American Movies* (New York: Random House, 1975);

Anthony Slide, *The Encyclopedia of Vaudeville* (Westport, Conn.: Greenwood Press, 1994);

Dickran Tashijian, *Skyscraper Primitives: Dada and the American Avant-Garde* (Middletown, Conn.: Wesleyan University Press, 1975);

Walter Terry, *The Dance in America*, revised edition (New York: Harper & Row, 1971);

Frank Tirro, *Jazz: A History* (New York: Norton, 1977);

Robert C. Toll, *On with the Show: The First Century of Show Business in America* (New York: Oxford University Press, 1976);

Steven Watson, *Strange Bedfellows: The First American Avant-Garde* (New York: Abbeville Press, 1991);

Arthur Frank Wertheim, *The New York Little Renaissance: Iconoclasm, Modernism, and Nationalism in American Culture, 1908–1917* (New York: New York University Press, 1976);

Irving Zeidman, *The American Burlesque Show* (New York: Hawthorn, 1967).

BUSINESS AND THE ECONOMY

Norman Beasley, *Main Street Merchant: The Story of J. C. Penney Company* (New York: Whittlesey House, 1948);

Ernest L. Bogart and Donald L. Kemmerer, *Economic History of the American People* (New York: Longmans, Green, 1942);

Richard O. Boyer and Herbert M. Morais, *Labor's Untold Story* (Pittsburgh: UERMWA, 1955);

John Brooks, *The Autobiography of American Business* (Garden City, N.Y.: Doubleday, 1974);

Keith L. Bryant Jr., ed., *Encyclopedia of American Business History and Biography: Railroads in the Age of Regulation, 1900–1980* (Columbia, S.C.: Bruccoli Clark Layman / New York: Facts On File, 1988);

Bryant, and Henry C. Dethloff, *A History of American Business* (Englewood Cliffs, N.J.: Prentice-Hall, 1983);

Vincent P. Carosso, *The Morgans: Private International Bankers* (Cambridge, Mass.: Harvard University Press, 1988);

Frank Barkley Copley, *Frederick W. Taylor: Father of Scientific Management*, volumes 1 and 2 (New York: Kelley, 1969);

John M. Dobson, *A History of American Enterprise* (Englewood Cliffs, N.J.: Prentice-Hall, 1988);

Melvyn Dubofsky, *We Shall Be All: A History of the Industrial Workers of the World* (Chicago: Quadrangle Books, 1969);

Foster Rhea Dulles, *Labor in America: A History* (New York: Crowell, 1949);

Joshua Freeman, et al., *Who Built America? Working People and the Nation's Economy, Politics, Culture, and Society*, volume 2 (New York: Pantheon, 1992);

Great Stories of American Businessmen (New York: American Heritage Publishing, 1972);

James R. Green, *The World of the Worker: Labor in Twentieth Century America* (New York: Hill & Wang, 1980);

Robert Lacy, *Ford: The Men and the Machine* (Boston: Little, Brown, 1986);

George S. May, ed., *Encyclopedia of American Business History and Biography: Banking and Finance, 1913–1989* (Columbia, S.C.: Bruccoli Clark Layman / New York: Facts On File, 1990);

David Montgomery, *The Fall of the House of Labor: The Workplace, the State, and American Labor Activism, 1865–1925* (Cambridge: Cambridge University Press, 1987);

Gareth Morgan, *Images of Organization* (Beverly Hills, Cal.: Sage, 1986);

Margaret Myers, *A Financial History of the United States* (New York: Columbia University Press, 1970);

Allan Nevins, *Ford: The Times, The Man, The Company* (New York: Scribners, 1954);

Harvey O'Connor, *Mellon's Millions: The Biography of a Fortune* (New York: John Day, 1993);

Glenn Porter, ed., *Encyclopedia of American Economic History: Studies of the Principal Movements and Ideas*, 3 volumes (New York: Scribners, 1980);

Edwin C. Rozwenc, ed., *Roosevelt, Wilson and the Trusts* (Boston: Heath, 1950);

Philip Taft, *Organized Labor in American History* (New York: Harper & Row, 1964).

EDUCATION

James D. Anderson, *The Education of Blacks in the South, 1860–1935* (Chapel Hill: University of North Carolina Press, 1988);

Barbara Beatty, *Preschool Education in America: The Culture of Young Children from the Colonial Era to the Present* (New Haven: Yale University Press, 1995);

Selma Cantor Berrol, *Julia Richman: A Notable Woman* (Philadelphia: Balch Institute Press, 1993);

Robert H. Bremner, *American Philanthropy* (Chicago: University of Chicago Press, 1960);

John Brubacher, *A History of the Problems of Education* (New York: McGraw-Hill, 1947);

Sol Cohen, ed., *Education in the United States: A Documentary History* (New York: Random House, 1974);

Lawrence A. Cremin, *American Education: The Metropolitan Experience, 1876–1980* (New York: Harper & Row, 1988);

Cremin, *The Transformation of the School: Progressivism in American Education, 1876–1957* (New York: Vintage, 1964);

Charles William Dabney, *Universal Education in the South* (Chapel Hill: University of North Carolina Press, 1936);

William Clyde DeVane, *Higher Education in Twentieth-Century America* (Cambridge, Mass.: Harvard University Press, 1965);

Raymond B. Fosdick, *The Story of the Rockefeller Foundation* (New Brunswick, N.J.: Transaction Publishers, 1989);

Patricia Albjerg Graham, *S.O.S.: Sustain Our Schools* (New York: Hill & Wang, 1992);

Carol Gruber, *Mars and Minerva: World War I and the Uses of the Higher Learning in America* (Baton Rouge: Louisiana State University Press, 1975);

Margaret A. Haley, *Battleground: The Autobiography of Margaret A. Haley,* edited by Robert L. Reid (Urbana: University of Illinois Press, 1982);

Louis R. Harlan, *Separate and Unequal: Public School Campaigns and Racism in the Southern Seaboard States, 1901–1915* (Chapel Hill: University of North Carolina Press, 1958);

Richard Hofstadter, *The Progressive Historians* (New York: Knopf, 1969);

Helen Lefkowitz Horowitz, *Campus Life: Undergraduate Cultures from the End of the Eighteenth Century to the Present* (Chicago: University of Chicago Press, 1987);

I. L. Kandel, *American Education in the Twentieth Century* (Cambridge, Mass.: Harvard University Press, 1957);

Herbert M. Kliebard, *The Struggle for the American Curriculum, 1893–1958* (New York: Routledge & Kegan Paul, 1987);

Edward A. Krug, *The Shaping of the American High School* (New York: Harper & Row, 1964);

Ellen Condliffe Lagemann, *The Politics of Knowledge: The Carnegie Corporation, Philanthropy, and Public Policy* (Chicago: University of Chicago Press, 1989);

Lagemann, *Private Power for the Public Good: A History of the Carnegie Foundation for the Advancement of Teaching* (Middletown, Conn.: Wesleyan University Press, 1983);

Christopher J. Lucas, *American Higher Education: A History* (New York: St. Martin's Press, 1994);

David A. Marcell, *Progress and Pragmatism: James, Dewey, Beard, and the American Idea of Progress* (Westport, Conn.: Greenwood Press, 1974);

Robert A. Margo, *Race and Schooling in the South, 1880–1950: An Economic History* (Chicago: University of Chicago Press, 1990);

James McLachlan, *American Boarding Schools: A Historical Study* (New York: Scribners, 1970);

Joel Perlmann, *Ethnic Differences: Schooling and Social Structure Among the Irish, Italians, Jews and Blacks in an American City, 1880–1935* (New York: Cambridge University Press, 1988);

Maxine Schwartz Seller, ed., *Women Educators in the United States, 1820–1993: A Bio-Bibliographical Sourcebook* (Westport, Conn.: Greenwood Press, 1994);

Richard Norton Smith, *The Harvard Century: The Making of a University to a Nation* (New York: Simon & Schuster, 1986);

Barbara Miller Solomon, *In the Company of Educated Women* (New Haven: Yale University Press, 1985);

David B. Tyack, *The One Best System: A History of American Urban Education* (Cambridge, Mass.: Harvard University Press, 1974);

Tyack and Elizabeth Hansot, *Managers of Virtue: Public School Leadership in America, 1820–1980* (New York: Basic Books, 1982);

Laurence R. Veysey, *The Emergence of the American University* (Chicago: University of Chicago Press, 1965);

Warren Weaver, *U.S. Philanthropic Foundations: Their History, Structure, Management, and Record* (New York: Harper & Row, 1967);

Robert Westbrook, *John Dewey and American Democracy* (Ithaca, N.Y.: Cornell University Press, 1991);

Alden Whitman, ed., *American Reformers* (New York: Wilson, 1985).

FASHION

Warren James Belasco, *Americans on the Road: From Autocamp to Motel, 1910–1945* (Cambridge, Mass.: MIT Press, 1979);

John Elting and Michael McAfee, eds., *Military Uniforms in America,* volume 4, *The Modern Era — From 1868* (Novato, Cal.: Presidio, 1988);

John Crosby Freeman, *The Forgotten Rebel: Gustav Stickley and His Craftsman Mission Furniture* (Watkins Glen, N.Y.: Century House, 1966);

William Dudley Hunt Jr., *Encyclopedia of American Architecture,* revised by Robert T. Packard and Balthazar Korab (New York: McGraw-Hill, 1994);

Edgar Kaufmann and Ben Raeburn, eds., *Frank Lloyd Wright: Writings and Buildings* (New York: Horizon, 1973);

Frances Kennett, *The Collector's Book of Fashion* (New York: Crown, 1983);

Coy L. Ludwig, *The Arts & Crafts Movement in New York State, 1890s–1920s* (Hamilton: Gallery Association of New York State, 1983);

Caroline Rennolds Milbank, *New York Fashion: The Evolution of American Style* (New York: Abrams, 1989);

Patricia Anne Murphy, *Cass Gilbert: Minnesota Master Architect* (Minneapolis: Minnesota University Gallery, 1980);

John Peacock, *20th Century Fashion: The Complete Sourcebook* (New York: Thames & Hudson, 1993);

Arthur J. Pulos, *American Design Ethic: A History of Industrial Design to 1940* (Cambridge, Mass.: MIT Press, 1983);

Beverly Russell, *Women of Design: Contemporary American Interiors* (New York: Rizzoli, 1992);

O. E. Schoeffler and William Gale, *Esquire's Encyclopedia of 20th Century Men's Fashions* (New York: McGraw-Hill, 1973);

Stephen W. Sears, *The American Heritage History of the Automobile in America* (New York: American Heritage Publishing, 1977);

Douglass Shand-Tucci, *Ralph Adams Cram: Life and Architecture* (Amherst: University of Massachusetts Press, 1995);

C. Ray Smith, *Interior Design in 20th-Century America: A History* (New York: Harper & Row, 1987);

Marie Via and Margaret Searle, eds., *Head, Heart and Hand: Elbert Hubbard and the Roycrofters* (Rochester, N.Y.: University of Rochester Press, 1994);

Marcus Whiffen and Frederick Koeper, *American Architecture, 1607–1976* (Cambridge, Mass.: MIT Press, 1981).

GOVERNMENT AND POLITICS

Ruth B. A. Bordin, *Woman and Temperance* (New Brunswick, N.J.: Rutgers University Press, 1990);

John D. Buenker, *The Income Tax and the Progressive Era* (New York: Garland, 1985);

Kendrick A. Clements, *The Presidency of Woodrow Wilson* (Lawrence: University of Kansas Press, 1992);

Robert D. Cuff, *The War Industries Board* (Baltimore: Johns Hopkins University Press, 1973);

Robert H. Ferrell, *Woodrow Wilson and World War I, 1917–1921* (New York: Harper & Row, 1985);

Ellen Fitzpatrick, *Endless Crusade: Women Social Scientists and Progressive Reform* (New York: Oxford University Press, 1990);

Eleanor Flexner, *Century of Struggle* (Cambridge, Mass.: Harvard University Press, 1975);

Anthony Gengarelly, *Distinguished Dissenters and Opposition to the 1919–1920 Red Scare* (Lewiston: Mellen Press, 1996);

Linda Gordon, *Pitied But Not Entitled* (Cambridge, Mass.: Harvard University Press, 1995);

Lewis L. Gould, *Reform and Regulation* (New York: Wiley, 1978);

Allen D. Grimshaw, ed., *Racial Violence in the United States* (Chicago: Aldine, 1969);

Ellis W. Hawley, *The Great War and the Search for a Modern Order*, second edition (New York: St. Martin's Press, 1992);

Samuel P. Hays, *The Response to Industrialism, 1885–1914* (Chicago: University of Chicago Press, 1957);

John Higham, *Strangers in the Land: Patterns of American Nativism* (New Brunswick, N.J.: Rutgers University Press, 1955);

Richard Hofstadter, *The Age of Reform: From Bryan to FDR* (New York: Random House, 1955);

John J. Johnson, *A Hemisphere Apart: The Foundation of United States Policy Toward Latin America* (Baltimore: Johns Hopkins University Press, 1990);

Maldwyn Allen Jones, *American Immigration* (Chicago: University of Chicago Press, 1960);

David M. Kennedy, *Over Here: The First World War and American Society* (New York: Oxford University Press, 1980);

William M. Leary Jr. and Arthur S. Link, eds., *The Progressive Era and the Great War, 1896–1920* (Arlington Heights, Ill.: AHM, 1978);

Arthur S. Link, *Woodrow Wilson and the Progressive Era, 1910–1917* (New York: Harper & Row, 1954);

Link and Richard L. McCormick, *Progressivism* (Arlington Heights, Ill.: Harlan Davidson, 1983);

S. D. Lovell, *The Presidential Election of 1916* (Carbondale: Southern Illinois Univeristy Press, 1980);

Alonso Aguilar Monteverde, *Pan-Americanism from Monroe to the Present* (New York: Monthly Review Press, 1968);

John L. Moore, ed., *Congressional Quarterly's Guide to U.S. Elections* (Washington, D.C.: Congressional Quarterly, 1994);

George E. Mowry, *The Era of Theodore Roosevelt and the Birth of Modern America: 1900–1912* (New York: Harper & Row, 1958);

Robert K. Murray, *Red Scare* (New York: McGraw-Hill, 1964);

Donald G. Nieman, *Promises to Keep: African-Americans and the Constitutional Order, 1776 to the Present* (New York: Oxford University Press, 1991);

Robert A. Pastor, *Limits to Friendship* (New York: Knopf, 1988);

James Oliver Robertson, *No Third Choice: Progressives in Republican Politics, 1916–1921* (New York: Garland, 1983);

W. J. Rorabaugh, *The Alcoholic Republic: An American Tradition* (Oxford: Oxford University Press, 1979);

Arthur M. Schlesinger Jr., ed., *History of American Presidential Elections, 1789–1968*, volume 3 (New York: Chelsea House/McGraw-Hill, 1971);

James P. Shenton, *Ethnicity and Immigration* (Washington, D.C.: American Historical Association, 1990);

Barbara J. Steinson, *American Women's Activism in World War I* (New York: Garland, 1982);

Ralph A. Stone, ed., *Wilson and the League of Nations* (Huntington, N.Y.: Krieger, 1978);

Barbara Tuchman, *The Zimmermann Telegram* (New York: Viking, 1958);

Josefina Zoraida Vazquez and Lorenzo Meyer, *The United States and Mexico* (Chicago: University of Chicago Press, 1985);

James Weinstein, *The Corporate Ideal in the Liberal State, 1900–1918* (Boston: Beacon, 1968);

John Womack Jr., *Zapata and the Mexican Revolution* (New York: Knopf, 1969).

LAW AND JUSTICE

Sidney H. Asch, *The Supreme Court and Its Great Justices* (New York: Arco, 1971);

Liva Baker, *The Justice from Beacon Hill: The Life and Times of Oliver Wendell Holmes* (New York: HarperCollins, 1991);

Alexander M. Bickel and Benno C. Schmidt Jr., *History of the Supreme Court of the United States: The Judiciary and Responsible Government, 1910–1921* (New York: Macmillan, 1984);

Homer Cummings and Carl McFarland, *Federal Justice: Chapters in the History of Justice and the Federal Executives* (New York: Macmillan, 1937);

William F. Furbath, *Law and the Shaping of the American Labor Movement* (Cambridge, Mass.: Harvard University Press, 1991);

John A. Garraty, ed., *Quarrels That Have Shaped the Constitution* (New York: Harper & Row, 1987);

Charles Goodell, *Political Prisoners in America* (New York: Random House, 1973);

James W. Hurst, *The Law of Treason in the United States* (Westport, Conn.: Greenwood Press, 1971);

John W. Johnson, *American Legal Culture, 1908–1940* (Westport, Conn.: Greenwood Press, 1981);

Earl W. Kintner and Joseph P. Bauer, *Federal Antitrust Law* (Cincinnati: Anderson, 1989);

Stephen M. Kohn, *American Political Prisoners: Prosecutions under the Espionage and Sedition Acts* (Westport, Conn.: Praeger, 1994);

Alpheus T. Mason, *The Supreme Court from Taft to Burger* (Baton Rouge: Louisiana State University Press, 1980);

Michael E. Parrish, *Felix Frankfurter and His Times: The Reform Years* (New York: Macmillan, 1982);

William Preston Jr., *Aliens and Dissenters: Federal Suppression of Radicals, 1903–1933* (Cambridge, Mass.: Harvard University Press, 1963);

Dawn Reilly and Norman Murphy, *The Supreme Court of the United States: Its Beginnings and Its Justices, 1790–1991* (Washington, D.C.: Commission on the Bicentennial of the United States Constitution, 1992);

David J. Rothman, *Conscience and Convenience: The Asylum and Its Alternatives in Progressive America* (Boston: Little, Brown, 1980);

Robert Schnayerson, *The Illustrated History of the Supreme Court of the United States* (New York: Abrams, 1986);

Bernard Schwartz, *The Law in America* (New York: American Heritage Publishing, 1974);

John E. Semonche, *Charting the Future: The Supreme Court Responds to a Changing Society, 1890–1920* (Westport, Conn.: Greenwood Press, 1978);

Philippa Strum, *Louis D. Brandeis: Justice for the People* (Cambridge, Mass.: Harvard University Press, 1984).

LIFESTYLES AND SOCIAL TRENDS

Paul Boyer, *Urban Masses and Moral Order in America, 1820–1920* (Cambridge, Mass.: Harvard University Press, 1978);

Norman H. Clark, *Deliver Us from Evil: An Interpretation of American Prohibition* (New York: Norton, 1976);

Melvyn Dubofsky, *Industrialism and the American Worker, 1865–1920* (Arlington Heights, Ill.: Harlan Davidson, 1985);

John Hope Franklin and Alfred A. Moss Jr., *From Slavery to Freedom: A History of African Americans* (New York: McGraw-Hill, 1994);

Joshua Freeman and others, *Who Built America? Working People and the Nation's Economy, Politics, Culture, and Society* (New York: Pantheon, 1992);

J. C. Furnas, *Great Times: An Informal Social History of the United States* (New York: Putnam, 1974);

Kenneth T. Jackson, *Crabgrass Frontier: Suburbanization in the United States* (New York: Oxford University Press, 1985);

Jacqueline Jones, *Labor of Love, Labor of Sorrow: Black Women, Work and the Family from Slavery to the Present* (New York: Basic Books, 1985);

Alan Kraut, *The Huddled Masses: The Immigrant in American Society, 1880–1921* (Arlington Heights, Ill.: Harlan-Davidson, 1982);

William Leach, *Land of Desire: Merchants, Power, and the Rise of a New American Culture* (New York: Random House, 1993);

Peter J. Ling, *America and the Automobile: Technology, Reform and Social Change* (Manchester, U.K.: Manchester University Press, 1990);

Rosalind Rosenberg, *Divided Lives: American Women in the Twentieth Century* (New York: Hill & Wang, 1992);

Susan Strasser, *Never Done: A History of American Housework* (New York: Pantheon, 1982).

MEDIA

Whitman Bassow, *The Moscow Correspondents: Reporting on Russia from the Revolution to Glasnost* (New York: Morrow, 1988);

Arthur Asa Berger, *The Comic-Stripped American: What Dick Tracy, Blondie, Daddy Warbucks and Charlie Brown Tell Us about Ourselves* (New York: Walker, 1973);

Meyer Berger, *The Story of the New York Times* (New York: Times Books, 1950);

Alfred A. Cornebise, *The Stars and Stripes: Doughboy Journalism in World War I* (Westport, Conn.: Greenwood Press, 1984);

George H. Douglas, *The Smart Magazine: Fifty Years of Literary Revelry and High Jinks at Vanity Fair, The New Yorker, Life, Esquire, and The Smart Set* (Hamden, Conn.: Archon Press, 1991);

Susan Douglas, *Inventing American Broadcasting, 1899–1922* (Baltimore: Johns Hopkins University Press, 1987);

Julia Edwards, *Women of the World: The Great Foreign Correspondents* (New York: Ivy Books, 1988);

Edwin Emery and Michael Emery, *The Press and America,* fourth edition (Englewood Cliffs, N.J.: Prentice-Hall, 1978);

Charles Forcey, *The Crossroads of Liberalism: Croly, Weyl, Lippmann, and the Progressive Era, 1900–1925* (New York: Oxford University Press, 1961);

John Hohenberg, *Foreign Correspondence: The Great Reporters and Their Times,* second edition (Syracuse, N.Y.: Syracuse University Press, 1985);

Lauren Kessler, *The Dissident Press: Alternative Journalism in American History* (Beverly Hills, Cal.: Sage, 1984);

Phillip Knightly, *The First Casualty: From the Crimea to Vietnam: The War Correspondent as Hero, Propagandist, and Myth Maker* (New York: Harcourt Brace Jovanovich, 1975);

Sidney Kobre, *Development of American Journalism* (Dubuque, Iowa: William C. Brown, 1969);

Richard Marschall, *America's Great Comic-Strip Artists* (New York: Abbeville Press, 1989);

Marion Marzolf, *Civilizing Voices: American Press Criticism, 1880–1950* (New York: Longman, 1991);

H. C. Peterson and Gilbert Fite, *Opponents of War, 1917–1918* (Seattle: University of Washington Press, 1968);

Theodore Peterson, *Magazines in the Twentieth Century* (Urbana: University of Illinois Press, 1964);

Ishbel Ross, *Ladies of the Press* (New York: Harper, 1936);

Michael Schudson, *Discovering the News: A Social History of American Newspapers* (New York: Basic Books, 1978);

W. A. Swanberg, *Citizen Hearst* (New York: Scribners, 1961);

Swanberg, *Pulitzer* (New York: Scribners, 1967);

John Tebbel, *Between Covers: The Rise and Transformation of Book Publishing in America* (New York: Oxford University Press, 1987);

Stephen Vaughn, *Holding Fast the Inner Lines: Democracy, Nationalism, and the Committee on Public Information* (Chapel Hill: University of North Carolina Press, 1980).

MEDICINE AND HEALTH

Theodora M. Abel, *Psychological Testing in Cultural Contexts* (New Haven: College and University Press, 1973);

N. J. Block and Gerald Dworkin, eds., *The IQ Controversy, Critical Readings* (New York: Pantheon, 1976);

James Bordley III and A. McGehee Harvey, *Two Centuries of American Medicine, 1776–1976* (Philadelphia: Saunders, 1976);

Mark Caldwell, *The Last Crusade: The War on Consumption, 1862–1954* (New York: Atheneum, 1988);

Bernard G. Campbell, *Humankind Emerging,* sixth edition (New York: HarperCollins, 1992);

Frederick F. Cartwright, *The Development of Modern Surgery from 1830* (New York: Crowell, 1967);

Ellen Chesler, *Woman of Valor: Margaret Sanger and the Birth Control Movement in America* (New York: Simon & Schuster, 1992);

Helen Clapesattle, *The Doctors Mayo* (Minneapolis: University of Minnesota Press, 1941);

William C. Cockerham, *Medical Sociology* (Englewood Cliffs, N.J.: Prentice Hall, 1989);

Alfred W. Crosby Jr., *Epidemic and Peace, 1918* (Westport, Conn.: Greenwood Press, 1976);

M. Patricia Donahue, *Nursing, The Finest Art* (Saint Louis: Mosby, 1985);

Donald H. Fleming, *William Henry Welch and the Rise of Modern Medicine* (Boston: Little, Brown, 1954);

John F. Fulton, *Harvey Cushing, A Biography* (Springfield, Ill.: Charles C. Thomas, 1946);

R. J. Herrnstein, *I.Q. in the Meritocracy* (Boston: Little, Brown, 1971);

Saul Jarcho and Gene Brown, eds., *Medicine and Health Care* (New York: Arno, 1977);

David M. Kennedy, *Birth Control in America: The Career of Margaret Sanger* (New Haven: Yale University Press, 1991);

James T. Patterson, *The Dread Disease: Cancer and Modern American Culture* (Cambridge, Mass.: Harvard University Press, 1987);

Nan Richardson, Catherine Chermayeff, and Thomas K. Walker, eds., *Medicine's Great Journey: One Hundred Years of Healing* (Boston: Little, Brown, 1992);

Robert G. Richardson, *Surgery: Old and New Frontiers* (New York: Scribners, 1968);

Evelyn Sharp, *The IQ Cult* (New York: Coward, McCann & Geoghegan, 1972);

Edward Shorter, *The Health Century* (New York: Doubleday, 1987);

Paul Starr, *The Social Transformation of American Medicine* (New York: Basic Books, 1982);

Elizabeth H. Thomson, *Harvey Cushing: Surgeon, Author, Artist* (New York: Collier, 1961);

Andrew C. Twaddle and Richard M. Hessler, *A Sociology of Health* (New York: Macmillan, 1987).

RELIGION

Ray H. Abrams, *Preachers Present Arms* (Scottsdale, Pa.: Herald Press, 1969);

Sydney H. Ahlstrom, *A Religious History of the American People* (New Haven: Yale University Press, 1972);

Bernham P. Beckwith, *The Decline of U.S. Religious Faith, 1912–1984* (Palo Alto, Cal.: Beckwith, 1985);

Ira V. Brown, *Lyman Abbott: Christian Evolutionist* (Cambridge, Mass.: Harvard University Press, 1953);

Jay P. Dolan, *The American Catholic Experience: A History from Colonial Times to the Present* (Garden City, N.Y.: Doubleday, 1985);

Edwin S. Gaustad, *A Religious History of America*, new revised edition (New York: HarperCollins, 1990);

James Hennesey, *American Catholics: A History of the Roman Catholic Community in the United States* (New York: Oxford University Press, 1981);

Arthur Hertzberg, *The Jews in America: Four Centuries of an Uneasy Encounter: A History* (New York: Simon & Schuster, 1989);

William R. Hutchinson, *The Modernist Impulse in American Protestantism* (Cambridge, Mass.: Harvard University Press, 1975);

Charles H. Lippy, ed., *Twentieth-Century Shapers of American Popular Religion* (New York: Greenwood Press, 1989);

Charles H. Lippy and Peter Williams, eds., *Encyclopedia of the American Religious Experience* (New York: Scribners, 1988);

C. Roland Marchand, *The American Peace Movement and Social Reform, 1898–1918* (Princeton: Princeton University Press, 1973);

George M. Marsden, *Fundamentalism and American Culture: The Shaping of Twentieth-Century Evangelicalism, 1870–1925* (New York: Oxford University Press, 1980);

Martin Marty, *Pilgrims in Their Own Land: 500 Years of Religion in America* (Boston: Houghton Mifflin, 1984);

Isidore S. Meyer, ed., *Early History of Zionism in America* (New York: Arno, 1977);

John F. Piper Jr., *The American Churches in World War I* (Athens: Ohio University Press, 1985);

Ernest R. Sandeen, *The Roots of Fundamentalism: British and American Millenarianism, 1800–1930* (Chicago: University of Chicago Press, 1970);

Timothy P. Weber, *Living in the Shadow of the Second Coming: American Premillennialism, 1875–1982*, revised edition (Grand Rapids, Mich.: Academie Books, 1983).

SCIENCE AND TECHNOLOGY

Isaac Asimov, *Eyes on the Universe: A History of the Telescope* (Boston: Houghton Mifflin, 1975);

Asimov, *Understanding Physics* (New York: Walker, 1966);

Marcia Bartusiak, *Thursday's Universe* (New York: Times Books, 1986);

Peter G. Bergmann, *The Riddle of Gravitation* (New York: Scribners, 1968);

Peter J. Bowler, *The Non-Darwinian Revolution* (Baltimore: Johns Hopkins University Press, 1988);

Barbara Lovett Cline, *The Questioners* (New York: Crowell, 1965);

Maitland Edey and Donald C. Johanson, *Blueprints: Solving the Mystery of Evolution* (Boston: Little, Brown, 1989);

Albert Einstein, *Relativity: The Special and General Theory,* fifteenth edition (London: Methuen, 1954);

Nathan G. Hale Jr., *Freud and the Americans: The Beginnings of Psychoanalysis in the United States, 1876–1917* (New York: Oxford University Press, 1971);

Fred Hoyle, *Astronomy* (Garden City, N.Y.: Doubleday, 1962);

Max Jammer, *The Conceptual Development of Quantum Mechanics* (New York: McGraw-Hill, 1966);

Stephen Kern, *The Culture of Time and Space, 1880–1918* (Cambridge, Mass.: Harvard University Press, 1983);

Daniel J. Kevles, *The Physicists: The History of a Scientific Community in Modern America* (New York: Knopf, 1971);

Robert Lacey, *Ford: The Men and the Machine* (Boston: Little, Brown, 1986);

Tom Lewis, *Empire of the Air: The Men Who Made Radio* (New York: HarperCollins, 1991);

Ian McNeil, *An Encyclopedia of the History of Technology* (London: Routledge, 1990);

Dorothy Ross, *The Origins of American Social Science* (New York: Cambridge University Press, 1991);

Emilio Segre, *From X-Rays to Quarks: Modern Physicists and Their Discoveries* (San Francisco: W. H. Freeman, 1980);

A. H. Sturtevant, *A History of Genetics* (New York: Harper & Row, 1965);

Michael J. H. Taylor and John W. R. Taylor, *Encyclopedia of Aircraft* (New York: Putnam, 1978);

James S. Trefil, *From Atoms to Quarks: An Introduction to the Strange World of Particle Physics* (New York: Scribners, 1980);

Mitchell Wilson, *American Science and Invention* (New York: Simon & Schuster, 1954);

Tibor Zoltai and James H. Stout, *Mineralogy: Concepts and Principles* (Minneapolis: Burgess, 1984).

SPORTS

Gerald Astor, *The PGA World Golf Hall of Fame Book* (New York: Prentice Hall, 1991);

Al Barkow, *The History of the PGA Tour* (New York: Doubleday, 1989);

Bud Collins and Zander Hollander, eds., *Bud Collins' Modern Encyclopedia of Tennis,* second edition (Detroit: Gale Research, 1994);

Allison Danzig, *The History of American Football: Its Great Teams, Players, and Coaches* (Englewood Cliffs, N.J.: Prentice-Hall, 1956);

Danzig, *The Racquet Game* (New York: Macmillan, 1930);

Danzig, *The Winning Gallery* (Philadelphia: United States Court Tennis Association of America, 1985);

Edward F. Dolan, *Great Moments in the Indy 500* (New York: Watts, 1982);

Marvin Drager, *The Most Glorious Crown* (New York: Winchester, 1975);

John Findling and Kimberly Pele, eds., *The Historical Dictionary of the Olympic Games* (Westport, Conn.: Greenwood Press, forthcoming 1996);

Nevin H. Gibson, *The Encyclopedia of Golf* (New York: A. S. Barnes, 1958);

Allen Guttmann, *The Olympics: A History of the Modern Games* (Urbana & Chicago: University of Illinois Press, 1994);

Zander Hollander, ed., *Modern Encyclopedia of Basketball* (New York: Four Winds, 1969);

William S. Jarrett, *Timetables of Sports History: Football* (New York: Facts On File, 1989);

Ivan N. Kaye, *Good Clean Violence: A History of College Football* (Philadelphia: Lippincott, 1973);

Graeme Kent, *Boxing's Strangest Fights* (London: Robson, 1991);

Frank G. Menke, *The Encyclopedia of Sports, Fourth Revised Edition* (New York: A. S. Barnes, 1969);

Douglas A. Noverr and Lawrence E. Ziewac, *The Games They Played; Sports in American History, 1865–1980* (Chicago: Nelson-Hall, 1983);

Gilbert Odd, *Encyclopedia of Boxing* (New York: Crescent, 1983);

Roberto L. Quercetani, *A World History of Modern Track and Field Athletics* (New York: Oxford University Press, 1964);

Benjamin G. Rader, *American Sports: From the Age of Folk Games to the Age of Televised Sports,* second edition (Englewood Cliffs, N.J.: Prentice Hall, 1990);

William H. P. Robertson, *The History of Thoroughbred Racing in America* (Englewood Cliffs, N.J.: Prentice-Hall, 1964);

John Rousmaniere, *America's Cup Book, 1851–1983* (New York: Norton, 1983);

Alex Sachare, ed., *The Official NBA Basketball Encyclopedia,* second edition (New York: Villard, 1994);

Jay Schleifer, *Indy! The Great American Race* (New Jersey: Crestwood House, 1995);

Robert Sommers, *The U.S. Open: Golf's Ultimate Challenge* (New York: Atheneum, 1987);

David Stirk, *Golf: the History of an Obsession* (Oxford: Phaidon, 1987);

Bert R. Sugar, *The Great Fights: a Pictorial History of Boxing's Greatest Bouts* (New York: Gallery, 1981);

Rich Taylor, *Indy: Seventy-five Years of Racing's Greatest Spectacle* (New York: St. Martin's Press, 1991);

John Thorn and Pete Palmer, *Total Baseball: The Official Encyclopedia of Major League Baseball,* fourth edition (New York: Viking, 1995);

Alan Trengove, *The Story of the Davis Cup* (London: Stanley Paul, 1985);

David Wallechinsky, *The Complete Book of the Olympics,* revised edition (New York: Viking, 1988);

A. B. C. Whipple, *The Racing Yachts* (Alexandria, Va.: Time-Life Books, 1978);

Suzanne Wilding and Anthony Del Balso, *The Triple Crown Winners: The Story of America's Ten Superstar Race Horses* (New York: Parents' Magazine, 1978).

CONTRIBUTORS

ARTS   CAROLYN KITCH
                                      Temple University

BUSINESS AND THE ECONOMY   ROBERT P. BATCHELOR
                                      Temple University and the History Factory

EDUCATION   HARRIETT WILLIAMS
                                      University of South Carolina

FASHION   JESSICA MARSHALL
                                      Fairfield, Connecticut
                                      SILVANA R. SIDDALI
                                      Harvard University

GOVERNMENT AND POLITICS   JOHN LOUIS RECHIUTTI
                                      Lawrence Technological University

LAW AND JUSTICE   G. JACK BENGE
                                      Santa Barbara, California

LIFESTYLES AND SOCIAL TRENDS   NANCY E. BERNHARD
                                      Somerville, Massachusetts
                                      DAVID MCLEAN
                                      Seattle, Washington

MEDIA   NANCY BERNHARD
                                      Somerville, Massachussetts

MEDICINE AND HEALTH   JOAN D. LAXSON
                                      Newton, Massachusetts

RELIGION   DAVID MCLEAN
                                      Seattle, Washington
                                      MONICA SIEMS
                                      University of California, Santa Barbara

SCIENCE AND TECHNOLOGY   JOHN LOUIS RECHIUTTI
                                      Lawrence Technological University

SPORTS   ADAM HORNBUCKLE
                                      Alexandria, Virginia
                                      MARTIN MANNING
                                      Woodbridge, Virginia

INDEX OF PHOTOGRAPHS

GENERAL INDEX

A

A. A. Houseman and Company 112

A. C. Fones Clinic, Bridgeport, Conn. 381

A. M. Radcliff (architectural firm) 186

"Aba Daba Honeymoon" 29

Abbe, Cleveland 520

Abbelen, Peter 479

Abbey Theatre, Dublin 25, 56

Abbott, Austin 461

Abbott, Charles C. 520

Abbott, E. G. 409

Abbott, Edith 159

Abbott, Lyman 449, 461–462

Abbott, Vaughn 461

ABC Powers 196, 210–211

Abel, John Jacob 407, 424, 518

Abortion 295

Abraham Lincoln 68

Abraham Lincoln: The Prairie Years (Sandburg) 71

Abraham Lincoln: The War Years (Sandburg) 71

Abrahams, Maurice 26

Abrams v. *United States* 215, 263, 290

Abstract art 41–43

Academy Awards (Oscars) 68, 70

Academy of the Natural Sciences 520

Acheson, Dean 286

Actors Equity Association 28, 38, 63

Actors Equity strike of 1919 36, 38, 63

Adams, A. Emmett 33

Adams, Abigail 221

Adams, Albert 402

Adams, Annette 260

Adams, Franklin P. 364

Adams, Henry 75, 161, 245, 339

Adams, Henry Carter 120

Adams, John 221, 226

Adams, Samuel Hopkins 402, 411, 413

Adams, W. S. 518

Adams Railroad Company 259

Adamson, William C. 227

Adamson Act of 1916 86, 100, 117, 122, 199, 227, 258, 288

Addams, Jane 155, 213, 316, 324, 333, 432, 442, 451, 472

Adler, Felix 159, 469

Adler, Jacob 56

The Adopted Son 32

The Adventures of Kathlyn 27, 50

Advertisement (Cowell) 54

Advertising 104–105, 116, 164, 187, 202, 317, 344, 347, 358, 402

Africa Times and Orient Review 330

African American suffrage 223, 245, 256, 288, 324

African Americans 34, 36, 38, 40, 44, 52–54, 59, 61, 68, 73–76, 102, 123, 129, 133, 146–148, 157–161, 206, 208, 223–224, 243, 250, 256, 260, 280, 288, 295, 302–303, 305–306, 308, 310, 314, 325, 330–331, 334, 336–337, 340, 351, 373–374, 386, 401, 442, 463, 467, 472–473, 480–481, 511, 518, 526, 533, 543, 547, 556

African Methodist Episcopal Church 336, 437, 442, 472–473, 479–481

African Methodist Episcopal Zion Church 472, 481

African Myths (Woodson) 158

Agassiz, Alexander 121

"Agitation Rag" 30

Agricultural education 133, 138, 148–150

Agricultural Historical Association 131

"Ah, Sweet Mystery of Life" 24

Ahern, Will 61

Aida (Verdi) 24

AIDS 389

Aiken, Conrad 28, 31, 33, 47, 476

Aked, Charles 435, 449, 452, 475

Akins, Zoë 55

Akron Indians 548

Akron University 547

Al Que Quiere! (Williams) 33

Alabama Stakes 550

Albee, E. F. 63

Albee, Fred H. 406, 409

Albert I of Belgium 369

Albert, Dr. Heinrich F. 215, 256

Alcock, John 494

Alcohol abuse 231, 283

Alden, Henry Mills 376

Alderman, Edwin 146

Aldington, Richard 47

Aldrich, Nelson W. 232, 249

Aldrich Plan 249

Aleichem, Sholem 56

Alexander, Archbishop 478

Alexander, Eleanor 300

Alexander, Grover Cleveland 564

Alexander Hamilton (Lodge) 245

Alexander's Bridge (Cather) 26, 65

"Alexander's Ragtime Band" 25, 52

Ali, Duse Mohammed 330

Ali, Noble Drew. *See* Drew, Timothy.

"Alice Blue Gown" 36

Alien Act of 1918 35

Alien Land Holding Bill of 1913 254

"All Alone" 25

All-American football team (1917) 74

Allds, Jotham P. 373

Allen, Dudley Peter 427

Allen, Forrest C. "Phog" 541
Allen, Frederick Lewis 349
Allenby, Edmund 459
Allied Powers (World War I) 83, 85, 93, 108, 111, 135, 200, 203, 207, 215–216, 241–242, 245–247, 291, 304, 352, 357–358, 367, 373, 395, 407, 449, 476, 501, 505, 512–513
Allison, James A. 534
Allison, William B. 232
Allston, John M. 189
Alpha and Beta intelligence tests (U.S. Army) 386, 440
Alrich, George L. 465
Altman, Benjamin 121
Always in Vogue (Chase) 368
Always the Young Strangers (Sandburg) 71
Amalgamated Clothing Workers of America 339
Amarilly of Clothes-Line Alley 34
Amateur Athletic Union (AAU) 528, 541–543, 553, 556–558
Amateur Fencers League of America 525
The Ambassador of Christ (Pope Pius X) 466
The Ambassadors (James) 76
Amberg, David M. 171
AME Review 433, 473
American Academy of Arts and Letters 71, 184
American Academy of Arts and Sciences 72, 517
American Arbitration Association 243
American Association for Labor Legislation 228–229, 390–391
American Association for the Advancement of Osteopathy 428
American Association for the Advancement of Science 515–516
American Association for the Hard of Hearing 384
American Association of Immunologists 381–382, 425
American Association of Industrial Physicians and Surgeons 383
American Association of University Professors (AAUP) 128–129, 134, 155
American Association of University Women 273
American Association of Variable Star Observers 515

American Association of Women 326
American Astronomical Society 516
American Automobile Association 534
American Bar Association (ABA) 280, 287–288
"American Beauty Rag" 27
American Bible Society 436, 454
American Cancer Society 381
American Car and Foundry Company 122
American Cast Iron Pipe Company 121
American Citizenship (Beard) 153
American City Government (Beard) 153
American Civil Liberties Bureau 452
American Civil Liberties Union 155, 270, 304
American Civil War 54, 68, 90, 132, 135, 158, 206, 231, 237, 246, 252, 289, 318–319, 340, 373, 377, 396, 414, 420, 427–428, 443, 461–462, 466, 470, 513
American College of Physicians 382
American College of Surgeons 381–383, 392–393, 424
American Communist Party 220
American Defense League 352
American Defense Society 62
American Dermatological Association 427
American Equal Rights Association 463
American Expeditionary Forces (AEF) 201, 204, 215–216, 246, 303, 319, 346–347, 349, 363, 374, 512
American Federation of Art 189
American Federation of Catholic Societies 435
American Federation of Labor (AFL) 87, 90, 96–100, 102, 105, 107, 113, 116–117, 127–128, 133, 155, 215, 226, 228, 332, 390–391
American Federation of Teachers (AFT) 128, 133, 155
The American Friend 468
American Friends Service Committee 436, 452, 467
American Government and Politics (Beard) 153
American Hebrew Medal 327
American Home Economics Association 322

American Institute of Architects 170, 184, 187, 189–190
American Institute of Electrical Engineers 493
American Institute of Mining Engineers 493
American Jewish Committee 329
American Journal of International Law 244
American Journal of Psychology 323
American Ladies' Tailors Association 164, 181
American Law Institute 293
American Law Review 289
American Lawn Bowls Association 528
American League (baseball) 527, 532, 536–541, 560–561, 564–566
American Legion 204, 220, 261, 545
American Liberty League 288
American Library Association 456
The American Magazine 71, 371
American Marconi Company 346
American Medical Association (AMA) 383, 386, 389–393, 402–404
— Council of Medical Education 381, 386, 392
— Council on Medical Education and Hospitals 380
— Council on Pharmacy and Chemistry 402
American Mercury 363
American Motors Corporation (AMC) 115
American Museum of Natural History, New York City 189
American Music Hall, Chicago 58
American Naturalist 507
"The American Newspaper" 344, 350
American Newspaper Guild 374
American Orthodox Church 440, 477
American Peace League 152
American Philological Association 161
American Philosophical Association 154
American Philosophical Society 516–517
American Professional Football Association 531
American Protective League 304, 307, 311, 352
American Psychological Association 129, 154, 323

American Public Health Association 382

American Railroad Company 259

American Railroad Express Company 259

American Red Cross 61, 146, 314, 320, 324, 334, 339, 364, 407, 427, 467–468, 550

American Red Cross Hospital, Neuilly, France 407

American Red Cross Nursing Service 396, 421

American Revolution 62, 270, 313

American School Board Journal 143

American School Citizenship League 152. *See also* American Peace League.

American Society of Civil Engineers 493

American Society of Composers, Authors, and Publishers (ASCAP) 29, 33, 38, 63, 255, 346

American Society of Mechanical Engineers 493

American Society of Orthodontists 383

American Telephone and Telegraph (AT&T) 87, 89, 99, 113, 292, 346, 348

American Tobacco Company 80, 123, 253, 265, 268, 292

American Union Against Militarism 310, 451

American Union Commission 461

American Unitarian Association 451

American Viscose Company 164

American Weekly 374

American Woman Suffrage Association 221, 463

American Zionist Medical Unit 461, 478

Americanism 89, 228, 239, 305, 339, 374, 440, 460

Americanization 38, 94, 129–130, 134, 156, 228, 315–316, 440–441, 460, 466–467

Americanization Committee, Cleveland 131. *See also* National Americanization Committee.

America's Coming-of-Age (Brooks) 37

Amherst College 126, 155, 244

Amory, Cleveland 363

Amoss, David Alfred 427

Amundsen, Roald 372, 489

Anarchism 60, 120, 192, 204, 208, 215, 220, 252, 260, 270, 300–301, 305, 328, 440–441, 445–447

"And the Green Grass Grew All Around" 26

Anderson, George M. 189

Anderson, James 146

Anderson, John F. 424

Anderson, Margaret 45, 47, 346, 374

Anderson, Maxwell 375

Anderson, Sherwood 31–32, 34–35, 45, 60

Anderson, Willie 567

Andrews, Fannie Fern Phillips 152

Anesthesia 392, 405, 424–425

Annotated Bible (Gaebelein) 465

Anthanasaw v. *United States* 283

Anthony, Susan B. 221, 335, 369, 463–464

Anthracite Coal Strike Committee 118

Anthracite coal strike of 1913 81

Anti-Alien Labor Law, Arizona 257

Anti-Saloon League 231, 254, 320

Anti-Semitism 112, 126, 256, 295, 329, 433, 435, 441–442, 464–465, 469

Antibiotics 385, 387

Antioch College 462

"Any Little Girl That's a Nice Little Girl Is the Right Little Girl for Me" 24

Apache tribe 245

Apfel, Oscar 28

The Apostle of Vengeance 31

Apostolic Times 480

Appeal to Reason 352

Appearances: Notes of Travel, East and West (Santayana) 476

Apple, Andrew T. 520

April Twilights (Cather) 65

The Arab 30

Arabic 198

Arbeiter und Soldenrat 357

Arbitration in the New Industrial Society (Kellor) 244

Arbuckle, Roscoe "Fatty" 31, 34, 49, 51

Arc de Triomphe, Paris 320

Archbald, Robert W. 274, 287, 294

Archbold, John D. 121

Archibald, George 524, 565

Arden, Elizabeth 164, 339

Arensberg, Louise 60

Arensberg, Walter 60

Ariadne auf Naxos (Strauss) 54

Arizona Constitution 193, 253

Arizona Employers' Liability 278

Arkansas Supreme Court 128

Arliss, George 49, 55–56, 61

Armistice Day (11 November) 203, 217, 220, 240, 357, 437, 456

Armory Show of 1913 27, 42–43, 72, 76, 178, 328, 363

Armour and Company 281

Armstrong, Edwin H. 490, 492, 505

Armstrong, Louis 53

Army of the Potomac 427

Arndt, Felix 32

Arnett, Benjamin W. 472

Arnstein, Julius "Nick" 58

Art Deco 171, 174, 178

Art Institute of Chicago 72

Art Nouveau 177–178, 188

Art of Love 294

Art Students League of New York 72, 370

Artful Kate 25

Arts and Crafts movement 174–175, 187–188

Arver v. *United States* 259

"As a Woman Sees It" (Dorr) 370

As It Is in Life 24

Asaf, George 30

ASCAP. *See* American Society of Composers, Authors, and Publishers.

Ash Can School 37, 40

Ashley, Clarence 161

Ashurst, Henry 100

Asian 366

Asinof, Eliot 560

Assemblies of God 434

Assembly-line production 82, 85–86, 89, 93, 95, 104, 166, 177, 301, 306, 370, 489–490, 493, 500

Associated Charities of Boston 340

Associated Press 345–346, 353, 355, 377

Association for the Study of Negro Life and History 158, 160

Association of American Painters and Sculptors 26, 38, 42–43

Association of American Physicians 415

Association of Experimental Pathology 381

Association of Immunologists 382

Association to Abolish War 451–453

Astaire, Adele 73–74

Astaire, Fred 48, 65, 73–74

Astor, John Jacob 339
Astor Ballroom, New York City 63
Astor family 367
Astor Hotel, New York City 164
Astor Theatre, New York City 28, 34
Astrology (racehorse) 562
Astronomical and Astrophysical Society of America 515
Astronomical Journal 520
"Athletics as Education and Athletics as Business" (Foster) 159
Atkinson, George F. 520
Atlanta Constitution 329
Atlanta Georgian 329
Atlanta Journal 329
The Atlantic Monthly 38, 46, 363, 375–376
Attell, Abe 543
Atteridge, Harold R. 29
"Au Revoir, But Not Goodbye, Soldier Boy" 33
Auburn University 547
Audley Farm, Va. 563
Auer, John 424
Aufderheide, May 25
Austin, Mary 24, 26, 32
The Autobiography of an Ex-Colored Man (Johnson) 26
Automobile Club of America 534
Automobile industry 80, 82, 85, 93–95, 104, 113–115, 148, 169, 172, 174, 177–178, 302, 307, 311–313, 338, 488–494, 499–500, 534
The Avenging Conscience 28
Avery, Martha G. M. 435
Avery, Oswald T. 424
Aviation 75, 82, 113–114, 168, 180, 255, 339, 372, 424, 491, 493–494, 510, 516, 519, 524–525
Avondale Presbyterian Church, Cincinnati 189
Aydelotte, Frank 159
Ayer, Nat D. 25
Ayres, Milan 140
Azora (Hadley) 54
Aztec Indians 44

B

B. Altman and Company 121
Babcock, Harry 557
"Babes in the Wood" 30, 58
Bach, Richard 189
Backyards, Greenwich Village (Sloan) 40, 72

Bacon, Augustus O. 297
Bacon, Sir Francis 510
Bacon, Frank 55, 63
Bacon, Henry 184
Baden-Powell, Sir Robert 301
Baekeland, Leo Hendrik 504
Baer, George F. 121
Bagnall, Robert 336
Baha, Abdul 433
Baha'i faith 433, 479
Baha'i Mother Temple, Wilmette, Ill. 433
The Baha'i Revelation 479
Bailey, William W. 520
Bailey v. Drexel Furniture Company 231, 269
Baker, Doc 548
Baker, E. G. "Cannonball" 527
Baker, Frank 539
Baker, George (Father Divine) 338, 433, 438
Baker, George F. 107
Baker, John Franklin "Home Run" 564
Baker, Newton D. 34, 157, 198, 241–242, 259, 318, 530, 538
Baker, Ray Stannard 354
Baker, William Henry 427
Balak, Victor 552
Balch, Emily Greene 120, 334, 471
Baldwin, Roger 270
Baldwin, T. A. 246
Balfour, Arthur 459
Balfour Declaration of November 1917 459, 478
Ball, Ernest R. 26
Ball, Robert 526
Ballets Russes 32, 43
Ballinger, Richard A. 234, 286
Ballinger-Pinchot Affair of 1909–1910 207, 232, 234, 286
Baltimore Evening News 374
Baltimore Sun 374
Bancroft, Hubert H. 339
Bancroft, John Sellers 520
Bandelier, Adolph F. 520
The Bank 30
Bank of California, San Francisco 122
Bank of England 266
Bank Street College of Education 157
Baptist Church 433, 435, 438, 440, 450, 452, 473–474, 477–479, 481
Baptist Home Mission 480
Bara, Theda 30–32, 35, 48–49, 75
Barber, J. Max 473

The Bargain 28, 50
Barnard College 150, 186, 517
Barnes, James 531, 550
Barnes, Roscoe Conkling 567
Barr, Amelia Edith Huddleston 75, 479
Barrell, Joseph 520
Barrett, Charlie 546
Barrett, Harrison D. 479
Barrows, Isabel Hayes Chapin 339
Barry, Jack 539
Barrymore, Ethel 55–56, 63, 74, 186
Barrymore, John 55–56, 74
Barrymore, Lionel 63, 68, 74
Barrymore family 55
Barthelmess, Richard 31, 35, 49
Barton, Bruce 347
Barton, Clara 339, 396, 427
Barton, Durstine, and Osborn (advertising agency) 347
Baruch, Bernard M. 109–110, 112–114, 202, 214, 260
A Basic History of the United States (Beard and Beard) 153
The Basket Woman (Austin) 24
Bates, Lindon Jr. 520
Baths of Caracalla 172
Batten, Samuel 474
Battle, Kathleen 53
Battle Creek Toasted Corn Flakes Company 384
The Battle Cry of Peace 30
"The Battle Hymn of the Republic" (Howe) 76
The Battle of Gettysburg 27
The Battle of the Sexes 28
Bauhaus School 167
Baum, L. Frank 75, 339
Baumann, Eulgen 415
Bayer Company 402
Bayes, Nora 52, 73
"Be Fair to Germany" (Rauschenbusch) 452
"Be My Little Baby Bumble Bee" 26
Beal, James Hartley 426
"Beale Street Blues" 32, 69
Bean, Leon Leonwood 92, 189
Beard, Charles Austin 120, 153–155, 337
Beard, Mary 153
The Bearded Bandit 26
The Beast of Berlin 355
Beattie, Bessie 370
"Beautiful Ohio" 34

Committee on Occupational Standards 333
The Common Law 289
Commonwealth Pier, Boston 388
Communism 97, 102, 203–204, 208, 215, 220, 392, 440–441, 445, 465, 478
Communist International 372
Communist Labor Party 220, 372
Complete Poems (Sandburg) 27, 71
Computing Tabulating Recording Company 518
Comstock, Anthony 294
Conant, Charles A. 121
Conant, James 135
Confederate army 252, 297–298
Conference on Faith and Order for North America (1916) 435
The Conflict (Phillips) 25
The Congo and Other Poems (Lindsay) 28
Congregation of Notre Dame 480
Congregationalism 435, 440, 449, 461, 479–481
Congregationalist 452
Congregationalist Church 447
Congress of Industrial Organizations (CIO) 117
Congress of Surgeons of North America Cancer Campaign Committee 412
Congress of the Toilers of the East 372
Congressional Government (Wilson) 247
Congressional Union for Woman Suffrage 222, 327, 334–335, 463
Conley, Jim 256, 295, 329
Conn, Herbert William 427
A Connecticut Yankee in King Arthur's Court (Twain) 76
Conrad, Joseph 363
Conservationism 307–308
Conservative Judaism 441, 460, 469
Constancy (Boyce) 31, 56
"Constitution and Discipline" (Jones) 468
Contemporaries (Steele) 56
Contemporary Verse 47
Converse, Frederick Shepherd 24, 54
Cook, George Cram 31, 38, 56, 60, 338
Cook, William W. 266
Cooke, Robert A. 424
Cookman Institute 336

Coolidge, Calvin 102, 242, 248, 260, 288, 305
Coolidge, William D. 386, 409, 424, 490, 513, 518
Coombs, Jack 539
Cooper, Miriam 30, 49, 68
Cooper, Theodore 121
Cooperative Safety Congress 381
Coppage v. *Kansas* 256
The Copperhead (Thomas) 55
Coppin, Fanny Muriel Jackson 479
Coquette 70
Corey, Herbert 357
Cornell University 127, 150, 242–243, 256, 520, 546, 557, 566
— Prudence Risley Hall 190
Cornhuskers (Sandburg) 34, 71, 75
Corning Glass Works 491
Corona Company 489
Corporate liberalism 205
Cosmopolitan 65, 376
Cosmopolitan Studios 74
Costello, Maurice 24, 49
Cottam, Harold 365
Coubertin, Pierre de 552, 554
Coulon, Johnny 543
Cournos, John 47
Couzens, James 94
The Coward 30
Cowell, Henry 54
Cowley, Malcolm 360
Cox, Catherine 420
Cox, James Middleton 374
Cox, Kenyon 43
Coykendall, Samuel D. 121
Crafts, Charley 59
Crafts, James M. 520
The Craftsman 175, 188
Craftsman Building, New York City 188
Craftsman, Inc. 188
Craig, Gordon 328
Craig, Ralph 553, 556
Cram, Ralph Adams 173, 185
Cram and Wentworth (architectural firm) 185
Cram, Goodhue and Ferguson (architectural firm) 165, 173, 185
Cramp, Charles H. 121
Crane, Hart 47, 60, 345
Crane, Joshua 559
Crane, Zenas 121
Crane and Company 121
Cravath, Paul D. 279
Cravath System 279

Craveth, Clifford Carlton "Cactus" 564
The Cream of the Jest (Cabell) 32
Creede (Colo.) *Chronicle* 377
Creel, George 33, 39, 62, 201, 215, 258, 266, 313, 347, 349, 354–355
Creel Committee. *See* United States — Committee on Public Information.
Creelman, James 376
Creole Jazz Band 53
Cret, Pasul Philippe 174
Crimean War 396
Criminal Anarchy Act of 1902, New York State 296
The Crisis 223, 252, 337, 344, 374
Crisp, Donald 28
Crocker, William 186
Croix de Guerre 65, 217, 310
Croly, Herbert 37, 346, 359–360
Crosby, Caresse. *See* Jacob, Mary Phelps.
Crosby, Fanny 479
Crowe, Samuel J. 424
Crowell, Thomas Y. 121
Crowninshield, Frank 345, 362–363, 367
The Crucifixion (Fuller) 40
Crump, E. H. "Boss" 69
Cubism 38–43, 175
Cubist Poems (Weber) 39
Cudell, Adolph 190
Culberson, Charles 215
Cullen, Countee 337
Cullen, Dr. Thomas S. 411
Cultural Nationalism 37
Cumberland College 547
Cummings, E. E. 46
Cummins, Albert 232
A Cup of Tea 186
Cupples, Samuel 121
The Cure 32
Curie, Pierre 505
Current Opinion 44
Currey, Margery 60
Curtis, C. H. K. 164
Curtis, Herbert D. 492
Curtis, Margaret 565
Curtis Publishing Company 344
Curtiss, Glenn 255, 494, 524
Cushing, Harvey Williams 386, 405–406, 407–408, 424
Custer's Last Raid 26
The Custom of the Country (Wharton) 27
Cutter, Ephraim 427
Cuyler, Francis 161

D

Dabney, Charles 146
Dadaism 41, 43
Daddy Long Legs 35–36
Dagenhart, Roland 268
Daily Graphic 356
Daily Mirror 356
Daily Sketch 356
Daisy Miller (James) 76
Dakin, Henry Drysdale 395, 424
Dana, Charles 377
Dana, Henry W. L. 137–138
Dana, John Cotton 178
"Dance and Grow Thin" 33, 44
The Dance of the Ages 44
Dandy, Walter E. 407, 424
Daniel Webster (Lodge) 245
Daniels, Bebe 32, 49
Danmark, Ribe 26
"Danny Boy" 27
Danzig, Allison 558
"Dardanella" 36
"The Darktown Strutter's Ball" 33
Darrach, James A. 190
Darrow, Clarence 90, 119, 296, 356
Dartiguenave, Sudre 209
Dartmouth College 66, 126, 159, 546
Darwin, Charles 271–272, 507
Darwinism 288, 443, 445, 461–462, 469, 474, 507
Darwinism and Human Life (Thompson) 507
"The Daughter of Rosie O'Grady" 34
Daughters of 1812 62
Daughters of the American Revolution (DAR) 62, 334
Daughters of Zion 460
— Hadassah Chapter 460
Daus, Rudolph L. 190
Davenport, C. B. 507
Davenport, Homer 376
Davenport, Ira 553
Davidson, Jo 328
Davidson College 246
Davies, Arthur B. 40, 42
Davies, Joseph E. 98
Davies, Marion 74
Davis, Andrew Jackson 479
Davis, Jackson 159
Davis, John William 269, 287–288
Davis, Katherine 338
Davis, Marguerite 425
Davis, Owen 55

Davis, Rebecca Harding 75, 369
Davis, Richard Harding 75, 361, 369, 376
Davis Cup 526–527, 555–556
Dawn O'Hara (Ferber) 25
Dawson, Joe 525, 535, 565
Day, Clinton 190
Day, Frank Miles 190
Day, William R. 269
Daylight Saving Time 202
A Day's Pleasure 35
Dayton Daily News 374
Dayton-Wright Airplane Company 113
Dean, George S. 190
Death Comes for the Archbishop (Cather) 66
"The Death of Rodriguez" (Davis) 369
"The Death of the Hired Man" (Frost) 67
De Booy, Theodoor 520
Debs, Eugene V. 37, 97, 193, 203, 215, 235, 237, 260, 270, 310
Declaration of London 196
Decoration Day 437
Deeds, Edward A. 114
De Forest, Lee 346, 362, 489, 505
Dehnert, Henry "Dutch" 542
DeKoven, Reginald 54
Delafield, Francis 427
Deland, Margaret 25, 31
Delano, Jane Arminda 396, 427
Delano, Ward P. 190
Delco 114–115
De Leon, Daniel 122, 249
The Delight Makers (Bandelier) 520
Dell, Floyd 56, 60, 344, 363
Delour, Pamela 44
DeMar, Clarence 524
Demby, Edward T. 437
DeMille, Cecil B. 28, 30–32, 34–35, 44, 49–51, 301
DeMille, William 69
Democracy and Education (Dewey) 132, 154, 156
Democratic National Convention, 1912 194, 236
Democratic National Convention, 1916 239
Democratic Party 67, 71, 90, 96, 99–100, 107–108, 117, 192, 194, 197, 204–207, 219–220, 225–227, 230–232, 235–242, 245, 247, 249, 265, 274, 287–288, 291, 323, 335, 374, 433, 473
"That Demon Rag" 26

Dempsey, William Harrison "Jack" 530, 533, 545, 552
Dempster, Carol 35, 49, 68
Demuth, Charles 41–42, 60, 75
Denishawn 43–44
Denishawn School of Dancing, Los Angeles 30, 39
DePalma, Ralph 535–536, 566
DePauw University 153
Depression of 1873 71
Depression of the 1890s 290, 474
Depression of the 1930s. *See* Great Depression.
Dere Mable (Streeter) 34
Des Imagistes 47
Desegregation 60
Desmond, Norma 70
De Sylva, B. G. 36
Detroit Evening News 368
Detroit Free Press 368
Detroit Public Library 187
Detroit Tigers 537–538, 560
Deutscher Werkbund 165–166, 178
Devanter, Willis Van 252
Devine, Edward T. 333
DeVinne, Theodore Lowe 376
Devore, Josh 540
Dewey, Evelyn 154
Dewey, Adm. George 358
Dewey, John 126, 128–129, 131–132, 134, 139, 141, 149, 154–156, 360, 417, 476
De Wolfe, Elsie 185–186, 189
Dewson, Molly 338
De Zayas, Marius 42
Diaghilev, Sergey 32, 43
Dial 507
Díaz, Aldolfo 92
Díaz, Porfirio 193, 209–210
Dickinson, Emily 28
Dictionary of the Bible 480
Diggs, Maury I. 294
Dillon, Jack 529
Dillon, Will 25
"The Dingbat Family" (Herriman) 345, 371
Dipley, Walter 543
Director's Liability Act of 1910 550
Directors Guild of America 68
Discourses and Sermons (Pope Pius X) 466
Distinguished Service Cross 396
Distinguished Service Medal 438, 477–478
Divine, Father. *See* Baker, George.
Dix, Dorothea 386

Dix, John A. 220
Dixon, Amzi 432, 444–445, 464
Dixon, Samuel G. 427, 520
Dixon, Thomas Jr. 67–68
Dobie, Gilmour 547
Dochez, Alphonse 424
Dochez, Raymond 424
Dr. Lafleur's Theory 24
Dodd, Mrs. John B. 300
Dodge, Edwin 328
Dodge, Grace Hoadley 340
Dodge, Henry 338
Dodge, Horace 177
Dodge, John 177, 338
Dodge, Josephine Marshall Jewell 338
Dodge, Mabel 60–61, 327–328
Dodge Motor Cars 491, 500
"The Dogin' Rag" 27
A Dog's Life 34
Dole, Charles 452
Dole, Larry 540
Dollar Diplomacy 81, 92, 208
Dollar Savings Bank, Pittsburgh 189
Dolliver, Jonathan P. 232, 297
Dolphin 195
A Dome of Many-Coloured Glass (Lowell) 26
Donaldson, Walter 34, 36
Donau (racehorse) 524, 565
Donerail (racehorse) 526, 565
Donovan, Michael Joseph 567
Donovan, Walter 29
"Don't Blame It All on Broadway" 27
Don't Change Your Husband 35, 44
D'Ooge, Martin Luther 161
Doolittle, Hilda (H.D.) 31, 47, 345
Dorais, Gus 546
Dorr, John Pixley 370
Dorr, Julian 370
Dorr, Rheta Childe 344, 369–370
Dos Passos, John 32, 46, 350
Dostoyevsky, Fyodor 361
Doubleday, Frank 376
Doubleday, Page, and Company 376
Dough and Dynamite 28
Douglas, George 362
Douglass, Frederick 463
Dove, Arthur 42
"Down Among the Sheltering Palms" 30
"Down by the Old Mill Stream" 24
Dramatists Guild 26, 38, 63
Draper, Andrew 159

Draper Gold Medal 517
The Dream Girl 31
"Dream On, Little Soldier Boy" 34
The Dreamy Kid (O'Neill) 36
Dreier, Mary 120, 243
Dreiser, Theodore 25–26, 28, 30, 34, 37, 39, 45, 60, 363
Dress 362
Dress and Vanity Fair 345
Dresser, Marie 302
Dressler, Marie 28, 48, 51
Drew, Howard P. 556
Drew, John 67
Drew, Timothy 433, 442
Drexel Building, New York City 190
Drexel Institute, Philadelphia 113
Drift and Mastery (Lippmann) 248, 360
Drinkwater, Charlotte 161
Drive for French War Babies 338
Drug abuse 255, 284, 402
Drummond, William 174
Dryden, John F. 122
Dual Alliance (World War I) 211
Dubofsky, Melvyn 100
Du Bois, W. E. B. 40, 146, 159, 223, 252, 300, 330, 337, 344, 374, 472–473
DuBose, William Porcher 479
Duchamp, Marcel 33, 42–43, 61
Duckering, F. W. 424
Dudley, William L. 520
Duffey, James 527
Duhring, Louis Adolphus 427
Du Maurier, Daphne 344
Dunbar, Paul Laurence 27
Duncan, Elizabeth 328
Duncan, Isadora 29, 33, 39, 43, 60, 74, 328
Duncan, James 558
Duncan, James A. 102
Duncan, Robert K. 521
Dunn, Johnny 36
Dunne, Finley Peter 24, 35
Du Pont, Pierre 114–115
Du Pont Company 87, 89, 111, 114–115, 292
Durack, Sarah 553
Durant, William C. "Billy" 114–115, 338
Durant Motors 115
Durante, Jimmy 59
Durham, Caleb W. 521
Durham, William 479
Durham System 521
Durstine, Roy 347

Duryea, Hiram 122
Duse, Eleanora 328
Dwight, James 567
Dying Swan (Pavlova) 43
"Dynamite Rag" 24

E

The Eagle's Mate 28
Eakins, Thomas 76
Earl, Mary 34
Earth Triumphant (Aiken) 28
Eastern League (basketball) 541
Eastman, Crystal 213, 347, 374
Eastman, George 424
Eastman, Max 56, 60, 328, 344, 347, 352, 374
Eastman Kodak Company 38, 48, 87, 89, 264
Eaton, Edith. *See* Sui Sin Far.
Ebert Prize 426
Eclectic Gothic architecture 185
Ecole des Beaux-Arts, Paris 168–171, 175, 184, 190
Econometrics Society 120
Economic Beginnings of the Far West (Coman) 121
An Economic Interpretation of the Constitution of the United States (Beard) 120, 153, 337
Economic Origins of Jeffersonian Democracy (Beard) 120, 153
Economides, Basile 282
Ecumenical Council of the Vatican (1870) 466
Eddington, A. S. 507
Eddy, Mary Baker 479
Edgewater People (Freeman) 34
Edison, Thomas Alva 48, 52, 493
Edison Pictures 44, 48, 67
Edison Records 52
Edsall, David Linn 424
"Education for Special Classes of Children" (Commission on Education) 127
The Education of Henry Adams (Adams) 75, 161
"Education of the Japanese" (NEA) 127
"Education of the Negro" (NEA) 127
The Education of the Negro Prior to 1861 (Woodson) 158
Edward, Prince of Wales (later Edward VII of Great Britain) 180, 356
Efficiency in the Household 322

Federal Council of Churches of Christ in America 434, 436, 439–440, 451–454, 478
— Commission on Peace and Arbitration 439, 451
— Committee on Industrial Conditions 456
— General Committee on Army and Navy Chaplains 454
— General War-Time Commission 436–438, 453–456, 478
— Joint Committee on War Production Communities 456
— Social Creed of the Churches 456
Federal Highway Act of 1916 199
Federal League 526–527, 532, 537–539, 561
Federal Reserve Act of 1913 81, 90–91, 195, 205, 225–226, 249, 255, 296
Federal Reserve Banks 81, 195, 226
Federal Reserve Board (FRB) 81, 90–91, 195, 226, 255
Federal Reserve System 81, 86, 90–91, 107, 262, 287, 291
Federal Theater Project 56
Federal Trade Commission (FTC) 85, 89, 98–99, 122, 226, 255, 262, 266, 287
Federal Trade Commission Act of 1914 82, 98, 196, 287
Federated Colored Catholics 436
Federation of American Zionists (FAZ) 434, 437, 459–460, 477–478
— Provisional Executive Committee for General Zionist Affairs 434, 459
Federation of State Medical Boards 380
"Felicity Rag" 25
Fellow-servant rule 275–277
Fellowship of Reconciliation 452–453
Fels, Joseph 122
Feminism 122, 133, 153, 324, 553
Fenway Park, Boston 525
Ferber, Edna 25, 32, 55, 74
Ferguson, Frank 185
Ferguson, W. S. 136
Fernald, Dr. Walter 273
Ferris, William H. 330
Fessenden, Reginald A. 505
A Feud in the Kentucky Hills 26
Fiddler on the Roof 56

Fidelity Manufacturing Company 268
Field, Stephen D. 521
Fields, Arthur 29
Fields, W. C. 28, 48, 57, 59, 63, 73–74
Fifth International Prophetic Conference (1914) 465
Fifty Years and Other Poems (Johnson) 33
Filene's department store 89
Fillmore, Millard 313
Final Report (Pershing) 246
The Financier (Dreiser) 26, 45
Fincke, William 453
Finding the Trail of Life (Jones) 467
The Finer Grain (James) 24
The Finished Mystery (Russell) 437, 455, 478
Finney, John Miller Turpin 424
Fire and Wine (Fletcher) 27
The Fire Chief's Daughter 24
First National Pictures 70
First Presbyterian Church, Coldwater, Mich. 243
First Presbyterian Church, New York City 477
Fish, Mrs. Stuyvesant 367
Fisher, Carl G. 501, 534
Fisher, Dorothy Canfield 26, 30, 46
Fisher, Fred 24, 27, 30, 32, 36
Fisher, H. C. "Bud" 345, 371
Fisher, Irving 120
Fisher, John 518
The Fisher-Maid 25
Fiske, Minnie Maddern 27, 49, 55–56, 61
Fitzgerald, F. Scott 350, 363
Fitzpatrick, John 102
Fitzsimmons, Robert 567
Five Men and Pompey (Benét) 30
Five-dollar day 87, 89, 93–95, 119
"Fizz Water (A Rag)" 29
Flagg, Ernest 170
Flagler, Henry M. 122
Flagons and Apples (Jeffers) 26
Fletcher, Art 540
Fletcher, John Gould 27, 30–31, 34, 47
Flexner, Abraham 159, 386, 403–404, 422, 424
Flexner, Simon 422, 424
Flexner Report 380, 386, 392, 403, 405, 424
The Floorwalker 31
Flower, Benjamin O. 122
Flynn, Elizabeth Gurley 120, 332

Foch, Ferdinand 216
Folies-Bergère, Paris 73, 319
Folks, Homer 333
Follis, Charles 567
Fonck, Rene 494
A Fool There Was 30
Foote, Irene. *See* Castle, Irene.
"For Me and My Gal" 33
For the Right (Rauschenbusch) 474
Foraker, Joseph Benson 249
Foran, Martin A. 241
Forbes, Bertie Charles 347
Forbes 347
Ford, Guy Stanton 159
Ford, Henry 89, 93–95, 119–120, 165, 169, 177, 198, 260, 301–302, 311–313, 348, 489–490, 498–500, 518
Ford, Webster. *See* Masters, Edgar Lee.
The Ford (Austin) 32
Ford Motor Company 82, 85, 87, 93–95, 114, 168–169, 177, 302, 313, 338, 495, 498, 500, 513
— Employees's Savings and Loan Association 94
— Highland Park plant, Mich. 89, 93–95, 104, 164, 172, 301, 498
— River Rouge plant, Detroit 166, 172
— Sociological Department 94–95, 302
Ford's Theater, Washington, D.C. 71
Forester, Frank 558
The Forester's Daughter (Garland) 28
Fort McHenry, Baltimore 466
Fortune 185
Forty-Five Minutes from Broadway (Cohan) 26, 58
La forza del destino (Verdi) 74
Fosbury, Richard 557
Fosdick, Harry Emerson 450, 477
Fosdick, Raymond B. 354
Foster, George Burnham 479
Foster, Herbert 159
Foster, Stephen 54
Foster, William 100, 102, 159
Fountain (Duchamp) 33, 42–43
Four Doctors (Sargent) 423
The Four Horsemen of the Apocalypse 51
Four Minute Men 313–314
Fourteen Points 202–203, 207, 217–218, 242, 247
Fourth Symphony (Ives) 54

Fowler, John W. 567
Fownes, W. C. Jr. 565
Fox, George 468
Fox, William 58
Fox Studio News 48
Fox tribe 339, 553, 563
Fox-trot 44
The Fra 187, 376
Francis Ferdinand, Archduke of Serbia 211, 242
Francis Ouimet Caddy Scholarship Fund 562
Frank, Leo M. 256, 295, 329–330, 433, 435, 442
Frank, Waldo 41, 375
Frank Leslie's Illustrated Weekly 376
Frankel, Charles 475
Frankel, Lee K. 333
Frankfurter, Felix 269, 360
Franklin and Marshall College 520
Franklin Park, Boston 561
Franklin Winslow Kane (Sedgwick) 24
Frederick, Christine 322
Free and Other Stories (Dreiser) 34
Free Negro Owners of Slaves in the U.S. (Woodson) 158
Freedman, Andrew 567
Freedom and Culture (Dewey) 155
Freeman, Legh Richmond 376
Freeman, Mary E. Wilkins 34
Freer, Charles Lang 122
Freer Gallery, Washington, D.C. 122
Fremstad, Olive 54
French, Daniel Chester 184
French Army 215, 224
Freud, Sigmund 37, 386, 417, 508–509
Frick, Henry Clay 122, 186, 189
Frick Collection 189
Friedman, Leo 24
Friedman, Max 543
The Friend 468
Friends Boarding School, Union Springs, N.Y. 467
The Friends Intelligencer 468
Friends Reconstruction Unit 452
Friends Review 468
Friends School, Providence, Rhode Island 467
Friends Service Committee 468
Frigidaire 115
Friml, Rudolph 58
Frohman, Charles 63, 76
Frohman, Daniel 55, 63
From the Manger to the Cross 25

Frost, James Marion 479
Frost, Robert 27–28, 31, 37, 47, 66–67, 476
Fruehauf, August 491
"Fulfilled Prophecy, A Potent Argument for the Bible" (Gaebelein) 465
Fuller, Meta Warrick 40
Fullerton, Hugh 541, 560
Fultz, David 537
Fundamentalism 270, 432, 440–441, 443–446, 459, 464–465
The Fundamentals 432, 441, 444–445, 464–465
Funeral March (Chopin) 74
Funk, Casimir 489
Funny Girl 58
Furber, Douglas 33
Furey, Jim 542
Furey, Tom 542
A Further Range (Frost) 67
Future of Electricity (Steinmetz) 488, 519
The Future of the American Jew (Kaplan) 470
Futurism 40–41

G

Gaebelein, Arno C. 444–445, 464–465
Gaidzik, George 564
Gaines, Wesley John 479
Gale, Zona 25, 34
Galileo 420
Gallaudet, Edward Miner 340
Gallaudet College. *See* National Deaf-Mute College, Washington, D.C.
Galsworthy, John 55
Galt, Francis L. 427
Galton, Francis 271
A Game of Golf (Ouimet) 562
Gans, Joe 567
Garden, Mary 32, 54
Garden City Golf Club, N.Y. 550
Gardner, Jimmy 543
Gardner, Robert A. 525, 566
Garfield, James 428
Garland, Hamlin 24–25, 28, 31, 45
Garland, Judy 73
Garrison, Lindley M. 198, 241
Garrison, William Lloyd 373
Garvey, Marcus 303, 330–331, 437, 442
Gary, Elbert H. 102
Gassed (Sargeant) 61

Gathercoal, E. N. 426
Gauguin, Paul 42
Gaynor, William J. 249
Gazette du Bon Ton 178
Geiger, Hans 518
Geiger counter 518
General Conference Mennonite Church 480
General Education Board (GEB) 145
General Electric (GE) 87, 89, 148, 348, 409, 424, 493, 514
General Motors (GM) 114–115, 177, 313, 338
General Motors Acceptance Corporation (GMAC) 115
General William Booth Enters into Heaven (Ives) 54
"General William Booth Enters into Heaven" (Lindsay) 39, 47
General William Booth Enters into Heaven and Other Poems (Lindsay) 27
Genetic Studies of Genius (Terman) 420
The "Genius" (Dreiser) 30, 39, 45
"Gentlemen's Agreement" of 1907 193
George, Ann 140
George, Henry 122, 286, 475
George, Walter 557
George J. Helmer Infirmary of Osteopathy 428
George Smith (racehorse) 528, 564, 566
George Washington (Lodge) 245
Georgetown University 367, 480
Georgia Jazz Band 52
Georgia State Penitentiary 253
Georgia Tech University 529, 547, 564, 566
Gerber, Alexander 36
German Americans 35, 62, 197, 231, 256, 306, 310, 321, 349, 351–352, 358, 440, 452, 473, 475, 479, 554
German Army 352, 357, 369, 455
German Atrocities (Hillis) 450
German Methodist Episcopal Church 464
"German War Practices" 355
"The German Whisper" 355
Geronimo 245
Gershwin, George 36, 38, 52, 57, 69, 73
Get Rich Quick (Cohan) 37
The Ghost of Rosy Taylor 34

Gruelle, Marcella 338
Gruening, Emil 427
A Guest of Honor (Joplin) 52–53
Guest, Edgar A. 31, 33
Guidelines on the Schools in Wartime 130
Guillén, Jorge 477
Guinn and Beale v. *United States* 223
Guiteau, Charles J. 428
Gulf Stream (Winslow) 76
USS *Gulflight* 197
Gulick, Luther Halsey 300, 567
Gullible's Travels (Lardner) 32
"Gum Shoe Fox Trot" 33
Gumberg, Alexander 371
The Gun Fighter 32
Gustav V of Sweden 563
Gutenberg, Beno 510
Guthe, Dr. Karl E. 161, 521
Guttmann, Allen 553
Gwyn-Jeffreys, Henry 490

H

H. D. *See* Doolittle, Hilda.
H. J. Heinz Company 89
Hackett, Francis 360
Hackett, James K. 27, 55–56, 61
Hadassah 339, 433, 460–461, 478
Hadley, Henry Kimball 54
Hagen, Walter 527, 531–532, 549–550, 566
"Hail, Hail, The Gang's All Here" 33
Haitian National Assembly 93
Hale, George Ellery 492, 495
Hale, William Bayard 358
Haley, Jack 59
Hall, Charles M. 521
Hall, G. Stanley 323, 419, 508
Halley's Comet 488
Halsted, William Stewart 407, 423
Halton, Frank 500
Hamilton, Alan McLane 428
Hammer v. *Dagenhart* 230, 259, 278, 287
Hammerstein, Oscar II 73
Hammond, Harriet D. 526
Hammond, James B. 122, 521
Hampton, Rob 27
Hampton Institute 146–147, 157, 160, 511
Hampton's Magazine 370
Hanaford, Phoebe 463
Hand, Learned 360
Handwerker, Ida 338

Handwerker, Nathan 338
Handy, W. C. 27, 29–30, 32, 34, 52, 68–69
Hanley, James F. 33
Hanly, J. Frank 199, 240
Hanson, Ole 102
Hanson, William F. 54
Hapgood, Hutchins 56, 60, 328
The Harbor (Poole) 30
Hard, William 370
Harding, Warren G. 203, 221, 238, 242, 245
Harlan, John Marshall 249, 297
Harlem Renaissance 38, 40, 69, 336, 374
"Harlem Strut" 33
Harlow, Robert "Bob" 549
Harper, Frances Ellen Watkins 76
Harper, James 122
Harper, John W. 122
Harper's Bazar 178, 189
Harper's Magazine 461
Harper's Monthly 71, 376
Harper's Weekly 286
Harriman, Mary Williamson 273
Harriman, W. Averell 113
Harris, Isaac 295
Harris, Joel Chandler 24, 34
Harrison, Benjamin 244, 297
Harrison, Hubert 336
Harrison Narcotic Act of 1914 284, 382–383
Harron, Robert 28, 49
Harroun, Ray 300, 524, 534, 536, 565
Hart, Lorenz 74
Hart, Lucy 428
Hart, William S. 28, 30–32, 49–50
Hartford Railroad 254
Hartley, Marsden 42, 60–61, 75
Harvard Lampoon 371, 476
Harvard Lampoon Castle, Cambridge, Mass. 190
Harvard Monthly 371, 476
Harvard University 47, 66, 126–127, 135–136, 138, 140–141, 145, 158–161, 245, 271, 289, 362, 371, 373, 375, 404, 468, 478, 481, 515, 525, 527, 546, 563, 565
— Harvard College 137, 244, 476
— Hasty Pudding theatricals 371
— Law School 244, 285, 289, 296, 360
— Medical School 133, 151, 383, 398, 405, 427
— Observatory 495, 515–516, 521

— Psychology Department 127
— Radcliffe College 152, 156, 159–160, 514
— School of Public Health 398
— Students' Army Training Corps 160
— Wolcott Gibbs Laboratory 515
The Harvester (Stratton-Porter) 25
Haskell Institute for Indians, Lawrence, Kans. 563
Hassam, Childe 42
Hastings, Thomas 164, 189
Hauge's Synod 435
Haughton, Percy 546
"Have a Heart" 32
Haverford College 467, 515
— Philosophy Department 468
Havez, Jean C. 27
Havre de Grace Racetrack, Baltimore 551
Hawaweeny, Raphael 480
Hay, John 33
Hay–Bunau-Varilla Treaty of 1903 502
Hay-Herrán Treaty of 1903 502
Hay-Pauncefote Treaty of 1901 254
Hayden, Scott 25, 27, 52, 76
Hayes, Alfred 332
Hayes, James P. 448
Hays, Gen. Will H. 49
Hays Office 49
Haywood, William "Big Bill" 60, 97, 120, 229, 259, 295, 310, 332
Head Start 157
Headwaiters and Sidewaiters Society 336
The Healer (Herrick) 25
Healy, Eliza 480
Healy, Patrick Francis 480
Heap, Jane 45
A Heap o' Livin' (Guest) 31
Hearst, William Randolph 65, 73–74, 167, 175, 329, 345–346
Hearst magazines 344
Hearst newspaper chain 350, 358–359, 369, 371, 376
Hearst-Selig Pictures 48
Heart o' the Hills 35
The Heart of Nora Flynn 31
Hearts Adrift 28, 70
Hearts of the World 34, 51, 68
Heaton, John 368
"Heaven Will Protect the Working Girl" 24
Hegeman, John Rogers 122
Heifetz, Jascha 34

Heindel, Max 480

Heins and La Farge (architectural firm) 185

Heisman, John W. 547, 564

Heisman Trophy 564

Held, Anna 73, 76

Held, Will 32

Helen of Troy (Teasdale) 25

Hellman, Lillian 56

Hello Broadway (Cohan) 58

"Hello, Central, Give Me 603" 25

Hell's Gate Railroad Bridge, New York City 166

Hell's Hinges 30, 50

Helmer, George Jacob 428

Hemingway, Ernest 46, 350, 352

Hench, Dr. Philip S. 415

Henderson, Charles Richmond 340

Henley Royal Regatta 527

Henri, Robert 37, 40, 71–72

Henry Phipps Psychiatric Clinic 417

Henry Street Settlement House, New York City 56, 334

Henry Street Visiting Nurse Service 421

Henry, O. (William Sydney Porter) 24–25, 27, 35, 76

Herbert, Fred 524

Herbert, Victor 24, 32, 36, 58, 63, 73, 346

Hermit (racehorse) 562

Heroin 255

Herrick, James Bryan 381, 408, 424

Herrick, Robert 24–25, 27–28

Herriman, George 345, 370–371

Herrmann, August Garry 536

Herron, S. D. 566

Hertz, Heinrich R. 505

Hertzsprung, Ejnar 490, 515–517

Hertzsprung-Russell Diagram 490, 516

Herzer, Wallie 26

Herzl, Theodor 464

Herzog, Charles 540

"The Hesitating Blues" 30, 69

Hess, Cliff 32, 34

Hess, Harry Hammond 510

Hess, Victor 498

Heubsch, B. W. 360

Hibernian Savings and Loan Association Building, San Francisco 190

Hickman, Art 36

Hickman, Howard 50

Hicks, Joseph L. 428

Higbee, Lenah S. 396

High Jinks (Friml) 58

Higham, John 243

"Hilarity Rag" 24

Hill, David B. 297

Hill, James J. 122

Hill, Joe 257, 331–332

Hill, John A. 122

Hill, Walter P. 159

Hill, William 488

Hillguit, Morris 434

Hillis, Newell Dwight 449–450

Hillquit, Morris 310, 336

Hillside School, Boston 161

Hilton, James 344

Hindenburg, Paul von 357–358

Hinkey, Frank 546

Hinks, Arthur R. 516

"Hinky-Dinky Parlez-vous" 34

Hippodrome, New York City 26, 44, 58, 62, 432

Hirsch, David 117

His Family (Poole) 32, 35, 75

His New Job 30

His Second Wife (Poole) 34

His Trust/His Trust Fulfilled 24

Hispanic Americans 102

Hiss, Philip Hanson Jr. 428

The Historical Outlook 130

A History of Genetics (Sturtevant) 518

History of Quakerism (Jones) 468

History of the American People (Wilson) 228

The History of the Negro Church (Woodson) 158

History Teacher's Magazine 130

"Hitchy Koo" 26

Hitler, Adolf 167, 357

Hoffman, Josef 166, 178

Hogan, James Joseph 567

Hogg, James S. 242

Hoke, Effie 282

Hoke v. *United States* 255, 282

Holiness Church of the Nazarene 479

Holladay, Paula 60

Holland, Edmund Milton 76

Holland, John P. 521

Hollerith, Herman 518

Holliday, James Wear 567

Holman, Nat 542–543

Holmes, John Haynes 434, 442, 451–453, 478

Holmes, Dr. Joseph Austin 80, 252

Holmes, Oliver Wendell Jr. 63, 220, 263, 269–271, 287–290, 352

Holocaust 465

Holt, Henry 67

Holy Koran (Drew) 442

Homans, J. 424

"Home Burial" (Frost) 67

Home economics 148–151, 159

Home Fires in France (Fisher) 46

Home Front Memo (Sandburg) 71

Home Missions Council 456

Home Monthly 65

Home, Sweet Home 28

Home Trade League of America 317

Homer, Louise 54

Homer, Winslow 40, 76

"Homesickness Blues" 32

Homestead strike of 1892 286

Honey and Salt (Sandburg) 71

Honorbilt Modern Homes 175

Hooker, John Daggett 495

Hooker Telescope 492

Hookworm 382, 398

Hoover, Herbert 83, 248, 293, 304, 468

Hopalong Cassidy (Mulford) 24

Hope, Eugenia Burns 338

Hope Diamond 338

Hope of Israel 464–465

Hoppe, Willie 564

Hopper, Edward 42, 72

Horine, George 525, 557

The Horrors of War 28, 51

Hortense Ward Act of 1913 121

Hoschna, Karl 76

"Hot House Rag" 29

Hotchkiss, Hazel V. 524, 531, 555, 565–566

Hotel Commodore, New York City 167

Hotel Marseilles, New York City 434

Hotel Pennsylvania, New York City 167

Hough, Henry Battle 375

Houghton Mifflin 361

USS *Housatonic* 200

House, Edward Mandell 198, 242–244, 247

House and Garden 367

The House in Good Taste (de Wolfe) 186

House of Morgan 93

The House of Orchids (Sterling) 25

House-Grey Memorandum of 1916 198

"The Housekeeper" (Frost) 67

Houston, David F. 120

How the Other Half Lives (Riis) 377

Jones, John Paul 532, 557
Jones, Lowell 468
Jones, Mary Hoxie 467–468
Jones, Robert Edmond 28, 56, 60
Jones, Rufus Matthew 436, 467–468
Jones, Sarah Hawkshurst Coutant 468
Jones, Sybil 467
Jones Act of 1917 200, 258
Joplin, Scott 24, 26, 33, 52–54, 76
Jordan, Eben 122
Jordan, Joe 24
Jordan, Marsh and Company 122
Joss, Adrian 567
Journal of Educational Psychology 126
Journal of Industrial Hygiene 383
Journal of Negro History 158
Journal of Pharmaceutical Sciences 426
Journal of the American Medical Association 381, 391, 402, 425
Journal of Urology 407
Joy, Charles 453
Joyce, James 35, 45, 47, 346
Judaism 38, 56, 106, 193, 206, 227, 315, 329, 432–435, 437, 440–442, 451, 456–457, 459–460, 464–465, 469–470, 477–478, 480
Judaism as a Civilization (Kaplan) 469–470
Judge, Jack 26
Judge 362
Judith of Bethulia 28, 68
Judson, Adoniram Brown 428
Judson, Edward 480
Jung, Carl 386
"The Junior College" (NEA) 127
"The Junior High School" (Commission on Education) 127
"Junk Man Rag" 27
Jurgen (Cabell) 35
Just Folks (Guest) 33
Just Nuts 32
Justice (Galworthy) 55, 347

K

Kahanamoku, Duke 525, 553
Kahn, Albert 164, 166, 168, 171–172
Kahn, Gus 30, 32–34, 36, 52
The Kaiser, Beast of Berlin 51, 355
"The Kaiser's Got the Blues" 34
Kalamazoo Daily Telegraph 333
Kalem Pictures 48

Kalich, Bertha 56
Kallikak family 386
Kansas City Police 279
Kansas City Star 310, 374, 376
Kansas State University 161
Kaplan, Rabbi Israel 469
Kaplan, Mordecai M. 433, 441, 460, 469–470
Kathleen Mavourneen 35
"Katzenjammer Kids" 345
Kay Bee Studio 31, 48
Kayhew, Mary Morton Kimball 340
Keane, John Joseph 480
Keating, Edward 268
Keating-Owen Act of 1916 199, 230, 258–259, 268–269
Keaton, Buster 34, 51, 59, 61
Kedrovsky, Father John 477
Keeler, Ruby 73
Keenan, Frank 50
Kehilath Jeshurun, New York City 469
Kehilla 469
Keith, Benjamin Franklin 63, 76
Keith's Theater, New York City 58
Keith-Albee Theatrical Production Company 58
Keller, Helen 301, 332
Kelley, Florence 333, 338, 422, 451
Kellogg, Arthur 333–334
Kellogg, Howard 445
Kellogg, Mary 333
Kellogg, Paul 333–334, 442
Kellor, Frances 243, 316
Kellor, Mary Sprau 243
Kelly, Billy 552
Kelly, Eddie 543
Kelly, Howard A. 409, 423
Kelly, J. P. 424
Kelmscott Press 187
Kemp, Thomas J. 295
Kempster, Walter 428
Kendall, Edward C. 415, 425
Kendrick, Jim 543
Kennedy, John F. 66
Kennedy, Paul 228
Kennedy, William K. 529
Kentucky Derby 524–528, 530, 550–552, 562–566
Kenyon, William 321
Keokuk Dam 81
Keppard, Freddie 53
Kerensky, Aleksandr 220
Kern, Jerome 29–30, 32–33, 52, 54, 57–58, 73

Kern-McGillicuddy Act of 1916 229
Kessler, David 56
Keswick Movement 480
Ketchel, Stanley 543
Kettering, Charles Franklin 80, 177, 488, 499
Key, Ellen 323
Keystone Comedies 27, 29, 50–51, 59
Keystone Studio 31, 48, 50–51
Kid, Dixie 543
Kid Auto Races at Venice, California 28
Kid Boots (Ziegfeld) 73
Kilbane, Johnny 525
Kilmer, Joyce 28, 61, 76
Kilpatrick, William Heard 139, 154, 159
King, Billie Jean 556
King, Martin Luther Jr. 339
King, Robert A. 34
King, Samuel A. 521
King Coal (Sinclair) 32
King Features Syndicate 345
King of Kings 50
"Kismet Rag" 27
Kitchenaid Company 120
Kiviat, Abel 557
"K-K-K-Katy" 34
Klaus, Frank 526
Klaw, Mark 63
Knapp, Willie 530
A Knight of the Road 25
Knight, Edgar 145
Knights of Columbus 434–435, 455–456
— Supreme Board of Directors 436, 455
— Commission on Religious Prejudices 435
Knights of Labor 118, 466
Knights of Mary Phagan 435
Knights of Pythias Band 69
Knopf, Alfred A. 74, 360
Knox, George William 480
Knox, Philander C. 92, 208
Koch, Robert 396, 420, 422
Kohlsatt, H. H. 534
Kohn, Julius A. 112
Kolehmainen, Johannes 553
Kolster, Frederick 518
Koren, Ulrik Vilhelm 480
Koster Theater, New York City 58
Kraenzlein, Alvin C. 554
"Krazy Kat" (Herriman) 345, 370–371

Maledon, George 298

Mallinson, Dr. W. L. 502

Mallon, Mary 296

Mallory, Molla. *See* Bjurstedt, Molla.

"Mama and Papa Blues" 32

The Man Against the Sky (Robinson) 31

The Man from Home 28

Man O'War (racehorse) 552

"The Man Who Owns Broadway" 58

"Mandy" 36

Manet, Edouard 42

Manhattan Bridge 121

Mann, Alonzo 295

Mann, Dr. Gustave 160

Mann, Horace 132, 462

Mann, James R. 192, 248, 252

Mann, Col. William D'Alton 363

Mann Act. *See* White Slave Traffic Act of 1910.

Mann-Elkins Act of 1910 80, 122, 192, 207, 227, 248, 252, 274, 292

Manning, Cardinal Henry 466

Mannock, Edward 494

"Maple Leaf Rag" 53, 76

Marching Men (Anderson) 32

Marconi, Guglielmo 366, 372, 505

Marconi Wireless Company 361–362, 365–366

Mare Island Marines 530

Maria Rosa 31

Marin, John 38, 40, 42

Marine, David 425

Marks, Jack 546

Marlowe, Julia 67

The Marne (Wharton) 34, 46

Marquand, John P. 344

Marquard, Rube 525, 540

Marquis, Don 374

Marsh, Mae 28, 30–31, 49, 68

Marshall, Gen. George 246

Marshall, Henry I. 26

Marshall, Thomas R. 194, 199, 273, 302

Marshall Field department store 104

Martin, Dr. Franklin 393

Martin, Louis 44

Martyn, Henry 298

Marvin, Pauline 50

Marx, Groucho 367

Marx, Harpo 367

Marx, Karl 117

Marx Brothers 59

Marxism 460

Mary Turner (Fuller) 40

Mason, Lowell 54

Mason, Max 513

USS *Massachusetts* 121

Massachusetts General Hospital 337, 424

Massachusetts House of Representatives 245

Massachusetts Institute of Technology (MIT) 89, 127, 133, 159–160, 166, 169, 171, 186, 398

— School of Architecture 190

Massachusetts Medical Society 273

Massachusetts National Guard 260

Massachusetts State Amateur Golf Championship 562

Massachusetts State Bar Association 289

Massachusetts State Legislature 296, 338

Massachusetts Supreme Court 289

Massachusetts Woman Suffrage Association 463

The Masses 37, 72, 328, 344, 352, 371, 374–375

Masters, Edgar Lee 30–31, 34–35, 45, 47, 74

Mathews, Shailer 436, 451, 458, 464, 478

Mathewson, Christy 526, 540

Matisse, Henri 26, 39, 42, 47

Matthew, Wentworth Arthur 437

Matthews, Artie 26, 30

Matthews, W. Somerset 344, 363

Maurer, Alfred 61

Maxim, Hiram S. 512, 521

Maxime's, Paris 319

Maxson, Dr. Henry Martin 155–156

Maxwell, James Clerk 505

Maxwell, Vera 44

Maxwell Car Company 312

Maybeck, Bernard 166, 175

Mayo, Dr. Charles Horace 389, 407, 413, 415–417

Mayo, Adm. Henry T. 195

Mayo, Dr. William James 389, 407, 415–416

Mayo, Dr. William Worrall 415

Mayo Clinic 382, 389, 407, 415–416

— Laboratory Division 415

Mayo family 382, 389–390

Mayo Foundation for Medical Education and Research 382, 389, 415

Maytime (Romberg) 58

McAdoo, William Gibbs 83, 91, 109, 172, 213

McCabe, John 527, 565

McCarron, Charles 32

McCarthy, Joseph 27, 34, 36

McClelland, John 563

McClement, John H. 114

McClure, S. S. 65

McClure's 65, 350

McCollum, Elmer Verner 425

McCormick, Joseph Medill 313

McCormick, Robert H. 521

McCormick, Robert R. 344, 348, 356, 374

McCoy, Al 527

McCoy, Bessie 76

McCoy, George Walter 425

McCrae, James 122

McCree, Junie 24

McCullough, John Griffin 122

McCutcheon, James 122

McDermott, John J. 524–525, 548, 565

McDonald, Henry 548

McDonald, Patrick J. 557

McGarvey, John William 480

McGee, W. J. 521

McGinnity, Joe 540

McGovern, Joseph Terrance 567

McGrath, Matthew 558

McGraw, John J. 540

McGraw-Hill Book Company 122

McInnis, John 539

McKay, Claude 337

McKean, Edward John 567

McKelway, Alexander J. 249, 340

McKim, Mead and White (architectural firm) 164, 167, 170, 172, 184, 186, 189

McKinley, William 48, 231, 241, 296, 376, 472

McLaughlin Motor Car Company 114

McLean, Edward 338

McLean, John R. 122, 376

McLean, Vinson 338

McLeod, Fred 550

McLoughlin, Maurice E. 525–526, 555–556, 565

McManigal, Ortie 90, 280

McMurry, Frank Morton 139

McNamara, James 80, 90, 229, 252, 280, 344, 356

McNamara, John J. 80, 90, 229, 252, 280, 344, 356

McPherson, Aimee Semple 437

McReynolds, James Clark 255

McSorley's Bar (Sloan) 40, 72
McTammany, John 521
The Meaning of Faith (Fosdick) 477
The Meaning of God in Modern Jewish Religion (Kaplan) 470
The Meaning of Prayer (Fosdick) 477
Meanwell, Walter 541
Measles 380, 385, 393, 421, 424
The Mechanical Factors of Digestion (Cannon) 424
The Mechanism of Mendelian Heredity (Morgan, Sturtevant, and Bridges) 418
Medal of Honor 217
Medical Education in the United States and Canada (Flexner). *See* Flexner Report. 404
Medill, Joseph 356
Meggido Mission Church 480
"Melancholy (My Melancholy Baby)" 26
Méliès 48
Mellanby, Edward 425
Meltzer, Samuel J. 424
A Memoir in the Form of a Novel (Santayana) 477
"Memories" 30
"Memphis Blues" 27, 69
Men, Women, and Ghosts (Lowell) 31
Mencken, H. L. 231, 313, 345, 350, 363, 369, 374
Mendel, Gregor 417, 501
Mendel, Lafayette Benedict 425
"Mending Wall" (Frost) 67
Mendl, Sir Charles 186
Mennonite Church of North America 436
Mennonites 452–453
Mennonitisher Friedensbote 480
Menorah Journal 469–470
Mental illness 235, 272–273, 315, 340, 386
The Merchant of Venice (Shakespeare) 33
Merchants and Manufacturers Association 280
Meredith, James "Ted" 553, 557
Meridian (racehorse) 524, 565
Merlin (Robinson) 33
Merril, Maud A. 420
Merrill, William H. 368
Messenger 336–337
Messiah College 481
Methodist Church 440, 443, 464

Methodist Episcopal Church 464–465, 481
— Missionary Society 465
Methodist General Conference 433
Methodist Protestant Church 480
MetLife Building, New York City. *See* Pan American Building, New York City.
Metro-Goldwyn-Mayer 73
Metropolitan 371
Metropolitan Amateur Golf Championship 549
Metropolitan Life Insurance 122, 385, 411
Metropolitan Life Insurance Building, New York City 171
Metropolitan Museum of Art, New York City 178, 189
Metropolitan Open 548
Metropolitan Opera, New York City 24–26, 28, 32–33, 35, 54, 62, 74, 367
Metropolitan Postgraduate School of Medicine, New York City 427
Mexican Army 210, 241
Mexican Constitution of 1917 211
Mexican Revolution 192, 291, 353, 369
Mexican-American War 212
Meyer, Adolf 417
Meyer, George 249
Meyer, George W. 25, 33
Meyer, Louis 444
Meyer, Max 180
Meyer, Stephen 94
Meyers, John 540
Miami Herald 344
Micheaux, Elder 438
Michelson, Albert 506
Michigan State College 502
Michigan State Hygiene Laboratory 397
Michigan State Normal School 368
Mickey 34
Mid-American Chants (Anderson) 34
Mid-Channel (Pinero) 55
Middlebury College 161
Midland 346
Midlothian Country Club, Chicago 549
Midnight Frolics (Ziegfeld) 44, 73
Midway Gardens, Chicago 165, 168, 171, 174
Mies van der Rohe, Ludwig 167
"Military Training in the Schools" (NEA) 127

Millay, Edna St. Vincent 33, 56, 60, 363
The Millennial Hope (Case) 458
Miller, Arthur 56
Miller, George Frazier 337
Miller, Joaquin 76
Miller, Kelly 473
The Miller of Old Church (Glasgow) 25
Millet, Francis D. 76
Millikan, Robert A. 489, 491, 497–498
Mills, Benjamin Fay 480
Mills, Darius Ogden 122
Mills' Hotels 122
Milton, John 374
Milwaukee Journal 374–375
Milwaukee Leader 270, 294, 344, 352
The Mind of Primitive Man (Boas) 489
Mindell, Fania 258, 303, 383, 419
Miner, Bill 253
Ministerial Association 300
"A Ministry of Reconciliation" (Fincke and Chaffee) 453
Minstrelsy 68–69, 73–75
Minter, Mary Miles 30, 34, 49
The Miracle Man 35
Miss Crittenden's English and French Boarding and Day School for Young Ladies and Little Girls 421
Miss Graham's Young Ladies' Boarding School 328
Miss 1917 65, 73
Mission Church of Simon of Cyrene, New York City 433, 442
Mission Style 176–177, 188
Missionary Review 480
Missouri National Guard 224
Missouri Plan 281
"Missouri Waltz" 29
Mr. Dooley Says (Dunne) 24
"Mr. Sky Pilot" 448
Mr. Smith Goes to Washington 51
Mistress Nell 30
Mitchel, John Purroy 122, 249, 478
Mitchell, John 118, 249
Mitchell, Lucy Sprague 156–157
Mitchell, Maggie 76
Mitchell, S. Weir 76
Mitchell, Wesley Clair 156
Mitropolsky, Stephen 480
Mix, Tom 24, 49–50
Modern dance 24, 30, 37, 43
Modern Dancing 64

National Americanization Committee 228, 243
National Arts Club, New York City 24, 72
National Association (baseball) 567
National Association for the Advancement of Colored People (NAACP) 30, 123, 146, 223–224, 252, 300, 308–309, 337, 344, 374–375, 473
National Association for the Study and Prevention of Infant Mortality 380, 399
National Association for the Study and Prevention of Tuberculosis 410
National Association of Directors of Research 128
National Association of Manufacturers 275
National Association of Professional Baseball Players 568
National Association of the Motion Picture Industry 305
National Association of Theatrical Producing Managers 63
National Association Opposed to Woman Suffrage 338
National Bank 107, 225
National Baptist Convention of America 435
National Baptist Convention U.S.A., Inc. 435
National Baptist Publishing Board 435
National Basketball League 542
National Birth Control League 419
National Board for Historical Service 135
National Board of Medical Examiners 383
National Canning Association 501
National Cash Register 89, 121, 148
National Catholic War Council 436, 438, 441–442, 454, 456, 465, 467
National Catholic Welfare Conference. See National Catholic War Council.
National Challenge Cup 529
National Child Labor Committee 87, 122, 249, 267
National City Bank 107, 123, 209, 225
National Civic Federation 118

National Collegiate Athletic Association 541
National Commission (baseball) 536–537
National Commission of Fine Arts 187
National Commission on Law Observance and Enforcement 293
National Committee on Mental Hygiene 386
National Committee on Public Morals 435
National Conference of Catholic Charities 432
National Conference of Social Work (1939) 334
National Congress on University Extensions 128
National Consumers' League 338
National Convention of Charities and Corrections 243
National Deaf-Mute College, Washington, D.C. 340
National Defense Act of 1916 199, 213, 257
National Defense Act of 1920 396
National Education Association (NEA) 127, 131, 133, 151, 159
— Committee on History and Education for Citizenship in Schools 131
— Department of Superintendents 160
National Education Day 128
National Emergency Committee on Nursing 396, 422
National Federation of Music Clubs 54
National Football League 548, 563
National Fraternal Council of Negro Churches 473
National History Review 135
National Institute of Arts and Letters 66, 72
National League (baseball) 532, 536, 538–541, 560, 564–568
National League for the Protection of Colored Women 243
National Medal of Science 518
National Men's Singles Championship 556
National Monetary Commission 296
National Negro Committee 223, 300
National Organization for Public Health Nursing 380, 421

National Packing Company 253
National Parks Service 257
National Pencil Factory 329
National Progressive Republican League 192–193, 207, 232, 248
National Prohibition Act of 1919. *See* Volstead Act of 1919.
National Safety Council 381
National Security League 159
National Service Committee 243
National Spiritualist Association 479
National Starch Company 122
National Superintendents' Association 155
National Tuberculosis Association 385, 411
National Urban League 223
National War Work Council 455
National Weekly 376
National Woman Suffrage Association 221, 369, 463
National Woman's Party 324, 335
National Women's Trade Union League 120
Nationalism 92, 134
Native American Church 480
Native Americans 54, 72, 298, 326, 553, 563
Nativism 62, 97, 102, 118, 129, 215, 227–228, 306, 316, 324, 326, 337, 339, 440, 467
Naughty Marietta (Herbert) 24, 58
Naumberg, Margaret 155, 160
Navin, Frank 537
Navratilova, Martina 556
Navy Cross 396
Nazimova, Alla 31
Nazism 322
Nearing, Dr. Scott 160
Nebraska State Journal 65
The Negro (Ransom) 473
Negro History Week 158
Negro Rhapsody (Gilbert) 54
Negro Training Schools, Tennessee 160
Negro Vaudeville Circuit 53, 60
Negro World 330
Neighborhood Playhouse, New York City 56
Neihardt, John G. 30
Nelson, Oscar "Battling" 543
Nelson, William Rockhill 249, 376
Neo-Gothic architecture 169
Nernst, Walther 514
Nestor, Agnes 106
Neurosurgery 405, 407

Osborn, Alex 347
Osborne, Thomas B. 425
Osgood, Howard 474
Oskar II 198
Osler, Sir William 423
Other Main-Travelled Roads (Garland) 24
Other People's Money and How Bankers Use It (Brandeis) 225
Others 47
Otis, Harrison Gray 90, 123, 249, 356, 376
Ott, Isaac 428
Ottoman Empire 218, 457, 459
Ouimet, Francis 526, 549, 561–562, 565
Ouimet, Louis 561
Ouimet, Wilfred 561
Our Christian Heritage (Pope Pius X) 466
Our Colored Fighters 355
Our Country (Strong) 481
Our Hope 444, 464–465
Our Mrs. McChesney (Ferber) 74
Our Slavic Fellow Citizens (Balch) 120
Out of Work: A Study of Employment Agencies (Kellor) 243
"Out, Out" (Frost) 67
Out There 61
Outlines of European History (Beard) 153
Outlook 273, 449, 461–462
"The Oven Bird" (Frost) 67
Over the Top 74
"Over There" 33, 35, 39, 52, 74, 303
Overman Act of 1918 202, 214
Ovid 294
Owen, Chandler 336
Owen, Robert L. 225–226, 268
Own Your Own Home (Lardner) 35
Oxford University
— Ruskin Hall 153

P

P. F. Collier and Son 376
Pace, Harry 69
Pacific Coast Hockey League 548
Pacific Coast League of Canada 527
Pacifism 51, 339, 351, 358, 374, 434, 436, 439, 441, 447, 449–453, 462, 468, 475, 478, 480
"Pack Up Your Troubles in Your Old Kitbag and Smile, Smile, Smile" 30

Packard Motor Company 494
Packard Motor Company Plant, Detroit 172
Paddock, Charles 556
Page, Walter Hines 123, 249, 376
Paine, Robert Treat 123, 340
The Palace Theatre, New York City 28, 58, 60, 76
Palais de Danse, New York City 44
Palmer, A. Mitchell 204, 220, 260, 268, 305
Palmer, Frederick 350, 353–354, 361
Palmer Raids 204, 220
Pan American Building, New York City 173
Panama Canal 81–82, 92, 166, 195–196, 245, 298, 301, 313, 368, 491, 502–503
Panama Canal Act of 1912 254
Panama-California Exposition of 1915, San Diego 166, 173, 175
Panama-Pacific Exposition of 1915, San Francisco 128, 178
— Palace of Fine Arts 166, 175
Pankhurst, Christabel 334
Pankhurst, Emmeline 296, 334, 370, 463
Pankhurst, Sylvia 334
Papanicolaou, George N. 425
Papke, Billy 526
Paramount Pictures 48. *See also* Lasky Feature Play Company.
Paris Peace Conference of 1919 152, 203, 217, 244, 360, 368, 373
Park, Roswell 428
Park Avenue Christian Church, New York City 185
Parke, Davis and Company 415
Parker, Dorothy 74
Parker, Francis 139
Parker, Dr. Horatio 26, 54, 76
Parker, Isaac C. 298
Parker, John J. 291
Parker, Junius 268
Parker, Morgan 425
Parker, Quanah 480
Parlin, Charles Coolidge 164
Parnell, Charles 184
Pasadena Star News 130
The Passing of the Great Race (Grant) 272, 322
Passing Shows (Shubert Brothers) 57
Pasteur, Louis 396
Pastor's Theater, New York City 58

Paterson Strike Pageant of 1913 60, 72, 301
Path of the Conquistadors (Bates) 520
Pathé Frères (movie company) 25, 48
Pathé's Weekly 25
Patou, Jean 181
Patria 31, 51, 65
Patriotic Service Leagues, Indiana 130
Patriotism and Religion (Mathews) 451, 478
Patten, Simon 334
Patterson, J. H. 121
Patterson, Joseph Medill 348, 356
Paul, Alice 222, 324, 327, 334–335
Pavlova, Anna 24, 43–44
The Pawnshop 31
Payne, Daniel 472
Payne-Aldrich Tariff of 1909 232–233, 249, 297
Peabody, George Foster 146, 160
Peace advocates 120, 420, 434–436, 438–440, 448–453, 456, 474, 481
"Peace and Plenty Rag" 36
Peace Mission Movement 438
Pearce, Louise 501
Pearce, Richard Mills 425
Pearl of the Army 31
Pearson's 345, 375
Pecci, Cardinal Gioacchino 466
Peck, Charles H. 425
Peck, George W. 376
Peg o' My Heart 27, 55
"Peggy" 36
Pegler, Westbrook 354
Peirce, Charles 154
Pell, Charles C. 527, 564
Pellagra 381, 398, 414
Pennell, V. H. 559
Pennsylvania Academy of Art 71–72
Pennsylvania Railroad 122, 164, 172, 308
Pennsylvania Railroad Station, New York City 164, 167, 172
Pennsylvania Society for the Prevention of Tuberculosis 410
Pennsylvania State College 138
Penrod (Tarkington) 28, 45
Pentecostal Testimony 479
Pentecostalism 434, 437–438, 479–480
The People, Yes (Sandburg) 71
The Perils of Pauline 28, 50

Riley, James Whitcomb 76, 338
Riley, William Bell 438, 446
Rinehart, Mary Roberts 361, 370
Ring, Jim 541
Ring Cycle (Wagner) 62
"A Ring on the Finger Is Worth Two on the Phone" 25
The Rink 31
Rio Rita 73
Ripostes (Pound) 26
The Rise of American Civilization (Beard and Beard) 153
The Rise of David Levinsky (Cahan) 32, 45
The Rising Tide (Deland) 31
Ritchie, Willie 525
Ritter, Mary 153
Ritz-Carlton Hotel, New York City 64
Rivers to the Sea (Teasdale) 30
Riverside Hospital, New York City 296
"The Road Not Taken" (Frost) 67
Roamer (racehorse) 551
Roberts, Ellis H. 123
Roberts, Lee S. 33
Roberts, Luckey 27
Robertson, William 160
Robeson, Paul 73–74
Robin Hood 70
Robinson, Boardman 371, 375
Robinson, Edwin Arlington 24, 31, 33, 47, 328
Robinson, Florence 151
Robinson, Harriet Jane 123
Robinson, Russel 24–26
Rochester Jeffersons 548
Rochester Theological Seminary 452, 473–475
"Rock-a-Bye Your Baby with a Dixie Melody" 34
Rockefeller, John D. 81, 88, 107, 119, 121–122, 229, 301, 338
Rockefeller, John D. Jr. 338
Rockefeller family 225
Rockefeller Foundation 121, 159, 301, 338, 381–382
Rockefeller Hospital, New York City 408
Rockefeller Institute for Medical Research 380, 409, 422, 424, 427
— War Demonstration Hospital 395
Rockefeller Sanitary Commission 380, 398
Rockne, Knute 546

Rodgers, Calbraith P. 524
Rodgers, Richard 74
Rodin, Auguste 42
Rodman, Henrietta 60
Rodman, William Louis 428
Roebling, Charles G. 123
Roentgen, William Conrad 409
Rogers, Charles Buddy 70
Rogers, Galbraith Perry 494
Rogers, Ginger 65
Rogers, James Gamble 166, 173
Rogers, Will 33, 57, 59, 73
Rolling Stones (Henry) 27
Roman Empire 457
The Romance of Elaine 30, 50
A Romance of the Redwoods 32
A Romance of the Western Hills 24
Romberg, Sigmund 32, 36, 44, 58
Roosevelt, Franklin D. 67, 71, 110, 113, 240, 243, 247, 292–293, 305, 327, 334, 355, 373–374
Roosevelt, Theodore 80, 92, 99, 118–119, 192–194, 199, 205–209, 225, 228, 232–239, 243, 245–247, 249, 254, 263–265, 286, 289, 291–292, 298, 318, 321, 323, 333, 337, 358–359, 368–370, 376, 391, 432, 439, 451, 459, 461, 466, 473, 478, 502, 545
Roosevelt, Theodore Jr. 300
Roosevelt Corollary of 1904 208
Roosevelt Dam 488
Root, Elihu 194, 234, 238–239, 248
Root, George Frederick 54
Rosalie (Ziegfeld) 73
Rose, Ed 33
Rose, Jack 254
Rose, Ralph Waldo 557, 567
Rose Bowl 528, 547
"Rose Room" 36
Rosenberg, Ethel 271
Rosenberg, Julius 271
Rosenfeld, Monroe H. 76
Der Rosenkavalier (Strauss) 54
Rosenthal, Herman "Beansie" 254
Rosenwald, Julius 113, 157
Ross, Edward Alsworth 119–120
Ross, Harold 347, 363–364
Ross, John Kenneth Leveson 552, 562
Rotch and Tilden (architectural firm) 185
Roth, Arthur V. 528
Rothapfel, Samuel F. "Roxy" 59
Rountree, John Wilhelm 468

Rous, Peyton 425
Roush, Ed 541
Rousseau, Henri 42
Rowntree, Leonard G. 407, 425
Royal, John M. 336
Royal and Ancient Golf Club of St. Andrews, Scotland 562
Royal Astronomical Society 517
The Royal Vagabond (Cohan) 58
Roycroft Press 187
Rubin, Lena 469
Rubinstein, Arthur 328
Rubinstein, Helena 166, 339
Ruby, Harry 36, 52
Ruether, Dutch 541
Ruggles of Red Gap (Wilson) 30
The Rules of Golf (Ouimet) 562
Runyon, Damon 353
Rush Hour, New York (Weber) 40
Ruskin, John 188
Russell, Bertrand 496
Russell, Charles Edward 345, 375
Russell, Charles Taze 432, 434, 437, 455, 478, 480
Russell, Henry Norris 490, 516
Russell, Lillian 39, 56, 62–63, 67
Russell, Linus Eli 428
Russell, Sidney 489, 519
Russellites. *See* Jehovah's Witnesses. 455
Russell's Paradox 496
Russian Orthodox Church 438, 440, 477, 480
Russian Revolutions of 1917 220, 271, 347, 370–373, 440, 477
The Russian Road to China (Bates) 520
Russian Symphony Orchestra 31
Russo-Japanese War 246, 369
Rutgers University 310
Ruth, George Herman "Babe" 528, 530, 532, 540, 559
Rutherford, Ernest 488, 492, 496–498, 518
Rutherford, Joseph 455, 478
Ryan, Elizabeth 556
Ryan, Father John A. 434, 456
Ryan, Patrick J. 558
Ryder, Albert Pinkham 42, 76
Ryerson, Donald 313

S

Saarinen, Eliel 171
Sabbath Prayer Book (Kaplan) 470
Sabine, Wallace C. 521

The Sense of Beauty (Santayana) 476
Serenata Morisca (Shawn and St. Denis) 44
Seton, Ernest Thompson 300
Settlement-house movement 56, 155, 159, 213, 334, 337–338, 432, 440, 442, 472
Seurat, Georges 42
The Seven Arts 37, 41, 46, 249, 371, 375–376
Seventeen (Tarkington) 31, 45
Seventh-Day Adventists 481
Seventh Street Hotel, Pittsburgh 189
Sever, James W. 409
Sex 156, 282, 294, 306, 356–357, 374, 509
Sex discrimination 87, 105, 107, 129, 150–151, 159, 221, 223, 306, 323, 326, 339, 370, 396, 462–464, 529, 550
Sex education 306, 418
"Sex Morality and Sex Hygiene" (NEA) 127
Seymour, Charles 242
Seymour, Horatio 368
Seymour, James Bentley "Cy" 568
Shackleford Good Roads Act of 1916. *See* Federal Highway Act of 1916.
Shahan, Thomas 432
Shakerism: Its Meaning and Message (White) 481
Shakers 481
Shanewis (Cadman) 54
Shannon, J. R. 29
Shapley, Harlow 491–492, 495
Shaw, Anna Howard 213, 249, 438, 440, 443, 463, 478, 480
Shawn, Ted 30, 39, 44, 61
Sheeler, Charles 41
Sheldon, Edward 55, 74
Shelly, Andrew B. 480
Shelton, Murray 546
Sheppard, Melvin 553, 557
Sheridan, Martin Joseph 568
Sherman, James S. 193–194, 237
Sherman, Lawrence Y. 238
Sherman, Gen. William Tecumseh 67, 184
Sherman Antitrust Act of 1890 80, 82, 98, 121, 192–193, 197, 207, 225–226, 245, 256, 264–265
Schick, Béla 490
Shields, Ren 76
Shilling, Carol H. 525, 565
"Shine On, Harvest Moon" 73

Shingle-style architecture 187
Shinn, Everett 40, 60, 72
Shipping Act of 1916 199, 215
Shirk, J. Marshall 190
Sho-Jo (Griffes) 54
Shoop, John D. 160
A Short History of the English Colonies (Lodge) 245
Shoulder Arms 34, 51
Show Boat 57, 73
Show Girl (Ziegfeld) 73
Shrady, John 428
Shubert, Lee 44
Shubert Brothers 25–26, 57–58, 63, 73
Sibelius, Jean 29
Sidgwick, Henry 469
Sikorsky, Igor 490
Silver, John 137
Simmons, Furnifold M. 108, 226
Simmons, Gertrude 160
Simmons, William Joseph 339, 435
Simmons College 337
Simpson, George 524, 548
Sin and Society 119
Sinclair, Harry 538
Sinclair, John 161
Sinclair, Upton 32, 35, 332, 347
Sing Sing prison 254
Singer Building, New York City 170
Singing Jailbirds (Sinclair) 332
The Single Hound (Dickinson) 28
Single Tax doctrine 122
Sioux tribes 245
Sir Barton (racehorse) 530, 552, 562–564, 566
Sister Carrie (Dreiser) 45
Sitter, Willem de 492
Siwanoy Golf Course, Bronxville, N.Y. 550
Six-dollar day 95
Sixes and Sevens (Henry) 25
Sixty-ninth Regiment Armory, New York City 42
Skinner, Otis 55
Slacker Raids 304, 311
Slaton, John M. 295, 329
Slavery 52, 68, 76, 118–119, 145–147, 157–158, 192, 223, 231, 300, 330, 340, 448, 462, 479–480
Slipher, Vesto M. 516–517
Sloan, Alfred P. 115
Sloan, Dolly 72
Sloan, Helen 72
Sloan, John 28, 37, 39–40, 60, 71–72

Sloane, A. Baldwin 24
Sloane Hospital for Women, New York City 296
Slosson, Edward 134
Slye, Maude 425
A Small Town Boy (Jones) 467
Smalley, George W. 377
Smallpox 129, 385
Smart Set 38, 46, 345, 349, 362–363, 374
Smiles (Ziegfeld) 33, 73
Smith, Alex 524, 548, 565
Smith, Alfred E. 220
Smith, Amanda 480
Smith, Bessie 52, 60
Smith, Charlotte 69
Smith, Eugene 140
Smith, Hannah Whitall 480
Smith, Harry B. 32
Smith, Jack 69
Smith, James Henry 558
Smith, John B. 521
Smith, Joseph Jr. 480
Smith, Joseph III 480
Smith, Joseph Fielding Sr. 480
Smith, Lottie 69
Smith, Macdonald 524, 548
Smith, Mamie 36
Smith, Pamela Colman 42
Smith, Rev. Paul 258
Smith, Russell 26, 34
Smith, S. L. 160
Smith, Thorne 34
Smith, Zilpha D. 333
Smith College 150
Smith-Hughes Act of 1917 83, 129, 148–149, 166, 178, 200
Smith-Lever Act of 1914 82, 148–149, 196, 224, 255
Smithsonian Institution 511
Smoke Bellew (London) 26
Smolny Institute, Russia 371
Snodgrass, Fred 540
"Snookey Ookums" 27
"Snookums Rag" 34
Social Aspects of Christianity (Ely) 474
Social Christianity 440
Social Darwinism 262
Social Gospel 249, 432–433, 439–443, 446, 454, 456, 472, 474–475, 479–481
"Social Ideals in English Letters" (Scudder) 478
The Social Principles of Jesus (Rauschenbusch) 440, 475
Social Security Act of 1935 334

Socialism 37, 56, 71–72, 99, 106–
107, 117, 206, 208, 215, 220,
232, 235, 249, 260, 270, 336,
344, 349, 351–352, 356, 371,
435, 440, 444–447, 460, 474, 478
Socialism and Character 478
Socialism: Promise or Menace (Ryan)
434
Socialist Labor Party 122, 237, 249
Socialist Party 37, 71, 97, 203, 215,
220, 235, 237, 240, 260, 270,
273, 294, 296, 336, 375, 418,
474, 478
Socialist Party of America 193,
220, 228, 235, 252, 310
Society for the Advancement of Ju-
daism (SAJ) 470
Society for the Collegiate Instruc-
tion of Women. *See* Radcliffe
College.
Society of American Artists 75
Society of American Fashions 165,
181
Society of Automobile Engineers
113
Society of Friends 153, 165, 324,
334, 434, 436, 449, 452, 467–468
Society of Independent Artists 32–
33, 38, 42–43, 72
Sockalexis, Lewis M. 568
Soddy, Frederick 498
The Solar System and Its Origins
(Russell) 516
A Soldier's Mother in France (Dorr)
370
Soldier's Pay (Faulkner) 46
Solidarity 332, 448
Solvay physics congresses 488, 498
Some Imagist Poets 47
Sometime (Friml) 58
A Son of the Middle Border (Garland)
45
Sonata Virginianesque (Powell) 54
The Song of Hugh Glass (Neihardt)
30
The Song of the Lark (Cather) 30,
39, 46, 66
Songs and Satires (Masters) 31
Songs for a Summer's Day (MacLe-
ish) 30
Songs for the New Age (Oppenheim)
28
The Sonnet 47
Sonnets and Other Verses (Santayana)
476
The Sorbonne 158
Sorg, Paul J. 374

The Souls of Black Folk (Du Bois)
146
Sousa, John Philip 26, 34, 36, 52,
61
South Atlantic League 560
South Philadelphia Hebrew Associ-
ation 542
South Sea Tales (London) 25
Southern Baptist Church 481
Southern Baptist Convention Sun-
day School Board 479
Southern Baptist Theological Semi-
nary 481
Southern Express Railroad Com-
pany 259
Southern League (baseball) 560
Southern Pacific Railroad 99, 253
Southern Railroad Express 253
Southern Sociological Congress
249
Southern States National Child
Labor Committee 267
Southern Women's Magazine 345
Southwestern Baptist Theological
Seminary 479
Spalding, Albert Goodwill 568
Spalding, John Lancaster 480
Spalding, Archbishop Martin 466
Spalding's Guide 541
Spanish-American War of 1898
48, 71, 209, 245–246, 358, 369,
420
Speaks, Oley 33
Speer, Robert E. 453, 478
Sperry, Elmer Ambrose 489, 519
Spirit of Emancipation 40
The Spirit of Freedom and Justice
(Ransom) 473
"The Spirit of John Brown" (Ran-
som) 473
The Spirit of '76 32, 62, 270
*Spiritual Reformers in the Sixteenth
and Seventeenth Centuries* (Jones)
468
Spiritualism 444
Spitzka, Edward Charles 428
The Spoilers 59
Spoon River Anthology (Masters) 30,
47, 74
Spooner, John C. 232
Springfield (Mass.) *Republican* 376
"Springtime Rag" 32
Spry, William 332
The Squaw Man 28
The Squirrel-Cage (Fisher) 26
Standard Oil 80, 121–122, 192,
263, 265, 292, 297

Stanford University 119, 128, 133,
142, 419, 525, 547
Stanford-Binet intelligence test
142, 386, 419–420
Stanley Company 499
Stanley Cup 529, 531–532, 548
Stanton, Charles E. 354
Stanton, Elizabeth Cady 221, 369,
463
Star Shoot (racehorse) 562
Star-Spangled Banner (dance) 33
"The Star-Spangled Banner" 62
Stark, E. J. Jr. 26, 29, 33
Stars and Stripes 347, 363–365
Starved Rock (Masters) 35
State College of Kentucky 417
State v. *Young* 223
Staten Island Marine Hospital 397
Stebbins, Lucy Ward 160
Steelworkers' strike of 1919 102–
103, 204, 220
Steele, Wilbur Daniel 34, 56
Stegner, Wallace 332
Steichen, Edward 39, 41, 61, 71
Steichen, Lillian 71
Stein, Gertrude 26, 28, 39, 47, 60,
328
Stein, Leo 328
Stein & Blaine 189
Steinmetz, Charles P. 488, 519
Steinmetz, E. M. A. 189
Steinway, Charles H. 123
Stella, Joseph 40, 42, 60
Stella Maris 34
Sterling, Andrew B. 24, 27, 30
Sterling, George 25
Sternaman, Dutch 546
Sterne, Maurice 328
Stevens, Raymond B. 98
Stevens, Wallace 43, 47, 475–476
Stevens Institute of Technology
514
Stevenson, Robert Louis 71, 137
Stewart, George A. 395
Stewart, John 161
Stewart, Lyman 444–445
Stewart, Milton 445
Stickley, Albert 188
Stickley, Charles 188
Stickley, Gustav 176, 187–188
Stieglitz, Alfred 24, 26, 29, 37, 39,
41–43, 47, 74, 328
Stiles, Charles Wardell 398
Stillman, James 107, 123
Stimson, Henry L. 234
Stirling, Alexa 566
Stock market crash of 1929 73

Terman, Lewis Madison 142–143, 401, 419–420
Terrible Threateners 352
Terrorism 90, 294, 445
Terry, Milton Spencer 481
Tess of the D'Urbervilles 27
Tess of the Storm Country 28, 70
Testimony Publishing Company 445
Tewanima, Louis 533, 553
Texas Review 346
Thais 32
"That Mysterious Rag" 26
Thaw, Harry K. 297
The Man Who Owns Broadway (Cohan) 58
The Palace, New York City 59
"The Trail of the Lonesome Pine" 27
The Theatre 55
Theatre Guild 35–36, 56, 60
Theobald, Stephen 432
A Theology for the Social Gospel (Rauschenbusch) 440, 475
The Theology of an Evolutionist (Abbott) 462
The Theory of the Leisure Class (Veblen) 181
Therbligs 116
"There's a Broken Heart for Every Light on Broadway" 30
"There's a Little Bit of Bad in Every Good Little Girl" 32
"They Didn't Believe Me" 29
They of the High Trails (Garland) 31
Third Symphony (Ives) 54
Thomas, Augustus 55
Thomas, Edward 66
Thomas, Lowell 355
Thomas, Norman 273
Thomas, Rene 527, 535, 565
Thomas, Wilbur 452
Thomas B. Jeffery Company 177
Thompson, Charles 29
Thompson, James Arthur 507
Thompson, Peter 180
Thompson, Robert 554
Thomson, Ernest A. 558
Thorndike, Edward L. 141–143, 156, 507
Thorpe, Charlotte Vieux 563
Thorpe, Hiram 563
Thorpe, James Francis "Jim" 339, 525, 532–533, 548, 553, 563
The Three Musketeers 70, 73
Three Soldiers (Dos Passos) 46
Thurman, Wallace 336
Tiernan, Michael Joseph 568

Tierney, Harry 36
Tiffany, Louis Comfort 167, 177
Tiger (Bynner) 27
"Tiger Rag" 33
Tilden, William "Big Bill" 552, 556
'Till I Come Back to You 34
" 'Till the Clouds Roll By" 33, 58
" 'Till We Meet Again" 33, 52
Tillie's Punctured Romance 28, 51
Tillman, Benjamin "Pitchfork Ben" 298
Time 477
Tin Pan Alley 38, 52, 54, 57, 69, 76
Tiqweth Israel — The Hope of Israel Monthly 464
The Titan (Dreiser) 28, 45
Titanic 76, 80, 253, 301, 339, 345, 350, 365–366, 372, 489, 506
Toklas, Alice B. 328
Tom Sawyer (Twain) 76
Tombaugh, Clyde 517
Tomlinson, Thomas Henry 428
Torrey, Reuben A. 444, 458, 464–465
Toscanini, Arturo 28
Toulouse-Lautrec, Henri de 42
Toward the Gulf (Masters) 34
Tower of Ivory (MacLeish) 33
The Town Down the River (Robinson) 24, 47
Town Topics 363
Toy, Crawford Howell 481
Toy Theater, Boston 26, 56
Tracey, William 24
Trading with the Enemy Act of 1917 83, 201
The Trail of the Lonesome Pine 31
The Tramp 30
Transcendentalism 340
Traphagen, Ethel 189
Trask, James Dowling 424
Travers, Jerome D. 528, 548, 562, 565–566
The Treason of the Senate (Phillips) 376
Treasure Island (Stevenson) 71, 137
Treat 'Em Rough (Lardner) 34
Treaty of Brest-Litovsk 370
Treaty of Versailles 97, 100, 204, 208, 217, 219–220, 242, 244–247, 261, 372, 440
The Tree of Life (Lowell) 34
Treemonisha (Joplin) 52–53
"Trees" (Kilmer) 76
Trees and Other Poems (Kilmer) 28
Triangle Film Corporation 31, 48

Triangle Shirtwaist Company, New York City 37, 164, 180, 228, 253, 295, 300, 338
Trier Township High School, Winnetka, Ill. 129
Trilling, Lionel 67
Trinity Church, Portland, Oregon 190
Triple Alliance 212
Triple Crown 532, 552, 562–564
Triple Entente 211
Il trittico (Puccini) 35, 54
The Troll Garden (Cather) 65
Trotsky, Leon 361
Trotter, William Monroe 473
True Heart Susie (Chaplin) 35
True Story 348, 360
Truman, Harry S 288, 319, 337
Trusts 37, 48, 55, 80, 82–83, 85–86, 88, 90, 98–99, 107–108, 122, 192–193, 197, 202, 205, 207, 225–226, 233–234, 236–237, 253, 262–266, 279, 289, 292, 296–297, 427, 528
Tuberculosis 159, 385, 406, 410–411, 419–420, 427–428
Tubman, Harriet 340
Tucker, Sophie 48, 69
Tuileries Gardens 320
Tulane University 16
— Medical School 151
Tunney, Gene 545
"The Turkey Trot" 26
The Turmoil (Tarkington) 30, 45
The Turn of the Screw (James) 76
Turner, B. B. 407
Turner, Florence ("The Vitagraph Girl") 49
Turner, Henry McNeal 481
Turner, Thomas Wyatt 436
Turns and Movies (Aiken) 31
Tuskegee Institute 123, 146–147, 157–158, 160–161, 250, 340, 511
Tutankhamen of Egypt 372
Tuxedo Brass Band 52
Tuxedo Club, Tuxedo Park, N.Y. 558
Twain, Mark (Samuel Langhorne Clemens) 31, 76
"Twelfth Street Rag" 32
The Twentieth Century Crusade 462
Twentieth Century Religion (Mills) 480
Twenty Years at Hull House (Addams) 432
Twenty-Five Years of American Education (Reisner) 132

291 41

291 gallery, New York City 24, 29

Typhoid fever 296, 380, 393, 395, 414, 420–421, 427

Typhus 388, 414

U

The U. P. Trail (Grey) 34

Ukrainian Americans 480

Ulysses (Joyce) 35, 45, 47, 346

Uncle Remus and the Little Boy (Chandler) 24

Uncle Remus Returns (Harris) 34

"Under the Bamboo Tree" 75

"Under the Yum Yum Tree" 24

Underground Railroad 462

Underwood, Benjamin Franklin 481

Underwood, Oscar W. 107–108, 226, 236

Underwood-Simmons Tariff Act of 1913 81, 85–86, 90, 108, 195, 226

Union Army 298, 466

Union Boat Club 527

Union League Club of Philadelphia 236

Union of American Hebrew Congregations 469

Union of Orthodox Rabbis 470

Union Oil 444

Union Pacific 50

Union Pacific Railroad 253

"The Union Scab" 332

Union Theological Seminary, New York City 477

Union Theological Seminary, Tokyo 480

Union Trust Company Bank, San Francisco 190

Unitarian Church 173, 434, 442, 450–453, 479–480

United Artists (UA) 70

United Booking Offices of America (UBO) 63

United Brotherhood of Carpenters and Joiners 96

United Brotherhood of Elevator and Switchboard Operators 336

United Civic League of New York 437

United Fruit 330, 348

United Managers' Protective Association 63

United Mine Workers (UMW) 81, 96–97, 99, 117–118, 220, 229, 249

United Negro Improvement Association 303

United Norwegian Synod 435

United Presbyterian Theological Seminary 465

United Press (UP) 353–355, 357

United Press International (UPI) 347

United States

— Aircraft Production Board 86, 113

— Alien Property Custodian 83

— Army 61, 142, 213, 215, 245–246, 263, 319, 347, 357, 383, 386, 393, 396, 409, 424, 436, 454–455, 513, 545–546, 565; *First Division* 216; *Second Division* 216; *Third Division* 216; *Twenty-Sixth Division* 21; *Ninety-Second Division* 309; *Ninety-Third Division* 224; *New York Fifteenth Regiment* 61; *328th Infantry Regiment, Company G* 217

— Army Aviation Service 201, 516

— Chaplain's Corps 455

— Army Engineer Service 452

— Army General Staff 246

— Army Medical Corps 452

— Army Nurse Corps 396

— Army Quartermaster Corps 452

— Army School of Nursing 383, 396

— Army Signal Corps 351, 511

— Army War College 246

— Board for Vocational Education 130, 148, 150

— Board of Censorship 347

— Board of Mediation and Conciliation 254

— Bureau of Corporations 196, 226, 255

— Bureau of Education 126–127, 130–131, 145, 149–150, 159, 228

— Bureau of Labor 276

— Bureau of Mines 80, 252

— Bureau of Naturalization 228

— Bureau of Standardization of Trades 116

— Bureau of the Census 382

— Children's Bureau 129, 230, 338, 381, 421, 424

— Circuit Court 255, 281

— Civilian Advisory Commission 113

— Coast Guard 197, 256

— Commerce Court 192, 274, 294

— Commission on Education 127, 130, 158

— Commission on Immigration 282

— Commission on Training Camp Activities 319, 354, 436

— Commission on Uniform Laws 268

— Committee on Public Information (Creel Commission) 35, 39, 62, 135, 201, 215, 258, 313, 347, 349, 352, 354–355, 375, 467

— Committee on Roads 501

— Congress 35, 71, 80–83, 86, 90, 97–98, 100–101, 107–109, 130, 135, 138, 148, 178, 192–204, 205, 207–208, 210, 212–213, 215, 217, 219, 221–234, 237, 240–241, 245, 247–248, 252–254, 256–261, 263, 265, 267–271, 274, 276, 282–285, 287–288, 290–292, 294–298, 300–303, 305, 308, 310, 316, 318, 320, 327, 335, 354–356, 359, 366, 374, 381–383, 389, 391–392, 396–397, 421–422, 437, 449, 454, 463–464

— Constitution 153, 199, 205, 215, 219, 227, 230–231, 245, 254–257, 259, 263, 267, 269–270, 273, 278, 282, 284, 287–291, 295, 326, 334, 473, 501; *Bill of Rights* 270; *First Amendment* 49, 270; *Fourth Amendment* 279; *Tenth Amendment* 259, 269; *Thirteenth Amendment* 270; *Fourteenth Amendment* 146, 279; *Fifteenth Amendment* 221, 463; *Sixteenth Amendment* 81, 86, 107, 194–195, 226, 263; *Seventeenth Amendment* 195, 221, 254, 263, 297; *Eighteenth Amendment* 83–84, 202–204, 231, 240, 245, 259–261, 263, 284–285, 303, 305, 320–321, 384, 443; *Nineteenth Amendment* 221, 223, 248, 260, 263, 324, 327, 335; *Twentieth Amendment* 292; *Twenty-First Amendment* 231

— Constitutional Convention 153, 221

— Council of National Defense 100, 109, 113, 117, 135, 199, 201, 213–214, 393

— Council of National Defense, Medical Division 383, 386, 396, 421

University of Minnesota 159, 381, 415, 547
— Medical School 389
University of Nebraska 65, 119, 246
University of North Carolina 161, 508
— Bureau of Extension 130
University of Notre Dame 526, 546
University of Oregon 529
University of Pennsylvania 160, 334, 427, 520, 547, 557, 563
— Law School 268, 547
— Medical School 151, 380, 425
University of Pittsburgh 566
University of Rochester 474
— Eastman School of Medicine and Dentistry 424
University of Southern California 556
The University of Today (Slosson) 134
University of Virginia 150, 246
— Medical School 151
University of Washington 547
University of Wisconsin 119, 127, 133, 138, 151
University of Wurzburg Physical Institute 409
University of Zurich 417
An Unseen Enemy 26
Unser, Al 536
Untermeyer, Samuel 225
Up From Slavery (Washington) 250, 330, 340
Upper Montclair Country Club, New Jersey 550
Upset (racehorse) 552
Urban, Joseph 73
Urbanization 37–38, 98, 205, 262, 307
"The U.S. Field Artillery March" (Sousa) 34
Utah State Penitentiary 331

V

The Vagabond 31
Van Alstyne, Egbert 30, 32
Van Amringe, John Howard 161
Van Anda, Carr 350, 372
Van Cott, Margaret Newton 481
Vanderbeck, Mrs. C. H. 566
Vanderbilt family 367
Van Devanter, Willis 297
Vandover and the Brute (Norris) 28
Vanity Fair 46, 58, 74, 345, 349, 362–363, 367

Van Osdel, Oliver 445
Van Slyke, Lucius Lincoln 425
Van Vechten, Carl 328
Van Vleck, John M. 521
Vanzetti, Bartolomeo 334
Vardon, Harry 526, 549, 562
Variety 25, 28, 31, 48, 59, 75
The Varmint (Johnson) 24
Vassar Training Camp 396
Vaudeville 25, 28–29, 38, 44, 51–54, 58–62, 69, 73, 76
Vaughan, Dr. Victor Clarence 397, 420–421
Vaughan, William 157
Vaughn, Jim 529
Vaughan family 157
The Vaunt of Man (Leonard) 26
Veblen, Thorstein 60, 181, 507
Vedder, E. B. 425
Venereal disease 319, 383, 386, 393, 398
The Venus Model 34
Verdi, Giuseppe 24, 59, 74
Verdict 376
Vernor, Dudleigh 26
Versailles Peace Conference of 1919. *See* Paris Peace Conference of 1919.
A Versatile Villain 27
Verses (Jewett) 31
Very Good, Eddie (Kern) 54, 58
Vicariate-Apostolic of North Carolina 466
Victor Ollnee's Discipline (Garland) 25
Victor Records 33, 44, 52
Victor Talking Machine Company 159, 302
Victorian architecture 168, 170, 176
Victorian art 178
Victorian design 168, 186
Victorian fashion 180
Villa, Francisco "Pancho" 75, 198, 211, 241, 246, 371
Villard, Henry 373
Villard, Oswald Garrison 344, 350, 373
Vionnet, Madeleine 181
Virginia (Glasgow) 27
Virginia Military Institute 150
Virginia Polytechnic Institute 157
The Virginian (movie) 28
Vitagraph Pictures 48
The Vixen 31

Vocational education 83, 126–127, 132–133, 148–149, 155, 159–161, 200, 243, 330
Vogel, Lucien 178
Vogue 166, 178, 181, 349, 362, 367
Voice of the Negro (Barber) 473
Volkenburg Browne, Ellen 60
Volkenburg Browne, Maurice 60
Volstead Act of 1919 84, 204, 261, 285, 305
Von Der Ahe, Christian Frederick Wilhelm 568
Von Tilzer, Albert 24, 32–33, 52
Von Tilzer, Harry 24–27, 30, 52
Vulcanite Portland Cement Company 122

W

Wabash College 541
Waddell, George Edward "Rube" 568
Wagner, Richard 54, 62
Wagner Act of 1935 63
Waite, Catherine 123
"Waiting for the Robert E. Lee" 26, 76
Wald, Lillian D. 396, 421–422, 451
Walden School 155, 160
Waldorf-Astoria Hotel, New York City 74
Walker, Sarah Breedlove "Madame C.J." 123
Walker Cup 562
Walker Theatre, Los Angeles 27
Walkowitz, Abraham 39
Waller, Fats 36
Wallon, Augustus 464
Wallon, Louis 464
Walter Dodge House, Los Angeles 175
Walter Reed Hospital, Washington, D.C. 396
Walters, Alexander 481
Walworth, Rev. Clarence 466
Wanamaker, John 103–105, 148
Wanamaker, Rodman 550
Wanamaker's department store 103, 317, 366, 550
War Aims Course 159
War and Laughter (Oppenheim) 31
"The War and the Schools" 135
War Brides 31, 51
The War Bride's Secret 51
War Camp Community Service 456
War Cloud (racehorse) 530
War Finance Corporation 83, 202

Whiting, Richard A. 33, 52

Whitman, Charles S. 239, 257

Whitman, Walt 71

Whitney, Gertrude Vanderbilt 29, 43, 72

Whitney, Warren 173

Whitney, Willis R. 89

Whitney Museum. *See* Whitney Studio Club.

Whitney Studio Club, New York City 29, 43, 72

Whitsitt, William Heth 481

Whitson, Beth Slater 24

Whitten-Brown, Arthur 494

Whittier, John Greenleaf 467

Whittier Settlement House, Jersey City, N.J. 337

"Who Is Santayana?" (Frankel) 475

Whoopie (Ziegfeld) 73

Whooping cough 385

Who's Who 127

"Whose Little Heart Are You Breaking Now?" 33

"Why Keep Me Waiting So Long?" 33

Why Marry? (Williams) 34–35, 75

Wickersham, George W. 292–293

Widdemer, Margaret 34, 75

Widener, Peter A. B. 123

Wiener Werkestätten 178

Wightman, Hazel Hotchkiss. *See* Hotchkiss, Hazel V.

Wilberforce University 472–473

Wilce, Dr. John W. 547

Wilcox, Ella Wheeler 76, 481

Wilcox, Howard 535, 566

The Wild Goose Chase 30

Wilde, Oscar 54, 361

Wildflower 28

Wilding, Tony 555

Wiley, Harvey W. 297

Wilhelm II of Germany 217, 449–450

Will Christ Come Again? (Case) 458, 478

Willard, Jess 528, 533, 545

Williams, Bert 59, 73

Williams, Claude "Lefty" 541, 560

Williams, Harry H. 26, 27, 36

Williams, Horatio B. 408

Williams, Jesse Lynch 34–35, 55, 75

Williams, Kathlyn 24, 27, 50

Williams, Kid 527

Williams, Leighton 474

Williams, Richard Norris II 529, 556, 566

Williams, Samuel M. 368

Williams, Tennessee 56

Williams, William Carlos 27, 33, 43, 47, 60

Williams, Wythe 353

Willis, John Henry 463

Wills, Maury 528

Willys-Overland Company 500

Wilson, Edith Bolling Galt 198, 247, 318

Wilson, Edmund 360

Wilson, Ellen Louise Axson 165, 247, 340

Wilson, Harry Leon 30

Wilson, Henry B. 355

Wilson, James 297, 511

Wilson, Louis B. 415

Wilson, William B. 99, 117, 194

Wilson, William L. 241

Wilson, Woodrow 33, 81–82, 85–88, 90–93, 96–102, 107–114, 116–117, 120, 130, 135, 138, 152, 157, 181, 194–204, 205, 207–220, 222, 225–231, 236–237, 239–248, 254–261, 263, 265, 268, 271, 274, 280, 285, 287, 291, 293, 295, 301–303, 305, 308, 310, 314, 316, 318, 321, 324, 332–335, 340, 346–347, 349, 354, 358–360, 368–371, 373, 384, 386, 391, 393, 421, 434–435, 437, 439–440, 449–451, 455–456, 459, 463–464, 466, 473, 477–478, 501, 545

Wilson Act of 1890 283

Wimbledon Tennis Tournament 555–556

Windy McPherson's Son (Anderson) 31

Winesburg, Ohio (Anderson) 35, 45

The Wings of the Dove (James) 76

The Winning of Barbara Worth (Wright) 25

Winona Bible Conference of 1911 433

Winter Garden Theatre, New York City 25, 36, 74

Winter in Taos (Dodge) 328

Wisconsin Supreme Court 277

Wisconsin Woman Suffrage Association 463

Wise, Rabbi Stephen S. 333, 440, 442, 451, 459–460, 478

"Wise Old Moon" 26

With the Allies (Davis) 369

Withers Stakes 550, 552

Witla, Eugene 39

Wobblies. *See* Industrial Workers of the World (IWW).

Wodehouse, P. G. 32–33, 58

The Woman God Forgot 32

A Woman of Fifty (Dorr) 370

A Woman of Genius (Austin) 26

The Woman Rebel 418

Woman suffrage 37, 48, 107, 120, 133, 168, 181, 201, 205, 208, 213, 221–223, 245, 248, 259, 262–263, 296, 298, 300, 303, 306, 320, 323–324, 326–327, 334, 344, 369–370, 373, 434, 438, 440, 443, 462–464, 478, 480

Woman Suffrage Party 327

Woman's Christian Temperance Union (WCTU) 152, 480

Woman's Medical College 421

Woman's Party 222–223, 327, 463. *See also* Congressional Union.

Woman's Peace Party 213, 310, 327

Woman's Research Foundation 335

Woman's Home Companion 345, 374

Women in Industry Service 325

Women in the War 131

Women's American Home Missionary Society 480

Women's Christian Temperance Union 152, 231, 443, 480

Women's Death Battalion, Russia 370

Women's Educational and Industrial Union 340

Women's Home and Foreign Missionary Society 479

Women's International League for Peace and Freedom 213

Women's National Bowling Association 529

Women's Suffrage Resolution of 1918 259

Women's Trade Union League (WTUL) 107

Women's Zionist Organization of America 460

Women's Wear Daily 164, 180, 344

The Wonderful Wizard of Oz (Baum) 75

Wood, Joe 539–540

Wood, Junius 353

Woodbury, Frank 488

Woodson, Carter Godwin 158, 160

Woollcott, Alexander 364

Woolworth, Rev. Clarence 466

Woolworth, Frank W. 170, 339

Woolworth Building (Marin) 40, 489

Woolworth Building, New York City 38, 80, 165, 170, 186, 339, 493

Woolworth stores 52, 170, 339, 360

Worcester Foundation 419

Worcester Polytechnic Institute 161

Word and Witness (Bell) 434

Wordsworth, William 67

Work, Henry Clay 54

Work 30

"Workers and Peasants Government" (Lenin) 371

Workingmens Building Association 340

Workmen's compensation 86, 100, 121, 205, 220, 229, 235–236, 238–239, 247, 256, 262, 275–278, 380, 390

Workmen's Compensation Act of 1916 199

World Conference of Friends (1937) 468

World Council of Churches 471

World Court 245, 293

"World Democracy and America's Obligation to Her Neighbors" (Speer) 453–454, 478

World Methodist Conference (1947) 473

World Missionary Conference (1910) 432

World Outlook 326

World Peace Congress 451

World Series. *See* Major League Baseball World Series.

World War I, battles 386, 472

— Aisne-Marne Offensive 202

— Battle of Belleau Wood 202, 246

— Battle of Château-Thierry 202, 246

— Battle of Saint-Mihiel 203, 216

— Battles of the Marne 202, 216, 246

— Battle of the Somme 512

— Meuse-Argonne Offensive 203, 216–217, 246, 319

World War I, causes 197, 200, 211–212, 242

World War I, fatalities 35, 216

World War I and African Americans 157, 224, 308, 351

— and agriculture 224

— and art 39, 42–43, 61

— and aviation 494

— and book publishing 361

— and business 86, 90, 93, 95, 99, 101, 109, 111–112, 114, 256, 260, 263, 269, 285

— and censorship 33, 201–202, 244, 270, 344, 347, 354

— and civil liberties 269

— and conscientious objectors 248, 259, 310–311, 436, 452–453, 455, 468

—and domestic politics 109, 114, 202, 213–215, 240, 246, 263, 270–271

— and the economy 85–87, 91, 93, 105, 108–111, 113, 263, 307

— and education 128, 130, 134–136, 138, 141–142, 144–145, 147, 150, 152–153, 159

— and fashion 166, 181–183

— and finance 196, 201, 213, 324, 513

  and foreign relations 201, 207, 242–244, 247, 291

— and foreign trade 82

— and German Americans 62, 351, 473, 475

— and immigration 228

— and intelligence testing 318, 386, 399

— and journalism 61, 71, 344, 346, 349, 354, 357–358, 360

— and labor 63, 87, 96–97, 100, 102, 114, 116–117, 215, 338, 373, 447, 456

— and law 262, 281

— and literature 39, 46–47, 61, 66–67, 319

— and medicine 385–386, 388, 390, 393–396, 405–407, 410–411, 416, 420–422

— and military draft 201, 213, 241, 259, 288, 294, 303–304, 310–311, 318, 393, 452, 538

— and military strategy 196–197, 200, 215–217, 241, 245–247, 513

— and motor vehicle industry 501

— and moving pictures 51, 68, 347

— and music 34–35, 39, 52, 62

— and nativism 129

— and newsreels 48, 351

— and pacifism 207, 241, 269–270, 310–311, 324, 327, 351, 361

— and peace advocates 120, 213, 294, 451–452

— and progressivism 439

— and prohibition 284–285

— and public opinion 93, 120, 185, 207, 213, 245, 249, 310, 334,

336, 347, 349, 351, 354, 358, 368–369, 373–374

— and radio 346–347, 362

— and rationing 168, 175, 304, 307

— and religion 434–435, 437, 439–442, 445, 447–459, 461–462, 465–468, 477–478

— and religious fundraising 456

— and scientific management 116

— and social relations 306, 314, 316

— and socialism 351

— and sports 532–533, 535, 538, 542, 545–546, 549–550, 554, 556, 559

— and technology 493, 513, 516

— and theater 59

— and war correspondents 61, 71, 346, 349–350, 352–354, 356–358, 361, 369–370, 374–376

— and weapons 491, 512, 514

— and women 213, 222, 324, 442

World War II 71, 102, 181, 246, 248, 271, 308, 355, 357–358, 365, 373, 465, 468, 514, 553, 564

World Women's Party 335

World Zionist Organization 459

World's Christian Fundamentals Association 438, 441, 446

World's Hard Court Championships 556

World's Parliament of Religions, Chicago (1893) 472

World's Work 376

Worth (racehorse) 565

Wounds from Blank Cartridges (Allen) 427

The Wrath of the Gods 28

Wright, Frank Lloyd 164–166, 168, 170–171, 174–176, 188

Wright, Harold Bell 25, 28, 31

Wright, Marc 557

Wright, Orville 113, 123, 180, 255, 521, 524–525

Wright, Richardson 367

Wright, W. C. 559

Wright, Wilbur 123, 180, 255, 340, 521, 524–525

Wylie, Elinor 26

Wyman, Walter 428

Wynn, Ed 48, 59, 63, 74

X

X rays 381, 385–386, 392, 394–395, 407–409, 424, 490, 498, 510